The Book of Saints

A Comprehensive Biographical Dictionary

Edited by Dom Basil Watkins, OSB
on behalf of the Benedictine monks of
St Augustine's Abbey, Ramsgate

Seventh edition
Entirely revised and reset

A & C Black • London

Seventh edition 2002
First published 1921
A & C Black Publishers Limited
37 Soho Square
London W1D 3QZ
www.acblack.com

ISBN 0-7136-5300-0

A & C Black uses paper produced with elemental chlorine-free pulp, harvested from managed sustainable forests.

A CIP catalogue record for this book is available from the British Library.

Printed by Graficas Zamudio Printek S.A.L.,
Vizcaya, Spain

Jacket illustrations:

St Patrick

Mosaic by Trevor Caley at Westminster Cathedral. Reproduced by kind permission of the cathedral administrator. Photograph taken by Peter Kowal. © Iconart

St Michael and St Gabriel

Icon by E. Bakalarz. Photograph taken by Peter Kowal. © Iconart

The Book of Saints

Contents

List of Illustrations

Every effort has been made to trace and acknowledge copyright owners. If any right has been omitted the publishers offer their apologies and will rectify this in subsequent editions following notification.

Introduction

This book contains entries for all those who have been formally canonized or beatified by the Roman Catholic Church to date, as well as for those who have had their local veneration approved by the Church as a whole and those who have been listed in the old Roman Martyrology. As well as these categories it also lists the more prominent of those local saints who have been venerated in the distant past, before the process of canonization was formalized, and who have not had their veneration approved by the Roman Magisterium. There are very many of these, most of whom are no longer liturgically honoured anywhere but who feature in historical records and local traditions.

In previous editions, entries under the same Christian name were listed by feast-day. Nowadays such a listing is not of any more use than random order, and the entries in this edition are listed in alphabetical order, as follows: firstly by the first word of the Christian name, then by surname (if any) or cognomen. Compound Christian names are hyphenated. There are no entries with surname first. Those entries for consecrated religious are by their names in religion, as given by the official documents published in Rome, even if they are better known by their baptismal names. Different religious congregations have differing traditions regarding surnames: the Franciscans tend to replace them by a cognomen derived from the person's place of birth and the Carmelites drop surnames altogether. For the purpose of listing, all surnames (where known) have been restored, e.g. 'Teresa-of-the-Child-Jesus Martin'. Names in bold type refer to individual saints or blesseds, and those in bold italics to those whose public veneration has been suppressed (especially in 1969). Those in text type are variant names of individuals listed elsewhere.

A name is given in the familiar English form or in the form most familiar in England, e.g. 'James' not 'Jacques', without any offence intended to national sensibilities. An exception is made for certain obsolescent English forms that are widely divergent from the original, e.g. 'Dionysius' is listed as such and not as 'Dennis', and 'Louis' not as 'Lewis'. Anglo-Saxon names have been generally left in the familiar Latinized forms rather than being rendered as they were actually pronounced, but dog-Latin versions of vernacular names have mostly been avoided (these usually add 'us' or 'is' to the end, e.g. 'Guerricus' for 'Guerric').

Geographical names are a delicate subject nowadays. Those in previous editions have been checked in a contemporary atlas, and many have had to be corrected. It is no longer assumed that readers are intimately familiar with the place names of any one country such as Italy or France. Again, any existing familiar English form as employed in the national media of the United Kingdom is used in preference, e.g. Cologne rather than Köln, Milan rather than Milano, and contemporary names are used in preference to historical ones (even at the risk of apparent anachronism). The names of Far Eastern saints and blesseds have been badly garbled in previous editions, being derived from Spanish or Portuguese transliterations rendered into Latin and thence into English, and these have been checked and corrected.

The entries for New Testament saints presume that the reader has access to a copy of the Bible, so no duplication at length of information available therein is attempted. All Old Testament characters have been deleted from the text, so as to avoid questions of biblical exegesis which are better dealt with elsewhere. Certain obscure consecrated religious whose veneration as blessed was never confirmed have also been deleted, together with several alleged saints the information on whom was inadequate.

This book is intended primarily to be a work of reference, which entails that a critical attitude is taken towards historical evidence (especially early legends). No attack on anybody's devotional attachments or practices is intended as a result.

Readers are welcome to draw attention to any mistakes or omissions.

Abbreviations

?	date or status uncertain
A.	Apostle
a	'ante' (before, in time)
Bl, BB	Blessed (single and plural)
B.	Bishop
C	century
Comp(s)	Companion(s)
c	'circa' (about, in time)
d.	died
D.	Deacon
Dr.	Doctor of the Church
F.	Founder of a religious congregation
L.	Lay person
M.	Martyr
P.	Secular priest
p	'post' (after, in time)
q.v.	which see
R.	Religious (in general, including hermits and consecrated virgins)
R(CP).	Passionist
R(CR).	Canon Regular of St Augustine
R(CSSR).	Redemptorist
R(OC).	Carmelite
R(OCart).	Carthusian
R(OCD).	Discalced Carmelite
R(OCist).	Cistercian
R(OCSO).	Cistercian of the Strict Observance
R(OFM).	Franciscan
R(OFM Conv).	Conventual Franciscan
R(OFM Cap).	Capuchin Franciscan
R(OP).	Dominican
R(OPraem).	Praemonstatensian (Norbertine)
R(OSA).	Augustinian Friar
R(OSB).	Benedictine
R(OSB Cam).	Camaldolese
R(OSB Oliv).	Olivetan
R(OSB Silv).	Silvestrine
R(OSB Vall).	Vallumbrosan
R(OSM).	Servite
R(SJ).	Jesuit
S.	Subdeacon
St, SS	Saint (single and plural)
T.	Tertiary (categorized as religious, above).
V.	Virgin Martyr

A

Aaron (St) *see* **Julius and Aaron**

Aaron (St) R. Jun 22
d. *p*552. A Briton who emigrated to Brittany, France, he became a hermit at what is now St Malo and attracted disciples who formed a monastery. St Malo himself joined this *c*550.

Aaron of Cracow (St) B. R(OSB). Oct 9
d. 1059. By tradition a monk at Cluny under St Odilo, he became the first abbot of the abbey of Tyniec, Poland, in 1040, then first archbishop of Cracow in 1046.

Aaron of Sandomir (Bl) *see* **Sadoc of Sandomir and Comps**

Abachum (St) *see* **Marius, Martha and Comps**

Abb *see* **Ebba**

Abban (St) R. Mar 16
C5th. A contemporary of St Patrick and a nephew of St Ibar, he founded Killabban Abbey in Co. Laois, Ireland.

Abban (St) R. Oct 27
C6th. St Kevin's nephew, he founded many monasteries in southern Ireland, notably Magh-Armuidhe (Adamstown) in Co. Wexford. (There are other SS Abban listed, but the evidence concerning all of them is hopelessly confused.)

Abbo of Auxerre (St) B. R(OSB). Dec 3
d. *c*860. Abbot of St Germain's Abbey at Auxerre, France, he became bishop of that city in 857 but resigned in 859.

Abbo of Fleury (St) R(OSB). Nov 13
?945–1004. From near Orléans, France, he became a child-oblate and monk at Fleury. He was famous as a scholar, and spent two years (985–7) as the head of the school at Ramsey Abbey, England, at the invitation of St Oswald, the founder. In 988 he became abbot of Fleury, and served as a mediator between the pope and the French king. He was killed in a riot at the monastery of La Réole in Gascony which he was attempting to reform, and was venerated (dubiously) as a martyr. He has left some writings.

Abbo of Metz *see* **Goeric**

Abdechalas (St) *see* **Simeon Barsabae and Comps**

Abdisho (Abdiesus, Ebedjesu) (St) M. May 16
C4th. One of those martyred in the persecution ordered by Shah Shapur II (who tried to eliminate Christianity from the Persian Empire between 341 and 380) he was either a deacon or a bishop of Kashkar in Mesopotamia. There might have been two martyrs of this name.

Abdon and Sennen (SS) MM. Jul 30
C3rd or C4th. Persians (noblemen, according to their unreliable acta), they were brought to Rome as prisoners of war and then helped imprisoned Christians and buried the bodies of martyrs. They were themselves martyred in the reign of either Decius or Diocletian (sources differ).

Abel of Lobbes (St) B. R. Aug 5
d. ?751. Either Anglo-Saxon or Irish, he went with St Boniface to Germany and was elected archbishop of Rheims, France. The archbishopric was occupied by an intruder, so he went to the abbey of Lobbes and became its abbot instead.

Abel of Sandomir (Bl) *see* **Sadoc of Sandomir and Comps**

Abercius (St) B. Oct 22
d. ?167. Asserted to have succeeded St Papias as bishop of Hierapolis in Phrygia, Asia Minor, he was imprisoned for campaigning against paganism but was released and died in peace. He composed his own epitaph, which was

discovered in 1882 and is an important early witness of the Church's dogmatic teaching.

Abibas (St) L. Aug 3
C1st. The legend is that he was the second son of the Gamaliel who taught St Paul (Acts 5:34; 22:3), became a Christian like his father and died aged 79. His alleged relics were found at Capergamala near Jerusalem in 415, together with those of SS Stephen, Gamaliel and Nicodemus.

Abibus (St) *see* **Samosata (Martyrs of)**

Abibus of Edessa (St) M. Nov 15
d. 322. A deacon of Edessa, Syria (now Urfa in Turkey), he was burnt during the reign of Licinius and buried with his friends, SS Gurias and Samonas.

Abilius of Alexandria (St) B. Feb 22
d. ?98. According to Eusebius (the only source), the first three bishops of Alexandria in Egypt were SS Mark, Anianus and Abilius, the last from 84.

Abilus-of-the-Cross Ramos y Ramos (Bl) *see* **Nicephorus Díez Tejerina and Comps**

Ablebert *see* **Emebert**

Abra (St) R. Dec 12
?342–360. The daughter of St Hilary of Poitiers, she took his advice to become a nun but died aged seventeen. She is venerated at Poitiers, France.

Abraham (Abraamios) of Arbela (St) M. B. Feb 4
d. ?346. A bishop of Arbela in Mesopotamia, he was killed at Telman in the reign of Shah Shapur II of Persia.

Abraham (Abraames) of Carrhae (St) B. Feb 14
d. ?422. A hermit of Syria, he converted a Lebanese village to Christianity by borrowing money to pay its taxes. Becoming bishop of Carrhae (Harran) in Mesopotamia, he gained influence over Emperor Theodosius II and his court, and died while visiting Constantinople.

Abraham of Clermont (St) R. Jun 15
d. *c*480. Born on the Euphrates river, during a persecution in Persia he went to Egypt but was abducted as a slave by brigands for five years. When he escaped he sailed to Gaul, where he became a hermit near Clermont-Ferrand, France. Lastly he became abbot-founder at the monastery of St Cyriac there. He is a patron against fever.

Abraham of Ephesus (St) B. Oct 28
C6th. Founder of the Abrahamite monastery by the Golden Gate at Constantinople, he became archbishop of Ephesus, Asia Minor, in ?542. Two of his homilies are extant.

Abraham Kidunaia (St) R. Mar 16
d. ?366. He fled from wealth and a prestigious marriage to become a hermit near Edessa, Syria, but was ordained for a town called Beth-Kiduna, which he completely converted to Christianity. St Ephrem was his friend and wrote his biography. (The stories concerning his niece Mary seem to be spurious.)

Abraham of Kratia (St) B. Dec 6
474–?558. Born in Emesa, Syria, when young he became superior of a monastery at Kratia in Bithynia, Asia Minor, and then bishop of the city. He fled twice, the second time to die in a monastery of the Holy Land.

Abraham the Poor (or Simple) (St) R. Oct 27
d. ?367. Born at Menuf, Egypt, he was a disciple of St Pachomius for twenty-three years before becoming a hermit in a cave for seventeen years. His veneration is popular in Egypt. He is not the Abraham who features in the writings of St John Cassian.

Abraham of Sandomir (Bl) *see* **Sadoc of Sandomir and Comps**

Abrahamite Monks (SS) MM. Jul 8
d. 830–840. The monastery of St Abraham of Ephesus in Constantinople was one of those which resisted the iconoclast heresy of the Imperial court, and Emperor Theophilus had a group of its monks executed in consequence.

Abran *see* **Gibrian**

Abrosimus (Abrosima) (St) M. Apr 22
d. 341. A Persian priest, he was stoned to death with a group of his people in the reign of Shah Shapur II.

Abrunculus (St) B. Apr 22
d. ?527. He was a bishop of Trier, Germany.

Absale (St) *see* **Lucius, Absale and Lorgius**

Abudimus (Abudemius) (St) M. Jul 15
C4th. From the Aegean island of Tenedos, Greece (now Bozcada in Turkey), he was martyred in the reign of Diocletian.

Abundantius (St) *see* **Abundius, Abundantius and Comps**

Abundantius (St) *see* **Leo, Donatus and Comps**

Abundius (St) *see* **Alexander, Abundius and Comps**

Abundius (St) *see* **Carpophorus and Abundius**

Abundius (St) *see* **Irenaeus and Abundius**

Abundius (St) *see* **Justus and Abundius**

Abundius, Abundantius and Comps (SS) MM. Sep 16
d. ?303. Their untrustworthy acta assert that Abundius was a priest who raised John, the son of a senator Marcian, from the dead. These three, together with Abundantius (a deacon) were then beheaded at Rignano near Florence, Italy, on the orders of Emperor Diocletian and their relics taken to Rome.

Abundius (Abundantius) of Como (St) B. Apr 2
d. ?469. A Greek, he became bishop of Como, Italy, in 449. As a capable theologian he was sent by Pope St Leo to Emperor Theodosius II on a mission which helped prepare for the Council of Chalcedon in 451. He is depicted with a deer, or in the act of resurrecting a dead child.

Abundius of Cordoba (St) M. P. Jul 11
d. 854. A parish priest of Ananelos near Cordoba when the Umayyad caliphs ruled Spain, he was involved with the 'martyr movement' and became embroiled in inter-religious polemic. He defended Christianity before the caliph's Islamic tribunal, was beheaded as a result and then fed to the dogs.

Abundius of Rome (St) L. Apr 14
d. ?564. Pope St Gregory the Great wrote about the humble and grace-filled life of this sacristan of St Peter's in Rome, and he is still veneratead there.

Acacius has many variants: Achatius, Achacius, Acathius, Achathius, Achates, Agatius or Agathius.

Acacius (St) *see* **Hirenarchus, Acacius and Comps**

Acacius (St) *see* **Patrick, Acacius and Comps**

Acacius Agathangelus (Thaumaturgus) (St) B. Mar 31
d. *p*251. According to his apparently genuine acta, he was a bishop of western Asia Minor who was arrested in the Decian persecution but who so impressed his judges with his defence of Christianity that he was set free. His veneration is very popular in the East.

Acacius of Amida (St) B. Apr 9
d. ?421. Bishop of Amida in Persia (now Diyarbakir in Turkish Kurdistan), he ransomed Persian prisoners of war from the proceeds of the sale of the sacred vessels of his cathedral. The Shah, Bahram V, was so impressed that he ceased to persecute his Christian subjects.

Acacius of Ararat and Comps Jun 22
The story of the Roman army officer Acacius and his ten thousand soldiers, allegedly martyred on Mount Ararat in Armenia, was popular in the Middle Ages. It is fiction and their cultus has been suppressed.

Acacius of Byzantium (St) M. May 8
d. ?303. A Cappadocian centurion in the Roman army in Thrace, he was tortured and beheaded at Byzantium (later Constantinople) in the reign of Diocletian. Emperor Constantine later built a basilica there in his honour.

Acacius of Miletus (St) M. Jul 28
d. *c*310. He was martyred at Miletus, Asia Minor, in the reign of Licinius.

Acca (St) B. R. Oct 20
*c*660–740. A Northumbrian disciple and companion of St Wilfrid on his journeys and appointed by him abbot of Hexham on the Tyne, England, he succeeded his master as bishop there in 709. Well educated for his time, he retired or was exiled in 732, but died at Hexham. St Bede dedicated several writings to him as a sign of friendship.

Accursius (St) *see* **Berard, Peter and Comps**

Acepsimas of Cyrrhus (St) R. Nov 3
C5th. A hermit, he lived in a cave near Cyrrhus near Antioch, Syria, for sixty years during the reign of Emperor Theodosius I.

Acepsimas of Hnaita and Comps (SS) B. MM. Apr 22
d. 376. An octogenarian bishop of western Persia, his genuine acta describe him being tortured and flogged to death in the reign of Shah Shapur II along with two priests named Aithalas and Joseph.

Acestes (St) M. Jul 2
C1st. The legend of the martyrdom of St Paul mentions Acestes and two other soldiers leading him to execution, who were converted by him and were themselves beheaded as a result.

Achacius or Achatius *see* **Acacius**

Achard *see* **Aichard**

Acharius (St) B. R. Nov 27
d. ?640. A monk at Luxeuil, France, under St Eustace and bishop of Noyon-Tournai from 621, he helped St Amandus of Elnone, oversaw the establishment of the diocese of Thérouanne near Calais and arranged that his friend St Omer was made the first bishop.

Ache and Acheul *see* **Acius and Aceolus**

Acheric and William (SS) RR(OSB). Nov 3
d. *p*860. These two hermits founded the monastery of Belmont in the Vosges mountains near Strasbourg, France.

Achilles (St) *see* **Felix, Fortunatus and Achilles**

Achilles (St) *see* **Nereus and Achilles**

Achilles and Amoes (SS) RR. Jan 17
C4th. The Byzantine liturgy call these two Egyptian desert fathers, mentioned by Rufinus, 'the flowers of the desert'.

Achilles of Alexandria (St) B. Nov 7
d. 313. Successor of St Peter the martyr as patriarch of Alexandria, Egypt, he ordained the heresiarch Arius. Nevertheless, he was praised by St Athanasius and despised by the schismatic Meletians for the orthodoxy of his doctrine.

Achilles Kiwanuka (St) M. Jun 3
d. 1886. He was a clerk in Buganda, Uganda, before becoming a courtier of King Mwanga, on whose orders he was martyred. *See* **Charles Lwanga and Comps**.

Achilles of Larissa (St) B. May 15
d. *c*330. Bishop of Larissa in Thessaly, Greece, he was apparently at the first ecumenical council of Nicaea. In 986 his city was sacked by Tsar Samuel of Bulgaria and his relics taken to Prespa.

Acindynus (St) *see* **Victor, Zoticus and Comps**

Acindynus, Pegasius, Aphthonius, Elpidephorus and Anempodistus (SS) MM. Nov 2
d. 345. Persian priests and clerics, they were martyred in the reign of Shah Shapur II.

Acisclus and Victoria (SS) MM. Nov 17
d. ?304. Siblings, they were martyred in Cordoba, Spain, probably in the reign of Emperor Diocletian. Their home became a church and they are now the principal patrons of the city.

Acisclus Piña Piazuelo (Bl) *see* **Hospitaller Martyrs of Spain**

Acius and Aceolus (SS) MM. May 1
d. ?303. A deacon and subdeacon respectively, they were martyred near Amiens, France, in the reign of Emperor Diocletian. Their veneration is popular there but their acta are unreliable.

Actinea and Graecina (SS) MM. Jun 16
C4th. They are martyrs associated with Volterra in Tuscany, Italy. The former was beheaded there in the reign of Emperor Diocletian.

Acutius *see* **Januarius**

Acyllinus (St) *see* **Scillitan Martyrs**

Ada (St) R. Dec 4
End C7th. She was an abbess of the nunnery of St Julien-des-Prés at Le Mans, France.

Adalar (Adalher) (St) M. R. Jun 5
d. 755. A monk, he was a companion and fellow-martyr of St Boniface at Dokkum, Netherlands. His shrine was at Erfurt, Germany, resulting in the tradition that he was the city's first bishop.

Adalard (Adalhard, Adelhard, Adelard, Alard) (St) R. Jan 2
?750–826. Grandson of Charles Martel, he was an adviser to Charlemagne. Entering the monastery of Corbie in Picardy, France, he became abbot in ?780 but was exiled from 814 to 821. He then founded New Corbie in Lower Saxony (now Corvey near Paderborn). He was an important figure in the Carolingian Renaissance, but opposed the universal imposition of the Benedictine rule for monasteries in the Empire being implemented by St Benedict of Aniane. Some of his writings survive.

Adalbald d'Ostrevant (St) M. L. Feb 4
d. 652. The son or grandson of St Gertrude the Elder, he was a Frankish courtier and married a Gascon lady called Rictrude. Some of her relatives disapproved and murdered him, and he was then venerated as a martyr. His wife and children (Maurontus, Clotsind, Eusebia and Adalsind) were also saints.

Adalbero of Augsburg (Bl)
B. R(OSB). Apr 28
d. 909. A nobleman and monk of Ellwangen near Ulm, Germany, he was an uncle of St Ulric. He restored the abbey of Lorsch and was made bishop of Augsburg in 887, becoming chief adviser of Arnulf of Bavaria, tutor to his son Louis and regent when the latter became Holy Roman Emperor as a child. He was well educated and a talented musician.

Adalbero of Liege (Bl) B. Jan 1
d. 1128. He was a bishop of Liege, Belgium, and founder of the abbey of St Giles there.

Adalbero II of Metz (Bl) B. Dec 14
d. 1005. Related to the dukes of Lorraine and educated at the Benedictine abbey of Gorze, he became bishop of Metz, France, in 984. He was zealous in spreading the new Cluniac monastic observance in his diocese. His cultus was not confirmed.

Adalbero of Würzburg (St) B. Oct 6
?1010–1090. A nobleman from Lambach near Linz, Austria, he was a student at Paris with St Altman of Passau. When he became bishop of Würzburg in 1045 he supported Pope St Gregory VII against Emperor Henry IV, which led to his exile to an abbey (which he had helped to found) in his native town. He died there and had his cultus approved in 1883.

Adalbert the Deacon (St) R. Jun 25
d. 705. A Northumbrian monk, he trained in Ireland under St Egbert of Iona and accompanied St Willibrord to Friesland in 690 as a deacon, the headquarters of his own mission later becoming the abbey of Egmond.

Adalbert of Magdeburg
(St) B. R(OSB). Jun 20
d. 981. Emperor Otto III chose this monk of Trier, Germany, to evangelize Kievan Rus, north of the Black Sea, but the embassy of 961 was a failure and he alone survived. He then became abbot of Weissenburg and first archbishop of Magdeburg in 968 with jurisdiction over the Sorb Slavs. He was a great patron of scholarship.

Adalbert (Vojtech) of Prague
(St) M. B. R(OSB). Apr 23
956–997. Born in Bohemia (Czech Republic) and educated by his namesake of Magdeburg, he became bishop of Prague in 983 but gave up and went to Rome to be a Benedictine. He tried and failed twice again, in the process preaching in Poland, Hungary and Kievan Rus, before being killed by the Old Prussians near Danzig (now Gdansk in Poland). He is called the apostle of the Catholic Slavs.

Adaldag (St) B. Apr 28
*c*900–988. He was a Saxon canon of Hildesheim, Germany, before becoming bishop of Bremen-Hamburg in 937. He was an effective missionary, and under him Denmark was arranged into four dioceses.

Adalgar (St) B. R(OSB). May 15
d. 909. He was a monk at Corvey before becoming bishop of Bremen-Hamburg (based at Bremen, Germany) in 889.

Adalgis (Algis) (St) R. Jun 2
d. ?686. An Irish monk, disciple of St Fursey, he became a missionary in Picardy, France. The village of St Algis is the site of his monastery.

Adalgis of Novara (St) B. Oct 7
d. *c*850. Allegedly from the Lombard royal family, he was an influential bishop of Novara near Milan, Italy, for twenty years.

Adalgott I (St) R(OSB). Oct 26
d. 1031. A monk of Einsiedeln, Switzerland, he became abbot of Disentis in 1016 and was involved in monastic and liturgical reform.

Adalgott II (St) B. R(OSB). Oct 3
d. 1165. A monk under St Bernard at Clairvaux, France, he became abbot of Disentis and bishop of Chur, Switzerland, in 1150. An excellent pastor, he founded a hospital for poor people.

Adalsind (St) R. Dec 25
d. ?715. A daughter of St Adalbald d'Ostrevent, she was a nun at Hamay-les-Marchiennes near Arras, France, where her sister St Eusebia was abbess.

Adam of Caithness (St) M. B. Sep 15
d. 1222. He was the Cistercian abbot of Melrose, Scotland, when he was made bishop of Caithness in 1213. His diocese was a long way from the centre of royal authority in Scotland, and when he tried to enforce laws previously neglected (including the payment of church tithes) he was

burned in his palace in a riot. His cultus was not confirmed.

Adam of Ebrach (Bl) R(OCist). Feb 25
d.1161. From near Cologne, he was a monk at Morimond, France, before becoming a Cistercian at Foligny and then abbot of Marmoutier. He became abbot-founder of Ebrach near Mannheim, Germany, in 1127 and later founded several daughter-abbeys. He was acquainted with St Hildegard of Bingen. His cultus has not been confirmed.

Adam of Fermo (St) R(OSB). May 16
d. *p*1212. A hermit, he became abbot of San Sabino on Monte Vissiano near Fermo, Italy, and his shrine is in that city's cathedral.

Adamnan of Coldingham (St) R. Jan 31
d. ?680. An Irish pilgrim, he became a monk at Coldingham in Scotland (near Berwick) under the abbess St Ebba, and his cultus was confirmed in 1898 for St Andrew's and Edinburgh.

Adamnan (Adam, Aunan, Eunan) of Iona (St) R. Sep 23
?625–704. From Co. Donegal, Ireland, he became abbot of Iona, Scotland, in 679 and supported the Roman observance of Easter against the Celtic one (without converting his monastery). He wrote a biography of St Columba, and was an influential lawgiver in Ireland.

Adauctus (St) M. Feb 7
d. 304. An Italian minister of finance to Emperor Diocletian at the latter's capital at Nicomedia, Asia Minor, he was executed after his religion was discovered. His fate was shared by the entire Phrygian town of Antandro which was burnt, and the two incidents are connected by Rufinus.

Adauctus (St) *see* **Felix and Adauctus**

Adauctus and Callisthene (SS) Oct 4
d. ?312. Father and daughter in Ephesus, Asia Minor. He was martyred in the reign of Emperor Maximinus Daza. She survived to live a life of charity.

Addai and Mari (SS) BB. Aug 5
C2nd. The apostles of Persia. The former was probably a missionary bishop of Edessa, Syria (now Urfa, Turkey). The latter has nothing reliable known about him, but is alleged to have founded the first church in the Persian Empire near Ctesiphon. The Chaldean eucharistic liturgy is named after them.

Adalgrin (Adegrin) (St) R(OSB). Jun 4
d. 939. A knight, he became a monk with St Odo at Baume-les-Messieurs in Burgundy, France, and was then a hermit nearby.

Adela of Blois (St) L. Feb 24
?1062–1137. Youngest daughter of William I of England, she married Stephen of Blois, France, became involved in French politics and (especially when widowed) endowed many monasteries and churches.

Adela of Messines (St) R(OSB). Sep 8
d. 1071. The widow of a count of Flanders, she became a nun at Messines near Ypres, Belgium, in 1067.

Adela of Pfalzel (St) R. Dec 24
?675–?734. Allegedly daughter of King Dagobert II of the Franks, when widowed she founded the nunnery of Pfalzel near Trier, Germany, and was its first abbess. Her cultus is unconfirmed.

Adelaide, Empress (St) L. Dec 16
*c*930–999. A daughter of the king of Burgundy and widow of Lothair II of Italy, she was rescued from persecution and married by Emperor Otto I. Again widowed (in 973), she was harassed by her son but became regent of the Holy Roman Empire when old before retiring to a nunnery. She was friendly with the abbots of Cluny, who supported her.

Adelaide (Aleydis) of Skarenbeke (St) R(OCist). Jun 15
d. 1250. A young Cistercian nun of La Cambre at Brussels, Belgium, she became blind, leprous and paralyzed and had to go into isolation from her community. She offered up her sufferings for souls in Purgatory and had visions of their being set free as a result. Her biography was written by a contemporary, and her cultus was confirmed in 1907.

Adelaide of Vilich (St) R(OSB). Feb 5
d. ?1015. Her father, the count of Gelder, founded the nunneries of Vilich near Bonn and Our Lady of the Capitol at Cologne, Germany, and she was abbess of each in turn. Her cultus was confirmed for Cologne in 1966.

Adelbert *see* **Adalbert**

Adelelm (Alleaume, Elesmes, Lesmes) of Burgos (St) R(OSB). Jan 30
d. 1097. Born near Poitiers, France, he became a soldier but met St Robert of Chaise-Dieu on returning from a pilgrimage to Rome and joined

his monastery. In 1079 he was sent to Burgos, Spain, and founded the monastery of St John outside the city walls with the help of the king and queen of Castile. A church dedicated to him stands on the site.

Adelhelm of Engelberg (Bl) R(OSB). Feb 25
d. 1131. A monk of Sankt-Blasien in the Black Forest, Germany, he was the founder of the abbey of Engelberg, Switzerland.

Adelhelm of Etival (St) R. Apr 27
d.1152. A Flemish disciple of St Bernard of Tiron, he founded the abbey of Etival-en-Charnie in the Jura, France.

Adelgott *see* **Adalgott**

Adelin *see* **Hadelin**

Adelina (St) R(OSB). Oct 20
d. 1125. A grand-daughter of King William I of England and sister of Bl Vitalis of Savigny, she became abbess of a nunnery in Normandy, France, which her brother had founded, later called Les Dames Blanches de Mortain.

Adelind (Bl) R(OSB). Aug 28
d. *c*930. As a widow she founded the nunnery of Buchau on the Federsee in Württemberg, Germany, later becoming a nun there herself.

Adeloga (Hadeloga) (St) R. Feb 2
d. ?745. A Frankish princess, she was the foundress and first abbess of the nunnery of Kitzingen in Bavaria, Germany. According to her unreliable C12th biography, she was the daughter of Charles Martel.

Adelphus of Metz (St) B. Aug 29
C5th. He has an ancient cultus at Metz, France, as a bishop there, but nothing is known of his life.

Adelphus of Remiremont (St) R. Sep 11
d. *c*670. A grandson of St Romaricus and his successor in 653 as abbot of Remiremont in the Vosges, France, he died at the abbey of Luxeuil.

Adeltrud *see* **Aldetrud**

Adeodatus *see* **Deusdedit**

Aderald (St) S. Oct 20
d. 1004. As archdeacon of Troyes, France, he led a pilgrimage to the Holy Land and then founded the abbey of the Holy Sepulchre at Samblières to house the relics that he had collected.

Adheritus (Abderitus, Adery) (St) B. Sep 27
C2nd. A Greek, he succeeded St Apollinaris as bishop of Ravenna, Italy. His shrine has been in the basilica of St Apollinaris in Classe there since the early Middle Ages.

Adilia *see* **Adela**

Adjutor (Ayutre) (St) R. Apr 30
d. 1131. The Norman lord of Vernon-sur-Seine, France, he went on the First Crusade, returned and became a monk at Tiron. Later he was a hermit near the monastery.

Adjutor (St) *see* **Priscus II of Capua and Comps**

Adjutor (St) *see* **Victurus, Victor and Comps**

Adjutus *see* **Avitus**

Adjutus (St) *see* **Berard and Comps**

Ado of Jouarre (St) R. Jan 31
d. *c*650. A disciple of St Columban, he was the founder of the double monastery of monks and nuns at Jouarre east of Paris, France. This was under the rule of an abbess, and was a model for many such monasteries in the early Middle Ages. The Rules of SS Benedict and Columban were combined in its customary.

Ado of Vienne (St) B. R(OSB). Dec 16
*c*800–875. A Burgundian monk of Ferrières, he became headmaster of the abbey school of Prüm near Trier, Germany, but the jealousy of some monks drove him away to Rome. He eventually became bishop of Vienne in 859, and did well. He compiled a martyrology which was a remote ancestor of the old Roman Martyrology, but seems unfortunately to have resorted to deliberate and unscrupulous forgery and invention to do so. The errors thus perpetrated have had a long history.

Adolf and John (SS) MM. Sep 27
d. *c*850. They were two brothers from Seville, Spain, who had a Muslim father and a Christian mother. They were martyred in Cordoba for refusing to accept Islam.

Adolf Kolping (Bl) P. Dec 4
1813–1865. Born near Cologne, Germany, he was initially a shoemaker working twelve hours a day but managed to study for the priesthood, being ordained in 1845. He was parish priest at the industrial town of Elberfeld, then became a

cathedral canon in 1849 and founded a Catholic association of apprentices, the 'Kolping Family'. This was a 'people's academy in the people's style', offering opportunities for study in a family environment and aiming at the intellectual and spiritual improvement of the working class. There were 26,000 members in Europe and America at his death. He was beatified in 1991.

Adolf Mukasa Ludigo (St) M. Jun 3
1886. He was originally a herdsman, then a martyr of Buganda, Uganda. *See* **Charles Lwanga and Comps**.

Adolf of Osnabrück (St)
B. R(OCist). Feb 11
?1185–1224. A nobleman of Westphalia, Germany, he resigned a canonry at Cologne to become a Cistercian at Camp. He became bishop of Osnabrück in 1216, and was known as 'the almoner of the poor' by his charity. Adolf Hitler (baptized a Catholic) was named after him.

Adria (St) *see* **Eusebius, Marcellus and Comps**

Adrian (St) *see* **Hermes, Adrian and Comps**

Adrian III, Pope (St) Jul 8
d. 885. He became pope in 884 and immediately set out for the diet of Worms, intending to seek aid from the Germans against the Muslims. He died on the way near Modena, Italy, and was buried at the abbey of Nonantola near Modena. His cultus was confirmed in 1892 for Nonantola.

Adrian and Eubulus
(SS) MM. Mar 5 and 7
d. 308. They went to visit the Christians in Caesarea in the Holy Land, were seized and then martyred two days apart (Adrian first).

Adrian of Canterbury (St) R. Jan 9
d. 710. An African abbot of Nerida near Naples, Italy, he was asked by Pope Vitalian to become archbishop of Canterbury but declined and nominated St Theodore of Tarsus instead. The pope sent him to England anyway, to help St Theodore and (according to St Bede) to keep an eye on him. He became abbot of SS Peter and Paul (later renamed after St Augustine) at Canterbury, established a famous school there and became known for his scholarship. His body was discovered in 1091 and his cultus established afterwards.

Adrian Fortescue (Bl) M. Jul 9
1476–1539. Born at Ponsbourne in Herts, England, he was a cousin of Anne Boleyn and was married to Anne Stonor. A Knight of St John, he refused the oath of supremacy to King Henry VIII and was beheaded on Tower Hill, London. He was beatified in 1895. *See* **England (Martyrs of)**.

Adrian van Hilvarenbeek (St) *see* **Gorinchem (Martyrs of)**

Adrian of May and Comps
(SS) MM. RR. Mar 4
d. ?875. A missionary bishop (possibly Irish), he was killed together with some English monks by the Danes on the Isle of May in the Firth of Forth, Scotland. Their connection with Hungary is mythical.

Adrian of Nicomedia (St) M. Sep 8
d. ?304. According to his legend he was a pagan army officer at the court of Emperor Diocletian at Nicomedia, Asia Minor, who helped Christian prisoners and was himself imprisoned. His work was taken up by his wife, St Natalia. All the prisoners being killed, she took his relics to Argyropolis from where others took them to Rome. He is a patron of butchers and soldiers, but his cultus was confined to local calendars in 1969.

Adrian of Wintershoven (St) M. R. Mar 19
d. ?668. A disciple of St Landoald, he was killed by robbers while begging for his community near Maastricht, Netherlands, and was subsequently locally venerated as a martyr.

Adrio, Victor and Basilla
(SS) MM. May 17
? They were martyred at Alexandria, Egypt, either by pagans or by Arians.

Adulf (St) *see* **Botolph and Adulf**

Adventor (St) *see* **Octavius, Solutor and Adventor**

Ae-; this prefix is often rendered **A-** or **E-**

Aedan *see* **Aidan**

Aedesius (St) M. Apr 8
d. ?306. A Lycian and brother of St Amphianus, he was at Alexandria, Egypt, studying philosophy in the reign of Galerius and rebuked a judge who was forcing consecrated virgins into prostitution. As a result he was tortured and drowned in the sea.

Aedh (Aod, Aedsind, Aidus) MacBricc (St) B. R. Nov 10
d. ?588. A disciple of St Illadan at Rathlihen in Offaly, Ireland, he founded several churches in his native Meath and was bishop there.

Aedh, Aedhan
Eighteen other Irish saints named Aedh and twenty named Aedhan are listed, but the historical evidence is hopelessly confused.

Aegidius *see* **Giles**

Aelgifu *see* **Elgiva**

Aelphege *see* **Elphege**

Aelred (St) R(OCist). Jan 12
1109–1167. A priest's son from Hexham in Northumberland, England, he became master of the palace of King David of Scotland before joining the Cistercians at Rievaulx, Yorks, in 1133. He became abbot of Revesby and then of Rievaulx in 1147, and combined personal austerity with gentleness in office. He has left several ascetical writings.

Aengus (Oengus, Oengoba) the Culdee (St) B. R. Mar 11
d. *c*830. The composer of a well-known metrical hymn to the saints called the Felire ('Festilogium'), he was alleged to have been a monk at Clonenagh in Co. Laois, Ireland, and became abbot-bishop there. Although famous in his day, there is no early biography of him nor any evidence of contemporary liturgical veneration.

Aeonius of Arles (St) B. Aug 18
d. *c*500. He became bishop of Arles, France, in ?494, and encouraged monasticism. He was succeeded by his friend St Caesarius.

Aeschilius *see* **Eskill**

Aethelgifu *see* **Ethelgiva** or **Elgiva**

Aethelhard *see* **Ethelhard**

Aetherius *see* **Etherius**

Aetius (St) *see* **Forty Martyrs of Sebaste**

Afan (St) B. Nov 16
C6th. Patron of Llanafan, Powys, Wales, he was alleged to have been a bishop of the Cunedda family.

Affrosa *see* **Daffrosa**

Afra of Augsburg (St) M. Aug 5
d. ?304. A martyr of Augsburg, Germany, with an ancient cultus, she probably died in the reign of Diocletian but the legend describing her as a Cypriot prostitute is worthless. A great abbey in the city was dedicated to her.

Afra of Brescia (St) V. May 24
? A martyr of Brescia, Italy, she is connected by an unreliable legend with SS Faustina and Jovita.

Africa (Martyrs of)
Under the Roman Empire, 'Africa' meant what is now the Maghreb. There were many martyrs there as it was a stronghold of Latin Christianity, and the following were listed in the old Roman Martyrology:

Apr 9
? 'Martyrs of Massyla' were praised by St Augustine and by Prudentius.

Oct 16
? A group of 220 were killed in unrecorded circumstances.

Oct 30
? A group of between 100 and 200 were killed in an early persecution.

Jan 6
d. *c*210. A group of both sexes was burnt in the reign of Septimus Severus.

Feb 11
d. ?303. The 'Guardians of the Holy Scriptures', who died rather than hand the sacred texts over to the authorities when this was required in the reign of Diocletian. (The willingness of others to obey led to the Donatist schism.)

Apr 5
d. 459. A large group was killed in the reign of King Genseric, an Arian Vandal. They were celebrating the Easter Mass, and the lector had his throat pierced by an arrow while intoning the 'Alleluia'.

Dec 16.
d. 482. A large group of women was killed in the reign of King Hunneric, an Arian Vandal.

Africanus (St) *see* **Terence, Africanus, Pompeius and Comps**

Africus (St) B? Nov 16
C7th. He is locally venerated in the Comminges near Toulouse, France. The tradition alleges him to have been a bishop zealous for orthodoxy, but there is no documentary evidence for this.

Agabius (St) B. Aug 4
d. *c*250. He is alleged to have been an early bishop of Verona, Italy, but his existence is uncertain.

Agabus (St) L. Feb 13
C1st. The church prophet mentioned in the Acts of the Apostles (9:28; 21:10–12), he is often depicted as a Carmelite because of a worthless medieval legend.

Agamund (St) *see* **Theodore of Crowland and Comps**

Aganus (St) R(OSB). Feb 16.
*c*1050–1100. He was an abbot of the monastery of St Gabriel at Airola in Campania, Italy.

Agape (St) *see* **Donatus, Sabinus and Agape**

Agape *see* **Faith, Hope and Charity**

Agape (St) *see* **Indes, Domna and Comps**

Agape, Chionia and Irene (SS) MM. Apr 3
d. ?304. Their legend states that they were three unmarried sisters who were in a group of martyrs burnt at Thessalonika, Greece, in the reign of Diocletian, except for Irene who was taken from the group and abused in a brothel for two days before being killed.

Agape of Terni (St) V. Feb 15
d. ?273. The unreliable legend of St Valentine of Terni alleges that he founded a community of virgins and that this martyr was one of them.

Agapitus (St) *see* **Bassus, Dionysius and Comps**

Agapitus (St) *see* **Eustace of Rome and Comps**

Agapitus (St) *see* **Sixtus II, Pope and Comps**

Agapitus I, Pope (St) Apr 22
d. 536. Born in Rome and archdeacon there, he was elected pope in May 535 and had to go on an embassy to Emperor Justinian in order to persuade him not to re-conquer Italy from the Ostrogoths. While in Constantinople he deposed Patriarch Anthimus for monophysitism and then died. His body was returned to Rome. Some of his letters survive.

Agapitus of Palestrina (St) M. Aug 18
d. ?274. He was allegedly a teenager aged fifteen who was martyred at Palestrina near Rome. He has an ancient cultus and is the city's patron, but his acta are unreliable.

Agapitus of Ravenna (St) B. Mar 16
C4th. He was an early bishop of Ravenna, Italy.

Agapitus of Synnada (St) B. Mar 24
C3rd. He was a bishop in Phrygia, Asia Minor.

Agapius (St) *see* **Aphrodisius, Caralippus and Comps**

Agapius (St) *see* **Bassa and Sons**

Agapius (St) *see* **Carterius and Comps**

Agapius (St) *see* **Timolaus, Dionysius and Comps**

Agapius of Caesarea (St) M. Nov 20
d. ?306. From Caesarea in the Holy Land, he had been imprisoned three times as a Christian and the fourth time was chained to a murderer to be thrown to the wild animals in the amphitheatre. His companion was pardoned but he refused to renounce his faith and was mauled by a bear. The next day he was weighted with stones and thrown into the sea.

Agapius of Cirta and Comps (SS) MM. Apr 29
d. ?259. The Spanish priests (or bishops) Agapius and Secundinus were exiled to Cirta in Numidia (now Algeria) in the reign of Valerian and were martyred there together with the virgins Tertulla and Antonia and a woman with her twins. (The old Roman Martyrology includes one Emilian, but he is not mentioned in the extant acta).

Agapius of Novara (St) B. Sep 10
d. 447. He succeeded St Gaudentius as bishop of Novara in Piedmont, Italy, in 417.

Agatha (St) M. Feb 5
? One of the most famous Latin virgin martyrs (also venerated in the East), she was killed at Catania, Sicily. Her unreliable legend states that her breasts were amputated as part of her martyrdom, and she is thus depicted with a knife or shears and with a plate holding her breasts. Her name is in the Roman Canon of the Mass, and she is the patroness of bell-founders, wet-nurses (of both because of her breasts) and of jewellers.

Agatha of Carinthia (St) L. Feb 5
d. 1024. Wife of Paul, count of Carinthia, she was devoted to her household duties and was patient in the face of her jealous husband's brutal abuse until she managed to convert him. She is venerated in Carinthia, Austria.

Agatha Jeon, Agatha Kim and **Agatha**

St Agatha, Feb 5

Kwon (St) *see* **Korea (Martyrs of)**
Agatha Lee (SS) There were four **Korean martyrs** (q.v.) with this name.

Agatha Lin (Zhao) (St) M. L. Jan 28
1817–1858. From Qinglong in Guizhou, China, when young she took a private vow of virginity and became a headmistress. She was beheaded with SS Jerome Lu (Tingmei) and Laurence Wang (Bing). *See* **China (Martyrs of)**.

Agatha Phutta (Bl) *see* **Thailand (Martyrs of)**

Agatha of Wimborne (St) R. Dec 12
d. *c*790. A nun of Wimborne in Dorset, England, she accompanied St Lioba to help St Boniface in his mission among the Germans.

Agathangelus and Cassian
(BB) MM. RR(OFM Cap). Aug 7
d. 1638. Two French Capuchins (the former from Vendôme, the latter from Nantes), they went to Egypt in the 1630s to help in ecumenical work with the Coptic Church. Failing in this because of the public immorality of some local Catholics, they went to Ethiopia disguised as Coptic monks. Their arrival was reported to the Negus (Emperor) Fasilidas by a German Protestant and they were stoned to death at Gondar after a three-day public ordeal during which they were offered their freedom if they accepted the doctrines of the native Ethiopian church. They were beatified in 1906.
Agathangelus of Ancyra (St) M. Jan 23
d. ?309. He was converted and baptized by St Clement of Ancyra when the latter was a prisoner at Rome, and accompanied him when he was allowed to go home. They were martyred at Ancyra, Asia Minor, but their acta are spurious.

Agathius *see* **Acacius**

Agatho (St) M. Dec 7
d. 250. He is apparently identical to St Besas, one of the companions of SS **Julian and Eunus** (q.v.).

Agatho (St) R. Oct 21
C4th. An Egyptian desert father, he is quoted in the *Apophthegmata Patrum.*

Agatho (St) *see* **Cyrion, Bassian and Comps**

Agatho, Pope (St) R? Jan 10
*c*577–681. Born in Palermo in Sicily, he may have been a Latin or Byzantine-rite monk before becoming pope in 678. His legates presided over the sixth ecumenical council at Constantinople against monothelitism in 680. He also restored St Wilfrid to the bishopric of York after the latter's diocese had been divided.

Agatho and Triphina (SS) MM. Jul 5
d. ?306. Nothing is known about these Sicilian martyrs, not even the sex of the latter-named.

Agathoclia (Agatholica) (St) M. Sep 17.
? The old Roman Martyrology describes her as the servant of a pagan woman who ill-treated her in order to force her to apostatize. She was eventually condemned and burnt. Possibly a Greek, she is the patron of Mequinenza in Aragón and has thus been described as a Spaniard.

Agathodorus (St) *see* **Basil, Ephrem and Comps**

Agathodorus (St) *see* **Carpus of Thyatira and Comps**

Agathonica (St) *see* **Bassa, Paula and Agathonica**

Agathonica (St) *see* **Carpus of Thyatira and Comps**

Agathonicus, Zoticus and Comps (SS) MM. Aug 22
C4th? The former was a patrician who was

martyred near Byzantium (later Constantinople) in the reign of Maximian Herculeus, while the latter were a philosopher and some of his disciples martyred at about the same time. A basilica was built in their honour at Constantinople.

Agathopodes (St) *see* **Philo and Agathopodes**

Agathopodes and Theodolus (SS) MM. Apr 4
d. 303. The former was a deacon and the latter a young lector of the church at Thessalonika, Greece. They were martyred in the reign of Emperor Maximian Herculeus for refusing to hand over the sacred texts.

Agathopus (St) *see* **Theodolus, Saturninus and Comps**

Ageranus (Ayran, Ayrman) and Comps (SS) MM. RR(OSB). May 21
d. 888. A monk of Bèze in the Côte d'Or, France, he was left behind with six others (Genesius, Bernard, Sifiard and Rodron, monks; Adalaric, a boy and Ansuinus, a priest) when his community fled on the invasion of Burgundy by the Norsemen in 886–889. They were massacred.

Agericus (Aguy, Airy) of Tours (St) R. Apr 11
d. *c*680. A disciple of St Eligius, he became abbot of the monastery of St Martin at Tours, France.

Agericus (Aguy, Airy) of Verdun (St) B. Dec 1
*c*521–591. Successor of St Desiderius as bishop of Verdun in 554, he was highly regarded by SS Gregory of Tours and Venantius Fortunatus, his contemporaries. He was buried in his own home, which became a church and then the Benedictine abbey of St Airy.

Aggaeus *see* **Haggai**

Agia (Aia, Austregildis, Aye) of Mons (St) R. Apr 18
d. ?714. She was the wife of St Hidulf, count of Hainault, Belgium. The couple decided to separate and become consecrated religious, so she entered a nunnery at Mons while he entered the abbey of Lobbes. She is venerated by the Beguines of Belgium.

Agia (Aia, Aye) of Orléans (St) L. Sep 1
C6th. From Orléans, France, she was the mother of St Lupus of Sens.

Agil (Aile, Ail, Aisle, Ayeul, Ely) (St) R. Aug 30
*c*580–650. A Burgundian nobleman, he became a monk at Luxeuil under St Columban and his successor St Eustace and accompanied the latter on a missionary journey to Bavaria in ?617. He then became the first abbot of Rebais near Paris, France.

Agilbert (Aglibert) (St) B. R. Oct 11
d. ?685. A Frankish monk and a biblical scholar who studied in Ireland, he went as a missionary to Wessex, England, and became bishop of Dorchester-on-Thames. The king of Wessex objected to his being unable to speak Old English and divided his diocese, so he left. He supported St Wilfrid at the synod of Whitby over the question of Roman versus Celtic church customs, then returned to France where he became bishop of Paris in 668. He was buried at the monastery of Jouarre.

Agilberta (Aguilberta, Gilberta) (St) R. Aug 10
d. *c*680. Second abbess of the Frankish monastery of Jouarre near Paris, France, from 660, she was related to SS Ado (the founder), Ebregisil of Meaux and Agilbert of Paris.

Agileus (St) M. Oct 15
d. *c*300. A martyr at Carthage in Roman Africa, he was highly venerated by the African and Roman churches. His relics were taken to Rome, and St Augustine preached an extant sermon in his honour.

Agilulf (St) B. Jul 9
d. *c*750. He became archbishop of Cologne in ?746. In the C11th he was confused with a monk martyred by barbarians and was hence listed as a martyr, and was also alleged to have been abbot of Stavelot-Malmédy, Belgium. Both of these assertions are false.

Aglibert (St) *see* **Agoard, Aglibert and Comps**

Agnellus of Naples (St) R. Dec 14
d. ?596. A hermit and then abbot of San Gaudioso near Naples, Italy, he is one of the patron saints of that city. The tradition is that he used to raise sieges by displaying a banner of the cross.

Agnellus of Pisa (Bl) R(OFM). Mar 13
1194–1235. From Pisa, Italy, he was received as a Franciscan by St Francis and sent by him firstly to found a house in Paris and then to be the first provincial superior in England.

Arriving at Dover in 1224, he founded a friary at Canterbury and also at Oxford, where he established a famous school and where he died. His cultus was confirmed in 1892 for Pisa.

Agnes (St) V. Jan 21
d. ?305. A Roman girl aged about twelve, she was martyred and buried on the Via Nomentana in Rome, where a basilica was built for her in the reign of Constantine. She is mentioned in the Roman canon of the Mass, was praised by Prudentius and SS Ambrose and Damasus and as a virgin martyr is a special guardian of chastity. This despite her age, as she had reached the age of consent for girls in the Roman Empire. Her acta are untrustworthy. Her attribute is a lamb (a pun on her name).

Agnes of Assisi (St) R(OFM). Nov 16
1197–1253. She was the younger sister of St Clare, whom she followed to the Benedictine convent of Panso near Assisi, Italy, when aged sixteen and thence to San Damiano. She was the first Poor Clare abbess of Monticelli at Florence, opened convents at Padua, Venice and Mantua and died at San Damiano three months after St Clare.

Agnes of Bagno (Bl) R(OSB Cam) Sep 4
d. ?1105. She was a Camaldolese nun at Santa Lucia near Bagno di Roma in Tuscany, Italy, and has her shrine at Pereto. Her cultus was confirmed in 1823.

Agnes of Bavaria (Bl) L. Nov 11
1525–1532. Daughter of Duke Ludwig IV of Bavaria, Germany, she was being educated at the Poor Clare convent of St James in Munich when she died, aged seven.

Agnes de Beniganim *see* **Josephine-Mary-of-St-Agnes Albiñana**

Agnes of Bohemia (St) R(OFM). Mar 2
1200–1282. Born at Prague, Czech Republic, she was the daughter of the king of Bohemia and was educated by the Cistercian nuns of Trzebnica, Poland. She refused to marry and, with the help of the pope, she founded and entered a Poor Clare convent at Prague which was staffed by five nuns sent by St Clare from Assisi. She remained there for the rest of her life, forty-six years, and was canonized in 1989.

Agnes Cao (Guiying) (St) M. L. Jan 25
1821–1856. From a Catholic family of Guizhou, China, she was orphaned when young, settled at Xingyi and was briefly married. In her widowhood she was a disciple of St Augustus Chapdelaine and helped the missionaries in Guangxi, China, as a catechist. She was martyred at Yaoshan by being stuffed into a cage which only permitted her to stand and being left to die. *See* **China (Martyrs of)**.

Agnes Kim (St) *see* **Korea (Martyrs of)**

Agnes-of-Jesus de Langeac
(Bl) R(OP). Oct 19
1602–1634. Born in Puy-en-Velay, France, when aged seven she set out to be a 'slave of the Holy Virgin' and joined the Dominicanesses at Langeac in 1623. She was made prioress, but was deposed through calumny. She was mystically involved in prayer for Fr Olier, Abbot of Pébrac (who opened the first seminaries in France) and was beatified in 1994.

Agnes Phila (Bl) *see* **Thailand (Martyrs of)**

Agnes of Poitiers (St) R. May 13
d. ?588. She was the adopted daughter of Queen St Radegund, and was made abbess of Holy Cross at Poitiers, France. St Caesarius of Arles provided her with a rule for her monastery, but she had to be deposed in 589 after a revolt among the nuns. She was a friend of St Venantius Fortunatus.

Agnes-of-St-Louis de Romillon (Bl) *see* **Orange (Martyrs of)**

Agnes Segni of Montepulciano
(St) R(OP). Apr 20
?1268–1317. From Tuscany, Italy, when aged nine she entered a nunnery at Montepulciano and went on to be founding superior of a Dominican nunnery in the city in 1306. She was a famous mystic, and is the patron of the city.

Agnes Takea (Bl) M. L. Sep 10
d. 1626. She was a Japanese, the wife of Bl Cosmas Takea, and was beheaded at Nagasaki in the 'Great Martyrdom' with BB Charles Spinola and Comps. *See* **Japan (Martyrs of)**.

Agnes (Le Thi) Thanh (St) M. Jul 12
d. 1841. Born of Christian parents at Bai-den, Vietnam, she was arrested for her faith and died in prison at Namdinh. *See* **Vietnam (Martyrs of)**.

Agnes of Venosa (Bl) R(OSB). Sep 4
d. ?1144. The story is that she was an erotic dancer sent by enemies of St William of Montevergine in order to compromise him. She repented and ended up as abbess of the Monteverginian nuns at Venosa, Italy.

Agoard, Aglibert and Comps (SS) MM. Jun 24
? The old Roman Martyrology lists them as having being martyred at Créteil near Paris, France, with a large number of others. Their date is unknown.

Agobard (St) B. Jun 6
?769–840. A Spanish refugee from the Arab invaders, he was a priest at Lyons, France, before becoming archbishop in 813. He was famous as a churchman, a politician and a liturgical theologian and has left many writings.

Agofred (St) R. Jun 21
d. 738. A monk of La Croix-St-Leuffroi near Evreux in Normandy, France, he was a brother of St Leutfrid.

Agrecius (Agricius) (St) B. Jan 19
d. ?335. Predecessor of St Maximinus as bishop of Trier, Germany, he was at the Council of Arles in 314. A biography of the C11th claimed that he obtained the Holy Coat (a garment venerated at Trier as having been worn by Christ) from St Helen in Jerusalem.

Agricola (St) M. Dec 3
? He was a martyr in Pannonia (modern Hungary) who is listed in the ancient martyrologies, but with no biographical details.

Agricola (St) *see* **Valentine, Concordius and Comps**

Agricola (St) *see* **Vitalis and Agricola**

Agricola of Avignon (St) B. Sep 2
*c*630–700. Patron of Avignon, France, since 1647, he was allegedly a monk at Lérins for sixteen years before becoming the coadjutor and successor of his father, St Magnus, as bishop of Avignon in 660. He founded a daughter house of Lérins in the city as well as a nunnery, and allegedly drove away a flock of storks by his blessing. His story is only documented from the C15th.

Agricola (Arègle, Agrèle) of Chalon-sur-Saône (St) B. Mar 17
d. 580. A bishop of Chalon-sur-Saône, France, he was praised by St Gregory of Tours for the austerity of his life.

Agricola of Nevers (St) B. Feb 26
d. ?594. He was bishop of Nevers, France, from *c*570.

Agricola of Tongres (St) B. Feb 5
d. 420. A C10th catalogue, transcribed from ancient diptychs, lists him as eleventh bishop of Tongres, France.

Agrippina (St) V. Jun 23
d. ?262. She was a Roman virgin martyr, perhaps of the reign of Valerian. There are competing shrines to her in Mineo, Sicily, and in Constantinople.

Agrippinus of Alexandria (St) B. Jan 30
d. *c*180. He was the ninth bishop of Alexandria, Egypt, after St Mark, according to Eusebius.

Agrippinus of Autun (St) B. Jul 9
d. 538. A bishop of Autun, France, he ordained St Germanus of Paris.

Agrippinus of Como (St) B. Jun 17
d. 615. He was a bishop of Como, Italy. His cultus is unconfirmed.

Agrippinus (Arpinus) of Naples (St) B. Nov 9
C2nd or C3rd. A bishop of Naples with an ancient cultus, his relics are under the cathedral's high altar together with those of SS Eutychius and Acutius (alleged companions of St Januarius).

Agritius *see* **Agrecius**

Aguy *see* **Agericus** or **Agrecius**

Aia *see* **Agia**

Aibert (Aybert) (St) R(OSB). Apr 7
*c*1060–1140. Born near Tournai, Belgium, he became a monk at St Crispin's Abbey there, was cellarer and provost for 23 years and then became a hermit. He celebrated two masses daily by choice, one for the living and one for the dead.

Aichard (Achard) of Clairvaux (Bl) R(OCist). Sep 15
d. *c*1170. He was professed as a monk at Clairvaux, France, by St Bernard, who sent him to help with several foundations and then made him novice-master at Clairvaux. Two of his writings survive in manuscript.

Aichard (Achard) of Jumièges (St) R. Sep 15
d. ?687. Born at Poitiers, France, the son of a Merovingian courtier, when young he became a monk at Ansion in Poitou. After 39 years

St Aidan of Lindisfarne, Aug 31

there he became abbot at Quinçay and then at Jumièges, where he succeeded St Philibert. His community there allegedly numbered almost a thousand.

Aidan (Maedoc) of Fearns
(St) B. R. Jan 31
d. 626. From Connaught, Ireland, he became a monk in his youth under St David in Wales before founding a monastery at Fearns in Co. Wexford and becoming its first superior and bishop. His biography is semi-legendary. He is the principal patron of the diocese of Fearns.

Aidan of Lindisfarne (St) B. R. Aug 31
d. 651. An Irish monk of Iona, Scotland, he was sent to evangelize Northumbria, England, in 635 at the request of its king, St Oswald. He founded a monastery at Lindisfarne and became bishop there, and his fruitful apostolate is described in St Bede's *Ecclesiastical History*. He also founded monasteries at Melrose, Hartlepool and Gateshead, thus introducing the Irish monastic tradition into Scotland and England. He died at Bamburgh, and is sometimes represented with a stag (owing to a legend that he saved a hunted deer by praying to make it invisible).

Aidan of Mayo (St) B. R. Oct 30
d. 768. He was a bishop of Mayo, Ireland.

Aignan *see* **Anianus**

Aigulf (Ayoul, Aueul, Aout, Hou) of Bourges (St) B. R. May 22
d. *p*835. A well-educated hermit, he was forced to become bishop of Bourges, France, against his will in 812.

Aigulf (Ayou, Ayoul) of Lérins
(St) M? R. Sep 3
*c*630–676. From Blois, France, the tradition is that he became a monk of Fleury and was sent to Montecassino in order to find the relics of St Benedict. This was because Fleury had just converted to the Benedictine observance. In *c*670 he was sent to be abbot of Lérins and to effect a similar conversion but some of the brethren there, resenting this, took him and four other monks to an island off Corsica and murdered them.

Ailbe (Ailbhe) of Emly (St) B. Sep 12
C6th. He was allegedly the first bishop of Emly in Co. Tipperary, Ireland.

Ailred *see* **Aelred**

Aimard *see* **Aymard**

Aimé *see* **Amatus**

Aimo (Aimonius) of Meda
(St) R. Feb 13
d. *c*790. He was the founder of St Victor's nunnery at Meda near Milan, Italy.

Aimo (Aymo, Haimo) of Savigny (St) R(OSB). Apr 30
d. 1173. From near Rennes, France, he entered the monastery of Savigny in Normandy but was suspected of having leprosy. To avoid dismissal he volunteered to nurse two leper-monks. Afterwards he was professed, ordained and became a monastic official. He suffered many trials and enjoyed mystical experiences.

Aimo Taparelli (Bl) R(OP). Aug 18
1395–1495. Born in Savigliano in Piedmont, Italy, of the family of the counts of Lagnasco, he became a Dominican and was appointed chaplain to Bl Duke Amadeus of Savoy. He was also inquisitor-general for Lombardy and Liguria. His cultus was confirmed in 1856 for Turin and the Dominicans.

Airald (Ayruld) (Bl) R(OCart) Jan 2
d. ?1156. A Carthusian prior of Portes near Belley, France, he was made bishop of St John of Maurienne in Savoy in 1132. His cultus was confirmed for Maurienne in 1863.

Airy *see* **Agericus**

Aisle *see* **Agilus**

Aithalas (St) *see* **Acepsimas of Hnaita and Comps**

Aizan and Sazan (SS) MM. Oct 1
d. *c*400. Two brothers, they were noblemen of Axum, Ethiopia, and allegedly became missionaries there and friends of St Athanasius.

Ajou *see* **Aigulf**

Ajutre *see* **Adjutor**

Alacrinus (Bl) B. R(OCist). Jan 5
d. 1216. He was a prior of the monastery of Casamari near Veroli, Italy, and was papal legate in Germany at the end of the C12th.
Aladius *see* **Albaud**

Alan of Lavaur (St) R. Nov 25
C7th. He was the founder and first abbot of the monastery of Lavaur in Gascony, France.

Alan and Alorus of Quimper
(SS) BB. Oct 26
C5th. Two Breton bishops, their cultus is ancient but they have left no biographical details.

Alan of Sassovivo (Bl) R(OSB). Jul 18
d. 1311. An Austrian monk, he made a pilgrimage to Rome for the jubilee of 1300 and joined the monastery of Sassovivo, becoming a hermit just before his death.

Alan de Solminihac (Bl) B. R(CR). Jan 3
1593–1659. A nobleman born in Périgord, France, when aged twenty he became the abbot of the decayed Augustinian abbey of Chancelade and seriously set out to reform it. In 1637 he became bishop of Cahors, and similarly worked to reform a degraded diocese and to fight the errors of Jansenism. He was beatified in 1981.

Alanus *see* **Almus**

Alaric (Adalric, Adalrai)
(St) R(OSB). Sep 29
d. 975. Son of a duke of Swabia, Germany, he was sent to be educated at the abbey of Einsiedeln, Switzerland. He became a monk there, and later a hermit on an island in the Zurich See.

Alban (St) M. Jun 20
C3rd or C4th. A pagan soldier at Verulamium in Roman Britain, he was converted to Christianity by a persecuted priest sheltering in his house and was martyred instead of him on a hill outside the town. The record of this, in Bede's *Ecclesiastical History*, is the only narrative witness to the Romano-British Church. Bede placed the martyrdom in the context of the persecution of Diocletian, but this has been doubted and that of Decius proposed. King Offa of Mercia later built an abbey on the site of the martyrdom, around which grew the city of St Alban's. His attribute is a cross on a pole.

Alban of Mainz (St) M. Jun 21
d. *c*400. A Greek priest of Naxos in the Cyclades, he was sent into exile by the Arians to Mainz, Germany, where he was a missionary. The local Arians killed him, and an abbey at Mainz was dedicated in his honour.

Alban-Bartholomew Roe
(St) M. R(OSB). Jan 31
d. 1642. Born in Suffolk, England, of Protestant parents, he went to Cambridge University, was converted at Douai and became a monk at Dieuleward (now Ampleforth) in 1612. He worked in London and the Home Counties from 1615 until he was executed at Tyburn with Bl

Richard Reynolds after a long imprisonment. He was canonized in 1970. *See* **England (Martyrs of)**.

Albaud (Aladius) (St) B. Oct 1
d. 520. He was a bishop of Toul, France, and built a church in honour of his predecessor, St Aper. This later became a Benedictine monastery.

Alberic of Bagno de Romana
(St) R(OSB Cam). Aug 29
d. *c*1050. He was a Camaldolese hermit at Bagno de Romana near Sarsina, Italy, and his shrine is at San Anastasio near Montefeltro.

Alberic of Cîteaux (St)
R(OCist). F. Jan 26
d. 1109. One of the three founders of the Cistercians, he was at first a hermit at Collan near Châlons-sur-Marne, France, then he followed St Robert to Molesmes in 1075 and became his prior there. They both went to Cîteaux in 1098. St Alberic was prior there as well, and succeeded St Robert as abbot in 1099.

Alberic Crescitelli (St) M. P. Jul 9
1863-1900. From near Benevento, Italy, he attended the Pontifical Seminary for Foreign Missions at Rome and, after being ordained in 1887, went as a missionary to Shanxi, China. He was captured in the Boxer Rebellion, tortured and dismembered. *See* **China (Martyrs of)**.

Alberic of Gladbach (St) R(OSB) Dec 24
C10th. A monk of the Bavarian abbey of Gladbach, Germany, he is also referred to as Albert in the sources.

Alberic of Stavelot-Malmédy
(St) R. Oct 28
d. 779. He is one of five abbots of the twin Belgian monasteries of Stavelot-Malmédy who are venerated as saints. *See* **Agilulf** and **Sigolin**.

Alberic of Utrecht (St) B. R. Nov 14
d. 784. A nephew of St Gregory of Utrecht, he became cathedral prior at Utrecht, Netherlands, and succeeded his uncle as bishop in 775. He was well educated, a successful missionary among the Germans and Frisians and was a friend of Alcuin.

Albert *see* **Autbert**

Albert *see* **Ethelbert**

Albert of Bergamo (St) T(OP). May 11
d. 1279. An Italian peasant farmer and a Dominican tertiary, he was persecuted by his wife and relatives for helping poor and destitute people. He died at Cremona, Italy, and had his cultus confirmed for there in 1728.

Albert of Bologna (Bl)
R(OSB Vall). May 20
d. 1245. A nobleman from Bologna, Italy, he joined a Vallumbrosan abbey nearby and became its abbot. The abbey was later named after him.

Albert of Butrio (St) R(OSB). Sep 5
d. 1073. He was the abbot-founder of the monastery of Butrio near Tortona in Piedmont, Italy.

Albert of Cashel (St) B. Jan 8
C7th. He is the patron of Cashel in Ireland, and has an unreliable extant biography. According to this, he was an Anglo-Saxon missionary in Ireland and Bavaria who visited Jerusalem and who died and was buried in Regensburg in Bavaria, Germany.

Albert Chmielowski (St)
T(OFM). F. Jun 17
1845–1916. Born at Igołomia in Russian Poland near Cracow (then under the Hapsburgs), he studied in Warsaw and St Petersburg but was involved in the Polish insurrection of 1863 against Russia and was exiled to Western Europe, where he studied painting. He found Christian faith in painting religious pictures and moved to Cracow where he shared his life and earnings from his painting with the poor. In 1880 he became a Franciscan tertiary, being called 'another Francis', and his followers became the 'Albertine Fathers and Sisters'. He was canonized in 1989.

Albert (Aribert) of Como
(St) B. R(OSB). Jun 3
d. ?1092. A bishop of Como, Italy, he had been a hermit at Rho and then monk and abbot of San Carpofero.

Albert of Csanad (St) R. May 28
d. ?1492. A Pauline monk of Hungary, he was a Latin poet and orator and died at the monastery of Bajcs.

Albert of Gambron (St) R. Dec 29
C7th. A Frankish courtier, he became a hermit and then founded the abbey of Gambron-sur-l'Authion, France, which incorporated the rules of SS Benedict and Columban into its customary.

Albert (Lambert) of Genoa (St) R(OCist). Jul 8
d. 1239. A lay brother at the Cistercian abbey of Sestri de Ponente near Genoa, Italy, he became a hermit nearby.

Albert the Great (St) B. Dr. R(OP). Nov 15
*c*1200-1280. A nobleman from Swabia, Germany, he joined the Dominicans while at the University of Padua, became a lecturer in theology at Cologne and Paris and recognized the genius of his pupil, St Thomas Aquinas. Then he became provincial superior of the Dominicans in Germany and bishop of Regensburg for two years from 1260. The rest of his life was spent teaching and writing in Cologne, where he was the pioneer in applying Aristotelianism to theology and where his immense output dealt with all contemporary branches of scholarship (hence his nickname, 'Doctor Universalis'). He was declared a doctor of the Church in 1931, being thus equivalently canonized, and is the patron of scientists.

Albert Hurtado Cruchaga (Bl) R(SJ). Aug 18
1901–1952. Born in Viña del Mar, Chile, of a poor family, he became a Jesuit in Santiago and chaplain of the youth movement of 'Catholic Action' there. In 1944 he started 'El Hogar del Christo', a series of homes for homeless people, and in 1947 he founded the 'Chilean Trade Union Association' in order to promote the Church's social teaching. Dying of pancreatic cancer, he was beatified in 1994.

Albert of Jerusalem (St) B. R(CR). F. Sep 25
?1149–1214. An Italian canon regular, he was in turn prior-general of the Augustinians, bishop of Bobbio and of Vercelli and, in 1205, Latin Patriarch of Jerusalem under Pope Innocent III. He established his residence at Acre, in the Holy Land, and helped St Brocard organize the hermits of Carmel, writing a rule for them. Thus he is the co-founder of the Carmelites. He was killed by a corrupt master of a hospital at Acre whom he had deposed.

Albert of Louvain (St) M. B. Nov 21
?1166–1192. Born at Keizersberg near Louvain, Belgium, he was elected bishop of Liege in opposition to Emperor Henry VI, who had his own candidate. The pope supported him and he was ordained at Rheims in 1192, but he was murdered by three German knights two months later and was regarded as a martyr.

Albert of Montecorvino (St) B. Apr 5
d. 1127. A son of Norman immigrants, he became bishop of Montecorvino near Salerno, Italy, but went blind when old and was provided with a coadjutor. The latter treated him with cruelty, which he bore with patience.

Albert of Pontida (Bl) R(OSB). Sep 5
d. 1095. A soldier of Bergamo, Italy, he was badly wounded and vowed that he would become a consecrated religious if cured. After a pilgrimage to St James at Compostela he founded the abbey of St James at Pontida outside Bergamo and put it under the Cluniac obedience. His relics, formerly enshrined at Bergamo, were returned to Pontida (which survives as a working monastery) in 1928.

Albert Quadrelli (St) B. Jul 4
d. 1179. Born at Rivolta d'Adda near Cremona, Italy, he was parish priest of his native town for 25 years before becoming bishop of Lodi in 1168.

Albert of Sassoferrato (Bl) R(OSB). Oct 25
d. 1330. He was a monk of Santa Croce di Tripozzo in the Marches, Italy, later a Camaldolese monastery, and had his cultus confirmed for the Camaldolese in 1837.

Albert of Trapani (St) R(OC). Aug 7
*c*1240-1307. From Trapani, Sicily, he joined the Carmelites there and went to Messina as a priest. He became provincial superior in 1296. His special work was the conversion of Jews to Christianity, at which he was very successful. His cultus was confirmed in 1454.

Albert of Trent (St) M. B. Mar 27
d. 1181. A bishop of Trent (now in Italy), he was killed in the wars between the Emperor Frederick Barbarossa and the north Italians and was later venerated as a martyr.

Albert of Vallombrosa (Bl) R(OSB Vall). Aug 1
d. 1094. A disciple of St John Gualbert at Vallombrosa, he was cellarer there for 40 years and also prior. His cultus was approved in 1602, together with that of **Rudolf** (q.v.).

Alberta (St) V. Mar 11
d. ?286. She was a virgin martyr of Agen, France, one of the first victims of the persecution in the reign of Diocletian.

Albertinus (St) R(OSB). Apr 13
d. 1294. He became a monk of Fonteavellana,

near Urbino, Italy, the chief monastery of a Benedictine congregation (united to the Camaldolese in 1570) in 1250 and served as prior general of said congregation from 1275. His cultus was confirmed in 1782.

Albeus *see* **Ailbe**

Albina (St) V. Dec 16
d. 250. A young woman, she was martyred at Caesarea in the Holy Land in the reign of Decius. However, the old Roman Martyrology states that she was martyred near Gaeta in the Campagna, Italy, where her ancient shrine is located. The Eastern tradition is that her body was miraculously transported there from Caesarea.

Albinus *see* **Alvitus**

Albinus (Aubin) of Angers
(St) B. R. Mar 1
469–550. From Vannes, France, he became a monk and abbot of Tincillac near Angers, then bishop of Angers in ?529. He played an important part at the third council of Orléans in 538. The abbey of St Aubin at Angers was dedicated to him, and he has a shrine and pilgrimage centre at St Aubin de Moeslain.

Albinus (Albuinus)
of Buraburg (St) B. R. Oct 26
d. *p*760. He was an English monk called Witta ('Blond'), who latinized his name when he went on the German mission with St Boniface. He became bishop of Buraburg in Hesse in 741.

Albinus of Lyons (St) B. Sep 15
d. 390. The successor of St Justus as bishop of Lyons after 381, he was alleged to have built the church of St Stephen there as his cathedral.

Albuin (St) B. Feb 5
d. ?1006. A nobleman of Carinthia, Austria, he became bishop of Säben in 977 and transferred the see to Brixen in the South Tyrol (now in Italy).

Alburga (St) R. Dec 25
d. *c*810. The half-sister of King Egbert of Wessex, England, she founded a nunnery at Wilton (Wilts) and became a nun there when widowed.

Alcmund (Alkmund, Alchmund)
of Hexham (St) B. Sep 7
d. 781. He was the seventh bishop of Hexham on the Tyne, England, from 767.

Alcmund of Northumbria
(St) M. Mar 19
d. *c*800. A royal prince of Northumbria, he was exiled in Scotland for years before being killed in Shropshire, England, in circumstances which led to his being venerated as a martyr, firstly at Lilleshall and then at Derby.

Alcuin (Flaccus Albinus) May 19
?735-804. Born in York, he was educated at the cathedral school and then became headmaster. While on a journey to collect the pallium for his archbishop from the pope he met Charlemagne at Parma, Italy, and was enlisted to found and run the palace school of the Frankish empire. When old he was made abbot of St Martin of Tours, despite not being a monk, and restored the observance there with the help of St Benedict of Aniane. A prolific writer, especially on theology and liturgy, he was listed as a beatus in the Gallican martyrology but has never had a cultus.

Alda (Aldobrandesca, Aude,
Blanca, Bruna) (Bl) T(OSB). Apr 26
1249-1309. A woman of Siena, Italy, with a very pious husband, when widowed she became a tertiary of the Humiliati (an extinct Benedictine congregation) and was devoted to penance and works of charity. Her veneration is popular in Siena but is unconfirmed.

Aldate (Eldate) (St) B? Feb 4
?C6th. Churches at Oxford and at Gloucester are dedicated to this saint but he has no reliable biographical details. Fanciful legends describe him as a West Briton fighting the Saxon invaders or as a bishop of Gloucester, but there is a suspicion that the name originally described a locality ('Old Gate').

Aldebrand (Hildebrand) (St) B. May 1
1119–1219. Born near Cesena, Italy, he became provost of Rimini where he preached vigorously against licentiousness and once had to flee for his life as a result. In 1170 he became bishop of Fossombrone, where he is the principal patron.

Aldegund (St) R. Jan 30
630-684. Sister of St Waldetrude, she was the abbess-founder of Maubeuge in Flanders, France.

Aldemar (St) R(OSB). Mar 24
d. *c*1080. From Capua, Italy, he became a monk of Montecassino and chaplain to the nuns at St Laurence's nunnery at Capua. His ability to perform miracles proved embarrassing and he was recalled to his abbey, but he later founded

and was superior of several monasteries such as Bucchianico in the Abruzzi, where his shrine is located. He loved animals.

Alderic (Aldric, Audry) of Le Mans (Bl) B. Jan 7
d. 856. Chaplain of Emperor Louis the Pious and bishop of Le Mans, France, from 832, he was a saintly bishop and a capable public official. Some of his writings are extant.

Alderic (Aldric, Audry) of Sens (St) B. R(OSB). Oct 10
790-841. A monk of Ferrières, he was a priest of the archdiocese of Sens, France, before becoming the master of the imperial palace and archbishop of Sens from 828. He was a zealous patron of ecclesiastical education.

Aldetrude (Adeltrude) (St) R. Feb 25
d. 696. Daughter of SS Vincent Madelgar and Waldetrude, she was sent as a girl to her aunt St Aldegund at Maubeuge in Flanders, France, and later became that nunnery's second abbess. She was succeeded by her sister St Madalberta. Her extant biography is unreliable.

Aldhelm (Adhelm) (St) B. R. May 25
639–709. Born in Wessex, England, he became a monk at Malmesbury, studied under St Adrian at Canterbury, became headmaster of the Malmesbury abbey school and then was made abbot in 675. He was made first bishop of Sherborne in 705 while remaining abbot of Malmesbury, where his shrine was established. The first English scholar of note, he wrote poetry in English and Latin (although none of his English work is extant). He loved books, and has been called the first English librarian.

Aldwyn (St) R.
C8th. This obscure abbot of Lincolnshire, England, has given his name to Coln St Aldwyn near Fairford (Glos). There is no evidence of any cultus.

Alena (St) V. Jun 18
d. *c*640. Born near Brussels, Belgium, of pagan parents and baptized without their knowledge, she was seized and killed while secretly going to Mass.

Aleth (Bl) L. Apr 4
d. 1105. Wife of Tecolin and mother of St Bernard of Clairvaux, she had her relics enshrined at Clairvaux, France, in 1250.

Alexander (St) M. B. Sep 21
C2nd. A bishop somewhere near Rome, he was known for performing miracles and was martyred on the Claudian Way about twenty miles from Rome. Pope St Damasus enshrined his relics in a Roman church.

Alexander (St) M. Jan 30
C3rd. The old Roman Martyrology listed him as an elderly martyr in the reign of Decius, but he may be the same as St Alexander of Jerusalem.

Alexander (St) M. Mar 27
C3rd. The old Roman Martyrology lists him as a soldier who was martyred in Pannonia (now in Hungary) in the reign of Maximian Herculeus, and he may be the anonymous martyr of Thrace (European Turkey) celebrated on May 13.

Alexander (St) *see* **Amantius, Alexander and Comps**

Alexander (St) *see* **Ammonius and Alexander**

Alexander (St) *see* **Epimachus and Alexander**

Alexander (St) *see* **Epipodius, Alexander and Comps**

Alexander (St) *see* **Gaius and Alexander**

Alexander (St) *see* **Hyacinth, Alexander and Tiburtius**

Alexander (St) *see* **Leontius, Attius and Comps**

Alexander (St) *see* **Mark, Alphius and Comps**

Alexander (St) *see* **Maximus, Claudius and Comps**

Alexander (St) *see* **Patermuthius, Copres and Alexander**

Alexander (St) *see* **Photinius, Sanctius and Comps**

Alexander (St) *see* **Priscus, Malchus and Alexander**

Alexander (St) *see* **Seven Brothers**

Alexander (St) *see* **Sisinnius, Martyrius and Alexander**

Alexander (St) *see* **Thalelaeus of Aegae and Comps**

Alexander (SS) *see* **Timolaus and Comps**

Alexander (St) *see* **Victor, Alexander, Felician and Longinus**

Alexander (St) *see* **Victor of Marseilles and Comps**

Alexander I, 'Pope' (St) M? May 3
d. ?113. He was listed by St Irenaeus as having been pope for about six years (other sources differ), but not a martyr. (The Roman church was probably still an informal federation of Christian synagogues at the time.) His acta as a martyr are fictitious.

Alexander, Abundius, Antigonus and Fortunatus (SS) MM. Feb 27
? They died either in Rome (according to the old Roman Martyrology), or in Thessaly (according to St Bede). Nothing else is known.

Alexander and Antonina (SS) MV. May 3
d. 313. Their legend states that the latter was a virgin of Byzantium (later Constantinople) who was condemned to be sexually abused in a brothel but was allowed to escape by the former, a soldier, who changed clothes with her. They were together tortured and burnt.

Alexander, Eventius and Theodolus (SS) MM. May 3
d. ?113. Roman martyrs, they were buried on the Via Normativa. The first was later confused with St Alexander I, Pope. Their cultus was confined to local calendars in 1969.

Alexander, Heraclius and Comps (SS) MM. Oct 22
? Their place and time is unknown. Their story is that St Alexander was a bishop who was successful in converting Jews and pagans and who was tortured and martyred together with St Heraclius, a soldier guard converted by his example, and others.

Alexander and Theodore (SS) MM. Mar 17
? Nothing is known about these martyrs.

Alexander and Theodolus (SS) MM. May 3
? They may be an erroneous duplicate of the above in the old Roman Martyrology.

Alexander Akimites (St) R. F. Jan 15
d. 430. A Greek monk in Syria, he founded a laura by the Euphrates which grew to number *c*400 monks. A great traveller, he later founded the 'Akoimetoi' (monks who celebrated the Divine Office in relays, day and night) and these became very influential in Constantinople.

Alexander of Alexandria (St) B. Feb 26
*c*250–328. Patriarch of Alexandria, Egypt, from 312, he condemned Arius (one of his clergy) for heresy and favoured the young St Athanasius, whom he ordained deacon. He was also faced with the schism of the rigorist Meletians. He died just after he and St Athanasius had attended the first ecumenical council at Nicaea (325), which definitively condemned Arianism. A few of his writings have survived.

Alexander Blake (Bl) M. L. May 4
d. 1590. He was a London ostler who was executed with Bl Nicholas Horner on the charge of having aided Bl Christopher Bales, a priest. He was beatified in 1987. *See* **England (Martyrs of)**.

Alexander Briant (St) M. R(SJ). Dec 1
?1561-1581. From Somerset, he converted while studying at Oxford and was ordained at Douai in 1578. He worked in Somerset until seized in London in 1581 and severely tortured in order to make him disclose the whereabouts of Fr Robert Parsons SJ. He took the Jesuit vows in prison before being tried and condemned for alleged complicity in a fictitious plot. He was executed at Tyburn with SS Ralph Sherwin and Edmund Campion and was canonized in 1970. *See* **England (Martyrs of)**.

Alexander Carbonarius of Comana (St) M. B. Aug 11
d. ?275. A philosopher who became a charcoal-burner as an exercise in humility, he was made bishop of Comana in Pontus, Asia Minor, on the recommendation of St Gregory Thaumaturgus and was martyred by being burnt. These events were described by St Gregory Nyssa.

Alexander of Constantinople (St) B. Aug 28
d. 336. Bishop of Constantinople from 313 to 336 during the Arian controversy, he was at the First Council of Nicaea in 325 and spoke out against Arius.

Alexander of Corinth (St) M. Nov 24
d. 361. He was martyred at Corinth, Greece, in the reign of Julian.

Alexander Crow (Bl) M. P. Nov 30
d. 1586. A shoemaker from York, he was ordained at Rheims and was a priest in

Yorkshire for two years before being seized while baptizing a child at South Duffield. He was executed at York and was beatified in 1987. *See* **England (Martyrs of)**.

Alexander of Fermo (St) M. B. Jan 11
d. *c*250. A bishop of Fermo near Ancona, Italy, he was martyred in the reign of Decius. His relics are enshrined in the cathedral there.

Alexander of Fiesole (St) M. B. Jun 6
d. *c*840. A bishop of Fiesole near Florence, Italy, he appealed to the emperor to restore certain properties of his diocese which had been alienated, and was consequently ambushed and drowned near Bologna by his opponents.

Alexander of Jerusalem (St) M. B. Mar 18
d. 251. A fellow student with Origen in Alexandria, he became bishop of his native city in Cappadocia, Asia Minor, and was imprisoned for his faith in the reign of Severus. He afterwards became coadjutor to Narcissus in Jerusalem, and this is the first recorded example of the transfer of a bishop and of coadjutorship. He founded a library and a school for the exiled Origen, and died in prison at Caesarea in the reign of Decius.

Alexander Rawlins (Bl) M. S. Apr 7
d. 1595. Possibly from Gloucestershire, he was educated at Rheims and ordained in 1590. He was captured and executed while on the York mission and was beatified in 1929. *See* **England (Martyrs of)**.

Alexander of Rome (St) M. Feb 9
? A Roman, he was martyred with thirty-eight companions.

Alexander Sauli (St) B. R. Oct 11
1534–1593. From Milan, Italy, he became a Barnabite priest and a zealous preacher and confessor, being for a time the spiritual director of St Charles Borromeo. He became superior of his congregation and was made bishop of Aleria in Corsica for twenty years in 1569, completely reforming the diocese. He was transferred to Pavia just before his death, and was canonized in 1904.

Alexander of Thessalonika (St) M. Nov 9
C4th. He was martyred at Thessalonika, Greece, in the reign of Maximian Herculeus.

Alexander of Trier (St) M. Oct 5
d. ?303. He was one of very many martyred at Trier, Germany, by the prefect Rictiovarus in the reign of Diocletian.

Alexander of Verona (St) B. Jun 4
C8th. Nothing is known about this bishop of Verona, Italy.

Alexandra (St) *see* **Theodotus of Ancyra and Comps**

Alexandra of Amisus and Comps (SS) MM. Mar 20
d. *c*300. A group of women of Amisus in Paphlagonia, Asia Minor, they were burnt in the reign of Diocletian. The companions were Claudia, Euphrasia, Matrona, Juliana, Euphemia, Theodosia and Derphuta with her sister.

Alexandria (Martyrs of)
The contests between paganism, heresy and Christianity were especially vicious at Alexandria, Egypt, during the Roman Empire, and many died in both official persecutions and in the rioting for which the city was notorious. The following anonymous groups were listed in the old Roman Martyrology:

Aug 10
d. 257. St Dionysius left a description of a violent persecution in the reign of Valerian, when inhuman tortures were used.

Feb 28
d. 260. Many Christians were considered to be martyrs who had died after nursing the sick during an epidemic in the reign of Valerian, in contrast with the pagans who abandoned them in fear.

Mar 21
d. 342. The Catholic churches were sacked on a Good Friday by the pagans and Arians during the reign of the Arian emperor Constantius, and many worshippers died. St Athanasius wrote about this.

Jan 28
d. 356. While St Athanasius was celebrating Mass, an Arian army officer ordered the congregation to be massacred. St Athanasius escaped.

May 13
d. 372. When St Athanasius was exiled for the fifth time by the Arian emperor Valens, many of his followers were killed, especially in the Theonas church.

Mar 17
d. 390. During the reign of Theodosius there was a riot between the Christians and the worshippers of Serapis, who had the main temple in the city. Many died, and the temple of Serapis was destroyed by Patriarch Theophilus in the following year.

Alexandrina di Letto (Bl) R(OFM). Apr 3
1385-1458. Born at Sulmona in the Abruzzi, Italy, she joined the Poor Clares as a teenager and founded her own nunnery at Foligno in 1423, being encouraged in this by the pope. This became the basis of a Franciscan reform movement.

Alexis Delgado (Bl) *see* **Ignatius de Azevedo and Comps**

Alexis Falconieri (St) R(OSM). F. Feb 17
1200-1310. *See* **Servites, Founders of**. He is patron of studies in the Servite order.

Alexis of Nagasaki (Bl) M. R(OP). Sep 10
d. 1622. A Japanese catechist and a Dominican novice, he was burnt in the 'Great Martyrdom' at Nagasaki with BB Charles Spinola and Comps. *See* **Japan (Martyrs of)**.

Alexis Nakamura (Bl) M. Nov 27
d. 1619. A Japanese layman of the family of the daimyos of Hirado, he was beheaded with Anthony Kimura and Comps at Nagasaki. *See* **Japan (Martyrs of)**.

Alexis of Rome Jul 17
? The cultus of this saint was suppressed for the Latin rite in 1969 owing to its being basically fictitious, although it remains popular in the East. The remote source seems to be a certain Mar Riscia, a holy man of Edessa, Syria (now Urfa in Turkey). The developed legend, which spread to the West on the opening of the Greek monastery of SS Boniface and Alexis in the C10th, concerns a Roman senator's son who fled his wedding to become a beggar and eventually returned home to live unrecognized as a menial beneath a staircase (which is his attribute).

Alexis Wu (St) *see* **Mark Tyeng and Comps**

Aleydis *see* **Adelaide**

Alfanus (Alphanus) (St) B. R(OSB). Oct 9
d. 1085. A monk of Montecassino, he became archbishop of Salerno, Italy, in 1058. He administered the last rites to Pope St Gregory VII.

Alferius (St) R(OSB). Apr 12
930–1050. A Norman nobleman of Salerno, Italy, he went on an embassy to France, fell ill at the abbey of Chiusa, recovered and became a monk at Cluny under St Odilo. The duke of Salerno obtained his return, and he founded the abbey of La Cava outside the city. This spawned hundreds of affiliated houses of the Cluniac observance in southern Italy. His cultus was confirmed in 1893 for La Cava.

Alfonso *see* **Alphonsus**

Alfred *see* **Altfrid**

Alfred the Great, King *Oct 26*
849–899. King of Wessex, England, he defeated the Danes at the nadir of Anglo-Saxon fortunes and thus ensured the future of the English church and nation. He was a patron of scholarship and translated patristic works into English, but his alleged attempt to re-found monastic life with monasteries at Athelney and Shaftesbury had minimal impact. The existence of this attempt, together with much concerning his alleged personal piety, depends on a late C10th biography the historicity of which is questionable. He had an informal cultus in England in the Middle Ages but this was never confirmed and is now extinct.

Alfred Parte Saiz (Bl) *see* **Dionysius Pamplona Polo and Comps**

Alfreda *see* **Etheldritha**

Alfrick (St) B. R(OSB). Nov 16
d. 1005. An abbot of Abingdon, England, he became bishop of Wilton in 990 and archbishop of Canterbury in 995. He proved himself an able pastor at the time of the Danish incursions.

Alfwold (St) B. R(OSB). Mar 26
d. 1058. A monk of Winchester, England, he became bishop of Sherborne in 1045 and propagated the veneration of SS Cuthbert and Swithin.

Algeric *see* **Agericus**

Alice *see* **Adelaide**

Alice Rich (Bl) R(OSB) *see* **Margaret and Alice Rich**

Alipius (Alypius) (St) B. Aug 15
d. *c*430. A friend and disciple of St Augustine, he was baptized with him in Milan, Italy, in 387. Afterwards they spent some time together as religious at his home town of Tagaste in Roman Africa before Alipius visited the Holy Land and then became bishop of Tagaste in 393. As such he was St Augustine's chief supporter.

Aliprand (Leuprand) (St) R. Jul 24
C8th. Of the Lombard royal family, he became abbot of St Augustine's in Ciel d'Oro at Pavia, Italy.

Alix le Clerc *see* **Mary-Teresa-of-Jesus Le Clerc**

Alkeld (Athilda) (St) V? Mar 27
?C10th. She has two Yorkshire, England, churches dedicated to her. An ancient painting depicts her as a girl being strangled by Vikings, but nothing else is known.

Alkmund *see* **Alcmund**

Allan *see* **Elian**

Alleaume *see* **Adelemus**

Alloyne *see* **Bavo**

Allucio (St) L. F. Oct 23
d. 1134. Born near Pescia in Tuscany, Italy, he was a herdsman before the town made him superior of the almshouse at Val di Nievole. His followers were called 'Brethren of St Allucio'. His cultus was confirmed in the C19th.

Allyre *see* **Illidius**

Almachus (Telemachus) (St) M. R. Jan 1
d. 391. An Eastern hermit, while in Rome he publicly protested against the gladiatorial contests in the amphitheatre. The prefect ordered him killed, and the emperor Honorius allegedly abolished such games as a consequence (if so, without full effect).

Almedha (Eled, Elevetha) (St) V. Aug 1
C6th. Allegedly a descendant of St Brychan, by tradition she was martyred on a hill outside Brecon, Wales.

Almirus (Almer, Almire) (St) R. Sep 11
d. *c*560. Born in the Auvergne, France, he was educated at the local monastery of Menat. There he met St Avitus and went with him to Micy near Orléans. He ended up as a hermit at Gréez-sur-Roc.

Almus (Alme, Alanus) (St) R(OCist). Jun 28
d. 1270. A Cistercian monk of Melrose, he became first abbot of Balmerino, Scotland.

Alnoth (St) M. R. Nov 25
d. *c*700. A cowherd at St Werburga's monastery at Weedon near Northampton, England, he became a hermit in Stowe Wood nearby but was killed by thieves and then venerated as a martyr. His wood has been grubbed up recently by a greedy farmer.

Alodia (St) see **Nunilo and Alodia**

Alonzo *see* **Alphonsus**

Alorus (St) *see* **Alan and Alorus**

Aloysius-Armand-Joseph Adam (Bl) *see* **John-Baptist Souzy and Comps**

Aloysius Batis Sainz (St) *see* **Mexico (Martyrs of)**

Aloysius Escalé Binefa (Bl) *see* **Philip-of-Jesus Munárriz Azcona and Comps**

Aloysius-Gonzaga Gonza (St) M. Jun 3
d. 1886. A page at the court of King Mwanga of Buganda, Uganda, he was imprisoned after being baptized and killed with a spear after a few weeks. *See* **Charles Lwanga and Comps**.

Aloysius Gonzaga (St) R(SJ). Jun 21
1568-1591. A nobleman born at Castiglione delle Stiviere in Tuscany, Italy, as a boy he was a page at the courts of Tuscany, Mantua and Spain but joined the Jesuits when aged seventeen despite his family's opposition. Professed in 1587, he was a disciple of St Robert Bellamine. He died at Rome of the after-effects of plague after nursing sufferers of that disease. Canonized in 1726, he is the protector of young students and patron of Christian youth. A contemporary likeness is extant.

Aloysius Guanella (Bl) P. F. Oct 27
1842–1915. A shepherd-boy on the Swiss border before he became a priest of Como, Italy, he was much influenced by St John Bosco and founded the 'Servants of Charity' and the 'Daughters of Our Lady of Providence' in order to relieve distress of any kind. He established his congregations in the United States to help Italian immigrants and wrote much on popular piety. He died at Como and was beatified in 1964.

Aloysius-Francis Lebrun (Bl) *see* **John-Baptist Souzy and Comps**.

Aloysius Lladó Teixidó and Aloysius Masferrer Vila (BB) *see* **Philip-of-Jesus Munárriz Azcona and Comps**

Aloysius Orione (Bl) P. F. Mar 12
1872–1940. Born in Tortona, Italy, he became a priest there after being influenced as a teenager by St John Bosco. He started his 'Little Work of Divine Providence' in order to help needy people, modelled on the charism of St

Joseph Cottolengo, and founded five religious congregations to help, namely the 'Sons', 'Hermits', and 'Brothers of Divine Providence'; the 'Little Sisters of Charity' and the 'Blind Sacramentine Sisters'. He also had world-wide missionary interests and worked for reunion with the Orthodox. He was beatified in 1980.

Aloysius-Mary Palazzolo
(St) P. F. Jun 15
1827–1886. From Bergamo, Italy, he was ordained in 1880 and proved to have a similar charism to that of St John Bosco. He was involved in the Christian education of children and adults, and also in caring for sick and poor people and for the children of manual workers. He founded the 'Poor Little Sisters' and the 'Brothers of the Holy Family' to further these ends. He was beatified in 1963.

Aloysius Rabatá (Bl) R(OC). May 11
*c*1430–1490. He became a Carmelite at Trapani, Sicily, and became superior of the friary at Randazzo. He was attacked, hit on the head and died later as a result, meanwhile refusing to identify his unknown assailant. His cultus was confirmed for the Carmelites in 1841.

Aloysius Scrosoppi (Bl) R. F. Oct 5
1804–1884. From Udine, Italy, he became a priest there and, with his brother Charles who was superior of the city's Oratory, started helping destitute girls. This led to the formation of the 'Sisters of Providence', who spread through Europe. He followed his brother into the Oratory and succeeded him as its superior, which he remained until it was suppressed by the Italian government. He was beatified in 1981.

Aloysius Stepinac (Bl) M. B. (Feb 10)
1898-1960. Born in Krašic, Croatia (then part of Hungary), he became a diocesan priest of Zagreb in 1930 and was energetically involved in charitable activities. He was made archbishop in 1937, and did not support the racist policies of the fascist government of Croatia established after the German invasion of Yugoslavia but tried to help its victims. After the Communist takeover in Yugoslavia he was tried in 1946 and sentenced to hard labour for sixteen years, commuted to house arrest in his home town in 1951. He was made a cardinal in 1953, and there is evidence that he was killed by poisoning. He was beatified as a martyr in 1998.

Aloysius Versiglia and Callistus Caravario (SS) MM. Feb 25
d. 1930. The former was born near Tortona, Italy, in 1885, joined the Salesians in 1885 and went to China in 1906. He became vicar-apostolic of Suzhou in 1921. The latter was from Lombardy, born in 1903, who joined the Salesians in 1918, went to China and became pastor of Linjou in 1928. While accompanying Bl Aloysius on a pastoral visit to that place with three young Christian women, his group was ambushed at Litaoqui by robbers intent on rape. The two men intervened, were beaten to death and their bodies burned. *See* **China (Martyrs of)**.

Aloysius Wulphy Huppy (Bl) *see* **John-Baptist Souzy and Comps**

Alpais of Cudot (Bl) L. Nov 3
d. 1211. Born in Cudot near Sens, France, she helped her peasant family on the farm until bedridden with leprosy while still a child. It was alleged that for a long time her only food was the Eucharist. Her patience and gentleness made such an impression that her cultus was informally maintained until confirmed for Sens in 1874.

Alphaeus (St) L. May 26
C1st. He was the father of St James the Less (*see* Matt 10:3). The legends concerning him are worthless.

Alphaeus and Zacchaeus
(SS) MM. Nov 17
d. 303. Cousins, they were beheaded in Caesarea in the Holy Land in the reign of Diocletian. The former was a local reader and exorcist, the latter was a deacon from Gadara (now in Jordan).

Alphege the Elder (or the Bald) (St) B. R(OSB). Mar 12
d. 951. He became a monk in unknown circumstances and was made bishop of Winchester, England, in 934. He was possibly related to St Dunstan whom he introduced to the monastic life and then ordained, together with St Ethelwold. ('Bald' refers to his tonsure, which was unusual in England at a time when monastic life had collapsed.)

Alphege the Martyr (St)
M. B. R(OSB). Apr 19
?954-1012. A monk of Deerhurst near Gloucester, England, he became bishop of Winchester in 984 and archbishop of Canterbury in 1005. When the Danes invaded in 1011 he refused to leave his people, and when held to ransom he refused to let the money of the poor be used. His captors soon lost

patience, pelted him with bones during a drunken feast at Greenwich and then killed him with an axe. This is a noteworthy example of a martyr witnessing to justice rather than strictly to faith.

Alphanus *see* **Alfanus**

Alpherius *see* **Alferius**

Alphius (St) *see* **Mark, Alphius and Comps**

Alphius, Philadelphus and Cyrinus (SS) MM. May 10
d. 251. They are patrons of Lentini in Sicily and have a popular cultus in Australia based on the shrine at Silkwood in Queensland. They were possibly brothers who were martyred in the reign of Decius.

Alphonsa-of-the-Immaculate-Conception Muttathupadathu (Bl) R(OFM). Jul 28
1910-1946. Born in Kudamaloor in Kerala, India, in the Malabarese rite, she avoided an arranged marriage as a teenager by burning her feet and was allowed to join the Poor Clares at Bharananganame in 1927. Initially healthy, her health quickly broke down for a period of five years until she was healed after asking the intercession of Bl Cyriac. She was then professed in 1935, but her health gave way again and the rest of her life was a physical torment. She was beatified in 1986.

Alphonsus of Astorga (St) B. R(OSB). Jan 26
C9th. A bishop of Astorga, Spain, on his retirement he joined the abbey of St Stephen de Ribas de Sil in Galicia.

Alphonsus-Mary Fusco (Bl) P. F. Feb 6
1839–1910. From Angri near Nocera, Italy, the only child of peasant farmers, he was ordained as a diocesan priest in 1863 and ministered in his home town. In 1878 he helped to found the congregation of the Baptistine Sisters of the Nazarene in order to teach and care for poor orphan children at their 'Little House of Providence'. Other houses were opened throughout Italy before his death. He was beatified in 2001.

Alphonsus Leziniana (St) M. R(OP). Jan 22
d. 1745. A Dominican from Navas del Rey near Valladolid, Spain, he was martyred in north Vietnam with SS Francis Gil and Comps. *See* **Vietnam (Martyrs of)**.

Alphonsus-Mary Liguori (St) B. Dr. R(CSSR). F. Aug 1
1696–1787. A nobleman born near Naples, Italy, he started his career as a lawyer but became a priest instead in 1726. The need to catechize the rural peasantry led him to found the 'Congregation of the Holy Redeemer' (Redemptorists) in 1749. He was forced to become bishop of Sant' Agata de' Goti for thirteen years in 1762, until his health failed and he returned to his congregation. He wrote much on theology, spirituality, ethics and history, was canonized in 1839 and declared a doctor of the Church in 1871.

Alphonsus de Mena (Bl) M. R(OP). Sep 10
d. 1622. Born at Logroño, Spain, he became a Dominican at Salamanca, went to Japan and was burnt at Nagasaki in the 'Great Martyrdom' with BB Charles Spinola and Comps. *See* **Japan (Martyrs of)**.

Alphonsus Miquel Garriga (Bl) *see* **Philip-of-Jesus Munárriz Azcona and Comps**

Alphonsus Navarete (Bl) M. R(OP). Jun 1
d. 1617. From Valladolid, Spain, he became a Dominican missionary in the Philippines and then the provincial vicar in Japan in 1611. After converting thousands to Christianity he was beheaded on the island of Takashima with BB Leo Tanaka and Ferdinand-of-St-Joseph Ayala. He was beatified in 1867. *See* **Japan (Martyrs of)**.

Alphonsus de Orozco (Bl). R(OSA). Sep 19
1500–1591. Born at Oropesa in Castile, Spain, as an undergraduate at Salamanca University he was inspired to become an Augustinian friar by the sermons of St Thomas of Villanueva. He was a preacher at the court of King Philip II and a prolific and important spiritual author in Spanish.

Alphonsus Pacheco (Bl) M. R(SJ). Jul 7
1550–1583. From Minayá in Catalonia, Spain, he joined the Jesuits in 1566 and became a missionary priest in Goa, Portuguese India. After a difficult career he was killed in the district of Salsette (near Bombay) with Bl Rudolf Acquaviva and Comps.

Alphonsus Rodriguez (St) R(SJ). Oct 30
1531–1617. From Segovia, Spain, he became a married wool-merchant but lost his family and joined the Jesuits as a lay brother when aged 44. He was doorkeeper of the college of Montesión at Palma on Mallorca from 1580 to 1604, and managed to edify the whole island by

the way he performed this duty. He was canonized in 1888.

Alphonsus Sorribes Teixidó (Bl) *see* **Philip-of-Jesus Munárriz Azcona and Comps**

Alphonsus de Vaena (Bl) *see* **Ignatius de Azevedo and Comps**

Alpinian (St) *see* **Martial of Limoges and Comps**

Alrick (St) R. Jun 30
C12th. He was a hermit and disciple of St Godric, who was with him when he died at Crowland, Lincs, England.

Altfrid (Alfred) (St) B. R(OSB). Aug 15
d. 874. A monk of Corvey in Lower Saxony, Germany, he became bishop of Hildesheim in 851 and was known in the Holy Roman Empire for his peace and goodwill. He supported monasticism, upheld canon law and was devoted to Our Lady.

Altheus *see* **Tathai**

Althryda *see* **Eheldritha**

Altigianus and Hilarinus
(SS) MM. Aug 23
d. 731. Two monks, they were killed in the Arab incursion into France at St-Seine-l'Abbaye, near Dijon.

Altinus (Attinus) (St) M? Oct 19
? He was connected with the churches of Orléans and Chartres, France, either as a C4th martyr or, in a spurious foundation legend, as a disciple of Christ who migrated to Gaul in the C1st.

Altmann (Bl) B. R(CR). Aug 8
*c*1020–1091. From Westphalia, Germany, he became a canon at Paderborn and then at Aachen, chaplain to Emperor Henry III and bishop of Passau in 1065. He supported Pope St Gregory VII against Emperor Henry IV and was exiled, but he maintained his influence. He was a zealous supporter of the Augustinian canons regular and founded and reformed several of their abbeys, including that of Göttweig where he was buried.

Alto (St) R. Feb 9
d. *c*760. A wandering hermit, possibly Irish, he settled in a wood near Augsburg, Germany, which the Frankish king Pepin gave to him and built a church which St Boniface consecrated in 750. This later became the abbey of Altomünster. His alleged relics are preserved there.

Aluinus *see* **Alvitus**

Alvarez of Cordoba (Bl) R(OP). Feb 19
d. *c*1430. A Dominican at Cordoba, Spain, from 1368, he was a successful preacher in Andalucia, France and Italy and his reform friary that he founded in 1423 became a noted centre of piety and scholarship. He opposed Peter de Luna, the last antipope of Avignon. His cultus was confirmed for Cordoba in 1741.

Alvarez Garcia (Bl) *see* **Peter Rodríguez and Comps**

Alvarez Mendez (Bl) *see* **Ignatius de Azevedo and Comps**

Alvitus (Avitus, Aluinus, Albinus) (St) B. R(OSB). Sep 5
d. ?1063. A relative of St Rudesind born in Galicia, Spain, he entered the Cluniac abbey of Sahagún and became bishop of León in 1057. He transferred St Isidore's relics from Seville (then under Muslim rule) to León.

Alypius the Stylite (St) R. Nov 26
d. ?625. From Adrianople in Paphlagonia, Asia Minor, he became a hermit nearby and allegedly spent fifty-three years as a stylite on a pillar. *See* **Stylianos**.

Amabilis of Riom (St) P. Jun 11
d. 475. Apparently he was cathedral precentor at Clermont-Ferrand, France, and then parish priest at Riom in the Auvergne. He is invoked against fire and snakes.

Amabilis of Rouen (St) R. Jul 11
d. ?634. A nun at Saint-Amand at Rouen, France, she was thought to be an Anglo-Saxon princess.

Amadeus degli Amedei
(St) R(OSM). F. Feb 17
d. 1265. *See* **Seven Holy Founders of the Servite Order**. He became superior of the foundation on Monte Senario at Florence in 1233.

Amadeus of Clermont
(Bl) R(OCist). Jan 14
d. *c*1150. Lord of Hauterives in Drôme, France, he joined the Cistercian abbey of Bonnevaux with sixteen of his vassals and went on to found four monasteries: Léoncel, Mazan, Montperoux and Tamis. He died at Bonnevaux.

Amadeus of Lausanne
(Bl) B. R(OCist). Jan 28
*c*1110–1159. Son of Bl Amadeus of Clermont, he was educated at Cluny and was at the court of Emperor Henry V before joining the abbey of Clairvaux under St Bernard. In 1139 he became abbot of Hautecombe in Savoy, he was made bishop of Lausanne in 1144 and became co-regent of Savoy and chancellor of Burgundy before he died. His eight sermons on Our Lady are dogmatically important.

Amadeus of Portugal (St) R(OFM). Aug 9
1420–1482. A Portuguese nobleman, he became a Hieronomyte but then decided to transfer to the Franciscans and became a lay brother at Assisi after much opposition. After being a hermit he was ordained and founded several reform friaries, these being united to the Franciscan Observants in 1568.

Amadeus IX of Savoy, Duke (Bl) L. Mar 30
1435–1472. Born at Thonon, he became reigning duke of Savoy (now in France) in 1455 and endeared himself to most of his subjects. A sufferer of epilepsy, he had to abdicate in favour of his wife but was the remote ancestor of the Italian royal family. He died at Vercelli, Italy. His cultus was confirmed for Savoy in 1677.

Amador *see* **Amator**

Amaethlu (Maethlu) (St) R. Dec 26
C6th. He was the founder of the church of Llanfaethlu on Anglesey, Wales.

Amandus of Bordeaux (St) B. Jun 18
d. ?431. He succeeded St Delphinus as bishop of Bordeaux (*c*404) and converted and catechized St Paulinus of Nola, who wrote about him.

Amandus of Elnone (St) B. Feb 6
?584–?676. Born near Nantes, France, after 15 years as a hermit at Bourges he visited Rome and was ordained as a missionary bishop. He worked in what is now French Flanders and in Belgium, founding many monasteries, and apparently became bishop of Tongeren-Maastricht. That he preached to the Slovenes in Carinthia, Austria, and to the Basques in Navarre, Spain and France, is uncertain. He died as a nonagenarian in retirement at Elnone near Tournai, Belgium, his best-known foundation. The place is now named St-Amand-les-Eaux after him.

Amandus of Lérins (St) R. Nov 18
d. 708. He succeeded the murdered St Aigulf as abbot of Lérins, France, in 676 and dealt firmly with the scandalous situation in the monastery.

Amandus (Amantius)
There are many obscure saints of this name in the period C4th–C7th; the following are identifiable:
1) ? A bishop of Avignon, France. Nov 4
2) d. 346. The first bishop of Strasbourg (now in France). Oct 26
3) C4th. A bishop of Rennes, France. Nov 13
4) C4th. A bishop of Worms, on the Rhine, Germany. Oct 26
5) C4th. A bishop of Rodez, France. Nov 4
6) C5th. A hermit in a Limousin forest, France. Oct 6
7) d. 515. The count of Grisalba near Bergamo, Italy. Apr 6
8) C6th. A Scottish hermit at Beaumont near Rheims, France. Jun 16
9) C6th. The abbot-founder of St-Amand-de-Coly, Limoges, France. Jun 25
10) d. 644. The abbot-founder of Moissac, France. Feb 6
11) C7th. The abbot-founder of Nantes, France. Feb 6
12) C7th. The abbot-founder of St-Amand-de-Boixe, France. May 22

Amantius (St) *see* **Getulius, Cerealis and Comps**

Amantius (St) *see* **Landoald and Amantius**

Amantius (St) *see* **Zoticus, Irenaeus and Comps**

Amantius, Alexander and Comps (SS) MM. Jun 6
? Traditionally Amantius was a bishop of Noyon, France, who evangelized around Carcassonne and who had three brothers who were priests. The four were martyred at Cannes near Caracassonne.

Amantius of Città del Castello (St) P. Sep 26
d. *c*600. He was a priest (and is now the patron) of Città del Castello near Perugia, Italy, and was a valued acquaintance of Pope St Gregory the Great.

Amantius of Como (St) B. Apr 8
d. 440. He succeeded St Provinus as bishop of Como, Italy.

Amarand (St) B. R. Nov 7
d. *p*725. An abbot of Moissac, he became bishop of Albi, France, at the end of the C7th.

Amaranthus (St) M. Nov 7
C3rd. He was mentioned by St Gregory of Tours as having been martyred at Albi, France, but details are lacking.

Amarinus (Amarian) (St) M. R. Jan 25
d. 676. Superior of a monastery in the Vosges, France, where the village of St Amarin is now situated, he was martyred with St Praejectus of Clermont.

Amasius (St) B. Jan 23
d. 356. A Greek refugee from the Arians, he became second bishop of Teano, Italy, in 346.

Amaswinthus (St) R. Dec 22
d. 982. He was abbot for 42 years of a monastery at Silva de Málaga in Andalucia, Spain.

Amata of Bologna (St) R(OP). Jun 10
d. 1270. A Dominican nun of St Sixtus at Rome, she was co-founder of the nunnery of St Agnes in Val di Pietro, Bologna, Italy.

Amata-of-Jesus de Gordon (Bl) *see* **Orange (Martyrs of)**

Amata of Joinville (St) R. Sep 24
C6th? Allegedly one of the seven saintly daughters of a count of Perthes who became hermits near Châlons-sur-Marne, France, she was at Joinville. The others were SS Francula, Hoilde, Liberia, Lutrud, Menehould and Pusinna.

Amator, Peter and Louis
(SS) MM. Apr 30
d. 855. They were martyred at Cordoba, Spain, under the Umayyad Emir for preaching in public. Amator was a priest from Martos near Cordoba, Peter was a monk and Louis was a layman.

Amator of Autun (St) B. Nov 26
C3rd. He was a bishop of Autun, France.

Amator of Auxerre (St) B. May 1
d. 418. He was bishop of Auxerre, France. His extant biography is unreliable.

Amator (Amador) of Guarda
(St) R. Mar 27
? There are several churches in Portugal dedicated to this hermit from near Guarda, who has been confused with St Amator of Rocamadour.

Amator (Amatre, Amadour) of Rocamadour (St) Aug 20
? An incorrupt body was found buried beneath the floor of the church of Our Lady of Rocamadour, France, in 1166, and a cultus of 'St Amadour' established. Nothing is known of him, and incorruption cannot now be accepted in itself as proof of sanctity. A common opinion is that he was a hermit.

Amatus of Nusco (St) B. R(OSB)? Aug 31
d. 1093. He was a bishop of Nusco near Naples, Italy. It has been alleged that he was a Benedictine monk beforehand.

Amatus (Amat, Amé, Aimé, Amado) of Remiremont (St) R. Sep 30
?567–?628. From Grenoble, France, he was a monk and hermit for over thirty years at the abbey of St Maurice of Agaune, Switzerland, before joining St Eustace at Luxeuil. There he inspired St Romaric to found the Columbanian double monastery of Remiremont in 620, and became its first abbot.

Amatus Ronconi (Bl) R(OSB). May 8
d. 1292. From near Rimini, Italy, he became a monk at the abbey of San Giuliano there after four pilgrimages to Compostela. His cultus was confirmed for Rimini in 1776.

Amatus of Sion (St) B. R. Sep 13
d. 690. Abbot of Agaune, he became bishop of Sion in the Valais, Switzerland (not of Sens, as claimed). A false accusation led to his banishment firstly to the abbey of Péronne and then to that of Breuil, where he died as a monk.

Ambicus, Victor and Julius
(SS) MM. Dec 3
C4th. They were martyred at the imperial capital of Nicomedia, Asia Minor, in the reign of Diocletian.

Ambrose of Agaune (St) R. Nov 2
d. 523. He was abbot of Agaune near St Moritz, Switzerland, not to be confused with another of the same name who died in 582.

Ambrose of Alexandria (St) L. Mar 17
d. *c*250. A rich nobleman of Alexandria, Egypt, he was a friend and patron of Origen and suffered a spell of imprisonment for his faith in the reign of Maximinus.

Ambrose Autpertus (St) R. Jul 19
d. ?778. From France, he was Charlemagne's tutor at the court of Pepin the Short but, while in the Duchy of Benevento, Italy, as the king's

envoy, he entered the abbey of St Vincent at Volturno and later became its abbot. He was highly rated as a biblical exegete in the Middle Ages.

Ambrose Barlow (St) M. R(OSB). Sep 10
d. 1641. From near Manchester, Edward Barlow was baptized as a Catholic, raised as a Protestant but re-converted and studied for the priesthood at Douai and Valladolid. He became a monk of St Gregory's at Douai in 1615 but transferred his stability to the Spanish abbey of Cellanova. He worked in southern Lancashire for twenty-four years and was imprisoned and released four times before being captured at Leigh and executed at Lancaster. He was canonized in 1970. *See* **England (Martyrs of)**.

Ambrose of Cahors (St) B. Oct 16
d. ?752. He was a bishop of Cahors, France, but resigned to be a hermit and died at a place in Berry now called St-Ambrose-sur-Arnon.

Ambrose Chevreaux (Bl) *see* **September (Martyrs of)**

Ambrose of Ferentino (St) M. Aug 16
d. ?303. He was a centurion martyred at Ferentino in central Italy in the reign of Diocletian, but his acta have their earliest documentary witness from the C14th.

Ambrose Fernandez (Bl)
M. R(SJ). Mar 14
1551–1620. From Sisto in Portugal, he went as a fortune-hunter to Japan but joined the Jesuits as a lay brother in 1577. He died of a stroke in the notorious prison of Suzuta at Omura and was beatified in 1867. *See* **Japan (Martyrs of)**.

Ambrose Kibuka (St) M. Jun 3
d. 1886. A page at the court of King Mwanga of Buganda, Uganda, he was burnt alive in the year after his baptism. *See* **Charles Lwanga and Comps**.

Ambrose of Milan (St) B. Dr. Dec 7
?339–397. Born in Gaul, where his father was praetorian prefect, he became a lawyer at Rome and then the governor of Liguria and Emilia while in his early 30s. He was based in Milan, Italy, the imperial capital in the West, at a time when the Church was disturbed by Arianism. While he was keeping order at the election of a new bishop he found himself elected by acclamation after a child shouted 'Ambrose for bishop!' Despite being unwilling and only a catechumen, he was ordained on Dec 7, 374, became a great pastor and was the most influential churchman of the time in Italy (the popes included). Well known for his charity, his writings, his ability in administration and his fervent opposition to Arianism, he also opposed the misuse of secular power, as in his famous rebuke of Emperor Theodosius I over a massacre at Thessalonika. He is one of the four great Latin Fathers and a doctor of the Church, and his attributes are a whip or a beehive (as a reference to the sweetness of his preaching).

St Ambrose of Milan, Dec 7

Ambrose of Saintes (St) B. Aug 28
d. *p*450. He was bishop of Saintes, France, for fourteen years and was the predecessor of St Vivian, who is venerated with him at La Rochelle.

Ambrose Sansedoni (Bl) R(OP). Mar 20
1220–1287. From Siena, he joined the Dominicans in 1237 and studied with St Thomas Aquinas under St Albert the Great at Cologne. A superb preacher (his vehemence was supposed to have hastened his death), he preached in Germany, France and Italy and was also master of the pope's palace. His attribute is a model of his native city, and his cultus was confirmed in 1622.

Ambrose of Sens (St) B. Sep 3
d. *c*450. All that is known is that he was bishop of Sens, France.

Ambrose Traversari (Bl)
R(OSB Cam). Nov 20
1376–1439. Born near Florence, Italy, he became a typical Renaissance scholar who studied under the Greek humanist Chrysoloras at Venice, but then he joined the Camaldolese at St Mary of the Angels at Florence in 1400. There he wrote much (especially in Greek), accumulated an important library and worked for the reconciliation of the patriarchate of Constantinople at the Council of Florence. In 1431 he became abbot-general of his order.

Amé *see* **Amatus**

Amedeus *see* **Amadeus**

Amelberga This has variants: Amalberga, Amalburga, Amalia, Amelia.

Amelberga of Maubeuge (St) R. Jul 10
d. 690. Born in Brabant in the Low Countries, she was a niece or sister of Bl Pepin of Landen, wife of Count Witger and mother of SS Gudula, Emebert and Reineldis. Witger became a monk at Lobbes and she became a nun at Maubeuge in Flanders, France.

Amelberga of Münsterbilzen
(St) R. Jul 10
d. ?772. She was clothed as a nun at Münsterbilzen in Belgium (near Maastricht, Netherlands), by St Willibrord. Her relics transferred to the abbey of St Peter at Ghent, Belgium, in 1073.

Amelberga of Susteren (St)
R(OSB). Nov 21
d. *p*900. Abbess of Susteren in Limburg, Netherlands, she educated two daughters of the king of Lorraine.

Amicus and Amelius (SS) MM. Oct 12
d. 773. Two Frankish knights, they died while on Charlemagne's campaign against the Lombards in north Italy and have a cultus at Mortara in Lombardy.

Amicus of Fonteavellana
(St) R(OSB). Nov 20
d. ?1045. After being a secular priest and a hermit he became a monk at St Peter's Abbey at Fonteavellana, Italy, which had just been founded by St Dominic of Sora and was subject to Montecassino. His cultus was fostered at the latter place. (St Peter's was not St Peter Damian's monastery.)

Ammia (St) *see* **Theodotus of Caesarea and Comps**

Ammianus (St) *see* **Theodore, Oceanus and Comps**

Ammon, Emilian, Lassa and Comps (SS) MM. Feb 9
? They were a group of 44 martyred at Membressa in Roman Africa.

Ammon, Theophilus, Neoterius and Comps (SS) MM. Sep 8
? They were a group of 25 martyred at Alexandria in Egypt.

Ammon, Zeno, Ptolemy, Ingen and Theophilus (SS) MM. Dec 20
d. 249. The first four were soldiers and the last a civilian, and they were at the trial of a Christian in Alexandria, Egypt, who was wavering. They gave vocal support and were themselves beheaded.

Ammon the Great (St) R. F. Oct 4
d. *c*350. One of the greatest Egyptian desert fathers, he came from a wealthy family who forced him to marry, but he and his wife lived in chastity for eighteen years before separating by mutual agreement in order to become consecrated religious. Ammon settled as a hermit at Nitria, on the western edge of the Delta, and eventually had up to 5000 monks around him. This monastic settlement attracted many educated people from Alexandria. It was not the present Wadi Natrun, which was another famous monastic settlement called Scetis.

Ammon of Heraclea and Comps (SS) MM. Sep 1
d. ?322. A deacon and forty young women whom he had converted, they were martyred at Heraclea in Thrace, European Turkey, in the reign of Licinius. Ammon was killed by a red-hot helmet put on his head.

Ammonaria, Ammonaria, Mercuria and Dionysia (SS) MM. Dec 12
d. *c*250. They were martyred in Alexandria, Egypt, in the reign of Decius. The two Ammonarias were teenagers, Mercuria was an old woman and Dionysia was the mother of a large family.

Ammonius (St) *see* **Dionysius and Ammonius**

Ammonius (St) *see* **Faustus, Didius and Comps**

Ammonius (St) *see* **Modestus and Ammonius**

Ammonius (St) *see* **Moseus and Ammonius**

Ammonius (St) *see* **Theodore of Pentapolis and Comps**

Ammonius and Alexander
(SS) MM. Feb 9
? They were martyred at Soli on Cyprus.

Amnichad (Amnuchad)
(Bl) R(OSB). Jan 30
d. 1043. Either Scottish or Irish, he became a monk and then a hermit at Fulda, Germany.

Amo (Amon) of Toul (St) B. Oct 23
C4th. He succeeded St Mansuetus as bishop of Toul, France.

Amor (St) *see* **Viator and Amor**

Amor (Amator, Amour) of Amorbach (St) R. Aug 17
C8th. He was a companion of St Pirmin in the latter's missionary work in Germany, and founded the abbey of Amorbach in Franconia.

Amor (Amour) of Aquitaine (St) R. Oct 8
C9th. Born in Aquitaine, France, he was a hermit at Maastricht, Netherlands, and founded the nunnery of Münsterbilzen near Liege, Belgium. He has been confused with St Amor of Amorbach.

Amparo Rosat y Balasch (Bl) *see* **Angela-of-St-Joseph Lloret Martí and Comps**

Ampelius (St) *see* **Saturninus, Dativus and Comps**

Ampelius of Milan (St) B. Jul 7
d. ?672. He was bishop of Milan while the Lombards were invading Italy, and had some good influence on them.

Ampelus and Gaius (SS) MM. Nov 20
d. ?302. Nothing is known of them, although they have been presumed to have been martyred at Messina, Sicily, in the reign of Diocletian.

Amphianus (Appian, Apian) (St) M. Apr 2
d. ?305. A young man of Lycia, Asia Minor, he went into the governor's house and interrupted his sacrifice to his domestic idols with a rebuke. For this he was tortured to death. His brother was St Aedisius.

Amphibalus (St) P. Jun 24
C3rd or C4th. He was the anonymous priest who was sheltered by St Alban and who diverted attention by borrowing and wearing his 'amphibalus' or cloak. This was mistakenly taken to be the name of the priest, who was also mistakenly alleged to have been martyred with St Alban.

Amphilochius (St) *see* **Philetus, Lydia and Comps**

Amphilochius of Iconium (St) B. Nov 23
c340–?395. A cousin of St Gregory Nazianzen, he studied with him and St Basil at Constantinople and was a lawyer in Constantinople before being made bishop of Iconium, Asia Minor (now Konya in Turkey) by St Basil in 373. He was one of the Cappodocian Fathers, opposing Arianism and Macedonianism and writing an important work on the divinity of the Holy Spirit against the latter. He also presided at the synod of Side, which condemned the Messalian assertion that prayer is the only means of salvation. Most of his writings have been lost.

Amphion of Nicomedia (St) B. Jun 12
d. *p*325. He was bishop of Epiphania in Cilicia during the persecution of Galerius, was later made bishop of Nicomedia, Asia Minor, and attended the First Council of Nicaea. He wrote against the Arians.

Ampliatus, Urban and Narcissus (SS) MM. Oct 31
C1st. They are mentioned in St Paul's letter to the Romans (16:8–12), and feature in the legends associated with St Andrew in Greece.

Amulwine (Amolvine) (St) B. R. Feb 7
d. *c*750. He succeeded St Erminus as abbot and regionary bishop of Lobbes near Charleroi, Belgium.

Amunia (St) R(OSB). Mar 11
d. ?1069. As a widow she joined her daughter St Aurea as a hermit affiliated to the abbey of Cogolla in La Rioja, Spain.

Anacharius (Aunacharius, Aunaire) of Auxerre (St) B. Sep 25
d. 604. From near Orléans, France, he was educated at the Burgundian court and became bishop of Auxerre in 561. He ordered the Divine Office to be recited in all his diocesan churches.

Anacharius-of-the-Immaculate Benito Nozal (Bl) *see* **Nicephorus Díez Tejerina and Comps**

Anacletus *see* **Cletus**

Ananias (St) M. Jan 25
C1st. He was the disciple who baptized St Paul (*see* Acts 9), and his legend states that he evangelized Damascus, Eleutheropolis (near Gaza) and other places before being martyred.

Ananias (St) *see* **Simeon Barsabae and Comps**

Ananias of Arbela (St) M. L. Dec 1
? He was martyred at Arbela, either the one in Persia or the one in north Mesopotamia.

Ananias of Phoenicia and Comps (SS) MM. Feb 25
d. ?298. A priest of Phoenecia (now the Lebanon), he was imprisoned in the reign of Diocletian and converted Peter his jailer and seven soldiers of the guard. They were all martyred together.

Anastasia (St) V. Dec 25
d. ?304. Traditionally she was martyred at Sirmium (now Srem Mitrovica in Serbia), but her acta are worthless and little is known of her. Her relics were taken to Constantinople and her cultus in Rome developed around her basilica by the Forum, where many Byzantine officials used to live. She was the only saint commemorated at Christmas, and her name is in the Roman Canon of the Mass.

Anastasia (St) *see* **Basilissa and Anastasia**

Anastasia and Cyril (SS) MM. Oct 28
d. ?253. Their dubious and distasteful story, recounted in the old Roman Martyrology, involves a Roman woman being publicly mutilated in the reign of Valerian and a bystander who had done her a kindness being martyred with her. There is doubt concerning their historical existence.

Anastasia the Patrician (St) R. Mar 10
C6th? Her fictitious story describes her as a noblewoman of Constantinople who caught the eye of Emperor Justinian and excited the jealousy of Empress Theodora. To get away from this she went to a nunnery in Alexandria, and then spent 28 years in Scythia (now Dobrudja, Romania) disguised as a male hermit. This is a fairly common stock theme in hagiography.

Anastasius (St) M. Dec 5
? Nothing is known about this martyr.

Anastasius (St) *see* **Cyriac, Paulillus and Comps**

Anastasius (St) *see* **Julian, Basilissa and Comps**

Anastasius (St) *see* **Marcellus and Anastasius**

Anastasius (St) *see* **Maximus the Confessor and Comps**

Anastasius I, Pope (St) Dec 19
d. 401. He became pope in 399. The old Roman Martyrology, St Jerome, St Augustine and St Paulinus of Nola all praised his poverty and pastoral concern. He held a synod against Origenism in 400 and was succeeded by his son, Innocent I.

Anastasius, Felix and Digna (SS) MM. Jun 14
d. 853. They were two monks and a nun of the double monastery of Tábanos, near Cordoba, Spain, in the time of the Muslim Umayyad emirs. Anastasius had been a deacon at a church in the city and Felix was a Berber monk from Asturias. They were executed for preaching at Cordoba.

Anastasius, Jucundus, Florus, Florianus, Peter, Ratites, Tatia and Tilis (SS) MM. Jan 6
C4th. They were martyred at Sirmium (now Srem Mitrovica in Serbia).

Anastasius, Placid, Genesius and Comps (SS) MM. Oct 11
? They were listed as martyrs in the old Roman Martyrology, but with no details.

Anastasius I of Antioch (St) B. Apr 21
d. 599. Patriarch of Antioch, Syria, he opposed the imperial innovations in Christology by Justinian and was exiled for 23 years by Justin II. He was restored by Maurice with the aid of St Gregory the Great. He is not to be confused with his namesake of Sinai.

Anastasius II of Antioch, the Younger (St) M. B. Dec 21
d. 609. He succeeded St Anastasius I as patriarch of Antioch, Syria, and was horribly murdered during a rebellion of the Syrian Jews against the tyrannical Emperor Phocas (who had ordered a persecution against them).

Anastasius of Brescia (St) B. May 20
d. 610. Bishop of Brescia in Lombardy, Italy, he helped to convert the Lombards from Arianism.

Anastasius of Camerino and Comps (SS) MM. May 11
d. 251. An army tribune involved in the persecution in the reign of Decius, he was converted by the courage of those being tortured under his authority. A few days after this he and his entire household were arrested and beheaded. Their shrine is at Camerino in the Marches, Italy.

Anastasius of Cluny (St) R(OSB). Oct 16
*c*1020–1085. A rich and well-educated Venetian, he became a monk at Mont-Saint-Michel in Normandy, France, but left because of a simoniac abbot and joined Cluny under St Hugh in 1066. He went to preach to the Muslims in Spain for seven years by order of the Pope in 1073, then returned to Cluny. Afterwards he was a hermit near Toulouse and died on his way back to Cluny again.

Anastasius Cornicularius (St) M. Aug 21
d. 274. According to his story (a duplication of that of St Anastasius of Camerino), he was an army officer ('Cornicularius' was a rank) who was converted by the example of St Agapitus at Salone near Palestrina, Italy, and was then martyred. The old Roman Martyrology, however, confused him with St Anastasius the Fuller in placing his martyrdom at Salona in Dalmatia, Croatia.

Anastasius of Esztergom (St) B. R(OSB). Nov 12
d. ?1037. A disciple of St Adalbert of Prague, he was abbot of Brevnov, Czech Republic, and then of Pannonhalma, Hungary, from 996 to 1006 at the invitation of King St Stephen. Then he was made archbishop of Esztergom and primate of Hungary.

Anastasius the Fuller (St) M. Sep 7
d. 304. A cloth-fuller from Aquileia near Venice, Italy, he moved to Salona, near Split, Croatia, and openly professed his faith during the persecution of Diocletian, even painting a cross on his front door. He was executed by drowning.

Anastasius of Lérida (St) May 11
? The patron of Lérida, Spain, he is claimed to have been a native of that city but may be a duplication of one of the martyrs called Anastasius.

Anastasius of Mar Saba and Comps (SS) MM. Mar 20
d. ?797. The archimandrite and brethren of the monastery of Mar Saba in the Judaean Desert, they were massacred by raiders. The monastery survives.

Anastasius of Pavia (St) B. May 30
d. 680. A convert from Arianism, he became bishop of Pavia near Milan, Italy, in 680.

Anastasius the Persian (St) M. Jan 22
d. 628. Magundat had been a soldier of the Persian Shah Chosroes II but he converted, was baptized as Anastasius and became a monk at Jerusalem. In the Persian invasion he was taken to the Shah at Caesarea and executed. His head was eventually enshrined in the Roman church of SS Anastasius and Vincent, but his cultus was confined to local calendars in 1969.

Anastasius of Sens (St) B. Jan 7
d. 977. Archbishop of Sens, France, from 968, he started building the cathedral there and was buried at the abbey of Saint-Pierre-le-Vif.

Anastasius the Sinaite (St) R. Apr 21
d. *c*700. A monk from the Holy Land, he became abbot of St Catherine's at Sinai and was prominent in the Christological controversies of the period, leaving many ascetical and theological works (all of which were later edited). The most famous of these is the *Hodegos* or *Guide*.

Anastasius of Suppentonia (St) R. Jan 11
d. *c*570. A notary of the Roman church, he became abbot of Suppentonia (Castel Sant'Elia) near Nepi, Italy. St Gregory the Great wrote that he and his monks died in quick succession 'at the summons of an angel' (probably from an epidemic).

Anastasius of Terni (St) B. Aug 17
d. ?553. He was bishop of Terni, near Rome, at the time when the Empire was re-conquering Italy from the Ostrogoths. The tradition was that he had been a Syrian hermit near Perugia, but this is thought to be the result of a confusion between a hermit-martyr and a bishop of Terni.

Anathalon (St) B. Sep 24
C1st. The worthless tradition is that St Barnabas sent him to become the first bishop of Milan, Italy, and that he died at Brescia.

Anatolia and Audax (SS) MM. Jul 9
d. *c*250. The former was a Roman girl, martyred near Rieti near Rome with a soldier

whom she had converted in prison. St Jerome wrote that she had a sister, Victoria, and that the two were martyred after being denounced by rejected suitors.

Anatolius (St) *see* **Eustace, Thespesius and Comps**

Anatolius (St) *see* **Photina and Comps**

Anatolius of Cahors (St) B? Feb 7
? He had a shrine at the abbey of Saint-Mihiel near Verdun, France, and his unreliable legend makes him a bishop of Cahors.

Anatolius of Constantinople
(St) B. Jul 3
d. 458. He was patriarch of Constantinople from 449.

Anatolius Kiriggwajjo (St) M. Jun 3
d. 1886. From a family of herdsmen, he became one of the pages of King Mwanga of Buganda, Uganda, and was martyred. *See* **Charles Lwanga and Comps**.

Anatolius of Laodecia (St) B. Jul 3
d. ?282. From Alexandria, Egypt, and head of the Aristotelian school there, he became bishop of Laodecia (Latakia, Syria) in 269. He was a great philosopher and mathematician, and his writings were commended by St Jerome.

Anatolius of Salins (St) B? R. Feb 3
? There is a church dedicated to this hermit where he lived at Salins in the Jura, France. His two legends make him either a Scots bishop of the C9th or a Galician bishop of the C4th.

Andéol *see* **Antiochus**

Andeolus (St) M. May 1
d. 208. His tradition is that he was a subdeacon of Smyrna (Izmir, Turkey), sent to France by St Polycarp and martyred near Viviers on the Rhône.

Andochius, Thyrsus and Felix
(SS) MM. Sep 24
C2nd. The first was a priest of Smyrna (Izmir, Turkey) and the second a deacon. The tradition is that they were sent by St Polycarp to Autun, France, where they lodged with Felix, a rich merchant whom they converted and with whom they were martyred.

Andrew (St) M. A. Nov 30
C1st. The elder brother of St Peter was the first-called of the Apostles (hence his Greek title of 'Protoclete') and features in the Gospels, but he did not become one of the 'Inner Council' of SS Peter, James and John. There is no scriptural evidence for his career after the resurrection. Patristic authors preserved the traditions that he evangelized Scythia (now the coast-lands of Romania) and the heartland of modern Greece, being martyred at Patras. The tradition that he was executed on a diagonal cross is late. Later authors, under the influence of disputes over ecclesiastical precedence, claimed him as the founder of the churches at Byzantium (i.e. Constantinople) and at Kiev. Hence he is the patron of the Patriarchate of Constantinople and of the Ukraine, as well as of Scotland. His alleged body has been at Amalfi, Italy, since it was stolen from Constantinople in 1210, but his head (formerly at Rome) has been returned.

St Andrew, Nov 30

Andrew (St) *see* **Hypatius and Andrew**

Andrew (St) *see* **Peter, Andrew and Comps**

Andrew (St) *see* **Stephen the Younger and Comps**

Andrew and Aponius (SS) MM. Feb 10
C1st. Their legend states that they were martyred at Bethlehem in the Holy Land at the same time as St James the Great.

Andrew, John, Peter and Anthony (SS) MM. Sep 23
d. 900. After the Muslim Aghlabids of Tunisia had conquered Syracuse in Sicily, they deported these four, then tortured and executed them.

Andrew Abellon (Bl) R(OP). May 15
1375–1450. He was the prior of the royal Dominican friary of St Mary Magdalen at Saint-Maximin, France, and also Aix-en-Provence (where he died) and at Marseilles. He was a talented painter. His cultus was confirmed in 1902 for Aix and the Dominicans.

Andrew Alricy and Andrew Angar (BB) *see* **September (Martyrs of)**

Andrew of Antioch (Bl) R(CR). Nov 30
1268–1348. A Norman descendent of Robert Guiscard who was born at Antioch, Syria, he became a Canon Regular of the Holy Sepulchre at Jerusalem. He died at Annecy, now in France, on an expedition to collect funds for the Levantine houses of his order.

Andrew Avellano (St) R. Nov 10
1521–1608. From Castronuovo near Naples, Italy, he became an ecclesiastical lawyer before joining the Theatines and had a very successful apostolate, especially in Lombardy where he became a friend and counsellor of St Charles Borromeo. Dying at Naples when about to say Mass, he was canonized in 1712 but his cultus was confined to local or particular calendars in 1969.

Andrew Bauer (Bl) *see* **Gregory Grassi and Comps**

Andrew Bessette (Bl) R. Jan 6
1845–1937. Born at Saint-Grégoire-d'Iberville in Quebec, Canada, he was a manual worker in the United States before joining the Congregation of the Holy Cross in 1870. For 34 years he did domestic work at the college at Côtes des Neiges and developed a great devotion to St Joseph, which bore fruit when he founded the sanctuary of St Joseph at Montreal in 1904. He was beatified in 1982.

Andrew Bobola (St) M. R(SJ). May 16
1592–1657. A Polish nobleman, he joined the Jesuits at Vilnius, Lithuania, in 1611 and spent his life reconciling Orthodox believers with the Catholic Church. He was captured by a gang of Cossacks at Ivanava near Pinsk, Bielarus, and was tortured and partially flayed before being killed. He was canonized in 1938.

Andrew Caccioli (St) R(OFM). Jun 3
1194–1254. From Spello near Assisi, Italy, he was a wealthy priest before becoming one of the first disciples of St Francis. He supported a strict interpretation of the Franciscan rule against the innovations of Br Elias and was persecuted and imprisoned as a result. He died at the friary he had founded at Spello, and his cultus was confirmed for there in 1738.

Andrew the Calabite (St) M. R. Oct 20
d. 766. A monk of Crete, he went to Constantinople and publicly denounced as heresy the iconoclastic policy of Emperor Constantine V. The latter had him tortured, then abandoned him to a mob of iconoclasts who paraded him through the city and lynched him.

Andrew Cheong (St) *see* **Korea (Martyrs of)**

Andrew Conti of Anagni (Bl) R(OFM). Feb 17
d. 1302. A nobleman from Anagni, Italy, he was a nephew of Pope Alexander IV but became a Franciscan lay brother and then a hermit in the Apennines, staying that way despite an offer to make him a cardinal. He was much troubled by demons, and is invoked against them. He died at Rome and his cultus was confirmed for Anagni in 1724.

Bl Andrew Bessette, Jan 6

Andrew Corsini (St) B. R(OC). Feb 4
1302–1373. A nobleman of Florence, Italy, he spent his early teens in hedonism but joined the Carmelites when aged sixteen and became austerely penitential all his life. He studied at Paris and Avignon, was made prior at Florence and became bishop of Fiesole nearby in 1360. He was charitable to the poor and an effective mediator between the warring factions of the time. He was canonized in 1724 and his cultus was confined to particular calendars in 1969.

Andrew of Crete (St) B. R. Jul 4
*c*660–740. From Damascus, Syria, he was a monk at Mar Saba and then at the Holy Sepulchre in Jerusalem. Then he became a deacon at Hagia Sophia at Constantinople and finally archbishop of Gortyna in Crete in 692. He wrote many homilies and panegyrics of saints, and invented the Byzantine liturgical hymn-form called the 'canon'.

Andrew Dotti (Bl) R(OSM). Aug 31
1256–1315. A nobleman and military officer from Borgo San Sepolcro, Italy, he joined the Servites with St Philip Benizi at Florence in 1278 and went on preaching expeditions with him. He died as a hermit at Vallucola near Montevecchio, and had his cultus confirmed for Borgo San Sepulcro and the Servites in 1806.

Andrew Duliou (Bl) *see* **Laval (Martyrs of)**

Andrew Dung Lac (St) M. P. Dec 21
1785–1839. A Vietnamese priest, he was beheaded with St Peter Thi. *See* **Vietnam (Martyrs of)**.

Andrew of Elnone (Bl) R. Feb 6
d. *c*690. He succeeded St Amand as abbot of Elnone near Tournai, Belgium, and their relics were enshrined together in 694.

Andrew Fardeau (Bl) *see* **William Repin and Comps**

Andrew-Charles Ferrari (Bl) B. Feb 2
1850–1921. From near Parma, Italy, he became a priest and the rector of the seminary there before becoming bishop of Como in 1891. He was made archbishop of Milan in 1894, taking the name Charles in honour of St Charles Borromeo, and proved a model bishop. He was loyal to the teachings of the Church at the time of the Modernist crisis, and sought to put them into practice at a time of great social change. He died of throat cancer and was beatified in 1987.

Andrew of Florence (St) B. Feb 26
d. ?407. He was either the predecessor or successor of St Zenobius as bishop of Florence, Italy, or there may have been two Andrews as such.

Andrew-Hubert Fournet
(St) P. F. May 13
1752–1834. Born at Saint-Pierre-de-Maillé near Poitiers, France, he became parish priest of his native town and served as such, at the risk of his life, through the French Revolution. He, with St Jane-Elizabeth Bichier des Ages, founded the 'Daughters of the Cross' for nursing and teaching in 1807. He died at La Puye and was canonized in 1933.

Andrew dei Franchi Boccagni
(Bl) B. R(OP). May 30
1335–1401. Born in Pistoia near Florence, Italy, he became a Dominican there and was made bishop in 1378. He resigned and went back to his old friary one year before he died. His cultus was confirmed for Pistoia in 1921.

Andrew de'Gallerani (Bl) R. F. Mar 19
d. 1251. A military officer of Siena, Italy, he accidentally killed a man whom he had heard blaspheming and was exiled. He lived a life of unusual penance and charity and was allowed to return, whereupon he founded the 'Brothers of Mercy' (who lasted until 1308). His cultus was confirmed for Siena in 1798.

Andrew Grasset de Saint-Sauveur (Bl) *see* **September (Martyrs of)**

Andrew Hibernon (Bl) R(OFM). Apr 18
1534–1602. Born near Murcia, Spain, of impoverished nobility, he worked to support his sister but was robbed of his savings and joined the Conventual Franciscans in reaction as a lay brother. However, he transferred to the Alcantarines (reformed Franciscans) at Elche, and converted many Muslims by his frank simplicity. He died while setting up a friary at Gandia, and was beatified in 1791.

Andrew Kaggwa (St) M. L. Jun 3
d. 1886. The royal band-master at the court of King Mwanga of Buganda, Uganda, he was baptized in 1881 and later beheaded. *See* **Charles Lwanga and Comps**.

Andrew Kim (St) M. P. Sep 20
d. 1846. A Korean nobleman, he was the first Korean to be ordained priest. This was at Macao, and on his return he was quickly arrested and executed. *See* **Korea (Martyrs of)**.

Andrew-Joseph Marchandon (Bl) *see* **John-Baptist Souzy and Comps**

Andrew of Montereale (Bl)
R(OSA). Apr 12
1397–1480. From Mascioni near Rieti, Italy, when aged fourteen he became an Augustinian friar at Montereale. He was an itinerant preacher in Italy and France and served as provincial superior of Umbria. He was noted for his fasting, and his cultus was confirmed for Rieti in 1764.

Andrew of Peschiera (Bl) R(OP). Jan 19
1400–1485. From Peschiera on Lake Garda near Verona, Italy, he became a Dominican at Brescia when aged fifteen, studied at Florence and then did missionary work in the Valtellina on the Swiss border. The 'Apostle of the Valtellina', his cultus was confirmed for Verona and Como in 1820.

Andrew of Phú Yên (Bl) M. L. Jul 26
?1625–1644. From Phú Yên in south Vietnam, he was converted by Fr de Rhodes, a famous Jesuit missionary in Vietnam, and became a catechist. In 1644 the king ordered foreign missionaries to be expelled and Christianity suppressed; Bl Andrew was ordered to be executed as an example by the city governor. He was beatified in 2000. *See* **Vietnam (Martyrs of)**.

Andrew of Rinn (Bl) M? L. Jul 12
1459–1462. This peasant toddler of Rinn near Innsbruck, Austria, was entrusted to an uncle by his mother when his father died. She later found his body hanging in a wood, and the uncle blamed itinerant Jews for his murder. This led to an anti-Semitic cultus which was confirmed by Pope Benedict XIV in 1752, although he refused to permit canonization.

Andrew of Sandomir (Bl) *see* **Sadoc of Sandomir and Comps**

Andrew the Scot (St) R. Aug 22
d. ?877. His dubious story is that he was a disciple of St Donatus of Fiesole and accompanied him from Ireland to Rome on pilgrimage. Then he became archdeacon at Fiesole near Florence, Italy, when his master was made bishop there.

Andrew de Soveral and Comps (BB) Oct 3
d. 1645. Jesuit missionaries from Portugal had started to evangelize the native peoples of Rio Grande do Norte, at the easternmost tip of Brazil, when the Dutch West India Company invaded in 1630 and established a government at Recife. The people of the two parishes at Natal and Cunhaú were brutally persecuted by the Calvinist Dutch. Those attending Mass at the chapel at Cunhaú were massacred with their priest, Bl Andrew, on July 16. Those of Natal were rounded up, taken to a site 20 km from the city and massacred with their priest, Bl Ambrose-Francis Ferro, after vicious tortures. The two priests and twenty-eight companions were beatified in 2000. (The official list of names is awaited.)

Andrew of Strumi (St)
R(OSB Vall). Mar 10
d. 1097. From Parma, Italy, he was a disciple of St Arialdus at Milan and became a monk at Vallombrosa in 1069. He was first abbot of the Vallumbrosan monastery at Strumi from 1085.

Andrew (Nguyen-kim) Thong
(St) M. L. Jul 15
c1790–1855. A Vietnamese catechist and village leader, he died on his way to exile at Mi-Tho. *See* **Vietnam (Martyrs of)**.

Andrew Tokuan (Bl) M. L. Nov 18
d. 1619. A Japanese layman born in Nagasaki, he was a member of the Confraternity of the Holy Rosary and was burnt alive with Bl Leonard Kimura for sheltering missionaries. He was beatified in 1867. *See* **Japan (Martyrs of)**.

Andrew the Tribune and Comps
(SS) MM. LL. Aug 19
d. ?303. Their story is that they were an officer and some men of Galerius's army on an expedition against the Persians. They were denounced as Christians, took refuge in the Taurus Mountains (in southern Asia Minor) but were followed and killed.

Andrew Trong (St) M. L. Nov 28
1817–1835. A Vietnamese soldier, he became a member of the Paris Mission Society and was beheaded at Hué. It is recorded that his mother caught his severed head. *See* **Vietnam (Martyrs of)**.

Andrew Tuong (St) M. L. Jun 16
1862. He was a Vietnamese layman and martyr. *See* **Vietnam (Martyrs of)**.

Andrew Wang (Tianqing) (St) *see* **Joseph Wang (Yumei) and Comps**

Andrew Wouters van Heynoert
(St) M. P. Jul 9
d. 1592. One of the martyrs of **Gorinchem** (q.v.), he was a secular priest at Heynoert near

Dordrecht, Netherlands, who had been living a scandalous life. When the Calvinist 'Sea-Beggars' captured him and tried to make him apostatize, however, he refused and was hanged with the other martyrs.

Andrew Yakichi (St) M. L. Oct 2
d. 1622. An eight-year-old, he was one of a family of four Japanese martyred at Nagasaki. His father Louis was burned, while he, his mother Lucy and brother Francis were beheaded. *See* **Japan (Martyrs of)**.

Andrew Yoshida (Bl) M. Oct 1
d. 1617. A Japanese layman, he was a member of the Confraternity of the Holy Rosary and was martyred at Nagasaki with Bl Caspar Hikojiro for sheltering missionaries. They were beatified in 1867. *See* **Japan (Martyrs of)**.

Andrew Zoerard (St) R. Jul 17
d. *c*1010. A Polish hermit, he was associated with a Benedictine monastery on the mountain of Zobar near Nitra, Slovakia, and was the spiritual father of St Benedict of Skalka. He was canonized in 1083.

Andronicus (St) *see* **Tharacus, Probus and Andronicus**

Andronicus and Athanasia
(SS) RR. Oct 9
C5th. They were a married couple of Antioch in Syria, the husband being a banker or silversmith. According to their story, when their children died they separated to become hermits in Egypt and, after many years, occupied adjoining cells without recognizing each other until Athanasia died. Their veneration is popular in Egypt and Ethiopia.

Andronicus and Junias
(SS) MM? May 17
C1st. They are mentioned by St Paul in his letter to the Romans (16:7). Other details are legendary.

Anectus (Anicetus) (St) M. Jun 27
d. 303. Cardinal Baronius, the reviser of the old Roman Martyrology, probably made a guess at placing this martyr at Caesarea in the Holy Land in the reign of Diocletian.

Anectus (St) *see* **Codratus of Corinth and Comps**

Anempodistus (St) *see* **Acindynus, Pegasius and Comps**

Anesius (St) *see* **Theodulus, Anesius and Comps**

Angadresima (Angadrisma, Angadreme) (St) R(OSB). Oct 14
d. ?695. Abbess of Oröer-des-Vierges near Beauvais, France, she was a cousin of St Lambert of Lyons and had been professed as a nun by St Ouen.

Angela-Mary Astorch (Bl)
R(OFM Cap). Dec 2
1592–1665. From Barcelona, Spain, she joined the Capuchin nuns there when aged sixteen and became abbess and novice-mistress. She drew up the constitutions for the Spanish Capuchinesses and founded the nunnery at Murcia, where she died. She was known for mystical graces, and was beatified in 1982.

Angela of Foligno (Bl) T(OFM). Jan 4
?1248–1309. She was a rich, self-indulgent married woman of Foligno near Rome, Italy, but converted and became a Franciscan tertiary before her husband and children all died. Then she lived a penitential life as the leader of a large group of tertiaries of both sexes, and had many supernatural and mystical experiences which she recounted to her confessor and which he published. Her cultus was confirmed in 1693.

Angela-of-the-Cross Guerrero Gonzalez (Bl) R. F. Mar 2
1846–1931. Born in Seville, Spain, she tried in turn to join the Carmelites and Sisters of Charity but her health failed her. Then she became a seamstress and eventually founded her own institute in 1875, the 'Society of the Cross', in order to help the poor in their own homes and to have a charism based on bearing one's cross in following Christ. She was beatified in 1982.

Angela-of-St-Joseph Lloret Martí and Comps (BB) MM. RR. Nov 20
1875–1936. Born near Alicante, Spain, she became superior-general of the 'Sisters of Christian Doctrine' who were devoted to catechesis. Their mother-house was suppressed in 1936 at the start of the Spanish Civil War, the seventeen sisters there were imprisoned for three months and then were executed in the autumn at Paterna. They were beatified in 1995. *See* **Spanish Civil War (Martyrs of)**.

Angela de'Merici (St) R. F. Jan 27
1474–1540. She was born on the shores of Lake Garda near Verona, Italy, was orphaned when young and then devoted herself to

educating girls and nursing sick women. She was joined by others, and thus was founded the congregation of the Ursulines in 1535. They were the first teaching order of women religious ever founded. She died at Brescia and was canonized in 1807.

Angela Salawa (Bl) R. Mar 12
1881–1922. Born near Cracow (then in Austria, now in Poland), she became a domestic servant there when aged sixteen. She took a private vow of chastity and did works of charity in her spare time, especially for the sick and wounded during the First World War. In 1917 her health started to fail and she retired to a shed where she spent five years in solitude before dying, offering her poverty and continual prayer for God's glory in the new nation of Poland and in the world. She was beatified in 1991.

Angela-Mary Truszkowska
(Bl) T(OFM). F. Oct 10
1825–1889. A Polish noblewoman born at Kalisz, then in Russian Poland, when young she devoted herself to caring for the poor and needy. A conversion experience in 1848 led her to try her vocation with the Visitation nuns. Failing, she founded the 'Felician Sisters' in 1855 (with a contemplative branch in 1860), and re-founded them in Austrian Galicia in 1865 after their suppression in Russia. The congregation has become international. She was beatified in 1993.

Angelelmus (Bl) B. Jul 7
d. 828. He may have been abbot of the monastery of SS Gervase and Protase at Auxerre, France, before he became bishop there in ?813.

Angelico (Fra) *see* **John Faesulanus**

Angelina of Marsciano (Bl) T(OFM). Jul 15
1377–1435. A noblewoman born at Montegiove in Umbria, Italy, she was married when fourteen and widowed when seventeen. She then founded a convent of Franciscan tertiaries at Foligno in 1397, became the superior and founded fifteen other houses of the new congregation by the time it received papal approval in 1428. Her cultus was confirmed for Foligno in 1825.

Angelus
This is the original Latin form of a name common in Latin countries: 'Angelo' in Italy, 'Ange' in France, 'Angel' in Spain and 'Anjo' in Portugal.

Angelus (St) *see* **Daniel, Samuel and Comps**

Angelus of Acquapagana (Bl) R. Aug 19
1271–1313. After being a Camaldolese monk at Val de Castro he became a Silvestrine hermit at Acquapagana near Camerino, Italy. His cultus was confirmed for Camerino in 1845.

Angelus Carletti (Bl) R(OFM). Apr 12
d. 1495. From Chivasso near Turin, Italy, he was a lawyer and senator of Monferrato but then became a Franciscan at Genoa instead. He filled important offices in his order, wrote a standard text on casuistry (the 'Summa Angelica'), preached among the Muslims and Waldenses and was known for effecting conversions. His cultus was confirmed for Monreale and Cuneo in 1753.

Angelus Conti of Foligno
(Bl) R(OSA). Aug 27
1226–1312. From Foligno, Italy, he became an Augustinian friar when aged twenty and was a friend of St Nicholas of Tolentino. He founded three houses of his order in Umbria, and his cultus was confirmed for Foligno in 1891.

Angelus Falcone of Acri (Bl)
R(OFM Cap). Oct 31
1669–1739. From Acri near Bisignano in Calabria, Italy, he became a Capuchin with difficulty in 1690 after failing twice in trying to become a consecrated religious. His career as a preacher was initially a failure, but then it succeeded spectacularly. He died at Acri and was beatified in 1825.

Angelus of Furci (Bl) R(OSA). Feb 6
1246-1327. From near Chieti in the Abruzzi, Italy, he became an Augustinian friar, studied theology at Paris and then had a life-long career as professor of theology at Naples University. He also served a term as his order's provincial, but refused to become a bishop. His cultus was confirmed for Naples and Vasto in 1888.

Angelus of Gualdo (Bl)
R(OSB Cam). Feb 14
?1265–1325. From Nocera in Umbria, Italy, when young he completed a barefoot penitential pilgrimage to Compostela in Spain before becoming a Camaldolese lay brother. He spent forty years immured in his cell and was known for his simplicity, innocence and gentleness. His cultus was confirmed for Nocera in 1825.

Angelus of Jerusalem (St)
M. R(OC). May 5
1145–1220. Born in Crusader Jerusalem of convert Jewish parents, he was one of the first hermits on Mount Carmel and was chosen to

obtain papal approval for the common rule written for them by St Albert. After visiting Rome he stopped to preach in Sicily and was killed by a man whose crimes he had denounced.

Angelus of Massaccio (Bl)
M. R(OSB Cam) May 8
d. 1458. A Camaldolese monk of Santa Maria di Serra in the Marches, Italy, he was killed by heretics called Fraticelli because of his preaching on Church dogma against them. His cultus was confirmed for Iesi in 1842.

Angelus-Augustine Mazzinghi
(Bl) R(OC). Oct 30
1377–1438. He became a Carmelite in his native city of Florence, Italy, and went on to be professor of theology, prior at Frascati and at Florence, and provincial superior. He was extremely edifying as a consecrated religious, and his cultus was confirmed in 1761 for Florence.

Angelus Orsucci (Bl) M. R(OP). Sep 10
1573–1622. From Lucca, Italy, he became a Dominican there, studied at Valencia and went to be a missionary in the Philippines and then in Japan. He was captured, imprisoned for four years in atrocious conditions at Omura and then burned at Nagasaki in the 'Great Martyrdom' with BB Charles Spinola and Comps. *See* **Japan (Martyrs of)**.

Angelus Scarpetti (Bl) R(OSA). Oct 1
d. *c*1306. From Borgo San Sepulcro in Umbria, Italy, he joined the Augustinian friars and was a fellow student of St Nicholas of Tolentino. He was known for his miracles, and one story was that he resurrected a man who had been executed despite his intercession for a pardon. The claim that he founded several friaries in England is not confirmed. His cultus was confirmed for Borgo San Sepulcro in 1921.

Angelus Sinesius (Bl) R(OSB). Nov 27
d. ?1386. Born at Catania, Sicily, he became a monk at the Benedictine abbey of San Nicolo del' Arena and went on to be abbot of La Scala in Palermo. As such he was influential in restoring the monastic observance in the Sicilian Benedictine monasteries.

Angelus Sostre Corporales (Bl) *see* **Hospitaller Martyrs of Spain**

Angilbert (St) R. Feb 18
*c*750–814. An important figure at the court of Charlemagne, he filled several major offices and was noted for his poetry as well as having two illegitimate sons by the emperor's daughter. The Emperor gave him the abbey of St Riquier, near Abbeville, France, as a reward and he converted from a rather dissipated life to being a reforming abbot, having about 300 monks in his community. He introduced the continual celebration of the Divine Office in relays, thus influencing later Cluniac custom.

Anglin (St) R. Oct 28
d. ?768. He was the tenth abbot of the great twin monasteries of Stavelot-Malmédy, Belgium. *See* **Sigolin**.

Angus *see* **Aengus**

Anianus (St) *see* **Demetrius, Anianus and Comps**

Anianus of Alexandria (St) B. Apr 25
C1st. Eusebius and the apocryphal Acts of St Mark describe him as a shoemaker who was second bishop of Alexandria, Egypt, after St Mark.

Anianus of Chartres (St) B. Dec 7
C5th. He was the fifth bishop of Chartres, France, but nothing else is known.

Anianus of Orléans (St) B. Nov 17
d. ?453. The fifth bishop of Orléans, France, it was left to him to organize the defences of the city at the approach of the Huns under Attila. He allegedly had a meeting with the latter and averted a siege.

Anicetus, Pope *Apr 17*
d. 166. A Syrian, by tradition he became pope in 155. He was visited by St Polycarp to discuss the date of Easter, and this is historically the first evidence for an individual bishop of Rome acting on his own authority. He also fought against the Gnostics. His cultus was suppressed in 1969 after he had been falsely celebrated as a martyr for centuries.

Anicetus, Photinus and Comps (SS) MM. Aug 12
d. ?305. They are known only through unhistorical acta, which describes them as martyrs of Nicomedia, Asia Minor, in the reign of Diocletian.

Anicetus Hryciuk (Bl) *see* **Podlasia (Martyrs of)**

Anicetus-Adolf Seco Gutierrez (St) *see* **Cyril-Bertrand Sanz Tejedor and Comps**

Aninus (St) R. Mar 16
? He is listed as a Syrian hermit of uncertain date known for his austerities and miracles.

Anne (St) L. Jul 26
C1st. The name of the mother of Our Lady is not mentioned in the New Testament, and the earliest reference to SS Joachim and Anne as being her parents is in the 'Protoevangelium of James', an apocryphal work written *c*170. St Anne's cultus emerged in the East in the C6th and in the West in the C8th, but it did not become general in the latter until the C14th. It then became very popular.

St Anne, Jul 26

Anne An (Jiao) (St) See next entry.

Anne An (Xin) and Companions
(SS) MM. Jul 11
1900. She was with St Mary An (Guo) her daughter-in-law, Anne An (Jiao) her grand-daughter-in-law and Mary An (Linghua) her granddaughter when they were seized by a gang of Boxers at their village in Anping county, southeastern Hebei, China. After being invited to abandon their faith they were killed. *See* **China (Martyrs of)**.

Anne-of-St-Basil Cartier (Bl) *see* **Orange (Martyrs of)**

Anne (Susanna) of Constantinople
(St) R. Jul 23
*c*840–918. Born in Constantinople, when she was in her early teens she was orphaned and was left a large fortune. Being pestered by men wanting to marry her for her money, she spent it in helping the poor and went to live fifty years as a hermit near Ephesus instead.

Anne-Mary Erraux (Bl) *see* **Valenciennes (Martyrs of)**

Anne-of-St-Bartholomew García
(Bl) R(OCD). Jun 7
1549–1626. From Almendral near Avila, Spain, she initially took part in her family's work of shepherding but then joined St Teresa's reformed convent at Avila as its first lay sister, becoming the founder's secretary and companion in her journeys to make foundations throughout Spain. In 1606 she was sent to introduce the reform into France as a choir nun, and was prioress at Pontoise and Tours. She founded the English convent at Antwerp, Belgium, in 1612 and died there. She has left some religious verse. She was beatified in 1917.

Anne-Rose Gattorno (Bl) R. F. May 6
1831–1900. From a rich family of Genoa in Italy, she married and had a family but lost her husband and her wealth. This led to a spiritual conversion and she became a Franciscan tertiary, receiving the stigmata in 1862. In 1866 she founded the 'Daughters of St Anne, Mother of Mary Immaculate' at Piacenza for active works of mercy. Her institution had become international by the time she died at Rome. She was beatified in 2000.

Anne Hamard (Bl) *see* **William Repin and Comps**

Anne-Mary Javouhey (Bl) R. F. Jul 15
1779–1851. From Jallanges in the Côte d'Or, France, when she was young during the French Revolution she used to shelter and care for persecuted non-juring priests. After the persecution had passed she founded the 'Sisters of St Joseph of Cluny' at Cabillon in 1805. This mother house was moved to Cluny seven years later, and the sisters started missionary work worldwide. She herself worked on the missions in West Africa and French Guiana for several years. She died in Paris and was beatified in 1950.

Anne Kim (St) *see* **Korea (Martyrs of)**

Anne-Alexander Lanfant (Bl) *see* **September (Martyrs of)**

Anne-Josephine Leroux (Bl) *see* **Valenciennes (Martyrs of)**

Anne Line (St) M. L. Feb 27
1565–1601. From a Calvinist family of Great Dunmow in Essex, she converted when aged twenty and was driven from home as a result. She married a fellow convert in 1585, but he was exiled and she was left destitute in 1594. Then she kept a safe house for priests in London and took private vows. After a raid during a Mass at her house she was arrested and hanged at Tyburn for sheltering priests. She was canonized in 1970. *See* **England (Martyrs of)**.

Anne Maugrin (Bl) *see* **William Repin and Comps**

Anne-of-St-Alexis Minutte (Bl) *see* **Orange (Martyrs of)**

Anne-of-the-Angels Monteagudo (Bl) R(OP). Jan 10
1601–1686. Born in Arequipa in Peru, she joined the Dominicanesses there in 1618. Believing that the monastery should be like a seminary of holiness for the laity, she got permission from the bishop to help those coming to her with prayers, advice and help. Her last decade was one of severe physical suffering , and she was beatified in 1985.

Anne Pak (St) *see* **Korea (Martyrs of)**

Anne (Anna) the Prophetess (St) Sep 1
C1st. *See* the Gospel of St Luke, 2:36–38 (other traditions are apocryphal).

Anne Schäffer (Bl) L. (Oct 5)
1882–1925. From Mindelstetten near Regensburg, Germany, she wished to become a missionary sister but scalded both legs with boiling lye while working in a laundry when aged 19. The injuries did not heal, leaving her bed-ridden. She recognized a call to share mystically in the sufferings of Christ crucified, and received the stigmata in 1910. Despite her infirmity she maintained an active apostolate through a voluminous correspondence. She died of a brain injury caused by falling out of bed, and was beatified in 1999.

Anne-Mary Taigi (Bl) L. Jun 9
1769–1837. She was the daughter of a chemist in Siena, Italy, and when her father's business failed she went to Rome to work as a domestic servant. She married a butler of the Chigi family, had seven children and lived the normal life of a married working-class woman. She reached a high degree of holiness, however, and had the charisms of prophecy and the reading of thoughts. Many high churchmen and noble seculars sought her advice. She was beatified in 1920.

Anne-Frances de Villeneuve (Bl) *see* **William Repin and Comps**

Anne Wang (St) *see* **Joseph Wang (Yumei) and Comps**

Anno of Cologne (St) B. Dec 4
*c*1010–1075. He was the son of a poor knight of Swabia, and when he became the prince-archbishop of Cologne, Germany, in 1056 many of that city despised him for it. However, he had a crowded, important and not always edifying career in the Church and in politics, and founded the abbey of Siegburg (which survives). He retired there to do strict penance for the last year of his life.

Anno of Herrieden (Bl) *see* **Cathold, Anno and Diethard**

Anno (Hanno, Annon) of Verona (St) B. May 13
d. 780. He was a bishop of Verona, Italy.

Annobert (Alnobert) (St) B. R. May 16
d. *p*689. A monk of Almenèches, he became bishop of Sées in Normandy, France, in 685.

Annunciata Cocchetti (Bl) R. F. Mar 23
1800–1882. From near Brescia, Italy, her family were rich but she was orphaned, moved to Milan and, on the advice of Fr Luke Passi, settled at Cemmo in the Camunico valley and opened a girls' school in 1831. In 1842 she joined the 'Teaching Sisters of St Dorothy', founded at

Venice by Fr Luke and, when he died, the bishop of Brescia encouraged her to found an independent congregation, the 'Sisters of St Dorothy at Cemmo', in 1866. She was beatified in 1991.

Ansanus the Baptizer (St) M. Dec 1
d. ?304. His story is that he was of the Anician family of Rome, became a Christian when aged twelve and was handed over to the authorities by his father. He escaped, and gained his nickname by converting many at Bagnorea and Siena before being recaptured and beheaded.

Ansbald (St) R(OSB). Jul 12
d. 886. A nobleman of Luxembourg, he became abbot of Prüm, Germany, in 860 and made the abbey famous for its observance. He is noted for re-building Prüm with the help of Emperor Charles the Fat after the Norsemen had burned it down.

Ansbert (St) B. R. Feb 9
d. 693. He was the chancellor at the court of the Merovingian king Clotaire III before becoming a monk at Fontenelle in Normandy, France, under St Wandrille, the founder. He was the third abbot, and became bishop of Rouen in 684. Pepin of Heristal banished him, and he died at the abbey of Hautmont.

Ansegis (St) R(OSB). Jul 20
*c*770–833. From near Lyons, France, he became a monk of Fontenelle in Normandy when aged eighteen, and was then chosen by Charlemagne to restore several abbeys, including Luxeuil and his own house. A great canonist, he wrote a collection of capitularies which was incorporated into the imperial law-code.

Anselm of Canterbury
(St) B. Dr. R(OSB). Apr 21
?1033–1109. From Aosta in Piedmont, Italy, he became a monk at Bec (now Le Bec-Hellouin), France, under Bl Herluin, then was abbot there and succeeded Lanfranc as archbishop of Canterbury, England, in 1093. He was soon exiled by King William II, however, and was at the council of Bari in 1098 where he helped to reconcile the Byzantine-rite bishops of the area of south Italy just conquered by the Normans. The next king, Henry I, invited him back but exiled him again after he disputed the king's right to invest bishops. He only returned permanently in 1106. His philosophical and theological work was a bridge between the patristic authors (especially St Augustine) and the scholastics, and is still of importance (especially his presentation of the 'ontological argument'). His biography was written by his secretary, a monk of Canterbury Cathedral called Eadmer. He was declared a doctor of the Church in 1720.

St Anselm of Canterbury, Apr 21

Anselm II of Lucca (St) B. R(OSB). Mar 18
1036–1086. Born at Mantua, Italy, he was chosen to be bishop of Lucca by his uncle, Pope Alexander II, but initially refused to be invested by Emperor Henry IV. Pope St Gregory VII later persuaded him to accept for a while, but then he fled his diocese and became a Cluniac monk at Polizone. The pope made him return, but his attempt to reform the cathedral canons at

Lucca caused them to rebel and he fled again. He then became the papal legate in Lombardy, and was a strong supporter of Pope St Gregory as well as being a noted scholar and canonist (a collection by him of canon laws is extant). He died at Mantua.

Anselm of Nonantola (St) R. Mar 3
d. 803. Duke of Friuli and brother-in-law of the Lombard King Aistulf, he became a monk and founded the abbeys of Fanano and Normantola, Italy, together with attached hospitals and hostels. Banished to Montecassino by the next king, Desiderius, after seven years he was restored by Charlemagne when the Lombard kingdom had been conquered by the Franks.

Anselm Polanco Fontecha and Philip Ripoll Morata
(BB) MM. BB. R(OSA) Feb 2
d. 1939. Bl Anselm was born near Palencia, Spain, joined the Augustinian friars and became bishop of Teruel in 1935. Bl Philip, his vicar-general, was born in Teruel. When the city was captured by the Republicans in 1938 during the Spanish Civil War, the two were imprisoned for 13 months. At war's end, they were taken hostage by disbanded soldiers and shot in a gorge near Gerona. They were beatified in 1995. *See* **Spanish Civil War (Martyrs of)**.

Ansfrid (Bl) B. R(OSB). May 3
d. 1010. Duke of Brabant in the Low Countries and an imperial knight, he founded the convent of Thorn in 992 for his wife and daughter, and became a monk at his other foundation of Heiligen. But he was made archbishop of Utrecht, Netherlands, in 994, which he remained until he went blind in 1006. Then he retired to Heiligen to die.

Ansgar (Anskar, Oscar) (St)
B. R(OSB). Feb 3
801–865. A nobleman from near Amiens, France, he was educated at the abbey of Corbie in Picardy when St Adelard was abbot and St Paschasius Radbert was schoolmaster. After becoming a monk there he was transferred to New Corbie in Lower Saxony, Germany (Corvey near Paderborn), whence he was taken by King Harold of Denmark to evangelize his subjects. After a missionary expedition to Sweden he was made first archbishop of Hamburg in 832 after the Franks conquered the Saxons, and his mission territory covered Denmark, Scandinavia and northern Germany as well. After Hamburg was destroyed by the Vikings in 845 his see was united to that of Bremen. His personal missionary efforts in Sweden met with initial success but with eventual failure, and Christianity was only firmly established there in the C11th. He died at Bremen and is the patron of Denmark.

Ansilio (St) R(OSB). Oct 11
d. late C7th. He was a monk of the abbey of Lagny near Meaux, France, where he had a cultus.

Ansovinus (St) B. Mar 13
d. 840. A hermit near Torcello, he accepted appointment as bishop of Camerino, Italy, on condition that he was exempt from having to support and provide soldiers (this was standard practice for bishops as feudal lords at the time).

Anstrude (Austrude, Austru)
(St) R. Oct 17
?645–?709. She was the second abbess of the nunnery of St John Baptist at Laon, France, after her mother St Salaberga, who had founded it. The mayor of the palace of the Merovingian king at the time was Ebroin, with whom she had very serious diffculties.

Ansuerus and Comps (SS)
MM. RR(OSB). Jul 15
d. 1066. A noble of Schleswig, he became a monk and then abbot of St Georgenburg near Ratzeburg south of Lübeck, Germany, which abbey became a centre of evangelization among the indigenous Slavs east of the river Elbe. He and 28 of his community were stoned to death in an anti-Christian rebellion by them.

Ansurius (Aduri, Asurius, Isauri) of Orense (St) B. R(OSB). Jan 26
d. 925. A bishop of Orense in Galicia, Spain, from 915, he helped to found the great abbey of Ribas de Sil and resigned to become a monk there in 922.

Anterus, Pope (St) Jan 3
d. 236. A Greek, he was pope for only a few weeks. There is no record of his having been a martyr. He was the first pope to be buried in the catacomb of St Callistus, and part of his epitaph survives.

Anthelm (St) B. R(OCart). Jun 26
1105–1178. A noble from Chignin in Savoy (now in France), he was ordained when young and became a Carthusian at Portes after a chance visit there. In 1139 he became prior of the Grande Chartreuse, and was instrumental in setting the Carthusians up as a separate

religious order. In 1152 he became prior of Portes, and he reluctantly became bishop of Belley in 1163. He was such a model bishop that he was universally loved in his diocese, but he showed his personal preference by visiting his original monastery whenever possible.

Anthes (St) *see* **Fortunatus, Gaius and Anthes**

Anthia (St) *see* **Eleutherius, Anthia and Comps**

Anthimus (St) *see* **Cosmas and Damian**

Anthimus of Nicomedia (St) M. B. Apr 27
d. 303. Bishop of Nicomedia, Asia Minor, he was martyred in the reign of Diocletian (whose capital the place was). There followed a pogrom of local Christians.

Anthimus of Rome (St) M. May 11
d. ?303. His story is that he was a priest of Rome who converted a prefect in the reign of Diocletian and was thrown into the Tiber. He escaped, but was beheaded.

Antholian and Comps (SS) MM. Feb 6
d. ?265. St Gregory of Tours mentions them as martyrs of Auvergne, France, in the reigns of Valerian and Gallienus. The companions were Cassius, Maximus, Liminius and Victorinus.

Anthonius *see* **Anthimus**

Anthony (St) *see* **Andrew, John and Comps**

Anthony (St) *see* **Bassus, Anthony and Protolicus**

Anthony (St) *see* **Irenaeus, Anthony and Comps**

Anthony (St) *see* **Julian, Basilissa and Comps**

Anthony (St) *see* **Melasippus, Carina and Anthony**

Anthony, Merulus and John
(SS) RR. Jan 17
C6th. St Gregory the Great wrote about these three monks of his monastery of St Andrew on the Coelian Hill in Rome, describing their virtues and miracles.

Anthony Auriel (Bl) *see* **John-Baptist Souzy and Comps**

Anthony Baldinucci (Bl) R(SJ). Nov 7
1665–1717. From Florence, Italy, he became a Jesuit in 1681 and was a home missionary in the Abruzzi and Romagna. He had some very unusual methods of preaching and of calling people to penance, such as whipping himself until bloody. Dying at Pofi, he was beatified in 1893.

Anthony Bannassat (Bl) *see* **John-Baptist Souzy and Comps**

Anthony Bonafaldi (Bl) R(OFM). Dec 1
?1402–1482. From Ferrara, Italy, he became a Franciscan there and was sent to the Holy Land. Having returned, he died at Contignola near Faenza, and his cultus was confirmed for Faenza in 1901.

Anthony Boucharenc de Chaumeils and Anthony de Bouzet (BB) *see* **September (Martyrs of)**

Anthony Chevrier (Bl) P. F. Oct 2
1826-1879. From Lyons, France, he became parish priest at St Andrew's there in 1860. Following the advice of St John Vianney to arrange for the catechizing of poor children for first communion, he founded the catechesis centre of 'La Providence du Prado', and tertiary Franciscan congregations of priests and sisters to run it. He also took charge of a new parish in the suburbs across the river Rhône, then in a separate diocese. He was beatified in 1986.

Anthony della Chiesa (Bl) R(OP). Jul 28
1394–1459. A nobleman from near Vercelli in Piedmont, Italy, after he became a Dominican he was prior of the friaries of Como, Savona, Florence, and Bologna and was a helper of St Bernardine of Siena in his apostolate. His cultus was confirmed for Vercelli in 1819.

Anthony-Mary Claret
(St) B. F. Oct 24
1807–1870. From Salent in Catalonia, Spain, he was a weaver before being ordained in 1835. He devoted himself to home missions, and the group of priests which helped him he formed into the 'Missionary Sons of the Immaculate Heart of Mary', nicknamed the 'Claretians'. He became bishop of Santiago de Cuba in 1850 and was appointed royal confessor to Queen Isabella II in 1856, in both offices having great difficulty from anti-clericalism. He and the queen both went into exile in 1868, and he died at Fontfroide in France after having attended the First Vatican Council and spoken in favour of papal infallibility. He was known for his

charisms of prophecy and miracles, and was canonized in 1950.

Anthony Correa (Bl) *see* **Ignatius de Azevedo and Comps**

Anthony-Mary Dalmau Rosich (Bl) *see* **Philip-of-Jesus Munárriz Azcona and Comps**

Anthony Daniel (Bl) *see* **John Brébeuf and Comps**

Anthony Daveluy and Comps (SS) MM. B. Mar 30
d. 1866. From Amiens, France, he was sent to Korea as a missionary priest, where he became coadjutor to Bl Simon Berneaux for twenty years and wrote many works in Korean. He was seized in Keutori, interrogated before the royal tribunal, imprisoned, tortured and killed with a sword. He had four companions: Peter Amaître, a priest aged 29 from Angoulême; Martin-Luke Huin, a priest aged 30 from Langres; Luke Hoang (Chai-ken), a Korean layman convert who had given much help to SS Simon and Anthony, especially in translating into Korean; and Joseph Chiang (Nak-syo), who was a Korean catechist aged 64. They were canonized in 1984. *See* **Korea (Martyrs of)**.

Anthony Deynan (St) M. T(OFM). Feb 6
d. 1597. A Japanese native of Nagasaki, he was an acolyte and a Franciscan tertiary who was crucified when aged thirteen. *See* **Paul Miki and Comps** and **Japan (Martyrs of)**.

Anthony Fantosati and Comp (SS) B. MM. RR(OFM). Jul 4
d. 1900. Born in 1842 at Santa Maria in Valle, Italy, he became a Franciscan at Spineta and went to China in 1867. After serving as a missionary in Hubei for eighteen years he was made Vicar-General of Upper Hubei and Vicar-Apostolic of South Hunan in 1892. During the Boxer uprising he was travelling by boat to Henyang with Joseph Gambaro, who was a Franciscan priest born near Novara, Italy, in 1869. They were ambushed and beaten to death. *See* **China (Martyrs of)**.

Anthony Fatati of Ancona (Bl) B. Jan 19
*c*1410–1484. Born at Ancona, Italy, he was in turn archpriest at Ancona, vicar-general of Siena, canon at St Peter's at Rome, bishop of Teramo and finally bishop of Ancona. He has a cultus in all these places.

Anthony Fernandez (Bl) *see* **Ignatius de Azevedo and Comps**

Anthony Fournier (Bl) *see* **William Repin and Comps**

Anthony Francisco (Bl) M. R(SJ). Jul 27
d. 1583. Born at Coïmbra, Portugal, he became a Jesuit in 1570. After being sent to India he took charge of the mission of Arlin on the island of Salsette, near Bombay, and was martyred with **Rudolph Acquaviva** (q.v.).

Anthony of Froidemont (St) R(OSB). Mar 9
C10th. A monk of Luxeuil, he became a hermit at Froidemont in Franche-Comté, France.

Anthony Fuster (Bl) R(OP). Apr 5
C14th. A disciple of St Vincent Ferrer, he was well known for reconciling enemies at Vich in Catalonia, Spain, and has a cultus there.

Anthony-of-St-Anne Galvão (Bl) R(OFM). (Dec 23)
1739-1822. From near São Paolo in Brazil, his family was wealthy and he became an Alcantarene Franciscan at Rio de Janeiro in 1760. In 1768 he was made preacher and public confessor at São Paolo, and founded the famous nunnery of Our Lady of Light in the city. He died and was buried there, and was beatified in 1998.

Anthony-Mary Gianelli (St) B. Jun 7
1789–1846. Born at Cereta near Genoa, Italy, of a poor family, he was ordained in 1812 after a benefactress paid for his education, and served as a parish priest before becoming bishop of Bobbio in 1838. He founded the 'Sisters of Our Lady of the Garden' and was a very successful bishop both pastorally and in administration. He died at Piacenza and was canonized in 1951.

Anthony González (St) *see* **Laurence Ruiz and Comps**

Anthony Grassi (Bl) P. Dec 13
d. ?1672. He was a priest of the Oratory at Fermo in the Marches, Italy, and was its superior from 1635 until his death. He had the charism of the reading of consciences and was a great spiritual director. One story is that his serenity of manner became more marked after he was struck by lightning. He was beatified in 1900.

Anthony the Great (St) R. Jan 17
?251–356. He is regarded as being the father of all monks. Born at Coma in Upper Egypt, he was

orphaned in his youth and gave away the property he inherited in order to become a hermit on the outskirts of his village. This was not unusual at the time, but he was the first in then going into the real desert and he spent a long time in seclusion fighting diabolic temptations. Afterwards he became famous throughout Egypt and beyond, and became a strong supporter of St Athanasius against the Arians. He gathered many disciples, having a more public base at Pispir on the Nile and also a completely isolated oasis retreat (the 'Inner Mountain') in the Eastern Desert, where he died and where the Coptic monastery bearing his name still flourishes. St Athanasius wrote his biography, which was translated into Latin and which introduced the monastic ideal to Rome. His attribute is the tau-cross and he is often represented with a pig (which symbolizes his temptations).

St Anthony, Jan 17

Anthony van Hornaer (St) *see* **Gorinchem (Martyrs of)**

Anthony Ishida and Comps
(BB) MM. Sep 3
d. 1632. A Japanese Jesuit, he was burned at Nagasaki with five companions: BB Bartholomew Guttierez, Vincent Carvalho and Francis-of-Jesus Ortega, Augustinians; Jerome-of-the-Cross de Torres, a secular priest, and Gabriel-of-St-Mary-Magdalen of Fonseca, a Franciscan lay-brother. They had been tortured for over a month beforehand in order to induce apostasy. *See* **Japan (Martyrs of)**.

Anthony Kauleas (St) B. Feb 12
829–901. From near Constantinople, he became a monk and abbot of the Theotokos monastery there before being appointed patriarch in 893, the second after Photius. He tried to reconcile the factions which had arisen in the time of the latter.

Anthony Kim (St) *see* **Korea (Martyrs of)**

Anthony Kimura and Comps
(Bl) M. L. Nov 27
1595–1619. Of the family of the daimyos of Hirado-jima and a relative of Bl Leonard Kimura, he was beheaded at Nagasaki (Japan) with ten companions: BB Thomas Koteda, Leo Nakanishi, Alexis Nakamura, Michael Sakaguchi, John Iwanaga, Bartholomew Seki, Matthias Nakano, Matthias Kozaka, Romanus Motayama and John Motayama. *See* **Japan (Martyrs of)**.

Anthony Kiuni (Bl) M. R(SJ). Sep 10
1572–1622. A Japanese, he became a Jesuit at Omura and was burned at Nagasaki during the 'Great Martyrdom' with Charles Spinola and Comps. **See Japan (Martyrs of)**.

Anthony of Korea (Bl) M. L. Sep 10
d. 1622. A Korean catechist helping the Jesuits in Japan, he was beheaded at Nagasaki during the 'Great Martyrdom' with Charles Spinola and Comps. *See* **Japan (Martyrs of)**.

Anthony of Lérins (St) R. Dec 28
d. *c*520. Born in Lower Pannonia (now Hungary), he was a hermit at several places in the Alps before he became a monk at Lérins, France.

Anthony of Lithuania and Comps (SS) MM. LL. Apr 14
d. 1342. Lithuania was the last country in Europe to embrace Christianity, and SS Anthony and John were officials of the court of the Grand Duke who had converted to the Christian faith while it was still pagan. They were crucified for refusing to eat meat on a day of abstinence prescribed by the Church. A bystander, St Eustace, was converted by the example of their fortitude and was himself martyred. The three are the patrons of Vilnius.

Anthony Llauradó Parisi (Bl) *see* **Hospitaller Martyrs of Spain**

Anthony Lucci (Bl) R(OFM). Jul 24
1681–1752. Born in the Abruzzi, Italy, he joined the Franciscans in 1698, studied at Naples and Rome and became a consultant for various dicasteries of the Curia at Rome. The Pope chose him to be bishop of Bovino, where he became known for his charity to the poor. He was bishop for 23 years, and was beatified in 1989.

Anthony Manzoni 'the Pilgrim'
(Bl) L. Feb 1
?1237–1267. Born at Padua, Italy, of a wealthy family, he distributed his inheritance to the poor and then spent the rest of his short life on continuous pilgrimage between Loreto, Rome, Compostela and the Holy Land. His family, including his two sisters who were nuns, considered him a disgrace for living in dire poverty whenever he was in Padua.

Anthony Martinez Gil-Leonis (Bl) *see* **Hospitaller Martyrs of Spain**

Anthony of Milan (Bl) *see* **Monaldus of Ancona and Comps**

Anthony-of-St-Dominic of Nagasaki (Bl) *see* **Dominic Castellet and Comps**

Anthony-of-St-Francis of Nagasaki (Bl) M. L. Aug 17
d. 1627. A Japanese catechist and a fellow worker with **Francis-of-St-Mary of Mancha** (q.v.), he was burned at Nagasaki with him and thirteen others. *See* **Japan (Martyrs of)**.

Anthony Neyrot (Bl) M. R(OP). Apr 10
d. 1460. From Rivoli near Turin, Italy, he became a Dominican but was captured by Muslim pirates on the way to Naples and taken to Tunis. There he apostatized to Islam and married but repented after a few months, put on his Dominican habit and publicly proclaimed Christ. He was stoned to death, and had his cultus confirmed for Turin in 1767.

Anthony Ono (Bl) M. L. Sep 10
d. 1622. A three-year-old, he was martyred during the 'Great Martyrdom' at Nagasaki with his father, Bl Clement Ono, and Charles Spinola and Comps. *See* **Japan (Martyrs of)**.

Anthony-Frederick Ozanam
(Bl) L. F. Sep 9
1813–1853. From Milan, Italy, he was brought up in Lyons, France, and went to Paris to study law in 1831. Two years later he started a lay society for practical work among the poor, which became the 'Society of St Vincent de Paul'. As well as law, he studied literature and became a Sorbonne professor in 1844, specializing in Dante. He was involved in many contemporary Catholic causes, and denounced both economic liberalism and socialism. He died at Marseilles and was beatified in 1997.

Anthony of Padua (St)
Dr. R(OFM). Jun 13
1195–1231. From Lisbon, Portugal, when young he joined the Canons Regular but transferred to the Franciscans at Coïmbra in 1212. He set off for the Maghreb in order to preach to the Muslims but illness and stormy weather brought him to Italy instead. He met St Francis, who helped him establish himself as a preacher against heresy and as a thaumaturge. He died at Padua and was canonized the following year, being especially popular in intercession as a finder of lost objects. In 1946 he was declared a doctor of the Church, being responsible for introducing Augustinian theology to the nascent Franciscans. He is represented with the Christ-Child and a lily.

St Anthony of Padua, Jun 13

Anthony Page (Bl) M. P. Apr 20
d. 1593. Born in Harrow in Middlesex, he studied at Oxford and Douai and was ordained at Soissons in 1591. On Candlemas in 1593 a great search for priests ordered for the North found him at Haworth Hall near York. He was executed at York and was beatified in 1987. *See* **England (Martyrs of)**.

Anthony de' Patrizzi (Bl) R(OSA). Apr 27
d. 1311. From Siena, Italy, he became an Augustinian friar at Monticiano and became the superior of the friary. His cultus was confirmed for the Augustinian friars in 1804.

Anthony Pavoni (Bl) M. R(OP). Apr 9
?1326-1374. From Savigliano south of Turin, Italy, he became a Dominican and superior of the friary in his native town before becoming inquisitor-general for Liguria and Piedmont. He was killed by Waldensian heretics at Bricherasio on leaving a church after preaching a sermon against them, and had his cultus confirmed for Turin and the Dominicans in 1856.

Anthony Perulles Estíval (Bl) *see* **Peter Ruiz de los Paños y Angel and Comps**

Anthony Primaldo and Comps
(BB) MM. Aug 14
d. 1480. The city of Otranto, on the heel of Italy, was briefly captured by the Ottoman Turks in 1480, and they gave the inhabitants the choice between conversion to Islam or death. Led by Bl Anthony, an elderly and pious artisan, eight hundred citizens chose death and were put to the sword with their bishop in the cathedral. The city never recovered. Their cultus was approved for Otranto in 1771.

Anthony-Mary Pucci (St) R(OSM). Jan 12
1819–1892. From Poggiole in Tuscany, Italy, he became a Servite in 1843 and was appointed parish priest of Viarregio. He was a model pastor, especially in his care for the poor and the sick, and was canonized in 1962.

Anthony (Nguyen-Huu) Quynh
(St) M. L. Nov 24
1768–1840. A Vietnamese physician, he became a catechist attached to the Paris Foreign Mission Society and was killed by strangling after two years' imprisonment. *See* **Vietnam (Martyrs of)**.

Anthony du Rocher (St) R. May 4
C6th. He was the abbot-founder of the abbey of St Julian at Tours, France, and then a hermit at a place called Le Rocher. The story that the disciple of St Benedict called St Maurus went on a mission to France, with St Anthony as a companion, is fictional.

Anthony Sanchez Silvestre (Bl) *see* **Hospitaller Martyrs of Spain**

Anthony Sanga (Bl) M. L. Sep 10
d. 1622. A Japanese catechist, he suffered in the 'Great Martyrdom' at Nagasaki with Charles Spinola and Comps. *See* **Japan (Martyrs of)**.

Anthony Schwartz (Bl) P. F. (Sep 15)
1852–1929. From a large family near Vienna, Austria, his father was a theatrical musician and he started a career as a singer but entered the Vienna seminary instead, being ordained in 1875. His work as a hospital chaplain gave him contact with the sufferings of young workers and apprentices, and he founded a religious community to help them: the 'Christian Workers of St Joseph Calasanz'. He aimed at their Christian and moral formation, publicly fought the way they were exploited and was one of the pioneers of the Church's social teaching as expressed in the encyclical *Rerum Novarum*. This caused controversy, which he avoided answering. He died at Vienna and was beatified in 1998.

Anthony Slomšek (Bl) B. (Sep 24)
1800-1862. From a peasant family of Slom in Stryia, Austria (now in Slovenia), he was ordained in 1824 and served as a parish priest and seminary spiritual director before being made bishop of Lavant in 1846. He transferred the see to Maribor in 1859 and was zealous for the evangelization of the Slovene people, as well as being visitor-apostolic for the declining Benedictine monasteries of central Europe. He died at Maribor and was beatified in 1999.

Anthony Suarez (Bl) *see* **Ignatius de Azevedo and Comps**

Anthony and John of Tlaxcala
(BB) MM. LL. Sep 23
?1516–1529. Native Mexicans born near Tlaxcala, Mexico, they were converted and set off to evangelize Oaxaca with a Dominican tertiary. They wished to destroy any idol they came across and, when they came to a village called Cuauhtinchán, Bl Anthony went into a temple to do so while Bl John waited outside. The residents beat the latter to death, and did the same to the former when he came out to remonstrate. They were beatified in 1990 with Bl Christopher.

Anthony Torriani of Amandola
(Bl) R(OSA). Jan 28
?1355–1450. Born at Amandola in the Marches, Italy, he became an Augustinian friar and a friend and disciple of St Nicholas Tolentino. His cultus was confirmed for Fermo in 1759.

Anthony Turner (Bl) M. R(SJ). Jun 20
d. 1679. From Dalby Parva, Leics, he was a graduate of Cambridge who became a Jesuit in

1653 and was executed at Tyburn with BB Thomas Whitbread and Comps. *See* **England (Martyrs of)**.

Anthony Turriani (Bl) R(OSA). Jul 24
d. 1694. Born at Milan, Italy, he became a physician there after studying at Padua. He joined the Augustinian friars and, after several apostolic journeys including one including three years spent at Compostela, Spain, he died at Aquila in the Abruzzi, Italy. His cultus was confirmed for Aquila in 1759.

Anthony-of-St-Bonaventure of Tuy (Bl) M. R(OFM). Sep 8
1588–1628. From Tuy in Galicia, Spain, he studied at Salamanca, became a Franciscan and went to Manila, Philippines. There he was ordained and went to Japan, where he reconciled over 2700 apostates before being burned alive at Nagasaki with BB Dominic Castellet and Comps. *See* **Japan (Martyrs of)**.

Anthony dei Vici (Bl) R(OFM). Feb 8
1391–1461. From Stroncone, Italy, he became a Franciscan lay brother when aged eleven. Despite his lowly status he was chosen to help Bl Thomas Bellacci in his work in Tuscany against the dualist heretics called the 'Fraticelli'. After more than a decade at this he was recalled to the friary of the Carceri at Assisi and lived a life of penance. His cultus was confirmed for Assisi and the Franciscans in 1687. In 1809 his relics were forcibly seized by the citizens of Stroncone.

Anthony Weerden (St) *see* **Gorinchem (Martyrs of)**

Anthony Yamada (Bl) M. L. Aug 19
d. 1622. He was a Japanese sailor on the ship taking BB Louis Flores and Comps to Japan, and was beheaded at Nagasaki with them. *See* **Japan (Martyrs of)**.

Anthony-Mary Zaccaria (St) P. F. Jul 5
1502–1539. From Cremona, Italy, he was medical student before becoming a secular priest. As such he was known for his enormous apostolic zeal, and the work that he undertook as a result probably shortened his life. In 1530 he founded the 'Clerks Regular of St Paul', usually known as the Barnabites as their headquarters in Milan were at the church of St Barnabas. He died at Cremona and was canonized in 1897.

Anthusa of Constantinople (St) R. Jul 27
C8th. A hermit, she became superior of a nunnery near Constantinople and openly defied the iconoclast edicts of Emperor Constantine V. She was interrogated by him and tortured, but the empress protected her from further harm and she lived to an advanced age.

Anthusa the Elder (St) *see* **Athanasius, Anthusa and Comps**

Anthusa the Younger (St) V. Aug 27
? She was martyred in Persia, traditionally by being sewn up in a sack and dropped into a well.

Antidius (Antel, Antible, Tude) (St) M. B. Jun 17
d. ?265. A disciple of St Froninus and his successor as bishop of Besançon, France, he was killed by invading barbarians at Ruffey.

Antigonus (St) *see* **Alexander, Abundius and Comps**

Antimus (St) R(OSB). Jan 28
C8th. He was apparently an abbot of the abbey of Brantôme in the Dordogne, France, founded by Charlemagne in 769 and destroyed by the Norsemen in 817.

Antinogenes (St) *see* **Victor, Stercatius and Antinogenes**

Antioch (Martyrs of)
The following anonymous groups were listed in the old Roman Martyrology as having been martyred at Antioch (Syria):

Dec 24
d. 250. Forty unmarried women were killed in the reign of Decius.

Mar 11
d. *c*300. Many in the reign of Maximian were viciously tortured to death.

Nov 6
d. 637. Ten (or more) were killed when the Muslims captured the city.

Antiochus (St) M. Dec 13
d. *c*110. He was martyred in the reign of Hadrian on the island off south-west Sardinia which now bears his name.

Antiochus (St) *see* **Nicostratus, Antiochus and Comps**

Antiochus and Cyriac (SS) MM. Jul 15
C3rd. Their legend alleges that Antiochus was a physician beheaded at Sebaste, Asia Minor, and when milk spurted from the neck instead of blood Cyriac, the executioner, was converted and was himself martyred. Nothing is actually known about them.

Antiochus (Andeol) of Lyons (St) B. Oct 15
C5th. A priest of Lyons, France, he was sent to Egypt to persuade St Justus, the city's bishop, to return after the latter had fled to become a monk. Failing in this, he became bishop himself.

Antipas (St) M. Apr 11
d. *c*90. See Rev 2: 13. He was the 'faithful witness' put to death at Pergamum, Asia Minor, but the allegations that he was bishop there and was martyred are unreliable.

Antonia of Brescia (Bl) R(OP). Oct 27
1407–1507. She became a Dominican nun at Brescia, Italy, when young, and was made prioress at Ferrara when aged 66. Her rule was just but also rigorous and she was deposed. She lived to her hundredth year, and her trials proved her patience and humility.

Antonia of Cirta (St) *see* **Agapius of Cirta and Comps**

Antonia of Florence (Bl) T(OFM). Feb 28
1400–1472. From Florence, Italy, she was widowed when young and became a Franciscan conventual tertiary. As superior of the convent at Aquila she introduced the original rule of the Poor Clares, and had St John Capestrano as a guide. She suffered much from a painful illness before she died. Her cultus was confirmed for Aquila in 1847.

Antonia Messina (Bl) V. May 17
1919–1935. Born near Nuoro in Sardinia, she was a pious child in the context of a traditional peasant society. She was out collecting firewood for the family's bread oven after Mass one Sunday when she was a victim of attempted rape and suffered fatal head injuries in defending her virginity. She was beatified in 1987.

Antonillus-Mary Calvo Calvo (Bl) *see* **Philip-of-Jesus Munárriz Azcona and Comps**

Antonina (St) *see* **Alexander and Antonina**

Antoninus (St) *see* **Aristeus and Antoninus**

Antoninus (St) *see* **Lucilla, Flora and Comps**

Antoninus (St) *see* **Lucy, Antoninus and Comps**

Antoninus (St) *see* **Marcellinus, Claudius and Comps**

Antoninus (St) *see* **Victor, Zoticus and Comps**

Antoninus of Caesarea and Comps (SS) MM. Nov 13
d. 297. They were martyred in the reign of Galerius at Caesarea in the Holy Land. Ennatha was a virgin and was burned, while Antoninus, Zebinas and Germanus were beheaded.

Antoninus Fontana (St) B. Oct 31
d. 660. He was bishop of Milan, Italy, for one year. St Charles Borromeo enshrined his relics.

Antoninus of Pamia (St) M. Sep 2
? The old Roman Martyrology lists an Antoninus martyred at 'Pamia'. This could be Apamea in Syria or Pamiers in France, both of which have a tradition concerning a martyr of this name.

Antoninus of Piacenza (St) M. Sep 30
C3rd. He is said to have been a soldier of the Theban Legion martyred at Piacenza, Italy. His alleged blood, kept in a phial, is claimed to have the same properties as that of St Januarius at Naples.

Antoninus Pierozzi (St) B. R(OP). May 10
1389–1459. From Florence, Italy, he became a Dominican at Fiesole and was made prior of the Minerva at Rome while still young. In 1436 he founded San Marco at Florence, and reluctantly became archbishop of the city in 1446. He was known to care for his people, especially the poor, and was a writer on moral theology and international law. Canonized in 1523, his cultus was confined to local calendars in 1969.

Antoninus of Sorrento (St) R(OSB). Feb 14
d. 830. A monk of one of the daughter-houses of Montecassino, he became a refugee hermit because of war until he settled at Sorrento, Italy, as abbot of the monastery of St Agrippinus. He is the patron of Sorrento.

Anysia (St) V. Dec 30
d. 304. According to her legend she was a young woman of Thessalonika, Greece, who was killed by a soldier after she refused to let him take her to a pagan sacrifice.

Anysius (St) B. Dec 30
d. ?407. The successor of St Ascholius as bishop of Thessalonika, Greece, he was the representative of Pope St Damasus in Illyria and a friend of SS Ambrose and John Chrysostom.

Août *see* **Augustus**

Apelles (Apellius), Lucius (Luke) and Clement (SS) MM. Apr 22
C1st. The old Roman Martyrology described them as 'from among the first disciples of Christ', usually equated with those mentioned in Rom 16:10, 21. The martyrology entry is duplicated for Sept 10, where the name of Clement is added. Traditionally St Apelles was bishop of Smyrna (Izmir, Turkey) and St Lucius bishop of Laodicea.

Aper (Apre, Epvre, Evre) (St) B. Sep 15
d. ?507. He became bishop of Toul, France, in 500. According to tradition he had been a lawyer from Trier before being ordained.

Aphrahat (Aphraates) (St) R. Apr 7
C4th. A Persian, he was a hermit firstly at Edessa and then at Antioch, Syria, and opposed Arianism in the reign of Valens. His identification with the famous Syriac patristic writer is uncertain.

Aphrodisius (St) *see* **Peter and Aphrodisius**

Aphrodisius, Caralippus, Agapius and Eusebius (SS) MM. Apr 28
C1st. Their worthless legend, recounted by St Gregory of Tours, makes Aphrodisius an Egyptian who sheltered the Holy Family during their flight into Egypt and who was martyred with the other three in Languedoc, France.

Aphrodisus of Alexandria and Comps (SS) MM. Apr 30
? A priest, he was martyred at Alexandria, Egypt, with about thirty of his people.

Aphthonius (St) *see* **Acindynus, Pegasius and Comps**

Apian *see* **Appian**

Apodemius (St) *see* **Zaragoza (Eighteen Martyrs of)**

Apollinaris (St) *see* **Cyriac and Apollinaris**

Apollinaris and Timothy (SS) MM. Aug 23
These two were venerated at Rheims, France. Apparently the former was St Apollinaris of Ravenna and the latter was St Timothy at Rome, and a local legend was invented to explain why they were celebrated on the same day at Rheims when their real identities had been forgotten.

Apollinaris the Apologist (St) B. Jan 8
d. *c*180. Claudius Apollinaris was a bishop of Hierapolis in Phrygia, Asia Minor, who wrote an *Apology for Christianity* dedicated to the emperor Marcus Aurelius as well as other works. None is extant. He was an effective opponent of Montanism.

Apollinaris of Montecassino (Bl) R(OSB). Nov 27
d. 828. A child-oblate at Montecassino, Italy, he became abbot there in 817. His relics survive in the rebuilt abbey.

Apollinaris Morel (Bl) *see* **September (Martyrs of)**

Apollinaris of Ravenna (St) M. B. Jul 23
C1st? The first bishop of Ravenna, Italy, he allegedly died from the effects of torture on an uncertain date and had his shrine established at Classe outside the city (where his basilica now stands). His acta, describing him as a disciple of St Peter, are fictions of the C7th and his cultus was confined to local calendars in 1969.

Apollinaris Sidonius *see* **Sidonius Apollinaris**

Apollinaris Syncletica (St) R. Jan 5
C4th? She is the heroine of a religious romance which alleges that she disguised herself as a boy in order to live undiscovered in the hermitage of one of the Egyptian saints called Macarius.

Apollinaris (Aiplonay) of Valence (St) B. Oct 5
d. *c*520. Elder brother of St Avitus of Vienne, he was a very successful bishop of Valence, France, and is the patron of that diocese.

Apolline *see* **Apollonia**

Apollo (St) R. Jan 25
?316–395. He spent forty years as a hermit in the Egyptian desert, and ended as superior of five hundred monks near Hermopolis. He gave public witness against Emperor Julian.

Apollo, Isacius and Crotates (SS) MM. Apr 21
They form part of the legend of St George, and are described as domestic servants of the empress Alexandra, wife of Diocletian, who were martyred at Nicomedia. The problem with this is that Alexandra never existed.

Apollonia of Alexandria (St) V. Feb 9
d. 249. An elderly deaconess of Alexandria, Egypt, she was martyred in the reign of Decius.

According to her legend she had her teeth torn out with pincers before being threatened with burning unless she apostatized. She replied by jumping into the fire. Her attribute is a tooth in pincers and she is invoked against toothache. Her cultus was confined to local calendars in 1970.

St Apollonia of Alexandria, Feb 9

Apollonia of Nagasaki (Bl) M. L. Sep 10
1622. A Japanese widow, she was beheaded at Nagasaki in the 'Great Martyrdom' with BB Charles Spinola and Comps. *See* **Japan (Martyrs of)**

Apollonius (St) *see* **Marcian, Nicanor and Comps**

Apollonius (St) *see* **Philemon and Apollonius**

Apollonius (St) *see* **Proculus, Ephebus and Apollonius**

Apollonius and Eugene (SS) MM. Jul 23
? Roman martyrs, the former was tied up and used as an archery target and the latter was beheaded.

Apollonius and Leontius
(SS) MM. BB. Mar 19
? These two were listed as martyred bishops in the Hieronomian martyrology, but nothing is known about them. They have been claimed for Braga in Portugal.

Apollonius of Alexandria and Comps (SS) MM. Apr 10
d. *c*250. A priest with five others, they were martyred at Alexandria, Egypt, in the reign of Decius.

Apollonius the Apologist
(St) M. L. Apr 18
d. ?190. A Roman senator, he was betrayed as a Christian by one of his slaves and beheaded. His 'apologia', or the defence of Christianity that he made at his trial, has survived in an Armenian text.

Apollonius of Benevento (St) B. Jul 8
d. *p*326. A bishop of Benevento, Italy, he went into hiding during the persecution of Diocletian.

Apollonius of Brescia (St) B. Jul 7
? The shrine of this alleged bishop of Brescia in Lombardy, Italy, is in the cathedral there. He is mentioned in the unreliable acta of SS Faustinus and Jovita.

Apollonius of Iconium (St) M. Jul 10
Early C4th. From Sardis, Asia Minor, he was flogged and crucified at Iconium (now Konya, Turkey).

Aponius (St) *see* **Andrew and Aponius**

Apphia (St) *see* **Philemon and Apphia**

Appian (St) *see* **Mansuetus, Severus and Comps**

Appian of Caesarea (St) M. Apr 2
d. 306. He was martyred at Caesarea in the Holy Land during the persecution of Galerius.

Appian of Commacchio (St) R. Mar 4
d. *c*800. From Liguria, Italy, he became a monk at the abbey of Ciel d'Oro at Pavia before going on to be a hermit at Commacchio on the Adriatic and evangelizing the surrounding area.

Apronia (Evronie) (St) R. Jul 15
C5th-C6th. From Trier, Germany, she was a sister of St Aper, bishop of Toul, who received her vows as a nun. She died at Troyes, France.

Apronian (St) M. Feb 2
d. ?304. According to his legend he was a Roman jailer who was converted when taking St Sisinnius before the tribunal, forthwith declared his new faith and was himself martyred. *See* **Saturninus and Sisinnius**.

Apuleius (St) *see* **Marcellus and Apuleius**

Aquila (St) *see* **Cyril, Aquila and Comps**

Aquila (St) *see* **Domitius of Caesarea and Comps**

Aquila (St) *see* **Severian and Aquila**

Aquila and Priscilla (SS) MM? Jul 8
C1st. What is known of them is found in the Acts of the Apostles. They were among the Jews banished from Rome by Emperor Claudius, and they set up as tent-makers at Corinth. St Paul lodged with them there (Acts 18:3) before (according to tradition) they returned to Rome in the reign of Nero and were martyred there.

Aquila of Alexandria (St) M. May 20
d. 311. An Egyptian in Alexandria, his legend states that he was ripped apart with iron wool-carding combs in the reign of Maximinus Daia. This was on the orders of the prefect Arianus, who converted and was martyred in the same persecution.

Aquilina (St) *see* **Niceta and Aquilina**

Aquilina of Byblos (St) V. Jun 13
d. 293. According to her unreliable acta, she was a twelve-year-old girl who was tortured and martyred at Byblos in the Lebanon.

Aquilinus (St) *see* **Heradius, Paul and Comps**

Aquilinus, Geminus, Eugene and Comps (SS) MM. Jan 4
d. ?484. Numbering seven, they were killed in Roman Africa by the Arian Vandal King Hunneric. Their acta are lost, but were known to St Bede in the C8th. The companions were Marcian, Quintus, Theodotus and Tryphon.

Aquilinus, Geminus, Gelasius and Comps (SS) MM. Feb 4
C3rd? They are listed as martyrs at 'Forum Sempronii' (a poor guess is that this is Fossombrone in central Italy), but nothing is known about them. The companions were Magnus and Donatus.

Aquilinus and Victorian (SS) MM. May 16
? They are listed by St Bede in his martyrology as having been martyred in Isauria, central Asia Minor, but nothing is known about them.

Aquilinus of Evreux (St) B. Oct 19
*c*620–695. From Bayeux, France, he was a soldier in the Frankish army for forty years. On his return from fighting the Visigoths, he and his wife agreed to spend their lives in works of charity and they moved to Evreux. St Aquilinus was soon made bishop there, but he avoided public life.

Aquilinus of Milan (St) M. Jan 29
C7th?. His history has been very badly confused. According to the tradition, he was a Bavarian priest at Cologne, Germany, who fled the likelihood of being made a bishop, went to Paris and then to Milan, Italy. He preached against the Manichaean heretics there and was killed as a result. However, the evidence suggests that he was of the C7th and was martyred by the Arian Lombards. His shrine is at Milan.

Arabia (St) *see* **Theusetas, Horres and Comps**

Arabia (Martyrs of) Feb 22
d. ?306. There was a noteworthy pogrom of Christians in the Roman province of Arabia during the reign of Galerius. This province was in south-west Syria, with Bostra as its capital.
Ararat (Martyrs of) *see* **Acacius and Comps**

Arator of Alexandria and Comps (SS) MM. Apr 21
? He was listed by the old Roman Martyrology as a martyred priest of Alexandria, Egypt, but nothing further is known about him. His companions were Felix, Fortunatus, Silvius and Vitalis.

Arator of Verdun (St) B. Sep 6
d. *c*460. He was the fourth bishop of Verdun, France.

Arbogast (St) B. Jul 21
d. ?678. Born in Aquitaine (not in the British Isles), he became a hermit in Alsace, France, and was forced to become the bishop of Strasbourg by the Frankish king. He was a wise

and humble bishop, who directed that he should be buried in the criminals' graveyard but who later had a church built over his grave. He is depicted as walking on a river.

Arcadius (St) M. Jan 12
d. ?302. A prominent Roman African citizen of Caesarea in Mauretania, near Algiers, he died after being slowly mutilated in the reign of Maximian Herculeus.

Arcadius, Probus and Comps (SS) MM. Nov 13
d. 437. They were from Andalucia, Spain, and were taken to Africa by the Arian Vandal King Genseric, where they were the first to be martyred in the Vandal persecution. The companions were the brothers Paschasius, Eutychian and Paulillus. Paulillus was a small child, and when he would not apostatize he was severely beaten and enslaved.

Arcadius of Bourges (St) B. Aug 1
d. ?549. Bishop of Bourges, France, he was at the council of Orléans in 538.

Arcanus (St) *see* **Giles and Arcanus**

Archangela Girlani (Bl) R(OC). Feb 13
1460–1494. From Trino, Italy, she became a Carmelite at Parma in 1477 and was the founding superior of the Carmel at Mantua. She was a model religious, and her cultus was confirmed for the Carmelites in 1864.

Archangelus Canetuli (Bl) R(CR). Apr 16
d. 1513. From Bologna, Italy, he became a Canon Regular and was known for his natural talents and his supernatural charisms. He died as archbishop-elect of Florence.

Archangelus Piacentini (Bl) R(OFM). Jul 30
d. 1460. From Calafatimi, Sicily, he was a hermit at Alcamo when Pope Martin V suppressed the hermitages of the island. He then joined the Franciscan Observants at Palermo, became provincial superior and helped them spread throughout Sicily. His cultus was confirmed for Mazzara in 1836.

Archangelus Tadini (Bl) P. F. (May 20)
1846–1912. From Verolanuova near Brescia, Italy, he was ordained for the diocese of Brescia in 1870 and became parish priest of Botticino Sera in 1887, where he remained for the rest of his life. He had a great interest in the welfare of factory workers, especially women, and founded the 'Worker Sisters of the Holy House of Nazareth' to help educate the latter. He was beatified in 1999.

Archelais, Thecla and Susanna (SS) VV. Jan 18
d. 293. They were refugees from persecution in Emilia, Italy, who fled to Nola in the Campagna, but there they were seized, and then tortured and beheaded at Salerno.

Archelaus (St) *see* **Quiriacus, Maximus and Comps**

Archelaus, Cyril and Photius (SS) MM. Mar 4
? Nothing is known about these martyrs.

Archelaus of Kashkar (St) B. Dec 26
d. ?278. Bishop of Kashkar in Mesopotamia, he is remembered as a great opponent of Manichaeism but the writings on the subject bearing his name are not by him.

Archippus (St) B? Mar 20
C1st. St Paul referred to him twice (Phil 2; Col 4:17). Derivative tradition considered him to be the first bishop of Colossae, Asia Minor.

Arcontius (St) *see* **Quintius, Arcontius and Donatus**

Arcontius of Viviers (St) M. B. Jan 19
C8th or C9th. A bishop of Viviers, France, he is recorded as having been killed by a mob for having defended the interests of his diocese.

Ardalion (St) M. L. Apr 14
d. *c*300. He is described as having been an actor somewhere in the East, who suddenly proclaimed himself a Christian while engaged in ridiculing Christianity on stage. His audience then arranged that he was roasted alive in the market-place. The same story is told about others, such as SS Genesius and Gelasius.

Ardan (Ardaing, Ardagne, Ardagnus) (St) R(OSB). Feb 11
d. 1058. He was an abbot of Tournus near Autun, France, and was remembered for his charity to the sufferers of a famine from 1030 to 1033.

Ardo (St) R(OSB). Mar 7
d. 843. From Languedoc, he was a monk of Aniane near Montpellier, France, when St Benedict of Aniane was abbot there. He became the school headmaster and St Benedict's secretary, travelling companion, biographer and successor as abbot when St Benedict went to Aachen. His cultus was peculiar to Aniane.

Arduin of Rimini (St) R. Aug 15
d. 1009. A priest of Rimini, Italy, he became a hermit and died at the monastery of San Gudenzio without taking vows there.

Arduin (Ardwyne, Ardoine) of Trepino (St) L? Jul 28
C7th? The patron saint of Ceprano in eastern Lazio, Italy, he is traditionally and improbably regarded as one of four Saxon pilgrims who died in the region.

Aredius (Yrieux) (St) R. Aug 25
d. 591. From Limoges, France, after service at the Frankish court he became the abbot-founder of the monastery of Atane in the Limousin, afterwards named St Yrieux after him. He was a noted evangelist throughout France. Other variants of his name are Yriez, Yriel, Ysary, Ysère and Ysèry.

Aredius (Arige, Aregius) of Lyons (St) B. Aug 10
d. *p*614. He was an outstanding archbishop of Lyons, France, although his political activities were questionable.

Aregle *see* **Agricola**

Aresius, Rogatus and Comps (SS) MM. Jun 10
? They were seventeen Roman African martyrs. Some martyrologies identify them with **Theodolus, Saturninus and Comps** (q.v.).

Aretas of Rome and Comps (SS) MM. Oct 1
? They are listed in the old Roman Martyrology as numbering five hundred and four and as having been martyred at Rome. One opinion is that they are a duplication of the martyrs of **Najran** (q.v.).

Aretius (Arecius, Aregius) and Dacian (SS) MM. Jun 4
? They were martyred at Rome and buried in the catacombs on the Appian Way.

Argariarga *see* **Osmanna**

Argeus, Narcissus and Marcellinus (SS) MM. Jan 2
d. 320. Their legend alleges that they were three brothers who joined the army of the emperor Licinius. St Marcellinus was only a boy and, when he refused to perform military duties, he was flogged, imprisoned and then thrown into the Black Sea at Tomi, on the coast of Romania. His brothers were beheaded.

Argymyrus (St) M. R. Jun 28
d. 858. Born near Cordoba, Spain, he became a high-ranking Muslim of that city but was dismissed from office on suspicion of being a secret Christian. Shortly afterwards he became a monk, openly renounced Islam, proclaimed Christ and was beheaded.

Ariadne (St) M. Sep 17
d. *c*130. Her legend states that she was the Christian slave of a Phrygian prince of Asia Minor who had her flogged for refusing to join the pagan celebration of his birthday. She ran away and took refuge in a cleft in a rock which miraculously opened and then closed, thus entombing her.

Arialdus (St) M. D. Jun 27
d. 1066. A deacon of Milan, Italy, with the support of the emperor he made a stand against the simony prevalent at the time, especially that of the reigning archbishop. He was excommunicated, imprisoned on an island in Lake Maggiore and then killed there by two priests supporting the archbishop. His cultus was confirmed for Milan in 1904.

Arian, Theoticus and Comps (SS) MM. Mar 8
d. ?311. Arian was the governor of Thebes, Egypt, and he and his four companions were converted at Alexandria after witnessing the martyrdom of SS Apollonius and Philemon. The presiding judge ordered them to be drowned in the sea.

Arigius (St) B. May 1
535–604. Bishop of Gap, France, for twenty years, he was a great pastor.

Arild (St) V. Oct 30
? The church at Oldbury-on-the-Hill in Gloucestershire, England, is dedicated to this saint, allegedly a local girl who died in defence of her chastity and who had a shrine at Gloucester Abbey.

Aristaeus and Antoninus (SS) MM. Sep 3
? They have been associated with Capua, Italy, but there is no local record of them there. The former is probably an Egyptian martyr and the latter a duplication of St Antoninus of Apamea.

Aristarchus of Thessalonika (St) M? B? Aug 4
C1st. He is the travelling companion and fellow-worker of St Paul, mentioned in Acts 20:4,

27;2 and Philem. 24. Legend makes him first bishop of Thessalonika, Greece, and a sharer in St Paul's martyrdom at Rome.

Aristides the Apologist (St) L. Aug 31
C2nd. A Athenian philosopher, he wrote an apology for Christianity to the emperor Hadrian in 125. This was preserved by being incorporated into the text of the story of Barlaam and Josaphat.

Aristion (St) M. Feb 22
C1st. Traditionally one of the seventy-two disciples, he was alleged to have been martyred either at Salamis in Cyprus or at Alexandria in Egypt.

Aristobolus (St) M. Mar 15
C1st. He is mentioned in St Paul's letter to the Romans (16:11), and is traditionally one of the seventy-two disciples. The legends identifying him with Zebedee the father of SS James and John, and placing him in Britain, are fictions.

Ariston and Comps (SS) MM. Jul 2
d. ?285. A group of ten (the others being Crescentian, Eutychian, Felicissimus, Felix, Justus, Marcia, Symphorosa, Urban and Vitalis), they were martyred in the Campagna, Italy, in the reign of Diocletian. Details are lacking.

Aristonicus (St) *see* **Hermogenes of Melitene and Comps**

Arius ('Macarius') of Petra (St) B. Jun 20
d. *c*350. Arius was a bishop of Petra (now in Jordan) who was present at the council of Sardica in 347. The Arians managed to get him exiled to Africa, where he died. He has never had a cultus, but Cardinal Baronius inserted him into the old Roman Martyrology and changed his name to Macarius to distinguish him from Arius the heresiarch. Perhaps he thought he was Scottish.

Armagilus (Armel, Ermel, Ermyn) (St) R. Aug 16
d. *c*550. Allegedly a cousin of St Sampson and born in south Wales, he was a missionary in Cornwall, England, where St Erme is named after him and in Brittany, France, where he founded monasteries at Saint-Armel-des-Boscheaux and Ploermel. He is represented holding the Devil on a chain or tied up with his priestly stole, and sometimes with armour under his vestments.

Armand *see* **Ormond**

Armentarius of Antibes (St) B. Jan 30
d. *p*451. The first bishop of Antibes in Provence, France, he has a church at Draguignan dedicated to him.

Armentarius of Pavia (St) B. Jan 30
d. ?711. As bishop of Pavia, Italy, he obtained the independence of his diocese from the archbishop of Milan.

Armogastes and Saturus (SS) MM. Mar 29
d. *p*460. Palace courtiers at Carthage in Roman Africa, they were singled out in the Arian persecution arranged by the Vandal King Genseric. They were tortured, put to work in the mines and then enslaved as cowherds but were not killed as their persecutors did not want them venerated as martyrs. The old Roman Martyrology added 'Archimimus and Masculas', but this is probably a garbled reference to St Armogastes: 'President of the Theatre, a native of Mascula'.

Armon *see* **Germanus of Auxerre**

Arnold de'Cattenei (St) M. R(OSB). Mar 14
1184–1254. From Padua, Italy, he joined the Benedictine abbey of St Justina there and became its abbot. The tyrant ruling the city persecuted him for a long time, then chained him up in prison at Asolo for eight years until he died. He was venerated as a martyr.

Arnold the Greek (St) L. Jul 8
d. *p*800. A Greek courtier of Charlemagne, he was famed for his charity to the poor and gave his name to the village of Arnoldsweiler near Aachen, Germany.

Arnold of Hiltensweiler (Bl) L. May 1
d. *p*1127. He was the obscure founder of the nunnery of Langnau near Bern, Switzerland, and appears to have been a knight who went on the First Crusade. His shrine was at Hiltensweiler.

Arnold Janssen (Bl) P. F. Jan 15
1837–1909. Born at Goch, Germany, after he was ordained he founded the 'Missionary Society of the Divine Word' in 1875 at Steyl in the Netherlands in order to help in foreign missions. He also founded two congregations for women: the 'Missionary Servants of the Holy Spirit' and the 'Servants of the Holy Spirit for Perpetual Adoration'. He was beatified in 1975.

Arnold Rèche (Bl) R. Oct 23
1838–1890. From near Metz, France, he became a coachman and muleteer in Charleville before joining the 'Brothers of the Christian Schools' in 1862. He taught at Rheims from 1863 to 1877, but found it hard to keep discipline. Then he was made novice-master at Thillois in 1877 and gave great edification. He became rector of the institute's retirement home in Rheims just before he died of a stroke, and was beatified in 1987.

Arnulf of Eynesbury (St) R? Aug 22
C9th. His alleged relics were venerated at Eynesbury ('Arnulfsbury') in Cambridgeshire, England. Claimed to have been a local Anglo-Saxon hermit, he may be a duplication of St Arnulf of Metz.

Arnulf of Gap (St) B. R(OSB). Sep 19
d. *c*1070. Born at Vendôme, France, he joined the abbey of the Holy Trinity there and became the bishop of Gap in 1063. He is the principal patron of the city.

Arnulf of Mainz (St) M. B. Jul 1
d. 1160. He was archbishop of Mainz, Germany, from 1153 until he was murdered by members of his church. He was venerated as a martyr.

Arnulf of Metz (St) B. Jul 18
?582–?641. A nobleman from near Nancy, France, he was a high official at the Frankish Austrasian court before he and his wife agreed to become consecrated religious. She became a nun, but he was made bishop of Metz, France, in 616 before he could join the monastery of Lérins. When he retired as bishop he became a hermit near Remiremont. He was the progenitor of the Carolingian dynasty.

Arnulf of Novalese (St)
M. R(OSB). Oct 31
d. *c*840. A monk of Novalese in Piedmont, Italy, he was killed in a Muslim raid.

Arnulf of Soissons (St) B. R(OSB). Aug 15
*c*1040–1087. From Flanders, for some years he was a soldier in the royal army of France and then became a hermit at the abbey of St Médard at Soissons, France. He was forced to become the city's bishop in 1081, but was expelled by a rival and retired to the abbey of Oudenbourg, Belgium, which he had founded.

Arnulf of Toul (St) B. Nov 15
d. 871. He was bishop of Toul, France, from 847.

Arnulf (Arnoul) of Villers
(Bl) R(OCist) Jun 30
d. 1228. Born at Brussels, Belgium, he was a self-indulgent young man but became a Cistercian lay brother at Villers in Brabant and spent his life in penance. He attained to a high level of contemplative prayer.

Arontius (Orontius) *see* **Honoratus, Fortunatus and Comps**

Arpinus *see* **Agrippinus**

Arsacius (Ursacius) (St) R. Aug 16
d. 358. His story is that he was a Persian soldier in the Roman army who converted and became a hermit in a tower overlooking Nicomedia, Asia Minor. He foretold the earthquake of 358 which destroyed the city, and was found dead in his tower by refugee citizens.

Arsenius (St) *see* **Heron, Arsenius and Comps**

Arsenius (St) *see* **Pelagius, Arsenius and Sylvanus**

Arsenius of Corfu (St) B. Jan 19
d. 959. Born in Constantinople of Jewish descent, he became the first bishop of Corfu, Greece, and is a patron of the island.

Arsenius the Great (St) R. Jul 19
d. ?449. A Roman of senatorial rank, he was chosen by Emperor Theodosius I to be the tutor of his mentally subnormal sons, Arcadius and Honorius, in 383. In 393 he fled to Egypt in disgust and became a monk and disciple of St John the Short at Scetis, where his erudition, austerity and silence enhanced his reputation among the native Copts. After Scetis was devastated by barbarians in 434 he moved to Troë near Memphis, where he died. He features in the *Apophegmata Patrum*.

Artald (Arthaud, Artaud)
of Belley (Bl) B. R(OCart). Oct 7
1101–1206. A courtier of Savoy (now in France), he became a Carthusian at Portes in 1120 and founded a monastery at Arvières-en-Valromey in 1140. He was appointed bishop of Belley in 1188, but resigned two years later and returned to Arvières where he died a centenarian. His cultus was approved for Belley in 1834.

Artaxus and Comps (SS) MM. Jan 2
C3rd or C4th. They were martyred at Sirmium (Srem Mitrovica in Serbia). The companions

were Acutus, Eugenda, Maximianus, Timothy, Tobias and Vitus.

Artemas of Lystra (St) B? Oct 30
C1st. One of St Paul's disciples (*see* Titus 3:12), he was traditionally the first bishop of Lystra, Asia Minor.

Artemas of Puteoli (St) M. Jan 25
? His legend, probably fictional, describes him as a schoolboy of Puteoli (Pozzuoli near Naples, Italy) who was stabbed to death by his pagan confreres with their pens. A similar story is told of others.

Artemius, Candida and Paulina (SS) MM. Jun 6
d. 302. The governor of a Roman prison and his wife and daughter, they were converted by St Peter the Exorcist and baptized by St Marcellinus. Artemius was beheaded and the two women were buried alive under a cairn.

Artemius of Clermont (St) B. Jan 24
d. 396. An imperial legate, he fell ill at Clermont-Ferrand, France, when on the way to Spain and eventually became bishop there.

Artemius the Great Martyr (St) M. Oct 20
d. 363. A high courtier under Emperor Constantine, he was made prefect of Egypt by Emperor Constantius. He was a zealous Arian and persecuted St Athanasius and the Orthodox in Egypt. There is no indication that he repented of this, but he was beheaded as a Christian in the reign of Julian and was venerated as a martyr.

Artemius of Sens (St) B. Apr 28
d. 609. From Sens, France, he became bishop of his city.

Artemon (St) M. P. Oct 8
d. ?305. A priest of Laodicea in Phrygia, Asia Minor, he was burned in the reign of Diocletian.

Arthelais (St) L. Mar 3
C6th. One of the patrons of Benevento, Italy, she was alleged to have fled there from Constantinople in order to escape the unwelcome attentions of Emperor Justinian.

Arthur Ayala Niño and Arthur Donoso Murillo (BB) *see* **Hospitaller Martyrs of Spain**

Asaph (St) B. R. May 5
d. *c*600. A monk, he was allegedly a disciple of St Kentigern and his successor as abbot and bishop at the place now named after him in north Wales. Many of his relatives also became saints, e.g. Deiniol and Tysilo.

Ascelina (St) R(OSB). Aug 23
1121–1195. A relative of St Bernard of Clairvaux, she was a nun at Boulancourt near Chaumont, France, and a noted mystic.

Ascholius (St) B. R. Dec 30
d. 383. A Cappadocian hermit, he became bishop of Thessalonika, Greece, in 380.

Asclas (St) M. Jan 23
d. ?287. He was martyred at Antinoë, Egypt, in the reign of Diocletian by being thrown into the Nile.

Asclepiades (St) B. Oct 18
d. 217. He succeeded St Serapion as bishop of Antioch, Syria, in 211, and is listed as a martyr. This seems to be because of his sufferings during the persecution in the reign of Septimus Severus.

Asclepiodotus (St) *see* **Maximus, Theodore and Asclepiodotus**

Asella (St) R. Dec 6
d. ?406. St Jerome wrote in praise of this Roman abbess, relating that she became a nun when aged ten and then a recluse in a small cell two years later. Disciples gathered around her and these became a sizeable community.

Asicus (Ascicus, Tassach) (St) B. Apr 27
d. *c*490. An early disciple of St Patrick in Ireland, he became first abbot and bishop of Elphin in Co. Roscommon, of which diocese he is the patron. He was a coppersmith and some examples of his handiwork survive.

Aspasius (St) B. Jan 2
d. *c*560. A bishop of Auch, France, he is recorded as having been at the councils held at Orléans in 533, 541 and 549. His cultus survives in the diocese of Meaux, especially at Melun.

Aspren (Aspronas) (St) B. Aug 3
C2nd? By tradition he was the first bishop of Naples, Italy, and was healed, baptized and ordained by St Peter. He seems to date from the end of the second century in reality.

Asteria (Hesteria) (St) V. Aug 10
d. ?307. According to her dubious acta she was a sister of St Grata who helped with the burial of

St Alexander and was martyred at Bergamo, Italy.

Astericus (Astricus, Ascrick)
(St) B. R(OSB). Nov 12
d. ?1035. A Czech, he accompanied St Adalbert on his Bohemian mission and became the first abbot of Brevnov. Having to flee to Hungary, he then became the first abbot of Pannonhalma (newly founded by St Stephen of Hungary) and also archbishop of Kalocsa. He was sent as ambassador to Rome, obtained the recognition of the Hungarian kingdom from Pope Sylvester II and brought back the 'Crown of St Stephen' for the coronation.

Asterius (St) M. P. Oct 21
d. ?223. A Roman priest, he buried the body of Pope St Callistus after the latter's martyrdom and was himself thrown into the Tiber at Ostia as a result by order of Emperor Alexander Severus. His body was recovered and enshrined in the cathedral at Ostia.

Asterius (St) *see* **Claudius, Asterius and Comps**

Asterius (St) *see* **Marinus and Asterius**

Asterius (St) *see* **Thalelaeus of Aegae and Comps**

Asterius of Amasea (St) B. Oct 30
d. *c*400. He was a bishop of Amasea in Pontus, Asia Minor, and a famous preacher. Twenty-one of his homilies are extant.

Asterius of Petra (St) B. Jun 10
d. *p*362. Formerly an Arian, he converted to orthodoxy, became bishop of Petra (now in Jordan) and published an account of the Arian machinations at the Council of Sardica (347). He was banished to Libya by Constantius, recalled by Julian and is last heard of in 362.

Astius (St) *see* **Peregrine, Lucian and Comps**

Asyncritus (St) *see* **Herodion, Asyncritus and Phlegon**

Athan *see* **Tathai**

Athanasia (St) R. Aug 14
d. 860. Born on the island of Aegina off Piraeus, Greece, of an ancient Greek family, she lost her first husband in warfare against the Muslims. She remarried, but the couple separated by mutual consent to become consecrated religious and she turned their former house into a convent which she ruled as abbess.

Athanasia (St) *see* **Andronicus and Athanasia**

Athanasius (St) *see* **Zozimus and Athanasius**

Athanasius, Anthusa and Comps (SS) MM. Aug 22
d. *c*257.According to the acta of St Anthusa (which resemble those of St Pelagia of Tarsus), Athanasius was a bishop of Tarsus in Cilicia who baptized Anthusa, a lady of Seleucia, and two of her slaves, Charisius and Neophytus. The three men were martyred in the reign of Valerian, while she lived for 23 years afterwards.

Athanasius of Alexandria
(St) B. Dr. May 2
?296–373. Born in Alexandria, Egypt, he became a deacon under St Alexander there and denounced Arius as a heretic. After having accompanied St Alexander to the Council of Nicaea in 325 he became patriarch himself in 328 and was the outstanding champion of Christ's divinity against Arianism. For this he was exiled five times between 336 and 366, initially to Trier, then to Rome (where he helped introduce an awareness of monasticism with his translation of the life of St Anthony and by taking two monks with him), and then to the Egyptian desert among the monks. He was an outstanding theologian, pastor and churchman and is a doctor of the Church.

Athanasius the Athonite
(St) R. F. Jul 5
*c*920–1003. From Trebizond (now Trabzon, Turkey), he became a monk on the Bithynian Olympus and then migrated to the colony of hermits on Mount Athos. There he founded the 'Great Laura', the first cenobitic monastery there, with the help of his friend the Emperor Nicephorus Phocas. This was the start of the great monastic republic of Athos, which survives, and he became superior of sixty communities on the mountain by the time of his death. He was killed when the dome of his monastery's church fell in.

Athanasius Bazzekuketta
(St) M. L. Jun 3
d. 1886. He was a page at the court of King Mwanga of Buganda, Uganda, and the royal treasurer. Baptized in 1885, he was martyred by order of the king a year later. *See* **Charles Lwanga and Comps**.

Athanasius of Jerusalem (St) M. D. Jul 5
d. 452. When the Council of Chalcedon condemned monophysitism in 451, the monophysites in Jerusalem deposed the bishop St Juvenal and intruded one Theodosius. St Athanasius, a deacon, protested at this and was beheaded by members of the garrison.

Athanasius of Modon (St) B. Jan 31
d. ?885. From Catania, Sicily, he fled to Patras in the Peloponnesus, Greece, when the Muslims invaded, became a monk of the Byzantine rite and then bishop of Modon (now Methoni, on the South-Western tip of the Peloponnesus).

Athanasius of Naples (St) B. Jul 15
832–872. Son of the duke of Naples, Italy, he was made bishop there when aged eighteen. After twenty years he was a target of extortion by his ruling relatives, who imprisoned and exiled him. He died at Veroli but his body was eventually transferred back to Naples.

Athanasius of Nicomedia (St) R. Feb 22
d. ?818. From Constantinople, he became abbot of the monastery of SS Peter and Paul near Nicomedia, Asia Minor, and gave witness against the iconoclast policy of Emperor Leo III. He suffered much as a result.

Athanasius of Sorrento (St) Jan 26
? He has a cultus at Sorrento, Italy, but nothing is known about him and he may be a duplicate of St Athanasius of Naples.

Athanasius Vidaurretta Labra (Bl) *see* **Philip-of-Jesus Munárriz Azcona and Comps**

Athelm of Canterbury (St)
B. R(OSB). Jan 8
d. 923. A paternal uncle of St Dunstan, he became a monk and then abbot of Glastonbury, England, before being made first bishop of Wells. In 914 he became archbishop of Canterbury.

Athenodorus (St) M. B. Oct 18
d. ?269. Born in Neocaesarea in Cappodocia, Asia Minor, he was a brother of St Gregory Thaumaturgus, was converted with him and studied with him under Origen at Caesarea in the Holy Land. He became bishop of an unknown town in Pontus and was martyred in the reign of Aurelian.

Athenodorus (St) M. Nov 11
d. ?304. According to the old Roman Martyrology he was martyred in Mesopotamia in the reign of Diocletian. He died after torture and before he could be executed; his would-be executioner dropped dead and no-one else dared to be the replacement.

Athenogenes (St) M. B. Jan 18; Jul 16
? The old Roman Martyrology listed him on January 18 as an old theologian burned in Pontus who left in writing a hymn that he sang at his martyrdom. St Basil identified this with the Byzantine vespers hymn, *Phos Hilaron*. He seems to be identical to the bishop martyred at Sebaste in Armenia with ten disciples in the reign of Diocletian and listed on July 16.

Atheus *see* **Tathai**

Athilda *see* **Alkeld**

Atilanus Cruz Alvarado (St) *see* **Mexico (Martyrs of)**

Attala (Attalus) of Taormina (St) R. Apr 3
d. *c*800. He was abbot of a monastery at Taormina, Sicily.

Attalas (St) R. Mar 10
d. 627. A Burgundian monk of Lérins, France, he transferred to Luxeuil under St Columban and accompanied him to Bobbio in Lombardy, Italy, where he helped him found the abbey there and succeeded him as abbot in 615. In his abbacy the monks of Bobbio rebelled against the severity of the Columbanian rule.

Attalia (Attala) (St) R. Dec 3
?697–741. A niece of St Ottilia, she became a nun and then abbess of St Stephen's nunnery at Strasbourg in Alsace, France.

Attalus (St) *see* **Photinus, Sanctius and Comps**

Attalus (St) *see* **Stephen, Pontian and Comps**

Atticus (St) M. Nov 6
? He was listed by the old Roman Martyrology as having been martyred in Phrygia, Asia Minor, but no details survive.

Atticus of Constantinople (St) B. Jan 8
d. 425. From Armenia and a former heretic, he opposed St John Chrysostom and became patriarch of Constantinople during the latter's second banishment and before his death. He did, however, restore Chrysostom's name to the diptychs, the lists of those commemorated in public prayers. Some of his letters survive.

Attilanus (St) B. R(OSB). Oct 5
d. ?916. From near Zaragoza, Spain, he became a monk and then prior at Moreruela under St Froilan as abbot. They were ordained together as bishops, Froilan of León and Attlianus of Zamora.

Attius (St) *see* **Leontius, Attius and Comps**

Atto of Oca-Valpuesta (St)
B. R(OSB). Nov 19
d. ?1044. A monk at Oña in Old Castile, Spain, under St Enneco as abbot, he was made bishop of Oca-Valpuesta.

Atto (Attho) of Pistoia (St)
B. R(OSB Vall). May 22
d. 1153. From either Badajoz, Spain, or Florence, Italy, he became a monk at Vallombrosa near the latter city and then abbot-general of the congregation of that name. He was made bishop of Pistoia, and wrote biographies of SS John Gualbert and Bernard degli Uberti.

Atto of Tordino (St) R(OSB). Nov 19
d. *p*1010. He was the first abbot of Tordino, a monastery founded by Montecassino near Teramo, Italy, in 1004.

Attracta (Athracht) (St) R. Aug 12
C5th? Possibly a contemporary of St Patrick in Ireland, she was a hermit at Killaraght on Lough Gara in Co. Sligo and then at Drum near Boyle in Co. Roscommon. Both places became nunneries under her direction.

Aubert *see* **Autbert**

Aubierge *see* **Ethelburga**

Aubin *see* **Albinus**

Auctus, Taurion and Thessalonica (SS) MM. Nov 7
? Nothing is known about these martyrs of Amphipolis near Thessalonika, Greece.

Audas (Abdas) and Comps
(SS) MM. May 16
d. 420. A Persian bishop with seven priests, nine deacons and seven virgins, they were martyred at the start of a general persecution in the Sassanid Persian Empire.

Audax (St) *see* **Anatolia and Audax**

Audifax (St) *see* **Marius, Martha and Comps**

Audöenus *see* **Ouen**

Audomarus *see* **Omer**

Audrey *see* **Etheldreda**

Augulus (Augurius, Aule) (St) M. B. Feb 7
d. ?303. He is listed as a bishop in the Hieonomian martyrology. Later writers place his martyrdom at London in the reign of Diocletian, or identify him with St Aule of Normandy.

Augurius (St) *see* **Fructuosus, Augurius and Eulogius**

Augusta (St) V. Mar 27
C5th. She was a daughter of a Teuton duke of Friuli, Italy, and when she converted to Christianity her father killed her himself. She has an ancient cultus at Serravalle near Treviso.

Augustalis (Autal) (St) B. Sep 7
d. *c*450. He was a bishop in Roman Gaul, possibly at Arles, France.

Augustina-of-the-Sacred-Heart Dejardin (Bl) *see* **Valenciennes (Martyrs of)**

Augustina Pietrantoni (St) R. Nov 12
1864–1894. Born at Tivoli near Rome to a large peasant family, she became a Sister of Charity and a nurse at the Santo Spiritu Hospital at Rome. The atmosphere in the hospital was anti-religious, and there she was fatally stabbed by a patient. She asked for mercy for him before she died, and was canonized in 1999.

Augustine and Paulinus
(SS) RR(OSB). Nov 5
C6th. According to the tradition of Montecassino, they were sent by St Benedict to found the monastery at Terracina between Rome and Naples, Italy.

Augustine, Sanctian and Beata (SS) MM. Sep 6
d. 273. They were Spaniards who fled during a persecution but were martyred at Sens, France.

Augustine Caloca Cortés (St) *see* **Mexico (Martyrs of)**

Augustine of Canterbury
(St) B. R. May 27
d. 604. He was prior of St Andrew's monastery on the Coelian Hill in Rome when he was sent

by Pope St Gregory the Great with forty companions to evangelize the pagan Anglo-Saxons in Britain. He was ordained bishop for the mission at Arles on the way. The missionaries landed at Ebbsfleet on Thanet in the kingdom of Kent in 597, converted the king, St Ethelbert, with many of his subjects and established the primatial English diocese at Canterbury. St Augustine succeeded in establishing the Latin Church in England, but failed to establish relationships with the Celtic Christians. He died shortly after St Gregory, and the two are venerated as the 'apostles of the English' There is no historical evidence that he was a Benedictine.

Augustine Cennini (Bl) *see* **Prague (Martyrs of)**

Augustine-Ambrose Chevreaux
(Bl) R(OSB). Sep 2
d. 1792. The last superior-general of the Maurist Benedictine congregation in France, he was imprisoned with many others at the Paris Carmel and killed in the September massacres after the French Revolution. *See* **September (Martyrs of)**.

Augustine-Joseph Desgardin (Bl) *see* **John-Baptist Souzy and Comps**

Augustine Fangi (Bl) R(OP). Jul 22
d. 1493. From Biella in Piedmont, Italy, he joined the Dominicans there and had a busy apostolic career united with physical sufferings until he died at Venice. He had his cultus confirmed for Biella in 1872.

Augustine of Hippo (St) B. Dr. F. Aug 28
354–430. He was born in Tagaste in Roman Africa, his mother (St Monica) was a fervent Christian but his father was a pagan. He trained as a rhetorician and practised that profession at Tagaste, Carthage, Rome and Milan. As a young man he was attracted to Manichaeism and fathered a child (St Adeodatus) out of wedlock. He was converted by the influence of St Ambrose of Milan and his mother's prayers, helped by St Paul's theology and the use of neo-platonic philosophy. Being baptized in Milan by St Ambrose in 387, he went back to Africa and lived in quasi-monastic seclusion with a few friends for three years until his ordination for the city of Hippo as priest and then as bishop. As a pastor his literary output was enormous (especially famous are his *Confessions*, *The City of God* and *The Trinity*), and his influence on Latin patristic and early medieval theology was absolute. His need to combat especially the heresies concerning grace of Donatism and Pelagianism led him to develop the doctrine of grace and free-will in a authoritative manner. Two letters of his advising religious communities were much later incorporated into a formal rule bearing his name, which became very popular in the Middle Ages. He is a doctor of the Church. His alleged relics are at Pavia, Italy.

St Augustine of Hippo, Aug 28

Augustine (Phan Viet) Huy
(St) M. L. Jun 13
d. 1839. A Vietnamese soldier, he was sawn in half with St Nicholas Thé. *See* **Vietnam (Martyrs of)**.

Augustine Kažotić (Bl) B. R(OP). Aug 8
1260–1323. From near Split in Dalmatia, Croatia, he became a Dominican, preached in Croatia and Hungary and was made bishop of Zagreb. He had the charisms of gentleness and healing. Later he was transferred to Lucera, Italy, for which place his cultus was confirmed in 1702.

Augustine Lee (St) *see* **Korea (Martyrs of)**

Augustine (Nguyen van)
Moi (St) M. T(OP). Dec 19
d. 1839. A poor Vietnamese labourer and a

Dominican tertiary, he was strangled at Ninh-Tai after refusing to trample on a crucifix. With him died SS Dominic (Bui van) Uy, Francis-Xavier (Ha Trong) Mau, Stephen (Nguyen van) Vinh and Thomas (Nguyen van) De. *See* **Vietnam (Martyrs of)**.

Augustine of Nicomedia (St) *see* **Flavius, Augustus and Augustine**

Augustine Novellus (Bl) R(OSA). May 19
d. 1309.From Taormina, Sicily, he obtained a degree in law at Bologna and became chancellor of the Kingdom of Sicily under King Manfred. Being left for dead after the battle of Benevento against Charles of Anjou led him to join the Augustinian friars as a lay brother, but he was soon persuaded to accept ordination and he eventually became his order's prior-general and the pope's confessor and legate. His cultus was confirmed for Siena, where he died, in 1759.

Augustine Ota (Bl) M. R(SJ). Sep 25
d. 1622. From Hirado-jima off Japan, he was a catechist before being imprisoned and beheaded at Iki. He became a Jesuit in prison. He was beatified in 1867. See **Japan (Martyrs of)**.

Augustine Pak (St) *see* **Korea (Martyrs of)**

Augustine-Emmanuel Philippot (Bl) *see* **Laval (Martyrs of)**

Augustine Roscelli (Bl) P. F. May 7
1818–1902. Born in Casarza Ligure, Italy, he was initially a shepherd but became a parish priest in Genoa in 1846 and spent innumerable hours in the confessional. He also set up a vocational training centre for young women with no other means of support apart from prostitution, and worked as chaplain in the city's orphanage and prison. He founded the 'Sisters of the Immaculata' to help him in 1876. He was beatified in 1995.

Augustine Ryou (St) *see* **Korea (Martyrs of)**

Augustine Schöffler (St) M. May 1
1822–1851. From Mittelbronn in Lorraine, France, he joined the 'Paris Society for Foreign Missions', was sent to Vietnam and was beheaded there. *See* **Vietnam (Martyrs of)**.

Augustine Webster (St)
M. R(OCart). May 4
d. 1535. A Carthusian at Sheen in Surrey, England, he was made prior of Axholme, Lincs. He visited the London Charterhouse together with St Robert Lawrence of Beauvale to consult its prior, St John Houghton, about the religious policy of King Henry VIII. They were arrested at the London Charterhouse, executed at Tyburn for denying the king's supremacy in spiritual matters and were canonized in 1970. *See* **England (Martyrs of)**.

Augustine Zhao Rong (St) M. P. Jul 9
1746–1815. From Wuchuan in Guizhou, China, he was a warden in a prison in which Christians were being held and was converted by their example. In 1781 he was ordained and went to do missionary work in western Sichuan. He was arrested in 1815 and, being already ill, died in prison after torture. *See* **China (Martyrs of)**.

Augustus (St) *see* **Flavius, Augustus and Augustine**

Augustus (St) *see* **Priscus II of Capua and Comps**

Augustus of Bourges (St) R. Oct 7
C6th. An abbot at Bourges, France, he was a friend of St Germanus of Paris and discovered the body of St Ursinus (the evangelizer of the district).

Augustus Chapdelaine (St) M. P. Feb 27
1814–1856. The ninth child of a peasant of Normandy, France, he joined the 'Paris Society of Foreign Missions' and went to China to be a missionary priest in Guangxi in 1852. He was captured at Xilin and was seriously tortured in order to induce apostasy. He died as a result in prison. *See* **China (Martyrs of)**.

Augustus-Andrew Martín Fernandez (St) *see* **Cyril-Bertrand Sanz Tejedor and Comps**

Aulaire *see* **Eulalia of Barcelon**a

Auld *see* **Aldate**

Aunaire *see* **Anacharius**

Aunemund (Annemond, Chamond) (St) B. Sep 28
d. 658. An archbishop of Lyons, France, he was a friend of St Wilfrid of York and gave him shelter for three years during one of his absences from England. He was murdered at Chalon-sur-Saône by order of Ebroin, the mayor of the Merovingian palace, in the presence of St Wilfrid. St Bede refers to him as Dalphinus in error.

Aurea of Boves (St) R. Oct 6
C8th. From Amiens, France, as a young girl she became a hermit at Boves and eventually superior of a large community there.

Aurea (Oria) of Cogolla
(St) R(OSB). Mar 11
?1042–1069. She was a hermit attached to the Benedictine abbey of San Millán de la Cogolla in Navarre, Spain, and had St Dominic of Silos as a spiritual director.

Aurea (Aura) of Cuteclara
(St) M. R. Jul 19
d. 856. She was a Muslim from Cordoba, Spain, who converted to Christianity when a widow and became a nun at Cuteclara for over twenty years. Her family denounced her as an apostate from Islam and she was beheaded.

Aurea of Ostia (St) V. Aug 24
d. *c*270. She has an ancient cultus at Ostia near Rome, but her acta are fictional.

Aurea of Paris (St) R. Oct 4
d. 666. A Syrian, she was appointed by St Eligius as superior of the nunnery of St Martial at Paris, France, in 633. She died in an epidemic with 160 of her community.

Aurelia and Neomisia (SS) LL. Sep 25
? Their story is that they were from Asia Minor and went on pilgrimage to the Holy Land and to Rome. At Capua, Italy, they were waylaid by pirates, but escaped under the cover of a thunderstorm, took refuge at Macerata near Anagni and died there.

Aurelia of Strasbourg (St) R(OSB). Oct 15
d. 1027. A French princess, she was attached to a Benedictine abbey at Strasbourg in Alsace, France, for 55 years as a hermit and had contact with St Wolfgang.

Aurelian of Arles (St) B. Jun 16
d. 551. Bishop of Arles, France, from 546, he was Pope Vigilius's legate for Gaul and founded two monasteries (one for each sex) at Arles. The customaries that he gave them were based on the rules of SS Caesarius and Benedict.

Aurelian of Limoges (St) B. May 10
C1st or C3rd. He was a disciple of St Martial of Limoges, France, and became bishop of that city.

Aurelius and Publius (SS)
MM. BB. Nov 12
C2nd. They were two bishops who wrote against the Montanists. Little else is known about them, and they were martyred either in Asia Minor or in Africa.

Aurelius of Armenia (St) B. Nov 9
d. 475. He was allegedly a bishop in Armenia who went into exile to Milan, Italy, and who brought the relics of St Dionysius of Milan with him.

Aurelius of Carthage (St) B. Jul 20
d. 429. Bishop of Carthage and metropolitan of Roman Africa, he was a friend of St Augustine of Hippo and an early opponent of Pelagianism. He asked the help of the civil authorities against the activities of the Donatists.

Aurelius of Cordoba (St) *see* **George, Aurelius and Comps**

Aurelius-Mary Villalón Acebrón and Comps (BB) MM. RR. Nov 16
d. 1936. Seven members of the 'Brothers of Christian Schools' who were teaching in the college of Almería, Spain, they were killed after the local 'Revolutionary Committee' ordered the liquidation of priests and religious. They were beatified in 1993. *See* **Spanish Civil War (Martyrs of)**.

Aureus, Justina and Comps
(SS) MM. Jun 16
C5th. Aureus was bishop of Mainz, Germany, and went into exile with his sister Justina when the Huns (or Vandals) invaded. They then returned and were massacred with the congregation while he was saying Mass.

Ausonius of Angoulême
(St) M. B. May 22
C1st or C3rd. He was claimed to be a disciple of St Martial of Limoges and first bishop of Angoulême, France.

Auspicius of Apt (St) B. Aug 2
ante C4th. He is the alleged first bishop of Apt, France.

Auspicius of Toul (St) B. Jul 8
d. ?475. Mentioned as bishop of Toul, France, by Sidonius Apollinaris, he had a shrine at Saint-Mansuy.

Auspicius of Trier (St) B. Jul 8
d. *c*130? Claimed to be the fourth bishop of Trier, Germany, in succession to St Maternus, he is probably a duplication of St Auspicius of Toul.

Austell (St) R? Jun 28
C6th. The town of St Austell in Cornwall,

England, possibly gets its name from a disciple of St Mewan who settled on the site.

Austin *see* **Augustine**

Austindus (St) B. R(OSB). Sep 25
d. 1068. From Bordeaux, he joined the abbey of Saint-Orens at Auch, France, became its abbot and entered it into the Cluniac congregation. In 1041 he became the city's archbishop and fought against simony.

Austreberta (St) R. Feb 10
?635–704. From near Thérouanne in Artois, France, she was the daughter of St Framechild and the count palatine Badefrid and was clothed as a nun at Ponthieu by St Omer. She became abbess of St Philibert's foundation at Pavilly in Normandy.

Austregildis *see* **Agia**

Austregisilus (Aoustrille, Outrille) of Bourges (St) B. May 20
551–624. From Bourges, France, he was educated as a courtier but became a monk at Saint-Nizier in Lyons instead, going on to become abbot there and bishop of Bourges in 612.

Austremonius (Stremoine) of Clermont-Ferrand (St) B. Nov 1
C1st or C3rd. Traditionally one of seven missionaries sent from Rome to evangelize Gaul, he preached in the Auvergne and became the first bishop of Clermont-Ferrand, France.

Austriclinian (St) *see* **Martial of Limoges and Comps**

Astrude *see* **Anstrude**

Autbert of Avranches (St) B Sep 10
d. *p*709. Bishop of Avranches, France, he founded the famous abbey of Mont-St-Michel off the coast of Normandy.

Autbert of Cambrai-Arras (St) B. Dec 13
d. ?669. Bishop of Cambrai-Arras, he was a great patron of monastic life and founded many monasteries in northern France, including the great abbey of St Vedast at Arras. His attribute is a baker's peel (bread shovel).

Autbert of Landevennec (St) R(OSB). Feb 1
d. 1129. A monk of Landevennec in Brittany, France, he became chaplain to the nunnery of St Sulpice near Rheims and has a cultus in that city.

Autbod (St) R. Nov 20
d. 690. An Irish missionary monk, he preached in northern France and became a hermit near Laon.

Autel *see* **Augustalis**

Authaire (Oye) (St) L. Apr 24
C7th. He was a palace courtier of the Merovingian King Dagobert I and father of St Ouen of Rouen, France.

Authbertus *see* **Autbert**

Autonomous (St) M. B. Sep 12
d. *c*300. According to the Byzantine tradition he was an Italian bishop who fled to Bithynia, Asia Minor, during the persecution by Diocletian. There he was martyred after success as a missionary.

Autor (Adinctor, Auteur) (St) B. Aug 9
C5th. A bishop of Metz, France, he had his shrine at the abbey of Marmoutier from 830.

Auxanus (Ansano) (St) B. Sep 3
d. 568. He was a bishop of Milan, Italy, where he has a popular cultus.

Auxentius (St) R. Feb 14
d. *c*470. A Persian born in Syria, he was a guard in the service of Emperor Theodosius II before becoming a hermit in Bithynia near Constantinople. He successfully defended his orthodoxy against false accusations at the Council of Chalcedon in 451.

Auxentius (St) *see* **Eustratius and Comps**

Auxentius of Mopsuestia (St) B. Dec 18
d. *p*321. A soldier in the army of Emperor Licinius, he was persecuted for refusing to join in pagan rites, but survived and went on to become bishop of Mopsuestia near Antioch, Syria.

Auxibius (St) B. Feb 19
C1st. He was traditionally baptized by St Mark and made first bishop of Soli in Cyprus by St Paul.

Auxilius (St) *see* **Basileus, Auxilius and Saturninus**

Auxilius, Isserninus and Secundinus (SS) BB. Dec 6
C5th. They were fellow missionaries with St Patrick in the evangelization of Ireland, and co-signatories with him of an extant decree

pointing out to the Irish clergy that appeals could be made to Rome against the judgments of the archbishop of Armagh.

Ava (Avia) (St) R(OSB). Apr 29
d. *p*845. A niece of King Pepin of the Franks, she was blind when young but was miraculously cured and went on to become abbess at the nunnery of Denain in Flanders, France.

Aventinus of Chartres (St) B. Feb 4
d. *c*520. He was the successor of his brother, St Solemnnis, as bishop of Chartres, France.

Aventinus of Larbouch (St) M. R. Jun 7
d. 732. Born at Bagnères in the Pyrenees, France, he became a hermit in the valley of Larbouche and was killed there by the Arabs.

Aventinus of Troyes (St) R. Feb 4
d. ?538. From central France, he was the almoner of St Lupus of Troyes, but left that city to become a hermit at the place later named St Aventin after him.

Avertanus (St) R(OC). Feb 25
d. 1380. Born in Limoges, France, he became a Carmelite lay brother there but died outside Lucca, Italy, while on a pilgrimage to the Holy Land with Bl Romeo.

Avitus (St) M. Jan 27
? The old Roman Martyrology lists an African martyr of this name, who may be linked with the St Avitus who is anachronistically celebrated as the apostle and first bishop of the Canaries.

Avitus I of Clermont (St) B. Aug 21
d. *c*600. He was a bishop of Clermont-Ferrand, France, and ordained Gregory of Tours as deacon.

Avitus II of Clermont (St) B. Feb 21
d. 689. He became bishop of Clermont-Ferrand, France, in 676, and was one of the great Frankish bishops of the Dark Ages.

Avitus (Avy) of Micy (St) R. Jun 17
d. ?530. A monk of Menat in Auvergne, France, he became abbot of Micy near Orléans and then was allegedly a hermit in the hills of Perche (west of Chartres) where he formed the disciples who joined him into a new monastery which he ruled. He is probably the 'Adjutus' listed in the old Roman Martyrology on Dec 19.

Avitus of Vienne (St) B. Feb 5
*c*450–519. From the Auvergne, France, he was the brother of St Apollinaris, bishop of Valence, and son of St Hesychius, bishop of Vienne. He succeeded the latter and was a popular bishop and writer, having also the respect of the ruling Arian Burgundians. He converted their king, St Sigismund, to orthodoxy from Arianism. Many of his letters survive.

Aybert *see* **Aibert**

Aye *see* **Agia**

Aymard of Cluny (Bl) R(OSB). Oct 5
d. 965. He was the successor in 942 of St Odo as abbot of Cluny in Burgundy, France, but went blind and resigned in favour of St Majolus ten years later. In his retirement he was noted for his patience.

Aymarus Vaz (Bl) *see* **Ignatius de Azevedo and Comps**

Azadanes and Azades
(SS) MM. Apr 22
d. 341–2. The former was a Persian deacon and the latter an important official at the court of the Persian Shah Shapur II. They were martyred with St Abdiesus.

Azas and Comps (SS) MM. Nov 19
d. *c*304. They were a group of about 150 soldiers martyred in Isauria, central Asia Minor, in the reign of Diocletian.

B

Babylas and Comps (SS) MM. Jan 24
d. *c*250. He was bishop of Antioch, Syria, and St John Chrysostom gave two homilies in his honour, asserting that he refused an emperor (possibly Philip the Arabian) admission to his cathedral. He died in chains while awaiting execution in the reign of Decius, and his relics were enshrined near the famous shrine to Apollo at Daphne near the city. His companions were three youths, Epolonius, Prilidian and Urban, who were pupils of his and who were also martyred.

Babilla *see* **Basilla**

Bacchus (St) *see* **Sergius and Bacchus**

Bademus (St) M. R. Apr 10
d. *c*380. A Persian, he founded and ruled a monastery near Beth Lapat and was martyred in the reign of Shah Shapur II.

Badilo (St) R(OSB). Oct 8
d. *c*870. A monk of Vézelay in Yonne, France, he became abbot of Leuze in Hainault, Belgium.

Badulf (Badour, Badolf) (St) R(OSB). Aug 19
d. *c*850. He was an abbot of Ainay near Lyons, France, and had a local cultus there.

Baglan (St)
? Apparently there were two Welsh saints of this name, perhaps of the C5th, but nothing is known about them.

Bain (Bagnus) (St) B. R. Jun 20
d. *c*710. A monk of Fontenelle in Normandy, France, under St Wandrille, he became bishop of Thérouanne (including Calais, of which he is the patron) in 685 for twelve years before returning to his abbey and becoming its abbot. Near the end of his life he was also made superior of Fleury, which Pepin had just restored.

Baisil
There is an ancient Anglican church with this dedication in the diocese of Llandaff in Wales, but there is no other evidence of such a saint (unless he is Boswell of Melrose).

Baithin (Comin) (St) R. Jun 9
d. ?598. Described as a cousin of St Columba, he succeeded him as abbot of Iona, Scotland.

Bajulus (St) *see* **Liberatus and Bajulus**

Balbina (St) V. Mar 31
d. *c*130. The old Roman Martyrology describes her as the daughter of the Roman martyr Quirinus, who was baptized by Pope St Alexander I, became a consecrated virgin and was buried after her martyrdom on the Appian Way near her father. All this, apart from her martyrdom, is unreliable. Her shrine was later established on the Aventine.

Balda (St) R. Dec 9
Late C7th. She was the third abbess of Jouarre near Meaux, France, and her shrine was established at the abbey of Nesle-la-Reposte near Troyes.

Baldegund (St) R. Feb 10
d. *c*580. She was an abbess of the ancient nunnery of the Holy Cross at Poitiers, France.

Balderic (Baudry) (St) R. Oct 16
C7th. A son of Sigebert I, king of Frankish Austrasia, he became the abbot-founder of Montfaucon in Champagne, France, and founded a nunnery at Rheims where his sister, St Bova, became a nun.

Baldji Oghlou Ohannes (Bl) *see* **Salvator Lilli and Comps**

Baldomer (Galmier) (St) R. Feb 27
d. *c*650. A locksmith at Lyons, France, he became a monk and sub-deacon at the monastery of St Justus there. He is a patron of locksmiths.

Baldred (St) B. Mar 6
C8th. He is alleged to have been the successor of St Kentigern Mungo as bishop of Glasgow, Scotland, before becoming a hermit on the Firth of Forth, but he has also been identified with St Balther.

Baldus *see* **Bond**

Baldwin (Baudoin) of Laon
(St) M. P. Oct 6
d. *c*680. Son of St Salaberga and brother of St Anstrude, he was an archdeacon at Laon, France, and was murdered in circumstances which led him to be venerated as a martyr.

Baldwin of Rieti (St) R(OCist). Jul 5
d. 1140. An Italian monk of Clairvaux under St Bernard and one of the latter's favourite disciples, he was sent to Rieti, Italy, to be abbot of San Pastore there. He is the town's principal patron.

Balin (Balloin) (St) R. Sep 3
C7th. One of four brothers who accompanied St Colman to Iona, Scotland. They were alleged to have been sons of a Saxon noble and their final settlement in Co. Galway, Ireland, was called Teachsachson ('House of the Saxons').

Balsamus (St) R(OSB). Nov 24
d. 1232. The tenth abbot of Cava near Salerno, Italy, he had his cultus approved in 1928.

Balthasar (St) *see* **Magi**

Balthasar Ravascieri of Chiavari (Bl) R(OFM). Oct 17
d. 1492. A Franciscan companion of Bl Bernardine of Feltre, he had his cultus confirmed for Pavia, Italy, in 1930.

Balthasar de Torres (Bl) M. R(SJ). Jun 20
1563–1626. Born in Granada, Spain, he became a Jesuit in 1579, taught theology at Goa, India, and Macao, China, and went to Japan in 1606. He was burned at Nagasaki with Francis Pacheco and Comps. *See* **Japan (Martyrs of).**

Balther (Baldred, Balred) (St) R. Mar 6
d. 756. A monk of Lindisfarne, he became a hermit at Tyninghame in East Lothian, Scotland, and then on Bass Rock. An odd legend has him miraculously moving an islet off the coast nearby for the greater safety of sailors. He shared a shrine at Durham with St Bilfrid.

Balthild *see* **Bathild**

Bandarid (Banderik, Bandery)
(St) B. Aug 9
d. 566. Bishop of Soissons, France, from 540 and founder of the abbey of Crépin (where he was buried), he was banished by King Clotaire I for seven years and worked anonymously in the garden of a British monastery (according to legend) before being discovered and recalled.

Banka *see* **Breaca**

Baptist or Baptista *see* **John-Baptist**

Barachisius (St) *see* **Jonas, Barachisius and Comps**

Baradates (St) R. Feb 22
d. *c*460. A famous Syrian hermit, he was praised in the contemporary *History of the Monks of Syria* by Theodoret of Cyrrhus. His asceticism was typical of Syrian monks, amounting to self-torture.

Barbara *Dec 4*
? According to her unreliable acta, first written in the C7th, she was a young woman who was imprisoned in a tower by her paranoid father who then had her condemned for becoming a Christian and was himself killed by lightning. The old Roman Martyrology placed these events at Nicomedia, Asia Minor, in ?303, but the story is now judged to be fictional and her cultus was suppressed in 1969. Her attribute is a tower.

Barbara Cho, Barbara Choi, Barbara Han, Barbara Kim, Barbara Ko, Barbara Kwon, Barbara Lee 1) and Barbara Lee 2) (SS) MM. *see* **Korea (Martyrs of)**

Barbara Cui (Lian) (St) M. Jun 15
1849–1900. A Catholic of Xiaotan in Hebei, China, she was the mother of two priests and was massacred by a gang of Boxers with another son and daughter-in-law and seven other Christians at Liushuitao. *See* **China (Martyrs of)**.

Barbasymas (Barbascemin) and Comps (SS) MM. Jan 14
d. 346. He was the bishop of Seleucia-Ctesiphon, the capital of the Sassanid Persian Empire and was imprisoned for eleven months with sixteen companions in the reign of Shah Shapur II. They were martyred after being tortured.

Barbatian (St) R. Dec 31
C5th. A priest of Antioch, Syria, he went to Rome and became known by Empress Galla Placidia who built a monastery for him at the

seat of imperial government at Ravenna and who employed him as an adviser.

Barbatus (Barbas) (St) B. Feb 19
?612–682. Born in Benevento, Italy, he became his city's bishop in 663. An opponent of monothelitism, he organized resistance in the siege by Emperor Constans II and later took part in the condemnation of that heresy by the Sixth Ecumenical Council at Constantinople. He had to help suppress a local snake cult adopted by Lombard immigrants, an interesting example of pagan survival in Italy.

St Barbara, Dec 4

Barbe *see* **Barbara**

Barbea (St) *see* **Sharbel and Barbea**

Barbolenus of Bobbio (St) R. Aug 31
d. *c*640. The fourth abbot of Bobbio in Lombardy, he conflated elements of the rule of St Benedict with the rule of St Columban previously used there (the abbey did not become fully Benedictine until the C10th).

Barbolenus of Paris (St) R. Jun 26
d. ?677. A monk of Luxeuil under St Columban, he became the first abbot of St Maur-des-Fossés near Paris, France, and was helped by St Fursey in founding many churches and hospitals in the diocese of Paris.

Bardo (St) B. R(OSB). Jun 10
982–1053. A monk of Fulda in Hesse, Germany, he served as abbot of Werden and then of Hersfeld before becoming archbishop of Mainz in 1031. He served as the imperial chancellor and was known for his love of the poor, of animals and also of rigorous penances which Pope St Leo IX advised him to mitigate.

Bardomian, Eucarpus and Comps (SS) MM. Sep 25
? They numbered 28 and they were martyred in Asia Minor, but nothing else is known.

Barlaam (St) M. Nov 19
d. *c*304. Martyred at Antioch of Pisidia, Asia Minor, in the reign of Diocletian, he was praised in an extant homily by St Basil.

Barlaam and Josaphat (SS) Nov 27
They are the main characters of a Christian adaptation of a Buddhist legend which is among the works attributed to St John Damascene and is possibly by him. They were inserted into the old Roman Martyrology in the C16th.

Barnabas (St) M. A. Jun 11
C1st. A Cypriot and the patron of Cyprus, he was a very early Christian disciple and shared St Paul's early career as a apostle (*see* Acts of the Apostles). Traditionally he died a martyr on Cyprus, although Milan implausibly claims him as its first bishop. He is liturgically celebrated as a apostle and his attribute is a pile of stones.

Barnabas of Sandomir (Bl) *see* **Sadoc of Sandomir and Comps**

Barnard (St) B. R(OSB). Jan 23
777–841. From near Lyons, France, he was educated at the court of Charlemagne and became a soldier but resigned, founded the abbey of Ambronay and became a monk and then abbot there in 803. He was made bishop of Vienne, France, in 810, and took part in attempts at church reform. His cultus was confirmed in 1903.

Barnoch *see* **Barrog**

Barontius and Desiderius (SS) RR. Mar 25
d. ?725. The former was a noble of Berry, France, who became a monk at Lonrey near Bourges but then travelled to Pistoia, Italy, to be a hermit as a result of a vision. The latter was his companion in his austere life there.

Barr *see* **Finbarr**

Barrfoin (Bairrfhionn, Barrindus) (St) B? R. May 21
C6th. The obscure information about him places him at St Columba's foundation at Drumcullen in Co. Offaly, Ireland, and then at Killbarron in Co. Donegal. A legend describes him voyaging to America and informing St Brendan of his discovery. He was possibly a bishop.

Barrog (Barrwg, Barnoch) (St) R. Sep 27
C7th. A disciple of St Cadoc, he was a hermit at Barry Island (which was named after him) near Cardiff, Wales.

Barsabas and Comps (SS) MM. Dec 11
d. ?342. A Persian abbot and his monks, they were martyred in the reign of Shah Shapur II. Possibly they are the same as those below or SS Simeon Barsabae and Comps.

Barsabas of Persepolis and Comps (SS) MM. Oct 20
d. ?342. A Persian abbot and his community of eleven monks, they were martyred near Persepolis in the reign of Shah Shapur II.

Barsanuphius and John (SS) RR. Apr 11
d. *c*540. They were famous recluses at a monastery near Gaza in the Holy Land, the latter being the disciple and secretary of the former. Many letters of direction of theirs survive, as their help was sought by all sorts of people, and their cultus in the East is popular.

Barsenorius (St) R. Sep 13
C7th. He was the successor as abbot to St Leutfrid at La-Croix-Saint-Leuffroi near Evreux, France, and had his shrine at Fécamp.

Barses (Barso, Barsas) (St) B. Jan 30
d. ?379. A bishop of Edessa in Syria (now Urfa in Turkey), he was exiled to the desert between Egypt and Libya by the Arian emperor Valens and died there.

Barsimaeus (Barsamja) (St) B. Jan 30
? According to the old Roman Martyrology he was a bishop of Edessa, Syria, martyred in the reign of Trajan. There is no independent evidence for this.

Bartholomea Bagnesi *see* **Mary-Bartholomea Bagnesi**.

Bartholomea Capitanio (St) R. F. Jul 26
1807–1833. Born at Lovere near Bergamo, Italy, she tried her vocation with the Poor Clares but discerned a more active vocation and so opened a school at home in 1824 and a hospital in 1826. She was also a correspondent on spiritual matters with the local young people and clergy. In 1832 she founded the 'Sisters of Charity of Lovere' together with St Vincenza Gerosa, and was the inspiration of her institute during the year before she died. She was canonized in 1950.

Bartholomew (St) M. A. Aug 24
C1st. He is listed among the twelve Apostles in the synoptic gospels and is identified with the Nathaniel in the first chapter of the gospel of St John. Nothing is known about his career, and the traditions are late and conflicting. Eusebius states that he was in 'India' before St Pantaenus, and the Roman tradition has him being martyred in Armenia. His alleged relics are enshrined on the eponymous island in the Tiber in Rome, and his attribute is a flaying-knife.

Bartholomew 'Aiutami-Cristo' (Bl) R(OSB Cam). Jan 28
d. 1224. From Pisa, Italy, he became a Carthusian lay brother at the monastery of St Frediano there. His nickname means 'Christ, help me', which he continually repeated. His cultus was confirmed for Pisa and the Camaldolese in 1857.

Bartholomew Amidei (St) *see* **Servites, Founders of**

Bartholomew Buonpedoni (Bl) P. Dec 14
d. 1300. Initially a secular servant at a Benedic-

St Bartholomew, Aug 24

tine abbey at Pisa, Italy, he then became a Franciscan tertiary before being ordained a priest of the diocese of Volterra when aged thirty. He was at the parish of Peccioli before contracting leprosy, and he spent the last twenty years of his life helping his fellow lepers. His cultus was confirmed for Colle di Val d'Elsa in 1910.

Bartholomew of Cervere (Bl)
M. R(OP). Apr 21
1420–1466. From Savigliano in Piedmont, Italy, he became a Dominican, taught theology at Turin and became the inquisitor for Piedmont. He was killed by heretics at Cervere near Fossano and had his cultus confirmed for the Dominicans in 1853.

Bartholomew Chieng (Moun-ho) and Comps (SS) MM. LL. Dec 13
d. 1866. They were seven Korean laymen who were martyred together. St Bartholomew was aged 65; St Peter Ni (Mieng-se), 50; St Peter Son (Syen-chi), 47; Peter Chyo (Hoa-se), 40 (these four had families); Joseph Han (Wen-sye), 38; Peter Cheng (Wen-chi), 21 and Joseph Cho (Youn-o), 17. *See* **Korea (Martyrs of)**.

Bartholomew Fanti (Bl) R(OC). Dec 5
1443–1495. From Mantua, Italy, he became a Carmelite there and became famous as a preacher and spiritual director of St John-Baptist Spagnuolo, among others. He also had the charism of healing. His cultus was confirmed for Mantua in 1909.

Bartholomew of Farne
(St) R(OSB). Jun 24
d. ?1193. A Dane from Whitby, England, he was ordained in Norway, became a monk at Durham and went on to be a hermit in St Cuthbert's cell on Farne Island. He died there after forty-two years.

Bartholomew Guttierez (Bl)
M. R(OSA). Sep 3
1538–1632. A Mexican, he became an Augustinian friar at Puebla in 1596, was ordained and was then sent to Manila in 1606. He became prior at Ukusi in Japan in 1612, and was an effective missionary until his betrayal and imprisonment in 1629. He was burned at Nagasaki with Bl Anthony Ishida and Comps. *See* **Japan (Martyrs of)**.

Bartholomew Jarrige de la Morélie de Biars (Bl) *see* **John-Baptist Souzy and Comps**

Bartholomew Laurel (Bl)
M. R(OFM). Aug 16
d. 1627. From Mexico City, he became a Franciscan lay brother, studied medicine in Manila from 1609 and went to Japan in 1622. He was burned at Nagasaki with Francis-of-St-Mary of Mancha and Comps. *See* **Japan (Martyrs of)**.

Bartholomew Longo (Bl) L. F. Oct 5
1841–1926. From the Campagna, Italy, he became a lawyer in Naples and married a widowed client who had property in the valley of Pompei near the city. There he founded a sanctuary to Our Lady 'of Pompei' in 1876 and worked hard to promote Marian devotions and to further charity, especially towards the children of prisoners. He founded the 'Daughters of the Rosary', a congregation of Dominican tertiaries. He was beatified in 1980.

Batholomew dos Mártyres
(Bl) B. R(OP). (July 16)
1514–1590. From Lisbon in Portugal, he became a Dominican in 1528, going on to teach philosophy and theology and being appointed the royal preacher. In 1559 he was ordained bishop of Braga, and set about reforming his large diocese. His theological writings have been of enduring influence. He died in retirement at the Dominican convent at Viana do Castelo and was beatified in 2001.

Bartholomew Mohyoye (Bl) M. Aug 19
d.1622. A Japanese sailor on the ship carrying BB Louis Flores and Comps to Japan, he was beheaded at Nagasaki with them. *See* **Japan (Martyrs of)**.

Bartholomew-Mary dal Monte (Bl) P. (24 Dec)
1726–1778. From Bologna, Italy, he was educated by the Jesuits there and became a priest after being inspired by St Leonard of Port-Maurice. He became a famous and effective home-missionary, preaching in about sixty Italian dioceses apart from his own, and was zealous against Jansenism and Enlightenment scepticism. He was merciful towards sinners, however. He died at Bologna and was beatified in 1997.

Bartholomew Osypiuk (Bl) *see* **Podlasia (Martyrs of)**

Bartholomew Pucci-Franceschi
(Bl) R(OFM). May 23
d. 1330. From Montepulciano, Italy, he was a wealthy married layman who obtained his wife's permission to become a Franciscan. A 'fool for Christ's sake', his cultus was confirmed for Montepulciano in 1880.

Bartholomew of Rossano (Bl) R. Nov 11
d. 1065. A Calabrian Greek from Rossano, Italy, he followed St Nilus to Grottaferrata near Frascati and is regarded as the second founder of this surviving Basilian monastery of the Italo-Greek rite. He was also a noted writer of Greek hymns.

Bartholomew of Sandomir (Bl) *see* **Sadoc of Sandomir and Comps**

Bartholomew Sheki (Bl) M. Nov 27
d. 1619. A Japanese layman of the family of the daimyos of Hirado-jima, he was beheaded at Nagasaki with Thomas Koteda and Comps. *See* **Japan (Martyrs of).**

Bartholomew Shichiyemon
(Bl) M. Sep 10
d. 1622. A Japanese layman, he was beheaded at Nagasaki with BB Charles Spinola and Comps in the 'Great Martyrdom. His son Peter was beheaded the next day with BB Caspar Koteda and Comps. *See* **Japan (Martyrs of)**.

Bartholomew Sonati (Bl) *see* **Prague (Martyrs of)**

Bartholomew of Tours (Bl)
B. R(OSB). Nov 11
d. 1067. Abbot of Marmoutier, he became bishop of Tours, France, in 1052 and had to fight against many difficulties. He tried hard but failed to reconcile the heretic Berengarius.

Bartholomew of Vicenza (Bl)
B. R(OP). Oct 23
*c*1200–1270. From Vicenza, Italy, he made his vows as a Dominican to St Dominic at Padua. He became Latin bishop of Limassol, Cyprus, in 1252 and bishop of Vicenza in 1256. His cultus was approved for Vicenza in 1793.

Bartholomew de Vir (Bl) R(OCist). Jun 26
d. 1157. Bishop of Laon, France, from 1113 to 1151, he helped St Norbert found the abbey of Prémontré and himself founded the Cistercian abbey of Foigny. He became a monk there after retiring as bishop.

Barulas (St) *see* **Romanus and Barulas**

Barypsabas (St) M. Sep 10
C1st. Allegedly an Eastern hermit who was martyred in Dalmatia, Croatia, his legend states

that he carried to Rome a jar containing some of the original blood that Christ shed on the cross.

Basil (St) *see* **Stephen the Younger and Comps**

Basil, Ephrem and Comps
(SS) MM. BB. Mar 4
C4th. A group of missionary bishops with a common cultus, Basil, Ephrem, Eugene, Agathodorus, Elpidius, Etherius and Gapito were martyred in the Crimea and the Ukraine while SS Nestor and Arcadius were martyred in Cyprus.

Basil of Aix (St) B. Jan 1
d. ?475. A priest of Arles, France, he became the second bishop of Aix-en-Provence.

Basil of Amasea (St) M. B. Apr 26
d 319. Bishop of Amasea in Pontus, Asia Minor, he was drowned in the Black Sea in the reign of Licinius for giving shelter to St Glaphyra. His acta are unreliable.

Basil of Ancyra (St) M. P. Mar 4
d. 362. A priest of Ancyra, Asia Minor (now Ankara in Turkey), he was a fervent opponent of Arianism and was tortured before being martyred in the reign of Julian.

Basil of Bologna (St) B. Mar 6
d. 335. He was ordained bishop of Bologna, Italy, by Pope St Sylvester in 315.

Basil the Elder and Emmelia (SS) LL. May 30
d. *c*370. The parents of SS Basil the Great, Gregory of Nyssa, Peter of Sebaste and Macrina the Younger as well as of six other children, they were distinguished lay people of Caesarea in Cappodocia, Asia Minor (now Kayseri in Turkey) who were exiled for a time in the reign of Galerius. St Basil was a lawyer whose mother was St Macrina the Elder. She was herself a disciple of St Gregory Thaumaturgus, a disciple of Origen.

Basil of Constantinople and Procopius Decapolita (SS) RR. Feb 27
d. *c*750. They were friends and monks of Constantinople and were imprisoned for witnessing against the iconoclast policy of the emperor Leo III. After his death they were released.

Basil the Great (St) B. Dr. R. F. Jan 2
*c*330–379. Born of a distinguished family at Caesarea in Cappodocia, Asia Minor (now Kayseri in Turkey), his parents, three siblings and paternal grandparents are also saints (*see* **Basil and Emmelia**). After studying at Constantinople and Athens he visited the famous monks of Egypt, Syria and the Holy Land before founding a monastery on the Iris river in Pontus. This led to the writing of his *Rules*, still standard for Eastern monasticism. In 370 he became metropolitan of Caesarea and spent the rest of his short life fighting against the Arianism which was being favoured by the imperial court at Constantinople. His influence was absolutely dominant in Cappodocia, and his writings helped establish the Catholic doctrine of the Trinity, especially as regards the divinity of the Holy Spirit. He also left a collection of letters which became standards in Greek rhetoric and edited the Byzantine eucharistic liturgy named after him. He is one of the four 'Great Doctors' in the West and one of the three 'Holy Hierarchs' of the East, being portrayed with a characteristic long dark beard.

Basil of Sandomir (Bl) *see* **Sadoc of Sandomir and Comps**

Basil the Younger (St) R. Mar 26
d. 952. A hermit living near Constantinople with the gift of prophecy, he was a refugee from torture as a suspected spy by the Muslims and died a centenarian. His biography, by his disciple Gregory, survives.

Basileus (St) *see* **Epictetus, Basileus and Aptonius**

Basileus (St) *see* **Jovinus and Basileus**

Basileus, Auxilius and Saturninus (SS) MM. Nov 27
? They were martyred at Antioch in Syria. Basileus was a bishop, but of where is unknown.

Basilian (St) *see* **Theotimus and Basilian**

Basilides (St) *see* **Theodolus, Saturninus and Comps**

Basilides, Cyrinus, Nabor and Nazarius *Jun 12*
Formerly listed in the old Roman Martyrology as having been martyred in the reign of Diocletian, they had their cultus suppressed in 1969. Basilides seems to be a duplicate of the one in the next entry, Cyrinus to be St Quirinus of Sisak and the last two to be unknown Milanese martyrs.

Basilides, Tripos, Mandal and Comps (SS) MM. Jun 10
d. 270–5. Numbering twenty-three, they were martyred on the Aurelian Way outside Rome in the reign of Aurelian.

Basilides of Alexandria (St) M. L. Jun 30
d. 205. A soldier of the guard of the prefect of Egypt, he defended St Potamioena the Elder from the hostility of the spectators when detailed to be her executioner and was converted. He was shortly afterwards martyred in the reign of Septimus Severus. His story is in the history by Eusebius.

Basiliscus (St) *see* **Cleonicus, Eutropius and Basiliscus**

Basiliscus of Comana (St) M. B. May 22
d. 312. Bishop of Comana in Pontus, Asia Minor, he was beheaded near Nicomedia in the reign of Maximin and his body was dumped into a river. It was recovered and taken back to Comana.

Basilissa (St) *see* **Callinica and Basilissa**

Basilissa (St) *see* **Julian, Basilissa and Comps**

Basilissa and Anastasia (SS) MM. Apr 15
d. ?68. Their legend has it that they were disciples in Rome of SS Peter and Paul, whose bodies they buried and who were themselves martyred in the reign of Nero. Their existence is doubtful.

Basilissa of Nicomedia (St) V. Sep 3
d. ?303. The old Roman Martyrology lists her as having been martyred in Nicomedia, Asia Minor, when aged nine after having converted the city governor during the reign of Diocletian. The story seems to be fictional.

Basilissa of Oehren (St) R(OSB). Dec 5
d. *c*780. She was abbess of Oehren near Trier, Germany.

Basilla (St) *see* **Adria, Victor and Basilla**

Basilla of Rome (St) V. May 20
d. 304. Her legend, which is a commonplace in hagiographical literature, states that she was a young Roman woman who was martyred after refusing to marry a pagan patrician to whom she had been betrothed.

Basilla of Smyrna (St) V. Aug 29
? The old Roman Martyrology lists her as having died at Smyrna (Izmir, Turkey), but other sources list Sirmium (now Srem Mitrovica in Serbia).

Basinus (St) B. R. Mar 4
d. ?705. The abbot of St Maximin's Abbey at Trier, Germany, he succeeded St Numerian as bishop of the city and was of great assistance to St Willibrord and his companion Saxon missionaries. He retired to his abbey in old age to die.

Basolus (Basle) (St) R. Nov 26
?555–620. From Limoges, he was a monk at Verzy near Rheims, France, before becoming a wonder-working hermit for forty years on a hill overlooking the city.

Bassa (St) *see* **Victor, Victorinus and Comps**

Bassa, Paula and Agathonica (SS) VV. Aug 10
? They are listed as having been martyred at Carthage in Roman Africa.

Bassa and Sons (SS) MM. Aug 21
d. 304. The wife of a pagan priest, she was martyred with her three sons, Theogonius, Agapius and Fidelis, at Larissa in Greece (not Edessa). Their cultus is ancient but their acta are unreliable.

Bassian (St) *see* **Cyrion, Bassian and Comps**

Bassian (St) *see* **Peter, Successus and Comps**

Bassian of Lodi (St) B. Jan 19
d. 413. A Sicilian bishop of Lodi in Lombardy, Italy, he was highly regarded by his friend St Ambrose whom he attended on his deathbed.

Bassus (St) *see* **Maximus, Bassus and Fabius**

Bassus, Anthony and Protolicus (SS) MM. Feb 14
? They were thrown into the sea at Alexandria, Egypt, in an imperial persecution, possibly with nine companions.

Bassus, Dionysius, Agapitus and Comps (SS) MM. Nov 20
? A group of forty-three, they were martyred at Heraclea in Thrace, European Turkey.

Bassus of Nice (St) M. B. Dec 5
d. *c*250. Bishop of Nice, France, he was killed by being pierced with two large nails.

Bathild (Balthild) (St) R. Jan 30
d. 680. A Saxon girl sold as a slave to the mayor (comptroller) of the palace of the Frankish king of Neustria, France, she ended up as queen by marrying King Clovis II in 649. She was regent from 656 (when her husband died) until 664 when her eldest son Clotaire III took power, and two other sons later became kings. She founded the abbey of Corbie and the double monastery (for nuns and monks) at Chelles and became a nun at the latter, the rule of which was derived from those of SS Columban and Benedict. Her contemporary biography is reliable.

Bathus, Wereka and Comps
(SS) MM. Mar 26
d. 370. They are listed as having been Goths who were burned in a church by their king, Jungerich or Athanaric, for having converted to Christianity. This was possibly in what is now Romania.

Baudacarius (St) R. Dec 21
d. 650. The relics of this monk of Bobbio in Lombardy, Italy, were enshrined there in 1483.

Baudelius (St) M. May 20
C2nd or C3rd. A married man from Orléans, France, he was a zealous Christian and was martyred at Nîmes. His cultus has left four hundred churches in France and north Spain dedicated to him.

Baudry *see* **Bauderic**

Bavo (St) R. Oct 1
?589–660. From Hesbaye near Liege, Belgium, he led an immoral life when young but was widowed and then converted to a life of penance by a sermon by St Amandus of Elnone. He founded an abbey (later named after him) on his property at Ghent and ended up as a hermit in a cell nearby. He is patron of the city.

Baya and Maura (SS) RR. Nov 2
C10th? They were hermits in Scotland, the latter being the disciple of the former and the founder of a nunnery. The details are obscure. St Baya may be St Begha or Bee, or the pair of them may be identical to SS Maura and Britta.

Bean (St) B. Oct 26
d. *p*1012. He was the first bishop of Mortlach, Scotland, which see was transferred to Aberdeen early in the C12th. There is confusion between him and other saints of the same name.

Beata (St) *see* **Augustine, Sanctian and Beata**

Beata (St) *see* **Cyril, Rogatus and Comps**

Beatrice (St) *see* **Simplicius, Faustinus and Beatrice**

Beatrice I of Este (Bl) R(OSB). May 10
?1191–1226. Daughter of the Marquis d'Este of Ferrara, Italy, she was orphaned as a child and ran away from home to become a Benedictine nun at Solarola near Padua when aged fourteen. She died aged twenty at the nunnery at Gemola which she had founded, and had her cultus confirmed for Ferrara in 1763.

Beatrice II of Este (Bl) R(OSB). Jan 18
d. 1262. A niece of the above, she lost her fiancé when young and then had founded for her the Benedictine nunnery of St Anthony at Ferrara, Italy, becoming a nun there in 1254. Her cultus was confirmed for Ferrara in 1774.

Beatrice d'Ornacieaux (Bl)
R(O Cart). Feb 13
d. 1309. She joined the Carthusian nuns at Parmenie when aged thirteen and had a mystical devotion to the Passion as well as suffering from diabolic manifestations. She died at the nunnery of Eymieux near Valence, France, which she had helped to found.

Beatrice da Silva Meneses
(St) R. Aug 16
1424–1490. A Portuguese noblewoman born at Ceuta in Morocco, when aged twenty she accompanied a Portuguese princess to the Spanish court at Toledo and quickly became a nun at the Cistercian nunnery of St Dominic of Silos there. Later she founded the Congregation of the Immaculate Conception ('Conceptionists'), which had the Benedictine rule under her but which was given the rule of St Clare after her death. She died at Toledo and was canonized in 1976.

Beatus (St) R. May 9
?. He is venerated as the apostle of Switzerland and his hermitage is pointed out at Beatenberg near Interlaken, Bern canton. Nothing certain is known of his life.

Beatus *see* **Beoadh**

Beatus of Liébana (St) R. Feb 19
d. 789. From Asturias, Spain, he was a monk of Liébana who fought against the Adoptionist heresy which was being propagated by Helipandus, archbishop of Toledo. After this was condemned he became abbot of Valcavado

and wrote a commentary on the Apocalypse. His cultus in Spain is unapproved.

Beatus of Trier (St) R. Aug 26
C7th. He was a hermit near Trier, Germany.

Becan (Began) (St) R. Apr 5
C6th. One of the 'twelve apostles of Ireland', he was a contemporary of St Columba and founded a monastery at Killbeggan in Co. Westmeath. This later became a Cistercian abbey.

Bede the Venerable (St) Dr. R. May 25
673–735. Born near Wearmouth in Sunderland, England, he was a child-oblate in the abbey there under St Benedict Biscop and was transferred to the foundation at Jarrow. There he remained all his life as a scholar and teacher of his brethren, becoming a polymath and one of the most learned men then in western Europe. In contrast he took part in no important events, apart from his ordination by St John of Beverley. His major work, the *Ecclesiastical History of the English People*, makes him the progenitor of English historiography and is the only coherent source for the early Anglo-Saxon Church. His works on biblical exegesis (his main interest) were very popular in the Middle Ages, and he also helped to establish the counting of years from the birth of Christ. His cultus was not fully established in England before the Reformation (hence some Protestants refer to him as 'Venerable Bede' instead of 'St Bede') but he was declared a doctor of the Church in 1899. His attribute is a water-jug.

Bede the Younger (St) R(OSB). Apr 10
d. 883. An important official at the court of Emperor Charles the Bald, he became a Benedictine at the abbey of Gavello south of Padua, Italy. He refused to become a bishop. His relics have been at the abbey of Subiaco since the C19th.

Bega (Begga) of Andenne (St) R. Dec 17
d. 693. Daughter of BB Pepin of Landen and Ida and sister of St Gertrude of Nivelles, she married Ansegis (son of St Arnulf of Metz) and was the mother of Pepin the Short, the founder of the Carolingian dynasty. As a widow she founded and governed a nunnery at Andenne on the Meuse, France.

Bega (Begu) of Hackness (St) R. Sep 6
d. *c*660. She was a nun at Hackness near Whitby, England, under St Hilda, and had her shrine at the abbey of Whitby. She has been confused with St Bega of St Bees.

Bega (Bee, Begh) of St Bees
(St) R. Oct 31
C7th. She was allegedly an Irish girl who fled a threatened marriage and founded a nunnery on St Bees Head in Cumbria, England.

Belina (St) V. Feb 19
d. 1135. From Landreville near Troyes, France, she was with her father's sheep when a local nobleman tried to seduce her and killed her when she refused. She was canonized in 1203.

Bellinus (St) M. B. Nov 26
d. 1151. Allegedly a German, as bishop of Padua, Italy, he energetically opposed simony and was hence assassinated.

Benedict
This name is in Latin, Benedictus; in Italian, Benedetto; in French, Benoît; in Spanish, Benito; in Portuguese, Bento; in Catalan, Benet; in German, Benedikt; in mediaeval English, Benet.

Benedict II, Pope (St) May 7
d. 685. A Roman, he was elected pope in 683 but his consecration was delayed a year while awaiting confirmation from the emperor in Constantinople. He then reigned for eleven months.

Benedict XI, Pope (Bl) R(OP). Jul 7
1240–1304. From Treviso, Italy, Nicholas Boccasini joined the Dominicans and became their ninth master-general before being made cardinal of Ostia and papal legate. He was elected pope in 1303. His cultus was confirmed for Perugia in 1736.

Benedict d'Alignan (Bl)
B. R(OFM). Jul 8
d. 1268. Reputed to have been a Benedictine abbot before becoming bishop of Marseilles, France, he made a pilgrimage to the Holy Land and, on his return, resigned and became a Franciscan.

Benedict of Angers (St) B. Jul 15
d. *c*820. He was a bishop of Angers, France.

Benedict of Aniane (St) R(OSB). Feb 11
*c*750–821. A Visigoth named Witiza, he served at the Frankish courts of Pepin and Charlemagne before becoming a monk near Dijon in 773. In 779 he founded his own abbey on his patrimony in the Aniane gorge in Languedoc, and this became the centre of reform of the monasteries in France and Germany under imperial encouragement. In

813 Emperor Louis the Pious built for him a model abbey called Kornelimünster near the imperial capital of Aachen. In 817 he presided at a synod of abbots at Aachen which imposed the Benedictine rule and a common customary on all the monasteries of the Empire, thus definitively establishing the Benedictines as a religious order.

Benedict of Arezzo (Bl) R(OFM). Aug 31
d. 1281. From Arezzo, Italy, and an early companion of St Francis of Assisi, he was one of the first Franciscan provincials and was sent to the Holy Land and to the Byzantine Empire. He gave a Franciscan habit to the emperor at Constantinople as a present.

Benedict of Benevento and Comps (SS) MM. RR(OSB Cam). Nov 12
d. 1005. From Benevento, Italy, he became a Camaldolese monk and went as a missionary to Poland with a companion named John. They settled at Miedzyrzec near Gniezno and were joined by Matthew, Isaac and Christian from the locality. The little community was massacred by robbers. Their cultus was confirmed in 1508.

Benedict Biscop (St) R. Jan 12
?628–?690. A Northumbrian noble, when a young man he made two pilgrimages to Rome and became a monk at Lérins during the second of them. Returning with St Theodore, he became abbot of St Peter's in Canterbury, England, and then founded the twin monasteries of Wearmouth and Jarrow (675–682) in Northumbria. In these he introduced Roman liturgical customs and chant and used the rule of St Benedict in compiling the customary. The abbeys became famous for scholarship of high quality (the library was probably the best in Anglo-Saxon England) and craft-work which (especially in stone and glass) was novel in Saxon England. He was the spiritual father of St Bede.

Benedict (Bénézet) of the Bridge (St) L. Apr 14
d. ?1184. A Savoyard shepherd, he apparently received a vision of an angel telling him to build a stone bridge over the Rhône at Avignon, France. This he did, with the help of the bishop and certain miracles.

Benedict of Cagliari (St) B. R(OSB). Feb 17
d. *p*1112. A monk of St Saturninus's Abbey at Cagliari, Sardinia, he was bishop of Dolia on the island from 1107 before returning to his abbey in 1112.

Benedict of Campania (St) R. Mar 23
d. *c*550. In his *Dialogues*, St Gregory the Great states that this hermit was thrown into a furnace somewhere in the Campania, Italy, by some Goths commanded by Totila and kept unharmed by a miracle.

Benedict de Castro (Bl) *see* **Ignatius Azevedo and Comps**

Benedict Crispus (St) B. Mar 11
d. 725. He was archbishop of Milan, Italy, from 680.

Benedict-Joseph Labre (St) L. Apr 16
1748–1783. From near Boulogne-sur-Mer, France, his family ran a shop but he tried his vocation with the Carthusians and Cistercians before becoming a pilgrim-beggar. He wandered from shrine to shrine in western Europe, living off alms but never accepting money. Being absolutely destitute and subject to serious privations, he is the best example in the West of the 'fool for Christ's sake' more familiar in the Russian tradition. He died in Rome and was canonized in 1883.

Benedict-of-St-Philadelphus Manassari (St) R(OFM). Apr 4
1526–1589. Nicknamed 'The Moor', he was born near Messina in Sicily of Negro serf parents. He became a hermit and then a Franciscan lay brother at Palermo. Starting as the cook, he went on to become an excellent superior and novice-master of the friary before becoming the cook again when old (which he preferred). He was canonized in 1807.

Benedict-Joseph-Labre Mañoso González (Bl) *see* **Hospitaller Martyrs of Spain**

Benedict of Mazerac (St) R. Oct 22
d. 845. From Patras, Greece, he fled as a refugee with ten companions to Nantes, France, and founded a small monastery at Mazerac nearby.

Benedict Menni (St) R. F. Apr 24
1841–1914. From Milan, Italy, he helped to transfer wounded soldiers from the railway station to the hospital run by the Hospitallers of St John of God in 1859, and this led him to join them in 1860. In 1866 he went to Barcelona to restore a children's' hospital and to found a badly needed mental hospital. He founded the 'Hospitaller Sisters' in 1880 and he founded their new Spanish province in 1884. He became superior-general in 1909 but had to resign owing to calumny which exiled him from Italy and Spain. He died in Paris and was canonized in 2000.

Benedict of Nursia (St)
R(OSB). F. Jul 11
*c*480–550. He is primarily celebrated as the compiler of the monastic rule named after him, in itself anonymous and based on an earlier document called the Rule of the Master (possibly also by him). An ancient tradition equates him with the hero of the second *Dialogue* of St Gregory the Great, which is the only biographical source and which (although not intended as historigraphical in genre) has an authentic historical background. The rule and dialogue lack cross-references. According to the latter he was a young man from Nursia (now Norcia in Umbria, Italy) who went to study at Rome but fled in disgust and became a hermit near the ruins of Nero's villa at Subiaco. There he established a monastic colony before moving to Montecassino about 530 and founding the abbey there, where he died. There is no evidence that he was ordained, and there are competing claims for his relics at Montecassino and Fleury, France. His rule gradually took precedence in the monasteries of Merovingian France and apparently became established in Saxon English monasticism through the agency of SS Wilfrid and Benedict Biscop. It was prescribed for the Carolingian Empire from 817 and was absolutely dominant in Western monasticism for over two centuries after, at a time when monasteries were the centres of the surviving civilization. For this reason St Benedict was declared patron of Europe in 1964. There is no evidence for his cultus at Rome before the C10th.

St Benedict of Nursia, Jul 11

Benedict de' Passionei
(Bl) R(OFM Cap). Apr 30
1560–1625. From Urbino, Italy, he was a lawyer there before joining the Capuchins at Fano in 1584. He was the companion of St Laurence of Brindisi in the latter's travels in Austria and Bohemia, but returned to Italy to die at Fossombrone. He was beatified in 1867.

Benedict Revelli (St) B. R(OSB). Feb 12
d. *c*900. He was allegedly a Benedictine monk before becoming a hermit on the island of Gallinaria in the Gulf of Genoa, Italy. In 870 he became the bishop of Albenga in Liguria.

Benedict Ricasoli (Bl) R(OSB Vall). Jan 20
d. 1107. From Coltiboni near Florence, Italy, he became a Vallumbrosan monk in a monastery founded by his parents and then a hermit. His cultus was confirmed for Fiesole in 1907.

Benedict of Sandomir (Bl) *see* **Sadoc of Sandomir and Comps**

Benedict of Sebaste (St) B. Oct 23
d. ?654. His dubious story alleges that he was a bishop of Sebaste (formerly Samaria) in the Holy Land who fled persecution by Emperor Julian and settled as a hermit at Quinçay near Poitiers, France. The site subsequently became an abbey.

Benedict of Skalka (St) R. May 1
d. 1002. Trained by St Andrew Zorard, he became a hermit on Mount Zobor near Nitra, Slovakia, and was famous for his austerity and prayerfulness. He was killed by marauders in 1012 and was canonized in 1083.

Benedict-of-the-Virgin-del-Villar Solana Ruiz (Bl) *see* **Nicephorus Díez Tejerina and Comps**

Benedict-of-Jesus Valdivieso Saez (St) *see* **Cyril-Bertrand Sanz Tejedor and Comps**

Benedicta (St) *see* **Priscus, Priscillian and Benedicta**

Benedicta and Cecilia (SS)
RR(OSB). Aug 17
C10th. These two daughters of St Zwentibold, king of Lorraine, were successive abbesses at Susteren, the nunnery founded for them by their father in the Rhineland, Germany.

Benedicta Cambiagio Frassinello
(Bl) R. F. May 10
1791–1858. From near Genoa, Italy, she married John-Baptist, a young farmer, and they mutually agreed to live in celibacy two years later. In 1825 she entered the Ursulines at Bressino and he the Somaschi as a lay brother, but she had to leave because of her health and settled at Pavia. There the bishop encouraged her to open an institute in 1828 to care for derelict girls and to turn them into respectable wives and mothers. Her husband left the Somaschi to help, which lost them the bishop's approval and they moved back to their old farm at Ronco and founded the 'Benedictine Sisters of Providence' for this work. She was beatified in 1987.

Benedicta Hyon (St) *see* **Korea (Martyrs of)**

Benedicta of Laon (St)V. Oct 8
? She was martyred near Laon, France, but further details are conflicting.

Benedicta of Rome (St) R. May 6
C6th. St Gregory the Great, in his fourth *Dialogue*, wrote that this nun of St Galla's nunnery in Rome had her death foretold to her by St Peter in a vision.

Benedicta of Sens (St)V? Jun 29
? The old Roman Martyrology listed her as a consecrated virgin near Sens, France. Later legends describe her as sister of SS Augustine and Sanctian from Spain, the three of them being martyred in Gaul in the reign of Aurelian.

Benedictine Martyrs of the Reformation (BB) MM. RR(OSB). Dec 1
d. 1539. Three Benedictine abbots, with two (possibly four) other monks, were executed during the dissolution of the monasteries in England and were beatified as martyrs in 1895. However, the abbots and their communities had signed the Oath of Supremacy demanded by King Henry VIII, and there is no record of their having publicly recanted. The wish to save their abbeys seems to have been their primary motivation in their vacillating attitude towards the government, and this was a factor in their favour at their beatification.

Bl Thomas Beche (or Marshall) became abbot of Colchester St John's in 1535 and refused to surrender his abbey. His private remarks showing his disgust at the government's religious policy were enough for him to be arrested and executed at Colchester, although the records of his trial (which survive) describe him as trying to explain these remarks away. It is clear, however, that he remained orthodox.

Bl Hugh Cook (or Faringdon) became abbot of Reading in 1520. What happened to him in 1539 is not very clear, and an anonymous pamphlet in his defence has been a major source. He was possibly implicated in the conspiracy of the Marquess of Exeter. He was executed with Bl John Eynon, parish priest of St Giles' in Reading, and Bl John Rugg, a retired prebendary of Chichester living at the abbey. These two are often claimed as monks, but there is no record of their having taken vows. The date of their execution is unknown.

Bl Richard Whiting became abbot of Glastonbury in 1525. He refused to surrender his abbey, and was executed on Tor Hill on November 15 with two of his brethren, Bl John Thorne, the treasurer, and Bl Roger James, the sacristan. The records are poor, but it seems that they were condemned at Wells for robbery, having concealed precious items in various places in the abbey in order to save them from seizure.

Bénézet *see* **Benedict of the Bridge**

Benignus (St) *see* **Evagrius and Benignus**

Benignus (St) *see* **John and Benignus**

Benignus (Benen) of Armagh
(St) B. Nov 9
d. ?466. St Patrick's favourite disciple and his psalm-singer, he evangelized Clare and Kerry and became abbot of Drumlease before succeeding St Patrick as archbishop of Armagh, Ireland. The legend connecting him with Glastonbury is worthless.

Benignus of Dijon (St) M. Nov 1
d. *c*270. Probably a martyr in the reign of Aurelian, he had an abbey erected over his shrine at Dijon, France. The legend connecting him with St Polycarp of Smyrna is worthless.

Benignus of Fontenelle (St) R. Mar 20
d. 725. Abbot of Fontenelle in Normandy, France, he was exiled thence to Flay near

Beauvais and was elected abbot there. After Charles Martel allowed him to return home he served as abbot of both monasteries.

Benignus of Milan (St) B. Nov 20
d. ?477. He was archbishop of Milan, Italy, when the Heruli, led by Odoacer, took the city.

Benignus of Todi (St) M. P. Feb 13
d. ?303. A priest of Todi in Umbria, Italy, he was martyred in the reign of Diocletian.

Benignus of Utrecht (St) B. Jun 28
C6th. He was a bishop mentioned in a decretal of Pope Pelagius II as wanting to resign, but it is not clear from which see. Chartres, France, is a possibility. He seems to have retired to Utrecht, Netherlands, where his shrine was established.

Benignus Visdomini (Bl)
R(OSB Vall) Jul 17
d. 1236. A priest of Florence, Italy, he became a monk at Vallombrosa after having repented of a sinful life, and went on to become abbot-general. However, contrition for his past led him to resign and die as a hermit.

Benignus of Wroclaw (St)
R(OCist). Jun 20
C13th. A Cistercian monk at Wroclaw, Poland, he was killed with many of his community in the Mongol incursion.

Benild (St) M. L. Jun 15
d. 853. A woman of Cordoba, Spain, when that was a Muslim city, she was inspired to speak out against Islam by the example of a priest being killed and was herself burned the following day. Her ashes were thrown into the Guadalquivir river in order to prevent their veneration.

Benildus Romançon (St) R. Aug 13
1805–1862. From Thuret near Clermont-Ferrand, France, he became a Brother of the Christian Schools and proved the feasibility of combining a career as a teacher with a life of prayer and of fidelity as a religious. He had an externally uneventful career as headmaster at Saugues, where he died. He was canonized in 1967.

Benincasa of La Cava (Bl)
R(OSB). Jan 10
d. 1194. He became the eighth abbot of his monastery of La Cava near Salerno, Italy, in 1171 and sent a hundred monks to occupy the new Sicilian royal monastery at Monreale. His cultus was confirmed in 1928.

Benincasa of Monticchiello
(Bl) R(OSM). May 11
1376–1426. From Florence, Italy, he became a Servite at Montepulciano and went on to be a lifelong hermit, firstly near Siena and then in an inaccessible cave at Monticchiello. His cultus was confirmed for the Franciscans in 1829.

Benjamin (St) M. D. Mar 31
d. ?431. A Persian deacon, he was imprisoned and released on condition that he ceased preaching. On his not obeying, he was tortured and killed in the reign of Shah Varanes by being impaled on a knotty stick inserted into his anus.

Benjamin-Julian Alfonsus Andrés (St) *see* **Cyril-Bertrand Sanz Tejedor and Comps**

Benjamin Cobos Celada (Bl) *see* **Hospitaller Martyrs of Spain**

Benno of Einsiedeln (Bl)
B. R(OSB). Aug 3
d. 940. Formerly a canon of Strasbourg, he settled at St Meinrad's former hermitage in Switzerland and thus founded the abbey of Einsiedeln, which survives. In 927 he became bishop of Metz, but his reforming zeal was objected to and he was attacked and blinded. He retired to Einsiedeln.

Benno of Meissen (St) B. Jun 16
1010–11106. Possibly from Hildesheim, Germany, and educated at the abbey there, he became a canon at Gozlar. Being made bishop of Meissen in 1066, he was almost alone among the German bishops in supporting Pope St Gregory VII against Emperor Henry VI. After the latter's submission he concentrated on evangelizing the Sorbs. He was canonized in 1523 and is patron of Munich.

Benno II of Osnabrück
(Bl) B. R(OSB). Jul 12
d. 1088. From Swabia, Germany, he became a monk at Reichenau where he was taught by Bl Herman the Cripple. Becoming archbishop of Osnabrück in 1067, he supported Pope St Gregory VII against Emperor Henry VI. He was also a noted architect. He retired to his monastic foundation of Iburg, where he died.

Bentivolius da Bonis (Bl)
R(OFM). Jan 2
d. 1232. From San Severino in the Marches, Italy, he was one of the earliest disciples of St Francis. His cultus was confirmed for San Severino in 1852.

Benvenuta Bojani (Bl) T(OP). Oct 30
d. 1292. The seventh of seven daughters of a noble couple of Cividale in Friuli, Italy, when young she became a Dominican tertiary and lived a severely penitential life in her parents' household, doing housework, praying and working miracles. Her cultus was approved for Udine in 1763.

Benvenutus Mareni (Bl) R(OFM). May 21
d. 1289. From Recanati near Loreto, Italy, he became a Franciscan lay brother and mostly worked in the kitchen. He was subject to supernatural phenomena. His cultus confirmed for Recanati in 1796.

Benvenutus Scotivoli (St)
B. R(OFM)? Mar 22
d. 1283. From Ancona, Italy, he studied law at Bologna with St Sylvester Gozzolini before becoming archdeacon of Ancona. He was made bishop of Osimo in 1264, which Ghibelline diocese he reconciled to the Papacy. The assertion that he was a Franciscan is based merely on a grey hood found in his tomb and is hardly adequate.

Beoadh (St) B. Mar 8
d. 518–525. Bishop of Adcarne in Co. Roscommon, Ireland, he has left his name to a famous early piece of Irish metalwork called the 'Bell of St Beoadh'.

Beoc (Beanus, Dabeoc, Mobeoc) (St) R. Dec 16
C5th or C6th. He founded a monastery on an island named after him in Lough Derg, Co. Donegal, Ireland.

Beocca, Ethor and Comps
(SS) MM. RR(OSB). Apr 10
d. 870. The Viking raids on Anglo-Saxon England in the C9th destroyed monastic life in the country. St Beocca was abbot of Chertsey in Surrey, and he and his community (allegedly about ninety) were massacred in a Danish raid up the Thames. *See* **Hedda and Comps**, **Tancred and Comps** and **Theodore of Crowland and Comps**.

Berach (Barachias) (St) R. Feb 15
C6th. He was a disciple of St Kevin before founding a monastery at Kilbarry in Co. Roscommon, Ireland, ruins of which survive.

Berachiel (St) *see* **Seven Archangels**

Berard of Carbio and Comps
(SS) MM. RR(OFM). Jan 16
d. 1220. They were sent by St Francis to convert the Muslims in Iberia and the Maghreb, and went from Italy to Coïmbra, Portugal. They started preaching in Seville, were driven out and tried again in Morocco, where they were beheaded. Berard, Otto and Peter were priests, and Adjutus and Accursius were lay brothers. The protomartyrs of the Franciscans, they were canonized in 1481.

Berard of Maris (St) B. Nov 3
d. 1130. He became cardinal-archbishop of Marsi east of Rome in 1109 (the cathedral of this diocese is at Pescina), and had his cultus there confirmed in 1802.

Berarius of Le Mans (St) B. Oct 17
d. *c*680. A bishop of Le Mans, France, he succeeded St Haduin.

Bercham *see* **Berthanc**

Bercharius (St) M. R. Oct 16
d. ?696. A monk originally of Luxeuil, France, he was made the first abbot of Hautvilliers at its foundation by St Nivard of Rheims. After going on pilgrimage to Rome and the Holy Land he founded an abbey at Moutier-en-Der but was stabbed one night by a monk whom he had rebuked, and died after expressing his forgiveness.

Bercthun (Bertin) of Beverley
(St) R. Sep 24
d. 733. A disciple of St John of Beverley, he was appointed first abbot of Beverley, Yorks, England, by him. The abbey was destroyed by the Vikings and not re-founded.

Berctuald *see* **Brithwald**

Beregisus (St) P. Oct 2
d. *p*725. As a priest he was the confessor of Pepin of Heristal, with whose help he founded the abbey of Saint-Hubert in the Ardennes, Belgium. It is not certain whether he became a monk or abbot there.

Berencardus (Berenger) (St)
R(OSB). May 26
d. 1293. From near Toulouse, France, he became a Benedictine at Saint-Papoul near Carcassonne, France, and served as novice-master, almoner and master of works. He was known for his charity and patience.

Berengarius of Formbach
(Bl) R(OSB). Oct 29
d. 1108. He became first abbot of Formbach in Bavaria, Germany, in 1094.

Berenice (St) *see* **Domnina, Berenice and Prosdoce**

Berlinda (Berlindis, Bellaude)
(St) R. Feb 3
d. 702. A niece of St Amandus, she became a nun at Moorsel near Alost, Belgium, and then a hermit at Meerbeke when her nunnery was destroyed.

Bernard, Mary and Grace
(SS). MM. Jun 1
d. *c*1180. Ahmed, Zoraida and Zaida were children of Mansur, the Muslim emir of Lérida in Catalonia, Spain. Ahmed converted, became a Cistercian monk named Bernard at Poblet near Tarragona and, when old, he tried to convert his siblings. He was successful with the two sisters, but a brother had the three of them executed as apostates from Islam.

Bernard of Arce (St) R. Oct 14
C9th. He was a pilgrim, either a Saxon or a Frank, who died as a hermit at Arpino in Campania, Italy, after having been to Rome and the Holy Land.

Bernard II of Baden (Bl) L. Jul 15
1428–1458. Margrave of Baden, Germany, he left his brother as regent and, as an ambassador of Emperor Frederick III, tried in several European courts to arrange a crusade against the Turks. He failed, died at Moncalieri in Piedmont, Italy, and had his cultus confirmed for there and for Turin in 1769.

Bernard of Bagnorea (St) B. Oct 20
d. *p*800. As bishop of Vulci in Tuscany, Italy, he transferred the see to Ischia di Castro.

Bernard Calvo (St) B. R(OCist). Oct 24
d. 1243. A Cistercian monk in Catalonia, Spain, he was the first abbot of Santas Creus near Tarragona before becoming bishop of Vich in 1233.

Bernard of Carinola (St) B. Mar 12
d. 1109. From Capua, Italy, he was the first bishop of Carinola in Campania, having transferred the diocese thereto from Forum Claudii in 1100 after thirteen years as a bishop. He was very old when he died.

Bernard of Clairvaux (St)
Dr. R(OCist.) Aug 20
1090–1153. A nobleman born near Dijon, France, in 1112 he joined the new abbey of Cîteaux with (it is asserted) thirty friends and relatives whom he had persuaded to enter. He was sent to be first abbot of the new foundation at Clairvaux in 1115 and transformed the struggling Cistercian congregation into a spectacular success, founding sixty-eight abbeys. He became one of the most famous and influential men in western Europe and was popular as an adviser of those in power, secular as well as ecclesiastical. His theological writings, of which the most famous are the *Treatise on the Love of God* and the *Commentary on the Song of Songs*, were highly influential and led him to be declared a doctor of the Church in 1830. He proclaimed the Second Crusade at Vézelay in 1146, and the disaster that this proved to be cast a shadow over his later life and vitiated his political judgment. He died at Clairvaux and was canonized in 1174. His attribute is a white dog.

Bernard Cucsac (Bl) *see* **September (Martyrs of)**

Bernard (Vu van) Due (St) M. P. Aug 1
1755–1838. A retired secular priest of Vietnam, he voluntarily gave himself up during the persecution of the Vietnamese church and was beheaded. *See* **Vietnam (Martyrs of)**.

Bernard Latini of Corleone
(Bl) R(OFM Cap). Jan 19
1605–1667. A shoemaker from Corleone in Sicily, he was reputed the best swordsman in the island before fatally wounding an opponent and taking sanctuary in the Capuchin church at Palermo. There he became a lay brother in 1632, and was famous for his austerity. He was beatified in 1768.

Bernard Lichtenberg (Bl) P. Nov 5
1875–1943. From Breslau, Germany (now Wroclaw, Poland), he became a parish priest in Berlin and provost of its cathedral in 1938. Active politically, he protested at the treatment of the Jews by the Nazis and they sent him to the concentration camp at Dachau. He died on the way and was beatified in 1996.

Bernard of Lippe (Bl) B. R(OCist.) Jan 23
d. 1217. Count of Lippe (a small German state near Hanover), he became a Cistercian monk and abbot of Dünemunde before being made bishop of Semgallen in Courland (now Latvia).

Bernard of Menthon (St) R(CR). May 28
d. ?1081. He was the vicar-general of the diocese of Aosta in the Alps, Italy, for forty years and was especially solicitous for the welfare of the many travellers crossing the mountain passes. He founded hospices, run by canons

regular, in the two passes now bearing his name. He died at Novara. A breed of dog is named after him, and he is the patron of mountaineers.

Bernard (or Berard) Paleara (St) B. R(OSB). Dec 19
d. 1122. A monk of Montecassino, he became bishop of Teramo, Italy, in 1115 and is that town's principal patron.

Bernard of Parma (St) B. R(OSB Vall). Dec 4
1055–1133. From Florence, Italy, he gave up brilliant prospects to became a monk at Vallombrosa and went on to become abbot-general of that congregation before being made a cardinal in 1097 and bishop of Parma in 1106. He was active against simony and schism, was exiled twice but was a great success as a bishop. He died at the abbey of Cavana, which he had founded.

Bernard the Penitent (Bl) R(OSB). Apr 19
d. 1182. A Provençal criminal, he was sentenced by his bishop to seven years' penance, which he spent on pilgrimage in Europe and to the Holy Land. He did this while wearing seven heavy iron rings around his body. Afterwards he became a hermit at Sithiu at Saint-Omer, France, and then a monk at the abbey there.

Bernard Peroni of Offida (Bl) R(OFM Cap). Aug 23
1604–1694. From near Ancona, Italy, he became a Capuchin lay brother at Offida, was some time at Fermo and then became the collector of alms at Offida. He was famous for his wisdom and working of miracles, and also for his concern for poor and sick people. He was beatified in 1795.

Bernard of Rodez (Bl) R(OSB). Jul 19
d. 1079. Abbot of St Victor at Marseilles, France, he was a friend of Pope St Gregory VII and St Hugh the Great, and was hence a leader in the Gregorian reform. He was made a cardinal and papal legate to Germany and then to Spain.

Bernard de Roquefort(Bl) *see* **William Arnaud and Comps**

Bernard Scammacca (Bl) R(OP). Feb 16
d. 1486. From Catania, Sicily, his family was wealthy and he was a delinquent youth until he was seriously wounded in a duel. Then he repented of his conduct, joined the Dominicans and did continuous penance for his past excesses. His cultus was approved for Catania in 1825.

Bernard-Mary-of-Jesus Silvestrelli (Bl) R(CP). Dec 9
1831–1911. A Roman, he tried to join the Passionists in 1853 but his health failed him. He entered successfully at Morrovalle near Macerta in 1856 in company with St Gabriel of Our Lady of Sorrows, having been ordained meanwhile. He was superior-general of his congregation from 1878 to 1907, was highly regarded by the popes and refused to become a cardinal out of humility. His retirement was spent at Moricone in the Sabine Hills, where he died of a fall. He was beatified in 1988.

Bernard of Tiron (St) R(OSB). F. Apr 14
1046–1117. From near Abbeville, France, he became a monk at St Cyprian's at Poitiers and was appointed prior of St Sabinus for twenty years. Then he became a hermit, was appointed abbot of St Cyprian's but went off to be a hermit again in a forest near Chartres. His disciples there formed the nucleus of the abbey of Tiron and a new congregation, the Tironensians, which was an attempt to restore the full observance of the Benedictine rule. They spread in France and were important in Scotland, but mitigated their observance and were eventually merged with the Maurists. His cultus was confirmed in 1861.

Bernard Tolomei (Bl) R(OSB Oliv). F. Aug 21
1272–1348. From Siena, Italy, and educated by an uncle who was a Dominican, he studied law and served the city in several offices, including that of mayor. In 1313 he became a hermit at Monteoliveto, ten miles from Siena, and there founded a new abbey. This was the start of the new congregation of the Olivetans. He and many of his monks died of the plague while nursing sufferers during an epidemic and his body was lost, which is why he was never canonized. His cultus was approved for Siena and the Olivetans in 1644.

Bernard of Valdeiglesias (St) R. Aug 20
d. *p*1155. He was a monk of Valdeiglesias in Galicia, Spain, and may have been a Cistercian.

Bernardine degl' Albizzeschi of Siena (St) R(OFM). May 20
1380–1444. From Massa Maritima, Italy, he became a Franciscan Observant in 1402. He preached his first sermon in 1417, and subsequently became the foremost Italian

missionary preacher of the C15th. His special subject was the Holy Name of Jesus, devotion to which he was instrumental in spreading. From 1438 to 1442 he was vicar-general of his order, and helped to improve its discipline. He died at Aquila and was canonized in 1450. His attribute is a plaque with the initials IHS, also three mitres at his feet (representing bishoprics that he had refused).

St Bernardine of Siena, May 20

Bernardine Amici of Fossa (Bl) R(OFM). Nov 27
d. 1503. From near Aquila, Italy, he became a Franciscan Observant in 1445 and, after serving in various administrative posts, became an itinerant preacher in Italy, Croatia and Bosnia. He died at Aquila, where his cultus was confirmed in 1828.

Bernardine Realino (St) R(SJ). Jul 2
1530–1616. From near Modena, Italy, he became a lawyer but joined the Jesuits in 1564. He was ten years at Naples, and then was the rector of the college at Lecce until his death. He was canonized in 1947.

Bernardine Tomitano of Feltre (Bl) R(OFM). Sep 28
1439–1494. From Feltre in the Dolomites, Italy, he became a Franciscan Observant and was a teacher before finding his vocation as a vehement preacher, especially against usury. As a practical aid against this he helped in the setting up of 'monti di pieta' (charitable lending-houses) in several Italian cities. His cultus was confirmed for Feltre and Pavia in 1728.

Bernger (Bl) R(OSB). Oct 29
d. 1108. He was first abbot of the abbey of Formbach in Bavaria, Germany, near Passau.

Berno (St) R(OSB). Jan 13
*c*850–927. A Burgundian, he became a monk at Autun and then abbot of Baume-les-Messieurs, where he restored the abbey and received the vows of St Odo. He founded three other abbeys before he founded Cluny in 910, where he was abbot until he was succeeded by St Odo in 926.

Bernold of Ottobeuren (Bl) R(OSB). Nov 25
d. *c*1050. He was a monk and thaumaturge of Ottobeuren in Bavaria, Germany.

Bernulf (St) B. Jul 19
d. 1054. He was a bishop of Utrecht, Netherlands, and was zealous for the reform of his diocese.

Bernwald (Berward) (St) B. R(OSB). Nov 20
*c*960–1022. The grandson of the count palatine of Saxony, Germany, he was imperial court chaplain and tutor of Emperor Otto III before being made bishop of Hildesheim in 993. He was an accomplished artist, being skilled in architecture, painting, sculpture and metal-working, and some of his work survives at Hildesheim. He apparently became a Benedictine monk before his death.

Beronicus, Pelagia and Comps (SS) MM. Oct 19
? They numbered fifty-nine and were martyred at Antioch, Syria, in an early persecution, but nothing else is known.

Bertellin *see* **Bettelin**

Bertha *see* **Rupert and Bertha**

Bertha of Avenay (St) M. R. May 1
d. *p*680. She was the founder and first abbess of Avenay near Rheims, France. Her unreliable legend describes her as the former wife of St Gundebert who was killed by her stepsons because of her generosity to the poor.

Bertha of Blangy (St) R. Jul 4
d. ?725. The daughter of a Frankish court official from Arras, France, when widowed she became a nun at her foundation at Blangy with her two daughters in ?686, and was subsequently abbess.

Bertha of Kent, Queen
d. 612. Oddly, the wife of King St Ethelbert had no medieval veneration as a saint despite the efforts of some Victorians in east Kent, England, to pretend otherwise (she is depicted as a saint in a C19th window at Ramsgate Abbey).

Bertha of Marbais (Bl) R(OCist). Jul 18
d. 1247. A relative of the count of Flanders, when widowed she became a Cistercian nun at Ayvrières and was then made first abbess of her family's foundation at Marquette near Lille, France. She has a local cultus in the diocese of Namur, Belgium.

Bertha of Vald'Or and Gombert
(SS) MM. RR. May 1
C10th. Gombert, the founder of a nunnery at Rheims, France, was living in chastity with Bertha, who was married to someone else at the time. But he was murdered, so Bertha founded the nunnery of Val d'Or at Avenay, became abbess there and was in turn killed by relatives of her husband. The two have a joint local cultus.

Berthald (Berthaud) (St) R. Jun 16
d. *c*540. A hermit in the Ardennes, Belgium, he was ordained by St Remigius.

Berthanc (St) B. Apr 6
d. *c*840. He is alleged to have been a monk at Iona, Scotland, and then bishop of Kirkwall in the Orkneys. His alleged tomb is located on the island of Inishmore in Galway Bay, Ireland, however.

Bertharius *see* **Betharius**

Bertharius of Montecassino
(St) M. R(OSB). Oct 22
d. ?884. Of the Frankish royal family, he became abbot of Montecassino, Italy, in 856 and was killed in the abbey church of Teano with several of his brethren by a Muslim raiding party. Some homilies and other writings of his survive. His cultus was approved in 1727.

Berthoald (St) B. Oct 13
C7th. He was a bishop of the united dioceses of Cambrai and Arras, France.

Berthold of Carmel (St) R(OC). Mar 29
d. ?1195. From Limoges, France, he studied at Paris and then went to the Holy Land as a crusader. There he joined the Latin-rite hermits who had settled on Carmel and was appointed their superior by his brother Aymeric, Latin patriarch of Jerusalem. This was the start of the Carmelite order.

Berthold of Engelberg (Bl) R(OSB). Nov 3
d. 1197. The third abbot of Engelberg, Switzerland, he was famous as a copier of books and encouraged studies in his monastery.

Berthold of Garsten (Bl) R(OSB). Jul 27
1090–1142. A nobleman born near Constance, Germany, he was widowed when aged thirty and became a monk at Sankt-Blasien in the Black Forest. Eventually he became first abbot of the new foundation of Garsten in Styria, Austria, which abbey he made rich and famous. Much of his time was spent in hearing confessions. His cultus was confirmed for Linz in 1970.

Berthold (Bertoldo) of Parma
(St) R(OSB). Oct 21
d. 1111. Born at Parma, Italy, his parents were Anglo-Saxon refugees from the Norman conquest of England. He spent his life as a lay brother serving in the nunnery of St Alexander in that city.

Bertilla of Chelles (St) R. Nov 5
d. ?705. A nun at Jouarre near Meaux, France, she served in various capacities there before becoming the first abbess of the great double monastery of Chelles which had been founded by Queen St Bathild with nuns from Jouarre. (The foundation was not initially Benedictine.) She was abbess for fifty years, during which the foundation was a great success and attracted many Anglo-Saxon vocations.

Bertilla of Maroilles (St) R. Jan 3
d. ?687. A married noblewoman, she and her husband St Walbert made a vow of continence. When she was widowed she became a hermit at Maroilles near Cambrai, France. Her daughters were SS Waldetrude and Aldegund.

Bertilo (Bl) M. R(OSB). Mar 26
d. *c*880. Abbot of the monastery of St Benignus at Dijon, France, he was killed with several of his community at the church's altar during a raid by Norsemen.

Bertin the Great (St) R. Sep 5
d. ?709. From near Constance, Germany, he became a monk at Luxeuil, France, under St Waldebert and went as a missionary to the Pas-de-Calais. Then he was made first abbot by St Omer of the new foundation of Sithiu, later named after him and now in the town of St Omer, and this was such a success that he made several further foundations. His attribute is a boat (since his monastery was then on an island in a fen).

Bertin the Younger (Bl) R. May 2
d. ?699. He was a monk at Sithiu at St Omer, France, during the abbacy of its founder, St Bertin the Great.

Bertoara (St) R. Dec 4
d. *p*614. She was abbess of the Columbanian nunnery of Our Lady of Sales at Bourges, France, for two years from 612.

Bertram *see* **Bettelin**

Bertram (Bertichramnus) of Le Mans (St) B. Jul 3
d. ?626. From Autun, France, he was educated by St Germanus at Paris, became archdeacon there and was then made bishop of Le Mans. He was interested in agriculture, viniculture and in being charitable to the poor.

Bertrand of Aquileia (St) M. B. Jun 6
1260–1350. From near Cahors, France, he was the papal auditor at Avignon before being made patriarch of Aquileia near Venice, Italy, in 1334. He was killed for opposing simony and the alienation of church property in his diocese.

Bertrand de Caupenne (Bl) *see* **September (Martyrs of)**

Bertrand of Comminges (St) B. Oct 16
d. 1123. A knight from Gascony, France, he became archdeacon of Toulouse and then bishop of Comminges in 1083. He restored the diocese (which is now united to Toulouse) during his fifty years as bishop.

Bertrand of Garrigue (Bl) R(OP). Sep 6
d. 1230. From Garrigue near Nîmes, France, he was a secular priest but became a Dominican under St Dominic and helped to found the friary at Paris. He was a constant companion of St Dominic before becoming the provincial for Provence. He died at Toulouse and his cultus was confirmed for Valence and the Dominicans in 1881.

Bertrand of Grandselve (Bl) R(OCist). Oct 23
d. 1149. Abbot of the Cistercian abbey of Grandselve near Toulouse, France, for twelve years, he was a noted visionary.

Bertrand (Bertram, Bertran, Ebertram) of St Quentin (St) R. Jan 24
C8th. He was a disciple of St Bertin who helped St Omer in the evangelization of Flanders, France, before becoming abbot of St Quentin.

Bertulf of Bobbio (St) R. Aug 19
d. 640. A Frank, he became a monk at Luxeuil under St Eustace and then went to Bobbio in Lombardy, Italy, where he succeeded St Attalas as abbot in 627. He managed to obtain papal dispensation for his abbey from episcopal jurisdiction, the first such case recorded.

Bertulf of Renty (St) R. Feb 5
d. ?705. A pagan from Germany, he went to Flanders, converted and became one of the clergy under St Omer. He founded the abbey of Renty, to which he retired.

Bertwin (St) B. Nov 11
d. ?698. An Anglo-Saxon monk, he was ordained as a missionary bishop and evangelized the territory around Namur, Belgium, where he founded the abbey of Malonne.

Besas (St) *see* **Julian, Cronion Eunus and Besas**

Bessarion the Great (St) R. Jun 17
C5th. There are several early Egyptian monks of this name who have been confused, but the one with this feast-day seems to have been a thaumaturge who founded a monastery on Mount Zion in Jerusalem. Another was a disciple of St Anthony and of St Macarius at Scetis.

Betharius (St) B. Aug 2
d. *c*623. He was bishop of Chartres, France, from 595, but the extant biography is unreliable.

Bettelin (Bethlin, Bethelm) (St) R. Sep 9
C8th. A disciple of St Guthlac, when his master died he and his companions joined the monastery founded at Crowland, Lincs, by the king of Mercia, England. A saint of this name was patron of Stafford.

Betto (St) B. R(OSB). Feb 24
d. 918. He was a monk of the abbey of St Columbus at Sens, France, before becoming bishop of Auxerre.

Beuno (St) R. Apr 21
d. *c*640. From Powys, Wales, he founded monasteries on the Welsh border at Llanfeuno and Llanymynech as well as that at Clynog Fawr in Gwent, which became one of the greatest in Wales. In legend he is associated with St Winefride.

Beuve *see* **Bova**

Bianor and Silvanus (SS) MM. Jul 10
C4th. They were beheaded in Pisidia, Asia Minor. Their acta are unreliable.

Bibiana (Vibiana, Vivian) (St) V. Dec 2
? She was a virgin martyred at Rome, where she has a basilica to which her cultus was confined in 1969. Her acta are completely worthless, being medieval romantic fiction, and the corresponding entries in the old Roman Martyrology are spurious. *See* **Dafrosa** and **Priscus, Priscillian and Benedicta**.

Bibiana Hampai (Bl) *see* **Thailand (Martyrs of)**

Biblig *see* **Byblig**

Biblis (St) *see* **Photinus, Sanctius and Comps**

Bicor (St) M. B. Apr 22
C4th. A Persian bishop, he was martyred in the reign of Shah Shapur II.

Bieuzy (Budoc) (St) M. R. Nov 24
C7th. A British disciple of St Guthlac, he followed his master to Brittany, France, and was martyred there. Further details are lacking.

Bilfrid (Billfrith) (St) R. Mar 6
C8th. A hermit of Lindisfarne in Northumberland, England, he was an expert goldsmith and worked on the binding of the Lindisfarne Gospels. His alleged relics were discovered in the C11th and were enshrined at Durham.

Bilhild (St) R. Nov 27
*c*630–*c*710. From near Würzburg, Germany, she was married to the duke of Thuringia and founded the nunnery of Altmünster at Mainz when widowed, becoming its abbess.

Birgitta *see* **Brigid of Sweden**

Birillus (St) B? Mar 21
d. ?90. His legend states that he accompanied St Peter to Italy from Antioch, Sicily, and was ordained by him as first bishop of Catania, Sicily. There is no historical evidence for this.

Birinus (St) B. Dec 3
d. *c*650. A priest of Rome who was possibly a monk, he volunteered to go to England as a missionary and was ordained bishop at Milan on the way. On arriving he converted King Cynegils of Wessex in 634. In 636 he established his cathedral at Dorchester on Thames (in a diocese which was the remote ancestor of the diocese of Lincoln) and evangelized the surrounding area, which was then the powerbase of the kingdom. He is known as the apostle of Wessex.

Birnstan (Birrstan, Brynstan)
(St) B. R(OSB). Nov 4
d. ?934. A disciple of St Grimbald, he succeeded St Frithestan as bishop of Winchester, England, and was devoted to praying for the souls in Purgatory.

Biteus *see* **Movean**

Bitheus and Genocus (SS) RR. Apr 18
C6th. All that is known is that they were British monks who accompanied St Finian to Ireland.
Blaan *see* **Blane**

Bladus (St) B. Jul 3
? He is claimed to be one of the early bishops of the Isle of Man.

Blesilla (St) R. Jan 22
363–383. Daughter of St Paula and a disciple of St Jerome, she was with her mother in the Holy Land but died at Rome aged twenty.

Blaise and Demetrius
(SS) MM. Nov 29
? They were martyred at Veroli, Italy, but nothing else is known.

Blaise (Blase) of Sebaste
(St) M. B. Feb 3
d. ?316. According to his legendary acta he was a bishop of Sebaste in Armenia who saved the life of a boy who was choking on a fish-bone and who was martyred in the reign of Licinius after being tortured with a wool-comb, which is his attribute. Thus a special 'Blessing of St Blaise' for diseases of the throat is available in the Latin rite on his feast-day. The crusaders popularized his cultus in the West.

Blaithmaic (Blathmac, Blaithmale) (St) M. R. Jan 15
d. ?823. An Irish abbot, he resigned and went to Iona, Scotland, where he was killed in the church during a Danish raid.

Blanca *see* **Alda**

Blanche *see* **Gwen**

Blanda (St) *see* **Calepodius and Comps**

Blandina (St) *see* **Photinus, Sanctius and Comps**

Blandina Merten (Bl) R. May 18
1883–1918. Born to a pious peasant family near Koblenz, Germany, she was a clever girl and obtained her teacher's certificate in 1902. Her character was such that she was nicknamed 'the angel' in all seriousness. She joined the Ursulines at Ahrweiler in 1908 and taught at Saarbrücken and Trier before dying of tuberculosis. She was beatified in 1987.

Blandinus (St) R. May 1
d. *p*650. He was the second husband of St Salaberga and the father of SS Anstudis and Baldwin of Laon. He had a cultus in the diocese of Meaux, France, centred on the village of St Blandin where he had allegedly been a hermit.

Blane (Blaan, Blain) (St) B. Aug 10
C6th. A disciple of SS Comgall and Canice in Ireland, he became a bishop in Scotland and was buried at a monastery he had founded at Dunblane.

Blath (Flora) (St) R. Jan 29
d. 523. The best known of the several saints of this name was a lay sister who served as a cook in St Brigid's nunnery at Kildare, Ireland, and who had a great reputation for holiness.

Bledrws (St)
? There is a church with this dedication in Dyfed, Wales, but no other record of a saint of this name exists.

Bleiddian *see* **Lupus of Troyes**

Blenwydd (St)
? There is a church with this dedication on Anglesey, Wales, but no other record of a saint of this name exists.

Blida (Blythe) (St) L.
?C11th. She was the mother of St Walstan and was probably the saint of the same name venerated at Martham in Norfolk, England.

Blidulf (Bladulf) (St) R. Jan 2
d. *c*630. This monk of Bobbio in Lombardy, Italy, is recorded as having opposed the Arianism of the Lombard king Ariovald.

Blinlivet (Blevileguetus) (St) B. R. Nov 7
C9th. He was a bishop of Vanne in Brittany, France, who resigned to become a monk at Quimperlé.

Blitharius (Blier) (St) R. Jun 11
C7th. A Scot, he accompanied St Fursey to France and settled as a hermit at Sézanne near Troyes.

Blitmund (St) R. Jan 3
d. *c*660. A monk of Bobbio in northern Italy under St Attalas, he accompanied St Walaricus to France. They founded the abbey of Leucone on the Somme, later renamed Saint-Valéry, and he was the second abbot.

Bobinus (St)B. R. Jan 31
d. ?766. From Aquitaine, France, he was a monk of Moutier-la-Celle who became bishop of Troyes in 760.

Bobo (Beuvon) (St) R. May 22
d. ?985. A Provençal knight who fought the Muslim pirates based at Fresnet in Provence, when old he became a hermit and died at Voghera near Pavia, Italy, while on one of his annual pilgrimages to Rome.

Bodagisil (St) R. Dec 18
d. 588. He had served as Frankish governor of Marseilles and of Swabia (Germany) when he became the abbot-founder of the monastery of St Ayold near Metz, France. He is praised by SS Venantius Fortunatus and Gregory of Tours.

Bodfan (Bobouan) (St) R. Jun 2
C7th. He is the patron of Aber in Gwynedd, Wales, and his legend states that an irruption of the sea which formed Beaumaris Bay led him, his father and eleven brothers to become monks at Bangor Isycoed, and that he went on to be a hermit on Bardsey.

Bodo (St) B. R. Sep 11
d. *p*670. From Toul, France, he and his wife were influenced by his sister St Salaberga to separate and become consecrated religious. He became a monk at Laon and founded three monasteries before being made bishop of Toul in 670.

Boethian (St) M. R. May 22
C7th. A disciple of St Fursey in Ireland, he went to France and founded the monastery of Pierrepont near Laon. He was killed by wrongdoers whom he had rebuked.

Boethius (St) M. L. Oct 23
*c*480–524. Anicius Manlius Torquatus Severinus Boethius was a Roman whose father was consul under King Theodoric the Ostrogoth, and who became consul himself in 510 after being educated at Athens and

Alexandria. He was a notable philosopher and his influence on medieval thought was profound. As well as attempting to translate all the works of Plato and Aristotle into Latin he wrote several extant original works, the most famous being *The Consolation of Philosophy* which he wrote in prison after being accused of treason by the king in 534. He was later executed at Pavia, for which city his cultus as a saint was confirmed in 1883, and is also venerated at the church of Santa Maria in Portico at Rome. His status as a martyr is dubious.

Bogumil (Theophilus) of Gniezno (St) B.R(OSB Cam). Jun 10
d. 1182. From Dobrow on the Wartha river, Poland, he studied in Paris and became parish priest of his home town before becoming archbishop of Gniezno. He failed to win over his clergy despite his wisdom and zeal, but he founded the Cistercian abbey of Coronowa. In 1172 he resigned and became a Camaldolese monk at Uniejow. His cultus was approved for Wloclawek in 1925.

Boisil *see* **Boswell**

Bolcan (Olcan) (St) B. Feb 20
d. *c*480. He was baptized by St Patrick and sent by him to study in Gaul before being ordained bishop of Derkan in Ulster, Ireland. There he founded an important school. He is not the same as the Bolcan who was venerated at Elphin.

Boleslava-Mary Lament (Bl) R. F. Jan 29
1862–1946. From Łowicz in Poland, in 1876 she went to Warsaw to work as a fine dressmaker but in 1892 started to care for derelict people. In 1903 her spiritual director, Bl Honoratus Koźmiński, advised her to go to Mohilev in Bielarus and found the 'Missionary Sisters of the Holy Family' to foster church unity with the Orthodox. They moved to St Petersburg in 1907, working with children and the poor until the Russian revolution exiled them. Some stayed behind clandestinely, but Bl Boleslava re-established the mother house at Białystok in Poland, where she had a stroke two years before she died. She was beatified in 1991.

Bolonia (St)V. Oct 16
d 362. A girl aged fifteen, she was allegedly martyred in the reign of Julian at a place north of Dijon, France, where the village of Sainte-Boulogne now is.

Bona *see* **Bova**

Bonadonna (Bl) *see* **Luchesius and Bonadonna**

Bonajuncta Monetti (St) R(OSM) F. Feb 17
d. 1257. *See* **Servites, Founders of**. When the seven started their foundation community on Mt Senario he had the task of collecting alms for them to live on. He was the second superior-general of the new order.

Bonaventure (St) B. R(OFM). Dr. Jul 15
1221–1274. From near Viterbo, Italy, he was baptized as John but was nicknamed 'Good Fortune' by St Francis, who cured him miraculously when he was a toddler. He became a Franciscan when aged twenty, studied at the University of Paris under Alexander of Hales and taught there until elected minister-general of his order in 1257. His work in establishing it earned him the title of 'Second Founder', and he wrote an authoritative life of St Francis in order to foster its unity. He was made cardinal-bishop of Albano in 1273 and died during the Council of Lyons, for which he had helped to prepare. He was canonized in 1482. As one of the foremost medieval scholastics and a great mystical writer he was declared a doctor of the Church in 1588.

Bonaventure Baduario (Bl) R(OSA). Jun 10
1332–1386. A nobleman of Peraga near Padua, Italy, he became an Augustinian friar and was general of his order before being made cardinal-priest of St Caecilia's church in Rome. He was killed with bow and arrow in Rome on the orders of a relative whom he had irritated.

Bonaventure Buonacorsi (Bl) R(OSM). Dec 14
d. 1313. From Pistoia in Tuscany, Italy, he was the leader there of the anti-papal Ghibelline party until he was converted in 1276 by St Philip Benizi, who was acting as a peace-maker between them and the pro-papal Guelfs. He joined the Servites and became a preacher of peace himself, being nicknamed 'the blessed. His cultus was approved for the Servites in 1822.

Bonaventure Gran (Bl) R(OFM). Sep 11
1620–1684. From near Barcelona, Spain, when his wife died he became a Franciscan at Escornalbu. His mystical charismata attracted attention, however, so he went to Rome and became the doorkeeper at St Isidore's friary. He

founded several Franciscan retreat-houses in and around Rome, and his advice was valued by popes and cardinals. He died at Rome and was beatified in 1906.

Bonaventure of Miyako
(St) M. T(OFM). Feb 6
d. 1597. A Japanese Franciscan tertiary and a catechist helping the Franciscan missionaries in Japan, he was crucified at Nagasaki with SS Paul Miki and Comps. *See* **Japan (Martyrs of)**.

Bonaventure of Potenza
(Bl) R(OFM). Oct 26
1651–1711. From Potenza in Lucania, Italy, he became a Franciscan at Nocera and was a home-missioner based initially at Amalfi, then at Ischia and at Naples. He died at Ravello and was beatified in 1775.

Bonaventure Tolomei
(Bl) R(OP). Dec 27
d. 1348. From Siena, Italy, he was a very pious child who had mystical charismata but changed as a teenager and indulged in four years of sexual immorality and sacrilege. Then he repented, went on pilgrimage on foot to the major shrines of western Europe and joined the Dominicans. He died while nursing sufferers of plague at Siena.

Bonaventure Tornielli (Bl)
R(OSM). Mar 31
1412–1491. From Forli, Italy, he became a Servite in 1448 and was a preacher in the Papal States and the Kingdom of Naples. He also served for a period as vicar-general of his congregation. He died at Udine, and his cultus was confirmed for Romagna and the Servites in 1911.

Bond (Baldus) of Sens (St) R. Oct 29
C7th. A Spaniard, he was admitted to public penance by St Artemius of Sens, France, and became a hermit there.

Bonet *see* **Bonitus**

Bonfilius of Foligno (St)
B. R(OSB). Sep 27
1040–1125. From Osimo near Ancona, Italy, he entered the abbey at Storace and became its abbot. He was made bishop of Foligno in 1078, but resigned in 1096 after a pilgrimage to the Holy Land and retired to die at the abbey of St Mary of La Fara near Cingoli.

Bonfilius Monaldi (St) R(OSM) F. Feb 17
d. 1262. *See* **Servites, Founders of**. He had a vision of Our Lady in the cathedral in Florence, Italy, which led him to inspire his six companions to join him in founding the new order, and he was the first superior-general.

Boniface (St) *see* **Callistus, Felix and Boniface**

Boniface (St) *see* **Dionysia, Dativa and Comps**

Boniface (St) *see* **Liberatus, Boniface and Comps**

Boniface I, Pope (St) Sep 4
d. 422. A Roman, he was elected pope in 418 but the electoral college had split and he was troubled by an anti-pope, Eulalius. He resisted Pelagianism, and letters to him on the subject by St Augustine survive.

Boniface IV, Pope (St) May 8
d. 615. From Valeria in the Abruzzi, Italy, he became pope in 608 and is remembered for dedicating the Roman Pantheon temple as a church (thus ensuring the building's survival). An unconfirmed tradition states that he had been a disciple of St Gregory and a monk at St Sebastian's.

Boniface and Thecla (SS) MM. Aug 30
d. *c*250. They were apparently martyred in the reign of Maximian at Hadrametum in Roman Africa (now Sousse in Tunisia). According to their dubious acta they were the parents of the **Twelve Brothers** (q.v.).

Boniface of Crediton (St) M. R. Jun 5
*c*680–754. A Saxon called Winfrith from Crediton in Devon, England, he became a child-oblate at a monastery in Exeter when aged five and, when professed, went to Nursling near Southampton to be school headmaster. There he became a priest in 710 and went on a missionary expedition to Friesland (now Netherlands and Germany) in 716 which was a failure. He went to Rome in 718 to get the pope's approval for his subsequent outstandingly successful missionary effort in Germany, which earned him the title of apostle of that country. He became missionary bishop in 723 with full jurisdiction, and set up new dioceses as well as founding many monasteries for both sexes based on the Benedictine ideal. Many Anglo-Saxon consecrated religious from England helped to fill these. He also helped to organize the Church in France. In 747 he was made archbishop of Mainz, Germany, but resigned in 752 to go on mission again in

St Boniface of Crediton, June 5

Friesland. He was killed with fifty-two companions at Dokkum by a gang of pagan robbers and was buried at his monastic foundation at Fulda in Bavaria, Germany.

Boniface Curitan (St) B. Mar 14
d. *c*660. Possibly a Roman, he became bishop of Ross, Scotland, and evangelized the native Picts and immigrant Scots from Ireland. He is alleged to have founded many churches and to have introduced Roman customs, as distinct from the Celtic ones.

Boniface of Ferentino (St) B. May 14
C6th. He is mentioned in the *Dialogues* of St Gregory the Great as a miracle-working bishop of Ferentino in Tuscany, Italy,

Boniface of Lausanne (St) B. Feb 19
d. 1265. From Brussels, Belgium, he was educated by the nuns at La Cambre near there, then studied and taught dogma firstly at the University of Paris and then at that of Cologne. In 1230 he became bishop of Lausanne but retired in 1239, whereupon he went back to La Cambre (by then Cistercian) as chaplain.

Boniface of Querfurt (St)
M. R(OSB Cam). Jun 19
d. 1009. From near Paderborn, Germany, he accompanied his relative Emperor Otto III to Rome and there was clothed as a Camaldolese monk by St Romuald. In 1004 he became archbishop of Magdeburg, Germany, with special responsibility for the Slavs and Balts of the German marches, and was killed with eighteen companions by pagan Prussians at Braunsberg (now Braniewo in Poland). He is also commemorated by error in the old Roman Martyrology on October 15 under his baptismal name of Bruno.

Boniface of Savoy (Bl)
B. R(OCart). Mar 13
d. 1270. Of the ducal family of Savoy, he was a Carthusian at the Grand Chartreuse before becoming bishop of Belley in 1232, episcopal administrator of Valence as well in 1239 and then archbishop of Canterbury, England, in 1241. He was very unpopular and experienced serious trouble trying to enforce his alleged rights of visitation, so he has never been venerated at Canterbury. He died while back in Savoy, was buried in Hautcombe abbey and had his cultus confirmed for Turin in 1830.

Boniface of Tarsus *May 14*
He was allegedly martyred at Tarsus at the start of the C4th, but his acta are fictitious and his cultus is unknown before the C9th. It was

suppressed in 1969. The church of SS Alexis and Boniface at Rome has his alleged relics.

Boniface of Valperga (Bl) B. R(CR). Apr 25
d. 1243. Initially a Benedictine at Fruttuaria, he transferred to the Augustinian canons regular to become prior at St Ursus at Aosta in the Italian Alps in 1212. He became bishop of Aosta in 1219, and had his cultus confirmed for that place in 1890.

Bonitus (Bont) of Clermont (St) B. R. Jan 15
?623–706. From Auvergne, France, he was the Frankish Austrasian king's chancellor and prefect of Marseilles before becoming bishop of Clermont-Ferrand in 690 for ten years. Then he became a monk at Manglieu near Clermont-Ferrand, and died at Lyons after a pilgrimage to Rome.

Bonitus of Montecassino (St) R(OSB). Jul 7
d. ?582. The tradition is that he was the fourth abbot of Montecassino after St Benedict and that when the Lombards sacked the abbey in *c*570 he and the surviving brethren took refuge in Rome with nothing with them but the manuscript of the rule of St Benedict. They then set up again as a monastery near the Lateran. This story has been used to assert the Benedictine character of Roman monasticism subsequently, but there is no evidence of a cultus of St Benedict at Rome before the C10th.

Bonizella Piccolomini (Bl) L. May 6
d. 1300. She is remembered at Siena, Italy, for having devoted herself and her wealth to helping the poor in the district of Belvederio after she was widowed.

Bononius of Lucedio (St) R(OSB). Aug 30
d. 1026. From Bologna, Italy, he was a Benedictine monk at St Stephen's there before travelling to Egypt to become a hermit. Returning, he became the abbot of Lucedio in Piedmont. A Camaldolese tradition makes him a disciple of St Romuald.

Bonosa (St) *see* **Eutropius, Zosima and Bonosa**

Bonosus and Maximian (SS) MM. Aug 21
d. 362. Two army officers of the Herculean cohort based at Antioch, Syria, they were tortured and beheaded on the orders of Emperor Julian after they refused to give up their cohort's banner bearing the chi-rho symbol in exchange for a pagan one.

Bonus and Comps (SS) MM. Aug 1
d. 257. A priest, he was martyred at Rome with eleven companions (Faustus, Maurus, Primitivus, Calumniosus, Joannes, Exuperius, Cyril, Theodore, Basil, Castilus and Honoratus) in the reign of Valerian.

Boris and Gleb (SS) MM. Jul 24
d. 1010. They were sons of St Vladimir the Grand Prince of Kiev, and when their father died they were killed by their brother Svyatopolk who wanted to succeed to the throne. Out of piety they refused either to fight for their rights or to allow themselves to be defended by their allies, and were thus venerated as 'passion bearers. In the Russian church this category of martyr does not need to die as a result of specific hatred of the faith, as distinct from martyrs in the West (but *see* **Alphege the Martyr**). In the West they used to be known as Romanus and David.

Bosa (St) B. R. Mar 9
d. 705. A monk of Whitby in Yorkshire, England, when St Hilda was abbess there, he was ordained bishop of York by St Theodore in 678 when St Wilfrid was in exile. He stepped down in favour of the latter in 686 but took his place again in 691. He was praised by St Bede.

Boisil (Boswell) (St) R. Feb 23
d. ?661. He was abbot of Melrose, Scotland, when SS Cuthbert and Egbert were monks there, and they (together with St Bede) held him in great esteem.

Botolph and Adulf (SS) RR. Jun 17
C7th. Their story is very confused and untrustworthy. According to it they were Saxon noble brothers who became monks in the Low Countries. Adulf allegedly became bishop of Maastricht (a confusion with another of the same name), while St Botolph returned to England and founded a monastery at 'Ikanhoe'. This was thought to have been near Boston ('Botolph's town'), but is now thought to be Iken in Suffolk. Many English churches were dedicated to him, especially at town gates (there are good examples in the City of London).

Botvid (St) M. L. Jul 28
d. 1100. A Swede from Södermanland west of Stockholm, Sweden, he became a convert in England and was a missionary back home until he was killed by a Finnish slave whom he had bought and was instructing.

Bova and Doda (SS) RR. Apr 14
C7th. They were sister and niece respectively of St Balderic, who founded a nunnery at Rheims, France, and made St Bova its first abbess. St Doda was apparently its second.

Bradan (St) B. Oct 20
C7th. A bishop of the Isle of Man, he gave his name to Kirkbraddan near Douglas.

Brannoc (St) R. Jan 7
C6th? The founder of a monastery at Braunton near Barnstaple in Devon, England, he seems to have come from south Wales (although the traditions are untrustworthy). *See* **Brynach**.

Branwalader (Brelade) (St) B. Jan 19
C6th? Allegedly a bishop in Jersey, he had his relics transferred to Milton Abbas in Dorset, England, in 935. Nothing is known about him.

Braulio-Mary Corres Diaz de Cerio (Bl) *see* **Hospitaller Martyrs of Spain**

Braulio of Zaragoza (St) B. R. Mar 26
?585–651. He was allegedly a monk at Zaragoza and a pupil and disciple of St Isidore of Seville. Becoming bishop of his native city in 631, he was one of the celebrated Iberian fathers and helped St Isidore in renewing the Visigothic Church in Spain. He wrote several hagiographical works and has left a collection of letters.

Breaca (Breage, Bray) (St) R. Jun 4
C5th. A disciple of St Brigid, she allegedly emigrated from Ireland to Cornwall, England, with some companions, initially landing at Hayle.

Bregwin (St) B. Aug 26
d. 764. He became the twelfth archbishop of Canterbury, England, in 761. A letter of his to St Lull of Mainz survives.

Brenach *see* **Brynach**

Brendan of Birr (St) R. Nov 29
d. ?573. A fellow disciple of St Brendan the Voyager under St Finian at Clonard, he founded a monastery at Birr near the town of the same name in Offaly, Ireland. St Columba was a great friend of his, and saw his soul going to heaven in a vision after his death.

Brendan the Voyager (St) R. May 16
?486–578. From Fenit in Co. Kerry, Ireland, he was educated under St Ita and was later a disciple of St Finian of Clonard and of St Jarlath of Tuam. He founded many monasteries in Ireland, chief of which became Clonfert in Co. Galway, on which he imposed a very austere rule of life. He is chiefly famous for his legendary voyage to the 'Isles of the Blessed', written down in the C11th, which has been claimed as a possible discovery of America. This is extremely unlikely, although its feasibility has been shown by a journey in a replica craft. He is a patron of sailors.

Bretannion (St) B. Jan 25
d. *c*380. Bishop of Tomi, on the coast of Romania, he was exiled by Emperor Valens for being anti-Arian but popular protest forced his recall.

Brian Lacey (Bl) M. Dec 10
1591. A Norfolk layman, he was hanged at Tyburn for sheltering priests together with St Eustace White and Comps. *See* **England (Martyrs of)**.

Briarch (St) R. Dec 17
d. ?627. From Ulster, he became a monk in Wales under St Tudwal and accompanied him to Brittany, France. He founded a monastery at Guingamp.

Briavel (St) R? Jun 17
? The old administrative capital of the Forest of Dean, England, is called St Briavel's but no record of such a saint has survived. That he was a hermit is a guess based on the locality.

Brice (Britius, Brixius) (St) B. Nov 13
d. 444. A disciple of St Martin of Tours at Marmoutier, as a priest he was ambitious and licentious but managed to be chosen as St Martin's successor as bishop of Tours, France, in 397. He was a bad bishop for twenty years until he was expelled and fled to Rome. There he repented, was allowed to return and was then such a success that he was honoured with popular and extensive veneration after his death.

Brictius (St) B. Jul 9
d. ?312. Bishop of Martola near Spoleto in Umbria, Italy, he was imprisoned in the persecution of Diocletian but survived and was venerated as a confessor, dying in the reign of Constantine.

Bride and Bridget *see* **Brigid**

Brieuc (Brioc) (St) R. May 1
*c*420–510. From north Dyfed, Wales, he was educated in Gaul by St Germanus of Auxerre

and became a missionary in his native territory until driven out by invasion. Then he went to Brittany, France, with many followers and founded two abbeys, at Tréguier and St Brieuc.

Brigid and Maura (SS) MM. Jan 28
? Their story is that they were the daughters of a Scottish chieftain who were martyred in Picardy, France, while on a pilgrimage to Rome. They are probably the same as **Maura and Britta** (q.v.).

Brigid of Fiesole (St) R. Feb 1
C9th. Allegedly a sister of St Andrew the Scot, she became a hermit in the Apennines near Florence, Italy, and was carried by angels to her brother's deathbed. The story is apparently fictional.

Brigid (Briga) of Kilbride
(St) R. Jan 21
C6th. Contemporary with her more famous namesake and according to tradition visited by her, she was venerated in the diocese of Lismore, Scotland.

Brigid (Bride) of Kildare (St) R. Feb 1
*c*450–?525. 'Mary of the Gael' was allegedly born near Dundalk, became a nun when young and is credited with founding the first nunnery in Ireland at Kildare. She is one of the most popular Irish saints and the junior patron of Ireland and very many legends have her as their subject. Her mercy and charity to the poor often feature in these. She is the special patron of those in the dairy industry and a cow is her attribute. Unfortunately the historical evidence for her is poor, and one scholarly opinion nowadays is that she never existed but was the Christianization of a pagan deity.

Brigid-of-Jesus Morello (Bl) R. F. Sep 4
1610–1679. A noblewoman of Rapallo near Genoa, Italy, she married and settled at Salsomaggiore near Parma but her husband died of illness after the hardships of the Spanish invasion of 1636 and she took a private vow of chastity in 1640. Then she was recommended as the right person to run a new boarding school for girls at Piacenza, and this led to the foundation of the 'Ursuline Sisters of Mary Immaculate' in 1649 for this sort of work. She died after being seriously ill for twenty-four years and was beatified in 1998.

Brigid (Birgitta) of Sweden
(St) R. F. Jul 23
1303–1373. A noblewoman born near Uppsala, Sweden, she married when aged fifteen and had a happy family life for twenty-eight years, having eight children. But her husband died when the couple were on a pilgrimage to Compostela and she started to live a visionary life of penance. Her account of her visions of Christ survive in Latin translation, having been edited by others. She founded the mother house of her new religious order of the Holy Saviour (the Brigettines) at Vadstena on the great lake of Vattern in 1344 and moved to Rome in 1350, where she died. She is depicted in the distinctive habit of her Order (itself a result of a vision), with a chain or a heart marked with a cross or with a pilgrim's staff and flask. She was declared a patron of Europe in 2000.

Brinstan *see* **Birnstan**

Brioc *see* **Brieuc**

Brithwold (Brihtwald, Berthwald, Berctuald) of Canterbury
(St) B. R. Jan 9
d. 731. A monk of Reculver, England, he became abbot there ?679 and then succeeded St Theodore as archbishop of Canterbury in 692.

Brithwold of Ramsbury
(St) B. R(OSB). Jan 22
d. 1045. A monk of Glastonbury, England, he became bishop of Ramsbury, Wiltshire, in 1005. He was a great benefactor of Malmesbury abbey and of his own monastery, where he was buried.

Brito (Britonius) (St) B. May 5
d. 386. Bishop of Trier, Germany, and metropolitan of Gaul, he fought Priscillianism but opposed the intervention of the secular power against that heresy.

Britwin (Brithwin, Brithun) of Beverley (St) R. May 15
d. ?733. Abbot of Beverley in Yorkshire, England, he was a friend and patron of St John of Beverley who joined his monastery after resigning as archbishop of York.

Brixius *see* **Brice**

Brocard (St) R(OC). Sep 2
d. 1231. He succeeded St Berthold as superior of the Frankish hermits on Carmel in the Holy Land and asked St Albert, Latin Patriarch of Jerusalem, to draw up a rule of life for them. This was the genesis of the Carmelites as a religious order. He was highly respected by the Muslims.

Bron (St) B. Jun 8
d. ?511. A disciple of St Patrick, he became bishop of Cassel Irra near Sligo, Ireland.

Bronach (Bromana) (St) R. Apr 2
? She is listed in the martyrologies of Tallaght and Donegal as a religious at Glen Seichis in Co. Down, Ireland, which is now called Kilbronach after her.

Bronislava (Bl) R(OPraem). Aug 30
1203–1259. She was a noblewoman from Kamien in Silesia, Poland, and her cousin was St Hyacinth of Cracow. In 1219 she became a Premonstratensian nun at Zwierzyniec near Cracow, and died as a hermit. Her cultus was confirmed for Cracow in 1839.

Brothen and Gwendolen (SS) Oct 18
C6th? They were once venerated in Wales but nothing is known about them. Brothen gave his name to Llanbrothen and Gwendolen possibly to several places such as Llanwyddelan and Dolwyddelan.

Bruno the Carthusian (St)
R(OCart). F. Oct 6
*a*1030–1101. From Cologne, Germany, he studied in France at Rheims and Paris, became a canon at Cologne and was then diocesan chancellor at Rheims. However, he left to become a hermit under St Robert of Molesmes and then withdrew with six companions to La Grande Chartreuse in the Alps near Grenoble in 1084, thus founding the Carthusian order of cenobitic hermits with the help of St Hugh of Grenoble, France. In 1090 Pope Bl Urban II, his disciple, called him to Rome to be his adviser but he was allowed to found another monastery at La Torre near Squillace in Calabria. He died in retirement there.

Bruno the Great (St) B. Oct 11
?925–965. The youngest son of Emperor Henry I, he was devoted to his studies when young and became the arch-chancellor of the Empire under his brother Emperor Otto I in 951. In 953 he became duke of Lorraine and simultaneously archbishop of Cologne, Germany, thus uniting the ecclesiastical and secular power in one person as the prince-bishop. This sort of arrangement survived in the Holy Roman Empire until Napoleon and in Bruno it worked well, although in later centuries it was the source of serious scandal. He raised educational standards, introduced the reform of Gorze to the monasteries in the diocese (he was commendatory abbot of Lorsch and Corvey) and was a central figure in the Ottonian imperial polity.

St Bruno the Carthusian, Oct 6

Bruno of Querfurt *see* **Boniface of Querfurt**

Bruno of Saxony and Comps *see* **Ebstorf (Martyrs of)**

Bruno of Segni (St)
B. R(OSB). Jul 18
?1050–1123. From near Asti in Piedmont, Italy, he studied at Bologna and disputed with Berengarius concerning the latter's denial of the Real Presence in the Eucharist. His work on this subject was definitive for centuries. In 1079 he became bishop of Segni and was then papal librarian and cardinal legate. He retired temporarily to Montecassino and became its abbot in 1107, but was recalled in 1111 and died at Segni. He was canonized in 1183.

Bruno Serunkuma (St) M. L. Jun 3
d. 1885. A soldier in the army of Mwanga, king of Buganda, Uganda, he was burnt alive a few weeks after his baptism. *See* **Charles Lwanga and Comps**.

Bruno of Würzburg (St) B. May 17
?1005–1045. Son of the Duke of Carinthia, he was an imperial counsellor before becoming bishop of Würzburg, Germany, in 1033. He founded many churches in his diocese and wrote several extant catechetical works. He was killed

by a collapsing balcony at a banquet with Emperor Henry III at Peusenbeug, Austria, while they were on an expedition to Hungary.

Brychan (St) L? Apr 6
? In legend he was a Welsh king associated with the region of Brecknock who had eleven sons and twenty-four daughters forming a clan of saints and who had other saints among his descendants. Nothing historical is known about him.

Brynach (Bernach, Brenach)
(St) R. Apr 7
C5th? He was possibly an Irishman who settled in Wales, building a hermitage at Carn Englyi (Mount Angel) overlooking Nefyn on the Lleyn peninsula. He may be identical to St Brannoc.

Brynoth (St) B. May 9
d. 1317. He was a bishop of Skara near the great lake Vänern in Sweden.

Budoc (Budeaux) (St) B. Dec 9
C7th? From Brittany, France, he was allegedly educated in Ireland and became abbot of Youghal near Cork before returning to Brittany and succeeding SS Samson and Maglorius as bishop of Dol. There are several places in Devon and Cornwall, England, named after him.

Buithe (Buite, Boethius) (St) R. Dec 7
d. 521. A Scot, he spent some time as a monk in Italy before returning to Scotland to evangelize the Picts. The place called Kirkbuddo near Forfar seems to be named after him.

Bulgaria (Martyrs of) (SS) MM. Jul 23
C9th. The Bulgars migrated across the Danube to their present homeland in 679, but their first great ruler was Khan Krum who came to power in 804. He attacked the Byzantine Empire and managed to defeat and kill Emperor Nicephorus I in battle in 811. During his campaigns many Byzantine civilians were apparently killed because they were Christians, and these were reckoned as martyrs. The Bulgars became Christian themselves in 865.

Burchard of Worms (St)
B. R(OSB). Aug 20
d. 1026. From Hesse, Germany, he studied at Koblenz, became a monk at Lobbes and was forced to become the bishop of Worms in 1006 by the emperor. He was famous as a compiler of canon law.

Burchard of Würzburg
(St) B. R. Oct 14
d. ?754. An Anglo-Saxon monk from Wessex, England, he joined St Boniface on mission in 732 and became the first bishop of Würzburg, Germany, in 741. He evangelized Franconia, founding many monasteries, and allegedly resigned in 753 to become a monk at Homburg before he died.

Burgundofara (Fara) (St) R. Dec 7
d. 657. The daughter of a Frankish courtier, she was cured of a chronic illness as a child by the prayers of St Columban and developed a monastic vocation. Her father wanted her to marry but could not break her resolve and ended up founding the nunnery of Faremoutiers near Meaux, France, for her. She was abbess there for thirty-seven years, and many Anglo-Saxon girls received their monastic training there. The old Roman Martyrology also listed her by error on April 3. SS Faro and Cagnoald were her brother and sister.

Burien (Buryan) (St) R? Jun 4
C6th. An Irish hermit, he or she is the patron of St Buryan in Cornwall, England, and may have been a hermit there.

Buzad Banfy (Bl) M. R(OP). Dec 8
d. 1241. A Hungarian count, he became a Dominican and was killed in church by the Mongols when they sacked Pest.

Byblig (Biblig, Peblig, Piblig, Publicius) (St) Jul 3
C5th? He gave his name to Llanbiblig near Caernarfon, Wales, but nothing is known about him.

C

Cadfan (St) R. Nov 1
Early C6th. From Brittany, France, he migrated to Wales and founded several monasteries, notably on Bardsey Island and at Tywyn.

Cadfarch (St) R. Oct 24
C6th. A monk of Bangor Isycoed, Wales, and a disciple of St Illtyd, he allegedly founded churches at Penegoes and Abererch.

Cadoc (Docus, Cathmael, Cadvael) (St) M. B. R. Jan 24
d. *c*580. Of the royal family of Morgannwg, Wales, he became a monk and founded the great monastery of Llancarfan near Cardiff in 518. After extensive travels he went to Brittany, France, with St Gildas in 547 and was a hermit on an island in the Morbihan until returning in 551. He allegedly became a bishop and was killed by the invading Saxons at 'Beneventum'. There is a church dedicated to another saint of the same name at Cambusland, Scotland.

Cadroe (Cadroel) (St) R(OSB). Mar 6
d. 976. The son of a Scottish prince, he was educated at Armagh, Ireland, travelled to England and France and became a monk at Fleury. He was abbot in turn of a new foundation at Waulsort on the Meuse and of a monastery at Metz.

Cadwalladr Fendigaid (St) L. Nov 12
d. ?682. The Gwledig (king) of the Cymri, he was a son of the great warrior of the same name who had helped defeat and kill St Edwin but had a reputation for disliking warfare. He had to fight for his people, however, but was badly defeated. Churches dedicated to him survive in Wales. In legend he was expected to return to help his countrymen in getting rid of the 'Sais' (Saxons), possibly owing to being confused with his father. He has also been confused with the Saxon St Caedwalla.

Caecilia, Caecilianus *see* **Cecilia, Cecilianus**

Caecilian (St) *see* **Zaragoza (Eighteen Martyrs of)**.

Caecilius (St) *see* **Torquatus, Ctesiphon and Comps**

Caecilius (Caecilian) of Carthage (St) P. Jun 3
C3rd. According to the old Roman Martyrology, he was a priest of Carthage who converted St Cyprian. The latter revered his memory, appropriating his name and taking care of his family after his death.

Caecilius López López (Bl) *see* **Hospitaller Martyrs of Spain**

Caedmon (St) R. Feb 11
d. *c*680. A Northumbrian shepherd, he worked for the monastery of Whitby in Yorkshire, England, before becoming a lay brother there under St Hilda. He was the first Christian Saxon poet, but only the fragment preserved by St Bede has survived.

Caedwalla of Wessex, King (St) L. Apr 20
659–689. King of Wessex, England, as a pagan Saxon he was typically cruel and conquered Surrey, Sussex and Kent. Then he was converted by St Wilfrid and went to Rome to be baptized by Pope St Sergius. He died less than a week after his baptism, and his relics are in St Peter's. There is no evidence of an ancient cultus.

Caelestine *see* **Celestine**

Caelian (St) *see* **Faustinus, Lucius and Comps**

Caellainn (Caoilfionn) (St) R. Feb 3
C6th? There is a church in Co. Roscommon, Ireland, dedicated to her and she is listed in the Donegal martyrology.

Caerealis (St) *see* **Getulius, Caerealis and Comps**

Caerealis (Cerulus, Celerius), Pupulus, Gaius and Serapion (SS) MM. Feb 28
? They were martyred at Alexandria, Egypt. Gaius was added to the group by Baronius when he revised the old Roman Martyrology.

Caerealis and Sallustia (SS) MM. Sep 14
d. 251. Husband and wife, they were catechized by Pope St Cornelius and martyred at Rome in the reign of Decius.

Caesarea (St) R. May 15
? She has a popular cultus based at a cave near Otranto in the heel of Italy, where she is alleged to have been a hermit after taking refuge from danger of molestation.

Caesareus (St) *see* **Victor, Zoticus and Comps**

Caesaria of Arles (St) R. Jan 12
d. *c*530. Sister of St Caesarius of Arles, France, she was abbess of a nunnery founded in the city for her by her brother. Her talents were praised by SS Gregory of Tours and Venantius Fortunatus.

Caesarius (St) *see* **Germanus, Theophilus and Comps**

Caesarius, Dacius and Comps (SS) MM. Nov 1
? A group of seven, they were martyred at Damascus, Syria.

Caesarius and Julian (SS) MM. Nov 1
? They were martyred at Terracina in Lazio, Italy, the former being an African deacon (with a church dedicated to him on the Appian Way at Rome) and the latter being a priest. Their date is unknown but they are in the earliest martyrologies.

Caesarius of Angoulême (St) D. Jan 29
C1st or C3rd. He is alleged to have been a deacon of Angoulême, France, under that city's first bishop, St Ausonius.

Caesarius of Arabissus (St) M. Dec 28
d. 309. He was considered to have atoned for a rather immoral life by being nailed to the stake and burned at Arabissus in Armenia in the reign of Galerius. He was the father of Eudoxius the Arian.

Caesarius of Arles (St) B. R. Aug 27
470–543. From Chalon-sur-Saône, France, he became a monk at Lérins in 490 and bishop of Arles in 500. A great bishop, he chaired several local councils of the Church, notably that of Orange in 529 which condemned semi-pelagianism. He founded his namesake nunnery at Arles, made his sister St Caesaria its abbess and drew up an influential rule for it. He is one of the best examples of how the leaders of the Church in western Europe had to take on much of the social and political responsibility for their people as the social structures of the Western Roman Empire fell into decay. He has left a collection of homilies.

Caesarius de Bus (Bl) R. F. Apr 15
1544–1607. Born near Avignon, France, he converted from a sinful life in 1574 and became devoted to preaching and catechesis in response to the Council of Trent. When aged 52 he was ordained and founded the Congregation of the Fathers of Christian Doctrine ('Doctrinarians') to this end. He was beatified in 1975.

Caesarius of Clermont (St) B. Nov 1
d. *p*627. He was a bishop of Clermont-Ferrand, France.

Caesarius Nazianzen (St) L. Feb 25
d. 369. He is known from the extant funeral oration given by his brother, St Gregory Nazianzen. A doctor of medicine at the court of Constantinople, he resisted attempts by Emperor Julian to convert him back to paganism. He remained a catechumen nearly all his life, however, until almost killed in an earthquake at Nicaea.

Caesarius Niño Pérez (Bl) *see* **Hospitaller Martyrs of Spain**

Caesidius and Comps (SS) MM. Aug 31
C3rd. The unreliable acta of St Rufinus describe him as that saint's son, one of a group martyred at Lake Fucino, east of Rome.

Caesidius Giacomantonio (St) M. R(OFM). Jun 4
1873–1900. From Fossa Aquilana, Italy, he became a Franciscan and was sent to China in 1899. There he was posted to Hengyang in southern Hunan, but after only a month there was attacked by a mob of Boxers and burnt alive with petrol. *See* **China (Martyrs of)**.

Cagnoald (St) B. R. Sep 6
d. ?635. Brother of SS Faro and Burgundofara, he was a monk at Luxeuil under St Columban before becoming bishop of Laon, France.

Caian (St) R. Sep 25
C5th. A reputed son or grandson of St Brychan, he gave his name to Tregaian on Anglesey, Wales.

Caidoc and Fricor (Adrian)
(SS) RR. Apr 1
C7th. Two Irishmen, they who evangelized the country of the Morini around Amiens, France. St Richarius, one of their disciples, founded a monastery which is now the village of Saint-Riquier near Abbeville and their relics are preserved there.

Caillin (St) B. Nov 13
C7th. A bishop in Ireland associated with St Aidan of Fearns, he was described as having made a stone circle out of some sceptical Druids.

Caimin (Cammin) of Inniskeltra (St) R. Mar 24
d. 653. He lived as a hermit on the island of Inniskeltra in Lough Derg, Ireland, and attracted many disciples by his austerity. He founded a monastery on the Island of Seven Churches, was associated with St Senan and copied out a psalter (part of which survives).

Cairlon (Caorlan) (St) R. Mar 24
C6th. An abbot in Ireland, he was allegedly restored to life by St Daig McCairill after having died. Later he became archbishop of Cashel.

Cairnech *see* **Carantac**

Caius *see* **Gaius**

Cajetan (St) R. F. Aug 7
1480–1547. A nobleman from Vicenza in Lombardy, Italy, he was in the curia at Rome from 1506 to 1517. On returning to Vicenza he organized charitable work for sick and poor people there and at Rome and Venice. In 1523, together with Peter Caraffa (bishop of Chieti and later Pope Paul IV) and others, he founded the Congregation of Clerks Regular or 'Theatines' for that work. This became one of the great congregations of the Counter-Reformation, rejecting support from benefices and becoming involved in missionary work and in the Tridentine liturgical reform. He died at Naples and was canonized in 1671.

Cajetan Catanoso (Bl) P. F. Sep 20
1879–1963. From near Reggio Calabria, Italy, his family were pious landowners. He was ordained in 1902 and became a parish priest in his city. He encouraged the devotion to the Holy Face, fostered priestly vocations and was keen on arranging parish missions. In 1935 he founded the 'Daughters of St Veronica, Missionaries of the Holy Face' for prayer, catechesis and charitable works. His beatification was in 1997.

Calais *see* **Carileff**

Calanicus (St) *see* **Florian, Calanicus and Comps**

Calepodius and Comps
(SS) MM. May 10
d. ?222–232. Romans, they were massacred by a pagan mob in the reign of Alexander Severus. Calepodius, the first to be killed, gave his name to a catacomb. Palmatius, of consular rank, was killed with his family and forty-two of his household, while the senator Simplicius was killed with sixty-five of his family and household. Also killed were a married couple, Felix and Blanda.

Caletricus (St) B. Sep 4
529–*c*580. He succeeded St Lubinus as bishop of Chartres, France, his native city, in ?557.

Calimerius (St) M. B. Jul 31
d. *c*190. A Greek, he was educated at Rome by Pope St Telesphorus and became bishop of Milan, Italy. He evangelized the Po valley before being martyred in the reign of Commodus by being dropped down a well. His relics are in his church at Milan.

Calixtus *see* **Callistus**

Callinica (Callinicus?) and Basilissa (SS) MM. Mar 22
d. 250. Two rich ladies (or possibly one with her manservant), they were martyred in Galatia, Asia Minor, after trying to help imprisoned Christians.

Callinicus (St) M. Jul 29
C3rd? He was burned at Gangra in Paphlagonia, Asia Minor, his native town. His acta are unreliable but his veneration is popular in the East.

Callinicus (St) *see* **Thyrsus, Leucius and Callinicus**

Calliope (St) M. Jun 8
d. 250? She was perhaps beheaded somewhere in Greece, but details are lacking and her acta are fictitious.

Calliopus (St) M. Apr 7
d. *c*303. He was crucified head-downwards at Pompeiopolis in Cilicia, Asia Minor, in the reign of Diocletian.

Callisthene (St) *see* **Adauctus and Callisthene**

Callistratus and Comps (SS) MM. Sep 26
d. *c*300. They were allegedly fifty soldiers killed in prison at Byzantium, possibly in the reign of Diocletian. Their acta are fictitious.

Callistus (Callista) (St) *see* **Evodius, Hermogenes and Callistus**

Callistus I, Pope (St) M. Oct 14
d. ?222. A slave at Rome before his emancipation, he was made deacon by Pope St Zephyrinus and had responsibility for the catacomb now named after him. He became pope in 217, and showed leniency in the controversy as to whether the Church could re-admit serious sinners to communion after penance. In this he was opposed by the rigorists, notably Tertullian and St Hippolytus. The latter, his bitter enemy, violently attacked him in writing in the *Philosophumena* and was made anti-pope against him. He died a martyr, but his acta are fictitious.

Callistus, Charisius and Comps (SS) MM. Apr 16
C3rd. A group of nine, they were thrown into the sea at Corinth, Greece.

Callistus, Felix and Boniface (SS) MM. Dec 29
? They are in all the Western martyrologies, but nothing is known about them.

Callistus and Mercurialis (St) M. Oct 15
d. 1003. From Huesca, Spain, they went to France and were killed in battle against Muslim raiders. They are venerated at Tarbes.

Callistus Caravario (St) *see* **Aloysius Versiglia**

Callixtus *see* **Callistus**

Calminius (Calmilius) (St) R. Aug 19
d. *c*690. From the Auvergne, France, he was governor of that region before becoming a hermit near Tulle and founding two monasteries.

Calocerus (St) M. Apr 18
? According to his late and unreliable acta, he was an official of Emperor Hadrian at Brescia, Italy, and was connected with SS Faustinus and Jovita.

Calocerus and Parthenius (SS) MM. May 19
d. 250. Roman brothers who were eunuchs in the palace of Tryphonia, wife of Emperor Decius, they were martyred in the persecution arranged by the latter.

Calocerus of Ravenna (St) B. Feb 11
d. *c*130. A disciple of St Apollinaris, he succeeded him as bishop of Ravenna, Italy.

Calogerus (St) R. Jun 18
d. ?486. A Greek, he became a monk at Rome and was a missionary on the Lipari Islands before becoming a hermit for thirty-five years near Girgenti, Sicily.

Calogerus (St) *see* **Gregory, Demetrius and Calogerus**

Calupan (St) R. Mar 3
d. 575. A monk of Méallet in the Auvergne, France, he became a hermit in a cave near his monastery.

Cambrai (Martyrs of) (BB) MM. RR. Jun 26
d. 1794. The convent of the Daughters of Charity at Arras was founded in 1656, and was running a girls' school and nursing in the town at the onset of the French Revolution in 1789. The sisters were allowed to carry on nursing in lay attire but were required to take the revolutionary oath in 1794. They refused, so were imprisoned and then guillotined at Cambrai. The superior was Mary-Magdalen Fontaine and the other three were Jane Gérard, Mary-Teresa Fantou and Mary-Frances Lanel. They were beatified in 1920. *See* **French Revolution (Martyrs of)**.

Camelian of Troyes (St) B. Jul 28
d. ?525. He succeeded St Lupus as bishop of Troyes, France, in 478.

Camerinus (St) *see* **Luxorius, Cisellus and Camerinus**

Camilla of Auxerre (St) R. Mar 3
d. ?437. From Civitavecchia, Italy, she became a disciple of St Germanus of Auxerre at Ravenna and accompanied his corpse back to Auxerre, France. Then she became a hermit nearby.

Camilla Gentili (Bl) M. May 18
C14th or C15th. Her cultus as a martyr was confirmed for Sanseverino, Italy, in 1841 and her relics are in the Dominican church there.

Camillus Constanzi (Bl) M. R(SJ). Oct 12
1572–1622. From Calabria, Italy, he became a Jesuit and went to Japan in 1605. In 1614 he was expelled to Macao but returned in disguise in 1621 and was caught and slowly burned at Hirado. *See* **Japan (Martyrs of)**.

Camillus de Lellis (St) R. F. Jul 14
1550–1614. From the Abruzzi, Italy, he became a soldier and proved to be a quarrelsome gambler. He set out to change his ways in 1575 and tried to become a Capuchin but a chronic, incurable infection in one leg prevented this and he went on to be the director of a Roman hospital instead. He founded a confraternity to help with the nursing, and was ordained in 1584. His confraternity became a religious order, the 'Clerks Regular of a Good Death, Ministers of the Sick' usually known as Camillans, and this was approved in 1591. He died at Rome, was canonized in 1746 and was declared to be the patron of sick people and their helpers in 1886.

Camin *see* **Caimin**

Campania (Martyrs of) (SS) MM. Mar 2
C6th. St Gregory the Great mentions several hundred killed during the Lombard invasion of southern Italy.

Candida (St) *see* **Artemius, Candida and Paulina**

Candida (St) *see* **Lucius, Rogatus and Comps**

Candida of Bañoles (St) R. Jan 27
d. ?798. She was the mother of St Emerius, the founder of the abbey at Bañoles near Gerona, Spain, and died as a hermit near the monastery.

Candida of Carthage (St) V. Sep 20
d. ?300. She was martyred at Carthage in Roman Africa, perhaps in the reign of Maximian Herculeus (although her dates are disputed).

Candida-Mary-of-Jesus Cipitria y Barriola (Bl) R. F. Aug 9
1845–1912. Born in Guipúzcoa, Spain, of a working class family, she founded the 'Daughters of Jesus' in Salamanca with an Ignatian charism in order to educate children of all backgrounds. A deep contemplative and lover of poverty, she had a universal interest in social justice and was beatified in 1996.

Candida the Elder (St) L. Sep 4
d. ?78. Her legend is that she welcomed St Peter when he was passing through Naples on his way to Rome and was miraculously cured of an illness by him. Then she converted St Aspren, the city's alleged first bishop. She probably never existed.

Candida of Rome (St) M. Aug 29
? She was one of a group of martyrs who were killed on the Ostian Way outside Rome. Her relics were enshrined in the church of St Praxedes in the C9th.

Candida of Whitchurch (St) Jun 1
? The shrine of St Candida at Whitchurch Canonicorum in Dorset is the only one to survive the Reformation with its relics intact. These were examined in 1900 and it was found that she was about forty. Nothing else is known about her.

Candida the Younger (St) L. Sep 10
d. ?586. A married woman with a family at Naples, Italy, she achieved sanctity as a wife and mother. Her relics were noted for exuding a liquid with miraculous properties.

Candidus (St) M. Oct 3
? He was martyred at a place called the 'Shaggy Bear' (ad Ursum Pileatum) on the Esquiline in Rome.

Candidus (St) *see* **Faustinus, Lucius and Comps**

Candidus (St) *see* **Fortunatus, Felician and Comps**

Candidus (St) *see* **Theban Legion**

Candidus, Piperion and Comps (SS) MM. Mar 11
d. 254–9. A group of twenty-two, they were martyred either at Carthage, Roman Africa, or at Alexandria, Egypt, probably in the reign of Valerian. Nothing further is known.

Candres (St) B. Dec 1
C5th. A missionary bishop, he worked in the territory around Maastricht, Netherlands, and has a local cultus at Rouen, France.

Canice (Canicus, Cainnech, Kenny, Kenneth) (St) R. Oct 11
?525–?600. The patron saint of Kilkenny,

Ireland, was born in Ulster and learned to be a monk under St Finian at Clonard, Co. Meath, and St Cadoc in Wales. He travelled extensively as a missionary in Scotland and Ireland, perhaps founding the monastic settlement at St Andrew's, Scotland, and that at Kilkenny as well as several others.

Canion (St) *see* **Priscus II of Capua and Comps**

Cannatus of Marseilles (St) B. Oct 15
C5th. He succeeded St Honoratus I as bishop of Marseilles, France.

Cannera (Cainder, Kinnera)
(St) R. Jan 28
d. *c*530. A hermit near Bantry, Ireland, she died while visiting St Senan on his island of Scattery in the Shannon estuary and was buried there.

Canog (Cynog) (St) M. Oct 7
d. ?492. The alleged eldest son of St Brychan, he was killed in a Saxon raid at Van, near Llanidloes in Powys, Wales, and buried at Merthyr Cynog. Several Welsh churches are dedicated to him, and he is known in Brittany as St Cenneur.

Cantian and Cantianilla (SS) MM. *see* **Cantius and Comps**

Cantidus, Cantidian and Sobel
(SS) MM. Aug 5
? They were martyred in Egypt, but nothing else is known.

Cantius and Comps (SS) MM. May 31
d. ?304. St Protus was the tutor of SS Cantius, Cantian and Cantianilla, three siblings of the Anicii family at Rome. They fled from Emperor Diocletian to Aquileia but were executed there on his orders. A panegyric in their honour by St Maximus of Turin survives.

Canute (Knut) IV, King of Denmark (St) M. Jan 19
1043–1086. An illegitimate son of King Sweyn III of Denmark and a great-nephew of King Canute the Great who ruled Denmark and England, he was a zealous Christian. When he became king himself he set out to establish the Church in Denmark according to canon law and also instigated missionary activity among the Balts. He tried twice to invade England. One of his innovations was the introduction and enforcement of church tithes, and this helped to foster a revolt led by his brother which ended in his being killed at Odense. Thus he was regarded as a martyr, and his shrine was established at the Benedictine abbey that he had founded there. He was canonized in 1101, but his cultus has been confined to local calendars since 1969.

Canute Franco Gómez (Bl) *see* **Hospitaller Martyrs of Spain**

Canute (Knut) Lavard (St) M. Jan 7
?1096–1131. He was duke of Schleswig (then part of Denmark) and a nephew of St Canute the King. He had to do much fighting against Scandinavian pirates and was also involved in missionary activity among the Slavs of eastern Holstein. He was a candidate for the Danish throne, and was assassinated as a result near Ringsted in a conspiracy headed by a relative who wished to supplant him. He was then venerated as a martyr and was canonized in 1169.

Capito (St) *see* **Meneus and Capito**

Capitolina and Erotheis
(SS) MM. Oct 27
d. 304. A lady and her maid, they were martyred at Caesarea in Cappodocia, Asia Minor, in the reign of Diocletian.

Capitolinus (St) *see* **Quintilis and Capitolinus**

Cappodocia (Martyrs of)
(SS) MM. May 23
d. 303. Many Christians were tortured and killed in a pogrom in Cappodocia, Asia Minor, in the reign of Galerius.

Caprasius of Agen (St) M. Oct 20
d. ?303. He was martyred at Agen on the Garonne, France, in the reign of Diocletian. His acta, including his connection with St Faith, are spurious.

Caprasius of Lérins (St) R. Jun 1
d. *c*430. He was a hermit on the Riviera island of Lérins, France, and was joined by SS Honoratus and Venantius. The three of them did a monastic tour of the East, and Venantius died in Greece. The other two returned to Lérins, where Honoratus founded the famous monastery and Caprasius succeeded him as abbot when he became bishop of Arles.

Caradoc (St) R. Apr 13
d. 1124. He was court harpist to King Rhys of Morgannwg, South Wales, before becoming a monk at Llandaff. He was ordained at Mynyw (St David's), and was a hermit on Barry Island

but was harassed by pirates and moved to St Ismael's cell near Haroldston in Pembrokeshire, where he died. His shrine is at St David's.

Caralippus (St) *see* **Aphrodisius, Caralippus and Comps**

Caran (St) B. Dec 24
C7th. He is in the Aberdeen breviary and there are traces of a cultus in eastern Scotland, notably at Anstruther in Fife where a fair used to be held in his honour.

Carantac (Carantog, Cairnach, Carnath) (St) R. May 16
C6th. He was a Briton who went with St Patrick to Ireland.

Carantoc (St) R. May 16
C6th. He founded the church at Llangranog near Cardigan, Wales, and was also associated with Crantock in Cornwall and Carhampton in Somerset, England. He has a cultus in Brittany and may be identical to St Carantac in Ireland.

Caraunus (Ceraunus, Chéron) (St) M. D. May 28
C5th. A deacon from Rome, he evangelized the region around Chartres, France, and was killed by robbers. An Augustinian monastery arose around his shrine.

Cardeña (Martyrs of) *see* **Stephen of Cardeña**

Carileff (Calais) (St) R. Jul 1
d. ?536. From Aquitaine, he was a companion of St Avitus of Micy before becoming a hermit on his own and founding a monastery at Anille in Maine, France. This abbey was later named St Calais after him.

Carina (St) *see* **Melasippus, Carina and Anthony**

Carissima of Albi (St) R. Sep 7
C5th. From Albi, France, she was a hermit in a forest nearby and then a nun at Vioux. Her relics are in the cathedral of Albi.

Caritas *see* **Faith, Hope and Charity**

Carloman, King (Bl) R. Aug 17
707–755. He was the eldest son of Charles Martel, and a younger brother was Pepin the Short. When his father died and he became king of Frankish Austrasia he helped in the foundation of many great monasteries and supported St Boniface in the German missions. He also tried to reverse his father's policy of using ecclesiastical lands as rewards for service to the king. He resigned in 747, became a monk and ended up in Montecassino, Italy, where he worked in the kitchen and as a shepherd. He was sent as a mediator between Pepin and the Lombards, but fell sick on the way and died at Vienne, France.

Carmelus Gil Arano (Bl) *see* **Hospitaller Martyrs of Spain**

Carmelus Volta (Bl) *see* **Emmanuel Ruiz and Comps**

Carnath, Carnech *see* **Carantac**

Carol Davy (Bl) *see* **William Repin and Comps**

Caroline Kóska (Bl) V. Nov 18
1898–1914. From near Tarnow in Austrian Galicia (now Poland), she was one of a peasant family who were a focus of devotional activity in her parish. She was a prayerful, hard-working and charitable child. When the Russian army invaded at the start of the First World War an enemy soldier seized her at her home and forced her into the forest in order to rape her. Her body was later found bearing the wounds of heroic resistance and with the throat cut, but with its virginity intact. She was beatified in 1987.

Caroline Lucas (Bl) *see* **William Repin and Comps**

Caron (St) Mar 5
? He is the patron of Tregaron in Dyfed, Wales, but nothing is known about him.

Carponius, Evaristus, Priscian and Fortunata (SS) MM. Oct 14
d. ?303. Their legend describes them as siblings who were martyred at Caesarea in the Holy Land in the reign of Diocletian. Their relics are at Naples, Italy.

Carpophorus (St) *see* **Four Crowned Martyrs**

Carpophorus (St) *see* **Rufus and Carpophorus**

Carpophorus and Abundius (SS) MM. Dec 10
d. 290–300. A priest and deacon, they were martyred in the reign of Diocletian, probably at Spoleto (or at Rome, but not at Seville).

Carpophorus of Como and Comps (SS) MM. Aug 7
d. ?295. A group of soldiers, they were martyred at Como, Italy, in the reign of Maximian Herculeus. The companions were Exanthus, Cassius, Severinus, Secundus and Licinius.

Carpus of Thyatira and Comps (SS) MM. Apr 13
d. 150 or 250. A bishop of Thyatira, Asia Minor, he was seized with his deacon Papylus, the latter's sister Agathonica and their servant Agathodorus. They were taken to Sardis (where the last-named was whipped to death) and then to Pergamos to be martyred, either in the reign of Marcus Aurelius or of Decius.

Carpus of Troy (St) B? Oct 13
C1st. He is mentioned by St Paul in II Tim 4:13 but nothing else is known. The Byzantine martyrology lists him as a bishop.

Carterius (St) M. Jan 8
d. 304. A priest, he was martyred at Caesarea in Cappadocia, Asia Minor, in the reign of Diocletian.

Carterius and Comps (SS) MM. Nov 2
d. ?315. They were ten soldiers burned at the stake at Sebaste in Armenia in the reign of Licinius. The companions were Styriacus, Tobias, Eudoxius, Agapius, Marinus, Oceanus, Eustratius, Nicopolitanus and Atticus.

Carthage the Elder (St) B. Mar 5
d. *c*540. He succeeded St Kieran as bishop of Ossory in Co. Offaly, Ireland, and may have been a son or grandson of King Aengus.

Carthage (Carthach Mochuda) the Younger (St) R. May 14
d. ?637. From Co. Kerry, Ireland, in 590 he founded a monastery at Rathin in Co. Westmeath and was abbot and bishop there (a common arrangement in the early Irish church). He wrote the monastery's rule in verse. The community was expelled in 635 and re-settled at Lismore, where it became famous as a place of studies. His cultus was confirmed in 1903 as the principal patron of Lismore.

Carthusian Martyrs
See **Augustine Webster**, **Humphrey Middlemore**, **James Walworth**, **John Davy**, ***John Houghton**, **John Rochester**, **Richard Bere**, **Robert Lawrence**, ***Robert Salt**, **Sebastian Newdigate**, ***Thomas Green**, **Thomas Johnson**, ***Thomas Redyng**, ***Thomas Scriven**, ***Walter Pierson**, **William Exmew**, ***William Greenwood**, and **William Horne** (all with separate entries). Those of the London Charterhouse who were starved to death at Newgate Prison are marked *.

Casdoe (St) *see* **Dadas, Casdoe and Gabdelas**

Casilda of Briviesca (St) R. Apr 9
d. *c*1050. From Toledo, Spain, and possibly a Muslim who converted to Christianity, she became a hermit near Briviesca in Burgos province. Her veneration is popular in Spain, especially at Burgos and Toledo.

Casimir of Poland (St) L. Mar 4
1458–1484. Born at Cracow, the third son of King Casimir IV of Poland, he was offered the crown of Hungary by a rebellious faction there in 1471 but refused to countenance the use of force and was briefly imprisoned by his disappointed father. As the heir to the Polish crown he was Grand-Duke of Lithuania and served as regent in the absence of his father for two years from 1481, but refused to marry as he wished to stay celibate. He died of tuberculosis at Hrodno, Bielarus, on a visit to Lithuania and was buried at Vilnius. He is one of the patrons of Poland, and his attributes are a crown and a lily.

Caspar (St) *see* **Magi**

Caspar Alvarez (Bl) *see* **Ignatius de Azevedo and Comps**

Caspar Bertoni (St) R. F. Jun 12
1777–1853. From Verona, Italy, he became a priest there in 1789 and founded a Marian oratory with some young people which became a focus of renewal for the diocese. He formed his priest-disciples into a congregation called the 'Stigmatine Fathers' in 1816. He was canonized in 1989.

Caspar de Bono (Bl) R. Jul 14
1530–1604. From Valencia, Spain, he became a silk merchant, then a soldier and finally a Minim friar. He served twice as corrector-provincial for the Spanish Minims and was beatified in 1786.

Caspar del Bufalo (St) R. F. Oct 21
1786–1836. From Rome, he was ordained there in 1808 and was exiled to Corsica for rejecting the Napoleonic polity. Returning in 1814, he went to Giano near Spoleto and

founded there the first house of the 'Missioners of the Precious Blood' for home-mission work in Italy. It was opposed, especially as regards its name, and was only approved after his death. He was canonized in 1955.

Caspar Cratz *see* **John Caspar Cratz**

Caspar Hikojiro (Bl) M. L. Oct 1
d. 1617. The housekeeper of Bl Alphonsus Navarrete, he was beheaded with Bl Andrew Yoshida at Nagasaki. *See* **Japan (Martyrs of)**.

Caspar Koteda and Comps
(Bl) MM. Sep 11
d. 1622. Of the family of the daimyos of Hirado, he worked as catechist for Bl Camillus Costanzo and was martyred at Nagasaki with two companions, BB Francis Takeya and Peter Shichiyemon (both children) on the day after the 'Great Martyrdom'. They were beatified in 1867. *See* **Japan (Martyrs of)**.

Caspar Maignien (Bl) *see* **September (Martyrs of)**

Caspar Páez Perdomo (Bl) *see* **Hospitaller Martyrs of Spain**

Caspar Sadamatsu (Bl) M. R(SJ). Jun 20
d. 1626. From Omura, Japan, he became a Jesuit lay brother in 1582 and worked as secretary for several Jesuit provincials in Japan. The last of these was Bl Francis Pacheco, with whom he was burned at Nagasaki. He was beatified in 1867. *See* **Japan (Martyrs of)**.

Caspar Stranggassinger
(Bl) R(CSSR). Sep 26
1871–1889. From Berchtesgaden in Bavaria, Germany, of a peasant family, he joined the Redemptorists at Gars in 1893 and was ordained two years later. He became the vice-rector of the trainee missionaries and a teacher of Latin, but he regarded his personal sanctification as his chief work. He died after a short illness and was beatified in 1988.

Caspar and Mary Vas
(BB) MM. TT(OFM). Aug 16
d. 1627. A Japanese married couple, they were Franciscan tertiaries who were martyred at Nagasaki with Francis-of-St-Mary of Mancha and Comps. *See* **Japan (Martyrs of)**.

Cassia (St) *see* **Sabina, Julian and Comps**

Cassian (St) *see* **Lucius, Rogatus and Comps**

Cassian (St) *see* **Peter, Marcian and Comps**

Cassian *see* **John Cassian**

Cassian of Autun (St) B. Aug 5
d. *c*350. An Egyptian (according to a C9th biography) and a noted thaumaturge, he became bishop of Autun, France, in 314.

Cassian of Benevento (St) B. Aug 12
d. *c*340. He was bishop of Benevento, Italy, and his relics are at St Mary's church there.

Cassian of Imola (St) M. Aug 13
d. ?304. His story is that he was the headmaster of a school at Imola near Ravenna, Italy, and that he was martyred in the reign of Diocletian by being handed over to his pagan pupils, who slowly stabbed him to death with their pens. This is according to Prudentius, but the same improbable fate is described of other martyrs and the cultus was confined to local calendars in 1969.

Cassian of Tangier (St) M. Dec 3
d. 298. During the trial of St Marcellus at Tangier in Roman Africa (now in Morocco) in the reign of Diocletian, Cassian as the recorder of the proceedings became indignant at the injustice being perpetrated, threw down his pen and declared himself to be a Christian. He was arrested and martyred a few weeks later. His acta are genuine, and he is mentioned in one of the hymns of Prudentius.

Cassian of Todi (St) M? B? Aug 13
C4th? He is alleged to have been the successor of St Pontian as bishop of Todi, Italy, and to have been martyred in the reign of Maximian Herculeus, but his acta are unreliable and he may be a duplicate of St Cassian of Imola.

Cassian Vaz López-Neto (Bl) *see* **Agathangelus and Cassian**

Cassius (St) *see* **Carpophorus of Como and Comps**

Cassius, Florentius and Comps (SS) MM. Oct 10
d. 303. They were martyred at Bonn, Germany, by the emperor Maximian Herculeus.

Cassius, Victorinus, Maximus and Comps (SS) MM. May 15
d. ?264. They were martyred by invading barbarians at Clermont-Ferrand, France.

Cassius of Narni (St) B. Jun 29
d. 558. He was bishop of Narni near Rome from

537. St Gregory the Great wrote of him with approbation.

Castor and Dorotheus (SS) MM. Mar 28
? They were martyred at Tarsus in Cilicia, Asia Minor, in an early persecution.

Castor and Stephen (SS) MM. Apr 27
? They were martyred at Tarsus in Cilicia, Asia Minor, in an early persecution, and may be the same as the previous.

Castor, Victor and Rogatian
(SS) MM. Dec 28
? All that is known is that they were martyred in Roman Africa.

Castor of Apt (St) B. Sep 2
d. *c*420. From Nîmes, France, he got married and settled at Marseilles but he and his wife separated to become consecrated religious and he founded a monastery at Manauque. Then he was forced to become the bishop of Apt. St John Cassian wrote the *Institutes* at his request.

Castor of Koblenz (Bl) P. Feb 13
C4th. According to his legend he was a Gascon who was ordained by St Maximinus of Trier and who evangelized the Moselle valley between there and Koblenz, Germany, settling at Karden. He is the patron of Koblenz.

Castora Gabrielli (Bl) T(OFM). Jun 14
d. 1391. She was a Franciscan tertiary married to a lawyer at Sant' Angelo in Vado, Umbria, Italy, and after she was widowed she gave her possessions to the poor and lived an ascetic life.

Castorius (St) *see* **Claudius, Nicostratus and Comps**

Castorius (St) *see* **Four Crowned Martyrs**

Castrensis (St) *see* **Priscus, Castrensis and Comps**

Castritian of Milan (St) B. Dec 1
d. 137. He is listed as bishop of Milan, Italy, from 95, the predecessor of St Calimerius.

Castulus (St) M. Mar 26
d. 288. An official at the Roman palace of Emperor Diocletian, he used to give refuge to persecuted Christians and was hence tortured, imprisoned and buried alive in a sand-pit. A cemetery and basilica were named after him.

Castulus (St) *see* **Saturninus, Castulus and Comps**

Castulus (St) *see* **Zoticus, Rogatus and Comps**

Castulus and Euprepis (SS) MM. Nov 30
? Nothing is known about these Roman martyrs.

Castus (St) *see* **Magnus, Castus and Maximus**

Castus (St) *see* **Marcellus, Castus and Comps**

Castus and Emilius (SS) MM. May 22
d. *c*250. They were burned at Carthage, Roman Africa, in the reign of Decius, having repented after apostatizing under torture. Both St Cyprian and St Augustine praised them.

Castus and Secundinus
(SS) BB? Jul 1
d. ?305. Their relics are at Gaeta near Naples, Italy. They are alleged to have been bishops but their acta are unreliable.

Catald (Cathal) (St) B. May 10
d. ?671. From Munster, Ireland, he was a pupil and then the headmaster of the monastery school at Lismore. He became bishop of Rachau, but went on a pilgrimage to the Holy Land. Then he was made bishop of Taranto in the heel of Italy on his way back, and is the principal patron of that diocese. Two different persons may have been conflated in this tradition.

Catellus (St) B. Jan 19
C9th. He was bishop of Castellamare south of Naples, Italy, and is the principal patron of that diocese.

Cathan (Catan, Chattan, Cadan) (St) B. May 17
C6th or C7th. He is alleged to have been a bishop on the Isle of Bute, Scotland, and to have been buried either at Kingarth there or at Tamlacht near Derry, Ireland. There may have been two saints of this name.

Catherine of Alexandria *Nov 25*
Her fictitious and fanciful acta describe her as having been martyred at Alexandria, Egypt, in the reign of Maxentius. Her alleged relics are at the monastery named after her at Sinai, but the first evidence of her cultus (which became very popular in the Middle Ages) dates from the C9th. Her attribute is a cartwheel with a spiked rim (the 'Catherine wheel'). Her cultus was suppressed in 1969.

St Catherine of Alexandria, Nov 25

Catherine of Bologna (St) R(OFM). Mar 9
1413–1463. From Bologna, Italy, she was a maid of honour at the ducal court of Ferrara and joined a group of Franciscan tertiaries there. In 1432 this became a Poor Clare house, and she became prioress of a foundation at Bologna in 1457. Her charism was expressed in prayer for the conversion of sinners, and the visions she had led her to write the *Revelations of the Seven Spiritual Weapons*. She was canonized in 1712. She is depicted holding the Christ-Child.

Catherine of Cardona (Bl) R(OC). May 21
1519–1577. A Spanish noblewoman born at Naples, Italy, she was at the court of King Philip II of Spain before becoming a hermit near Roda in Andalucia. After twenty years she became a recluse at a Carmelite convent, and St Teresa of Avila wrote approvingly of her.

Catherine Cheong (St) *see* **Korea (Martyrs of)**

Catherine Cittadini (Bl) R. F. (Dec 14)
1801–1857. From Bergamo, Italy, she was orphaned when young and settled at Somasca with her sister. There they started a boarding school for girls, which act eventually led to the foundation of the congregation of the Ursuline Sisters of Somasca. This is now established worldwide. She was beatified in 2001.

Catherine Coltenceau (Bl) *see* **William Repin and Comps**

Catherine-Mary Drexel (St) R. F. Mar 3
1858–1955. Born in Philadelphia, USA, she was the heiress to a banking fortune and a city socialite but was inspired to donate her wealth to missionary work among Native and African Americans. Pope Leo XIII asked her to found her own congregation, and she set up the 'Blessed Sacrament Sisters for Indians and Coloured People' at her family's summer mansion at Torresdale. She made 49 foundations as well as setting up the Xavier University at New Orleans in 1915. Her canonization was in 2000.

Catherine of Genoa (St) L. Sep 15
1477–1510. She was a noblewoman of the Fieschi family of Genoa, Italy. The man she married when aged sixteen lived a profligate life, and her own life was empty before she had a sudden conversion and became absorbed in piety and charitable works. Her husband started sharing her interests after he went bankrupt, and they worked in a local hospital until he died and she became its director. She was a famous mystic (the 'Apostle of Purgatory') and her experiences are described in the *Vita e dottrina* (of which she was not the final editor, as it was published forty years after her death). She was canonized in 1737.

Catherine Jarrige (Bl) T(OP). Jul 4
1754–1836. Born near St Flour in the Massif Central, France, she grew up as a lacemaker and entered the Dominican Third Order at Mauriac where she begged for poor people. After the Revolution she helped the non-juring clergy in many ways, and also worked in rebuilding the Church after the Terror. She was beatified in 1996.

Catherine-of-Jesus de Justamond (Bl) *see* **Orange (Martyrs of)**

Catherine Labouré (St) R. Nov 28
1806–1875. A farmer's daughter from the Côte d'Or, France, she became a Sister of Charity of St Vincent de Paul in 1830 and lived a very

ordinary life until she died at the Enghien-Reuilly convent at Paris. She had a series of private visions of Our Lady, however, who instructed her in the design of, and devotion to, the 'Miraculous Medal'. This has became popular throughout the Church. She was canonized in 1947.

Catherine Lee (St) *see* **Korea (Martyrs of)**

Catherine Mattei (Bl) T(OP). Sep 4
1486–1547. From Racconigi near Cuneo in Piedmont, Italy, she was a daughter of a blacksmith and became a Dominican tertiary while working as a weaver at home. She set out to imitate the life of her namesake of Siena and received the stigmata, but was persecuted and fled to Carmagnola, where she died. Her cultus was confirmed for the Dominicans in 1808.

Catherine of Nagasaki (Bl) M. L. Sep 10
d. 1622. She was a Japanese widow who was beheaded in the 'Great Martyrdom' at Nagasaki, together with BB Charles Spinola and Comps. *See* **Japan (Martyrs of)**.

Catherine of Pallanza (Bl)
R(OSA). Apr 6
?1437–1478. From Pallanza near Novara, Italy, she became a hermit in the mountains above Varese near Milan when she was fourteen. She attracted disciples and founded the Augustinian nunnery of S. Maria del Monte. Her cultus was confirmed for Milan in 1769.

Catherine of Parc-aux-Dames
(Bl) R(OCist). May 4
C13th. She was a Jewish girl from Louvain, Belgium, called Rachel, and her father often entertained the chaplain of the Duke of Brabant at home and indulged in polemical discussions with him. Listening to these led to a conversion and she left home when aged twelve, was baptized and joined the nearby Cistercian nunnery of Parc-aux-Dames. She became famous as a thaumaturge.

Catherine dei Ricci (St) T(OP). Feb 2
1522–1590. A noblewoman of Florence, Italy, she became a Dominican regular tertiary at Prato and served as novice-mistress and prioress, being influenced by Savanarola. She was a great mystic, having visions of the Passion and receiving the stigmata as well as being a thaumaturge. Thousands of people of all kinds visited her at her convent to seek her help. She died at Prato and was canonized in 1712.

Catherine of Siena (St)
T(OP). Dr. Apr 29
1347–1380. From Siena, Italy, she was the twenty-fifth child of a wool-dyer. Having made a vow of chastity when aged seven, she became a Dominican tertiary when aged fifteen, remaining at her parents' home and gathering all sorts of people as disciples by the example of her sanctity. She helped the poor of the city, nursed plague victims, lived a heroically penitential life and was very effective in converting obdurate sinners. The unity and welfare of the Church was her special concern, and she persuaded Pope Gregory XI to return to Rome from Avignon in 1376 and also tried to heal the subsequent Great Schism. Apart from over four hundred letters she wrote a *Dialogue* which is of first importance in mystical theology. She died at Rome, whither she had been summoned by the pope, and was canonized in 1461. In 1939 she was declared patron of Italy and was declared a doctor of the Church in 1970 and a patron of Europe in 2000.

St Catherine of Siena, Apr 29

Catherine Soiron (Bl) *see* **Compiègne (Martyrs of)**

Catherine of Sweden (St) R. Mar 24
?1331–1381. A Swede, the fourth child of St Brigid, she married a German nobleman who

was a life-long invalid. They lived in continence until he let her go to her mother in Rome in 1349. She accompanied her mother's body back to the Bridgettine nunnery at Vadstena in 1373 and became its abbess (her husband having died in 1351). In 1379 she obtained papal recognition of the Bridgettines and also promoted her mother's canonization. Her cultus was confirmed in 1484.

Catherine Tanaka (Bl) M. L. Jul 12
d. 1626. The wife of Bl John Tanaka, she was beheaded at Nagasaki, Japan, with Mancius Araki and Comps. *See* **Japan (Martyrs of)**.

Catherine (Kateri) Tekákwitha (Bl) R. Apr 17
1656–1680. A Native American, her father was an Iroquois and her mother was a Christian Algonquin. Born in what is now New York State, USA, she was orphaned when aged four and baptized by missionaries when aged twenty. Her family disapproved and she fled to French Canada (now Quebec), where she took a vow of virginity and became known for her prayer, work and asceticism. She died at Sault aged twenty-four and was beatified in 1980.

Bl Catherine Tekákwitha, Apr 17

Catherine Thomás (St) R(CR). Apr 5
1533–1574. An orphan girl of Valdemuzza on Majorca, Spain, she kept the sheep of an uncle who abused her before she joined the Canonesses of St Augustine at Palma when aged sixteen. She became a 'fool for Christ's sake' and was subject to mystical and diabolic phenomena, allegedly being continually in ecstasy at the end of her life. She was canonized in 1930.

Catherine du Verdier de la Sorinière (Bl) *see* **William Repin and Comps**

Catherine Volpicelli (Bl) R. F. Dec 28
1839–1894. From a rich family of Naples, Italy, she was initially a socialite but turned to a life of prayer and was inspired by a French pious association, the 'Apostleship of Prayer'. In 1874 she founded the 'Servants of the Sacred Heart' at Naples. She died there and was beatified in 2001.

Cathold, Anno and Diethard (BB) RR. Sep 29
Late C8th. They were three monks who evangelized the area around Eichstätt, Germany.

Catulinus and Comps (SS) MM. Jul 15
? They were martyred at Carthage, Roman Africa, and St Augustine preached a surviving panegyric on St Catulinus, a deacon. His companions were Januarius, Florentius, Pollutana, Julia and Justa. Nothing else is known about them.

Catus (St) *see* **Paul, Gerontius and Comps**

Cawrdaf (St) R. Dec 5
C6th. He was a monk at Llantwit Major, Wales, under St Illtyd after having been the ruler of Brecknock.

Ceadda *see* **Chad**

Ceallach (Kellach) of Killala (St) B. R. May 1
C6th. Of the Connaught, Ireland, royalty, he was educated by St Kieran at Clonmacnoise, became bishop of Killala, Co. Mayo, and ended up as a hermit. He has been claimed as a martyr. There were several other saints of the same name.

Ceallach McAedh (St) B. R? Apr 1
d. 1129. Possibly an Irish monk of Glastonbury, England, he studied at Oxford. When he became archbishop of Armagh, Ireland, in 1106 he was the last appointed by hereditary succession, as he initiated a reform of the Irish church which

was continued by St Malachy, his successor whom he had chosen.

Cearan (Ciaran) the Devout (St) R. Jun 14
d. 870. He was abbot of Bellach-Duin, now Castlekeeran in Co. Cavan, Ireland.

Ceccard of Luna (St) M. B. Jun 16
d. *c*860. Bishop of Luna in Tuscany, Italy, he rebuked the inhabitants of Massa-Carrara for immoral behaviour and they killed him. His cultus was confirmed for Massa in 1832.

Cecilia (St) V. Nov 22
C2nd or C3rd. One of the most celebrated of the Roman virgin martyrs, she is commemorated in the Roman canon of the Mass. Her acta are legendary, however, and all that is known for certain is that she was buried in the cemetery of St Callistus. She is traditionally associated with SS Valerian and Tiburtius, and the alleged relics of the three of them are at St Cecilia's in Trastevere. She is the patron of musicians and is usually depicted with a musical instrument.

Cecilia (St) *see* **Benedicta and Cecilia**

Cecilia Butsi (Bl) *see* **Thailand (Martyrs of)**

Cecilia Romana (St) *see* **Diana, Cecilia and Amata**

Cecilia Ryou (St) *see* **Korea (Martyrs of)**

Cedd (St) B. Oct 26
d. 644. A Nothumbrian and monk of Lindisfarne whose brother was St Chad, he was sent by St Finan to help in evangelizing Mercia, England, before being consecrated bishop of the East Saxons at London in 654. He founded monasteries at Tilbury and Bradwell, Essex, attended the Synod of Whitby (at which he renounced the Celtic rite) and founded a monastery (initially Celtic) at Lastingham near Malton, Yorks, to which he retired to die. (None of his monasteries survived the Viking incursions.)

Ceferino *see* **Zephyrinus**

Ceitho (St) R. Nov 1
C6th. Traditionally one of five saintly brothers ('Pumsaint') of the Cunedda family to whom the church at Llanpumpsaint near Carmarthen, Wales, was dedicated, he founded the church at Llangeitho in Dyfed.

Celerina (St) *see* **Laurentinus, Ignatius and Celerina**

Celerinus (St) L. Feb 3
d. *p*250. Grandson of St Celerina and one of the famous confessors of the Roman African church, he was imprisoned and tortured while on a visit to Rome in the reign of Decius. His later career is unknown but a church was dedicated to him at Carthage.

Celestine (St) *see* **Saturninus, Neopolus and Comps**

Celestine I, Pope *Apr 6*
d. 432. A Roman priest from the Campagna, he succeeded St Boniface I as pope in 422. He supported the campaign of St Germanus of Auxerre against Pelagianism, sent St Palladius to evangelize Ireland and confirmed the condemnation of Nestorius through his legates at the Council of Ephesus in 431. His cultus was suppressed in 1969.

Celestine V, Pope *see* **Peter Celestine**

Cellach (St) B. R. Apr 1
C9th. An archbishop of Armagh, Ireland, an abbot of Iona and the founder of the monastery of Kells, all sharing this name, were possibly the same person. There are over thirty other Irish saints with the same name, most of whom are probably duplicates.

Celloch *see* **Mochelloc**

Celsus *see* **Ceallach**

Celsus (St) *see* **Nazarius and Celsus**

Celsus and Clement (SS) MM. Nov 21
? Only the names are known of these Roman martyrs.

Celsus of Antioch (St) *see* **Julian, Basilissa and Comps**

Censurius of Auxerre (St) B. Jun 10
d. 486. He succeeded St Germanus as bishop of Auxerre, France, in 448, built a church in his honour there and was himself buried in it.

Centolla and Helen (SS) MM. Aug 13
d. ?304. They were martyred near Burgos, Spain, in the reign of Diocletian.

Ceolfrid (Geoffrey) (St) R. Sep 25
?642–716. A Northumbrian monk at the Yorkshire, England, monastery of Gilling, he transferred to the monastery of Ripon where he became novice-master. In 672 he transferred again to Wearmouth-Jarrow at the invitation of

St Benedict Biscop, the founder, and eventually became abbot of the twin monasteries. St Bede was one of his monks. He arranged the production of the *Codex Amiatinus* as a gift to the pope, and this survives at Florence as the oldest single-volume copy of the Vulgate and a witness of the high artistic standards of Saxon monasticism. He resigned in 716 and died at Langres, France, while on a pilgrimage to Rome.

Ceollach (St) B. Oct 6
C7th? He is recorded as a monk of Iona, Scotland, who was briefly bishop of Mercia before returning to his monastery and then going back to Ireland.

Ceolwulf (St) R. Jan 15
d. 764. A king of Northumbria, England, from 729 and a patron of monasticism, he was failure as a ruler and so abdicated and became a monk at Lindisfarne. There he allegedly provided the means for the community to drink alcohol at their meals. St Bede dedicated his *Ecclesiastical History* to him.

Cera (Ciar, Cyra, Cior, Ceara, Kiara) (St) R. Jan 5
C7th. A Co. Tipperary, Ireland, abbess, she had two nunneries, at Kilkeary near Nenagh and at Tehelly.

Ceratius (Cérase) (St) B. Jun 6
d. ?455. The cultus of this bishop of Grenoble, France, was confirmed in 1903.

Ceraunus (Ceran) of Paris (St) B. Sep 27
d. *p*614. A bishop of Paris, France, his shrine was formerly in the church of St Geneviève there.

Cerbonius (St) B. Oct 10
d. *c*580. A Roman African bishop, he was a refugee from the Vandals and settled at Populonia in Tuscany, Italy, allegedly becoming bishop there. The Lombards exiled him to Elba, where he died. He is the patron of Massa Maritima, into which diocese his own has been incorporated.

Cerneuf *see* **Serenus**

Ceslaus (St) R(OP). Jul 17
?1184–1242. From Kamien, Poland, he was a canon at Cracow before becoming a Dominican at Rome under St Dominic with St Hyacinth, his brother. He was made the provincial of Poland at Breslau in Silesia (now Wroclaw in Poland), preached in Silesia and Bohemia and was the spiritual director of St Hedwig of Silesia. He was a leader in the city's successful resistance to the Mongols in their incursion of 1240. His cultus was confirmed for Wroclaw in 1712.

Cettin (Cethagh) (St) B. Jun 16
C5th. A disciple of St Patrick, he was a missionary bishop in the counties of Roscommon and Meath, Ireland. 'Cethagh' may have been a separate person.

Cewydd (St) Jul 1
C6th. He was based in Anglesey , Wales, and has a forty-day weather legend told about him similar to that of St Swithin.

Ch- *see* **C-**, **K-**, if names spelt thus initially are not found.

Chad (Ceadda) (St) B. R. Mar 2
d. 672. From Northumbria, England, and brother of St Cedd, he was educated at Lindisfarne under St Aidan and in Ireland before becoming abbot of the Columbanian monastery of Lastingham founded by his brother. During one of St Wilfrid's exiles he was made archbishop of York but was removed by St Theodore of Canterbury when St Wilfrid returned and went to Lichfield in 669 to evangelize the Mercians. He died there, and part of his relics are now at his namesake cathedral at Birmingham. His attributes are a church and a vine.

Chaeremon (St) *see* **Gaius, Faustus and Comps**

Chaeremon of Nilopolis and Comps (SS) Dec 22
d. *p*250. A very old bishop of Nilopolis, Egypt, when the Decian persecution was instigated he took to the hills with some companions. They were never seen again and were probably eaten by animals or enslaved by nomads (the Sahara desert was greener in those days.)

Chaffre *see* **Theofrid**

Chagnoald (Chainoald, Cagnou) (St) B. Sep 6
d. 633. Brother of SS Faro and Fara and a disciple of St Columban, he helped the latter to found the abbey of Bobbio in Lombardy, Italy, before becoming bishop of Laon, France.

Chalcedon (Martyrs of) (SS) MM. Sep 24
d. 304. They numbered forty-nine and were martyred at Chalcedon, across the Bosporus from Byzantium (Constantinople). Possibly they were the city's church choir.

Chamond (Annemond)
(St) M. B. Sep 28
d. 657. He was at the court of King Clovis II of the Franks before becoming archbishop of Lyons, France, but was assassinated by order of Ebroin, mayor of the palace. St Wilfrid was present at the enshrining of his relics.

Charalampias and Comps
(SS) MM. Feb 18
d. 203. A priest, he was martyred at Magnesia, Asia Minor, in the reign of Septimus Severus with two soldiers and three women.

Charbel (St) M. Sep 5
d. 107. He was martyred at Antioch, Syria, in the reign of Trajan, and his veneration is popular among the Maronites.

Charbel Malkhlouf (St) R. Dec 24
1828–1898. A Maronite of Lebanon born at Beqa Kafra, he became a monk at Annaya in 1848 and was then a hermit for twenty-three years. He was greatly devoted to the Eucharist, and became revered in the region by Muslims as well as Christians. He was canonized in 1977.

Charisius (St) *see* **Athanasius, Anthusa and Comps**

Charisius (St) *see* **Callistus, Charisius and Comps**

Charitina (St) V. Oct 5
d. ?304. She died under torture in the reign of Diocletian, probably at Amisus on the south coast of the Black Sea.

Chariton (St) *see* **Zeno and Chariton**

Charity (St) *see* **Faith, Hope and Charity**

Charles-Anthony-Nicholas Ancel (Bl) *see* **John-Baptist Souzy and Comps**

Charles Bérard de Pérou (Bl) *see* **September (Martyrs of)**

Charles of Blois (Bl) T(OFM). Sep 29
?1319–1364. A nephew of King Philip VI of France, he married Joan of Brittany in 1341and thus became Duke of Brittany. He spent the rest of his life fighting in defence of his title against his uncle, John de Montfort, apart from nine years spent in the Tower of London. He was killed in battle. His cultus was forbidden in 1368, but confirmed for Blois and St Brieuc in 1904.

Charles Borromeo (St) B. Nov 4
1538–1584. From Rocca d'Arona near Lake Maggiore, Italy, his uncle was Pope Pius IV and he was made a curial cardinal and archbishop of Milan in 1560 when aged only twenty-two and not yet a priest. He was secretly ordained bishop in 1563 to avoid pressures to marry, became papal Secretary of State and was instrumental in the Counter-Reformation (especially in the Tridentine reform of the curia). In 1565 he became bishop of Milan which was in a state of serious decay as a diocese. The rest of his life was spent in renewing it thoroughly and he became the greatest bishop of his day in Italy, with enormous influence. He was canonized in 1610.

Charles Carnus (Bl) *see* **September (Martyrs of)**

Charles Cho (St) *see* **Korea (Martyrs of)**

Charles-Renatus Collas de Bignon (Bl) *see* **John-Baptist Souzy and Comps**

Charles Eraña Guruceta and Comps (BB) MM. LL. Sep 18
1884–1936. From Guipúzcoa, Spain, he became a lay Marianist and ran a prestigious school in Madrid. After the start of the Civil War he tried to find help from other Marianist communities in Ciudad Real, but these had been dispersed and he was arrested with two confreres: Bl Fidelis Fuidio Rodriguez and Bl Jesus Hita Miranda. They were martyred on different dates and were beatified in 1995. *See* **Spanish Civil War (Martyrs of)**.

Charles Garnier (Bl) *see* **John Brébeuf and Comps**

Charles the Good (Bl) M. Mar 2
d. 1127. A son of St Canute, king of Denmark, he went with his uncle Robert II on crusade to the Holy Land and succeeded him as count of Flanders in 1119. He was a wise and careful ruler, with a special concern for the poor, and was killed at Bruges, Belgium, in a conspiracy by some magnates. His cultus was confirmed for Bruges in 1883.

Charles the Great ('Charlemagne')
(Bl) L. Jan 28
742–814. The son of Pepin the Short, he became king of the Franks in 768 and was crowned as the first Holy Roman Emperor in 800 by Pope St Leo III. He was successful in founding a great empire in the West around his capital at Aachen, and tried hard to raise the standards of Church and state therein. But the

political foundations were inadequate and his empire did not long survive his death. His cultus was approved for Aachen in 1165 and was popular in the north of Germany and of France in the Middle Ages, partly owing to anti-papal nationalist sentiment. Pope Benedict XIV confirmed it in the C18th, despite the emperor's immoral private life and his unsoundness concerning the dogmatic validity of icons. He is the principal patron of Metten Abbey.

Charles le Gué (Bl) *see* **September (Martyrs of)**

Charles-Arnold Hanus (Bl) *see* **John-Baptist Souzy and Comps**

Charles-of-St-Andrew Houbin (Bl) R(CP). Jan 5
1821–1893. From near Maastricht, Netherlands, he joined the Passionists at Tournai in 1846, was ordained in 1852 and was then sent to London. He went to Dublin in 1857, where he spent the rest of his life (apart from 1866-74 at Sutton, Surrey, in England). He sometimes had to spend all day in the confessional, such were the numbers coming to him, and converted many sinners and lapsed Catholics both in Britain and in Ireland. He had a great zeal for the sanctification of Ireland as a means to the conversion of Britain and prayed always for the unity of the Church. His beatification was in 1988.

Charles Hurtel (Bl) *see* **September (Martyrs of)**

Charles Hyen (St) *see* **Korea (Martyrs of)**

Charles Leisner (Bl) P. Aug 12
1915–1945. From Rees on the Rhine, Germany, he was involved in underground Catholic youth work under the Nazis at Münster. After being ordained deacon he was sent to the concentration camp at Dachau for criticizing Hitler in 1941 and was secretly ordained priest there in 1944. He died of tuberculosis just after his liberation and was beatified in 1996.

Charles Lwanga and Comps (SS) MM. Jun 3
1885–7. The evangelization of kingdom of Buganda (the core of modern Uganda) started with the exploration of the area by the British in the latter part of the C19th, and saw competition between Catholic and Protestant missionaries in setting up local churches. In October 1885 the new Kabaka (king) Mwanga, who was an extremely corrupt and vicious young man, ordered the assassination of James Hannington, the newly arrived Anglican missionary bishop. Then he ordered a general persecution of his Christian subjects in May 1886, mainly because the Christians among his page-boys (Charles Lwanga was their leader) objected to being the casual targets of his licentiousness. Twenty-two Catholics, mostly courtiers aged between 13 and 30, were killed by being dismembered and burned alive before the Kabaka's overthrow in September 1888. They were canonized in 1964, and are the proto-martyrs of sub-Saharan Africa. A number of Protestants were killed as well. *See* **Uganda** in lists of national martyrs in appendix.

Charles-Joseph-Eugene de Mazenod (St) B. F. May 21
1782–1861. From Aix-en-Provence, France, of a family in the high civil service, he was exiled by the French Revolution and was ordained on his return in 1811. He founded the 'Missionary Oblates of Mary Immaculate' in order to promote popular missions and to preach to the poor, and was made bishop of Marseilles in 1837. He thoroughly reformed his diocese. His canonization was in 1995.

Charles Meehan (Bl) M. R(OFM). Aug 12
1640–1679. An Irish Franciscan, he was on his way home from Bavaria (where he had taken refuge from persecution) but his ship was wrecked on the north Welsh coast and he was executed at Ruthin despite never having been a priest in Wales or England (he may have worked in Scotland). He was beatified in 1987. *See* **Wales (Martyrs of)**.

Charles Melchiori of Sezze (St) R(OFM). Jan 7
1613–1670. From Sezze in the Campagna, Italy, he became a Franciscan in 1635 and famous for mystical experiences. It was alleged that he bore a visible wound caused by a ray of light from a consecrated host piercing his heart in 1648. He wrote several treatises on the spiritual life and also an autobiography. He died at Rome and was canonized in 1959.

Charles Navarro Miquel (Bl) *see* **Dionysius Pamplona Polo and Comps**

Charles Régis de la Calmette (St) *see* **September (Martyrs of)**

Charles-Emmanuel Rodrígues Santiago (Bl) L. Jul 13
1918–1963. The 'Lay Apostle of the Liturgy' was born at Caguas, Puerto Rico, and had a

hard childhood marked by the destitution of his family after a fire and by the onset of ulcerative colitis. The latter interfered with his formal education but he was a voracious seeker after knowledge and became deeply committed to propagating the understanding of the church's liturgy. While working as an office clerk he edited a magazine on the subject and organized many initiatives to further his life's aim. He died of rectal cancer and was beatified in 2001.

Charles of Sayn (Bl) R(OCist). Jan 29
d. ?1215. A soldier, he became a Cistercian monk at Himmerod, Belgium, in 1185 and died there after having served as abbot of Villers in Brabant from 1197 to 1209. Villers became a famous abbey under him. He has an unconfirmed cultus among the Cistercians.

Charles Spinola and Comps
(SS) MM. Sep 10
d. 1622. An Italian nobleman born at Prague, he became a Jesuit in 1584 and was on the Japanese missions from 1594 to 1618. Then he was seized, imprisoned for four years and finally burned alive in the 'Great Martyrdom' at Nagasaki with twenty-two companions (seven Jesuits, six Dominicans, three Franciscans and six lay people), after having to watch twenty-nine others being beheaded. *See* **Japan (Martyrs of)**.

Charles Steeb *see* **John-Henry-Charles Steeb**

Charles Veret (Bl) *see* **September (Martyrs of)**

Charlotte-of-the-Resurrection Thouret (Bl) *see* **Compiègne (Carmelite Martyrs of)**

Chef *see* **Theodore**

Chelidonia (St) R(OSB). Oct 13
d. 1152. From the Abruzzi, Italy, when young she became a hermit in a cave called the 'Morra Ferogna' near Tivoli and was clothed as a Benedictine nun at St Scholastica's nunnery at Subiaco nearby. She continued as a hermit, however. Her relics are in her abbey church and she is one of the patrons of Subiaco.

Chely *see* **Hilary of Mende**

Cheron *see* **Caraunus**

Cherubin Testa (Bl) R(OSA). Feb 20
1451–1479. He was an Augustinian friar at Avigliana in Piedmont, Italy, and his cultus was confirmed for the Augustinian friars in 1865.

Chi Zhuzi (St) M. L. Jul ?
1882–1900. From a peasant family of Dezhao in Hebei, China, he became a catechumen but his parents objected when the Boxer Uprising took place. He fled to a Catholic area, where he initially failed to find acceptance because he was unbaptized, and worked as a servant. His parents ordered him to return home but he met a Boxer gang on the way and was dismembered. *See* **China (Martyrs of)**.

Chilian *see* **Kilian, Colman and Totnan**

Chillien (Killian, Chilianus)
(St) R. Nov 13
C7th. An Irish missionary in Artois, France, he was a relative of St Fiacre and had his shrine at Aubigny near Arras.

China (Martyrs of) MM. Nov 13
Christianity has been in China for over a thousand years, but the Catholic Church only started getting established there with the arrival of the Portuguese in the region in the early sixteenth century. The Jesuits gained influence at the court of the Ming emperors, but Christianity was not easily compatible with the Confucianism of the State. When the Manchus overthrew the Ming dynasty in 1643 there was a wave of persecution. The protomartyr of the Chinese church was Bl Francis de Capillas who was martyred in Fujian in 1648. The Jesuits regained some influence at court, but persecution was renewed in 1717 and continued intermittently until the Western powers enforced toleration in the Treaty of Nanking in 1842. In 1900, as the Empire was decaying, there was a two-month long xenophobic outburst, mostly in north-central areas, called the Boxer Rebellion. About 30,000 Catholics were massacred during this, mostly in the provinces of Hebei and Hunan. A total of 120 martyrs, natives and missionaries, were canonized in 2000 (St John-Gabriel Perboyre was canonized in 1996.) *See* lists of national martyrs in appendix.

Chionia (St) *see* **Agape and Chionia**

Chl- also *see* **Cl-**, **Kl-**

Chr- also *see* **Cr-**

Christeta (St) *see* **Vincent, Sabina and Christeta**

Christian (St) *see* **Benedict of Benevento and Comps**

Christian of Auxerre (Bl) B. Nov 22
d. ?873. He was a bishop of Auxerre, France.

Christian of Clogher (St) B. Jun 12
d. 1138. The brother of St Malachy of Armagh, he became bishop of Clogher in Co. Tyrone, Ireland, in 1126. His shrine was at Armagh.

Christian of Mellifont (Bl) R(OCist). Mar 18
d. 1186. Giolla Croist O'Conarchy was an Irish priest from Bangor, Ireland, who became a Cistercian monk at Clairvaux under St Bernard and was sent to found the abbey of Mellifont in Co. Louth, Ireland, in 1142. The Cistercians became the dominant monastic order in Ireland. He may have served as bishop of Lismore, but he died at his abbey.

Christian of Prussia (Bl) B. R(OCist). Dec 4
d. 1245. A Cistercian monk, possibly from the abbey of Oliva near Gdansk, Poland, he went to evangelize Prussia in 1207 when it was still an independent nation and was consecrated the first missionary bishop of Prussia in 1215. He was only partially successful, and he helped to introduce the Teutonic Knights after a pagan reaction. These went on to exterminate the Prussians in course of time.

Christiana of the Cross *see* **Oringa**

Christiana of Dendermonde (St) R. Jul 24
C7th. Allegedly a Saxon king's daughter, she was a hermit at Dickelvenne, south of Ghent, Belgium, and had her shrine at Dendermonde near Antwerp, of which place she is the patron.

Christiana of Georgia *see* **Nino**

Christicola *see* **Cele-Christ**

Christina the Astonishing (Bl) R. Jul 24
1150–1224. From near Liege, Belgium, she was orphaned in 1165 and had a cataleptic fit in 1182 which initiated a series of unbelievable mystical phenomena which lasted for the rest of her life (hence her nickname). These were recorded by a Dominican before she died at a convent at St Truiden.

Christina of Bolseno (St) V. Jul 24
? She was possibly a Roman who was martyred at Bolseno in Tuscany, Italy. Her acta are legendary and have been confused with the fantastic stories concerning a probably fictional 'Christina of Tyre'. Her attributes are an arrow and a millstone. Her cultus was confined to local calendars in 1969.

Christina Bruzo (Bl) R. Nov 6
1242–1312. From Stommeln near Cologne, Germany, she was a Beguine at Cologne before becoming the housekeeper of the parish priest at Stommeln. From age eleven she was subject to an extraordinary series of mystical and paranormal phenomena which were recorded by a Dominican. Her cultus was confirmed for Cologne in 1908.

Christina Camozzi (Bl) R(OSA). Feb 13
1435–1456. From Porlezza on Lake Lugano, Italy, she was the daughter of a doctor and led a worthless life until a sudden conversion caused her to become an Augustinian nun in 1454. She nursed in a hospital at Spoleto and practised extreme mortifications. Her cultus was confirmed for the Augustinians in 1834. (She is sometimes surnamed 'Visconti' in error).

Christina Ciccarelli (Bl) R(OSA) Jan 18
1481–1543. From Luco de Marsi in the Abruzzi, Italy, she became an Augustinian nun and prioress at Aquileia. Her cultus was confirmed for that place in 1841.

Christina of Markyate (Bl) R(OSB). Dec 5
?1097–?1161. A noblewoman of Huntingdon, England, she wished to become a nun but was prevented by her parents until she fled and became a hermit at Markyate near St Alban's. Her disciples there formed a new nunnery under the authority of the abbey at the latter place. Her cultus was unconfirmed.

Christina the Persian (St) V. Mar 13
C5th. A young Persian woman, she was whipped to death in the reign of Shah Shapur II.

Christinus of Gniezno (St) *see* **Benedict of Gniezno and Comps**

Christinus Roca Huguet (Bl) *see* **Hospitaller Martyrs of Spain**

Christopher (St) M. Jul 25
? The old Roman Martyrology lists him as a martyr in Lycia, Asia Minor, in the reign of Decius. Nothing is known about him but many fanciful legends have been attached to his name. The most familiar has him as a giant carrying the Christ-child across a river, and this is how he is usually represented. His cultus was confined to local calendars in 1969 but he remains a popular patron of travellers.

St Christopher, July 25 *(see p. 117)*

Christopher (St) *see* **Leovegild and Christopher**

Christopher Bales (Bl) M. P. Mar 4
d. 1590. From Coniscliffe west of Darlington in Co. Durham, England, he was educated at Rome and Rheims and ordained priest at Douai in 1587. The next year he went to England and after two years was seized and hanged, drawn and quartered at Fleet Street in London. He was beatified in 1929. *See* **England (Martyrs of)**.

Christopher Buxton (Bl) M. P. Oct 1
d. 1588. From Tideswell in Derbyshire, England, he was educated at Rheims and Rome and ordained priest in 1586. He was hanged, drawn and quartered at Canterbury and was beatified in 1929. *See* **England (Martyrs of)**.

Christopher of Guardia
(St) M. Sep 25
d. ?1490. From Guardia near Toledo, Spain, he was alleged to have been kidnapped by renegade Jews at Toledo and crucified at Guardia. The Jews were under serious pressure in Spain at the time and were about to be expelled by Ferdinand and Isabella. His cultus was confirmed in 1805.

Christopher Maccassoli
(Bl) R(OFM). Mar 11
d. 1485. A nobleman from Milan, Italy, he became a Franciscan and eventually re-founded a friary at Vigevano near Milan. He was sought out by thousands for help and advice. His cultus was confirmed for Vigevano in 1890.

Christopher Magallanes Jara (St) *see* **Mexico (Martyrs of)**

Christopher of Milan (Bl) R(OP). Mar 1
d. 1484. From Milan, Italy, he became a Dominican and was a preacher famous in the Republic of Genoa and the Duchy of Milan. He had a friary founded for him at Taggia near Ventimiglia, where he died. His cultus was confirmed for Ventimiglia and the Dominicans in 1875.

Christopher Robinson
(Bl) M. P. (Mar)
d. 1607. From near Carlisle, he was ordained at Rheims in 1592 and was a priest in Cumbria for five years before being captured at Penrith. He was executed at Carlisle on an uncertain date and was beatified in 1987. *See* **England (Martyrs of)**.

Christopher of Romandiola
(Bl) R(OFM). Oct 31
?1172–1272. A parish priest of the diocese of Cesena, Italy, at Romandiola, he became one of the early Franciscans after St Francis visited his village and was one of the first of the order in Gascony, France. He died at Cahors and his cultus was confirmed for there in 1905.

Christopher of Sandomir (Bl) *see* **Sadoc of Sandomir and Comps**

Christopher of Tlaxcala
(Bl) M. L. Sep 23
*c*1514–1527. A native Mexican born near Tlaxcala and converted by the Franciscans, he had a father who objected to his evangelizing. On a family feast day the latter was encouraged by one of his wives to beat Bl Christopher badly and to throw him on a bonfire. He died that night, after having thanked his father for the gift of martyrdom. He was beatified in 1900 with BB Anthony and John.

Christopher Wharton
(Bl) M. P. Mar 28
d. 1600. From Middleton near Ilkley in Yorkshire, England, he was a nephew of the first Lord Wharton and a fellow of Trinity College, Oxford before his conversion. He was ordained at Rheims in 1584 and was a priest in Yorkshire until he was captured at Carlton Hall near Leeds and executed at York. He was beatified in 1987. *See* **England (Martyrs of)**.

Chrodegang of Metz (St) B. Mar 6
d. 766. From near Liege, Belgium, he was the chief minister for Charles Martel from 737 and was made bishop of Metz, France, while retaining his secular office in 742 after Pepin had become ruler. He introduced the Roman liturgy to his diocese (displacing the Gallican rite), founded and restored several monasteries (notably Gorze) and organized his cathedral chapter into a canonry living a common life under a rule. This last innovation was extremely influential. He died at Metz and his shrine was at Gorze until destroyed in the French Revolution.

Chrodegang of Sées (St) M. B. Sep 3
d. 775. The brother of St Opportuna, he became bishop of Sées in Normandy, France, but was assassinated by a relative to whom he had entrusted the administration of the diocese while on pilgrimage to Rome.

Chromatius of Aquileia
(St) B. Dec 2
d. ?407. Bishop of Aquileia, Italy, from 387, he was associated with the ascetic community there headed by St Jerome and Rufinus. He was consecrated bishop by St Ambrose in ?387, and loyally defended St John Chrysostom when the latter was exiled. He was a great theologian but little of his writings survives.

Chromatius of Rome (St) L. Aug 11
C3rd. He was allegedly prefect of Rome and father of St Tiburtius of Rome.

Chronan *see* **Cronan**

Chrysanthus and Daria (SS) MM. Oct 25
d. *c*300. They were martyrs buried on the Salarian Way at Rome but nothing else is known about them. Their legend describes them as a married couple, an Egyptian husband and a Greek wife, who were buried alive in a sandpit at Rome in the reign of Numerian (d. 284). There was no persecution during this emperor's reign. Their cultus was confined to particular calendars in 1969.

Chrysogonus (St) M. Nov 24
d. ?304. He was martyred at Aquileia near Venice, Italy, and has a basilica at Rome but nothing else is known about him. His association with St Anastasia is legendary. Since 1969 his cultus is confined to his basilica, although he is mentioned in the Roman canon of the Mass.

Chrysolius (St) M. B? Feb 7
C4th. From Armenia, he was a refugee from the persecution of Diocletian and was a missionary in what is now Belgium until martyred. His relics are at Bruges, Belgium.

Chrysologus *see* **Peter Chrysologus**

Chrysophorus (St) *see* **Victor, Zoticus and Comps**

Chrysostom *see* **John Chrysostom**

Chrysotelus (St) *see* **Parmenius and Comps**

Chuniald and Gislar (SS) PP. Sep 24
C7th. They were missionary priests, possibly from Scotland or Ireland, who were based at Salzburg, Austria, and helped St Rupert of Salzburg to evangelize the surrounding areas.

Cian (St) R. Dec 11
C6th. He was a hermit near Caernarfon, Wales, and was possibly a servant of St Peris beforehand.

Cianan *see* **Kenan**

Ciaran *see* **Kieran**

Ciaran (Kieran, Kyran) the Younger (St) R. Sep 9
d.?556. From the region of Connaught, Ireland, he was trained in the monastic life by St Finian of Clonard and became the abbot-founder of Clonmacnois in West Meath, on the Shannon. For this influential monastery he drew up an extremely austere monastic rule, known as 'the Law of Kieran'.

Cicely *see* **Cecilia**

Cicco of Pesaro (Bl) T(OFM). Aug 4
d. 1350. From Pesaro, Italy, he became a Franciscan tertiary and a hermit nearby. His cultus was confirmed for Pesaro in 1859.

Cilinia (St) L. Oct 21
d. *p*458. The mother of St Principius of Soissons and of St Remigius of Rheims, she died at Laon, France.

Cillene (St) R. Jul 3
d. ?752. An Irish monk, he became abbot of Iona, Scotland, in 726.

Cindeus (St) M. Jul 11
d. *c*300. A priest of Pamphylia, Asia Minor, he was burned alive in the reign of Diocletian.

Cinnia (St) R. Feb 1
C5th. A princess of Ulster, Ireland, she became a nun near Clogher after having been baptized by St Patrick, who also received her vows.

Cisellus (St) *see* **Luxorius, Cisellus and Camerinus**

Cissa (St) R. Sep 23
Late C7th. He was a monk-hermit in Northumbria, England, most probably at Lindisfarne.

Ciwa *see* **Kigwe**

Clair *see* **Clarus**

Clare Agolanti (Bl) T(OFM). Feb 10
?1282–?1346. A noblewoman of Rimini, Italy, she married twice and lived a sinful and worthless life as a wife. But her second husband died and her father and brother were killed in civil disturbances, after which she converted, became a Franciscan tertiary, founded the nunnery of Our Lady of the Angels at Rimini and henceforth lived a life of rigorous penance. Her cultus was confirmed for Rimini in 1784.

Clare of Assisi (St) R(OFM). F. Aug 11
?1194–1253. A beautiful young noblewoman from Assisi, Italy, she ran away from home to join St Francis and to follow his ideals. He heard her vows as a nun in 1212, found a refuge for her at the Benedictine nunnery of St Paul's in Assisi and then obtained a house by the church of St Damian for her and her sister St Agnes in 1215. She governed this first nunnery of the Poor Clares in absolute poverty for forty years, and was as much instrumental in spreading the Franciscan ideal as St Francis herself. She is often represented holding a monstrance, in reference to a story that she saved her nunnery from a raid by mercenary soldiers by exposing the Blessed Sacrament to them.

Clare Bosatta de Pianello
(Bl) R. Apr 20
1858–1887. From Pianello Lario near Como, Italy, in 1877 she joined the 'Daughters of Our Lady of Providence' which had just been founded by Bl Aloysius Guanella at the Sacred Heart Hospital there. In 1886 she moved to Como and became the superior-general, but did not live long as such. She was devoted both to the interior life and to caring for the elderly and orphans. Her beatification was in 1991.

Clare Gambacorta (Bl) R(OP). Apr 17
1362–1419. Daughter of the ruler of Pisa, Italy, and sister of Bl Peter Gambacorta, she was a widow at fifteen and tried to join the Poor Clares. Her father prevented this, but allowed her to become a Dominican nun in 1378. She became the prioress of her own foundation in the city and set out to reform her order. Her cultus was confirmed for Pisa and the Dominicans in 1830.

Clare-of-the-Cross of Montefalco (St) R(OSA). Aug 17
?1275–1308. From Montefalco near Spoleto, Italy, she became a Franciscan tertiary hermit with her sister at Montefalco but her sister founded the Augustinian nunnery of the Holy Cross in 1290 and she became the second

St Clare of Assisi, Aug 11

abbess. (The circumstances of their change in rule are obscure). She was a great mystic with a special devotion to the Passion, and the Instruments of the Passion were allegedly visible on her heart (probably scar-tissue caused by heart attacks) when this was examined after her death. She was canonized in 1881.

Clare Yamada (Bl) M. Sep 10
d. 1622. She was beheaded in the 'Great Martyrdom' at Nagasaki, Japan, with her husband, Bl Dominic Yamada, and Charles Spinola and Comps. *See* **Japan (Martyrs of)**.

Claritus (Chiarito) Voglia (Bl) L. May 6
*c*1300–1348. A nobleman of Florence, Italy, he founded the 'Chiarito' convent of Augustinian nuns in the city in 1342, which his wife joined and which he worked for as a domestic until his death of the plague.

Clarentius of Vienne (St) B. Apr 26
d. *c*620. He succeeded St Etherius as bishop of Vienne, France.

Clarus (St) M. B. Jun 1
? Apparently a missionary bishop, he was sent from Rome to evangelize Aquitaine, France, where he was martyred. He is not the same as St Clarus of Nantes.

Clarus (St) R. Nov 4
d. ?875. Allegedly from Rochester in Kent, England, he went to France and became a hermit near Cherbourg. Then he wandered about and ended up near Beauvais, where he was killed by a noblewoman after he had rejected her advances. His shrine was at his namesake village of Saint-Clair-sur-Epte and he is invoked against sore eyes (probably because of his name: 'Clear').

Clarus of Marmoutier (St) R. Nov 8
d. 397. From Tours, France, he was a monk at Marmoutier under St Martin and became a hermit nearby.

Clarus of Nantes (St) B. Oct 10
? He was a bishop of Nantes, by tradition a disciple of St Peter and apostle of Armorica, Brittany, France. He was more likely of the C3rd.

Clarus of Seligenstadt (St) R(OSB). Feb 1
d. ?1048. A monk of Seligenstadt near Mainz, Germany, he became a hermit for thirty years nearby and became known for his austerities and his motto: 'Christ, and him crucified'.

Clarus of Vienne (St) R. Jan 1
d. *c*660. From near Vienne, France, he became a monk at the monastery of St Ferreol and then abbot of St Marcellus at Vienne. His cultus was confirmed in 1903.

Classicus (St) *see* **Lucius, Sylvanus and Comps**

Clateus of Brescia (St) M. B. Jun 4
? He was allegedly a bishop of Brescia, Italy, who was martyred in the reign of Nero. This is unhistorical.

Claud *see* **Claudius**

Claudia (St) L. Aug 7
C1st. She is mentioned in St Paul's second letter to Timothy (4:21), but her story is otherwise fictional.

Claudia (St) *see* **Alexandra of Amisus and Comps**

Claudia (St) *see* **Theodotus of Ancyra and Comps**

Claudia Thévenet *see* **Mary-of-the-Incarnation Thévenet**

Claudian (St) *see* **Papias, Diodorus and Comps**

Claudian (St) *see* **Victor, Victorinus and Comps**

Claudian (St) *see* **Victorinus, Victor and Comps**

Claudius (St) *see* **Lucillan, Claudius and Comps**

Claudius (St) *see* **Marcellinus, Claudius and Comps**

Claudius, Asterius, Neon and Comps (SS) MM. Aug 23
d. 303. Three brothers of Aegea in Cilicia, Asia Minor, they were betrayed as Christians by their step-mother (who coveted their property) and were either crucified or beheaded. Traditionally associated with them are Donvina (a mistake for 'Domina') and Theonilla.

Claudius, Crispin and Comps (SS) MM. Dec 3
? Nothing is known about these African martyrs. The companions were Magina, John and Stephen.

Claudius, Hilaria and Comps (SS) MM. Dec 3
d. ?283. Allegedly a military tribune at Rome, his wife, two sons (Jason and Maurus) and seventy soldiers, they feature in the legendary acta of SS Chrysanthus and Daria.

Claudius, Justus, Jucundinus and Comps (SS) MM. Jul 21
d. 273. They were eight companions of St Julia, martyred with her at Troyes, France, in the reign of Aurelian. Their shrine was at the abbey of Jouarre near Meaux.

Claudius, Lupercus and Victorius (SS) MM. Oct 30
d. *c*300. Sons of the centurion St Marcellus, they were beheaded at León, Spain, in the reign of Diocletian.

Claudius, Nicostratus and Comps (SS) MM. Jul 7
d. ?288. They are in the unreliable acta of St Sebastian as having been martyred at Rome on the same day as that saint, but are probably identical with the Four Crowned Martyrs of Pannonia. They seem to be listed again by the old Roman Martyrology on Nov 8. The companions are Castorius, Victorinus and Symphorian.

Claudius Béguignot (Bl) *see* **John-Baptist Souzy and Comps**

Claudius of Besançon (St) B. R. Jun 6
d. ?696. From Franche-Comté, France, he was initially a soldier but became a priest and a canon of Besançon. The he became a monk at Condat in the Jura, was made abbot and introduced the rule of St Benedict there. In 685 he became bishop of Besançon but remained abbot of his monastery, to which he retired to die and which was later named St Claud after him.

Claudius Bochot, Claudius Cagnières des Granges, Claudius Cayx-Dumas, Claudius Chaudet and Claudius Colin (BB) *see* **September (Martyrs of)**

Claudius la Colombière (St) R(SJ). Feb 15
1641–1682. From near Grenoble, France, he became a Jesuit at Avignon in 1659 and went on to be the superior of the house at Paray-le-Monial. There he was the spiritual director of St Margaret-Mary Alacoque, and helped her in fostering the devotion to the Sacred Heart. He went to England in 1676 as the Duchess of York's chaplain, but was banished as a result of the Oates plot. He died at Avignon and was canonized in 1992.

Claudius Dumonet (Bl) *see* **John-Baptist Souzy and Comps**

Claudius Fontaine (Bl) *see* **September (Martyrs of)**

Claudius Granzotto (Bl) R(OFM). Sep 2
1900–1947. Born in S. Lucia del Piave, Italy, he left school when young, served in the army and then obtained a diploma in sculpture from Venice's Academy of Fine Arts. After working in his own studio for four years he joined the Franciscans in order to unite his art to holiness. He became a model friar as well as a sculptor with great spiritual and human sensitivity. He died of a brain tumour and was beatified in 1994.

Claudius-Joseph Jouffret de Bonnefont and Claudius Laplace (BB) *see* **John-Baptist Souzy and Comps**

Claudius Laporte and Claudius Marmotant (BB) *see* **September (Martyrs of)**

Claudius-Barnabas Laurent de Mascloux (Bl) *see* **John-Baptist Souzy and Comps**

Claudius Mayneud de Bisefranc and Claudius Ponse (BB) *see* **September (Martyrs of)**

Claudius Richard (Bl) *see* **John-Baptist Souzy and Comps**

Claudius Rousseau (Bl) *see* **September (Martyrs of)**

Clear *see* **Clarus**

Cledog *see* **Clydog**

Cledwyn (Clydwyn) (St) L. Nov 1
C5th. The patron of Llandegwyn in Clwyd, Wales, was alleged to have been the eldest son of St Brychan and to have succeeded him as ruler of Brecknock.

Cleer (Clether) (St) R. Oct 23
d. *c*520. A Welsh nobleman, he emigrated to Cornwall, England, and settled at the place near Liskeard where St Cleer's chapel and well now are. He is possibly identical with the patron of St Clether, a village near Camerton in the same county.

Clement (St) *see* **Apelles, Lucius and Clement**
Clement (St) *see* **Celsus and Clement**

Clement I, 'Pope' (St) M. Nov 23
d. ?101. By tradition he was the third successor of St Peter and pope for about a decade. The Roman church was most probably an informal federation of Christian synagogues at the time with no one overall leader, however. His letter to the church at Corinth, in which he attempted to settle some disputes there in the name of the Roman church, survives as one of the most important sub-apostolic writings. The so-called 'second letter' is not by him. He is mentioned in the Roman canon of the Mass and is venerated as a martyr, but nothing is known for certain about his life and his acta are unreliable. His alleged relics were brought to Rome from the Crimea by SS Cyril and Methodius. His attribute is an anchor.

Clement of Alexandria *Dec 4*
d. ?217. Titus Flavius Clemens succeeded Panthenus as the head of the catechetical school at Alexandria, Egypt, and had Origen as a pupil. As is witnessed by his surviving writings, he set out to reconcile Christianity and classical scholarship. He was listed in the old Roman Martyrology until 1751, when Cardinal Baronius deleted his name on the grounds of heterodoxy.

Clement of Ancyra (St) M. B. Jan 23
d. 309. Bishop of Ancyra, Asia Minor (now Ankara in Turkey), he was martyred in the reign of Diocletian. His acta are unreliable.

Clement of Cordoba (St) M. Jun 27
d. ?298. He was martyred at Cordoba, Spain, in the reign of Diocletian, and was associated with St Zoilus.

Clement Díez Sahagún (Bl) *see* **Hospitaller Martyrs of Spain**

Clement of Dunblane (St) B. R(OP). Mar 19
d. 1258. He was clothed as a Dominican by St Dominic, preached in Scotland, introduced his order to that country and became bishop of Dunblane.

Clement of Elpidio (Bl) R(OSA). Apr 8
d. 1291. From Osimo, Italy, he became an Augustinian friar and was made superior-general in 1270. He drew up written constitutions which were approved in 1287, and is thus regarded as the order's second founder. His cultus was approved for Orvieto and the Augustinian friars in 1572.

Clement-Mary Hofbauer (Dvorak) (St) R(CSSR). Mar 15
1751–1820. The son of a Czech grazier of Tasswitz in Moravia, Czech Republic, he was a baker before becoming a hermit in 1775. Going to Rome, he was clothed as a consecrated religious at Tivoli near Rome. He joined the Redemptorists at Rome in 1783 and was sent to found a house at Vienna. This proving impossible, he established himself in Warsaw in 1787 with immediate success, and became vicar-general for Middle-Europe in 1793. The house at Warsaw was closed by Napoleon in 1807 and he went back to Vienna for the rest of his life, where he was very popular as a preacher and missioner, being nicknamed the 'Apostle of Vienna'. He was canonized in 1909.

Clement of Ireland (St) P. Mar 20
d. *p*828. From Ireland, he succeeded Alcuin as the head of the palace school under the emperors Charlemagne and Louis the Pious. He wrote an extant analysis of grammatical technique.

Clement Kyuyemon (Bl) M. L. Nov 1
d. 1622. From Arima in Japan, he was the housekeeper of Bl Paul Navarro, wrote his biography and was martyred with him and his two companions at Shimabara. *See* **Japan (Martyrs of)**.

Clement Marchisio (Bl) P. F. Sep 20
1833–1903. A Piedmontese, he was ordained in 1856 and became the parish priest of Rivalba near Turin in 1860, where he stayed for 43 years. He was concerned for young people, especially for teenage girls moving to the towns from the villages in order to find a living. He built a hospital for them, trained such girls in weaving as a alternative to prostitution and founded the 'Daughters of St Joseph' to help him in 1877. He was beatified in 1984.

Clement of Metz (St) B. Nov 23
? He is claimed as the first bishop of Metz, France, having been sent there as a missionary from Rome.

Clement of Ohrid and Comps (SS) B. R. Jul 17
d. 916. Clement, Nahum, Gorazd, Angelarius and Sabas were priests assisting SS Cyril and Methodius on the mission to the Slavs of Great Moravia (roughly the present-day Czech Republic), but were expelled when the Latin clergy of the neighbouring German dioceses procured the suppression of the mission in 885. They migrated to Bulgaria, which had accepted

Christianity in the Byzantine rite through their khan Boris, and founded a monastery at Ohrid (now in the republic of Macedonia). This became the main centre for the development of the infant Bulgarian church, and Clement became its first archbishop. He was the first author (as distinct from translator) to write in Church Slavonic, helped by Nahum, and the five are considered the apostles of Bulgaria and of Macedonia.

Clement Ono (Bl) M. L. Sep 10
d. 1622. A Japanese, he was martyred in the 'Great Martyrdom' at Nagasaki with his three-year-old son, Bl Anthony Ono and Charles Spinola and Comps. *See* **Japan (Martyrs of)**.

Clement of Sandomir (Bl) *see* **Sadoc of Sandomir and Comps**

Clement of Syracuse (St) R. Mar 5
d. *c*800. He was an abbot of St Lucy's abbey at Syracuse, the oldest Western-rite abbey on Sicily.

Clementina Nengapeta Anuarite (Bl) V. Dec 1
1941–1964. She was born near Isiro in north-eastern Belgian Congo (now Congo-Kinshasa) to an animist family but was baptized in 1943, went in 1953 to the school run by the Sisters of the Holy Family at the Bafwabaka mission and joined them as a sacristan and cook. After the independence of the Congo there was civil war, and the Simba faction seized the mission at the end of 1964. Thirty-four of the native sisters were rounded up and taken to Isiro to provide sexual relief for the soldiers, and Clementina was chosen by the commandant. She resisted on the grounds of her consecration and he beat her to death. She was beatified in 1985.

Clementinus, Theodotus and Philomenus (SS) MM. Nov 14
? They were martyred at Heraclea in Thrace, European Turkey, but nothing is known about them.

Cleomenes (St) *see* **Theodolus, Saturninus and Comps**

Cleonicus, Eutropius and Basiliscus (SS) MM. Mar 3
d. ?308. They were in a group of forty or fifty martyred in Pontus, Asia Minor (the south coast of the Black Sea), in the reign of Diocletian. Most seem to have been soldiers but several were crucified and these would have been slaves. They were associated with St Theodore Stratelates.

Cleopatra (St) L. Oct 19
d. 319. A widow in the Holy Land, her story is that she obtained the body of St Varus, who had been martyred in the reign of Diocletian and enshrined it at her home in Dar'ā, Syria. That same day her twelve-year-old son died and appeared to her in a vision with the saint.

Cleophas (St) M? Sep 25
C1st. He was one of the two disciples who met Christ on the road to Emmaus (Luke 24). That is all that is known about him, but the old Roman Martyrology stated that he was martyred by the Jews in his house at Emmaus. He has been identified with Alphaeus, the father of St James the Less, and Hegesippus stated that he was a brother of St Joseph. Both of these suppositions lack foundation.

Clerus (St) M. D. Jan 7
d. *c*300. He was a deacon martyred at Antioch, Syria.

Cletus, 'Pope' (St) Apr 26
C1st. Allegedly the second successor of St Peter as pope (according to St Irenaeus), he is identical to St Anacletus. (The latter originated from the two versions of the name in the papal lists being taken to be different people.) His cultus was suppressed in 1969 but he is mentioned in the Roman canon of the Mass.

Clicerius of Milan (St) B. Sep 20
d. ?438. Nothing is known about this bishop of Milan, Italy.

Clinus (St) Mar 30
? Allegedly a Greek and a monk of Montecassino, Italy, he became the superior of the daughter house of St Peter in the Forest near Pontecorvo.

Clodoald (Cloud) (St) R. Sep 7
d. *c*560. A grandson of King Clovis (France), he was educated by St Clotilde but he fled to Provence when his two brothers were murdered and became a hermit. He eventually became the abbot-founder of the abbey named after him near Paris.

Clodulf (Clou) of Metz (St) B. Jun 8
605–?667. He succeeded his father St Arnulf as bishop of Metz, France, in ?656. He was allegedly bishop for forty years, but the evidence is against this.

Cloelia Barbieri (St) R. F. Jul 13
1847–1870. From near Bologna, Italy, she lost her father early in life and had a pious but

poverty-stricken childhood. Despite having little education she taught the basics to the local poor children and also nursed, attracting several poor young women as helpers. When she was 21 she started the 'Minim Sisters of Our Lady of Sorrows' with four of them under the patronage of St Francis of Paola. She died two years later of tuberculosis as a result of her being malnourished as a child, and was canonized in 1989.

Clotilde (St) L. Jun 3
?474–545. Born at Lyons, France, she was a daughter of the king of Burgundy and married Clovis, the king of the Franks. She was instrumental in his conversion to Catholicism in 496, which event was of the first importance for the future of the Church in the West. She was widowed in 511, and died by St Martin's tomb at Tours.

Clotilde-of-St-Francis-Borgia Paillot (Bl) *see* **Valenciennes (Martyrs of)**

Clotsind (Glodesind) (St) R. Jun 30
?635–714. Daughter of SS Adalbald and Rictrude, she was educated at the nunnery of Marchiennes near Douai, France, by her mother the abbess and founder, and succeeded her as abbess.

Clou *see* **Clodulf**

Cloud *see* **Clodoald**

Clydog (Scledog, Clitanus, Cleodius) (St) L. Nov 3
C6th? He was allegedly a descendent of St Brychan and was killed at Clodock near the Black Mountains in Herefordshire, England.

Cocca (Cucca, Cuach) (St) R. Jun 29
? She is the patron of Kilcock in Co Kildare, Ireland.

Codratus *see* **Quadratus**

Codratus of Corinth and Comps (SS) MM. Mar 10
d. ?258. He was martyred at Corinth, Greece, in the reign of Valerian with Dionysius, Cyprian, Anectus, Paul and Crescens. The Byzantine martyrology lists another sixteen names.

Coemgen *see* **Kevin**

Cogitosus (St) R. Apr 18
C8th? Apparently a monk at Kildare, Ireland, he is the traditional author of the biography of St Brigid.

Cointha (Quinta) (St) M. Feb 8
d. 249. She was a native Egyptian martyred at Alexandria in the reign of Decius, allegedly by being dragged through the city tied to a horse's tail.

Colan *see* **Gollen**

Colette Boilet (St) R(OFM). Mar 6
1381–1447. From Corbie in Picardy, France, she was a carpenter's daughter who tried her vocation as a Benedictine and then as a Beguine before becoming a hermit at Corbie. Finally she recognized her true vocation as being that of restoring the Poor Clares to their original charism, especially as regards absolute poverty. She was made their superior by the anti-pope at Avignon in 1406 and established her Colettine reform in France, Germany and the Low Countries, founding seventeen new convents. She also helped St Vincent Ferrer in his work against the Great Schism. Dying at Ghent, she was canonized in 1807. Her attribute is a lamb, and she is depicted as a Poor Clare with bare feet (one of the distinguishing features of her reform).

Colgan the Wise (St) R. Feb 20
d. ?796. He was abbot of Clonmacnois in Co. Offaly, Ireland, and a friend of Alcuin. A prayer composed by him survives.

Collen (St) May 21
? Nothing is known about the patron of Llangollen, Wales, except that he is also associated with Cornwall.

Colman
This name was extremely popular in the early Irish church. There are ninety-six saints with it in the Donegal martyrology, two hundred and nine in the Book of Leinster and others recorded elsewhere. Many of these are apparently duplicates.

Colman (St) *see* **Kilian, Colman and Totnan**

Colman of Armagh (St) R. Mar 5
C5th. He was a disciple of St Patrick and was buried by him at Armagh, Ireland.

Colman of Cloyne (St) B. R. Nov 26
*c*530–606. From Cork, Ireland, when a young man he was the royal bard at the court of Cashel but was baptized in middle age by St Brendan and became a monk and a priest. He preached in Munster, founded the abbey at Cloyne in Co. Cork and became its first bishop. His cultus was approved in 1903 as the principal patron of the diocese of Cloyne.

Colman of Dromore (St) R. Jun 7
C6th. Either from Argyll or Ulster (there are two traditions), he became the abbot-founder and bishop of Dromore in Co. Down, Ireland, and was allegedly the teacher of St Finian of Clonard. His cultus was approved in 1903 as principal patron of the diocese of Dromore.

Colman Elo (St) R. Sep 26
d. *c*610. A nephew of St Columba, he was the abbot-founder of monasteries at Muckamore in Co. Antrim, Ireland, and at Lynally ('Land-Elo') in Co. Offaly. He is the reputed author of the *Alphabet of Devotion*.

Colman of Glendalough (St) R. Dec 12
d. 659. He is listed as an abbot of Glendalough in Co. Wicklow, Ireland.

Colman of Kilroot (St) B. R. Oct 17
C6th. A disciple of St Ailbe of Emly, he was abbot-bishop of Kilroot near Carrickfergus in Co. Antrim, Ireland.

Colman of Lindisfarne (St) B. R. Feb 18
d. ?676. From the region of Connaught, Ireland, he was a monk of Iona, Scotland, before becoming third abbot-bishop of Lindisfarne, England. He refused to accept the Roman traditions prescribed by the Synod of Whitby in 664, and went back to Ireland with his community. There he founded a monastery on Inishboffin off the coast of Co. Mayo, but had to found another at Mayo for his Saxon monks as they did not get on with their Irish brethren. St Bede and Alcuin wrote in praise of him.

Colman of Lismore (St) B. R. Jan 23
d. ?702. He became abbot-bishop of Lismore in Co. Waterford, Ireland, in 698. Under his care the abbey, with its school, reached the height of its prosperity.

Colman Macduagh (St) B. R. Oct 29
d. ?632. A nobleman of Ireland (Macduagh means 'Son of Duac'), he was a hermit on Arranmore island in Co. Donegal and at Burren in Co. Clare before founding the monastery of Kilmacduagh in Co. Galway and becoming its abbot-bishop. He is the principal patron of the diocese.

Colman (Columban) Mc O'Laoighse (St) R. May 15
C6th. A disciple of St Columba at Iona and of St Fintan of Cloneagh, he founded the monastery of Oughaval in Co. Offaly, Ireland.

Colman McRoi (St) R. D. Jun 16
C6th. A disciple of St Columba, he was the abbot-founder of the monastery of Reachrain on the island of Lambay in Co. Dublin, Ireland.

Colman of Senboth-Fola (St) R. Oct 27
d. *c*632. He was an abbot associated with St Aidan of Ferns in Co. Wexford, Ireland.

Colman (Coloman) of Stockerau (St) M. Oct 13
d. 1012. He was a pilgrim from Ireland or Scotland passing through Austria on his way to the Holy Land, and because he could not speak German he was seized as a spy, tortured and hanged at Stockerau near Vienna. Then he was honoured as a saint because his body (now at the abbey of Melk) worked miracles. He is a minor patron of Austria.

Colmoc *see* **Colman of Dromore**

Coloman of Ungvar (Bl) R. Jun 28
d. *c*1510. A Hungarian Pauline monk at Ungvar (now Uzhhorod in Ukraine), he was a thaumaturge famous for healing the blind, the lame and lepers.

Columba (Columb) (St) V? Sep 17
? There are two places in Cornwall, England, named after this saint, who is alleged to have been a young woman martyred by a pagan ruler.

Columba of Cordoba (St) M. R. Sep 17
d. 853. From Cordoba, Spain, she became a nun at Tábanos but her monastery was destroyed by the Muslims and she went back to Cordoba. There she was urged to convert to Islam but reviled Muhammad instead and was beheaded.

Columba Gabriel (Bl) R(OSB). F. Sep 24
1858–1926. A Pole, born in what is now Ivanovo-Frankivsk in the Ukraine, she became a Benedictine nun at Lviv in 1882. Distinguished by her prayer, purity and love of neighbour, she was made abbess in 1897 but had to move to Rome in 1900 in order to escape unwelcome attention. In 1908 she founded the 'Benedictine Sisters of Charity', an active sisterhood which spread through Italy and to Romania and Madagascar. She was beatified in 1993.

Columba Guardagnoli (Bl) T(OP). May 20
1467–1501. From Rieti in Umbria, Italy, she became a Dominican tertiary at Perugia, founded the convent of St Catherine there and won the respect of all in the city, including its

rulers. She was alleged to have incurred the enmity of Lucrezia Borgia, however. Her cultus was confirmed for Perugia and Rieti in 1627.

Columba (Colum, Colm, Columcille) of Iona (St) R. Jun 9
?521–597. The 'Apostle of Scotland' was of the Clan O'Neill and was born at Gartan in Co. Donegal, Ireland. He studied under St Finian at Clonard, became a monk at Glasnevin and founded monasteries at Derry and Durrow. he emigrated with twelve companions to Iona in Scotland in 563, not as a penance (as the story goes) but as part of the Irish settlement of Dalriada (Argyll) which had begun about 525. Iona became the greatest monastery in north Britain, and for thirty-four years he evangelized the Picts, Strathclyde Britons and Lothian Saxons as well as his fellow Irish settlers ('Scots'), the four races which made up the future kingdom of Scotland. The monastery's influence extended to Northumbria. His biography was written by St Adamnan, and part of the Book of Psalms which he copied (the 'Cathach') survives.

Columba Kim (St) *see* **Korea (Martyrs of)**

Columba McCrimthain (St) R. Dec 12
d. 548. A disciple of St Finian of Clonard from Leinster, he became abbot of a Munster, Ireland, monastery called Tyrdaglas.

Columba Marmion (Bl) R(OSB). Jan 30
1858–1923. He was born at Dublin, Ireland, of an Irish father and French mother, and initially became a diocesan priest. However, in 1886 he became a monk at the Benedictine abbey of Maredsous in Belgium and helped found the abbey of Keizersberg in Louvain. In 1909 he was elected as abbot of Maredsous and became well known as a spiritual director and retreat-giver; his conferences were published and are regarded as spiritual classics. He had to oversee the forced formation of the Maredsous congregation of Benedictines as a result of the disruptions of the First World War. He died in an influenza epidemic and was beatified in 2000.

Columba of Sens (St) V. Dec 31
d. 273. A Spanish refugee from persecution, with other Spaniards she was martyred at Meaux, France, in the reign of Aurelian. Her shrine was at Sens before the Huguenots destroyed it. Her acta are not reliable.

Columban (St) R. Nov 23
?543–615. From Leinster, Ireland, he was a monk at Bangor in Co. Down under St Comgall before becoming a wandering missionary with several companions *c*580. Passing through England and Brittany, he founded the great monastery of Luxeuil in Burgundy in 591 and was abbot for twenty years. His extremely austere rule there became very influential among the rural Frankish nobility, but started to be mitigated soon after his death by insertions from the Benedictine rule. He offended the Frankish court by outspoken criticism of its morals and the local church hierarchy by his insistence on the Celtic observance in his houses, and he was forced into exile in 610. In ?612 he founded the monastery of Bobbio in Lombardy, Italy, where he died. He has left several writings.

Columban of Ghent (St) R. Feb 2
d. 959. He was an Irish hermit at Ghent, Belgium.

Columban the Younger (St) R. Nov 21
d. *p*616. He was a disciple of St Columban and a monk at Luxeuil, France.

Columbinus of Lure (St) R. Sep 13
d. *c*680. He succeeded St Deicola as abbot of Lure in Burgundy, France.

Columbus of Fréjus (Bl) R(OP). Nov 8
d. 1229. A Dominican, he was prior of Toulouse and of Montpellier and died while preaching at Fréjus, France. His shrine is in the cathedral there.

Comgall (St) R. May 10
?520–?602. An Ulsterman, he became a monk at Clonenagh under St Fintan and founded the great monastery of Bangor in Co. Down, Ireland, in ?555. He imposed a severe rule, but the house became a source of many missionary monks such as St Columban. He seems to have travelled to Scotland, Wales and Cornwall but he died at Bangor. His cultus was confirmed in 1903.

Comgan of Killeshin (St) R. Feb 27
d. ?565. He was abbot of Killeshin in Co. Laois, Ireland.

Comgan of Loch Alsh (St) R. Oct 13
C8th. An Irish prince who was a brother of St Kentigern, he emigrated to Scotland with his nephew St Fillan and they became monks on Loch Alsh in Ross. He was buried on Iona.

Cominus
There has been serious confusion between various saints of this name, especially in Ireland.

Cominus of Catania (St) M. May 1
d. 270. He was martyred at Catania, Sicily.

Compiègne, Carmelite Martyrs of (BB) MM. RR(OCD). Jul 17
d. 1794. The Carmel at Compiègne was established in 1641 but it was suppressed in 1790 after the French Revolution and the sisters were forced to disperse and live in the town. They tried to maintain their common life as far as possible, however, and this was charged against them by the local Jacobins. Sixteen of them were taken to Paris, tried and guillotined. They were the superior, Teresa-of-St-Augustine Lindoin, twelve choir sisters, a novice and two externs (the Soiron sisters, Teresa and Catherine). They were beatified in 1906. *See* **French Revolution (Martyrs of)**.

Conald *see* **Chuniald**

Conall (Coel, Conald) (St) R. May 22
C7th. He was abbot of the monastery of Inniscoel in Co. Donegal, Ireland, where there is a holy well named after him.

Conan (St) B. R. Jan 26
d. ?648. From Ireland, he was a monk of Iona, Scotland, and allegedly became bishop of Sodor (the Hebrides) and the Isle of Man.

Concessa (St) M. Apr 8
? She was a martyr venerated at Carthage, Roman Africa.

Concessus (St) *see* **Demetrius, Concessus and Comps**

Concordia (St) *see* **Hippolytus of Rome**

Concordius (St) *see* **Valentine, Concordius and Comps**

Concordius (St) *see* **Zeno, Concordius and Theodore**

Concordius of Spoleto (St) M. Jan 1
d. 175. He was allegedly a sub-deacon of Rome martyred at Spoleto, Italy, in the reign of Marcus Aurelius.

Condedus (Condé, Condède) (St) R. Oct 21
d. *c*690. An Anglo-Saxon, he became a hermit at Fontaine-de-Saint-Valéry on the Somme, France, joined the abbey of Fontenelle in 673 but became a hermit again on an island in the Seine near Caudebec called Belcinac. This has since eroded away.

Congan *see* **Comgan**

Congar *see* **Cumgar**

Conindrus (St) *see* **Romulus and Conindrus**

Conleth (St) B. R. May 4
d. ?519. A hermit at Oldconnell in Co. Kildare, Ireland, he allegedly knew St Brigid and became spiritual director of her nunnery at Kildare. He was eventually made its first bishop and was known as a skilled metalworker, copyist and illuminator. He is the principal patron of the diocese of Kildare.

Connat (Comnatan) (St) R. Jan 1
d. *c*590. She was abbess of the nunnery at Kildare, Ireland.

Conogan (Guenegan) (St) B. R. Oct 16
d. 460. A hermit, he succeeded St Corentin as bishop of Quimper in Brittany, France, and is still venerated there. His name means 'White', so it is 'Albinus' in Latin.

Conon (St) *see* **Papias, Diodorus and Comps**

Conon, Father and Son (SS) MM. May 29
d. 275. They were allegedly tortured to death at Iconium, Asia Minor (now Konya in Turkey) in the reign of Aurelian. Their relics are at Naples. They are unknown in the East.

Conon the Gardener (St) M. Mar 6
d. 250. His story is that he was from Nazareth in the Holy Land and was a gardener at Mandona in Pamphylia, Asia Minor, before being martyred in the reign of Decius.

Conon of Nesi (St) R. Mar 28
d. 1236. He was abbot of the Byzantine-rite monastery of Nesi, Sicily.

Conor O'Devany (Bl) M. B. R(OFM). Jun 20
d. 1611. He was the Franciscan bishop of Down and Conor, Ireland, and was hanged at Dublin with Bl Patrick O'Loughlan, a fellow Franciscan priest. They were beatified in 1992. *See* **Ireland (Martyrs of)**.

Conrad of Bavaria (Bl) R(OCist). Feb 14
?1105–1154. The son of a duke of Bavaria, Germany, he studied at Cologne but became a monk at Morimond before transferring to Clairvaux under St Bernard. He went to the

Holy Land to be a hermit, but died at Modugno in Apulia, Italy, on his way back to visit St Bernard on his deathbed. His cultus was confirmed for Molfetta in 1832.

Conrad Birndorfer of Parzheim (St) R(OFM Cap). Apr 21
1818–1894. From a peasant family at Parzheim in Bavaria, Germany, he became a Capuchin lay brother in 1849 and spent over forty years as doorkeeper at his friary at Altötting. He had the charism of prophecy and discernment of consciences, and was famous for the charitable care he took of callers. He was canonized in 1934.

Conrad Bosinlother (Bl) M. R(OSB). Jan 15
d. 1145. From near Trier, Germany, he became a monk at Siegburg and then abbot of Mondsee in Austria. He set out to reform the abbey and to restore its rights of tithe and was murdered by some nobles at Oberwang as a result. He was venerated at his abbey as a martyr and his relics enshrined in 1682, but his cultus is almost extinct.

Conrad of Constance (St) B. Nov 26
d. 975. A nobleman, he became bishop of Constance, Germany, in 934. He managed to go on pilgrimage to the Holy Land three times and to avoid involvement in secular politics, an unusual feat for a bishop in the Ottonian Empire. He was canonized in 1123.

Conrad of Frisach (Bl) R(OP). Nov 24
d. 1239. A university doctor at Bologna, Italy, he was received as a Dominican by St Dominic and sent to Germany. He died at Magdeburg.

Conrad of Heisterbach (Bl) R(OCist). Nov 25
d. *c*1200. He was a soldier and an official at the court of the Margrave of Thuringia, Germany, before he became a Cistercian at Heisterbach.

Conrad of Hildesheim (Bl) R(OFM). Apr 14
*c*1190–? From Italy, he was among the earliest disciples of St Francis and was sent by him to establish the Franciscans in north Germany. He did so at Hildesheim, where his cultus survived until the Reformation.

Conrad Miliani of Ascoli (Bl) R(OFM). Apr 19
1234–1289. From Ascoli Piceno, Italy, he joined the Franciscans together with the future Pope Nicholas IV and was sent to evangelize the Muslims in Libya. He survived this and was teaching theology in Paris when called to Rome by his confrere who had become pope. He died on the way, at Ascoli.

Conrad Nantwin (Antwin) (Bl) M. L. Aug 1
d. 1286. A pilgrim to Rome, he was passing through Wolfrathshausen near Munich, Germany, when he was seized and burned at the stake by the bailiff of the local lord. There is a church dedicated to him there and a local cultus which has been approved.

Conrad O'Rourke (Bl) *see* **Patrick O'Healey**

Conrad of Offida (Bl) R(OFM). Dec 14
?1237–1306. From Offida near Ascoli Piceno, Italy, he joined the Franciscans in 1251, became a hermit near Ancona and served as priest in that town. He was sympathetic to the eremitic and spiritual aspects of the Franciscan charism. He died at Bastia in Umbria while preaching and had his cultus confirmed for the Franciscans in 1817.

Conrad of Ottobeuren (Bl) R(OSB). Jul 27
d. 1227. He was abbot of Ottobeuren in Bavaria, Germany, from 1191, and rebuilt his abbey only to have it burn down in 1217. He rebuilt it again, and it survives as a working monastery. His cultus is unconfirmed.

Conrad of Piacenza (St) T(OFM). Feb 19
1290–1354. A nobleman of Piacenza, Italy, while out hunting he started a forest fire for which a poor man was blamed and executed. In reparation he gave away his possessions, let his wife join the Poor Clares and became a hermit and a Franciscan tertiary. Initially living near Piacenza, he ended up at Noto in Sicily where he lived for thirty years.

Conrad (Cuno) Pfullingen (St) M. B. Jun 1
d. 1066. A Swabian nobleman, he was appointed bishop of Trier, Germany, by his uncle St Annon, who was archbishop of Cologne. But this violated the rights of the Trier cathedral chapter and he was seized on his way to Trier, thrown over the battlements of the castle of Uerzig and stabbed to death.

Conrad of Seldenbüren (Bl) R(OSB). May 2
d. 1126. From near Zurich, Switzerland, he founded the abbey of Engelberg in the canton of Unterwalden and became a lay brother there.

Being sent to Zurich to defend his abbey's property, he was murdered by the opposition and was afterwards venerated as a martyr.

Conrad of Zähringen (Bl) B. R(OCist). Sep 30
d. 1227. A son of the count of Urach near Stuttgart, Germany, he became a canon at Liege, Belgium, before becoming a Cistercian monk at Villers near Brussels. He was abbot there in 1209, at Clairvaux in 1214, at Cîteaux in 1217 and was then made cardinal-bishop of Porto, near Rome, in 1219. He served a papal legate in Languedoc during the Albigensian Crusade (1224–6) and died at Bari in Italy.

Conradin of Brescia (Bl) R(OP). Nov 1
d. 1429. From Bornato near Brescia, Italy, he became a Dominican at Padua in 1413 and went on to be prior at Bologna. There he was imprisoned twice by the Guelphs for supporting the Pope.

Conran (St) B. Feb 14
? The legend concerning a bishop of the Orkney Islands, Scotland, with this name is worthless.

Consortia (St) R. Jun 22
d. 570? Her story is that she founded a nunnery which had been endowed by the Frankish king Clotaire in return for her having miraculously healed his daughter. She was venerated at Cluny, France, but nothing is known for certain about her.

Constabilis (St) R(OSB). Feb 17
?1060–1124. From Lucania, he became a child-oblate and monk at the abbey of Cava near Salerno, Italy, with St Leo as his abbot. In 1122 he became abbot himself and allegedly founded the town of Castelabbate (of which he is the patron). His cultus was confirmed in 1893.

Constance Meunier (Bl) *see* **Compiègne (Carmelite Martyrs of)**

Constant (St) M. R. Nov 18
d. 777. He was a hermit on the shore of Lough Erne in Co. Fermanagh, Ireland, and was murdered in circumstances which led him to be venerated as a martyr.

Constantia (St) *see* **Felix and Constantia**

Constantian of Javron (St) R. Dec 1
d. 570. From the Auvergne, France, he became a monk at Micy near Orléans and then founded the abbey of Javron near Le Mans.

Constantine (St) *see* **Seven Sleepers**

Constantine I, Emperor (St) L. May 21
d. 337. The son of Constantius Chlorus and St Helena, he was educated at the court of Diocletian and was proclaimed emperor after the sudden death of his father at York in 306. This led to civil war which he won in the West by the battle of the Milvian Bridge in 312, having fought under a Christian standard. The following year he promulgated the Edict of Milan, giving peace and protection to the Church. He had to intervene in the Arian controversy which followed, however, and called and presided over the first ecumenical council at Nicaea in 325. In 330 he established Constantinople as a new Christian capital for the Empire, which remained the greatest city in Christendom for a thousand years. He was only baptized on his deathbed and the nature of his personal commitment to Christianity has been debated. He is venerated in the East as the Thirteenth Apostle.

Constantine of Beauvais (St) B. R. Jun 15
d. ?706. Allegedly a monk at Jumièges under St Philibert, he became bishop of Beauvais, France.

Constantine of Carthage (St) Mar 11
? The old Roman Martyrology lists him as a 'confessor at Carthage, Roman Africa', which implies that he witnessed to the faith in a persecution and survived.

Constantine of Cornwall (St) R? Mar 9
d. ?576. A village near Falmouth in Cornwall, England, and an island near Padstow are named after this alleged Cornish king who became a hermit. His story is unhistorical.

Constantine of Gap (St) B. Apr 12
d. 529. He was the first bishop of Gap, France.

Constantine of Montecassino (St) R(OSB). Jul 21
d. *c*560. He is traditionally the successor of St Benedict as abbot of the monastery of Montecassino, Italy.

Constantine II of Scotland, King (St) M. L. Apr 2
d. 874. He died fighting pagan Danish invaders, was buried at Iona and locally venerated as a martyr.

Constantinople (Martyrs of)
The old Roman Martyrology listed three anonymous groups of martyrs at Constantinople:

Mar 30
d. 353–9. The Orthodox who were killed in the reign of the Arian emperor Valens.

Feb 8
d. 485. The community of the Dion monastery, who were massacred during the Acacian schism for delivering the notice of excommunication to Patriarch Acacius.

Jul 8
d. 832. The Abrahamite monks who were killed in the reign of the iconoclast emperor Theophilus for defending the validity of icons.

Constantius (St) *see* **Maxentius, Constantius and Comps**

Constantius of Ancona (St) L. Sep 23
C6th. He was the sacristan at St Stephen's church in Ancona, Italy, where his veneration is still popular.

Constantius of Aquino (St) B. Sep 1
d. *c*520. Bishop of Aquino, Italy, he is mentioned with approbation in the *Dialogues* of St Gregory the Great.

Constantius Bernocchi (Bl) R(OP). Feb 25
1410–1481. From Fabriano in the Marches, Italy, he became a Dominican at Ascoli when aged fifteen and went on to teach theology at Bologna and Florence. He served as prior of various friaries, including that of Ascoli where he died. His cultus was confirmed for Ascoli in 1811.

Constantius Bojko (Bl) *see* **Podlasia (Martyrs of)**

Constantius of Perugia and Comps (SS) MM. Jan 29
d. 170. Allegedly the first bishop of Perugia, Italy, he was killed with many of his people in the reign of Marcus Aurelius. Their acta are not reliable. *See* **Simplicius, Constantius and Victorian**.

Constantius Roca Huguet (Bl) *see* **Hospitaller Martyrs of Spain**

Constantius of Rome (St) P. Nov 30
C5th. He is listed in the old Roman Martyrology as a priest of Rome who opposed the Pelagians and was persecuted by them.

Contardo d'Este (St) L. Apr 16
d. 1249. A nobleman of Ferrara, Italy, he set out on a pilgrimage to Compostela but only got as far as Broni near Tortona where he died destitute.

Contardo Ferrini (Bl) T(OFM). Oct 17
1859–1902. From Milan, Italy, he took degrees in civil and canon law at Pavia University before teaching at Messina, Mutina and finally again at Pavia. He was a Franciscan tertiary, a member of the Society of St Vincent de Paul, a friend of the future Pope Pius XI and a model of a Catholic university professor. He died at Suna on Lake Maggiore and was beatified in 1947.

Contestus of Bayeux (St) B. Jan 19
d. *c*510. He became bishop of Bayeux, France, in 480.

Conus of Cardossa (St) R(OSB). Jun 3
d. *c*1200. From Diano in Lucania, Italy, he became a monk at Cardossa nearby. His relics were enshrined at Diano and his cultus was confirmed for there in 1871.

Convoyon (St) R(OSB). Jan 5
d. 868. From Brittany, France, he was archdeacon of Vannes but then became a hermit, a monk at Glanfeuil and finally the abbot-founder of St Saviour's at Redon. He was driven from his monastery by the Norse and died in exile. His cultus was confirmed for Redon in 1866.

Conwall (Conval) (St) R. Sep 28
d. *c*630. From Ireland, he was apparently at Iona, Scotland, before helping St Kentigern to evangelize Strathclyde.

Copres (St) *see* **Patermuthius, Copres and Alexander**

Corbinian (St) B. Sep 8
670–730. A Frank from near Fontainebleau, France, he became a hermit and then went to Rome in 709. There he was made a missionary bishop for Bavaria, Germany, by the pope in 717, and established himself at Freising. He founded the abbey of Obermais, where he died.

Corbmac of Durrow (St) R. Jun 21
C6th. He was a disciple of St Columba, who put him in charge of his foundation at Durrow in Co. Offaly, Ireland.

Cordula *Oct 22*
Her story is part of the fictional cycle of legends associated with St Ursula and her cultus was suppressed in 1969.

Cordula-of-St-Dominic Barré (Bl) *see* **Valenciennes (Martyrs of)**

Corebus (St) B. M. Apr 18
d. ?117–138. His story is that he was a prefect at Messina, Sicily, who was converted by St Eleutherius and martyred in the reign of Hadrian. The acta of St Eleutherius are fiction, however, and St Corebus probably never existed.

Corentin (St) R. May 1
? A Cornish hermit, he became a bishop in Brittany, France, perhaps at Quimper where he is venerated. The village of Cury in the Lizard in Cornwall, England, is named after him.

Corfu (Martyrs of) MM. Apr 29
C1st. The 'Seven Robbers' were allegedly converted by St Jason (*see* Acts 17:5) and martyred on the island of Corfu. The Byzantine martyrology lists them as Euphrasius, Faustian, Inischolus, Januarius, Mannonius, Massalius and Saturninus.

Cormac (St) R. Dec 12
C6th. An abbot somewhere in Ireland, he is remembered because he was a friend of St Columba and visited him on Iona, Scotland.

Cormac McCullinan (St) B. Sep 14
d. 908. He was apparently first bishop of Cashel in Co. Tipperary, Ireland, and was chosen as king of Munster in 902. He was killed in battle. The *Psalter of Cashel*, compiled by him, still exists.

Cornelia (St) *see* **Theodolus, Anesius and Comps**

Cornelius (St) *see* **Stephen, Pontian and Comps**

Cornelius, Pope (St) M? Sep 16
d. 253. He became pope in 251 after a fourteen-month vacancy caused by the Decian persecution. One of his most serious problems concerned the re-admission to communion of those who had apostatized during that persecution, and he advocated a lenient policy towards these. A rigorist faction denied that such people could be forgiven, however, and it elected Novatian as anti-pope. Cornelius's policy prevailed, helped by the support of such as St Cyprian of Carthage, and Novatian was excommunicated (his sect, however, survived for a long time). The persecution was revived and St Cornelius was exiled to Civita Vecchia where he died. There is no evidence that he was actually a martyr, although St Cyprian described him as such. His tomb in Rome is extant and he is mentioned in the Roman canon of the Mass. His attribute is a cow or a cow's horn (a pun on his name).

St Cornelius, Sep 16

Cornelius of Caesarea (St) B? Feb 2
C1st. He was the centurion baptized by St Peter at Caesarea in the Holy Land (Acts 10), and was traditionally regarded as the first bishop of that city.

Cornelius McConchailleach
(St) B. R(CR). Jun 4
?1120–1176. Born in Ireland, he became an Augustinian canon regular at Armagh in 1140 and went on to become abbot in 1151 and archbishop in 1174. He died at Chambéry in Savoy, France, on his way back from a pilgrimage to Rome and has a popular cultus there.

Cornelius van Wijk (St)
M. R(OFM). Jul 9
d. 1572. From Wijk bij Duurstede near Utrecht, Netherlands, he became a Franciscan at Gorinchem and was hanged at Briel with eighteen companions. *See* **Gorinchem (Martyrs of)**.

Corona (St) *see* **Victor and Corona**

Corona of Elche (St) R(OSB)? Apr 24
? She was a nun at Elche near Valencia, Spain.

Cosmas and Damian (SS) MM. Sep 26
d. ?303. Their story is that they were Arab brothers who practised medicine and who did not charge for their services (hence their nickname of 'Anargyrioi', or 'Moneyless', in the East). According to tradition, they were martyred at Cyrrhus near Antioch, Syria, in the reign of Diocletian and their relics were taken to Rome. Their cultus was extremely popular in the West in the Middle Ages and they are mentioned in the Roman canon of the Mass. Their attribute is an item of medical equipment (e.g. a mortar and pestle). Their acta are legendary, and assert that they were martyred with their mother Theodora and their brothers Anthimus, Euprepius and Leontius.

Cosmas of Aphrodisia (St) M. B. Sep 10
d. 1160. From Palermo, Sicily, he became bishop of Aphrodisia and died of ill-treatment during the Muslim conquest of his city.

Cosmas Brun Arará (Bl) *see* **Hospitaller Martyrs of Spain**

Cosmas Takeya (St) M. T(OFM). Feb 6
d. 1597. A Japanese Franciscan tertiary, he was an interpreter for the Franciscan missionaries and was crucified at Nagasaki with St Paul Miki and Comps. *See* **Japan (Martyrs of)**.

Cosmas Takeya Sozaburo
(Bl) M. Nov 18
d. 1619. A Korean, he was taken to Japan as a prisoner of war. While there he joined the Confraternity of the Holy Rosary and sheltered Bl John of St Dominic, for which he was burned at Nagasaki with BB Leonard Kimura and Comps. *See* **Japan (Martyrs of)**.

Cosmo de Carbognano *see* **Gomidas**

Cottidus, Eugene and Comps
(SS) MM. Sep 6
? They are listed as having been martyred in Cappodocia, Asia Minor, Cottidus being a deacon, but nothing is known.

Craton and Comps (SS) MM. Feb 25
d. ?273. Allegedly a philosopher and rhetorician from Athens, he was teaching in Rome when he was converted by St Valentine of Terni and martyred with his family in the reign of Aurelian.

Credan (St) R. Aug 19
d. *c*780. He was abbot of Evesham near Worcester, England, in the reign of King Offa of Mercia.

Crescens (St) B? Jun 27
C1st. He was a disciple of St Paul, who referred to him as having gone to Galatia in Asia Minor (2 Tim 4:10). Thus he is traditionally the first bishop of the Galatians and was martyred there in the reign of Trajan. There are other traditions, seriously confused and unreliable, associating him with Vienne in France and Mainz in Germany (apparently as a result of confusing Galatia with Gaul).

Crescens (St) *see* **Codratus of Corinth and Comps**

Crescens (St) *see* **Symphorosa of Tivoli and Comps**

Crescens (St) *see* **Valerian, Urban and Comps**

Crescens of Myra (St) M. Apr 15
? He was burned at the stake at Myra in Lycia, Asia Minor.

Crescens of Rome and Comps (SS) May 28
d. ?244. He was tortured and burned at Rome with Dioscorides and Paul. The old Roman Martyrology added Helladius, who was not of the group.

Crescentia (St) *see* **Vitus, Modestus and Crescentia**

Crescentia Hoss *see* **Mary-Crescentia Hoss**

Crescentian (St) *see* **Ariston and Comps**

Crescentian (St) *see* **Hilaria, Digna and Comps**

Crescentian (St) *see* **Valerian, Urban and Comps**

Crescentian, Victor, Rosula and Generalis (SS) MM. Sep 14
d. ?258. They are alleged to have been martyred in Carthage, Roman Africa, with St Cyprian.

Crescentian of Rome (St) M. Nov 24
d. 309. He was racked in the presence of SS Cyriac, Largus and Smagagdus at Rome, dying as a result in the reign of Maxentius.

Crescentian of Saldo (St) M. Jun 1
d. ?287. He was allegedly a soldier beheaded at Saldo in Umbria, Italy, but he may not have existed.

Crescentian of Sassari (St) M. May 31
d. *c*130. He was martyred at Sassari, Sardinia, in the reign of Hadrian, being associated with SS Gabinus and Crispulus. His veneration is still popular there.

Crescentiana (St) M. May 5
C5th? A church in Rome was dedicated to her by the end of the C5th, but nothing else is known.

Crescentio (St) *see* **Narcissus and Crescentio**

Crescentius (St) M. Sep 14
d. *c*300. An eleven-year-old son of St Euthymius, he fled with his father to Perugia, Italy, in the persecution of Diocletian but was brought back to Rome when orphaned to be tortured and beheaded.

Crescentius (St) *see* **Dominic, Victor and Comps**

Crescentius (St) *see* **Gaius and Crescentius**

Crescentius (St) *see* **Maxentius, Constantius and Comps**

Crescentius *see* **Crescens**

Crescentius of Florence (St) S. Apr 19
d. ?396. He was a sub-deacon to St Zenobius at Florence, Italy, and a disciple of St Ambrose.

Cresconius (St) *see* **Valerian, Urban and Comps**

Crete (Martyrs of) *see* **Theodulus, Saturninus and Comps**

Crewenna (St) R. Feb 1
C5th. She accompanied St Breaca from Ireland to Cornwall, England, and left her name to Crowan near Helston.

Crispin (St) *see* **Claudius, Crispin and Comps**

Crispin (St) *see* **Julius, Potamia and Comps**

Crispin and Crispinian (SS) MM. Oct 25
d. ?285. Brothers who were shoemakers, they were allegedly beheaded at Soissons, France, in the reign of Diocletian but were probably Roman martyrs whose relics were transferred. Their veneration was popular during the Middle Ages (one legend had them living at Faversham in Kent, England) but has faded away. They were patrons of shoemakers and their attributes are shoes or cobbling tools.

Crispin of Ecija (St) M. B. Nov 19
C4th. A bishop of Ecija in Andalucia, Spain, he was beheaded in the reign of Maximian Herculeus.

Crispin Fioretti of Viterbo (St) R(OFM Cap). May 23
1668–1750. From Viterbo, Italy, he became a Capuchin lay brother there and worked as a cook. Later he was at Tolfa, then at Rome and Albano and finally he died at Rome where his cultus is extremely popular. He had great spiritual wisdom, was heroic in nursing sick people and called himself the 'Capuchin's donkey'. He was canonized in 1982.

Crispin of Pavia (SS) BB. Jan 7
Pavia in Lombardy, Italy, has two saints among its bishops called Crispin. The first was bishop for thirty-five years in the first half of the C3rd, and the second was bishop during the pontificate of St Leo the Great and signed the acts of the Council of Milan in 451. The latter seems to have the feast day listed.

Crispina (St) M. Dec 5
d. 304. A married woman with several children from Thagura in Numidia, Roman Africa, she refused to offer pagan sacrifice and was tortured and beheaded in the reign of Diocletian. Her acta are genuine, and St Augustine preached two sermons about her.

Crispulus (St) *see* **Gabinus and Crispulus**

Crispulus and Restitutus (SS) MM. Jun 10
C1st? They were possibly martyred at Rome in the reign of Nero. The old Roman Martyrology depends on Rabanus Maurus in assigning them to Spain, however.

Crispus (St) *see* **John and Crispus**

Crispus and Gaius (SS) MM? BB? Oct 4
C1st. They were the only ones that St Paul baptized at Corinth (1Cor 1:14), Crispus being ruler of the synagogue (Acts 18:8) and Gaius being probably referred to by St Paul as 'my host' (Rom 16:23) and by St John as 'dearly beloved' in his third letter. Traditionally they became bishops of Aegina and Thessalonika, Greece, respectively and were martyred.

Cristiolus (St) R. Nov 3
C7th. The brother of St Sulian, he was the

founder of several churches, notably Llangristiolus on Anglesey, Wales.

Croidan, Medan and Degan (SS) RR. Jun 4
C6th. They were three disciples of St Petroc in Cornwall, England.

Cronan Beg (St) B. Jan 7
C7th. His surname means 'Little'. He was bishop at Aendrum in Co. Down, Ireland.

Cronan of Roscrea (St) R. Apr 28
d. ?626. From Munster, he founded several monasteries, notably Roscrea in Co. Tipperary, Ireland.

Cronan the Tanner (St) R. Jun 3
d. 617. He was a disciple of St Kevin at Glendalough, Ireland.

Cronan the Wise (St) B. Feb 9
C8th? His nickname came from his ability to systematize Irish canon law. He was probably the same as St Roman, bishop of Lismore. Allegedly he concealed his identity to become a monk at Iona but was recognized by St Columba there.

Cronidas (St) *see* **Philetus, Lydia and Comps**

Cronion (St) *see* **Julian, Cronion and Comps**

St Cross
Churches with this dedication in England are commemorating not a saint but the cross of Christ.

Crotates (St) *see* **Apollo, Isacius and Comps**

Crowland (Martyrs of) *see* **Theodore of Crowland and Comps**

Crummine (St) B. Jun 28
C5th. A disciple of St Patrick, he was made bishop by him of Lackan in Co. Westmeath, Ireland.

Ctesiphon (St) *see* **Torquatus, Ctesiphon and Comps**

Cuan (Mochua) (St) R. Dec 24
d. ?657. From the region of Connaught, Ireland, he was a warrior before he became a monk and founded the monasteries at Timahoe in Co. Laois and at Derinish in Co. Cavan, where he died. There are more than fifty other Irish saints of the same name (many duplicates).

Cuby *see* **Cybi**

Cucuphas (Cugat, Guinefort) (St) M. Jul 25
d. 304. A Punic nobleman from Scillis in Roman Africa, he went to Spain and was martyred near Barcelona. On the site arose the abbey of St Cugat del Valles, and he became one of the most popular of the Spanish martyrs. Prudentius wrote some poetry in his honour.

Culmatius (St) *see* **Gaudentius and Culmatius**

Cumgar (Cungar, Cyngar, Congar, Docuinus, Doguinus) (St) R. Nov 7
C6th or C8th. A Celtic monk, he founded a monastery at Congresbury in Somerset, England, and was buried there (the name means 'Cumgar's tomb'). His C12th biography is unreliable and confuses him with other Welsh saints having similar names.

Cumine the White (St) R. Feb 24
d. 669. An Irish abbot of Iona, Scotland, he wrote a biography of St Columba.

Cummian (Cumian, Cummin) of Bobbio (St) B. R. Jun 9
d. *c*720. An Irish bishop, he went on pilgrimage and ended up at Bobbio in Lombardy, Italy, where he became a monk.

Cummian Fada (St) R. Nov 12
d. 662. A monk at Clonfert, Ireland, he went on to be the abbot-founder of the monastery of Kilcummin in Co. Offaly. He was noted for defending the Roman computation of Easter against the Celtic one traditional at the time in Ireland.

Cunegund *see* **Kinga**

Cunegund the Empress (St) R(OSB). Mar 3
d. 1039. She was married to Emperor St Henry II in 999, and helped to found the new diocese of Bamburg and the nunnery of Kaufungen. A year after she was widowed she entered the latter as a nun, in 1025. It has been claimed that the marriage was not consummated (there were no children) and she has been liturgically celebrated as a virgin as a result.

Cunera (St) Jun 12
? This saint has a cultus (once popular in Germany) based at Rhenen in the Netherlands. Her story is worthless legend, derived perhaps from the murder of a servant girl by her mistress in the Middle Ages.

Cunibert of Cologne (St) B. Nov 12
d. ?663. A Frankish courtier from Moselle, France, he became archdeacon of Trier, Germany, and then archbishop of Cologne in 623. He was regent of Frankish Austrasia while King St Sigebert III was a minor and founded many churches and monasteries. His shrine is at Cologne. His extant medieval biographies are unreliable.

Cunibert of Maroilles (St) R. Sep 16
d. *c*680. He succeeded St Humbert as abbot of Maroilles near Cambrai, France.

Cuno of Einsiedeln (Bl) Mar 8
d. *p*978. Son of St Gerold, he was a monk with his brother Bl Ulric at the Swiss abbey of Einsiedeln and has a cultus there.

Curcodomus (St) D. May 4
C3rd. A Roman deacon, he became a helper of St Peregrinus, first bishop of Auxerre, France.

Curé d'Ars *see* **John-Mary Vianney**

Curig (St) B. Jun 16
C6th. He is alleged to have been bishop of Llanbadarn in Wales but there is confusion between several saints of this name. There are several churches with this dedication.

Curitan *see* **Boniface**

Curonotus of Iconium (St) M. B. Sep 12
d. *c*258. Bishop of Iconium, Asia Minor (now Konya in Turkey), he was martyred in the reign of Valerian.

Cury *see* **Corentin**

Cuthbert of Canterbury (St) B. R. Oct 26
d. 758. A monk of Lyminge in Kent, England, he became bishop of Hereford in ?736 and archbishop of Canterbury in 740. He was a correspondent of St Boniface in Germany. His cultus was unconfirmed.

Cuthbert of Lindisfarne (St) B. R. Sep 4
d. 687. Possibly of Saxon parents (this is uncertain), he was a shepherd until he became a monk at Melrose, Scotland, in 651, which abbey followed Celtic traditions. He was guest-master at Ripon, England, until that monastery converted to Roman practices, upon which he returned to Melrose and became prior there and then at Lindisfarne. He accepted the verdict of the Synod of Whitby in 664 and helped convert his monastery to Roman customs, however, then he went to Farne as a hermit in 676. In 684 he was made bishop of Lindisfarne, but resigned and returned to Farne just before he died. His relics were eventually enshrined at Durham in 995 and became the most popular focus of pilgrimage in the North of England in the Middle Ages. They were left in situ at the Reformation. He is depicted holding the severed head of St Oswald and accompanied by the swans and otters that he befriended as a hermit.

St Cuthbert of Lindisfarne, Sep 4

Cuthbert Mayne (St) M. P. Nov 30
1544–1577. From near Barnstaple in Devon, England, his family was Protestant and he became an Anglican minister but he converted while studying at Oxford and was eventually ordained at Douai. In 1575 he went to Cornwall but was captured within a year and executed at Launceston. The protomartyr of the English seminaries, he was canonized in 1970. *See* **England (Martyrs of)**.

Cuthburga and Quenburga (SS) R. Aug 31
d. ?725. They were sisters of the king of Wessex, England. Cuthburga married Aldfrid, a son of King Oswy of Northumbria, in 688 but apparently the marriage was not consummated and he allowed her to become a nun at Barking under St Hildelid. Then she became the abbess-founder (allegedly with her sister) of the great double monastery of Wimborne in Dorset, which later took an active part in the mission to the Germans by St Boniface.

Cuthman (St) R. Feb 8
C9th. He was a hermit at Steyning in Sussex, England, and when the church there was granted to the French abbey of Fécamp they appropriated his relics.

Cutias (St) *see* **Maximus, Claudius and Comps**

Cybar *see* **Eparchius**

Cybi (Cuby) (St) R. Nov 8
C6th. He was abbot-founder of a monastery at Caer-gybi (Holyhead) on Anglesey, Wales. The popularity of his ancient veneration is evidenced by churches dedicated to him at Llangibby, Gwent, at Llangybi, Gwynedd, and at Tregony, Landulph and Cuby in Cornwall. The legends about him are unreliable.

Cynderyn *see* **Kentigern**

Cyneburga *see* **Kyneburga**

Cynfarch *see* **Kingsmark**

Cynfran (St) Nov 11
C5th. One of the sons of St Brychan, he is the patron of Llysfaen in Gwynedd, Wales, where he has a holy well.

Cynllo (St) Jul 17
C7th. Traditionally a brother of St Teilo, he has several churches dedicated to him in Wales.

Cynog *see* **Canog**

Cynwl (St) R. Apr 30
C6th. Brother of St Deiniol of Bangor, he was a hermit of Wales who had several churches dedicated to him.

Cyprian (St) *see* **Codratus of Corinth and Comps**

Cyprian (St) *see* **Felix, Cyprian and Comps**

Cyprian (St) *see* **Sabinus and Cyprian**

Cyprian and Justina *Sep 26*
d. ?303. The legend is that Cyprian was a pagan astrologer who tried to seduce Justina, a Christian maiden, and was converted by her instead, both of them being beheaded at Nicomedia, Asia Minor, in the reign of Diocletian. The story is fictional and the cultus was suppressed in 1969.

Cyprian of Brescia (St) B. Apr 21
d. 582. A bishop of Brescia, Italy, he has his shrine in that city.

Cyprian of Carthage (St) M. B. Sep 16
*c*200–258. Thascius Cecilianus Cyprianus was a Roman African lawyer who became a Christian in ?245 and bishop of Carthage in 248. He was one of the earliest Latin church fathers, writing numerous theological treatises and letters. His support for the lenient policy of Pope St Cornelius in dealing with the lapsed was decisive against the rigorist party led by Novatian, but he erred in teaching that the baptism of heretics is invalid. He went into hiding during the persecution of Decius but was seized and martyred in the reign of Valerian. His acta are genuine, and he is mentioned in the Roman canon of the Mass.

Cyprian Subran (St) R. Dec 9
d. 586. Originally a monk at Périgueux in the Dordogne, France, he became a hermit nearby at the place where the village of Saint-Cyprien now is.

Cyprian Tansi (Bl) R(OCSO). (Jan 20)
1903–1964. He was an Igbo from a farming family of the Aguleri region near Onitsha in Nigeria. He was brought up as an animist but was baptized when aged nine and went on to be ordained as the second indigenous priest of the Onitsha diocese in 1937. He was appointed the parish priest of Dunukofia, where his zeal and example led to a major increase in vocations. In response to his bishop's wish that a contemplative monastery be founded in his diocese, he became a Cistercian at Mount St Bernard near Leicester, England, in 1950. He was shocked when the decision was taken in 1963 to make the foundation in Cameroon instead, but accepted this and was about to become novice-master there when he died at Leicester of an aneurysm. He was beatified in 1998.

Cyprian of Toulon (St) B. R. Oct 3
d. *c*545. A monk at St Victor's Abbey at Marseilles, France, he was a disciple of St Caesarius of Arles and wrote his biography. He became bishop of Toulon in 516 and vigorously opposed the local semi-Pelagians.

Bl Cyprian Tansi, Jan 20 *(see p. 137)*

Cyr *see* **Quiricus and Julitta**

Cyra (St) *see* **Marana and Cyra**

Cyrenia and Juliana (SS) MM. Nov 1
d. 306. They were burned at Tarsus in Cilicia, Asia Minor, in the reign of Maximian.

Cyria (St) *see* **Zenais, Cyria and Comps**

Cyriac, Cyriaca
These names are also spelt Quiriacus, Quiriaca; or Kyriacus, Kyriaca; or Kiriacus, Kiriaca; or Dominicus, Dominica. The last pair are the Latin equivalents.

Cyriac (St) *see* **Antiochus and Cyriac**

Cyriac (St) *see* **Exuperius, Zoë and Comps**

Cyriac (St) *see* **Florentius, Julian and Comps**

Cyriac (St) *see* **Orentius, Heros and Comps**

Cyriac (St) *see* **Paul and Cyriac**

Cyriac (St) *see* **Paul, Lucius, and Cyriac**

Cyriac (St) *see* **Tarcisius, Zoticus and Comps**

Cyriac and Apollinaris (SS) MM. Jun 21
? They are listed as Roman African martyrs but nothing else is known.

Cyriac and Julitta *see* **Quiricus and Julitta**

Cyriac, Largus, Smaragdus and Comps (SS) MM. Aug 8
d. ?304. They were martyred and buried on the Ostian Way outside Rome, perhaps in the reign of Diocletian. There is a church in Rome dedicated to St Cyriac but the acta are unreliable and nothing else is known. The cultus was confined to particular calendars in 1969.

Cyriac and Paula (SS) MV. Jun 18
d. 305. They were stoned to death at Malaga, Spain, in the reign of Diocletian.

Cyriac, Paulillus and Comps (SS) MM. Dec 19
d. 303. They were martyred at Nicomedia, Asia Minor, in the reign of Diocletian. Listed also are Secundus, Anastasius and Sindimius. Nothing else is known.

Cyriac (Quiriacus) of Ancona (St) M? B? May 4
? The unreliable acta of this patron of Ancona, Italy, describe him as a bishop of Jerusalem martyred in the reign of Julian. Jerusalem had no bishop of this name, so (if he existed) he was perhaps a bishop of Ancona martyred while on a pilgrimage in the Holy Land.

Cyriac-Elias-of-the-Holy-Family Chavarra (Bl) B. F. Jan 3
1805–1871. Born near Changanachary in Kerala, India, he was ordained in the Malabar rite in 1829 and started a religious foundation at Mannanam in 1831. This prospered, its work being preaching, spiritual missions and teaching in seminaries, and six other houses for men and one for women were also opened. There was a schism in the Malabar rite when an Assyrian bishop arrived in 186, and Cyriac was made Vicar-Apostolic to counter this. He purified the Malabar liturgy as well as writing much. He was beatified in 1986.

Cyriac of Constantinople (St) B. Oct 27
d. 606. He was the sacristan at Hagia Sophia in Constantinople before becoming patriarch there in 595.

Cyriac the Great (St) R. Sep 29
448–556. One of the famous monks of the Judaean Desert, as a teenager he went from Corinth to the Holy Land and became a monk under SS Euthymius and Gerasimus. During his long life (he died a centenarian) he opposed the Origenist errors popular among monks in the

Holy Land at the time. His stone-built cell survives in the desert at Sousakim where he spent the latter years of his life as the only hermit able to survive in such a barren place, the driest in the Holy Land (just west of the southern part of the Dead Sea). His biography was written by Cyril of Scythopolis.

Cyriac of Nicomedia and Comps (SS) MM. Apr 7
? These eleven are listed as having been martyred at Nicomedia, Asia Minor.

Cyriaca (St) *see* **Photina and Comps**

Cyriaca of Nicomedia and Comps (SS) VV. May 19
d. 307. Six maidens, they were burned at Nicomedia, Asia Minor, in the reign of Galerius.

Cyriaca (Dominica) of Rome (St) L. Aug 21
d. 249. She is described in the legend of St Laurence as a wealthy Roman widow who used to shelter persecuted Christians and whose house he used when distributing alms.

Cyril (St) *see* **Anastasia and Cyril**

Cyril (St) *see* **Archelaus, Cyril and Photius**

Cyril (St) *see* **Paul, Cyril and Comps**

Cyril (St) *see* **Primus, Cyril and Secundarius**

Cyril, Aquila and Comps (SS) MM. Aug 1
? The companions were Peter, Domitian, Rufus and Menander. Cyril seems to have been a bishop of Tomi (on the Black Sea coast of Romania), Peter was a duplicate of the apostle and Rufus was a martyr of Rome. The group was erroneously associated with Philadelphia in Asia Minor.

Cyril and Methodius (SS) RR. Feb 14
d. 869 and 885. The 'Apostles of the Slavs' were brothers from Thessalonika, sons of a government official. Constantine was a brilliant student at Constantinople and became a priest and a professor at the university there. Methodius became a provincial governor and ended up in a monastery on the Bithynian Olympus. In 863 they went to evangelize Moravia, a Slav kingdom (now part of the Czech republic), for which they translated the Scriptures and liturgical texts into Slavonic. This caused opposition from the local Latin clergy so they went to Rome for approval. There Constantine became a monk with the name Cyril and quickly died. Methodius got the necessary approval and returned to Moravia as bishop and legate, but continued to be opposed by the German clergy for his remaining sixteen years. His work was initially successful but not lasting in Moravia. It bore greater fruit in the other Slavic lands, and the brothers were declared co-patrons of Europe with St Benedict in 1980.

Cyril, Rogatus and Comps (SS) MM. Mar 8
? They are listed as Roman African martyrs with Cyril as a bishop, but nothing is known. Also listed are Felix, another Rogatus, Beata, Herenia, Felicity, Urban, Silvanus and Mamillus.

Cyril of Alexandria (St) B. Dr. Jun 27
?376–444. From Alexandria, Egypt, he was a nephew of Patriarch Theophilus and became patriarch himself in 412. He fought the surviving paganism in Egypt (with violent results) and strongly opposed the Christological teachings of Nestorius, Patriarch of Constantinople. These were condemned at the Council of Ephesus in 431, at which he presided and which marked the height of the Egyptian Church's influence. He was a great theologian and one of the greatest Eastern fathers, being venerated as the chief teacher of the Coptic and Ethiopian churches. He was declared a doctor of the Church in 1882.

Cyril of Antioch (St) B. Jul 22
d. *c*300. He became patriarch of Antioch, Syria, in 280 and endured the persecution of Diocletian, but seems not to have been a martyr.

Cyril of Caesarea (St) L. May 29
d. ?251. His story is that he was a boy at Caesarea in Cappadocia, Asia Minor, who converted without his father's knowledge and who was thrown out of his home and tortured as a result. He does not seem to have been a martyr.

Cyril of Constantinople (St) R(OC?). Mar 6
1138–1234. A Greek from Constantinople, he became a priest but fled to the Holy Land to avoid the troubles caused by the Fourth Crusade. He became a hermit on Mount Carmel but the story that he became a Carmelite prior-general is a fabrication. There are writings mistakenly attributed to him.

Cyril of Gortyna (St) M. B. Jul 9
d. 250. He was an elderly bishop of Gortyna in Crete martyred in the reign of Decius.

Cyril of Heliopolis (St) M. D. Mar 29
d. ?362. A deacon of Heliopolis (Baalbek) in Lebanon, he destroyed some idols there and was disembowelled by the townsfolk as a result in the reign of Julian. The city remained a pagan stronghold for another century.

Cyril of Jerusalem (St) B. Dr. Mar 18
?315–386. From near Jerusalem, he became bishop of that city *c*350. He firmly opposed the Arians and spent a total of seventeen years in exile as a result. His fame derives from his set of catechetical lectures given in Lent to those being baptized at Easter, which led to his being declared a doctor of the Church in 1882.

Cyril of Sandomir (Bl) *see* **Sadoc of Sandomir and Comps**

Cyril-Bertrand Sanz Tejedor and Comps (SS) MM. RR. Oct 9
d. 1934. The Brothers of the Christian Schools had a school at Turón in Spain, south of the Sierra Nevada and, on October 8, Innocent-of-Mary-Immaculate Canoura Arnau, a Passionist priest, had come to hear confession and to say Mass. While assembled to celebrate Mass he and eight Brothers were seized by Republicans, taken to the cemetery where graves had been dug, and shot. Cyril had been Rector for two years; Marcian-Joseph López López was the sacristan and cook; Julian-Alfred Fernández Zapico prepared the pupils for First Communion; Victorianus-Pius Bernabé Cano was the choirmaster; Benjamin-Julian Alfonsus Andrés and Innocent-of-Mary-Immaculate Canoura Arna had just made final vows, and there were three juniors: Augustus-Andrew Martín Fernandez, Benedict-of-Jesus Valdivieso Saez and Anicetus-Adolf Seco Gutierrez. They were canonized in 1999. *See* **Spanish Civil War (Martyrs of)**.

Cyril of Trier (St) B. May 19
C5th. The relics of this bishop of Trier, Germany, are at the abbey church of St Matthias in that city.

Cyrilla of Cyrene (St) M. Jul 5
d. *c*300. An old widow of Cyrene, Libya, she died under torture in the reign of Diocletian.

Cyrilla of Rome (St) V. Oct 28
d. ?269. She was allegedly the daughter of St Tryphonia and features in the legendary acta of St Laurence. Nothing is known about her.

Cyrinus (St) *see* **Alphius, Philadelphus and Cyrinus**

Cyrinus (St) *see* **Basilides, Cyrinus and Comps**

Cyrinus, Primus and Theogenes (SS) MM. Jan 3
d. 320. They are listed as three soldiers who were martyred at Cyzicus on the Sea of Marmara, Asia Minor. However, the listing in the old Roman Martyrology seems to be a garbled rendering of 'At Cyzicus, at the entrance of the Hellespont, the memory of the martyr Theogenes'.

Cyrinus of Rome (St) M. Oct 25
d. *c*300. He was martyred at Rome in the reign of Diocletian and is mentioned in the fabricated acta of Pope St Marcellinus.

Cyrion, Bassian, Agatho and Moses (SS) MM. Feb 14
? Martyrs of Alexandria, Egypt, they were listed together because they were all burned at the stake. Respectively they were a priest, lector, exorcist and layman.

Cyrion and Candidus (SS) *see* **Forty Martyrs of Sebaste**

Cyrus and John (SS) MM. Jan 31
d. ?303. A physician and a soldier who had met in the desert after fleeing persecution in Alexandria, Egypt, they returned to the city to assist an imprisoned woman and her three daughters and were themselves martyred. Their shrine near Canopus became famous and they are among the most popular martyrs of the Coptic Church.

Cyrus of Carthage (St) B? Jul 14
? When Cardinal Baronius revised the old Roman Martyrology he inserted this otherwise unknown bishop on the basis of a reference in Possidus's biography of St Augustine where the latter is described as giving a sermon on his feast-day. 'Cyrus' may simply be a copyist's error for 'Cyprian'.

Cythinus (St) *see* **Scillitan Martyrs**

D

Dabeoc *see* **Beoc**

Dabius (Davius) (St) R. Jul 22
? An Irish priest who worked in Scotland, he may be identical to St Movean. Several churches in Scotland are dedicated to him.

Dacian (St) *see* **Aretius and Dacian**

Dacius (St) *see* **Caesarius, Dacius and Comps**

Dadas (St) *see* **Maximus, Quintilian and Dadas**

Dadas, Casdoe and Gabdelas
(SS) MM. Sep 29
*c*310–368. A married noble Persian couple and (probably) their son, they were at the court of Shah Shapur II and were martyred after vicious tortures.

Dafrosa (Affrosa) (St) M? Jan 4
? According to the worthless acta of St Bibiana, Dafrosa was her mother and was martyred at Rome in the reign of Julian. She probably never existed.

Dagan *see* **Decuman**

Dagobert II of Austrasia
(St) M. L. Dec 23
652–679. A son of King St Sigisbert III of Frankish Austrasia, he was banished after his father's death to an Irish monastery in 656 but recalled and made king in 675. He founded several abbeys. He was killed by order of Ebroin, the mayor of the palace, at Stenay near Verdun and afterwards popularly regarded in Lorraine as a martyr.

Daig (Dagaeus, Daganus) McCairill (St) B. R. Aug 18
d. 586. A disciple of St Finian, he founded a monastery at Inishkeen in Co. Louth, Ireland, and became its abbot-bishop. He was a famous maker of sacred objects in metal.

Dallan Forgaill (St) M. R. Jan 29
d. 598. A relative of St Aidan of Ferns, he was from the region of Connaught, Ireland, and became a famous scholar. His most famous work is a poem in honour of St Columba, *Ambra Choluim Kille*. He was killed by pirate raiders.

Dalmatius of Constantinople
(St) R. Aug 3
d. *c*440. Originally a soldier in the bodyguard of Emperor Theodosius I at Constantinople, he became a monk in that city and was made archimandrite of all its monasteries by the Council of Ephesus.

Dalmatius Moner (Bl) R(OP). Sep 26
1291–1341. From near Gerona, Spain, he became a Dominican there and led an extremely austere life in the friary, refusing all positions of responsibility. His cultus was confirmed for Gerona in 1721.

Dalmatius of Pavia (St) M. B. Dec 5
d. 304. From a pagan noble family at Monza near Milan, he was a missionary in north Italy until he was made bishop of Pavia. That was in the year before he was martyred in the reign of Maximian Herculeus.

Dalmatius of Rodez (St) B. Nov 13
d. 580. He became bishop of Rodez, France, in 524 and had to defend his people against persecution by the Arian Visigoths.

Damascus (Martyrs of) *see* **Emmanuel Ruiz and Comps**

Damasus, Pope (St) Dec 11
?304–384. Born in Rome of Spanish parents, he became a deacon at the Spanish church of St Laurence there and went on to be elected pope in 366. (The election was violently contested and there was an anti-pope, Ursicinus.) He effectively opposed heresies such as Arianism and Apollinarianism, revised the Roman liturgy and restored many churches and catacombs,

composing famous inscriptions for martyrs' tombs therein. Also he commissioned his friend St Jerome to revise the Latin New Testament, which eventually resulted in the latter producing the Vulgate edition of the Bible.

Damhnade (Damnat) (St) R. Jun 13
? She had a popular cultus centred on the counties of Cavan and Fermanagh, Ireland, but nothing is known for certain about her.

Damian (SS) MM. Feb 12
? There were apparently two martyrs confused in the old Roman Martyrology on this date. The first was a soldier martyred in Roman Africa or at Alexandria and the second was a Roman whose relics were taken from St Callistus's catacombs to Salamanca, Spain.

Damian (St) *see* **Cosmas and Damian**

Damian *see* **Dyfan**

Damian dei Fulcheri (Bl) R(OP). Oct 26
*c*1400–1484. From Finario near Savona in Liguria, Italy, he became a Dominican there and went on to preach throughout northern Italy. He died at Reggio d'Emilia and had his cultus confirmed for Savona and the Dominicans in 1848.

Damian Nam (St) *see* **Korea (Martyrs of)**

Damian of Pavia (St) B. Apr 12
d. ?715. As a priest of Pavia, Italy, he opposed the Monothelites at the synod of Milan in 680, which influenced the third ecumenical council of Constantinople in condemning that heresy. In ?685 he was made bishop, and was a peacemaker between the Lombards and the emperor.

Damian Vaz (Bl) *see* **Peter Rodriguez and Comps**

Damian-Joseph de Veuster
(Bl) R. May 10
1840–1889. Born at Tremelo, Belgium, he followed his brother in becoming a 'Picpus Father' in 1859 and went to Hawaii in 1864 (when it was still an independent country). He was on a mission on the 'Big Island' when the government announced a policy of deporting all lepers to a concentration camp at Kalaupapa on Molokai. He volunteered to join them in 1873, caught leprosy himself and died there sixteen years later. He was beatified in 1995.

Damian Yamichi (Bl) M. Sep 10
d. 1622. He was a Japanese layman beheaded in the 'Great Martyrdom' at Nagasaki with his five-year-old son, Michael Yamichi, and Charles Spinola and Comps. *See* **Japan (Martyrs of)**.

Daniel (St) *see* **Elias, Jeremias and Comps**

Daniel and Verda (SS) MM. Feb 21
d. 344. A priest and a laywoman, they were martyred in Persia in the reign of Shah Shapur II.

Daniel (Deiniol) of Bangor
(St) B. R. Sep 11
d. 584. He founded the monasteries at Bangor in Gwynedd and at Bangor Isycoed in Clwyd, Wales, and allegedly became first bishop of the former place in 516. The cathedral and many Welsh churches are dedicated to him.

Daniel of Belvedere and Comps (SS) MM. RR(OFM). Oct 10
d. 1227. This group of early Franciscan missionaries were sent to Morocco by Br Elias in order to convert the Muslims there. Daniel was the leader, having been the provincial superior of Calabria, Italy, and the others were Samuel, Angelus, Domnus, Leo, Nicholas and Hugolin. They arrived at Ceuta, preached in public and were initially arrested and imprisoned as insane. Later it was demanded that that they convert to Islam and, on their refusal, they were beheaded. They were canonized in 1516.

Daniel Brottier (Bl) R. Feb 28
1876–1936. From La Ferté-Saint-Cyr near Blois, France, he was ordained and joined the 'Congregation of the Holy Spirit and the Immaculate Heart of Mary' at Orly in 1903 in order to become a missionary. His first posting to Senegal ruined his health very quickly, however, and he had to return in 1906. Then he organized home support for the missions, founding the *Souvenir Africain* periodical and collecting money for the building of Dakar Cathedral. He also started the 'National Union of Combatants' for war veterans and restored a famous orphanage in Paris. He died of typhoid and was beatified in 1984.

Daniel Comboni (Bl) B. F. Oct 10
1831–1881. Born in Limone sul Garda, Italy, of very poor parents, he became a priest in Verona and dedicated his life to evangelizing Africa. He went to Khartoum, Sudan, in 1854 as a missionary but returned to Europe in 1864 in order to plead for the missions, in the process founding the 'Verona Fathers' in 1867 and the 'Missionary Sisters of Verona' in 1872. In 1877 he was made Vicar Apostolic of Central Africa. He died at Khartoum and was beatified in 1996.

Daniel of Gerona (St) M. R. Apr 29
C9th. His story is that he was from Asia Minor, was a hermit at Gerona, Spain, in the reign of Charlemagne and was martyred. There is no historical evidence for any of this.

Daniel Karmasz (Bl) *see* **Podlasia (Martyrs of)**

Daniel of Padua (St) M. D. Jan 3
d. 168. His story is that he was a convert Jewish deacon who helped St Prosdocimus, the first bishop of Padua, Italy, before being martyred. His alleged relics were found and enshrined in the C11th.

Daniel-Andrew des Pommerayes (Bl) *see* **September (Martyrs of)**

Daniel of Sandomir (Bl) *see* **Sadoc of Sandomir and Comps**

Daniel the Stylite (St) R. Dec 11
d. 493. From near Samosata on the upper Euphrates, Syria, he started as a monk there but visited St Simeon the Elder on his pillar near Antioch in 452 and resolved to imitate him. This he did near Constantinople, where Emperor Leo I built him a series of pillars on which he lived for thirty-three years until his death. He was forcibly ordained in situ and descended to the ground only once in that time in order to rebuke the Monophysite Emperor Basiliscus. He was the oracle of the whole city.

Daniel of Venice (St)
T(OSB Cam). Mar 31
d. 1411. A merchant from Germany, he set up house near the Camaldolese monastery at Murano in Venice, Italy, and lived under their rule as a hermit while continuing his business and giving the proceeds to the poor. He was killed by robbers.

Daniel (Deiniol, Deyniolen) the Younger (St) R. Nov 22
d. 621. Abbot of Bangor Isycoed near Wrexham, Wales, he seems to have escaped the sack of his monastery by the king of Northumbria in 616 during which two thousand monks were alleged to have been killed.

Darerca (Diar-Sheare) (St) L. Mar 22
C5th? Traditionally St Patrick's widowed sister, she allegedly had fifteen sons ten of whom became bishops in Ireland. Her name means 'Firm Love'.

Daria (St) *see* **Chrysanthus and Daria**

Darius, Zosimus, Paul and Secundus (SS) MM. Dec 19
? They were martyred at Nicaea, Asia Minor, but nothing else is known.

Darlugdach (Dardulacha, Derlugdach) (St) R. Feb 1
d. ?524. She allegedly succeeded St Brigid as second abbess of Kildare, Ireland.

Dasius, Zoticus, Gaius and Comps (SS) MM. Oct 21
d. ?303. Fifteen soldiers, they were martyred at Nicomedia, Asia Minor, in the reign of Diocletian.

Dasius of Dorostorum (St) M. Nov 20
d. ?303. A Roman soldier, he refused to take part in the pagan celebration of Saturnalia and was martyred at Dorostorum in Moesia, Bulgaria. His relics are at Ancona, Italy, and his acta may derive from genuine sources.

Dathus (Datus) (St) B. Jul 3
d. 190. According to his legend he became bishop of Ravenna, Italy, in the reign of Commudus after the miraculous appearance of a dove over his head. His existence is doubtful.

Datius (Dativus), Julian, Vincent and Comps (SS) MM. Jan 27
d. 427-531. They were martyred in Roman Africa by the Arian Vandals.

Datius, Reatrus (Restius) and Comps (SS) MM. Jan 27
? They were martyred in Roman Africa.

Datius of Milan (St) B. Jan 14
d. 552. A friend of Cassiodorus, he became bishop of Milan, Italy, after 530 but fled to Constantinople after his diocese was overrun by the Arian Ostrogoths. There he died after defending Pope Vigilius in the 'Three Chapters' controversy.

Dativa (St) *see* **Dionysia, Dativa and Comps**

Dativus (St) *see* **Nemesian and Comps**

Dativus (St) *see* **Saturninus, Dativus and Comps**

David (St) B. R. Mar 1
d. *c*600. The fame of the patron saint of Wales rests entirely on the polemical biography of Rhygyfarch, bishop of St David's, which was written *c*1090. It sets out to defend the independence of his diocese against the claims of

Canterbury and is unreliable, being full of obvious anachronisms. It seems evident, however, that the saint was a great monastic founder, establishing a monastery at Mynyw (Menevia) where the city named after him now is and becoming its first bishop (being mentioned as present at the synod of Brefi in 545). The monks there followed an extremely austere rule. His cultus was approved in 1120 and his shrine became a great pilgrimage-centre. The relics preserved there have recently been shown not to be his. His attribute is a leek, or a daffodil (perhaps a pun on his name).

David *see* **Boris and Gleb**

David Carlos Marañón (Bl) *see* **Dionysius Pamplona Polo and Comps**

David Galvan Bermúdez (St) *see* **Mexico (Martyrs of)**

David Gonson (Bl) M. Jul 12
d. 1541. A son of Vice-Admiral Gonson (or Gunston), he was a knight of St John of Jerusalem at Clerkenwell, London, and was hanged, drawn and quartered at Southwark for refusing to accept King Henry VIII's spiritual supremacy. He was beatified in 1929. *See* **England and Wales (Martyrs of).**

David of Himmerod (Bl) R(OCist). Dec 11
d. 1179. From Florence, Italy, he became a Cistercian monk at Clairvaux, France, under St Bernard in 1131 and was sent to Germany in 1134 to found the abbey of Himmerod near Trier.

David Lewis (St) M. R(SJ). Aug 27
1616–1679. From Gwent, Wales, he was educated at Abergavenny, became a convert, studied for the priesthood at Rome and became a Jesuit in 1644. He worked in South Wales for thirty-one years from 1648, based at Cwm in Gwent and using the alias 'Charles Baker'. As a result of the Oates plot he was executed at Usk and was canonized in 1970. *See* **Wales (Martyrs of)**.

David Oghou David (Bl) *see* **Salvator Lilli and Comps**

David Roldán Lara (St) *see* **Mexico (Martyrs of)**

David of Sandomir (Bl) *see* **Sadoc of Sandomir and Comps**

David of Scotland, King *May 24*
?1085–1153. Scotland's greatest king was the son of Malcolm III and St Margaret of Scotland and began his reign in 1124. He was arguably responsible for making Scotland into a modern nation by reforming the legal system and public administration and encouraging trade and the foundation of towns. He also reformed the Scottish church, established a system of dioceses and founded many famous monasteries. He was famously pious and correct in his private life. His shrine was at Dunfermline Abbey and he was venerated there until the Reformation, but his cultus was never confirmed.

David of Thessalonika (St) R. Jun 26
d. ?540. From Mesopotamia, he was a hermit outside Thessalonika, Greece, for seventy years. His alleged relics have been at Pavia, Italy, since 1054.

David Uribe Velasco (St) *see* **Mexico (Martyrs of)**

David of Västermanland (St) B? R(OSB). Jul 15
d. *c*1080. According to the unreliable details concerning him, he was an English Cluniac Benedictine who joined the mission in Sweden headed by St Sigfrid and eventually founded a Benedictine abbey at Monkentorp (the last allegation is anachronistic). He is alleged to have been the first bishop of Västerås.

Davinus the Pilgrim (St) R. Jun 3
d. 1051. An Armenian, he was on a pilgrimage to Rome and Compostela when he stopped off for a while as a hermit at Lucca, Italy. There he fell ill and died.

Day (St) Jan 18
? There is a church dedicated to this unknown saint (possibly identical to St Deicola) near Redruth in Cornwall, England.

Dé *see* **Aidan of Fearns**

Declan McErc (St) B. R. Jul 24
C5th. The first bishop of Ardmore in Co. Waterford, Ireland, he has been claimed as having been a missionary in Ireland before St Patrick but his biography is legendary.

Decorosus (St) B. Feb 15
d. 695. From Capua, Italy, he became bishop there in 660. His shrine is at the cathedral.

Decuman (Dagan) (St) M. R. Aug 27
d. 706. According to his late biography he was

a Welsh nobleman who settled as a hermit at the place near Watchet in Somerset, England, later named after him. He was then murdered.

Deel (Deille) *see* **Deicola**

Degadh *see* **Dagaeus**

Degenhard (Bl) R(OSB). Sep 3
d. 1374. A monk at Niederaltaich in Bavaria, Germany, after a while he left to be a hermit with BB Otto and Hermann, also of that abbey, who had established their cell at Frauenau. Later they moved to Breitenau on the Danube.

Deicola (St) R. Jan 18
d. ?625. An Irish monk of Bangor, he accompanied St Columban to Burgundy and helped him to found the abbey of Luxeuil. When Columban was exiled Deicola was too old to travel and founded the abbey of Lure in the Vosges instead. His name has many variants: Deicolus, Desle, Dichul, Deel, Delle, Deille.

Deifer (St) R. Mar 7
C6th. He founded a monastery at Bodfari near Denbigh, Wales.

Deiniol *see* **Daniel of Bangor**

Delphina of Signe (Bl) T(OFM). Dec 9
?1283–?1358. A noblewoman of Provence, France, she married St Elzear of Sabran in 1299 but they agreed not to consummate the marriage and became Franciscan tertiaries. In 1317 they went to the court of Naples, Italy, where she made friends with the queen. When she was widowed in 1323 she returned to Provence and lived in absolute poverty. She was buried at Apt, and her cultus was confirmed in 1694.

Delphinus of Bordeaux
(St) B. Dec 24
d. 404. Bishop of Bordeaux, France, from 380, he fought the Priscillianists and was instrumental in converting St Paulinus of Nola.

Demetria (St) V. Jun 21
d. ?363. The worthless acta of St Bibiana allege that Demetria was her sister. She probably never existed.

Demetrian (St) B. R. Nov 6
d. ?912. From Ketheria (Khytri) near Nicosia, Cyprus, when his wife died he became a monk and then bishop of Ketheria. His veneration is very popular on Cyprus.

Demetrius (St) M. Aug 14
? He is listed in the old Roman Martyrology as a Roman African martyr but there is no other record of him.

Demetrius (St) *see* **Blaise and Demetrius**

Demetrius (St) *see* **Gregory, Demetrius and Calogerus**

Demetrius, Anianus, Eustosius and Comps (SS) MM. Nov 10
? They are listed as a group of twenty-three martyred at Antioch, Syria, Demetrius being a bishop and Anianus his deacon.

Demetrius, Concessus, Hilary and Comps (SS) MM. Apr 9
? A very unlikely group of martyrs, listed together although apparently from different places.

Demetrius, Honoratus and Florus (SS) MM. Dec 22
? They are listed as having been martyred at Ostia near Rome, and may be the same as SS Demetrius and Honorius.

Demetrius and Honorius
(SS) MM. Nov 21
? They are listed as Romans who were martyred at Ostia.

Demetrius of Alexandria (St) B. Oct 9
d. 231. He became patriarch of Alexandria, Egypt, in 189. Under him the catechetical school reached the height of its fame, being traditionally associated with Origen who was his friend. However, he had him banished after they fell out when Origen was irregularly ordained in the Holy Land.

Demetrius of Thessalonika
(St) M. D. Oct 8
d. ?303. He was probably a deacon who was martyred at Sirmium (Srem Mitrovica in Serbia) in the reign of Diocletian. His cultus flourished in Thessalonika, of which city he is the patron and where the legend grew up of his having been a military hero. As such he is one of the most popular saints in the Orthodox Church, being nicknamed the 'Great Martyr'. He is represented on horseback fighting a dragon, distinguishable from St George in having a red horse instead of a white one.

Demetrius of Tbilisi (Bl) *see* **Thomas of Tolentino and Comps**

Democritus, Secundus and Dionysius (SS) MM. Jul 31
? Nothing is known about these martyrs. They have been described as being from Phrygia, Asia Minor, or Roman Africa.

Denis, Dennis
These are the traditional French and English versions of 'Dionysius'. They are only used nowadays in reference to certain Western saints, however, and the original name has been preferred in this book.

Denise *see* **Dionysia**

Dentlin (Dentelin, Denain) (St) L. Mar 16
C7th. The son of SS Vincent Madelgar and Waldetrude, he was seven years old when he died and was buried at Rees near Cleves, Germany. A local cultus grew up in response to miracles at his tomb.

Deochar (Theotker, Gottlieb) (St) R(OSB). Jun 7
d. ?832. He was a monk at Fulda and a disciple of Alcuin at the court of Charlemagne before becoming a hermit at Herrieden in Franconia, Germany. There he became the first abbot of an abbey founded for him by Charlemagne.

Deodatus of Blois (St) R. Apr 24
C6th? From Blois, France, he became a hermit at the place where the abbey and village of Saint-Dyé-sur-Loire later grew up. His biographies are legendary.

Deodatus of Lagny (St) R. Feb 3
C8th. He was a monk of Lagny, to the east of Paris, France.

Deodatus of Jointures (St) B? R. Jun 19
d. *p*680. He was the abbot-founder of the Columbanian abbey of Jointures in the Vosges, France, where the town of Saint-Dié now stands. Asserted to have been a bishop, he has been confused with St Deodatus of Nevers.

Deodatus (Dié, Didier, Dieu-Donné, Adéodat) of Nevers (St) B? R. Jun 19
d. 679. He was allegedly bishop of Nevers, France, for three years from 655 before becoming a hermit at Jointures in the Vosges, where he founded a monastery later named after him. It was alleged that he was also the hermit-founder of the monastery of Ebersheimmünster near Strasbourg, Alsace, France.

Deodatus of Nola (St) B. Jun 27
d. 473. He succeeded St Paulinus as bishop of Nola, Italy, in 431.

Deodatus de Ruticinio (St) *see* **Nicholas Tavelić and Comps**

Deodatus of Sora (St) Sep 27
? Nothing is known of this saint, who has a cultus in the diocese of Sora in Lazio, Italy.

Deogratias (St) B. Mar 22
d. 457. After the Arian Vandals had driven St Quodvultdeus into exile there was no Catholic bishop in Carthage, Roman Africa, until St Deogratius was elected in 456. He died after a year. As bishop, he helped the prisoners brought back by the Vandals after they had sacked Rome, selling all that the local church possessed in order to do so.

Deogratias Palacios (Bl) *see* **Vincent Soler and Comps**

Derfel Gadarn (St) R. Apr 5
C6th. He was a Welsh warrior before he became a monk at St Illtyd's monastery at Llantwit Major. Later he was a hermit at Llandderfel near Bala, Gwynedd, and a wooden image of him as a soldier on a horse was an object of pilgrimage in the Middle Ages until it was burned with Bl John Forest at Smithfield by order of Thomas Cromwell in 1538.

Dermitius O'Hurley (Bl) M. B. Jun 20
d. 1584. He was archbishop of Cashel, Ireland, and was tortured and hanged in the reign of Queen Elizabeth I. He was beatified in 1992. *See* **Ireland (Martyrs of)**.

Dermot (Diarmis, Diarmaid) the Just (St) R. Jan 10
C6th. From the region of Connaught, Ireland, he founded a monastery and school on the island of Innisclothran in Co. Longford, which became a great pilgrimage centre.

Derphuta (St) *see* **Alexandra of Amisus and Comps**

Deruvianus *see* **Dyfan**

Derwa *see* **Dyfan**

Desideratus of Bourges (St) B. May 8
d. 550. He was a Frankish courtier and succeeded St Arcadius as bishop of Bourges, France, in 543.

Desideratus (Désiré) of Clermont (St) B. Feb 11
d. 602. He succeeded St Avitus as bishop of Clermont-Ferrand, France.

Desideratus of Fontenelle (St) R. Dec 18
d. *c*700. He was a son of St Waningus, the founder of Fécamp Abbey, and became a monk at Fontenelle in Normandy, France.

Desideratus of Gourdon (St) R. Apr 30
d. ?569. He was a hermit at Gourdon near Chalon-sur-Saône, France.

Desiderius (St) *see* **Barontius and Desiderius**

Desiderius (St) *see* **Januarius of Benevento**

Desiderius, Pope *see* **Victor III**

Desiderius of Auxerre (St) B. Oct 27
d. ?625. He succeeded St Anacharius as bishop of Auxerre, France, and is often confused with St Desiderius of Vienne.

Desiderius of Cahors (St) B. Nov 15
d. 655. A Gallo-Roman nobleman, he was at the Frankish court before succeeding St Rusticus, his murdered brother, as bishop of Cahors, France, in 630. Some of his letters survive.

Desiderius of Langres and Comps (SS) M. B. May 23
d. 364 or 411. Perhaps from Genoa, he became bishop of Langres, France, and was killed with many of his people in a barbarian incursion. It is unclear who the barbarians were: either Alemans in 364 or Vandals in 411. He is alleged to have been killed in their camp after going there to beg mercy for his city.

Desiderius of Lonrey (St) R. Oct 19
d. ?705. A monk and disciple of St Sigiranus at Lonrey near Bourges, France, he became a hermit at La Brenne nearby.

Desiderius Rhodonensis (St) M. B? Sep 18
d. *c*670. He was allegedly a bishop ambushed and murdered by robbers near Belfort in Alsace, France.

Desiderius (Didier) of Thérouanne (St) B. R(OCist)? Jan 20
d. 1194. Bishop of Thérouanne near Saint-Omer, France, he founded the Cistercian abbey of Blandecques nearby and retired to another Cistercian monastery before dying, so the Cistercians have claimed that he was one of them. His cultus has not been confirmed.

Desiderius of Vienne (St) M. B. May 23
d. 608. From Autun, he became bishop of Vienne, France, in 596 and was a correspondent of Pope St Gregory the Great, but was persecuted and exiled by Queen Brunhilde. He was eventually stoned to death at her instigation and that of an enemy bishop of Lyons at the place now called Saint-Didier-sur-Chalaronne.

Deusdedit (Adeodatus), Pope (St) Nov 8
d. 618. A Roman, he became pope in 615 during the Lombard invasions and was remembered for his concern for the sick during an epidemic. He favoured the secular clergy, and there is no evidence that he had been a monk as has been claimed. The error probably arises from confusion with Deusdedit of Montecassino.

Deusdedit of Brescia (St) B. Dec 10
d. *c*700. Bishop of Brescia, Italy, he played a leading part in the Monothelite controversy in Italy.

Deusdedit of Canterbury (St) B. Jul 14
d. 664. A Saxon called Frithona, he succeeded St Honorius as archbishop of Canterbury, England, the first native to do so. Little is known of his episcopacy.

Deusdedit of Montecassino (St) M. R(OSB). Oct 9
d. 834. A monk of Montecassino, Italy, he became abbot in 828 and became known for his almsgiving. The Duke of Benevento tried to extort the abbey's property by ill-treating and imprisoning him, and he apparently starved to death in prison.

Deusdedit of Rome (St) L. Aug 10
C6th. A Roman shoemaker, contemporary of St Gregory the Great, he is described by him as giving to the poor every Sunday whatever was left over from his week's earnings after paying for the bare necessities of life.

Devereaux *see* **Dubricius**

Devinicus (Denick, Teavneck) (St) B? Nov 13
C6th. From Aberdeen, Scotland, he was associated with the missionary work of SS Columba and Machar and evangelized

Caithness. He may have been a bishop. His tomb was at Banchory-Devenick near Aberdeen.

Devota (St) V. Jan 27
d. 303. From Corsica, she died on the rack in the reign of Diocletian and is the patron of Corsica and Monaco. Her relics are at Monaco.

Dewi *see* **David**

Deyniolen *see* **Daniel the Younger**

Diaconus ('Deacon') (St) M. D. Mar 14
C6th. He was mentioned by St Gregory the Great as a deacon who was killed with two monks in the province of Marsi, Italy, by the invading Lombards. Thus he is listed as 'Deacon'.

Diana, Cecilia and Amata (BB). RR(OP). Jun 9
C13th. They were the founders of the first Dominican nunnery at Bologna. Diana de Andelo was a native noble girl who entered a local convent, was abducted by her parents but returned and helped transfer the community to Valle di San Pietro. Amata and Cecilia Romana came from the St Sixtus nunnery in Rome to introduce the Dominican rule there. Cecilia had been personally acquainted with St Dominic. Their cultus was confirmed for Bologna and the Dominicans in 1891.

Dichu (St) L. Apr 29
C5th. His story is that he was an Ulster, Ireland, pig-farmer, the son of a chieftain, who opposed St Patrick at his landing but changed his mind, became his first convert and gave him the land at Saul, Co. Down, for his first church. His later life is obscure.

Dichul *see* **Deicola**

Dictinus of Astorga (St) B. Jul 24
d. 420. A Priscillianist born in Spain of Greek parents, he fell under the influence of St Ambrose, recanted of his heresy at a synod at Toledo in 400 and then became bishop of Astorga.

Didacus *see* **Diego**

Didier *see* **Desiderius**

Didius (St) *see* **Faustus, Didius and Comps**

Didymus (St) *see* **Diodore, Diomedes and Didymus**

Didymus (St) *see* **Theodora and Didymus**

Dié *see* **Deodatus**

Diego
This is a corrupt form of the Spanish name for St James (Jacob); the original Sant Iago became San Diego. In modern times it has been latinized to Didacus. The Portuguese version is 'Diogo'.

Diego Andrade (Bl) *see* **Ignatius de Azevedo and Comps**

Diego de Azevedo (Bl) B. Feb 6
d. 1207. The provost of the cathedral at Osima, Spain, he collaborated with his bishop to establish the cathedral chapter under the rule of St Augustine and obtained a canonry for St Dominic. He became bishop in 1201 and went to Denmark and then to Rome on a royal mission with the latter. Being prevented by the pope from resigning as bishop, he was involved in preaching to the Albigenses with St Dominic before returning to Spain. The assertion that he became a Cistercian is false.

Diego Carvalho (Bl) M. R(SJ). Feb 22
1578–1624. From Coïmbra, Portugal, he became a Jesuit in 1594, went to Goa in 1600 and to Japan as a priest in 1609. In 1623 he was arrested with a number of his people, taken to Sendai and immersed in the icy waters of a river until he died of hypothermia. He was beatified in 1867. *See* **Japan (Martyrs of)**.

Diego-of-Cadiz García Molina (Bl) *see* **Hospitaller Martyrs of Spain**

Diego López Caamaño (Bl) R(OFM Cap). Mar 24
1743–1801. From Cádiz, Spain, he became a Capuchin at Seville in 1759 and preached throughout Spain, especially in Andalucia, giving more than 20,000 sermons. He also had a fruitful ministry in the confessional. He died at Ronda and was beatified in 1894.

Diego Oddi (Bl) R(OFM). (Jun 3)
1839–1919. From a poor peasant family of Vallinfreda in Lazio, Italy, he was influenced by Bl Marianus of Roccacasale into becoming a Franciscan at Bellegra in 1871. He begged for alms for his friary in the Subiaco region for forty years, and became known for continuous prayer, penance and cheerfulness. He was beatified in 1999.

Diego Pérez (Bl) *see* **Ignatius Azevedo and Comps**

Diego of San Nicolás (St)
R(OFM). Nov 12
*c*1400–1463. From a poor family at San Nicolás del Puerto near Seville, Spain, he became a Franciscan lay brother at Arrizafa and was appointed guardian of the friary on Fuerteventura in the Canaries in 1445. He was sent to Rome in 1450 and nursed the sick in an epidemic there. He died at Alcalá, back in Spain, and was canonized in 1588. His cultus was confined to local calendars in 1969.

Diego-Aloysius de San Vitores and Peter Calungsod (BB)
MM. R(SJ). Apr 2
1627–1672. A nobleman born at Burgos, Spain, the former became a Jesuit in 1640 and went to be a missionary in the Philippines in 1662. In 1668 he went to Guam and baptized 3,000 in three years. The latter was a young Filipino catechist who accompanied him. There were disturbances between the natives and immigrant Filipinos, however, causing anti-Christian agitation owing to which many lapsed. BB Diego and Peter visited one such lapsed Christian native, baptized his baby daughter with the consent of the mother and were killed as a result. Bl Diego was beatified in 1985, and Bl Peter in 2000.

Diego Ventaja Milán and Emmanuel Medina Olmos (BB) MM. BB. Aug 30
d. 1936. They were the bishops of Almería and Guadix, Spain, and were killed after the 'Revolutionary Committee' of Almería ordered the liquidation of priests and religious. They were beatified together in 1993. *See* **Spanish Civil War (Martyrs of)**.

Diemut (Diemuda) (Bl) R(OSB). Mar 29
d. *c*1130. A nun at Wessobrun in Bavaria, Germany, she became a hermit while still a nun of the monastery and worked at copying manuscripts (some survive).

Diethard (Bl) *see* **Cathold, Anno and Comps**

Dietrich (St) *see* **Ebstorf (Martyrs of)**

Dieudonné *see* **Deusdedit** or **Adeodatus**

Digain (St) R. Nov 21
C5th. Allegedly the son of a Cornish ruler, he founded the church at Llangernw in Clwyd, Wales.

Digna (St) *see* **Anastasius, Felix and Digna**

Digna (St) *see* **Hilaria, Digna and Comps**

Digna and Emerita (SS) VV. Sep 22
d. ?259. Their story is that they were Roman maidens who were martyred in the reign of Valerian, being hanged by their hair and burned with torches until they died. The two names may refer to a single person.

Digna of Todi (St) R. Aug 11
d. early C4th. A maiden of Todi in Umbria, Italy, she took to the mountains to escape the persecution of Diocletian and died a hermit.

Diman (Dimas, Dima) Dubh (St) B. R. Jan 6
d. 658. His surname means 'Black'. A monk and disciple of St Columba, he became abbot-bishop of Connor in Co. Antrim, Ireland. The Roman church addressed a letter to him and to other Irish bishops in 640 concerning Pelagianism and the date of Easter.

Dimbalac Oghlou Wartavar (Bl) *see* **Salvator Lilli and Comps**

Dimitri *see* **Demetrius of Thessalonika**

Dingad (St) R. Nov 1
C5th. One of the sons of St Brychan, he became a hermit and founder of the church at Llandovery in Dyfed, Wales.

Diocles (St) *see* **Zoëllus, Servilius and Comps**

Diocletius (St) *see* **Sisinius, Diocletius and Florentius**

Diodore (St) *see* **Lucy, Antoninus and Comps**

Diodore (St) *see* **Papias, Diodore and Comps**

Diodore, Diomedes and Didymus (SS) MM. Sep 11
? They are listed as martyrs of Laodicea (Latakia) in Syria.

Diodore, Marianus and Comps (SS) MM. Dec 1
d. 283. Roman martyrs of the reign of Numerian, they are described as a priest, deacon and congregation who were discovered by the authorities while assembled for prayer in the catacomb of SS Chrysanthus and Daria and who were then walled up and left to die.

Diodore and Rhodopianus
(SS) MM. DD. May 3
Early C4th. Two deacons, they were martyred at Aphrodisiopolis in Caria, Asia Minor, in the reign of Diocletian.

Diogenes (St) *see* **Timothy and Diogenes**

Diogo *see* **Diego**

Diomedes (St) *see* **Diodorus, Diomedes and Comps**

Diomedes, Julian and Comps
(SS) MM. Sep 2
? They are merely listed as having been burned, drowned, beheaded or crucified without any other details. The others are Philip, Eutychian, Hesychius, Leonides, Philadelphus, Menalippus and Pantagapes.

Diomedes Anargyrus (St) M. Aug 16
d. 300–311. From Tarsus in Cilicia, Asia Minor, according to his story he was a physician and practised among the poor free of charge (hence his surname meaning 'Moneyless'). He was seized at Nicaea, Asia Minor, but died while being taken to Nicomedia, where his body was beheaded.

Diomma (St) R. May 12
C5th. The patron of Kildimo in Co. Limerick, Ireland, is alleged to have been the teacher of St Declan of Ardmore and other saints, but details are lacking.

Dion (St) *see* **Lucy, Antoninus and Comps**

Dionysia
This name is familiarly rendered as 'Denise'.

Dionysia (St) *see* **Ammonaria, Ammonaria, Mercuria and Comps**

Dionysia (St) *see* **Peter, Andrew and Comps**

Dionysia, Dativa and Comps
(SS) MM. Dec 6
d. 484. According to Victor of Utica, who wrote an account of the persecution in Africa under the Arian Vandal king Hunneric, this group included the widow Dionysia, her sister Dativa and her small son Majoricus who were all burned at the stake. Emilian, a physician, and Tertius, a monk, were flayed alive and Boniface and others were killed in ingenious ways.

Dionysius
In the Middle Ages this name was usually rendered in English as Dennis (from the French Denis). 'Sydney' is a corrupt form of 'Saint Denis'.

Dionysius (St) *see* **Codratus of Corinth and Comps**

Dionysius (St) *see* **Democritus, Secundus and Dionysius**

Dionysius (St) *see* **Hilary, Tatian and Comps**

Dionysius (St) *see* **Lucillian, Claudius and Comps**

Dionysius (St) *see* **Seven Sleepers**

Dionysius (St) *see* **Socrates and Dionysius**

Dionysius, Pope (St) Dec 30
d. ?268. A Roman, he became pope in ?259 and successfully restored the church's life after the persecution of Valerian. He opposed the heresies of Sabellius and of Paul of Samosata.

Dionysius and Ammonius
(SS) MM. Feb 14
? They were apparently beheaded at Alexandria, Egypt.

Dionysius and Dionysius (SS) *see* **Timolaus and Comps**

Dionysius, Emilian and Sebastian (SS) MM. Feb 8
? The old Roman Martyrology lists them as Armenian monks but nothing is known about them.

Dionysius, Faustus, Gaius, Peter, Paul and Comps (SS) MM. Oct 3
d. ?257. From Alexandria, Egypt, they were banished to Libya in 250 in the Decian persecution, then brought back and martyred in the reign of Valerian. There is confusion over the identities of each, despite their insertion into the old Roman Martyrology by Cardinal Baronius. Dionysius seems to be the patriarch of Alexandria and Faustus and Gaius the same as **Gaius and Faustus** (q.v.).

Dionysius and Privatus (SS) MM. Sep 20
? They are listed as martyrs of Phrygia, Asia Minor.

Dionysius and Redemptus
(SS) MM. RR(OCD). Nov 29
d. 1638. Dionysius-of-the-Nativity Berthelot

was a French navigator and cartographer who became a Carmelite at Goa, India, in 1635, was ordained in 1638 and sent on a Portuguese embassy to Aceh. This was a fervently Muslim kingdom on the north tip of Sumatra. Redemptus-of-the-Cross Rodriguez da Cunha, a Portuguese lay brother, went with him. The delegation was not well received and they were killed. They were beatified in 1900.

Dionysius of Alexandria (St) B. Nov 17
d. 265. From Alexandria, Egypt, he was a pupil of Origen and was his successor as head of the catechetical school of Alexandria before becoming patriarch in 248. He was exiled in the reign of Decius and again in that of Valerian but succeeded in remaining in control of his diocese. He was a great theologian and controversialist, but only the fragments preserved by Eusebius survive of his writings.

Dionysius the Areopagite
(St) M? B? Oct 9
d. ?95. Converted by St Paul at Athens (Acts 17:34), he traditionally became first bishop of Athens and was martyred. In the Middle Ages he was deliberately confused with St Dionysius of Paris, and also the works by the C5th mystical writer now called 'Pseudo-Dionysius' were ascribed to him. The identity of the latter is wholly unknown.

Dionysius of Augsburg (St) M. B. Feb 26
d. ?303. His story, from the C8th acta of St Afra, describes him as her uncle who was baptized by St Narcissus and who became the first bishop of Augsburg in Bavaria, Germany. He was possibly martyred in the reign of Diocletian.

Dionysius the Carthusian
(Bl) R(OCart). Mar 12
1402–1471. From Flanders, he obtained his doctorate at Cologne University when aged twenty-one and became a Carthusian at Roermond, Netherlands, in 1423. There he remained until his death, except for a period at a new foundation at 's Hertogenbosch. He was a great and prolific mystical writer, being nicknamed the 'Ecstatic Doctor'. His cultus has not been confirmed.

Dionysius of Corinth (St) M? B. Apr 8
d. *c*170. Succeeding St Primus as bishop of Corinth, Greece, he had great authority in the Church of his day and wrote many letters to other local churches, including that of Rome. Only fragments of these survive. The Byzantine martyrology lists him as a martyr but the old Roman Martyrology does not.

Dionysius Duval (Bl) *see* **September (Martyrs of)**

Dionysius Fujishima (Bl) M. R(SJ). Nov 1
d. 1622. Of a noble Japanese family near Arima, he became a Jesuit novice and was martyred with Bl Paul Navarro (q.v.). *See* **Japan (Martyrs of)**.

Dionysius of Milan (St) B. May 25
d. ?359. The successor of St Protasius as bishop of Milan, Italy, in 351, he defended St Athanasius against the Arian Emperor Constantius and was thus exiled to Cappodocia with St Eusebius of Vercelli. He died there but St Ambrose had his relics brought back to Milan by St Aurelius of Armenia.

Dionysius Pamplona Polo
and Comps (BB) MM. RR. Sep 22
d. 1936. From Teruel province, Spain, he joined the Piarists and became parish priest at Peralta de la Sal in Huesca (the birthplace of their founder, St Joseph Calasanz). He, five of his brethren there and seven other Piarists were shot in Monzón prison during the Civil War and were beatified in 1995. *See* **Spanish Civil War (Martyrs of)**.

Dionysius (Denis) of Paris
and Comps (SS) MM. Oct 9
d. *c*250. According to St Gregory of Tours (the sole source), Denis was sent from Rome with five other missionary bishops to evangelize Gaul and became the first bishop of Paris, France. In the reign of Decius he was beheaded with his two companions, Rusticus and Eleutherius, at a place near the city where the abbey named Saint-Denis after him was later founded. In the C9th Hilduin, abbot of Saint-Denis, forged a set of acta linking the saint to St Dionysius the Areopagite and to the author of an anonymous C5th spiritual author now called the 'Pseudo-Dionysius'. This conflation of three separate persons led to a popular cultus in the Middle Ages. He is depicted as a headless bishop.

Dionysius of Rome (St) M. May 12
d. 304. He was allegedly the uncle and guardian of St Pancras and went with him to Rome. They were seized and St Dionysius died in prison in the reign of Diocletian, being listed as a martyr.

Dionysius Ssebuggwawo (St) M. Jun 3
d. 1885. A servant of King Mwanga of Buganda, Uganda, he was caught teaching the catechism by the latter and was killed with a spear. He was the first victim of the Ugandan persecution. *See* **Charles Lwanga and Comps**.

Dionysius of Vienne (St) B. May 8
d. *p*193. Allegedly one of the ten missionaries sent from Rome to Gaul with St Peregrinus, he succeeded St Justus as bishop of Vienne, France. He was not a martyr.

Dioscorides (St) *see* **Crescens of Rome and Comps**

Dioscorides of Smyrna (St) M. May 10
? He was martyred at Smyrna, Asia Minor (now Izmir, Turkey).

Dioscorus (St) *see* **Heron, Arsenius and Comps**

Dioscorus (St) *see* **Themistocles and Dioscorus**

Dioscorus (St) *see* **Victorinus, Victor and Comps**

Dioscorus of Kynopolis (St) M. May 18
d. ?305. A lector at Kynopolis, Egypt, he was burned to death with red-hot plates.

Diruvianus *see* **Dyfan**

Disibod (Disen) (St) B. R. Sep 8
d. *c*700. Allegedly an Irish bishop, he went to Germany with some companions and evangelized the area around Mainz. Near there he founded a monastery later called Disenberg which, as a nunnery, became famous as the home of St Hildegard. Her biography of him is historically worthless.

Dismas *see* **Good Thief**

Diuma (St) B. Sep 7
C7th. An Irish priest, he accompanied St Cedd to Mercia, England, and was later a missionary bishop there. St Bede wrote highly of him.

Dizier *see* **Desiderius**

Docco *see* **Cumgar**

Dochow (Dochau, Dogwyn)
(St) B? R. Feb 15
d. ?473. According to the biography of St Samson, he was a Welsh monk who founded a monastery in Cornwall, England. In the Ulster Annals he is mentioned as a bishop.

Docus *see* **Cadoc**

Doda (St) *see* **Bova and Doda**

Dodo of Asch (Bl) R(OPraem). Mar 30
d. 1231. He married against his better judgement before becoming a Premonstratensian at Mariengaard and later a hermit at Assen in Friesland, Netherlands. He practised incredible austerities and was reputed to have received the stigmata. He was killed by a falling wall.

Dodo of Lobbes (St) R. Oct 1
d. *c*750. From near Laon, France, he was a child-oblate at the abbey of Lobbes, Belgium, under St Ursmar, became a monk there and was later abbot of Wallers-en-Faigne.

Dodolin of Vienne (St) B. Apr 1
C7th. He was bishop of Vienne, France.

Dogfan (Dyfan, Docwan)
(St) M. R. Jul 13
C5th. Of the family of St Brychan, he founded the church at Llanrhaiadr yn Mochnant, Wales, and was killed by pagan Saxons at Merthyr Dyfan near Cardiff.

Dogmael (St) R. Jun 14
C5th–C6th. The patron of St Dogmael's, across the river from Cardigan, Wales, seems to have founded a monastery there as well as in Anglesey and in Brittany.

Domangard (Donard) (St) R. Mar 24
d. *c*500. In St Patrick's time he was a hermit on Slieve Donard in the Mourne Mountains of Co. Down, Ireland.

Dometius *see* **Domitius**

Dominator of Brescia (St) B. Nov 5
d. ?495. He was a bishop of Brescia in Lombardy, Italy.

Dominic
This is from the Latin Dominicus, which is the equivalent of the Greek name Cyriac.

Dominic and Gregory
(BB) RR(OP). Apr 26
d. 1300. Two Spanish Dominicans, they were preaching in the Somontano district of Aragón, Spain, north-east of Zaragoza. During a thunderstorm they sheltered under a rock on a mountainside near Perarú but this was struck by lightning, fell and buried them. Their shrine is at Besians near Barbastro, and their cultus was confirmed for Barbastro in 1854.

Dominic, Victor and Comps
(SS) MM. Dec 29
? Nothing is known about these Roman African

martyrs. The companions are Primian, Lybosus, Saturninus, Crescentius, Secundus and Honoratus.

Dominic-of-the-Mother-of-God Barberi (Bl) R(CP). Aug 27
1792–1849. From a peasant family near Viterbo, Italy, he became a Passionist in 1815 and served as superior at Lucca from 1831 and as provincial of south Italy from 1833. In 1841 he was sent to England as superior of his order's first house in England, at Aston, Staffs. He was hoping for the imminent conversion of the country as a whole and this, together with his unprepossessing appearance and poor English, led him to be treated with hostility by native Catholics and Protestants alike. His personal holiness inspired many individual conversions to the Roman Catholic Church, however, including that of John Henry Newman. He was taken ill on a train, died at Reading and was beatified in 1963.

Dominic of Brescia (St) B. Dec 20
d. ?612. He succeeded St Anastasius as bishop of Brescia, Italy. His relics were enshrined by St Charles Borromeo.

Dominic de la Calzada (St) R. May 12
d. 1109. From Vitoria in the Basque Country, Spain, he became a hermit in Rioja after failing to become a monk at Valvanera. The work he took up was building a bridge, causeway and hospice as part of a pilgrim route to Compostela passing near his hermitage on the Oja River and the site, now called La Calzada ('The Causeway'), itself became a pilgrimage centre.

Dominic Cam (St) M. T(OP). Mar 11
1859. He was a martyred Vietnamese priest and Dominican tertiary. *See* **Vietnam (Martyrs of)**.

Dominic Castellet and Comps (BB) MM. Sep 8
d. 1628. They were a group of twenty-two martyred at Nagasaki, Japan. Eleven were burned alive: Bl Dominic was from near Barcelona, Spain, and, on becoming a Dominican, was sent to Japan where he became vicar-provincial; martyred with him were two Dominican lay brothers, Thomas-of-St-Hyacinth of Nagasaki and Anthony-of-St-Dominic of Nagasaki; two Franciscans, Anthony-of St-Bonaventure of Tuy and Dominic of Nagasaki, and six lay people: Louise of Omura, Michael Yamada, John Tomachi, John Inamura, Paul Aibara and Matthew Alvarez. Eleven were beheaded: Dominic, Michael, Paul and Thomas Tomachi (sons of John Tomachi); Laurence Yamada (son of Michael Yamada); Romanus and Leo Aibara (sons of Paul Aibara); Louis, Francis and Dominic Nihachi (father and two sons), and James Hayashi. *See* **Japan (Martyrs of)**.

Dominic Collins (Bl) M. R(SJ). Jun 20
d 1602. A Jesuit lay brother, he was hanged at Cork. *See* **Ireland (Martyrs of)**.

Dominic of Comacchio (Bl) R(OSB). Jun 21
d. *p*820. According to the Venetian traditon, he was a monk of Comacchio near Venice who went on pilgrimage to the Holy Land, managed to steal the relics of St Mark from Alexandria, Egypt, and then brought them back to Venice.

Dominic (Dinh) Dat (St) M. Jul 18
d. 1839. A Vietnamese soldier, he was strangled. *See* **Vietnam (Martyrs of)**.

Dominic Fernandez (Bl) *see* **Ignatius de Azevedo and Comps**

Dominic de Guzman (St) R(OP). F. Aug 8
1170–1221. From Caleruega near Burgos, Spain, he became a canon regular at Osma Cathedral and went with his bishop, Bl Diego de Azevedo, to the south of France in 1202 in order to help the evangelical campaign against the Albigenses (which later turned into a crusade). The experience convinced him of the necessity of preaching the faith to ordinary people. The two of them opened a nunnery at Prouille for women converts from the Albigenses in 1206, which was the start of the Dominican order. This, the 'Friars Preachers', was approved in 1216 and was sent all over Europe by St Dominic in order to preach and teach. Together with the Franciscans it represented a radical departure from the previously accepted norms of consecrated life which presumed stability in a monastery. The friars proved ideally suited to the urban civilization developing in the high Middle Ages, especially in the new universities. St Dominic died at Bologna after much journeying in western Europe and was canonized in 1234. He is represented as an elderly Dominican holding a lily, or with a dog or a rosary.

Dominic (Nguyen van) Hanh (St) M. R(OP). Aug 1
1772–1838. He was a Vietnamese Dominican priest. *See* **Vietnam (Martyrs of)**.

St Dominic de Guzman, Aug 8 *(see p. 153)*

Dominic Henares (St) M. B. R(OP). Jun 25
d. 1838. A Spanish Dominican, he became the coadjutor bishop of the apostolic vicar for Vietnam, St Ignatius Delgado, in 1803. He was seized and beheaded with his catechist, St Francis Chieu, at Nam Dinh. *See* **Vietnam (Martyrs of)**.

Dominic Huyen (St) M. Jun 5
d. 1862. He was a Vietnamese lay martyr. *See* **Vietnam (Martyrs of)**.

Dominic Ibáñez de Erquicia
(St) M. R(OP). Sep 28
1589–1633. Born in San Sebastian, Spain, he became a Dominican missionary in the Philippines and spent a decade as Vicar Provincial in Japan before being martyred in Nagasaki with St Francis Shoyemon. He was canonized in 1987. *See* **Japan (Martyrs of)**.

Dominic-of-the-Blessed-Sacrament Iturrate Zubero (Bl) R. Apr 7
1901–1927. Born in Dima in the Basque Country, Spain, he joined the Trinitarians in 1914, was sent to Rome in 1919 and was ordained in 1925. A model religious, he had strong devotions to the Blessed Sacrament and to Our Lady and wished to go on the foreign missions. However he was appointed master of students at Cordoba instead and, while still in Rome, contracted tuberculosis and returned to Spain to die. He was beatified in 1983.

Dominic Jorjes (Bl) M. Mar 14
d. 1619. A soldier from Portugal, he settled in Japan and became the housekeeper of Bl Charles Spinola. He was burned alive at Nagasaki with Bl **Leonard Kimura and Comps** (q.v.). *See* **Japan (Martyrs of)**.

Dominic (Pham trong) Kham
(St) M. T(OP). Jan 13
d. 1859. He was a Vietnamese lay martyr. *See* **Vietnam (Martyrs of)**.

Dominic Lentini (Bl) P. (Feb 25)
1770–1828. From a poor family of Lauria in Basilicata, Italy, he was ordained priest in 1794 and served as parish priest of his native town all his life. His life was manifestly centred on the Eucharist, on evangelical poverty and on prayer and he was totally dedicated to evangelization in his district. He was effective in converting sinners because he obviously practised what he preached, and was devoted to Our Lady of Sorrows. He also set out to teach an authentic Christian culture to the young people who gathered at his house. He was beatified in 1997.

Dominic Loricatus (St) R. Oct 14
995–1060. From Umbria, Italy, he spent his life doing penance for his parents who had given a deerskin to the local bishop to obtain his ordination. He never exercised his priestly functions, wore a coat of mail next to his skin (hence his surname), recited the Psalter once a day and fasted on bread and water. At first he was a hermit in Umbria, then a disciple of St Peter Damian at Fonteavellano and finally prior of a monastery at Frontale.

Dominic Magoshichi de Hyuga
(Bl) T(OP). Sep 12
d. 1622. A Japanese catechist and Dominican tertiary, he was burned alive at Omura with Bl **Thomas Zumarraga and Comps** (q.v.). *See* **Japan (Martyrs of)**.

Dominic Mao (St) M. Jul 16
d. 1862. He was a Vietnamese lay martyr. *See* **Vietnam (Martyrs of)**.

Dominic Mau (St) M. R(OP). Nov 5
d. 1858. He was a Vietnamese priest martyr. *See* **Vietnam (Martyrs of)**.

Dominic of Nagasaki (Bl)
M. R(OFM). Sep 8
d. 1628. A Japanese catechist, he took vows as

a Franciscan while in prison at Omura with Bl Anthony of St Bonaventure and was burned with him at Nagasaki. *See* **Dominic Castellet and Comps** and **Japan (Martyrs of)**.

Dominic-of-the-Holy-Rosary of Nagasaki (Bl) R(OP). Sep 10
d. 1622. A Japanese catechist and a Dominican novice, he was beheaded during the 'Great Martyrdom' at Nagasaki. *See* **Charles Spinola and Comps** and **Japan (Martyrs of)**.

Dominic Nakano (Bl) M. Sep 10
d. 1622. The nineteen-year-old son of Bl Matthias Nakano, he was beheaded at Nagasaki, Japan, in the 'Great Persecution'. *See* **Charles Spinola and Comps** and **Japan (Martyrs of)**.

Dominic Nihachi (Bl) Sep 8
d. 1628. He was a toddler aged two when he was beheaded with his father and brother at Nagasaki, Japan. *See* **Dominic Castellet and Comps** and **Japan (Martyrs of)**.

Dominic Nguyen, Dominic Nhi and Dominic Ninh (SS) MM. Jul 16
d. 1862. They were Vietnamese lay martyrs. *See* **Vietnam (Martyrs of)**.

Dominic Pitarch Gurrea (Bl) *see* **Hospitaller Martyrs of Spain**

Dominic of Sandomir (Bl) *see* **Sadoc of Sandomir and Comps**

Dominic Savio (St) L. Mar 9
1842–1857. The son of a blacksmith at Riva de Chieri in the Piedmont, Italy, he became a pupil of St John Bosco (who wrote his biography). He died at Mondonio aged fourteen, having shown evidence of high sanctity, and is the youngest non-martyr so far canonized (in 1954).

Dominic Shobyoye and Comps (Bl) Sep 16
d. 1628. A Japanese layman, he was beheaded at Nagasaki with Michael Himoyona and the latter's son, Paul. *See* **Japan (Martyrs of)**.

Dominic of Silos (St) R(OSB). Dec 20
*c*1000–1073. From Rioja, Spain, he became a monk and prior of San Millán de Cogolla in the kingdom of Navarre but was exiled after quarrelling with the king. The king of Castile welcomed him and sent him to restore the abbey of Silos (now named after him) which he achieved with great success. Under him the abbey became famous for the production of manuscripts, and was also involved in the ransoming of prisoners taken by the Muslims. At his shrine Bl Jane de Aza de Guzman prayed for a child whom she named Dominic in gratitude. He later founded the Dominicans.

Dominic of Sora (St) R(OSB). Jan 22
951–1031. From Foligno, Italy, he became a priest at his home town and the abbot-founder of several monasteries in middle Italy, including Sora in Lazio where he died.

Dominic Spadafora (Bl) R(OP). Oct 3
d. 1521. From Palermo, Sicily, he joined the Dominicans after being a student at Padua and became a famous preacher in Italy. He died in the friary he had founded at Montecerignone near San Marino and had his cultus confirmed for Montefeltro in 1921.

Dominic Toai (St) M. Jun 5
d. 1862. He was a Vietnamese lay martyr. *See* **Vietnam (Martyrs of)**.

Dominic Tomachi (Bl) M. Sep 8
d. 1628. He was sixteen when he was beheaded with his three brothers at Nagasaki. Their father, Bl John Tomachi, was burned. *See* **Dominic Castellet and Comps** and **Japan (Martyrs of)**.

Dominic Trach (St) M. R(OP). Sep 18
1792–1842. He was a Vietnamese priest and Dominican tertiary beheaded in north Vietnam. *See* **Vietnam (Martyrs of)**.

Dominic Tuoc (St) M. T(OP). Apr 2
d. 1839. A Vietnamese priest and a tertiary of the Dominicans, he died in prison from wounds inflicted on him and was canonized in 1988. *See* **Vietnam (Martyrs of)**.

Dominic (Buy van) Uy (St) M. T(OP). Dec 19
1813–1839. He was a nineteen-year-old Vietnamese catechist and Dominican tertiary who was beheaded at Ninh-Tai in north Vietnam. With him died SS Augustine (Nguyen van) Moi, Francis-Xavier (Ha Trong) Mau, Stephen (Nguyen van) Vinh and Thomas (Nguyen van) De. *See* **Vietnam (Martyrs of)**.

Dominic (Dominguito) de Val (St) M. Aug 31
d. 1250. A seven-year-old altar boy, he was allegedly kidnapped by some Jews at Zaragoza, Spain, and nailed to a wall. The popularity of his veneration was certainly aided by anti-Semitism, and this is one of the reported attacks

on children by individual Jewish psychopaths which helped in the dissemination of the 'blood libel' against Jews as a whole.

Dominic Vernagalli (Bl) R(OSB Cam). Apr 20
d. 1218. From Pisa, Italy, he became a Camaldolese monk at the abbey of St Michael there and founded a hospital attached to the monastery. His cultus was confirmed for the Camaldolese in 1854.

Dominic (Nguyen van) Xuyen (St) M. R(OP). Nov 26
1788–1839. He was a Vietnamese Dominican beheaded with St Thomas Du. *See* **Vietnam (Martyrs of)**.

Dominic Yamada (Bl) M. Sep 10
d. 1622. He was beheaded with his wife, Bl Clare, in the 'Great Martyrdom' at Nagasaki, Japan. *See* **Charles Spinola and Comps** and **Japan (Martyrs of)**.

Dominica *see* **Cyriaca**

Dominica Ogata (Bl) M. L. Sep 10
d 1622. She was a Japanese laywoman beheaded at Nagasaki, Japan, in the 'Great Martyrdom'. *See* **Charles Spinola and Comps** and **Japan (Martyrs of)**.

Dominica of Tropea (St) M? Jul 6
? Cardinal Baronius inserted this saint into his revision of the old Roman Martyrology. She was alleged either to have been martyred on the banks of the Euphrates and to have had her body carried by angels to Tropea in the Campagna, Italy, or to have been a native of the latter place martyred there. She was unknown in Tropea before the C16th and seems to be a version of an apocryphal martyr of Nicomedia called Cyriaca.

Domitian (St) *see* **Cyril, Aquila and Comps**

Domitian (St) *see* **Eutychius and Domitian**

Domitian and Hadelin (SS) RR. Jun 15
d. *c*690. Monks of Lobbes, Belgium, they were disciples there of St Landelin and were also apparently associated with the abbey of Crépin near Cambrai, France.

Domitian of Châlons (St) B. Aug 9
C4th? He succeeded his teacher St Donatian as third bishop of Châlons-sur-Marne, France.

Domitian of Lérins (St) R. Jul 1
?347-440. An orphan from Rome, he became a monk at Lérins (off the Riviera coast, France) and later founded the abbey of St Rambert-de-Joux near Belley. The sources referring to him are very unreliable.

Domitian of Maastricht (St) B. May 7
d. *c*560. From France, he was bishop of Tongeren, Belgium, and transferred his see to Maastricht, Netherlands. He evangelized the Meuse valley and has his shrine at Huy, Belgium.

Domitilla *see* **Flavia Domitilla**

Domitius of Amiens (St) R. Oct 23
C8th. A canon of the cathedral of Amiens, France, he became a hermit at Saint-Acheul.

Domitius of Caesarea and Comps (SS) MM. Mar 23
d. 361. His story is that he was a Phrygian who heckled the pagan ceremonies held in a theatre in the presence of Emperor Julian, possibly at Caesarea in the Holy Land. He was beheaded, allegedly together with Pelagia, Aquila, Eparchius and Theodosia although these probably do not belong with him.

Domitius the Illustrious (St) M. R. Jul 5
d. ?362. His dubious story is that he was a Persian hermit walled up in his cave near Cyrrhus, Syria, by order of Emperor Julian. He was probably a Persian or Phrygian monk stoned in the pagan reaction of the time, and identical to his namesakes of Caesarea and Nisibis.

Domitius of Nisibis and Comps (St) M. R. Aug 7
C4th. He was allegedly a Persian monk martyred at Nisibis in Mesopotamia with two disciples in the reign of Julian, but is probably a duplicate of Domitius of Caesarea.

Domna (St) *see* **Indes, Domna and Comps**

Domneva *see* **Ermenburga**

Domnina of Anazarbus (St) M. Oct 12
d. 303. She was alleged to have died in prison from the effects of beating and torture at Anazarbus in Cilicia, Asia Minor.

Domnina, Berenice and Prosdoce (SS) MM. Oct 4
d. 303–310. A mother with her two daughters from Antioch, Syria, they allegedly fled to

Edessa (now Urfa in Turkey) to escape persecution but were seized and drowned themselves on the way back in order to escape abuse by their escorting soldiers. Such action is now condemned as suicide by the Church.

Domnina of Terni and Comps (SS) MM. Apr 14
d. ?269. They are listed in the old Roman Martyrology as having been martyred at Terni in Umbria, Italy, but may belong to Teramo instead.

Domninus (St) *see* **Marcellinus, Vincent and Domninus**

Domninus (St) *see* **Philemon and Domninus**

Domninus, Silvanus, Philotheus, Theotimus and Comps (SS) MM. Nov 5
? Associated with Emesa, Syria, the first two were a young physician and a bishop who were condemned together to slavery in the mines but were martyred a while apart. The others were martyred perhaps in the reign of Maximian.

Domninus, Victor and Comps (SS) MM. Mar 30
d. ?304. They are two separate groups, listed together. Domninus, Philocalus, Achaicus and Palotinus seem to have been martyred at Thessalonika, Greece, in the reign of Maximian Herculeus. Victor and ten others were martyred elsewhere, the place being now unknown. Domninus is listed twice in error in the old Roman Martyrology, also on October 1st.

Domninus of Grenoble (St) B. Nov 5
C4th. He was the alleged first bishop of Grenoble, France.

Domninus of Parma (St) M. Oct 9
d. 304. From Parma, Italy, he fled the persecution of Diocletian but was pursued and beheaded nearby at Borgo San Donnino, where his shrine now is.

Domnio of Bergamo (St) M. Jul 16
d. ?295. He was martyred at Bergamo in Lombardy, Italy, in the reign of Diocletian.

Domnio of Rome (St) P. Dec 28
C4th. A Roman priest, he is remembered because SS Jerome and Augustine wrote in his praise.

Domnio of Salona and Comps (SS). Apr 11
? According to his historically worthless legend he was one of the seventy-two disciples of Christ and was sent by St Peter to evangelize Dalmatia (now part of Croatia), where he became first bishop of Salona (now a suburb of Split) and was martyred with many others. He was probably martyred in the reign of Diocletian.

Domnoc *see* **Modomnock**

Domnolus of Le Mans (St) B. R. May 16
d. 581. Abbot of a monastery near Paris, France, he became bishop of Le Mans in 559 and was a founder of many monasteries, churches and charitable institutions.

Domnus (St) *see* **Daniel, Samuel and Comps**

Domnus of Vienne (St) B. Nov 3
d. 657. He succeeded St Desiderius as bishop of Vienne, France, and was noted for ransoming captives taken in the wars of the period.

Donald (Donivald) (St) R. Jul 15
C8th. He is alleged to have lived as a religious with his nine daughters in Glen Ogilvie near Coupar Angus, Scotland. The 'Nine Maidens' went to Abernethy after he died.

Donard *see* **Domangard**

Donas *see* **Donatian**

Donat (Dunwyd) (St) Aug 7
? There is nothing known about the patron of St Donat's, on the coast of Glamorgan, Wales.

Donata *see* **Scillitan Martyrs**

Donata and Comps (SS) MM. Dec 31
? The alleged relics of these early Roman woman martyrs were in the catacombs of the Via Salaria. Listed also are Paulina, Rustica, Nominanda, Serotina and Hilaria.

Donatian, Praesidius and Comps (SS) MM. Sep 6
d. ?484. An account survives by Victor of Utica of the persecution of the Catholics in ex-Roman Africa by Hunneric, Arian king of the Vandals. Almost five thousand were exiled in one year. These bishops of what is now Tunisia were driven into the desert to die, the others being Mansuetus, Germanus and Fusculus, while Laetus was burned.

Donatian and Rogatian (SS) MM. May 24
d. 299. They were martyred at Nantes, France, in the reign of Diocletian.

Donatian of Châlons-sur-Marne
(St) B. Aug 7
C4th? He was the second bishop of Châlons-sur-Marne, France.

Donatian (Donas) of Rheims (St) B. Oct 14
d. 390. From Rome, he became bishop of Rheims, France, in 360. In the C9th his relics were taken to Bruges, Belgium, of which place he became the patron.

Donatilla (St) *see* **Maxima, Donatilla and Secunda**

Donatus (St) *see* **Aquilinus, Geminus and Comps**

Donatus (St) *see* **Epiphanius, Donatus and Comps**

Donatus (St) *see* **Hermogenes, Donatus and Comps**

Donatus (St) *see* **Leo, Donatus and Comps**

Donatus (St) *see* **Mansuetus, Severus and Comps**

Donatus (St) *see* **Polyeuctus, Victorius and Donatus**

Donatus (St) *see* **Primus and Donatus**

Donatus (St) *see* **Quintius, Arcontius and Donatus**

Donatus (St) *see* **Restitutus, Donatus and Comps**

Donatus and Felix (SS) *see* **Twelve Brothers**

Donatus and Hilarinus
(St) BM. Aug 7
d. C4th. Their acta are unreliable. Donatus was the second bishop of Arezzo in Tuscany, Italy, but through confusion with another of the same name was listed as a martyr. He had no connection with Hilarinus, who was a martyr of Ostia. Their cultus was confined to local calendars in 1969.

Donatus, Justus, Herena and Comps (SS) MM. Feb 25
d. *c*250. A group of fifty, they were martyred in Roman Africa in the reign of Decius.

Donatus, Sabinus and Agape
(SS) MM. Jan 25
? They are listed in the old Roman Martyrology but nothing is known about them.

Donatus, Secundian, Romulus and Comps (SS) MM. Feb 17
d. 304. A group of eighty-nine, they were killed at Porto Gruaro (the old Concordia) near Venice, Italy, in the reign of Diocletian.

Donatus of Besançon (St) B. Aug 7
d. *c*660. Educated at the monastery of Luxeuil, he became bishop of Besançon, France, in 624 and founded a pair of monasteries for monks and nuns there. His 'Rule for Virgins' relies on the rules of SS Benedict and Columban.

Donatus of Corfu (St) Oct 29
? All that is known about this extremely dubious saint is that his alleged relics were brought to Corfu, Greece, by a refugee priest from Asia Minor in *c*600 and were enshrined at Kassiopi at the instigation of St Gregory the Great.

Donatus of Euraea (St) B. Apr 30
d. late C4th. Bishop of Euraea in Epirus (now Albania), he was mentioned by the Church historian Sozomen.

Donatus of Fiesole (St) B. Oct 22
d. 874. From Scotland or Ireland, he was returning from a pilgrimage to Rome when he was made bishop of Fiesole near Florence, Italy, in ?829. He was a literary scholar, and cared for other pilgrims.

Donatus of Orléans (St) R. Aug 19
d. ?535. From Orléans, France, he became a hermit near Sisteron in Provence, France, and has his shrine there.

Donatus of Ripacandida
(St) R(OSB). Aug 17
1179–1198. From Ripacandida in Basilicata, Italy, of which place he is the patron, he became a monk at the Monteverginian abbey of St Onuphrius at Petina in 1194.

Donatus of Sandomir (Bl) *see* **Sadoc of Sandomir and Comps**

Donnan of Eigg and Comps
(SS) MM. RR. Apr 17
d. ?618. Allegedly a monk of Iona, Scotland, under St Columba, he became abbot-founder of a daughter monastery on the island of Eigg nearby. The entire community of fifty-three was

allegedly massacred on Easter Sunday by Danish raiders. His existence is suspect.

Donvina (St) *see* **Claudius, Asterius and Comps**

Dorbhene (St) R. Oct 28
d. 713. Abbot of Iona, Scotland, he was descended from a brother of St Columba and copied out St Adamnan's life of the latter. This copy is extant.

Dorcas *see* **Tabitha**

Doris *see* **Dorothy**

Dorotheus (St) *see* **Castor and Dorotheus**

Dorotheus and Gorgonius
(SS) MM. Sep 9
d. 303. They were among the first victims of the persecution ordered by Diocletian, being the palace-master and chamberlain at the emperor's capital at Nicomedia, Asia Minor. Their martyrdom by strangling is recorded by Eusebius. Their cultus was confined to particular calendars in 1969.

Dorotheus of Gaza (St) R. Jun 5
d. *c*640. He was the abbot of a monastery near Gaza in the Holy Land, a popular ascetical writer and the teacher of St Dositheus.

Dorotheus of Tyre (St) M. B. Jun 5
d. ?362. His life is obscure, but it is alleged that he was a priest of Tyre, Lebanon, who was exiled in the reign of Diocletian, then made bishop on his return and finally beaten to death at Varna, Bulgaria, in the reign of Julian.

Dorotheus the Younger (St) R. Jun 5
C11th. From Trebizond, now Trabzon on the Black Sea coast of Asia Minor, he became a monk at Samsun along the coast after he lost his wife and then founded the monastery of Khiliokomos nearby.

Dorothy (Dorothea, Dora) *Feb 6*
She was alleged to have been martyred at Caesarea in Cappodocia, Asia Minor, in the reign of Diocletian but her acta are a romantic fiction and she is unknown in the East. Her cultus, formerly very popular in the West, was suppressed in 1969. She is represented with roses or apples.

Dorothy (St) *see* **Euphemia, Dorothy and Comps**

St Dorothy, Feb 6

Dorothy of Montau (St) R. Oct 30
1336–1394. A peasant girl from Montau in Teutonic (later East) Prussia, she married a wealthy swordsmith of Danzig (now Gdansk in Poland) called Albert. They had nine children, and she changed his harsh character by means of patience and prayer. After his death she became a hermit at Marienwerder (now Kwidzyn in Poland). Her cultus survived the Second World War in Poland and was confirmed in 1976.

Dorymedon (St) *see* **Trophymus, Sabbatius and Dorymedon**

Dositheus of Gaza (St) R. Feb 23
d. *c*530. A rich young man, he became a convert at Jerusalem and then a monk near Gaza in the monastery of St Dorotheus, who became his teacher. His poor health prevented him from practising austerities and his brethren did not think much of him, but St Dorotheus recognized and described his abandonment of self-will. He died soon after entering.

Dositheus Rubio Alonso (Bl) *see* **Hospitaller Martyrs of Spain**

Dotto (St) R. Apr 9
C6th? He is listed as an abbot of the Orkneys, Scotland.

Douceline *see* **Dulcelina**

Drausinus (Drausius) of Soissons (St) B. Mar 7
d. ?576. He became bishop of Soissons, France, in 658 and managed to persuade Ebroin, the tyrannical mayor, i.e. comptroller, of the Merovingian palace, to help build a nunnery at Soissons when better known for pillaging such places. Hence he is invoked against the plotting of enemies, and St Thomas of Canterbury is alleged to have prayed at his shrine before returning to England and his martyrdom.

Dreux *see* **Drogo**

Drillo *see* **Trillo**

Drithelm (St) R. Aug 17
d. *c*700. According to the *Ecclesiastical History* of St Bede he was a Northumbrian who had a vision of hell and became a monk at Melrose, Scotland, as a result, living a life of penance in a cell near the monastery in order to avoid what he had seen.

Droctoveus (Droctonius, Drotté) (St) R. Mar 10
d. *c*580. He was a disciple of St Germanus of Paris before becoming abbot of St Symphorian's Abbey at Autun, France. His former master then appointed him first abbot of his new monastery at Paris, later called Saint-Germain-des-Prés.

Drogo of Baume (Bl) R(OSB). Apr 2
C10th. After a worldly life he became a monk at Fleury on the Loire, France, and ended up as a lay brother at Baume-les-Messieurs in Burgundy. There he was the monastery shepherd.

Drogo (Dreux, Druon) of Sebourg (St) R. Apr 16
d. 1186. A Fleming from Artois, France, he lost his parents when aged twenty and, after disposing of his property, became a wandering shepherd and apparently went on pilgrimage to Rome nine times. Eventually he settled as a hermit near Sebourg in Hainault and lived on bread and water for forty-five years.

Drostan (St) R. Jul 11
d. *c*610. From Ireland, he was a monk at Iona under St Columba and first abbot of Deer near Aberdeen. He is venerated as one of the apostles of Scotland and has a holy well near Aberdour.

Drusus (St) *see* **Lucian, Metrobius and Comps**

Drusus (or Drusina), Zosimus and Theodore (SS) MM. Dec 14
? They were martyred in Syria, probably at Antioch since St John Chrysostom preached an extant homily on their feast day there.

Druthmar (St) R(OSB). Aug 13
d. 1046. A monk of Lorsch near Worms, Germany, he was appointed abbot of Corvey in Lower Saxony by Emperor St Henry II (the abbey was degenerate and the previous abbot had been deposed). He re-established monastic discipline and the monastery had a good reputation under him.

Dubricius (Dubric, Dyfrig, Devereux) (St) B. R. Nov 14
d. ?545. One of the founders of monasticism in Wales, he established monasteries in the Wye Valley area from bases at Henllan and Moccas. He had jurisdiction over Caldey, appointed St Samson abbot there and later ordained him bishop. By tradition he was first bishop of Llandaff and then of Caerleon. He died on Bardsey.

Dubtach of Armagh (St) B. Oct 7
d. ?513. He was archbishop of Armagh, Ireland, from 497.

Dubtach (Duthac) of Ross (St) B. Mar 8
d. 1065. A missionary bishop in Ross, Scotland, he had his shrine at Tain, which was a famous pilgrimage centre before the Reformation.

Dula (St) V. Mar 25
? Her story is that she was a slave girl sold to a pagan soldier at Nicomedia, Asia Minor. She refused to be his concubine, as was his right under Roman law, and he killed her in anger.

Dulas of Zepherinum (St) M. Jun 15
d. 300. His real name was Tatianus (the nickname 'Dulas' means 'servant'). He was imprisoned at Zepherinum in Cilicia, Asia Minor, and was savagely tortured over two days because he mocked the pagan gods. He died of the effects while being taken away for execution. His acta are reliable.

Dulcard (St) R. Oct 25
d. 584. A monk at Micy near Orléans, France, he became a hermit near Bourges where the village of St Doulchard is now situated.

Dulcelina (Douceline) (St) T(OFM). Sep 1
?1214–1274. From Digne, France, she founded a house of Beguines (Franciscan tertiaries living in community but without a perpetual vow of obedience) at Hyères in Provence in *c*1230. Then she made other foundations at Aix and at Marseilles, where she died.

Dulcidius (Dulcet, Doucis) of Agen (St) B. Oct 16
d. *c*450. He succeeded St Phoebadius as bishop of Agen, France.

Dulcissima of Sutri (St) V? Sep 16
? She is the patron of Sutri near Rome but nothing is known about her.

Dunawd (St) R. Sep 7
d. *p*602. Allegedly a refugee from Strathclyde, he was the abbot-founder of the great monastery at Bangor-Isycoed near Wrexham, Wales, and was present at the second meeting of the British bishops with St Augustine in 602.

Dunchadh of Clonmacnoise (St) R. Jan 16
d. 988. From Westmeath, Ireland, he was a hermit near the monastery of Clonmacnoise before becoming abbot there in 969. He died in retirement at Armagh.

Dunchadh (Dumhaid) of Iona (St) R. May 25
d. 717. He was abbot of Iona, Scotland, from 710, when Roman customs were finally accepted at that monastery in place of the Celtic ones.

Dunstan of Canterbury (St) B. R(OSB). May 19
909-988. From a noble family of Somerset, England, he was educated by the monks at Glastonbury, which was possibly the only monastery in England where any sort of monastic life had survived the Danish incursions. He became a royal courtier but made private monastic profession and returned to Glastonbury as a hermit, where he practised the crafts of metalwork, manuscript illumination and embroidery for which he became famous. He was appointed abbot of Glastonbury by the king in 943 and made the abbey a centre of monastic renewal, introducing the Benedictine rule. His monastic zeal was increased by a period of exile at Ghent, where he saw the effects of continental monastic reform. After his recall in 957 this zeal bore fruit in collaboration with SS Ethelwold and Oswald, the three founding and reforming many monasteries and promulgating the 'Regularis Concordia' for their common observance. He became bishop of Worcester in 957 and archbishop of Canterbury in 960 and had great influence in affairs of state. Also the English custom of having cathedral priories was instigated by him, and he may have introduced monks at Canterbury Cathedral, where he died. He is often depicted holding the Devil by the nose with a pair of pincers.

St Dunstan, May 19

Dwynwen (St) R. Jan 25
d. *c*460. Of the family of St Brychan, she settled as a hermit at Llanddwyn on Anglesey. The place became a great pilgrimage centre before the Reformation. The saying 'Nothing wins hearts like cheerfulness' is attributed to her, and she is the Welsh patron of true lovers.

Dwynwen *see* **Theneva**

Dyfan (Deruvianus, Damian) (St) M. May 26
C2nd. According to his worthless legend he was sent to Britain as a missionary by Pope St Eleutherius at the request of the fictional King St Lucius. The place called Merthyr Dyfan near Cardiff, Wales, indicates that he may have been a genuine saint of unknown date, and he may be the same as an otherwise unknown St Derwa recorded in Cornwall.

Dyfnan (St) R. Apr 24
C5th. One of the sons of St Brychan, he founded the church at Llandyfnan in Anglesey, Wales.

Dyfnog (St) R. Feb 13
C7th. He formerly had a popular cultus in Clwyd, Wales.

Dyfrig *see* **Dubricius**

Dympna (Dymphna) (St) V. May 15
? Her fanciful legend describes her as an Irish princess who fled with a priest from her incestuous father to Gheel near Antwerp, Belgium, where they were killed by their pursuers. The story was invented for some relics found there in the C13th, and insane people were alleged to be cured at her shrine. She became their patron and a great mental hospital was built that same century at Gheel.

E

Ead- *see* **Ed-**

Eadgith *see* **Edith**

Eanswith (Eanswida) (St) R. Sep 12
d. *c*640. A grand-daughter of King St Ethelbert of Kent, England, she was first abbess of a nunnery (the first in Saxon England) founded for her in 630 by her father the king at Folkestone. It was destroyed by the Danes in 867 but re-founded as a cell of Canterbury Cathedral Priory and transferred to the site of the present Anglican town church of SS Mary and Eanswith in 1137 after incursions by the sea. Her alleged relics were rediscovered in that church in 1885 and are still there.

Easterwine *see* **Esterwine**

Eata (St) R. Oct 26
d. ?686. A disciple of St Aidan, he became abbot of Melrose in Scotland (a Celtic monastery) and received St Cuthbert as a monk there. After the council of Whitby he accepted the Roman observances and became the first English bishop of Lindisfarne. He was made bishop of Hexham on a division of his diocese in 678, was at Lindisfarne 681–5 and then left that see to St Cuthbert when he went back to Hexham.

Ebba the Elder (St) R. Aug 25
d. 683. Sister of SS Oswald and Oswy, kings of Northumbria, England, with the help of the latter and with the guidance of St Cuthbert she became a nun and founded the double monastery of Coldingham in Scotland, near Berwick-on-Tweed. This had a similar structure to that at Whitby. She was known for her holiness, but not for her administrative ability and the monastery was a failure.

Ebba the Younger and Comps
(SS) MM. RR. Aug 23
d. *c*870. According to Matthew Paris (the only source) she was the abbess of Coldingham in Berwickshire, Scotland. During a Danish raid she cut off her upper lip in order to reduce the likelihood that she would be raped, and persuaded her community to do the same. The Danes burned the nunnery with the nuns inside.

Ebbo (St) B. R. Aug 27
d. *c*740. From Tonnerre near Troyes, France, he became a monk at Sens and then bishop there in 709. He organized a successful resistance to a Muslim raid in 725, and retired to be a hermit at Arces before he died.

Eberhard *see* **Everard**

Ebontius (Pontius, Ponce, Ebon)
(St) B? R(OSB)? Oct 3
d. 1104. According to his legend, which may be fictional, he was a French monk from Garonne who became abbot of St Victorian in Aragón, Spain, and then the first bishop of Barbastro after that place was captured from the Muslims.

Ebregisil of Cologne *see* **Evergisil**

Ebregisil of Meaux (St) B. Aug 31
C7th. A bishop of Meaux, France, he was a brother of St Agilberta of Jouarre and died at her abbey.

Ebrulf (Évroul) of Beauvais
(St) R. Jul 25
d. *c*600. From Beauvais near Paris, France, he became a hermit and introduced monastic life into his native district, founding the abbey of St-Fuscien-aux-Bois. His dates are uncertain.

Ebrulf (Évroul) of Ouche
(St) R. Dec 29
?617–706. From Bayeux in Normandy, France, he was at the Merovingian court before becoming a monk at Deux Jumeaux near his native city. Later he became abbot-founder of Ouche (later named after him) and also founded some smaller monasteries. The historian Oderic Vitalis was a monk under him.

Ebstorf (Martyrs of) (SS) Feb 2
d. 880. In the winter of 880 the Norsemen were raiding Lower Saxony, Germany, and Duke Bruno of Saxony led the army of King Louis III against them. The army was caught by snow on the Lüneberg Heath, ambushed and massacred. The Duke and four bishops were among those who died. They were venerated as martyrs at Ebstorf until the Reformation.

Ecclesius (St) B. Jul 27
d. 532. Bishop of Ravenna, Italy, from 521, he started the construction of the basilica of St Vitalis there and is commemorated by a mosaic therein.

Echa (Etha) (St) R. May 5
d. 767. He is referred to as a monk who became a hermit at Crayk near Easingwold in Yorkshire, England.

Edan *see* **Aidan**

Edana (Etaoin) (St) R. Jul 5
? This obscure Irish nun is patron of several places in western Ireland and possibly lived near Carrick-on-Shannon. She may be identical to St Modwenna.

Edbert of Lindisfarne (St) B. R. May 6
d. 698. A monk of Lindisfarne in Northumbria, England, he succeeded St Cuthbert as abbot-bishop there in 688 and became famous for his knowledge of the Bible. St Bede praised his learning. His shrine was later at Durham.

Edbert of Northumbria, King (St) R. Aug 20
d. 768. He succeeded St Ceolwulf as king of Northumbria, England, in 737 and ruled for twenty-one years. Then he abdicated, became a priest at York and spent the decade before his death in prayer and penance.

Edburga
This name has many variants, e.g. Iderberga, Edberga, Eadburga, Ideberga, Idaberga.

Edburga of Bicester (St) R. Jul 18
Late C7th. Possibly a daughter of King Penda of Mercia, England, she was a nun at Aylesbury and had a shrine at Bicester, Oxon.

Edburga of Lyminge (St) R. Dec 13
C7th. She was a nun at Lyminge in Kent, England.

Edburga of Thanet (St) R. Dec 12
d. 751. Of the Wessex, England, royalty, she was a disciple of St Mildred and was probably her successor when she became abbess at Minster-in-Thanet. She rebuilt the church there and corresponded with St Boniface in Germany, whom she helped by sending books, vestments and money.

Edburga of Winchester (St) R. Jun 15
d. 960. Daughter of King Edward the Elder and grand-daughter of King Alfred the Great, she was placed as a child-oblate at the Nunminster at Winchester, England, which nunnery had been founded by the latter king's widow. She had a pilgrimage shrine at Pershore Abbey.

Edeyrn (St) R. Jan 6
C6th. This legendary saint, venerated in Brittany, France, is described as a hermit there who had been associated with King Arthur.

Edfrith of Leominster (St) R. Oct 26
d. ?675. A monk of Northumbria, England, he was involved in the mission to Mercia and founded the monastery at Leominster.

Edfrith of Lindisfarne (St) B. R. Jun 4
d. 721. He became bishop of Lindisfarne in Northumbria, England, in 698, and seems to have been the writer and illuminator of the *Lindisfarne Gospels*.

Edgar the Peaceful, King of England *Jul 8*
943–975. He became king in 959 and his reign was marked by a great revival in the Church, especially in its monastic life. This was spear-headed by St Dunstan, his friend and adviser. He took a nun, St Wulftrude, as mistress and St Edith of Wilton was their daughter. He apparently had a cultus at Glastonbury Abbey but this was never approved.

Edigna (Bl) R. Feb 26
d. 1109. According to her unreliable legend she was a French royal princess who fled to avoid marriage and lived as a hermit in a hollow lime tree at Puch in Bavaria, Germany. Her popular cultus is unconfirmed.

Edilburga *see* **Ethelburga**

Ediltrudis *see* **Etheldreda**

Edistius (St) M. Oct 12
d. ?303. He was martyred at Ravenna, Italy, in the reign of Diocletian.

Edith of Polesworth (St) R(OSB). Jul 15
d. ?925. She was allegedly the daughter of King

Edward the Elder of England and was widowed after marrying a Danish leader. Then she became a nun (and possibly abbess) at Polesworth, Warks. She has been seriously confused with others of the same name.

Edith Stein *see* **Teresa-Benedicta-of-the-Cross Stein**

Edith of Wilton (St) R(OSB). Sep 16
961–984. Daughter of King Edgar of England and of the nun St Wulftrude, she was taken to Wilton Abbey in Wiltshire as a baby and never left it. She was professed as a nun when aged fifteen, and refused either to become an abbess or to become queen when her father died. St Dunstan was at her deathbed.

Edmigius Primo Rodríguez (Bl) *see* **Aurelius-Mary Villalón Acebrón and Comps**

Edmund, King (St) M. Nov 20
849-870. King of East Anglia, England, from ?855, he was killed after being taken prisoner in a Danish incursion, allegedly because of his faith. He is often depicted pierced with arrows, as according to tradition his captors used him for target practice before beheading him. The place where this happened is described as 'Hellesdon', which seems to be a field near Bradfield St Clare in Suffolk rather than the town in Norfolk. The place nearby where he was buried became a great abbey around which the town of Bury St Edmunds grew.

Edmund Arrowsmith
(St) M. R(SJ). Aug 28
d. 1628. From a recusant farming family at Haydock near St Helens, Lancs, he studied at Douai, was ordained priest in 1612 and went on the Lancashire mission the following year. In 1623 he became a Jesuit. He was hanged, drawn and quartered at Lancaster and was canonized in 1970. *See* **England (Martyrs of)**.

Edmund Bojanowski (Bl) L. F. (Aug 17)
1814–1871. A Polish nobleman from Grabónog in the German Empire, after his university studies he devoted his life to works of charity in the rural areas of his ancestral locality. After founding a home for orphans he attracted some young women as disciples from the local peasantry, and thus founded the 'Sisters, Servants of Mary Immacuate' in 1858.This had 22 houses in Poland at the time of his death. He was beatified in 1999.

Edmund Campion (St) M. R(SJ). Dec 1
?1540–1581. From London, he was a pupil at Christ's Hospital there, then a brilliant student at St John's College at Oxford. He became an Anglican deacon before he converted, whereupon he studied at Douai and at Rome where he became a Jesuit. He was ordained at Prague and was one year on the English mission where he was a great success. Then he was betrayed, tortured and hanged, drawn and quartered at Tyburn. He was canonized in 1970. *See* **England (Martyrs of)**.

Edmund Duke and Comps
(Bl) MM. PP. May 27
d. 1590. From Kent, he was educated at Rheims and ordained at Rome in 1589. He went to the North with BB Richard Hill (a Yorkshireman ordained at Laon), John Hogg and Richard Holliday. The four young priests were immediately seized and executed at Durham. They were beatified in 1987. *See* **England (Martyrs of)**.

Edmund Gennings
(St) M. P. Dec 10
d. 1591. From Lichfield, Staffs, he was an English convert who studied at Rheims and was ordained priest there in 1590. He was quickly captured on his return to England together with St Polydore Plasden during Mass at the house of St Swithin Wells in Gray's Inn Road, London. He was hanged, drawn and quartered at Gray's Inn Fields with St Swithin and was canonized in 1970. *See* **England (Martyrs of)**.

Edmund Rich B. Nov 16
1180–1242. From a family of shopkeepers at Abingdon on the Thames, England, he was a student at Oxford and Paris before becoming professor of philosophy at Oxford in 1219. He became a canon of Salisbury Cathedral in 1222 and was made archbishop of Canterbury in 1233. His reforming zeal for justice and good ecclesiastical discipline made him unpopular with the king, his own cathedral priory and the papal legate among others so he secretly went into exile in 1250 to the Cistercian abbey of Pontigny, France. He died at Soissy, an Augustinian monastery, but his shrine was at Pontigny. The Cistercian claim that he became a monk of theirs seems to be false. There is a college at Oxford named after him.

Edmund Sykes (Bl) M. P. Mar 23
d. 1588. The son of an English merchant in Leeds, he was ordained at Rheims in 1581 and was a priest in York for four years before being deported. On his return there he was betrayed by his brother and was executed. He was beatified in 1987. *See* **England (Martyrs of)**.

Ednot (St) B. R(OSB). Oct 19
d. 1016. A monk at Worcester, England, and a disciple of St Oswald of York, he became abbot of Ramsey and bishop of Dorchester-on-Thames in 1006. He was killed in a Danish raid up the river.

Edsin (St) B. Oct 28
d. 1050. After having been chaplain to the king of Denmark and bishop of Winchester, England, he became archbishop of Canterbury in 1038. As such he crowned St Edward the Confessor.

Edward II, King of England
1307–27. After his revolting murder at Berkeley Castle the body of this worthless king was acquired by the abbot of Gloucester with the intention of establishing it as a focus of pilgrimage to his abbey. His intention was so successful that the abbey was able to rebuild its church (now the cathedral) with the profits. This is a good example of the abuses that caused the act of canonization to be removed from the power of local churches and to be reserved to the Papacy.

Edward Bamber (Bl) M. P. Aug 7
d. 1646. From a recusant family near Poulton, Lancs, he studied at St Omer and Seville and was ordained at Cadiz in 1626. He was a priest in Lancashire for sixteen years before his capture during the Interregnum, and he was executed at Lancaster with BB Martin Woodcock and Thomas Whitaker. They were beatified in 1987. *See* **England (Martyrs of)**.

Edward Barlow *see* **Ambrose Edward Barlow**

Edward Bautista Jímenez (Bl) *see* **Hospitaller Martyrs of Spain**

Edward Burden (Bl) M. P. Nov 29
d. 1588. A convert graduate of Oxford from Co. Durham, he was ordained at Rheims and was a priest at York, becoming known for his kindness and gentleness. He was executed there and was beatified in 1987. *See* **England (Martyrs of)**.

Edward Campion (Bl) M. P. Oct 1
d. 1588. From Ludlow, Shrops, he studied at Jesus College at Oxford but converted, studied at Rheims and was ordained in 1587. He was executed at Canterbury and was beatified in 1929. *See* **England (Martyrs of)**.

Edward Catherick (Bl) M. P. Apr 13
d. 1642. From Carlton near Richmond, Yorks, he was educated at Douai and was on the English mission from 1635. He was executed at York and was beatified in 1929. *See* **England (Martyrs of)**.

Edward Cheevers (Bl) *see* **Matthew Lambert and Comps**

Edward Coleman (Bl) M. L. Dec 3
d. 1678. A Suffolk landowner, he was educated at Peterhouse in Cambridge but became a convert and the secretary of the Duchess of York (the sister-in-law of King Charles II). He was the first victim of the Oates plot, being executed at Tyburn on the charge of conspiring with foreign powers to re-establish the Catholic church in England. *See* **England (Martyrs of)**.

St Edward the Confessor, Oct 13

Edward the Confessor, King of England (St) L. Oct 13
1003–1066. Born at Islip near Oxford, a son of King Ethelred the Unready, he spent much of his youth in exile at Normandy before becoming king in 1042. He was pious, generous and

unambitious and was respected for his unworldliness and chastity (the rumour had it that his marriage was not consummated), but he lacked the ruthlessness, ambition and consistency needed for a successful contemporary ruler. He was more interested in prayer and hunting than in government but his reign was afterwards remembered for its prosperity, peace and justice. He founded Westminster Abbey, where he was buried and where his relics were enshrined on this date in 1162, the year after his canonization. They remain in situ. The depiction on the Bayeux Tapestry of a fair-haired man with a long beard is probably based on his actual appearance. His cultus was confined to particular calendars in 1969.

Edward Fulthrop (Bl) M. L. Jul 4
d. 1597. A Yorkshire landowner, he converted and was executed at York as a result together with BB Henry Abbot, Thomas Bosgrave and William Andleby. He was beatified in 1929. *See* **England (Martyrs of)**.

Edward James (Bl) M. P. Oct 1
d. 1588. From the village of Breaston near Derby, he was a student at St John's College in Oxford but converted and studied at Rheims and Rome. He was ordained priest in 1583, was executed at Chichester, Sussex, and was beatified in 1929. *See* **England (Martyrs of)**.

Edward Jones (Bl) M. P. May 6
d. 1590. A convert from somewhere in the diocese of St Asaph, Wales, he studied at Rheims and was ordained in 1588, being captured two years later and executed in Fleet Street, London. He was beatified in 1929. *See* **England (Martyrs of)**.

Edward the Martyr, King of England (St) M. L. Mar 18
d. 979. The son of Edgar the Peaceful, he succeeded him as king in 975 when aged thirteen. He was murdered at Corfe by a faction favouring his younger brother (a later allegation blamed his stepmother) and buried at Wareham, Dorset. He did not die for the faith but the injustice of his death and his remembered goodness led to popular veneration and his relics were transferred to Shaftesbury Abbey. They are now at the Orthodox monastery at Brookwood, Surrey.

Edward Oldcorne (Bl) M. R(SJ). Apr 7
d. 1606. From York, he was ordained priest at Rome and became a Jesuit in 1587. He was on mission in the Midlands from 1588 to 1606 and was executed at Worcester for alleged involvement in the Gunpowder Plot together with Bl Ralph Ashley. He was beatified in 1929. *See* **England (Martyrs of)**.

Edward Osbaldeston (Bl) M. P. Nov 16
1560–1594. Of the Lancashire gentry, he was born at Osbaldeston Hall near Blackburn and was ordained at Rheims in 1585. He was a priest in Yorkshire but was betrayed by a renegade priest who saw him in an inn at Tollerton. He was executed at York and beatified in 1987. *See* **England (Martyrs of)**.

Edward Poppe (Bl) P. (Jun 10)
1890–1924. From Moerzeke in Flanders, Belgium, he became a parish priest at Ghent before serving as rector of a religious community in his home region and then as director of clerics fulfilling their military service. His lifelong interest was the re-evangelization of Flanders in the face of the growing secularization of society, and he wrote much to this end. He was beatified in 1999.

Edward Powell (Bl) M. P. Jul 30
d. 1540. A Welshman, he became a fellow of Oriel College in Oxford and a canon of Salisbury Cathedral, being known for his writings against Luther. As one of advisers of Queen Catherine of Aragon he opposed the spiritual claims of King Henry VIII and was imprisoned for six years before being hanged, drawn and quartered at Smithfield, London, with BB Richard Featherston and Thomas Abel. He was beatified in 1886. *See* **England (Martyrs of)**.

Edward Ripoll Diego (Bl) *see* **Philip-of-Jesus Munárriz Azcona and Comps**

Edward-Joseph Rosaz (Bl) B. F. Mar 3
1830–1893. Born at Susa in Piedmont, Italy, he was ordained in 1854 and became a cathedral canon, the seminary rector and chaplain to nuns and prisoners. To help the poor and children of the diocese he founded the 'Franciscan Missionary Sisters of Susa' in 1870. He became bishop in 1878 and proved to be a truly great pastor, being devoted to the Eucharist, Our Lady and the pope. His personal spirituality was based on 'lectio divina'. He was beatified in 1991.

Edward Shelley (Bl) M. L. Aug 30
d. 1588. A landowner of Warminghurst in Sussex, he was hanged at Tyburn for sheltering priests along with St Margaret Ward and BB John Roche, Richard Flower, Richard Leigh and Richard Martin. He was beatified in 1929. *See* **England (Martyrs of)**.

Edward Stransham (Bl) M. P. Jan 21
d. 1586. From Oxford, he was a student at St John's College there but converted, studied at Douai and Rheims and was ordained in 1580. From the following year he was on mission in London and Oxford until he was captured and executed at Tyburn. He was beatified in 1929. *See* **England (Martyrs of)**.

Edward Thwing (Bl) M. P. Jul 27
1560–1600. Related to St John of Bridlington and to Bl Thomas Thwing, he was born at Heworth Hall in Yorks and became Professor of Hebrew and Greek at the college at Rheims before being ordained at Laon in 1597. He was a priest in Lancashire before being captured and executed at Lancaster with Bl Robert Nutter. He was beatified in 1987. *See* **England (Martyrs of)**.

Edward Waterson (Bl) M. P. Jan 8
d. 1593. A convert from London, he studied at Rheims and was ordained in 1592. He was immediately captured on his return to England and executed at Newcastle. He was beatified in 1929. *See* **England (Martyrs of)**.

Edwen (St) R. Nov 6
C7th. The patron of Llanedwen in Anglesey, Wales, is alleged to have been either a daughter of St Brychan or of King St Edwin of Northumbria when he was a pagan prince staying as a guest in Wales.

Edwin, King (St) M. L. Oct 12
d. 633. He was king of Northumbria, England, from 616, when he seized the throne after the death of King Ethelfrith in battle. Then he married St Ethelburga of Kent and was baptized by St Paulinus, her chaplain, in 627 after much hesitation. He was killed on Hatfield Chase fighting an alliance of the pagan Mercian King Penda and the Christian Welsh King Cadwalladr and was venerated as a martyr. He was succeeded in due course by St Oswald, the exiled son of Ethelfrith.

Edwold (St) R. Aug 29
C9th. He was allegedly King St Edmund of East Anglia, England, and was a hermit near Cerne Abbas in Dorset, where his shrine was established.

Efflam *(Inflannan)* (St) R. Nov 6
d. *c*700. His story is that he was an Irish nobleman who fled his home to escape marriage and became abbot-founder of a monastery at Plestan near St Brieuc in Brittany, France.

Egbert of Iona (St) R. Apr 24
d. 729. An Anglo-Saxon monk from Lindisfarne, he went to Ireland to study at an unidentified monastery called 'Rathmelsigi' and remained there, helping to inspire missionary monks to go to the Germanic countries. Then he went to Iona, Scotland, and tried to introduce the Roman observance. He eventually succeeded, it being alleged that he died on the first Easter Sunday celebrated there on the date given by the Roman calculation.

Egbert of Ripon (St) R. Mar 18
d. *c*720. A monk, probably of the abbey at Ripon in Yorkshire, England, he was venerated there from *c*1000.

Egbert of York (St) B. Nov 19
d. 766. Brother of King Edbert of Northumbria, he became bishop of York, England, in 732 and founded the famous cathedral school there which had Alcuin as its most famous pupil. He was a friend of St Bede. He joined his brother in retirement in a monastery when the latter abdicated in 758.

Egdunus and Comps (SS) MM. Mar 12
d. 303. They were martyred at Nicomedia, Asia Minor, in the reign of Diocletian by being hanged head-downwards over a fire.

Egelnoth *see* **Ethelnoth**

Egelwin (Ethelwin) (St) L. Nov 29
C7th. A prince of Wessex, England, he lived as an invalid at Athelney in the Somerset marshes before an abbey was founded there, where his shrine was later established.

Egidius *see* **Giles**

Egil (Aeigilus) (St) R(OSB). Dec 17
d. 822. A monk of Fulda in Bavaria, Germany, he was appointed abbot after the emperor Charlemagne deposed his violent predecessor in 817. He restored the tranquillity of the house and prepared it for the magnificence of his successor, St Rabanus Maurus.

Egilhard (St) M. R(OSB). May 25
d. 881. Abbot of Charlemagne's model monastery of Kornelimünster near Aachen, Germany, he was killed by the Norse at Berchem, Belgium, and venerated as a martyr.

Egilo (Egilon, Eigil) (St) R(OSB). Jun 28
d. 871. Abbot of Prüm near Trier, Germany, he had St Humphrey as one of his monks. He restored the abbey of Flavigny near Dijon and

founded that of Corbigny near Nevers, both in France.

Egino (Bl) R(OSB). Jul 15
d. 1120. From Augsburg in Bavaria, Germany, he was received as a child-oblate at the abbey of SS Ulric and Afra there. As a monk he sided with the pope in his conflict with the emperor and was expelled by his abbot in 1098. He was recalled in 1103, became abbot himself in 1106 but was persecuted by a simonical bishop and fled to Rome in 1120. He died at the Camaldolese monastery at Pisa on his way back.

Egwin (St) B. R? Dec 30
d. 717. An Anglo-Saxon nobleman and possibly a monk, he became bishop of Worcester, England, in 692 but was driven away by a hostile faction. He was reinstated after going to Rome for vindication, and probably founded Evesham Abbey where his shrine was established.

Egypt (Martyrs and Confessors)
The old Roman Martyrology listed two anonymous groups of martyrs and confessors of Egypt:

Jan 5
d. 303. Many were killed in the Thebaid in the reign of Diocletian.

May 21
d. *c*357. During the Arian controversy many bishops and priests were sent into exile from Alexandria.

Eigrad (St) R. Jan 6
C6th. A brother of St Sampson, he was a monk under St Illtyd and settled on Anglesey, Wales.

Eilan *see* **Elian**

Eingan (Einion, Eneon, Anianus) (St) R. Feb 9
C6th. Alleged to have been a Cumbrian prince, he settled as a hermit at Llanengan on the Lleyn Peninsula, Wales.

Einhilde and Roswinda (SS) RR. Dec 13
C8th. They were nuns under St Ottilia at Hohenburg near Regensburg in Bavaria, Germany, Roswinda possibly being her sister. Einhilde went on to be abbess of Niedermünster nearby.

Ekbert (Egbert) (St) R. Nov 25
d. 1075. A monk of Gorze near Metz, France, he became abbot of Münsterschwartzach in Bavaria, Germany.

Ekhard (St) R. Jun 28
d. 1084. A cathedral canon at Halberstadt near Magdeburg, Germany, he retired to Huysburg nearby and founded a monastery there.

Ela Longsword (Bl) R(CR). Feb 1
d. 1261. The widow of an earl of Salisbury, England, she was a disciple of St Edmund Rich and founded a Carthusian monastery at Hinton, Somerset, as well as an Augustinian nunnery at Lacock where she became abbess.

Elaeth the King (St) R.
C6th. A Strathclyde British chieftain and bard, he was exiled to Wales by the Picts and became a monk under St Seirol on Anglesey, where he founded Amlwch church. Some of his poetry is extant.

Elaphius (St) B. Aug 19
d. 580. He became bishop of Châlons-sur-Marne, France, in 572. He died on a journey to Spain which according to St Gregory of Tours was an embassy, but later tradition describes him as looking for the relics of St Eulalia at Mérida.

Eldad or Eldate *see* **Aldate**

Eldrad *see* **Heldrad**

Eleazar (St) *see* **Minervus, Eleazar and Comps**

Eleazar *see* **Elzear**

Eleazar de Sabran (St) L. Sep 27
1286–1323. A nobleman from Provence, France, married to Bl Delphina of Signe, he held the barony of Ansouis at home as well as the county of Ariano in the kingdom of Naples. He went to the latter as tutor to the king's son, served as regent of the kingdom and died in Paris as its ambassador. He was noted for his honesty, penance and prayer at a time when these qualities were not common among his class. He was canonized in 1369.

Elefreda *see* **Etheldritha**

Elerius (St) R. Nov 3
C6th. He is mentioned in the legend of St Winifred as her spiritual director and biographer as well as the founder of her nunnery at Gwytherin in Clwyd, Wales.

Elesbaan (Caleb), Negus (St) L. Oct 27
d. ?555. He was the Negus (king) of Axum in Ethiopia after that country became Christian

and campaigned against the Jewish king of the Himyarites in the Yemen after the latter persecuted his Christian subjects. He abdicated to become a monk, allegedly at Jerusalem but actually near Axum. His name was inserted into the old Roman Martyrology although he was almost certainly a Monophysite.

Elesmes *see* **Adelelmus**

Eleuchadius of Ravenna (St) B. Feb 14
C2nd. A Greek, he was converted by St Apollinaris of Ravenna, Italy, and was bishop-administrator for him in his absence. Then he succeeded St Adheritus as bishop and is alleged to have introduced the practice of the Divine Office to the West.

Eleusippus (St) *see* **Speusippus, Eleusippus and Comps**

Eleutherius (St) *see* **Dionysius of Paris and Comps**

Eleutherius, Pope *May 26*
d. 189. A Greek deacon of Rome, he succeeded St Soter as pope in ?174. Very little is known about him, and the story that he sent missionaries to Britain is a myth. His cultus was suppressed in 1969.

Eleutherius, Anthia and Comps (SS) MM. Apr 18
d. 117–138. They were alleged to have been an Illyrian bishop, his mother and eleven others who were martyred in the reign of Hadrian. Their acta are completely worthless, however, being medieval Byzantine fiction.

Eleutherius and Leonides (SS) MM. Aug 8
? They were burned, possibly at Byzantium (later Constantinople) but nothing is known for certain.

Eleutherius of Auxerre (St) B. Aug 16
d. 561. He was bishop of Auxerre, France, from 532.

Eleutherius of Byzantium (St) M. B. Feb 20
d. *c*310. Allegedly a bishop and martyr of Byzantium (later Constantinople), he is usually identified with St Eleutherius of Tarsia.

Eleutherius of Nicomedia and Comps (SS) MM. Oct 2
d. ?303. He was allegedly a soldier-martyr at Nicomedia, Asia Minor, but his acta are unreliable and he may be the same person as his namesakes of Byzantium and Tarsia.

Eleutherius of Rocca d'Arce (St) R. May 29
? The principal patron of Rocca d'Arce near Aquino, Italy, he was a hermit there who was alleged to have been an English pilgrim and a brother of SS Grimwald of Pontecorvo and Fulk Scotti.

Eleutherius of Spoleto (St) R. Sep 6
d. *c*590. Abbot of a monastery at Spoleto, Italy, he was a thaumaturge and had some of his miracles described by St Gregory the Great (who himself experienced a cure). He migrated to Rome and became a monk at St Gregory's monastery of St Andrew's.

Eleutherius of Tarsia (St) M. Aug 4
d. *c*310. He was a martyr of Tarsia in Bithynia, Asia Minor, and had a pilgrimage-shrine there as well as a church in Constantinople. His acta are unreliable.

Eleutherius of Tournai (St) M? B. Feb 20
d. ?531. From Tournai, Belgium, he became bishop there (possibly the first) in 486 and evangelized the Franks settling in the area. He allegedly died as a result of being attacked by some local Arians, but the extant biographies are unreliable.

Elevetha *see* **Almedha**

Elfleda of Glastonbury (St) R. Oct 23
d. ?936. An Anglo-Saxon noblewoman, she became a hermit near Glastonbury, England. St Dunstan was one of her admirers as a boy.

Elfleda (Ethelfleda) of Romsey (St) R(OSB). Oct 29
d. *c*1000. Daughter of Earl Ethelwold, the founder of the nunnery of Romsey in Hampshire, England, she became a nun there and eventually abbess.

Elfleda (Ethelfleda, Edilfleda, Elgiva) of Whitby (St) R. Feb 8
653–714. Daughter of King Oswy of Northumbria, she was placed in the nunnery at Hartlepool as a toddler under St Hilda in thanksgiving for her father's victory over King Penda of Mercia in battle in 654. She went to Whitby with St Hilda, succeeded her as abbess and became extremely influential in her kingdom (she helped reconcile SS Wilfrid and Theodore and was close to St Cuthbert).

Elfrick *see* **Alfrick**

Elgar (St) R. Jun 14
d. *c*1100. From Devon, England, he was allegedly kidnapped by Danes, taken to Ireland and forced to work as a public executioner. After he escaped he settled as a hermit on Bardsey off the Lleyn Peninsula, Wales.

Elgiva (St) R(OSB)? May 18
d. 944. Wife of King Edmund of Wessex, England, (921–946) and mother of Kings Edwy and Edgar, she re-founded the nunnery at Shaftesbury and retired to die there, possibly as a nun. She was praised by William of Malmesbury. There is some confusion over her identity.

Elian (Eilan, Allan) (St) R. Jan 13
C6th. A Cornishman or Breton related to St Ismael, he was associated with Llaneilian on Anglesey and with Llaneilan near Conway, both places in Wales with famous holy wells, as well as with the church of St Allen near Truro in Cornwall, England. He has been confused with St Hilary.

Elias *see* **Peleus, Nilus and Comps**

Elias, Jeremias, Isaias, Samuel and Daniel (SS) MM. Feb 16
d. 309. Five Egyptians, they went to visit some fellow Christian countrymen who had been condemned to the mines in Cilicia, Asia Minor. On the way back they were seized and beheaded at Caesarea in the Holy Land. Eusebius was there at the time and wrote a graphic account of the martyrdom.

Elias, Paul and Isidore (SS) MM. Apr 17
d. 856. Elias was a priest of Cordoba, Spain, under Muslim rule and was killed with two young men, allegedly monks, whom he was directing. St Eulogius left an eye-witness account of the martyrdom.

Elias of Cologne (Bl) R(OSB). Apr 16
d. 1042. Traditionally an Irishman, he was a hermit before becoming abbot of the Scottish abbey of St Martin at Cologne, Germany, in 1020, and later also of the abbey of St Pantaleon.

Elias Facchini (St) *see* **Gregory Grassi and Comps**

Elias of Jerusalem (St) *see* **Flavian and Elias**

Elias Leymarie de Laroche (Bl) *see* **John-Baptist Souzy and Comps**

Elias-del-Socorro Nieves (Bl) M. R(OSA). Oct 11
1882–1928. From a peasant family of Guanajuato State, Mexico, despite tuberculosis he became an Augustinian friar at Yurira in 1904 and was ordained in 1916. In 1921 he was put in charge of an extremely poor rural parish until 1927, when the 'Christero' guerrilla movement against the persecution of the church by the government broke out. He was ordered by the latter to move to a city so as to be under observation but took to the hills instead and continued his rural ministry in secret. After fourteen months he was captured with two ranchers by a military patrol, recognized as a priest and shot with them. He was beatified in 1997.

Elias of Sandomir (Bl) *see* **Sadoc of Sandomir and Comps**

Elias Spelaiotes (St) R. Sep 11
?865–?960. From Reggio di Calabria, Italy, he became a monk when aged nineteen and died as a hermit in a cave at Meliculla (his surname means 'Troglodyte'). He has been confused with Elias of Thessalonika.

Elias of Syracuse (St) B. R? Aug 26
d. ?664. Allegedly a monk of Syracuse, Sicily, he succeeded St Zosimus as bishop there.

Elias of Thessalonika (St) R. Aug 17
823–903. From Sicily, he was enslaved after the Muslim conquest of the island in 831 but was released and visited the holy places of the East before founding a monastery at Salianae in Calabria, Italy. He died at Thessalonika on his way to Constantinople.

Eligius Herque du Roule (Bl) *see* **September (Martyrs of)**

Eligius (Eloi, Eloy) of Noyon (St) B. Dec 1
588–660. From a lowly background at Limoges, France, owing to his talent he became the royal goldsmith and minter at the Frankish court at Paris and endowed many churches and monasteries such as Solignac. In 640 he left his post to become a priest, was made bishop of Noyon and evangelized French and Belgian Flanders. He had an extremely popular cultus in the Middle Ages. Some pieces of precious metalwork allegedly by him survived to the French Revolution, but all but one fragment were then destroyed.

Elijah *see* **Elias**

Eliantius *see* **Lantfrid, Waltram and Comps**

Elined *see* **Almedha**

Eliphius (Eloff) (St) M. Oct 16
d. 362. Allegedly from Ireland or Scotland, he was martyred at Soulosse near Saint-Dié, France, and had his relics taken to Cologne, Germany, in the C10th.

Elizabeth (St) L. Nov 5
C1st. What is known about the mother of St John the Baptist is limited to the Gospel of St Luke.

Elizabeth Achlin 'the Good'
(Bl) T(OFM). Nov 25
1386–1420. From Waldsee in Württemberg, Germany, she became a Franciscan tertiary in 1400 and was a prodigious faster as well as a mystic and stigmatic. In 1403 she joined a community at Reute nearby and died there. Her cultus was confirmed for Constance in 1766.

Elizabeth-Anne Bayley Seton
(St) R. F. Jan 4
1774–1821. From New York, she was a devout member of the Episcopalian Church until she was widowed with five children in 1804. Then she converted, was confirmed at Baltimore in 1806 and went on to found the first indigenous American sisterhood, the 'Sisters of Charity of St Joseph'. They worked to build up a parochial school system in the USA. She died near Baltimore and was canonized in 1975.

Elizabeth Canori Mora (Bl) T. Feb 4
1779–1825. A Roman, she married a young lawyer but he soon abandoned her with two daughters. This meant she had to earn her own living, but still managed to care for other needy families. She became a Trinitarian tertiary in 1807. Her husband repented shortly after her death and became a priest of the Franciscan Conventuals, as she had predicted. She was beatified in 1994.

Elizabeth-of-the-Trinity Catez (Bl) R(OCD) Nov 8
1880–1906. From near Bourges, France, she early recognized a Carmelite vocation and made a private vow of chastity when aged 14. She joined the Carmel at Dijon in 1901 and died of tuberculosis five years later, but her experience of contemplative prayer in the meantime led her to develop her doctrine of the indwelling of the Holy Trinity in the praying subject. She was beatified in 1984.

Bl Elizabeth-of-the-Trinity Catez, Nov 8

Elizabeth Cheong (St) *see* **Korea (Martyrs of)**

Elizabeth-Teresa-of-the-Heart-of-Jesus Consolin (Bl) *see* **Orange (Martyrs of)**

Elizabeth Ferrer Sabría (Bl) *see* **Angela-of-St-Joseph Lloret Martí and Comps**

Elizabeth of Hungary
(St) T(OFM). Nov 17
1207–1231. Born at Presburg in Hungary (now Bratislava in Slovakia), she was a daughter of King Andrew II and a niece of St Hedwig. When aged fourteen she married Ludwig IV, landgrave of Thuringia, Germany, and was happily married with three children until he died on crusade at Otranto. Then she was dispossessed (but was granted the city of Marburg) and became a Franciscan tertiary, living in poverty while helping the destitute. She was canonized in 1235. She is often depicted with her cloak full of roses.

Elizabeth of Hungary, the Younger
(St) R(OP). May 6
d. 1338. Daughter of King Andrew III of Hungary, she refused to marry a son of the king of Bohemia and became a Dominican nun at

Töss near Zürich, Switzerland. She was the last of the Arpad dynasty which had included King St Stephen, and the Hungarian crown went to the House of Anjou as a result.

Elizabeth-Bartholomea Picenardi (Bl) T(OSM). Feb 20
1428–1468. From Mantua, Italy, when she lost her mother she became a Servite tertiary and collected a group of disciples from the Mantuan nobility, thus founding a new nunnery. Her cultus was confirmed in 1804 for Cremona, Mantua and the Servites.

Elizabeth of Portugal
(St) T(OFM). Jul 4
1271–1336. Daughter of the king of Aragon, when aged twelve she married King Denis of Portugal who was a capable ruler but an immoral and selfish person. At his dissolute court she gave an example of Christian rectitude and charity and tried to make peace between the Iberian kingdoms. As a widow she became a Franciscan tertiary at a Poor Clare convent at Coïmbra. She was canonized in 1625.

Elizabeth Qin (Bian) and Simon Qin (Qunfu) (St) MM. LL. Jul 19 and 17
1846 and 1886–1900. She was a widow of Nanpeiluo in Hebei, China, with six children. After the Boxer rebellion they moved to Liucan for safety but were betrayed. As they fled, St Simon, a son, was caught and killed; St Elizabeth was shot dead with two daughters two days later (another son had already been killed). *See* **China (Martyrs of)**.

Elizabeth Renzi (Bl) R. F. Aug 14
1786–1859. From near Rimini, Italy, she joined the Augustinians at Pietrarubbia in 1807 but the community was suppressed in 1810 and she returned home. In 1824 she started to teach at the secondary school at Corriano, which lacked qualified teachers. To run it properly she eventually founded the 'Pious Teachers of Our Lady of Sorrows', which was approved as a diocesan institute with a charism based on the Seven Sorrows of Our Lady. Dying at Corriano, she was beatified in 1989.

Elizabeth-Rose of Rozoy
(St) R(OSB). Dec 13
d. 1130. A nun of Chelles near Paris, France, she was the abbess-founder of the nunnery at Rozoy near Sens.

Elizabeth of Schönau (St) R(OSB). Jun 18
1126–1164. When aged twelve she entered the Benedictine (not Cistercian) nunnery at Schönau near Bonn, Germany. After being professed in 1147 she became subject to visions which were described in the biography written by her brother Egbert, who was abbot of a neighbouring monastery. Some of these, such as those concerning St Ursula, seem to have been delusions but she was humble and bore her ill-health with patience. She became abbess in 1157.

Elizabeth Vendramini
(Bl) T(OFM). F. Apr 2
1790–1860. Born at Bassani near Vicenza, Italy, she refused to marry and, when aged 27, devoted herself to being 'poor with the poor' in order to help them and to find God in them. She went to Padua in 1828 and founded the 'Elizabethines', which were Franciscan tertiaries with St Elizabeth of Hungary as their patron. She was beatified in 1990.

Elid (Lide, Illog) (St) R. Aug 8
C7th. He was a hermit on the island of St Helen's in the Isles of Scilly, and ruins of a small monastery survive there. He may be the same as the patron of Hirnant in Powys, Wales.

Ellyw *see* **Almedha**

Elmo *see* **Erasmus or Peter Gonzalez**

Eloff *see* **Eliphius**

Eloi *see* **Eligius**

Eloquius (Eloque) of Lagny (St) R. Dec 3
d. *c*660. A disciple of St Fursey, he succeeded him as abbot of Lagny near Paris, France.

Elphege *see* **Alphege**

Elpidephorus (St) *see* **Acindynus, Pegasius and Comps**

Elpidius (St) *see* **Basil, Ephrem and Comps**

Elpidius (St) *see* **Priscus II of Capua and Comps**

Elpidius, Marcellus, Eustochius and Comps (SS) MM. Nov 16
d. 362. According to their story, Elpidius was an official at the court of the Arian emperor Constantius. After the accession of the pagan emperor Julian he was martyred with several companions in an unknown place, by being tied to the tails of unbroken horses and thus dragged about before being burned alive. The problem with this story is that any high official

at court at that time was most likely to have been an Arian himself, and hence would not have been regarded as a Catholic martyr. Also, Julian's policy was to avoid martyring Christians.

Elpidius of Cappadocia (St) R. Sep 2
C4th. There are two villages called Sant' Elpidio near Fermo in the Marches, Italy, and these are alleged to have been the sites of monasteries founded by a hermit from Cappodocia, Asia Minor.

Elpidius of Lyons (St) B. Sep 2
d. 422. He succeeded St Antiochus as bishop of Lyons, France. His shrine there (with many others in France) was destroyed by Calvinists in 1562.

Elpis *see* **Faith, Hope and Charity**

Elric *see* **Aldericus**

Elstan (St) B. R(OSB). Apr 6
d. 981. A monk under St Ethelwold at the latter's new foundation at Abingdon on the Thames, England, he was initially the cook and was noted for blind obedience. He succeeded the founder as abbot and was made bishop of Ramsbury in 970.

Elvan and Mydwyn (SS) Jan 1
C2nd. They were allegedly two Britons sent by a British king to Pope St Eleutherius to ask for a mission to Britain, to which they were themselves appointed. The story is fictional.

Elwin (Elvis) (St) R. Feb 22
C6th. He was allegedly one of the companions of St Breaca and may be the patron of St Allen near Truro in Cornwall, England, but the tradition is seriously confused.

Elwin *see* **Ethelwine**

Elzear *see* **Eleazar**

Emebert (Ablebert) (St) B. Jan 15
C7th? He has a cultus in Flanders, France, but is difficult to identify, being either a bishop of Cambrai in the mid C7th or a son of St Amelberga of Mauberge and a regionary bishop of Brabant who died *c*710.

Emerentiana (St) V. Jan 23
? She is a Roman martyr of unknown date but ancient cultus. Her unreliable legend describes her as being stoned to death after being discovered praying at the tomb of St Agatha, her recently martyred foster-sister. Her cultus was confined to local calendars in 1969.

Emeric of Hungary (St) L. Nov 4
1007–1031. Son of King St Stephen and crown-prince of Hungary, he was tutored by St Gerard Sagredo and gave promise of being a model ruler but died before his father in a hunting accident. A pagan reaction followed. He was canonized with his father in 1083.

Emeric de Quart (Bl) B. Aug 1
d. 1318. He became bishop of Aosta in the Alps, Italy, in 1301, and had his cultus confirmed for there in 1881.

Emerita (St) *see* **Digna and Emerita**

Emeritus (St) *see* **Saturninus, Dativus and Comps**

Emerius (St) R. Jan 27
C8th. A Frenchman, he became the abbot-founder of the abbey of Bañoles near Gerona in Catalonia, Spain.

Emeterius *see* **Hemiterius**

Emidius *see* **Emygdius**

Emilas and Jeremias (SS) MM. Sep 15
d. 852. Brothers from Cordoba, Spain, they preached against Islam in Arabic and were killed as a result in the reign of the Umayyad emir Abderrahman II. Emilas was a deacon.

Emilian (St) *see* **Agapius of Cirta and Comps**

Emilian (St) *see* **Ammon, Emilan and Comps**

Emilian (St) *see* **Dionysia, Dativa and Comps**

Emilian (St) *see* **Dionysius, Emilian and Sebastian**

Emilian Zariquiegui Mendoza (Bl) *see* **Aurelius-Mary Villalón Acebrón and Comps**

Emilian de Cogolla (St) R. Nov 12
d. 574. Initially a poverty-stricken shepherd in La Rioja, Spain, he became a hermit and then a priest of the church at Berceo near Tarazona. He went back to being a hermit, however, gathered a large number of disciples and thus founded the monastery of La Cogolla ('The Cowl'). He is a minor patron of Spain, having been invoked in the wars against the Moors.

Emilian (Aemilio) of Combes
(St) R. Jan 7
d. 767. From Vannes in Brittany, France, he became a monk at Saujon near Saintes and then a hermit in the forest of Combes near Bordeaux.

Emilian of Cyzicus (St) B. Aug 8
d. *c*820. A bishop of Cyzicus on the south shore of the Sea of Marmara, Asia Minor, he died in exile for opposing iconoclasm.

Emilian of Lagny (St) R. Mar 10
d. 675. An Irishman, he became a monk and then abbot of Lagny near Paris, France.

Emilian of Rennes (St) R. Oct 11
? He is listed in the old Roman Martyrology as a hermit at Rennes in Brittany, France, but there is no record of him locally and he is possibly a duplication of St Melanius of Rennes.

Emilian of Silistria (St) M. Jul 18
d. 362. He was martyred at Silistria, Bulgaria, in the reign of Julian.

Emilian of Vercelli (St) B. Sep 11
d. 520. He had been a hermit for forty years when he became bishop of Vercelli in Piedmont, Italy, and went on to die a centenarian.

Emiliana (St) R. Jan 5
C6th. She was a paternal aunt of St Gregory the Great, who described her as living in community with two other maiden aunts (Amita and Tarsilla) in their own house at Rome.

Emiliana (St) V? Jun 30
? There is a church dedicated to her in Rome but nothing is known of her and there is a suspicion that the dedication originally came from a street name.

Emilius (St) *see* **Castus and Emilius**

Emilius (St) *see* **Marcellus, Castus and Comps**

Emilius, Felix, Priam and Lucian
(SS) MM? May 28
? There are churches in Sardinia dedicated to these presumed martyrs but nothing is known about them.

Emily Bicchieri (Bl) R(OP). Aug 19
1238–1314. From Vercelli, Italy, she induced her father to found a Dominican nunnery there and she became the first superior. She had the charism of prophecy. Her cultus was confirmed for Vercelli in 1769.

Emily de Rodat *see* **Mary-Emily de Rodat**

Emily Tavernier Gamelin
(Bl) R. F. (Sep 23)
1800–1851. From Montreal, Canada, when aged twenty-three she married and had three children, but her entire family was dead by the time she was twenty-seven. Then she dedicated herself to alleviating human misery in all its forms, and gathered many disciples. In 1844 these became the 'Sisters of Providence' with herself as superior, and this congregation has become international in scope after her death of cholera. She was beatified in 2001.

Emily de Vialar (St) R. F. Aug 24
1797–1856. From Gaillac near Albi, France, she lost her mother when still a child and kept house for her father until she was thirty-five while devoting herself to prayer and works of charity. Then she received a large inheritance and set about founding the 'Sisters of St Joseph of the Apparition' locally in 1832. She lost her money and also her prestige in Albi after a disastrous missionary expedition to Algiers but managed to establish a house at Marseilles in 1852. By the time she died her institute had spread through Europe and to Africa and Asia. She was canonized in 1951.

Emma *see* **Gemma**

Emmanuel (St) *see* **Quadratus, Theodosius and Comps**

Emmanuel Alvarez (Bl) *see* **Ignatius de Azevedo and Comps**

Emmanuel Buil Lalueza (Bl) *see* **Philip-of-Jesus Munárriz Azcona and Comps**

Emmanuel of Cremona (Bl) B. Feb 27
d. 1298. He became bishop of Cremona, Italy, in 1291 but resigned and retired to the Cistercian monastery of Adwert in Friesland, Netherlands, in 1195. There is no evidence that he then took vows and the assertion that he was a monk there before he became a bishop is certainly false. He had a local cultus at Adwert.

Emmanuel Domingo y Sol
(Bl) P. F. Jan 25
1836–1909. Born at Tortosa, Spain, where he spent his life, he was ordained in 1860. Then he started the first Spanish Catholic newspaper directed at young men and founded the 'Institute of Diocesan Worker Priests' in order to give reparative adoration to the Blessed Sacrament as the centre of the priest's life and

to encourage priestly vocations. This spread to Portugal, Italy and the USA. He also founded three congregations of sisters and the Pontifical Spanish College in Rome. Extremely charitable to everyone, especially to the poor and despised, he was beatified in 1987.

Emmanuel Fernández and Emmanuel Pacheco (BB) *see* **Ignatius de Azevedo and Comps**

Emmanuel González García
(Bl) B. F. Jan 4
1877–1940. From Seville, Spain, he was ordained in 1901 and became a parish priest at Huelva where he developed a strong devotion to reparation to Jesus in the Blessed Sacrament. To this end he founded the 'Eucharistic Missionaries of Nazareth' and several lay societies. In 1920 he was made bishop of Malaga, but had to go into exile in 1931 as a result of the Spanish Civil War. He died at Palencia and was beatified in 2001.

Emmanuel Jímenez Salado (Bl) *see* **Hospitaller Martyrs of Spain**

Emmanuel López Orbara (Bl) *see* **Hospitaller Martyrs of Spain**

Emmanuel Martin Sierra (Bl) *see* **Vincent Soler and Comps**

Emmanuel Martínez Jarauta (Bl) *see* **Philip-of-Jesus Munárriz Azcona and Comps**

Emmanuel Medina Olmos (Bl) *see* **Diego Ventaja Milán and Comps**

Emmanuel Morales (St) *see* **Mexico (Martyrs of)**

Emmanuel (Le van) Phung
(St) M. Jul 31
?1796–1859. From Dan-nuoc in Vietnam, he became a catechist and was executed by strangling near Chaudoc. *See* **Vietnam (Martyrs of)**.

Emmanuel Rodríguez (Bl) *see* **Ignatius de Azevedo and Comps**

Emmanuel Ruiz and Comps
(BB) MM. Jul 10
d. 1860. After the Crimean War there was great hostility shown to the Middle Eastern Christians in the Ottoman Empire. The Druzes in the Lebanon indulged in a pogrom of their Christian neighbours, and when news of this reached Damascus a Muslim mob sacked the Christian quarter and massacred about four thousand with the connivance of the authorities. A community of eight Franciscans and three Maronite brothers who had taken refuge with them were offered the choice of conversion to Islam or death, and were killed after their refusal. They were Emmanuel Ruiz (superior of the friary), Carmelus Volta, Engelbert Kolland, Francis Pinazo d'Arpuentes, Nicanor Ascuenius, Nicholas Alberca, John-James Fernandez and Peter Soler (Franciscans); Francis, Mooti and Raphael Massabki (Maronite brothers). They were beatified in 1926.

Emmanuel Segura López (Bl) *see* **Dionysius Pamplona Polo and Comps**

Emmanuel Torras Sais (Bl) *see* **Philip-of-Jesus Munárriz Azcona and Comps**

Emmanuel (Nguyen van) Trieu
(St) M. P. Sep 17
?1756–1798. A Vietnamese with Christian parents, he became a soldier but left the army, was ordained priest and worked with the missionaries of the Paris Mission Society. While visiting his mother he was arrested and beheaded. *See* **Vietnam (Martyrs of)**.

Emmelia (St) *see* **Basil the Elder and Emmelia**

Emmeram (Haimhramm)
(St) M. B. Sep 22
d. *c*690. According to his unreliable biography, he was from Poitiers, France, and was on his way through Bavaria, Germany, on a missionary journey to the Avars when he was persuaded by the duke to stay at Regensburg and become its bishop. Then at the start of a journey to Rome he was waylaid by the duke's son who accused him of seducing a sister of his and ordered him to be blinded and deprived of his extremities. He died later as a result, was buried at Regensburg and was venerated as a martyr at the abbey that was founded at his shrine.

Emygdius (Emidius) (St) M? B? Aug 9
d. ?303. He is alleged to have been a bishop and martyr at Ascoli Piceno, Italy, but his acta are unreliable. He has a cultus in California as a protector against earthquakes.

Encratia (Engracia) (St) V. Apr 16
d. ?304. Her story is that she was a maiden who was tortured at Zaragoza, Spain, by being disembowelled and having one breast cut off.

Although regarded as a martyr she apparently survived this treatment.

Enda (Eanna) (St) R. F. Mar 21
d. *c*530. Brother of St Fanchea, he is regarded as Ireland's earliest founder of monasteries, the principal one being Killeaney on Inishmore in the Aran Islands. He had many disciples who went on to become great monastic founders, such as SS Brendan and Finian.

Endellion (St) R. Apr 29
C6th? Sister of St Nectan of Hartland, she was allegedly one of the descendants of St Brychan. Many legends are attached to her name, and part of her shrine survives at Endellion near Bodmin in Cornwall, England.

Eneco (Enneco, Iñigo) (St) R(OSB). Jun 1
d. 1057. From Calatayud near Zaragoza, Spain, he became a Cluniac monk at the Aragonese abbey of San Juan de la Peña and went on to become a hermit. The king appointed him abbot of Oña near Burgos, which abbey he elevated to great splendour. He won the respect of Jews and Muslims and was canonized in 1259.

Enfleda (St) R. Nov 24
d. ?704. Daughter of King St Edwin of Northumbria, England, and St Ethelburga, after the death of her father she was taken to Kent by her mother and later married King Oswy of Northumbria. As queen she was a great help to St Wilfrid, and as a widow she became a nun at Whitby under her daughter St Elfleda.

Engelbert *see* **Angilbert**

Engelbert of Cologne (St) M. B. Nov 7
?1186–1225. A son of the Count of Berg, as a child he became cathedral provost of Cologne, Germany, in 1203 but was excommunicated in 1206 for rebellion against the emperor and went on the Albigensian Crusade as an atonement. He became archbishop of Cologne in 1216 and (despite being a typical prince-prelate) he supported the secular clergy, restored monasteries and encouraged the new orders of friars. In 1221 he served as administrator of the Empire. He was killed on the orders of a nephew whom he had rebuked for plundering the nunnery of Essen and was venerated as a martyr.

Engelbert Kolland (Bl) *see* **Emmanuel Ruiz and Comps**

Engelmer (St) M. R. May 14
d. 1096. From a poor peasant family near Passau in Bavaria, Germany, he became a hermit but was killed by robbers and venerated as a martyr.

Engelmund (St) R. Jun 21
d. ?739. Allegedly the abbot of an unknown English monastery, he went to Friesland to help St Willibrord and died at Velsen near Amsterdam, Netherlands.

Enghenedl (St) R? Sep 30
C7th. Nothing is known about this founder of the church of Llanynghenedl near Holyhead, Wales.

England (Martyrs of) May 4
d. 1535–1681. From the Reformation to the C19th the Catholic Church was proscribed in England and Wales. The first 160 years of this period saw systematic persecution as government policy, initially under King Henry VIII who ruthlessly dealt with those who refused to accept his claim to spiritual supremacy. Martyrdoms were especially common under Queen Elizabeth I and King James I, but continued until the end of the C17th. All sorts of people suffered in various different places but the majority of them were regular and secular priests. This is because to work as a priest in England and Wales while having been ordained abroad was declared treason by statute, and the punishment specified for traitors was usually applied to condemned priests. This was to be half-asphyxiated by hanging, then to be disembowelled and dismembered while still alive. The Catholic laity were usually persecuted by the levy of fines because the government appreciated the extra revenue. Of the martyrs (including those of Wales), fifty-four were beatified in 1886, nine in 1895, one hundred and thirty-six in 1929 and eighty-five in 1987. So far forty-two have been canonized, including four Welsh martyrs (forty in 1970 and SS John Fisher and Thomas More in 1935), leaving a total of 242 beatified (including two Welsh martyrs). Before 2001 the forty saints of 1970 were celebrated together on Oct 25, but then one feast-day was established for all the English martyrs and the Welsh ones celebrated separately. *See* lists of national martyrs in appendix.

Englatius (Englat, Tanglen)
(St) B? R? Nov 3
d. 966. He lived at Tarves near Aberdeen, Scotland, and has been described as an abbot and a bishop.

Engratia (St) *see* **Fructus, Valentine and Engratia**

Enguerrammus (Angilram) (St) R(OSB). Dec 9
d. 1045. Of a humble family, he was in turn schoolboy, monk and abbot at Saint-Riquier near Abbeville, France, and was nicknamed 'the Learned Abbot' by his contemporaries. His Latin verse was of high quality.

Ennatha (St) *see* **Antoninus of Caesarea and Comps**

Ennodius (St) B. Jul 17
473–521. Magnus Felix Ennodius was a Gallo-Roman nobleman from Arles, France, who became a professor of rhetoric at Milan, Italy, and lived a carefree married life until a serious illness caused a conversion. His wife became a nun and he was ordained, being made bishop of Pavia near Milan in 510. He was a poet and hymnographer and also a papal legate at Constantinople during the reign of the Monophysite emperor Anastasius I.

Enoch *see* **Kennocha**

Enoder (Cynidr, Keneder) (St) R. Apr 27
C6th. Allegedly a grandson of St Brychan, he is commemorated by Llangynidr in Powys, Wales, and possibly by St Enoder in Cornwall, England. He is venerated in Brittany as St Quidic.

Enodoch (Wenedoc) (St) R. Mar 7
d. *c*520. An alleged descendant of St Brychan whose traditions are extremely confused, even the sex of this saint (who may simply be a duplicate of St Enoder) is uncertain.

Enogatus (St) B. Jan 13
d. 631. He was a bishop of Aleth near St Malo, France.

Eoban (St) M. B. R. Jul 7
d. 754. Allegedly an Irishman who became a monk in England, he helped St Willibrord and then St Boniface on their missions, was made bishop of Martelaar, Netherlands, by the latter and was martyred with him at Dokkum. His shrine was at Erfurt in Thuringia, Germany.

Eochod (St) R. Jan 25
d. 597. One of the twelve Irish monks who accompanied St Columba to Iona, Scotland, he later evangelized the Picts of Galloway.

Eogan *see* **Eugene**

Eosterwine *see* **Esterwine**

Epagathus (St) *see* **Photinus, Sanctus and Comps**

Epaphras (St) M? B? Jul 19
C1st. He is mentioned by St Paul in his Letter to the Colossians (Col 1:7, 4:12, also Philem 23), and is hence traditionally regarded as bishop of Colossae and a martyr there. This is not certain.

Epaphroditus (St) M? B? Mar 22
C1st. He is referred to by St Paul (Phil 2:25) as having been sent to the Philippians and hence has been traditionally regarded as the first bishop of Philippi in Greek Macedonia. He may be the same person as the first bishops listed for Andriaca in Lycia, Asia Minor, and Terracina in Italy, as all three are each alleged to have been among the seventy-two disciples of Christ.

Eparchius (St) *see* **Domitius of Caesarea and Comps**

Eparchius (Cybar) (St) R. Jul 1
?504–581. A nobleman from Périgord, France, he became a monk at Sessac and then a hermit at Angoulême in 542.

Ephebus (St) *see* **Proclus, Ephebus and Apollonius**

Ephesus (Martyrs of) (SS) MM. RR. Jan 12
d. ?762. In his revision of the old Roman Martyrology Cardinal Baronius listed forty-two monks of a monastery at Ephesus, Asia Minor, who were killed on the orders of Emperor Constantine V for opposing his iconoclast policy. Baronius's literary source for this entry is now unknown, but it might have been referring to **Stephen, Basil and Comps** (q.v.).

Ephrem (St) *see* **Basil, Ephrem and Comps**

Ephrem the Syrian (St) D. Dr. R. Jun 9
?306–373. A convert from Nisibis in Mesopotamia, it is probable that he was headmaster of the catechetical school there before the city was annexed by the Persian Empire in 363. Then he and most of the Christian population became refugees, and he settled at Edessa (now Urfa in Turkey) where he became a monk and a deacon. He was the most prolific and famous of the Syrian Fathers, being especially known for his biblical commentaries and the Syriac hymns which he wrote to encourage the Catholic faith and to oppose Arianism (Arius had apparently invented the genre of popular hymns in the contemporary

vernacular). The Mariological hymns are especially important dogmatically. He also led relief efforts in a famine which ravaged the district just before his death in his cell. He was declared a doctor of the Church in 1920.

Ephysius (St) M. Jan 15
d. ?303. He is alleged to have been martyred at Cagliari, Sardinia, in the reign of Diocletian but his acta are a worthless forgery. Nevertheless his veneration is popular on the island.

Epicharis (St) M. Sep 27
d. *c*300. She is alleged to have been a Roman senator's wife who was martyred at Byzantium (later Constantinople).

Epictetus (St) *see* **Martial, Saturninus and Comps**

Epictetus, Jucundus, Secundus, Vitalis, Felix and Comps
(SS) MM. Jan 9
d. ?250. They are listed as twelve Roman African martyrs, possibly of the Decian persecution as St Cyprian wrote of a bishop called Epictetus.

Epigmenius (St) M. P. Mar 24
d. *c*300. Listed as a Roman priest martyred in the reign of Diocletian, he is probably the same as St Pigmenius.

Epimachus and Alexander
(SS) MM. Dec 12
d. *c*250. They were tortured and burned at Alexandria, Egypt, in the reign of Decius. Epimachus is also listed in error in the old Roman Martyrology on May 10 together with St Gordian.

Epiphana (St) M? Jul 12
? An alleged martyr of Sicily, she is mentioned only in the unreliable acta of St Alphius.

Epiphania (St) R. Oct 6
c. *c*800. A nun at Pavia near Milan, Italy, she was allegedly the daughter of a Lombard king.

Epiphanius, Donatus, Rufinus, Modestus and Comps (SS) MM. Apr 7
? Nothing is known of these martyrs, except that Epiphanius was a Roman African bishop and that there were seventeen in the group.

Epiphanius and Isidore
(SS) MM. Aug 4
? The relics of these alleged martyrs were sent to Empress Galla Placidia by Emperor Theodosius II and enshrined in the cathedral at Besançon, France. They were thrown away in the French Revolution.

Epiphanius of Pavia (St) B. Jan 21
?439–?497. From Pavia (then called Ticinum) near Milan, Italy, he became bishop there in 467. The city was destroyed by Odoacer in 476, and Epiphanius was largely responsible for rebuilding it and renaming it Pavia. He travelled to Lyons to secure the release of thousands of Italians from captivity. He died at Pavia and his relics were taken to Hildesheim, Germany, in 962.

Epiphanius of Salamis
(St) B. R. May 12
?315–403. A native of the Holy Land, he became a monk when young and founded a monastery near Eleutheropolis east of Gaza. He was a zealous opponent of heresy, especially of Arianism and Origenism, and his 'Panarion' or handbook of heresies became famous. He became bishop of Salamis in Cyprus in 367. When old he was deceived by Patriarch Theophilus of Alexandria and joined in the deposition of St John Chrysostom at Constantinople, but became aware of the deception and died on the voyage back to Cyprus.

Epiphanius-of-St-Michael Sierra Conde (Bl) *see* **Nicephorus Díez Tejerina and Comps**

Epipodius, Alexander and Comps (SS) MM. Apr 22
d. 178. Two young men and thirty-four others, they were martyred at Lyons, France, in the reign of Marcus Aurelius.

Epistemis (St) *see* **Galation and Epistemis**

Epitacius, Basileus and Aptonius
(SS) MM. BB. May 23
C1st? They are early martyrs. The first-named is identified with the first bishop of Tuy in Galicia, Spain, and the second with a bishop of Braga in Portugal. The traditions are confused.

Epolonius (St) *see* **Babylas and Comps**

Eptadius (St) R. Aug 24
*c*490–550. From near Autun, France, he was married but became a penitent after an illness. To avoid being ordained he fled and eventually joined a monastery that he had founded at Cervon, where his shrine was later established.

Epvre *see* **Aprus**

Equitius (St) R. Aug 11
d. *c*540. He is the subject of the first book of the *Dialogues* of St Gregory the Great, the only evidence of his existence, and is described as a monk who founded a large number of monasteries for men and women in the ancient province of Valeria east of Rome. His headquarters were at what is now Pescara.

Erasma (St) *see* **Euphemia, Dorothy and Comps**

Erasmus of Antioch (St) M. Nov 25
? He is listed as having been martyred at Antioch, Syria, but may be a duplicate of St Erasmus of Formia.

Erasmus (Elmo, Erarmo, Ermo) of Formia (St) M. B. Jun 2
d. ?303. A bishop of Formia near Gaeta, Italy, he was martyred in the reign of Diocletian and had his relics taken to Gaeta when his town was destroyed in a Muslim raid in 842. This is all that is known. A large amount of legendary material has been added to his story, however, and this led to his veneration being very popular in the Middle Ages. He is the patron of sailors, and is depicted being martyred by having his intestines wound out with a windlass.

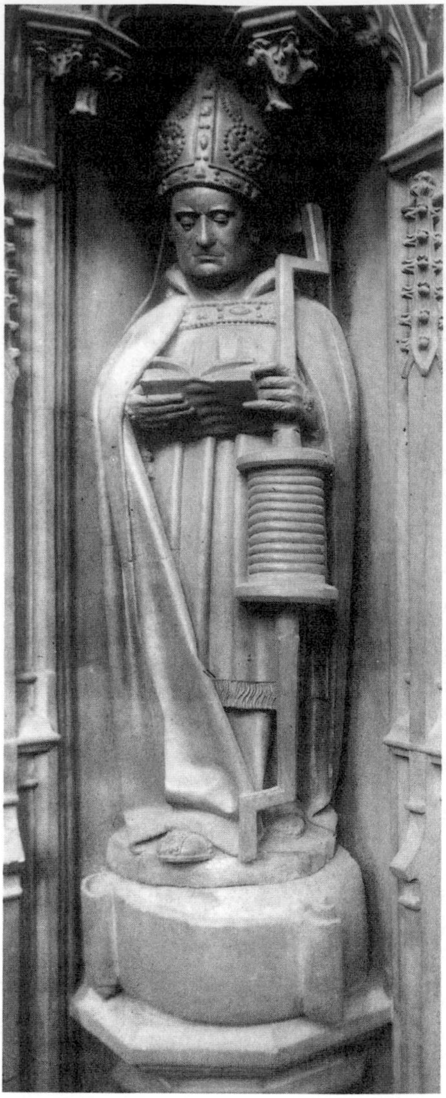
St Erasmus, Jun 2

Erastus (St) M? B. Jul 26
C1st. The city treasurer of Corinth, Greece, when St Paul was there, he is mentioned in Acts 19:22, Rom 16:23 and 2 Tim 4:20. Later traditions conflict: the Eastern tradition is that he became bishop of Caesarea Phillipi in the Holy Land, while the Roman tradition is that he became bishop of Philippi in Greek Macedonia and was martyred.

Erbin (Ervan, Erbyn, Erme, Hermes) (St) Jan 13
C5th? He seems to have been related to a Cornish ruler and is commemorated by the village of St Ervan near Newquay in Cornwall, England.

Ercongotha (St) R. Jul 7
d. 660. Daughter of King Erconbert of Kent, England, and Queen St Sexberga, she became a nun at Faremoutiers-en-Brie, France, under St Ethelburga, her aunt. She died young.

Erconwald (Erkenwald) (St) B. Apr 30
d. 693. Allegedly of the royal family of East Anglia, England, he became the abbot-founder of Chertsey in Surrey and founded a nunnery at Barking in Essex where his sister, St Ethelburga, became abbess. He was made bishop of London by St Theodore of Canterbury in 675 and died at Barking. His shrine at St Paul's cathedral in London was destroyed in the Reformation.

Erembert (St) B. R. May 14
d. ?672. From near Paris, France, he became a monk at Fontenelle in Normandy in *c*640 and bishop of Toulouse in 656. In 668 he retired back to his abbey.

Eremberta (St) R. Oct 16
Late C7th. St Wulmar, her uncle, was an abbot near Boulogne, France, and founded the nunnery of Wierre for her to serve as abbess.

Erentrude (Ermentrude) (St) R. Jun 30
d. ?718. A sister or niece of St Rupert of Salzburg, Austria, she became abbess of the nunnery of Nonnberg at Salzburg which he had founded for her.

Erfyl (Eurfyl) (St) R. Jul 5
? She is the patron of Llanerfyl in Powys, Wales.

Ergnad (Ercnacta) (St) R. Jan 8
C5th. Allegedly clothed as a nun by St Patrick, she is associated with Duneane in Co. Antrim, Ireland.

Ergoule *see* **Gudula**

Erhard (St) B. R. Jan 8
d. ?686. He was a missionary bishop working around Regensburg in Bavaria, Germany. His origin is uncertain, and he possibly became a Columbanian monk. He founded seven monasteries. His extant biography is unreliable.

Eric of Perugia (Bl) L. Mar 13
d. 1415. A Danish pilgrim, he died in a hospital at Perugia, Italy, and was imaginatively alleged to have been a prince (or even a king) back home.

Eric IX of Sweden, King
(St) M. L. May 18
d. 1160. He became king of Sweden in 1150 but his reign is not well documented. He was alleged to have been a protector of the Church and a just ruler and was nicknamed the 'Lawgiver'. In 1157 he started the Swedish conquest and colonization of Finland, which was later (and with little justification) called a missionary crusade. He was apparently killed in a brawl after attending church at Uppsala by rebels led by a Danish invader and was regarded as a martyr. He is the patron of Sweden.

Erizzo (Bl) R(OSB Vall). Feb 9
d. 1094. From Florence, Italy, he was the first disciple of St John Gualbert who founded the Vallumbrosan order. He himself became its fourth abbot-general, and his cultus was confirmed for the Vallumbrosans in 1600.

Erkembodo (St) R. Apr 12
d. 734. Allegedly an Irishman, he succeeded St Bertin the Great as abbot of Sithiu at Saint-Omer, France, at which abbey the Benedictine rule had replaced that of St Columban. He established the abbey's greatness, and became bishop of Thérouanne nearby in 722 while retaining the abbacy.

Erlafrid (St) R(OSB). Nov 6
d. *p*830. Count of Calw near Stuttgart, Germany, he founded the abbey of Hirschau near Nuremberg and became a monk there.

Erlembald Cotta Jun 27
d. 1075. A knight of Milan, Italy, he was involved in a struggle for church reform against a corrupt and simoniac archbishop and was killed as a result in a brawl. For this reason he was venerated as a martyr and his relics enshrined in 1095, but his character was not edifying and Baronius deleted him from the old Roman Martyrology.

Erluf (St) M? B. Feb 10
d. 830. Probably from Ireland, he became bishop of Werder near Berlin, Germany. It is uncertain as to whether he was killed by pagans or died in peace.

Ermel *see* **Armagillus**

Ermelinda (St) R. Oct 29
d. ?595. She was a hermit at Meldaert near Brussels, Belgium, where a nunnery was later founded. Her extant biography is legendary.

Ermenburga ('Domneva')
(St) R. Nov 19
d. *c*700. A princess of Kent, England, she married a prince of Mercia and was the mother of three royal Saxon abbesses: Mildred, Milburga and Mildgytha. When an old widow she founded a nunnery at Minster in Thanet, Kent, but resigned as abbess in favour of her daughter Mildred. Her nickname is a corruption of Domna (i.e. Lady) Ebba and is preserved in the name of the locality of Ebbsfleet where St Augustine landed.

Ermengard (Bl) R(OCist)? Jun 1
?1067–1147. From Angers, France, she married a duke of Brittany but was widowed. Allegedly she was clothed as a Cistercian nun by St Bernard before her death, but this is unlikely as the early Cistercian order rejected any affiliation with consecrated women religious.

Ermengilda (Ermenhilda)
(St) R. Feb 13
d. *c*700. Daughter of King Erconbert of Kent, England, and Queen St Sexburga, she married King Wulfhere of Mercia and was mother of St Werburga. When widowed she became a nun at Minster in Sheppey, Kent, under her mother, and succeeded her as abbess before moving to Ely and becoming abbess there.

Ermengol *see* **Hermengaudius**

Ermengytha (St) R. Jul 30
d. *c*680. A sister of St Ermenburga, she was a nun under her at Minster in Thanet, Kent, England.

Ermin (St) B. R. Apr 25
d. 737. From near Laon, France, as a priest he became a monk at Lobbes near Charleroi, Belgium, and succeeded St Ursmar as abbot and bishop there in 711.

Erminfrid (St) R. Sep 25
d. *c*670. A Frankish courtier, he became a monk at Luxeuil under St Waldebert and later founded the abbey of Cusance in Burgundy, France.

Erminold (Bl) M. R(OSB). Jan 6
d. 1121. A nobleman, he was a child-oblate at the abbey of Hirschau near Nuremberg in Bavaria, Germany, and was chosen first superior of the new foundation of Prüfening by the bishop of Bameberg in 1114. Because of his alleged severity, one of the lay brothers of the monastery hit him with a piece of timber and he died as a result. He was then venerated as a martyr.

Ernest (St) R(OSB). Nov 7
d. 1148. An abbot of Zwiefalten in Swabia, Germany, he resigned in 1146 and went on the disastrous Second Crusade. He then allegedly preached in Persia and Arabia, was tortured to death at Mecca and had his body rescued by an Armenian priest. The story is unlikely. Although he would have met that fate if he were caught in Mecca, there would not have been any Christians there to notice.

Ernin (Ernan) (St) R. Nov 2
C6th. A British emigrant, he became a hermit in Brittany, France, died at Locarn and had his shrine established there. There are several other saints with the same name, notably an alleged nephew of St Columba, a Welsh monk on Bardsey and several Irish monks.

Erney (St)
There is a church dedicated to this unknown saint at Landrake near Saltash in Cornwall, England.

Erotheis (St) *see* **Capitolina and Erotheis**

Erotis (Eroteis) (St) M. Oct 6
C4th. She is listed as having been burned alive, possibly in Greece although she may be a duplicate of St Erotheis.

Erth (Herygh, Urith) (St) Oct 31
C6th. Allegedly a brother of SS Uny and Ives, he emigrated to Cornwall, England, from Ireland and gave his name to the village of St Erth near St Ives.

Ervan *see* **Armagillus or Erbin**

Eskil (St) M. B. Jun 12
d. *c*1080. He allegedly accompanied St Sigfrid on a missionary expedition to Sweden from England and became bishop of Strängnäss near Stockholm. He protested at a pagan festival being held by some apostate converts of his and they stoned him.

Esterwine (St) R. Mar 7
d. 688. A courtier of Northumbria, England, he became a monk at the abbey at Wearmouth founded by St Benedict Biscop, his relative. When the latter retired as abbot in 684, he succeeded him but died before him.

Eternus (St) B. Jul 15
d. *p*600. He was a bishop of Evreux, France.

Etha *see* **Echa**

Ethbin (St) R. Oct 19
d. *c*600. Allegedly from Britain, he was educated in Brittany, France, by St Sampson and became a monk at Taurac in 554. The Franks raided the abbey and dispersed the community in 556, whereupon he went to Ireland and became a hermit (allegedly near Kildare).

Ethelbert and Ethelred
(SS) MM. LL. Oct 17
d. 670. Great-grandsons of St Ethelbert of Kent, England, and brothers of St Ermenburga, they had a claim to the Kentish throne and so were murdered by the chief counsellor of King Egbert at Eastry near Sandwich. The king founded Minster Abbey for their sister in expiation and their shrine was eventually established at Ramsey Abbey near Peterborough. Their status as martyrs is highly dubious.

Ethelbert of East Anglia, King
(St) M. L. May 20
d. 794. As king of East Anglia, England, he was about to marry a daughter of King Offa of Mercia but was ordered killed near Hereford by his future mother-in-law. His body was transferred to that city and he became one of several Saxon royals venerated as martyrs despite the secular nature of their deaths. His shrine was at Hereford Cathedral until the Reformation.

Ethelbert of Kent, King (St) L. Feb 25
560–616. He married Bertha, a Christian Frankish princess, and so knew about Christianity when he received St Augustine and his missionary companions at Ebbsfleet in Thanet, England, in 597. His baptism followed, although not immediately, and was the first of a Saxon king. He went on to found the cathedral at Canterbury (fairly certainly not as a monastery) on the site of his palace as well as monasteries outside the city at Canterbury (St Augustine's) and at Rochester. He was notable in not forcing conversion on his subjects, but his personal example bore fruit.

Ethelburga of Barking (St) R. Oct 11
d. ?675. She fled home, allegedly at the last Anglian royal court, to avoid marriage and St Erconwald, her brother, founded a nunnery for her at Barking in Essex, England. She was too young to become abbess, so St Hildelid was fetched from France to stand in until she was fit to govern. When she took over she proved a great success.

Ethelburga (Aubierge) of Faremoutiers (St) R. Jul 7
d. ?664. An illegitimate daughter of King Anna of East Anglia, she became a nun at Faremoutiers-en-Brie, France, and was the third abbess after Burgundofara and Sethrida.

Ethelburga of Lyminge (St) R. Apr 5
d. ?647. Daughter of King St Ethelbert of Kent, England, she married King St Edwin of Northumbria and took with her St Paulinus, who became bishop of York. There was a pagan reaction after her husband's death in battle and the two fled back to Kent, where she became abbess-founder of a nunnery at Lyminge near Folkestone in 660. This was destroyed by the Vikings but a new church (which survives) was built in 965 adjacent to the old, apparently incorporating the niche of her original shrine in its south wall. This can still be examined.

Ethelburga of Wessex (St) *see* **Ina and Ethelburga**

Etheldreda (Ethelreda, Ediltrudis, Audrey) (St) R. Jun 23
d. 679. Daughter of Anna, king of East Anglia, and sister of SS Ethelburga, Sexburga and Withburga, she married twice but allegedly refused to consummate either marriage. The second time she was supported by St Wilfrid, who encouraged her to become a nun at Coldingham in 672. She then founded a great double monastery at Ely, and her pilgrimage-shrine at the cathedral there was popular in the Middle Ages. Her hand survives in the Catholic church at Ely, and her attribute is a budding rod or lily. The word 'tawdry' is a corruption of 'St Audrey' and refers to the quality of the merchandise once sold in her honour at Ely.

Etheldritha (Ethelfreda, Alfreda, Althryda) (St) R. Aug 2
d. ?834. A daughter of King Offa of Mercia, England, she became a hermit at Croyland, Lincs, a century after St Guthlac settled on that island in the Fens. The monastery there, with her shrine, was destroyed by the Vikings in 870.

Etheldwitha (Ealsitha), Queen of England (St) R. Jul 20
d. 903. She was married to King Alfred the Great of England and, after his death, retired to the nunnery of Nunaminster which she had founded at Winchester.

Ethelfleda *see* **Elfleda**

Ethelgitha (St) R. Aug 22
d. *c*720. She is listed as an abbess somewhere in Northumbria, England.

Ethelgiva (St) R. Dec 9
d. 896. Daughter of Alfred the Great, king of England, she became abbess of Shaftesbury, Dorset, which was founded by her father. It was one of a pair of monastic foundations which were an attempt to re-start monastic life in England after the Vikings had destroyed it, and was more successful than its counterpart for men at Athelney.

Ethelnoth the Good (St) B. Oct 30
d. 1038. A monk of Glastonbury, he became archbishop of Canterbury, England, in 1020 and enshrined St Alphege there.

Ethelred *see* **Aelred**

Ethelred (St) *see* **Ethelbert and Ethelred**

Ethelred of Mercia, King (St) R. May 4
d. 716. King of Mercia, England, he abdicated to became a monk at his foundation at Bardney near Lincoln and went on to become its abbot. The monastery was re-founded in Norman times and survived as a mitred abbey until the Dissolution, but never amounted to much.

Ethelwin of Lindsey (St) B. May 3
d. ?692. He became the second bishop of Lindsey, Lincolnshire, England, in ?680.

Ethelwold (Oldilwald) of Farne (St) R. Mar 23
d. 699. A monk of Ripon in Yorkshire, England, as a hermit he took over St Cuthbert's cell on Farne Island after the latter's death and died there himself.

Ethelwold (Aedilauld) of Lindisfarne (St) B. R. Feb 12
d. *c*740. A disciple of St Cuthbert, he was abbot of Melrose, Scotland, before he became bishop of Lindisfarne.

Ethelwold of Winchester (St) B. R(OSB). Aug 1
912–984. From Winchester, England, he was a royal courtier with St Dunstan, was ordained with him and became a monk of Glastonbury under him. In 955 he became abbot-restorer of Abingdon near Oxford and bishop of Winchester in 963. He ejected the secular canons from his cathedral and replaced them with monks, and he also helped to re-found or restore many other monasteries: Chertsey, Peterborough, Thorney, Croyland, Winchester-Newminster and Ely. In this he worked with SS Dunstan and Oswald to re-establish monastic life in England after the Danish devastations and was the traditional author of the *Regularis Concordia*, the agreed standard of observance for the country's monasteries. He was also known as a craftsman.

Ethenia and Fidelmia (SS) RR. Jan 11
d. 433. Their story is that they were daughters of a ruler in Ireland who were converted and clothed as nuns by St Patrick near the palace of the Connaught kings and died immediately after receiving their first Holy Communion. Their shrine was at Armagh.

Etherius (St) *see* **Basil, Eugene and Comps**

Etherius of Auxerre (St) B. Jul 27
d. 573. He was bishop of Auxerre, France, from 563.

Etherius (Alermius) of Lyons (St) B. Aug 27
d. 602. He was an adviser of the king of Burgundy before becoming bishop of Lyons, France. As such he received St Augustine and companions as guests on their way to England.

Etherius of Nicomedia (St) M. Jun 18
d. ?303. He was martyred at Nicomedia, Asia Minor, in the reign of Diocletian.

Etherius of Vienne (St) B. Jun 14
C6th. He was a bishop of Vienne, France.

Ethernan (St) B. R. Dec 3
? From Scotland, he was a missionary in Buchan and around Aberdeen after being educated in Ireland.

Ethernascus *see* **Ernan**

Ethor (St) *see* **Beocca, Ethor and Comps**

Etto (Hetto) (St) B. R. Jul 10
d. *c*670. Allegedly from Ireland, he became a missionary bishop based near Cambrai, France, where he is venerated.

Eubulus (St) *see* **Adrian and Eubulus**

Eucarpius (St) *see* **Trophimus and Eucarpius**

Eucarpus (St) *see* **Bardomian, Eucarpus and Comps**

Eucharius of Trier (St) B. Dec 8
? Traditionally the first bishop of Trier, Germany, he is alleged to have been sent there by St Peter but is more likely to have been of the C3rd.

Eucherius of Lyons (St) B. R. Nov 16
d. 449. From a patrician family of Lyons, France, he was married but his wife died, whereupon he became a monk at Lérins and wrote some extant ascetical works. He became archbishop of Lyons in ?432 and was friendly with many of the great Gallo-Roman churchmen of the time. He retired to be a hermit in 441.

Eucherius of Orléans (St) B. R. Feb 20
d. ?738. From Orléans, France, he was well educated, especially in theology, and became a monk at Jumièges near Rouen in 714. He became bishop of Orléans in 721 and opposed Charles Martel's policy of sequestering Church property to help support his fight against the Arab invaders and to reward his followers. Thus he was exiled in 737, first to Cologne, Germany, and then to the vicinity of Liege, Belgium, where he died at the abbey of St Truiden.

Eudo (Eudon, Eudes, Odo) (St) R. Nov 20
d. *c*760. He was trained as a monk at Lérins before becoming the abbot-founder of Corméry-en-Velay in the Massif Central, France.

Eudocia (St) M. Mar 1
d. ?98–117. Allegedly originally a Samaritan prostitute at Heliopolis (Baalbek) in the Lebanon, she converted, became a penitent and was beheaded in the reign of Trajan.

Eudoxius (St) *see* **Carterius and Comps**

Eudoxius, Zeno, Macarius and Comps (SS) MM. Sep 5
d. ?311. A group of soldiers, they refused to join in a pagan sacrifice at Melitene in Armenia and were martyred in the space of about a fortnight. Their number is alleged to have been over a thousand but this is not likely.

Eufred (St) R. Oct 11
C7th. Allegedly a monk somewhere in the region of Asti near Turin, Italy, he has a shrine in Alba Cathedral nearby.

Eugendus (Oyend) (St) R. Jan 1
*c*450–?510. He was a child-oblate aged seven at Condat Abbey in the Jura, France, near Geneva and later became abbot. The site is now the town of Saint-Claude.

Eugene (St) *see* **Apollonius and Eugene**

Eugene (St) *see* **Aquilinus, Geminus and Comps**

Eugene (St) *see* **Basil, Ephrem and Comps**

Eugene (St) *see* **Cottidus, Eugene and Comps**

Eugene (St) *see* **Eustratius, Auxentius and Comps**

Eugene (St) *see* **Lucilla, Flora and Comps**

Eugene (St) *see* **Mardonius, Musonius and Comps**

Eugene (St) *see* **Paul, Cyril and Comps**

Eugene (St) *see* **Paul, Tatta and Comps**

Eugene (St) *see* **Symphorosa of Tivoli and Comps**

Eugene (St) *see* **Vindemilalis, Eugene and Longinus**

Eugene and Macarius (SS) MM. PP. Dec 20
d. 362. Two priests of Antioch, Syria, in the reign of Julian, they were whipped, exiled to Roman Arabia (southern Syria) and beheaded on their return.

Eugene I, Pope (St) Jun 2
d. 657. A Roman priest, he was elected to replace Pope St Martin in 654 while the latter was in exile in the Crimea for opposing the Monothelite teaching of Emperor Constans II. Becoming pope in reality the following year with the death of the exile, he continued the policy of opposition and was only saved from the fate of his predecessor by the preoccupation of the emperor with the Muslims.

Eugene III, Pope (Bl) R(OCist). Jul 8
d. 1153. Born near Pisa, Italy, as Peter Paganelli, he was in the diocesan curia of Pisa before becoming a monk at Clairvaux in France under St Bernard in 1135. He was appointed as first abbot of the new Cistercian abbey of Tre Fontane near Rome and was elected pope in 1145. But the Romans wanted to establish a republic without having the pope as secular ruler, so he had to flee the city and stay away for most of his pontificate. St Bernard wrote an ascetical treatise for him, *De Consideratione*. He allowed St Bernard to preach the Second Crusade, and his political judgement after the disaster that that proved to be was sounder than that of his old master. He died at Tivoli and his cultus was confirmed for the Cistercians and locally for Rome in 1872.

Eugene (Eoghan, Euny, Owen) of Ardstraw (St) B. Aug 23
C6th. Allegedly the first bishop of Ardstraw in Co. Tyrone, Ireland, he is apparently commemorated by Uny Lelant on St Ives Bay in Cornwall, England, and is also known in Brittany. He is the principal patron of the diocese of Derry, Ireland.

Eugene-of-the-Sacred-Heart Bossilkov (Bl) M. B. R(CP). Nov 13
1900–1952. From a Latin-rite peasant family of Belene near Pleven, Bulgaria, he joined the Passionists at Ere in Belgium in 1919 and, after his ordination at Nikopol in 1926 and his theological education at Rome, became a parish priest of the Nikopol diocese in Bulgaria. He became bishop in 1946, just after the Communist takeover of the country. The government policy was to destroy the Latin-rite Church, which involved the expulsion of all foreign missionaries, confiscation of property and the suppression of religious institutions. In 1952 he was arrested, interrogated with torture and executed at Sofia after a show trial. He was beatified in 1998.

Eugene of Carthage and Comps (SS) MM. Jul 13
d. 505. Becoming bishop of Carthage, Roman Africa, in 481, he was almost immediately driven into the desert with many of his people

Bl Eugene-of-the-Sacred-Heart Bossilkov, Nov 13 *(see p. 185)*

by the conquering Arian Vandals. With him were his archdeacon and deputy, Salutaris and Muritta. After being allowed to return twice, he was at last exiled to Albi, France, in 496. They were venerated as martyrs on account of their sufferings but did not die for the faith.

Eugene of Florence (St) D. Nov 17
d. 422. A disciple of St Ambrose of Milan, he became a deacon at Florence, Italy, under St Zenobius.

Eugene of Milan (St) B. Dec 30
? He is listed as a bishop of Milan, Italy, but with no indication of date.

Eugene of Paris (St) M. Nov 15
d. ?280. He accompanied St Dionysius from Rome to Paris, France, and was martyred at Deuil nearby. The assertion that he became archbishop of Toledo in Spain is fictitious, and his alleged relics there are spurious.

Eugene Ramirez Salazar (Bl) *see* **Hospitaller Martyrs of Spain**

Eugene of Toledo (St) B. R. Nov 13
d. 657. A Visigothic nobleman from Toledo, Spain, he became a monk and abbot at the Encratia monastery at Zaragoza and succeeded another of the same name as archbishop of Toledo in 646. He revised the local Gothic rite (now long extinct as such) and wrote some extant poetry.

Eugenia of Alsace (St) R. Sep 16
d. 735. Daughter of a duke of Alsace, she succeeded her aunt St Ottilia as abbess of Odilienberg near Strasbourg, France.

Eugenia Joubert (Bl) R. Jul 2
1876–1904. Born in Yssingeaux near Le Puy, France, she entered the 'Holy Family of the Sacred Heart', newly founded by Mary Ignatius Melin at Le Puy. Their charism was devotion to the Sacred Heart as the bond of community life and to catechetical instruction of poor people. She ended up in Liege, Belgium, following the way of spiritual childhood (especially in obedience and humility), and was beatified in 1994.

Eugenia Pico (Bl) R. (Sep 7)
1867–1921. From Crescenzago near Milan, Italy, she was the daughter of a musician who abandoned his family. Despite being raised in a corrupt and irreligious environment, she early received an urge to prayer. As a result, she ran away from home when aged 20 and joined the new 'Congregation of the Little Daughters of Sacred Hearts of Jesus and Mary' in Parma. In 1911 she became the Superior General, and was always faithful to her life's intention to 'suffer, be silent and love'. She was beatified in 2001.

Eugenia of Rome (St) V. Dec 25
d. ?257. She was martyred in the reign of Valerian and was buried on the Via Latina in Rome. Her fictitious acta describe how she disguised herself as a monk, became an abbot and was only exposed when she was accused of the impossible act of fornicating as a man with a woman. Such a story is a stock tale in early hagiography.

Eugenian (St) M. B? Jan 8
C4th? He was martyred at Autun, France, allegedly as a bishop who had fought against Arianism.

Eugraphus (St) *see* **Mennas, Hermogenes and Eugraphus**

Eugyppus (St) P. Jan 15
d. ?511. A Roman African, he was ordained priest at Rome, accompanied St Severinus on his missionary journey to Noricum (modern Austria) and was his biographer.

Eulalia (Aulaire, Aulazie, Olalla) of Barcelona (St) V. Feb 12
d. ?304. Allegedly a native of Barcelona, Spain, who was martyred in the reign of Diocletian, she has acta which are derived from those of St Eulalia of Mérida. This leads to the conclusion that she is a duplicate of the latter. Her veneration is still popular (especially in her city).

Eulalia of Mérida (St) V. Dec 10
d. ?304. The most famous virgin martyr of Spain, she is mentioned by St Augustine and has a hymn in her honour written by Prudentius. She was allegedly burned at the stake at Mérida when aged thirteen in the reign of Diocletian, but her acta are unreliable.

Eulampia, Eulampius and Comps (SS) MM. Oct 10
d. 310. They were martyred at Nicomedia, Asia Minor, in the reign of Galerius. Their unreliable acta describe them as young children, brother and sister, whose example converted a couple of hundred soldiers who were also martyred.

Eulogius of Alexandria (St) B. R. Sep 13
d. 607. A Syrian monk and abbot at Antioch, he became Melkite patriarch of Alexandria, Egypt, in 580. St Gregory the Great was his friend and correspondent and informed him of the sending of St Augustine and companions to England in a surviving letter.

Eulogius of Constantinople and Comps (SS) MM. Jul 3
d. 363–370. They numbered twenty-two and were martyred at Constantinople in the reign of Valens for opposing Arianism.

Eulogius of Cordoba (St) M. P. Mar 11
d. 859. Priest and seminary director of Cordoba, Spain, when that city was the capital of the Umayyad emirate, he was involved in the contemporary 'martyr movement' from 850 to 856 when several Christians courted martyrdom by publicly denouncing Islam. He wrote an account of them (*Memorial of the Saints*) in which he tried to defend their status as martyrs (the Church does not approve martyrdom resulting from gratuitously offensive behaviour towards non-Christians). He was about to become bishop of Toledo when he was executed for protecting St Leocritia, a young woman who had converted from Islam.

Eulogius of Edessa (St) B. May 5
d. *p*381. A priest of Edessa in upper Mesopotamia (now Urfa, Turkey), he was banished to the Egyptian Thebaid by Emperor Valens for opposing Arianism but recalled and made bishop after the latter's death in 375.

Eulogius (St) *see* **Fructuosus, Augurius and Eulogius**

Eumenes (St) B. Sep 18
C7th. Bishop of Gortyna in Crete, he was exiled to the Egyptian Thebaid for opposing Monothelitism and died there. His relics were returned, and the miracles associated with them gave him the nickname 'Wonderworker'.

Eunan of Raphoe (St) B? Sep 23
C7th. Patron of the former diocese of Raphoe in Co. Donegal, Ireland, he is probably identical with St Adamnan of Iona.

Eunician (St) *see* **Theodulus, Saturninus and Comps**

Eunomia (St) *see* **Hilaria, Digna and Comps**

Euny *see* **Eugenius**

Euphebius of Naples (St) B. May 23
? Nothing is known about this bishop of Naples, Italy.

Euphemia (St) *see* **Alexandra of Amisus and Comps**

Euphemia, Dorothy, Thecla and Erasma (SS)VV. Sep 3
? They were allegedly very early martyrs at Aquileia, Italy, and are venerated at Venice and in its former Adriatic possessions as well as at Ravenna.

Euphemia of Altomünster (Bl) R(OSB). Jul 17
d. 1180. A daughter of a count of Andechs in Bavaria, Germany, and sister of St Mechtild of Diessen, she became a nun and then abbess of Altomünster near Augsburg.

Euphemia of Chalcedon (St) V. Sep 16
d. ?307. Her acta are fictitious but she was certainly martyred at Chalcedon (across the Bosphorus from Constantinople) as a church was built on the site of her martyrdom in the reign of Constantine, and it was in this church that the ecumenical council of Chalcedon was held in 451. She is one of the most popular virgin-martyrs in the East but her cultus was confined to local calendars in the West in 1969.

Euphrasia (St) R. Mar 13
d. *c*420. From Constantinople and related to the

imperial family, when she lost her father at seven years of age she went to Egypt with her mother to join the Pachomian nuns at Tabennesis in the Thebaid. They took her but not her patrimony, which she left with her mother until the latter died. Then the emperor offered to marry her off, but she refused, asked him to give her fortune to charity and stayed in the nunnery until she died, aged about thirty. She has an early biography.

Euphrasia (St) *see* **Alexandra of Amisus and Comps**

Euphrasia (St) *see* **Theodotus of Ancyra and Comps**

Euphrasia-of-the-Immaculate-Conception Brard (Bl) *see* **Compiègne (Carmelite Martyrs of)**

Euphrasia Pelletier *see* **Mary-of-St-Euphrasia Pelletier**

Euphrasius (St) M? B? Jan 14
? He is listed as a bishop of Roman Africa and may be identical with Eucrathius, a correspondent of St Cyprian, or may have been a bishop martyred by the Arian Vandals.

Euphrasius (St) *see* **Corfu (Martyrs of)**

Euphrasius (St) *see* **Torquatus, Ctesiphon and Comps**

Euphrasius-of-the-Merciful-Love de Celis Santos (Bl) *see* **Nicephorus Díez Tejerina and Comps**

Euphronius of Autun (St) B. Aug 3
d. *p*475. He became bishop of Autun, France, in 460 and was one of the greatest bishops of Gaul in the C5th. He was a friend of St Lupus of Troyes, and a letter of his to him survives.

Euphronius of Tours (St) B. Aug 4
530–573. A nephew of St Gregory of Langres, he became bishop of Tours, France, in 556 and was remembered for helping to rebuild the city when it burned down.

Euphrosyne (St) R. Jan 1
? Her legend describes her as a young woman of Alexandria, Egypt, who joined a monastery as a monk to escape marriage and lived as such for many years, her sex only being discovered when she was dying. Her historical existence is doubtful as the story is a common one in hagiography, and other examples of it feature St Pelagia the Penitent and St Eugenia of Rome.

Euplus (St) M. Aug 12
d. 304. A native of Catania, Sicily, he was found in possession of a copy of the Gospels in contravention of an edict of persecution issued by Emperor Diocletian. He was tortured in order to induce apostasy before being martyred. His acta are genuine.

Euporus (St) *see* **Theodolus, Saturninus and Comps**

Euprepia (St) *see* **Hilaria, Digna and Comps**

Euprepis (St) *see* **Castulus and Euprepis**

Euprepius (St) M. Aug 21
d. ?303. He is described in the legendary acta of SS Cosmas and Damian as a companion martyr.

Euprepius of Verona (St) B. Sep 27
C3rd? He is venerated as the first bishop of Verona, Italy. A worthless tradition describes him as appointed by St Peter.

Eupsychius of Caesarea (1) (St) M. Sep 7
d. *c*130. He is alleged to have been martyred at Caesarea in Cappodocia, Asia Minor, in the reign of Hadrian.

Eupsychius of Caesarea (2) (St) M. Apr 7
d. 362. A young nobleman of Caesarea in Cappodocia, Asia Minor, when the emperor Julian visited the city he was arrested on a charge of having helped to destroy the temple of Fortune there and was then tortured and beheaded.

Eurfyl *see* **Erfyl**

Eurgain (St) R. Jul 30
C6th. Daughter of a nobleman of Glamorgan, Wales, she became the patron of Llantwit Fardre near Llantrisant.

Eurosia (Orosia) (St) V. Jul 25
d. 714. According to her legend she was from Bayonne in France (or from Bohemia) and was martyred at Jaca in the Aragonese Pyrenees, Spain, by Arab invaders. Despite doubts about her existence her cultus is popular and was confirmed for Jaca in 1902.

Eusebia of Bergamo (St) V. Oct 29
Late C3rd. She was martyred at Bergamo in Lombardy, Italy, in the reign of Maximian Herculeus.

Eusebia of Hamay (St) R. Mar 16
d. *c*680. Eldest daughter of SS Adalbald and Rictrude, as a child she was placed by her mother in the nunnery founded and run by St Gertrude, her grandmother, at Hamay near Douai, France. She became abbess when aged twelve (a typical example of hereditary succession in Frankish monasticism) but her mother thought that she was too young for the responsibility and she and her community moved to the nunnery at Marchiennes. Later, when she was more grown-up, they returned home to Hamay.

Eusebia of Saint-Cyr and Comps (SS) MM. RR(OSB). Sep 20
d . 838? According to their legend, they were the abbess and community of thirty-nine nuns of the nunnery of Saint-Cyr in Marseilles, France, who were massacred by Muslim pirates.

Eusebius (St) *see* **Aphrodisius, Caralippus and Comps**

Eusebius (St) *see* **Felix and Eusebius**

Eusebius (St) *see* **Gaius, Faustus and Comps**

Eusebius (St) *see* **Philip, Severus and Comps**

Eusebius, Pope (St) Aug 17
d. 310. A Greek, he was pope for only a few months during a violent controversy at Rome over the reconciliation of those who had apostatized in the recent persecution. He died in exile in Sicily.

Eusebius, Marcellus and Comps (SS) MM. Dec 2
d. 254–259. They were martyred at Rome in the reign of Valerian. Eusebius, a priest, was beheaded with Marcellus (his deacon), Neon and Mary; Adria and Hippolytus were whipped to death; Paulina died under torture and Maximus was thrown into the Tiber.

Eusebius, Neon, Leontius, Longinus and Comps (SS) MM. Apr 24
? They are listed as numbering forty in the Western tradition, nine in the Eastern, and have been incorporated into the legend of St George as witnesses of his martyrdom who were themselves martyred.

Eusebius, Nestabus, Zeno and Nestor (SS) MM. Sep 8
d. 362. They helped to destroy the main pagan temple at Gaza in the Holy Land during the reign of the emperor Julian and were lynched as a result by the townsfolk. Nestor was spared by the mob after the initial beating because of his good looks, but he died as a result of his wounds. Gaza remained a stronghold of paganism until its suppression in the Roman Empire later in the century.

Eusebius, Pontian, Vincent and Peregrine (SS) MM. Aug 25
d. ?192. Their relics were given to Vienne, France, by Pope St Nicholas in 863, and that is all that is known about them. Their acta are untrustworthy.

Eusebius of Africa and Comps (SS) MM. Mar 5
? They are listed as martyrs of Roman Africa.

Eusebius of Antioch (St) R. Jan 23
C4th. He was a Syrian hermit on Mt Coryphe near Antioch (now in Turkey).

Eusebius of Aschia (St) R. Feb 15
d. *p*400. He was a hermit at Aschia near Cyrrhus, Syria.

Eusebius of Bologna (St) B. Sep 26
d. *c*400. A friend of St Ambrose of Milan, he became bishop of Bologna, Italy, about 370. He opposed Arianism, and discovered the alleged relics of SS Vitalis and Agricola.

Eusebius Codina Millá (Bl) *see* **Philip-of-Jesus Munárriz Azcona and Comps**

Eusebius of Cremona (St) R. Mar 5
d. ?423. From Cremona, Italy, he went to join his friend St Jerome at Bethlehem in 393. He was involved in the Origenist controversy and defended St Jerome's views on this at Rome. He succeeded his friend as abbot of the Latin monastery at Bethlehem which establishment, however, did not last for long. There is an unsupported tradition that he founded the abbey of Guadelupe in Spain.

Eusebius of Esztergom (Bl) R. F. Jan 20
d. 1270. A cathedral canon of Esztergom, Hungary, he resigned and went to become a hermit in the forest of Pisilia, then in southern Hungary. There he was inspired to organize his fellow hermits into a new cenobitic congregation, the 'Hermits of St Paul', using the Augustinian rule. These spread through the Hapsburg Empire and Poland, but were virtually wiped out in the Napoleonic period and only survive in Poland. He has a cultus in Hungary but was not officially beatified.

Eusebius Forcades Ferraté (Bl) *see* **Hospitaller Martyrs of Spain**

Eusebius of Milan (St) B. Aug 12
d. 465. Probably a Greek, he succeeded St Lazarus as bishop of Milan, Italy, in 450 and was a zealous opponent of Monophysitism.

Eusebius of Murano (Bl)
R(OSB Cam). Feb 10
d. 1501. A Spanish nobleman, he was an ambassador at Venice, Italy, when he decided to become a Camaldolese monk at St Michael's monastery on the island of Murano.

Eusebius of Phoenecia (St) M. Sep 21
? He is listed as such as a martyr, but with no other details.

Eusebius of Rome (St) P. Aug 14
C4th. A parish priest, he was allegedly under house arrest in the reign of Constantius for opposing Arianism. His house became the present Roman church named after him. His acta are a forgery.

Eusebius of St Gall (St)
M. R(OSB). Jan 31
d. 884. An Irish pilgrim, he became a monk at the abbey of St Gall, Switzerland, and went on to become a hermit on the Victorsberg in Graubünden. There he was killed by a peasant with a scythe, allegedly because he had criticized the local lack of religion, and was venerated as a martyr.

Eusebius of Samosata
(St) M. B. Jun 21
d. *c*380. Bishop of Samosata, Syria, from 361, he was a friend and colleague of SS Basil and Gregory Nazianzen in their fight against Arianism. He was exiled to what is now Bulgaria by the emperor Valens in 373, but recalled on his death. He was killed at a place called Dolichium when an Arian woman dropped a brick on his head from the town wall.

Eusebius of Vercelli (St) B. Aug 2
?283–371. From Sardinia, he became a cleric in Rome and was made bishop of Vercelli in Piedmont, Italy, in 340. He was the first bishop in the West to organize his cathedral clergy under a monastic rule. In 355 he refused to consent to the exile of St Athanasius for opposing Arianism and was himself exiled to the East, spending some time in Egypt, but he was allowed to return by Emperor Julian in 363 and then worked to get rid of Arianism in the Western church. He died in peace.

Eusignius (St) M. Aug 5
d. 362. Allegedly aged one hundred and ten and with sixty years of army service behind him, he was beheaded at Antioch, Syria, in the reign of Julian for refusing to offer pagan sacrifice.

Euspicius (St) R. Jul 20
d. *c*500. A priest of Verdun, France, he persuaded King Clovis the Frank not to sack that city, then followed him to Orléans and founded the abbey of Micy near there on a property donated by the king.

Eustace (St) M? Oct 12
? He is listed in the old Roman Martyrology as a priest and confessor of Syria but the Bollandists considered that he was more likely to have been an Egyptian martyr.

Eustace (St) *see* **Valerian, Urban and Comps**

Eustace, Thespesius and Anatolius (SS) MM. Nov 20
d. 235. They were martyred at Nicaea, Asia Minor, in the reign of Maximinus Thrax.

Eustace Félix (Bl) *see* **September (Martyrs of)**

Eustace of Flay (St) R(OCist). Sep 7
d. 1211. From near Beauvais, France, he became a priest there but then joined the Cistercian abbey of Flay nearby and went on to become its abbot. He was involved in the Albigensian crusade, and was papal legate in England in the reign of King John.

Eustace of Lithuania (St) *see* **Anthony of Lithuania and Comps**

Eustace of Luxeuil (St) R. Mar 29
d. 629. A disciple of St Columban at Luxeuil, Burgundy, France, he became abbot in 613 when his master was forced into exile. He was allegedly in charge of six hundred monks, and under him the monastery became a great source of bishops and saints.

Eustace of Naples (St) B. May 10
C3rd. He was the seventh bishop of Naples, Italy, and his cultus was confirmed for there in 1884.

Eustace of Rome and Comps *Sep 20*
d. ?118. Their unreliable legend states that he was a Roman army officer with his wife Theopistes and two sons, Agapitus and

Theopistus. He was converted by seeing a stag with a crucifix between its antlers while out hunting and was martyred with his family in the reign of Hadrian. There is no historical evidence for their existence, and their cultus was suppressed in the Roman rite in 1969.

Eustace White and Comps
(St) M. P. Dec 10
d. 1591. From Louth, Lincs, he was a convert who trained for the priesthood at Rheims and at Rome. Ordained in 1588, he went to work in the West Country but was quickly seized at Blandford Forum and was hanged, drawn and quartered at Tyburn, London, together with St Polydore Plasden. With them were hanged BB Brian Lacey, John Mason and Sidney Hodgson. He was canonized in 1970. *See* **England (Martyrs of)**.

Eustadiola (St) R. Jun 8
d. 690. A noblewoman of Bourges, France, when widowed she used her wealth to restore churches and became the abbess-founder of Moyenmoutier in her city.

Eustathius of Ancyra (St) M. Mar 29
? According to his legend he was tortured and thrown into the local river at Ancyra, Asia Minor (now Ankara in Turkey), but was saved by an angel and died in peace.

Eustathius of Antioch (St) B. Jul 16
d. ?335. From Side in Pamphylia, Asia Minor, he became bishop of Beroea, Syria, in 270 and patriarch of Antioch in 323. He was present at the Council of Nicaea and opposed the Arians in his preaching and writing. In 331 he was deposed by an Arian synod at Antioch and died in exile at Trajanopolis in Thrace. This led to a long-term schism at Antioch.

Eusterius (St) B. Oct 19
C5th. He is listed as the fourth bishop of Salerno, Italy.

Eustochium Bellini of Padua
(Bl) R(OSB). Oct 13
1444–1469. Born to a nun in the degenerate Benedictine nunnery of St Prosdocimus at Padua, Italy, she was brought up there until a more observant community of nuns took over and she asked to become a nun with them. Although normally gentle and pious, she was subject to violent outbursts of hysteria and was thus suspected of witchcraft and of being possessed by a demon. Hence she was starved, ill treated, imprisoned and almost burned as a witch, which treatment she bore with patience and humility during her periods of lucidity. She was professed after the chaplain intervened in her favour, and then gained the respect of her community before she died. It was then discovered that she had burned the name of Jesus into the top of her breasts. She is locally venerated at Padua.

Eustochium of Bethlehem
(St) R. Sep 28
*c*370–419. The third and favourite daughter of St Paula, when her father died she and her mother toured the monastic sites in Egypt and then settled at Bethlehem with St Jerome. She helped him with his literary work, for example in his Vulgate translation of the Bible, and succeeded her mother as abbess at the nunnery that the latter had founded. She died there, in Bethlehem, and the Latin nunnery did not long survive her.

Eustochium Calafató
(St) R(OFM). Feb 16
1437–1468. A noblewoman of Messina, Sicily, she became a Poor Clare there in 1446 when only a child, and obtained permission from the pope in 1457 to found a nunnery of the Franciscan Observants at Montevergine in the city. She was canonized in 1988.

Eustochium of Tarsus (St) V. Nov 2
d. 362. From Tarsus in Cilicia, Asia Minor, she refused to sacrifice to Aphrodite in the reign of Julian and died under torture.

Eustochius (St) *see* **Elpidius, Marcellus and Comps**

Eustochius of Tours (St) B. Sep 19
d. 461. He succeeded St Brice as bishop of Tours, France, in 444.

Eustolia and Sosipatra (SS) RR. Nov 9
d. 610 and 625 resp. They may both have been daughters of Emperor Maurice at Constantinople (582–602), although Eustolia is alleged to have been born at Rome. They founded and entered a nunnery at Constantinople.

Eustorgius I of Milan (St) M? B. Sep 18
d. *p*331. A Greek, he became archbishop of Milan, Italy, in 315 and was zealous against Arianism. A remark in a letter of St Athanasius indicates that he may have been martyred as a result.

Eustorgius II of Milan (St) B. Jun 6
d. 518. A Roman priest, he became archbishop of Milan, Italy, in 512. He was especially

charitable to the poor, and ransomed many of his people captured by barbarian invaders.

Eustorgius of Nicomedia and Comps (St) MM. Apr 11
d. ?300. A priest of Nicomedia, Asia Minor, he was martyred with Nestor, Filonus and Ceremonius, probably in the reign of Diocletian.

Eustosius (St) *see* **Demetrius, Anianus and Comps**

Eustratius and Comps (SS) MM. Dec 13
d. ?302. According to their legend, Eustratius was an Armenian noble who was arrested in the reign of Diocletian. Auxentius, a priest, and Mardarius, a friend, interceded for him and were beheaded. His servant, Eugene, was tortured to death and converted a soldier, Orestes, by his example. The latter was taken to Sebaste with Eustratius and both were burned, on a gridiron and in a furnace respectively.

Eustreberta *see* **Austreberta**

Euthalia of Lentini (St) V. Aug 27
? She has a cultus as a virgin martyr at Lentini near Catania, Sicily, but her existence is doubtful.

Euthymius of Alexandria (St) M. D. May 5
? He is listed as a deacon and martyr of Alexandria, Egypt.

Euthymius Aramendía García (Bl) *see* **Hospitaller Martyrs of Spain**

Euthymius the Great (St) R. Jan 20
378–473. From Melitene in Armenia, he became a priest and monk and had supervision of the monasteries of his native district. He went to Jerusalem in 406 and became one of the greatest of the fathers of the Judaean desert, founding several lauras. He opposed Nestorianism and Monophysitism and was a bulwark of orthodoxy in the Holy Land after the Council of Chalcedon, when the Monophysites seized the bishopric of Jerusalem. He induced the empress Eudoxia not to support them and helped to restore the bishop Juvenal to his position. His biography was written by St Cyril of Scythopolis, and he is highly venerated in Eastern monasticism.

Euthymius the New (St) R. Oct 15
d. 886. As distinct from 'the Great', he was from Galatia, Asia Minor. He left his wife and family to become a monk at Thessalonika, Greece, and then on the Bithynian Olympus. Later he was on Athos, where he restored the monastery of St Andrew (later a Russian skete) and founded a nunnery at Thessalonika. He died on Athos.

Euthymius of Nicomedia (St) M. Dec 24
d. 303. He was martyred at Nicomedia, Asia Minor, the capital of the emperor Diocletian, after giving moral support to others facing martyrdom.

Euthymius of Perugia (St) L. Aug 29
d. ?303. A Roman, he fled with his wife and his son, St Crescentius, during the persecution of Diocletian. He died at Perugia and is venerated there. His acta are untrustworthy.

Euthymius of Sardis (St) M. B. R. Mar 11
d. ?829. A monk before he became bishop of Sardis, Asia Minor, he was present at the second ecumenical council of Nicaea in 787 which upheld the adoration of icons. The emperor Theophilus tried to restore iconoclasm and exiled Euthymius for twenty-nine years, after which he was whipped to death.

Eutropia (St) M. Oct 30
d. ?253. She is listed as a Roman African martyr, probably of the reign of Valerian.

Eutropia (St) *see* **Lybe, Leonis and Eutropia**

Eutropia (St) *see* **Nicasius, Eutropia and Comps**

Eutropia of Auvergne (St) L. Sep 15
C5th. Mentioned by Sidonius Apollinaris, she is listed as a charitable widow of the Auvergne, France.

Eutropius (St) *see* **Cleonicus, Eutropius and Basiliscus**

Eutropius (St) *see* **Tigrius and Eutropius**

Eutropius, Zosima and Bonosa (SS) MM. Jul 15
d. *p*273. They were martyred at Ostia at the mouth of the Tiber, Italy, in the reign of Aurelian.

Eutropius of Orange (St) B. May 27
d. *p*475. From Marseilles, France, he became bishop of Orange when that place had been devastated by the Visigoths and is described as supporting himself by farming. He is the source of a fictitious story concerning the first bishop of Orange (allegedly with the same name).

Eutropius of Saintes (St) M? B. Apr 30
? He is venerated as the first bishop of Saintes, France, and is alleged to have been a companion-martyr of St Dionysius of Paris.

Eutyches (St) *see* **Januarius of Benevento**

Eutyches (St) *see* **Maro, Eutyches and Victorinus**

Eutychian (St) *see* **Arcadius, Probus and Comps**
Eutychian (St) *see* **Ariston and Comps**

Eutychian (St) *see* **Diomedes, Julian and Comps**

Eutychian (St) *see* **Straton, Philip and Eutychian**

Eutychian, Pope (St) M? Dec 8
d. 283. Apparently from Tuscany, Italy, he is venerated as a martyr but nothing further is known about him.

Eutychius (St) *see* **Honorius, Eutychius and Stephen**

Eutychius (St) *see* **Placid, Eutychius and Comps**

Eutychius (St) *see* **Timothy, Polius and Eutychius**

Eutychius and Domitian
(SS) MM. Dec 28
? They are listed as a priest and his deacon who were martyred at Ancyra, Asia Minor (now Ankara in Turkey).

Eutychius and Florentius
(SS) RR. May 23
C6th. They were two monks who settled at Valcastoria near Norcia, Italy, and who were praised by St Gregory the Great.

Eutychius, Plautus and Heracleas
(SS) MM. Sep 29
? They are listed as martyrs of Thrace (south-eastern Balkans but the location is not exactly known).

Eutychius of Alexandria and Comps (SS) MM. Mar 26
d. 356. He was a sub-deacon of Alexandria, Egypt. When St Athanasius, patriarch of the city, was exiled in 356 for his anti-Arian views, one George (an Arian cleric) was set up as an anti-patriarch and instigated serious violence against the orthodox. Many were killed or seized and sent into exile, including Eutychius who was on the way to the mines as a prisoner when he died of exhaustion.

Eutychius (Oye) of Cádiz (St) M. Dec 11
C4th. He is venerated as a martyr at Cádiz, Spain, but nothing is certainly known about him. He may have been martyred at Mérida instead.

Eutychius of Constantinople
(St) B. R. Apr 6
d. 582. A monk from Amasea on the Black Sea coast of Asia Minor, he became patriarch of Constantinople in 553, dedicated the new church of Hagia Sophia there and was chairman at the fifth ecumenical council which was called in response to the continuing problem of the Monophysites. He opposed the emperor Justinian's plans to reconcile them and was exiled for twelve years.

Eutychius of Ferentino (St) M. Apr 15
? This unknown martyr at Ferentino in the Roman Campagna was mentioned by St Gregory the Great in his *Dialogues* as having appeared to St Redemptus, bishop of the place, in a vision.

Eutychius the Patrician and Comps (SS) MM. Mar 14
d. 741. They were the numerous victims of a massacre of Christians by Muslim Arabs at Carrhae in upper Mesopotamia (near Urfa in Turkey), which is the same place as the Haran associated with the patriarch Abraham.

Eutychius the Phrygian (St) L. Aug 24
C1st. According to the apocryphal acta of St John, he was a disciple of St Paul who attached himself to St John, was with him at Patmos and who died in peace after being tortured for the faith. His identification with the young man who fell from a window at Ephesus (Acts 20) is based merely on the names being the same.

Eutychius of Rome (St) M. Feb 4
d. ?303. He was martyred at Rome in the reign of Diocletian. His acta are lost, but the inscription composed for his tomb by Pope St Damasus has survived and it asserts that he was imprisoned for twelve days without food and then thrown into a well.

Euvert *see* **Evortius**

Evagrius (St) *see* **Priscus, Crescens and Evagrius**

Evagrius and Benignus
(SS) MM. Apr 3
? They were martyred at Tomi in Scythia, on the coast of Romania.

Evagrius, Priscian and Comps
(SS) MM. Oct 14
? They were martyred in Syria, or possibly at Rome.

Evagrius of Constantinople
(St) B. Mar 6
d. *c*380. He became archbishop of Constantinople in 370 for the few remaining Catholics in the city, after two decades during which the incumbent was an Arian. He was soon exiled by the emperor Valens and the place and time of his death are unknown.

Eval (Uvol, Urfol) (St) B? Nov 20
C6th. The patron of St Eval's, on the coast of Cornwall, England, near Newquay, is alleged to have been a bishop locally.

Evan (Inan) (St) R. Aug 18
C9th. He was a hermit in Ayrshire, Scotland, and a church is dedicated to him at Beith.

Evangelist and Peregrine
(SS) RR(OSA). Mar 30
d. *c*1250. Noblemen of Verona, Italy, they were school-friends who entered the local Augustinian friary together, were granted similar charisms in working miracles and died within a few hours of each other. Their cultus was approved for the Augustinian friars in 1837.

Evaristus (St) *see* **Carponius, Evaristus and Comps**

Evaristus (St) *see* **Theodolus, Saturninus and Comps**

Evaristus, 'Pope' *Oct 26*
d. ?107. He traditionally had Hellenic-Jewish ancestry but nothing is known for certain about him. Like all the early popes he used to have a cultus as a martyr, but this was suppressed in 1969.

Evasius of Asti (St) M. B. Dec 1
d. ?362. Allegedly the first bishop of Asti in Piedmont, Italy, the untrustworthy and late accounts given of him describe him as being driven from his diocese by Arians and being killed at Casale Monferrato in the reign of Julian.

Evasius of Brescia (St) B. Dec 2
? He is listed as the first bishop of Brescia, Italy.

Eve of Liege (Bl) R(OCist)? Mar 14
d. ?1266. A hermit at Liege, Belgium, allegedly affiliated to the Cistercians, she took over the work of campaigning (with success) for the institution of the feast of Corpus Christi when Bl Juliana of Cornillon died. Her cultus was confirmed for Liege in 1902.

Evellius (St) M. May 11
d. ?66. Allegedly a counsellor of Nero who was converted by the example of the first martyrs of Rome, he is connected in legend with St Torpes. They were supposedly martyred at Pisa but their existence is questionable.

Eventius (St) *see* **Alexander, Eventius and Theodolus**

Eventius (St) *see* **Zaragoza (Eighteen Martyrs of)**

Everard
This name is also rendered variously as Eberhard, Everhard, Evard, Erhard, Erard.

Everard of Einsiedeln
(Bl) R(OSB). Aug 14
d. 958. Of the ducal family of Swabia in Germany, he was provost of the cathedral chapter at Strasbourg when, in 934, he joined his friend Bl Berno at the latter's new monastery at Einsiedeln, Switzerland, and took over as first abbot on his death. He finished the construction of the abbey.

Everard Hanse (Bl) M. P. Jul 31
d. 1581. From Northamptonshire, he was educated at Cambridge and became an Anglican minister before his conversion. Then he was ordained priest at Rheims in 1581 and was captured and executed at Tyburn, London, immediately on his return to England. On the scaffold he was heard to say 'Oh, happy day!'. He was beatified in 1886. *See* **England (Martyrs of)**.

Everard of Mons (Bl) R(OCist). Mar 20
d. *c*1150. Count of Mons, Belgium, he repented of a war-crime and, as penance, went on pilgrimage to Jerusalem, Rome and Compostela before getting a job as pig-keeper at the Cistercian abbey of Morimond. He was recognized, persuaded to become a monk and went on to found the monasteries of Einberg and Mont-Saint-George. He has a cultus among the Cistercians.

Everard of Rohrdorf (Bl) R(OCist). Apr 14
1160–1245. A nobleman of Baden, Germany,

he became a Cistercian monk at Salem and was made abbot in 1191. He was influential at the imperial court as well as being highly regarded by the popes, and his abbey was responsible for seven Cistercian nunneries founded during his abbacy. He retired as abbot before he died.

Everard of Salzburg (St)
B. R(OSB). Jun 22
1085–1164. From Nuremberg, Germany, he was educated at the abbey of Michelberg at Bamberg, became a canon at the cathedral there but joined the abbey of Prüfenig instead in 1125. He became abbot of Biburg in 1133 and bishop of Salzburg, Austria, in 1147. He was a leading supporter of the pope during the investiture controversy.

Everard of Schaffhausen
(Bl) R(OSB). Apr 7
1018–1078. Count of Nellenburg, he was related to Pope St Leo IX and to Emperor St Henry II. In 1050 he founded Schaffhausen Abbey on the Rhine (now in Switzerland) and became a monk there. His wife founded a nunnery nearby. The abbey was the nucleus of what is now the capital of a Swiss canton.

Everard of Tütenhausen (St) L. Sep 12
d. ?1370. A shepherd, he has his shrine at Tütenhausen in Bavaria, Germany. His popular cultus has not been confirmed.

Evergisil of Cologne (St) B. Oct 24
d. ?591. He became archbishop of Cologne in 580, was highly respected at the Merovingian court and went as an ambassador to Visigothic Spain. In the old Roman Martyrology and in local legend he is duplicated by an alleged bishop of Cologne of the same name who was killed by robbers in 455. This person does not seem to have existed.

Everild (Averil) (St) R. Jul 9
Late C7th. From the Wessex, England, nobility, she ran away from home and was clothed as a nun with two companions by St Wilfrid, possibly at a place now called Everingham near Market Weighton in Yorkshire.

Evermarus (St) M. L. May 1
d. *c*700. He was a Frisian pilgrim murdered by robbers at Rutten near Tongeren, Belgium.

Evermod (St) B. R(OPraem). Feb 17
d. 1178. A disciple of St Norbert, he became a Premonstratensian canon at Antwerp, Belgium, before becoming superior of Gottesgnaden in 1134 and of Magdeburg, Germany in 1138. He evangelized the Slavs on the Elbe and became bishop of Ratzeburg near Lübeck, Germany, in 1154. As such he encouraged the dispossession of the native Slavs by inviting Saxons to colonize the area.

Evermund (Ebremund) (St) R. Jun 10
d. *c*720. A Frankish courtier, he and his wife decided to become religious and he founded several monasteries, notably Fontenay-Louvet near Alençon in Normandy, France. He ended up as abbot of Montmaire nearby, and his wife became a nun at one of his foundations.

Evilasius (St) *see* **Fausta, Evilasius and Maximus**

Evincius-Richard Alonso Uyarra (Bl) *see* **Aurelius-Mary Villalón Acebrón and Comps**

Evodius, Hermogenes and Callistus (Callista) (SS) MM. Apr 25
? The old Roman Martyrology lists these thrice. On August 2 they are listed as the three sons of St Theodota, a martyr of Nicaea. On April 25 and September 2 they are listed as having been martyred at Syracuse and Callistus is feminized to Callista. No acta exist mentioning their martyrdom at Syracuse, and Nicaea is possibly correct.

Evodius of Antioch (St) M? B. May 6
d. ?64. He was the first bishop of Antioch, Syria, after St Peter and was the predecessor of St Ignatius. There is no evidence that he was martyred.

Evodius of Le Puy (St) B. Nov 12
d. *p*560. He was a bishop of Le Puy, France.

Evodius of Rouen (St) B. Oct 8
d. 550. A Frankish archbishop of Rouen, France, he had his relics transferred to Braine near Soissons four hundred years after he died.

Evortius (Euvert) (St) B. Sep 7
d. *c*340. A Roman sub-deacon, he became bishop of Orléans, France. The Augustinian abbey of Saint-Euvert was built to house his shrine.

Evroul *see* **Ebrulf**

Ewald the Dark and Ewald the Fair (SS) MM. RR. Oct 3
d. ?695. Brothers from Northumbria, England, they were educated in Ireland, became monks and went on a missionary journey to Lower

Saxony, Germany. Shortly after they started their apostolate they were martyred together at Aplerbeke near Dortmund, Germany. Their nicknames refer to the colour of their hair.

Exanthus (St) *see* **Carpophorus of Como and Comps**

Expeditus (St) *see* **Hermogenes of Melitene and Comps**

Exuperantia (St) R? Apr 26
? She has a cultus at Troyes, France, and had allegedly been a hermit, but nothing is known about her.

Exuperantius (St) *see* **Sabinus, Exuperantius and Comps**

Exuperantius of Cingoli (St) B. Jan 24
C5th. Allegedly from Roman Africa, he was a bishop of Cingoli near Ancona, Italy.

Exuperantius of Ravenna (St) B. May 30
d. 418. He was bishop of Ravenna, Italy, from 398.

Exuperia (St) *see* **Symphronius of Rome and Comps**

Exuperius (St) *see* **Theban Legion**

Exuperius (Hesperus), Zoë, Cyriac and Theodolus (SS) MM. May 2
d. ?127. A married Phrygian couple and their two sons, they were slaves of a rich pagan native of Attalia in Pamphylia, Asia Minor, during the reign of Hadrian and were allegedly thrown into a furnace when they refused to take part in a thanksgiving sacrifice for the birth of a son to their master.

Exuperius (Soupire, Spire) of Bayeux (St) B. Aug 1
d. ?405. He became bishop of Bayeux, France, *c*390. His shrine was established at Corbeil.

Exuperius (Soupire) of Toulouse (St) B. Sep 28
d. 411. Bishop of Toulouse, France, from ?405, he was a friend of St Jerome and was remembered for his charity to the poor in the Holy Land and in Egypt as well as back home to those dispossessed by the barbarian invasions.

Ezechiel Moreno y Diaz (St) B. R(OSA). Aug 19
1848–1906. From Alfaro in the Ebro valley, Spain, he joined the Augustinian Recollects when aged sixteen and was a missionary in the Philippines from 1869 to 1885. Then, after some time in Spain, he went to Colombia in 1888. He became bishop of Pasto, where he was much revered. He was canonized in 1992.

F

Fabian (St) *see* **Stephen, Pontian and Comps**

Fabian, Pope (St) M. Jan 20
d. 250. He succeeded St Antheros as pope in 236 and had a peaceful pontificate until his arrest at the start of the persecution of Decius and his subsequent death in prison. He was praised by St Cyprian, his contemporary. Part of his relics were taken to the basilica of St Sebastian which led to the two being celebrated together liturgically until 1969, when their celebrations were separated.

Fabiola (St) L. Dec 27
d. 399. A Roman noblewoman, she was married to a worthless husband and so divorced him and re-married. This caused scandal to the Church, so she did public penance after being widowed and became a disciple of St Jerome, founding a hospital in the city with St Pammachius. In 395 she went to the Holy Land and tried to become a nun with St Jerome at Bethlehem, but he was not willing and she returned home and founded a hospice for pilgrims arriving at Rome. She was extremely popular among the common people of the city.

Fabius (St) *see* **Maximus, Bassus and Fabius**

Fabius of Caesarea (St) M. Jul 31
d. 300. A soldier, he was beheaded at Caesarea in Mauretania, Roman Africa, in the reign of Diocletian for refusing to carry the vexillum (standard) which had pagan symbols on it.

Fabrician and Philibert
(SS) MM. Aug 22
? These alleged martyrs are venerated at Toledo, Spain.

Fachanan of Kilfenora
(St) B. R. Dec 20
C6th. The principal patron of the diocese of Kinfenora in Co. Clare, Ireland, may be the same person as Fachanan of Ross.

Fachanan of Ross (St) B? R. Aug 14
Late C6th. He was allegedly the first bishop of Ross (Ross Carbery) in Co. Cork, Ireland, and founded a monastic school there at which St Brendan taught. He is the principal patron of the diocese of Ross.

Faciolus of Poitiers (St) R(OSB). Sep 7
d. *c*950. He was a monk at the abbey of St Cyprian at Poitiers, France.

Facundinus (St) B. Aug 28
d. *c*620. He was a bishop of Taino in Umbria, Italy, and is venerated in the diocese of Nocera.

Facundus and Primitivus
(SS) MM. Nov 27
d. *c*300. From León, Spain, they were beheaded at a place in the region where the abbey and then the town of Sahagún grew up, the name being a corruption of St Facundus.

Fagan *see* **Fugiatus**

Fagildus (St) R(OSB). Jul 25
d. 1086. He was abbot of the Benedictine abbey of St Martin at Compostela, Spain.

Failbhe the Little (St) R. Mar 10
674–754. He was abbot of Iona, Scotland, for seven years.

Failbhe McPipan (St) R. Mar 22
d. *c*680. He was the predecessor of St Adamnan as abbot of Iona, Scotland. There are about twenty other Scottish and Irish saints listed with this name.

Faith, Hope and Charity
(SS) VV. Aug 1
d. ?120. In Greek they are Pistis, Elpis and Agape; in Latin, Fides, Spes and Caritas. Their unreliable legend describes them as children, daughters of St Wisdom (Sophia or Sapientia), who were martyred with their mother at Rome in the reign of Hadrian.

Faith (Foy) of Conques (St) V. Oct 6
C3rd. From Agen on the Garonne, France, she was martyred there in the reign of Maximian Herculeus. Her shrine was established at the abbey of Conques where her golden reliquary made in 949 is a rare survival. Part of her relics was taken to Glastonbury, giving rise to a cultus in England and to several church dedications. Her legends are fictitious. Her attribute is a gridiron.

Fal *see* **Fidolus**

Falco of Cava (St) R(OSB). Jun 6
d. 1146. He became a Benedictine at Cava near Salerno, Italy, under St Peter and was prior of the daughter house of Cirzosimo before succeeding St Simeon as abbot in 1141. His cultus was confirmed for Cava in 1928.

Falco of Maastricht (St) B. Feb 20
d. 512. He was bishop of Maastricht, Netherlands, from 495.

Falco of Palena (St) R. Aug 9
d. 1440. A Calabrian, he became a hermit in the Abruzzi, Italy, and has his shrine at Palena. His cultus was confirmed for Valva and Solmona in 1893.

Famian (Gebhard) (St) R(OCist). Aug 8
*c*1090–1150. From Cologne, he became a pilgrim and went to Rome, the Holy Land and finally to Compostela, Spain, near where he became a hermit for twenty-five years. When the Cistercian abbey of Osera was founded he joined it, but went on another pilgrimage to the Holy Land and died at Gallese in Umbria, Italy, on his way back. His name was only given to him after death, and refers to the fame deriving from miracles at his shrine.

Fanchea Garbh (St) R. Jan 1
d. ?585. From near Clogher in Co. Louth, Ireland, she was the sister of St Endeus and was abbess-founder of nunneries at Rossory in Co. Fermanagh and at Killany in Co. Louth, being buried at the latter.

Fandilas (St) M. R. Jun 13
d. 853. An Andalucian, he was abbot of Peñamelaria near Cordoba, Spain, the capital of the Umayyad emirs. He was beheaded for preaching the futility of Islam.

Fantinus of Syracuse (St) L. Jul 24
d. ?303. From Syracuse, Sicily, he was converted by a hermit and converted his parents in turn, but they were martyred in the reign of Diocletian and he fled to Calabria, dying at Gioja.

Fantinus the Younger (St) R. Aug 30
d. *p*980. He was a Byzantine-rite abbot in Calabria, Italy, but his monastery was destroyed in a Muslim raid and he went to Corinth, Greece, and then to Larissa, dying at Thessalonika.

Fara *see* **Burgundofara**

Farannan (St) R. Feb 15
d. *c*590. From Ireland, he was a disciple of St Columba on Iona but returned to Ireland and became a hermit at Allernan (named after him) in Co. Sligo.

Faro (St) B. Oct 28
d. ?675. Brother of SS Burgundofara and Cagnoald, he was a Frankish courtier who rose to the position of royal chancellor before he and his wife separated to become religious. It is uncertain which monastery he was in before he became bishop of Meaux, France, in 626. As such he was a great supporter of monasticism.

Fastred de Cavamiez (Bl) Apr 21
d. 1163. From Cambron, Belgium, he became a Cistercian monk in France at Clairvaux under St Bernard and was made abbot of the new foundation of Cambron near Cambrai, France, in 1148. He became abbot of Clairvaux in 1157 and that of Cîteaux in 1162. He died in Paris, being attended on his deathbed by the pope and the French king.

Fausta (St) L. Dec 19
C3rd? She was allegedly the widowed mother of St Anastasia.

Fausta, Evilasius and Maximus (SS) MM. Sep 20
d. 303. According to their story, Fausta was a teenager who was ordered to be tortured by Evilasius, a pagan magistrate. She converted him by her fortitude, and they then converted a praetor, Maximus, in the same way. The three were martyred at Cyzicus on the Sea of Marmara, Asia Minor, in the reign of Diocletian.

Faustian (St) *see* **Corfu (Martyrs of)**

Faustina (St) *see* **Liberata and Faustina**

Faustina Kowalska *see* **Mary-Faustina Kowalska**

Faustinian (St) B. Feb 26
C4th. A bishop of Bologna, Italy, allegedly the second, he restored the life of his diocese after the persecution of Diocletian and then fought against Arianism.

Faustinus (St) *see* **Florentius, Julian and Comps**

Faustinus (St) *see* **Simplicius, Faustinus and Beatrix**

Faustinus and Jovita *Feb 15*
C2nd. Allegedly two brothers who were noblemen of Brescia, Italy, they were beheaded there in the reign of Hadrian. Their acta are unreliable and their cultus, although ancient, was suppressed in 1969.

Faustinus, Lucius and Comps (SS) MM. Dec 15
? Nothing is known about these Roman African martyrs. The companions were Candidus, Caelian, Mark, Januarius and Fortunatus.

Faustinus, Timothy and Venustus (SS) MM. May 22
d. ?362. They were martyred at Rome in the reign of Julian.

Faustinus of Brescia (St) B. Feb 16
d. 381. He succeeded St Ursicinus as bishop of Brescia in Lombardy, Italy, *c*360 As an alleged descendant of Faustinus and Jovita (q.v.) he compiled (or invented) their acta.

Faustinus Míguez (Bl) R. (Mar 8)
1831–1925. From the province of Orense in Spain, he joined the Piarists at Madrid and taught in various schools for almost fifty years, being inspired by the example of St Joseph Calasanz. He was also skilled in herbal medicine, founding a laboratory for research therein. Noting the illiteracy and marginalisation of many poor young women in contemporary Spanish society, he founded the 'Calasanctian Institute of the Daughters of the Divine Shepherdess' in 1885 to help with their education. Dying at Getafe, he was beatified in 1998.

Faustinus Oteiza Segura (Bl) *see* **Dionysius Pamplona Polo and Comps**

Faustinus Perez García (Bl) *see* **Philip-of-Jesus Munárriz Azcona and Comps**

Faustinus of Rome and Comps (SS) MM. Feb 17
? They numbered forty-five and that is all that is known for certain, although the old Roman Martyrology placed them at Rome.

Faustinus of Todi (St) L. Jul 29
C4th. This alleged disciple of St Felix of Martano has a church dedicated to him at Spoleto, Italy, and is venerated at Todi. He apparently died in peace after standing up for his faith during persecution.

Faustinus Villanueva Igual (Bl) *see* **Hospitaller Martyrs of Spain**

Faustus (St) M. Jul 16
d. *c*250. A Greek, he was martyred in an unknown place by being crucified and being used for archery practice. Allegedly he took five days to die.

Faustus (St) *see* **Bonus and Comps**

Faustus (St) *see* **Dionysius, Faustus and Comps.** (The old Roman Martyrology equated this Faustus with Faustus of Alexandria and with the Faustus in **Gaius, Faustus and Comps.**)

Faustus (St) *see* **Gaius, Faustus and Comps**

Faustus (St) *see* **Timothy and Faustus**

Faustus, Didius, Ammonius and Comps (SS) MM. Nov 26
d. ?311. Allegedly numbering six hundred and sixty, they were martyred in Egypt in the reign of Galerius. Faustus was a priest of Alexandria. Also listed are the bishops Phileas, Hesychius, Pachomius and Theodore.

Faustus, Macarius and Comps (SS) MM. Sep 6
d. 250. They numbered twelve and were beheaded at Alexandria, Egypt, in the reign of Decius.

Faustus of Alexandria (St) M. D. Nov 19
C4th. The deacon of St Dionysius of Alexandria and his companion in exile, he was martyred in extreme old age in the reign of Diocletian.

Faustus of Constantinople (St) R. Aug 3
C5th. A monk at Constantinople, he was allegedly the son of St Dalmatius.

Faustus of Milan (St) M. Aug 7
d. *c*190. He was allegedly a soldier martyred at Milan, Italy, in the reign of Commodus.

Faustus of Montecassino
(St) R(OSB)? Feb 15
C6th. According to the fictitious *Life of St Maurus* written in France in the C9th, he was a disciple of St Benedict at Montecassino, Italy, and one of the companions who went with St Maurus to France. He probably never existed.

Faustus of Riez (St) B. R. Sep 28
?408–490. From Brittany, France, he became a monk at Lérins and its abbot in 433. He was made bishop of Riez in 459, became very influential and fought against Pelagianism and Arianism. For this he was exiled. He was the most distinguished defender of semi-Pelagianism against the teachings on grace of St Augustine.

Faustus of Rome and Comps
(SS) MM. Jun 24
? A group of twenty-four unknown Roman martyrs, they may be identical with SS Lucilla, Flora and Comps (who numbered the same).

Faustus of Syracuse (St) R. Sep 6
d. ?607. Abbot of St Lucy's Abbey at Syracuse, Italy, he was the teacher of St Zosimus.

Febronia (St) M. R. Jul 25
d. ?304. According to her story she was a young nun of a nunnery at Nisibis in upper Mesopotamia (now on the border between Syria and Turkey) who was left behind with two others when the community fled the persecution of Diocletian. She was singled out to be tortured by the removal of the usual appendages before being beheaded. Her acta were allegedly written by one of the companions. There is doubt as to her having existed.

Fechin (St) R. Jan 20
d. ?665. From Sligo, Ireland, he was the abbot-founder of several monasteries, the greatest being at Fore in Westmeath. He is commemorated in Scotland by Ecclefechan near Lockerbie and by St Vigean's church at Arbroath.

Fedlemid *see* **Phelim**

Feighin *see* **Fechin**

Felan *see* **Foelan**

Fele *see* **Fidolus**

Felicia Meda (Bl) R(OFM). Oct 5
1378–1444. From Milan, Italy, she became a Poor Clare there in 1400 and was made abbess in 1425. Proving a success, she was sent to Pesaro to found a new nunnery in 1439. Her cultus was approved in 1812.

Felicia de Montmorency
(Bl) R(OV). Jun 6
1600–1666. A Frenchwoman born at Rome, she became a nun of the Visitation at Autun, France while its founder, St Jane Frances de Chantal, was still alive.

Felician (St) *see* **Fortunatus, Felician and Comps**

Felician (St) *see* **Hyacinth, Quintius and Comps**

Felician (St) *see* **Primus and Felician**

Felician (St) *see* **Severinus, Exuperus and Felician**

Felician (St) *see* **Victor of Marseilles and Comps**

Felician, Philippian and Comps (SS) MM. Jan 30
? They are listed as a group of one hundred and twenty-six Roman African martyrs.

Felician of Foligno (St) M. B. Jan 24
d. 251. From Foligno, Italy, he became a rhetorician at Rome but was sent back as bishop by Pope St Victor I. He evangelized Umbria but was arrested when very old in the reign of Decius and died on the road to Rome where he was to have been martyred. He is listed twice in error in the old Roman Martyrology, also on Oct 20.

Felician of Sandomir (Bl) *see* **Sadoc of Sandomir and Comps**

Felicinus *see* **Felix of Verona**

Felicissima (St) *see* **Gracilian and Felicissima**

Felicissimus (St) *see* **Ariston and Comps**

Felicissimus (St) *see* **Rogatian and Felicissimus**

Felicissimus (St) *see* **Sixtus II and Comps**

Felicissimus, Heraclius and Paulinus (SS) MM. May 26
d. 303. They were martyred in the reign of Diocletian, probably at Todi, Italy since their shrine is there.

Felicissimus of Perugia (St) M. Nov 24
d. ?303. He was martyred at Perugia, Italy, probably in the reign of Diocletian.

Felicity (St) *see* **Cyril, Rogatus and Comps**

Felicity (St) *see* **Perpetua, Felicity and Comps**

Felicity of Padua (St) R. Mar 26
C9th? She has a shrine at St Justina's Abbey at Padua, Italy, and was possibly a nun in that city.

Felicity Pricet (Bl) *see* **William Repin and Comps**

Felicity of Rome (St) M. Nov 23
d. ?165. She was an early martyr of Rome who was buried on the Via Salaria, and may be the Felicity mentioned in the Roman canon of the Mass (usually taken to be the companion of St Perpetua). Her unreliable acta describe her as a widow martyred with her seven sons, and the old Roman Martyrology mistakenly equates these with the **Seven Brothers** (q.v.). Her cultus was confined to local calendars in 1969.

Felicula (St) *see* **Vitalis, Felicula and Zeno**

Felicula of Rome (St) V. Jun 13
d. ?90. According to her legend, which is probably fictional, she was the foster-sister of St Petronilla and, after the latter's martyrdom in the reign of Diocletian, was left in prison without food or drink for a fortnight and then thrown into a ditch to die.

Felim (Fidlemin) (St) B. Aug 9
C6th. Allegedly a disciple of St Columba, he founded a monastery at Kilmore in Co. Cavan, Ireland, and is the principal patron of the diocese of Kilmore.

Felinus and Gratian (SS) MM. Jun 1
d. 250. They were soldiers martyred at Perugia, Italy, in the reign of Decius. Their shrine is at Arona on Lake Maggiore.

Felix (St) *see* **Anastasius, Felix and Digna**

Felix (St) *see* **Andochius, Thyrsus and Felix**

Felix (St) *see* **Arator of Alexandria and Comps**

Felix (St) *see* **Ariston and Comps**

Felix (St) *see* **Calepodius and Comps**

Felix (St) *see* **Callistus, Felix and Boniface**

Felix (St) *see* **Cyril, Rogatus and Comps**

Felix (St) *see* **Emilius, Felix and Comps**

Felix (St) *see* **Epictetus, Jucundus and Comps**

Felix (St) *see* **Florentius and Felix**

Felix (St) *see* **George, Aurelius and Comps**

Felix (St) *see* **Hilary, Tatian and Comps**

Felix (St) *see* **Isaurus, Innocent and Comps**

Felix (St) *see* **Januarius, Marinus and Comps**

Felix (St) *see* **John de Atarés and Comps**

Felix (St) *see* **Julius, Potamia and Comps**

Felix (St) *see* **Lupicinus and Felix**

Felix (St) *see* **Martial, Saturninus and Comps**

Felix (St) *see* **Nabor and Felix**

Felix (St) *see* **Narcissus and Felix**

Felix (SS) *see* **Nemesian and Comps (two of them)**

Felix (SS) *see* **Saturninus, Dativus and Comps (two of them)**

Felix (St) *see* **Scillitan Martyrs**

Felix (St) *see* **Seven Brothers**

Felix (St) *see* **Theodolus, Anesius and Comps**

Felix (St) *see* **Twelve Brothers**

Felix (St) *see* **Valerian, Urban and Comps**

Felix (St) *see* **Verulus, Secundinus and Comps**

Felix (St) *see* **Zaragoza (Eighteen Martyrs of)**

Felix (St) *see* **Zoëllus, Servilius and Comps**

Felix I, Pope *May 30*
d. 274. Allegedly a Roman, he became pope in 269. A letter forged by the Apollinarians in

condemnation of the heresy of Paul of Samosata was accepted by the council of Ephesus as being by him. He had been venerated as a martyr, but apparently in mistake for another Felix and his cultus was suppressed in 1969.

Felix II, Anti-pope (St) M? Jul 29
d. 365. He was archdeacon to Pope Liberius when the latter was exiled in 355 by Emperor Constantius for opposing Arianism. He was then elected as anti-pope by the Arian faction at Rome and was confirmed in office by the council of Sirmium. When Pope Liberius returned, he was driven into exile. The old Roman Martyrology listed him as a valid pope and also as a martyr, owing to the unreliable tradition that he opposed the emperor and was killed as a result. His cultus was confined to local calendars in 1969.

Felix II, Pope (St) Mar 1
d. 492. An alleged ancestor of St Gregory the Great, he became pope in 483 and firmly opposed Monophysitism. In 484 he condemned the *Henoticon*, an Imperial decree issued by Emperor Zeno and Patriarch Acacius of Constantinople in order to try to reconcile the Monophysites. This initiated the 'Acacian schism' between the two churches, which lasted until 518. He is sometimes wrongly listed as 'Felix III' because of Felix II, Anti-pope.

Felix III, Pope (St) Sep 22
d. 530. From near Benevento, Italy, he became pope in 526 and was remembered for his generosity to the poor of Rome. He approved the council of Orange in 529, which promulgated important doctrine on grace and original sin. He is sometimes wrongly listed as 'Felix IV' because of Felix II, Anti-pope.

Felix and Adauctus (SS) MM. Aug 30
d. ?304. Their legend, which seems to be an embellishment of the inscription composed for their tomb on the Ostian Way at Rome by Pope St Damasus, is that the former was a Roman priest who had been condemned and was being taken to his place of execution. An unknown bystander was led by his example to proclaim his faith and was martyred with him (the name meaning 'the one added'). Their cultus was confined to local calendars in 1969.

Felix and Augebert (SS) MM. Aug 30
C7th. They were two English slaves sold in France and brought to Rome, where St Gregory the Great ransomed them and had them educated in a monastery so as to be able to send them on his proposed mission to England. They were ordained, Felix as a priest and Augebert as a deacon, but were killed by pagans in Champagne, France, before they could do any work on St Augustine's mission.

Felix and Constantia (SS) MM. Sep 19
C1st? They are listed as martyrs of Nocera, Italy, in the reign of Nero, but which Nocera (in Campania or in Umbria) is disputed and there are two sets of relics.

Felix, Cyprian and Comps
(SS) MM. BB. Oct 12
d. ?484. Two bishops and allegedly 4966 Roman African Catholics, they were driven into the desert in modern Algeria by the Arian Vandal king Hunneric. There they died of privation, were eaten by wild animals or were killed or enslaved by the local Berbers. Their fate is recorded by Victor of Utica, their contemporary.

Felix and Eusebius (SS) MM. Nov 5
C1st? They were allegedly martyred at Terracina between Rome and Naples.

Felix and Fortunatus (SS) MM. Jun 11
d. 296. They were martyred at Aquileia near Venice, Italy, in the reign of Diocletian, and were allegedly two brothers from Vicenza.

Felix, Fortunatus and Achilles (SS) MM. Apr 23
d. ?212. A priest and two deacons, they were allegedly sent by St Irenaeus of Lyons to evangelize the district of Vienne, France, and were martyred in the reign of Caracalla. Their acta are unreliable.

Felix and Gennadius (SS) MM. May 16
? They had their shrine at Uzalis in Roman Africa, but nothing is known about them.

Felix and Januarius (SS) MM. Jan 7
? They were martyred at one of the cities called Heraclea in the East, not the one near Cadiz, Spain, where they are venerated.

Felix, Julia and Jucunda (SS) MM. Jul 27
? Erroneously listed in the old Roman Martyrology as martyrs at Nola near Naples, Italy, the first is the famous Felix of Nola while the other two seem to be martyrs of Nicomedia, Asia Minor.

Felix, Luciolus, Fortunatus, Marcia and Comps (SS) MM. Mar 3
? A group of forty martyrs, claimed for Roman Africa on slender grounds.

Felix and Maurus (SS) MM. Jun 16
C6th. From Caeasarea in the Holy Land, Maurus was a priest and Felix was his son. They went to Rome on pilgrimage and settled as hermits at a place near Terni now called San Felice after the son, who became famous as a thaumaturge.

Felix and Regula (SS) MM. Sep 11
C3rd. They have a popular local cultus at Zürich, Switzerland. According to their untrustworthy legend they were a brother and sister who took refuge there in the reign of Maximian but who were discovered and beheaded.

Felix, Symphronius, Hippolytus and Comps (SS) MM. Feb 3
? They were possibly martyred in Roman Africa, if they existed at all. It is suspected that they are a duplication of other martyrs.

Felix of Africa and Comps (SS) MM. Mar 23
C5th. They are listed as twenty-four Roman African martyrs.

Felix Amoroso of Nicosia (Bl) R(OFM Cap). Jun 1
1715–1787. From Nicosia, Sicily, he was an apprentice shoemaker and tried and failed several times to become a consecrated religious. Finally he became a lay brother in the Capuchin friary at his home town and went begging for funds for its maintenance. He helped poor and sick people, reconciled habitual sinners and was beatified in 1888.

Felix of Bologna (St) B. Dec 4
d. 429. A deacon at Milan, Italy, under St Ambrose, he later became bishop of Bologna.

Felix of Bourges (St) B. Jan 1
d. *c*580. He was a bishop of Bourges, France.

Felix of Cantalice (St) R(OFM Cap). May 18
1515–1587. From a peasant family near Cantalice in Apulia, Italy, he started out as a farm labourer but became a Capuchin lay brother at Anticoli in 1543. In 1547 he went to the friary at Rome and begged daily for funds for its support for forty years. He became friendly with SS Charles Borromeo and Philip Neri, was especially attached to children and was an example of spiritual joy (being nicknamed 'Deogratias' from his constantly saying 'Thanks be to God'). He was the first Capuchin to be canonized, in 1712.

Felix of Como (St) B. Jul 14
d. *c*390. He was consecrated bishop of Como, Italy, allegedly the first one there, by his friend St Ambrose.

Felix of Dunwich (St) B. Mar 8
d. 647. From Burgundy, France, he became a missionary bishop. In 630 he went to East Anglia, England, with its king St Sigebert (who had been baptized in exile) and became the 'Apostle of the East Angles' with the support of St Honoratus of Canterbury. He was a great success as a preacher, and established his base at Dunwich on the coast of Suffolk. This walled city has now been washed away by the sea and the church of St John, thought to have been his cathedral, was lost in 1540. His copy of the Gospels, written in *c*630, survived as the *Red Book of Dunwich* at Eye Priory and then at the magistrates' court at Eye before allegedly being cut up for tags at a local mansion in the mid-C19th. He is depicted with three rings on his right hand.

Felix of Fondi (St) R. Nov 6
C6th. A monk at Fondi near Terracina, Italy, he was highly regarded by St Gregory the Great, his contemporary. His monastery has been claimed as Benedictine.

Felix of Fritzlar (St) M? R. Jun 5
d. *c*790. A monk of Fritzlar in Hesse, Germany, he was allegedly martyred by the militantly pagan Saxons in their resistance to the Franks.

Felix of Metz (St) B. Feb 21
C2nd? He is the alleged third bishop of Metz, France. The existence of that diocese is only certain from the C4th, however, and the earlier traditions may be fictitious.

Felix of Montecassino (Bl) R(OSB). Mar 23
d. *c*1000. He was an ordinary Benedictine monk of Montecassino, Italy, but owing to miracles at his tomb at Chieti the bishop there enshrined his relics for veneration.

Felix of Nantes (St) B. Jul 7
d. 584. He was bishop of Nantes, France, for about thirty-three years.

Felix of Nicosia *see* **Felix Amoroso**

Felix of Nola (1) (St) P. Jan 14
d. *c*250. Born at Nola near Naples, Italy, his father was a soldier from Syria. He became a priest of Nola and was especially helpful to St Maximus the bishop when the persecution by

Decius broke out. He had to suffer much himself, and was thus sometimes celebrated as a martyr. St Paulinus of Nola had a great devotion to him and wrote in his honour, which led to his cultus being one of the most popular in south Italy. However it was confined to local calendars in 1969.

Felix of Nola (2) (St) M. B. Nov 15
d. ?287. The principal patron of Nola near Naples has been claimed as the famous St Felix, ordained as the town's first bishop and martyred with thirty companions. It is now considered more likely that they were two separate people.

Felix O'Dullany (Bl) B. R(OCist). Jan 24
d. 1202. An Irish Cistercian monk, probably of Jerpoint in Co. Kilkenny, he became bishop of Ossory in 1178. He has a cultus among the Cistercians.

Felix of Pavia (St) M. B? Jul 15
? This alleged bishop and martyr has a cultus at Pavia, Italy, but is otherwise unknown and may be the same as St Felix of Spoleto.

Felix of Pistoia (St) R? Aug 26
C9th? Allegedly an early hermit of Pistoia in Tuscany, Italy, his alleged relics were found there in 1414. His existence is doubtful.

Felix of Rhuys (St) R(OSB). Mar 4
d. 1038. From near Quimper in Brittany, France, he became a hermit on Ushant Island and afterwards a Benedictine monk at Fleury. In 1025 he became abbot-restorer of Rhuys, a great Breton monastery which had been founded by St Gildas but had then been destroyed by the Norse.

Felix of Rome (St) P. Jan 14
? A Roman priest, he has been confused with St Felix of Nola.

Felix of Seville (St) M. D. May 2
? He is a martyred deacon venerated at Seville, Spain.

Felix of Spoleto (St) M. B. May 18
d. ?304. He was bishop either of Spoleto, Italy, or of Spello nearby and was martyred in the reign of Diocletian.

Felix of Sutri (St) M. P. Jun 23
d. 257. A priest from Sutri near Viterbo, Italy, he had his face smashed in with a heavy stone at Civita Castellana nearby in the reign of Valerian.

Felix of Thibiuca (St) M. B. Oct 24
d. 303. Bishop of Thibiuca in Roman Africa, he refused to hand over his church's copies of the Scriptures for destruction as required by an edict of Diocletian. Thus he was taken to Carthage, exiled to Italy and beheaded at Venosa. The old Roman Martyrology listed four spurious companions: Adauctus (*see* **Felix and Adauctus**), Januarius, Fortunatus and Septimus (*see* **Twelve Brothers**).

Felix of Thynissa (St) M. Nov 6
? A Roman African, he died in prison awaiting martyrdom at Thynissa near Annaba, Algeria. St Augustine preached a sermon in his honour.

Felix of Trier (St) B. Mar 26
d. *c*400. He was consecrated bishop of Trier, Germany, by his friend St Martin of Tours in 386. However, those clerics who had elected him had also asked Maximus, the usuring emperor, for the death of the heretic Priscillian. So St Felix was refused communion by the pope and St Ambrose of Milan and resigned as a result, although his personal holiness was not in question.

Felix-of-the-Five-Wounds Ugalde Irurzun (Bl) *see* **Nicephorus Díez Tejerina and Comps**

Felix of Valois (St) R. F. Nov 20
?1127–?1212. According to his legend he was a hermit near Meaux, France, who founded the Trinitarian order with St John of Matha in order to redeem Christians taken prisoner by Muslim raiders. The early Trinitarians kept no records, a defect which their successors made up for by forgery, and so his existence is dubious. His cultus was confirmed for the Trinitarians and for Spain in 1666, extended to the entire Latin church in 1694 but confined again to local calendars in 1969.

Felix of Verona (St) B. Jul 19
? He was allegedly an early bishop of Verona, Italy.

Feock (St) Feb 2
? There is a place near Truro in Cornwall, England, called Feock but who this commemorates is entirely unknown, even as to gender.

Ferdinand of Aragon (St) B. Jun 27
C13th. Related to the Aragonese royal family, then ruling the kingdom of Naples, Italy, he became bishop of Caiazzo near Capua and has his shrine at Cornello.

Ferdinand-of-St-Joseph Ayalà (Bl) M. R(OSA). Jun 1
1575–1617. From near Ciudad Real, Spain, he became an Augustinian friar and went to Japan via Mexico in 1605 as vicar provincial of the Augustinian mission there. He worked at Osaka and was beheaded at Omura, being beatified in 1867. *See* **Japan (Martyrs of)**.

Ferdinand-Mary Baccilieri (Bl) P. F. (Jul 13)
1821–1893. From Campodoso near Modena, Italy, he tried his vocation with the Jesuits before being ordained as a diocesan priest of Bologna in 1844. In 1851 he was made parish priest of Galeazza, where he remained for forty-one years, the rest of his life. In order to educate poor girls of the parish he founded the 'Mantellate Servite Sisters of Rome' in 1866, and this has since become an international congregation. He was beatified in 1999.

Ferdinand of Portugal (Bl) M. L. Jun 5
1402–1443. Born at Santarém in Portugal, a son of the king, he became master-general of the Knights of Aviz, a military order affiliated to the Cistercians. He went on an expedition to Morocco to seize Tangiers in 1437, but this was routed and he was taken hostage with some others. The Portuguese refused a treaty and he died at Fez after five years' brutal slavery. His cultus was confirmed in 1470, and he is nicknamed 'the Constant' or 'the 'Standard-bearer'.

Ferdinand Sanchez (Bl) *see* **Ignatius de Azevedo and Comps**

Ferdinand III of Spain, King (St) L. May 30
1198–1252. King of Castile from 1217, he united his kingdom with that of León in 1230 and was able to follow up the crushing defeat of the Muslims by the Spanish Christians at Los Navos de Tolosa in 1212 by conquering Cordoba (1236), Murcia, Jaen, Cadiz and finally Seville in 1249. He consolidated his conquests by founding many Church institutions (including the university of Salamanca), by practising tolerance towards his new Muslim and Jewish subjects (although not towards heretics) and by aiming at doing no injustice to anyone. He lived extremely frugally and penitentially, died at Seville and had his cultus confirmed for Spain in 1655.

Feredarius (St) R. May 18
d. *p*863. From Ireland, he became abbot of Iona, Scotland, in 863 and oversaw the transfer of the relics of St Columba to Ireland because of the danger of Norse raids.

Fergna the White (St) R. Mar 2
d. 637. He was related to St Columba and succeeded him as abbot of Iona, Scotland.

Fergus (Fergustus, Ferguisius) of Downpatrick (St) B. Mar 30
C6th. He was allegedly bishop of Downpatrick, Ireland, but the traditions concerning him are vague and conflicting and he may be the same as St Fergus of Glamis.

Fergus (Fergustian) of Glamis (St) B. Nov 27
d. *p*721. An Irish missionary bishop, he worked in the regions of Strathearn, Caithness and Buchan in Scotland and died at Glamis near Forfar. He signed the acta of a Roman council in 721, describing himself as a Pict.

Fernando *see* **Ferdinand**

Ferran *see* **Ferdinand**

Ferreolus and Ferrutio (SS) MM. PD. Jun 16
d. ?212. According to their legend, they were Gallo-Romans who studied at Athens, Greece, and at Smyrna (now Izmir, Turkey), and were converted by St Polycarp. Returning as priest and deacon, they were sent by St Irenaeus of Lyons to evangelize the region around Besançon, France, where they were martyred after thirty years.

Ferreolus (Fergéol) of Grenoble (St) M. B. Jan 16
d. *c*670. Bishop of Grenoble, France, he was allegedly killed by order of Ebroin, the mayor of the palace of the Neustrian kingdom. He had his cultus confirmed in 1907.

Ferreolus of Limoges (St) B. Sep 18
d. ?591. Bishop of Limoges, France, he was admired by St Gregory of Tours but his extant biography is fictitious.

Ferreolus of Uzès (St) B. Jan 4
d. 581. From Narbonne, France, he became bishop of Uzès near Avignon but was exiled by the king for three years, allegedly because he tried to convert the Jews of his diocese. He wrote a rule for a monastery that he founded (this relies in part on the rule of St Benedict).

Ferreolus of Vienne (St) M. Sep 18
d. ?304. A Roman army officer, traditionally the commanding officer of **St Julian of Brioude** (q.v.), during a persecution (probably by Diocletian) he was imprisoned for his faith in a

latrine pit at Vienne, France, but escaped through the sewer. He was recaptured and beheaded.

Ferrutio (St) *see* **Ferreolus and Ferrutio**

Ferrutius of Mainz (St) M. Oct 28
? A Roman soldier stationed at Mainz, Germany, he tried to resign rather than take part in the prescribed pagan rituals but was imprisoned instead at Kastel nearby and died of ill-treatment.

Festus (St) *see* **Januarius of Benevento**

Festus (St) *see* **John and Festus**

Festus *see* **Faustus**

Fiace (Fiech) (St) B. R. Oct 12
C5th. A bard of Ireland, he was baptized and consecrated bishop for Leinster by St Patrick, in whose honour he wrote an extant hymn. He founded a monastery at Sletty near Carlow, where he was buried.

Fiachan (Fianchine) (St) R. Apr 29
C7th. From Munster, Ireland, he was a monk at Lismore and a disciple of St Carthage the Younger.

Fiacre (Fiacrius, Fiaker, Fèvre) (St) R. Aug 30
d. *c*670. From Ireland, he became a hermit at Kilferagh (named after him) in Co. Kilkenny before emigrating to France and becoming a hermit at Breuil near Meaux on a site given to him by the local bishop, St Faro. His cell grew into an abbey. His veneration is still popular and he is a patron of gardeners (his attribute is a spade) and of men suffering from venereal disease (he had no time for women).

Fibitius (St) B. Nov 5
d. *c*500. He was abbot of a monastery at Trier, Germany, before becoming bishop there.

Fidelis (St) M. Mar 23
? A Roman African martyr, he may be one of the companions of the St Felix listed on the same date.

Fidelis of Como (St) M. Oct 28
d. ?304. A soldier, he was martyred at Samolito near Como in Lombardy, Italy. Most of his relics were taken to Milan by St Charles Borromeo, but some remain at Como.

Fidelis of Edessa (St) *see* **Bassa and Sons**

Fidelis Fuidio Rodriguez (Bl) *see* **Charles Eraña Guruceta**

Fidelis of Mérida (St) B. Feb 7
d. *c*570. From somewhere in the Middle East, he went to Spain on a mercantile expedition. Then he settled at Mérida and was trained by St Paul, the bishop there, as his successor.

Fidelis Roy of Sigmaringen (St) M. R(OFM Cap). Apr 24
1577–1622. From Sigmaringen in southern Germany, he travelled widely as tutor to a young nobleman before qualifying as a lawyer and doing much work for the poor at Ensisheim in Alsace. Then he became a Capuchin at Freiburg-in-Breisgau in 1612 and was appointed head of the mission to Graubünden canton in Switzerland by the newly founded Roman congregation of Propaganda Fide in 1622. The area was fanatically Protestant but his success was startling, so the Zwinglian preachers asserted that he was an agent of the Hapsburgs. As a result he was murdered in the church at Seewis near Chur. Canonized in 1746.

Fidelmia (St) *see* **Ethenia and Fidelmia**

Fidentian (St) *see* **Secundus, Fidentian and Varicus**

Fidentius and Terence (SS) MM. Sep 27
? The alleged relics of these martyrs were discovered at Todi, Italy, in the C12th and are venerated there. Nothing is known about them and their acta are fictitious.

Fidentius of Padua (St) M? B? Nov 16
C2nd? He has a cultus at Padua but nothing is known about him. Traditionally he was a martyr, and Cardinal Baronius listed him as a bishop in his revision of the old Roman Martyrology (it is unclear why).

Fides *see* **Faith**

Fidleminus *see* **Phelim**

Fidolus (Phal) (St) R. May 16
d. *c*540. The son of a Roman official in Auvergne, France, he was captured and sold as a slave by the invading Franks but redeemed by Aventinus, an abbot of a monastery near Troyes. Fidolus later became abbot himself at the place, later named Saint-Phal after him.

Fidweten (Fivetein, Fidivitanus) (St) R(OSB). Dec 11
d. ?888. He was a monk at Redon in Brittany, France, and a disciple of St Convoyon there.

Fiech *see* **Fiace**

Fillan (St) R. Feb 3
d. *c*750. He was allegedly born in Ireland, a son of St Kentigern and nephew of St Comgan, and was a monk with the latter at Lochalsh before becoming a missionary around St Fillans west of Crieff, Scotland.

Fillan *see* **Foillan**

Fina *see* **Seraphina**

Finan *see* **Finian**

Finan of Aberdeen (St) R. Mar 18
C6th. Apparently from Wales (Llanffinnan on Anglesey is probably named after him), he was a missionary around Aberdeen, Scotland.

Finan Cam (St) R. Apr 7
C6th. From Munster, Ireland, he was a disciple of St Brendan at Clonfert before founding his own monastery at Kinnitty in Co. Offaly.

Finan of Lindisfarne (St) B. R. Feb 17
d. 661. An Irish monk of Iona, he was chosen by his brethren to succeed St Aidan as bishop of Lindisfarne. He continued the evangelisation of Northumbria, England, in partnership with its king St Oswin and founded monasteries at Gilling, Tynemouth and Whitby. He also sent missionaries to Mercia and East Anglia, consecrating St Chad for the Mercian mission. He was a staunch upholder of Celtic church traditions.

Finbar (Findbar, Barr) (St) B. R. Sep 25
C6th. A native of the region of Connaught, Ireland, he became a hermit at Gougane Barra and founded a monastery on the site of Cork (of which city he is considered the first bishop). The island of Barra in the Western Isles, Scotland, is named after him. His name means 'Blond'. He is the principal patron of the diocese of Cork.

Findan (Fintan) (St) R(OSB). Nov 15
d. ?876. From Leinster, Ireland, he was captured by Norse raiders and taken to the Orkneys to be a slave but escaped and went on pilgrimage to Rome. Then he became a monk at Farfa nearby before ending up as a hermit at the abbey of Rheinau on the Rhine in Zürich canton, Switzerland, for twenty-two years.

Findbarr *see* **Finian**

Fingar (Gwinear), Phiala and Comps (SS) MM. Dec 14
C5th. Brother and sister from Ireland, they were allegedly killed with their companions at Gwinear near Hayle in Cornwall, England. Fingar seems to have been a hermit in Brittany previously, as Plouvinger there is named after him and he is venerated there.

Finian (Finnian) of Clonard (St) B. R. Dec 12
d. ?549. From Myshall near Carlow, Ireland, he was a monk in Wales for some time before returning to Ireland and founding many monasteries and churches. The greatest of these was Clonard in Meath which became the foremost school in Ireland, famous for its biblical exegesis. Among its pupils were the so-called 'Twelve Apostles of Ireland', who helped to establish Christianity thoroughly in Ireland after the death of St Patrick's generation. He is the principal patron of the diocese of Meath.

Finian Lobur (St) R. Mar 16
d. ?560. He was allegedly made abbot of a monastery at Swords north of Dublin, Ireland, by St Columba, but the traditions concerning him are extremely confused.

Finian (Finbar, Winnin) of Moville (St) B. R. Sep 10
?493–579. Born near Strangford Lough in Co. Down, Ireland, he studied under St Colman and also under St Ninian at Whithorn, Scotland, before making a pilgrimage to Rome and being ordained there. When he returned he brought back some biblical manuscripts, which allegedly led to the famous incident of the psalter of St Columba. He founded the great monastery of Moville in Co. Down and became abbot-bishop there. He has been wrongly identified with St Frigidian of Lucca.

Finlugh (Finlag) (St) R. Jan 3
C6th. A brother of St Fintan of Doon, it is alleged that he was a disciple of St Columba in Scotland before being made abbot of a monastery founded by the latter at Tamlaght Finlagan in Co. Derry, Ireland.

Fintan of Clonenagh (St) R. Feb 17
d. 603. From Leinster, Ireland, and a disciple of St Columba at Terryglass, he became a hermit at Clonenagh in Co. Laois and founded a monastery for the disciples who came to him. Allegedly the austerity of this was such that neighbouring monasteries objected.

Fintan of Doon (St) R. Jan 3
C6th. A disciple of St Comgall at Bangor, he founded a monastery at Doon in Co. Limerick, Ireland, where his holy well is still a focus of veneration.

Fintan Munnu (St) R. Oct 21
d. ?635. Reputedly the most austere of Irish saints, he was under St Comgall at Bangor, was briefly at Iona and then apparently founded a monastery at Kilmun (named after him or another of the same name) near Dunoon on the Firth of Clyde, Scotland. Later he went back to Ireland and founded another monastery at Taghmon near Wexford, also named after him. He defended the Celtic calculation of the date of Easter. Apparently he suffered a very serious skin disease.

Fintan of Rheinau *see* **Findan**

Fionnchu (St) R. Nov 28
C6th. He succeeded St Comgall as abbot of Bangor, Co. Down, Ireland.

Firmatus and Flaviana (SS) MM. Oct 5
? They are venerated as martyrs at Auxerre, France, but nothing is known about them.

Firmian (Fermanus, Firminus) (St) R(OSB). Mar 11
d. *c*1020. He was abbot of the Benedictine monastery of St Sabinus at Piceno near Fermo in the Marches, Italy.

Firmin of Amiens I (St) M. B. Sep 25
C4th. The reputed first bishop of Amiens, France, and a martyr, he is described as being from Pamplona in Spanish Navarre and a convert of St Saturninus of Toulouse.

Firmin of Amiens II (St) B. Sep 1
C4th. The reputed third bishop of Amiens, France, he is alleged to have been a son of a convert of the first bishop (also called Firmin). It is possible that these two bishops were the same person.

Firmin of Amiens, Abbot (St) R? Mar 11
? In his revision of the old Roman Martyrology Cardinal Baronius inserted an abbot of Amiens called Firmin. No such saint has ever been venerated there, and he seems to have conflated Firmian of Piceno and Firmin, third bishop of Amiens.

Firmin of Armenia (St) *see* **Orentius, Heros and Comps**

Firmin of Mende (St) B. Jan 19
? He was the third bishop of Mende in the Massif Central, France.

Firmin of Metz (St) B. Aug 18
d. ?496. He succeeded St Adelphus as bishop of Metz, France, but the statements about him are confused.

Firmin of Uzès (St) B. Oct 11
516–553. From Narbonne, France, he was educated by an uncle who was bishop of Uzès near Avignon and succeeded him as bishop in 538.

Firmin of Verdun (St) B. Dec 5
d. 486. From Toul, France, he became bishop of Verdun.

Firmin of Viviers (St) B. Mar 29
C6th. He was a bishop of Viviers, France.

Firmina of Amelia (St) V. Nov 24
d. ?303. From Rome, she died under torture at Amelia in Umbria, Italy, in the reign of Diocletian.

Firmus (St) M. Jun 1
d. *c*290. He was an Eastern martyr, possibly of Egypt.

Firmus (St) *see* **Fortunatus, Felician and Comps**

Firmus (St) *see* **Gorgonius and Firmus**

Firmus (St) *see* **Orentius, Heros and Comps**

Firmus and Rusticus (SS) MM. Aug 9
d. *c*290. They were allegedly two related citizens of Bergamo in Lombardy, Italy, who were martyred at Verona in the reign of Maximian, but their acta are not authentic and they may have been African martyrs whose relics were taken to Verona.

Firmus of Tagaste (St) B. Jul 31
Early C4th. St Augustine wrote of him that he was 'firm by name but firmer by faith' because he endured torture rather than give up a fugitive sought by the authorities. On the basis of this Cardinal Baronius inserted his name into the old Roman Martyrology.
First Martyrs of Rome *see* **Protomartyrs of Rome**

Flannan (St) B. R. Dec 18
C7th. An Irish monk, he was ordained in Rome and was the first bishop of Killaloe in Co. Clare,

Ireland, founded by St Lua. He was also a hermit for a while on the Flannan Islands, west of Lewis in the Western Isles, Scotland. He is the principal patron of the diocese of Killaloe.

Flavia (St) *see* **Placid, Eutychius and Comps**

Flavia Domitilla, Euphrosyna and Theodora *May 12*
d. *c*100. The first-named was a great-niece of the emperors Titus and Domitian. She married St Flavius Clemens and was exiled to Pantelleria for her faith. If she is identical with the 'Domitilla Junior' mentioned by Eusebius, her husband was her uncle and she was exiled to Ponza Island, off Terracina. According to the unreliable acta of SS Nereus and Achilleus she was martyred at the latter place with two foster-sisters. There may be two martyrs of the same name, and the confusion helped lead to the cultus being suppressed in 1969.

Flavian (St) *see* **Montanus, Lucius and Comps**

Flavian and Elias (SS) BB. Jul 20
d. 512 and 518 resp. They were the patriarchs of Antioch and of Jerusalem and were exiled to Petra, Jordan, by the Monophysite emperor Anastasius I. Flavian had refused to commit himself to opposing the council of Chalcedon and was deposed, and Elias had supported him by refusing communion to the intruded patriarch Severus. Elias did not accept the council himself, however, and he is not venerated by the Orthodox. They died in exile and were inserted into the Roman Martyrology despite being under contemporary Roman excommunication for having accepted the *Henoticon.*

Flavian of Acquapendente (St) M. Dec 22
d. 362. Alleged to have been a prefect of Rome, in the reign of Julian he was branded on the forehead as a slave and exiled to Acquapendente in Tuscany, Italy, where he died. His acta are untrustworthy.

Flavian (Flavinian, Flavius) of Autun (SS) BB. Jul 20
d. ?544 and 614. The fifteenth and the twenty-first bishops of Autun, France, both called Flavian, are listed as saints.

Flavian of Civitavecchia (St) M. Jan 28
d. ?304. A deputy prefect of Rome, he was beheaded at Civitavecchia in the reign of Diocletian.

Flavian of Constantinople (St) M. B. Feb 18
d. 449. A priest of Constantinople, he became patriarch there in 446 and made an enemy of Chrysaphius, a palace eunuch and adviser of Emperor Theodosius II, by refusing to make a donation to him on his election. Then Flavian denounced the Monophysitism of the monk Eutyches, who claimed to be interpreting the teaching of St Cyril of Alexandria, in 448 and informed Pope St Leo. The latter replied with his famous 'Tome' (an encyclical letter). Then his enemies at home and Dioscorus, the patriarch of Alexandria, arranged for a council at Ephesus in 449, the so-called 'Robber Synod', at which Flavian was deposed and so badly beaten that he died three days later. He was vindicated at the Council of Chalcedon in 451, which accepted the Tome of Leo and definitively rejected Monophysitism.

Flaviana of Auxerre (St) *see* **Firmatus and Flaviana**

Flavius, Augustus and Augustine (SS) MM. May 7
d. *c*300. The bishop of Nicomedia, Asia Minor, and his two brothers, they were martyred in the reign of Diocletian (whose capital the place was). Eastern sources list the brothers as Marcellinus, Macrobius and Eutyches.

Flavius Argüeso González (Bl) *see* **Hospitaller Martyrs of Spain**

Flavius of Autun *see* **Flavian**

Flavius Clemens (St) M. Jun 22
d. 96. Brother of the emperor Vespasian and uncle of Titus and Domitian, he allegedly married his niece **Flavia Domitilla** (q.v.). He was consul with Domitian in 95, who had him executed in the following year for 'atheism' and 'Jewish customs'. This has been taken to refer to his conversion to Christianity.

Flocellus (Floscellus, Flocel) (St) M. Sep 17
d. *c*170. From near Coutances, France, he was a teenager who was tortured and thrown to the wild animals in the amphitheatre (allegedly at Autun) in the reign of Marcus Aurelius.

Flora (St) *see* **Lucilla, Flora and Comps**

Flora *see* **Blath**

Flora and Mary (SS) VV. Nov 24
d. 856. They were two young women of

Cordoba, Spain, when that city was the capital of the Umayyad emirate, and had Muslim fathers and Christian mothers. After choosing Christianity they were condemned as apostates under Islamic law and beheaded after a long imprisonment.

Flora of Beaulieu (Bl) R. Jun 11
d. 1347. From the Auvergne, France, when aged fourteen she joined the Hospitaller nuns of St John at Beaulieu near Rocamadour. She suffered some very interesting mystical and psychological phenomena associated with her spiritual sufferings.

Florence *see* **Florentina, Florentia or Florentius**

Florentia (Florence) (St) *see* **Tiberius, Modestus and Florentia**

Florentian (St) *see* **Valerian, Urban and Comps**

Florentina (Florence) (St) R. Jun 20
d. ?636. From Cartagena, Spain, she was the sister of SS Leander, Fulgentius and Isidore. The family was orphaned when she was little and she was educated by St Leander, who wrote a rule for a monastic foundation that she made. She died at Ecija.

Florentinus (Florentius), Hilary and Aphrodisius (SS) MM. Sep 27
?C5th. They are listed as hermits killed in Roman Gaul by invading barbarians, at a place which has been claimed as Sion in Valais, Switzerland, Sémont near Autun, Suint in the Charolais or Simond near Dijon (all in France).

Florentinus Asensio Barroso (Bl) M. B. Aug 9
1877–1936. Born near Valladolid, Spain, he was ordained in 1901 and became a lecturer in theology at the university there before being made the parish priest of the cathedral. He was a prolific and effective preacher and also confessor to consecrated religious, and was appointed the bishop of Barbastro at the start of 1936. The city was ruled by anti-clerical republicans and, despite his goodwill and collaboration, he was imprisoned in July and tortured and mutilated before being shot. He was beatified in 1997. *See* **Spanish Civil War (Martyrs of)**.

Florentinus Felipe Naya (Bl) *see* **Dionysius Pamplona Polo and Comps**

Florentinus of Trier (St) B. Oct 16
C4th. He is alleged to have been the successor of St Severianus as bishop of Trier, Germany, but there is serious doubt concerning the existence of both.

Florentius (St) R. Sep 22
C5th. From Bavaria, Germany, he became a disciple of St Martin of Tours, who ordained him and sent him to evangelize Poitou, France. He eventually settled as a hermit on the Loire river near Angers, and the disciples who gathered around him he formed into the monastery later known as Saint-Florent-le-Vieil.

Florentius (St) *see* **Cassius, Florentius and Comps**

Florentius (St) *see* **Catulinus, Januarius and Comps**

Florentius (St) *see* **Eutychius and Florentius**

Florentius (St) *see* **Sisinius, Diocletius and Florentius**

Florentius and Felix (SS) MM. Jul 25
d. 235. Two Roman soldiers, they were martyred at Furcona near Aquila, Italy, in the reign of Maximinius Thrax.

Florentius, Geminianus and Saturus (SS) MM. Apr 6
?C4th. They were martyred at Sirmium (now Srem Mitrovica, Serbia).

Florentius, Julian, Cyriac, Marcellinus and Faustinus (SS) MM. Jun 5
d. 250. They were beheaded at Perugia, Italy, in the reign of Decius.

Florentius (Flann) of Bangor (St) R. Dec 15
C7th. He was abbot of Bangor in Co. Down, Ireland.

Florentius of Carracedo (St) R(OSB). Dec 10
d. 1156. He was abbot of the monastery of Carracedo in El Bierzo, a region in León province, Spain, and his veneration is still popular locally. The monastery became Cistercian after his death.

Florentius Dumontet de Cardaillac (Bl) *see* **John-Baptist Souzy and Comps**

Florentius of Orange (St) B. Oct 17
d. ?526. He was a bishop of Orange near Avignon, France.

Florentius of Seville (St) P. Feb 23
d. ?485. He was a priest of Seville, Spain.

Florentius of Strasbourg (St) B. Nov 7
d. ?693. From Ireland, he went to Alsace, France, in 664 and founded a monastery at Haslach in the Black Forest, Germany. In 678 he became bishop of Strasbourg and established an Irish monastery there. He is called the 'Apostle of Alsace'.

Florentius of Thessalonika (St) M. Oct 13
d. 312. He was burned at the stake at Thessalonika, Greece, in the reign of Maximinus Daza.

Florentius of Trechâteaux (St) M. Oct 27
d. ?261. He was allegedly martyred by the invading Allemani at Arc sur Tille near Dijon in Burgundy, France, and his shrine established in a monastery named Trechâteaux nearby.

Florentius of Vienne (St) M? B. Jan 3
Late C4th? The old Roman Martyrology lists him as a bishop of Vienne, France, who was martyred in the reign of Gallienus ?275, and he is locally venerated as a martyr-bishop. But the list of bishops there puts him in the C4th and mentions him attending a council in 374.

Florian (St) M. May 4
d. 304. According to his legend he was a Roman officer who was thrown off the bridge at Lorch in Austria and drowned in the reign of Diocletian. His shrine is at Linz, part of his alleged relics are at Cracow, Poland, and he is the patron of Upper Austria. The facts are seriously confused, however, and more than one person of the name is involved in them.

Florian, Calanicus and Comps (SS) MM. Dec 17
d. ?637. Numbering sixty, they were soldiers captured by the Muslim Arab invaders at Eleutheropolis in the Holy Land (near Gaza) and massacred after refusing to apostatize.

Floribert of Ghent (St) R. Nov 1
d. *c*660. He was appointed by St Amandus as abbot of the two new monasteries at Ghent, Belgium, of Blandinsberg and St Bavon's.

Floribert of Liege (St) B. Apr 27
d. 746. He was the son of St Hubert and succeeded him as bishop of Liege, Belgium. He has been confused with St Floribert of Ghent.

Florida Cevoli (Bl) R(OFM Cap). Jun 12
1685–1767. Born of a noble family in Pisa, Italy, at the age of eighteen she entered the Capuchin Poor Clares of Citta di Castello. Her novice mistress was St Veronica Giuliani, who became abbess in 1716. Bl Florida was made the prioress, and became abbess in turn in 1727. She encouraged a stricter observance and was well known in the neighbourhood for her charity. She was beatified in 1993.

Florinus (St) P. Nov 17
C7th. He was a parish priest in the Graubünden, Switzerland, and some of his relics are at his namesake church at Koblenz, Germany. His extant biographies are unreliable.

Florius (St) *see* **Lucian, Florius and Comps**

Florus (St) *see* **Demetrius, Honoratus and Florus**

Florus, Laurus, Proculus and Maximus (SS) MM. Aug 18
C2nd? Their Byzantine legend, possibly fictional, describes the first two as Illyrian brothers who were stonemasons and who were employed by the last two to build a temple. When it was finished they were all converted, so they then dedicated the building as a church and were thrown down a dry well as a result.

Florus (Flour) of Lodève (St) B. Nov 3
d. 389. He was the first bishop of Lodève near Montpellier, France and has his shrine at Saint-Flour in the Massif Central.

Flos (St) *see* **Stephen, Pontian and Comps**

Flosculus (Flou) of Orléans (St) B. Feb 2
d. *p*480. He was bishop of Orléans, France. and a contemporary of Sidonius Apollinaris.

Flour *see* **Florus of Lodève**

Foellan (Foilan, Fillan) (St) R. Jan 9
C8th. From Ireland, he went to Scotland with St Kentigerna, his mother, and St Comgan, a relative, and became a missionary monk there. He died at Strathfillan in Perthshire.

Foillan (St) M. R. Oct 31
d. ?655. Brother of SS Fursey and Ultan, whom he accompanied to England from Ireland, he

became abbot of a Celtic-rite monastery at Burgh Castle near Great Yarmouth, Norfolk, and helped to evangelize East Anglia. When his monastery was destroyed in a raid by King Penda of Mercia he went to the Low Countries, founded a monastery at Fosses in Brabant, Belgium, and was the spiritual director of the nunnery at Nivelles. He was murdered by robbers in the forest of Soignies and venerated as a martyr.

Folcwin (St) B. Dec 14
d. 855. He became bishop of Thérouanne near Calais, France, in ?816. His shrine was established at the abbey of St Bertin at St Omer.

Forannan (St) B. R(OSB). Apr 30
d. 982. A bishop in Ireland, he emigrated and eventually became a monk at the abbey of Waulsort near Dinant, Belgium. In 962 he became abbot and successfully introduced the reform of Gorze into his own abbey.

Fort (St) M. B. May 16
C1st? He is allegedly the first bishop of Bordeaux, France, and a martyr.

Fortchern (St) B. R. Feb 17
C6th? Allegedly a convert of St Lornan, he succeeded him as bishop of Trim in Co. Meath, Ireland, but retired to be a hermit.

Fortis Gabrielli (Bl) R(OSB). May 13
d. 1040. From Gubbio in Umbria, Italy, he became a hermit in the mountains near Scheggia but later joined the new foundation at Fontavellana. His cultus was approved for Gubbio in 1756.

Fortunata (St) *see* **Carponius, Evaristus, Priscian and Fortunata**

Fortunata Viti *see* **Mary-Fortunata Viti**

Fortunatus (St) *see* **Alexander, Abundius and Comps**

Fortunatus (St) *see* **Arator of Alexandria and Comps**

Fortunatus (St) *see* **Faustinus, Lucius and Comps**

Fortunatus (St) *see* **Felix and Fortunatus**

Fortunatus (St) *see* **Felix, Fortunatus and Achilles**

Fortunatus (St) *see* **Felix, Luciolus and Comps**

Fortunatus (St) *see* **Felix of Thibuca**

Fortunatus (St) *see* **Hermagoras and Fortunatus**

Fortunatus (St) *see* **Honoratus, Fortunatus and Comps** and **Twelve Holy Brothers**

Fortunatus (St) *see* **Verulus, Secundinus and Comps**

Fortunatus (St) *see* **Vitalis, Revocatus and Fortunatus**

Fortunatus, Felician, Firmus and Candidus (SS) MM. Feb 2
? They are originally listed in the martyrology of Usuard but nothing is known about them.

Fortunatus, Felix and Comps (SS) MM. Feb 26
? Nothing is known about this group of twenty-nine martyrs.

Fortunatus, Gaius and Anthes (SS) MM. Aug 28
d. 303. They were martyred at Salerno, Italy, in the reign of Diocletian and have a popular local veneration there. Their acta are unreliable. Fortunatus may be the one of the same name associated with the 'Twelve Holy Brothers'.

Fortunatus and Lucian (SS) MM. Jun 13
? They were Roman African martyrs, but their acta have been lost.

Fortunatus and Marcian (SS) MM. Apr 17
? They are probably martyrs of Roman Africa, not (as asserted) of Antioch.

Fortunatus of Naples (Bl) B. Jun 14
d. *c*350. A bishop of Naples, Italy, he fought against Arianism and had his cultus confirmed in 1841.

Fortunatus the Philosopher (St) B. Jun 18
d. ?569. From Vercelli, Italy, he became the bishop of an unknown north Italian diocese but was driven into exile by the Lombard invasion. He settled at Chelles near Paris, France, and was much admired for his scholarship (for example by St Germanus of Paris). He has been confused with St Venantius Fortunatus.

Fortunatus of Rome (St) M. Oct 15
? He was martyred at Rome and buried on the Aurelian Way.

Fortunatus of Todi (St) B. Oct 14
d. 537. From Poitiers, he became bishop of Todi in Umbria, Italy, and is remembered for saving his city from being sacked by the army of Totilla the Goth.

Fortunatus of Torrita (St) P. Jun 1
d. *c*400. A parish priest of Torrito near Spoleto, Italy, he was remembered for earning his living by manual labour and for being extremely charitable to the poor.

Forty Martyrs of Sebaste *Mar 10*
d. 320. They were forty soldiers killed by order of the emperor Licinius at Sebaste in Armenia (now Sivas in Turkey). According to their story they were left naked for a night in winter on a frozen lake with a heated bath-house on its shore for any who apostatized. One did apostatize, but his place was taken by one of the guards who was converted by the heroism of the rest. At daybreak all were dead except the youngest, St Melito, who was carried by his mother following the cart full of corpses until he also died and she added his body to the rest. This martyrdom is mentioned by Sozomen and preached upon by SS Basil, Gregory of Nyssa, Gaudentius of Brescia and other patristic writers. The cultus is very popular in the East but was suppressed in the Roman rite in 1969.

Foster *see* **Vedast**

Four Crowned Martyrs (SS) M. Nov 8
There are two groups of martyrs with this title. One group of soldiers was allegedly martyred at Albano, Italy, about 305, namely Secundus, Severian, Carpophorus and Victorinus, and the other group somewhere in Lower Pannonia (around Belgrade in Serbia), namely Claudius, Nicostratus, Symphorian, Castorius and Simplicius. The latter group were stonemasons who refused a commission to carve a statue of the god Aesculapius and were martyred at the request of the retired emperor Diocletian. The relics of four only of these were taken to Rome, and they were later confused with the Albano group. Their acta are of great value but their cultus was confined to local or particular calendars in 1969.

Fourteen Holy Helpers *Aug 8*
There was a popular medieval devotion to these saints as especially helpful in time of need. They were St Giles and the martyrs SS Acacius of Ararat, Barbara, Blaise of Sebaste, Catherine of Alexandria, Christopher, Cyriac of Rome, Dionysius of Paris, Erasmus of Formiae, Eustace of Rome, George, Margaret, Pantaleon and Vitus. Their collective cultus was suppressed in 1969.

Foy *see* **Faith**

Fragan and Gwen (Blanche) (SS) Jul 5
C5th. A married couple, they were among the Britons who colonized Brittany, France, to get away from the disorder consequent upon the departure of the Roman army from Britain. Their offspring were SS Winwaloe, Jacut and Guithern, and they have churches dedicated to them in Brittany.

Franca of Fermo (St) R. Oct 1
C11th. She was a hermit at home at Fermo, Italy.

Franca Visalta (St) R(OCist). Apr 26
1170–1218. From Piacenza, Italy, when aged only seven she entered the Benedictine nunnery of St Sixtus there, was professed when aged fourteen and became the abbess in ?1198. Apparently she was too severe and was deposed, so she became a Cistercian nun in 1215. Then she was made abbess of the nunnery at Pittoli.

Frances d'Amboise (Bl) R(OC). Nov 4
1427–1485. A noblewoman of Brittany, France, she married its duke who was a depressive, jealous and dissolute character, and eventually reformed him by prayer and patience. She introduced the Carmelite nuns to Brittany, founded a nunnery at Nantes, became a nun there herself in 1460 when widowed and was made prioress in 1476.

Frances-of-the-Sacred-Heart-of-Jesus Aldea Araujo (Bl) *see* **Rita-Dolores Pujalte Sánchez**

Frances-of-Sales Aviat (St) R. F. Jan 10
1844–1914. Born near Châlons-sur-Marne, France, she left home in 1866, went to Troyes and teamed up with Fr Aloysius Brisson who had a mission to children working in factories. On the advice of the superior of the local Visitation convent they founded the 'Oblate Sisters of St Francis de Sales' in 1868, which spread through France despite opposition. But they were suppressed by an anti-clerical government in 1903 and she moved the mother house to Padua, Italy, where she died. She was canonized in 2001.

Frances Bellanger and Frances Bonneau (BB) *see* **William Repin and Comps**

Frances Bisoka (Bl) M. T(OP). Aug 16
d. 1627. A Japanese Dominican tertiary, she used to shelter missionaries in her house and was hence burned alive at Nagasaki with BB

Francis-of-St-Mary of Mancha and Comps. *See* **Japan (Martyrs of).**

Frances Bussa de' Leoni of Rome (St) T(OSB). Mar 9
1384–1440. A noblewoman of Rome, she was married for forty years from 1396 and reputedly never had an argument with her husband. She was a model wife and mother of six children, and obtained her husband's consent to live in continence and to practise contemplative prayer in 1414. She had many mystical experiences as well as many trials, such as the death of five of her children, her husband's banishment and the confiscation of their property. When she was widowed in 1436 she joined the house of regular Benedictine oblates that she had founded at Tor de' Specci ('Tower of Mirrors') in 1433. Her biography was written by her spiritual director and refers to her special devotion to, and awareness of, her guardian angel. She is a patron of motorists and of Benedictine oblates.

Frances-Xavier Cabrini (St) R. F. Dec 22
1850–1917. From near Lodi in Lombardy, Italy, the thirteenth child of her family, she became a teacher at a parish orphanage at Codogno in 1874 and founded the mother-house there of the 'Missionary Sisters of the 'Sacred Heart' three years later. This became a diocesan institute of Lodi in 1880 and she hoped to send her sisters to China, but the pope advised her to concentrate on the United States where the Italian immigrants were in danger of losing their faith. She went with the first group of sisters to New York in 1889 and continued taking new groups across regularly, year by year. She ended up founding sixty-seven religious institutes to be run by her congregation as schools, hospitals and orphanages in Europe and in both of the Americas. Eventually she became a citizen of the USA and died of malaria at one of her hospitals in Chicago. She was canonized in 1946.

Frances-Anne-of-the-Sorrowing-Virgin Cirrer Carbonell (Bl) R. Feb 27
1781–1855. Born at Sencelles on Majorca, Spain, of a peasant family, she had lost all her near relatives by the time she was forty. While running her farm she catechized children and practised penance and humility. Joining the Sisters of Charity in 1851, she carried on catechising and nursing in the parish and became the superior of her community. She died of a stroke immediately after Mass and was beatified in 1989.

Frances Lecroix (Bl) *see* **Valenciennes (Martyrs of)**

Frances Mézière (Bl) *see* **Laval (Martyrs of)**

Frances Michau, Frances Michineau and Frances Pagis (BB) *see* **William Repin and Comps**

Frances of Rome *see* **Frances Bussa de'Leoni**

Frances Suhard (Bl) *see* **William Repin and Comps**

Frances Tréhet (Bl) *see* **Laval (Martyrs of)**

Francis Alvarez (Bl) *see* **Ignatius de Azevedo and Comps**

Francis Aranha (Bl) *see* **Rudolph Acquaviva and Comps**

Francis Arias Martín (Bl) *see* **Hospitaller Martyrs of Spain**

Francis of Assisi (St) D. R(OFM). F. Oct 4
1181–1226. The son of a rich merchant of Assisi in Umbria, Italy, he was baptized as John but was nicknamed 'Frenchy', possibly because he could speak French. He joined his father's business and lived a carefree life until a spiritual conversion led him to a life of prayer and penance. His father disinherited him and he professed a state of absolute poverty for two years, restoring the chapels of St Damian and the 'Portiuncula' in his home town, before founding the Friars Minor in 1209. These were characterized by spiritual joy and complete poverty, individual and collective. He gathered five thousand disciples in ten years but the institutionalisation of such a charism proved very difficult, and these difficulties persisted long after his death. His rule received papal approval in 1215, however, and his friars established themselves throughout western Europe, especially in university towns. They were ideally suited to the new urban environment. In 1219, after the first solemn chapter of his order at Assisi, he went to Egypt to try and convert the Muslims but was rebuffed with courtesy. He received the stigmata on Mount Alvernia (the first recorded case) in 1224, and died as a deacon. 'Il Povarello' (the 'Poor Little Man') is the most popular saint of the second Christian millennium, although sentiment has rather obscured the starker aspects of his prophetic and apocalyptic witness.

St Francis of Assisi, Oct 4

Francis Balmain (Bl) *see* **September (Martyrs of)**

Francis Bell (Bl) M. R(OFM). Dec 11
1591–1643. A Worcestershire landowner, he was baptized as Arthur. Studying at Valladolid, he became a Franciscan, was ordained at Salamanca and was in turn chaplain to nuns in the Spanish Netherlands, superior of Douai friary, professor of Hebrew and first Provincial of the new Scottish province. Returning to England in 1634, he was seized by Parliamentary troops at Stevenage during the Civil War and was executed at Tyburn. He was beatified in 1987. *See* **England (Martyrs of)**.

Francis-Xavier-Mary Bianchi
(St) R. Jan 31
1743–1815. From Arpino in eastern Lazio, Italy, he became a Barnabite and was ordained priest Naples in 1767 in the face of his family's opposition. He was professor of theology at Naples University from 1778 and was also a noted spiritual director, but his main interest was in helping poor and derelict people, especially girls being forced into prostitution by poverty, and did so with such zeal and austerity that he ruined his health and lost the use of his legs from 1804. Nicknamed the 'Apostle of Naples', he died there and was canonized in 1951.

Francis Blanco (St) M. R(OFM). Feb 6
d. 1597. From Monterey in Galicia, Spain, he studied at Salamanca and became a Franciscan at Villapando. Initially he worked as a missionary in Mexico, then at Manila and finally in Japan from 1594. He was crucified at Nagasaki and was canonized in 1862 with SS Paul Miki and Comps. *See* **Japan (Martyrs of)**.

Francis de Borja (St) R(SJ). Oct 10
1510–1572. A nobleman from Gandía near Valencia, Spain, he was related to the notorious Italian Borgia family. Educated at the court of the emperor Charles V, he married in 1529 and was occupied as a courtier and in administering his estate at Gandía until he was widowed in 1546. The sight of his wife's body caused a spiritual conversion and he then became a Jesuit. He was elected superior-general of the Society in 1665 and made his chief work its development and strengthening, at which he was so successful that he became one of the most important figures of the Counter-Reformation. He founded new missions in the Americas, established the Jesuits in Poland and helped in the foundation of the German College in Rome. He died at Rome and was canonized in 1671, but his cultus was confined to particular calendars in 1969.

Francis Piani of Calderola
(Bl) R(OFM). Sep 13
d. 1407. From Calderola near Camerino, Italy, as a Franciscan he was a successful preacher and had the charism of reconciling enemies. He died at Colfano and had his cultus confirmed for Camerino in 1843.

Francis-Xavier Can (St) M. L. Nov 20
803–1837. From Sou Mieng in north-west Vietnam, he was a catechist helping the missionary priests of the Paris Society and was strangled in prison. *See* **Vietnam (Martyrs of)**.

Francis-Ferdinand de Capillas
(St) M. R(OP). Jan 15
1607–1648. From Palencia, Spain, he became a Dominican at Valladolid and was sent to Manila, Taiwan and finally Fujian province in China. He was successful as a missionary, but when the Manchus invaded he was tortured and beheaded as a spy at Fuan. He was canonized in 2000 as one of the martyrs of China, and is the protomartyr. *See* **China (Martyrs of)**.

Francis Caracciolo (St) R. F. Jun 4
1563–1608. From a noble Neapolitan family, he was born in the Abruzzi, Italy, and seems to have suffered from a severe skin disease when young. This healed after he decided to become a priest and, after his ordination in 1588, he founded the congregation of the 'Minor Clerks Regular' at Naples with John Adorno. Perpetual adoration of the Blessed Sacrament was one of its main duties. He was the first superior-general of the new order, founded many houses and died at Agnone while establishing a house there. He was canonized in 1807, but his cultus was confined to local or particular calendars in 1969.

Francis Carceller Galindo (Bl) *see* **Dionysius Pamplona Polo and Comps**

Francis the Carpenter (St) M. L. Feb 6
1597. A Japanese baptized by the Franciscans in Nagasaki, he came to watch the martyrdom of SS Paul Miki and Comps. He was seized and killed with them. *See* **Japan (Martyrs of)**.

Francis Castan Messeguer (Bl) *see* **Philip-of-Jesus Munárriz Azcona and Comps**

Francis-Louis Chartier (Bl) *see* **William Repin and Comps**

Francis (Do van) Chieu
(St) M. Jun 25
1796–1838. A Chinese catechist in Vietnam, he was arrested and beheaded with St Dominic Henares. *See* **Vietnam (Martyrs of)**.

Francis Choi (St) *see* **Korea (Martyrs of)**

Francis Coll (Bl) R(OP). F. Apr 2
1812–1875. From Vich in Catalonia, Spain, he joined the Dominicans just in time for their 38-year suppression in Spain. After 10 years as an exclaustrated priest-religious he obtained Petrine faculties as a roving missionary and spent 23 year preaching in Catalonia, mostly on the mysteries of the Rosary. He founded the 'Dominican Sisters of the Annunciation' in 1856 to teach in rural areas. Dying after some years of senile decay, he was beatified in 1979.

Francis-Mary Croese of Camporosso
(St) R(OFM Cap). Sep 20
1804–1866. From a peasant family near Ventimiglia, Italy, he became a Capuchin lay brother at the friary at Genoa in 1821 and was there for forty years as the almsgatherer. He died of cholera while nursing victims of an epidemic and was canonized in 1962.

Francis Dardin (Bl) *see* **September (Martyrs of)**

Francis Diaz del Rincón
(St) M. R(OP) Oct 28
1713–1748. From Seville, Spain, he became a Dominican at Ecija and was sent to China in 1736. He worked in the Fujian mission until he was captured and executed in prison. *See* **Francis Serrano Frias and Comps**.

Francis Dickenson (Bl) M. Apr 30
d. 1590. A Yorkshireman and a convert, he studied for the priesthood at Rheims and was ordained in 1589. He was quickly captured on his return to England and hanged, drawn and quartered at Rochester, Kent. He was beatified in 1929. *See* **England (Martyrs of)**.

Francis Duchesne (Bl) *see* **Laval (Martyrs of)**

Francis Dumasrambaud de Calandelle (Bl) *see* **September (Martyrs of)**

Francis Faà di Bruno (Bl) P. F. Mar 27
1825–1888. Born at Alessandria in Piedmont, Italy, he was in the officer corps of the army of the Kingdom of Sardinia for seven years before obtaining a doctorate in mathematics at Paris and becoming a lecturer at Turin University in 1856. He was a man of many talents, being an inventor, sacred musician and writer as well as a mathematician. Being inspired by St John Bosco, he was ordained in Rome in 1876 and founded the 'Little Sisters of Our Lady of Suffrage' in 1881 together with a church of the same name at Turin, so that the Office of the Dead could be said continually for the souls in Purgatory. He was beatified in 1988.

Francis-Anthony Fasani
(St) R(OFM Conv). Nov 27
1681–1742. From Lucera in Apulia, Italy, he became a Franciscan Conventual, went on to be provincial superior and introduced necessary reforms. Based mainly at Lucera, he became known for the grace of levitation in prayer. He died there and was canonized in 1986.

Francis of Fermo (Bl) *see* **Monaldus of Ancona and Comps**

Francis Fogolla (St) *see* **Gregory Grassi and Comps**

Francis François (Bl) *see* **John-Baptist Souzy and Comps**

Francis-Isidore Gagelin (St) M. P. Oct 17
1799–1833. From near Besançon, France, he joined the Paris Foreign Mission Society and was sent to Vietnam in 1822, being ordained priest on his arrival. He worked there until a persecution broke out, upon which he gave himself up to the governor of Bong Son and was strangled at Hue. *See* **Vietnam (Martyrs of)**.

Francis Galvez and Comps
(Bl) M. R(OFM). Dec 4
1567–1623. From Utiel near Valencia, Spain, he became a Franciscan at Valencia in 1591, went to Manila in 1609 and was in Japan for two years from 1612 until persecution broke out. He returned secretly in 1618 and was eventually burned alive at what is now Tokyo with BB Jerome de Angelis and Simon Yempo. He was beatified in 1867. About fifty were executed with them, but documentation is lacking in their cases. *See* **Japan (Martyrs of)**.

Francis Gárate (Bl) R(SJ). Sep 9
1857–1929. Born in Guipozcoa, Spain, he joined the Jesuits as a lay brother in 1874 and ended up as the gatekeeper of the University College of Deusto at Bilbao. His life and the way he performed his duties there for 41 years led him to be beatified in 1985.

Francis de Geronimo (St) R(SJ). May 11
1642–1716. From near Taranto in Apulia, Italy, he was educated by the Jesuits, ordained priest in 1666 and became a Jesuit in 1670. The rest of his life was spent as a preacher in south Italy, especially in Naples where he gathered huge congregations and converted many obdurate sinners. He also had great care for poor people (which the city did not lack). He was canonized in 1839.

Francis Gil de Frederich
(St) M. R(OP). Jan 22
1702–1745. From Tortosa, Spain, he became a Dominican at Barcelona and was sent firstly to the Philippines and then to north Vietnam in 1732. There he was captured, imprisoned for several years and beheaded at Checo. *See* **Vietnam (Martyrs of)**.

Francis Hébert (Bl) *see* **September (Martyrs of)**

Francis Hunot (Bl) *see* **John-Baptist Souzy and Comps**

Francis Ingleby (Bl) M. P. Jun 3
d. 1586. Born at Ripley, Yorks, he studied at Oxford and the Inner Temple, then at Douai, and was ordained at Laon. After two years as a priest at York the deference he was being shown in social intercourse with Catholics gave him away and he was executed at York. He was beatified in 1987. *See* **England (Martyrs of)**.

Francis Jaccard (St) M. Sep 21
1799–1838. From Savoy, he became a priest of the Society of Foreign Missions at Paris and was sent to south Vietnam in 1826. He was martyred by being garotted. *See* **Vietnam (Martyrs of)**.

Francis Kuhyoye and Francis Kurobyoye (BB) *see* **Francis-of-St-Mary of Mancha and Comps**

Francis Lefranc, Francis le Livec de Tresurin and Francis Londiveau (BB) *see* **September (Martyrs of)**

Francis Magellanes (Bl) *see* **Ignatius de Azevedo and Comps**

Francis-of-St-Mary of Mancha and Comps (BB) MM. Aug 16
d. 1627. He was burned alive at Nagasaki with Bartholomew Laurel (a Mexican Franciscan), Caspar Vas (a Japanese doctor who was a Franciscan tertiary, in whose house Bl Francis was captured), and Anthony-of-St-Francis of Nagasaki, a Japanese catechist. Beheaded with them were Mary Vas (Caspar's wife) and six Franciscan tertiaries: Louis Matsuo, a neighbour of the Vas couple; Francis Cuhyoye, baptized in prison; Thomas Jinyemono, formerly a domestic worker for the Jesuits; Luke Sukuyemon, a builder of hiding places; Michael Kizayemon, another carpenter; and Martin Gomez, who had concealed fugitive Franciscans. On the same day or on the previous one, four Dominican tertiaries were burned: Francis Kurobyoye, a catechist; Gaius Jinyemon, formerly a Buddhist monk from Korea; Mary-Magdalen Kiyota, from a daimyo's family, and Frances Bisoka. They were beatified in 1867. *See* **Japan (Martyrs of)**.

Francis and Jacinta Marto
(BB) LL.
1908–1919 and 1910–1920 resp. They were children of a peasant family of Aljustrel near Fátima, Portugal, and were keeping a flock of sheep with their cousin, Lucia de Jesus, on May 13, 1917 when they saw an apparition of the Blessed Virgin Mary. This apparition was repeated once a month for five months, and led to the founding of the famous Marian shrine of Fátima. Bl Francis died at home eighteen

BB Francis and Jacinta of Fatima

months later, and Bl Jacinta died at Lisbon two years and four months later. They were beatified in 2000.

Francis Massabki (Bl) *see* **Emmanuel Ruiz and Comps**

Francis-Xavier (Ha Trong) Mau (St) M. T(OP). Dec 19
d. 1839. A north Vietnamese catechist and a Dominican tertiary, he was executed at Ninh-Tai in north Vietnam with SS Augustine (Nguyen van) Moi, Dominic (Bui van) Uy, Stephen (Nguyen van) Vinh and Thomas (Nguyen van) De. *See* **Vietnam (Martyrs of)**.

Francis Mayaudon (Bl) *see* **John-Baptist Souzy and Comps**

Francis Méallet de Fargues (Bl) *see* **September (Martyrs of)**

Francis Migoret Lambeardière (Bl) *see* **Laval (Martyrs of)**

Francis Monnier (Bl) *see* **September (Martyrs of)**

Francis de Montmorency-Laval (Bl) B. May 6
1623–1708. A nobleman born near Evreux, France, he was ordained when aged 24, renounced his patrimony and became Vicar-Apostolic of New France (Canada and Louisiana) in 1658. He founded the diocese and seminary of Quebec in 1674 and was the first bishop until his retirement in 1684. He was beatified in 1980.

Francis de Morales (Bl) M. R(OP). Sep 10
d. 1622. From Madrid, he became a Dominican and worked on the Satsuma mission in Japan for twenty years. In 1608 he went to Fushimi and thence to Nagasaki in 1614, where he was burned with BB Charles Spinola and Comps in the 'Great Martyrdom'. *See* **Japan (Martyrs of)**.

Francis-of-St-Bonaventure of Musashino (Bl) M. R(OFM). Sep 12
d. 1622. A Japanese catechist from Musashino near Tokyo, he worked with Bl Apollinaris Franco, became a Franciscan in prison and was burned with him at Omura. *See* **Thomas-of-the-Holy-Spirit Zumarraga and Comps** and **Japan (Martyrs of)**.

Francis of Nagasaki (St) M. T(OFM). Feb 6
d. 1597. A Japanese doctor of medicine from Miyako, he was a Franciscan tertiary and helped the missionaries as a catechist. Crucified at Nagasaki with SS Paul Miki and Comps, he was canonized with them in 1862. *See* **Japan (Martyrs of)**.

Francis Néron *see* **Peter-Francis Néron**

Francis Nihachi (Bl) M. L. Sep 8
d. 1628. A Japanese five-year-old, he was beheaded at Nagasaki with his father, Louis, and his brother, Dominic. *See* **Dominic Castellet and Comps** and **Japan (Martyrs of)**.

Francis-of-Jesus Ortega (Bl) M. R(OSA). Sep 3
d. 1632. From Villamediana near Palencia, Spain, he became an Augustinian friar at Valladolid in 1614, went to Mexico in 1622 and thence to Japan with Bl Vincent Carvalho by way of Manila, Philippines. He was burned at Nagasaki. *See* **Anthony Ishida and Comps** and **Japan (Martyrs of)**.

Francis d'Oudinote la Boissière (Bl) *see* **John-Baptist Souzy and Comps**

Francis Pacheco and Comps (SS) MM. RR(SJ). Jun 20
1566–1626. A Portuguese, he became a Jesuit at Lisbon and was sent to Macao in 1592. He worked in Japan and served as rector of the college at Macao until he finally returned to Japan in 1617 to work in secret as provincial and as administrator of the diocese of Arima. He

was burned alive at Nagasaki with Balthasar de Torres (Spanish Jesuit); John-Baptist Zola (Italian Jesuit); Caspar Sadamatsu (Japanese Jesuit lay brother); Vincent Caum (Korean); Peter Rinsei, Michael Tozo, Paul Shinsuke and John Kisaku (Japanese). The last five became Jesuits in prison before their martyrdom. They were beatified in 1867. *See* **Japan (Martyrs of)**.

Francis Page (Bl) M. R(SJ). Apr 20
d. 1602. Born at Antwerp, his family was from Harrow in Middlesex, England. After his conversion he studied at Douai, was ordained in 1600, quickly captured on his return to England and became a Jesuit in prison before his execution at Tyburn, London. He was beatified in 1929. *See* **England (Martyrs of)**.

Francis-of-Jesus-Mary-and-Joseph Palau y Quer
(Bl) R(OC). F. Mar 20
1811–1872. Born at Aytona near Lérida, Spain, he overcame family opposition to enter the Barcelona Carmel in 1832. But this was burned down in an anti-clerical riot before he was ordained in 1836, so he spent the next four years as an itinerant preacher in Spain. When this became too dangerous he went into exile in France, but he returned to Barcelona in 1851 to open a school of adult catechesis. This in turn was suppressed in 1854 and he returned to preaching throughout Catalonia and the Balearics. At Ciudadela in Majorca he founded the 'Tertiary Sisters of Carmel', which later split to become the 'Carmelite Missionaries' and the 'Teresan Carmelite Missionaries', also the 'Carmelite Tertiary Brothers of Charity' (which became extinct in the Civil War). He died at Tarragona and was beatified in 1988.

Francis of Paola (St) R. F. Apr 2
1416–1507. From a poor family of Paola in Calabria, Italy, when aged thirteen he started living as a hermit on the coast nearby. He established a monastery for the disciples who had gathered around him in 1454, and thus founded the new order of Minim Friars. The name means 'the least', and they obliged themselves to a perpetual Lent by a fourth religious vow. The pope ordered him to go to Plessis-les-Tours in France to assist King Louis XI on his deathbed in 1482 and he was prevented from returning by the king's successors, who valued his holiness. He died at Plessis, was canonized in 1519 and was declared patron of seafarers in 1943.

Francis-of-St-Michael of Parilla (St) M. R(OFM). Feb 6
d. 1597. From near Valladolid, Spain, he became a Franciscan lay brother and went with St Peter-Baptist of San Esteban from Manila, Philippines, to Japan in 1593. They were captured at Osaka three years later, crucified at Nagasaki and canonized in 1862. *See* **SS Paul Miki and Comps** and **Japan (Martyrs of)**.

Francis Patrizi (Bl) R(OSM). May 12
d. 1328. From Siena, Italy, he was inspired by a sermon of a Servite friar, Bl Ambrose Sansedoni, and was received into that order by St Philip Benizi after his mother died. He had the charism of reconciling enemies. Dying in Siena, he had his cultus approved for there in 1743.

Francis Peltier (Bl) *see* **William Repin and Comps**

Francis Perez Godoy (Bl) *see* **Ignatius de Azevedo and Comps**

Francis of Pesaro (St) T(OFM). Aug 13
d. 1350. He was a Franciscan tertiary at Pesaro, Italy, and lived an austere life as a hermit there. His cultus was confirmed for Pesaro in 1859.

Francis Pinazo d'Arpuentes (Bl) *see* **Emmanuel Ruiz and Comps**

Francis-Xavier Ponsa Casallach (Bl) *see* **Hospitaller Martyrs of Spain**

Francis de Posadas (Bl) R(OP). Sep 20
1644–1713. From Aracoeli near Cordoba, Spain, he became a Dominican in his native town and spent his life giving missions throughout southern Spain before dying at Aracoeli. He was beatified in 1818.

Francis Regis Clet (St) M. R. Feb 18
1748–1820. From Grenoble, France, he joined the 'Congregation of the Mission' (the Lazarists) and went on to be the director of the seminary at the mother house in Paris. After the French Revolution broke out he was sent to China in 1791 and worked there under great difficulty for thirty years in Hubei before being seized, tortured and garroted at Hangzhou. *See* **China (Martyrs of)**.

Francis-Joseph de la Rochefoucault Maumont (Bl) *see* **September (Martyrs of)**

Francis Rod (St) *see* **Gorinchem (Martyrs of)**

Francis Ronci (Bl) R(OSB). Jun 4
1223–1294. From Abriola in Basilicata, Italy, he was one of the first disciples of Peter Celestine (later Pope St Celestine V) at the

latter's hermitage at Morone near Sulmona. He became the first general of the new Celestine congregation (now extinct) in 1285, and seems to have been made a cardinal a month before he died.

Francis-Mary Roura Farró (Bl) *see* **Philip-of-Jesus Munárriz Azcona and Comps**

Francis de Sales (St) B. Dr. F. Jan 24
1567–1622. A nobleman from near Annecy in Savoy (now in France), he was a law student at Paris and Padua before becoming a priest in 1593. Over the next four years he set about reconciling the Calvinist inhabitants of the Chablis to the Church, with enormous success (he allegedly made over eight thousand converts), and was made coadjutor bishop of Geneva in 1599. He was never able to visit the Calvinist stronghold of Geneva city. In 1602 he became bishop, and excelled as a pastor and a spiritual writer. He took care over the standard of his clergy and their preaching, founded a seminary at Annecy and became beloved by his people. His most famous writing is the *Introduction to the Devout Life*. He became acquainted with St Jane de Chantal in 1604 and helped her to found the Visitation order of nuns. He died at Lyons, was canonized in 1665, declared a doctor of the Church in 1877 and patron of journalists in 1923.

Francis-Xavier Seelos (Bl) R(CSSR) Oct 5
1819–1867. From Füssen in Bavaria, Germany, he early received a vocation to provide spiritual care for German-speaking migrants to the USA and joined the Redemptorists at New York in 1843. After being ordained in Baltimore in 1844 he was based at Pittsburgh and the cities in Maryland before serving as an itinerant preacher in the eastern USA. He died of yellow fever at New Orleans and was beatified in 2000.

Francis Serrano Frias and Comps (SS) MM. RR(OP). Oct 28
1691–1748. From Granada, Spain, he became a Dominican there and was sent to Fujian in China in 1725. In 1746 he was imprisoned, and strangled in prison two years later at Fuzhou. St Francis was made titular bishop of Tipasa while in custody. With him were martyred SS Joachim Royo Pérez, John Alcober Figura and Francis Diaz del Rincón. *See* **China (Martyrs of)**.

Francis Shoyemon (St) R(OP). Sep 28(d. n. Aug 14)
d. 1633. A Japanese catechist, priest and Dominican novice, he was martyred at Nagasaki with St Dominic Ibáñez de Erquicia and was canonized in 1987. *See* **Japan (Martyrs of)**.

Francis Solano (St) R(OFM). Jul 14
1549–1610. From Montilla in Andalucia, Spain, he became a Franciscan Observant there in 1569 and went to South America after twenty years of apostolic activity in Spain. He worked among the native Americans on the Plata estuary as well as with the colonists in Peru, at Trujillo and at Lima. He died at Lima and was canonized in 1726.

Francis Spinelli (Bl) P. F. Feb 6
1853–1913. From Milan, Italy, he became a diocesan priest at Bergamo in 1875 and founded the 'Sisters, Adorers of the Blessed Sacrament' with Catherine Comensoli in 1882. They suffered serious difficulties and accusations, so moved to Rivolta in the diocese of Cremona in 1889. The bishop there learned that the charges against them were false and approved the foundation. Bl Francis' motto was 'Love the Eucharist, take care of the poor, and forgive everything.' He was beatified in 1992.

Francis Takea (Bl) M. L. Sep 11
d. 1622. A Japanese twelve-year-old, the son of Bl Thomas Takea, he was beheaded at Nagasaki with Bl Caspar Koteda. *See* **Japan (Martyrs of)**.

Francis Taylor (Bl) M. L. Jun 20
d. 1621. A Dublin alderman, he died in prison and was beatified in 1992. *See* **Ireland (Martyrs of)**.

Francis Titelmans (Bl) R(OFM Cap). Oct 4
d. 1537. He was a university student at Louvain, Belgium, before he joined the Capuchins, and became a nurse at St James's Hospital at Rome.

Francis (Phan van) Trung (St) M. Oct 6
1825–1858. From Phan Xa in Vietnam, he became the equivalent of a corporal in the army and was beheaded at An Hoa. *See* **Vietnam (Martyrs of)**.

Francis Vareilhe-Duteil (Bl) *see* **September (Martyrs of)**

Francis Venimbene of Fabriano (Bl) R(OFM). Apr 22
1251–1322. From Fabriano, Italy, the son of a doctor of medicine, he became a Franciscan in 1267 and a disciple of St Bonaventure. He founded the first Franciscan library near his native city, and had his cultus confirmed for there in 1775.

Francis Xavier (St) R(SJ). Dec 3
1506–1552. Born at the family castle at Xavier in the kingdom of Navarre (now in Spain), as his father was a courtier he was sent to study at Paris University. There he became a companion of St Ignatius Loyola and was with him in taking vows as the first Jesuits at Montmartre in 1534. He was sent as a missionary to Goa, India, in 1541, and worked in south India and Ceylon (Sri Lanka) until 1545. Then he was in Malaya, the East Indies and south Vietnam until 1548, whereupon he went to Japan. There he made *c*2000 converts (the start of Christianity in Japan) in Kyushu and especially on Hirado-jima. The number of Japanese Christians reached six figures in a generation. In 1552 he set out on a journey to China but never got there, dying on the island of Shangchuan near Hong Kong. He is arguably the most successful missionary that the Church of the second millennium has had. He was canonized in 1602 and is joint patron of foreign missions with St Teresa of Lisieux.

Francis Yakichi (Bl) *see* **Louis Yakichi and Family**

Francis Zhang (Rong) (St) *see* **Gregory Grassi and Comps**

Franco (Francus) of Assergi
(St) R(OSB). Jun 5
d. ?1275. From near Assergi in the Abruzzi, Italy, he was a Benedictine at Colimento for twenty years before becoming a hermit near Assergi for the last fifteen years of his life.

Franco Lippi (Bl) R(OC). Dec 11
d. 1291. From near Siena, Italy, when young he became the leader of a group of troublemakers but had to flee retribution and then joined a gang of robbers in the mountains. He was a brigand until the age of fifty but then he was blinded in a fight, repented, went on a penitential pilgrimage to Compostela and received papal absolution as well as getting his sight back. Then he became a Carmelite lay brother at Siena. He was already aged over sixty-five but gained a reputation for holiness before he died.

Francoveus (Franchy) (St) R. May 16
C7th. From Amagne near Rheims, France, he became a monk at Saint-Martin-de-la-Bretonnière but was the target of spite from his fellow monks. The monastery was destroyed and he became a hermit near Nevers, but went back to his home village to die.

Francula (St) *see* **Amata of Joinville**

Fraternus of Auxerre (St) M? B. Sep 29
d. *c*450. A bishop of Auxerre, France, by tradition he was martyred by invading barbarians on the day of his consecration.

Fredegand (Fregaut) (St) R. Jul 17
d. *c*740. Possibly an Irish companion of St Foillan and a fellow missionary with St Willibrord, he was the first abbot of Kerkelodor near Antwerp, Belgium.

Frederick Albert (Bl) P. F. Sep 30
1820–1876. Born at Turin, Italy, he became priest of the parish of St Charles there and proved a model pastor. He founded the 'Sisters of St Vincent de Paul of the Immaculate Conception' in order to help the children left roaming the streets by working parents or through being abandoned. He refused to become a bishop out of humility. He was beatified in 1984.

Bl Frederick Janssoone, Aug 4

Frederick Janssoone (Bl) R(OFM). Aug 4
1838–1916. Born near Dunkirk, France, he joined the Franciscans at Amiens in 1864. Ordained in 1870, he immediately had to serve as chaplain in the Franco-Prussian War and then was vicar-superior in the Holy Land from

1875 to 1888. Then he went to Canada for 28 years, where he was on mission in all parts of the country and succeeded to such an extent that he has been called one of its apostles. He died at Montreal and was beatified in 1988.

Frederick of Liege (St) B. May 27
d. 1121. He became bishop of Liege, Belgium, in 1119 in place of a deposed simoniac bishop. He was a success, but was persecuted by partisans of his rival and was allegedly poisoned by them.

Frederick of Regensburg
(Bl) R(OSA). Nov 29
d. 1329. From a poor family of Regensburg in Bavaria, Germany, he became a lay brother at the Augustinian friary there and was the carpenter and chopper of firewood. His cultus was approved for Regensburg in 1909.

Frederick Rubio Alvarez (Bl) *see* **Hospitaller Martyrs of Spain**

Frederick (Fridrich) of Utrecht
(St) M. B. Jul 18
d. 838. Grandson of a king of the Frisians, he became bishop of Utrecht, Netherlands, in 820. He was especially keen to prohibit those marriages between near relatives which were forbidden by the Church, and was murdered as a result in a church at Maastricht.

Frediano *see* **Frigidian**

Fremund (St) M? R. May 11
d. 866. He was venerated at Dunstable Priory near Luton, England, and was possibly a Saxon hermit who was killed during a Danish incursion.

French Revolution (Martyrs of)
1792–4. The 'Ancien Régime' of the French monarchy was overthrown in May 1789. The Catholic Church was established by law before then in France, but had had its life perverted by the corruptions inherent in the determination to maintain a feudally structured society in the face of accelerating social change. Especially, the higher clergy and monastic religious enjoyed excessive income as being of noble status while the ordinary parish clergy were often poorly supported in all ways, material and spiritual. The initial reaction of the revolutionaries was to reform the Church, but this quickly involved demands that church people subscribe by oath to the new arrangements. Resistance to this and other measures led to a massacre by the mob in Paris in September 1792, and several other massacres during the 'Terror' in 1794 when the aim had changed to the dechristianisation of the country. *See* lists of national martyrs in the appendix.

Friard and Secundel (SS) R. Aug 1
d. ?577. They were hermits on an island in the Loire near Nantes, France, who evangelized the surrounding area.

Fricor (St) *see* **Caidoc and Fricor**

Frideswide (St) R. Oct 19
d. ?735. According to her C12th biography she was the daughter of a Saxon ruler in the middle Thames valley, England, who founded a nunnery on the site of what is now Christ Church in Oxford. Before the Reformation this was an Augustinian priory named after her, and the church (the present Anglican cathedral) contains fragments of her shrine. She has a holy well at Binsey, and is the patron of the city and university of Oxford.

Fridigand *see* **Fredegand**

Fridolin (St) R. Mar 6
C6th or C7th. An Irish missionary monk, he founded an abbey at Säckingen, Germany, on the right bank of the Rhine east of Basel, and is venerated as the apostle of the Upper Rhine region.

Frigidian (Frediano, Frigidanus) of Lucca (St) B. Mar 18
d. ?588. According to his questionable C11th biography, he was an Irishman who went on pilgrimage to Rome, became a hermit on Monte Pisano and was then made bishop of Lucca, Italy. He allegedly formed the city's clergy into a community of canons regular and rebuilt the cathedral after it had been burnt by the Lombards. His veneration is very popular in Lucca.

Frithbert (Fridebert) of Hexham (St) B. Dec 23
d. 766. He succeeded St Acca as bishop of Hexham in Northumbria, England, in 732.

Frithestan (St) B. R(OSB). Sep 10
d. ?933. A disciple of St Grimbald at Winchester, he was consecrated bishop of that city in 909 by St Plegmund, archbishop of Canterbury.

Frodobert (St) R. Jan 8
595–673. From Troyes, France, he was a monk at Luxeuil before becoming abbot-founder of Moutier-la-Celle near his native city.

Frodulf (Frou) (St) Apr 21
d. *c*750. A disciple of St Medericus, he became a monk at Autun, France, but had to flee an incursion by the Arabs and settled as a hermit at Barjon to the north of Dijon.

Froilán (St) B. R(OSB). Oct 3
d. 1006. From Lugo in Galicia, Spain, when aged eighteen he teamed up with St Attilanus in restoring monastic life at Moreruela near León. He founded other monasteries in the region, at a time when most of Spain was still Muslim, and went on to become bishop of León.

Fromund (St) B. Oct 24
d. *p*690. He was abbot of a monastery at Coutances, France, before becoming bishop there.

Froninus of Besançon (St) B. May 10
C4th. A bishop of Besançon, France, he was buried in the basilica of St Stephen which he had built.

Fronto (St) *see* **Zaragoza (Eighteen Martyrs of)**

Fronto and George (SS) BB? Oct 25
? They appear to have been early missionaries at Périgneux, France, but their legend is unreliable.

Fronto of Nitria (St) R. Apr 14
? He is listed as a monk of Nitria in Egypt, but his period is uncertain.

Frowin II of Engelberg
(Bl) R(OSB). Mar 7
d. 1178. A Benedictine monk of Sankt-Blasien in the Black Forest, Germany, he became abbot of Engelberg, Switzerland, in 1143. He founded a monastic school there, built up the famous library and was known as a chronicler and as a spiritual author.

Frowin of Salom (Bl) R(OCist). Feb 17
d. 1165. A Cistercian monk at Bellevaux in Savoy, he was the abbot-founder of Salom near Constance, Germany, and was a companion of St Bernard when the latter was preaching the disastrous Second Crusade in Germany.

Fructulus (St) *see* **Lucius, Sylvanus and Comps**

Fructuosa (St) *see* **Restitutus, Donatus and Comps**

Fructuosus of Braga (St) B. R. Apr 16
d. 665. He was of the reigning Visigothic nobility in Spain but went off to be a hermit in the mountains near Astorga. There he founded the Complutum monastery, for which he wrote a rule, and was abbot until going back to being a hermit. He also founded nine other monasteries for his disciples. Against his will he was made archbishop of Braga, Portugal, in 656.

Fructuosus of Tarragona
and Comps (SS) MM. Jan 21
d. 259. The bishop of Tarragona, Spain, and two deacons, Augurius and Eulogius, they were burned at the stake in the reign of Valerian. Their acta seem to be genuine.

Fructus (Frutos), Valentine and
Engratia (SS) MM. RR. Oct 25
d. ?715. Siblings, they were living as religious at Sepúlveda near Segovia, Spain, when the Arabs invaded. Valentine and Engratia were killed, but Fructus escaped and died as a hermit. They are the patrons of Segovia.

Frugentius of Fleury (St) M. R. Sep 3
d. 675. He was traditionally a companion of St Aigulf of Lérins, France, and was killed with him.

Frumentius and Aedisius (SS) BP. Oct 27
End C4th. They were probably brothers and the former, at least, was from Tyre, Lebanon. They were wrecked on the Eritrean coast while on a voyage on the Red Sea and were taken to Axum inland (now Tigre, Ethiopia), which was the capital of a powerful kingdom. They became courtiers of influence, and St Frumentius applied to St Athanasius, patriarch of Alexandria, Egypt, for a bishop for the country. He was consecrated himself, while St Aedisius was ordained priest. They firmly established the Church in Axum, and the present Ethiopian Orthodox Church is the direct descendent. Thus they are venerated as the apostles of Ethiopia.

Frumentius and Frumentius (SS) *see* **Victorian, Frumentius and Comps**

Fugatius and Damian (SS) PP. May 26
?C2nd. According to their fictional story, they were missionaries sent to Britain by Pope St Eleutherius. Their names are also given as Phaganus and Diruvianus, Fagan and Deruvian, Ffager and Dyfan. The latter has been confused with a possibly genuine St **Dyfan** of the Cardiff area (q.v.).

Fulbert (St) B. Apr 10
*c*960–1028. From Italy, he studied in France at the abbey of Rheims under Gerbert (the future

Pope Sylvester II), and was the headmaster of the cathedral school of Chartres (one of the few centres of learning in Western Europe at the time) before becoming the city's bishop in 1007. He was a great scholar as well as an outstanding bishop and monastic reformer, being especially favourable to the Cluniacs.

Fulcran (St) B. Feb 13
d. 1006. He became bishop of Lodève near Montpellier, France, in 949 and was known for his public firmness. A casual remark of his that a bishop who had converted to Judaism deserved to be burned resulted in just that, so he undertook serious penances in expiation.

Fulgentius of Affligem
(Bl) R(OSB). Dec 10
d. 1122. A Walloon, he became a monk at the Benedictine abbey of St Airy at Verdun, France, but his community was scattered in the disorder consequent on the investiture controversy and he eventually became abbot of Affligem, Belgium.

Fulgentius-of-the-Heart-of-Mary Calvo Sánchez (Bl) *see* **Nicephorus Díez Tejerina and Comps**

Fulgentius of Ecija (St) B. Jan 16
d. ?633. Brother of SS Isidore, Leander of Seville and Florentina, he became bishop of Ecija in Andalucia, Spain. He has been confused with St Fulgentius of Ruspe.

Fulgentius of Ruspe (St) B. Jan 1
462–527 or 468–533. A Roman African nobleman of Carthage, he became abbot of the monastery of Byzacene but fled the Vandal invasion and went to Rome. On his return he became bishop of Ruspe in 502 or 507, and was exiled twice again by the Arian Vandals to Sardinia. There he wrote much, being one of the most important theologians in the Western church in the C6th and a disciple of St Augustine and also writing on the history of the Vandal persecutions. He died at Ruspe.

Fulk of Castrofuli (St) L. May 22
d. *p*600. According to his dubious legend he was an English pilgrim who died as a result of nursing sufferers of an epidemic at Castrofuli near Arpino in western Lazio, Italy. He is patron of Castrofuli and his cultus was confirmed in 1572.

Fulk of Fontenelle (St) R(OSB). Oct 10
d. 845. He was abbot of Fontenelle in Normandy, France.

Fulk (Foulques, Fulco) of Neuilly (Bl) P. Mar 2
d. 1201. He became parish priest of Neuilly-sur-Marne near Paris, France, in 1191 and was famous for his penitential sermons. Pope Innocent III commissioned him to help preach the Fourth Crusade, but he died and was buried at Neuilly-sur-Marne before it set out on its disastrous and disgraceful expedition to Constantinople. His cultus has not been confirmed.

Fulk Scotti (St) B. R(CR). Oct 26
1164–1229. Born at Piacenza, Italy, of Scottish parents, he became an Augustinian canon there and was made bishop in 1210. He was transferred to Pavia in 1216.

Fulrad (St) R. Jul 16
d. 784. A rich nobleman from Alsace, he joined the great abbey of St Denis near Paris, France, and became its abbot in 750. As such he was a leading clerical courtier of the Carolingian court, serving as grand almoner under Charlemagne.

Fursey (St) R. Jan 16
d. ?648. An Irish monk, he founded a monastery on an island in Lough Corrib called Rathnat before emigrating to England and founding another in the abandoned Roman fort at Burgh Castle near Great Yarmouth, Norfolk. Then he went to France and founded a third at Lagny near Paris. He died at Forsheim in Picardy. His spiritual ecstasies were famous and were mentioned by St Bede.

Fusca and Maura (SS) MM. Feb 13
d *c*250. A fifteen-year-old girl of Ravenna, Italy, and her nurse, they were martyred there in the reign of Decius.

Fuscian (St) *see* **Victoricus, Fuscian and Gentian**

Fusculus (St) *see* **Donatian, Praesidius and Comps**

Fymbert (St) B. Sep 25
C7th. A bishop of the kingdom of Dalriada in the west of Scotland, he was allegedly consecrated by St Gregory the Great.

Fyncana and Fyndoca
(SS) VV? Oct 13
? They are listed in the Aberdeen Breviary and had a cultus at Echt near Brechin, Scotland, but nothing is known about them.

G

Gabdelas (St) *see* **Dadas, Casdoe and Gabdelas**

Gabinus (St) M. Feb 19
d. ?295. A Roman martyr, he was allegedly from Dalmatia (now part of Croatia) and a relative of the emperor Diocletian as well as a brother of Pope St Gaius and father of St Susanna. His acta are unreliable, however.

Gabinus and Crispulus (SS) MM. May 30
d. *c*130. They were martyred at Porto Torres near Sassari, Sardinia, in the reign of Hadrian and are venerated as the protomartyrs of Sardinia.

Gabriel the Archangel (St) Sep 29
The 'Angel of the Annunciation' is mentioned in the Bible at Dn 8:16, 9:21 and Lk 1:26–38 and is venerated together with SS Michael and Raphael.

Gabriel Desprez de Roche (Bl) *see* **September (Martyrs of)**.

Gabriel Ferretti (Bl) R(OFM). Nov 12
1385–1456. From Ancona, Italy, a relative of the counts of Ferretti, he became a Franciscan there, founded several new friaries and served as provincial of the Marches. His cultus was confirmed for Ancona in 1753. He was responsible for promoting the 'Franciscan Crown', a type of rosary.

Gabriel-of-St-Mary-Magdalen of Fonseca (Bl) M. R(OFM). Sep 3
d. 1632. A Spanish Franciscan lay brother, in 1612 he was sent to Manila, Philippines, and, after studying medicine there, went to Japan secretly. He worked among the persecuted Christian community as a doctor until he was captured and burned alive at Nagasaki with BB Anthony Ishida and Comps. *See* **Japan (Martyrs of)**.

Gabriel of Ise (St) M. T(OFM). Feb 6
d. 1597. He was a Japanese Franciscan tertiary crucified with SS Paul Miki and Comps. *See* **Japan (Martyrs of)**.

Gabriel Lalement (Bl) *see* **John Brébeuf and Comps**

Gabriel-Mary Nicolas (Bl) R(OFM). Aug 27
1463–1532. From near Clermont-Ferrand, France, he tried to become a Franciscan Observant but was refused admission to several friaries before being accepted at Notre-Dame-de-la-Fon near La Rochelle. He became the confessor of St Jane of Valois and helped her to found the order of the Annonciades in 1532. His cultus was approved in 1647.

Gabriel Perboyre *see* **John-Gabriel Perboyre**

Gabriel Pergaud (Bl) *see* **John-Baptist Souzy and Comps**

Gabriel-of-Our-Lady-of-Sorrows Possenti (St) R(CP). Feb 27
1838–1862. From Assisi, Italy, he was educated at Spoleto by the Jesuits and received a religious vocation after two serious illnesses. He joined the Passionists at Morovalle near Macerata in 1856 but only lived for another six years. Dying at Isola in the Abruzzi, he was remembered for heroic self-denial in small things and was canonized in 1920 after many miracles at his tomb. His cultus was confined to local or particular calendars in 1969.

Gabriel-John Taurin Dufresse (St) M. B. Sep 14
1750–1815. From near Clermont-Ferrand, France, he joined the Paris Society for Foreign Missions in 1774 and went to Sichuan province in China in 1777. In 1800 he was made titular bishop of Tabraca and apostolic administrator of the area, while being in continual danger of arrest as an enemy alien. He was finally

betrayed by a native Christian and hanged at Chengdu. *See* **China (Martyrs of)**.

Gabrielle Androuin (Bl) *see* **William Repin and Comps**

Gabrielle-Josephine Bonino
(Bl) R. Feb 8
1843–1906. Born in Savigliano in Piedmont, Italy, she tried her vocation twice in cloistered orders before founding the 'Sisters of the Holy Family' in 1880 to catechize orphans and to nurse poor sick people. Her charism was based on the Holy Family of Nazareth. She was beatified in 1995.

Gaetana Sterni (Bl) R. F. (Nov 26)
1827–1889. She was born at Cassola near Vicenza in Italy, but the family was at Bassano when her father died. She married when aged fifteen, but was a pregnant widow after eight months and then lost the baby. She then tried for a religious vocation, but her mother died and she had to take care of her younger siblings before finally being able to take charge of the town's poor-house in 1853. In 1860 she made religious profession and so founded the 'Daughters of the Divine Will', which has spread worldwide. She died at Bassano and was beatified in 2001. Her name is a feminine version of 'Cajetan'.

Gaiana (St) *see* **Rhipsime, Gaiana and Comps**

Gaius (St) *see* **Ampelus and Gaius**

Gaius (St) *see* **Caerealis, Pupulus and Comps**

Gaius (St) *see* **Crispus and Gaius**

Gaius (St) *see* **Dasius, Zoticus and Comps**

Gaius (St) *see* **Dionysius, Faustus and Comps**

Gaius (St) *see* **Fortunatus, Gaius and Anthes**

Gaius (St) *see* **Hermes, Haggai and Gaius**

Gaius (St) *see* **Hermogenes of Melitene and Comps**

Gaius, Pope *Apr 22*
d. 296. Nothing is known about him. He features in the acta of St Susanna and of St Sebastian, both of which are unreliable, and he is not listed as a martyr in the early records. Fragments of the Greek epitaph on his tomb in the cemetery of Callistus are extant. His cultus was suppressed in 1969.

Gaius and Alexander (SS) MM. Mar 10
d. *c*172. They had been opponents of Montanism in Phrygia, Asia Minor, before being martyred at Apamea (now Dinar, Turkey), in the reign of Marcus Aurelius.

Gaius and Crescentius
(SS) MM. Apr 16
C4th. They are listed by the old Roman Martyrology as two of the martyrs of Zaragoza, Spain, but they died in peace after a long imprisonment in the reign of Diocletian.

Gaius, Faustus and Comps
(SS) MM. Oct 4
C3rd. They are listed as clerical disciples of St Dionysius of Alexandria, Egypt, who were persecuted in the reign of Valerian. Gaius and Faustus seem to be listed also in the old Roman Martyrology on October 3 in error. The others were: Eusebius, a deacon who later became bishop of Laodicea (Latakia in Syria); Chaeremon, who had already suffered in the reign of Decius and who was exiled; and Lucius, about whom nothing is known.

Gaius and Leo (SS) MM. Jun 30
? They are listed as a priest and sub-deacon respectively, and were martyred either in Rome or in Roman Africa.

Gaius Jinyemon (Bl) M. T(OP). Aug 16
d. 1627. A Japanese (or Korean) born of a Christian parents on the island of Amakusa near Nagasaki, he became a Dominican tertiary and was martyred with BB Francis-of-St-Mary of Mancha and Comps. *See* **Japan (Martyrs of)**.

Gaius of Korea (Bl) M. T(OP). Nov 15
d. 1624. Originally a Korean Buddhist monk, he migrated to Japan as a Christian, helped the Dominican missionaries in Kyushu as a catechist and became a Dominican tertiary. He was burned at Nagasaki. *See* **Japan (Martyrs of)**.

Gaius of Milan (St) B. Sep 27
C1st? He is alleged to have succeeded St Barnabas as second bishop of Milan, Italy, and to have baptized St Vitalis with his sons, SS Gervase and Protase. There is no evidence of a diocese at Milan before 200 and so his existence is doubtful. St Charles Borromeo enshrined his relics in 1571.

Gaius of Nicomedia and Comps (SS) MM. Mar 4
d. ?254–259. He was possibly an official of the imperial palace at Nicomedia, Asia Minor, and was drowned in the sea there. His twenty-seven (or thirty-seven) companions were soldiers. Their date is uncertain.

Gajanus (St) M. Apr 10
C4th? He is listed as having been martyred in Dacia (western Romania) or, more likely, in Thrace (then the lands between the Danube and the Aegean).

Galata (St) *see* **Hermogenes of Melitene and Comps**

Galation (Galacteon) and Epistemis (SS) MM. Nov 5
d. ?251. According to the legend the former was a Christian who converted his pagan wife whereupon both entered monasteries and were martyred in the reign of Decius at Emesa (now Homs in Syria). They never existed, and their story was a Christianization of the pagan fable of Clitophon and Leucippe.

Galdinus della Sala (St) B. Apr 18
*c*1100–1176. A nobleman of Milan, Italy, he became a diocesan priest and then archdeacon. In 1161 he fled the city at the approach of the army of Emperor Frederick Barbarossa, but was made cardinal archbishop in 1165 in his absence. On his return he found the city mostly in ruins and was instrumental in encouraging its rebuilding. He was a great preacher and peacemaker, and died immediately after preaching a homily. He is the third most highly venerated saint of the Milanese church after SS Ambrose and Charles Borromeo.

Galganus (St) R. Dec 5
d. 1181. From Siena, Italy, he was a worldly young man but converted and became a hermit on Monte Siepe nearby. He was popular in the city and a church was built on the site of his cell. This became a Cistercian monastery in 1201, which probably explains the false claim that he had been a Cistercian monk.

Gall (St) R. Oct 16
*c*550–?645. A monk of Bangor, Ireland, he went with St Columban to England and France and helped him to found the abbey of Luxeuil in Burgundy. When his master was exiled to Italy he withdrew to be a hermit at a site in Switzerland where the great abbey of St Gall was founded after his death. The territory of this was an independent principality of the Holy Roman Empire, and survives as the Swiss canton of St Gall. The canton of Apenzell ('Abbot's Cell') was the abbot's private territory round his summer palace. The abbey's library was of very great importance.

Gall of Clermont (St) B. Jul 1
?489–554. From Clermont-Ferrand, France, he became a monk and chief cantor in the Frankish Austrasian palace chapel. In 527 he succeeded St Quinctian as bishop of his native city. He taught St Gregory of Tours, his nephew.

Galla (St) R. Oct 5
d. *c*550. A Roman noblewoman, she was the sister-in-law of Boethius. Being widowed one year after her marriage, she became a hermit at the Vatican and practised severe austerities before dying of breast cancer. She is briefly described by St Gregory the Great.

Gallgo (St) Nov 27
C6th. He is the patron of Llanallgo on the coast of Anglesey, Wales.

Gallicanus Avinius (St) L. Jun 25
d. ?362. A Roman consul and commander of the campaign against the Persians in the reign of Constantine, he converted in 330, retired to Ostia and built a church and hospital there. The old Roman Martyrology describes him as later being exiled to Alexandria and being martyred there in the reign of Julian, but this is false.

Gallicanus of Embrun (St) B. Jun 25
d. *p*541. He was bishop of Embrun, France.

Galmier *see* **Baldomerus**

Galnutius *see* **Winwaloe**

Gamaliel (St) L. Aug 3
C1st. He is the Jewish lawyer who taught St Paul (*see* Acts 22:3) and who intervened in favour of SS Peter and John (*see* Acts 5:34–9). A very doubtful tradition makes him a convert, and his even more doubtful relics were found near Jerusalem in 415. *See* **Abibas**.

Gamelbert (Bl) P. Jan 27
720–800. From a rich family at Michelsbuch near Augsburg in Bavaria, Germany, he was a soldier in the Frankish army before he became parish priest of his native village. He was remembered for his severe asceticism and his effective missionary activity. His cultus was confirmed for Augsburg in 1909.

Gamo (St) R. May 30
C8th. He was abbot of Brétigny near Noyon, France.

Gandulf Sacchi (Bl) R(OFM) Apr 3
d. 1260. From Binasco near Milan, Italy, he was one of the earliest Franciscans and spent his life preaching in Sicily. He died as a hermit at Polizzi Generosa near Palermo and had his cultus confirmed in 1621.

Gangulf of Varennes (St) M. R. May 11
720–760. A nobleman from Varennes-sur-Amance in Burgundy, France, according to his story he was a courtier and soldier until his wife's adultery persuaded him to become a hermit on his home estate. His wife's lover killed him, and the miracles at his tomb led him to be venerated as a martyr.

Garbh *see* **Fanchea**

Garbhan (St) R? Mar 26
C7th? Nothing certain is known about the patron of Dungarvan in Co. Waterford, Ireland.

Garcia of Artanza (St) R(OSB). Sep 29
d. ?1073. From near Burgos, Spain, he became monk and abbot of Artanza in Old Castile and was one of the chief counsellors of the Castilian king. Typically for the period in Spain, he fought with the king against the Muslims several times.

Garcia d'Aure (Bl) *see* **William Arnaud and Comps**

Garcia Rodriguez (Bl) *see* **Peter Rodriguez and Comps**

Garembert *see* **Warembert**

Garibald of Regensburg (St) B. Jan 8
d. 762. He was ordained as first bishop of Regensburg in Bavaria, Germany, by St Boniface *c*740, and seems to have been a monk in that city beforehand.

Garmier *see* **Baldomer**

Garmon *see* **Germanus**

Garnet *see* **Gervadius**

Gaspar *see* **Caspar**

Gaston *see* **Vedast**

Gatian of Tours (St) B. Dec 18
d. ?337. He was allegedly a disciple of St Dionysius of Paris and the first bishop of Tours, France.

Gaucherius (Gaultier, Walter) de Meulan (St) R(CR). Apr 9
d. 1140. The abbot-founder of the monastery of Augustinian canons at St John of Aureil near Limoges, France, he also helped his friend St Stephen Muret with the latter's new foundation at Grandmont. He died after falling off his horse.

Gaudentia and Three Comps (SS) VV. Aug 30
? They are listed in the old Roman Martyrology as having been Roman martyrs, but more ancient sources do not list them as martyrs and nothing is known about them.

Gaudentius, Culmatius and Comps (SS) MM. BD. Jun 19
d. 364. They are listed by the old Roman Martyrology as a bishop of Arezzo, Italy, and his deacon, late martyrs in the reign of Valentinian I. With them were killed Andrew a layman, his wife and children and fifty-three companions.

Gaudentius of Brescia (St) B. Oct 25
*c*360–*c*410. He was adopted and educated by St Philastrius of Brescia, became a monk at Caesarea in Cappodocia, Asia Minor, but was forced to return and become bishop of Brescia, Italy, on his foster-father's death in 387. He went to Constantinople in 405 to plead the cause of St John Chrysostom but was harshly received, imprisoned and deported. He is chiefly remembered for his paschal sermons.

Gaudentius of Gniezno (St) B. R(OSB). Jan 5
d. ?1008. He was the younger brother of St Adalbert of Prague, and the two were monks together at St Alexius's abbey at Rome. They went on mission to Prussia, where St Adalbert died in a massacre which St Gaudentius escaped. He was later made bishop of Gniezno in Poland by Emperor Otto III.

Gaudentius of Novara (St) B. Jan 22
d. 417. From Ivrea near Turin, Italy, and a refugee from his city, he was sheltered by St Laurence of Novara and became a disciple of St Eusebius of Vercelli. After administering the dioceses of Novara and Vercelli while the former was in exile, he became bishop of Novara in 379. The Canons Regular of the Lateran venerated him as the first organizer of community life among cathedral clergy.

Gaudentius of Ossero (St) B. R. Jun 1
d. 1044. Bishop of Ossero on the island of Cres, Croatia, he journeyed to Rome in order to appeal against his enemies. On the way back he fell ill at Ancona, Italy, resigned in 1042 and became a monk under St Peter Damian.

Gaudentius of Rimini (St) M. B. Oct 14
d. *c*360. Apparently from Ephesus, Asia Minor, he became a priest at Rome in 332 and bishop of Rimini, Italy, in 346. He opposed the Arians at the Council of Sirmium in 357 and was killed by them shortly afterwards.

Gaudentius of Verona (St) B. Feb 12
d. ?465. He was a bishop of Verona, Italy.

Gaudiosus of Brescia (St) B. Mar 7
d. ?445. He was a bishop of Brescia, Italy, and has his shrine there.

Gaudiosus of Naples (St) B. Oct 27
d. ?455. A bishop of Abitina in Roman Africa (and hence nicknamed 'the African'), he was exiled by the Arian Vandals in 440 and founded a monastery at Naples.

Gaudiosus of Salerno (St) B. Oct 26
C7th. A bishop of Salerno, Italy, he has his shrine at Naples.

Gaudiosus of Tarazona (St) B. R. Nov 3
d. ?585. A monk under St Victorian at Asen in the Pyrenean valley of the Esera in Huesca province, Spain, he became bishop of Tarazona (not Tarragona) near Zaragoza in 565.

Gaufrid (Bl) R. Sep 9
d. 1139. A disciple of Bl Vitalis and his successor as abbot of Savigny near Avranches in Normandy, France, in 1122, he oversaw the spread of the new Savignac monastic congregation in Normandy, England and Ireland. It numbered twenty-nine abbeys at his death but the congregation later amalgamated with the Cistercians.

Gaugeric (Gau, Géry) (St) B. Aug 11
d. ?635. From near Trier, Germany, he was ordained priest there and became bishop of Cambrai, France, in ?586. He was bishop for about four decades.

Gausmar (Bl) R(OSB). Jun 3
d. 984. He was abbot of St Martin's abbey at Savigny, France, from 954.

Gauzelin of Toul (St) B. Sep 7
d. 962. A Frankish noble, he became bishop of Toul, France, in 922 and supported the contemporary monastic reform movements.

Gebetrude (Gertrude) (St) R. Nov 7
d. ?675. She was abbess of Remiremont in the Vosges, France.

Gebhard of Constance (St) B. Aug 27
949–995. From the family of the counts of Bregenz, he was made bishop of Constance, Germany, in 979 by Emperor Otto II. He used his patrimony to found the Benedictine abbey of Petershausen near Constance, where he was buried. He has a cultus in Constance.

Gebhard of Salzburg (Bl) B.

Gebizo (St) R(OSB). Oct 21
d. ?1087. From Cologne, Germany, he became a monk at Montecassino, Italy, under Abbot Desiderius (the future Pope St Victor III) in 1076. The false assertion that he was entrusted with responsibility of crowning the king of Croatia by the pope is based on a confusion with a bishop of the same name. There has never been a liturgical cultus.

Gebuin of Lyons (St) B. Apr 18
d. 1080. Archbishop of Lyons, France, he was involved in the reforms of Pope St Gregory VII.

Gedeon of Besançon (St) B. Aug 8
d. ?796. He became bishop of Besançon, France, in 790.

Gelasinus (Gelasius) of Heliopolis (St) M. Aug 26
d. 297. According to his legend he was an actor at Heliopolis (Baalbek) in the Lebanon who was taking part in a comic parody of Christian baptism when he suddenly converted, announced seriously that he was a Christian himself and was stoned to death by the audience. He is probably identical with St Genesius the Comedian and the same story is alleged of other saints, but Heliopolis was a pagan stronghold for as long as paganism was tolerated and was a likely setting for such an incident.

Gelasius (St) *see* **Aquilinus, Geminus and Comps**

Gelasius (St) *see* **Theodulus, Saturninus and Comps**

Gelasius I, Pope (St) Nov 21
d. 496. Born at Rome of Roman African parents, he became pope in 492. He was a vigorous pope, fighting the Pelagians and

Manichaeans and upholding the Roman position as regards the continuing Acacian schism with Constantinople concerning Monophysitism. Some letters and treatises of his survive but he was not the author of the sacramentary named after him. Parts of this *Leonine Sacramentary* may, however, derive from him and many of his letters survive.

Gelasius of Armagh (St) B. R. Mar 27
1087–1174. The son of a bard, he became abbot of the Columban monastery of Derry, Ireland, and was made archbishop of Armagh in 1138, being allegedly the first Irish bishop to whom the pallium was sent. He consecrated St Laurence O'Toole as archbishop of Dublin in 1162 and made obeisance to the English King Henry II in 1172.

Gemellus of Ancyra (St) M. Dec 10
d. 362. For publicly rebuking the emperor Julian he was flayed and crucified at Ancyra, Asia Minor (now Ankara in Turkey), and was the last Roman martyr to be crucified.

Geminian (St) *see* **Lucy and Geminia**n

Geminian of Modena (St) B. Jan 31
d. 348. From near Modena, Italy, he became that city's bishop after 341 and had St Athanasius as a guest when the latter was on his way to exile in Gaul. He is the principal patron of the city.

Geminus (St) R. Oct 9
d. ?815. He was a monk at a monastery near Narni in Umbria, Italy, but it is not clear of which rite. He gave his name to San Gemini near Terni.

Geminus (St) *see* **Aquilinus, Geminus, Eugene and Comps**

Geminus (St) *see* **Aquilinus, Geminus, Gelasius and Comps**

Gemma Galgani (St) L. Apr 11
1878–1903. From Camigliano near Lucca, Italy, she lost her mother when she was seven and spent the rest of her short life at Lucca in intense suffering, both mental and physical. She never married and was under the spiritual care of the Passionists, although her desire to become a Passionist nun was frustrated by her physical ailments. She enjoyed spiritual peace in the face of her difficulties and was the subject of extraordinary supernatural phenomena, including the stigmata which recurred between 1899 and 1901. These phenomena caused adverse comment, but she was canonized in 1940.

St Gemma Galgani, Apr 11

Gemma of Goriano Sicoli (Bl) R. May 12
d. 1249. Initially a shepherdess, she was a hermit at Goriano Sicoli near Solmona in the Abruzzi, Italy, for forty-two years. Her cultus was approved for Sulmona and Valva in 1890.

Gemma (Hemma, Emma) of Gurk (St) R(OSB). Jun 29
d. 1045. Closely related to Emperor St Henry II, as a widow she founded a double monastery at Gurk in Carinthia, Austria, and became a nun there. Her cultus was confirmed for Gurk in 1938.

Gemus (St) R. Mar 19
? He had his shrine at Hürbach in Alsace, France, and was alleged to have been a monk, possibly of Moyenmoutier.

Genebald of Laon (St) B. Sep 5
d. ?555. The first bishop of Laon, France, consecrated by his relative St Remigius, he was married and continued to live with his wife in defiance of Church law. As a result of the scandal he resigned and spent seven years living as a penitential hermit.

Genebrard *see* **Gerebern**

Generalis (St) *see* **Crescentian, Victor and Comps**

Generosa (St) *see* **Scillitan Martyrs**

Generosus of Saint-Jouin-de-Marnes (St) R. Jul 16
d. ?682. He was abbot of Saint-Jouin-de-Marnes in Poitou, France.

Generosus of Tivoli (St) M. Jul 17
? His shrine is under the high altar of the cathedral at Tivoli near Rome, but nothing is known about him.

Genesius (St) *see* **Anastasius, Placid and Comps**

Genesius (Genès) of Arles
(St) M. Aug 25
d. ?303. Formerly a soldier, he was appointed notary by the magistrates of Arles, France. As a catechumen he refused to copy an edict of persecution against the Christians and fled, but caught and beheaded. He probably died in the reign of Maximian Herculeus.

Genesius of Clermont (St) B. Jun 3
d. 662. Bishop of Clermont-Ferrand, France, he was exceptionally popular and his people thwarted his wish to retire and become a hermit.

Genesius the Comedian
(St) M. Aug 25
d. ?300. He is probably the same as St **Gelasinus of Heliopolis** (q.v.). His story is identical except that it is set in Rome, and is told of at least three other martyrs.

Genesius of Lyons (St) B. R. Nov 1
d. ?679. A monk of Fontenelle in Normandy, France, he was prior there before he became a royal court-chaplain and was made bishop of Lyons in 658. He died at Chelles while making a visitation of the nunnery there.

Genistus of Aynac
(St) M. R(OSB). Apr 30
d. *c*1100. A Benedictine monk of Beaulieu near Limoges, France, he was killed by his nephew at Aynac-en-Quercy, near Cahors, of which place he is the patron.

Genevieve of Paris (St) R. Jan 3
?422–500. She is the patron of Paris, France, but the details of her life are controversial. According to the traditional version she was from Nanterre near Paris and became a friend of St Germanus of Auxerre when aged seven. Then she became a consecrated virgin when aged fifteen, moved to Paris and encouraged its people in the face of danger from the Huns and the Franks. She is depicted as a shepherdess holding a candle with a coin hanging from her neck. The Devil may be shown trying to extinguish the former, and an angel preventing him. Her shrine at Paris was in what is now the Pantheon, and was destroyed in the French Revolution.

Genevieve Torres Morales
(Bl) R. F. Jan 4
1870–1956. Born in Almenara in Castile, Spain, she was orphaned when aged eight and lost a leg five years later. She lived in a 'Mercy Home' run by the Carmelites of Charity, where she learnt self-abandonment to the will of God and also sewing. Lack of a leg precluded a vocation to an existing congregation, so in 1911 she founded 'Religious of the Sacred Heart of Jesus and the Holy Angels' to help poor women unable to live on their own. This spread from Valencia throughout Spain. She was beatified in 1995.

Gengulf *see* **Gangulf**

Genitus (St) *see* **Genulf of Cahors**

Gennadius (St) *see* **Felix and Gennadius**

Gennadius of Astorga (St)
B. R(OSB). May 25
d. ?936. A monk at Argeo near Astorga, Spain, he became the abbot-restorer of San Pedro de Montes and was a propagator of the Benedictine rule in León and Galicia. In ?895 he became bishop of Astorga for six years before retiring to be a hermit at San Pedro.

Gennadius of Constantinople
(St) B. Aug 25
d. 471. An able biblical exegete in the Antiochian tradition and a strong opponent of Alexandrian Christology, he became patriarch of Constantinople in 458. He deposed Timothy the Cat, the first monophysite patriarch of Alexandria.

Gennard (St) R. Apr 6
d. 720. He was a Frankish Neustrian courtier before he became a monk at Fontenelle in Normandy, France, under St Wandrille. He served for a period as abbot of Saint-Germer-de-Fly near Beauvais.

Gennaro *see* **Januarius**

Gennys *see* **Germanus of Auxerre**

Genocus (St) *see* **Blitheus and Genocus**

Genovefa *see* **Genevieve**

Gentian (St) *see* **Victoricus, Fuscian and Gentian**

Gentilis Finaguerria (Bl)
M. R(OFM). Sep 5
d. 1340. From Matelica in the Marches, Italy, he joined the Franciscans there and spent some

time on Mt Alvernia before setting out as a missionary to the Muslims of the Middle East. He got to Persia before he was killed.

Genuinus (Ingenuin) and Albinus (SS) BB. Feb 5
C7th and C11th resp. The former was a bishop of Sabion (which no longer exists) near Brixen in South Tyrol, Italy, while the latter was a bishop of Brixen. They have a joint local cultus.

Genulf (Genou) of Cahors (St) B. Jan 17
Mid C3rd. According to his story, he was sent from Rome with St Genitus, his father, to evangelize the area round Cahors, France. He became the city's first bishop but was persecuted, fled to Berry and became a hermit at Celles-sur-Nahon. It seems that two saints of the same name were conflated.

Geoffrey *see* **Agofredus, Ceolfred** or **Godfrey**

George, Aurelius, Natalia, Felix and Liliosa (SS) MM. Jul 27
d. ?852. George was from Bethlehem, a monk of Mar Saba who went to Spain to collect funds for his monastery. At Cordoba, ruled by the Umayyad emir Abd-er-Rahman II, he was seized on a charge of speaking against Islam together with two married couples, Aurelius and Natalia with Felix and Liliosa. He was offered his freedom as an alien but chose to be executed with the others.

George of Amastris (St) B. R. Feb 21
d. ?825. A native of Kromna near Amastris on the Black Sea coast, Asia Minor, he was first a hermit on Mount Sirik, then a monk of Bonyssa and finally bishop of Amastris. He successfully defended his city against Muslim attack.

George of Antioch (St) M. B. R. Apr 19
d. 814. A monk, he became bishop of Antioch in Pisidia, Asia Minor, and attended the second ecumenical council of Nicea, which condemned iconoclasm in 787. He was banished by Emperor Leo V, who was trying to reverse that decision, died in exile and was venerated as a martyr.

George Beesley (Bl) M. P. Jul 1
1563–1591. From Goosnargh, Lancs, England, he was ordained at Rheims in 1587 and was arrested at Croydon races after being seen dressed up and wearing a pistol. He was viciously tortured and executed at Tyburn with Bl Montford Scott, and was beatified in 1987. *See* **England (Martyrs of)**.

George Douglas (Bl) M. P. Dec 12
d. 1587. A teacher from Edinburgh, Scotland, he was converted and ordained in Paris in 1574. He was a priest in York until his execution there, and was beatified in 1987. *See* **England (Martyrs of)**.

George Edme René (Bl) *see* **John-Baptist Souzy and Comps**

George Errington (Bl) M. L. Nov 29
1554–1596. Born in Hirst Castle near Ashington, Northumberland, he was educated at Oxford and was repeatedly arrested for helping with the importation of priests and Catholic books. He was finally condemned for this and executed at York, being beatified in 1987. *See* **England (Martyrs of)**.

George Gervase (Bl) M. R(OSB). Apr 11
d. 1608. From Bosham, Sussex, when young he went privateering with Francis Drake in the West Indies but turned to the priesthood, was educated at Douai and ordained there in 1603. There he also became a Benedictine. After being on mission in England he was condemned and executed at Tyburn, London. He was beatified in 1929. *See* **England (Martyrs of)**.

George Girous (Bl) *see* **September (Martyrs of)**

George the Great (St) M. Apr 23
d. *c*300. One of the most popular saints in Christendom, he was fairly certainly a martyr at Diospolis (Lydda or Lod) in the Holy Land, possibly in the reign of Diocletian. All the other legends attached to his name are fictitious. His cultus as a soldier-saint, always popular in the East, spread to the West by the C7th and was greatly encouraged by the Crusaders. For obscure reasons he displaced St Edward the Confessor as major patron of England and is also a patron of Aragón, Portugal, Germany, Genoa, Venice and Ferrara. His shrine at Lod survives in the custody of the Greek Orthodox. He is familiarly depicted as a knight mounted on a white horse and killing a dragon with a lance. (If the horse is red, the depiction is of St Demetrius.)

George Haydock (Bl) M. P. Feb 12
1527–1584. From Cottam Hall near Preston, Lancs, he studied at Douai and was ordained at Rheims. Being betrayed soon after his arrival at London, he was executed at Tyburn with BB James Fenn, Thomas Hemerford, John Nutter and John Munden. He was beatified in 1987. *See* **England (Martyrs of)**.

St George the Great, Apr 23

George Limniotes (St) M. R. Aug 24
d. *c*730. An iconodule hermit on the Bithynian Olympus (a great monastic centre in Asia Minor near Constantinople), he was allegedly aged ninety-five when he had his hands and nose cut off in the reign of the iconoclast emperor Leo III.

George of Lodève (St) B. R(OSB). Feb 19
d. ?884. From near Rodez, France, he became a Benedictine at Conques but his monastery was destroyed by the Norse in 862 and he became a monk at Vabres near Rodez instead. When quite old he was made bishop of Lodève.

George Matulewicz (Bl) B. Jan 27
1871–1927. From near Kaunas in Lithuania (then in the Russian Empire), after his ordination he taught at Kielce, Poland and at St Petersburg. In 1909 he joined the Marian Clerks Regular, which the Russian government was suppressing, and re-formed them in secret. In 1911 he became the Superior General and opened noviciate houses in Poland, Lithuania, Switzerland and the USA for Poles and Lithuanians. He became bishop of Vilnius in 1918, but Poland annexed the city in 1920 and he resigned to become the Apostolic Visitor of newly independent Lithuania. Having organized the national Church, he died at Kaunas and was beatified in 1987.

George of Mitylene
(SS) BB. Apr 7, Feb 1, Feb 1
There are three bishops of Mitylene on Lesbos, one of the Aegean islands, who are venerated as saints. 'The Elder' was bishop from 763 to 816, and died in exile for opposing iconoclasm. 'The Younger' succeeded him, and 'the Third', a brother of the latter, was bishop for a year, 843–4.

George Napper (Bl) M. P. Nov 9
d. 1610. From Holywell, then just outside Oxford, he was at Corpus Christi College in Oxford before his conversion. He then studied at Douai, was ordained there in 1596 and worked in Oxfordshire until he was condemned and executed at Oxford. He was beatified in 1929. *See* **England (Martyrs of)**.

George Nichols (Bl) M. P. Jul 5
d. 1589. A convert graduate of Oxford, he was ordained at Rheims in 1581 and was a priest in Oxfordshire. Being seized at the Catherine Wheel Inn with BB Humphrey Pritchard, Thomas Belson and Richard Yaxley, he was executed with them at Oxford and was beatified in 1987. *See* **England (Martyrs of)**.

George of Périgueux (St) *see* **Fronto and George**

George Preca (Bl) P. T(OC). F. Jul 26
1880–1962. Born at Valletta, Malta, he was ordained in 1906 and quickly gathered a group of young disciples which led to the foundation of the 'Society of Christian Doctrine'. This is a lay society dedicated to catechesis which has spread worldwide. He became a Carmelite tertiary in 1918 and was beatified in 2001.

George Swallowell (Bl) M. L. Jul 26
d. 1594. From near Durham, he became an Anglican minister and a schoolmaster before his conversion. As a result he was condemned and executed at Darlington, and was beatified in 1929. *See* **England (Martyrs of)**.

George of Vienne (St) B. Nov 2
d. ?699. Bishop of Vienne, France, whose relics were discovered in 1251, he was alive at the end of the C7th or slightly later.

Georgia (St) R. Feb 15
d. *c*500. A young woman, she became a hermit at Clermont-Ferrand, France.

Geralach (St) R. Jan 5
d. *c*1170. A soldier from Valkenburg near Leyden, Netherlands, he led a dissipated life until his wife died tragically, whereupon he converted and became a hermit in a hollow oak at his native village. His life of penance was very austere, and he seems to have been in contact with St Hildegard concerning spiritual matters.

Gerald of Aurillac (St) L. Oct 13
855–909. Count of Aurillac in the Massif Central, France, he had a long illness when he was young and this gave him a taste for a life of prayer. He remained a layman instead of taking vows (exceptional for someone with such a disposition at the time) but did not marry and used his wealth for charity. He founded a Benedictine abbey on his estate at Aurillac, where he was buried.

Gerald of Béziers (St) B. R(CR). Nov 5
d. 1123. An Augustinian canon regular, he became bishop of Béziers near Montpellier, France, and was remembered for spending most of his income on the poor.

Gerald of Braga (St) B. R(OSB). Dec 5
d. 1109. From near Cahors in Gascony, France, he became a Benedictine at Moissac. In time he became chief cantor at Toledo cathedral, Spain, and was made archbishop of Braga in Portugal in 1096, thus re-establishing the church hierarchy in Portugal after the period of Muslim rule.

Gerald of Clairvaux (Bl) R(OCist). Oct 16
d. 1177. From Lombardy, he became a Cistercian monk at Fossanova in the Roman Campagna and went on to be abbot. In 1170 he became abbot of Clairvaux, France, and was killed at the abbey of Igny by a rebellious monk while on a canonical visitation.

Gerald of Mâcon (St) B. R(OSB). May 29
d. 927. A bishop of Mâcon, France, for forty years, he founded the abbey of Brou near Chartres and retired to die as a monk there.

Gerald of Mayo (St) B? R. Mar 13
d. 732. A Northumbrian Saxon monk of Lindisfarne, after the Synod of Whitby abolished the Celtic rite in England, he accompanied St Colman and the other monks who did not accept this decision to Inishboffin off the coast of Co. Mayo, Ireland. When that new monastery had to be split because the Saxons and Irish could not get on, St Gerald became abbot (and possibly bishop) of the foundation for the Saxons at Mayo. He probably lived long enough to witness the Roman rite being accepted there, too.

Gerald of Ostia (St) B. R(OSB). Feb 6
d. 1077. He was prior of Cluny before being made bishop of Ostia near Rome by Pope Alexander II in succession to St Peter Damian. He served as papal legate, and was imprisoned by Emperor Henry V in the investiture controversy. He is the principal patron of Velletri.

Gerard of Brogne (St) R(OSB). Oct 3
d. 959. From Brogne near Namur, Belgium, he became a soldier and a courtier of the count of Namur. Being sent on an embassy to the French king in 918, he stayed in Paris and became a monk at the Benedictine abbey of St Denis. He returned home to his own estate at Brogne in 914 and became abbot-founder of a monastery there (now the village of St Gérard), which became the centre of a monastic reform movement in the Low Countries and northern France during his twenty-two years as abbot. He was known for his equable disposition.

Gerard Cagnoli (Bl) R(OFM). Jan 2
1270–1345. A nobleman from near Pavia in Lombardy, Italy, he became a hermit on Mount Etna in Sicily and then a Franciscan lay brother. He worked as a cook, and was the recipient of many supernatural graces. His cultus was confirmed for Palermo in 1908.

Gerard of Clairvaux (Bl) R(OCist). Jan 30
d. 1138. One of the brothers of St Bernard of Clairvaux, France, and apparently the favourite one, he was a soldier when St Bernard became a monk but was wounded and decided to become a monk himself. He entered Cîteaux, went to Clairvaux when his brother was made abbot there and became the cellarer. He died before St Bernard, who preached an extant panegyric in his honour.

Gerard of Galinaro (St) L. Apr 28
d. ?639. Traditionally he died at Galinaro near Sora in eastern Lazio, Italy, and was one of four English pilgrims who died in the area (the others being Arduin, Bernard and Hugh). It is doubtful that they ever existed.

Gerard of La Charité (St) R(OSB). Dec 6
d. 1109. The first prior of the new Cluniac monastery of La-Charité-sur-Loire near Nevers, France, he founded several other Cluniac monasteries in France and went on to be abbot of Soigny. However he retired to return to La-Charité as an ordinary monk.

Gerard de Lunel (St) T(OFM). May 24
1275–1298. Allegedly a French pilgrim, he died as a hermit and Franciscan tertiary at Monte Santo near Ancona, Italy, on his way back from the Holy Land. His cultus was approved for Fermo in 1742.

Gerard Majella (St) R(CSSR). Oct 16
1725–1755. From Muro Lucano in Basilicata, Italy, he trained and worked as a tailor before joining the Redemptorist noviciate at Deliceto as a lay brother. Initially it was thought that he was not much use except in tailoring, but his amazing austerity and virtue were soon recognized and St Alphonsus ordered that he be professed early. The rest of his short life before his death of tuberculosis at Caposele contained a well-authenticated series of supernatural events including prophecies, the reading of consciences, bilocations and multiplication of food. He was canonized in 1904.

Gerard Mecatti of Villamagna (Bl) R. May 13
1174–1245. From a poor family at Villamagna near Florence, Italy, he was a knight's equerry on crusade on the Holy Land and was captured. Being ransomed, he became a penitential hermit back home in Villamagna with (apparently) a period serving as a Knight Hospitaller at Jerusalem. His cultus was approved for Florence and the Knights in 1833.

Gerard of Potenza (St) B. Oct 30
d. 1119. From Piacenza, Italy, he became a diocesan priest and then bishop of Potenza in Basilicata.

Gerard (Collert) Sagredo (St) M. B. R(OSB). Sep 24
d. 1046. The 'Apostle of Hungary' was from Venice, and was a monk at St George's abbey in that city. He was passing through Hungary on a pilgrimage to the Holy Land when he was detained by King St Stephen, who was in the process of Christianizing his kingdom. He became the tutor of the king's son, St Emeric (who died young), and was made the first bishop of Csanad in 1035. After the king's death there was a pagan reaction during which St Gerard was killed at what is now Budapest and his body thrown into the Danube.

Gerard of Sauve-Majeure (St) R(OSB). Apr 5
d. 1095. From Corbie in Picardy, France, he became a monk at the abbey there and, after pilgrimages to Rome and Palestine, became abbot of St Vincent at Laon in 1074. He was expelled by an usurper and founded the abbey of Sauve-Majeure near Bordeaux, which became the centre of a group of reformed monasteries. He introduced the Benedictine custom of saying Mass for a deceased monk for thirty successive days after the death.

Gerard Tintorio (Bl) L. Jun 6
d. 1207. A wealthy young merchant citizen of Monza in Lombardy, Italy, he used his wealth in founding a hospital where he served as a nurse. His cultus was approved for Monza in 1582.

Gerard of Toul (St) B. Apr 23
d. 994. From Cologne, he became bishop of Toul, France, in 963. He rebuilt the cathedral and founded monasteries which attracted Greek and Irish monk-scholars, thus much improving the standard of religion in the diocese. His successor went on to become Pope St Leo IX, and canonized him.

Gerardesca (Bl) R(OSB Cam). May 29
d. *c*1260. A noblewoman of Pisa, Italy, she married but persuaded her husband to become a Camaldolese monk at San Salvio there. She then lived as a hermit in a hut outside the monastery gate, being under the obedience of the monastic superior. Her cultus was confirmed for Pisa and the Camaldolese in 1856.

Gerasimus of the Jordan (St) R. Mar 5
d. *c*475. From Lycia, Asia Minor, he became a monk in the Holy Land and a disciple of St Euthymius the Great. He founded a great monastery on the Jordan on the traditional site of Christ's baptism near Jericho. The story about a lion becoming the companion of St Jerome after being done a kindness really refers to him, as ignorant Western pilgrims confused the two names in the Middle Ages.

Gerbald, Reginhard, Winebald and Worad (BB) MM. RR(OSB). May 25
d. 862. Monks of the abbey of St Bertin at St Omer, France, they were killed in a raid by the Danes.

Gerbold (St) B. R. Dec 5
d. *c*690. He was abbot-founder of Livray before becoming bishop of Bayeux, France.

Gerbrand (Bl) R(OCist). Oct 13
d. 1218. Abbot of the Cisterican monastery of Klaarkamp in Friesland, Netherlands, he founded another Cistercian abbey at Bloemkamp in 1191. He died at Foigny near Laon, France, when returning from a general chapter of his congregation, and had a cultus there.

Gerebald (St) B. Jun 12
d. 885. He became bishop of Châlons-sur-Marne, France, in 864.

Gerebern (Gerebrand)
(St) M? P? May 15
C7th. According to the unreliable legend of St Dympna, he was an old Irish priest who went with her to Belgium and was martyred with her. His alleged shrine is at Sonsbeck near Xanten on the lower Rhine, Germany.

Geremar (Germer) (St) R. Sep 24
d. ?658. From Beauvais, France, he was a Frankish courtier but retired to the abbey of Pentale on the Seine with his wife's consent. There he became abbot but some of the monks thought him too severe and tried to kill him, whereupon he resigned to be a hermit in a cave nearby. In 655, however, he founded an abbey between Beauvais and Rouen which was afterwards named Saint-Germer after him.

Gereon (St) M. Oct 10
C3rd? His extremely confused mediaeval legend featuring a legion of 678 soldiers martyred near Cologne, Germany, is merely an amplification of the story of the Theban Legion. There may originally have been two soldiers of this name, martyred at Xanten and at Bonn, or only one.

Gerin (Garin, Werin) (St) M. L. Oct 2
d. 676. Brother of St Leodegar, he was arrested with him by order of Ebroin, the mayor of the palace of the Merovingian kingdom, and was stoned to death near Arras, France, on suspicion of conspiracy against the king.

Gerius *see* **Gerard de Lunel**

Gerland of Caltagirone (St) R. Jun 18
C13th. Allegedly a German knight of one of the military orders (Templars or Hospitallers), he has his shrine at Caltagirone in Sicily.

Gerland of Girgenti (St) B. Feb 25
d. 1104. Allegedly born at Besançon, France, and a relative of Robert Guiscard the Norman adventurer, he became bishop of Girgenti in Sicily after the Normans had conquered that island from the Muslims, and worked to restore Christianity there.

German *see* **Jermyn**

Germana (Germaine) Cousin
(St) L. Jun 15
1579–1601. From Pibrac near Toulouse, France, she was a daughter of a labourer who lost his wife and re-married. Her step-mother despised her, and used the excuse of a serious skin disease to banish her from the house and to force her to sleep in a barn with the sheep for which she had to care. Despite the hardship, dirt and neglect she developed a full prayer life and was charitable to those in a similar state. Her step-mother eventually relented and allowed her back into the house, but she preferred to continue sleeping with the sheep and died alone with them. She was canonized in 1867.

Germanicus of Smyrna (St) M. Jan 19
d. 156. A young man of Smyrna (now Izmir, Turkey), he was thrown to the wild animals in the amphitheatre at the same games as featured the martyrdom of St Polycarp. The circular letter by the local church describing their martyrdoms survives.

Germanus (St) *see* **Antoninus of Caesarea and Comps**

Germanus (St) *see* **Donatian, Praesidius and Comps**

Germanus (St) *see* **Peregrine, Lucian and Comps**

Germanus (St) *see* **Saturninus, Neopolus and Comps**

Germanus (St) *see* **Servandus and Germanus**

Germanus and Randoald
(SS) MM. RR. Feb 21
d. ?677. The former was from Trier, Germany, and became a monk near Remiremont in the Vosges, France, and then at Luxeuil under St Waldebert. He later became abbot of Grandval near Moutier in the Jura canton, Switzerland, and had St Randoald as his prior. They were killed by a local ruler for defending the peasantry against unjust extortion.

Germanus, Theophilus, Caesarius and Vitalis (SS) MM Nov 3
d. 250. They were martyred at Caesarea in Cappodocia, Asia Minor, in the reign of Decius.

Germanus of Auxerre (St) B. Jul 31
?378–448. A nobleman from Auxerre, France, he studied law at Rome and was made governor of his native province by the emperor Honorius. In 418 he seems to have had a spiritual conversion and became bishop of his native city, and as such he visited Britain twice (in 429 and 447) to help defeat the Pelagian heresy. He died at the imperial capital of Ravenna while appeasing the emperor for a rebellion that had occurred in Brittany.

Germanus of Besançon (St) M. B. Oct 11
d. *c*390. The successor of St Desideratus as bishop of Besançon, France, he was allegedly martyred by Arian heretics.

Germanus of Capua (St) B. Oct 30
d. ?545. Bishop of Capua, Italy, he was sent to Constantinople by Pope Hormisdas to try and resolve the Acacian schism, and apparently met with ill-treatment. St Gregory the Great mentions him in his *Dialogues* as a friend of St Benedict, who had a vision of his soul at his death.

Germanus of Constantinople
(St) B. May 12
?674–740. From a patrician family, he became a priest at Constantinople and then bishop of Cyzicus on the Sea of Marmara, Asia Minor. In 715 he became patriarch of Constantinople, and energetically defended the dogmatic validity of icons against the iconoclast policy of Emperor Leo III. He was forced to resign and died in exile on his family estate. Some of his writings survive.

Germanus of Man (St) B. R. Jul 3
d. ?474. Allegedly a nephew of St Patrick and a missionary monk in Ireland, Wales and Brittany, he became bishop of the Isle of Man in about 466. A village in the north of the island is named after him and there are churches dedicated to him in north and mid Wales, but he has been often confused with St Germanus of Auxerre.

Germanus of Montfort (St) R(OSB). Nov 1
?906–1000. From Montfort near Malines, France, he studied at Paris, became a priest and then joined the monastery of Savigny. He was made prior of Talloires near Annecy in Savoy but ended his life as a hermit nearby. His relics were enshrined by St Francis de Sales in 1621, and his cultus was confirmed for Annecy in 1889.

Germanus of Paris (St) B. R. May 28
?496–576. From near Autun, France, he became a priest there and was abbot of a local monastery before becoming bishop of Paris and royal chaplain in 555. He had a good influence on the violent and immoral Merovingian royal family, and King Childebert I was impressed enough to found an abbey for him later known as Saint-Germain-des-Près. He was remembered for his charity to the poor.

Germanus-of-Jesus-and-Mary Pérez Gímenez (Bl) *see* **Nicephorus Díez Tejerina and Comps**

Germanus the Scot (St) M. B. May 2
d. *c*460. According to his unreliable acta, he was from Scotland or Ireland and was converted by St Germanus of Auxerre, whose name he took. He then became a missionary bishop and was martyred near Dieppe, France.

Germerius of Flay (St) R. Sep 24
d. *c*660. A Frankish courtier from Vardes, France, as such he founded a monastery at St-Pierre-aux-Bois and then became abbot of St-Samson-sur-Risle. Then he was a hermit for several years before becoming abbot-founder of Flay.

Germerius of Toulouse (St) B. May 16
d. ?560. From Angoulême, France, he became bishop of Toulouse in ?511.

Germoc (St) B? R. Jun 24
C6th. Of the Irish nobility, an alleged brother of St Breca, he founded a church where the village of Germoe now is near Helston in Cornwall, England, and is also venerated in Brittany.

Gero (St) B. Jun 28
d. 976. He was made archbishop of Cologne, Germany, in 969, and founded the abbey of Münstergladbach (which survives).

Gerold of Cologne (St) M. Oct 7
C13th. From Cologne, Germany, he led a life of ascetic pilgrimage between the major shrines of Christendom until he was killed by robbers near Cremona, Italy. He has a cultus there and at Cologne.

Gerold of Einsiedeln (St) R. Apr 19
d. 978. A nobleman of the Voralberg, Austria, he gave his lands to the Swiss abbey of Einsiedeln (where his sons, BB Cuno and Ulric, were monks) and became a hermit nearby where there is a village named after him.

Gerold of Evreux (St) B. R. Jun 14
d. 806. A courtier under Charlemagne, he became a monk and abbot at Fontenelle in Normandy, France, and was made bishop of Evreux in 787. However he resigned and returned to his monastery to die.

Gerontius (St) *see* **Paul, Gerontius and Comps**

Gerontius (Gerent), King
(SS) LL. Aug 10
C6th. One of the two was allegedly a king of Devon, England, when that was still under Celtic rule, and died in battle against the Saxons

in ?508. He and his wife Enid feature in many legends. Another of the same name was allegedly a king of Cornwall and died in ?596. Either could have given his name to the village of Gerrans near Truro, Cornwall.

Gerontius of Cervia (St) M. B. May 9
d. ?501. A bishop of Cervi near Ravenna, Italy, he was killed at Cagli near Urbino on his way back from a visit to Rome, possibly by robbers. He was venerated as a martyr.

Gertrude of Altenberg
(Bl) R(OPraem). Aug 13
1227–1297. Daughter of Ludovic IV, landgrave of Thuringia, Germany, and of St Elizabeth of Hungary, she was educated at the Premonstratensian nunnery at Altenberg in Thuringia and became abbess there in 1248. She was abbess for half a century.

Gertrude Comensoli (Bl) R. F. Feb 18
1847–1903. From near Brescia, Italy, she tried to join the Sisters of Charity when aged fifteen but her health quickly broke down. Then she lived in poverty for twenty years, doing domestic work and hoping to found a congregation of adorers of the Blessed Sacrament. This she did at Bergamo. They were called the 'Sacramentines' and supported themselves by teaching, moving to Lodi in 1891. She died at Bergamo and was beatified in 1989.

Gertrude the Elder (St) R. Dec 6
d. 649. A widow, she was the abbess-founder of the nunnery of Hamay near Douai, France.

Gertrude the Great (St) R(OSB). Nov 16
?1256–1302. Allegedly from Eisleben near Halle, Germany, when aged five she became a child oblate at the nunnery of Helfta nearby and went on to become a nun there. (The nunnery appears to have been Benedictine but pretending to be Cistercian for political reasons). From 1281 she had a continuous succession of mystical experiences and visions of Christ, especially during the Divine Office, and her writings derived from them helped to establish the devotion to the Sacred Heart. Her cultus was confirmed in 1677, and she is the patron of the West Indies. Her attribute is a flaming heart (she may be depicted with a mouse in mistake for Gertrude of Nivelles).

Gertrude of Nivelles (St) R. Mar 17
626–659. Daughter of Pepin of Landen and Bl Ida, when aged twenty she was made first abbess of the nunnery founded at Nivelles, Belgium, by her mother. She was known for her knowledge and charity at a time when both were in short supply, and became one of the most popular saints of the Middle Ages. Her attribute is a mouse, against which animal she is invoked.

Gertrude van Oosten
('of the East') (Bl) R. Jan 6
d. 1358. A domestic servant, she was jilted and so became a Beguine at Delft, Netherlands, instead. She reached an advanced degree in the spiritual life and received the stigmata. Her nickname allegedly derived from her favourite hymn: *The day breaks in the East*. Her cultus is not confirmed.

Gertrude of Remiremont (St) R. Nov 7
d. *c*690. Sister of St Adolf and grand-daughter of St Romaricus, she was educated at the nunnery of Saint-Mont near Remiremont in the Vosges, France, became a nun there and succeeded her aunt as abbess in ?654. Her cultus was approved in 1051.

Gerulf (St) M. L. Sep 21
?732–?750. According to the legend, he was the teenage son of the mayor of Merendree near Ghent, Belgium, and was killed by his godfather (who hoped to acquire his inheritance) on their way home from his confirmation. These circumstances led him to be venerated as a martyr.

Geruntius of Italica (St) M. B. Aug 25
d. ?100. According to the unreliable local tradition he was a bishop of Italica near Seville, Spain, who was martyred in the apostolic age. He is commemorated in the Mozarabic rite.

Geruntius of Milan (St) B. May 5
d. *c*470. He succeeded St Eusebius as bishop of Milan, Italy, in ?465.

Gervadius (Gerardin, Gernard,
Garnet) (St) R. Nov 8
C10th. An Irish monk, he became a hermit in a cave on the seashore at Drainie near Elgin, Scotland.

Gervase and Protase (SS) MM. Jun 19
C2nd? The relics of these supposed martyrs were discovered in Milan, Italy, in 386, during the episcopacy of St Ambrose. He mentioned the discovery in his letters, writing that the bloodstains were still visible on the bones, and proclaimed them to be the protomartyrs of Milan. Almost nothing was remembered of them at the time and their traditional acta are spurious. There is a suspicion that what was

actually discovered was a stone-age burial dressed with red ochre. Their cultus was confined to local calendars in 1969.

Gervase-Protase Brunel (Bl) *see* **John-Baptist Souzy and Comps**

Gervase of Sandomir (Bl) *see* **Sadoc of Sandomir and Comps**

Gerwin of Oudenburg
(St) R(OSB). Apr 17
d. 1117. From Flanders, he had been a pilgrim to the Holy Land before becoming a monk at Saint Winoc's Abbey at Corbie near Amiens, France. Then he became a hermit near the abbey of Oudenburg near Ostend, Belgium, serving as abbot there for a time.

Gerwin (Gervinus) of Rheims
(St) R(OSB). Mar 3
d. 1075. From Rheims, France, he was educated at the cathedral school there and became a cathedral canon. Then he became a Benedictine monk at Verdun and later abbot of St Riquier near Abbeville. A friend of St Edward the Confessor, he was a good preacher and was passionately attached to the Divine Office and to collecting Greek and Latin manuscripts.

Gery *see* **Gaugeric**

Getulius, Amantius, Caerealis and Primitivus (SS) MM. Jun 10
d. *c*120. According to their story, Getulius was the husband of St Symphorosa and Amantius was his brother. The other two were army officers sent to arrest them who were converted by them instead, and the four were beaten to death at Tivoli near Rome in the reign of Hadrian.

Gezzelin (Gotzelin, Joscelin)
(St) R. Aug 6
d. 1138. A hermit at Schlebusch near Cologne, Germany, he allegedly worked as a builder for the Cistercian abbey of Himmerod and imitated some early Syrian monks in never sleeping under a roof. He had his shrine at Luxembourg.

Ghebre Michael *see* **Michael Ghebre**

Ghislain (Gislenus, Guislain)
(St) R. Oct 9
d. *c*680. A hermit in a forest near Mons, Belgium, he became the abbot-founder of a monastery which became known as St Ghislain. For it he wrote a rule which was not replaced by that of St Benedict until 930.

Gibard (Gibert) (St) M. R(OSB). Apr 7
d. ?888. He was abbot of Luxeuil in Burgundy, France, when a Norse raiding party sacked the monastery. He and his community fled but were caught and massacred.

Gibitrude (St) R. May 8
d. ?655. She was a nun at Faremoutiers-en-Brie, France.

Gibrian and Siblings (SS) RR. May 8
d. *c*510. They were a Irish family of five brothers and three sisters: Gibrian, Tressan, Helan, Germanus, Petran, Franca, Promptia and Possenna. They were alleged to have migrated to Brittany and then to the region of Châlons-sur-Marne, France, where they became hermits.

Gilbert of Dornoch (St) B. Apr 1
d. 1245. Bishop of Caithness, Scotland, from 1225, he built the cathedral at Dornoch and was also of great service to the Scottish kings in their struggle to preserve the integrity of their nation. He is the most recent pre-Reformation Scotsman to have been canonized.

Gilbert Fautrel (Bl) *see* **September (Martyrs of)**

Gilbert of Hexham *see* **Tilbert**

Gilbert Lanchon (Bl) *see* **September (Martyrs of)**

Gilbert of Neuffontaines
(St) R(OPraem). Jun 6
d. 1152. A nobleman from the Auvergne, France, after coming back from the Second Crusade he and his wife became Premonstratensians and he became the abbot-founder of Neuffontaines near Clermont-Ferrand in 1151.

Gilbert of Sempringham
(St) R. F. Feb 4
1083–1189. Son of a Norman knight from Sempringham in Lincolnshire, England, he became parish priest there in 1123. He organized a group of seven women of the village into a religious community and thus founded the Gilbertines, the only religious order to have been founded in England. It was based on the pattern of a double monastery of nuns following the Benedictine rule and of canons following that of St Augustine, sharing a church. Twenty-two of these were founded in eastern England (not all with nuns), and he was the master-general until he went blind. He died in extreme old age, and his

shrine was a focus of pilgrimage at the great double monastery with its vast church (of which only crop marks remain) near the surviving parish church at Sempringham.

Gildard (Godard) (St) B. Jun 8
d. ?514. He was bishop of Rouen, France, for about fifteen years. He died about five years before St Medard was consecrated as bishop, yet the old Roman Martyrology repeated a worthless story that the two shared the same birthday, day of consecration and day of death.

Gildas the Wise 'Badonicus'
(St) R. Jan 29
d. *c*570. A Strathclyde Briton, he went to Wales as a refugee and became a monk under St Illtyd. Later he was a hermit on Flat Holm in the Bristol Channel and then emigrated to Brittany, France, and became a hermit on the peninsula of Rhuis near Vannes. He wrote *De Excidiis Britanniae* concerning the tribulations afflicting his fellow Britons as a result of the Saxon invasions and how these were justified given their immoral way of life. This work is a unique survival of, and witness to, post-Roman Christian British culture.

Gilduin (St) R(OSB)? Jan 27
1052–1077. A son of the count of Dol in Brittany, France, he was made a canon of St Samson's church there when very young and was elected bishop in 1076. He refused out of humility, persuaded Pope St Gregory VII at Rome to accept his refusal and died on the journey back. He is venerated at Chartres, where the tradition is that he became a monk.

Giles
This is the English form of the Latin Aegidius, Italian Egidio, French Gilles and Spanish and Portuguese Gil.

Giles (St) R. Sep 1
C8th. Very little is certainly known about him, yet he became one of the most popular saints of the Middle Ages (as witnessed by about 160 churches being dedicated to him in England) and many spurious legends were invented about him. He was possibly a Provençal who became a hermit and founded a monastery where the town of Saint-Gilles near Nîmes, France, now stands. This became a famous pilgrimage site. He is a patron saint of cripples, beggars and blacksmiths, has a deer or a crutch as an attribute and may be depicted with an arrow embedded in him. His cultus was confined to local calendars in 1969.

Giles and Arcanus (SS)
RR(OSB). Sep 1
d. *c*1050. The former was Spanish and the latter Italian, and they founded an abbey at the present Borgo San Sepolcro, Italy, to house the relics that they had acquired in the Holy Land.

Giles of Assisi (Bl) R(OFM). Apr 23
d. 1262. He became the third disciple of St Francis of Assisi in 1209 and preached unsuccessfully to the Muslims of Tunis (the very early Franciscans thought that they could evangelize the Muslims). Then he became a hermit in Italy and died at Perugia.

Giles de Bello of Laurenzana
(Bl) R(OFM). Jan 28
?1443–1518. From Laurenzana in Basilicata, Italy, he was a farm worker before becoming a Franciscan lay brother there and living as a hermit in the grounds of the friary. He was known for his love of animals. His cultus was approved for Matera in 1880.

Giles of Castañeda (Bl) R(OCist) Sep 1
d. ?1203. He was abbot of the Cistercian monastery of Castañeda in Asturias, Spain, and is venerated in the diocese of Astorga.

Giles-Mary-of-St-Joseph
Pontillo (St) R(OFM). Feb 7
1729–1812. Born in poverty at Taranto, Italy, he joined the Alcantarene Franciscans as a lay brother in 1754 and was at St Pascal's Hospice in Naples as a cook, mendicant and porter for 53 years. Although illiterate he was an advanced contemplative and his nights of prayer before the Blessed Sacrament enabled him to inspire even the noble and learned who talked with him. He was canonized in 1996.

Giles of Santarem (Bl) R(OP). May 14
1185–1265. A Portuguese, he studied medicine at Coïmbra, Paris and Toledo and was reputed to have practised black magic. He converted however, joined the Dominicans at Palencia, Spain, became the provincial superior for Spain and was based at Santarem, near Lisbon, when he died. His cultus was confirmed for Lisbon in 1748.

Giles of Saumur (Bl) B. Apr 23
d. 1266. Chaplain to St Louis IX, king of France, he went on crusade and became bishop of Damietta in the Egyptian delta in 1343, a brief responsibility as the Crusader attempt to conquer that city was a pathetic failure. In 1245 he became the Latin bishop of Tyre, Lebanon, instead, but died at Dinant in Belgium.

Girald (Girard, Giraud) of Fontenelle (St) R(OSB). Dec 29
d. 1031. A Benedictine monk of Lagny, he became abbot of Saint-Arnould near Chartres, France, and then of Fontenelle in Normandy, where he was killed by a rebellious monk.

Girald of Salles (Bl) R(CR). Oct 23
d. 1120. From near Bergerac, France, he was a canon regular there and a disciple of Bl Robert of Arbrissel. He founded two nunneries and seven monasteries and was buried at one of the latter, Châtelliers near Poitiers.

Girard de Bazonches (St) R(OSB). Nov 4
d. 1123. He was a Benedictine monk of St Aubin at Angers, France.

Gisella (Gizella, Gisele) (Bl) R. May 7
d. ?1095. Wife of King St Stephen and thus the first queen of Hungary, she may have been a sister of Emperor St Henry II. She helped the king in his policy of christianizing Hungary, so she was ill-treated and imprisoned in the pagan reaction after his death in 1038. She allegedly became a nun at Niedernburg near Passau in Bavaria, Germany, in 1042 and died as abbess.

Gislar (St) *see* **Chuniald and Gislar**

Gistilian (Gistlian) (St) B? R. Mar 2
C5th–C6th. An uncle of St David, he was a monk at Menevia when that monastery was transferred to the site of the present St David's, Wales.

Gladys (St) R. Mar 29
C5th. Allegedly one of the daughters of St Brychan, she was the wife of St Gundleus and mother of St Cadoc. She became a hermit after being widowed, and her name is associated with Gelligaer in eastern Glamorgan, Wales.

Glaphyra (St) V. Jan 13
d. ?324. A slave in domestic service to Constantia, wife of Emperor Licinius, she fled to St Basil, bishop of Amasea, when the emperor tried to seduce her. They were seized but she died on the way to her execution.

Glastian (St) B. Jan 28
d. 830. The patron of Kinglassie in Fife, Scotland, he interceded for the Picts when they were conquered by the Scots who had migrated to what is now Scotland from Ireland in the C6th.

Gleb (St) *see* **Boris and Gleb**

Glodesind *see* **Clotsind**

Glodesind of Metz (St) R. Jul 27
d. *c*600. A noblewoman from Metz, France, she overcame her father's opposition to become a nun at Trier, Germany, and founded a nunnery there.

Glunshallaich (St) R. Jun 3
C7th. He is recorded as having been a penitent who was converted by St Kevin and buried in the same grave with him at Glendalough, Ireland.

Gluvias (Glywys) Cerniw (St) R. May 3
C6th. Allegedly a brother of St Cadoc, he seems to have founded a monastery in Cornwall, England, and to have been martyred. Coedcerniw near Newport, Gwent, and Gluvian near St Coulomb Major, Cornwall, seem to commemorate him.

Glyceria (St) V. May 13
d. ?177. According to her story, she was a young woman who broke a statue of Zeus at Heraclea on the European coast of the Sea of Marmara during a pagan festival and was thrown to the wild animals during the games.

Glycerius of Milan (St) B. Sep 20
d. ?438. He was an archbishop of Milan, Italy.

Glycerius of Nicomedia (St) M. Dec 21
d. 303. A priest at Nicomedia, Asia Minor, he was burned at the stake in the reign of Diocletian.

Glywys *see* **Gluvias**

Goar (St) R. Jul 24
Late C6th? A secular priest from Aquitaine, France, he became a hermit on the Rhine between Koblenz and Bingen, Germany. Charlemagne built a pilgrimage church on the site of his cell. His C8th biography is fictitious.

Goban (Gobain) (St) R. Jun 20
d. *c*670. From Ireland and a disciple of St Fursey, he was a monk under him at Burgh Castle in Suffolk, England, before both fled to France in the face of a Mercian incursion. He became a hermit on the river Oise near Laon, where the village of Saint-Gobain now stands.

Goban Gobhnena (St) R. May 23
C6th or C7th. He is mentioned in the biography of St Laserian as a hermit at Tascoffin in Co. Limerick, Ireland.

Gobnata (Gobnet) (St) R. Feb 11
C6th? St Abban allegedly founded a nunnery at Ballyvourney near Macroom in Co. Cork, Ireland, and appointed her as abbess. She still has a holy well there.

Gobrain (St) B. R. Nov 16
630–725. A monk of Brittany, France, he became bishop of Vannes in 686 but resigned in 717 in order to be a hermit.

Godard *see* **Godehard**

Godebertha (St) R. Apr 11
d. *c*700. From near Amiens, France, she became a nun and abbess of a new nunnery at Noyon under the patronage of St Eligius, the bishop there. He wrote a rule for the foundation.

Godehard (Godard, Gothard)
(St) B. R(OSB). May 5
961–1038. From near Passau in Bavaria, Germany, his father was a servant of the canons at the secularized monastery of Niederaltaich so he joined them. In 996 he became their superior and re-introduced the monastic life there and in other monasteries in a similar state in several German dioceses, being asked to do so by Emperor St Henry II. He became bishop of Hildesheim in 1022. The famous St Gothard's Pass in the Alps seems to be named after him.

Godeleva (Godliva) (St) M. L. Jul 6
1040–1070. From near Boulogne, France, she married Bertulf van Gistel, a Flemish nobleman, and was viciously treated by him and his mother. She put up with it with patience, prayer and works of charity until he had her strangled. Later he did penance for this, went on crusade and became a monk. His castle at Gistel near Ostend, Belgium, became a nunnery.

Godfrey
The Latin Godefridus has many vernacular variants: Godefrid, Geoffrey, Jeffrey, Gotfrid, Goffry, Gottfried, Geoffroy, Gioffredo, Gaufrid, Geofroi, Goffredo, Gofrido, etc.

Godfrey of Amiens (St)
B. R(OSB). Nov 8
?1066–1115. From near Soissons, France, he became a child-oblate at the abbey of Mont-Saint-Quentin when aged five, was made abbot of Nogent-sous-Coucy in 1096 and bishop of Amiens in 1104. He was a great enemy of simony and clerical concubinage and was known to be austere with himself and others. His people would not allow him to resign to become a Carthusian.

Godfrey van Duyen (St) M. P. Jul 9
d. 1572. A secular priest and a former headmaster of a school at Paris, he was one of the **Gorinchem martyrs** (q.v.).

Godfrey of Kappenberg
(Bl) R(OPraem). Jan 13
1097–1127. Count of Kappenberg in Westphalia, Germany, and a substantial landowner, he was inspired by St Norbert to become a Premonstratensian monk and to convert his castles at Kappenberg, Ilmenstadt and Varlar into abbeys of the order. This was despite the violent opposition of his family, although his wife, brother and two sisters followed his example.

Godfrey of Loudun (Bl) B. Aug 3
d. 1255. From near Le Mans, France, he became bishop there in 1234 and was very active pastorally. He founded the Carthusian monastery of Parc d'Orgues and was buried there, his body having been brought back from Anagni, Italy, where he had died on a visit to the pope.

Godfrey of Merville
(St) R(OFM). Jul 9
d. 1572. Custodian of the Franciscan friary at Gorinchem, he was one of the **Gorinchem martyrs** (q.v.).

Godo (Gond) (St) R. Jul 24
d. *c*690. From Verdun, France, he was a nephew of St Wandrille and one of the founding monks of Fontenelle. Later he was the abbot-founder of Oyes in Brie, west of Paris, later named after him.

Godric (St) R(OSB). May 21
?1069–1170. From Walpole in Norfolk, England, he had an adventurous life as a seafarer and pilgrim before settling down as a hermit at Finchale (pronounced 'Finkle') on the Wear, being under the obedience of the cathedral priory at Durham. He was there for sixty years, becoming famous for his familiarity with wild animals as well as for his austerity and supernatural gifts and thus resembling the later Russian hermit saints. His biography was written by Reginald of Durham and some of his poems survive.

Godwin (St) R. Oct 28
d. *c*690. He was abbot of the great twin monasteries of Stavelot-Malmédy, Belgium. *See* **Sigolin**.

Goeric (Abbo) (St) B. Sep 19
d. 647. He succeeded St Arnulf as bishop of Metz, France, in 627. Other details are untrustworthy.

Goeznoveus (Goueznou, Gwyddno, Guinon, Winoc) (St) B. R. Oct 25
d. 675. From Cornwall, he was a brother of St Maughan. Emigrating to Brittany, France, he became a hermit near Brest and later bishop of the surrounding region of Léon. He died when a workman dropped a hammer on his head at Quimperlé.

Gofor (St) May 9
? He is the patron of Llanover near Abergavenny in Gwent, Wales.

Gohard (St) M. B. Jun 25
d. 843. Bishop of Nantes, France, from 838, he was killed during a Norse raid on the city while he was celebrating Mass. Many of his congregation, as well as other monks and priests, died in the attack.

Gollen (Collen, Colan) (St) R? May 21
C7th? He is the patron of Llangollen in Clwyd, Wales, but details of his life have been obscured by legend.

Golvin (Golwen) (St) B. R. May 21
C7th? Born near Brest in Brittany, France, of poor British immigrants, he became a hermit and later bishop of Léon. He died at Rennes, where his shrine was established.

Gombert (St) *see* **Bertha of Val d'Or and Gombert**

Gomer *see* **Gummarus**

Gomidas Keumurjian (Bl) M. P. Nov 5
?1656–1707. From Constantinople, he was an Armenian and became a priest of the Armenian patriarchate in that city. He and his family were reconciled to the Catholic church in 1696, which caused him to be regarded as a schismatic by his fellow Armenians. The Ottoman authorities were informed that he was an agent of hostile Christian powers and he was beheaded outside Constantinople, being beatified in 1929.

Gondulf (St) B. Sep 6
d. 823. He became bishop of Metz, France, in ?816, and has his shrine in Gorze Abbey.

Goneri (St) R. Jul 18
C6th. When the Saxons invaded Britain he was one of the refugees who fled to what is now Brittany, France, by tradition in a stone boat (thus he is a patron of sailors). Then he became a hermit, latterly near Tréguier.

Gonsalvo *see* **Gundesalvus**

Gontram *see* **Gunthamnus**

Gonzaga Gonza *see* **Aloysius-Gonzaga Gonza**

Good Thief, The (St) Mar 25
d. ?33. The repentant crucified thief described in the Passion narrative of St Luke's Gospel is traditionally given the name of Dismas. A number of fictitious legends feature him.

Goran (Woran) (St) R. Apr 7
C6th. He apparently lived near Bodmin in Cornwall, England, before St Petrock, and several Cornish churches are dedicated to him. He has a holy well at Gorran.

Gorazd (St) *see* **Clement of Ohrid and Comps**

Gordian (St) *see* **Valerian, Macrinus and Gordian**

Gordian of Rome (St) M. May 10
d. ?362. He was allegedly martyred at Rome in the reign of Julian, and his relics were placed in the same tomb as those of St Epimachus. This gave rise to their spurious acta and an erroneous entry in the old Roman Martyrology. Their cultus was confined to local calendars in 1969.

Gordian of Sandomir (Bl) *see* **Sadoc of Sandomir and Comps**

Gordius (St) M. Jan 3
d. 304. A centurion in the Roman army at Caesarea in Cappodocia, Asia Minor, he refused to take part in pagan sacrifice and was cashiered. Then he proclaimed Christ during a festival in honour of Mars and was martyred in the reign of Diocletian. St Basil preached a panegyric in his honour.

Gorgonia (St) L. Dec 9
d. ?375. Sister of St Gregory Nazianzen and daughter of SS Gregory Nazianzen the Elder and Nonna, she married and had three children, being remembered as a model wife and mother. Her brother gave an extant oration at her funeral, which is the only source concerning her life.

Gorgonius (St) M. Sep 9
? He was possibly a Roman martyr of the C3rd

or was the same as the Gorgonius mentioned below, or might have been martyred at Nicomedia in the reign of Diocletian with several companions. The evidence is badly confused. He was buried at Rome and is the patron of Minden, Germany, where some of his alleged relics were enshrined.

Gorgonius and Firmus (Firminus) (SS) MM. Mar 11
C3rd. They were martyred either at Nicaea in Bithynia, Asia Minor, or at Antioch, Syria.

Gorinchem (Gorkum) (Martyrs of) (SS) MM. Jul 9
d. 1572. Nineteen priests and religious, they were hanged by Calvinists at the ruined Augustinian monastery of Briel at Gorinchem near Dordrecht, Netherlands. Eleven were Franciscan Observants from the friary at Gorinchem, two were Premonstratensians, one was a Dominican, one was an Augustinian canon and four were secular priests. The town had been captured by Calvinist forces in rebellion against the Spanish government and the nineteen were imprisoned, harshly treated and interrogated in order to obtain their apostasy. They were offered their liberty in exchange for denying the Papal primacy and the Real Presence in the Eucharist, and were executed when they refused. This was despite the objections of the Prince of Orange, leader of the rebellion. They were canonized in 1867. *See* **Netherlands** in lists of national martyrs in appendix.

Gorman (St) B. R(OSB). Aug 28
d. 965. A Benedictine monk of Reichenau near Constance, Germany, he became a missionary and bishop of Schleswig (then in Denmark, now in Germany).

Gormcal (St) R. Aug 5
d. 1016. Abbot of Ardoilen in Co. Galway, Ireland, he was famous for his spiritual advice.

Gosbert (St) B. R(OSB). Feb 13
d. ?859. A disciple of St Ansgar, he became bishop of Osnabrück in Lower Saxony, Germany. He had trouble from the Danes and from the resentments caused by the forced conversion of the local Saxons, but he was not a martyr.

Goscelin (Goslin, Gozzelin) (St) R(OSB). Feb 12
d. 1153. He was abbot of San Solutore near Turin, Italy, from 1147.

Goswin (St) R(OSB). Oct 9
1086–1165. From Douai, France, he studied at Paris (where he opposed Abelard) and became a teacher of theology in his home town. In 1113 he became a Benedictine at Anchin nearby, and was abbot there from 1133. He was known as a reformer of monastic discipline, and his abbey was a famous source of illuminated manuscripts.

Gothard *see* **Godehard**

Gottschalk (St) M. L. Jun 7
d. 1066. The son of a Slav prince from what is now Mecklenburg, Germany, he was educated as a Christian at Lüneburg but apostatized after his father was killed by Christian Saxon settlers. He spent some time in Denmark and England, married a relative of King Canute and reconverted. He managed to establish himself as ruler over the Slavs to the east of Lübeck, and made it his policy to Christianize them with the aid of German missionaries and by founding monasteries. This was seen as part of German colonialism and was not popular, so there was a pagan reaction during which he was killed at Lenzen on the Elbe. That he was martyred for the faith has been questioned.

Govan (Goven, Cofen) (St) R. Jun 20
C6th. A hermit, probably a disciple of St Ailbe, he had a stone cell halfway down the cliff at St Govan's Head near Pembroke, Wales. After his death this was converted into a chapel, which survives and is one of the most evocative survivals of British eremitic monasticism.

Grace (St) *see* **Bernard, Mary and Comps**

Grace (St) *see* **Probus and Grace**

Gracilian and Felicissima (SS) MM. Aug 12
d. ?304. According to their untrustworthy legend, the former was in prison awaiting martyrdom at Falerna near Rome when he healed the latter, a blind girl, and hence converted her to Christianity. They were beheaded on the same day.

Graecina (St) *see* **Actinea and Graecina**

Grata (St) L. May 1
C4th or C8th. She is venerated at Bergamo, Italy, but the traditional details of her life are incoherent. There may have been two of the same name.

Gratia of Kotor (Bl) R(OSA). Nov 16
1438–1509. From Cattaro in Venetian Dalmatia (now Kotor in Montenegro), he fished in the Adriatic Sea for thirty years before

becoming an Augustinian lay friar. He had the charism of infused knowledge. He died at Murano near Venice and had his cultus confirmed for Kotor in 1889.

Gratian *see* **Gatian**

Gratian (St) *see* **Felinus and Gratian**

Gratus (St) *see* **Julius, Potamia and Comps**

Gratus of Aosta (St) B. Sep 7
d. *c*470. A bishop of Aosta in the Alps, Italy, he is patron of that place.

Gratus of Chalon-sur-Saône
(St) B. Oct 8
d. ?506. He was bishop of Chalon-sur-Saône, France.

Gratus of Oléron (St) B. Oct 11
d. ?506. He was the first bishop of the extinct diocese of Oléron in the Pyrenees, France.

Great Martyrdom at Nagasaki
(BB) MM. Sep 10
d. 1622. On this date 23 missionaries and native Christians were burned alive at Nagasaki in Japan, and 29 were beheaded. Those burned were eight Jesuits, six Dominicans, three Franciscans and five housekeepers of the missionaries, while those beheaded were two Dominicans, a Jesuit and 26 relatives of other martyrs. Two struggled from the fire only to be thrown back on it, and these were not beatified.

Gredifael (St) R. Nov 13
C7th. He accompanied St Paternus from Brittany to Wales, being either Breton or Welsh himself. He is alleged to have been an abbot at Whitland in Dyfed.

Gregory I 'the Great', Pope
(St) Dr. R. Sep 3
*c*540–604. Born in Rome of a wealthy patrician family, he was prefect of Rome from 571 but converted the family mansion into a monastery (St Andrew on the Coelian Hill) after his father's death and became a monk there in 575. Then he became archdeacon of the Roman church and was its representative at Constantinople from 579 to 585. (The Byzantine Eucharistic liturgy of the pre-sanctified bears his name). He became pope in 590, and proved to be one of the greatest. The city of Rome had lost its economic and political reasons for existence and he became the de facto local ruler, supporting the population from the landed patrimony of the papacy, especially in Sicily. He revised the Roman liturgy and wrote voluminously, especially on pastoral matters (being later declared a doctor of the Church), but as the first monk-pope he favoured his fellow monks at the expense of the secular clergy and this was resented. He had to pay off the Arian Lombards but oversaw the conversion of the Arian Visigoths and is especially famous for instigating the mission to the Anglo-Saxons through St Augustine and his successors at Canterbury, England. A medieval legend that he received his doctrine directly from the Holy Spirit led him to be depicted with a dove near his ear. The famous *Dialogues* may not be by him.

St Gregory the Great, Sep 3

Gregory II, Pope (St) Feb 13
669–731. A Roman, he was educated at the Lateran and was the archivist of the Roman church before he was elected pope in 715. He had to resist the religious policies of Emperor Leo III, who enforced iconoclasm in the Byzantine Empire in 726. For the German missions he consecrated SS Boniface and Corbinian and he fostered monastic life everywhere in the West. For this reason he used to be falsely claimed as a Benedictine.

Gregory III, Pope (St) Nov 28
d. 741. A Syrian, he became pope in 731 and immediately had to resist the strongly implemented iconoclastic policies of the emperor Leo III. Also the Lombards took Ravenna, the capital of the local Imperial province, in 734 and threatened finally to

conquer Rome. He appealed for help to Charles Martel, thus forming the historically important link between the Papacy and the Frankish kingdom which led to the Carolingian Empire.

Gregory VII, Pope (St) R(OSB). May 25
?1021–1085. Hildebrand was from Soana in Tuscany, Italy, and was educated at the Roman Cluniac monastery of St Mary on the Aventine where his uncle was superior. In time he became a monk and was made abbot of St Paul-outside-the-Walls in 1059. He was one of the leading figures in the reform movement in the Roman church, serving five popes as archdeacon before becoming pope himself in 1073. The thrust of his reform was against lay investiture, simony and clerical concubinage but this conflicted with the way the Church had been financed in other countries, especially in Germany, and he came into bitter conflict with Emperor Henry IV. Despite the famous penance by the latter at Canossa in 1077 Gregory was finally driven into exile and died at Salerno. His work made possible the power of the medieval Papacy, and he was canonized in 1606.

Gregory X, Pope (Bl) Jan 28
1210–1276. Theobald Visconti was from Piacenza, Italy, but became archdeacon at Liege, Belgium. He helped preach a crusade to try to save the remnant Latin Christian outposts in the Holy Land, and was elected pope in 1271 while at Acre there. He was not yet a priest. He convened the second ecumenical council of Lyons, which resulted in the brief reunification of the Latin and Byzantine Churches. His cultus was confirmed for Arezzo (where he had died) and Piacenza in 1713.

Gregory, Demetrius and Calogerus (SS) Jun 18
C5th. A bishop, archdeacon and abbot from Roman Africa, they were exiled by the Arian Vandals and settled at Fragalata near Messina, Sicily. They are patrons of that place.

Gregory of Auxerre (St) B. Dec 19
?455–?540. He became the bishop of Auxerre, France, in ?527.

Gregory Barbarigo (Barbardico) (St) B. Jun 18
1625–1697. A nobleman from Venice, he became bishop of Bergamo, Italy, in 1657, cardinal in 1660 and was transferred to Padua in 1664. He reformed his diocese as directed by the Council of Trent, was famous for the scale of his charity and was zealous for the re-unification of the Eastern and Western churches and for the support of Christians under Muslim rule. He was canonized in 1960 but had his cultus confined to local calendars in 1969.

Gregory of Besians (Bl) *see* **Dominic and Gregory**

Gregory of Burtscheid (St) R. Nov 4
d. 1002. Abbot of the Eastern-rite monastery of Cerchiara in Calabria, Italy, he fled to Rome from Muslim raids and met Emperor Otto III in Rome. They became friends, went back to Germany together and founded the Eastern-rite abbey of Burtscheid near Aachen, where St Gregory was first abbot. This was a centre of Byzantine cultural influence in the Ottonian Empire.

Gregory Celli of Verucchio (Bl) R(OSA). May 4
d. 1343. From Verucchio near Rimini, Italy, he became an Augustinian friar at a friary founded in his home town by his mother. He was expelled for some unknown but unjust reason and was hospitably received at the Franciscan friary at Monte Carnerio near Rieti. His cultus was confirmed for Rieti in 1769.

Gregory Chirivás Lacambra (Bl) *see* **Philip-of-Jesus Munárriz Azcona and Comps**

Gregory Decapolites (St) B. R. Nov 20
C9th. From the Isaurian Decapolis in central Asia Minor, he was in turn a monk, a bishop and a pilgrim but was remembered for going to Constantinople to oppose the iconoclast policy of Emperor Leo III. He had to suffer much as a result.

Gregory of Einsiedeln (St) R(OSB). Nov 8
d. 996. An Anglo-Saxon, he became a monk in Rome while on pilgrimage, stopped off at the abbey of Einsiedeln, Switzerland, on his way back and joined the community in 949. He became abbot and oversaw the period of the abbey's greatest splendour, reforming it along the lines being established at the time in England by St Dunstan.

Gregory of Elvira (St) B. Apr 24
d. ?394. Bishop of Elvira, which diocese was the precursor of Granada, Spain, he was a forceful opponent of Arianism and was one of the few bishops who refused the compromise of the council of Rimini in 359. He allegedly allied himself with the schism of Lucifer of Cagliari, but without himself lapsing from communion

with Rome. No Luciferian influence is detectable in his surviving writings.

Gregory Escrivano (Bl) *see* **Ignatius de Azevedo**

Gregory Girgenti (St) B. Nov 23
d. ?638. A monk of the Byzantine rite from Girgenti, Sicily, for a long time he was a monk in the lauras of the Levant before being made bishop of his home town by St Gregory the Great. A commentary on *Ecclesiastes* by him survives.

Gregory Grassi and Comps
(SS) MM. RR(OFM). Jul 9
d. 1900. He was the vicar-apostolic of northern Shanxi in China. During the Boxer Rebellion he and twenty-five of his people were executed at Taiyuan at the orders of the governor of the province. The others were Francis Fogolla OFM, his coadjutor and vicar-general for Tianjin; two priests, Elias Facchini and Theodoric Balat, OFM; a lay brother, Andrew Bauer; seven Franciscan Missionaries of Mary: Mary-Adolphine Dierkx, Mary-of-Peace-Giuliani, Mary-Hermina-of-Jesus Grivot, Mary-Amandina Jeuris, Mary-of-the-Holy-Birth Kerguin, Mary-of-St-Justus Moreau and Mary-Clare Nanetti; five Franciscan tertiary seminarians: John Zhang (Huan), Patrick Dong (Bodi), John Wang (Rui), Philip Zhang (Zhihe) and John Zhang (Jingguang); five other tertiaries: Thomas Shen (Jihe) (a manservant), Simon Chen (Ximan) (a lay catechist), Peter Wu (Anbang) (a servant), Francis Zhang (Rong) (a farmer), Matthew Feng (De) (a night watchman at the cathedral) and Peter Zhang (Banniu) (a servant at the cathedral), James Ysn (Guodong) (a cook), James Zhao (Quanxin) (a manservant) and Peter Wang (Erman) (a cook) were also killed. *See* **China (Martyrs of)**.

Gregory the Illuminator (St) B. Sep 30
*c*240–332. The details of the life of the 'Apostle of Armenia' are not well established, but it seems certain that he was a missionary to the independent kingdom of Armenia who converted Tiridat, the king, and became the first bishop of the new Armenian Church at Ashtishat (now Etchmiadzin). The Armenian legends concerning him are numerous and fanciful.

Gregory of Langres (St) B. Jan 4
d. 539. As the governor of the district around his native city of Autun, France, he was feared for his severity. He lost his wife, was ordained and made bishop of Langres and then became known for his gentleness and understanding. He was the father of St Tetricius and a great-uncle of St Gregory of Tours.

Gregory Makar (St) B. Mar 16
d. *c*1000. A hermit at Pithiviers near Orléans, France, he was allegedly an Armenian nobleman who had been made coadjutor bishop of Nicopolis and who then fled the attention he received.

Gregory Nazianzen the Elder
(St) B. Jan 1
?276–374. From Arianzos in Cappodocia, Asia Minor, he was a pagan civil servant until he was converted by his wife, St Nonna, in 325. Their three children, Gregory, Caesarius and Gorgonia, all became saints. He became bishop of Nazianzos nearby in 328, but joined a heterodox sect until he was converted to orthodox Christianity in 361 by his son Gregory, who became his coadjutor in 372. He died when almost a centenarian.

Gregory Nazianzen 'the Theologian' (St) B. Dr. R. Jan 2
329–389. The elder son of St Gregory Nazianzen the Elder, he studied law for ten years in Athens, during which he formed a close friendship with St Basil. They were briefly together at the latter's monastery on the Iris in Pontus, but then he went to Nazianzos to be a diocesan priest under his father, the bishop there, in 361. St Basil mistakenly consecrated him bishop of a hamlet called Sasima in 372 as a political move, but St Gregory did not accept this (his temperament did not fit him to public office) and he became coadjutor to his father instead. In 380 he was made patriarch of Constantinople in order to restore the Church there after the Arian ascendancy at court, but he resigned after only one month and went home to retirement. In that time he preached his *Theological Orations* which, together with his other writings, show him to be one of the most important of the Eastern Fathers and have given him the status of doctor of the Church. His feast-day was May 9 before 1969 but he is now celebrated with St Basil.

Gregory of Nyssa (St) B. Mar 9
d. ?395. A younger brother of St Basil, he married and was a teacher of rhetoric before becoming a priest. In 372 he was consecrated bishop of Nyssa in Cappodocia, Asia Minor, by his brother for political reasons (St Basil, as metropolitan of Caesarea, wanted as many suffragan bishops as possible to help him in his struggle with the Arian court). As such he was initially not a success and was exiled, as the

Arians were dominant in his diocese and he was not temperamentally suited to public life, but he was able to return in 379 and became the mainstay of orthodoxy in the region after St Basil's death. His theological writings are lucid and profound and he is one of the three 'Cappodocian Fathers' with SS Basil and Gregory Nazianzen but has not been declared a doctor of the Church, possibly because he accepted certain of Origen's speculations which were later condemned.

Gregory of Ostia (St) B. R(OSB). May 9
d. ?1044. Benedictine cardinal bishop of Ostia near Rome, he was papal legate in the Spanish kingdoms of Castile and Navarre. He died at Logroño and has a popular cultus in Navarre and Rioja. His extant biography has many contradictions and is unreliable.

Gregory of Spoleto (St) M. Dec 24
d. ?303. He was allegedly a priest martyred in the reign of Diocletian at Spoleto, Italy, but his acta are unreliable and his existence is not certain.

Gregory of Terracina (St)
R(OSB). Dec 12
d. *c*570. He is mentioned in the second *Dialogue* of St Gregory the Great as a disciple of St Benedict who became a monk at Terracina in eastern Lazio, Italy, with his brother, St Speciosus.

Gregory Thaumaturgus (St) B. Nov 17
?213–270. From Pontus, Asia Minor, he was a disciple of Origen and became bishop of Neocaesarea in that province in 240. The story is that there were seventeen Christians in the town then and only seventeen pagans left when he died. His surname means 'the Wonder-worker'. One of his close disciples was St Macrina the Elder, St Basil the Great's paternal grandmother. A little of his writings survives. His cultus was confined to particular calendars in 1969.

Gregory of Tours (St) B. Nov 17
540–594. From Clermont-Ferrand, France, he was educated by his uncle St Gall who was bishop there, and became bishop of Tours in 573. He was one of the most influential men in the Merovingian kingdom, and his chronological and hagiographical writings are important historical sources for the period.

Gregory of Utrecht (St) R. Aug 25
?707–776. From Trier, Germany, he met St Boniface as a child and became a monk under him. They were friends, and St Boniface made him abbot of St Martin's at Utrecht, Netherlands. He was administrator of the Utrecht diocese for twenty-two years, although he was never consecrated bishop. His abbey became a great missionary centre in his time.

Grimbald (St) R(OSB). Jul 8
d. 901. A monk and prior at the Benedictine abbey of St Bertin at St Omer, France, he was invited to England as a teacher by King Alfred the Great in 885 as part of that king's effort to restore the cultural and religious life of the country after the Danish incursions. He apparently refused to become archbishop of Canterbury and eventually became first superior of Winchester– Newminster. This was later the Benedictine abbey of Hyde (where his shrine was established), but at the time it was a house of canons and not a monastery.

Grimonia (Germuna) (St) V. Sep 7
C4th? She was allegedly an Irish girl who fled to Gaul to avoid marriage but who was pursued and killed at La-Capelle-en-Thiérache north of Laon. The story seems to be fictitious.

Grimwald of Pontecorvo (St) P. Sep 29
d. *p*1137. This archpriest of Pontecorvo in eastern Lazio, Italy, was traditionally an Englishman.

Grimwald-of-the-Purification Santamaria (Bl) R(CP). Nov 18
1883–1902. Born in Pontecorvo, Italy, he joined the Passionists there in 1889. His short religious life was outwardly ordinary and he was never ordained, but he had a developed sense of God's presence and was heroically virtuous. He died of meningitis and was beatified in 1995.

Grwst (St) R. Dec 1
C7th. He is the patron of Llanrwst, Clwyd, Wales.

Guala Roni (Bl) B. R(OP). Sep 3
d. 1244. From Bergamo, Italy, he became one of St Dominic's first disciples in Italy there and was the founding superior of the friaries at Brescia and Bologna. He became bishop of Brescia in 1228, but resigned in 1242 because of civil disturbances and retired to the Vallumbrosan monastery at Astino, where he died. His cultus was confirmed for Bergamo and Brescia in 1868.

Gualfard (Wolfhard) (St)
R(OSB Cam). May 11
d. 1127. From Augsburg, Germany, he was a

saddler and migrated to Verona, Italy, in 1096. The citizens started treating him as a holy man, so he fled and became a hermit in a marsh by the river until he was discovered, whereupon he became a recluse at the church of the Camaldolese monastery of San Salvatore.

Gualterus *see* **Walter**

Guarin (Warin) of Corvey
(Bl) R(OSB). Sep 26
d. 856. Apparently a son of St Ida of Herzfeld and brother of the duke of Saxony, he became abbot of Corvey near Paderborn, Germany, in 826.

Guarin (Warin) of Palestrina
(St) B. R(CR). Feb 6
d. 1159. From Bologna, Italy, he became an Augustinian canon regular at Mortara in 1104 and was elected bishop of Pavia in 1144. He absolutely refused to accept, but was forced by the pope to become cardinal bishop of Palestrina instead.

Guarin (Guerin) of Sion
(St) B. R(OCist). Jan 6
1065–1150. Originally a monk at Molesmes, France, he became abbot of Aulps near Geneva, Switzerland, and arranged that monastery's affiliation to Clairvaux. Later he became bishop of Sion in the Swiss canton of Valais. He died at Aulps and was buried there.

Guasacht O'Maelchu (St) B. Jan 24
C4th. A son of the man under whom St Patrick had been a slave in Ireland, he was one of the latter's first converts and was made first bishop of Granard in Co. Longford.

Gudelia (St) M. Sep 29
d. *c*340. She is listed as a young woman who was scalped and nailed to a tree by order of Shah Shapur II of Persia.

Gudula (Goule) (St) R. Jan 8
d. 712. Daughter of St Amelberga, she was educated by St Gertrude at Nivelles, Belgium, and, after the latter died, lived a life of prayerful seclusion near her parents' home at Merchtem near Brussels. She is the patron of Brussels. Her attribute is a lantern.

Gudwal (Curval) (St) B. R? Jun 6
C6th. Apparently a Welsh monk who founded a monastery in Cornwall, England, he may be identical to the missionary in Brittany, France, who was claimed as the successor of St Malo at Aleth. His shrine is at Blandinberg near Ghent, Belgium.

Guenhael (St) R. Nov 3
d. *c*550. Born in Brittany, France, he was educated at Landevenec under St Winwaloe and became abbot there himself in due course. His name means 'White Angel'.

Guennin (St) B. Aug 19
C7th. This bishop of Vannes in Brittany, France, has his shrine in the cathedral there.

Guerembald (St) R(OSB). Nov 10
d. 965. A monk of Hirsau near Stuttgart, Germany, he refused the bishopric of Speyer out of humility.

Guerric of Igny (Bl) R(OCist). Aug 19
?1080–?1155. From Tournai, Belgium, he studied at the cathedral school there and went on to be a canon and headmaster. On a visit to St Bernard at Clairvaux he was inspired to stay and to become a Cistercian, and was sent by the latter to be the first abbot of Igny near Rheims, France. His many writings on monastic spirituality are still popular.

Guesnoveus (Gouernou) (St) B. Oct 25
d. 675. A bishop of Quimper in Brittany, France, he died in retirement at a monastery that he had founded near Brest.

Guethenoc (St) *see* **Jacut and Guethenoc**

Guevrock (Gueroc, Kerric) (St) R. Feb 17
C6th. He went with St Tadwall from Wales to Brittany, France, and succeeded him as abbot of Locquirec near Morlais, where his shrine was established. He helped St Paul of Léon to administer his diocese.

Guibert (St) R(OSB). May 23
d. 962. A noble of Lorraine, he was a soldier before becoming a hermit on an estate of his at Gembloux near Brussels, Belgium. He turned this into a monastery but became a monk at Gorze near Metz, France, where he died but which he had to leave several times in order to defend his foundation in lawsuits. His shrine is at Gembloux.

Guido *see* **Guy**

Guingar *see* **Fingar**

Guingaloc (Guignole, Guinvaloeus) *see* **Winwaloe**

Guinizo (St) R. May 26
d. *c*1050. From Spain, he became a Benedictine at Montecassino, Italy, and remained as a

hermit on the mountain after the abbey buildings were raided and destroyed.

Guinoch (St) B. Apr 13
d. *c*838. A bishop in Scotland, he was venerated in Buchan which was probably his mission territory.

Guislain *see* **Ghislain**

Guitmar (St) R(OSB). Dec 10
d. ?765. He was fourth abbot of Saint-Riquier near Abbeville, France.

Gulstan (Gustan, Constans)
(St) R(OSB). Nov 29
d. *c*1010. He was a Benedictine at the abbey of St Gildas at Rhuys in Brittany, France, under St Felix.

Gumesind (Gomez) and Servusdei (Servideus) (SS) MM. Jan 13
d. 852. The former was a parish priest, the latter a monk, and they were beheaded at Cordoba, Spain, in the reign of Abd-er-Rahman II.

Gummar (Gomer) (St) R. Oct 11
?717–774. A military officer at the Frankish court, he had a wife who was extravagant and malicious and he separated from her after a long period of endurance in order to become a hermit. The present town of Lier near Antwerp, Belgium, grew up round his hermitage.

Gundebert (St) M. R. Apr 20
8th cent. Tradition describes him as a Frankish courtier who was the brother of St Nivard and the husband of St Bertha of Avenay. He separated from his wife, became a monk, crossed over to Ireland and was killed in his monastery there by marauders.

Gundebert (Gumbert) of Ansbach (St) R. Jul 15
C8th. A nobleman of Germany, he became abbot-founder of the monastery of Ansbach.

Gundebert (Gumbert, Gondelbert) of Sens (St) B. Feb 21
d. *c*676. A bishop of Sens, France, he resigned and retired into the Vosges mountains where he founded the abbey of Senones (*c*660).

Gundechar (Bl) B. Aug 2
1019–1073. From Eichstätt in Bavaria, Germany, he was educated at the cathedral school there and was court chaplain to the empress before becoming bishop of his home town. The *Pontifical* which he drew up is still preserved and is of great historical interest.

Gundekar (St) *see* **Waccar, Gundekar and Comps**

Gundelind (Guendelind)
(St) R. March 28
d. *c*750. She was a daughter of the duke of Alsace and a niece of St Ottilia, whom she succeeded as abbess of the nunnery of Niedermünster near Strasbourg, France.

Gundenis (St) V. July 18
d. 203. She was a young woman martyred at Carthage, Roman Africa, in the reign of Septimus Severus.

Gundisalvus of Amarante
(Bl) R(OP). Jan 16
1187–1259. From the Vizela valley near Braga, Portugal, he became parish priest at Rivas de Vizela but went on pilgrimage for fourteen years and was rejected by his vicar when he returned. Then he became a hermit at Amarante near Oporto, and later joined the Dominicans while remaining a hermit. His cultus was approved in 1560.

Gundisalvus Fusai (Bl) M. R(SJ). Sept 10
1582–1622. A Japanese, he held a high office at the court of his daimyo but attached himself to the Jesuit missionaries in Kyushu after his baptism. He was imprisoned at Omura and there received into the Society of Jesus by Bl Charles Spinola, with whom he was burnt alive in the 'Great Martyrdom' at Nagasaki. *See* **Japan (Martyrs of)**.

Gundisalvus Garcia (St) M. R(OFM). Feb 6
1556–1597. Born at Bassein, Burma, of a Portuguese father and Canarese mother, he was firstly a catechist for the Jesuits, then he ran a flourishing business in Japan and finally he joined the Franciscans at Manila as a lay brother in 1591. He returned to Japan as a translator for St Peter Baptist, with whom he was crucified at Nagasaki together with SS Paul Miki and Comps. *See* **Japan (Martyrs of)**.

Gundisalvus Gonzalo Gonzalo (Bl) *see* **Hospitaller Martyrs of Spain**

Gundisalvus Hendriquez (Bl) *see* **Ignatius de Azevedo**

Gundisalvus of Lagos (Bl) R(OSA). Oct 21
d. 1422. From Lagos in Portugal, he became an Augustinian friar and was famous as a great

preacher throughout Portugal. He died at Torres Vedras and his cultus was approved for Lisbon in 1778.

Gundisalvus of Las Junias (St) R(OCist). Oct 10
d. ?1163. He was the first superior of the Cistercian abbey of Las Junias in Portugal, founded from the abbey of Osera in 1135.

Gundulf of Bourges (St) B. Jun 17
C6th. He had a cultus at Bourges, France, as an alleged bishop of Milan who had died there, and may have been a bishop somewhere in Gaul.

Gunifort of Pavia (St) M. Aug 22
? He was allegedly from the British Isles and was martyred at Pavia, Italy. His legend resembles that of St Richard the King.

Gunther (Bl) R(OSB). Oct 9
955–1045. A cousin of St Stephen of Hungary and ancestor of the princes of Schwarzburg in Thuringia, Germany, he began life as an ambitious nobleman but was reformed by St Godehard of Hildesheim and became a monk at Niederaltaich in Bavaria. His ambitious nature reasserted itself, however, and he had himself made abbot of Göllingen, but proved a failure and returned to Niederaltaich. Then he lived as a hermit for twenty-eight years in the mountains of Bakony in Hungary.

Gunthiern (St) R. Jul 3
d. *c*500. A Welsh prince, he became a hermit at Kervegnac in Brittany, France.

Gunthild (St) R. Dec 8
d. *c*748 A nun of Wimborne in Dorset, England, at the request of St Boniface she migrated to Germany, where she was abbess of a nunnery in Thuringia and inspector of all the schools founded by the Anglo-Saxon nuns in Germany.

Guntram (Gontram), King (St) L. Mar 28
d. 592. King of Burgundy, France, he divorced his wife and over-hastily ordered the execution of his physician. Then he was overcome with remorse and lamented these sins for the rest of his life. He was also a good and popular king, and on his death was the object of popular veneration.

Gurias and Samonas (SS) MM. Nov 15
d. 305. They were beheaded at Edessa in Syria (now Urfa in Turkey) in the reign of Diocletian.

Gurloes (St) R(OSB). Aug 25
d. 1057. A Benedictine monk, he was the prior of Redon abbey near St Nazaire, France, before becoming the first abbot of Quimperlé in Brittany.

Gurval *see* **Godwall**

Guthagon (St) R. Jul 3
C8th? He has his shrine at Oostkerke near Ostend, Belgium, and his dubious tradition describes him as an Irish hermit in exile.

Guthlac (St) R. Apr 11
673–714. He had been a soldier in the Mercian army before joining the double monastery of Repton in Derbyshire, England. Then he became a hermit at Crowland, an island in the Lincolnshire Fens, where he apparently made a cell out of a sarcophagus excavated from a tumulus by treasure-hunters. There he spent the last fifteen years of his life. At a later period the abbey of Crowland was erected nearby but this was not on the site of his cell, the remains of which were wantonly destroyed in the C19th.

Guy
This is the English form of the Latin Vitus, and also of Guido. Variants in other languages are: Gui, Gwin, Guidone, Viton, Wido, Witen, Wit, Wye, Wyden.

Guy of Acqui (Bl) B. Jun 2
d. 1070. He was bishop of Acqui in Monferrato, Piedmont, Italy, from 1034. His cultus was confirmed for Acqui in 1853.

Guy of Anderlecht (St) L. Sep 12
d. ?1012. Surnamed 'the Poor Man of Anderlecht' he was a labourer from near Anderlecht, Belgium, who served as sacristan at Laeken before going on pilgrimage to Rome and Holy Land. On his return, sick and exhausted, he was admitted to the public hospital at Anderlecht and died there. His extant biography is late and unreliable.

Guy of Baume (St) R(OSB). Jun 18
d. *p*940. He succeeded Bl Berno as abbot of Baume in the Jura, France, but about the year 940 he resigned and retired to a hermitage near Fay-en-Bresse.

Guy-Mary Conforti (Bl) B. R. F. Nov 5
1865–1931. Born near Parma, Italy, he was influenced by the life of St Francis Xavier and, after becoming a cathedral canon, founded the 'Xavieran Missionaries' in 1895 in order to send missionaries to China. He took vows

himself in 1902 and became bishop of Parma in 1907, founding the Pontifical Missionary Union in 1916 and finally visiting China in 1928. He died exhausted, beloved by his city, and was beatified in 1996.

Guy of Durnes (Bl) R(OCist). Sep 23
d. ?1157. A monk of Clairvaux, he was one of St Bernard's favourite disciples and was sent to be abbot-founder of Our Lady of Cherlieu in the diocese of Besançon, France. At the request of St Bernard he revised the Cistercian chant, which revision was approved in the general chapter of 1150.

Guy Maramaldi (Bl) R(OP). Jun 25
d. 1391. A noble from Naples, he became a Dominican, taught philosophy and theology, established a friary at Ragusa (now Dubrovnik in Croatia) and died as the inquisitor-general for the Kingdom of Naples. His cultus was confirmed in 1612.

Guy of Pomposa (St) R(OSB). Mar 31
d. 1046. From Ravenna, Italy, he was a hermit before he became a Benedictine at the abbey of Pomposa near Ferrara. Then he was made prior of St Severus at Ravenna and abbot of Pomposa. He loved the study of sacred subjects, and St Peter Damian gave lectures on the Bible to his monks for two years at his request. Towards the end of his life he was fiercely, though unjustly, persecuted by the bishop of Ravenna.

Guy Vignotelli (Bl) R(OFM). Jun 16
?1185–1245. A rich citizen of Cortona, Italy, he gave up his wealth on hearing a sermon by St Francis of Assisi and was received as a Franciscan tertiary by the latter. He became a priest and lived the rest of his life as a hermit near Cortona.

Gwen (St) *see* **Fragan and Gwen**

Gwen of Cornwall (St) L. Oct 18
C5th. According to legend she was the sister of St Nonna (and therefore an aunt of St David), the wife of St Solomon I and the mother of St Cybi. She is associated with the village of St Wenn near St Coulomb Major in Cornwall, England.

Gwen (Candida, Blanche) of Talgarth (St) M. Oct 18
d. ?492. Allegedly a daughter of St Brychan, she was killed by the Saxons at Talgarth in Powys, Wales.

Gwendolen *see* **Gundelind**

Gwendolen (St) *see* **Brothen and Gwendolen**

Gwenfaen (St) R.
? The church at Rhoscolyn on Anglesey, Wales, is dedicated to him and he has a holy well nearby. Nothing else is known.

Gwenhael *see* **Guenhael**

Gwerir (St) R. Apr 4
? He was a hermit near Liskeard in Cornwall, England, and King Alfred was allegedly cured of a serious illness at his grave. His cell was occupied by St Neot after his death.

Gwrnerth (St) *see* **Llewellyn and Gwrnerth**

Gwynllyw (St) R. Mar 29
d. *c*500. Gwynllyw is anglicized as Woollos. He is alleged to have been the husband of St Gladys and the father of St Cadoc, and to have died as a hermit in Wales. There is an Anglican cathedral dedicated to him at Newport, Gwent.

Gyavira (St) M. June 13
d. 1886. Known as the 'good runner of messages', he was killed by order of King Mwanga of Buganda (Uganda). *See* **Charles Lwanga and Comps**.

H

Habakuk *see* **Abachum**

Habentius (St) *see* **Peter of Cordoba and Comps**

Habet-Deus (St) B. Feb 17
d. *c*500. Bishop of Luna in Tuscany, Italy, an ancient city now in ruins, he was probably a Roman African bishop who had been exiled by the Arian Vandals. He has a cultus at Sarzana near La Spezia.

Hadelin (St) *see* **Domitian and Hadelin**

Hadelin of Celle (St) R. Feb 3
d. *c*690. From Gascony, France, he accompanied St Remaclus first to Solignac and then to Maestricht and Stavelot. He became a hermit near Dinant, Belgium, and helped to found the abbey of Celle near Liege, where he died.

Hadelin (Adelheim) of Sées
(St) B. R(OSB). Nov 10
d. *c*910. A monk and abbot of St Calais near Le Mans, France, he became bishop of Sées in Normandy in ?884.

Hadeloga *see* **Adeloga**

Hadrian *see* **Adrian**

Haduin (Harduin) (St) B. Aug 20
d. ?653. A bishop of Le Mans, France, he founded several monasteries (notably that of Évron).

Hadulf (St) B. May 19
d. ?728. He was simultaneously the abbot of Saint-Vaast and bishop of Arras-Cambrai in Flanders, France.

Hadulf (St) *see* **Waccar, Gundekar and Comps**

Haggai (St) *see* **Hermes, Haggai and Gaius**

Haimo *see* **Aimo**

Hainmar (St) M. B. Oct 28
d. ?731. He was bishop of Auxerre, France, from 717, but was executed after quarrelling with the Frankish king.

Hallvard Vebjörnsson (St) M. L. May 15
d. ?1043. The son of a farmer near Drammen, Norway, and a cousin of the king, he was allegedly killed for defending from persecution a woman who had appealed to him for help. He is the patron saint of Oslo.

Hannibal-Mary de Francia
(Bl) P. F. Jun 1
1851–1927. A nobleman born in Messina, Sicily, he was ordained in 1878 and was parish priest at Case Avignone (a very poor place) where he founded orphanages for boys and girls. He became a cathedral canon and the seminary's spiritual director in 1882, and went on to found the 'Daughters of Divine Zeal' (1887) and the 'Rogationists of the Heart of Jesus' (1897). To spread the work of 'Rogare' (petitioning the Sacred Heart) he also founded secular institutes for clerics and lay people. He was beatified in 1990.

Harduin of León (St) B. Nov 29
C7th. He was a bishop of St Pol-de-Léon in Brittany, France, and his name has many versions, e.g. Ouardon, Wardon, Hoarzon, Huardo.

Hardulf (St) R? Aug 21
? The church at Breedon-on-the-Hill in Leicestershire, England, was dedicated to this saint, of whom nothing is known. He may be identical with the hermit of Bredon (or Breedon) mentioned in the biography of St Modwenna.

Harmon *see* **Germanus of Auxerre**

Harold of Gloucester (St) M. Mar 25
d. 1168. He was a boy alleged to have been killed by Jews at Gloucester, England. His veneration was never approved.

Hartmann (Bl) B. R(CR). Dec 23
d. 1164. From near Passau, Austria, he was educated at the Augustinian monastery there and became the superior of the cathedral chapter of Salzburg in 1122 when it was reorganized under the Augustinian rule. He was superior of two other Augustinian houses before becoming bishop of Brixen in South Tyrol in 1140. He had the respect of Emperor Frederick Barbarossa and of the pope as well as of the poor people of his diocese. He founded the famous Augustinian monastery of Neustift near Brixen, and had his cultus confirmed for the latter place in 1784.

Hartwig (Bl) B. Jun 14
d. 1023. He was archbishop of Salzburg, Austria, from 991.

Haruch (St) B. R(OSB). Jul 15
d. *c*830. He was abbot of Amorbach and then bishop of Verden near Bremen, Germany.

Hatebrand (St) R(OSB). Jul 30
d. 1198. A Frieslander, he became a Benedictine at Utrecht, Netherlands, and went on to be made abbot of Oldenklooster near Groningen in his native land in 1183. As such he revived Benedictine monachism throughout Friesland.

Hathawulf *see* **Hadulf**

Hatto (Bl) R(OSB). Jul 4
d. 985. A Swabian nobleman, he left all his property to the Benedictine abbey of Ottobeuren in Bavaria, Germany, and became a monk there. Afterwards he lived as a hermit, but the abbot thought that he was showing too much attachment to his former property and recalled him to community life. He readily obeyed.

Heart-of-Jesus Gómez Vives (Bl) *see* **Angela-of-St-Joseph Lloret Martí and Comps**

Hebed-Jesus *see* **Abdiesus**

Hedda of Peterborough and Comps (SS) MM. RR(OSB). Apr 9
d. 870. The abbot of Peterborough, England, and eighty-four monks of his community were slain by the Danes in a raid and subsequently venerated as martyrs (although they were probably not killed for their faith).

Hedda of Winchester (St) B. R. Jul 7
d. 705. An Anglo-Saxon monk and abbot, probably of Whitby, he was made bishop of Dorchester-on-Thames near Oxford, England, in 676 and transferred the see to Winchester. He was a great benefactor of the abbey of Malmesbury and the chief adviser of the king of Wessex.

Hedwig (Jadwiga) of Poland (St) L. Jul 17
1373-1399. Being the younger daughter of King Louis I of Hungary and thus a descendent of Charles of Anjou, she was elected and crowned Queen of Poland in 1384 when aged ten. In 1386 she was married to Jogaila, Grand Duke of Lithuania, thus uniting the two countries under one rule. Lithuania was still pagan, the last country in Europe to be so, and Jogaila's baptism before his marriage started its conversion. St Hedwig, a woman of extraordinary piety and kindness, encouraged this by her patronage of religion and scholarship and her work established the Polish-Lithuanian state as a power in Europe under her successors, the Jagiełłonian dynasty. She was also the founder of the Jagiełłonian University at Cracow, which became a major repository of Polish culture. Dying at Cracow, she was canonized in 1997.

Hedwig (Jadwiga) of Silesia (St) L. Oct 16
?1174–1243. Born at Andechs in Bavaria, Germany, but of Moravian descent, she was a daughter of the duke of Croatia and an aunt of St Elizabeth of Hungary. She was educated at the Benedictine nunnery of Kitzingen and married the Piast prince of Silesia, head of the Polish royal family, at the age of twelve. She bore him seven children who later caused great anxiety to their parents. The couple fostered religious life in Silesia, bringing in the orders of friars and founding the Cistercian nunnery at Trzebnica as the first nunnery in the country. Under their rule the imposition of German culture in Silesia was well advanced. She retired to Trzebnica in her widowhood but never took vows as a nun. She was canonized in 1267.

Hegesippus (St) C. Apr 7
d. *c*180. A Jewish convert from Jerusalem, he spent twenty years in Rome. Reputed the father of ecclesiastical history, he was the first to trace the succession of bishops of Rome from St Peter to his own day. Only a few chapters of his work survive. It was commended by Eusebius and by St Jerome, who knew it well and made use of it.

Heimerad (St) R. Jun 28
d. 1019. From Messkirch in Baden, Germany, he was a serf who became a priest and was chaplain to the lady of his manor before becoming a wandering pilgrim. He eventually

settled at Hasungenberg near Kassel as a hermit, and became famous for his miracles, asceticism and odd behaviour. His popular local cultus has not been confirmed.

Helan (St) R. Oct 7
C6th. An Irish monk, he emigrated to France with (allegedly) six brothers and three sisters and settled near Rheims as a missionary priest during the episcopate of St Remigius.

Heldrad (Eldrad) (St) R(OSB). Mar 13
d. ?842. From Provence, France, he spent his large fortune in charity and then went on pilgrimage to Rome. After many wanderings he joined the abbey of Novalese in the Italian Alps below Mont-Cenis pass, and became abbot for thirty years. He built much, including a hospice at the summit of the pass, and augmented the library. His cultus was approved in 1904.

Helen *see* **Alena**

Helen (St) *see* **Centolla and Helen**

Helen of Auxerre (St) L. May 22
d. *p*418. A young woman, she is mentioned in the acta of St Amator of Auxerre, France, as being present with him at his death.

Helen Duglioli (Bl) L. Sep 23
1472–1520.From Bologna, Italy, she married against her own inclinations in order to please her mother, yet lived a happy married life for thirty years. After her husband's death she occupied herself completely with works of charity. Already revered during her life, she was the object of a popular cultus after her death which was confirmed for Bologna in 1828.

Helen the Empress (St) Aug 18
*c*250–330. From Bithynia in Asia Minor (certainly not from Britain), she became the wife of Constantius Chlorus (who divorced her) and the mother of the emperor Constantine. She became a Christian after the Edict of Milan in 313 and afterwards lived mostly at Rome. She helped to build many churches there and in the Holy Land and made a famous visit to Jerusalem during which (according to a later tradition) she found the True Cross. Her porphyry sarcophagus is still extant in the Vatican Museum.

Helen Enselmini (Bl) R(OFM). Nov 4
d. 1242. From Padua, Italy, when aged twelve she became a Poor Clare nun at Arcella near her native city. It was alleged that her only food for months on end was the Eucharist. Before her

St Helen the Empress, Aug 18

death she became blind and dumb. Her cultus was approved for Padua in 1695.

Helen Guerra (Bl) R. F. Dec 23
1835–1914. The founder of the 'Sisters of St Zita', also called the 'Handmaids of the Holy Spirit', she was born and died at Lucca in Tuscany, Italy. She had a strong devotion to the Holy Spirit and to the propagation of the faith, and taught St Gemma Galgani. Her congregation is prominent in mission territories.

Helen (Ilona) of Hungary (Bl) R(OP). Nov 9
d. *c*1270. A Dominican nun at Veszprém, Hungary, she was the novice mistress of St Margaret of Hungary and was reputed to have the stigmata. She has an unconfirmed cultus in Hungary and in the Dominican order.

Helen (Heliada) of Ohren (St) R. Jun 20
d. *c*750. She was abbess of the nunnery of Ohren at Trier, Germany.

Helen (Yolanda, Iolantha) of Poland (Bl) R(OFM). Mar 6
d. 1298. A daughter of the king of Hungary and a niece of St Elizabeth, in 1256 she married King Boleslas V of Poland, after whose death in 1129 she lived as a Poor Clare at Gniezno. Her cultus was approved for Gniezno in 1827.

Helen of Skövde (St) M. L. Jul 31
d. *c*1160. A Swedish noblewoman, when left a widow she spent her fortune on the poor and on the Church, still in the process of being established in Sweden. In a family feud connected with a pagan reaction she was waylaid on her way to the church at Skövde and murdered.

Helen Valentini (Bl) T(OSA). Apr 23
d. 1458. Married to a knight of Udine near Venice, Italy, she was known in her city both for her devotion to her husband and large family for twenty-five years and for her charity and austerities as an Augustinian tertiary after her husband's death. Her cultus was confirmed for Udine in 1848.

Helentrude (St) R. May 31
d. *c*950. She was a hermit at Neuenheerse in Westphalia, Germany, and features in the legends concening St Ursula.

Heliconis (Helconides) (St) M. May 28
d. ?250. A woman from Thessalonika, she was seized at Corinth, Greece, and beheaded in the reign of Decius.

Helier (Helerous) (St) M. R. Jul 16
d. ?558. From Tongeren near Liege, Belgium, he went to live as a hermit on the island of Jersey and was murdered by robbers whom he was endeavouring to convert.

Helimenas (St) *see* **Parmenius and Comps**

Heliodorus (St) *see* **Mark, Alphius, and Comps**

Heliodorus, Dausa, Mariahle, Abdiso and Comps (SS) MM. Aug 20
d. 362. Of a group of 9000 Christians being deported by the Persians, 300 were selected by Shah Shapur II and invited to apostatize. Two hundred and seventy-five refused and were martyred, including **Abdicius** (q.v.).

Heliodorus, Desan, Marjab and Comps (SS) MM. Apr 9
d. ?355. Heliodorus was a bishop in Mesopotamia who was martyred with two priests and many of his people in the persecution of Shapur II, Shah of Persia.

Heliodorus, Venustus and Comps (SS) MM. May 6
C3rd. They are listed as seventy-seven who were martyred in the reign of Diocletian. Heliodorus and seven others seem to have been martyred in Africa, and St Ambrose claimed the greater part of the rest for Milan.

Heliodorus of Altinum (St) B. Jul 3
?332–390. A Dalmatian, when young he became a close friend of St Jerome whom he followed to the Holy Land and helped in the preparation of the Vulgate, financially and otherwise. Later he settled in Aquileia, Italy, and was made bishop of Altinum near Venice, a small town since destroyed. He was a great bishop and a brave opponent of Arianism.

Heliodorus of Magidus and Comps (SS) MM. Nov 21
d. *c*270.They were martyred at Magidus in Pamphylia, Asia Minor, in the reign of Aurelian.

Helladius (St) *see* **Crescens of Rome and Comps**

Helladius (St) *see* **Theophilus and Helladius**

Helladius of Auxerre (St) B. May 8
d. 387. Bishop of Auxerre, France, for thirty years, he converted St Amator, his eventual successor, to a devout life.

Helladius of Toledo (St) B. R. Feb 18
d. 632. From Toledo, Spain, he was a military officer at the Visigothic court before joining the abbey of Agali (Agallia) near Toledo, going on to become its abbot in 605. He was made archbishop of Toledo in 615.

Hemiterius and Cheledonius
(SS) MM. March 3
C4th? Allegedly two soldiers, they were martyred at Calahorra in Old Castile, Spain. Their acta have been lost, but both Prudentius and St Gregory of Tours mention them.

Hemma *see* **Gemma**

Hemma, Empress (Bl) R. Jan 31
?808–876. Wife of Emperor Louis the German and mother of Bl Irmengard and Emperor Charles the Fat, she became the abbess-founder of the nunnery of Obermünster near Regensburg, Germany.

Hemming (Bl) B. May 22
d. 1366. From Bälinge, Sweden, he became bishop of Turku in Finland (then Åbo, the capital of Swedish-ruled Finland). He and St Brigid held each other in esteem.

Henedina (St) *see* **Justa, Justina and Henedina**

Henrietta-of-Jesus de Croissy (Bl) *see* **Compiègne (Carmelite Martyrs of)**

Henrietta-of-the-Annunciation Faurie (Bl) *see* **Orange (Martyrs of)**

Henry
Originally a Teutonic name, it was rendered into Henricus in Latin and common vernacular variants are: German, Heinrich; French, Henri; Danish, Eric; Spanish and Portuguese, Enrique; Hungarian, Emeric; Italian, Enrico, Arrigo or Amerigo (whence America).

Henry II, Emperor (St) L. Jul 13
973–1024. The last emperor of the Saxon dynasty was born in Bavaria, Germany, educated by St Wolfgang of Regensburg and, as duke of Bavaria, was elected emperor in 1002 on the death of Otto III. He was crowned by the pope in 1014. With his wife St Cunegund he tried hard to establish peace and prosperity in the Empire through the proper establishment of the Ottonian system of administration, which gave an important role to bishops and monasteries. He was genuinely interested in the welfare of the Church, was determined in the imposition of ecclesiastical discipline where needed and favoured the Benedictine reform movements, especially of Gorze. His grants to the imperial bishops enabled them to function as secular rulers and he founded the see of Bamberg out of his own patrimony (his marriage was childless, which led to the legend that it had not been consummated). His justice, tempered with mercy, made him a popular ruler. Much legendary material was added to his biography after his death and before he was canonized in 1146, including the story that he had tried to become a Benedictine (which led to his being declared patron of Benedictine oblates by Pope St Pius X).

Henry Abbot (Bl) M. L. Jul 4
d. 1597. From Howden, Yorks, he was a layman who converted and was hanged at York for this reason with BB Edward Fulthrop, Thomas Bosgrave and William Andleby. He was beatified in 1929. *See* **England (Martyrs of)**.

Henry Betrán Llorca (Bl) *see* **Hospitaller Martyrs of Spain**

Henry of Bonn (Bl) M. L. Oct 18
d. 1147. A German nobleman, he set out on the Second Crusade in 1147, but stopped off to help the Portuguese conquer Lisbon from the Muslims. He died in the fighting and was venerated as a martyr.

Henry Canadell Quintana (Bl) *see* **Dionysius Pamplona Polo and Comps**

Henry of Clairvaux (Bl) R(OCist). Jul 14
d. 1189. From Marcy in Burgundy, France, he became a Cistercian monk at Clairvaux in 1155 and abbot there in 1176. He was involved in trying to convert the Albigenses in southern France, and helped preach the Third Crusade in Germany (which took place after his death).

Henry of Cologne (Bl) R(OP). Oct 23
d. 1225. One of the earliest Dominicans, he was recruited as a student at the university of Paris and became the first prior of the friary at Cologne, Germany.

Henry of Coquet (St) R. Jan 16
d. 1127. A Dane by birth, he went into exile and became a hermit on Coquet Island off the coast of Northumberland, England. The island belonged to the priory of Tynemouth to which he was affiliated, and he was buried in the priory church when he died.

Henry Ermès (Bl) *see* **September (Martyrs of)**

Henry Gallus of Albano (Bl)
B. R(OCist). Jul 4
d. 1188. A French Cistercian, he became cardinal bishop of Albano, Italy, in 1179 and died at Arras, France.

Henry Luzeau de la Mullonière and Henry Millet (BB) *see* **September (Martyrs of)**

Henry Morse (St) M. R(SJ). Feb 1
1549–1645. A convert from Brome in Suffolk, after working as a lawyer in London he studied for the priesthood at Douai and in Rome. Returning to England in 1624, he became a Jesuit in prison at York in 1626 and then worked in London and as a military chaplain in the Low Countries. He was selfless in caring for victims of the plague in London of 1636, catching it and then recovering. Imprisoned in 1638 on the testimony of an informer, he was released, worked in various parts of the country, re-arrested nine years later and executed at Tyburn. An attractive character, he was canonized in 1970. *See* **England (Martyrs of)**.

Henry de Ossó y Cervelló
(Bl) P. F. Jan 27
1840–1896. Born near Tortosa, Spain, as a priest of that diocese he was inspired by St Teresa of Avila and became an proponent of her teaching on prayer. He founded the 'Society of St Teresa of Jesus' in order to catechize young women and girls and was also involved in other foundations and in publication. He was beatified in 1979.

Henry Rebuschini (Bl) R. May 10
1860–1938. From the shores of Lake Como, Italy, his family was wealthy and initially opposed his vocation to the priesthood. However, after being at university, in the army and in a family silk factory as an accountant he tried to become a diocesan priest but was prevented by illness. Then he joined the Camillans in 1887 at Verona, was ordained by the future Pope St Pius X in 1889 and settled at the Cremona community from 1899 until his death, being superior for eleven years. He was a true contemplative as well as a server of sick people, and was beatified in 1997.

Henry Samson (Bl) *see* **September (Martyrs of)**

Henry Suso (Bl) R(OP). Jan 23
?1295–1366. From Constance, Germany, he became a Dominican when young, was prior in several friaries and was an excellent spiritual director. He was one of the greatest Dominican mystics and his *Book of the Eternal Wisdom*, a classic of German mysticism, is still read. He died at Ulm and his cultus was approved for the Dominicans in 1831.

Henry (Rigo) of Treviso (Bl) L. Jun 10
d. 1315. From Bozen (Bolzano) in South Tyrol, he moved to Treviso near Venice, Italy, and worked as a labourer after his family died. When old he lived on alms. His cultus was confirmed for Treviso in 1750.

Henry of Uppsala (St) M. B. Jan 19
d. ?1156. The details of the career of the English 'Apostle of Finland' are obscure. One manuscript connects him with a trip that Nicholas Brakspear (the future Pope Adrian IV) made to Scandinavia. Made bishop of Uppsala in Sweden in ?1152, he was helped in his missionary activity by King St Eric IX. He then went to Finland as a member of a colonizing expedition led by the same king and was murdered by a Finn in unclear circumstances. He was regarded as a martyr and was canonized in 1158.

Henry Walpole (St) M. R(SJ). Apr 7
1558–1595. From Docking, Norfolk, before his conversion he was educated at Norwich, Cambridge (Peterhouse) and Gray's Inn. Then he studied for the priesthood at the English College at Rome, where he became a Jesuit in 1584 before his ordination in 1588. He was an army chaplain in the Netherlands and a seminary teacher in Spain before he went to England, but was arrested the day after his arrival at Bridlington in Yorkshire. He was executed at York and was canonized in 1970. *See* **England (Martyrs of)**.

Henry Webley (Bl) M. L. Aug 28
d. 1588. A layman from Gloucestershire, he was arrested at Chichester in Sussex for harbouring a priest and executed at Mile End Green in East London with Bl William Dean. He was beatified in 1987. *See* **England (Martyrs of)**.

Henry Zdick (Bl) B. R(OPraem). Jun 25
d. 1150. A son of King Vratislav I of Bohemia, he became bishop of Olmouc, Czech Republic, in 1126. In 1137 he went to the Holy Land and became a Premonstratensian at Jerusalem. On his return to his diocese he introduced the Premonstratensians in many places and founded the abbey of Strahov at Prague for them.

Heraclas (St) B. Jul 14
d. 247. Brother of St Plutarch the martyr, he was a philosophy student at Alexandria, Egypt, was converted by Origen and succeeded him as head of the catechetical school there. He became patriarch in 231.

Heracleas (St) *see* **Eutychius, Plautus and Heracleas**

Heraclides (St) *see* **Plutarch of Alexandria and Comps**

Heraclius (St) *see* **Alexander, Heraclius and Comps**

Heraclius (St) *see* **Felicissimus, Heraclius and Paulinus**

Heraclius (St) *see* **Paul, Heraclius and Comps**

Heraclius (St) *see* **Priscus II of Capua and Comps**

Heraclius and Zosimus (SS) MM. Mar 11
d. ?263. They were martyred at Carthage, Roman Africa, in the reign of Valerian and Gallienus.

Heraclius of Sens (St) B. Jun 8
d. ?515. From Sens, France, he became bishop there and was one of those present in the cathedral of Rheims at the baptism of Clovis in 496. He was buried at his monastic foundation of St John the Evangelist at Sens.

Heradius, Paul, Aquilinus and Comps (SS) MM. May 17
d. 303. These seven were listed as having been martyred at 'Noviodunum' in the reign of Diocletian. The place is traditionally identified with Nyon on the lake of Geneva, Switzerland, but seems rather to have been near Galați in Romania.

Herais *see* **Irais**

Herbert of Derwentwater (St) R. Mar 20
d. 687. A hermit on an island (later named after him) in Derwent Water in the Lake District, England, he was a friend of St Cuthbert and by tradition, died on the same day as him.

Herbert Hoscam (St) B. Aug 20
d. 1180. From England, he became archbishop of Conza di Campania, Italy, and is the patron of that place.

Herbert (Haberne, Herbern) of Tours (St) B. R. Oct 30
? He was allegedly an abbot of Marmoutier and afterwards archbishop of Tours, France, but his dates are uncertain.

Herculanus of Brescia (St) B. Aug 12
d. *c*550. He was a bishop of Brescia in Lombardy, Italy.

Herculanus of Perugia (St) B. Nov 7
d. 549. The unreliable tradition of Perugia, Italy, celebrates two bishops of this name, one martyred in the reign of Domitian (feast day Mar 1), and the other killed by the soldiers of the Ostrogothic leader Totilla. The former is probably a duplicate of the latter.

Herculanus of Piegare (Bl) R(OFM). Jun 1
d. 1541. From Piegare near Perugia, Italy, he became a Franciscan at Sarteano and was famous as a preacher throughout Italy. He died near Lucca and had his cultus confirmed for Massa de Carrara in 1860.

Herculanus of Porto (St) M. Sep 5
d. ? 180. He was martyred at Porto near Rome, probably in the reign of Marcus Aurelius.

Herculanus of Rome (St) M. Sept 25
C2nd. He is mentioned in the untrustworthy acta of Pope St Alexander I as a Roman soldier who was converted by that pope and martyred shortly afterwards.

Herebald (Herband) (St) R. Jun 11
C8th. There is a church in Brittany, France, dedicated to this local hermit, an alleged Anglo-Saxon exile.

Herena (St) *see* **Donatus, Justus and Comps**

Herenia (St) *see* **Cyril, Rogatus and Comps**

Hereswitha (St) R Sep 3
d. *c*690. A princess of Northumbria, England, a sister of St Hilda and mother of SS Sexburga, Withburga and Ethelburga, she spent the last years of her life as a nun at Chelles, France.

Heribald (St) B. R(OSB). Apr 25
d. *c*857. He was a Benedictine monk and abbot of St Germanus at Auxerre, France, before becoming bishop of the same city.

Heribert (St) B. Mar 16
d. 1021. From Worms, Germany, he was educated at the monastic school of Gorze,

became the chancellor of Emperor Otto III and was made archbishop of Cologne in 998. A great churchman, well informed and enterprising, he was buried at the abbey he founded at Deutz on the Rhine. His extant bull of canonization is a forgery.

Herlinda and Relinda (SS) RR. Oct 12
d. *c*745 and 750 resp. They were educated at the nunnery at Valenciennes, France, and their father, an Austrasian noble, founded for them the nunnery of Maaseik, Belgium, north of Maastricht. They became respectively first and second abbesses, and were friends of SS Willibrord and Boniface.

Herluin (Bl) R(OSB). Aug 26
d. 1078. From Normandy, France, he was brought up to be a knight and served the count of Brionne before deciding to become a monk. He became abbot-founder of a monastery on his own estate at Bonneville, which moved to a new site on the banks of the river Bec in 1040. One of the first novices was Bl Lanfranc, and later St Anselm joined. Under these three men Bec became arguably the greatest centre of learning of western Christendom at the time. Herluin's relics are extant at Bec.

Bl Herluin of Bec, Aug 26

Herluka (St) R. Apr 18
d. 1127. She was initially a nun at Epfach, but was expelled for supporting the papacy against the Emperor and transferrred to Bernried near Augsburg, Germany.

Hermagoras and Fortunatus (SS) MM. Jul 12
d. ?66. According to their spurious legend, St Hermagoras was a disciple of St Mark, by whom he was appointed first bishop of Aquileia, Italy, only to be beheaded in the reign of Nero with his deacon, Fortunatus.

Herman *see* **Germanus**

Herman 'Contractus' of Reichenau (Bl) R(OSB). Sep 24
1013–1054. A nobleman's son who was severely crippled (hence his nickname), when aged seven he became a child oblate at the abbey of Reichenau on the Rhine, Germany, above Basel. He became a polymath and a famous religious poet, knowing Greek and Arabic and writing on theology, astronomy, mathematics and history. His cultus was confirmed in 1863.

Herman of Heidelberg (Bl) R(OSB). Sep 3
d. ?1326. He became a Benedictine monk at Niederaltaich in Bavaria, Germany, in 1320 and went on to be a hermit at Rinchnach (near Passau), where there is a local cultus.

Herman Joseph of Steinfeld (St) R(OPraem). Apr 7
*c*1150–1241. From Cologne, when aged seven he began to have mystical experiences which made him famous throughout Germany. Joining the Premonstratensians at Steinfeld in the Eifel, he served as sacristan, gained his nickname through a mystical marriage to Our Lady and helped propagate the spurious legend of St Ursula. He has left some mystical writings, and had his cultus confirmed in 1958.

Hermas (St) M? B? May 9
C1st. A Roman, he was mentioned by St Paul in his Letter to the Romans (16:14). A Byzantine tradition makes him a bishop of Philippi and a martyr.

Hermas, Serapion and Polyaenus (SS) MM. Aug 18
? They were listed as Roman martyrs who were dragged by their feet over rough ground by a pagan mob until they died, but the first seems to be the Hermes celebrated on Aug 28 and the other two to be from Alexandria.

Hermas (St) *see* **Nicander and Hermas**

Hermellus *see* **Hermylus**

Hermenegild the Goth (St) M. L. Apr 13
d. 586. Son of Leovigild, the Visigothic king of Spain, he married a Frankish Catholic princess

and was a subsidiary ruler at Seville. He became a Catholic and rebelled against his father, but was captured and executed. St Gregory the Great alleged that this was as a result of his conversion, but this is not confirmed by other contemporary authors. His cultus was confined to local calendars in 1969.

Hermenegild of Salcedo (St) R(OSB). Nov 5
d. 953. A Benedictine of Salcedo in the diocese of Tuy in Galicia, Spain, he was one of those under St Rudesind who helped to spread to spread the Benedictine rule throughout the region.

Hermengaudius (Armengol) (St) B. Nov 3
d. 1035. Bishop of Urgell in the Pyrenees, Spain, from 1010 till 1035, he built the cathedral and gave its canons a rule of life based on that of St Augustine.

Hermenland (Hermeland, Herblain, Erblon) (St) R. Mar 25
d. *c*720. He had been a cup-bearer at the Frankish royal court before he became a monk at Fontenelle in Normandy, France, under St Lambert. Then he became the first abbot of a daughter foundation on the island of Aindre in the estuary of the Loire near Nantes, where the suburb of St Herblain now stands.

Hermes (St) *see* **Philip, Severus and Comps**

Hermes (St) *see* **Publius, Victor and Comps**

Hermes, Adrian and Comps (SS) MM. Mar 1
d. *c*290. According to the old Roman Martyrology they were twenty-six who were martyred at Marseilles, France, in the reign of Maximian Herculeus. They are now generally identified with the Massylitan martyrs on whose feast-day St Augustine delivered a discourse. The original reading of the martyrology was Massylis (Marula) in Numidia, Roman Africa, the spelling of which is very similar to the Latin Massilia (Marseilles).

Hermes, Haggai and Gaius (SS) MM. Jan 4
d. *c*300. There is some uncertainty as to where these martyrs were killed. The old Roman Martyrology listed them as dying at Bologna in the reign of Maximian but this is not the city in Italy, where the former feast in their honour was abolished in 1914. It could have been Bologna, a town of Mycia, Asia Minor, or Bononia on the Danube.

Hermes of Rome (1) and Comps (SS) MM. Aug 28
C3rd? According to the very dubious acta of Pope St Alexander, they were Romans martyred with him in the reign of Hadrian. Their cultus, however, (which was confined to local calendars in 1969) was both ancient and widespread.

Hermes of Rome (2) (St) M. Dec 31
d. *c*270. Listed as a Roman exorcist, he is believed to have been martyred in the reign of Aurelian but may be the same as the Hermes, companion of Haggai and Gaius.

Hermias (St) M. May 31
d. 170. A veteran soldier, he was martyred at Comana in Cappodocia, Asia Minor (not in Pontus, as Baronius had had inserted in the old Roman Martyrology) and has a prominent place in the Byzantine liturgy.

Hermione (St) V. Sep 4
d. ?117. One of the daughters of Philip the Deacon, she is mentioned in the Acts of the Apostles (21:9) as a prophetess and, by tradition, died a martyr at Ephesus.

Hermippus and Hermocrates (SS) *see* **Hermolaus, Hermippus and Hermocrates**

Hermogenes (St) *see* **Evodius, Hermogenes and Callistus**

Hermogenes (St) *see* **Mennas, Hermogenes and Eugraphus**

Hermogenes (St) *see* **Peter and Hermogenes**

Hermogenes, Donatus and Comps (SS) MM. Dec 12
? Twenty-four martyrs, they are merely listed as having been driven into a marsh and there left to perish of cold and exhaustion. No other details are known.

Hermogenes of Melitene and Comps (SS) MM. Apr 19
C4th. Armenian martyrs, they are believed to have died at Melitene (although they have no cultus in the East). The companions are Gaius, Expeditus (or Elpidius), Aristonicus, Rufus and Galata. The cultus of St Expeditus as a patron against procrastination dates from C17th Germany.

Hermogius (St) B. R(OSB). Jun 26
d. ?942. From Tuy in Galicia, Spain, he founded the abbey of Labrugia in 915 and became a

bishop. He was taken prisoner by the Muslims and brought to Cordoba, but was subsequently released. His nephew, the boy St Pelagius, was kept there as a hostage. He then resigned and became a monk at Ribas del Sil.

Hermolaus, Hermippus and Hermocrates (SS) MM. Jul 27
d. ?305. According to the tradition Hermolaus, an old priest of Nicomedia, Asia Minor, converted St Pantaleon the imperial physician and was martyred with him and with the two brothers Hermippus and Hermocrates.

Hermylus and Stratonicus (SS) MM. Jan 13
d. 315. Hermylus, a deacon of Singidunum (near Belgrade, Yugoslavia), and Stratonicus, his servant, were drowned in the Danube in the reign of Licinius. Their acta are, however, unreliable.

Herodion, Asyncritus and Phlegon (SS) MM. Apr 8
C1st. St Paul refers to them in his letter to the Romans (Rom 16:11), the first as his relative. Their legends allege that they became become bishops: Herodion of Neopatras in Thessaly, Asyncritus of Marathon and Phlegon of Hyrcania.

Heron (St) *see* **Plutarch of Alexandria and Comps**

Heron, Arsenius, Isidore and Dioscorus (SS) MM. Dec 14
d. 250. The first three were burned to death at Alexandria, Egypt, in the reign of Decius. Dioscorus, a boy, was merely whipped and set free.

Heron of Antioch (St) M? B. Oct 17
d. ?136. A disciple of St Ignatius of Antioch, Syria, he succeeded him as bishop in ?116. He is doubtfully listed as a martyr.

Heros (St) *see* **Orentius, Heros and Comps**

Herulf (Hariolf) (St) B. R. Aug 13
d. 785. A son of the count of Ellwangen near Ulm, Germany, he became a monk at St Gall and later founded an abbey at Ellwangen in 764. Afterwards he became bishop of Langres, France.

Herundo (St) *see* **Romula, Redempta and Herundo**

Hervey the Blind (St) R. Jun 17
d. ?575. The son of a Welsh minstrel at the Frankish court at Paris, France, and blind from birth, he was taken as a child to Brittany, where he grew up to become a teacher and a minstrel himself. Though blind he became abbot of Plouvien, whence he migrated with part of his community to Lanhouarneau. He is still a popular saint in Brittany and is represented as a blind man being led about by a wolf.

Hervey of Tours (St) R. Apr 16
d. 1021. From near Tours, France, he became treasurer of the abbey of St Martin there and went on to be a hermit.

Hesperius *see* **Exuperius**

Hesychius (St) *see* **Diomedes, Julian and Comps**

Hesychius (St) *see* **Faustus, Didius and Comps**

Hesychius (St) *see* **Hieron, Nicander and Comps**

Hesychius (St) *see* **Peregrine, Lucian and Comps**

Hesychius (St) *see* **Torquatus, Ctesiphon and Comps**

Hesychius of Antioch (St) M. Nov 18
d. ?303. A Roman soldier and officer, master of the palace at Antioch, Syria, he threw away his military belt (part of his insignia) and proclaimed himself a Christian when the emperor Maximian ordered a persecution. As a punishment for this he was dressed as a woman and drowned in the River Orontes.

Hesychius of Durostorum (St) M. Jun 15
d. ?302. A Roman soldier, he was martyred at Durostorum (now Silistra in Bulgaria) with St Julian.

Hesychius of Gaza (St) R. Oct 3
d. ?380. A disciple of St Hilarion, he became a monk under him at Majuma near Gaza in the Holy Land. He followed his master in the latter's attempts to find solitude and, when Hilarion fled to Sicily, Hesychius spent three years searching for him. At Hilarion's death in 311 he took the body back to Majuma, where he lived until his own death.

Hesychius of Vienne (St) B. Mar 16
d. *c*490. A senator, he became bishop of Vienne, France, and was the father of St Avitus, his successor.

Hewald *see* **Ewald**

Hia *see* **Ia**

Hidulf of Lobbes (St) R. Jun 23
d. ?707. Count of Hainault and an Austrasian courtier, he married St Aye but they became consecrated religious by mutual consent. He entered the abbey of Lobbes near Charleroi, Belgium, which he had helped to found.

Hidulf of Trier (St) B. R. Jul 11
d. 707. From Regensburg in Bavaria, Germany, he became a monk at Trier and was later ordained as a regionary bishop. In ?676 he resigned and became abbot-founder of Moyenmoutier in the Jura, France. When he died he was abbot both of this and of Bonmoutier (afterwards called Saint-Dié) nearby.

Hierlath *see* **Jarlath**

Hieron, Nicander, Hesychius and Comps (SS) MM. Nov 7
d. *c*300. A group of thirty-three, they were martyred at Mitilene in Armenia in the reign of Diocletian.

Hieronides, Leontius, Serapion and Comps (SS) MM. Sep 12
d. *c*300. Hieronides was a very old deacon, and Leontius and Serapion were brothers. They were thrown into the sea at Alexandria, Egypt, in the reign of Diocletian with Seleucus (not, as listed, Selesius), Valerian and Straton.

Hieronymus *see* **Jerome**

Hierotheus (St) B. Oct 4
? It is likely that the alleged teacher and friend of St Dionysius the Areopagite either never existed or was of the C4th or the C5th. He has been claimed as bishop of Athens, of Jerusalem or of Segovia in Spain (the last is certainly false).

Hieu (St) R. Sep 2
d. *c*657. A young woman of Northumbria, England, she was allegedly the first nun in that kingdom, being clothed by St Aidan at Hartlepool. She became abbess there but left and founded a nunnery at a place near Tadcaster, Yorks, later called Healaugh after her. She is alleged by some to be identical with St Bega.

Hilaria (St) *see* **Claudius, Hilaria and Comps**

Hilaria (St) *see* **Donata, Paulina and Comps**

Hilaria, Digna and Comps (SS) MM. Aug 12
d. *c*304. Hilaria, alleged to be the mother of St Afra of Augsburg, was seized with her three maids while visiting her tomb and burned alive. The companions (Quiriacus, Euprepia, Eunomia, Quiriacus, Largio, Crescentian, Nimmia, Juliana and another twenty) were Roman martyrs buried on the Ostian Way who allegedly died on the same day.

Hilarinus (St) *see* **Altigianus and Hilarinus**

Hilarinus (St) *see* **Donatus and Hilarinus**

Hilarinus of Perse (St) M. P. Jun 15
C8th. A secular priest and schoolmaster in the Frankish Empire, he was killed by marauders at his base at Perse on the Lot River, France. His cultus was confirmed for Rodez in 1883.

Hilarion (St) *see* **Proclus and Hilarion**

Hilarion the Great (St) R. Oct 21
?291–?371. From Gaza in the Holy Land, he became a Christian and a disciple of St Anthony the Great while studying at Alexandria, Egypt. On his return to Gaza he was the first local Christian hermit in the desert nearby, but attracted so many disciples that he was able to found several monasteries. The latter part of his life was occupied with escaping from the crowds who followed him on account of his miracles. He lived on Mt Sinai, also in Egypt, Sicily, Dalmatia and finally on Cyprus, where he died at Paphos. His cultus in the Latin rite was confined to particular calendars in 1969.

Hilary (St) *see* **Demetrius, Concessus and Comps**

Hilary (St) *see* **Florentinus, Hilary and Aphrodisius**

Hilary (St) *see* **Valentine and Hilary**

Hilary (Hilarus), Pope (St) Feb 28
d. 468. From Sardinia, he held high office in the Roman curia under St Leo the Great, who sent him as papal legate to the 'Robber Synod of Ephesus' in 449 (from which he narrowly escaped with his life). He became pope in 461, and fought energetically against the Nestorian and Monophysite heresies. Under him the first recorded synod was held at Rome.

Hilary, Tatian, Felix, Largus and Dionysius (SS) MM. Mar 16
d. ?284. Hilary was a bishop of Aquileia, Italy,

Tatian was his deacon and the others were laymen. They were allegedly beheaded in the reign of Numerian.

Hilary of Arles (St) B. R. May 5
*c*400–449. From Lorraine, France, while still a pagan he held an important office in the local administration until St Honoratus, a relative, invited him to visit his monastery recently founded at Lérins. He was baptized and became a monk there, and when St Honoratus became archbishop of Arles he accompanied him as his secretary. He succeeded to the bishopric and was zealous in trying to establish metropolitan authority over other bishops of Gaul, which led him to be rebuked by Pope St Leo the Great. However his personal sanctity led him to be venerated even before his death.

Hilary of Carcassonne (St) B. Jun 3
C4th? He was bishop of Carcassonne, France.

Hilary Delgado Vílchez (Bl) *see* **Hospitaller Martyrs of Spain**

Hilary of Galeata (St) R. May 15
d. 558. A hermit near Faenza in Tuscany, Italy, he gathered his disciples into a new monastery called Galeata (afterwards known as Sant' Ilaro della Paglia). Initially this had a rule of which he was the author, but later it became Camaldolese.

Hilary-Mary Llorente Martín (Bl) *see* **Philip-of-Jesus Munárriz Azcona and Comps**

Hilary of Mende (St) B. Oct 25
d. 535 From Mende in the Massif Central, France, he became a hermit under the influence of the monastery of Lérins (where he spent some time) and founded a monastery before being made bishop of his native city.

Hilary of Pavia (St) B. May 16
d. 376. Bishop of Pavia near Milan, Italy, he was an opponent of Arianism.

Hilary of Poitiers (St) B. Dr. Jan 13
?315–?368. Of a pagan patrician family at Poitiers, France, he studied rhetoric and philosophy and married young. Shortly afterwards he became a Christian and was elected bishop of Poitiers in 353. He fought energetically against the Arianism of Emperor Constantius and was exiled to Phrygia, Asia Minor, for four years in 356. There he was able to study the theology of the Eastern fathers and to write his magisterial work on the Trinity. After his return he continued his powerful defence of the Nicene creed as well as introducing into the West much of Eastern trinitarian and christological thought, including the explanation of the divinity of Christ. He was declared a doctor of the Church in 1851.

Hilary of Toulouse(St) B. May 20
C4th. He was bishop of Toulouse, France.

Hilary of Volturno (St) R(OSB). Nov 21
d. ?1045. From Matera in Basilicata, Italy, he was abbot of St Vincent's Abbey at Volturno on the Gulf of Gaeta from 1011 to 1045. He revived the former splendour of his monastery.

Hilda (St) R. Nov 17
614–680. From Northumbria, England, and a relative of King St Edwin, she was baptized as a child in 631 by St Paulinus and became a nun at Hartlepool when aged thirty-three under the guidance of St Aidan. She became abbess in 649, and went on to become the first abbess of the double monastery (with monks and nuns) at Whitby in 657. The monastery held to the Celtic rule and liturgy and she herself was a determined opponent of the Romanizing policy of St Wilfrid. However the monastery was the venue of the Synod of Whitby, called by King Oswy in 664 in order to make a definitive choice between Roman and Celtic observances, and she and her community abided by its decision to prescribe the Roman rite. She died after a long illness.

Hildebert Ghent (St) M. R. Apr 4
d. 752. Abbot of the monastery of St Peter at Ghent, Belgium, he was killed by iconoclast fanatics for his defence of the validity of sacred images and was venerated as a martyr.

Hildebrand *see* **Gregory VII, Pope**

Hildebrand (Bl) *see* **Stephen and Hildebrand**

Hildegard, Empress (Bl) L. Apr 30
758–783. A daughter of the duke of Swabia, Germany, in 771 she married Charlemagne after he had repudiated his previous wife. They had eight children during their twelve years of marriage. She befriended St Lioba and is alleged to have founded Kempten abbey near Mainz, Germany, where she was buried.

Hildegard of Bingen (St) R(OSB). Sep 17
1098–1179. The 'Sibyl of the Rhine' was from Böckelheim in the Palatinate, Germany, and became a child-oblate at the nunnery at

Diessenberg when aged eight. As a young woman she was made superior there, and moved the community to Rupertsberg near Bingen in ?1147. She had mystical experiences from childhood and started publishing these when aged forty, becoming the first great German mystic. She denounced the vices of society and of the famous with fearlessness and justice, and her writings (which are prophetic, doctrinal and speculative) led her to be accused by numerous enemies. However she was defended by St Bernard and by his disciple, Pope Bl Eugene III. There has been much modern interest in her writings, music and art and several works have been translated into English (some tendentiously) and her music performed.

Hildegrin (St) B. Jun 19
d. ?827. He was a younger brother of St Ludger, and they worked together on the Saxon mission. He became bishop of Châlons-sur-Marne (France) in ?802, but retired when old to the abbey of Verden in Lower Saxony. There is no good evidence that he became a monk there.

Hildegund of Mehren (St)
R(OPraem). Feb 6
d. 1183. Wife of a count of Arnsberg, Germany, when widowed she founded a Premonstratensian nunnery at Mehren in the Eifel, entered as a nun with her daughter in the face of vehement family opposition and became prioress.

Hildegund 'Joseph' of Schönau
(Bl) R(OCist). Apr 20
d. 1188. Her romantic story, which may have an element of truth (unlike others with a similar plot), describes her as having made a pilgrimage from her native Rhineland to the Holy Land with her father while disguised as a boy. Then she entered the Cistercian abbey of Schönau near Heidelberg as a male novice, died as such and was only revealed as a woman after her death. Despite being in the Cistercian martyrology she has not had her cultus approved.

Hildelith (Hildilid, Hildeltha)
(St) R. Mar 24
d. ?717. Possibly an Anglo-Saxon princess, she became a nun either at Chelles or at Faremoutiers-en-Brie in France (there being no nunneries in England at the time). She was recalled to England by St Erconwald to train her sister, St Ethelburga of Barking. When the latter became abbess Hildelith stayed on as one of her nuns and eventually succeeded her. A great abbess and a cultured woman, she was admired by SS Aldhelm, Bede and Boniface.

Hildemar of Arrouaise (Bl)
M. R(CR). Jan 13
d. ?1097. A German, he was a court chaplain to King William I of England before becoming a hermit at Arrouaise in Artois, France, in 1087. He was joined by many disciples for whom he founded the influential monastery of Arrouaise under the Augustinian rule for canons regular. He was killed by an assassin who posed as a novice.

Hildemar of Beauvais (St)
B. R(OSB). Dec 10
d. *p*844. A monk of Corbie, he became bishop of Beauvais, France, in 821.

Hildemarca (St) R. Oct 25
d. *c*670. A nun at St Eulalia's monastery at Bordeaux, France, she was appointed first abbess of Fécamp by St Wandrille, the founder.

Hilduard (Hilward, Garibald)
(St) B. R. Sep 7
d. *c*750. A missionary bishop in Flanders, he founded the abbey at Dikelvenne on the Schlede above Ghent, Belgium.

Hillonius *see* **Tilio**

Hiltrude (St) R. Sep 27
*c*740–*c*790. Daughter of the count of Poitou, France, she became a hermit attached to the abbey of Liessies which her father had founded and which had her brother as abbot.

Hiltutus *see* **Illtyd**

Himelin (St) R. Mar 10
d. *c*750. An Irish (or Scottish) priest, he died at Vissenaken near Louvain, Belgium, on his return from a pilgrimage to Rome. He is still venerated locally.

Himerius (Immer, Imier) (St) R. Nov 12
d. *c*610. A missionary monk in the Jura, he has a town in Bern canton, Switzerland, named St Imier after him.

Himerius of Amelia (St) B. Jun17
d. *c*560. A Calabrian hermit, he was made bishop of Ameila in Umbria, Italy. He was described as a very austere man, primarily with himself and also with others. His relics were taken to Cremona in 995, where he is venerated as a principal patron.

Hipparchus (St) *see* **Samosata (Martyrs of)**

Hippolytus (St) *see* **Eusebius, Marcellus and Comps**

Hippolytus (St) *see* **Felix, Symphronius and Comps**

Hippolytus of Antioch (St) M. Jan 30
? He was martyred at Antioch, Syria, but the details given in the old Roman Martyrology are borrowed from the story of St Hippolytus of Rome.

Hippolytus of Belley (St) B. R. Nov 28
d. ?775. A monk at St Claude in the Jura, France, he became bishop of Belley in 755 but resigned and returned to his abbey.

Hippolytus Galantini (Bl)
T(OFM). F. Mar 20
1565–1619. From Florence, Italy, he was a silk-weaver. When eleven years old he started to help priests in catechizing children and was imitated in this by others, whom he formed into the congregation of Italian Doctrinarians. It soon spread throughout Italy. He died at Florence and was beatified in 1825.

Hippolytus of Porto *Aug 22*
He is a duplication of St Hippolytus of Rome, the confusion having arisen through the latter having a basilica dedicated to him at Rome. The old Roman Martyrology listed him as a bishop of Porto martyred by drowning in the reign of Alexander. This assertion is false, and his cultus was suppressed in 1969.

Hippolytus of Rome (St) M. Aug 13
d. ?235. A native priest of Rome, he supported the rigourist faction over the question as to whether the Church could absolve those guilty of serious sin. He was the bitter enemy of Pope St Callistus I, and caused himself to be elected anti-pope. With St Pontian he was exiled to the Sardinian mines and was there probably reconciled to the Church before his martyrdom. He is one of the most important ecclesiastical writers of his time. His story has been overlaid by spurious legends, however, such as the one that connects him with the death of St Laurence. St Concordia (a genuine martyr about whom nothing is known) was also falsely linked with him and they (with companions) were celebrated with a common feast before 1969.

Hirenarchus (Irenarchus), Acacius and Comps (SS) MM. Nov 27
d. ?305. Acacius, a priest, was martyred with seven women at Sebaste in Armenia, Asia Minor. Hirenarchus was a hostile pagan who was converted by witnessing their courage and was martyred with them.

Hoger (St) B. R(OSB). Dec 20
d. ?916. A monk of Corvey, he succeeded St Adalgar as bishop of Hamburg-Bremen in 909, and upheld diocesan and monastic discipline at a time of barbarian incursions.

Holy Land (Martyrs of) (SS)
There are five groups of anonymous martyrs of the Holy Land listed in the old Roman Martyrology.

May 28
d. *c*410. There was a massacre of monks by Bedouin early in the reign of the emperor Theodosius II.

Feb 19
d. ?509. There was a raid by Bedouin allied to Persia and many hermits and monks were slaughtered.

May 16
d. ?614. Forty-four monks of the laura of Mar Saba were massacred during the invasion by Shah Chosroes II of Persia.

Jun 22
d. ?614. Allegedly 1480 were massacred at Samaria or in its neighbourhood during the same Persian invasion.

Aug 16
? A group of thirty-three martyrs, about whom no details are known.

Hoilde (St) *see* **Amata of Joinville**

Homobonus (St) L. Nov 13
d. 1197. A merchant of Cremona, Italy, he was famous in his city for his scrupulous honesty, his model family life and his charity to the poor. He died during Mass and was canonized within two years.

Honestus (St) M. Feb 16
d. 270. From Nîmes, France, he was converted, ordained and sent into Spain as a missionary by St Saturninus of Toulouse. He appears to have been martyred at Pamplona in Spanish Navarre, but rival claims have been made for Toulouse and Amiens.

Honorata (St) R. Jan 11
d. *c*500. The sister of St Epiphanius, bishop of Pavia, Italy, she was a nun at Pavia when the soldiers of Odoacer, the king of the Heruli, kidnapped her. She was ransomed by her brother and returned to Pavia.

Honoratus (St) *see* **Demetrius, Honoratus and Florus**

Honoratus (St) *see* **Dominic, Victor and Comps**

Honoratus, Fortunatus, Arontius and Sabinian (SS) MM. Aug 27 and Sep 1
d. 303. They were beheaded at Potenza (Italy) in the reign of Maximian, and are one of the groups commemorated under the title of 'The Twelve Brothers'.

Honoratus of Amiens (St) B. May 16
d. *c*600. From near Amiens, France, he became bishop there. The church and street of St Honoré in Paris take their name from him.

Honoratus of Arles (St) B. Jan 16
*c*350–429. Born probably in Lorraine of a Roman consular family, he converted from paganism in his youth and went to the East to study monasticism. Returning to the West, he founded a famous monastery on the Mediterranean island of Lérins, France. He was forced to accept the archbishopric of Arles in 426, but died three years later.

Honoratus of Fondi (St) R. Jan 16
C6th. The abbot-founder of the monastery of Fondi on the border between Lazio and Campania, Italy, he has a biography in the *Dialogues* of St Gregory the Great.

Honoratus Koźmiński of Biała Podlaska (Bl) R(OFMCap) Oct 13
1829–1916. Born near Lublin, Poland, he studied architecture at Warsaw and lost his faith in the process. But then he was imprisoned for a few months in 1846 on suspicion of conspiracy against the Russian government, caught typhoid and got his faith back. Once released, he joined the Capuchins in Warsaw and was ordained in 1852, becoming well known as a preacher, confessor and prison chaplain. His friary was suppressed after the Polish rebellion of 1863 and he ended up in a prison-friary at Nowa Miasto, where he died. He was beatified in 1988.

Honoratus I of Marseilles (St) B. Aug 31
d 492. A disciple of St Hilary of Arles, France, he became bishop of Marseilles in 475.

Honoratus II of Marseilles (St) B. Aug 31
d. *c*950. A bishop of Marseilles, France, he introduced the Benedictine rule to the ancient abbey of St Victor there.

Honoratus of Milan (St) B. Feb 8
d. 570. He became bishop of Milan, Italy, in 567 but fled into exile when the Lombards captured the city in 569 and died at Genoa.

Honoratus of Toulouse (St) B. Dec 21
C3rd. From Navarra, Spain, he succeeded St Saturninus as bishop of Toulouse, France.

Honoratus of Vercelli (St) B. Oct 28
*c*330–415. From Vercelli, Italy, he was educated there by St Eusebius, became a monk and accompanied his master into exile at Scythopolis in the Holy Land in 355. In 396 he was elected bishop of his native city on the recommendation of St Ambrose, whom he assisted on his deathbed.

Honoré *see* **Honoratus of Amiens**

Honorina (St) V. Feb 27
? She is an early martyr of Gaul but her acta have been lost. Her veneration is ancient in Normandy, France.

Honorius (St) *see* **Demetrius and Honorius**

Honorius (St) *see* **Mansuetus, Severus and Comps**

Honorius, Eutychius and Stephen (SS) MM. Nov 21
d. *c*300. They were martyred at Asta in Andalucia,Spain, in the reign of Diocletian.

Honorius of Brescia (St) B. Apr 24
d. ?586. A hermit near Brescia, Italy, he became bishop there in 577.

Honorius of Buzançais (Bl) M. Jan 9
d. ?1250. From Buzançais in Berry, France, he was a rich and charitable cattle merchant. On his return from a journey he found that he had been robbed by his servants and, when he remonstrated with them, they killed him at Parthenay in Poitou. There he is venerated as a martyr.

Honorius of Canterbury (St) B. R. Sep 30
d. 653. A Roman monk, he joined the mission of St Augustine in England in 601 and succeeded St Justus as archbishop of Canterbury in 627, being consecrated at Lincoln by St Paulinus. He himself ordained as bishops St Felix for the East Angles and St Ithamar (the first native bishop) for Rochester. His attribute is a baker's peel (shovel), often with loaves upon it.

Honorius-of-the-Sorrowing-Virgin Carracedo Ramos (Bl) *see* **Nicephorus Díez Tejerina and Comps**

Hope (St) *see* **Faith, Hope, and Charity**

Hormisdas, Pope (St) Aug 6
d. 523. From Frosinone in Lazio, Italy, he succeeded St Symmachus as pope in 514. He is best remembered for the profession of faith called the *Formula of Hormisdas* which was accepted in the East in the reign of Justin I (519), thus ending the Acacian schism. His son, St Silverius, became pope in 536.

Hormisdas the Persian (St) M? Aug 8
d. 420. A young Persian nobleman who held the office of satrap, he refused to apostatize and was degraded by Shah Bahram to the rank of army camel-driver and subsequently either executed or exiled.

Horres (St) *see* **Theusetas, Horres and Comps**

Horsiesius (Orsisius) (St) R. Jun 15
d. *c*380. A favourite disciple of St Pachomius in Egypt, after his master died in an epidemic he succeeded him as superior of the cenobites of Tabennesis. Meek and gentle, he oversaw the expansion of the congregation but lacked leadership qualities and resigned in favour of St Theodore after a revolt by some of the monks in 351. He became superior again when St Theodore himself died in 368. He is the author of an ascetical treatise which St Jerome translated into Latin.

Hortulanus (St) *see* **Valerian, Urban and Comps**

Hosanna Cosie (Bl) T(OP). Apr 27
d. 1565. Catherine was the daughter of Orthodox parents in Montenegro but became a Catholic at Cattaro (then under Venetian rule, now Kotor in Montenegro) and became a Dominican tertiary, taking the name of Hosanna. Her cultus was confirmed for Kotor in 1928.

Hospitius (St) R. May 21
d. *c*580. From Nice, France, he became a hermit nearby at the place now named Cap-Saint-Hospice after him.

Hospitaller Martyrs of Spain
(BB) MM. RR. Jul 30
d. 1936. In the year of the outbreak of the Civil War in Spain seventy-one Hospitallers of St John were shot by the Republicans. They were from Toledo, Tarragona, Barcelona, Madrid and Castile and also included seven Colombians who had been studying at Ciempozuelos at Madrid and who were seized at Barcelona when trying to return home. They were beatified in 1992. *See* **Spanish Civil War (Martyrs of)**.

Hroznata (Bl) M. R(OPraem). Jul 19
1160–1217. A Czech nobleman, he was a courtier of King Ottokar the Great of Bohemia before the death of his wife and baby son. Then he founded the Premonstratensian abbey of Teplá near the Bavarian border and became a monk there. He was seized by some local nobles who coveted the monastery's lands and died of starvation in a dungeon, being subsequently venerated as a martyr. His cultus was approved for Prague in 1897.

Hubert (Hugbert) of Brétigny
(St) R. May 30
d. ?714. At the age of twelve he entered the abbey of Brétigny near Soissons, France, despite the opposition of his family. There he led a severely ascetical life.

Hubert of Liege (St) B. R. Nov 3
d. 727. A Frankish courtier, he was widowed and (according to his late biography) was converted while he was out hunting in circumstances similar to those narrated of St Eustace and others. Then he is alleged to have become a hermit in the Ardennes or a monk at Stavelot. Eventually he succeeded St Lambert as bishop of Maastricht in about 706 and transferred the see to Liege in Belgium, being the first bishop there. He is venerated as the apostle of the Ardennes, which was a remaining stronghold of paganism.

Hugh of Ambronay (St) R(OSB). Oct 21
C9th–10th. He was abbot of the Benedictine monastery of Ambronay near Belley, France.

Hugh of Anzy-le-Duc (St)
R(OSB). Apr 20
d. *c*930. From Poitiers, France, he became a monk at St Savin's Abbey nearby and was later sent to several monasteries to revive their monastic observance. Latterly he helped Bl Berno to found the abbey of Cluny, and died as prior of Anzy-le-Duc.

Hugh of Bonnevaux (Bl) R(OCist). Apr 1
d. 1194. A nephew of St Hugh of Grenoble, he became a Cistercian at Mézières. He was made abbot of Leoncel in 1163, and transferred to Bonnevaux in the Jura, France, in 1169. He had unusual powers of divination and exorcism, but is chiefly remembered as the mediator between Pope Alexander III and Emperor Frederick Barbarossa.

Hugh Canefro (St) P. Oct 8
1168–1230. He was a chaplain of the Knights of St John of Jerusalem at Genoa, Italy.

Hugh Faringdon (Bl) *see* **Benedictine Martyrs of the Reformation**

Hugh of Fosse (Bl) R(OPraem). Feb 10
d. 1164. From Fosse near Namur, Belgium, he was chaplain to the bishop of Cambrai before becoming a monk at Prémontré under St Norbert, whose companion and assistant he became and whom he succeeded as abbot of Prémontré and superior general of the Premonstratensian order. His cultus was confirmed for Namur in 1927.

Hugh the Great (St) R(OSB). Apr 29
1024–1109. A nobleman from Samur, France, he became a monk at Cluny in 1039 and was elected abbot in 1049 when aged twenty-five. He was abbot for sixty years, and during this period was the adviser of nine popes, was consulted and revered by all the sovereigns of western Europe and governed over 1000 monasteries and dependent houses of the Cluniac congregation. The vast abbey church at Cluny, at 169m long the biggest in Europe until the new St Peter's in Rome, was consecrated in 1095. An extremely gifted man, he retained his humility and charity, founding a leper-hospital at Marcigny at which he nursed the inmates himself. He was canonized in 1120.

Hugh Green (Bl) M. P. Aug 19
d. 1642. From London, he was educated at Peterhouse, Cambridge before his conversion. Then he studied for the priesthood at Douai, was ordained there in 1612 and worked in Dorset before being captured and hanged at Dorchester. *See* **England (Martyrs of)**.

Hugh of Grenoble (St) B. R(OSB). Apr 1
1053–1132. From Châteauneuf d'Isère, France, when aged twenty-five he became a lay canon at Valence and was made bishop of Grenoble in 1080. Convinced of his own inefficiency in the struggle especially against simony and clerical concubinage, he resigned and became a monk at the austere monastery of Chaise-Dieu. Pope St Gregory VII refused his resignation, however. He gave to St Bruno the land for his new monastery at Grande Chartreuse.

Hugh of Lincoln (St) B. R(OCart). Nov 17
1140–1200. From near Grenoble, France, he became a canon regular locally but joined the Carthusians at Chartreuse in 1160. In 1175 he was invited by King Henry II of England to make the first English Carthusian foundation at Witham in Somerset, which he did in the face of many difficulties. He was made bishop of Lincoln in 1181, and governed justly and wisely. He began the present cathedral of Lincoln and defended and befriended the Jews of the city. He died at London while on an embassy to France, and the kings of England and Scotland helped to carry his body back to Lincoln. Canonized in 1220, he is usually depicted as a bishop but sometimes as a Carthusian, in either case accompanied by a pet swan (or with seven stars about him, in mistake for St Hugh of Grenoble).

Hugh of Lincoln, the Lesser
(St) M. Aug 18
d. 1255 A boy of Lincoln, England, when aged nine he was murdered and thrown down a well. After a judicial inquiry, headed by King Henry III, eighteen Jews were executed for having allegedly killed 'Little Hugh' in a parody of the Crucifixion. His veneration was very popular in the Middle Ages but was an expression of anti-Semitism (paralleled by at least twelve cases of similar alleged ritual murders elsewhere) and was never officially confirmed.

Hugh dei Lippi-Uguccioni
(St) R(OSM). F. Feb 17
d. 1282. He accompanied St Philip Benizi to France and Germany and was vicar-general of the order in Germany for eight years. He died on Mt Senario, Italy. *See* **Servites, Founders of**.

Hugh of Mâcon (Bl) B. R(OCist). Oct 10
d. 1151. A Cistercian monk under St Stephen Harding, he became abbot of Pontigny in 1114 and bishop of Auxerre, France, in 1137, the first Cistercian to be made a bishop.

Hugh More (Bl) M. L. Aug 28
d. 1588. From Grantham in Lincolnshire, he was educated at Oxford and at Gray's Inn, London, before becoming a convert at Rheims. He was hanged as a result at Lincoln's Inn Fields in London and beatified in 1929. *See* **England (Martyrs of)**.

Hugh of Noara (St) R(OCist). Nov 17
d. *p*1172. He was the first abbot of the Cistercian abbey of Noara, Sicily.

Hugh of Rouen (St) B. R. Apr 9
d. 730. A Frankish nobleman, when very young he apparently became a monk at either Fontenelle or Jumièges. Then he became vicar-general of Metz, France, and was then made bishop of Rouen and of Paris, also abbot of Fontenelle and of Jumièges. Before his death, however, he resigned all these offices and died at Jumièges as a simple monk.

Hugh of Sassoferrato (Bl) R(OSB Silv). Sep 19
d. *c*1290. From Serra San Quirico near Camerino, Italy, after studying at Bologna he became a monk under St Silvester, whose devoted disciple he was. He died at Sassoferrato, and his cultus was approved for Nocera in 1717.

Hugh Taylor (Bl) M. P. Nov 26
1562–1585. From Durham, he was ordained at Rheims and was seized and executed at York soon after his arrival there. He was the first victim of the law of 1585 which defined as treason the entry into England by those who had been ordained abroad. He was beatified in 1987. *See* **England (Martyrs of)**.

Hugolin (St) *see* **Daniel, Samuel and Comps**

Hugolin of Gualdo (Bl) R(OSA). Jan 1
d. 1260. He was allegedly founder and first prior of the Augustinian friary at Gualdo in Umbria, Italy, and had his cultus approved in 1919. There is evidence that he was a Benedictine and that his monastery became Augustinian after his death.

Hugolin Magalotti (Bl) T(OFM). Dec 11
d. 1373. From Camerino, Italy, he became a Franciscan tertiary and a hermit there. His cultus was confirmed for Camerino in 1856.

Hugolin Zefferini (Bl) R(OSA). Mar 22
d. *c*1470? An Augustinian friar who lived at Cortona (or perhaps Mantua) in Italy, he had his cultus confirmed for Cortona in 1804.

Humbeline (St) R(OSB). Feb 12
1092–1135 A younger sister of St Bernard of Clairvaux, she married a rich Burgundian nobleman and was leading a worldly life when a visit to her brother in Clairvaux resulted in her spiritual conversion. She obtained her husband's consent to become a nun, entered the Benedictine nunnery of Jully-les Nonnais near Troyes, France, and became abbess there. She died in St Bernard's arms at Jully. Her cultus was approved in 1763.

Humbert of Marolles (St) R(OSB). Mar 25
d. *c*680. A disciple of St Amandus, he became the joint founder and first abbot of the abbey of Marolles near Cambrai, France.

Humbert of Romans (Bl) R(OP). Jul 14
d. 1277. The fifth master general of the Dominicans was born near Valence, France, at which city he died. He was particularly successful in the development of his order's foreign missions and in the ordering of courses of studies among the Dominicans.

Humbert III of Savoy (Bl) L. Mar 4
1136–1188. A count of Savoy and ancestor of the former Italian royal house, he had Bl Amedius of Lausanne as a tutor and succeeded to the throne at the age of thirteen. Later he retired to the Cistercian abbey of Hautcombe, but left to return to power and to get married for state reasons (he was three, perhaps four times married). He returned to the monastery after an heir was born, however, and the Cistercians claimed that he became a monk. His cultus was confirmed for Turin, Italy, in 1838.

Humiliana de' Cerchi (Bl) T(OFM). May 19
1220–1246. From Florence, Italy, she married at the age of sixteen. After the early death of her husband she became the first Franciscan tertiary at Florence, as her being the mother of two little girls prevented her from joining the Poor Clares. Her cultus was approved for Florence in 1694.

Humilis Pirozzo of Bisignano (Bl) R(OFM). Nov 27
1582–1637. From Bisignano in Calabria, Italy, he became a Franciscan lay brother and was so widely known for his sanctity that he was called to Rome, where Popes Gregory XV and Urban VIII consulted him. He was beatified in 1882.

Humilitas (or Rosanna) (St) R(OSB Vall). F. May 22
1226–1310. From Faenza in the Romagna, Italy, when aged fifteen she was compelled to marry a frivolous young man named Ugoletto. After nine years of marriage he became seriously ill, recovered, converted, became a monk and allowed Humilitas to become a nun. She first lived as a hermit near the Vallumbrosan monastery of St Apollinaris where her husband was a monk and later (persuaded by the Vallumbrosan superior-general) founded and governed the first two houses of Vallumbrosan nuns. Her cultus was confirmed for Faenza and Florence in 1720.

Humphrey *see* **Onuphrius**

Humphrey Middlemore (Bl) M. R(OCart). Jun 19
d. 1535. A Carthusian monk of the London Charterhouse, he was hanged at Tyburn with two of his brethren, BB Sebastian Newdigate and

William Exmew, for denying the royal supremacy in spiritual matters of King Henry VIII. He was beatified in 1886. *See* **England (Martyrs of)**.

Humphrey Pritchard (Bl) M. L. Jul 5
d. 1589. He was a Welsh employee at the Catherine Wheel Inn at Oxford, which was a local centre of Catholic activity. When the place was raided he was seized with BB Thomas Belson, George Nichols and Richard Yaxley and was executed at Oxford. He was beatified in 1987. *See* **England (Martyrs of)**.

Humphrey (Hunfried) of Thérouanne (St) B. R(OSB). Mar 8
d. 871. He was a monk at the Benedictine abbey of Prüm in the Eifel, Germany, at the time of its greatest splendour, and became bishop of Thérouanne near St Omer, France, as well as abbot of St Bertin. He was a source of strength and comfort to his people during the Norse invasions which devastated his diocese.

Huna (St) R. Feb 13
d. *c*690. He was a monk at Ely, England, under St Etheldreda, whom he helped on her deathbed. Afterwards he became a hermit on a nearby island in the Fens and died there.

Hunegund (St) R. Aug 25
d. *c*690. According to her biography she was from near Homblières in Picardy, France, was forced to marry against her wishes but made a private vow of virginity. She persuaded her husband to accompany her to Rome, where she arranged to be clothed as a nun by Pope St Vitalian. They returned home and she entered the nunnery at Homblières, while her former betrothed became a priest and chaplain there.

Hunfried *see* **Humphrey**

Hunger (St) B. Dec 22
d. 866. Bishop of Utrecht, Netherlands, from 856, during the Norse invasions he fled to the abbey of Prüm in the Eifel, Germany, and died there.

Hunna (St) L. Apr 15
d. 679. A relative of the duke of Alsace, she lived at Hunnaweyer near Strasbourg, France, and was nicknamed 'the holy washerwoman' because she used to wash the clothes of the poor. She was canonized in 1520.

Hyacinth (St) *see* **Protus and Hyacinth**

Hyacinth (St) *see* **Zoticus, Irenaeus and Comps**

Hyacinth, Alexander and Tiburtius (SS) MM. Sep 9
? Their shrine is at Fara in the Sabine country, about thirty miles from Rome, and they are alleged to have been martyred somewhere nearby.

Hyacinth, Quintus, Felician and Lucius (SS) MM. Oct 29
? They were listed as martyred somewhere in Lucania, Italy.

Hyacinth of Amastris (St) M. Jul 17
? He cut down a tree sacred to a pagan god, was tortured as a result and died in prison at Amastris in Paphlagonia, Asia Minor.

Hyacinth of Caesarea (St) M. Jul 3
d. *c*120. From Caesarea in Cappodocia, Asia Minor, he allegedly became a chamberlain of the emperor Trajan. When his faith was discovered he was imprisoned and offered as sustenance only meat consecrated to idols. This he refused and died in consequence of starvation.

Hyacinth Castañeda (St) M. R(OP). Nov 7
d. 1773. From Setavo near Valencia, Spain, he became a Dominican, was sent to China and then to Vietnam. There he was beheaded. *See* **Vietnam (Martyrs of)**.

Hyacinth Cormier (Bl) R(OP). May 21
1832–1916. From Orléans, France, he joined the Dominicans and became master-general in 1904. He oversaw the spread of his Order, promoted Thomism and founded the Angelicum in Rome in 1908. A noted ascetic writer of gentleness, firmness and wisdom based on a charism of liturgical prayer and sacred study, he faithfully interpreted the Church's teaching during the Modernist crisis. He was beatified in 1994.

Hyacinth Hoyuelos González (Bl) *see* **Hospitaller Martyrs of Spain**

Hyacinth Odrowaz (St) R(OP). Aug 17
1185–1257. Nicknamed 'the Apostle of Poland', he was from Silesia and became a canon of Cracow, Poland, before becoming a Dominican in Rome under St Dominic. In three missionary journeys he is alleged to have travelled through Poland, Scandinavia, Russia and as far as Tibet and China. The details of his life are, however, very uncertain. He died at Cracow, was canonized in 1594 and had his cultus confined to particular calendars in 1969.

Hyacinth Orfanel (Bl)
M. R(OP). Sep 10
1578–1622. From near Valencia, Spain, he became a Dominican at Barcelona, was sent to Japan and was burned alive at Nagasaki in the 'Great Martyrdom' after many years on mission there. *See* **Charles Spinola and Comps** and **Japan (Martyrs of)**.

Hyacinth of Porto Romano
(St) M. Jul 26
d. ?110. His existence as a martyr in the reign of Trajan is certain, but his acta are thoroughly untrustworthy. He is connected with Porto Romano, Italy.

Hyacintha de Mariscotti
(St) T(OFM). F. Jan 30
1585–1640. A noblewoman of Viterbo, Italy, when aged twenty she lost her lover, a marquis, who married her younger sister. In reaction she became such a nuisance that her family pressured her into entering the convent of Franciscan tertiaries at Viterbo. There she began by scandalously ignoring the rule, was converted to a better life but relapsed. Finally, over a period of twenty-four years, she gave herself up to a life of heroic humility, prayer, patience and incredible penances. She founded the 'Sacconi', an oblate nursing sisterhood now suppressed, and was canonized in 1807. She is liturgically celebrated as a virgin, which she was not.

Hydroc (St) R? May 5
C5th. He is the patron saint of Lanhydrock near Bodmin in Cornwall, England.

Hygbald (Hugbald, Higbald, Hybald) (St) R. Sep 18
d. *c*690. An abbot of a monastery somewhere in Lincolnshire, England, he has several churches dedicated to him there.

Hyginus, 'Pope' *Jan 11*
d. ?142. He was traditionally pope from 138, but this is uncertain. It is also doubtful as to whether he died a martyr. His cultus was suppressed in 1969.

Hypatius (St) *see* **Leontius, Hypatius and Theodulus**

Hypatius (St) *see* **Lucillian, Claudius and Comps**

Hypatius and Andrew (SS) MM. Aug 29
d. 735. Allegedly from Lydia, Asia Minor, Hypatius was a bishop and Andrew a priest. At Constantinople they were tortured, strangled and burned under a pile of icons by order of Emperor Leo III because of their opposition to his policy of iconoclasm.

Hypatius of Chalcedon (St) R. Jun 17
d. *c*450. A Phrygian, when aged nineteen he became a hermit, first in Thrace, European Turkey, and then at Chalcedon opposite Constantinople, where he became abbot of a flourishing laura. He was a determined opponent of Nestorianism.

Hypatius of Gangra (St) M. B. Nov 14
d. ?325. A bishop of Gangra in Paphlagonia, Asia Minor, he attended the council of Nicaea and was a prominent defender of the divinity of Christ. When on his way home he was stoned to death by a mob of Novatian heretics.

Hyperechios (St) R. Aug 7
? A desert father of Egypt, he has had about 160 of his apophthegmata preserved.

Hywyn (St) R. Jan 6
d. *p*516. Probably a companion of St Cadfan on his return journey from Brittany to Cornwall and Wales in 516, he is alleged to have been the founder of Aberdaron in Gwynedd. Several churches in western England known as St Owen's or St Ewen's possibly have him as patron.

I

Ia (Hia, Ives) (St) V. Feb 3
d. 450. From Ireland, a sister of St Ercus, she allegedly accompanied SS Fingar, Piala and other missionaries to Cornwall, England, and was martyred on the Hayle estuary. St Ives in Cornwall is named after her, but not St Ives near Cambridge. She is also linked with Plouyé in Brittany, France.

Ia and Comps (SS) MM. Aug 4
d. 360. A Greek slave (the name means 'Violet'), he or she was martyred in Persia with many other Christian captives (the figure usually given is nine thousand) during the persecution of Shah Shapur II. Their acta are lost.

Iago *see* **James**. (This obsolete Spanish form is now found only in the form Santiago = St James.)

Ibar (Iberius, Ivor) (St) R. Apr 23
C5th. From Ulster, he was a missionary in southern Ireland, allegedly just before St Patrick but becoming part of the latter's episcopal organization as bishop of Begerin, an island in Co. Wexford.

Ida of Boulogne (Bl) L. Apr 13
d. 1113. A noblewoman from Bouillon, Belgium, she was the wife of the count of Boulogne and mother of the famous crusaders Godfrey de Bouillon and King Baldwin of Jerusalem. She was extremely generous to several monasteries in the Low Countries.

Ida of Herzfeld (St) R. Sep 4
d. ?813. A great-granddaughter of Charles Martel, she was happily married but was widowed when still young. She then founded the nunnery of Herzfeld in Westphalia, Germany, where she died after a life of charity. She was the mother of St Guarin of Corvey.

Ida of Leeuw (Bl) R(OCist). Oct 30
d. *c*1260. From Leeuw, Belgium, she became a Cistercian nun at La Rameé in Brabant and was locally famous as a mystic. She has an unconfirmed cultus in Belgium.

Ida of Louvain (Bl) R(OCist). Apr 13
d. *c*1300. From Louvain, Belgium, she became a Cistercian nun at Roosendael near Mecheln and, according to her dubious biography, was subject to extraordinary mystical phenomena.

Ida (Itta, Iduberga) of Nivelles (Bl) R. May 8
d. 652. The wife of Bl Pepin of Landen, when widowed in 640 she became the founding superior of the nunnery at Nivelles, Belgium. St Gertrude, her daughter, succeeded her as abbess. Another of the same name was a nun at La Ramée who died in 1231 (feast-day there, Dec 12; the cultus of both is unconfirmed).

Ida of Toggenburg (Bl) R(OSB). Nov 3
?1156–?1226. According to her unreliable legend, she was the wife of a count of Toggenburg (otherwise unknown), was thrown by him through a castle window after suspicion of adultery and eventually obtained his permission to become a nun at Fischingen in Thurgau canton, Switzerland.

Idaberga *see* **Edburga** or **Isberga**

Idesbald (Bl) R(OCist). Apr 18
1100–1167. From Flanders, as a young man he was at the court of the count before becoming a canon at Veurne near Ostend, Belgium, in 1135. He left to become a Cistercian at the abbey of Duenen nearby, where he was abbot for twelve years. His cultus was confirmed for Bruges in 1894.

Ignatia-of-the-Blessed-Sacrament Pascual Pallardó (Bl) *see* **Angela-of-St-Joseph Lloret Martí and Comps**

Ignatius of Africa (St) *see* **Laurentinus, Ignatius and Celerina**

Ignatius of Antioch (St) M. B. Oct 17
d. ?107. Nicknamed Theophorus ('God-bearer'), he became bishop of Antioch, Syria, in ?69 but nothing is known about his career. In the reign of Trajan he was arrested, taken to Rome and thrown to the wild animals in the amphitheatre during public games. On the way there he wrote seven letters, which are still extant and are of great doctrinal value. His name is mentioned in the Roman canon of the Mass.

Ignatius de Azevedo and Comps (BB) MM. RR(SJ). Jul 15
d. 1570. A group of forty Portuguese and Spanish Jesuit missionaries, they were on their way to Brazil and the West Indies when their ship was boarded by Calvinist Huguenot pirates near the Canary Islands. Ignatius was the superior, from Coïmbra, Portugal, where he had joined the Jesuits in 1548. The leader of the pirates had them massacred, and their cultus was confirmed for Brazil in 1854. *See* **Canary Islands** in lists of national martyrs in appendix.

Ignatius Balocco of Santhiá (Bl) R(OFM Cap). Sep 22
1686–1770. From near Vercelli, Italy, he became a secular priest there in 1710 and then joined the Capuchins in 1716, being attracted by the charism of obedience. He spent his life at the Turin friary, serving as novice-master and also as a military chaplain, and was known for performing miracles. He was beatified in 1966.

Ignatius Cadello Peis of Làconi (St) R(OFM Cap). May 12
1701–1781. From Làconi in Sardinia, his parents were poor but he had a remarkable religious devotion as a child. He became a Capuchin lay brother at Cagliari and was occupied throughout his life in domestic work and in begging for the maintenance of his friary. Being illiterate he loved to listen to the gospels, especially to the Passion of Christ, and received the charisms of prophecy and the working of miracles. He was canonized in 1951.

Ignatius Casanovas Perramon (Bl) *see* **Dionysius Pamplona Polo and Comps**

Ignatius of Constantinople (St) Bp. Oct 23
?799–877. Son of the Byzantine emperor Michael I, he was castrated and forced to become a monk when his father was deposed in 813. He founded three monasteries in the Prinkipio islands before being appointed patriarch of Constantinople in 846. Standing firm against corruption in high places, he openly refused holy communion to Bardas Caesar (brother of the empress) on account of his public incest. Abdicating in 858, he was replaced by Photius but reinstated after nine years, remaining patriarch until his death.

Ignatius Delgado y Cebrián (St) M. B. R(OP). Jul 12
1761–1838. A Spanish Dominican on the Vietnamese missions, he worked there for nearly fifty years, being made titular bishop of Mellipotamo and appointed vicar apostolic of 'East Tonkin'. He was seized during a persecution, put into a small cage exposed to the elements and left to die. *See* **Vietnam (Martyrs of)**.

Ignatius Falzon (BI) (TOFM) Jul 1
1813–1865. Born at Valletta, Malta, he obtained a doctorate in civil and canon lw but did not feel called to become a lawyer or a priest. Instead, he dedicated his life to catechetical instrument among the British armed forces stationed on the island. He was pioneer and advocate of ecumenism and became a Franciscan tertiary. He was beatified in 2001.

Ignatius Franczuk *see* **Podlasia (Martyrs of)**

Ignatius Jorjes (Bl) M. Sep 10
d. 1622. The four-year-old son of Dominic Jorjes and Isabel Fenandez, he was beheaded with his mother at Nagasaki, Japan, during the 'Great Persecution'. *See* **Charles Spinola and Comps** and **Japan (Martyrs of)**.

Ignatius Kim (St) *see* **Korea (Martyrs of)**

Ignatius of Loyola (St) R(SJ). F. Jul 31
1491–1556. Born on the family estate at Loyola in the Basque Country, Spain, he was a page at the Spanish court and then a soldier. He was seriously wounded in the siege of Pamplona in 1521 during the conquest of the kingdom of Navarre, and during his convalescence was converted to the idea of serving the Church. Preparing himself by a retreat at Montserrat and Manresa, he wrote his classic work on spirituality *The Book of Spiritual Exercises*. Wishing to found a religious confraternity, he gathered a few companions while in Paris and they took their first vows together at the church of Montmartre in 1534. This was the start of the Society of Jesus, the aim of which was to work for the greater glory of God under the obedience of the pope. He was elected the first superior-general in 1541, which he remained until his death at Rome. By

then his Society had over 100 houses in twelve provinces throughout the world. He was canonized in 1622.

Ignatius Maloyan (Bl) M. B. (Jun 11)
1869–1915. An Armenian Catholic from Mardin, Turkey, he became a monk and priest of Bzommar monastery in Lebanon and ministered to the small Catholic Armenian population in Egypt from 1897 to 1910. In 1911 he was made archbishop fo his home town and re-evangelized a decayed diocese. In 1915 he and most of the Armenian population of Mardin were rounded up by the Turkish authorities and offered the choice of conversion to Islam or death (contrary to Shahira law). On the archbishop's refusal, after being tortured he was marched into the desert with 440 Armenians and some other Christians. They were massacred at a place called Chikhan; Bl Ignatius (alone) was beatified in 2001.

Ignatius Mangin and Comps
(SS) MM. Jul 20
d. 1900. The Boxer Rebellion in China caused the deaths of about 5,000 Catholics in south-eastern Hebei. Notable among the massacres was that at Zhujiahe, a walled town and Catholic centre where many refugees had gathered. The parish priest there was St Ignatius, from Verny, France, who was born in 1857 and became a Jesuit in 1875. He was sent to China in 1882. St Paul Denn, from Lille, France, who had become a Jesuit in 1872 when aged 25, joined him at Zhujiahe with many of his people from Gucheng. A government army, sympathetic to the Boxers, helped to besiege and take the town in the morning. The Boxers massacred the congregation at the church before setting fire to it, killing both priests there and over 2,000 lay people there and elsewhere. St Mary Zhu (Wu), a fifty-year-old housewife, was notable in being shot while shielding St Ignatius. Fifty-one survivors of the church massacre, including nineteen-year-old St Peter Zhu (Rixin), were killed in the afternoon. *See* **China (Martyrs of)**.

Ignatius Rice (Bl) R. F. May 5
1762–1844. A businessman of Waterford, Ireland, he lost his wife when he was aged twenty-seven with a small daughter, and thereupon devoted himself to charitable works. The Protestant government had a policy of repressing Catholic education so he sold his business, opened a school and founded the 'Congregation of Christian Brothers' on Salesian principles in 1820. He was beatified in 1996.

Ignatius Tejero Molina (Bl) *see* **Hospitaller Martyrs of Spain**

Ildephonsus-of-the-Cross Garcia Nozal (Bl) *see* **Nicephorus Díez Tejerina and Comps**

Ildephonsus Schuster (Bl)
B. R(OSB). Aug 30
1880–1954. A Roman, he became a Benedictine monk in 1896 at the local abbey of St Paul outside the Walls and was elected abbot in 1918. He served in the Curia, especially in liturgical matters, and became cardinal-archbishop of Milan in 1929. He denounced Fascism and proposed holiness as a good for all and the only way to human happiness. He was beatified in 1996.

Ildephonsus of Toledo (St) B. Jan 23
607–667. Nephew of St Eugene of Toledo, Spain, he was born in that city and studied at Seville under St Isidore. Then he joined the monastery at Agli on the Tagus near Toledo, becoming abbot there, and was made archbishop of Toledo in 657. He revised the Spanish liturgy and was a capable writer, chiefly on the subject of Our Lady.

Illidius (Allyre) (St) B. Jul 7
d. 385 The fourth bishop of Clermont-Ferrand, France, he was much admired by St Gregory of Tours.

Illog *see* **Ellidius**

Illtyd (Illtut) (St) R. Nov 6
d. ?505. He is one of the most famous of the saints of Wales but his extant biography contains much legendary material. Becoming a monk under St Cadoc, he went on to found the influential monastery of Llanilltyd Fawr (Llantwit Major) near Cardiff. This was the source of many Welsh saints of the period. He is alleged to have died near Dol in Brittany.

Illuminata (St) L. Nov 29
d. *c*320. She has a cultus as a virgin at Todi in Umbria, Italy.

Illuminatus the Franciscan
(St) R(OFM). May 11
d. *c*1230. An alleged disciple of St Francis of Assisi, he is often confused with his homonym of Sanseverino.

Illuminatus of Sanseverino
(St) R(OSB). May 11
d. *c*1000. From Sanseverino in the Marches, Italy, he became a Benedictine monk at the abbey of San Mariano there.

Bl Ildephonsus Schuster, Aug 30 *(see p. 275)*

Imelda Lambertini (Bl) R(OP). May 12
d. 1333. Allegedly from the noble family of Lambertini at Bologna, Italy, she was educated at the Dominican nunnery at Valdipietra there and seems to have joined the community. Her story is that she received her first Holy Communion in a miraculous manner at the age of eleven (under the canonical age for communion at the time) and died enraptured as a result the same day. Her cultus was confirmed for Bologna in 1826.

Imelin *see* **Emilian**

Imma (Immina) (St) R(OSB). Nov 25
*c*700. She was abbess of the Franconian monastery of Karlburg, Germany, but her shrine was in her native Würzburg.

Ina and Ethelburga (SS) RR? Sep 8
d. 727. Ina was king of Wessex, England, from 688 until 726 and restored the abbey of Glastonbury. Then he abdicated, made a pilgrimage to Rome with his queen, Ethelburga, and founded a hospice there for other English pilgrims. They died there, allegedly as consecrated religious.

Inan *see* **Evan**

Indaletius (St) *see* **Torqatus, Ctesiphon and Comps**

Indes, Domna, Agape and Theophila (SS) MM. Dec 28
d. 303. They were martyred at Nicomedia, Asia Minor, in the reign of Diocletian.

Indract (St) M. Feb 5
d. *c*700. An old legend describes him as an Irish chieftain who was returning from a pilgrimage to Rome when he was killed by pagan Saxons with his sister St Dominica (Drusa) and others near Glastonbury, England, where their relics were enshrined. A later, spurious legend describes them as contemporaries of St Patrick there.

Inés, Inez *see* **Agnes**

Inés de Beniganim *see* **Josephine-Mary-of-St-Agnes Albiñana**

Ingen (St) *see* **Ammon, Zeno and Comps**

Ingenuin *see* **Genuinus**

Iñigo *see* **Eneco**

Inischolus (St) *see* **Corfu, Martyrs of**

Injuriosus and Scholastica (SS) LL. May 25
d. *c*550.They were allegedly a senator of Auvergne, France, and his wife who lived the whole of their married life as brother and sister (without consummating their marriage).

Innocent (St) *see* **Isaurus, Innocent and Comps**

Innocent (St) *see* **Theban Legion**

Innocent I, Pope *Jul 28*
d. 417. From Albano near Rome, he succeeded his father Anastasius I as pope in 402. The outstanding event of his pontificate was the sack of Rome by Alaric the Goth in 410. He confirmed the acts of two African synods against the Pelagians and supported the deposed St John Chrysostom. His cultus was suppressed in 1969.

Innocent V, Pope (Bl) R(OP). Jun 22
1245–1277. From Tarentaise in Burgundy, France, he became a Dominican and was well known as a theologian and as a preacher. He was made archbishop of Lyons in 1272, and during his episcopate the second ecumenical council of Lyons was held in which he took a prominent part. As cardinal of Ostia he was made pope in 1276, but died only a few months later. His cultus was confirmed in 1898.

Innocent XI, Pope (Bl) Aug 12
1611–1689. From Como, Italy, he was elected pope in 1676. Outstanding for his charity, evangelical simplicity and poverty, he withstood the autocracy of King Louis XIV of France, struggled to stop nepotism, encouraged an exemplary life among the clergy and furthered catechetical instruction. He condemned Jansenism, Quietism and corrected the teaching of Molinos on grace. He was beatified in 1956.

Innocent, Sebastia (Sabbatia) and Comps (SS) MM. Jul 4
? A group of thirty-two, they were martyred at Sirmium (now Srem Mitrovica in Serbia).

Innocent-of-Mary-Immaculate Canoura Arna (St) *see* **Cyril-Bertrand Sanz Tejedor and Comps**

Innocent of Le Mans (St) B. Jun 19
d. 559. He was bishop of Le Mans, France, for over forty years.

Innocent Scalvinoni of Berzo
(Bl) R(OFM Cap). Mar 3
1844–1890. Raised as a child at Berzo near Brescia, Italy, he became a secular priest and curate for his home town in 1867. Then he joined the Capuchins in 1874, becoming assistant novice-master and public preacher and confessor. His body was returned to Berzo after he died and he was beatified in 1964.

Innocent of Tortona (St) B. Apr 17
d. *c*350. From Tortona, Italy, he was imprisoned and whipped in the reign of Diocletian, barely escaping death. After Constantine gave peace to the Church he was ordained and became bishop of his native city in ?326.

Innocents, The Holy (SS) MM. Dec 28
C1st. The male children in Bethlehem and the area around it whose massacre was ordered by Herod (Matt. 2: 1–18) have been liturgically venerated as martyrs from a very early date. The Gospel does not specify their number and this has led to the multiplication of their relics in many churches. They are depicted as a large number of small boys being killed by soldiers in various ways while their mothers utter protest.

Iphigenia (St) L. Sep 21
C1st. According to an apocryphal work, she was a young woman of Ethiopia (now Nubia, in northern Sudan) who was converted by St Matthew the apostle.

Iphigenia-of-St-Matthew de Gaillard (Bl) *see* Orange (Martyrs of)

Irais (Herais, Rhais) (St) V. Sep 22
d. *c*300. A maiden of Alexandria or of Antinoe, Egypt, she was beheaded in the reign of Diocletian.

Irchard (St) B. Aug 24
C7th. An apostle of the Picts and disciple of St Ternan, he was born in Galloway, Scotland, and is alleged to have been ordained bishop in Rome by St Gregory the Great.

Ireland (Martyrs of)
(BB) MM. Jun 20
d. 1579–1654. After the nadir of English fortunes in Ireland in the reign of Henry VIII, the policy of conquest that followed assumed that English culture and the Protestant church would be imposed on the native Irish. The number of the resultant victims of massacre, starvation and dispossession runs into seven figures, but the number of those martyred strictly for the faith is relatively low and 282 have been identified. The main periods of persecution were under Queen Elizabeth I and by Oliver Cromwell. Seventeen martyrs were beatified in 1992, comprising four bishops, two secular priests, five religious and six lay people. *See* lists of national martyrs in appendix.

Irenaeus (St) *see* **Quintian and Irenaeus**

Irenaeus (St) *see* **Theodore of Pentapolis and Comps**

Irenaeus (St) *see* **Zoticus, Irenaeus and Comps**

Irenaeus and Abundius
(SS) MM. Aug 26
d. ?258. According to their legend, they were martyrs of Rome who were drowned in a public sewer during the persecution of Valerian.

Irenaeus, Anthony, Theodore, Saturninus, Victor and Comps
(SS) MM. Dec 15
d. ?258. A group of twenty-two Romans, they were martyred in the reign of Valerian.

Irenaeus and Mustiola (SS) MM. Jul 3
d. 273. Irenaeus, a deacon, and Mustiola, a noblewoman, were martyred at Chiusi in Tuscany, Italy, in the reign of Aurelian for having ministered to other martyrs and having buried their bodies.

Irenaeus, Peregrine and Irene
(SS) MM. May 5
d. *c*300. They were burned at the stake at Thessalonika, Greece, in the reign of Diocletian.

Irenaeus of Lyons (St) M? B. Jun 28
*c*130–200. From Asia Minor and a disciple of St Polycarp (himself a pupil of St John the apostle), he migrated to Gaul and became bishop of Lyons in ?178. According to tradition he was a martyr but there is no evidence of this. He is the first of the Western Fathers (although he wrote in Greek), and his writings (especially his work *Against the Heretics*) are a very early testimony to the teachings of the apostles and the traditions of the early Church. His theological writings emphasise the importance of both Old and New Testaments, the unity of the gospels and the idea of the recapitulation of human nature in Christ.

Irenaeus of Sirmium (St) M. B. Mar 25
d. 304. A bishop in Pannonia, he was martyred in the reign of Diocletian at Sirmium (Srem Mitrovica in Serbia). His acta are authentic.

Irene (St) *see* **Agape, Chionia and Irene**

Irene (St) *see* **Irenaeus, Peregrine and Comps**

Irene (St) *see* **Sophia and Irene**

Irene of Santarém (St) R. Oct 20
? According to her legend she was a C7th nun near the city named Santarém after her in Portugal, but it seems that she is a duplicate of the St Irene in **Agape, Chionia and Irene**.

Irenion (St) B. Dec 16
d. 389. He was bishop of Gaza in the Holy Land in the reign of Theodosius I.

Irmengard (Bl) R(OSB). Jul 17
d. 866. Daughter of Emperor Louis the German, she was appointed by her father first abbess of Frauenwörth in the Chiemsee, Bavaria, Germany. Her cultus was confirmed for Munich and Freising in 1928.

Irmgard (Bl) R? Sep 4
Late C11th. According to her unreliable biography, she was a noblewoman who became a hermit at Süchteln, Germany and later at Cologne, where she died. Her historical identity is disputed.

Irmina (St) R. Dec 30
d. 708. Her unreliable C12th biography alleges the following. She was a daughter of King Dagobert II of Austrasia, and when aged fifteen she was engaged to marry but on the day of her wedding her betrothed died. She then persuaded her father to build the nunnery of Ohren near Trier for her. She was generous to both Celtic and Saxon missionary monks and built Echternach for St Willibrord in 698. She died at the monastery of Weissenburg, also founded by her father.

Isaac (St) *see* **Benedict of Benevento and Comps**

Isaac of Constantinople (St) R. May 30
d. *c*410. He publicly denounced the Arian emperor Valens at Constantinople, narrowly escaped death as a result and then became abbot-founder of the Dalmatian monastery, the oldest in the city. The cathedral at St Petersburg is dedicated to him.

Isaac (Isacius) of Cyprus
(St) M. B. Sep 21
? He was listed by the old Roman Martyrology as a bishop of Cyprus who was martyred.

Isaac of Gniezno (St) *see* **Benedict of Gniezno and Comps**

Isaac the Good (Bl) B. R(OSB). Jul 18
d. 880. He was entrusted with the task of re-founding the monastery of St Benignus at Dijon, France, by Emperor Charles the Bald after its destruction by the Norse, and was made bishop of Langres in 859.

Isaac the Great (1) (St) B. Sep 9
350–440. Son of St Nerses the Great, he succeeded his father as Armenian Katholikos of Etchmiadzin and was the real founder of the Armenian national church, obtaining independence from the metropolitan of Caesarea. He translated a large part of the Bible with St Mesrop, founded monasteries and was practically the only ruler of the Armenians after the Persians had deposed their king.

Isaac the Great (2) (St) B. May 13
d. *c*460. From Amida in Syria, he became abbot of a monastery near Antioch. He is the traditional author of a set of ascetical writings which remain popular in monastic circles, especially in the East. However the author of these seems to have been a Nestorian bishop of Nineveh who died ?595.

Isaac Jogues (St) *see* **John de Brébeuf and Comps**

Isaac of Monteluco (St) R. Apr 11
d. *c*550. A Syrian monk, he fled from the Monophysites and founded a laura at Monteluco near Spoleto in Umbria, Italy. He was one of the restorers of eremitical life in C6th Italy.

Isaac of Tabanos (St) M. R. Jun 3
825–852. From Cordoba, Spain, he became very proficient in Arabic and was made a notary under the Muslim government there. He resigned in order to become a monk at Tabanos nearby, but in a public debate at Cordoba he denounced Muhammed and was executed.

Isabella *see* **Elizabeth**

Isabella Fernandez (Bl) M. Sept 10
d. 1622. A Spanish lady, widow of Dominic Jorjes, she was beheaded with her son Ignatius at Nagasaki in the 'Great Martyrdom' for having given shelter to Bl Charles Spinola. *See* **Japan (Martyrs of)**.

Isabella of France (Bl) L. Feb 26
d. 1270 The only sister of King St Louis of France, she refused to marry the emperor of

Germany and, after the death of her mother Blanche of Castile, founded the convent of Poor Clares at Longchamps near Paris. There she lived under the rule without, however, taking vows. She was beatified in 1520.

Isacius (St) *see* **Apollo, Isacius and Crotates**

Isaias, Sabas and Comps (SS) MM. Jan 14
d. 309. Thirty-eight monks on Mt Sinai, they were massacred by Bedouin raiders. There was another massacre at Raithu on the Red Sea in 371, and another on Sinai in the C5th.

Isaias Boner (Bl) R(OSA). Feb 8
d. 1471. From Cracow, Poland, he studied theology at the university there, joined the Augustinian friars at Kasimiercz and was chiefly employed in teaching scripture, which he did with great zeal and success. His cultus is unconfirmed.

Isaias of Sandomir (Bl) *see* **Sadoc of Sandomir and Comps**

Isarnus (Ysarn) of Toulouse (St) R(CR). Sep 24
d. 1048. From near Toulouse, France, he joined the Augustinian monastery of St Victor at Marseilles, going on to become abbot. His reform of the monastery was imitated by other houses. He was famous for his charity, especially towards criminals.

Isaurus, Innocent, Felix, Jeremias and Peregrine (SS) MM. Jun 17
? From Athens, they are listed as having hidden in a cave at Apollonia in Macedonia, Greece, during one of the persecutions. On being discovered they were beheaded.

Isberga (Idaberga, Itisberga) (St) R. May 21
d. *c*800. A supposed sister of Charlemagne, she was a nun at Aire in the Artois, France, and is patron of that region.

Ischyrion and Comps (SS) MM. Jun 1
d. 250. He was the procurator of an Egyptian official (possibly in Alexandria) who had him castrated and impaled for the faith in the reign of Decius. The old Roman Martyrology listed five companions, and listed him also on Dec 22 in error.

Isfried (Bl) B. R(OPraem). Jun 15
d. 1204. He was a Premonstratensian at Kappenberg before being made bishop of Ratzeburg, Germany, in 1180, and was influential in support of the German drive to colonize the Slav lands east of the Elbe. His cultus was approved for the Premonstratensians in 1725.

Isidora the Simple (St) R. May 1
d. ?365. A nun at Tabennesi monastery in Egypt, she was a 'fool for Christ's sake' who was despised by her community. When her true holiness was revealed she fled to the desert to avoid being honoured, and died there.

Isidore (St) *see* **Elias, Paul and Isidore**

Isidore (St) *see* **Epiphanius and Isidore**

Isidore (St) *see* **Heron, Arsenius and Comps**

Isidore of Alexandria (St) M. Feb 5
? The old Roman Martyrology placed him at Alexandria, Egypt, but he is probably a duplicate of Isidore of Chios.

Isidore of Antioch (St) M. B. Jan 2
? When Cardinal Baronius revised the old Roman Martyrology he inserted this saint because of a note in the Hieronomian martyrology which read: 'In Antiochia Siridoni episcopi eiusdem loci'. No such bishop is known.

Isidore Bakanja (Bl) M. L. Aug 12
*c*1887–1909. Born in north-east Belgian Congo (now Congo Kinshasa), he became a Christian in his native village but was the only one to do so, so in order to make contact with other Christians he went to work on a rubber plantation. He was devoted to the scapular and the Rosary and, when refusing to desist from these, was ordered flogged by an atheist Belgian planter. He died six months later as a result, aged about 21 and after 30 months as a Christian. He was beatified in 1994.

Isidore Bover Oliver (Bl) *see* **Peter Ruiz de los Paños y Angel and Comps**

Isidore of Chios (St) M. May 15
d. ?251. He was martyred on Chios in the Aegean Sea, Greece, in the reign of Decius.

Isidore the Egyptian (St) R. Jan 15
d. 404. An Egyptian priest, he was in charge of the hospice for pilgrims at Alexandria. In defending St Athanasius he suffered much at the hands of the Arians. Accused of Origenism by St Jerome and others, he fled to Constantinople where he was befriended by St John Chrysostom.

Isidore the Farmer (St) R. May 15
d. 1170. A native of Madrid, Spain, married to St Mary Toribia de la Cabeza, he spent his whole life working in the fields on an estate just outside the city. Canonized in 1622, he is the patron of Madrid. His feast-day is given as May 10 in error in the old Roman Martyrology.

Isidore-of-St-Joseph de Loor (Bl) R(CP). Oct 6
1881–1916. Born near Ghent, Belgium, he was a very pious child with a devotion to the Passion. Joining the Passionists at Ere near Tournai, he was such a faithful religious that he was called an exemplar of the Passionist rule and of charity. He died in tranquil agony of pleurisy and was beatified in 1984.

Isidore Martínez Izquierdo (Bl) *see* **Hospitaller Martyrs of Spain**

Isidore of Nitria (St) B. Jan 2
C4th. Mentioned by St Jerome as 'a holy venerable bishop' who had welcomed him to Egypt, he may have been identical with St Isidore of Pelusium.

Isidore of Pelusium (St) R. Feb 4
d. *c*450. A famous Egyptian abbot of a monastery at Pelusium (east of Port Said), he was much admired by St Cyril of Alexandria. A great number of his letters are still extant.

Isidore of Seville (St) B. Dr. Apr 4
*c*560–636. From Cartagena, Spain, and brother of SS Leander, Fulgentius and Florentina, he was educated by St Leander and succeeded him as bishop of Seville in 600. He presided over several synods, reorganized the Spanish church, encouraged monastic life (he wrote an influential rule), completed the Mozarabic liturgical rite, was responsible for the decree of the council of Toledo in 633 and was himself an encyclopedic writer on theology, scripture, biography, history, geography, astronomy and grammar. He was declared a doctor of the Church in 1722, and his attribute is a swarm of bees or a hive.

Ismael (St) B. Jun 16
C6th. A disciple of St Teilo, he was ordained bishop of Menevia in Dyfed, Wales, by him. He is patron of several churches in the region.

Ismael (St) *see* **Manuel, Sabel and Ismael**

Isnard (Bl) R(OP). Mar 22
d. 1244. From Chiampo near Vicenza, Italy, he was professed as a Dominican by St Dominic in 1219 and was the founder and first prior of the friary at Pavia. It is written of him that, in spite of his ascetic life, he was excessively fat and people used to ridicule him about it when he was preaching. His cultus was confirmed for Pavia in 1919.

Issell *see* **Teilo**

Isserninus (St) *see* **Auxilius, Isserninus and Secundinus**

Issey *see* **Teilo**; perhaps also a Cornish variant of **Ita**

Ita (Ytha, Meda) (St) R. Jan 15
d. *c*570. From Drum in Co. Waterford, Ireland, she founded the nunnery at Killeedy in Co. Limerick, attracted a large number of disciples and taught several saints as children (St Brendan, for example). Her extant biographies are full of incredible anecdotes.

Ithamar (St) B. Jun 10
d. ?656. A native of Kent, England, he was the first Anglo-Saxon to be made bishop when he succeeded St Paulinus at Rochester.

Itta *see* **Ida of Nivelles**

Ivan (St) R. Jun 24
C9th. From Dalmatia, Croatia, he was a hermit at Karlstein in Bohemia (Czech Republic). He was offered a high position at court but refused, returned to his solitude and was murdered by peasants. His name is Slavic for John.

Ives *see* **Ia** or **Ivo**

Ivetta (Jutta) (Bl) R. Jan 13
1158–1228. When she was left a widow with two children at the age of eighteen she started nursing lepers at the hospice at Huy near Liege, Belgium, before becoming a hermit for more than forty years. She was famous for discernment of spirits and gifts of counsel.

Ivo (St) B. Apr 24
? According to his medieval legend he was a Persian bishop who became a hermit near where the town of St Ives in Cambridgeshire, England, now stands. (The town with the same name in Cornwall is not named after him but after St Ia).

Ivo of Chartres (St) B. R(CR). May 23
*c*1040–1115. The provost of the Augustinian canons regular of Saint-Quentin, he was made bishop of Chartres, France, in 1091. He was

renowned for his knowledge of canon law, on which he wrote much, and was consulted by the king on difficult canonical questions. Upright and just, he opposed the rapacity of contemporary ecclesiastical dignitaries.

Ivo Guillon de Keranrum and Ivo Rey de Kervisic (BB) *see* **September (Martyrs of)**

Ivo (Yvo) Hélory (St) L. May 19
1253–1303. From near Tréguier in Brittany, France, he studied at Paris and Orléans and practised law in his native city and at Rennes, both in the ecclesiastical and in the civil courts. He defended the poor and unprotected as well as the rich and was called 'the Advocate of the Poor'. He was canonized in 1347 and is patron of lawyers.

Ivor *see* **Ibar**

J

Jacinta Marto (Bl) *see* **Francis and Jacinta Marto**

Jacob *see* **James**

Jacobinus de'Canepaci
(Bl) R(OC). Mar 3
1438–1508. From Vercelli, Italy, he was a Carmelite lay brother there and had his cultus approved for Vercelli and the Carmelites in 1845.

Jacobinus (Jacopone) da Todi
(Bl) R(OFM). Dec 25
*c*1230–1306. From Todi in Umbria, Italy, he became a prosperous married lawyer but his wife died in 1268 and his grief triggered a conversion. Becoming a 'fool for Christ's sake', he eventually became a Franciscan famous for the writing of 'laudi' and joined the Spiritual faction of the order. This faction was becoming heterodox on the question of Christ's material poverty. He wrote against Pope Boniface VIII on the subject and was imprisoned and excommunicated as a result. He has a popular cultus at Todi that has not been confirmed (in this case, confirmation has probably been withheld).

Jacut and Guethenoc (SS) RR. Feb 8
C5th. Sons of SS Fragan and Gwen and brothers of St Gwenaloe, they were disciples of St Budoc and fled with him to Brittany, France, to escape the Saxons.

Jader (St) *see* **Nemesian and Comps**

Jadwiga *see* **Hedwig**

Jambert of Canterbury (St) B. R. Aug 12
d. 792. Abbot of St Augustine's abbey at Canterbury, England, he succeeded St Bregwin as archbishop there.

James
This is the English form of Jacob, which is notably corrupted in other vernaculars also: Giacomo in Italian; Jacques in French; Jaume in Catalan; Iago in Portuguese; Jaimc, Santiago or Diego in Spanish. (The last is listed separately.)

James Andrade (St) *see* **Ignatius de Azevedo and Comps**

James André (Bl) *see* **Laval (Martyrs of)**

James-Hilary Barbal Cosán
(St) M. R. Jan 18
1898–1937. From near Urgell in Catalonia, Spain, he joined the 'Brothers of the Christian Schools' at Mollensa in 1916 and taught Spanish and primary catechesis at Pibrac in France from 1926 (despite being deaf). In 1934 he went back to Calat in Spain as a cook and then moved to Tarragona. He was seized and imprisoned there in August 1936 at the start of the Spanish Civil War and was executed six months later. He was canonized in 1990. *See* **Spanish Civil War (Martyrs of)**.

James Bell (Bl) M. L. Apr 10
1521–1584. From Warrington, Cheshire, he was educated at Oxford and was ordained in the reign of Queen Mary. Initially conforming to the state church under Elizabeth, he repented and was reconciled to the Catholic Church. For this he was hanged at Lancaster and was beatified in 1929. *See* **England (Martyrs of)**.

James Benfatti (Bl) B.R(OP). Nov 26
d. ?1328. From Mantua, Italy, he became a Dominican, a teacher of theology and a great preacher. He became bishop of Mantua in 1303, and as such was nicknamed 'Father of the Poor'. His cultus was confirmed for Mantua and the Dominicans in 1859.

James Berthieu (Bl) M. R(SJ). Jun 8
1838–1896. From near St Flour, France, he was a parish priest there from 1864 until he joined the Jesuits in 1873 and was sent to Madagascar. He was a missionary first on Nosy Borah off the east coast and then on the main

island. The French conquered the island and overthrew the monarchy and government in 1895, but the following year there was a rebellion which proved anti-Christian. Bl James was seized at Ambohibernasoandro immediately after saying Mass, stripped, beaten to death and his body thrown into a river. He was beatified in 1965.

James-Philip Bertoni (Bl) R(OSM). May 30
?1444–1483. From Faenza, Italy, when aged nine he joined the Servites there and was procurator of the friary from the time of his ordination until his death. His cultus was confirmed for Faenza in 1761.

James Bianconi of Mevania (Bl) R(OP). Aug 23
d. 1301. From Mevania (now Bevagna) near Spoleto, Italy, he was the founder and first prior of the Dominican friary in his native city. His cultus was confirmed for Spoleto in 1674.

James Bird (Bl) M. L. Mar 25
1573–1592. From Winchester, when aged nineteen he was hanged there for being reconciled to the church and was beatified in 1929. *See* **England (Martyrs of)**.

James of Bitetto (Bl) R(OFM). Apr 27
d. ?1485. Surnamed alternatively 'of Slavonia', 'of Illyricum', 'of Zara' or 'of Dalmatia', he was from Šibenik in Dalmatia, Croatia, and became a Franciscan lay brother at Zadar. Most of his life was spent at the friary of Bitetto near Bari, Italy. His cultus was approved for Bitetto in 1700.

James Bonnaud (Bl) *see* **September (Martyrs of)**

James Burin (Bl) *see* **Laval (Martyrs of)**

James Buzabaliao (St) M. Jun 3
d. 1886. A soldier of King Mwanga of Buganda, Uganda, and a son of the royal bark-cloth maker, he was baptized in 1885 and burned alive at Namuyongo in the following year. *See* **Charles Lwanga and Comps**.

James Cagnot (Bl) *see* **John-Baptist Souzy and Comps**

James Carvalho (Bl) M. R(SJ). Feb 25
d. 1624. A Portuguese Jesuit, he was on the Japanese missions and was slowly killed with sixty other Christians at Sendai by being immersed in the icy waters of a river. He (alone) was beatified in 1867.

James Capoccio (Bl) R(OSA). Mar 14
d. 1308. From Viterbo, Italy, he became an Augustinian friar there and taught theology with considerable success, being nicknamed 'Doctor Speculativus'. He became bishop of Benevento in 1302 and was transferred to Naples in 1303. His cultus was confirmed for Naples in 1911.

James Chastan (Bl) *see* **Lawrence Imbert and Comps**

James Cinti of Cerqueto (Bl) R(OSA). Apr 17
d. 1367. From Cerqueto near Perugia, Italy, he joined the Augustinian friars at the latter city. His cultus was approved for Perugia in 1895.

James of Città delle Pieve (Bl) R(OSM). Jan 15
d. 1304. A Servite friar from Chiusi near Montepulciano, Italy, he restored a ruined hospital near Città delle Pieve and was nicknamed 'Almsgiver'. The hospital's revenue was appropriated by the bishop of Chiusi, who had Bl James killed when the latter won an appeal to Rome. His cultus was confirmed for Città del Piave in 1806.

James Claxton (Bl) M. P. Aug 28
d. 1588. A Yorkshireman, he was educated at Rheims and ordained there in 1582. He was hanged at Isleworth, Middlesex, and was beatified in 1929. *See* **England (Martyrs of)**.

James Cusmano (Bl) P. F. Mar 14
1834–1888. Born in Palermo, Sicily, he became a physician at Palermo University and set out to use his skills to treat bodies and souls together. He treated the poor without charge, and was ordained to the diocese in 1883. In 1883 he founded the 'Sisters, Servants of the Poor' and in 1888 the 'Brothers, Missionary Servants of the Poor', with a charism of genuine humility in helping orphans and poor and derelict people. He was beatified in 1983.

James the Deacon (St) R. D. Aug 17
d. *p*663. An Italian monk and deacon, he was a companion of St Paulinus in the mission to Northumbria, England. When the latter fled with Queen St Ethelburga in the pagan reaction after the death of King St Edwin, St James remained to care for the infant church from a base at Catterick. When King St Oswald came to the throne, missionaries were sent for from Iona instead to carry on the work, but St James survived to attend the Synod of Whitby in 663.

James Denji (Bl) M. L. Aug 19
d. 1622. A Japanese sailor on board the ship of Bl Joachim Hirayama Diaz, he was beheaded at Nagasaki with BB Louis Flores and Comps. *See* **Japan (Martyrs of)**.

James Duckett (Bl) M. L. Apr 19
d. 1602.From Skelsmergh near Kendal in Cumbria, he became a convert and settled as a bookseller in London where he specialized in printing and selling Catholic books. He was regularly imprisoned for this, for nine years in total, until priestly vestments were found on his premises and he was hanged at Tyburn. He was beatified in 1929. *See* **England (Martyrs of)**.

James Dufour (Bl) *see* **September (Martyrs of)**

James Falgarona Vilanova (Bl) *see* **Philip-of-Jesus Munárriz Azcona and Comps**

James Fenn (Bl) M. Feb 12
d. 1584. From Montacute near Yeovil in Somerset, he was educated at Oxford, became a schoolmaster and got married. On his wife's death he studied at Rheims and was ordained priest in 1580. Four years later he was martyred at Tyburn with BB George Haydock, John Munden, John Nutter and Thomas Hemerford, and was beatified in 1929. *See* **England (Martyrs of)**.

James Friteyre-Durvé (Bl) *see* **September (Martyrs of)**

James Galais (Bl) *see* **September (Martyrs of)**

James Gangala of the Marches (St) R(OFM). Nov 28
1394–1476. From a poor family of the Marches, Italy, he studied law but became a Franciscan instead at Assisi. His penances were extreme. A companion missionary of St John Capistrano in the countries of the Holy Roman Empire and a fellow supporter of Franciscan reform, it is alleged that he preached daily for forty years. He was canonized in 1726.

James Gapp (Bl) M. R. Aug 23
1897–1943. Born in Tyrol, Austria, of the working class, he entered the Marianists in 1921 and worked as a priest in their schools, also helping unemployed people. A strong opponent of the Nazis, after 1938 he went into exile in France and then in Spain, whence he was abducted, taken to Berlin and guillotined. He was beatified in 1996.

James Gengoro (Bl) M. L. Aug 18
d. 1620. A Japanese toddler aged two, son of BB Thomas and Mary Gengoro, he was crucified with his parents and Bl Simon Kiyota Bokusai at Kokura and was beatified in 1867. *See* **Japan (Martyrs of)**.

James Gorobioye (St) R(OP). Sep 28 (d. n. Aug 17)
d. 1633. A Japanese born near Omura, he became a Dominican missionary priest in Taiwan and Manila before being martyred at Nagasaki with his assistant, St Michael Kurobioye. He was canonized in 1987. *See* **Japan (Martyrs of)**.

James the Great (St) A. Jul 25
d. 44. A son of Zebedee and Salome, he was brother of St John the Evangelist and was called with him to the apostolate by Christ. He was quickly martyred after the Resurrection by order of King Herod Agrippa (Acts 12:2), the only apostle whose martyrdom is mentioned in the New Testament. A C9th legend, developed under Cluniac influence, makes him apostle of Spain and specifies Compostela in Galicia as the place where his body is enshrined. This legend spread throughout western Europe, so that Compostela became the most famous place of pilgrimage in Christendom after Jerusalem and Rome. He is the patron saint of Spain, and his attribute is a scallop shell.

James Griesinger (Bl) R(OP). Oct 11
1407–1491. From Ulm, Germany, he was a soldier before he became a Dominican lay brother at Bologna, Italy, in 1441. The rest of his life was spent in painting on glass, for which he had a great talent. His cultus was confirmed for Bologna in 1825.

James Guidi of Certaldo (Bl) R(OSB Cam). Apr 13
d. 1292. The son of a knight of Volterra near Rome, he joined the Camaldolese Benedictine abbey of St Justus at Volterra and was there for sixty years, during forty of which he acted as parish priest of the abbey church. His father and his brother joined the abbey as lay brothers. Twice he refused the abbacy, then acquiesced but quickly resigned.

James Hayashi (Bl) M. T(OP). Sep 8
d. 1628. A Japanese Dominican tertiary, he was beheaded at Nagasaki with BB Dominic Castellet and Comps. *See* **Japan (Martyrs of)**.

James Hourrier (Bl) *see* **September (Martyrs of)**

St James the Great, Jul 25 *(see p. 285)*

James Intercisus (St) M. L. Nov 27
d. 421. A Persian Christian courtier of high rank, he apostatized to keep the favour of Shah Yezdegird but repented and was martyred by having his extremities slowly cut off in over twenty pieces in the reign of the next shah, Bahram V. Then he was beheaded, along with many others. His surname means 'cut up'.

James Kern (Bl) R(OPraem). (Oct 20)
1897–1924. A Viennese, he entered the archdiocesan minor seminary in 1908 but was drafted into the Austrian army in 1915 and was very seriously wounded in the chest on the Italian front. After the war he continued his seminary studies but decided to replace a Norbertine who had apostatized and so entered the abbey of Geras in 1920. He was allowed to be ordained while still a junior in 1922, but his old war wound became infected and he died during surgery on the day fixed for his solemn profession. He was beatified in 1998.

James Kisai (St) M. R(SJ). Feb 6
d. 1597. A Japanese Jesuit lay brother, he worked for the Jesuit missionaries at Osaka as catechist and domestic servant, and was crucified at Nagasaki with SS Paul Miki and Comps. *See* **Japan (Martyrs of)**.

James Lacops (St) M. R(OPraem). Jul 9
d. 1572. A native of Oudenaarde near Ghent, Belgium, he became a Premonstratensian canon at Middelburg but apostatized in 1566, subsequently writing and preaching against the Church. However, he repented, returned to his abbey and was martyred by Calvinists with the group at **Gorinchem** (q.v.).

James Laigneau de Langellerie (Bl) *see* **William Repin and Comps**

James de la Lande (Bl) *see* **September (Martyrs of)**

James-Desiderius Laval (Bl) R. Sep 9
1803–1864. Born in Normandy, France, he became a doctor of medicine and a village practitioner but was then ordained when aged 35. He went as a missionary to Mauritius, where he was for 23 years, being called a 'second Peter Claver' because of his work among the employees of the sugar industry there. He became a Holy Ghost Father and was beatified in 1979.

James Ledoyen (Bl) *see* **William Repin and Comps**

James Lejardinier des Landes (Bl) *see* **September (Martyrs of)**

James the Less (St) A. May 3
d. ?62. Alternatively surnamed 'the Younger' or 'the Just', he was related to Christ and was one of the Twelve. After the Resurrection he became the first bishop of Jerusalem, being mentioned by Eusebius, and is the putative author of one of the canonical letters. According to tradition he was martyred at Jerusalem by being thrown from a pinnacle of the temple, stoned and then finally killed with the fuller's club which is his attribute.

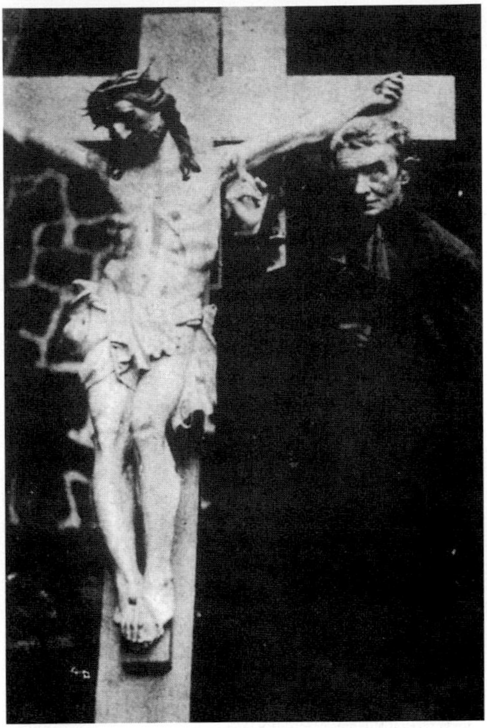

Bl James Desiderius Laval, Sep 9

James-Robert de Lezardière (Bl) *see* **September (Martyrs of)**

James Lombardie (Bl) *see* **John-Baptist Souzy and Comps**

James de Lubersac, James Menuret and James le Meunier (BB) *see* **September (Martyrs of)**

James Morelle Dupas (Bl) *see* **John-Baptist Souzy and Comps**

James (Do May) Nam
(St) M. P. Aug 12
d. 1838. A Vietnamese priest attached to the Paris Mission Society, he was beheaded with St Michael My. *See* **Vietnam (Martyrs of)**.

James of Nisibis (St) B. Jul 15
C4th. He ranks second to St Ephrem among the Syrian Fathers, but not much is known about him except that he took part in the first ecumenical council of Nicaea in 325 as bishop of Nisibis.

James of Numidia (St) *see* **Marianus, James and Comps**

James de Oldo (Bl) T(OFM). Apr 19
d. 1404. From Lodi, Italy, he married and for a time gave himself up to a life of pleasure. Being converted during a time of plague, he became a Franciscan tertiary together with his wife, turned his house into a church and was eventually ordained.

James of Padua (Bl) *see* **Thomas of Tolentino and Comps**

James of Persia (St) M. P. Apr 22
C4th. A Persian, he was martyred in the reign of Shah Shapur II.

James Rabé (Bl) *see* **September (Martyrs of)**

James Retouret (Bl) *see* **John-Baptist Souzy and Comps**

James Salès and William Saltemouche (BB) MM. RR(SJ). Feb 7
d. 1593. A Jesuit priest and lay brother respectively, they conducted a mission at Aubenas in the Cévennes, France. Bl James attacked Protestant teaching in his sermons, with such success that a company of Huguenot raiders kidnapped them and took them before a kangaroo court of Calvinist ministers. After a heated theological discussion Bl James was shot and Bl William was stabbed to death. They were beatified in 1926.

James Salomone (Bl) R(OP). May 31
1231–1314. A nobleman from Venice, Italy, he became a Dominican there and was at several friaries of the order until he died of cancer at Forli. His cultus was approved in 1526.

James of Samosata (St) *see* **Samosata (Martyrs of)**

James of Sandomir (Bl) *see* **Sadoc and Comps**

James of Sasseau (St) R(OSB). Nov 19
d. *c*865. Originally an army officer at Constantinople, after travelling widely he came to France, was ordained at Clermont and became a monk at Bourges. Later he was a hermit at Sasseau.

James Schmid (Bl) *see* **September (Martyrs of)**

James of Strepa (Bl) B. R(OFM). Oct 21
*c*1350–?1409. A Pole from Galicia, he became a Franciscan and worked very successfully as vicar-general of the Franciscan missions

St James the Less, May 3 *(see p. 286)*

among the Orthodox and pagans of what is now the western Ukraine. In 1392 he became archbishop of Halicz, based at Lemberg (now Lviv). His cultus was approved for Lviv in 1791.

James the Syrian (St) R. Aug 6
d. *p*500. He was a Syrian hermit at Amida (now Diyarbakir in Turkey).

James of Tarantaise (St) B. Jan 16
d. ?429. From Syria, he became a monk at Lérins, France, under St Honoratus and was a missionary in Savoy, becoming the first bishop of Tarentaise.

James Thompson (alias Hudson) (Bl) M. P. Nov 28
d. 1582. From York, he was educated for the priesthood at Rheims, ordained in 1581 and hanged the following year at York. He was beatified in 1895. *See* **England (Martyrs of)**.

James of Toul (St) B. Jun 23
d. 769. Probably from near Chaumont, France, it is alleged that he was a monk of Hornbach near Metz before he became bishop of Toul in 756. He was a great benefactor of monasteries, and died praying before the tomb of St Benignus at Dijon while returning from a pilgrimage to Rome.

James of Voragine (Bl) B. R(OP). Jul 13
*c*1230–1298. From Varezze (Voragine) near Savona, Italy, he became a Dominican in 1244, was provincial superior of Lombardy from 1267 to 1286 and became archbishop of Genoa in 1292. He is famous as the author of *The Golden Legend*, a major source-book for study of the medieval mind and its interests. His cultus was confirmed for Genoa and Savona in 1816.

James Walworth (Bl) M. R(OCart). May 11
d. 1537. A monk of the London Charterhouse, he was hanged in chains at York in the reign of Henry VIII and was beatified in 1886. *See* **England (Martyrs of)**.

James Yan (Guodong) and James Zhao (Quanxin) (SS) *see* **Gregory Grassi and Comps**

Jane
Many feminine versions of 'John' have developed independently in the various vernaculars. For the purpose of this book they are all listed under 'Jane', although 'Joan' and 'Jean' are English alternatives. Other forms are: in Italian, Giovanna; in French, Jeanne; in

Spanish, Juana; in Portuguese and Catalan, Joana.

Jane Antida Thouret (St) R. F. Aug 24
1765–1828. From near Besançon, France, the daughter of a tanner, she joined the 'Sisters of Charity of St Vincent de Paul' in 1787 but was forced to return home on the outbreak of the French Revolution. Then she started a school of her own for poor girls at Besançon, and attracted so many helpers in this and in other works of charity that she formed them into a new 'Institute of Sisters of Charity'. She died at Naples and was canonized in 1934.

Jane of Arc *see* **Joan of Arc**

Jane de Aza de Guzman (Bl) L. Aug 8
d. *c*1200. The mother of St Dominic was born at the family castle of Aza south of Burgos, Spain. She married Felix de Guzman, had two sons and a daughter and then conceived the future founder of the Dominicans after praying before the shrine of St Dominic of Silos. Her cultus was confirmed for Palencia, Osma and the Dominicans in 1828.

Jane of Bagno (Bl)
R(OSB Cam). Sep 4
d. ?1105. From Fontechiuso in Tuscany, Italy, she became a Camaldolese lay sister at Santa Lucia near Bagno. Her cultus as patron of Bagno was approved for Borgo San Sepolcro in 1823.

Jane Beretta Molla (Bl) L. Apr 28
1922–1962. Born near Milan, Italy, she became a doctor and specialized in paediatrics at the University of Milan from 1952, considering the practice of medicine to be a missionary vocation. Married in 1955, she developed a fibroma of the uterus during her third pregnancy and insisted that the life of the child should be saved rather than hers if a choice were necessary. This was done, and she died seven days after the birth of a healthy baby. She was beatified in 1994.

Jane-Elizabeth Bichier des Ages (St) R. F. Aug 26
1773–1832. A noblewoman born at the Château des Ages near Poitiers, France, she became a disciple of St Andrew Fournet at Saint-Pierre-de-Maillé after the Revolution and (in spite of grave difficulties at the outset) founded the 'Congregation of the Daughters of the Cross of St Andrew' for teaching and nursing in hospitals. She died at Paris and was canonized in 1947.

Jane-Mary Bonomo (Bl) R(OSB). Mar 1
1616–1670. Born at Asiago, near Vicenza, Italy, she was educated by the Poor Clares at Trent, became a Benedictine at Bassano in 1622 and fell into supernatural ecstasy for the first time at the ceremony of profession. She was novice mistress and was abbess three times, but was bitterly persecuted by some members of her own community. She was beatified in 1783.

Jane Bourigault (Bl) *see* **William Repin and Comps**

Jane-of-the-Cross Delanoue
(St) R.F. Aug 16
1666–1732. The twelfth child of a man who ran a small business in the village of Fenet near Angers, France, she had a pious childhood but her father died and she took over the business. This left little time for piety and she became avaricious, but after an extraordinary supernatural vision she began to help poor women and sick persons. For their care she founded and joined the institute of the 'Sisters of St Anne'. She died at Fenet and was canonized in 1982.

Bl Jane-of-the-Cross Delanoue, Aug 16

Jane Fouchard (Bl) *see* **William Repin and Comps**

Jane-Frances Frémiot de Chantal (St) R. F. Dec 12
1572–1641. From Dijon, France, she married the Baron de Chantal in 1592. They were happily married for eight years and had four

children before he died as the result of a hunting accident. Then she became the disciple and friend of St Francis de Sales, who described her as 'the perfect woman'. Under his guidance she founded the new order of the Visitation, chiefly for widows and for women unsuited to the austerities of the older religious orders. Sixty-six nunneries were established during her lifetime, the last years of which were a period of intense suffering in body and in mind. Dying at Moulins, she had her shrine established at Annecy and was canonized in 1767.

Jane Gérard (Bl) *see* **Cambrai (Martyrs of)**

Jane Gourdon, Jane Gruget and Jane-Mary Leduc (BB) *see* **William Repin and Comps**

Jane de Lestonnac (St) R. F. Feb 2
1556–1640. A noblewoman from Bordeaux, France, with a Calvinist mother, she married and had a family but her husband died when she was forty-six. Then she tried and failed to join a nunnery affiliated to the Cistercians, whereupon she set about founding a new religious institute for the education of girls in order to combat Calvinism. This was approved in 1607, and the first house of the 'Daughters of Our Lady of Bordeaux' was opened at Bordeaux. The order spread rapidly, some thirty houses being founded, and she was the superior-general. As the result of a calumny and intrigue on the part of one of the sisters she was deposed and spent some years in seclusion but was vindicated before she died. She was canonized in 1949.

Jane-Mary de Maillé (Bl) T(OFM). Mar 28
1331–1414. A noblewoman born near Tours, France, she married the Baron de Sillé with whom she lived in virginity for sixteen years. After his death in 1362 she joined the Franciscan tertiaries and retired to Tours, where she spent the rest of her life in poverty and deprivation owing to persecution by her husband's relatives. Her cultus was confirmed in 1871.

Jane-Frances-of-the-Visitation Michelotti (Bl) R. F. Feb 1
1843–1888. Born at Annecy, Savoy (now in France), from an early age she dedicated herself to caring for poor sick people in their homes, especially after she moved to Turin in 1871 and came under the influence of St John Bosco. In 1875 she founded the 'Little Servants of the Sacred Heart', whose fourth vow is to serve sick poor people without charge. She was beatified in 1975.

Jane Monnier and Jane Onillon (BB) *see* **William Repin and Comps**

Jane (Vanna) of Orvieto
(Bl) T(OP). Jul 23
d. 1306. From near Orvieto, Italy, she entered the convent of Dominican tertiaries there. Her familar name is a diminutive of 'Giovanna'. Her cultus was approved for Orvieto in 1754.

Jane of Portugal (Bl) R(OP). May 12
1452–1490. Born at Lisbon, a daughter of King Alphonsus V of Portugal, she entered the Dominican nunnery at Aveiro near Oporto in 1473. The king prevented her from taking vows, however, until a male heir was born in 1485. She had much trouble because of this. Her cultus was confirmed for Coïmbra in 1693.

Jane-Mary-of-St-Bernard de Romillon (Bl) *see* **Orange (Martyrs of)**

Jane-Mary Saillard d'Epinatz (Bl) *see* **William Repin and Comps**

Jane Scopelli (Bl) R(OC). Jul 9
?1428–1491. From Reggio d'Emilia, Italy, she founded the Carmelite nunnery there and was the first superior. She refused all endowments except those freely given to the nuns as alms. Her cultus was confirmed for Reggio and the Carmelites in 1771.

Jane of Signa (Bl) R. Nov 17
d. 1307. From Signa near Florence, Italy, she was a poor sheep-farmer's daughter and a shepherd herself before she became a hermit for forty years near her home village. Several religious orders claimed her as a tertiary, but there is no evidence that she was linked to any of them. Her cultus was approved for Florence in 1798.

Jane Soderini (Bl) T(OSM). Sep 1
1301–1367. From Florence, Italy, she was educated by St Juliana Falconieri and became a Servite tertiary through his guidance. Her cultus was confirmed for Florence in 1827.

Jane Thomas (Bl) *see* **William Repin and Comps**

Jane of Toulouse (Bl) T(OC). Mar 31
d. 1286. A noblewoman of Toulouse, France, she was affiliated to the Carmelite order by St Simon Stock while continuing to live with her parents and is thus considered the first Carmelite tertiary. She spent her time and resources in training young candidates for the

Carmelite friars. Her cultus was confirmed for Toulouse in 1895.

Jane of Valois (St) R(OFM). F. Feb 4
1464–1505. She was a daughter of King Louis XI of France, who despised her for her bodily deformity and married her off to the duke of Orléans (afterwards King Louis XII). Her husband obtained a decree of nullity of marriage on the grounds of constraint, so she retired to her castle at Bourges. There, with her confessor Bl Gabriel-Mary Nicolas, she founded the order of nuns of the Annunciation ('Annunciades') which were more involved in works of active charity than the Poor Clares. She took vows but did not live in community. She was canonized in 1949.

Jane-Baptist Varrano (Bl) R(OFM). May 31
1458–1527. Born at Camerino, Italy, daughter of the Duke of Varrano, she became a Poor Clare at Urbino in 1481 and was made abbess of the nunnery of St Claire, founded by her father, in 1499. Her cultus was confirmed for Camerino in 1843.

Jane Véron (Bl) *see* **Laval (Martyrs of)**

Januaria (St) *see* **Paul, Heraclius and Comps**

Januaria (St) *see* **Scillitan Martyrs**

Januarius (St) *see* **Catulinus and Comps**

Januarius (St) *see* **Corfu (Martyrs of)**

Januarius (St) *see* **Faustinus, Lucius and Comps**

Januarius (St) *see* **Felix and Januarius**

Januarius (St) *see* **Felix of Thibiuca**

Januarius (St) *see* **Marcellus of Tangier**

Januarius (St) *see* **Paul, Gerontius and Comps**

Januarius (St) *see* **Protus and Januarius**

Januarius (St) *see* **Seven Brothers**

Januarius (St) *see* **Severus, Securus and Comps**

Januarius (St) *see* **Sixtus II and Comps**

Januarius, Marinus, Nabor and Felix (SS) MM. July 10
? Nothing is known about these Roman African martyrs.

Januarius, Maxima and Macaria (SS) MM. Apr 8
? Nothing is known about these Roman African martyrs. Their names are sometimes given as 'Januarius, Maximus and Macarius' (three men instead of a man and two women).

Januarius and Pelagia (SS) MM. July 11
d. 320. They were beheaded at Nicopolis in Lesser Armenia, Asia Minor, in the reign of Licinius.

Januarius (Gennaro) of Benevento (St) M. B. Sep 19
d. 304. Bishop of Benevento, Italy, he was beheaded at Pozzuoli near Naples in the reign of Diocletian and his body was eventually enshrined at Naples, of which city he is the patron. The yearly liquefaction of a solid kept in two vials and alleged to be his blood is a phenomenon well-attested since the C15th and for which no conclusive scientific explanation has been found. A legend, now discredited but popular in the Middle Ages, linked him with the following: Festus, his deacon; Desiderius, reader; Sosius, deacon of the church of Misenum; Proculus, deacon of Pozzuoli, and two other Christians: Eutyches and Acurius. The existence of these is very doubtful and the joint cultus was suppressed in 1969.

Januarius Sánchez Delgadillo (St) *see* **Mexico (Martyrs of)**

Januarius-Mary Sarnelli (Bl) R(CSSR) Jun 30
1702–1744. A nobleman of Naples, Italy, he met St Alphonsus Liguori while nursing in a hospital and they became lifelong friends. As a parish priest he tried to help young prostitutes. He became a Redemptorist in 1733, preached popular missions and helped the spread of the Congregation. He was beatified in 1996.

Japan (Martyrs of) (SS and BB) MM. Feb 6
d. 1597–1637. The start of the Catholic Church in Japan was marked by the arrival of St Francis Xavier in 1549. Missionary activity was successfully carried on by the Portuguese and Spanish, especially in the island of Kyushu (which became the centre of Japanese Christianity), and this was helped by the

chaotic state of the country at the time and the lack of an effective central government. Many local rulers ('daimyos', sometimes incorrectly referred to as 'kings') converted, and inspired their subjects to do so. There was predictable hostility from the established religions of Buddhism and Shinto, and Japanese suspicion of the motivations of the foreign missionaries and their overseas sponsors. The first edict of persecution was in 1587, and the first mass execution in 1597 (*see* **Paul Miki and Comps**). A period of peace followed the establishment of strong central government with the Tokugawa shogunate in 1600, but persecution returned in 1612 and was violent from 1617, especially in Nagasaki. The complete suppression of the Church became government policy, and this was successful after the Shimabara Uprising was crushed in 1638. The country was completely isolated from foreign influence until the C19th, and the only Christians remaining by then were about 15,000 secret worshippers in Kyushu. *See* lists of national martyrs in appendix.

Jarlath (Hierlath) of Armagh
(St) B. Feb 1
d. *c*480. A disciple of St Patrick, he succeeded St Benignus as archbishop of Armagh, Ireland.

Jarlath of Tuam (St) B. R. Jun 6
d. *c*550. The founder and first abbot-bishop of Tuam in Co. Galway, Ireland, he established a monastic school there which became famous. St Brendan the Voyager and St Colman of Cloyne were pupils. He is the principal patron of the diocese of Tuam.

Jarman *see* **Germanus**

Jason (St) B? Jul 12
C1st. The Acts of the Apostles (17:5–9) refer to St Paul staying at his house in Thessalonika, Greece, and he is also mentioned in the letter to the Romans (16:21). The Byzantine martyrology describes him as a bishop of Tarsus in Cilicia, Asia Minor, who evangelized Corfu and died there. The old Roman Martyrology mistakenly confused him with the Mnason mentioned in Acts (21:16).

Jason (St) *see* **Claudius, Hilaria and Comps**

Jeremias (St) *see* **Elias, Jeremias and Comps**

Jeremias (St) *see* **Emilas and Jeremias**

Jeremias (St) *see* **Isaurus, Innocent and Comps**

Jeremias (St) *see* **Peter, Wallabonsus and Comps**

Jeremias Oghlou Boghos (Bl) *see* **Salvator Lilli and Comps**

Jeremias of Sandomir (Bl) *see* **Sadoc of Sandomir and Comps**

Jeremias of Wallachia (Bl)
R(OFM Cap). Mar 25
1556–1625. Born in Wallachia (now Romania), he went on pilgrimage to Italy when aged 21 but was robbed on the way and could only continue by begging and casual farm-work. Arriving at Bari, he went to Naples where he became a Capuchin lay brother in 1578. He used to nurse the sick and obtained the power to heal by signing with the cross; he also had the charisms of prophecy and the reading of consciences. Despite his illiteracy he was sought out by the well-educated. He was beatified in 1983.

Jermyn (German) Gardiner
(Bl) M. Mar 7
d. 1544. Educated at Cambridge, he became secretary to Stephen Gardiner, bishop of Winchester, and was executed at Tyburn with BB John Larke and John Ireland for denying the royal supremacy. He was beatified in 1886. *See* **England (Martyrs of)**.

Jerome (St) R. Dr. Sep 30
?341–420. Eusebius Hieronymus Sophronius was born at Stridon, near Ljubljana in Slovenia), studied in Rome (where he acquired a passion for classical literature) and was baptized there in 366. He was then with an ascetic community of friends (including Rufinus) at Aquila before going to the East in 373, travelling to Antioch (where he learned Greek, Hebrew and the practice of Biblical exegesis) and spending two years at the Syrian monastic colony at Chalcis. Returning to Rome in 382 he became secretary to Pope St Damasus, who entrusted to him the task of revising the Latin text of the New Testament. This eventually resulted in the Vulgate edition of the Bible, translated from the original Hebrew and Greek. He made enemies, and left with SS Paula and Eustochium to found a Latin monastery at Bethlehem in 386, where he died. Continually involved in controversy, he was a fierce polemicist and an unforgiving opponent (as is revealed in his surviving letters). He was the greatest Biblical scholar after Origen, being unusual among the Fathers for his knowledge of Hebrew, and has been venerated as a doctor

St Jerome, Sep 30

of the Church since the C8th. In the Western artistic tradition he is often shown with a lion in mistake for St Gerasimus. He did not compile the martyrology named after him.

Jerome de Angelis (Bl) M. R(SJ). Dec 4
d. 1623. From Castrogiovanni in Sicily, he became a Jesuit at Messina and went with Bl Charles Spinola to Japan. He worked for twenty-two years in various parts of Japan and was finally betrayed and burned alive at what is now Tokyo together with BB Francis Galvez and Simon Yempo. *See* **Japan (Martyrs of)**.

Jerome Emiliani (St) P. F. Feb 8
1481–1537. From Venice, Italy, as a young man he was an army officer and served in the his city's campaign of conquest of its hinterland. Being taken prisoner, he was set free after praying to Our Lady and became a priest as a result in 1518. He was fervent in wishing to help the poor, sick and orphans of Venice and elsewhere and so founded several orphanages and hospitals in northern Italy and started a religious society (the 'Servants of the Poor') to look after them. The first house of this was at Somascha near Milan, and it was raised to the status of a religious congregation (the 'Clerks Regular of Somascha') after his death. He died of an infection contracted while nursing at Bergamo, was canonized in 1767 and was declared the patron of orphans and street children in 1928.

Jerome Ghirarducci (Bl) R(OSA). Mar 3
d. 1369. From Rencanati near Ancona, Italy, he became an Augustinian friar and a peacemaker between rival factions in and around his native town. His cultus was confirmed for the Augustinians in 1804.

Jerome Hermosilla (St) M. B. R(OP). Nov 1
d. 1861. From La Calzada near Ciudad Real, Spain, he became a Dominican and went to Manila where he was ordained priest and sent to the mission of Vietnam in 1828. He succeeded St Ignatius Delgado as vicar-apostolic of 'East Tonkin' and was himself arrested, tortured and beheaded. *See* **Vietnam (Martyrs of)**.

Jerome Lu (Tingmei) (St) M. L. Dec 14
1811–1857. A convert schoolteacher from Langtai in Guizhou, China, he worked as a catechist and was beheaded at Mokou with SS Laurence Wang, Bing) and Agatha Lin, Zhao). *See* **China (Martyrs of)**.

Jerome Ochoa Urdangarin (Bl) *see* **Hospitaller Martyrs of Spain**

Jerome of Pavia (St) B. July 19
d. 787. He was an obscure bishop of Pavia, Italy, whose cultus was confirmed for there in 1888.

Jerome Ranuzzi (Bl) R(OSM). Dec 12
d. 1455. From Sant' Angelo in Vado near Urbino, Italy, he became a Servite and superior of the friary at his home town. As the personal adviser of the duke of Urbino he was nicknamed 'the Angel of Good Counsel'. His cultus was approved for Sant' Angelo in Vado in 1775.

Jerome-of-the-Cross de Torres (Bl) M. T(OFM). Sep 3
d. 1632. A Japanese secular priest, he had been educated in the seminary of Arima and ordained at Manila. Returning to Japan in 1628, he was burned alive with BB Anthony Ishida and Comps. *See* **Japan (Martyrs of)**.

Jerome of Vallombrosa (Bl) R(OSB Vall). Jun 18
d. 1135. A monk at Vallombrosa near Florence, Italy, he was a hermit for thirty-five years, allegedly subsisting for that time on bread and water only.

Jerome Weerden (St) R(OFM). Jul 9
1522–1572. From Weert in the Netherlands, he was a Franciscan missionary in the Holy Land for several years before becoming the vicar of the friary at Gorinchem under St Nicholas Pieck. He was a powerful preacher against Calvinism, and was one of the **Gorinchem martyrs** (q.v.).

Jesus Gesta de Piquer (Bl) *see* **Hospitaller Martyrs of Spain**

Jesus Hita Miranda *see* **Charles Eraña Guruceta**

Jesus Méndez Montoya (St) *see* **Mexico (Martyrs of)**

Jesus-Augustine Viela Ezcurdia (Bl) *see* **Philip-of-Jesus Munárriz Azcona and Comps**

Joachim (St) L. Jul 26
C1st. This is the name given to the father of Our Lady in the apocryphal gospel of James, although other sources name him as Heli, Cleopas, Eliacim, Jonachir or Sadoc. Nothing whatever is known about him. He has been commemorated liturgically in the East from early times but in the West only since the C16th.

Joachim of Fiore (Bl) R(OCist). Mar 30
*c*1130–1202. From near Cosenza in Calabria, Italy, after a pilgrimage to the Holy Land he became a Cistercian at Sambucina and was made abbot of Corazzo in 1176. In 1192 he left to become a hermit and founded a reformed abbey at Fiore, the start of a new Cistercian congregation. He was a prolific ascetical and biblical writer, and his commentary on the Apocalypse gave him the nickname of 'the Prophet'. After his death this work became the basis of heretical speculations on the part of some of his own congregation and by the Franciscan Spirituals, and his popular cultus was never confirmed.

Joachim Hirayama-Diaz (Bl) M. L. Aug 19
d. 1622. A Japanese ship's captain, he was hired to take BB **Louis Flores** (q.v.) and Peter Zuñiga to Japan. The ship was captured by Dutch privateers, brought to Hirado and her company taken to Nagasaki. Bl Joachim was burned with the two missionaries while the rest were beheaded. *See* **Japan (Martyrs of)**.

Joachim Hao (Kaizhi) (St) M. L. May 29
1782–1839. A craftsman of Guizhou, China, he was converted in Guiyang and exiled to Mongolia for eighteen years. After assisting the authorities during a Mongol rebellion he was allowed to return to Guiyang, but was later arrested, tortured and executed. *See* **China (Martyrs of)**.

Joachim Royo Pérez (St) M. R(OP). Oct 28
1691–1748. From Teruel, Spain, he became a Dominican at Valencia and was sent to China in 1715. He worked in secret in Jiangxi and Zhejiang, but was captured and executed after two years in prison. *See* **Francis Serrano and Comps**.

Joachim Sakakibara (St) M. T(OFM). Feb 6
d. 1597. A Japanese doctor, he worked with the Franciscan missionaries as a catechist and was crucified at Nagasaki with SS Paul Miki and Comps. *See* **Japan (Martyrs of)**.

Joachim of Sandomir (Bl) *see* **Sadoc of Sandomir and Comps**

Joachim-of-St-Anne Wall
(St) M. R(OFM). Aug 22
d. 1679. From a recusant family near Preston, Lancs, John Wall was educated at Douai and in Rome and became a Franciscan at Douai in 1651. In 1656 he returned to England and worked in Warwickshire and Worcestershire until he was arrested and executed as a result of the Oates plot. He was canonized in 1970. *See* **England (Martyrs of)**.

Joan of Arc (St) V. May 30
1412–143. Nicknamed 'the Maid of Orléans' or 'La Pucelle', she was the daughter of a peasant born at Domrémy in the Champagne, France. When aged seventeen, while keeping her father's sheep, she heard supernatural voices commanding her to take up arms and lead the French army against the English invaders then besieging Orléans. She left home disguised as a man, convinced the Dauphin of her sincerity and enabled him to be crowned as King Charles VII by her rapid military successes. As she herself had predicted, however, she was captured by the Burgundians and handed over to the English. Then she was tried by an ecclesiastical court, condemned as a heretic and burnt at the stake at Rouen. The case was re-tried in 1456 and she was declared innocent. She was canonized in 1920 and declared patroness of France in 1922. Problems exist, however, as to the 'heavenly' inspiration of her military career. She claimed that St Margaret of Antioch and St Catherine of Alexandria spoke to her but these persons never existed. She is usually depicted as a young woman in contemporary plate armour.

Joanna (St) L. May 24
C1st. The wife of Chuza, steward of the tetrarch Herod Antipas, she is mentioned by the Gospel of St Luke (8:3) as one of the women followers who ministered to the needs of Christ.

Joannicius the Great (St) R. Nov 4
750–846. From Bithynia, Asia Minor, he was a soldier in the imperial bodyguards of emperors Leo III and Constantine V and supported their iconoclast policies. He converted, however, became a hermit on the Bithynian Olympus when aged forty and was thenceforth an energetic defender of icons. He was also known as a prophet and thaumaturge.

Joanninus de San Juan (Bl) M. Jul 15
d. 1570. A nephew of the captain of the ship which carried BB **Ignatius de Azevedo and Comps** (q.v.), he volunteered to join them in their martyrdom and was thrown into the sea.

Joaquina Vedruna de Mas
(St) R. F. Aug 28
1783–1854. A Spanish noblewoman, she was widowed in the Napoleonic wars and went to live at Vich in Catalonia where she founded the 'Carmelite Sisters of Charity'. They spread throughout Spain and South America. She died of cholera at Barcelona and was canonized in 1959.

Joavan (St) B. Mar 2
d. *c*570. Allegedly from Ireland, he was educated in Britain and migrated to Brittany, France, to be with his uncle St Paul of Léon, whom he succeeded as bishop of St Pol de Léon.

Jodoc *see* **Judoc**

John
This is the most popular name in Christendom. The original Hebrew has been Hellenized and Latinized into Joannes, whence the numerous variants in all languages. Examples are: Italian, Giovanni; French, Jean; Spanish, Juan; Portuguese, Joan; Dutch, Jan; German, Johann; Russian, Ivan. There are also numerous diminutive forms, e.g. Italian, Giovannino, Nanino; Spanish, Juanito; French, Jeanin; Old English, Johnikin. The name is often used in combination with others, especially in the Latin countries, e.g. Gianpier, Gianluigi, Jean-Benoit, Jean-François, Juan-José, Juan-Maria.

John I, Pope (St) M. May 18
d. 526. A Tuscan, he became a priest at Rome and was made pope in 523. The city was then part of the Ostrogothic kingdom of Italy and was ruled by Theodoric, an Arian. It was known, however, that the Empire was planning a reconquest of Italy, and Pope John was ordered to go on an embassy to the emperor Justin I in 526 in order to try and forestall this and to ask for an end to imperial sanctions against Arians. On his return Theodoric imprisoned him on suspicion of having conspired with the emperor and he died of ill-treatment in custody.

John XXIII, Pope (Bl) (Jun 3)
1881–1963. Angelo Roncalli was born at Sotto il Monte near Bergamo, Italy, of a peasant family, entered the seminary in 1892 and was ordained in 1904. In 1925 he was made Apostolic Visitor to Bulgaria, and to Turkey and Greece in 1935. In 1944 he became Nuncio in France, and was made Cardinal Patriarch of

Venice in 1953. He was elected Pope in 1958, and the way he performed his duties earned him the nickname of 'Good Pope John'. He initiated the revision of the code of Canon Law but is most famous for his convening of the Second Vatican Council. He died when the council was still in session, and was beatified in 2000.

Bl John XXIII, Jun 3

John and Benignus (SS) R. Jul 21
d. 707. Allegedly twin brothers, they were monks of Moyenmoutier in the Vosges, France, under St Hidulf.

John and Crispus (SS) MM. Aug 18
? According to the old Roman Martyrology they were Roman priests who used to bury the bodies of martyred Christians, because of which they themselves suffered martyrdom. Their names are taken from the untrustworthy acta of SS Simplicius, Faustinus and Beatrix.

John and Festus (SS) MM. Dec 21
? They are listed in the old Roman Martyrology as having been martyred in Tuscany, Italy, but details are lacking.

John and James (SS) MM. Nov 1
d. ?344. They were Persian martyrs of the reign of Shah Shapur II. John is listed as a bishop.

John and Paul (SS) MM. June 26
? They were martyred at Rome but not (as asserted in their spurious acta) in the reign of Julian. Their names occur in the Roman canon of the Mass and there is a basilica dedicated to them on the Coelian Hill, to which their cultus has been confined since 1969.

John, Sergius and Comps
(SS) MM. RR. Mar 20
d. 796. A group of twenty monks of the laura of St Sabas in the Judaean Desert, they were killed in a Bedouin raid on the monastery. Many more were wounded and a few escaped. One of the last, called Stephen the Poet, wrote a detailed account of the event.

John Adams (Bl) M. P. Oct 8
d. 1586. A convert from Dorset, he was ordained at Rheims and seized at Winchester on his third missionary journey to England. He was executed at Tyburn with BB Robert Dibdale and John Love and was beatified in 1987. *See* **England (Martyrs of)**.

John-Jesus Adradas Gonzalo (Bl) *see* **Hospitaller Martyrs of Spain**

John the African (St) *see* **Claudius, Crispin and Comps**

John Agramunt Riera (Bl) *see* **Dionysius Pamplona Polo and Comps**

John Alcalde Alcaldo (Bl) *see* **Hospitaller Martyrs of Spain**

John Alcober Figuera
(St) M. R(OP). Oct 28
1694–1748. From Gerona, Spain, he became a Dominican at Granada and was sent to China in 1728. For sixteen years he worked in the province of Fujian but was arrested in 1746 and strangled in prison at Fuzhou. *See* **Francis Serrano and Comps**.

John Almond (St) M. P. Dec 5
?1577–1612. From Allerton near Liverpool, he was educated for the priesthood at Rheims and Rome. Ordained in 1598, he worked on the English mission from 1602 and was highly regarded. Executed at Tyburn, London, he was canonized in 1970. *See* **England (Martyrs of)**.

John the Almsgiver (St) B. R. Jan 23
d. ?616. Son of a governor of Cyprus, he lost his family, became a monk and went on to become Melkite patriarch of Alexandria in ?608. At this time the Egyptian church was completely split between the majority Monophysite Copts and the minority Orthodox Melkites. He gained the

admiration of both factions by his policy of liberal and systematic almsgiving and by his personal integrity (it being rumoured that he never spoke an idle word). He was exiled just before his death by the Persian conquest of Egypt.

John Amias (alias Anne)
(Bl) M. P. Mar 15
d. 1589. From near Wakefield, Yorks, he was a married clothes-seller but his wife died and he went on to study at Rheims for the priesthood. Ordained in 1581, he was executed at York with Bl Robert Dalby. He was beatified in 1929. *See* **England (Martyrs of)**.

John Andrzejuk (Bl) *see* **Podlasia (Martyrs of)**

John-Juvenal Aneina (Bl) B. Sep 12
1545–1604. From Fossano in Piedmont, Italy, he became professor of medicine at the university of Turin and was posted to the Savoyard Embassy at Rome. There he came under the influence of St Philip Neri, joined the Oratory in 1575 and was sent to Naples to open a new oratory there. He was noted especially for his work for the poor. Finally he was made bishop of Saluzzo in 1602 and set out on his first episcopal visitation. On his return to Saluzzo he was poisoned by a friar whose immorality he had rebuked. He was beatified in 1869.

John Angelo Porro
(Bl) R(OSM). Oct 24
d. 1504. From Milan, Italy, he became a Servite and, after some time spent at Monte Senario, worked in Milan until the end of his life. His cultus was confirmed for Milan in 1737.

John Angeloptes (St) B. Nov 27
d. 433. Bishop of Ravenna, Italy, from 430, he was nicknamed 'Angeloptes' (meaning 'the man who saw an angel') because, according to his legend, an angel only visible to him came and assisted him once in celebrating Mass.

John de Atarés and Comps
(SS) R. May 29
d. *c*750. A hermit in a cell under a huge rock near Jaca in the Aragonese Pyrenees, Spain, he was joined by two brothers from Zaragoza, Votus and Felix. Later their cell became the abbey of La Peña ('The Rock'), which was important in the formation of the Christian kingdoms of Navarre and Aragón.

John Aubert (Bl) *see* **September (Martyrs of)**

John of Autun (St) B. Oct 29
? Nothing is known about this bishop of Autun, France.

John of Avila (St) P. May 10
d. 1569. The 'Apostle of Andalucia' was born at Almodóvar del Pinar near Cuenca, Spain, and studied law at Salamanca and theology at Alcalá. He was about to leave for the New World after being ordained, but was detained by the archbishop of Seville and spent the forty years of his priestly career evangelizing Andalucia. He was a famous preacher, writer (his ascetical writings, especially his letters, are among the classics of Spanish literature) and spiritual director (he directed SS Teresa of Avila, Francis Borgia, John of God and Louis of Granada). He died at Montilla and was canonized in 1970.

John de Baeza (Bl) *see* **Ignatius de Azevedo and Comps**

John Baixeras Berenguer (Bl) *see* **Philip-of-Jesus Munárriz Azcona and Comps**

John Bangue (Bl) *see* **September (Martyrs of)**

John the Baptist (St) M. Jun 24
C1st. The career of the last of the prophets and the forerunner of Christ is described in the four Gospels, where he is presented as modelled on Elijah (in his clothing, for example). He is also mentioned by Josephus. There has been much scholarly speculation on the wider context of his ministry in contemporary Jewish society, and on a possible link with the Essenes of Qumran. Patristic tradition maintained that St John was freed from original sin and sanctified in his mother's womb, hence his birthday is liturgically celebrated with a higher dignity than the day of his beheading (Aug 29). The fate of his relics, especially of his head, is confused by conflicting traditions after the destruction of his alleged tomb at Samaria in the reign of Julian. The earliest of these describes his head being found at Emesa (now Homs) in Syria and being venerated at the great basilica at Damascus, which is now the Umayyad mosque there. His attribute is a lamb.

John Bassand (Bl) R(OSB). Aug 26
1360–1445. From Besançon, France, he became an Augustinian canon regular there but quickly passed over to the Celestine Benedictines (now extinct) at Paris. He was spiritual director of St Colette while founding a monastery at Amiens and was later the provincial superior of France. He made great

St John the Baptist, Jun 24 *(see p. 297)*

efforts to establish his congregation in Aragón, Italy and England (with no success in the latter case) and died near Aquila in Italy.

John of Bastone (Bl) R(OSB Silv). Mar 24
d. 1290. He was one of the first disciples of St Sylvester at Montefano and had his cultus confirmed for Fabriano, Italy, in 1772.

John and Peter Becchetti (BB) R(OSA). Aug 11
C13th. When St Thomas Becket was exiled by King Henry II, other members of his family were also banished, and one branch allegedly became the Becchetti of Fabriano, Italy. These two Augustinian friars were descended therefrom. Bl John allegedly taught at Oxford. Their cultus was approved for the Augustinian friars in 1835.

John Beche (Bl) *see* **Benedictine Martyrs of the Reformation**

John-Peter-of-St-Anthony Bengoa Aranguren (Bl) *see* **Nicephorus Díez Tejerina and Comps**

John Benincasa (Bl) R(OSM). May 11
1376–1426. From Florence, Italy, he became a Servite friar at Montepulciano and became a hermit, latterly at Monticelli where he died. He was not related to St Catherine of Siena.

John Benoît (Bl) *see* **September (Martyrs of)**

John Berchmans (St) R(SJ). Nov 26
1599–1621. From Diest in Brabant, Belgium, the son of a shoemaker, he studied at Mechelen and entered the Jesuits there at the age of seventeen, being sent to Rome for his novitiate. His short life of twenty-two years was remarkable for the heroic fidelity with which he kept even the most trivial points of regular observance, and yet he had great serenity. He was canonized in 1888 and is the patron of young altar-servers.

John of Bergamo (St) B. Jul 11
d. *c*690. Bishop of Bergamo, Italy, from ?656, he was famous for his scholarship and his success in resisting Arianism. The letters BM for 'Bonae Memoriae' ('of good memory') were added to his name in an early list and these were later misread as 'Beati Martyris' ('of the Blessed Martyr'), hence the spurious tradition of his martyrdom.

John Bernard (Bl) *see* **September (Martyrs of)**

John of Beverley (St) B. R. May 7
d. 721. From Harpham near Driffield in Yorkshire, England, he studied at Canterbury under SS Adrian and Theodore before becoming a monk at Whitby. Eventually he was ordained bishop of Hexham, whence he was transferred to York. He ordained St Bede to the priesthood and was the founder of Beverley Abbey, to which he retired in 717. This abbey did not survive the Vikings.

John-Mary Boccardo (Bl) P. F. Nov 20
1848–1913. From Turin, Italy, he became a diocesan priest there in 1871 and was a seminary spiritual director before being made parish priest of Pancalieri in 1882. Two years later there was a cholera epidemic there which left many children and old people with no-one to care for them, so he founded a hospice and a congregation of 'Poor Daughters of St Cajetan' which spread throughout Italy. He was both cheerful and devoted to arduous penance. Dying at Pancalieri, he was beatified in 1998.

John Bodey (Bl) M. L. Nov 2
d. 1583. From Wells, Somerset, and a fellow of New College, Oxford, he became a convert and studied law at Douai. Returning to England he worked as a schoolmaster, was condemned for repudiating the royal supremacy in spiritual matters and was hanged at Andover, Hants. He was beatified in 1929. *See* **England (Martyrs of)**.

John-Louis Bonnard (St) M. P. May 1
1824–1852. A French missionary priest who belonged to the Paris Society of Foreign Missions, he was beheaded in central Vietnam. *See* **Vietnam (Martyrs of)**.

John Bonnel de Pradal (Bl) *see* **September (Martyrs of)**

John Bosco (St) R. F. Jan 31
1815–1888. The son of a peasant from near Castelnuovo d'Asti in Piedmont, Italy, he became a diocesan priest at Turin in 1841 and began his life's work of educating boys. From the first he had a clear programme of education, namely to educate through love and to induce the boys to love their teachers, their studies and all the conditions surrounding their education. He gathered disciples and founded a new institute which received papal approval in 1860. This was dedicated to Our Lady, Help of Christians and St Francis of Sales, hence the name of 'Salesians'. It grew rapidly and spread throughout Europe and the foreign missions. He also formed a new sisterhood on the same pattern for the education of girls, the 'Daughters of Mary Auxiliatrix'. He died at Turin and was canonized in 1934.

John Boste (St) M. P. Jul 24
1543–1594. From Dufton near Appleby in Cumbria, he studied at the Queen's College, Oxford, converted in 1576 and then studied for the priesthood at Rheims. Ordained in 1581, he worked in northern England for twelve years until his execution at Durham. He was canonized in 1970. *See* **England (Martyrs of)**.

John Bottex (Bl) *see* **September (Martyrs of)**

John Bourdon (Bl) *see* **John-Baptist Souzy and Comps**

John Bousquet (Bl) *see* **September (Martyrs of)**

John de Brébeuf and Comps
(SS) MM. RR(SJ). Oct 19
1596–1649. From Condé-en-Brie in Normandy, France, he joined the Jesuits at Rouen in 1617 and was a missionary priest in the French colony of Quebec from 1625. There he worked among the native Huron nation for thirty-four years. The Hurons were the target of a policy of extermination by the Iroquois, their mortal enemies, and he and seven other Jesuits fell into the hands of the latter. They were very slowly tortured to death by cutting and burning (eyeballs were replaced by burning coals) and the bits left of their bodies were eaten. The other seven were Isaac Jogues (killed in 1646), Anthony Daniel, Gabriel Lalement, Charles Garnier, Noel Chabanel, John Lalande and Renatus Goupil.

John Bretton (Bl) M. L. Apr 1
1529–1598. A well-known recusant and family man of Sandal Magna, Yorks, he was condemned for 'using seditious words against the Queen'. However he was offered a reprieve in exchange for his apostasy, which he refused. He was executed at York, and was beatified in 1987. *See* **England (Martyrs of)**.

St John Bosco, Jan 31

John of Bridlington *see* **John Thwing**

John de Britto (St) M. R(SJ). Feb 4
1647–1693. From Lisbon, Portugal, he became a Jesuit in 1662 and soon afterwards was sent to southern India. He worked in what are now Kerala and Tamil Nadu, modelling his behaviour on that of the Brahmin caste in an attempt to make contact with the nobility. His methods were unconventional and enlightened in many other respects. He was captured, tortured and expelled in 1687 but returned in 1689 as superior of the Jesuit mission in India. He persuaded the rajah of Siruvalli to abandon polygamy, but one of the dismissed wives persuaded her relative, the rajah of Marava, to initiate a persecution and John was martyred at Oriyur. He was canonized in 1947.

John-Baptist de Bruxelles (Bl) *see* **John-Baptist Souzy and Comps**

John Bufalari of Rieti (Bl) R(OSA). Aug 9
d. *c*1350. From Castel Porziano near Rome, he became an Augustinian friar at Rieti. His cultus was approved for the Augustinian friars in 1832.

John-Baptist Bullaker (Bl) M R(OFM). Oct 12
d. 1642. The son of a physician at Midhurst in Sussex, he was baptized as Thomas. Studying at Valladolid, he joined the Franciscans at Abroya, was ordained and sent to Plymouth. He was caught on his arrival but released and had a ministry of eleven years before being caught saying Mass in London by the Parliamentary authorities during the Civil War. He was executed at Tyburn and was beatified in 1987. *See* **England (Martyrs of)**.

John Buonagiunta (St) *see* **Seven Holy Founders**

John Buoni (Bl) R(OSA). F. Oct 23
d. 1249. From Mantua, Italy, he was a travelling jester with a flair for obscenity who was popular at various Italian courts, but converted in 1208 after a severe illness and became a penitential hermit near Cesena. Disciples gathered to him, and these were given the Augustinian rule by the pope. His group united with others to form the order of Augustinian friars, often referred to as 'hermits' as a result of their origins. His cultus was approved in 1483.

John Burali of Parma (Bl) R(OFM). Mar 20
1209–1289. From Parma, Italy, he became a Franciscan and taught theology at Bologna and Naples. He was seventh minister-general of the Franciscans from 1247 to 1257 and visited the Franciscan provinces of various countries (including England). He also went to Constantinople as papal legate. He died in retirement at Greccio, and had his cultus confirmed for Camerino and the Franciscans in 1777.

John-Anthony Burró Más (Bl) *see* **Hospitaller Martyrs of Spain**

John Burté (Bl) *see* **September (Martyrs of)**

John Calabria (St) S. F. Dec 4
1873–1954. Born at Verona, Italy, of a poor family, he was ordained there in 1901 and founded a refuge for poor and derelict children in 1907 which became known as the 'Opus Dei'. This moved to San Zenone in Monte the next year, and he organized his helpers as the 'Poor Servants and Handmaids of Divine Providence' in 1914. He also organized a corresponding extern society in 1944. Dying at Verona, he was canonized in 1999.

John Calabytes (St) R. Jan 15
d. *c*450. His romantic legend, probably the source of the similar one concerning St Alexis, is as follows. From Constantinople, the twelve-year-old child of a nobleman, he ran away from home to be a monk at Gomon on the Bosporus. After six years he returned home incognito, so changed in appearance that his parents did not recognize him. He then lived on their charity in a small hut (his surname is Greek for 'hut dweller') outside the gate of their mansion, and only revealed himself to them as their son just before he died.

John Camillus 'the Good' (St) B. Jan 10
d. *c*660. A friend of St Gregory the Great, he became bishop of Milan, Italy, in 649 and resided there, the first bishop to do so since the invasion of the Arian Lombards seventy years previously. He fought the Arian and Monothelite heresies.

John Capeau (Bl) *see* **September (Martyrs of)**

John of Capistrano (St) R(OFM). Oct 23
1386–1456. From Capistrano in the Abruzzi, Italy, he became a lawyer and was governor of Perugia in the Papal States. When aged thirty he separated from his wife, joined the Franciscans and (influenced by St Bernardine of Siena) became a famous preacher. He was made papal inquisitor in 1426 and prompted a reform of his order. In 1431 he became minister-general

of the Observants, and was papal legate to many European states and in the Holy Land. He took measures against the Czech Hussites and the Jews (for which he has been criticized), and led a crusade to help the Hungarians against the Turks in 1455. He died near Belgrade and was canonized in 1724.

John of Caramola (Bl) R(OCist). Aug 26
d. 1339. From Toulouse, France, he was a hermit on Monte Caramola in the Basilicata, Italy, before becoming a Cistercian lay brother at the abbey of Sagittario near Naples.

John Carey (Bl) M. L. Jul 4
d. 1594. He was the Irish servant of Bl Thomas Bosgrave and was martyred at Dorchester, Dorset, with him and with BB John Cornelius and Patrick Salmon. They were beatified in 1929. *See* **England (Martyrs of)**.

John Caron (Bl) *see* **September (Martyrs of)**

John Cassian (St) R. Jul 23
?360–?433. From Scythia (probably Dobruja in Romania), when young he became a monk at Jerusalem with his friend Germanus but they then went to stay in Egypt from 386, visiting the various monastic centres. Thus he was able to gather the material for his two seminal works on monastic spirituality, the *Institutes* and the *Conferences*, which had a profound influence on Western monasticism (St Benedict recommended them in his rule). They were at Constantinople in 400, where St John was ordained deacon by St John Chrysostom, and were sent to Rome to seek help when the latter was exiled. In 414 St John founded two monasteries for men and women at Marseilles, where he died. He attacked St Augustine's teaching on grace on the basis that it denied free will, and hence has historically been regarded with a little suspicion by the Church.

John of Cetina and Peter de Dueñas (BB) M. R(OFM). May 22
d. 1397. Franciscans of Spain, they were sent to the Muslim kingdom of Granada in order to try and evangelize the inhabitants and were predictably killed. Their cultus is unconfirmed.

John of Chalon-sur-Saône
(St) B. May 9
d. ?475. He was the third bishop of Chalon-sur-Saône, France, having been ordained as such by St Patiens of Lyons.

John Charton de Millou (Bl) *see* **September (Martyrs of)**

John Chen (Xianheng) (St) M. L. Feb 18
1820–1862. From Chengdu in Sichuan, China, he moved to Guiyang to help a destitute sister and was converted there. As a lay catechist he helped St John-Peter Néel and was seized and beheaded with him and SS John Zhang (Tianshen), and Martin Wu (Xuesheng) at Kaiyang. *See* **China (Martyrs of)**.

John-Baptist Chieng (Seung-yen) (St) *see* **Peter Choi (Chi-chieng) and Comps**

John of Chinon (St) R. Jun 27
C6th. A Breton, he became a hermit at Chinon near Tours, France, and was the spiritual adviser of Queen St Radegund.

John Chozaburo and Comps
(Bl) M. T(OSA). Sep 28
d. 1630. A Japanese Augustinian tertiary, he helped Bl Bartholomew Gutierrez as a catechist and was beheaded at Nagasaki with five other tertiaries: BB Laurence Hachizo, Mancius Ichizayemon, Michael Sukizayemon, Peter Kuhyoye and Thomas Kahyoye. They were beatified in 1867. *See* **Japan (Martyrs of)**.

St John Chrysostom, Sep 13

John Chrysostom (St) B. Dr. Sep 13
?347–407. From Antioch, Syria, he was a hermit-monk in his youth but the austerity ruined his digestion and he became a priest of the city in 386. The sermons that he gave in the

great basilica there made him famous, and are the best extant examples of the Antiochian school of biblical exegesis. They gave him his surname 'Golden Mouth'. In 398 he was made patriarch of Constantinople and was zealous in reforming church life there, but this made enemies at the Imperial court and he was deposed and exiled at the 'Synod of the Oak' in 403 at the instigation of Theophilus, Patriarch of Alexandria. Returning by popular acclaim two months later, he was finally exiled to Armenia after he had offended the Empress and died at Pityus in Colchis, Georgia. He allegedly revised the Byzantine liturgy that now bears his name and was the most prolific of the Eastern doctors of the Church. His iconic representation shows him with a weak, wispy beard and is possibly based on his real appearance.

John Chugoku (Bl). M. R(SJ). Sep 10
d. 1622. From Yamaguchi in Japan, he worked with Bl Charles Spinola as a cathechist and was received by him as a Jesuit in the prison at Omura. He was the only Jesuit beheaded at Nagasaki in the 'Great Martyrdom'. *See* **Japan (Martyrs of)**.

John Cini 'Soldato' or 'Stipendario' or 'della Pace' (Bl) T(OFM). Nov 12
d. 1433. A nobleman of Pisa, Italy, as a soldier he was one of a gang that attacked a group of priests. Afterwards, remorseful, he became a Franciscan tertiary in 1396 and founded several charitable organizations as well as a confraternity of flagellants. His cultus was approved for Pisa in 1856.

John Climacus (St) R. Mar 30
570–649 or 525–605. From the Holy Land, he became a monk at St Catherine's monastery at Sinai and spent some time as a hermit before becoming abbot when aged seventy-five. He went back to being a hermit four years later. His fame, and his surname, derive from his popular ascetical work *The Ladder of Perfection*, which is still prescribed reading for monks of the Byzantine rite during Lent.

John Codinachs Tuneu (Bl) *see* **Philip-of-Jesus Munárriz Azcona and Comps**

John of Cologne (St) M. R(OP). Jul 9
d. 1572. From Cologne, Germany, he became a Dominican and parish priest of Hoornaer in the Netherlands and was one of the **Gorinchem martyrs** (q.v.).

John Colombini (Bl) L. F. Jul 31
*c*1300–1367. From Siena, Italy, he became an important figure in that city and was its first magistrate, being described as ambitious, avaricious and bad-tempered. While reading the story of St Mary of Egypt he was suddenly converted and eventually formed a small society of lay persons called Jesuati devoted to penance and deeds of charity. He has left a collection of letters.

John-Joseph-of-the-Cross Colosinto (St) R(OFM). Mar 5
1654–1734. From the island of Ischia near Naples, Italy, he became an Alcantarine Franciscan in 1670. He was superior of the new friary at Piedimonte di Alife before becoming superior of the new Italian branch of the Alcantarines in 1702. Dying at Naples, he was canonized in 1839.

John-Baptist Con (St) M. L. Nov 8
1805–1840. A Vietnamese married man, he was beheaded with SS Joseph (Nguyen Dinh) Nghi and Comps. *See* **Vietnam (Martyrs of)**.

John of Constantinople (St) R. Apr 27
d. 813. Abbot of the monastery of the Cathares at Nicaea near Constantinople, he was a firm opponent of the Iconoclast emperor Leo III, by whom he was imprisoned and exiled.

John-Nicholas Cordier (Bl) *see* **John-Baptist Souzy and Comps**

John of Cordoba (St) *see* **Adolf and John**

John-Charles Cornay (St) M. Sep 20
1809–1837. From Loudun near Poitiers, France, he joined the Paris Society of Foreign Missions and worked in Vietnam. He was seized at Ban No, kept in a cage for three months and brutally treated before being beheaded. *See* **Vietnam (Martyrs of)**.

John Cornelius (Bl) M. R(SJ). Jul 4
d. 1594. Born at Bodmin, Cornwall, of Irish parents, he was a fellow of Exeter College, Oxford, before studying for the priesthood at Rheims and then at Rome, where he was ordained in 1583. He worked for ten years on mission at Lanherne in Cornwall, became a Jesuit in 1594 and was martyred at Dorchester, Dorset, with BB John Carey, Patrick Salmon and Thomas Bosgrave. They were beatified in 1929. *See* **England (Martyrs of)**.

John de Craticula (St) B. R(CR). Feb 1
1098–1163. From Châtillon in Brittany, France, he allegedly was an Augustinian canon at Bourgmoyen in Blois and a friend of St

Bernard. He became bishop of Aleth, which see he transferred to Saint-Malo, and also abbot of the Augustinian abbey of Guingamp. His surname, 'of the Grating', derives from the metal railings that surrounded his shrine. He was not a Cistercian monk at Clairvaux under St Bernard and abbot-founder of Buzay and Bégard, as this was a separate person.

John of the Cross *see* **John-of-the-Cross de Yepes**

John Damascene (St) R. Dr. Dec 4
?676–749. Born in Damascus when that city was the capital of the Umayyad caliphate and where his father was the representative of the Christians at the court of the caliph, he was educated by a Sicilian monk who had been brought to Syria as a slave. After succeeding his father at court he became a monk at the laura of St Sabas in the Judaean Desert, where his writings made him the last of the Eastern fathers, influential in the mediaeval West as well as in the Byzantine East. He was the author of the first real compendium of theology, the *Fountain of Wisdom*, as well as of numerous liturgical hymns and of effective polemic against the iconoclast policy of Emperor Leo III. He was proclaimed a doctor of the Church in 1890.

John Dat (St) M. P. Oct 28
1764–1798. From north Vietnam, he was ordained in 1798 and beheaded that same year after three months' imprisonment. *See* **Vietnam (Martyrs of)**.

John Davy (Bl) M. R(OCart). Jun 8
d. 1537. A Carthusian monk at the London Charterhouse, he was starved to death with six others of his community at Newgate Prison where they were imprisoned for resisting the claims to spiritual supremacy of King Henry VIII. *See* **England (Martyrs of)**.

John-of-the-Cross Delgado Pastor (Bl) *see* **Hospitaller Martyrs of Spain**

John Díaz Nosti (Bl) *see* **Philip-of-Jesus Munárriz Azcona and Comps**

John Diego (Bl) R. Dec 9
*c*1474–1529. Born at Cuahtitlán near Mexico City, he was a married native Mexican but the couple had taken a vow of celibacy before the wife died in 1529. He saw a vision of Our Lady on a hill called Tepeyac, Guadalupe, in 1531, who told him to tell the bishop to build a church on the site. Three days later, in a second vision, she told him to pick wildflowers for the bishop which became roses on delivery. His cloak had developed an image of Our Lady on it, which is venerated at the shrine at Guadalupe. He became a hermit at the shrine, and his cultus was confirmed in 1990.

John Dominici (Bl) B. R(OP). Jun 10
?1356–1419. From Florence, Italy, he became a Dominican there in ?1373 and was involved in a contemporary restoration of discipline in his order. He was made vicar-general of the reformed friaries of Italy, and was made cardinal archbishop of Ragusa (now Dubrovnik in Croatia) in 1408, serving as papal legate in Bohemia and Hungary and converting many Hussites. He was also a leader in the healing of the Great Schism in the Western Church. He died at Buda, Hungary, and his cultus was confirmed for Florence and the Dominicans in 1832.

John Duckett (Bl) M. P. Sep 7
d. 1644. From near Sedbergh, Yorks, a relative of Bl James Duckett, he was educated for the priesthood at Douai and ordained in 1639. He was on mission at Durham, and was executed at Tyburn, London, with Bl Ralph Corby. He was beatified in 1929. *See* **England (Martyrs of)**.

John of Dukla (St) R(OFM). Jul 10
1414–1484. From a bourgeois family at Dukla near Tarnow, Poland, when young he was a hermit there before joining the Conventual Franciscans at Lemberg, now Lviv in Ukraine) in 1440. He was a preacher and local superior until he transferred to the Observants in 1463, and then spent the rest of his life ministering and preaching to the Germans in Lviv, where he died. His relics were taken from there back to Dukla after 1945, and he was canonized in 1997.

John Duns Scotus (Bl) R(OFM). Nov 8
1266–1308. Born in Duns, Berwickshire, Scotland, he became a Franciscan when aged fifteen and went to Oxford and Paris to study. He lectured on the 'Sentences of Lombard' and became the last of the great mediaeval scholastics (he is nicknamed 'Doctor Subtilis'). He became regent master in Paris in 1305 and went to lecture in Cologne before he died. His cultus was confirmed for the Franciscans in 1993.

John Duval (Bl) *see* **September (Martyrs of)**

John-Baptist Duverneuil (Bl) *see* **John-Baptist Souzy and Comps**

John Echarri Vique (Bl) *see* **Philip-of-Jesus Munárriz Azcona and Comps**

John-Baptist Egozcuezábel Aldaz (Bl) *see* **Hospitaller Martyrs of Spain**

John of Egypt (St) *see* **Cyrus and John**

John of Emesa (St) H. Jul 21
C6th. From Emesa (now Homs) in Syria, as a monk he went with St Simeon Salus to Jerusalem and ended up as a disciple of St Gerasimus.

John Eudes (St) P. F. Aug 19
1601–1680. From Ri near Alençon, France, he became a priest at Caen and entered the Oratory there in 1625. In 1633 he started his enormously successful career as a parish missionary, but soon appreciated the need for properly educated priests and tried to found a seminary at Caen. This was opposed, so he left the Oratory and founded the secular 'Society of Jesus and Mary' in 1643 in order to found and run seminaries. In 1641 he also founded the 'Sisterhood of our Lady of Charity of the Refuge' to care for repentant former prostitutes. A fervent propagator of the devotion to the Sacred Heart, the liturgical celebration and doctrinal foundations of which he helped to establish, he was well-known as an ascetic writer on this and other topics. He died at Caen and was canonized in 1925.

John the Evangelist (St) A. Dec 27
d. *c*100.From Galilee, the son of Zebedee and brother of St James the Great, he was a fisherman until called to be an apostle. The author of the fourth gospel, he is usually identified with 'the Disciple whom Jesus loved' mentioned therein and also wrote three canonical letters. The tradition that he was 'John the Elder' of Patmos, author of the book of Revelation, has been disputed since patristic times. By tradition also he was based at Ephesus after the Resurrection and died there of natural causes. One legend holds that he survived being boiled in oil at Rome before his exile to Patmos, and this event was sometimes depicted in the Middle Ages. His attribute is an eagle, also a chalice with a serpent crawling out of it.

John Eynon (Bl) *see* **Benedictine Martyrs of the Reformation**

John Faesulanus (St) R(OP). Feb 18
1387–1455. He is universally known as 'Fra Angelico'. Born near Florence, Italy, he became

St John the Evangelist, Dec 27

a Dominican at Fiesole in 1407, was at San Marco in Florence and died at La Minerva at Rome. His fame rests on his talent for religious painting, considered to be one of the greatest known in Western Europe. He was declared patron of artists in 1984, thus being effectively canonized.

John-Anthony Farina (Bl) B. F. (Mar 4)
1803–1888. From Gambellara near Vicenza in Italy, he was ordained as a diocesan priest of Vicenza in 1827. He was a good teacher, and worked in the seminary and as a headmaster before founding a school for poor girls in Vicenza in 1831. In 1836 he founded the 'Sisters, Teachers of St Dorothy and Daughters of the Sacred Hearts of Jesus and Mary', and in 1850 was chosen as bishop of Treviso. He was transferred to Vicenza in 1850, and died of a stroke there. His compassion for poor people and his enlightened opinions on education and the teaching profession made him outstanding among C19th bishops, and he was beatified in 2001.

John Felton (Bl) M. L. Aug 8
d. 1570. Born at Bermondsey in London of a Norfolk family, he was living at Southwark when the Bull of Pope St Pius V excommunicating Queen Elizabeth reached London. He attached a copy to the door of the bishop of London's house, for which act he was executed in the churchyard of St Paul's Cathedral. He was beatified in 1886. *See* **England (Martyrs of)**.

John Fenwick (Bl) M. R(SJ). Jun 20
d. 1679. From Durham, he was educated at Saint-Omer and became a Jesuit in 1656. He was martyred at Tyburn, London, with BB **Thomas Whitbread and Comps** (q.v.). *See* **England (Martyrs of)**.

John-James Fernandez (Bl) *see* **Emmanuel Ruiz and Comps**

John Fernandez of Braga and John Fernandez of Lisbon (BB) *see* **Ignatius de Azevedo and Comps**

John Finch (Bl) M. L. Apr 10
d. 1584. He farmed at Eccleston in Lancashire before being executed at Lancaster for being reconciled to the Church and for sheltering priests. He was beatified in 1929. *See* **England (Martyrs of)**.

John Fingley (Bl) M. P. Jun 6
d. 1586. From Barmby near Howden, Yorks, he studied at Cambridge and Douai, was ordained at Rheims and spent four years as a priest at York before his execution with Bl Francis Ingleby. He was beatified in 1987. *See* **England (Martyrs of)**.

John Fisher (St) M. B. Jun 22
1469–1535. From Beverley, Yorks, the son of a draper, he went to Cambridge University and eventually became its chancellor, doing much to further its growth and development. In 1504 he became bishop of Rochester and was the only one of the English hierarchy seriously to oppose King Henry VIII's wish to divorce Queen Catherine of Aragón. He also refused to take the Oath of Supremacy. As a result he was condemned for treason and beheaded on Tower Hill, having been created a cardinal shortly beforehand. He was canonized in 1969. His portrait is extant. *See* **England (Martyrs of)**.

John Forest (Bl) M. R(OFM). May 22
d. 1538. Apparently from Oxford and educated there, he became a Franciscan Observant at Greenwich in 1491 and was chosen as the confessor of Queen Catherine of Aragón, first wife of King Henry VIII. He opposed the queen's divorce and the king's supremacy in spiritual matters, so was very slowly burned to death at Smithfield. He was beatified in 1886. *See* **England (Martyrs of)**.

John Goizet (Bl) *see* **September (Martyrs of)**

John-Mary Gallot (Bl) *see* **Laval (Martyrs of)**

John-Baptist-of-the-Conception García (St) R. F. Feb 14
1561–1613. From near Toledo, Spain, he became a Trinitarian there in 1580 and founded a reformed house of that Order at Valdepeñas in 1597. This was the start of the 'Discalced Trinitarians', which reform received papal approval in 1636. He had to endure the bitter opposition of the 'unreformed', but 34 monasteries had adopted his rule at the time of his death. He died at Cordoba and was canonized in 1975.

John Gavan (Bl) M. R(SJ). Jun 20
d. 1679. A Londoner, he was educated at Saint-Omer and became a Jesuit in 1660. He was martyred at Tyburn, London, with BB **Thomas Whitbread and Comps** (q.v.). *See* **England (Martyrs of)**.

John of Ghent (Bl) R(OSB). Sep 29
d. 1439. A Benedictine of the abbey of Sainte-Claude in the Jura, France, he was with St Joan of Arc and is known as 'the Hermit of St Claude'.

John of Gniezno (St) *see* **Benedict of Gniezno and Comps**

John of God (St) R. F. Mar 8
1495–1550. From Montemor-o-Novo near Evora, Portugal, he became a mercenary soldier in 1522 and fought for Spain in Europe, lapsing from his faith in the process. Then he was a shepherd before re-converting in about 1535 and working as a pedlar of religious items and books. He opened a shop in Granada but suffered a nervous breakdown through guilt about his past. Bl John of Avila calmed him and inspired him to look after deprived people, so he founded a hospital at Granada in 1540 where he nursed the sick and which was the beginning of the new order of Brothers Hospitallers (Brothers of St John of God), which was approved in 1572 after his death. He was canonized in 1690 and declared patron of sick people and of hospitals in 1886.

John González of Sahagún
(St) R(OSA). Jun 12
1419–1479. From Sahagún near León, Spain, he studied at Salamanca and Burgos and was ordained in 1445, becoming a cathedral canon at Burgos. He initially held several benefices but his conscience led him to resign all but one, that of a chapel at Salamanca where he worked as a priest. He became an Augustinian friar in 1463, serving as novice-master and prior. His preaching and example, especially against sexual relations outside marriage, caused a great change in the social life of Salamanca but he was eventually poisoned by a woman who blamed him for the loss of her lover. He was canonized in 1690, but his cultus was confined to local calendars in 1969.

John of Gorze (St) R. Feb 27
d. ?975. A nobleman from near Metz, France, after administrating his large estates for some years he made a pilgrimage to Rome and then restored the abbey of Gorze and became a monk there in 933. The emperor Otto I sent him to Cordoba, Spain, for two years as ambassador to the Ummayad Caliph Abd-er-Rahman III, and then he became abbot of Gorze in 960. He initiated a reform movement there which was very influential among the Benedictine monasteries of northern Europe.

John of the Goths (St) B. Jun 26
d. *c*800. He was bishop of the Goths left behind in what is now the Crimea when their kinsfolk migrated to Europe to escape the Huns. He was a noted opponent of iconoclasm. Driven from the Crimea by the invading Khazars, he died in exile.

John of Grâce-Dieu (Bl)
R(OCist). Apr 20
d. 1280. A Benedictine monk of St Denis near Paris, France, before becoming a Cistercian, he was successively abbot of Igny, of Clairvaux in 1257 and of Grâce-Dieu in ?1262.

John Gradenigo (Bl) R(OSB). Dec 5
d. 1025. A Venetian nobleman, he became a monk at Cuxa in Roussillon, France, with his friend St Peter Urseolo. After a life of many difficulties he died as a hermit near Montecassino, Italy.

John Grande (St) R. Jun 3
1546–1600. From Carmona near Seville, Spain, he dealt in linen before he became a hermit at Marcena nearby. Later he left his cell to work in the prisons and hospitals at Xeres, where a recently opened hospital was entrusted to his care. This he handed over to St John of God, joining the latter's new order at Granada, and he continued to care for prisoners and sick people until he died at Xeres. He used to call himself 'Grande Pecador' ('Great Sinner') as a pun on his name. He was canonized in 1996.

John Grove (Bl) M. L. Jan 24
d. 1679. He was a servant of Bl William Ireland, with whom he was martyred at Tyburn for alleged complicity in the Oates Plot. *See* **England (Martyrs of)**.

John Gruyer (Bl) *see* **September (Martyrs of)**

John Gualbert (St) R(OSB Vall). F. Jul 12
d. 1073. A nobleman of Florence, Italy, as a young man he spent his time in worldly amusements until one Good Friday when he forgave his brother's murderer and then saw the image of Christ on a crucifix miraculously bow its head in acknowledgment of his charity. Thereupon he became a monk at San Miniato del Monte at Florence, but left in order to avoid being made abbot and founded the monastery of Vallombrosa ('Shady Valley') near Fiesole. This grew into a powerful Benedictine congregation which survives, based chiefly in Tuscany and Lombardy. He died at Passignano, one of his own foundations, was canonized in 1193 and had his cultus confined to local or particular calendars in 1969.

John-Baptist Guillaume (Bl) *see* **John-Baptist Souzy and Comps**

John Guilleminet (Bl) *see* **September (Martyrs of)**

John Haile (Bl) M. P. May 4
d. 1535. The vicar of Isleworth in Middlesex, he was martyred at Tyburn with St John Houghton and Comps. *See* **England (Martyrs of)**.

John Hambley (Bl) M. P. (Mar)
d. 1587. Born near Bodmin in Cornwall, he was ordained at Laon, France, and worked in Dorset before being captured. He promised to conform and was released, but continued as a priest in Wiltshire until his re-capture and execution at Salisbury. He was beatified in 1987. *See* **England (Martyrs of)**.

John Hewitt (alias Savell or Weldon) (Bl) M. P. Oct 5
d. 1588. A Yorkshireman, he was educated at Gonville and Caius College, Cambridge, and studied for the priesthood at Rheims. Ordained in 1586, he was hanged at Mile End Green in London and beatified in 1929. *See* **England (Martyrs of)**.

John Hoan (St) M. May 26
?1789–1861. From Kim-long in Vietnam, he was ordained priest and worked zealously as a missionary until he was beheaded near Doug-Hoi. *See* **Vietnam (Martyrs of)**.

John Hogg (Bl) *see* **Edmund Duke and Comps**

John Houghton (St) M. R(OCart). May 4
d. 1535. From Essex, he was a secular priest before he became a Carthusian and prior of the London Charterhouse. He and his community were unusual among English consecrated religious in refusing to assent to the Acts of Succession and Supremacy of King Henry VIII, and he was executed at Tyburn in his religious habit together with SS Augustine Webster and Robert Lawrence (fellow Carthusians) and with St Richard Reynolds and Bl John Haile. These were the protomartyrs of the English reformation. He was canonized in 1970. *See* **England (Martyrs of)**.

John Hunot (Bl) *see* **John-Baptist Souzy and Comps**

John the Iberian (St) R. Jul 12
d. ?1002. His surname derives from an old name for Georgia, and he was a royal adviser there. With his wife's consent he and his son St Euthymius became monks on Mt Olympus in Bithynia, Asia Minor, and then migrated to Mt Athos, where they founded the monastery of Iviron ('the Iberian'). This became a treasure-house of Georgian culture which still exists (although the monks are now Greek).

John Inamura (Bl) M. T(OP). Sep 8
d. 1628. He was a Japanese tertiary burned at Nagasaki. *See* **Dominic Castellet and Comps** and **Japan (Martyrs of)**.

John Ingram (Bl) M. P. Jul 26
d. 1594. From Stoke Edith in Herefordshire, he studied at New College, Oxford, and then (as a convert) at Rheims and at Rome. After his ordination in 1589 he worked in Scotland until his execution at Gateshead. *See* **England (Martyrs of)**.

John Ireland (BB) M. P. Mar 7
d. 1544. He was chaplain to St Thomas More before being made rector of Eltham, Kent. He was executed at Tyburn with BB Jermyn Gardiner and John Larke, and was beatified in 1929. *See* **England (Martyrs of)**.

John Iwanaga (Bl) M. L. Nov 27
d. 1619. He was of the family of the daimyos of Hirado-jima and was beheaded at Nagasaki, Japan. *See* **Anthony Kimura and Comps** and **Japan (Martyrs of)**.

John Jannin (Bl) *see* **September (Martyrs of)**

John-Francis Jarrige de la Morélie du Breuil (Bl) *see* **John-Baptist Souzy and Comps**

John Jones (alias Buckley) (St) M. R(OFM). Jul 12
1559–1598. From Clynog Fawr in Gwynedd, Wales, he became a Franciscan Observant at Pontoise, France, was ordained at Rome and worked on the London mission from 1592 until 1597. He was martyred at Southwark and canonized in 1970. *See* **England (Martyrs of)**.

John-Joseph Jugé de Saint-Martin (Bl) *see* **John-Baptist Souzy and Comps**

John Kearney (Bl) M. R(OFM). Jun 20
d. 1653. A Franciscan priest, he was hanged at Clonmel in the persecution by Cromwell. *See* **Ireland (Martyrs of)**.

John Kemble (St) M. P. Aug 22
1599–1679. From near Hereford, he studied for the priesthood at Douai, was ordained there and worked on the missions of Monmouthshire and Herefordshire for fifty-three years. When aged eighty he was hanged, drawn and

quartered at Hereford as a result of the Oates plot. He was canonized in 1970. *See* **England (Martyrs of)**.

John of Kenty *see* **John Wacienga**

John (Leo?) Kinuya (St) M. T(OFM). Feb 6
d. 1597. A Japanese silk-weaver from Miyako, he was baptized and became a Franciscan tertiary shortly before his crucifixion at Nagasaki. The sources differ as to his Christian name. *See* **Paul Miki and Comps** and **Japan (Martyrs of)**.

John Kisaku (Bl) M. R(SJ). Jun 20
d. 1626. A Japanese Jesuit novice, he was burnt alive at Nagasaki. *See* **Francis Pacheco and Comps** and **Japan (Martyrs of)**.

John Kolobos ('the Short')
(St) R. Sep 15
C5th. From Basta in Lower Egypt, he became a disciple of St Poemen at Scetis and was one of the most attractive characters among the desert fathers, being described as short-tempered and proud by nature but gentle and humble by grace. He was also famous for his absent-mindedness. In obedience to his master he regularly watered a walking-stick which, when it sprouted, was called 'the tree of obedience'.

John of Korea (Bl) M. L. Sep 10
d. 1622. A boy of twelve, son of Bl Anthony of Korea, he was beheaded with his mother, Bl Mary, and his brother, Bl Peter, in the 'Great Martyrdom' at Nagasaki, Japan. His father was burned. *See* **Japan (Martyrs of)**.

John-Baptist Laborier du Vivier (Bl) *see* **John-Baptist Souzy and Comps**

John le Laisant (Bl) *see* **September (Martyrs of)**

John de la Lande (Bl) *see* **John Brébeuf and Comps**

John-Michael Langevin (Bl) *see* **William Repin and Comps**

John Lanier (Bl) *see* **September (Martyrs of)**

John Lantrua of Triora
(Bl) M. R(OFM). Feb 13
1760–1816.From Triora in Liguria, Italy, when aged seventeen he became a Franciscan and volunteered to go to China after having been guardian of the friary at Velletri near Rome. At that time the Church was being persecuted there, and he worked successfully in Shanxi and Hubei in the face of many dangers and hardships after his arrival in 1799. Eventually he was seized and executed by strangulation at Changsha in Hubei, and was beatified in 1900. *See* **China (Martyrs of)**.

John Larke (Bl) M. P. Mar 7
d. 1544. He was rector of St Ethelburga's, Bishopsgate, London, then of Woodford, Essex, and finally of Chelsea, to which parish he was nominated by St Thomas More. He was executed at Tyburn with BB John Ireland and Jermyn Gardiner and was beatified in 1886. *See* **England (Martyrs of)**.

John-Mary du Lau d'Alleman, John de Lavèze Belay and John Lecan (BB) *see* **September (Martyrs of)**

John of La Verna (Bl) R(OFM). Aug 13
1259–1322. From Fermo, Italy, he became a Franciscan in 1272 and thereafter lived a semi-eremitical life at La Verna, his base for evangelizing the surrounding district. He was famous for his gift of infused knowledge. His cultus was approved for Arezzo and the Franciscans in 1880.

John Lee and John-Baptist Lee (SS) *see* **Korea (Martyrs of)**

John-Baptist Lego (Bl) *see* **William Repin and Comps**

John Legrand and John Lemaitre (BB) *see* **September (Martyrs of)**

John-of-the-Mother-of-God Leonardi (St) R. F. Oct 9
1542–1609. From near Lucca, Italy, he became a pharmacist's apprentice there but also studied for the priesthood and was ordained in 1571. He worked with great zeal in prisons and in hospitals and, founded the 'Clerks Regular of the Mother of God' (approved in 1593) with the help of two laymen and some priests. He is also considered one of the founders also of the College of Propaganda Fide for Foreign Missions in Rome, and was appointed Visitor of the Vallombrosan and Monteverginian monks when these needed reform. He died at Rome and was canonized in 1938.

John Leroy (Bl) *see* **September (Martyrs of)**

John Licci (Bl) R(OP). Nov 14
1400–1511. From Caccamo near Palermo, Sicily, he became a Dominican at Palermo and

died at the age of one hundred and eleven. His cultus was confirmed for Palermo in 1753.

John of Lithuania (St) *see* **Anthony of Lithuania and Comps**

John Lloyd (St) M. P. Jul 22
d. 1679. From Brecon in Powys, Wales, he was educated for the priesthood at Valladolid, Spain, was ordained in 1653 and was then on mission in Wales. He was executed at Cardiff with Bl Philip Evans as a result of the Oates plot and was canonized in 1970. *See* **Wales (Martyrs of)**.

John Lobedau (Bl) R(OFM). Oct 9
d. 1264. From Toru, Poland, he became a Franciscan there and then at Chełmno. His cultus was approved for Poland in 1638.

John Lockwood (alias Lascelles) (Bl) M. Apr 13
1561–1642. From Sowerby, Yorks, he studied for the priesthood at Rome, was ordained in 1597 and was on the English missions from 1598. He was aged eighty-one when he was hanged, drawn and quartered at York, and was beatified in 1929. *See* **England (Martyrs of)**.

John of Lodi (St) B. R(OSB). Sep 7
d. 1106. From Lodi Vecchio in Lombardy, Italy, after being a hermit for some years he became a monk at the abbey of Fontavellana under St Peter Damian, whose biography he wrote. He became prior of the abbey in 1072 and bishop of Gubbio in 1105.

John-Baptist Loir (Bl) *see* **John-Baptist Souzy and Comps**

John Love (Bl) M. P. Oct 8
d. 1586. He was born on London Bridge and was ordained at the English College at Rome. He then spent 30 months in London as a priest before being captured and executed at Tyburn with BB Robert Dibdale and John Adams. He was beatified in 1987. *See* **England (Martyrs of)**.

John-Baptist Luo (Tingyin) (St) M. L. Jul 29
1825–1861. A prosperous farmer at Qingyian in Guizhou, China, he was converted and moved to Yaojiaguan. There he administered the finances of the new seminary. He was beheaded with SS Joseph Zhang (Wenlan), Paul Chen (Changpin) and Martha Wang (Luo). *See* **China (Martyrs of)**.

John of Lycopolis (St) R. Mar 27
?305–394. One of the most famous of the Egyptian desert fathers, he was born near Asyut and was a carpenter before becoming a hermit when aged twenty-five in a cave in the cliffs overlooking the valley of the Nile at Lycopolis. He was there for forty years and became famous as a prophet, being consulted by the emperor Theodosius I as well as by many other people of all kinds, and his fame spread throughout the Roman Empire.

John-Baptist Machado (Bl) M. R(SJ). May 22
1580–1617. From Terceira, one of the Azores, he became a Jesuit at Coïmbra, Portugal, and went to Japan in 1609. He was beheaded at Nagasaki with Bl Peter of the Assumption and was beatified in 1867. *See* **Japan (Martyrs of)**.

John Macias (St) R(OP). Sep 18
1585–1645. From Ribera del Fresno in Extremadura, Spain, he emigrated to the New World as a servant, worked on a cattle ranch and gained a fortune which he gave to the poor when he became a Dominican lay brother at Lima, Peru. He was the door-keeper there for the rest of his life, and was canonized in 1975.

John Maki (Bl) M. L. Sep 7
d. 1627. An adopted son of Bl Louis Maki, he was burnt alive at Nagasaki, Japan, with his father and Bl Thomas Tsuji. *See* **Japan (Martyrs of)**.

John Marchand (Bl) *see* **September (Martyrs of)**.

John Marinoni (Bl) R. Dec 10
1490–1562. From Venice, Italy, he was a canon of St Mark's cathedral there but resigned to join the Theatines under St Cajetan in 1530. He was a ubiquitous preacher, the exclusive theme of his sermons being Christ crucified. He refused the archbishopric of Naples, the city in which he died. His cultus was confirmed for Naples and the Theatines in 1764.

John Mark (St) B. Sep 27
C1st. The old Roman Martyrology listed him as a bishop of Byblos, Lebanon, but the consensus of biblical scholars identifies him with St Mark the evangelist. *See* Acts 12:25.

John Mason (Bl) M. L. Dec 10
d. 1591. A layman from Kendal in Cumbria, he was condemned for sheltering priests and was hanged at Tyburn with SS Eustace White and Comps. He was beatified in 1929. *See* **England (Martyrs of)**.

John Matashichi (Bl) M. L. Aug 19
d. 1662. He was a sailor on the ship carrying BB Louis Flores and Comps. *See* **Japan (Martyrs of)**.

John of Matera (St) R(OSB). Jun 20
d. 1139. From Matera in Basilicata, Italy, when young he was a monk in a Benedictine monastery but his austerity was not popular. He next went to the monastery at Montevergine under St William, the founder, but left to become a popular preacher at Bari. Finally he settled at Pulsano near Monte Gargano where he established an abbey, the first of a series of foundations which became the new Benedictine Congregation of Pulsano (now extinct). He died at Pulsano.

John of Matha (St) R. F. Feb 8
1160–1213. From Provence, France, he studied at Paris and later founded the order of Trinitarians for the redemption of Christian captives enslaved by Muslims. This was approved in 1209. There are no trustworthy records of his life, and the story that he ransomed many captives himself at Tunis is unsupported by any evidence. He died at Rome and his cultus was approved in 1666, but was confined to local calendars in 1969.

John de Mavorga (Bl) *see* **Ignatius de Azevedo and Comps**

John-Baptist Mazzuconi
(Bl) M. P. Mar 25
1826–1855. From near Milan, he was ordained in 1852 and was one of the first graduates of the new Pontifical Institute for Overseas Missions. His group was sent to Woodlark Island in Melanesia off New Guinea, where they had a very difficult time (the natives threatened to eat them). In 1855 he was so badly affected by an ulcerative disease that he was sent to Sydney to recuperate for six months. On his return he found that his fellows had themselves left for Sydney. His ship struck coral off the island and a gang of natives boarded with an initial show of friendship, but they killed Bl John-Baptist with an axe before killing everybody else on board and plundering the ship. He was beatified in 1984.

John Ménard (Bl) *see* **William Repin and Comps**

John-Baptist Menestrel (Bl) *see* **John-Baptist Souzy and Comps**

John of Montemarano
(St) B. R(OSB)? Aug 17
d. ?1094. From near Montemarano in Campagna, Italy, he probably became a monk of Montecassino before being made bishop of Montemarano in 1074 by Pope St Gregory VII. His cultus was approved for Nusco in 1906.

John of Montfort (Bl) L. May 24
d. 1177/8. A nobleman from Voralberg, Austria, and Knight Templar of Jerusalem, he was wounded in a battle there against the Muslims and was taken to Cyprus, where he died at Famagusta. He had a cultus at Cyprus while the Latin church existed there, which was only until the Ottoman conquest.

John de Montmirail (Bl) R(OCist). Sep 29
1165–1217. The lord of Montmirail near Châlons-sur-Marne, France, he was a married soldier with a family but obtained his wife's consent to become a Cistercian at Longpoint, where he died. He has a cultus, approved in 1891, among the Cistercians and in several French dioceses.

John Mopinot (Bl) *see* **John-Baptist Souzy and Comps**

John Motoyama (Bl) M. L. Nov 27
d. 1619. He was of the family of the daimyos of Hirado-jima and was beheaded at Nagasaki, Japan. *See* **Anthony Kimura and Comps** and **Japan (Martyrs of)**.

John-Martin Moyë (Bl) P. F. May 4
1730–1793. From Lorraine, France, he became a diocesan priest of Metz in 1754 and founded the 'Sisters of Divine Providence' in 1762 in order to catechize in rural areas. In 1773 he joined the Paris Society of Missions and went to Chengdu in Sichuan, China, for eleven years. He baptized over 20,000 in the region and founded an institute of Chinese Christian virgins for nursing and catechesis. He returned exhausted, moved his earlier congregation to Trier and died there of typhus, being beatified in 1955.

John Munden (Bl) M. P. Feb 12
d. 1584. From Maperton, Dorset, he studied at New College, Oxford, became a schoolmaster, went to Rheims and to Rome for his seminary studies and was ordained in 1582. He was martyred at Tyburn with BB George Haydock, James Fenn, John Nutter and Thomas Hemerford, and was beatified in 1929. *See* **England (Martyrs of)**.

John-Mary Muzeyi (St) M. L. Jun 3
d. 1887. A native of Buganda, Uganda, he baptized many about to die and was beheaded in the persecution of Mwanga. *See* **Charles Lwanga and Comps**.

John Naizen (Bl) M. L. Jul 12
d. 1626. He was a wealthy Japanese layman from Arima. When the persecutors threatened him with the prostitution of his wife, Bl Monica Naizen, he apostatized for a while but repented and was burned alive at Nagasaki. His wife and child, Bl Louis Naizen, were beheaded. *See* **Mancius Araki and Comps** and **Japan (Martyrs of)**.

John-Baptist Nam (Thiong-sam)
(St) M. L. Mar 6
d. 1866. A mandarin of Seoul, Korea, and a royal chamberlain, he was a humble man and highly regarded by the people. However he was charged with apostasy from the national religion, tortured for information on other Christians and executed. He was canonized in 1984. *See* **Korea (Martyrs of)**.

John I of Naples (St) B. Jun 22
C5th. Bishop of Naples, Italy, he transferred the body of St Januarius from Puteoli to Naples.

John IV of Naples (St) B. Jun 22
d. 835. Bishop of Naples, Italy, he is locally known as 'the Peacemaker'.

John-Baptist Nativelle (Bl) *see* **September (Martyrs of)**.

John-Peter Néel (St) M. P. Feb 18
1832–1862. A French missionary priest of the Paris Foreign Missions Society, he was working in Guizhou province in China when he was arrested with SS John Chen (Xianheng), John Zhang (Tianshen) and Martin Wu (Xuesheng). He was tied to a horse's tail by his hair and dragged about before being beheaded with the others at Kaiyang. *See* **China (Martyrs of)**.

John Nelson (Bl) M. R(SJ). Feb 3
d. 1578. From Skelton near York, he entered the seminary at Douai when aged forty and was ordained in 1575. He was sent to London but was quickly arrested and executed at Tyburn, becoming a Jesuit beforehand. *See* **England (Martyrs of)**.

John Nepomucene (St) M. P. May 16
*c*1340–1393 (or 1383). From Nepomuk near Plzen in Bohemia (now the Czech Republic), he became a canon of Prague and eventually court chaplain and confessor to Queen Sophie, second wife of the dissolute King Wenceslaus IV. He was of a retiring disposition, and repeatedly refused bishoprics which were offered to him. By order of the king he was drowned in the river at Prague, by tradition because he refused to reveal to the king what he had heard from the queen in sacramental confession. He was canonized in 1729.

John-Nepomucene Neumann
(St) B. R(CSSR). F. Jan 5
1811–1860. From Prachatice near Plzen (Czech Republic), he became a missionary priest in the Buffalo district of New York State, USA in 1836. In 1840 he became a Redemptorist at Baltimore and was made bishop of Philadelphia in 1852. He had great care for the proper establishment of the Church in a developing society through the ministry of preaching, the education of youth (he increased the number of pupils at parish schools twenty-fold), the building of churches (eighty, plus the cathedral), the fostering of good liturgy and, above all, care of orphans and the poor. He also founded the 'Sisters of the Third Order of St Francis' and brought in many teaching orders. He was canonized in 1977.

John Ni (Youn-Il) (St) M. L. Jan 20
d. 1867. A Korean lay catechist with a family, he was tortured and beaten before being beheaded. *See* **Korea (Martyrs of)**.

'John' of Nicomedia (St) M. Sep 7
d. 303. A 'Christian of secular dignity', he tore down and ripped up Diocletian's edict of persecution against the Christians when this was publicly exhibited at Nicomedia, Asia Minor. For this he was tortured and burned alive. His true name is unknown; 'John' is the arbitrary Latin appellation, 'Eleutherius' the Byzantine.

John Norton (Bl) *see* **Thomas Palaser and Comps**

John Nutter (Bl) M. P. Feb 12
d. 1584. From near Burnley, Lancs, he was a fellow of St John's College, Cambridge, before converting, studying for the priesthood at Rheims and being ordained in 1581. He was executed at Tyburn, London, with BB George Haydock, James Fenn, John Munden and Thomas Hemerford. *See* **England (Martyrs of)**.

John Ogilvie (St) M. R(SJ). Mar 10
*c*1580–1615. He is the only canonized martyr of the Scottish Reformation. Apparently from

Drum-na-Keith in Strathisla, Banffshire, he was a Calvinist before converting while attending the Scottish College at Louvain in 1596. He became a Jesuit at Brno in 1599 and worked in the Czech lands and in France until 1613. Then he returned to Scotland, worked in and around Edinburgh and Glasgow and was captured at the latter place. For eight days and nights on end he was tortured and forcibly kept from sleep so that he should reveal the names of other Catholics. He was also offered his freedom and preferment in exchange for reverting to Protestantism, but refused and was hanged at Glasgow. He was canonized in 1976.

John Oldrati of Meda (St) R. F. Sep 26
d. ?1159. A nobleman from Meda near Milan, Italy, he was a diocesan priest before becoming a hermit at Rodenario near Como. There he founded the religious order of the Humiliati from an existing penitential confraternity, using the rule of St Benedict and including monks, nuns and tertiaries. He died at Milan. His order was suppressed in 1571.

John-of-St-Dominic of Omura
(Bl) M. R(OP). Mar 19
1619. A martyr of the Japanese missions, he died in prison at Omura. *See* **Japan (Martyrs of)**.

John of Oosterwijk (St)
M. R(OSA). Jul 9
d. 1572. A Dutchman, he became an Augustinian canon regular at Briel near Gorinchem and was director and confessor of a local community of Augustinian nuns. When the town was captured by Calvinist rebels he was hanged with the **Gorinchem martyrs** (q.v.) in the ruins of his sacked monastery.

John de Ortega (St) R. Jun 2
d. *c*1150. A diocesan priest of Burgos, Spain, he went on several pilgrimages to the Holy Land, Rome and Compostela before becoming a hermit at Ortega near Burgos. He helped St Dominic de la Calzada in building bridges, hospices and roads for the Compostela pilgrims. He is venerated at Burgos.

John Paine (St) M. P. Apr 20
d. 1582. A convert from near Peterborough, he was educated for the priesthood at Douai where he was ordained in 1576. He was based at Ingatestone in Essex until he was betrayed, and was executed at Chelmsford. He was canonized in 1970. *See* **England (Martyrs of)**.

John Pak (St) *see* **Korea (Martyrs of)**

John of Parma (St) R(OSB). May 22
d. ?982. From Parma, Italy, he became a cathedral canon there when young and allegedly made six pilgrimages to Jerusalem, where he became a monk. Then he became abbot of the Cluniac monastery of St John's at Parma in 973.

John of Pavia (St) B. Aug 27
d. 813.He was bishop of Pavia near Milan, Italy, from 801.

John Pelingotto (Bl) T(OFM). Jun 1
1240–1304. From Urbino, Italy, the son of a merchant, he became a Franciscan tertiary and spent his whole life in prayer and works of charity. His cultus was approved for Urbino in 1918.

John of Penna (Bl) R(OFM Conv). Apr 3
d. 1271. From Penna San Giovanni near Fermo, Italy, he became a Franciscan at Recanati near Ancona, where he died after founding several friaries in Provence, France, over a period of twenty-five years. His cultus was confirmed for Fermo and the Franciscan Conventuals in 1806.

John-Gabriel Perboyre (St) M. R. Sep 11
1802–1840. From near Montaubin, France, he joined the Vincentians there in 1818 and, after being ordained in 1825, was rector of the seminary at St Flour for ten years. Then he heard that his brother had died on mission in China and offered to replace him. He worked in Henan province until he was seized, imprisoned, given 110 strokes of a bamboo cane (which should have killed him) and strangled while tied to a cross at Wuchang. He was canonized in 1996. *See* **China (Martyrs of)**.

John of Perugia and Peter of Sassoferrato (BB) MM.
RR(OFM). Sep 3
d. 1231. These two Franciscan friars were sent by St Francis of Assisi in 1216 to preach to the Muslims in Spain. They worked in the district between Teruel and Valencia until they were seized in a mosque at Valencia and, on refusing to apostatize, were beheaded. Their cultus was approved for Valencia and Teruel in 1783.

John-Baptist Petrucci (Bl) *see* **Prague (Martyrs of)**

John Phillipot (Bl) *see* **September (Martyrs of)**

John-Baptist Piamarta (Bl) P. F. Apr 26
1841–1913. From a poor family in Brescia, Italy, he was ordained as a diocesan priest there in 1865. The state of the local proletariat inspired him to found the 'Istituto Artigianelli' in order to give boys (especially destitute ones) a Christian and professional training appropriate to the new industrial society. Also, noting the desperate poverty of the peasantry in assets and in knowledge, he helped found an agricultural colony at Remedello in order to propagate more effective agricultural techniques. To propagate these works he founded the 'Congregation of the Holy Family of Nazareth' and (with his mother) the 'Humble Servants of the Lord' for women. He died at Remedello and was beatified in 1997.

John Pibush (Bl) M. Feb 18
d. 1601. From Thirsk, Yorks, he studied at Rheims and was ordained in 1587. Most of his time in England subsequently was spent in prison, and he was executed at Southwark. He was beatified in 1929. *See* **England (Martyrs of)**.

John Plessington (St) M. P. Jul 19
d. 1679. From near Garstang, Lancs, he was educated for the priesthood at Valladolid, Spain, and was ordained at Segovia in 1662. He worked at Holywell in Clwyd, Wales, and then on the Wirral, but was hanged at Chester as a result of the Oates plot. He was canonized in 1970. *See* **England (Martyrs of)**.

John Pontus (Bl) *see* **September (Martyrs of)**

John del Prado (Bl) M. R(OFM). May 24
d. 1636. From near León, Spain, he joined the Franciscan Observants at Salamanca while studying theology there. Being sent to Morocco in order to minister to Christian slaves he was seized, tortured, burned and killed with a heavy stone along with two other Franciscans at Marrakesh. He was beatified in 1728.

John-of-Saint-Martha of Prados (Bl) M. R(OFM). Aug 16
1578–1618. From near Tarragona, Spain, he became a Franciscan priest and was sent to Japan in 1606 where he became fluent in Japanese. Arrested at Omura in 1615, he was imprisoned for three years before being beheaded at Miyako. He was beatified in 1867. *See* **Japan (Martyrs of)**.

John Quéneau and John Rateau (BB) *see* **September (Martyrs of)**

John of Ratzeburg (St) M. B. Nov 10
d. 1066. Allegedly an Anglo-Saxon from Lothian, Scotland, he became a missionary in Germany and was appointed bishop of Ratzeburg near Bremen. He worked in Mecklenberg and was martyred by native pagan Slavs during an uprising. He was also a missionary in Iceland.

John of Ravenna (St) B. Jan 12
d. 494. Bishop of Ravenna, Italy, from 452, he allegedly saved his city from destruction by Attila the Hun and mitigated its misery when it was captured by Theodoric, king of the Ostrogoths.

John-Francis Regis (St) R(SJ). Dec 31
1597–1640. From Fontcouverte near Narbonne, France, at the age of eighteen he became a Jesuit and was ordained in 1631. He was an indefatigable missionary among the rural population of Languedoc and Auvergne, making numerous conversions among the Huguenots. He also worked to help prisoners and prostitutes and established many confraternities of the Blessed Sacrament. Dying while preaching a mission at La Louvesc, he was canonized in 1737.

John-George Rehm (Bl) *see* **John-Baptist Souzy and Comps**

John of Réôme (St) R. Jan 28
425–539. From Dijon, France, when aged twenty he became a hermit at Réôme (now Ménétreux) but attracted disciples and, when these became too many, fled secretly and became a monk at Lérins. When he was exposed and recalled to Réôme he regulated his monastery according to the customs of Lérins and thus became one of the pioneers of monastic life in the West.

John de Ribera (St) B. Jan 6
1532–1611. From Seville, Spain, he was a son of the duke of Alcalá, viceroy of Naples. Educated at the university of Salamanca, he was ordained priest in 1557 and remained at the university as professor of theology. His talents became widely known and gained him the respect of Pope Pius V and of King Philip II of Spain. He became bishop of Badajoz, but was quickly transferred to Valencia as titular Latin Patriarch of Antioch and was made viceroy of that province. His life's work was to convert the Muslims remaining there.

John Rigby (St) M. L. Jun 21
d. 1600. Born at Harrock Hall near Wigan, Lancs, he went into domestic service for a recusant family at Sawston Hall in Cambridgeshire. There he was converted, but was arrested when testifying in favour of his employer and was condemned for being reconciled to the Church. He was executed at Southwark and canonized in 1970. *See* **England (Martyrs of)**.

John Righi of Fabriano (Bl)
R(OFM). Mar 11
1469–1539. From Fabriano in the Marches, Italy, he became a Franciscan and lived as a hermit at Massaccio. His cultus was approved for Iesi in 1903.

John Roberts (St) M. R(OSB). Dec 10
?1577–1610. From Trawsfynydd in Gwynedd, Wales, he was brought up nominally a Protestant but (like many contemporary Welshmen) had little identification with the English church. He studied at St John's College, Oxford and was about to become a student of law in 1598. He was received into the Church in Paris while on holiday, however, and went to Valladolid, Spain, to study for the priesthood. There he joined the Benedictines and was professed as a monk at Compostela in 1600. In 1602, after his ordination, he started work on the English mission. Six or seven times he was imprisoned and released, and during the plague of 1603 his services to the sick in London made him famous. Meanwhile he helped Dom Augustine Bradshaw in the founding of St Gregory's at Douai (now Downside abbey). He was captured while saying Mass, executed at Tyburn, London, and canonized in 1970. *See* **England (Martyrs of)**.

John Robinson (Bl) M. P. Oct 1
d. 1588. From Ferrensby near Knaresborough, Yorks, after losing his wife he went to Rheims to study for the priesthood and was ordained there in 1585. He was executed at Ipswich and was beatified in 1929. *See* **England (Martyrs of)**.

John Roche (alias Neale)
(Bl) M. Aug 30
d. 1588. An Irish waterman on the Thames, he was condemned to death for rescuing a fugitive priest and was executed at Tyburn, London, with St Margaret Ward and BB Edward Shelley, Richard Flower, Richard Leigh and Richard Martin. He was beatified in 1929. As depicted, he always wears Elizabethan working man's dress and carries an oar or a small boat. *See* **England (Martyrs of)**.

John Rochester (Bl)
M. R(OCart). May 11
d. 1537. From Terling near Witham, Essex, he became a Carthusian at the London Charterhouse and was executed at York with Bl James Walworth. He was beatified in 1886. *See* **England (Martyrs of)**.

John of Rome (1) (St) M. Jun 23
d. 362. A Roman priest, he was beheaded in the reign of Julian. The relic venerated as the head of John the Baptist at the English church in Rome of San Silvestro in Capite is probably his.

John of Rome (2) (St) *see* **Abundius, Abundantius and Comps**

John of Rome (3) (St) *see* **Anthony, Merulus and John**

John-Baptist de Rossi (St) P. May 23
1698–1764. From Voltaggio near Genoa, Italy, he became a Roman priest in 1721 and canon of Santa Maria in Cosmedin in 1737. His main work as missionary and catechist was among the teamsters, farmers and herdsmen of the Campagna, and among the sick and prisoners of the city. He died at Remo and was canonized in 1881.

John Rugg (Bl) *see* **Benedictine Martyrs of the Reformation**

John van Ruysbroeck (Bl) R(CR). Dec 2
1293–1381. From Ruysbroeck near Brussels, Belgium, he became a priest and a canon of Saint Gudule at Brussels and founder and first prior of the Augustinian monastery of Groenendael in 1343. His fame rests on his spiritual writings, which show him to be an important mediaeval mystic. His cultus was confirmed for Mechelen in 1908.

John of Sahagún *see* **John González of Sahagún**

John de Saint-Clair (Bl) *see* **September (Martyrs of)**

John of Salerno (Bl) R(OP). Aug 29
*c*1190–1242. From Salerno, Italy, he became a Dominican under St Dominic and founded the friary of Santa Maria Novella at Florence in 1221. His cultus was approved for Florence in 1783.

John-Baptist de la Salle (St) P. F. Apr 7
1651–1719. From Rheims, France, he was made a cathedral canon in 1667 and was ordained in

1678, after which he became chaplain to the 'Sisters of the Holy Infant'. These ran schools for girls, and he decided to devote his life to founding a similar institute for teaching boys. His ideas were original enough to meet serious opposition (no member of the institute was to be ordained, for example) but he started the noviciate of the 'Brothers of the Christian Schools' in 1691 and opened the first school at Paris in 1698. He died in retirement at the noviciate at St Yon and was canonized in 1900.

John Sánchez Munárriz (Bl) *see* **Philip-of-Jesus Munárriz Azcona and Comps**

John of Sandomir (1) and John of Sandomir (2) (BB) *see* **Sadoc of Sandomir and Comps**

John Sandys (Bl) M. P. Aug 11
d. 1586. A Lancastrian convert and Oxford graduate, he was ordained at Rheims and worked in Gloucester. While visiting the Anglican Dean of Lydney (an old friend who did not know of his conversion) he was seized and suffered a botched execution at Gloucester. He was beatified in 1987. *See* **England (Martyrs of)**.

John de San Martin (Bl) *see* **Ignatius de Azevedo and Comps**

John Sarkander (St) M. P. Mar 17
1576–1620. From Skoczów near Katowice, Poland (but then in Austrian Silesia), he became a diocesan priest of Olomouc in the Czech lands and was attached to the church at Holešov, which was on an estate owned by a Catholic but surrounded by lands of Protestant nobles. He converted many Hussites and Bohemian Brethren but was unjustly accused as a result by the said nobles of conspiring to bring Polish troops into the country at the start of the Thirty Years' War. He was ordered to reveal what he heard in confession from the patron of his church and, on refusing, was racked, tortured with burning pitch and left to die in prison. He was canonized in 1995.

John Savine (Bl) *see* **September (Martyrs of)**

John the Saxon (Bl) M. R(OSB). Feb 22
d. 895. Apparently from Lower Saxony, he was a monk in some French abbey and was allegedly invited by King Alfred to England in order to help carry out the king's desire to restore monastic life in the country after the devastation of the Danes. He was appointed abbot of the new royal foundation at Athelney, which failed in its intended function as a focus of renewal. Two French monks of his own community murdered him one night in church. This story depends on a late C10th source and its historicity has been questioned.

John-Baptist Scalabrini
(Bl) B. F. Jun 1
1839–1905. From near Como, Italy, he became a diocesan priest there in 1863 and was a parish priest and seminary rector before being made bishop of Piacenza in 1876. He was zealous for all aspects of his responsibility as bishop, especially as regards catechesis and the implementation of the Church's social teaching. Noting that Italian emigrants to the New World were in danger of losing their faith, he founded two congregations of 'Missionaries of St Charles' (the Scalabrinians) to care for them there and also inspired St Francis-Xavier Cabrini in her similar work. He died at Piacenza and was beatified in 1997.

John Seconds and John Séguin (BB) *see* **September (Martyrs of)**

John Shert (Bl) M. May 28
d. 1582. From near Macclesfield, Cheshire, he was at Brasenose College, Oxford, before his conversion and later studied at Douai and Rome. He was ordained in 1576, went back to England in 1579 and was executed at Tyburn, London, with BB Thomas Ford and Robert Johnstone. He was beatified in 1886. *See* **England (Martyrs of)**.

John Shoun (Bl) M. L. Nov 18
d. 1619. A Japanese from Miyako, he was baptized by the Jesuits at Nagasaki and was a member of the confraternity of the Holy Rosary. He was burned alive at Nagasaki. *See* **Leonard Kimura and Comps** and **Japan (Martyrs of)**.

John the Silent (St) B. R. May 13
454–558. Born at Nicopolis in Armenia, when aged nineteen he became a monk in a monastery that he founded there and was chosen bishop of Colonia when aged twenty-eight. He resigned after nine or ten years and anonymously entered the laura of St Sabas in the Judaean Desert, Holy Land. There he spent the rest of his life, part of it as a hermit walled up in his cell.

John Simon (Bl) *see* **September (Martyrs of)**

John Slade (Bl) M. L. Oct 30
d. 1583. Possibly from Manston, Dorset, he studied at New College, Oxford, became a schoolmaster and was martyred at Winchester for denying the royal supremacy in spiritual matters. He was beatified in 1929. *See* **England (Martyrs of)**.

John Soan de Goto (St) M. R(SJ). Feb 6
d. 1597. A Japanese Jesuit lay brother, he was a catechist at Osaka and was crucified at Nagasaki when aged eighteen. *See* **Paul Miki and Comps** and **Japan (Martyrs of)**.

John Sordi Cacciafronte
(Bl) M. B. R(OSB). Mar 16
d. 1183. From Cremona, Italy, he became a Benedictine at the abbey of St Laurence there and was made abbot in 1155. He sided with the pope against the emperor Frederick I Barbarossa, by whom he was banished from his abbey. Then he lived as a hermit near Mantua until he was made bishop there in 1174, transferring to Vicenza in 1177. He was killed by a man whom he had excommunicated for embezzling episcopal revenues, and had his cultus confirmed for Vicenza in 1824.

John Soreth (Bl) R(OC). Jul 30
*c*1420–1471 From Caen in Normandy, France, he became a Carmelite and was their prior-general from 1451. He was a forerunner of St Teresa in trying to reform his order and to admit nunneries, but with scant success. He allegedly died at Angers from eating unripe mulberries and had his cultus confirmed for the Carmelites in 1865.

John Southworth (St) M. P. Jun 28
d. 1654. From Lancashire, he studied for the priesthood at Douai, was ordained in 1619 and went to England, working firstly in Lancashire and then in London. The way he helped sufferers of the plague epidemic of 1636 was specially noteworthy. He was imprisoned in 1627 but subsequently released, only to be executed at Tyburn during the Commonwealth. He was canonized in 1970 and has his shrine in Westminster Cathedral. *See* **England (Martyrs of)**.

John-Baptist Souzy and Comps
(BB) MM. Aug 28
d. 1794–5. During the French Revolution the 'Constitutive Assembly' required all priests to take an oath to the Civil Constitution, and those who refused (the 'non-jurors') were treated as enemies of the state. In 1794, 829 priests and religious were concentrated on two former slave ships in the mouth of the Charente river with the eventual intention of taking them to Guiana. Bl John Baptist, a priest of La Rochelle, was appointed their vicar-general. They were packed together so that they had to stand most of the time and were starved and brutally treated. After ten months 547 had died, mostly from disease. John-Baptist was beatified in 1995, together with a selection of sixty-three companions from thirteen other dioceses besides La Rochelle and twelve religious institutes. *See* **French Revolution (Martyrs of)**.

John Soyemon (Bl) M. L. Aug 19
d. 1662. He was a scribe on the ship carrying BB Louis Flores and Comps. *See* **Japan (Martyrs of)**.

John-Baptist Spagnoli
of Mantua (Bl) R(OC). Mar 20
1447–1516. His family was from Spain but he was born at Mantua, Italy, and studied at Padua. In 1463 he joined the Carmelites at Ferrara and became the superior-general of the order in 1513. He was famous as a Latin poet, having written over 50,000 lines of Latin verse, and is a good example of contemporary Christian humanism in Italy. His cultus was confirmed for Mantua and the Carmelites in 1885.

John the Spaniard (Bl)
R(OCart). Jun 25
1123–1160. From Almanza near León, Spain, as a boy he travelled to France and studied at Arles. Then he became a Carthusian at Montrieu, was transferred to the Grande Chartreuse under St Anthelmus and finally became first prior of the new foundation at Reposoir near Lake Geneva. He drew up the first constitutions for the Carthusian nuns. His cultus was approved for the Carthusians in 1864.

John Speed (alias Spence) (Bl) M. L. Feb 4
d. 1594. From Durham, he was martyred there for sheltering priests and was beatified in 1929. *See* **England (Martyrs of)**.

John-Henry-Charles Steeb
(Bl) P. F. Dec 15
1775–1856. From Tübingen, Germany, his family were wealthy Lutherans and he went to Verona in Italy to study. There he was reconciled to the Church, was ordained and led a life involved in helping sick people, in catechesis and in education. To these ends he founded the 'Sisters of Mercy' with Sr Luiga Poloni. He died at Verona and was beatified in 1975.

John Stone (St) M. R(OSA). May 12
d. 1538. An Augustinian friar at Canterbury, he was executed there for denying the royal supremacy in spiritual matters of King Henry VIII and was canonized in 1970. *See* **England (Martyrs of)**.

John Storey (Bl) M. Jun 1
?1504–1571. From the North of England, he became a doctor of law at Oxford University, was the principal of a hall of studies there, married after 1547 and became a member of parliament and vicar-general of the London diocese in 1553. During the reign of Edward VI he went abroad but returned on the accession of Queen Mary, only to be imprisoned on the accession of Queen Elizabeth. He escaped to the Low Countries but was followed by Elizabeth's secret agents, kidnapped, brought back to England and executed at Tyburn for alleged treason. He was beatified in 1886.

John Sugar and Robert Grissold
(BB) MM. P. L. Jul 16
d. 1604. From Wimbourne near Wolverhampton, Bl John had been an Anglican catechist before studying at Oxford and becoming a vicar at Cannock. After his conversion he was ordained at Rheims in 1601 and was a priest for the poor Catholics around what is now West Midlands, being sheltered by Bl Robert (a gentleman-retainer at a Broadway household). They were seized near the latter's home at Rowington and were executed at Warwick, being beatified in 1987. *See* **England (Martyrs of)**.

John of Syracuse (1) (St) *see* **Andrew, John and Comps**

John of Syracuse (2) (St) B. R. Oct 23
d. ?609. He was bishop of Syracuse, Sicily, from 595.

John the Syrian of Pinna
(St) R. Mar 19
C6th. He was listed by the old Roman Martyrology as a Syrian monk who settled at Pinna near Spoleto, Italy, where he was abbot of a large monastic colony for forty-four years. It is possible that he was a refugee from Monophysite persecution.

John Talbot (Bl) *see* **Thomas Palaser and Comps**

John Tanaka (Bl) M. L. Jul 12
d. 1626. A Japanese layman, he sheltered Bl Balthasar de Torres, was seized with his wife, Bl Catherine Tanaka, as a result and, after a long imprisonment at Omura, was burned alive at Nagasaki. *See* **Mancius Araki and Comps** and **Japan (Martyrs of)**.

John Tavalli of Tossignano
(Bl) B. R. Jul 24
d. 1446. From Tossignano near Imola, Italy, he studied at the university of Bologna, joined the order of the Gesuati and became bishop of Ferrara in 1431. He produced an Italian translation of the Bible.

John Tessier (Bl) *see* **September (Martyrs of)**

John Baptist (Dinh van) Thanh
(St) M. L. Apr 28
d. 1840. A native catechist in Vietnam, he was attached to the Society of Foreign Missions. *See* **Vietnam (Martyrs of)**.

John the Thaumaturge (St) B. Dec 5
d. *p*750. Bishop of Polyboton in Phrygia, Asia Minor, he was one of the most strenuous champions of orthodoxy against the iconoclast emperor Leo III and his fame as a wonder-worker was such that the emperor did not dare to persecute him.

John Theristus (St) R. Feb 24
1049–1129. He was born in Palermo, Sicily, after his mother had been captured and enslaved in a raid on Calabria by the Sicilian Muslims. When aged fourteen he escaped to Calabria and became a Basilian monk at Stilo, going on to be abbot. His surname ('Mower') refers to his allegedly having miraculously cut a large hay field in a short time.

John Thorne (Bl) *see* **Benedictine Martyrs of the Reformation**

John Thules and Roger Wrenn
(Bl) M. P. Mar 18
d. 1616. The son of a schoolmaster at Whalley, Lancs, the former studied at Rheims and Rome and was ordained at Rome in 1592. Arrested soon after his return to England, he escaped and was a priest in Lancashire until his recapture. He escaped briefly again from Lancaster Castle with the latter (a recusant weaver from Chorley) but they got lost outside the town, were picked up and then executed together at Lancaster. They were beatified in 1987. *See* **England (Martyrs of)**.

John Thwing (St) R(CR). Oct 11
d. 1379. He had been a student at Oxford

university before he joined the Augustinian canons at Bridlington in Yorkshire, England, and was prior there for seventeen years. Little else is known about him. He was canonized in 1401.

John of Tlaxcala (Bl) *see* **Anthony and John of Tlaxcala**

John of Todi (St) *see* **Marcellinus, Mannea and Comps**

John Tomachi (Bl) M. T(OP). Sep 8
d. 1628. A Japanese married layman with four sons, he was a very active Christian and was a Dominican tertiary. He was burned alive at Nagasaki while his sons were beheaded. *See* **Dominic Castellet and Comps** and **Japan (Martyrs of)**.

John-Baptist Triquerie (Bl) *see* **Laval (Martyrs of)**

John-Nepomuk von Tschinderer und von Gleifheim (Bl) B. Dec 4
1777–1860. From Bozen in Tyrol, Austria (now in Italy), he became in turn a priest of Innsbruck, a canon of Trent (1827), auxiliary bishop of Voralberg (1832) and bishop of Trent in 1835. A model bishop in all aspects of his ministry, he built or restored over sixty churches, showed great interest in the seminary, was attentive to social problems and to the needs of the disadvantaged and had a great love for the pope and the Church's magisterium He was beatified in 1995.

John-Baptist Turpin du Cormier (Bl) *see* **Laval (Martyrs of)**

John of Tuy (St) R. Jun 24
C9th. A native of Galicia, Spain, he lived as a hermit near Tuy and his shrine is in the Dominican church there.

John of Valence (Bl) B. R(OCist). Apr 26
d. 1145. From Lyons, France, he was a canon there and became a Cistercian monk at Clairvaux after a pilgrimage to Compostela. Then he became first abbot of Bonnevaux on the Loire and was made bishop of Valence in 1141, despite his extreme reluctance. His cultus was approved in 1901.

John of Vallombrosa (Bl)
R(OSB Vall). Mar 10
d. *c*1380. From Florence, Italy, he became a monk at the Vallumbrosan monastery of the Holy Trinity there. However he became fascinated in black magic, became a practitioner of it and was then enslaved by depravity. He was found out, initially denied involvement but then confessed and was imprisoned in a filthy cell. Then he became truly penitent and reduced himself to a skeletal state by voluntary fasting, so that his brethren begged him to return to community life. He preferred to remain in prison until his death, however, living to a very old age and reaching great holiness. He was an elegant writer and a friend of St Catherine of Siena. His cultus is unconfirmed.

John-Baptist Velázquez Peláez (Bl) *see* **Hospitaller Martyrs of Spain**

John of Vercelli (Bl) R(OP). Dec 1
d. 1283. From Mosso Santa Maria near Vercelli, Italy, he studied at Paris and taught law there and at Vercelli. He then joined the Dominicans and eventually became their master-general in 1264. He was commissioned by the pope to draw up the schema for the second ecumenical council of Lyons. His cultus was confirmed for Vercelli and the Dominicans in 1903.

John-Baptist Vernoy de Montjournal (Bl) *see* **John-Baptist Souzy and Comps**

John of Verona (St) B. Jun 6
C7th. He succeeded St Maurus as bishop of Verona, Italy.

John of Vespignano (Bl) L. Apr 9
d. 1331. From Vespignano near Florence, Italy, during the local armed conflicts of the period he cared for the refugees who had fled to Florence. His cultus was approved for there in 1800.

John-Baptist Vianney (St) P. Aug 4
1786–1859. From near Lyons, France, as a teenager he was a farm-hand but he began studying for the priesthood when aged nineteen. This he found extremely difficult, but he managed to be ordained in 1815 and was made parish priest of Ars in 1818. This was a near-derelict rural parish of a sort common in post-revolutionary France, and he was there for the rest of his life. He restored the life of the parish to full vigour and became famous for prophecy, reading of consciences and supernatural knowledge as well as for being the target of diabolical manifestations. All kinds of people from all over the world asked him to hear their confessions, and during the last ten years of his life he had to spend from sixteen to eighteen hours a day in the confessional. He was canonized in 1925, being declared the patron of parish priests. He is commonly known as the 'Curé d'Ars' (priest of Ars).

John de Villette (Bl) *see* **September (Martyrs of)**

John of Vilnius (St) *see* **Anthony of Lithuania and Comps**

John Vincent (St) B. R(OSB). Dec 21
d. 1012. From Ravenna, Italy, he was a bishop of a diocese in the area before becoming a hermit on Monte Pirchiano. He attracted disciples, thus founding the abbey of St Michael of Chiusa.

John Wacienga (St) P. Dec 23
1390–1473. From Kenty in Silesia, Poland, he graduated from the university of Cracow and was appointed professor of theology there. For some time he took charge of a parish but, fearing the responsibility, returned to his biblical teaching and continued with this until his death. He habitually shared his earnings with the poor. He was canonized in 1767.

John Wall *see* **Joachim-of-St-Anne Wall**

John Wang (Guiju) (St) *see* **Joseph Wang (Guixin) and John Wang (Guiju)**

John Wang (Rui) (St) *see* **Gregory Grassi and Comps**

John of Warneton (Bl) B. R(CR). Jan 27
d. 1130. From Warneton near Ypres, Belgium, he was a disciple of St Ivo of Chartres and became a canon regular at Mont-Saint-Eloi near Arras, France. Eventually he was appointed bishop of Thérouanne and accepted only when directed to do so by the pope. He founded eight monasteries. Though he had a reputation for strictness he was noticeably merciful in dealing with a group of troublemakers who had conspired against his life as a result of his campaign against simony.

John-Baptist Wu (Mantang) (St) *see* **Paul Wu (Anju) and Comps**

John Wu (Wenyin) (St) M. L. Jul 5
1850–1900. From Dongertou in Hebei, China, he was a leader in his village until an attack by Boxers. He was taken before the magistrate, tortured to induce apostasy and executed. *See* **China (Martyrs of)**.

John Yago (Bl) M. L. Aug 19
d. 1662. He was a sailor on the ship carrying BB **Louis Flores and Comps** (q.v.).

John-of-the-Cross de Yepes (St) R(OCD). Dr. Dec 14
1542–1591. Born at Fontiveros near Avila, Spain, he was apprenticed to a silk-weaver but became a Carmelite at Medina in 1562. From 1564 he studied theology at Salamanca, where he fell under the influence of St Teresa of Avila. As a result he opened the first house of the Discalced reform for men at Duruelo in 1568. From 1572 to 1577 he was St Teresa's confessor but was then seized, imprisoned and viciously treated by Carmelite opponents of the reform at Toledo. This led to the definitive separation of the Discalced from the 'Calced' Carmelites in 1578. He was then made prior successively of several houses and visitor of the Andalucian province in 1585. The last years of his life were again a period of humiliation,misunderstanding and physical suffering. He died in obscurity at Ubeda. His fame rests on his mystical writings which contain a thorough exposition of empirical mysticism, besides being classics of Spanish literature. He was canonized in 1726 and declared a doctor of the Church in 1926.

John de Zafra (Bl) *see* **Ignatius de Azevedo and Comps**

John Zakoly (Bl) B. R. Feb 3
d. 1494. Bishop of Csanad, Hungary, he entered the Pauline order and died as prior of the monastery of Diosgyör.

John Zedazneli (St) R. Nov 4
C6th. He was the leader of a group of Syrian monks who helped to evangelize Georgia and who introduced the monastic life there.

John Zhang (Huan) and John Zhang (Jingguang) (SS) *see* **Gregory Grassi and Comps**

John Zhang (Tianshen) (St) M. L. Feb 18
1805–1862. From Kaiyang in Guizhou, China, he was a married carpenter and lay catechist who helped St John-Peter Néel and was beheaded at Kaiyang with him and SS John Chen (Xianheng) and Martin Wu (Xuesheng). *See* **China (Martyrs of)**.

John-Baptist Zhao (Mingxi) (St) *see* **Peter Zhao (Mingzhen) and John-Baptist Zhao (Mingxi)**

John-Baptist Zhu (Wurui) (St) M. L. Aug 18
1883–1900. From Green Grass River Village in Qin County, Hebei, China, the same county

where SS Ignatius Mangin and Companions were massacred, he escaped his village when it was besieged by the Boxers but was caught by government troops who handed him over to the rebels to be beheaded. *See* **China (Martyrs of)**.

John-Baptist Zola (Bl) M. R(SJ). Jun 15
1576–1626. From Brescia, Italy, he became a Jesuit in 1595, went to India in 1602 and then to Japan in 1606. Banished to China in 1614 he returned, was seized and then burned alive at Nagasaki. He was beatified in 1867. *See* **Francis Pacheco and Comps** and **Japan (Martyrs of)**.

Jolenta *see* **Helen of Poland**

Jonas, Barachisius and Comps (SS) MM. Mar 29
d. 327. Brothers from Beth-Asja in Persia, they were martyred in the reign of Shah Shapur II for refusing to convert to Zoroastrianism. There is an extant eye-witness account of the tortures that they suffered, which were examples of the contemporary Persian inventiveness in such matters. There were nine companions.

Jonas the Gardener (St) R. Feb 11
C4th. A monk of Demeskenyanos in Egypt under St Pachomius, he was the gardener of the community for eighty-five years, working during the day and plaiting ropes and singing psalms at night. He lived on raw vegetables and vinegar.

Jonas (Yon) of Paris (St) M. P. Sept 22
C3rd. An alleged companion or disciple of St Dionysius of Paris, France, he preached in the area around the city and was martyred.

Jonatus (St) R. Aug 1
d. *c*690. A monk at Elnone near Tournai, Belgium, under St Amandus, he was abbot first of Marchiennes from ?643 and then of Elnone from ?652.

Jorand (St) R(OSB). Nov 2
d. 1340. He was a monk-hermit at Kergrist in Brittany, France, and was later at Saint Juhec in Pedernec.

Jordan-of-St-Stephen Ansalone (St) M. R(OP). Sep 28
1598–1634. Born near Agrigento, Italy, he became a Dominican missionary in the Philippines and was two years in Japan before being martyred at Nagasaki. He was canonized in 1987. *See* **Japan (Martyrs of)**.

Jordan Forzatè (Bl) R(OSB). Aug 7
?1158–1248. From Padua, Italy, he became a monk and then abbot of the Benedictine abbey of St Justina there and was appointed governor of the city by Emperor Frederick II. A local tyrant then imprisoned him for two years. He died at Venice and is venerated in the region.

Jordan of Pisa (Bl) R(OP). Mar 6
d. 1311. He became a Dominican at Pisa, Italy, in 1280, studied at Paris and then became a famous preacher at Florence. He started using the local vernacular in his sermons instead of Latin and is thus reckoned as one of the founders of the Italian language. His cultus was approved for Pisa and the Dominicans in 1833.

Jordan of Saxony (Bl) R(OP). Feb 14
d. 1237. A German nobleman, he became a Dominican under St Dominic himself in 1220, attending the first general chapter of the order at Bologna while still a novice. He was later elected second master-general and oversaw the rapid expansion of the new order throughout Germany and into Denmark. He was a powerful preacher, and one of his sermons persuaded St Albert the Great to become a Dominican. He was shipwrecked and drowned when on a voyage to the Holy Land. His cultus was confirmed for the Dominicans in 1828.

Josaphat (St) *see* **Barlaam and Josaphat**

Josaphat Kuntsevich (St) M. B. R. Nov 12
1584–1623. From Wołodimir in Poland, he became a monk of the Byzantine rite when aged twenty and abbot of Vilnius in 1614. He devoted himself to the work of promoting the unity of the local Orthodox with the Catholic church, which had been arranged in the Union of Brest-Litovsk in 1596. He became archbishop of Polatsk in Bielarus in 1618 where he continued his work, defending the rights of the Byzantine-rite Catholics against the Latin-rite Polish clergy. There was an Orthodox reaction and the setting up of a rival hierarchy sponsored by Russia, and he was murdered at Vitebsk by a mob of Cossacks. He was the first Eastern-rite Catholic to be formally canonized in 1867, and his cultus was extended to the Latin rite in 1882.

Joscio (Josbert, Valbebertus) (Bl) R(OSB). Nov 30
d. 1186. His strange legend is that he was a Benedictine monk of Saint Bertin at St Omer, France, who was especially devoted to the 'Ave Maria'. After his death a rose-bush grew out of his mouth and the name of Mary was written

on the leaves. If this has any foundation at all it possibly derives from the patterns produced by leaf-miner caterpillars working on a rose-bush on his grave.

Joseph
The spelling is similar in most modern languages except the Italian Giuseppe and the Spanish José. In both Italy and Spain the name is frequently joined to that of Our Lady: Giuseppe-Maria, José-Maria. The feminine form takes the following variants: Italian: Giuseppa, Giuseppina; Spanish: Josefa, Josefina; French: Josephine. The last is used in this book.

Joseph Abibos (St) R. Sep 15
d. *c*590. One of the thirteen Syrian disciples of St John Zedazneli in Georgia, he became abbot of Alaverdi.

Joseph Allemano (Bl) P. F. Feb 16
1851–1926. From near Turin, Italy, he became a diocesan priest there in 1873 and worked in the junior seminary of Our Lady of Consolation, which he made into a special centre of Marian devotion. He gave the students the example of his uncle, St Joseph Cafasso, to follow and later founded the 'Missionaries of Our Lady of Consolation' for both sexes (male in 1910, female in 1910). He was canonized in 1990.

Joseph-Mary Amorós Hernández (Bl) *see* **Philip-of-Jesus Munárriz Azcona and Comps**

Joseph de Anchieta (Bl) R(SJ). Jun 9
1534–1597. Born in the Canary Islands, he went to Portugal in order to join the Jesuits and was sent to Brazil in 1553. He became the 'Apostle of Brazil', baptizing an enormous number of native Americans and serving as Provincial for the Jesuits of the entire colony for ten years. The city where he died, near Rio de Janeiro, is named Anchieta after him. He was beatified in 1980.

Joseph (Josippus) of Antioch
(St) M. D. Feb 15
? A deacon, he is listed as having been martyred with seven companions at Antioch, Syria.

Joseph of Arimathea (St) L. Mar 17
C1st. A member of the Jerusalem Sanhedrin, he is presented in the Gospels as a secret disciple who arranged Christ's burial. Later spurious legends concerning him are numerous. At the church of St Laurence in Genoa, Italy, is kept the 'Sacro Catino' in which he is alleged to have caught Christ's blood at the crucifixion, and he is also connected with the foundation of the church at Glastonbury, England (the 'Holy Thorn' there allegedly being his staff which took root).

Joseph-Mary Badía Mateai (Bl) *see* **Philip-of-Jesus Munárriz Azcona and Comps**

Joseph Baldo (Bl) P. F. Oct 24
1843–1915. From near Verona, he became a diocesan priest there, was deputy rector of the seminary for eleven years and then became parish priest of Ronchi a Athesim. This was a rustic place, poor and ignorant, but he improved all aspects of parish life for the 38 years he was there. In 1894 he founded the 'Poor Daughters of St Joseph' to take care of the elderly and children. He died slowly over two years, as he had prayed for, and was beatified in 1989.

Joseph Barsabas 'the Just'
(St) M? B? Jul 20
C1st. He was the losing candidate when St Matthias was chosen as an apostle in order to replace Judas Iscariot (Acts 1:23). A dubious tradition describes him as a martyr and a bishop of Eleutheropolis near Gaza. He is sometimes depicted as a child holding stones or loaves, or blowing soap bubbles.

Joseph Bécavin (Bl) *see* **September (Martyrs of)**

Joseph-Mary Blasco Juan and Joseph Brengaret Pujol (BB) *see* **Philip-of-Jesus Munárriz Azcona and Comps**

Joseph Cafasso (St) P. Jun 23
1811–1860. From Castelnuovo d'Asti, Italy, he was ordained in 1833 and three years later became professor of moral theology at the ecclesiastical college at Turin. In 1846 he was appointed superior of the college, which he remained until his death. He led a very penitential life and was famed for his skill in hearing confessions. He was canonized in 1947.

Joseph Calasanz (St) R. F. Aug 25
1557–1648. A nobleman from Peralta de la Sal near Barbastro, Spain, he was ordained a diocesan priest of Urguel and was engaged in pastoral work until he was directed to go to Rome in 1592 by a supernatural vision. There he joined the Confraternity of Christian Doctrine for the free education of poor and homeless children, and gradually organized it

into a religious society called Le Scuole Pie (Clerks Regular of Religious Schools) whose members became known as Scolopi or Piarists. The new congregation had to pass through a period of violent persecution, mainly from other religious engaged in similar work. When old he was unjustly accused of maladministration and removed as superior for a period. He died at Rome and was canonized in 1767.

Joseph (Hoang Luong) Canh
(St) M. T(OP). Sep 5
1765–1838. A Vietnamese doctor of medicine and a Dominican tertiary, he was beheaded in 1838. *See* **Vietnam (Martyrs of).**

Joseph Chang (St) *see* **Korea (Martyrs of)**

Joseph Chiang (Nak-syo) (St) *see* **Anthony Daveluy and Comps**

Joseph Cho (Youn-o) (St) *see* **Bartholomew Chieng (Moun-ho) and Comps**

Joseph-Benedict Cottolengo
(St) P. F. Apr 30
1786–1842. From Bra near Turin, Italy, he became a canon of Corpus Domini at Turin. In 1827 he opened a small shelter near his church for sick and derelict people, and in 1832 he transferred this to Valdocco, calling it the 'Little House of Divine Providence'. The 'Piccola Casa' soon grew into an extensive settlement, comprising asylums, orphanages, hospitals, schools, workshops and almshouses of all descriptions and catering for all needs. To meet the large daily expenditure needed to maintain all these institutions he relied almost entirely on alms, keeping no books of accounts and making no investments, and his trust in Divine Providence never failed him once. Throughout his life he was primarily a man of prayer. Dying at Chieri, he was canonized in 1934.

Joseph-Mary-of-Jesus Cuartero Gascón (Bl) *see* **Nicephorus Díez Tejerina and Comps**

Joseph Desa of Cupertino
(St) R(OFM Conv). Sep 18
1602–1663. From Cupertino near Brindisi, Italy, he tried his vocation as a religious at several places but failed because of his poor intelligence. Finally he became a lay tertiary of the Conventual Franciscans at Grotella and worked as a stable-hand until his spiritual charisms became manifest and he was professed and ordained. Thenceforward his life was marked by a series of frequent, remarkable and well-authenticated praeternatural incidents, such as the public manifestations of his power of levitation (he would fly from the church door to the altar over the heads of the worshippers. Once he flew to an olive tree and remained kneeling on a branch for half an hour). However he remained humble, gentle and cheerful. The publicity embarrassed his brethren and raised suspicions, and he was examined by the Inquisition and kept in remote friaries until he died at Osimo. He was canonized in 1767 and his cultus confined to particular calendars in 1969.

Joseph Desideri of Leonissa
(St) R(OFM Cap). Feb 4
1556–1612. From Leonessa near Rieti, Italy, he became a Capuchin at Assisi in 1574 and was sent to Constantinople to minister to Christian slaves there. After two years, having already been imprisoned for preaching to Turks, he tried to enter the palace to preach to the Sultan and was almost tortured to death before returning to Italy in 1589. Then he spent twenty years as a missionary among poor people before dying of cancer at Amatrice. He was canonized in 1745.

Joseph Diaz Sanjurjo (St)
M. B. R(OP). Jul 20
1857. The Spanish vicar apostolic of Central Tonkin in Vietnam, he was beheaded. *See* **Vietnam (Martyrs of)**.

Joseph-Richard Díez (Bl) *see* **Vincent Soler and Comps**

Joseph-Benedict Dusmet
(Bl) B. R(OSB). Sep 25
1818–1894. A nobleman born in Palermo, Sicily (his father was from the Low Countries), he entered the abbey of La Scala in 1833. After becoming abbot of Caltanisetta in 1852 and of St Nicholas at Catania in 1858, he was made archbishop of Catania in 1867 and Apostolic administrator of Caltagirone in 1885. He implemented Pope Leo XIII's scheme to re-found the Benedictine college of St Anselm's at Rome and was made a cardinal in 1888. Dying at Catania, he was beatified in 1988.

Joseph-Mary Escrivá de Ballaguer (Bl) P. F. Jun 26
1902–1925. Born in Barbastro, Spain, he became a secular priest in Zaragoza in 1925. In 1928 he founded in Madrid 'Opus Dei', a secular institute dedicated to offering a way of sanctification to lay people through the exercise of one's ordinary work in the world and

Bl Joseph-Mary Escrivá, Jun 26

through exercising one's family, social and personal obligations. He also founded the Society of the Cross for priests in 1943. He died in Rome and was beatified in 1994.

Joseph-of-the-Sacred-Heart Estalayo García (Bl) *see* **Nicephorus Díez Tejerina and Comps**

Joseph Falcoz (Bl) *see* **September (Martyrs of)**

Joseph Fernández (St) M. R(OP). Jul 24
1775–1838. A Spanish Dominican, he was sent to Vietnam in 1805 and became vicar-provincial in Tonkin, north Vietnam, where he was beheaded. *See* **Vietnam (Martyrs of)**.

Joseph Ferrer Esteve (Bl) *see* **Dionysius Pamplona Polo and Comps**

Joseph Figuero Beltrán (Bl) *see* **Philip-of-Jesus Munárriz Azcona and Comps**

Joseph-Isabel Flores Varela (St) *see* **Mexico (Martyrs of)**

Joseph Freinademetz (Bl) R. Jan 28
1851–1908. Born near Brixen, Tyrol (now in Italy), he was ordained in 1875 and joined the Society of the Divine Word at its foundation by Bl Arnold Janssen. In 1879 he went to China and spent 28 years there, first in Hong Kong and then in the new vicariate of South Shandong. He was beatified in 1975.

Joseph of Freising (Bl) B. R. Jan 17
d. 764.The founder of the monastery of Isen near Munich, Germany, he became third bishop of Freising in 764. His shrine is at Isen.

Joseph Gambaro (St) *see* **Anthony Fantosati and Joseph Gambaro**

Joseph Gérard (Bl) R. May 29
1831–1914. Born at Bouxières-aux-Chênes in Lorraine, France, he joined the Oblates of Mary Immaculate in 1851 and went to South Africa two years later. He was ordained at Pietermaritzburg in 1854 and worked with the Irish and Xhosas. Then, from 1864, he became the 'Apostle of the Basutos' and worked in Lesotho until he died at a mission there called Roma. He was beatified in 1988.

Joseph Gros (Bl) *see* **September (Martyrs of)**

Joseph Han (Wen-sye) (St) *see* **Bartholomew Chieng (Moun-ho) and Comps**

Joseph (Do Quang) Hien
(St) M. R(OP). May 9
d. 1840. A Vietnamese Dominican priest, he was beheaded at Nam-Dinh. *See* **Vietnam (Martyrs of)**.

Joseph (Doan Trinh) Hoan
(St) M. P. May 26
1861. He was a Vietnamese secular priest. *See* **Vietnam (Martyrs of)**.

Joseph the Hymnographer
(St) R. Jun 14
*c*810–886. From Syracuse in Sicily, he was a refugee from the invading Muslims and became a monk at Thessalonika. Moving to Constantinople, he then served as treasurer of Hagia Sofia and is famous for the writing of hymns for the Byzantine liturgy and office.

Joseph Imbert (Bl) *see* **John-Baptist Souzy and Comps**

Joseph (Nguyen Duy) Khang
(St) M. Nov 6
1832–1861. From Tra-vi in the province of Nam-Dinh, Vietnam, he was a servant of St

Jerome Hermosilla whom he tried to rescue from prison. Caught in the attempt, he was punished with one hundred and twenty lashes and, after other tortures, was beheaded. *See* **Vietnam (Martyrs of)**.

Joseph Lambton (Bl) M. P. Jul 31
1568–92. A Yorkshire landowner from Malton, he was ordained at Rome and returned to England with five other priests, arriving at Newcastle. Such an arrival could not be concealed and he was quickly captured and executed. He was beatified in 1987. *See* **England (Martyrs of)**.

Joseph (Nguyen van) Luu
(St) M. L. May 2
*c*1790–1854. A Vietnamese catechist, he was born at Cai-nhum and died in prison at Vinh-long. *See* **Vietnam (Martyrs of)**.

Joseph Ma (Taishun) (St) M. L. Jul ?
1840–1900. From Qianshengzhuang in Hebei, China, during the Boxer uprising he was caught by a gang hiding in the fields, taken to Wanglajia and tied to a tree. He was invited to apostatize and, on his refusal, was then beheaded. *See* **China (Martyrs of)**.

Joseph Manyanet Vives (Bl) R. F. Dec 17
1833–1901. From Tremp near Urgell in Catalonia, Spain, after his ordination he gathered priests and clerics at Tremp as the 'Sons of the Holy Family' in order to teach and catechize. They opened schools throughout Catalonia. He also founded the 'Daughters of the Holy Family'. He was beatified in 1984.

Joseph Marchand (St) M. P. Nov 30
1803–1835. From Passavant near Besançon, France, he joined the Paris Society for Foreign Missions and was sent to Vietnam. He was seized in Annam and died while bits of his flesh were being torn off with red-hot pincers. *See* **Vietnam (Martyrs of)**.

Joseph Marello (St) B. F. May 30
1844–1895. From Turin, Italy, he was ordained a diocesan priest of Asti in 1868. He attended the First Vatican Council in 1869, and the proclamation of St Joseph as the patron of the universal Church led him to found the 'Oblates of St Joseph' in 1878. These were lay brothers who did domestic work, taught catechism to children and assisted with the liturgy in parish churches. (Priests were received from 1883.) In 1888 he became the bishop of Acqui, and died in 1895. He was canonized in 2001.

Joseph Mkasa (St) M. L. Jun 3
d. 1885. Majordomo to King Mwanga of Buganda, Uganda, he reproached him for ordering the killing of the newly-arrived Anglican missionary bishop James Hannington. He was executed as a result. *See* **Charles Lwanga and Comps**.

Joseph Mora Velasco (Bl) *see* **Hospitaller Martyrs of Spain**
Joseph Moreau (Bl) *see* **William Repin and Comps**

Joseph Moscati (St) L. Nov 16
d. 1927. From Benevento, Italy, he became a famous doctor of medicine at Naples and a professor at the university there. Famous for his medical research, he also spent much of his time and resources in caring for poor people in the slums of the city. He was canonized in 1987.

Joseph Nascimbeni (Bl) P. F. Jan 21
1851–1922. Born on the shore of Lake Garda, Italy, he became a diocesan priest of Verona in 1874 and took on the parish of Castelleto (*c*900 people) in 1884. He was there for 45 years, fostering the apostolate of the laity, renewing the liturgical life and founding the 'Poor Sisters of the Holy Family' (Franciscan tertiaries) with M. Mary Mantovani. By his death this had 1,200 members. He died of a stroke and was beatified in 1988.

Joseph (Nguyen van) Nghi and Comps (St) M. P. Nov 8
d. 1840. A Vietnamese priest of the Paris Mission Society, he was beheaded with four companions: John-Baptist Con, Martin (Ta Duc) Tinh, Martin Tho and Paul (Nguyen) Ngan. *See* **Vietnam (Martyrs of)**.

Joseph Oriol (St) P. Mar 23
1650–1702. From a poor family of Barcelona, Spain, he managed to become a priest and a doctor of theology despite his poverty and was made a canon of Santa Maria del Pino in his native city. He lived on bread and water for twenty-six years while maintaining a very active apostolate, being particularly successful with soldiers and children. He was canonized in 1909.

Joseph-Mary Ormo Seró (Bl) *see* **Philip-of-Jesus Munárriz Azcona and Comps**

Joseph-of-Jesus-and-Mary Osés Sainz (Bl) *see* **Nicephorus Díez Tejerina and Comps**

Joseph Oviefve (Bl) *see* **September (Martyrs of)**

Joseph of Palestine 'the Count' (St) L. Jul 22
d. ?356. A Jewish disciple of Rabbi Hillel at Tiberias in the Holy Land, he was ruler of the synagogue there before being baptized at Tarsus in 326. Being made an imperial official by Emperor Constantine, he lived at Scythopolis and built many churches. His name was inserted into the old Roman Martyrology by Cardinal Baronius, but he has never had a cultus.

Joseph the Patriarch (St) L. Mar 19
C1st. The foster-father of Christ and the husband of Our Lady is only known from the gospels of Matthew and Luke. Since he is not mentioned in the narratives of Christ's passion it is believed that he was then already dead. His veneration was widespread in the East from early times, and grew in the West from the C14th. He was declared patron of the universal Church in 1870 and is also patron of workers (as such he has a subsidiary feast on May 1) and of those seeking a holy death. His attribute is a lily, and he is also depicted with carpenter's tools.

Joseph Pavón Bueno (Bl) *see* **Philip-of-Jesus Munárriz Azcona and Comps**

Joseph Pazery de Thorame (Bl) *see* **September (Martyrs of)**

Joseph-Sebastian Pelczar (Bl) B. Mar 28
1842–1924. Born in Korczyna in Austrian Galicia, now Poland, he became a diocesan priest of Przemysl in 1864. He was a professor at the seminary and Rector of the Jagiełłonian University at Cracow before being made auxiliary bishop of his diocese in 1890, and was made diocesan bishop the following year. He was especially careful in the formation of his priests, believing that only holy priests could produce lasting apostolic fruit. He was beatified in 1991.

Joseph Pellé (Bl) *see* **Laval (Martyrs of)**

Joseph-Mary Peris Polo (Bl) *see* **Peter Ruiz de los Paños y Angel and Comps**

Joseph of Persia (St) M. P. Apr 22
d. 376. He was martyred with St Acepsimas in the reign of the Persian Shah Shapur II.

Joseph-Mary Pignatelli (St) R(SJ). Nov 28
1737–1811. A nobleman from Zaragoza, Spain, he became a Jesuit at Tarragona when aged fifteen and went on to teach at Manresa, Bilbao and Zaragoza. After the Jesuits were expelled from Spain, he was in charge of the juniors in exile on Corsica and then at Ferrara, Italy. Finally, after the suppression of the Society in 1773, he was at Bologna for twenty years, helping with the livelihoods of his secularized brethren and counselling them. At the same time he worked hard for the restoration of the Society, and was allowed to open a quasi-novitiate in1799. In 1804 he became the first Italian provincial of the restored Jesuits: 'the link between the old and the new'. He died at Rome and was canonized in 1954.

St Joseph the Patriarch, Mar 19

Joseph Rada (Bl) *see* **Vincent Soler and Comps**

Joseph Rim (St) *see* **Korea (Martyrs of)**

Joseph-Mary Robles Hurtado (St) *see* **Mexico (Martyrs of)**

Joseph-Cecil Rodríguez Gonzalez (Bl) *see* **Aurelius-Mary Villalón Acebrón and Comps**

Joseph-Mary Ros Florensa (Bl) *see* **Philip-of-Jesus Munárriz Azcona and Comps**

Joseph-Mary Rubio Peralta (Bl) R(SJ). May 2
1864–1929. Born near Granada, Spain, he became a parish priest there, then a teacher in the seminary and a member of the diocesan curia. He joined the Jesuits in 1906 and stayed at Matáro near Barcelona until his death. He was a model religious, and very charitable, being beatified in 1985.

Joseph Ruiz Cuesta (Bl) *see* **Hospitaller Martyrs of Spain**

Joseph-Mary-of-Jesus-Dying Ruiz Martínez (Bl) *see* **Nicephorus Díez Tejerina and Comps**

Joseph of St Hyacinth (Bl) M. R(OP). Sep 10
d. 1622. From near Jaén, Spain, he was provincial vicar of the Dominican missions in Japan and was fluent in Japanese. He was burnt alive in the 'Great Martyrdom' at Nagasaki. *See* **Charles Spinola and Comps**.

Joseph Sala Picó (Bl) *see* **Peter Ruiz de los Paños y Angel and Comps**

Joseph of Sandomir (Bl) *see* **Sadoc of Sandomir and Comps**

Joseph (Pham Trong) Ta (St) M. Jan 13
1859. He was a Vietnamese layman and martyr. *See* **Vietnam (Martyrs of)**.

Joseph (Le Dang) Thi (St) M. L. Oct 24
d. 1860. Captain in the royal Vietnamese army, he was garrotted at An-hoa. *See* **Vietnam (Martyrs of)**.

Joseph-Mary Tomasi (St) P. Jan 3
1649–1713. Born at Licata in Sicily, a son of the duke of Palermo, he joined the Theatines and was based at Rome, where he devoted his scholarly talents to the methodical study of the liturgy and produced several very valuable works on the subject. He was the confessor of the future Pope Clement XI, and after the papal election ordered him to accept under pain of mortal sin. The new pope thereupon made Joseph a cardinal. He was in the habit of teaching the catechism to the children in his titular church's parish. He died at Rome and was canonized in 1986.

Joseph Tovini (Bl) T(OFM). Jan 16
1841–1897. From Cividate Camuno near Brescia, Italy, he studied law at the University of Padua and worked at Brescia where he married (the couple had ten children). He became mayor of his home town in 1871 and was later a councillor for Brescia. As such he made positive efforts to promote the Church's witness in lay life at a period when anti-clericalism was fashionable. He was involved in many social, charitable and especially educational projects and was also a Franciscan tertiary. He died at Brescia and was beatified in 1998.

Joseph Tuan (St) M. Jan 7
1862. A Vietnamese layman and martyr. *See* **Vietnam (Martyrs of)**.

Joseph Tuc (St) M. Jan 6
1862. A Vietnamese layman and martyr. *See* **Vietnam (Martyrs of)**.

Joseph (Nguyen Dinh) Uyen (St) M. T(OP). Jul 3
1778–1838. A Vietnamese catechist, he died in prison. *See* **Vietnam (Martyrs of)**.

Joseph Vaz (Bl) B. Jan 16
1651–1711. The 'Apostle of Ceylon (Sri Lanka)' was born in Portuguese Goa, India, and became a missionary priest there. In 1687 he went to Jaffna. The Portuguese had been expelled from Ceylon fifty years previously by the Calvinist Dutch and the resident Catholic population had had no priest since then. He soon had to flee to the inland kingdom of Kandy (then still independent) and was imprisoned, but won a rain competition with the local Buddhist clergy and was given faculties by the king in 1696. Then he was appointed vicar-general, organized the missions, translated religious works into Sinhala and negotiated terms with the Dutch government. He was beatified in 1995.

Joseph (Dang Dinh) Vien (St) M. P. Aug 21
1786–1838. A Vietnamese priest, he was

beheaded at Hung-An. *See* **Vietnam (Martyrs of)**.

Joseph Wang (Guixin) and John Wang (Guiju) (SS) MM. LL. Jul 13
1875 and 1863–1900. First cousins of the Double-Tomb Village in Hebei, China, during the Boxer Uprising they were in an inn while on a journey when they were recognized as Catholics. St John was killed at once, but St John was taken before the county prefect. The latter was sympathetic and promised him his freedom if he would apostatize, but he refused and was handed over to the Boxers to be killed. *See* **China (Martyrs of)**.

Joseph Wang (Yumei) and Comps (SS) MM. LL. Jul 21
d. 1900. He was the 77-year-old leader of the Catholic community at Machiachuang in Hebei, China, and was seized by a Boxer gang at the entrance to his village with SS Anne Wang and Lucy Wang (Wang) with her nine-year-old son, St Andrew Wang (Tianqing). He was killed on this date, while the other three were killed on the following day. *See* **China (Martyrs of)**.

Joseph-Mary de Yermo y Parres (St) P. F. Sep 20
1851–1914. Born in Mexico City of wealthy parents, he became a diocesan priest at León in Guanajuato in 1879. Taking over 'El Calvario', a poor chapel in the suburbs, he turned it into a centre of perpetual adoration and evangelical charity. In 1885 he founded 'Servants of the Sacred Heart and the Poor' to help destitute people after finding two dead babies half-eaten by animals while walking by the river. He also founded a school for the Tarahumara nation in the north of Mexico and a refuge for destitute women in Los Angeles, where he died. He was canonized in 2000.

Joseph Yuan (Gengyin) (St) M. L. Jul 20
1853–1900. From Hui in Hebei, China, he was on his way to the market town of Dayin when he met a gang of Boxers who tried to make him worship in the town temple. On his refusal he was killed. *See* **China (Martyrs of)**.

Joseph Yuan (Zaide) (St) M. L. May 9
1766–1817. From a Catholic family of the Peng district of Sichuan, China, he was ordained in 1795 and worked in the north-eastern part of Sichuan until he was betrayed by an adulterous woman whom he had rebuked. He was executed at Hezhou after prolonged tortures in prison.

Joseph Zhang (Dapeng) (St) M. L. Feb 2
1754–1815. From Duyun in Guizhou, China, he became a silk merchant at Guiyang and was baptized in 1800. He worked as a lay catechist until he was betrayed by his brother-in-law during a persecution and executed at Xijiaotang. *See* **China (Martyrs of)**.

Joseph Zhang (Wenlan) (St) M. L. Jul 29
1831–1861. From a Catholic family of Sichuan, he was admitted to the seminary at Yaojiaguan in the province of Guizhou but was beheaded a year later with SS Paul Chen (Changpin), John-Baptist Luo (Tingying) and Martha Wang (Luo). *See* **China (Martyrs of)**.

Josephine-Mary-of-St-Agnes Albiñana (Bl) R(OSA). Jan 21
1625–1696. From near Valencia, Spain, she became an Augustinian nun at Benigamin. She was beatified in 1888, and is commonly known as 'Inés de Benigamin'.

St Josephine Bakhita, Feb 8

Josephine Bakhita (St) R. Feb 8
1869–1947. Born in the Sudan, she was kidnapped when aged six and sold as a slave five times before being bought in Khartoum by the Italian consul. She went back to Italy with him and became the governess of a friend's daughter. They were both entrusted to the Canossian Sisters in Venice, where Josephine was baptized in 1890 and took vows in 1896. She worked in Schio as cook, seamstress and

porter and died there after dictating her memoirs. She was canonized in 2000.

Josephine-Mary Barrera Izaguirre (Bl) *see* **Mary-Gabrielle de Hinojosa Naveros and Comps**

Josephine Naval Girbés (Bl) L. Dec 24
1820–1893. From Algemesí near Valencia, Spain, she lived and died there. Her mother died when she was thirteen, so she turned to Our Lady and became a model of the 'parish lady', always helping in the life of the parish and basing her own life of prayer on the liturgical cycle. She ran a free needlework school at her home. Her beatification was in 1988.

Josephine Vannini (Bl) R. F. Oct 16
1859–1911. Born in Rome, she was orphaned and tried to join the Daughters of Charity but her health prevented this. In 1891 she met Bl Louis Tezza, procurator general of the Camillans, who encouraged her to found a female branch of his order. This she did, adding a fourth vow of service to the sick even at risk to one's life. The 'Daughters of St Camillus' had spread to France, Belgium and Argentina before she died. She was beatified in 1994.

Josse *see* **Judoc**

Jovinian (St) M. May 5
d. *c*300. He was with St Peregrinus of Auxerre on mission, was a church reader at Auxerre, France, when the latter was bishop there, survived him and is believed to have been martyred.

Jovinus (St) *see* **Peter, Marcian and Comps**

Jovinus and Basileus (SS) MM. Mar 2
d. ?258. They were martyred at Rome in the reign of Gallienus and Valerian and were buried on the Latin Way.

Jovita (St) *see* **Faustinus and Jovita**

Jucunda (St) *see* **Felix, Julia and Jucunda**

Jucunda of Reggio (St) R. Nov 25
d. 466. A consecrated virgin of Reggio in Aemilia, Italy, she was a disciple of St Prosper, bishop of that city.

Jucundian (St) M. Jul 4
? He is listed as a Roman African who was martyred by being thrown into the sea.

Jucundinus (St) *see* **Claudius, Justus and Comps**

Jucundus (St) *see* **Epictetus, Jucundus and Comps**

Jucundus of Bologna (St) B. Nov 14
d. 485. He was a bishop of Bologna, Italy.

Jude (Thaddeus) (St) A. Oct 28
C1st. One of the Twelve, he was brother of St James the Less and therefore related to Christ. One of the canonical letters is attributed to him. The traditions concerning his later career are confused and unreliable, including the one that he was martyred in Persia with St Simon the Zealot. This legend has led to the two apostles sharing a feast-day. He is the patron of difficult or hopeless cases or problems.

Judicael, King of Brittany (St) R. Dec 17
*c*590–658. As a royal prince he became a monk at the monastery of St Meen near Rennes, France, but was elected king of Brittany and married in 630. He retired to become a monk again in 642 after a successful reign.

Judith (St) *see* **Salome and Judith**

Judoc (Jodoc, Josse), King of Brittany (St) Dec 13
d. ?668. Brother of St Judicael, King of Brittany, when the latter abdicated he was the successor for a few months. Then he fled with twelve companions and ended up as a hermit at St Josse (named after him) near Boulogne-sur-Mer, France. His veneration was popular in medieval England and some relics were enshrined at Winchester.

Julia (St) V. Oct 7
d. *c*300. She was martyred in the reign of Diocletian, either in Egypt or in Syria.

Julia (St) *see* **Catulinus, Januarius and Comps**

Julia of Arezzo (Bl) R(OSB Cam). Dec 15
? She was a Camaldolese nun at Arezzo, Italy.

Julia Billiart (St) R. F. Apr 8
1751–1816. From Cuvilly in Picardy, France, the daughter of a shopkeeper, she took a vow of chastity when aged fourteen and worked in helping and teaching the poor. In 1774 she saw an assault on her father and became bedridden by hysterical paralysis. However she became a mystic, attracted disciples and supported the 'non-juring' clergy during the French Revolution. Moving to Amiens to escape persecution, she formed a sisterhood for the

education of girls in 1803 (later to become the 'Institute of Notre Dame of Namur'), and was cured of her paralysis in 1804. She moved the mother-house of her institution to Namur in Belgium, died there and was canonized in 1970.

Julia of Certaldo (Bl) T(OSA). Feb 15
1319–1367. From Certaldo near Florence, Italy, as a teenager she was a domestic servant but became an Augustinian tertiary at Florence when aged eighteen. Returning to her native town, she lived as a hermit in a cell next to the church of SS Michael and James. Her cultus was confirmed for Florence in 1819.

Julia of Corsica (St) V. May 22
C5th. Her story is that she was a young noblewoman of Carthage in Roman Africa who was sold as a slave by the Vandals when they captured that city. The ship on which she was being taken to Gaul was wrecked on Corsica while a pagan festival was taking place and, after being rescued, she refused to join in the festivities and was crucified on the northern tip of the island. She is the patron of Corsica.

Julia of Lisbon (St) *see* **Verissimus, Maxima and Julia**

Julia of Mérida (St) V. Dec 10
d. ?304. She was martyred with St Eulalia at Mérida, Spain, in the reign of Diocletian.

Julia-of-Jesus de la Neuville (Bl) *see* **Compiègne (Carmelite Martyrs of)**

Julia of Nicomedia (St) *see* **Felix, Julia and Jucunda**

Julia of Troyes (St) V. Jul 21
d. *p*272. According to her story she was a young woman of Troyes, France, who was beheaded there in the reign of Aurelian. Her acta are a forgery.

Julia of Zaragoza (St) *see* **Zaragoza (Eighteen Martyrs of)**

Julian (St) M. Mar 23
? The old Roman Martyrology listed him as a confessor but it appears certain that he was also a martyr. Nothing more is known about him.

Julian (St) *see* **Caesarius and Julian**

Julian (St) *see* **Datius, Reatrus and Comps**

Julian (St) *see* **Diomedes, Julian and Comps**

Julian (St) *see* **Julius of Novara**

Julian (St) *see* **Lucian, Maximian and Julian**

Julian (St) *see* **Macarius and Julian**

Julian (St) *see* **Macrobius and Julian**

Julian (St) *see* **Modestus and Julian**

Julian (St) *see* **Montanus, Lucius and Comps**

Julian (St) *see* **Peter, Julian and Comps**

Julian (St) *see* **Publius, Julian and Comps**

Julian (St) *see* **Quintian, Lucius and Comps**

Julian (St) *see* **Sabinus, Julian and Comps**

Julian (St) *see* **Symphorosa**

Julian (St) *see* **Theodore, Oceanus and Comps**

Julian, Basilissa and Comps
(SS) MM. Jan 9
d. ?302. Their story is that they were a married couple who took vows of celibacy and turned their house into a refuge for the poor and homeless. As a widower Julian was martyred at 'Antioch' (probably Antinoe in Egypt is meant) in the reign of Diocletian with four companions: Anthony, a priest; Anastasius, a new convert; Marcionilla, a married woman and Celsus, her little son. The legend is a romantic story with a possible foundation in fact.

Julian, Cronion Eunus and Besas (SS) MM. Feb 27
d. 250. Julian, a citizen of Alexandria, Egypt, was accused of being a Christian and, having gout, was carried to the law court by his two Christian slaves. One apostatized through fear but the other, Cronion Eunus, was martyred with his master. They were paraded on camels through Alexandria, whipped and burned to death. Besas, a sympathetic soldier, was killed by the mob for having tried to help them. These details were preserved by St Dionysius of Alexandria.

Julian, Eunus, Macarius and Comps (SS) MM. Oct 30
d. ?250. They are listed in the old Roman Martyrology as martyrs of Alexandria in Egypt, but SS Julian and (Cronion) Eunus are dupli-

cated on Feb 27 and St Macarius on Dec 8. The duplication was caused by the insertion of a group of sixteen including the above-mentioned.

Julian, Marcian and Comps (SS) MM. Aug 9
d. 730. When Emperor Leo III instituted his iconoclast policy at Constantinople one of its first public manifestations was the removal and destruction of the great icon of Christ over the Bronze Gate of the imperial palace. The soldier sent to accomplish this was lynched by a group of about ten citizens who were seized and executed either at once or eight months later. The companions are: Alexis, Demetrius, James, John, Leontius, Marcella, Peter and Photius.

Julian of Anazarbus (St) M. Mar 16
d. ?302. A senator of Anazarbus in Cilicia, Asia Minor, in the reign of Diocletian he was tortured, sewn up in a sack with scorpions and vipers and thrown into the sea at Aegae. His body was recovered and enshrined at Antioch, Syria, where St John Chrysostom gave a sermon in his honour.

Julian of Apamea (St) B. Dec 9
C3rd. Bishop of Apamea in Syria, he took part in the Montanist controversy.

Julian of Brioude (St) M. Aug 28
C3rd. From Vienne, France, he was an imperial army officer and a secret Christian. On the outbreak of persecution, probably under Decius, he fled but surrendered to his pursuers and had his throat cut near Brioude. His shrine became the most famous one in Auvergne.

Julian of Caesarea (1) (St) M. Aug 25
? Cardinal Baronius listed him as a Syrian priest martyred at 'Caesarea', but on poor evidence.

Julian of Caesarea (2) (St) M. Feb 17
d. 308. According to Eusebius he was a Cappodocian (from Asia Minor) who was visiting Caesarea in the Holy Land when St Pamphilus and his ten companions were being martyred. He offered himself to the executioners to make up the number of twelve and was roasted to death over a slow fire.

Julian of Cagliari (St) M. Jan 7
? His alleged relics were discovered and enshrined at Cagliari, Sardinia, in 1615 and he was equated with the Julian mentioned in the old Roman Martyrology on this date.

Julian Carrasquer Fos (Bl) *see* **Hospitaller Martyrs of Spain**

Julian Cesarello de Valle (Bl) R(OFM). May 11
? He was born and died at Valle in Istria (near Rovinj in Croatia), where his tomb is venerated. Nothing is known about him. His cultus was approved in 1910.

Julian of Cuenca (St) B. Jan 28
?1127–?1208. From Burgos, Spain, he was appointed bishop of Cuenca in 1196 after that city was taken from the Muslims by the kingdom of Castile in 1177. He allegedly spent all his spare time earning money for poor people by the work of his hands, and is the principal patron of the diocese of Cuenca.

Julian of Edessa (St) R. Jun 9
d. *c*370. A captive from Italy, he was sold into slavery at Baalbek in Lebanon and led an immoral life with his master while the latter was alive. On regaining his freedom he entered a monastery near Edessa in Mesopotamia (now Urfa in Turkey) under St Ephraem, whose biography he wrote.

Julian of Egypt and Comps (SS) Feb 16
? It is alleged that he was the leader of 5,000 martyrs in Egypt, but nothing is known for certain. One source-text substitutes 'militibus' for 'millibus', i.e. 'five soldiers' not 'five thousand persons'.

Julian-Alfred Fernández Zapico (St) *see* **Cyril-Bertrand Sanz Tejedor and Comps**

Julian Hédouin (Bl) *see* **September (Martyrs of)**

Julian the Hospitaller (St) L. Feb 12
? His legend, which was very popular in the Middle Ages, is as follows: Julian killed his own parents in error, went to Rome with his wife to obtain absolution and, on their return home, built a hospice on a river bank where they looked after the poor and the sick and ferried travellers across the river. He is for this reason a patron of boatmen, innkeepers and travellers. The story is fictitious and seems to be a variant of that of SS Julian and Basilissa.

Julian le Laisant (Bl) *see* **September (Martyrs of)**

Julian of Lyons (St) M. Feb 13
? He is listed in the old Roman Martyrology as having been martyred at Lyons, France, although Nicomedia is a possible alternative.

Julian Majali (Bl) R(OSB). Oct 4
d. 1470. A Benedictine of San Martino delle Scale in Sicily, he was held in great esteem by popes and kings. Six years before his death he became a hermit.

Julian of Le Mans (St) B. Jan 27
C3rd? He is traditionally the first bishop of Le Mans, France, and is patron of several churches in England.

Julian-of-St-Augustine Martinet (Bl) R(OFM). Apr 8
d. 1606. From Medinaceli near Soria, Spain, after being twice rejected by the Franciscans he was finally admitted as a lay brother near Segovia. He accompanied the Franciscan preachers on their home-missions, and used to ring a handbell through the streets of the places visited in order to summon people to the public sermon. He died at Alcalá de Henares and was beatified in 1825.

Julian Massey (Bl) *see* **September (Martyrs of)**

Julian Maunoir (Bl) R(SJ). Jan 28
1606–1683. From near Avranches, France, he became a Jesuit in 1625 and hoped to go to Canada. However he became a missionary in Brittany for forty years instead, learning the Breton language well enough to preach in it and allegedly reconciling 30,000 people to the faith in two years. Previously the Bretons had been neglected by the French-speaking clergy, but he was joined by several secular priests in his work. He died exhausted at Plévin and was beatified in 1951.

Julian Moreno (Bl) *see* **Vincent Soler and Comps**

Julian-Francis Morin de la Girardière and Julian Moulé (BB) *see* **Laval (Martyrs of)**

Julian of Norwich *May 13*
d. ?1416. The famous mystic of Norwich, the author of *Revelations of Divine Love*, has formerly been listed as a beata. She has been quoted in the Catholic Catechism with an attribution referring to her as 'Dame', however, which is a definitive indication that she has no approved cultus.

Julian Palazaola Artola (Bl) *see* **Hospitaller Martyrs of Spain**

Julian of Perugia (St) *see* **Florentius, Julian and Comps**

Julian the Poor *see* **Julian the Hospitaller**

Julian Poulain de Launay (Bl) *see* **September (Martyrs of)**

Julian Sabas (St) R. Jan 17
d. 377. From Baalbek, Lebanon, he became a hermit of Osrhoene in Mesopotamia. He visited Antioch to help the church there after the expulsion of St Meletius and also spent some time at Sinai. St John Chrysostom and Theodoret of Cyrrhus have left accounts of his life.

Julian of Sora (St) M. Jan 27
d. *c*150. A Dalmatian, he was seized at Atina in eastern Lazio, Italy, while on a journey, then tortured and beheaded in the reign of Antoninus Pius. His shrine is at Sora.

Julian of Toledo (St) B. R. Mar 8
d. 690. He was a monk at Zaragoza, Spain, under St Eugene, whom he succeeded as abbot in the same monastery and then as archbishop of Toledo in 680. He was the first archbishop to exercise primacy over the whole Iberian peninsula. Besides presiding over several national councils and revising and developing the Mozarabic liturgy, he was a voluminous writer (few of his writings survive).

Juliana (St) *see* **Alexandra, Claudia and Comps**

Juliana (St) *see* **Cyrenia and Juliana**

Juliana (St) *see* **Hilaria, Digna and Comps**

Juliana (St) *see* **Leo and Juliana**

Juliana (St) *see* **Paul and Juliana**

Juliana and Sempronia (SS) VV. Jul 27
d. 303? They are principal patrons of Matarone in Catalonia, Spain, and their legend alleges that they buried St Cucuphas. Despite doubts as to their having existed, their cultus was confirmed in 1850 for Barcelona.

Juliana of Bologna (St) L. Feb 7
d. 435. She is described by St Ambrose of Milan as a married woman of Bologna, Italy, who gave permission for her husband to leave her and become a priest, and who then devoted herself to bringing up her four children and to the service of the church and the poor.

Juliana of Collalto (Bl) R(OSB). Sep 1
d. 1262. A noblewoman from near Treviso, Italy, when aged ten she entered the Benedictine

nunnery at Salarola but transferred to Gemmola in 1222 with Bl Beatrix of Este. In 1226 she became the abbess-foundress of SS Biagio and Cataldo at Venice. Her cultus was approved for Venice in 1753.

Juliana of Cornillon (Bl) R(OSA). Apr 5
1192–1258. From Rutten near Liege, Belgium, she became an Augustinian nun and prioress at Cornillon. As such she successfully promoted the institution of the feast of Corpus Christi, her greatest achievement, but was slandered as a false visionary and driven from her nunnery. Recalled by the bishop of Liege, she was expelled permanently in 1248. She took refuge at the Cistercian nunnery of Salzinnes and, when this place was burned, became a hermit at Fosses. Her cultus was confirmed locally in 1869.

Juliana Falconieri (St) T(OSM). Jun 19
1270–1341. A noblewoman of Florence, Italy, her uncle St Alexis Falconieri was a co-founder of the Servite Friars and she became a tertiary when aged sixteen. In 1304 the community of Servite tertiaries known as the 'Mantellate', of which she was the first superior, was formally established and admitted into the order by St Philip Benizi. She was canonized in 1737 and her cultus was confined to local calendars in 1969.

Juliana of Nicomedia (St) V. Feb 16
d. 305. The old Roman Martyrology listed her as having been martyred at Nicomedia, Asia Minor, but it is possible that she was martyred near Naples (perhaps at Cumae, where her relics are allegedly enshrined). The details are seriously confused.

Juliana of Pavilly (St) R(OSB). Oct 11
d. *c*730. A servant girl, she became a nun at Pavilly in Normandy, France, under St Benedicta and succeeded her as abbess. She is called 'the Little Sister of Jesus'.

Juliana Puricelli (Bl) R(OSA). Aug 14
1427–1501. From Busto Arsizio near Milan, Italy, she became an Augustinian nun and the first companion of Bl Catherine da Pallanza at the Sacro Monte sopra Varese, where she died. Her cultus was approved for Milan in 1769.

Juliette Kim (St) *see* **Korea (Martyrs of)**

Juliette-of-St-Francis Verolot (Bl) *see* **Compiègne (Carmelite Martyrs of)**

Juliot (St) Jun 26
? Nothing is known about the patron of the Anglican church at Luxulyan in Cornwall, England, who has been confused with the Julitta in 'Quiricus and Julitta'.

Julitta (St) *see* **Quiricus and Julitta**

Julitta (St) *see* **Theodotus, Thecusa and Comps**

Julitta of Caesarea (St) M. Jul 30
d. 303. A rich citizen of Caesarea in Cappodocia, Asia Minor, she was cheated out of her property by a pagan and, on her appealing to the magistrates, was denounced as a Christian and burned.

Julius (St) *see* **Ambicus, Victor and Julius**

Julius (St) *see* **Paul, Gerontius and Comps**

Julius I, Pope (St) Apr 12
d. 352. A Roman, he was pope from 337 and supported the exiled St Athanasius, whom he defended against his Arian accusers. The letter he wrote to the East on this occasion is one of the most important dogmatic statements of the Roman see. He also built several churches in Rome.

Julius, Aaron and Comps (SS) MM. July 1
d. ?304. According to tradition they were martyred at Caerleon in Gwent, Wales, in the reign of Diocletian. They are included in St Bede's martyrology and (with St Alban) are the only martyrs known of the Romano-British church.

Julius, Potamia, Crispin, Felix, Gratus and Comps (SS) MM. Dec 5
d. 302. Twelve Roman Africans, they were martyred at Thagura in Numidia in the reign of Diocletian.

Julius Álvarez Mendoza (St) *see* **Mexico (Martyrs of)**

Julius of Durostorum (St) M. May 27
d. ?302. A veteran Roman soldier, he was martyred at Durostorum on the Danube (now Silistra in Romania) in the reign of Diocletian, together with other soldiers.

Julius of Gelduba (St) M. Dec 20
? He is listed as having been martyred at 'Gelduba', in Thrace (possibly in Bulgaria).

Julius-of-the-Sacred-Heart Mediavilla Concejero (Bl) *see* **Nicephorus Díez Tejerina and Comps**

Julius of Novara (St) P. Jan 31
d. *p*390. He was a priest from Aegina, Greece, and, with his brother Julian (a deacon), was authorized by the emperor Theodosius I to convert the pagan temples around Lake Maggiore, Italy, into churches.

Julius Pazery de Thorame (Bl) *see* **September (Martyrs of)**

Julius of Rome (St) M. Aug 19
d. ?190. An alleged Roman senator, he is mentioned in the unreliable acta of SS Eusebius, Pontian and Comps. There is no historical evidence for his existence.

Junian (St) R. Oct 16
C5th. He was a hermit at the place now called St Junien after him near Limoges, France.

Junian of Mairé (St) R. Aug 13
d. 587. He had been a hermit at Chaulnay before becoming the abbot-founder of Mairé in Poitou, France.

Junias (St) *see* Andronicus and Junias

Juniper Serra (Bl) R(OFM). Aug 28
1713–1784. Born in Majorca, he joined the Franciscans at Palma in 1730 and went to Mexico in 1749 to teach in the Apostolic College there and to go on mission. In 1769 Spain started the conquest of California, then inhabited by people of many different nations, mostly living as hunter-gatherers. He went with the army and founded nine missions, including San Francisco and San Diego (around which the namesake cities grew). He had a great devotion to the well-being of the natives but shared the contemporary views of their culture, which has been unfairly held against him. He died at Carmel, CA and was beatified in 1988.

Jurmin (St) L. Feb 23
C7th. A prince of East Anglia, England, he was a son or (more likely) a nephew of King Anna (d. 654). His relics were eventually enshrined at Bury St Edmunds.

Just (St)
? The patron of St Just near Land's End in Cornwall, England, may be identical with Justus of Beauvais or with Ust, or may be an unknown.

Justa (St) *see* **Catulinus, Januarius and Comps**

Justa, Justina and Henedina (SS) MM. May 14
d. ?130. They are alleged to have been martyred somewhere on Sardinia in the reign of Hadrian, and are venerated on that island.

Justa and Rufina (SS) MM. Jul 19
d. ?287. According to their unreliable acta, they were two sisters of Seville, Spain, who worked as potters and who were martyred in the reign of Diocletian. They are the principal patrons of Seville. Early sources list them as 'Justus and Rufina' (i.e. as a man and woman).

Justin (St) *see* **Maxentius, Constantius and Comps**

Justin (St) *see* **Symphorosa**

Justin of Chieti (St) B? Jan 1
d.?540. He has an ancient cultus at Chieti near Pescara, Italy, and may have been a bishop there.

Justin-of-St-Gabriel-and-Our-Lady-of-Sorrows Cuesta Redondo (Bl) *see* **Nicephorus Díez Tejerina and Comps**

Justin de Jacobis (St) B. R. Jul 31
1800–1860. From San Fele in Basilicata, Italy, he became a Vincentian and was superior of various communities in central Italy. In 1839 he was made prefect-apostolic of his congregation's mission in Ethiopia, and adapted his way of life to that of the country. This won him the respect of much of the native Monophysite church, but the government suspected him to be a foreign agent and he was imprisoned twice. In 1848 he was made bishop and vicar-apostolic at Massawa. He founded many missions, established a native Catholic clergy and allegedly converted about 12,000, among them Bl Michael Ghebre. He died at Halai in Eritrea and was canonized in 1975.

Justin of Louvre (St) M. Aug 1
d. ?290. A little boy, he is alleged to have been martyred at Louvre near Paris, France. He may be identical with St Justus of Beauvais, for their two stories seem to have a common source.

Justin Martyr (St) M. Jun 1
*c*100–165. The first Christian philosopher was from a pagan family of Nablus in the Holy Land and studied philosophy at Ephesus. The great philosophical systems of the time failed to convince, however, and he was eventually converted to Christianity when aged about thirty. He was subsequently at Rome, where he

was martyred. His acta are genuine. Of his many writings only two, *Apologies for the Christian Religion* and his *Dialogue with Trypho* survive.

Justin Orona Madrigal (St) *see* **Mexico (Martyrs of)**

Justin of Rome (St) M. Sep 17
d. 259. A Roman priest, he allegedly buried the bodies of martyrs such as St Laurence and was martyred himself. His relics were transferred to Freising in Germany.

Justina (St) *see* **Aureus, Justina and Comps**

Justina (St) *see* **Cyprian and Justina**

Justina (St) *see* **Justa, Justina and Henedina**

Justina Bezzoli (Bl) R(OSB). Mar 12
d. 1319. From Arezzo, Italy, when aged thirteen she became a Benedictine nun at St Mark's nunnery there but transferred to that of All Saints, also Benedictine. Later she lived as a hermit at Civitella, and finally returned to community life at All Saints. Her cultus was confirmed for Arezzo in 1890.

Justina of Byzantium (St) V. Nov 30
? She is listed as having been martyred at Byzantium, but there is doubt about this.

Justina of Padua (St) V. Oct 7
d. *c*300. She was a virgin-martyr of Padua, Italy, in the reign of Diocletian. Her acta (a medieval forgery) linked her with St Prosdocimus, the alleged disciple of St Peter. Her veneration spread throughout Italy on account of the famous Benedictine abbey dedicated to her at Padua. She is depicted as a young woman with both breasts pierced by one sword.

Justinian (Iestin) of Ramsey
(St) M. R. Aug 23
C6th. From Brittany, he became a hermit on the island of Ramsey near St David's, Wales, and was murdered by robbers. Many legends feature him; he is also claimed for the Isle of Man.

Justus (St) M. July 14
? He is listed as a Roman soldier martyred at Rome (or perhaps at 'New Rome', meaning Constantinople).

Justus (St) *see* **Ariston, Crescentian and Comps**

Justus (St) *see* **Claudius, Justus and Comps**

Justus (St) *see* **Donatus, Justus and Comps**

Justus (St) *see* **Macarius, Rufinus and Comps**

Justus *see* **Ust**

Justus and Abundius (SS) MM. Dec 14
d. 283. They were beheaded at Baeza near Jaén, Spain, in the reign of Numerian, allegedly after a futile attempt to burn them.

Justus and Pastor (SS) MM. Aug 6
d. ?304. They were two brothers, aged respectively thirteen and nine, who were whipped and beheaded at Alcalá, Spain, in the reign of Diocletian.

Justus of Beauvais (St) M. Oct 18
C3rd? A child aged nine, he is alleged to have been martyred at Beauvais, France, but his acta are fictional and he is probably derived from another saint of the same name.

Justus of Canterbury (St) B. R. Nov 10
d. 627. A Roman monk, he was one of those sent by St Gregory the Great in 601 to reinforce the mission to the Anglo-Saxons. He became bishop of Rochester, England, in 604 and he succeeded St Mellitus at Canterbury in 624.

Justus of Lyons (St) B. R. Sep 2
d. 390. A deacon of Vienne, France, he became bishop of Lyons in 350. In 381 he fled secretly to Egypt and became a monk, refusing to return when his whereabouts were discovered by his people and preferring to die there.

Justus Ranfer de Brenières (St) *see* **Simon Berneaux and Comps**

Justus of Susa (St) M? R? Oct 17
C10th? He is the principal patron of Susa in Piedmont, Italy, where his body was found in 1087. A monastery was built around his shrine. His dubious legend states that he was a monk killed by marauders at Oulx nearby. His cultus was confirmed in 1903.

Justus of Trieste (St) M. Nov 2
d. 303. From Trieste, Italy, he was martyred in the reign of Diocletian by being drowned in the sea.

Justus of Urgell (St) B. May 28
d. *p*527. He is the first recorded bishop of Urgell in Catalonia, Spain. St Isidore wrote about him,

and he himself wrote a commentary on the *Song of Songs*.

Justus of Vienne (St) B. May 6
d. ?968. He was bishop of Vienne, France.

Juthware (St) V? Jul 1
C7th. Many odd legends concern her, such as the one that she was beheaded by her father who found that her underwear was moist and suspected promiscuity, the moisture having been caused by a cheese poultice prescribed in malice by her stepmother. She may have been a Briton living in Devon, England, before the incursions of the Saxons. Her attribute is a cheese.

Jutta *see* **Ivetta**

Jutta (Judith) of Disenberg
(Bl) R(OSB). Dec 22
d. 1136. A noblewoman, she became a hermit in a cell near the monastery-church of Disenberg on the Rhine, Germany, where she was entrusted with the education of St Hildegarde. Other disciples came to her and she formed them into a Benedictine community, which she ruled for twenty years.

Jutta (Julitta) of Heilingenthal
(St) R(OCist). Nov 29
d. *c*1250. She was the leader of a sorority of pious women at Essleben near Würzburg, Germany, before becoming founder and first abbess of the Cistercian nunnery of Heilingenthal in 1234. A relic of her arm with a golden cup attached for sick people to drink from was locally famous.

Jutta of Sangerhausen (St) R. May 5
d. 1250. A noblewoman of Thuringia, Germany, she was widowed by her husband's death on crusade and, after providing for her children, became a hermit at Kulmsee in Prussia (now Chełmża in Poland).

Juvenal of Narni (St) B. May 3
d. 369. First bishop of Narni in central Italy, he was allegedly ordained by Pope St Damasus. His biographers have confused him with other saints of the same name and so there is no certainty as to the details of his career. His cultus was confined to local calendars in 1969.

Juvenal II of Narni (St) B. May 7
C6th? Allegedly a bishop of Narni, Italy, he may be identical with his namesake. His reputed shrine is at Benevento.

Juvenal Aneina *see* **John-Juvenal Aneina**

Juventinus and Maximinus
(SS) MM. Jan 25
d. 363. They were officers in the army of Emperor Julian and, when they criticized the laws against Christians and refused to sacrifice to idols, were degraded, imprisoned, whipped and finally beheaded at Antioch, Syria.

Juventius (St) M. Jun 1
? The relics of this Roman martyr were transferred in the C16th to the Benedictine abbey of Chaise-Dieu, Evreux, France.

Juventius of Pavia (St) B. Feb 8
C1st? The tradition is that St Hermagoras, bishop of Aquileia and disciple of St Mark, sent SS Syrus and Juventius to evangelize Pavia, Italy, of which city the latter became the first bishop. The old Roman Martyrology listed him a second time with St Syrus on Sept 12.

K

Kanten (Cannen) (St) R. Nov 5
C8th. He allegedly founded a monastery at Llanganten near Builth Wells in Powys, Wales.

Karantoc *see* **Carantac**

Kateri Tekákwitha *see* **Catherine Tekákwitha**

Kea (Kay, Kenan, Quay)
(St) B? R. Nov 5
C6th. The details of his life are very uncertain, but he was apparently a Welsh monk who migrated to Cornwall (he gave his name to Landkey near Barnstaple in Devon) and then to Brittany, France, where he is known as St Quay.

Kebius *see* **Cuby**

Kellach *see* **Ceallach**

Kenan (Cianan) of Duleek
(St) B. R. Nov 24
d. *c*500. From Meath, Ireland, and allegedly a disciple of St Martin of Tours, he became bishop of Duleek near Drogheda and built Ireland's first stone cathedral.

Kenelm (St) M? L. Jul 17
d. 821. Historically he was a son of King Coenwulf of Mercia, England (d. 821), and appears to have died before his father, possibly in battle. The abbey at Winchcombe (then Mercia's capital) contained his shrine and inspired the entirely spurious medieval legend that he had succeeded his father as king when aged seven and was murdered in the forest of Clent in the Black Country by order of his sister. He was venerated as a martyr, but this veneration did not survive the suppression of the abbey (east of the present parish church) except for a passing interest among certain Victorian romantic medievalists.

Kennera (St) R. Oct 29
? Apparently a hermit at Kirkinner near Wigtown, Scotland, she has been connected with the spurious legends concerning St Ursula and St Regulus of Patras.

Kenneth (Kened, Cenydd)
the Lame (St) R. Aug 1
C6th. A nobleman of Wales and a disciple of St Illtyd, he founded a monastery at Senghenydd ('St Kenneth') near Caerphilly. The boundary-bank of this mostly survives, although now only enclosing a mining village. He founded another monastery at Llangenydd in the Gower and later emigrated to Brittany, France, being associated with Ploumelin there.

Kenneth *see* **Canice**

Kennocha (Kyle, Enoch)
(St) R. Mar 25
d. 1007. A nun of Fife, Scotland, she gave her name to a former railway terminus in Glasgow.

Kentigern Mungo (St) B. R. Jan 13
d. ?603. The surname Mungo means 'darling'. The late sources assert that he settled as a missionary monk on the Clyde, on the site of the present city of Glasgow, Scotland, and was ordained first bishop of the Strathclyde Britons in ?540. Driven into exile, he preached around Carlisle and then went to Wales to stay with St David at Menevia. Tradition alleges that he founded the monastery of Llanelwy (St Asaph), but if anything he was only its abbot for a time. In ?573 he was able to return to Scotland, initially to near Dumfries but then back to Glasgow where he died.

Kentigerna (St) R. Jan 7
d. 734. Daughter of a prince of Leinster, Ireland, and mother of St Coellan, as a widow she left Ireland and became a hermit on the island of Inchcailloch in Loch Lomond, Scotland, where a ruined church is dedicated to her.

Kerric *see* **Guevrock**

Kerrier *see* **Kieran**

Kessog (Mackessog) (St) M? B. R. Mar 10
d. *c*560. A nobleman from Cashel in Co. Tipperary, Ireland, he became a missionary bishop in Scotland, working in and around Dumbartonshire. It is not certain where he died, but one tradition alleges that he was martyred at Luss on Loch Lomond.

Kester *see* **Christopher**

Keverne (St) Nov 18
C6th. The patron of St Keverne near Falmouth in Cornwall, England, was either the same as St Kieran or a friend of his.

Kevin (Coemgen, Caoimhghin) (St) R. Jun 3
d. ?618. From the ruling family of Leinster, Ireland, he was educated by St Petroc of Cornwall (who was then in Ireland) and became the abbot-founder of Glendalough in Co. Wicklow. This is perhaps the most famous and beautiful of the ancient Irish monastic sites. His extant biographies are full of untrustworthy legends (which may be based on actual facts, however). He is the principal patron of Dublin, and his attribute is a blackbird which allegedly nested in his hand.

Kew (Kigwe, Kywe, Ciwa) (St) R. Feb 8
C5th? The patron of the village of St Kew near Camelford in Cornwall, England, is probably the same as St Ciwa, a C6th or C7th saint of Gwent, Wales.

Keyne (Ceinwen) (St) R. Oct 8
C5th. From Wales, she was allegedly a daughter of St Brychan and became a hermit near Liskeard in Cornwall, England, where there is a village and holy well named after her. The town of Keynsham in Somerset is not so named, however.

Khodianin Oghlou Kadir (Bl) *see* **Salvator Lilli and Comps**

Kieran (Kiernan, Kyran, Ciaran) (St) B. Mar 5
d. *c*530. Styled 'the first-born of the saints of Ireland', he was from Ossory, Co. Offaly, and was probably ordained bishop by St Patrick. He is wrongly identified with St Piran of Cornwall, but the tradition that he was the first bishop of Ossory and the founder of the monastery of Saighir is ancient. He is the principal patron of the diocese of Ossory.

Kilda (St)
The famously isolated Scottish island is named after a wholly unknown saint.

Kilian *see* **Chillien**

Kilian (Chilian), Colman and Totnan (SS) MM. RR. Jul 8
d. ?689. They left Ireland as missionary monks and settled near Würzburg in Franconia, Germany, where they converted the duke. Kilian became that city's first bishop but the three were allegedly killed on the orders of the duke's former wife whom he had had to divorce because she was his brother's widow.

Kilian of Inishcaltra (St) R. Jul 29
C7th. Abbot of a monastery on the island of Inishcaltra in Lough Dearg, Ireland, he wrote a life of St Brigid.

Kinga (Cunegund) of Poland (St) T(OFM). Jul 24
d. 1292. A niece of St Elizabeth of Hungary and great-niece of St Hedwig, she was married to Boleslav V, Prince of Cracow, Poland, and allegedly lived with him in celibacy. The couple tried hard to alleviate the sufferings caused by the Mongol incursions, and she died as a Franciscan tertiary in the nunnery she had founded at Sandecz. Her cultus was confirmed in 1690, and she is one of the patrons of Poland.

Kinemark (Cynfarch) (St) R. Sep 8
C5th? There are churches in Wales dedicated to this alleged emigrant Scottish nobleman.

Kitt *see* **Christopher**

Kizito (St) M. Jun 3
d. 1886. At fourteen he was the youngest of those martyred by King Mwanga of Buganda (Uganda). *See* **Charles Lwanga and Comps**.

Klaus *see* **Nicholas**

Korea (Martyrs of) Sep 20
The Church in Korea was not initially set up by missionaries but by native lay people who had become familiar with the Jesuit mission at the court of the Ming emperor at Beijing, China. Many scholars of the Silhak (or 'practical wisdom') school of Korean philosophy at Seoul, the capital, took to Christianity in the C18th because of the obvious superiority of Western technology as a product of Christian belief. But Christianity was incompatible with State Confucianism, and the first persecution was in 1801. In 1837 the first missionaries, of the Paris Society of Foreign Missions, entered the country to organize the Church which had slowly spread from Seoul. A formal edict of persecution was issued in response in 1839,

and St Laurence Imbert and two priest companions were seized, imprisoned, tortured and solemnly beheaded near Seoul. Thousands of native Korean Catholics were killed then and during a second persecution after 1866, of all ages and social classes, priests as well as lay people. A hundred and three of these were canonized in 1984. *See* lists of national martyrs in appendix.

Košice (Martyrs of) (SS)
MM. RR(SJ). Sep 7
d. 1619. Mark Körösy was a Croatian nobleman, born at Kriin in 1582 and, as a priest, becoming a member of the cathedral chapter of Esztergom. He was sent to Kassa in Imperial Hungary (now Košice in Slovakia) in order to administer the property of a defunct Benedictine abbey.

Stephen Pongrácz was a Transylvanian nobleman, born in 1582, who entered the Jesuit noviciate at Brno in 1602 and was sent to Kassa as chaplain to the Imperial Hungarian troops and to the few Magyar Catholics in the town.

Melchior Grodziecky was a Polish nobleman from Silesia, born in 1584, who entered the Brno noviciate in 1603 and was sent to Kassa as chaplain to the Czech and Polish soldiers and to the Slovak civilians.

Kassa as a town was solidly Calvinist, and when the Calvinist prince of Transylvania rebelled against the Emperor in 1619 and besieged it, the townsfolk betrayed the garrison. The town council asked for the death of the three priests, and they were tortured first in order to induce their apostasy. SS. Mark and Stephen were beheaded, but St Melchior was castrated, roasted upside-down until his abdomen burst and then thrown alive into a ditch with the bodies of the other two, where he lingered for twenty hours. They were canonized in 1995.

Kouradji Oghlou Ziroun (Bl) *see* Salvator Lilli and Comps

Kybi *see* **Cuby**

Kyneburga, Kyneswith and Tibba (SS) RR. Mar 6
d. *c*680. The first two were daughters of King Penda of Mercia, England, famous for his fierce opposition to Christianity. The former was the first abbess of Cyneburgecaester (now Castor near Peterborough) and was succeeded by her sister. Tibba may have been a relative of theirs who joined them at the nunnery. Their relics were eventually enshrined together at Peterborough Abbey.

Kyneburga of Gloucester
(St) M. Jun 25
? Her story was that she was a princess who fled to escape marriage and became the domestic servant of a baker at Gloucester, England, only to have the latter's wife murder her out of jealousy. She had a local cultus at Gloucester

Kyran *see* **Kieran**

Kyrin *see* **Boniface**

L

Lactan McCorpe (St) R. Mar 19
d. 672. From near Cork, Ireland, he was educated at Bangor under St Comgall and was sent by him as abbot-founder of Achadh-Ur (now Freshford) in Co. Kilkenny.

Ladislas (Lancelot, Laszlo), King of Hungary (St) L. Jun 27
1040–1095. King of Hungary, he annexed Dalmatia and Croatia from the Byzantine Empire and thus helped to establish the borders that his country had until the First World War. His enlightened government with regard to the affairs of both Church and state made him one of the great national heroes of Hungary. He fought successful wars against the Poles, Russians and Cumans and died while preparing to take part in the First Crusade as supreme commander. He was canonized in 1192.

Ladislas of Gielniow (Bl) R(OFM). Sep 25
1440–1505. A Pole, he joined the Franciscan Observants at Warsaw and eventually became their provincial superior. As such he sent Franciscan missionaries to Lithuania and occupied himself in preaching throughout Poland. He died at Warsaw and had his cultus confirmed for Poznan in 1750.

Laetantius (St) *see* **Scillitan Martyrs**

Laetus (St) *see* **Donatian, Praesidius and Comps**

Laetus (St) *see* **Vincent and Laetus**

Laetus (Lié) (St) R. Nov 5
d. 533. He was a hermit north of Orléans, France, at the place now called St Lié after him.

Laicin *see* **Molagga**

Lamalisse (St) R. Mar 3
C7th. A hermit, he allegedly gave his name to the village of Lamlash on the island of Arran, Scotland.

Lambert and Valerius (Bellere, Berlher) (SS) RR. Oct 9
d. *c*680. They were disciples of St Ghislain near Mons, Belgium.

Lambert of Lyons (St) B. R. Apr 14
d. 688. From Flanders, he was a Frankish courtier before becoming a monk at Fontenelle in Normandy, France, under St Wandrille, whom he succeeded as abbot in 666. He became bishop of Lyons in 678.

Lambert of Maastricht (St) M. B. R? Sep 17
?635–?709. From Maastricht, Netherlands, he became bishop of that city in 670 but was exiled by Ebroin, mayor of the Frankish palace, in 675. He lived at the abbey of Stavelot for seven years, allegedly as a monk, before being recalled by Pepin the Short. He helped St Willibrord with his missionary work, and was murdered at the altar of the church at Liege (then a village) because of a vendetta.

Lambert Péloguin (St) B. R(OSB). May 26
*c*1080–1154. From Bauduen in north Provence, France, he became a Benedictine at Lérins and was made bishop of Vence near Nice in 1114.

Lambert of St Bertain (Bl) R(OSB). Jun 22
d. 1125. He was a child-oblate at the Benedictine abbey of St Bertin at St Omer, France, and eventually became its abbot. He joined the abbey to the Cluniac congregation and finished its church.

Lambert of Zaragoza (St) M. Apr 16
d. *c*900. He was allegedly a servant killed somewhere near Zaragoza, Spain, by his Muslim master when the Moors ruled there.

Landelin (St) R. Jun 15
?625–686. A Frankish nobleman from Bapaume near Arras, France, he was educated

by St Aubert of Cambrai but became a brigand. Repenting, he became the abbot-founder of Lobbes near Charleroi, Belgium, in 654 and then founded three other abbeys, the last being Crépy near Laon, France, where he died.

Landeric (Landry) of Meaux (St) B. R. Apr 17
C7th. The eldest son of SS Vincent Madelgar and Waldetrude, he was bishop of Meaux near Paris, France, from 641 to 650 but resigned to succeed his deceased father as abbot of Soignies.

Landeric of Novalese (St) M. R(OSB). Jun 10
d. ?1050. A parish priest in the valley of the Arc in Savoy (now France), he became a Benedictine monk at Novalese and was drowned in the river by some malefactors whom he had reprimanded.

Landeric of Paris (St) B. Jun 10
d. ?661. Bishop of Paris, France, from 650, he founded the 'Hôtel-Dieu', the first hospital in Paris.

Landoald and Amantius (SS) PD. Mar 19
d. ?668. Their historically worthless legend alleges that they were a Roman priest and deacon who were sent by the pope to evangelize what is now Belgium, founding the church at Wintershoven near Tongeren.

Landrada (St) R. Jul 8
d. *c*690. She was the abbess-founder of the nunnery at Munsterbilzen near Tongeren, Belgium.

Landulf Variglia (St) B. R(OSB). Jun 7
1070–1134. From Asti in Piedmont, Italy, he became a Benedictine at Ciel d'Oro (Pavia) and was made bishop of Asti in 1103.

Lang Yang (St) Jul 20
1900. A woman catechumen, she was a victim of the Boxers in south-eastern Hebei, China. *See* **China (Martyrs of)**.

Lantfrid, Waltram and Elilantus (BB) RR. Jul 10
d. *p*770. Three brothers, they founded the abbey of Benediktbeuren near Munich, Germany, and succeeded one another as abbots. St Lantfrid, the first, was still alive in 770.

Lanuin (Bl) R(OCart). Apr 14
d. 1120. A disciple of St Bruno, he went with his master to Calabria, Italy, and succeeded him as prior of the Carthusian monastery which they founded at Torre near Squillace. He was also appointed visitor-apostolic of all the monastic houses in Calabria. His cultus was confirmed for Squillace in 1893.

Lanzo (Bl) R(OSB). Apr 1
d. *c*1100. A monk at Cluny, he was chosen to be the prior of the first Cluniac monastery in England, founded by William de Warenne at Lewes in Sussex. Starting with himself and three other monks, he established the new priory of St Pancras as one of the five greatest of the Cluniac congregation with a church (the largest in Sussex) modelled on that of Cluny.

Largio (St) *see* **Hilaria, Digna and Comps**

Largus (St) *see* **Hilary, Tatian and Comps**

Largus (St) *see* **Cyriac, Largus and Comps**

Lasar (Lassar, Lassera) (St) R. Mar 29
C6th. A niece of St Fortchern, she was educated by SS Finan and Kiernan at Clonard, Ireland, and became a hermit in Meath. Her name means 'Flame'.

Laserian (Molaise) (St) B? R. Apr 18
d. 639. He was the founder of the monastery and diocese of Leighlin in Co. Carlow, Ireland, as well as Inishmurray in Co. Sligo, and was allegedly appointed as apostolic legate to Ireland by the pope. He promoted the Roman observance of the date of Easter in place of the traditional Celtic one. He is the principal patron of the diocese of Leighlin.

Lassa (St) *see* **Ammon, Emilian and Comps**

Laszlo *see* **Ladislas**

Latinus of Brescia (St) B. Mar 24
d. ?115. He is alleged to have succeeded St Viator as third bishop of Brescia, Italy, and to have been imprisoned and tortured in the persecution of Domitian, but this tradition is unreliable.

Laudo *see* **Lauto**

Laura of Cordoba (St) M. R. Oct 19
d. 864. According to her legend, she was a widow of Cordoba, Spain, who became a nun at Cuteclara, succeeded St Aurea as abbess and was boiled in pitch by the Muslim authorities. The whole story is probably fictional.

Laura Vicuña (Bl) R. Jan 22
1891–1904. Born at Santiago in Chile, her father died in 1893 and the family eventually settled at Junín de los Andes in Argentina in 1900. She failed to join the Sisters of Mary Auxililatrix which ran her school, but she took private vows and consecrated her life to God in 1903 in exchange for the conversion of her mother. Sickness followed and she died the next year aged twelve. She was beatified in 1988.

Laurence of Africa (St) *see* **Martial, Laurence and Comps**

Laurence Bai (Xiaoman)
(St) M. L. Feb 25
1821–1856. A labourer from a very poor family of Guizhou, China, he moved to Yaoshan in Guangxi in 1851 and was converted by St Augustine Chapdelaine. He was beheaded after being tortured. *See* **China (Martyrs of)**.

Laurence Bâtard (Bl) *see* **William Repin and Comps**

Laurence of Brindisi *see* **Laurence Russo of Brindisi**

Laurence of Canterbury (St) B. R. Feb 2
d. 619. One of the monks sent on the English mission with St Augustine by Pope St Gregory the Great, he was sent back to Rome to report to St Gregory on progress and to bring back reinforcements. Becoming St Augustine's successor as archbishop of Canterbury in 604, he had to face the pagan reaction in Kent under Eadbald and thought of escaping to France but was allegedly rebuked by St Peter in a dream and eventually converted Eadbald. He is depicted as a bishop holding a whip or displaying the marks of a whipping.

Laurence Giustiniani (St) B. Sep 5
1381–1455. A nobleman of Venice, Italy, when aged nineteen he became a secular canon at San Giorgio in Alga, which he made into the centre of a congregation. In 1433 he was made bishop of Castello. This diocese was united with the patriarchate of Grado and the see transferred to Venice in 1451, thus making him the first patriarch of that city. His writings on mystical contemplation were popular. He was canonized in 1690 and his cultus was confined to local calendars in 1969.

Laurence-of-St-Nicholas Hachizo
(Bl) M. T(OSA). Sep 28
d. 1630. A Japanese Augustinian tertiary, he was condemned for having sheltered the Augustinian missionaries and was beheaded at Nagasaki with BB John Chozaburo and Comps. *See* **Japan (Martyrs of)**.

Laurence Han (St) *see* **Korea (Martyrs of)**

Laurence Humphrey (Bl) M. L. Jul 7
1571–1591. A native of Hampshire and a convert, he was only twenty years of age when he was hanged, drawn and quartered at Winchester for becoming a Catholic. He was beatified in 1929. *See* **England (Martyrs of)**.

Laurence (Nguyen van) Huong (St) M. P. Apr 27
?1802–1856. A Vietnamese priest, he was beheaded near Ninh-biuh. *See* **Vietnam (Martyrs of)**.

Laurence the Illuminator (St) B. R. Feb 3
d. 576. A Syrian layman he fled to Rome to avoid Monophysite persecution, was ordained there and founded a monastery near Spoleto, Italy. He was chosen bishop of that city in 552, but later resigned and founded the abbey of Farfa in the Sabine hills near Rome. Renowned as a peacemaker, he was also famous for healing blindness, both spiritual and physical (hence his surname).

Laurence Imbert and Comps
(SS) MM. Sep 20
d. 1839. From Aix-en-Provence, France, he joined the Paris Society of Foreign Missions and worked firstly as a missionary priest in China and then as a bishop in Korea. He was tortured to death with Peter Maubant and James Chastan, missionary priests of the same society. *See* **Korea (Martyrs of)**.

Laurence Loricatus (Bl) R(OSB). Aug 16
d. 1243. From Apulia, Italy, he became a soldier but accidentally killed a man and made a pilgrimage to Compostela in reparation. Then he settled as a penitential hermit in a cave near the Benedictine abbey at Subiaco in 1209. His surname derives from the coat of mail which he wore next to his skin. His shrine is at Sacro Speco (Subiaco) and his cultus was confirmed in 1778.

Laurence Majoranus (St) B. Feb 7
d. ?546. Bishop of Siponto, Italy, from 492, he founded the famous sanctuary of St Michael on Monte Gargano. His city is now replaced by Manfredonia, of which place he is the patron.

Laurence dei Mascoli
(Bl) R(OFM). Jun 6
1476–1535. A nobleman from Villamagna in

the Abruzzi, Italy, he became a Franciscan and was a very successful preacher. He died at Ortona and his cultus was confirmed for there in 1923.

Laurence Nerucci (Bl) *see* **Prague (Martyrs of)**

Laurence Ngon (St) M. May 22
d. 1862. He was a Vietnamese layman and martyr. *See* **Vietnam (Martyrs of)**.

Laurence of Novara and Comps (SS) MM. Apr 30
d. ?397. He is described as having migrated from the West (Spain or France?) to Piedmont, Italy, and to have become a diocesan priest under St Gaudentius, bishop of Novara. He was massacred with a group of children whom he was instructing.

Laurence O'Toole (Lorcan Ua Tuathail) (St) B. R(CR). Nov 14
1128–1180. From Co. Kildare, Ireland, when young he became a monk at Glendalough and was made abbot at the age of twenty-five. In 1162 he became archbishop of Dublin and was faced with the English invasion in 1170, being much involved in negotiating on behalf of the Irish with King Henry II of England. He attended the Third Lateran Council at Rome in 1179, was made papal legate in Ireland and carried out many reforms in his diocese, where he introduced the Arrouasian canons regular (following their rule himself). He died at the Augustinian abbey of Eu in Normandy while on an embassy to the English king and was canonized in 1226.

Laurence the Portuguese (Bl) R.
d. *c*14th. A Hieronomyte monk, his cultus was confirmed for Lisbon, Portugal, in 1820.

Laurence Richardson (alias Johnson) (Bl) M. P. May 30
d. 1582. From Great Crosby, Lancs, he was educated at Brasenose College, Oxford, and, after his conversion, studied for the priesthood at Douai. Ordained in 1577, he worked in Lancashire, was martyred at Tyburn, London, with St Luke Kirby and BB Thomas Cottam and William Filby and was beatified in 1886. *See* **England (Martyrs of)**.

Laurence of Rippafratta (Bl) R(OP). Sep 28
d. 1457. From Rippafratta in Tuscany, Italy, he became a Dominican at Pisa under Bl John Dominic and was made novice-master at Cortona. SS Antoninus of Pierozzi and 'Fra Angelico' were among his novices, also Bl Benedict of Mugello. His cultus was approved for the Dominicans in 1851.

Laurence Rokuyemon (Rokusuke) (Bl) M. L. Aug 19
d. 1622. He was a Japanese merchant on the ship carrying BB Louis Flores and Comps. *See* **Japan (Martyrs of)**.

Laurence of Rome (St) M. D. Aug 10
d. 258. In the patristic era he was probably the most famous of the Roman martyrs, as is evidenced by the writings of SS Ambrose, Leo the Great, Augustine and Prudentius. His martyrdom must have deeply impressed the contemporary Roman Christians, and Prudentius described it as the death of idolatry in Rome (which from that time began to decline). His acta are unreliable, however, having been written at least a century after his death. They claim that he was one of the deacons of Pope St Sixtus II when that pope was beheaded, and was himself martyred three days later by being roasted alive on a gridiron. It is more likely that he was beheaded. He was buried on the Via Tiburtina, where his basilica now stands, and is mentioned in the Roman canon of the Mass. His attribute is a gridiron.

Laurence Ruiz and Comps (SS) MM. RR(OP). Sep 29
d. 1637. Four Dominicans and two laymen, they went on a missionary expedition to Japan from Manila in 1636. The Japanese had closed their country and were in the process of extirpating the native Christians, and the group were captured immediately on arrival, tortured in prison and executed by being hanged head-down in pits and left to die. St Anthony González was born at León, Spain, in 1593; St William Courtet was born at Sérignan, France, in 1590; St Michael de Aozaraza was born at Oñate, Spain, in 1637 and died in prison on the 24 September; St Vincent-of-the-Cross Shiwozuka was a native Japanese who lapsed in prison but subsequently repented. The laymen were St Laurence Ruiz, a family man from Manila, and St Lazarus of Kyoto, a Japanese translator who also lapsed briefly under torture. They were canonized in 1987, with ten others. *See* **Japan (Martyrs of)**.

Laurence Russo of Brindisi (St) R(OFM Cap). Dr. Jul 21
1559–1619. From Brindisi, Italy, he joined the Capuchins at Venice, was ordained in 1582 and became a famous preacher in north Italy, south

Germany and the lands of the Habsburgs. There he fought militant Protestantism from 1599 until 1602, when he became the Capuchin vicar-general. Then he was appointed the military chaplain of the imperial army fighting against the Turks in Hungary, and contributed to its success by his prayers and shrewd military advice. In 1606 he was sent back to Germany to establish the Capuchins there, was greatly favoured by the Catholic courts of central Europe and was entrusted with important diplomatic missions. He died at Lisbon during one of these, was canonized in 1881 and was declared a doctor of the Church (arguably the least famous) in 1959, mainly because of his contributions to Mariology.

Laurence-Mary-of-St-Francis-Xavier Salvi (Bl) R(CP). Jun 12
1782–1856. Born at Rome, he joined the Passionists at Monte Argentario in 1801 and had a fruitful apostolate of retreats and missions in central Italy, being also a member of the Passionist curia at Rome. His preaching was inspired by a great devotion to the Infant Jesus, and he held a series of prayer-meetings to him at Viterbo to free the city from cholera. He then died of a stroke at Vetralla nearby, where his shrine is, and was beatified in 1989.

Laurence Wang (Bing) (St) M. L. Dec 14
1802–1857. From a Catholic family of Guiyang, China, he became a prosperous farmer and a catechist in Guizhou. He was beheaded at Mokou with SS Jerome Lu (Tingmei) and Agatha Lin (Zhao). *See* **China (Martyrs of)**.

Laurence Yamada (Bl) M. T(OP). Sep 8
d. 1628. A Dominican tertiary, son of Bl Michael Yamada, he was beheaded at Nagasaki with BB Dominic Castellet and Comps. *See* **Japan (Martyrs of)**.

(?) Laurent (Bl) *see* **September (Martyrs of)**

Laurentia (St) *see* **Palatias and Laurentia**

Laurentina-of-St-Stanislaus Prin (Bl) *see* **Valenciennes (Martyrs of)**

Laurentinus (St) *see* **Pergentinus and Laurentinus**

Laurentinus, Ignatius and Celerina (SS) MM. Feb 3
C3rd. Roman African martyrs, mentioned by St Cyprian in one of his letters, they were two uncles and an aunt of St **Celerinus** (q.v.).

Laurentinus Sossius (Bl) M. Apr 15
d. 1485. A boy aged five, he was allegedly killed by renegade Jews on Good Friday at Valrovina near Vicenza, Italy, and had his cultus approved for Vicenza in 1867.

Laurianus-of-Jesus-Crucified Proaño Cuesta (Bl) *see* **Nicephorus Díez Tejerina and Comps**

Laurianus of Seville (St) M? B? Jul 4
d. ?544. What is doubtfully alleged about him was that he was a Hungarian who was made archbishop of Seville, Spain, and was martyred at Bourges, France.

Laurus (Léry) (St) R. Sep 30
C7th. From Wales, he emigrated to Brittany and founded a monastery at a place later known as St Léry.

Laurus (St) *see* **Florus, Laurus and Comps**

Lauto (Laudo, Laudus, Lô) of Coutances (St) B. Sep 22
d. ?568. He was bishop of Coutances in Normandy, France, from 528, and his family estate is now the village of St Lô.

Laval (Martyrs of) (BB) Jun 19
d. 1794. They were nineteen martyrs of the French Revolution. At Laval, on Jan 21, thirteen secular priests and one conventual Franciscan were guillotined for refusing to subscribe to the Civil Constitution of the Clergy. Frances Mézière was a teacher guillotined at Laval on Feb 5; Frances Tréhet and Jane Véron were Sisters of Charity executed at Ernée on Mar 13 and Mar 20 respectively; Mary-of-St-Monica Lhuilier was a lay sister of the Sisters Hospitaller of the Mercy of Jesus and was executed at Laval on Jun 25, and John Burin was a merchant shot as a priest in an ambush at Champgenéteux on Oct 17. They were beatified together in 1955. *See* **French Revolution (Martyrs of)**.

Lawdog (St) Jan 21
C6th. He is the patron of four churches in south-west Wales, and may be the same as St Lleuddad.

Lazarus (St) B? Jul 29
C1st. He was the disciple and friend who was raised from the dead by Christ (John 11). According to a Greek tradition he became bishop of Kition in Cyprus. The French legend which connects him with Marseilles is traceable only to the C11th, and has no historical foundation whatsoever. It probably arose from

confusion with an early bishop of Aix with the same name.

Lazarus (St) *see* **Zanitas and Comps**

Lazarus of Kyoto (St) *see* **Laurence Ruiz and Comps**

Lazarus of Milan (St) B. Feb 11
d. *c*450 He was the archbishop of Milan, Italy, when the Ostrogoths took the city. His feast day is an example of the old Milanese tradition of not keeping saints' days in Lent, which practice is now generally followed by the Roman rite.

Lazarus Múgica Goiburu (Bl) *see* **Hospitaller Martyrs of Spain**

Lazarus Tiersot (Bl) *see* **John-Baptist Souzy and Comps**

Lazarus Zographus (St) R. Feb 23
d. ?867. From Armenia, he became a monk at Constantinople. A talented painter (hence his Greek surname, 'the Painter'), he used to restore defaced icons in the reign of the iconoclast emperor Theophilus. For this he was allegedly tortured, but after the final abandonment of iconoclasm he became an ambassador to Rome, dying on Cyprus on his way there.

Lea (St) R. Mar 22
d. 384. A wealthy Roman widow, she joined the community of St Marcella and was later elected abbess. In her humility she used to perform various menial domestic duties for her nuns (that this was considered worthy of note indicates the class structure of contemporary Roman monasticism).

Leafwine *see* **Lebuin**

Leander (St) B. Feb 27
550–600. The elder brother of SS Fulgentius, Isidore and Florentina, when young he became a monk at Seville, Spain, and was later sent to Constantinople on a diplomatic mission. There he met St Gregory the Great, whose close friend he became and whose *Moralia* were published at his request. On his return to Spain he became archbishop of Seville in 579, and proved to be a great pastor. He revised the Spanish liturgy, converted St Hermenegild (and thus started the conversion of the Visigoths from Arianism) and was responsible for convening two national synods at Toledo in 589 and 590. He also founded the episcopal school of Seville and wrote a monastic rule. His attribute is a flaming heart.

Lebuin (Leafwine) (St) R. Nov 12
d. ?775. A monk of Ripon, England, he went to the Netherlands on mission in 754 and was sent by St Gregory of Utrecht to the dangerous borderlands between the Franks and Saxons, where he founded the church at Deventer. His personal bravery won him the respect of the Saxons (although they preferred to stay pagan). *See* **Livin**.

Leger *see* **Leodegar**

Lelia (St) R. Aug 11
C6th? She seems to have lived at a very early period and has given her name to several places in Ireland, such as Killeely near Limerick.

Leo (St) M. B. Mar 14
? The old Roman Martyrology listed him as a bishop martyred in the Agro Verano, Rome. Nothing else is known about him. He may have been a victim of the Arians.

Leo (St) *see* **Daniel, Samuel and Comps**

Leo (St) *see* **Gaius and Leo**

Leo I, Pope 'the Great'
(St) Dr. Nov 10
d. 461. Probably from Tuscany, Italy, he became a priest at Rome and was archdeacon under two popes. He was made pope himself in 440 and emphasized his jurisdiction and responsibility as the successor of St Peter by fighting heretical tendencies in other churches, especially Nestorianism and Monophysitism in the East. His celebrated 'Tomos' or dogmatic letter, which he sent to Flavian the patriarch of Constantinople, was acclaimed as the teaching of the Church at the council of Chalcedon in 451. It summarized the exact Catholic position concerning the twofold nature and one person in Christ, as against the extreme positions of these two heresies, but was rejected especially by the church in Egypt which went into schism. He negotiated with Attila the Hun outside Rome in 452, apparently persuading him not to besiege the city, but had to endure its sack by Genseric the Vandal in 455. He was proclaimed a doctor of the Church in 1754.

Leo II, Pope (St) Jul 3
d. 683. A Sicilian, he became pope in 681. He governed the church for only two years, and the outstanding event of his pontificate was his acceptance of the decrees of sixth ecumenical council of Constantinople which condemned Monothelitism and Pope Honorius I for accepting it.

Leo III, Pope (St) Jun 12
d. 816. A Roman, he became pope in 795 but was attacked by a mob, imprisoned and maltreated in 799. He escaped and asked for help from Charlemagne, who re-established order in Rome. Subsequently he crowned Charlemagne as emperor of the West in St Peter's on Christmas Day, 800, thereby founding the Holy Roman Empire and ushering in the Middle Ages. Leo refused to add the 'filioque' to the Nicene creed. He was canonized in 1673.

Leo IV, Pope (St) R(OSB). Jul 17
d. 855. A Roman and a monk of the Benedictine abbey of San Martino, he was chosen pope in 847. In response to the Muslim threat he finished enclosing the Vatican with a wall, thus creating the 'Leonine city'. Through his prayers and exhortations to the city militia, the Muslim raiders from Calabria were utterly routed at Ostia. His benefactions to churches take up many pages in the *Liber Pontificalis*. The English king Alfred visited Rome in 853, and Leo was his sponsor at his confirmation.

Leo IX, Pope (St) Apr 19
1002–1054. Bruno of Dagsburg was from Alsace, a cousin of the emperor Conrad, and was made bishop of Toul, France, in 1026. In 1048 he was elected pope and immediately started the reform of the Roman curia with the help of his spiritual adviser Hildebrand, the future Pope St Gregory VII. He fought simony, lay investiture and clerical concubinage and condemned Berengar and his eucharistic doctrine. He went to war with the Normans in southern Italy, was taken prisoner at Benevento and released but shortly afterwards died before the high altar in St Peter's. One of his advisers was Humbert who overreached his authority as papal legate at Constantinople and precipitated the definitive schism with the patriarch, Michael Cerularius, in 1054.

Leo, Donatus, Abundantius, Nicephorus and Comps
(SS) MM. Mar 1
? A group of thirteen, they were possibly martyred in Roman Africa.

Leo and Juliana (SS) MM. Aug 18
? Despite their listing in the old Roman Martyrology, they do not belong together. Leo was martyred at Myra in Lycia, Asia Minor, and Juliana at Strobylum. Juliana may be the same as the martyr of Ptolemais (*see* **Paul and Juliana**).

Leo and Paregorius (SS) MM. Feb 18
d. *c*260. They were martyred at Patara in Lycia, Asia Minor. Their alleged acta seem to be a pious romance.

Leo Aybara (Bl) M. T(OP). Sep 8
d. 1628. A Japanese catechist and Dominican tertiary, he was beheaded at Nagasaki with BB Dominic Castellet and Comps. *See* **Japan (Martyrs of)**.

Leo Carentanus (St) M? B? Mar 1
?856–900. According to his untrustworthy story, he was from Carentan in Normandy, France, and was bishop of Rouen before becoming a missionary in the Basque Country. He was allegedly beheaded by pirates near Bayonne, of which city he is now the patron.

Leo of Catania 'the Thaumaturge' (St) B. Feb 20
703–787. A priest of Ravenna, Italy, he became bishop of Catania, Sicily, and was respected by the emperors at Constantinople for his learning. His biography has been embellished with many unreliable anecdotes.

Leo II of Cava (Bl) R(OSB). Aug 19
1239–1295. He became the fifteenth abbot of the Benedictine abbey of La Cava near Naples, Italy, in 1268. His cultus was approved for there in 1928.

Leo Inchausti (Bl) *see* **Vincent Soler and Comps**

Leo Karasumaru (St) M. T(OFM). Feb 5
d. 1597. From Korea, he was a Shinto priest before his conversion and became the first Franciscan tertiary in Japan. He helped the Franciscan missionaries as a catechist and was crucified at Nagasaki. *See* **Paul Miki and Comps** and **Japan (Martyrs of)**.

Leo of Lucca (St) R(OSB). Jul 12
d. 1079 From Lucca, Italy, he became a Benedictine at the abbey of La Cava near Naples under its founder St Alferius, and succeeded him as abbot in 1050. His cultus was approved for La Cava in 1893.

Leo Luke (St) R. Mar 1
d. *c*900. He became abbot of a Byzantine-rite monastery at Corleone, Sicily, and also has a cultus in Calabria. He died a centenarian after eighty years of monastic life.

Leo of Melun (St) Nov 10
? The subject of an ancient cultus at Melun near

Paris, France, he is now considered to be identical with Pope St Leo I.

Leo Nakanishi (Bl) M. L. Nov 27
d. 1619. A Japanese layman, he was related to the daimyos of Hirado-jima and was beheaded at Nagasaki with BB Thomas Koteda and Comps. *See* **Japan (Martyrs of)**.

Leo of Nonantula (St) R(OSB). Nov 20
d. 1000. He was abbot of the Benedictine monastery of Nonantula near Modena, Italy.

Leo of Saint-Bertin (Bl) R(OSB). Feb 26
d. 1163. A Flemish nobleman, he was appointed abbot of Lobbes in 1131 and of the great abbey of St Bertin at St Omer, France, in 1138. There he ruled for twenty-five years. In 1146 he joined the second crusade, reached Jerusalem and, on his return, brought with him the alleged relic of Christ's blood which has since been venerated at Bruges.

Leo Satsuma (Bl) M. T(OFM). Sep 10
d. 1622. A Japanese Franciscan tertiary, he was a catechist and was burned alive in the 'Great Martyrdom' at Nagasaki with Bl Charles Spinola and Comps. *See* **Japan (Martyrs of)**.

Leo of Sens (St) B. Apr 22
d. 541. Bishop of Sens, France, for twenty-three years, he was the patron of St Aspasius.

Leo Sukuyemon (Bl) M. L. Aug 19
d. 1622. He was the Japanese pilot of the ship carrying BB Louis Flores and Comps. *See* **Japan (Martyrs of)**.

Leo Tanaka (St) M. Jun 1
d. 1617. He worked with the Jesuit missionaries as a catechist and was beheaded at Nagasaki with Bl Alphonsus Navarete. *See* **Japan (Martyrs of)**.

Leo of Troyes (St) R. May 25
d. *c*550. He succeeded St Romanus as abbot of the monastery of Mantenay near Troyes, France.

Leobald (Liebault) (St) R. Aug 8
d. 650. He was a monk at Orléans, France, before becoming abbot-founder of Fleury (now called Saint-Benoît-sur-Loire) nearby.

Leobard (Liberd) (St) R. Jan 18
d. 593. A hermit at Tours, France, he was affiliated to the abbey of Marmoutier and lived in a cell nearby for twenty-two years as a disciple of St Gregory of Tours.

Leobin (Lubin) (St) B. Sep 15
d. ?556. His family were peasants from Poitiers, France, and he became a hermit when young. Then he became a priest, then abbot of Brou and finally bishop of Chartres.

Leocadia (Locaie) (St) V. Dec 9
d. ?303. The old Roman Martyrology listed her as a young woman of Toledo, Spain, who was condemned to death and died in prison in the reign of Diocletian. Her cultus there is older than the C6th.

Leocritia (Lucretia) (St) V. Mar 15
d. 859. A young woman of Cordoba, Spain, she was driven from home by her Muslim parents when she converted to Christianity and was sheltered by St Eulogius. Both were flogged and beheaded.

Leodegar (Leger) (St) M. B. Oct 2
?616–678. He was educated at the Frankish court and then by his uncle, the bishop of Poitiers. In 653 he was made abbot of a monastery in that city, where he introduced the Benedictine rule. *c*hosen as bishop of Autun in 659 by St Bathilde the queen regent, he reformed his diocese but was also involved in secular matters, especially at court. This led him to incur the enmity of Ebroin, mayor of the palace, who had him degraded, imprisoned in the monasteries of Luxeuil and Fécamp, blinded and finally murdered. He is popularly venerated in France as St Leger, but the famous horse-race at Doncaster, England, has no connection with him. He is depicted with the instruments of his martyrdom (drill, bodkin, fish-hook) or with his eyes, tongue and other parts of his face on a plate.

Leonard of Avranches (Bl) B. Mar 4
d. ?614. As a young man he was a notorious brigand but was converted (mainly through the prayers of his mother) and later became bishop of Avranches, France.

Leonard Casanova of Port Maurice (St) R(OFM). Nov 26
1676–1751. From Imperia-Porto-Maurízio on the Riviera, Italy, he was a brilliant student at Rome and became a Franciscan Observant there. Soon after his ordination he began his career as a home missionary especially in Tuscany, spreading the devotions to the Blessed Sacrament, to the Sacred Heart, to the Immaculate Conception and especially to the Stations of the Cross. He is alleged to have established the last in five hundred and seventy-two places, including the Coliseum in Rome. He

was a prolific ascetical writer and his works filled thirteen volumes. In 1744 he was sent to restore the discipline of the Franciscans in Corsica, was recalled to Rome in 1751 but died on the night after his arrival. He was canonized in 1867.

Leonard of Cava (Bl) R(OSB). Aug 18
d. 1255. He became eleventh abbot of La Cava near Salerno, Italy, in 1232. His cultus was confirmed for there in 1928.

Leonard Kimura and Comps (BB) MM. Nov 18
d. 1619. A Japanese nobleman, and convert, he became a Jesuit tertiary and was burned alive at Nagasaki with BB Andrew Tokuan, Cosmas Takeya, Dominic Jorge and John Shoun. *See* **Japan (Martyrs of)**.

Leonard Murialdo (St) P. F. Mar 30
1828–1890. From Turin, Italy, after obtaining his doctorate at the university there and being ordained he devoted himself to the education of poor boys. In this he was an associate of St John Bosco, and was also a contemporary of SS Joseph Cafasso and Joseph Cottolengo. He founded the 'Pious Society of St Joseph' to care for young apprentices in 1873, and became heavily involved in the emergent Catholic worker movement. In many ways he sought to implement the Church's social teaching as later summarized in the encyclical *Rerum Novarum* of 1891. He died at Turin and was canonized in 1970.

Leonard of Noblac (St) R. Nov 6
C6th? According to his legend, for which no evidence exists before the C11th, he was a Frankish courtier converted by St Remigius of Rheims. He became a monk at Micy near Orléans and later a hermit in the forest of Noblac nearby. His veneration was very popular in the West during the Middle Ages, and the town and forest of St Leonard's in Sussex, England, are named after him. His attribute is a set of fetters or a lock.

Leonard of Reresby (St) L. Nov 6
C13th. A local tradition of Thryberg near Rotherham in Yorkshire, England, describes him as going on crusade, being taken prisoner by the Muslims and then being miraculously transported (shackles and all) back home only to die almost immediately after his arrival.

Leonard of Vandoeuvre (St) R. Oct 15
d. *c*570. A hermit, he was the abbot-founder of Vandoeuvre, now the village of St Leonard aux Bois near Le Mans, France.

Leonard Vechel (St) M. Jul 9
d. 1572. From 's-Hertogenbosch, Netherlands, he studied at Louvain and became parish priest of Gorinchem, where he was noted for his opposition to Calvinism. He was one of the **Gorinchem martyrs** (q.v.).

Leonian (St) R. Nov 6
d. *c*570. From what is now Hungary, he was taken as a captive to Gaul and, on regaining his freedom, became a hermit near Autun, France. Later he joined the abbey of St Symphorian there. His cultus was approved in 1907.

Leonidas of Alexandria (St) M. Apr 22
d. 202. The father of the famous exegete Origen and himself a distinguished philosopher, he was martyred at his native city of Alexandria, Egypt, in the reign of Septimus Severus.

Leonidas of Antinoë and Comps (SS) MM. Jan 28
d. 304. They were martyred at Antinoë in Egypt in the reign of Diocletian, and probably included SS **Philemon and Apollonius** (q.v.).

Leonides (St) *see* **Diomedes, Julian and Comps**

Leonides (St) *see* **Eleutherius and Leonides**

Leonilla (St) *see* **Speusippus, Eleusippus and Comps**

Leonis (St) *see* **Lybe, Leonis and Eutropia**

Leonore (Lunaire) (St) B.R. Jul 1
d. *c*570. A son of a king of Brittany, France, he was born in exile in Wales, was educated by St Illtyd and ordained bishop by St Dyfrig. Crossing to Brittany (then ruled by his brother), he founded the monastery of Pontual near St Malo.

Leontius (St) *see* **Apollonius and Leontius**

Leontius (St) *see* **Eusebius, Neon and Comps**

Leontius (St) *see* **Hieronides, Leontius and Comps**

Leontius, Attius, Alexander and Comps (SS) MM. Aug 1
d. *c*300. Three citizens of Perga in Pamphylia, Asia Minor, with six farm labourers (Cindeus, Mnesitheus, Cyriacus, Menaeus, Catunus and Eucleus) they set about destroying the altar of

Artemis there and were executed as a result in the reign of Diocletian.

Leontius, Hypatius and Theodulus (SS) MM. Jun 18
d. ?135. They were Greeks martyred at Tripoli, Lebanon.

Leontius, Maurice, Daniel and Comps (SS) MM. Jul 10
d. *c*320. Numbering forty-five, they were martyred at Nicopolis in Armenia under the emperor Licinius and were among the last martyrs of the great persecution.

Leontius of Aegae (St) M. Sep 27
? He is listed in the old Roman Martyrology as having been martyred with SS Cosmas and Damian, but probably never existed.

Leontius of Caesarea (St) B. Jan 13
d. 337. Bishop of Caesarea in Cappodocia, Asia Minor, he was at the council of Nicaea in 325 and was zealous against Arianism, being commended by St Athanasius.

Leontius the Elder (St) B. Aug 21
d. ?541. He was the predecessor of St Leontius the Younger as bishop of Bordeaux, France.

Leontius of Fréjus (St) B. Dec 1
d. ?432. St John Cassian dedicated his first ten *Conferences* to him. He became bishop of Fréjus, France, in ?419.

Leontius Pérez Ramos (Bl) *see* **Philip-of-Jesus Munárriz Azcona and Comps**

Leontius of Saintes (St) B. Mar 19
d. 640. Bishop of Saintes, France, he was a friend of St Malo and welcomed him as an exile from Brittany.

Leontius the Younger (St) B. Jul 11
*c*510–565. A soldier, he fought the Visigoths and then married and settled at Bordeaux, France. However he was forced to become bishop and governor of that city, his wife becoming a nun.

Leopardin (St) M. R. Nov 24
C7th. Abbot of the monastery of St-Symphorien-de-Vivarais near Bourges, France, he was assassinated on the orders of the wife of the patron of his abbey and locally venerated as a martyr. .

Leopardus (St) M. Sept 30
d. 362. A servant or slave in the household of the emperor Julian, he was probably executed at Rome. His shrine was established at Aachen, Germany.

Leopold II 'the Good', Margrave of Austria (St) L. Nov 15
1073–1136. Born at Melk, Austria, and a grandson of Emperor Henry III, he became fourth Margrave of Austria in 1096. Austria at that time was a German borderland flanked by the non-German kingdoms of Bohemia and Hungary, and his successful reign of forty years helped to establish it as a power-base which was later built upon by the Hapsburgs. He founded many religious houses as a part of his plan to establish German culture on a secure foundation there, of the Benedictines and Cistercians as well as of the new friars.

Leopold Croci of Gaiche (Bl) R(OFM). Apr 2
1732–1815. From Gaiche near Perugia, Italy, he became a Franciscan and was professor of philosophy and theology and apostolic missionary for the Papal States. During the Napoleonic period he was compelled to abandon his Franciscan habit when aged seventy-seven and become a parish priest. He died at Monteluco and was beatified in 1893.

Leopold Mandić (St) R(OFM Cap). Jun 30
1866–1942. Born at Castelnovo, Italy, of Croat parents, he joined the Capuchins when aged eighteen and especially exercised his priestly vocation in Padua through the sacrament of penance. He was also involved in fostering unity between the Catholic Church and the Orthodox of the Slavic rites. He was canonized in 1983.

Leothad of Auch (St) R. Oct 23
d. 718. A Frankish nobleman, he became a monk and then abbot of Moissac near Montauban, France, before being made bishop of Auch.

Leovigild and Christopher (SS) MM. RR. Aug 20
d. 852. They were two monks of monasteries near Cordoba, Spain, and were beheaded at that city by the Muslim authorities.

Lesbos (Martyrs of) VV? Apr 5
? Five martyrs (possibly virgins) are listed in the old Roman Martyrology as having been martyred on the Aegean island of Lesbos.

Lesmes *see* **Adelelm**

Letard *see* **Liudhard**
Leu *see* **Lupus of Sens**

Leuchteldis *see* **Lufthild**

Leucius (St) *see* **Peter, Severus and Leucius**

Leucius (St) *see* **Thyrsus, Leucius and Callinicus**

Leucius of Brindisi (St) B. Jan 11
d. ?180. The alleged first bishop of Brindisi, Italy, he is said to have arrived as a missionary from Alexandria but may have done so instead as relics, having died as an Egyptian bishop. Or he may have been the Leucius of Brindisi of the C5th mentioned by St Gregory the Great.

Leudomer (Lumier) of Chartres (St) B. Oct 2
d. ?585. He was a bishop of Chartres, France.

Leutfrid (Leufroy) (St) R. Jun 21
d. 738. From Évreux, France, he founded a monastery near there later called La-Croix-St-Leufroy and was allegedly abbot for forty-eight years. He is usually depicted surrounded by the poor children whom he liked to befriend.

Levan (Selyf, Selevan) (St) R. Jun 8
C6th. The patron of St Levan near Penzance in Cornwall, England, where his chapel and well survive, is alleged to have been associated also with Killeevan in Co. Monaghan, Ireland. He has been confused with St Solomon III of Brittany, and is probably the same as the Selyf of Lansallos.

Lewina (St) V? Jul 24
C5th. She was first mentioned in 1058, when her alleged relics were transferred from Seaford in Sussex, England, to Berg near Brussels, Belgium. She was allegedly a British maiden martyred by the Saxon invaders and venerated at Seaford, but was probably the result of a fraud instead.

Lezin *see* **Lucinius**

Liafdag (St) M. B. Feb 3
d. *c*980. A Frieslander, he was consecrated missionary bishop of Ripen in Jutland in 948 but was killed by pagans after working in Denmark and Norway.

Libentius (Liawizo) (St) B. Jan 4
938–1013. From Swabia, Germany, he became bishop of Hamburg-Bremen in 988 and is regarded as one of the apostles of the Slavs (whose boundary was then the Elbe). He was driven into exile by the Danes.

Liberalis (St) P. Apr 27
d. *c*400. A priest of the district around Ancona, Italy, he fought Arianism and was persecuted as a result. His shrine is at Treviso.

Liberata and Faustina (SS) RR. Jan 18
d. 580. Two sisters of Como, Italy, they founded a nunnery in that city and have their shrine at the cathedral.

Liberata of Pavia (St) R. Jan 16
C5th. Sister of SS Epiphanius and Honorata of Pavia, Italy, she was a consecrated virgin living with her parents.

Liberatus and Bajulus (SS) MM. Dec 20
? Nothing is known about these Roman martyrs.

Liberatus, Boniface and Comps (SS) MM. RR. Aug 17
d. 483. Liberatus was abbot of Capsa in Roman Africa and was martyred with several of his community at Carthage on the orders of King Hunneric the Vandal. Boniface was a deacon, Servus and Rusticus were sub-deacons, Rogatus and Septimus were monks and Maximus was a child being educated in the monastery.

Liberatus da Lauro Brumforti (Bl) R(OFM). Sep 6
d. 1258. From San Liberato in the Marches, Italy, he became a Franciscan at Suffiano and introduced a reform there which set out to restore the initial austerity of his order. His cultus was approved for Camerino in 1731.

Liberatus Weiss and Comps (Bl) MM RR(OFM). Mar 3
d. 1716. Liberatus was from Austria, Samuel Marzorati was from Piedmont and Michael-Pius a Zerbo was from Lombardy. The three Franciscan friars went on mission to Ethiopia, meeting up in Cairo and travelling to Gondar (then the capital). They were initially welcomed, but the Negus was overthrown in a coup shortly after their arrival and the new regime arrested them on doctrinal grounds. They were questioned on the two natures of Christ (the Ethiopian church is Monophysite), the value of circumcision (traditional in Ethiopia), and the use of unleavened bread in the Eucharist (considered heretical there) and, on giving the Catholic position on these, were stoned to death. They were beatified in 1988.

Liberia (St) *see* **Amata of Joinville**

Liberius of Ravenna (St) B. Dec 30
d. *c*200. He was allegedly one of the first bishops of the diocese of Ravenna, Italy.

Liberius Wagner (Bl) M. P. Dec 9
1593–1631. From Mühlhausen near Gotha, Germany, he was initially a Protestant but was converted by the Jesuits at Würzburg, Bavaria, and went on to become parish priest at Altenmünster nearby. His successful attempts to convert the local Protestants incurred enmity, which motivated his being betrayed to the invading Swedes in the Thirty Years' War. He was imprisoned and tortured for five days before his execution at Schonungen, and was beatified in 1974.

Libert (Lietbert) of Cambrai
(St) B. Jun 23
d. 1076. Bishop of Cambrai, France, from 1076, he went on pilgrimage to the Holy Land but failed to get there and built the abbey of the Holy Sepulchre instead on his return. He excommunicated the lord of Cambrai and was brutally persecuted as a result.

Libert of St Truiden (St) M. R. Jul 14
d. 783. From Mechelen, Belgium, he was educated by St Rumbold there, became a monk and transferred to the abbey of St Truiden. He was killed in a raid by the Norsemen.

Liborius (St) B. Jul 23
d. 390. Bishop of Le Mans, France, from 348, he is the patron of Paderborn, Germany, as his relics were transferred there in 836. His cultus was confined to local calendars in 1969.

Licerius (Lizier) (St) B. Aug 27
d. ?548. A Spaniard, he emigrated to France and became bishop of the Conserans region of the Pyrenees in 506.

Licinius (St) *see* **Carpophorus of Como and Comps**

Licinius (Lézin) of Angers
(St) B. R. Nov 1
d. ?616. A Frankish courtier and count of Anjou, he became a monk near Angers, France, and was chosen bishop of that city in 586. He was consecrated by St Gregory of Tours. Later he tried to resign but his people would not let him.

Lidanus (St) R(OSB). Jul 2
1026–1118. From the Abruzzi, Italy, he became the abbot-founder of the Benedictine abbey of Sezze on the Pontine Marshes, of which place he is the patron. His was one of many attempts to drain the marshes, which task was only accomplished in the C20th. When old he retired to Montecassino.

Lide *see* **Elid**

Lidwina *see* **Lydwina**

Lié *see* **Laetus** or **Leo**

Liephard (St) M. B. Feb 4
d. 640. An Englishman and perhaps a bishop, he was alleged to have been the companion of King Cadwalla on the latter's pilgrimage to Rome. On the return journey he was killed near Cambrai, France.

Ligorius (St) M. R. Sept 13
? He is listed in the Roman Martyrology as an Eastern hermit who was killed by a pagan mob, but no details are known. His shrine is at Venice, Italy.

Liliosa (St) *see* **George, Aurelius and Comps**

Limbania (St) R(OSB). Aug 15
d. 1294. From Cyprus, she became a Benedictine nun at Genoa, Italy, and then a hermit in a cave below the city church of St Thomas. The claim that she was an Augustinian seems to derive from this church having become such in 1509.

Limnaeus (St) *see* **Thalassius and Limnaeus**

Linus, 'Pope' (St) M? Sep 23
d. ?79. Traditionally (according to St Irenaeus) he succeeded St Peter as pope in 67. There is no historical evidence that he was a martyr, and his cultus was suppressed in 1969. He continues to be mentioned in the Roman canon of the Mass, however.

Lioba (St) R. Sep 28
d. ?781. A relative of St Boniface, she became a nun at Wimborne in Dorset, England, under St Tetta, entered into correspondence with him in Germany and, at his request, collected a group of nuns and went to join him on mission in 748. He made her abbess of a new nunnery at Tauberbischofsheim and also supervisor of the daughter houses founded therefrom. Thus she was an important source of the Benedictine contribution to the foundation of German Christian culture and civilization. She had been abbess for thirty-eight years before she resigned just before her death.

Liphard (Lifard) (St) R. Jun 3
d. ?550. An alleged brother of St Leonard of Noblac, he had been a judge at Orléans, France, before becoming a hermit when aged fifty and eventually the abbot-founder of the monastery of Meung-sur-Loire.

Litteus (St) *see* **Nemesian and Comps**

Liudger *see* **Ludger**

Liudhard (Letard) (St) B? Feb 24
d. *c*600. A Frank, allegedly bishop of Scnlis, hc became the chaplain of Queen Bertha of Kent, England, after she married King St Ethelbert. The latter remained a pagan until the arrival of St Augustine, and St Liudhard seems to have made no attempt at missionary work, although the extant church of St Martin at Canterbury was possibly his chapel.

Liutwin (St) B. R. Sep 29
d. ?713. He had been founder and monk of a monastery at Mettlach near Trier, Germany, before becoming bishop of the latter place.

Livin (Lebwin, Lievin) (St) M? B? Nov 12
d. *c*650. His extant biography is a forgery, and it is suspected that he is the same person as Lebuin of Deventer. According to his traditional story he was an Irishman, ordained by St Augustine of Canterbury, who crossed over to Flanders to become a successful missionary and to be martyred near Aalst, Belgium.

Lizier *see* **Licerius**

Lleudadd (Laudatus) (St) R. Jan 15
C6th. He was allegedly a Welshman who was abbot of Bardsey, Gwynedd, before emigrating to Brittany, France, with St Cadfan, but some scholars maintain his identity with St Lauto of Coutances.

Llewellyn (Llywelyn) and Gwrnerth (SS) RR. Apr 7
C6th. They were monks at Welshpool, Wales, and afterwards on Bardsey.

Llibio (St) R. Feb 28
C6th. He is the patron of Llanllibio on Anglesey, Wales.

Lô *see* **Lauto**

Loarn (St) B. Aug 30
C5th. From western Ireland and a disciple of St Patrick, he has been described as a regionary bishop of Downpatrick.

Locaie *see* **Leocadia**

Lolan (St) B. Sep 2
d. ?1034. He was a bishop in Scotland, possibly at Kincardine near Stirling. A worthless legend describes him as a C5th missionary from Galilee in the Holy Land.

Lollian (St) *see* **Samosata (Martyrs of)**

Loman (Luman) (St) B. Feb 17
d. *c*450. He is alleged to have been a nephew of St Patrick and thc first bishop of Trim in Meath, Ireland, but may have been of the C7th.

Lombards (Martyrs under the) (SS) Mar 2
d. ?579. A group of eighty, they were killed by the invading Lombards in Campania, Italy, for 'refusing to adore the head of a goat', according to the old Roman Martyrology. They are also mentioned by St Gregory the Great.

Lomer (Laudomarus, Launomar) (St) R. Jan 19
*c*490–593. He was a shepherd-boy near Chartres, France, before becoming a priest and then a hermit. He formed his disciples into the monastery of Corbion near Chartres and died a centenarian.

Longinus (St) M? Mar 15.
C1st. The soldier who pierced the side of Christ hanging on the cross (John 19:34) is traditionally referred to by this name, and is alleged to have been from Cappodocia, Asia Minor, and to have been martyred there. He is depicted with his spear, the head of which became a famous relic in the Middle Ages. The centurion who acknowledged Christ crucified to be the son of God is also called Longinus (Matt 27:54).

Longinus (St) *see* **Eusebius, Neon and Comps**

Longinus (St) *see* **Orentius, Heros and Comps**

Longinus (St) *see* **Victor of Marseilles and Comps**

Longinus (St) *see* **Vindemnialis, Eugene and Longinus**

Lonochil (Longis, Lenogisil) and Agnofleda (SS) Apr 2
d. 653 and 638. According to their legend, the former was a priest who founded a monastery

St Longinus, Mar 15 *(see p. 351)*

at the place now called St Longis near Le Mans, France. The latter made a vow of virginity and appealed to his protection and both were slandered as a result, only to have their innocence proved miraculously.

Lorgius (St) *see* **Lucius, Absalom and Lorgius**

Lothar (Loyer) (St) B. R. Jun 14
d. ?756. From Lorraine, he founded a monastery near Argentan, France, at a place later called St-Loyer-des-Champs. Afterwards he was bishop of Sées for thirty-two years.

Louis
The original Frankish name of Khlodovekh (Clovis in Latin) has given rise to two distinctive modern forms: Louis in French and Ludwig in German. The former is more familiar in English and has been preferred in this book (the traditional English form of Lewis is obsolescent). The modern Latin form is Ludovicus, and Aloysius is also a derivative (but listed separately).

Louis Allemand (Bl) B. Sep 16
d. 1450. From the upper Rhône valley, he was made archbishop of Arles, France, in 1423 and cardinal shortly afterwards. He was leader of the anti-papal party at the council of Basel which had gathered to try to end the Western Schism, and consecrated the antipope Felix V. As a result he was deprived of the cardinalate and excommunicated by Pope Eugenius IV, but Pope Nicholas V restored him and for the rest of his life he involved himself only with his duties as a bishop. He was austere in his private life. Dying near Arles, he was beatified in 1527.

Louis Baba (Bl) M. R(OFM). Aug 25
d. 1624. A Japanese catechist, he accompanied Bl Louis Sotelo to Spain when the latter was deported. Returning to Japan, he was arrested and became a Franciscan in prison at Omura before being burned alive at Shimabara with BB Michael Carvalho and Comps. *See* **Japan (Martyrs of)**.

Louis Barreau de la Touche and Louis Barret (BB) *see* **September (Martyrs of)**

Louis Beaulieu (St) *see* **Simon Berneaux and Comps**

Louis and Mary Beltrame Quattrocchi (BB) LL
1880–1951 and 1884-1965 resp. Louis was born in Catania, Sicily, grew up in Urbino, Italy, obtained a degree in law at Rome and became a senior civil servant. He married Mary, a Florentine of the noble Corsini family, in 1905. The couple had two sons, one who became a diocesan priest and the other a Trappist monk, and two daughters, one who became a Benedictine nun. Louis died of a heart attack and Mary of old age. The God-centred witness of their family life led them to be chosen as the first married couple to be beatified together, in 2001.

Louis-Remigius Benoist (Bl) *see* **September (Martyrs of)**

Louis Bertrán (1) (St) R(OP). Oct 9
1526–1581. From Valencia, Spain, a relative of St Vincent Ferrer, he became a Dominican in 1544 and was master of novices at Valencia before being sent to South America in 1562. There he was a missionary among the native peoples of what are now Colombia and Panama

and also on the Leeward Islands. He was alleged to have the gift of tongues when preaching to them. After seven years of great success he was recalled to Valencia, where he died. He was canonized in 1671 and is the patron of Colombia.

Louis Bertrán (2) and Comps
(Bl) M. R(OP). Jul 29
d. 1627. From Barcelona, Spain, a relative of the St Louis Bertrán who went to Colombia, he became a Dominican, was sent to the Philippines in 1618 and then to Japan. He was burned alive with BB Mancius-of-the-Holy-Cross of Omura and Peter-of-the-Holy-Mother-of-God of Arima at Omura, and they were beatified in 1867. *See* **Japan (Martyrs of)**.

Louis Bonnard *see* **John-Louis Bonnard**

Louis Boubert (Bl) *see* **September (Martyrs of)**

Louis (Ludwig) von Bruck
(St) M. L. Apr 30
d. 1429. A boy born of Swiss parents at Ravensburg near Constance, Germany, he was allegedly murdered by renegade Jews at Easter.

Louis of Cordoba (St) *see* **Amator, Peter and Louis**

Louis Correa (Bl) M. R(SJ). Jul 15
d. 1570. A Jesuit student, he was born at Evora in Portugal and martyred with Bl **Ignatius de Azevedo and Comps** (q.v.).

Louis le Danois (Bl) *see* **September (Martyrs of)**

Louis Flores and Comps
(Bl) M. R(OP). Aug 19
1570–1622. From Antwerp, Belgium, he emigrated with his parents to Mexico, joined the Dominicans and became novice-master. In 1602 he went to the Philippines, and set out for Japan in 1620 with Bl Peter Zuñiga, an Augustinian missionary, on a ship captained by Bl Joachim Hirayama Diaz. This was captured by Dutch privateers en route and handed over to the Japanese authorities. The ship's company were tortured, imprisoned for two years and finally executed at Nagasaki. The three mentioned were burnt. Beheaded were eleven Japanese crew and passangers: Anthony Yamada, Bartholomew Mohyoye, James Denji, John Matashichi, John Soyemon, John Yago, Laurence Rokusuke, Leo Sukuyemon, Mark Shinyemon, Paul Sankichi, Thomas Koyanagi and a Spanish passenger, Michael Díaz Hori. *See* **Japan (Martyrs of)**.

Louis IX of France, King (St) L. Aug 25
1214–1270. Born at Poissy near Paris, he became king of France under the regency of his mother, Blanche of Castile, in 1226. He reigned for forty-four years and was successful in subverting the previous arbitrary and corrupt feudal system of local courts of law by establishing the Crown as the administrator of proper justice (especially for the poor and weak). He supported and implemented measures of Church reform, was especially generous to the mendicant orders and founded many ecclesiastical institutions, the most famous being the Sainte-Chapelle in Paris built for his large collection of relics. He was a devoted husband and father of eleven children, and was famously austere and prayerful in his private life. His domestic military campaigns had some success, but he led two crusades which were disasters. He was captured and ransomed during the first, to Damietta in Egypt, and died of dysentery during the second, to Tunis. He was canonized in 1297, and is usually depicted with a cross, crown of thorns or other emblems of Christ's Passion and with the royal fleur-de-lys as his emblem.

Louis François and Louis Gastineau (BB) *see* **Laval (Martyrs of)**

Louis Gaultier, Louis Hurtrel and Louis Longuet (BB) *see* **September (Martyrs of)**

Louis-Mary Grignion de Montfort (St) P. T(OP). Apr 28
1673–1716. From a poor Breton family, he completed his priestly studies with the aid of a benefactor and was ordained in 1700. In 1705 he became a home missionary in north-western France and was known for his childlike devotion to Our Lady and to the Rosary (he was a Dominican tertiary) as well as for his fervent opposition to Jansenism. He became hospital chaplain at Nantes in 1715, and founded there the 'Sisters of Divine Wisdom' for teaching and nursing and the 'Company of Mary' for missionary work. He died at St-Laurent-sur-Sèvre and was canonized in 1947. His mariological writings, especially his 'True Devotion to the Blessed Virgin', remain influential and controversial.

Louis Ibaraki (St) M. Feb 5
1585–1597. A Japanese boy aged twelve, he served at Mass for the Franciscan missionaries in Kyushu and was crucified at Nagasaki. *See*

Paul Miki and Comps and **Japan (Martyrs of)**.

Louis Kawara (Bl) M. R(SJ). Sep 10
d. 1622. He was a page at the court of Michael, the Christian daimyo of Arima, Japan, but was exiled when the latter apostatized. He became a Jesuit under Bl Charles Spinola and burned alive with him at the 'Great Martyrdom' at Nagasaki. *See* **Japan (Martyrs of)**.

Louis Maki (Bl) M. L. Sep 7
d. 1627. He was burned alive at Nagasaki, Japan, with his adopted son, Bl John Maki, and Bl Thomas Tsuji for allowing the latter to celebrate Mass in his house. *See* **Japan (Martyrs of)**.

Louis Matsuo (Bl) M. T(OFM). Aug 17
d. 1627. He was a Japanese Franciscan tertiary beheaded at Nagasaki. *See* **Francis-of-St-Mary of Mancha and Comps** and **Japan (Martyrs of)**.

Louis Maudit (Bl) *see* **September (Martyrs of)**

Louis Morbioli (Bl) T(OC). Nov 16
1439–1495. From Bologna, Italy, as a young man he led an immoral life but was converted by sickness at Venice, became a Carmelite tertiary and lived as a wayfarer, teaching Christian doctrine to the young and begging alms which he gave to the poor. He died at Bologna and had his cultus confirmed for there in 1842.

Louis-Zepherinus Moreau
(Bl) B. F. May 24
1824–1901. From Beçancour in Quebec, Canada, one of a large peasant family, as a priest he became the cathedral master of ceremonies and chancellor of the diocesan curia. In 1852 he moved to the new diocese of St Hyacinth, and became its bishop in 1876. He fostered all aspects of Church life with great loyalty to the magisterium and devotion to the Sacred Heart, and founded the 'Sisters of St Martha' in 1890 to work as domestics in seminaries and schools. He wrote about 20,000 letters as bishop. He was beatified in 1987.

Louis Naizen (Bl) M. L. Jul 12
1619–1626. A Japanese boy aged seven, son of BB John and Monica Naizen, he was beheaded with them at Nagasaki. *See* **Mancius Araki and Comps** and **Japan (Martyrs of)**.

Louis Nihachi (Bl) M. T(OP). Sep 8
d. 1628. A Japanese Dominican tertiary, he was beheaded at Nagasaki with his two sons, Francis and Dominic, for having given shelter to missionaries. *See* **Dominic Castellet and Comps** and **Japan (Martyrs of)**.

Louis Palmentieri of Casoria
(Bl) R(OFM). F. Mar 30
1814–1885. From near Naples, Italy, he joined the Franciscans in 1832 and became a priest and teacher. In 1887 he had a mystical experience (his 'cleansing') and dedicated himself to caring for the poor and infirm after it. He established a friary of strict observance in Naples, and his co-workers became the 'Brothers of Charity' (1859) and the 'Sisters of St Elizabeth' (1862). He was beatified in 1993.

Louis Pavoni (Bl) P. F. Apr 1
1784–1849. From Brescia, Italy, he spent his entire life there, becoming a diocesan priest in 1807. His concern for young people led him to found the institute of the 'Sons of Mary Immaculate' to help care for them. He was beatified in 1947.

Louis Rigot (Bl) *see* **September (Martyrs of)**

Louis Sasada (Bl) M. R(OFM). Aug 25
d. 1624. Son of Bl Michael Sasada, he accompanied Bl Louis Sotelo to Mexico when the latter was deported from Japan, became a Franciscan there and was ordained at Manila in the Philippines in 1622. He then returned to Japan and was burned alive with **Michael Carvalho and Comps** (q.v.).

Louis Sotelo (Bl) M. R(OFM). Aug 25
d. 1624. A nobleman from Seville, Spain, he became a Franciscan at Salamanca, was sent to Manila in the Philippines in 1601 and to Japan in 1603. He was deported in 1613 and went back to Spain but returned in 1622, was arrested at Nagasaki and burned alive with Michael Carvalho and Comps. *See* **Japan (Martyrs of)**.

Louis Tezza (Bl) R. (Sep 26)
1841–1923. From Conegliano near Treviso, Italy, he early recognized a vocation to serve sick people and joined the Camillans at Verona in 1850. In 1871 he was sent to make a new province of his congregation in France, and in 1891 he became the vicar-general of the Camillans. He helped Bl Josephine Vannini found the 'Daughters of St Camillus' as the female branch of the Camillans. In 1900 he went to refound the Camillans at Lima in Peru, where he stayed until his death. He was beatified in 2001.

Louis (Ludwig) IV of Thuringia
(Bl) L. Sep 11
1200–1227. Landgrave of Thuringia, Germany, and husband of St Elizabeth of Hungary, he was a capable ruler and a brave knight and died at Otranto while following the emperor Frederick II on crusade. His cultus has not been confirmed.

Louis of Toulouse (St) B. R(OFM). Aug 19
1274–1297. Son of Charles II of Anjou, king of Naples, he was great-nephew of St Louis of France and of St Elizabeth of Hungary. Probably born at Nocera, Italy, he grew up in Provence, France, and was sent as a hostage to Aragón, Spain, in 1288, spending seven years at Barcelona. He was appointed bishop of Toulouse, France, just before his release, reluctantly accepted but became a Franciscan just before his ordination and consecration. He died six months later at Brignoles and was canonized in 1317.

Louis Yakichi (Bl) M. L. Oct 2
d. 1622. A Japanese, he tried to rescue Bl Louis Flores from prison on Hirado-jima and was burned alive at Nagasaki with his wife, Lucy, and his two sons, Andrew and Francis. He was beatified in 1867. *See* **Japan (Martyrs of)**.

Louise degl' Albertoni (Bl)
T(OFM). Jan 31
1474–1533. A Roman noblewoman, as a widow with three children she became a Franciscan tertiary and spent the rest of her life in works of charity. Her cultus was approved locally for Rome in 1671.

Louise Bessay de la Voûle and Louise-Amata Dean de Luigné (BB) *see* **William Repin and Comps**

Louise-of-St-Francis-of-Assisi Ducrez (Bl) *see* **Valenciennes (Martyrs of)**

Louise de Marillac (St) R. F. Mar 15
1591–1660. Born in Paris, she wanted to become a nun but married instead on the advice of her confessor. Being widowed in 1625,she spent the rest of her life in working with St Vincent de Paul in founding the 'Sisters of Charity'. The sisters took their vows for the first time in 1638, and she was their superior until she died at Paris. She was canonized in 1934.

Louise-Teresa de Montaignac de Chauvence (Bl) R. F. Jun 27
1820–1885. Born at Le Havre, France, of an old noble family, when aged eighteen she consecrated herself to the Hearts of Jesus and Mary and set out to further devotion thereto. Setting up house at Montluçon, she founded the 'Pious Union of Oblates of the Sacred Heart of Jesus' (approved 1874) which taught girls, ran orphanages, helped in poor parishes and fostered devotion to the Sacred Heart. She was beatified in 1990.

Louise of Omura (Bl) M. L. Sep 8
d. 1628. She was the eighty-year-old Japanese housekeeper of Bl Dominic Castellet and was burned with him at Nagasaki. *See* **Japan (Martyrs of)**.

Louise Poirier and Louise Raillier de la Tertinière (Bl) *see* **William Repin and Comps**

Louise of Savoy (Bl) R(OFM). Jul 24
1462–1503. Daughter of Bl Amadeus IX, Duke of Savoy, and cousin of Bl Joan of Valois, she was married when aged seventeen and widowed at twenty-seven. Then she joined the Poor Clares at Orbe and was employed in collecting food for the community, which she did with a cheerful spirit (a noblewoman doing such a thing was a wonder in those days). Her cultus was approved for Turin in 1839.

Loup *see* **Lupus of Troyes**

Lua (Lugid, Molua) (St) R. Aug 4
?554–?609. Allegedly from Limerick, Ireland, he became a disciple of St Comgall and founder of many monasteries (the legendary number is 120), notably that at Killaloe in Co. Clare where St Flannan was his disciple. His rule was extremely austere but he had great tenderness for people and animals.

Lubin *see* **Leobin**

Lubbock
There is no such saint. References to 'St Lubbock's Day' are obsolete slang for the August bank holiday in England, which had been instituted by one Sir John Lubbock.

Lucanus of Gascony (St) M. Oct 30
C5th. He is alleged to have been martyred at Lagny near Paris, France, where his relics were enshrined.

Lucentia (St) L. May 18
*c*900? She has a local cultus based on her shrine at Provins in Champagne, France, and is alleged to have been a lay woman there who lived in continual prayer and fasting and who made a living from spinning wool.

Lucerius (St) R. Dec 10
d. 739. He became a child oblate at the abbey of Farfa near Rome under its restorer St Thomas of Maurienne, whom he eventually succeeded as abbot.

Luchesius and Bonadonna
(BB) TT(OFM) Apr 28
d. *c*1260. From Poggibonsi near Siena, Italy, they were a married couple. He was in business as a grocer, money-changer and corn merchant, but they became Franciscan tertiaries in ?1221 and led penitential lives as hospital nurses. It is not certain that they were the first such tertiaries, as has been claimed.

Luchtighern *see* **Louthiern**

Lucian (St) *see* **Emilius, Felix and Comps**

Lucian (St) *see* **Fortunatus and Lucian**

Lucian (St) *see* **Peregrine, Lucian and Comps**

Lucian, Florius and Comps
(SS) MM. Oct 26
d. *c*250. They were martyred at Nicomedia, Asia Minor, in the reign of Decius, but their acta are unreliable.

Lucian, Maximian and Julian
(SS) MM. Jan 8
d. *c*290. According to their unreliable legend they were Roman missionaries martyred at Beauvais, France.

Lucian, Metrobius, Paul, Zenobius, Theotimus and Drusus
(SS) MM. Dec 24
? They were martyred at Tripoli, Libya.

Lucian of Antioch (St) M. P. Jan 7
d. 312. Possibly from Edessa (now Urfa in Turkey), where he was educated as a scripture scholar, he became a priest and teacher of exegesis at Antioch, Syria. He especially opposed the allegorizing tendencies of Alexandrian exegesis, and the leaders of the Arian heresy in the C4th regarded him as their greatest master. In 304 he was seized, taken to Nicomedia and put in prison, where he died of torture after nine years. He was highly regarded by St John Chrysostom and St Jerome.

Lucian of Beauvais (St) M. Jan 8
C3rd? He was allegedly a missionary martyred at Beauvais, France, but was probably a duplicate of the above.

Lucidius (St) B. Apr 26
C4th? A bishop of Verona, Italy, he was listed as being famous for a life of prayer and study.

Lucidus (St) R(OSB). Jul 28
d. ?938. A Benedictine monk near Aquara in the Valley of Diano near Salerno, Italy, he became a hermit at Santa Maria dell' Albaneta and had his cultus confirmed for Diano and Aquara in 1880.

Lucilla, Flora, Eugene, Antoninus, Theodore and Comps
(SS) MM. Jul 29
d. *c*260. According to their unreliable acta they were a group of twenty-three who were martyred at Rome in the reign of Gallienus, but seem rather to have been confused duplications of the following: Faustus of Rome and Comps; Lucy, Antoninus and Comps; Lucy of Rome and Comps. Ancient records seem to have been badly muddled.

Lucilla (St) *see* **Nemesius and Lucilla**

Lucillian, Claudius, Hypatius, Paul and Dionysius (SS) MM. Jun 3
d. 273. The first was allegedly a convert in his old age at Byzantium who was crucified there with four young men. An embellishment alleges that he was their father and that Paula of Byzantium was their mother. They were probably martyred elsewhere and their relics brought to Constantinople (as Byzantium later became).

Lucina (three of the same name) (SS) Jun 30
There seem to have been three Roman martyrs of this name: (1) Of apostolic times, mentioned in the spurious acta of SS Processus and Martinianus; (2) In the reign of Decius, *c*250; (3) Linked with St Sebastian and other martyrs in the reign of Diocletian. The first is commemorated on June 30.

Lucinus (Lezin) of Angers
(St) B. Feb 13
d. ?618. A Frankish courtier, he became bishop of Angers, France.

Luciolus (St *see* **Felix, Luciolus and Comps**

Lucius (St) *see* **Apelles, Lucius and Clement**

Lucius (St) *see* **Faustinus, Lucius and Comps**

Lucius (St) *see* **Gaius, Faustus and Comps**

Lucius (St) *see* **Hyacinth, Quintus and Comps**

Lucius (St) *see* **Montanus, Lucius and Comps**

Lucius (St) *see* **Nemesian and Comps**

Lucius (St) *see* **Paul, Lucius and Cyriac**

Lucius (St) *see* **Ptolemy, Lucius and Companion**

Lucius (St) *see* **Quintian, Lucius and Comps**

Lucius (St) *see* **Saturninus, Castulus and Comps**

Lucius (St) *see* **Theodosius, Lucius and Comps**

Lucius, Absalon and Lorgius (SS) MM. Mar 2
? The old Roman Martyrology lists these as having been martyred at Caesarea in Cappodocia, Asia Minor.

Lucius, Rogatus, Cassian and Candida (SS) MM. Dec 1
? They were martyrs of Rome.

Lucius, Silvanus, Rutilus, Classicus, Secundinus, Fructulus and Maximus (SS) MM. Feb 18
? They were allegedly Roman African martyrs. When Cardinal Baronius revised the old Roman Martyrology, he stated that he inserted them on the evidence of reliable manuscripts. Such have not survived.

Lucius I, Pope *Mar 4*
d. 254. He succeeded St Cornelius as pope in 253, but was immediately exiled and died at Rome on his return after eight months. St Cyprian referred to him as a martyr, but this is false and his cultus was suppressed in 1969.

Lucius of Adrianople and Comps (SS) MM. B. Feb 11
d. 350. Bishop of Adrianople near Constantinople, he was a vigorous opponent of Arianism and was twice exiled by Emperor Constantius before being restored by the council of Sardica in 347. Then he was imprisoned during a purge of supporters of St Athanasius ordered by the emperor and died in prison. Some of his people were killed in the disturbances.

Lucius of Britain, King (St) Dec 3
d. ?200. According to the legend, first recorded in the C6th, this king of Britain asked Pope St Eleutherius to send missionaries to Britain, founded the dioceses of London and Llandaff and eventually went as a missionary himself to Switzerland. This story is romantic fiction, based on the story of King Agbar IX of Edessa (now Urfa in Turkey). The latter was also known as Lucius, and he also asked Pope St Eleutherius for missionaries to be sent to his country.

Lucius of Cyprus and Comps (SS) MM. Aug 20
? According to the unreliable story in the old Roman Martyrology he went from Cyrene to Cyprus, and this implies an identity with Lucius of Cyrene.

Lucius of Cyrene (St) B? May 6
C1st. He was one of the prophets and teachers mentioned in Acts 13:1 as being in the church at Antioch when Paul and Barnabas were set apart for their apostolate. His surname led to the tradition that he was the first bishop of Cyrene in Libya.

Lucretia *see* Leocritia

Lucretia of Mérida (St) V. Nov 23
d. 306. She was martyred at Mérida, Spain.

Lucy, Antoninus, Severinus, Diodore, Dion and Comps (SS) MM. Jul 6
They result from an apparent duplication in the old Roman Martyrology of Lucilla, Flora and Comps.

Lucy and Geminian *Sep 16*
d. *c*300. According to their untrustworthy acta they were a 75-year-old Roman widow and a catechumen martyred together in the reign of Diocletian. Their cultus was suppressed in 1969.

Lucy Broccadelli (Bl) T(OP). Nov 15
1476–1544. From Narni in Umbria, Italy, after three years of unconsummated marriage to a Milanese nobleman she became a Dominican regular tertiary at Viterbo. In 1494 she became the first prioress of the new nunnery at Ferrara and received the stigmata two years later, but she was hopeless as a superior and was deposed. Then she was treated with serious cruelty by her successor, and lived on in uncomplaining obscurity for thirty-nine years. Her cultus was confirmed for the Dominicans, Ferrara, Narni and Viterbo in 1710.

Lucy Bufalari (Bl) R(OSA). Jul 27
d. 1350. From Castel Ponziano near Rome, a sister of Bl John Bufalari of Rieti, she became an Augustinian nun at Amelia and went on to be prioress. She is a patron against demonic possession. Her cultus was confirmed for the Augustinians in 1832.

Lucy of Caltagirone (Bl) R(OFM). Sep 26
d. ?1304. From Caltagirone, Sicily, she became a Poor Clare at Salerno and had her cultus approved for there in 1514.

Lucy Filippini (St) R. Mar 25
1672–1732. From Tarquinia in Lazio, Italy, when aged sixteen she became a consecrated religious under the guidance of the bishop of Montefiascone near Viterbo. In 1692 she started helping Bl Rosa Venerini in her work of teaching poor girls, but took over the enterprise in the diocese of Montefiascone and founded her own community in 1704. This was summoned to Rome, where it became the Pontifical Institute of Religious Teachers or 'Filippini'. She died at Montefiascone and was canonized in 1930.

Lucy de Freitas (Bl) M. L. Sep 10
d. 1622. A Japanese woman married to a Portuguese, she gave shelter to missionaries and was hence burned alive in the 'Great Martyrdom' at Nagasaki, Japan. *See* **Japan (Martyrs of)**.

Lucy Khambang (Bl) *see* **Thailand (Martyrs of)**

Lucy Kim (1), Lucy Kim (2) and Lucy Pak (SS) *see* **Korea (Martyrs of)**

Lucy of Rome and Comps (SS) MM. Jun 25
They are an apparent duplication in the old Roman Martyrology of Lucilla, Flora and Comps.

Lucy of Settefonti (Bl) R(OSB Cam). Nov 7
C12th. From Bologna, Italy, she became a Camaldolese nun (considered the first such by the Camaldolese) at Settefonti nearby.

Lucy of Syracuse (St) V. Dec 13
d. 304. She is one of the most famous of the Western virgin-martyrs and her name is in the Roman canon of the Mass, but her acta are not reliable (despite ante-dating the C6th). She was martyred at Syracuse, Sicily, in the reign of Diocletian but her shrine is at Venice. Her attribute is her pair of gouged-out eyes.

Lucy Wang (Cheng) and Comps (SS) MM. LL. Jun 28
d. 1900. She was born in 1882 at Laochuntan in Hebei, China, but was orphaned and was brought up at the Catholic orphanage at Wangla. The village was invaded by a gang of Boxers and all the Catholics massacred, but she and three other orphan girls were initially kept alive. The others were Mary Fan (Kun), aged sixteen from Daji, Mary Chi (Yu), aged fifteen from the same place and Mary Zheng (Xu) aged eleven from Kou. The Boxers spent four days trying to persuade them to apostatize and to marry, but they refused and were massacred. *See* **China (Martyrs of)**.

Lucy Wang (Wang) (St) *see* **Joseph Wang (Yumei) and Comps**

Lucy Yakichi (Bl) *see* **Louis Chakichi**

St Lucy of Syracuse, Dec 13

Lucy Yi (Zhenmei) (St) M. L. Feb 19
1813–1862. From a Catholic family of Mianyiang in Sichuan, China, when young she took a private vow of virginity and worked as a schoolteacher and lay catechist. She moved to Guiyang and taught at a convent there, but was seized upon meeting St John-Peter Néel and

companions as prisoners on the road near Kaiyang. She was beheaded the next day. *See* **China (Martyrs of)**.

Ludger (Liudger) (St) B. Mar 26
d. 809. A Frisian from near Utrecht, Netherlands, he was educated under St Gregory there and under Alcuin at York, England. After his ordination at Cologne in 777 he was a missionary in Friesland and in what is now Lower Saxony and Westphalia under the imperial patronage of Charlemagne. He spent some time as a refugee from the Saxons at the abbey of Montecassino in Italy, but did not take vows as a monk. In 804 he became first bishop of Münster, and is hence called the apostle of Westphalia.

Ludmilla (St) M. L. Sep 16
d. 921. The wife of the first Christian duke of Bohemia, she was entrusted with the education of St Wenceslas, her grandson. The latter's mother, her daughter-in-law, resented her influence and had her strangled by hired assassins at Tetin, her private estate. Her shrine was at Prague, Czech Republic.

Ludolf of Corvey (St) R(OSB). Aug 13
d. 983. He became abbot of Corvey near Paderborn, Germany, in 971 and revived the monastic school at that famous abbey.

Ludolf of Ratzeburg (St)
B. R(OPraem. Mar 29
d. 1250. A Premonstratensian canon, he became bishop of Ratzeburg near Lübeck, Germany, and imposed the rule of his order on his cathedral chapter. He was imprisoned and badly treated by the secular ruler, dying as a result.

Ludwin (Leodewin) (St) B. R. Sep 29
d. 713. Educated under St Basinus, his uncle and bishop of Trier, Germany, he married when young but his wife died so he then founded the abbey of Mettlach and became a monk there. Later he became bishop of Trier himself.

Lufthild (St) R. Jan 23
d. ?850. She is locally venerated around Cologne, Germany, and is alleged to have been a hermit on the Lüftelberg.

Luke (St) *see* **Parmenius and Comps**

Luke (St) *see* **Silvanus, Luke and Mucius**

Luke Alonso (St) M.
R(OP). Sep 28 (d. n. Oct 19)
1594–1633. From Asturias, Spain, he became a Dominican missionary in the Philippines and in the north of Honsu, Japan, before being martyred at Nagasaki with his assistant, St Matthew Kohioye. He was canonized in 1987. *See* **Japan (Martyrs of)**.

Luke Banabakintu (St) M. L. Jun 3
d. 1886. A native of Buganda, Uganda, he was baptized in 1881 and burned alive at Namuyongo. *See* **Charles Lwanga and Comps**.

Luke Belludi (Bl) R(OFM). Feb 17
1200–1285. He became a Franciscan at Padua, Italy, under St Francis himself, and was the intimate associate of St Anthony of Padua. On his own death he was laid in the empty tomb from which the body of St Anthony had been transferred. His cultus was confirmed for Padua in 1927.

Luke Bojko *see* **Podlasia (Martyrs of)**

Luke the Evangelist (St) Oct 18
C1st. A Greek doctor of medicine at Antioch, Syria, he wrote the third gospel and the Acts of the Apostles. The autobiographical passages in the latter describe how he accompanied St Paul on some of the latter's missionary journeys, and he is referred to in St Paul's letter to the Colossians (4:14). Nothing is known about his life after the ending of Acts, and there is no evidence that he was martyred. A C6th legend asserts that he painted the original of the *Hodegetria* icon of Our Lady, and several surviving Byzantine icons have been traditionally claimed as his work. In 2001, his alleged relics at Padua, Italy, were DNA-tested and found to be probably genuine. His attribute is an ox.

Luke Hoang (Chai-ken) (St) *see* **Anthony Daveluy and Comps**

Luke Kirby (St) M. P. May 30
?1548–1582. From Richmond in Yorkshire, he was probably educated at Cambridge. After his conversion he studied for the priesthood at Rome and Douai, returned to England in 1580 and was immediately arrested on landing at Dover. He was seriously tortured in the Tower of London before being executed at Tyburn with BB Laurence Richardson, Thomas Cottam and William Filby. He was canonized in 1970. *See* **England (Martyrs of)**.

Luke Kiyemon (Bl) M.
T(OFM). Aug 16
d. 1627. A Japanese Franciscan tertiary, he was beheaded at Nagasaki with BB Francis-of-St-Mary of Mancha and Comps. *See* **Japan (Martyrs of)**.

Luke (Vu Ba) Loan (St) M. P. Jun 5
1756–1840. An elderly priest of north Vietnam, he was beheaded. *See* **Vietnam (Martyrs of)**.

Luke of Sandomir (Bl) *see* **Sadoc of Sandomir and Comps**

Luke (Pham Trong) Thin
(St) M. Jan 13
1859. He was a Vietnamese layman and martyr. *See* **Vietnam (Martyrs of)**.

Luke the Younger (St) R. Feb 7
d. ?946. From a peasant family of Aegina, Greece, he became a monk at Athens and a hermit near Corinth before dying on a mountain in Phocis which was later called 'Soterion' after the miracles that he worked. These also gave him the nickname 'the Thaumaturge'.

Lull (St) B. R. Oct 16
?710–786. A monk of Malmesbury, England, he was a relative of St Boniface and joined him in Germany in 725, becoming his archdeacon and chief assistant. He was sent to Rome in 751, and on his return Boniface ordained him as regionary bishop and his coadjutor at Mainz. He took over as bishop when Boniface left for Friesland and his murder, and founded the monastery of Hersfeld where his shrine now is.

Lunaire *see* **Leonorius**

Luperculus (Lupercus) (St) M. B. Mar 1
d. *c*300. He is alleged to have been a bishop of Eauze (an extinct French diocese near Lourdes) who was martyred in the reign of Diocletian, but may be a duplicate of one of the Zaragoza martyrs. He is venerated in the diocese of Tarbes.

Lupercus (St) *see* **Claudius, Lupercus and Victorius**

Lupercus (St) *see* **Zaragoza (Eighteen Martyrs of)**

Luperius (St) B. Nov 15
C6th or C8th. Nothing is known about this bishop of Verona, Italy.

Lupicinus and Felix (SS) BB. Feb 3
C5th. They are listed as bishops of Lyons, France, but without any further information except that the former died in 486.

Lupicinus of Condat (St) R. Mar 21
d. *c*480. Brother of St Romanus of Condat, with him he founded two monasteries in the Jura, France, Condat (now the town of St Claude) and Lauconne.

Lupicinus of Verona (St) B. May 3
C5th. He was a bishop of Verona, Italy.

Lupus (St) *see* **Saturninus and Lupus**

Lupus of Bayeux (St) B. Oct 25
d. *p*465. He was bishop of Bayeux, France.

Lupus of Chalon (St) B. Jan 27
d. *c*610. Bishop of Chalon-sur-Saône, France, he was famous for helping people in trouble. A letter of St Gregory the Great addressed to him in 601 survives.

Lupus of Lyons (St) B. Sep 25
d. 542. A monk of a monastery near Lyons, France, he became archbishop of that city and had to cope with the annexation of the kingdom of Burgundy by the Franks in 534.

Lupus of Novae (St) M. Aug 23
? He was listed as being a slave of St Demetrius of Thessalonika and a martyr in that city, but this is false. He had a basilica at Novae near Svishtov in Bulgaria, and was probably martyred in the area.

Lupus of Sens (St) B. Sep 1
d. 623. A monk of Lérins, he became bishop of Sens, France, in 609.

Lupus of Soissons (St) B. Oct 19
d. *c*540. This bishop of Soissons, France, was a nephew of St Remigius of Rheims.

Lupus of Troyes (St) B. Jul 29
384–478. From Toul, France, he married a sister of St Hilary of Arles but they separated by mutual consent after seven years and he became a monk at Lérins. He was made bishop of Troyes in 426. He allegedly accompanied St Germanus of Auxerre to Britain to help combat Pelagianism, and allegedly saved his city from being sacked by Attila the Hun. Both of these assertions are probably false.

Lupus of Verona (St) B. Dec 2
? Nothing is known about this bishop of Verona, Italy.

Lutgard (St) R(OCist). Jun 16
1182–1246. From Tongeren, Belgium, she became a Benedictine nun there when aged twenty, and transferred to the Cistercian nunnery of Aywières in 1208 in order to escape being made abbess. She was favoured with

apparitions of Christ, Our Lady and of many saints and is outstanding among the women mystics of the Middle Ages. She went blind eleven years before her death.

Lutrud (St) *see* **Amata of Joinville**

Luxorius, Cisellus and Camerinus (SS) MM. Aug 21
d. ?303. A soldier and two boys, they were beheaded in Sardinia in the reign of Diocletian and have their shrine at Pisa.

Lybe, Leonis and Eutropia (SS) VV. Jun 15
d. 303. The first two were sisters who were beheaded and burned alive respectively, and the last was a girl aged twelve who was used as an archery target. They were martyred at Palmyra, Syria, in the reign of Diocletian.

Lybosus (St) *see* **Dominic, Victor and Comps**

Lycarion (St) M. Jun 7
? He is listed as an Egyptian martyr.

Lydia (St) *see* **Philetus, Lydia and Comps**

Lydia Purpuraria (St) L. Aug 3
C1st. From Thyatira, Asia Minor (now Akhisar in Turkey), a city famous for its dye-works, she was a dealer in Tyrian purple dye (hence her surname). While at Philippi in Macedonia she became St Paul's first convert in Europe (Acts 16:14–15).

Lydwina (Bl) L. Apr 14
1380–1433. The daughter of a labourer from Schiedam, Netherlands, she was a pretty girl but prayed that she would be disfigured in order to avoid marriage. So she broke a rib while skating when aged sixteen and suffered complications which left her bedridden, gangrenous and in agony for the rest of her life (over forty years). She had mystical visions and ecstasies, allegedly took no food except the Eucharist and reached a high level of contemplative prayer. Her cultus was confirmed for Haarlem in 1890.

Lyé *see* **Leo or Laetus**

Lyons and Vienne (Martyrs of) *see* **Photinus, Sanctius and Comps**

Lythan (St) R? Sep 1
? He is the patron of St Lythan's near Cardiff, Wales.

Lyutius (St) R(OSB). Jul 28
d. ?1038. Allegedly a monk of Montecassino, Italy, who died as a hermit at La Cava, he may be identical with St Lucidus of Aquara.

M

Mabyn (Mabon, Mabenna) (St) Sep 21
C6th. The patron of St Mabyn's near Bodmin in Cornwall, England, was allegedly one of the daughters of St Brychan. There are other Welsh saints of similar names, and they are not clearly distinguished. One was the founder of Llanfabon, Glamorgan, and another was associated with Ruabon, Clwyd.

Macaille (St) B. Apr 25
d. ?489. A disciple of St Mel, he became bishop of Croghan in Co. Offaly, Ireland, and allegedly assisted his master in clothing St Brigid as a nun. He has been confused with St Machai of Bute.

Macaria (St) *see* **Januarius, Maxima and Macaria**

Macarius (St) *see* **Eudoxius, Zeno and Comps**

Macarius (St) *see* **Eugene and Macarius**

Macarius (St) *see* **Faustus, Macarius and Comps**

Macarius and Julian
(SS) MM. Aug 12
? They are listed by the old Roman Martyrology as martyrs of Syria, but earlier martyrologies list them as confessors.

Macarius, Rufinus, Justus and Theophilus (SS) MM. Feb 28
d. *c*250. These alleged potters were martyred in the reign of Decius, either at Rome (according to the old Roman Martyrology) or at Alexandria, Egypt.

Macarius of Alexandria (1)
(St) M. Dec 8
Listed as a martyr of Alexandria, Egypt, he seems to be a triplicate of his namesake in **Macarius of Alexandria (2) and Comps** and **Macarius, Rufinus and Comps**

Macarius of Alexandria (2) and Comps (SS) MM. Oct 30
d. *c*250. They are listed as martyrs of Alexandria, Egypt, by the old Roman Martyrology, but seem to be duplicates of **Macarius, Rufinus and Comps**.

Macarius the Alexandrian
(St) R. Jan 2
*c*300–390. He was a sweet-maker at Alexandria, Egypt, before his conversion *c*340, and became one of the great desert fathers of Nitria on the western edge of the Nile Delta. A famous athletic ascetic, he became the priest and superior of the hermit colony of the Cells nearby and was a friend of his namesake of Scetis. He was allegedly also a monk under St Pachomius for a while, but the other Tabennesiote brethren disapproved of his asceticism.

Macarius of Antioch (St) B? Apr 10
d. 1012. Allegedly from Antioch in Pisidia, Asia Minor, and bishop there, he resigned and travelled westward as a pilgrim, ending up at Ghent, Belgium, and dying in a hospice there during an epidemic. His biography is a forgery.

Macarius the Great (St) R. Jan 15
*c*300–390. The founder of the monastic colony at Scetis (now the Wadi-el-Natrun in Egypt) was apparently a native Egyptian camel-driver associated with the natron trade before he settled as a monk in this rift-valley in the desert when aged about thirty. He was there for about sixty years, and attracted thousands of disciples. Scetis became the stronghold of Coptic monasticism, as distinct from the more intellectual Greek monasticism at Nitria, and the site of his cell is still marked by a functioning monastery. A collection of ascetical homilies have been traditionally attributed to him, although he is not the author. With his Alexandrian namesake he was banished for a while by the Arians after the death of St Athanasius.

Macarius of Jerusalem
(St) B. Mar 10
d. ?335. Bishop of Jerusalem from 314, he oversaw the construction of the Anastasis and Martyrion at the site of Calvary. According to legend this involved his identifying the True Cross found by St Helen. He was present at the first Council of Nicaea.

Macarius of Petra *see* **Arius**

Macarius of Sandomir (Bl) *see* **Sadoc of Sandomir and Comps**

Macarius the Scot (Bl) R(OSB). Dec 19
d. 1153. From Scotland (or Ireland), he emigrated to Germany and became first abbot of St James's monastery at Würzburg.

Macarius the Thaumaturge
(St) R. Apr 1
d. 830. Abbot of Pelecetes near Constantinople, he upheld the validity of icons and was hence persecuted by the Iconoclast emperors Leo V and Michael II. After several years in prison he died in exile.

Macartan (Aedh mac Cairthinn) (St) B. Mar 24
d. ?505. He was an early disciple of St Patrick, by whom he is alleged to have been ordained bishop of Clogher, Ireland. He is the principal patron of the diocese of Clogher.

Maccabean Martyrs (SS) Aug 1
d. ?168 BC. Apart from the archangels, these were the only persons in the Old Testament (2 Mac 6 and 7) who had a liturgical cultus in the Western Church. Their alleged relics were in the church of St Peter ad Vincula in Rome, but in the 1930s they were discovered to be dogs' bones and removed. Their cultus was confined to local calendars in 1969.

Maccaldus *see* **Maughold**

Maccallin (Malcallan)
(St) R(OSB). Jan 21
d. 978. An Irishman, he went on pilgrimage to St Fursey's shrine at Péronne near Amiens, France, and entered the Benedictine abbey of Gorze. Then he became a hermit, and ended up as abbot of Waulsort near Dinant, Belgium.

Maccallin (Macallan, Macculin Dus) (St) B. R. Sep 6
d. ?497. Bishop of Lusk in Co. Dublin, Ireland, he apparently visited Scotland and founded some monasteries there.

Macdara (St) R.
? He gave his name to St Macdara's Island off the coast of Co. Galway, Ireland, on which there is a ruined church. He was probably a hermit there.

Macedo (St) *see* **Philetus, Lydia and Comps**

Macedonius, Patricia and Modesta (SS) MM. Mar 13
d. ?304. The old Roman Martyrology listed these as a married couple and their daughter who were martyred at Nicomedia, Asia Minor, but it is doubtful that they were related. Earlier martyrologies listed a group of twenty-two.

Macedonius, Theodulus and Tatian (SS) MM. Sep 12
d. 362. When emperor Julian restored paganism as the state religion, the temple at Meros in Phrygia, Asia Minor, was reopened and its idols restored. These three broke into the temple, destroyed the idols and were consequently slowly roasted to death on gridirons.

Macedonius II of Constantinople
(St) B. Apr 25
d. 516. He was appointed patriarch of Constantinople in 496 and insisted on the acceptance of the council of Chalcedon. This was politically inexpedient at the time, and he died in exile at Gangra.

Macedonius Kritophagos
(St) R. Jan 24
d. *c*430. One of the more famous of the Syrian ascetical hermits, for forty years he wandered around Syria without ever sleeping under a roof. Only when he grew old did he start sleeping in the huts of the peasants. His surname refers to his diet of barley.

Maceratus (St) see **Peregrine, Maceratus and Viventius**

Machabeo (Gilda-Marchaibeo)
(St) R. Mar 31
1104–1174. He was abbot of the monastery at Armagh, Ireland, from 1134.

Machai of Bute (St) R. Apr 25
C5th. He was apparently a disciple of St Patrick who settled as a hermit on the island of Bute, Scotland.

Machan (St) B. Sept 28
? From Scotland, he was consecrated as a missionary bishop (allegedly at Rome) and died at Campsie near Stirling.

Machar (Mochumna) (St) B? R. Nov 12
C6th. An Irish nobleman, he was baptized by St Colman and became a disciple of St Columba at Iona, Scotland. Then he was sent with twelve companions to convert the Picts, and allegedly founded the church at Old Aberdeen.

Machudd (Machell) (St) R. Nov 15
C7th. He was abbot-founder of the monastery of Llanfechell on Anglesey, Wales.

Machutus *see* **Malo**

Mackessog *see* **Kessog**

MacNissi (St) B. Sep 3
d. 514. He was allegedly baptized as an infant by St Patrick, who then ordained him bishop when he grew up. He was the abbot-founder of a monastery (probably at Kells) which was the progenitor of the diocese of Connor in Co. Antrim, Ireland. He is the principal patron of the diocese.

Macra (St) V. Jan 6
d. 287. From Rheims, France, she was martyred at Fismes nearby on the orders of the prefect Rictiovarus at a time before the general persecution of Christianity was ordered by Diocletian. She was severely tortured, and her attribute is the pair of pincers which was used on her.

Macrina *see* **Margaret**

Macrina the Elder (St) L. Jan 14
d. *c*340. The paternal grandmother of SS Basil and Gregory of Nyssa, she was a native of Neocaesarea in Pontus, Asia Minor, and as a young woman was a disciple of St Gregory Thaumaturgus, the bishop there. During the persecution ordered by Diocletian she and her husband hid for over seven years in a forest on their land near the shore of the Black Sea. They returned home in 311, but were further persecuted under Licinius. She taught St Basil as a boy.

Macrina the Younger (St) R. Jul 19
?327–379. Grand-daughter of St Macrina the Elder, she was the eldest daughter of SS Basil the Elder and Emmelia and sister of SS Basil the Great and Gregory of Nyssa. She helped her parents to educate her younger brothers and sisters, and then became a nun with her mother at a nunnery they founded on the Iris river.

Macrinus (St) *see* **Valerian, Macrinus and Gordian**

Macrobius (St) *see* **Sabinus, Julian and Comps**

Macrobius and Julian
(SS) MM. Sep 13
d. ?321. The old Roman Martyrology has a confused entry for these two, who were martyred in the reign of Licinius. The first was apparently a Cappodocian from Asia minor martyred at Tomi on the Black Sea, Romania, and the latter was apparently martyred in Galatia, Asia Minor. They seem to be duplicated in **Valerian, Macrinus and Gordian**.

Macull *see* **Maughold**

Madalberta (St) R. Sep 7
d. 706. Daughter of SS Vincent Madelgar and Waldetrude, she was educated by her aunt St Aldegund at her nunnery at Maubeuge in Flanders, France. She became a nun there, and succeeded her sister St Aldetrude as abbess in 697.

Madeleine *see* **Mary-Magdalen**

Madelgisil (Mauguille) (St) R. May 30
d. ?655. An Irish monk and a favourite disciple of St Fursey, he was a monk for several years at St Riquier near Abbeville, France, before becoming a hermit at Monstrelet, where he died.

Maden (Madern, Madron) (St) R. May 17
d. ?545. From Cornwall, England, he became a hermit there and in Brittany, France. The chapel with its holy well at Madron, Cornwall, is on the alleged site of his hermitage and is still a place of pilgrimage.

Madir *see* **Hemiterius**

Madoes (Madianus) (St) R? Jan 31
? The patron of St Madoes near Perth, Scotland, may be identical with St Aidan of Ferns. Another tradition alleges that he was a missionary in Scotland with St Boniface Curitan. It seems impossible to disentangle the facts from the legendary accretions.

Madrun (Materiana) (St) R. Apr 9
C5th. She was a Welsh or Cornish saint to whom some churches in Wales (such as the one at Trawsfynydd) are dedicated, and who is associated with Minster near Camelford in Cornwall, England.

Maedhog (Aedhan, Mogue) (St) R. Apr 11
C6th. He was the abbot-founder of Clonmore in Co. Carlow, Ireland, and was associated with SS Oncho and Finan.

Maedoc (Modoc, Aedan, Edan, Aidus) *see* **Aidan**

Mael (Mahel) (St) R. May 13
C6th. A Breton and a disciple of St Cadfan, he accompanied his master from Brittany, France, to Wales and became a hermit on Bardsey.

Maelmuire (Marianus) O'Gorman (St) R. Jul 3
d. *p*1167. An abbot of Knock in Co. Louth, Ireland, he wrote a list of saints for Ireland in Irish verse.

Maelrhys (St) R. Jan 1
C6th. Probably a Breton, he was a hermit on the island of Bardsey, Wales.

Maelruan (St) R. Jul 7
d. 792. Abbot-founder of the monastery of Tallaght near Dublin, Ireland, he helped to compile the martyrologies of Tallaght and Oengus. Other writings of his are extant.

Maelrubha (St) R. Apr 21
d. ?724. A monk of St Comgall's monastery at Bangor in Co. Down, Ireland, he migrated to Iona, Scotland, and later founded a church at Applecross on the western coast of Ross in the Highlands. His cultus was confirmed in 1898.

Maethlu *see* **Amaethlu**

Mafalda (Bl) R(OCist). May 2
1184–1257. Daughter of King Sancho I of Portugal, when aged twelve she was married to King Henry I of Castile but the marriage was later nullified on account of consanguinity. She then became a nun at Arouca near Oporto in 1216, which nunnery became Cistercian in 1222. Her cultus was confirmed for Portugal in 1792.

Magdalen *see* **Mary-Magdalen**

Magdalveus (Madalveus, Mauvé) (St) B. Oct 5
d. ?776. From Verdun, France, he became the city's bishop in ?736 after having been a monk at St Vannes.

Magenulf *see* **Meinulf**

Magi (SS) Jan 6
C1st. The story in Matthew's gospel (Matt. 2) concerning the visit of some Persian wise men to Christ as a baby in Bethlehem does not specify their number. That they were three is an ancient tradition, probably deriving from the three gifts. The tradition that they were kings is from the C6th, probably from Ps 72:10, and the names Balthasar, Caspar and Melchior are from the C8th. Their alleged shrine is at Cologne, Germany, and they are usually depicted as being of different races and ages so as to represent all of humanity.

Magina (St) *see* **Claudius, Crispin and Comps**

Maginus (Magí) (St) M. Aug 25
d. *c*304. From Tarragona, Spain, he was a missionary in the hills behind that city and was beheaded in the reign of Diocletian.

Maglorius (Maelor, Magloire) (St) B. Oct 24
d. ?575. From Glamorgan, Wales, he was educated under St Illtyd and emigrated to Brittany with St Sampson, his relative. There he became abbot of Lammeur, while Samson became abbot and then bishop of Dol. Maglorius succeeded him as bishop, but later resigned and founded a monastery on Sark in the Channel Islands. There he died.

Magneric of Trier (St) B. Jul 25
d. 596. A Frank, he succeeded St Nicetius as bishop of Trier, Germany, in ?566 and was a friend of St Gregory of Tours.

Magnoaldus *see* **Magnus**

Magnobod (Maimboeuf) (St) B. Oct 16
d. *c*670. A Frankish nobleman, he was elected bishop of Angers, France, and was famous for his miracles.

Magnus (St) M. Jan 1
? He is listed as a martyr in the old Roman Martyrology, but with no details.

Magnus (St) *see* **Aquilinus, Germinus and Comps**

Magnus (St) *see* **Saturninus, Castulus and Comps**

Magnus (St) *see* **Sixtus II, Pope and Comps**

Magnus, Castus and Maximus (SS) MM. Sep 4
? They probably belong with SS **Rufinus, Silvanus and Comps of Ancyra**, and have been separated in error.

Magnus of Anagni (St) M? B? Aug 19
The old Roman Martyrology listed him as a

bishop martyred in the reign of Decius, but he is a mistaken duplication of St Andrew the Tribune. The original entry for the latter was 'Andreas Tribunus Magnus Martyr (the Great Martyr)', but an early scribe inserted a comma after 'Tribunus' and thus created a fictitious entry. The fiction was later padded out with worthless acta.

Magnus of Avignon (St) B. Aug 19
d. ?660. His story is as follows. From Avignon, France, he was governor of that city but his wife died and he followed the example of St Agricola, his son, became a monk at Lérins and was made bishop of Avignon in 656. His existence is doubtful, as he is first mentioned in a document of 1458 and there is no evidence of an early cultus. There was, however, a bishop named Magnus at the council of Chalon-sur-Saône in 630.

Magnus of Eraclea (St) B. Oct 6
d. *c*660. A Venetian, he became bishop of Oderzo near Treviso, Italy, but the Lombards destroyed his city in 638 and he moved the bishopric to the new city of Eraclea, nearer the Adriatic and named after the emperor Heracleus. This in turn is now only a village.

Magnus (Magnoaldus, Maginold, Mang) of Füssen (St) R. Sep 6
d. ?666. Nothing is known for certain about the abbot-founder of Füssen in the Bavarian Alps, Germany, although he has been falsely described as a fellow-missionary with SS Columbanus and Gall.

Magnus of Milan (St) B. Nov 5
d. 525. Not much is known about him, except that he became archbishop of Milan in *c*520.

Magnus of Orkney (St) M. Apr 16
?1076–1116. Son of an earl of the Orkneys, Scotland, when they were part of Norway, he was forced by the king to go raiding but refused to fight and fled to the court of Scotland. There he lived a life of penance, but later returned to share the government of the earldom with Hakon, his cousin. The latter had him murdered. The motive was political, but he was regarded as a martyr and his shrine is in Kirkwall cathedral. His attribute is an axe or club.

Maguil *see* **Madelgisilus**

Maharshapur (St) M. Oct 10
d. 421. A Persian nobleman, after three years' imprisonment in the reign of Shah Varanes V he was thrown into an oubliette and left to die of starvation.

Maidoc (Madoc) (St) B? Feb 28
There are several Welsh and Irish saints with this name, and they are not easy to tell apart. The name itself is a variant of Aidan, especially used for St Aidan of Ferns, and other forms are: Aidnus, Edan, Aldus, Edus, Eda, Maidoc, Maedoc, Modoc, Modog, Moedoc, Moeg, Mogue and Madog. The patron of Llanmadog in Gower, Wales, seems to be a C6th bishop, and has his feast-day on this date.

Maidoc (Mo-Mhaedog) (St) R. Mar 23
C5th. He was abbot of Fiddown in Co. Kilkenny, Ireland.

Maildulf (St) R. May 17
d. 673. An Irish monk who emigrated to England, he founded the abbey of Malmesbury, Wilts, had St Aldhelm among his disciples and died there. The abbey was re-founded after the Viking period.

Maimbod (St) M. R. Jan 23
d. *c*880. An Irish missionary monk, while on his way to Rome he was allegedly killed by robbers near Besançon, France, and is venerated locally.

Mainard (Bl) R(OSB). Dec 10
d. 1096. He was abbot-founder of the Benedictine monastery and congregation of the Holy Cross at Sassovivo near Foligno, Italy.

Mainchin (St) B? R. Jan 2
C7th? The principal patron of the city and diocese of Limerick, Ireland, may have been the first bishop there, or a monastic founder in the vicinity.

Maine (Mewan, Méen) (St) R. Jun 21
d. ?617. He was a Welsh or Cornish disciple of St Samson, whom he accompanied to Brittany, France. There he founded a monastery at the place now called St Méen near Rennes.

Majolus (Maieul) of Cluny (St) R(OSB). May 11
?906–994. The fourth abbot of Cluny was from Avignon, France, and became archdeacon of Mâcon after being educated at Lyons and while still very young. To escape being made bishop of Besançon he became a monk at Cluny, and was shortly afterwards made coadjutor to the blind St Aymard. In 965 he succeeded as abbot, and under him the Cluniac congregation spread

throughout western Europe. He was the friend of emperors Otto I and II, and several times refused the papacy. He died at Souvigny.

Majoricus (St) *see* **Dionysia, Dativa and Comps**

Malachy O'More (Maolmhaodhog ua Morgain) (St) B. Nov 3
1094–1148. From Armagh, Ireland, he was ordained by St Cellach and was successively vicar-general to the latter, abbot of Bangor, bishop of Connor and Down and archbishop of Armagh from 1132. In 1137 he resigned and made a pilgrimage to Rome, visiting St Bernard at Clairvaux. The pope made him apostolic legate for Ireland with powers to correct abuses. He was a great restorer of the Church in Ireland, finished the replacement of the Celtic liturgy by the Roman and founded Mellifont (the first Cistercian abbey in Ireland) in 1142. He died at Clairvaux on his way back from another visit to Rome, allegedly in St Bernard's arms, and was canonized in 1190. The spurious 'prophecies of the popes' attributed to him were first found in Rome four centuries later.

Malachy of Sandomir (Bl) *see* **Sadoc of Sandomir and Comps**

Malard (St) B. Jan 15
d. *p*650. This bishop of Chartres, France, was present at the council of Chalon-sur-Saône in 650.

Malchus (St) *see* **Priscus, Malchus and Alexander**

Malchus of Chalcis (St) R. Oct 21
d. *c*390. A Syrian monk at Chalcis near Antioch, after about twenty years of monastic life he was kidnapped by the Bedouin and sold as a slave. His master gave him another captive, already married, to be his wife but they lived in continence until they managed to escape after seven years. He returned to Chalcis, where St Jerome knew him and wrote his biography.

Malchus of Waterford (St) B. R(OSB)? Apr 10
d. *p*1132. An Irishman, he was educated at Winchester, England, allegedly became a monk there and was consecrated as first bishop of Waterford by St Anselm. He was one of the consecrators of St Malachy O'More. His life has been confused with those of several of his namesake contemporaries.

Malo (Machutis, Maclou) (St) B. Nov 15
d. *c*640. Possibly from Wales, he became a monk under St Brendan and eventually migrated to Brittany, France, with a group of missionaries. He settled near the site of the town of St Malo, of which he is recognized as the first bishop. For a time he was banished and resided at Saintes.

Mamas (Mammas, Mamans) (St) M. Aug 17
d. ?275. A shepherd of Caesarea in Cappodocia, Asia Minor, he was martyred in the reign of Aurelian. His cultus is popular in the East, but his acta are not reliable.

Mamelta (St) M. Oct 17
d. ?344. Her story is that she was a Zoroastrian priestess at Bethfarme in Persia who was converted and baptized, but was recognized as a Christian by her white baptismal garment. A mob stoned her and drowned her in a lake.

Mamertinus (St) R. Mar 30
d. ?462. A pagan converted by St Germanus of Auxerre, France, he became a monk in that city and went on to be abbot.

Mamertus of Vienne (St) B. May 11
d. 475. He was archbishop of Vienne, France, from 461, and introduced the Rogation Days before the Ascension as liturgical acts of supplication in times of great difficulty for his city. These were taken up by the Roman rite, but have now been abolished.

Mamilian (Maximilian) (St) M. Mar 12
? Nothing is known for certain about this Roman martyr.

Mamilian I of Palermo (St) B. Jun 16
d. ?312. He was allegedly a bishop of Palermo, Sicily, who was imprisoned and tortured in the persecution of Diocletian but who escaped, fled to Rome and died at Porto nearby. He may be identical with Mamilian II.

Mamilian II of Palermo (St) B. Sep 15
d. 460. A bishop of Palermo, Sicily, he was allegedly exiled by the Arian king Genseric and settled on the island of Montecristo off Tuscany. There he died.

Mamillus (St) *see* **Cyril, Rogatus and Comps**

Mammea *see* **Mannea**

Manahen (St) May 24
C1st. He is mentioned in the Acts of the

Apostles (13:1) as a courtier of King Herod Antipas and as a prophet. He is alleged to have died at Antioch, Syria.

Manak (St) R. Oct 14
C6th. He was abbot of Holyhead, Wales, with some connection with St Cybi, but apparently died in Cornwall, England. Manaccan near Falmouth seems to be named after him, or may be commemorating a female hermit (the alleged sister of St Levan).

Mancius Araki Ky-uzaburo and Comps (Bl) MM. LL. Jul 8
d. 1626. A Japanese layman, he was seized with eight others for giving shelter to missionaries working in Kyushu and was imprisoned at Omura. There he died of tuberculosis but his body was burned with the other men of the group, including his brother Matthias Araki Hyozaemon and also his cousin Peter Araki Chobyoye as well as John Tanaka and John Naizen. Susanna Chobyoye (Peter's wife), Catharine Tanaka (John Tanaka's wife) and Monica and Louis Naizen (John Naizen's family) were beheaded. *See* **Japan (Martyrs of)**.

Mancius of Évora (St) M. Mar 15
C5th (or 6th?). From Rome, he appears to have been bought as a slave by Jewish traders and taken to Évora, Portugal, where he was tortured and killed by his masters.

Mancius Ichizayemon (Bl) M. T(OSA). Sep 28
d. 1630. A Japanese Augustinian tertiary, he was beheaded at Nagasaki with BB John Chozaburo and Comps. *See* **Japan (Martyrs of)**.

Mancius-of-the-Holy-Cross of Omura (Bl) M. R(OP). Jul 29
d. 1627. An old Japanese catechist, he was burnt alive at Omura and became a Dominican just beforehand. *See* **Louis Bertrán and Comps** and **Japan (Martyrs of)**.

Mancius-of-St-Thomas Shibata (Bl) M. R(OP). Sep 12
d. 1622. A Japanese catechist, he was burnt alive with Bl **Thomas Zumarraga and Comps** (q.v.), and became a Dominican in prison beforehand. *See* **Japan (Martyrs of)**.

Mancus (St) *see* **Winnow, Mancus and Myrbad**

Mandal (St) **Basilides, Tripos and Comps**

Manehild (Ménéhould) (St) R. Oct 14
d. *c*490. She was the youngest of seven sisters, all of whom are honoured as saints in different parts of Champagne, France, and is the patron of the town of Ste Ménéhould.

Manettus (Manetius, Manetto) dell' Antella (St) R(OSM). F. Feb 17
d. 1268. *See* **Servites (Founders of)**. He became provincial of Tuscany and then fourth general of the order. He attended the council of Lyons in 1246, and at the request of St Louis introduced the order into France. He resigned in favour of St Philip Benizi and retired to Mt Senario in the year before he died.

Manez (Mannes, Manes) de Guzmán (Bl) R(OP). Jul 30
d. 1268. An elder brother of St Dominic, he was born at Calaruega in Old Castile, Spain. He joined the original sixteen Dominicans in 1216, was later the prior at Paris and founded a Dominican nunnery at Madrid. His cultus was approved for the Dominicans in 1834.

Manire (St) B. Dec 19
? He was allegedly a missionary bishop in Deeside and in the nearby mountains of north-west Scotland.

Mannea (St) *see* **Marcellinus, Mannea and Comps**

Mannonius (St) *see* **Corfu (Martyrs of)**

Mannus *see* **Magnus**

Mansuetus (St) *see* **Donatian, Praesidius and Comps**

Mansuetus (St) *see* **Papinianus and Mansuetus**

Mansuetus, Severus, Appian, Donatus, Honorius and Five Comps (SS) MM. Dec 30
d. ?483. The old Roman Martyrology lists these as having been martyred at Alexandria, Egypt, during the Monophysite reaction against the council of Chalcedon.

Mansuetus of Milan (St) B. Feb 19
d. *c*690. From Rome, he became archbishop of Milan, Italy, in ?672. He was one of the leaders of the Western campaign against Monothelitism.

Mansuetus (Mansuy) of Toul (St) B. Sep 3
d. *c*350. He allegedly became the first bishop of

Toul, France) in 338, but his extant biography is fictitious.

Manuel *see* **Emmanuel**

Manuel, Sabel and Ismael
(SS) MM. Jun 17
d. 362. Persian noblemen, they were sent by the Shah to Emperor Julian at Chalcedon to negotiate for peace. The tradition is that Julian, finding that they were Christians, had them beheaded and that this was one of the proximate causes of the war that led to the emperor's death in battle.

Mappalicus and Comps
(SS) MM. Apr 17
d. 250. Protomartyrs of the Decian persecution in Roman Africa, they suffered at Carthage and were commended by St Cyprian.

Maprilis (St) *see* **Martial, Saturninus and Comps**

Marana and Cyra (SS) RR. Aug 3
C5th. Two women of Beroea, Syria, they became hermits together and allegedly only spoke on the day of Pentecost. They have no cultus in the East.

Marcella of Rome (St) L. Jan 31
325–410. A Roman noblewoman, she was widowed when young. Under the direction of St Jerome, who was her guest for three years, she then devoted herself to the study of the Bible, to prayer and to works of charity. Her house became a centre of activity for several like-minded ladies of the Roman nobility. She had given away her wealth by the time Alaric the Goth sacked Rome, but the invaders thought that she had hidden it and whipped her. This caused her death shortly afterwards.

Marcella (St) *see* **Plutarch of Alexandria and Comps**

Marcella-of-St-Thomas Navarro (Bl) *see* **Angela-of-St-Joseph Lloret Martí and Comps**

Marcellian (St) *see* **Mark and Marcellian**

Marcellian (St) *see* **Secundian, Marcellian and Verian**

Marcellina (St) R. Jul 17
*c*330–398. She was the elder sister of St Ambrose of Milan and he dedicated several of his writings to her, notably his treatise *On Virginity* Pope Liberius heard her vows as a consecrated virgin at Rome in 353, but she later lived with her brothers at Milan, Italy, where her shrine is.

Marcellina Darowska (Bl) R. F. Jan 5
1827–1911. Born in the Ukraine, she was of the 'kresy' (borderland) Polish gentry. Her father forced her to marry, but she was early widowed and helped found the 'Sisters of the Immaculate Conception' at Jazlowiec (near Lviv, now in the Ukraine) in 1860. She was convinced that a morally healthy society depended on the regeneration of the family, helped by the education of women. In fifty years as superior she opened seven other convents with schools, but her work and her ancestral culture were destroyed by the Second World War and by the Soviets. She was beatified in 1996.

Marcellinus (St) *see* **Argeus, Narcissus and Marcellinus**

Marcellinus (St) *see* **Florentius, Julian and Comps**

Marcellinus, Pope Apr 26
d. 304. Virtually nothing certain is known about his life, most of which was spent in a period when the Church was not being persecuted. He allegedly complied with the order of the emperor Diocletian in 303 to worship pagan gods, together with several prominent members of his clergy, and had his name left out of the list of popes compiled by Pope St Damasus. Later apologists over-compensated and invented the story of his remorse and subsequent martyrdom, for which there is no contemporary evidence. His cultus was suppressed in 1969.

Marcellinus, Claudius, Cyrinus and Antoninus (SS) MM. Oct 25
d. 304. The spurious legend of the martyrdom of Pope St Marcellinus lists these as his fellow martyrs.

Marcellinus (Marcellus), Mannea, John, Serapion, Peter and Comps
(SS) MM. Aug 27
d. ?303. According to their authentic acta, this family comprising a tribune, his wife and three sons were arrested with a bishop, three priests, eight laymen and another woman. They together formed the entire Christian population of a small place now thought to be Oxyrinchus in Egypt, and were taken to Thmuis and beheaded.

Marcellinus and Peter (SS) MM. Jun 2
d. 304. Marcellinus was a priest and Peter probably an exorcist, both of the Roman clergy. Their extant acta are unreliable, but they were certainly greatly venerated by the contemporary Romans since they are commemorated in the Roman canon of the Mass and Emperor Constantine built a basilica (remains of which survive) over their tombs.

Marcellinus, Vincent and Domninus (SS) Apr 20
d. ?374. They were African missionaries who worked in Dauphine, France. St Marcellinus was ordained first bishop of Embrun near Gap by St Eusebius of Vercelli. St Vincent succeeded St Domninus as bishop of Digne, where their shrine is.

Marcellinus of Ancona (St) B. Jan 9
d. ?566. From Ancona, Italy, he became bishop there in *c*550 and is mentioned in the *Dialogues* of St Gregory the Great.

Marcellinus-Joseph-Benedict Champagnat (St) R. F. Jun 6
1789–1840. Born in the Loire valley, France, the son of a miller, while studying in the Lyons seminary (in company with SS John Vianney and Peter Chanel) he was involved in the discussions over the foundation of the Marist Fathers. He was ordained in 1816, and founded the Marist Brothers after giving the last rites to a dying boy who was completely ignorant of Church teaching. He himself became a Marist Father when that institute was approved in 1836. He was canonized in 1999.

Marcellinus (Marchelm, Marculf) of Deventer (St) R. Jul 14
d. ?762. An Anglo-Saxon, he followed St Willibrord to the Netherlands and was a missionary in Overijssel together with St Lebuin. In 738 he accompanied St Boniface to Rome. He died at Oldenzaal, but his shrine was established at Deventer.

Marcellinus of Ravenna (St) B. Oct 5
Late C3rd? Traditionally the second or third bishop of Ravenna, Italy, he allegedly succeeded St Agapitus.

Marcellinus the Tribune (St) M. Apr 6
d. 413. Tribune and secretary of state of Emperor Honorius, he was sent by the latter to Africa to resolve the Donatist schism. He tried to enforce with severity the decisions of a synod at Carthage against the Donatists, but they intrigued against him and managed to have him executed without trial. St Augustine was his friend, and dedicated his work *De Civitate Dei* to him.

Marcellus (St) *see* **Elpidius, Marcellus and Comps**

Marcellus (St) *see* **Eusebius, Marcellus and Comps**

Marcellus *see* **Marcellinus**

Marcellus (St) *see* **Publius, Julian and Comps**

Marcellus (St) *see* **Sabinus, Exuperantius and Comps**.

Marcellus I, Pope (St) Jan 16
d. 309. He was pope for only one year and was apparently exiled by the usurper Maxentius, but there is no proof that he was a martyr. An unreliable legend alleges that he was forced to work in the stables of the public post service. His cultus was confined to local calendars in 1969.

Marcellus and Anastasius (SS) MM. Jun 29
d. 274. Roman missionaries, they were martyred at Argenton near Bourges, France, in the reign of Aurelian. Marcellus was beheaded and Anastasius whipped to death.

Marcellus and Apuleius (SS) MM. Oct 7
? They were martyred at Capua, Italy, but no details are extant and their cultus was confined to local calendars in 1969.

Marcellus, Castus, Emilius and Saturninus (SS) MM. Oct 6
? The shrine of these martyrs, who were possibly Roman Africans, was at Capua, Italy.

Marcellus Akimetes (St) R. Dec 29
d. ?485. From Apamea, Syria, he joined the monks who were called the Akimetes ('non-sleepers') because they recited the divine office in relays non-stop, day and night. He became the third abbot of their chief abbey at Constantinople, and under his rule they grew in numbers and influence. He was present at the council of Chalcedon.

Marcellus of Apamea (St) M. B. Aug 14
d. 389. From Cyprus, where he was governor, he was made bishop of Apamea, Syria, after the

death of his wife in 381. He had to enforce the decree of Emperor Theodosius I prohibiting paganism and was overseeing the burning of the temple at Aulona when he was thrown into the flames by its infuriated congregation.

Marcellus Callo (Bl) M. L. Mar 19
1921–1945. Born in Rennes, France, he joined the 'Young Christian Workers' in 1936 and worked for a printing company. He was a model Christian working man. In 1943 he shared the fate of many in occupied Europe in being seized and deported to Thuringia in Germany as a forced worker for the German war effort. He gave witness to his faith there which led the Nazis to send him to the concentration camp at Mauthausen, where he died. He was beatified as a martyr in 1987.

Marcellus of Die (St) B. Apr 9
d. 474. From Avignon, France, he was educated by his brother St Petronius, bishop of Dié near Valence (not of Saint-Die), and succeeded him as bishop. He had much difficulty with the Arians, and died after a long episcopate.

Marcellus Gaucher Labiche de Reignefort (Bl) *see* **John-Baptist Souzy and Comps**

Marcellus of Lyons (St) M. P. Sep 4
d. ?178. A priest of Lyons, France, he was imprisoned but escaped, was recaptured and then buried up to his waist on the banks of the Saône and left to die. It is alleged that he survived three days.

Marcellus of Nicomedia
(St) M. P. Nov 26
d. 349. A priest of Nicomedia, Asia Minor, during the reign of the emperor Constantius he was seized by Arians and thrown over a precipice.

Marcellus of Paris (St) B. Nov 1
d. *c*430. A bishop of Paris, France, he was buried in the old Christian cemetery outside the walls of the city and the locality is now called St Marceau.

Marcellus Spinola y Mestre
(Bl) B. F. Jan 19
1835–1906. After a childhood spent in various Spanish ports he became a parish priest at Seville in 1866, going on to become a cathedral canon and then auxilliary bishop. He became bishop of Malaga in 1886 and then archbishop of Seville in 1896. He worked to put the Church's social teaching into practice, as had been set out in the encyclical *Rerum Novarum*, and founded the 'Handmaids of the Immaculate Virgin and the Divine Heart'. He was made a cardinal just over a month before he died. He was beatified in 1987.

Marcellus of St Gall (St) R(OSB). Sep 27
d. ?869. A 'Scot' (from Ireland or Scotland), he became a monk at St Gall, Switzerland, and was the tutor of Bl Notker Balbulus.

Marcellus of Tangier (St) M. Oct 30
d. 298. A centurion of the Roman army stationed at Tangier, Roman Africa, he refused to join in the celebration of the emperor's birthday because this involved a pagan sacrifice. He discarded his weapons and insignia, declared himself a Christian and was then tried and executed. His acta are genuine. The notary was St Cassian, who refused to write the official report of the case and who was also martyred in consequence. His alleged relics were enshrined at León, Spain, in the late C15th, and the unreliable Spanish tradition makes him the father of twelve martyrs: Claudius, Lupercius, Victoricus, Facundus, Primitivus, Faustus, Januarius, Martial, Hemeterius, Chelidonius, Servandus and Germanus.

Marcellus of Trier (St) M. B. Sep 4
? This alleged martyr-bishop of Trier in Germany (or of Tongeren in Belgium) was listed in the old Roman Martyrology despite being seemingly a C10th invention.

Marchelm *see* **Marcellinus**

Marcia (St) *see* **Ariston and Comps**

Marcia (St) *see* **Felix, Luciolus and Comps**

Marcia (St) *see* **Zenais, Cyria and Comps**

Marcian (St) *see* **Abundius, Abundantius and Comps**

Marcian (St) *see* **Aquilinus, Geminus and Comps**

Marcian (St) *see* **Fortunatus and Marcian**

Marcian (St) *see* **Julian, Marcian and Comps**

Marcian (St) *see* **Mark, Marcian, and Comps**

Marcian (St) *see* **Martyrius and Marcian**

Marcian (St) *see* **Nicander and Marcian**

Marcian (St*)* *see* **Peter, Marcian and Comps**

Marcian, Nicanor, Apollonius and Comps (SS) MM. Jun 5
d. ?304. They were listed in the old Roman Martyrology as having been martyred in Egypt in the reign of Diocletian, but their acta are worthless and they may be garbled duplicates of **Nicander and Marcian** (q.v.).

Marcian of Auxerre (St) R. Apr 20
d. *c*470. A peasant from Bourges, France, he became a lay brother at the abbey of SS Cosmas and Damian at Auxerre and looked after the cows.

Marcian of Constantinople (St) P. Jan 10
d. ?471. Born in Rome, he was brought up in Constantinople where he was ordained. He was appointed treasurer of the church of Hagia Sofia and as such he arranged for the building of several lesser churches, notably that of the Anastasis. He was wrongly suspected of Novatianism and was persecuted as a result.

Marcian of Cyrrhus (St) R. Nov 2
d. 387. He left the emperor's court at Constantinople and gave up a brilliant military career in order to become a hermit in the desert of Chalcis in Syria. He had several well-known disciples.

Marcian of Iconium (St) M. Jul 11
d. 243. He was a young man martyred at Iconium in Lycaonia, Asia Minor, and his tongue was cut out before his execution in order to stop him praying aloud.

Marcian-Joseph López López (St*)* *see* **Cyril-Bertrand Sanz Tejedor and Comps**

Marcian of Pamplona (St) B. Jun 30
d. ?757. The signature of this bishop of Pamplona, Spain, appears on the decrees of the sixth council of Toledo in 737.

Marcian (Mariano) of Ravenna (St) B. May 22
d. ?127. He allegedly became the fourth bishop of Ravenna, Italy) in 112.

Marcian of Saignon (St) R. Aug 25
d. 485. From the Vaucluse, France, he was the abbot-founder of St Eusebius's Abbey at Apt.

Marcian of Syracuse (St) M. B. Jun 14
d. ?255. According to the Sicilian legend, 'the first bishop of the West' was sent to Syracuse by St Peter himself and was been thrown from a tower by a Jewish mob. It is more likely that he was a bishop of the C3rd.

Marcian of Tortona (St) B. Mar 6
d. ?120. The tradition is that he was a disciple of St Barnabas and was first bishop of Tortona in Piedmont, Italy, for forty-five years before being martyred in the reign of Hadrian. He is probably identical with St Marcian of Ravenna.

Marciana (St*)* *see* **Susanna, Marciana and Comps**

Marciana of Caesarea (St) V. Jan 9
d. ?303. She was a consecrated virgin of Mauritania (now Morocco), was accused of having shattered a statue of the goddess Diana and was thrown to the wild animals in the amphitheatre. There she was gored to death by a bull. Her relics were transferred to Toledo, Spain, where she has been falsely claimed as a native.

Marciana of Toledo (St) V. Jul 12
d. ?303. The old Roman Martyrology listed her as having been martyred at Toledo, Spain, but she is identical with St Marciana of Caesarea.

Marcionilla (St*)* *see* **Julian, Basilissa and Comps**

Marcius (Mark, Martin) of Montecassino (St) R(OSB)? Oct 24
d. ?679. This hermit at Montecassino, Italy, was mentioned by St Gregory the Great in his dialogue concerning St Benedict. The Cassinese tradition is that he became a monk at the abbey and then a hermit again on Monte Massico near Mondragone, where he died.

Marcolino Ammani (Bl) R(OP). Jan 24
1317–1397. From Forli, Italy, he became a Dominican there when very young and was a model religious, but it was only after his death that his brethren realized how heroic was his sanctity. His cultus was confirmed for Forli in 1750.

Marculf (St) R. May 1
d. 558. From Bayeux, France, he was the abbot-founder of a monastery of hermit-monks on the Egyptian model at Nanteuil. His relics were enshrined at Corbigny near Nevers in 898, and after the French kings were crowned at Rheims they used to go there, touch the relics and then themselves allegedly be able to heal by touch those suffering from scrofula ('the king's evil'). The shrine was predictably destroyed in the French Revolution.

Mard *see* **Medard**

Mardarius (St) *see* **Eustratius and Comps**

Mardonius (St) *see* **Migdonius and Mardonius**

Mardonius, Musonius, Eugene and Metellus (SS) MM. Jan 24
? They were burnt at the stake somewhere in Asia Minor.

Mareas (St) M. B. Apr 22
d. 342. A Persian bishop, he was martyred in the reign of Shah Shapur II together with twenty-one other bishops, nearly two hundred and fifty priests, many monks and nuns and a large number of lay people. The church of Persia was brought to the verge of extinction by this persecution, which was motivated by the suspicion that Christians were fifth-columnists loyal to the Roman Empire.

Margaret-Mary Alacoque (St) R. Oct 16
1647–1690. From L'Hautecourt in Burgundy, France, she became a Visitation nun at Paray-le-Monial in 1671 and then had a series of visions of Christ which led her to start work at the spreading of public and liturgical devotion to the Sacred Heart in 1675. This caused violent opposition from her own community and from outside, especially from Jansenist circles, but her humility prevailed over this and over the serious personality disorders witnessed to by her autobiography. The modern popularity of the devotion to the Sacred Heart derives from her. She was canonized in 1920, and has a flaming heart as her attribute.

Margaret-of-St-Sophia d'Albarède (Bl) *see* **Orange (Martyrs of)**

Margaret (Marina) of Antioch Jul 20
d. ?303. She is allegedly (and probably accurately) described as a maiden of Antioch in Pisidia, Asia Minor, martyred in the reign of Diocletian. Her acta are worthless, being exaggerated legend, but she is one of the most popular of virgin-martyrs and her cultus is very ancient. In the East she is known as Pelagia. Part of her legend involves her being swallowed and regurgitated by a dragon before being beheaded, and she is often depicted with such. Her cultus was suppressed in 1969.

Margaret the Barefooted (St) L. Aug 27
d. 1395. A peasant girl of Sanseverino near Ancona, Italy, when aged fifteen she married a fairly prosperous man of that town. She had great sympathy for the poor, and in solidarity with them always went barefoot whatever the weather. Her husband regarded this as an insult to his dignity, and treated her with contempt and cruelty for years.

Margaret di Bartolomeo of Cortona (St) T(OFM). Feb 22
1247–1297. From Laviano in Tuscany, Italy, a farmer's daughter, she was the mistress of a young nobleman for nine years but he was murdered and she repented after seeing his decomposing corpse. After publicly confessing her sins in the church of Cortona she placed herself under the direction of the Franciscans there and became a penitential tertiary, founding a hospital where she (and a community of other tertiaries that she had founded) nursed. She was involved in the city's political affairs and was much slandered, but was nevertheless in receipt of supernatural charismata. She was canonized in 1728.

Margaret Bays (Bl) L. Jun 26
1815–1879. Born at Siviriez in Fribourg, Switzerland, she lived there all her life as a dressmaker, being involved in the social works of mercy and in evangelization through the media. She was miraculously cured of intestinal cancer at the moment that the dogma of the Immaculate Conception was pronounced in 1854, and thereupon received the stigmata and a mystical experience of the Passion every Friday. Being centred on God made her profoundly humble, however, and she was beatified in 1995.

Margaret Bermingham (Bl) M. L. Jun 20
d. 1584. An Irish widow, she was betrayed by her son and spent three years in prison before dying of hardship. She was beatified in 1992. *See* **Ireland (Martyrs of)**.

Margaret-of-St-Augustine Bonnet (Bl) *see* **Orange (Martyrs of)**

Margaret Bourgeoys (St) R. F. Jan 19
1620–1700. From Troyes, France, she went to Canada (then a French colony) as tutor to the children of the French garrison of Montreal. In 1688 she founded the congregation of the 'Sisters of Notre Dame de Montreal' in order to teach in the colony, for which work she obtained royal approval. Her congregation subsequently spread to the United States, receiving papal approval in 1889. She was canonized in 1982.

Margaret of Città-di-Castello
(Bl) T(OP). Apr 13
1287–1320. Born to a noble family at Méldola near Forli, Italy, she was blind and deformed and her shamed parents kept her locked up until she was aged twenty. Then they took her to the shrine at Città-di-Castello hoping for a cure, and abandoned her there when this was not forthcoming. She was rescued and sheltered by several families in the city, being usually occupied in looking after children, and became a Dominican tertiary. She is the earliest person formally beatified (in 1609) who has not yet been canonized.

Margaret Clitherow (St) M. L. Mar 25
1556–1586. Born in York, she became a Catholic shortly after she married and was imprisoned for two years as a consequence. On her release she began to shelter priests in her house. This caused her to be arrested again and put on trial, but she refused to plead in order to protect those she had helped. The legal penalty specified for this was to be laid down on the ground and pressed with heavy weights, which penalty was imposed on her at York. She died as a result. She was canonized in 1970, and is depicted as an Elizabethan housewife kneeling or standing on the heavy door on which the weights had been piled. *See* **England (Martyrs of)**.

Margaret Colonna (Bl) R(OFM). Dec 30
d. 1284. Daughter of Prince Odo Colonna of Palestrina, Italy, she turned the family castle on a mountainside above the city into a Poor Clare nunnery which she joined, and for which her brother, Cardinal James Colonna, wrote a mitigated version of the Franciscan rule. Her cultus was confirmed locally for Rome in 1847.

Margaret Ebner (Bl) R(OP).
1291–1351. Born at Donauwörth in Bavaria, Germany, she became a Dominican nun and died at Medingen. Her cultus was confirmed for Augsburg in 1979.

Margaret of England
(Bl) R(OCist). Feb 3
d. 1192. She was born in Hungary but her mother was probably English and related to St Thomas of Canterbury. After her mother had died in the Holy Land she made a pilgrimage to our Lady of Montserrat near Barcelona and then joined the Cistercian nuns at Sauve-Benite near Le Puy, France.

Margaret of Hungary (St) (OP). Jan 18
1252–1270. Daughter of Bela IV, king of Hungary, she founded a Dominican nunnery on an island in the Danube near Budapest and herself joined it. Her life there was famously penitential and she was canonized in 1943.

St Margaret of England, Feb 3

Margaret of Lorraine
(Bl) R(OFM). Nov 6
1463–1521. A daughter of a duke of Lorraine, she married the duke of Alençon, France, in 1488 and had three children, but he died in 1492. After she had brought up her children she founded a Poor Clare nunnery at Argentan and became a nun there herself in 1519. Her cultus was confirmed for Sées in 1921.

Margaret of Louvain (Bl) V. Sep 2
1207–1225. Her nickname in Belgium is 'the Humble'. According to the unreliable account of the Cistercian Caesarius of Heisterbach, she was from Louvain and was working as a maidservant at an inn there which was raided by robbers. They murdered her employers, abducted her and then killed her when she refused to marry one of them on account of her wanting to become a Cistercian nun. Her cultus is unconfirmed.

Margaret Pole (Bl) M. L. May 28
1471–1541. She was a Plantagenet, a niece of Edward IV and Richard III, and married Sir Reginald Pole. They had five children before she was widowed. Then she was created Countess of Salisbury in her own right and appointed governess to Princess Mary, daughter of King Henry VIII. When her son Cardinal Pole opposed the royal supremacy in spiritual matters and refused to return to England, Henry revenged himself on her, holding her in the Tower of London for two years. Finally she was condemned for high treason by 'Bill of Attainder', beheaded on Tower Hill and beatified in 1886. *See* **England (Martyrs of)**.

Margaret and Alice Rich
(SS) RR(OSB). Aug 24
d. 1257 and 1270. Sisters of St Edmund of Canterbury, as teenagers they were placed by him in the Benedictine nunnery at Catesby, Northants, England, after the prioress had a vision instructing her to accept them without a dowry. Margaret later became prioress, but the tradition that Alice succeeded her is based upon a chronicler's error. The nunnery became a major centre of devotion to St Edmund. Their cultus has not been confirmed.

Margaret Rivière and Margaret Robin
(BB) *see* **William Repin and Comps**

Margaret of Savoy (Bl) T(OP). Nov 23
d. 1464. A daughter of Duke Amadeus II of Savoy, she was born at Pinerolo near Turin, Italy, and married the marquis of Montferrat in 1403. In 1418 she was widowed and, influenced by St Vincent Ferrer, became a Dominican tertiary. She founded a nunnery at Alba in Liguria in 1426 and became first prioress there. Her cultus was confirmed for Alba and Savoy in 1669.

Margaret of Scotland (St) L. Nov 16
1046–1093. Her father was a son of King Edmund Ironside of England and her mother was a Hungarian princess reputed to be related to St Stephen of Hungary. She was born in Hungary but grew up in the court of St Edward the Confessor. At the Norman conquest she tried to flee back to Hungary but her ship was wrecked off Scotland and she became the queen-consort of King Malcolm III of Scotland instead in 1070. The eldest son of her large family became King David I, one of Scotland's greatest kings. She was pious, charitable and just and, among other good works, founded the great Benedictine abbey of Dunfermline as a royal mausoleum. She was canonized in 1251.

Margaret Ward (St) M. L. Aug 30
d. 1588. A lay woman from Congleton in Cheshire, she was in domestic service with a recusant family in London. She helped to arrange the escape of a priest from the Bridewell prison, but a rope used was traced to her and she was severely tortured before being hanged at Tyburn. She was canonized in 1970. *See* **England (Martyrs of)**.

Margaritus Flores García (St) *see* **Mexico (Martyrs of)**

Mari (St) *see* **Addai and Mari**

Maria *see* **Mary**

Mariana *see* **Mary-Anne**

Marianus (St) *see* **Diodore, Marianus, and Comps**

Marianus *see* **Marcian of Auxerre**

Marianus (St) *see* **Victor, Alexander and Marianus**

Marianus, James and Comps
(SS) MM. Apr 30
d. 259. They were martyred at Lambesa in Numidia (Roman Africa, now Algeria). Marianus was a reader and James a deacon, and their acta are authentic.

Marianus of Entreaigues
(St) R. Aug 19
d. ?515. A biography of this hermit in the forest of Entreaigues near Evaux-les-Bains, France, was written by St Gregory of Tours.

Marianus-of-Jesus Euse
Hoyos (Bl) P. Jul 13
1845–1926. From a peasant family of Yarumal in Colombia, he was ordained at Medellin in 1872 and became parish priest of Angostura in 1878. He proved an exemplary pastor, his

ministry being based on continuous prayer and asceticism. He was beatified in 2000.

Marianus of Roccacasale
(Bl) R(OFM). (May 30)
1778–1866. From Roccacasale near L'Aquila, Italy, he was a shepherd before becoming a Franciscan at Arischia for twelve years from 1802. Then he transferred to Bellegra and was the receptionist there for the rest of his life, manifesting a special love for poor people. He was beatified in 1999.

Marianus Scotus (Moelbrigte)
(Bl) R(OSB). Dec 22
d. 1086. From Ireland, he became a monk, migrated to Cologne, Germany, in 1056, became a hermit at Fulda and finally went to Mainz in 1069. He wrote a *Chronicle of the World*. His real name meant 'servant of Brigid'.

Marianus Scotus (Muirdach MacRobartaigh) (Bl) R(OSB). Feb 9
d. 1088. From Donegal, Ireland, he went on pilgrimage to Rome but was side-tracked and became a monk at Michelsberg near Bamberg, Bavaria, in 1067. He transferred to Regensburg and became abbot-founder of the abbey of St Peter there in 1078, thus originating the congregation of 'Scottish' monasteries in south Germany. His hobby was copying manuscripts.

Marina
This is the Latin form of the Greek name Pelagia, a fact which has caused a few duplicates in extant martyrologies.

Marina (St) V? Jun 18
? In the ancient martyrologies she is listed also as Mary, Marina or even Marinus (which would make her a male). She is moreover listed simply as a consecrated virgin, not as a martyr. She has been identified with St Margaret or with St Pelagia the Penitent, and her legend served as a model for those of SS Euphrosyne, Theodora and others. The old Roman Martyrology listed her as a martyr at Alexandria, Egypt.

Marina of Omura (St) M. T(OP). Sep 28
d 1634. A Japanese Dominican tertiary, she was burnt alive at Nagasaki and was canonized in 1987. *See* **Japan (Martyrs of)**.

Marina of Orense (St) V. Jul 18
? Her relics are at Orense in Galicia, Spain, but nothing is known about her. Cardinal Baronius added her to the old Roman Martyrology.

Marinus (St) R. Sep 4
C4th? According to the unreliable tradition he was a stonemason from an island off the coast of Dalmatia, Croatia, who was ordained deacon by St Gaudentius of Rimini and who died as a hermit on the site of the capital of the tiny Republic of San Marino, which is named after him.

Marinus *see* **Amarinus**

Marinus (St*) see* **Januarius, Marinus and Comps**

Marinus and Asterius (SS) MM. Mar 3
d. 262. Marinus was a Roman soldier stationed at Caesarea in the Holy Land who was about to be promoted to the rank of centurion, but he was denounced as a Christian by a jealous rival and immediately martyred. Asterius (or Astyrius) was a senator who buried the body. It is uncertain as to whether he was also martyred.

Marinus, Theodotus and Sedopha (SS) MM. Jul 5
? They were martyred at Tomi on the Black Sea coast of Romania.

Marinus, Vimius and Zimius
(SS) RR(OSB). Jun 12
d. *p*1000. The 'Three Holy Exiles' were Benedictine monks of the 'Scots' (i.e. Irish) abbey of St James at Regensburg, Bavaria, who became hermits at Griesstetten in *c*1000.

Marinus of Anazarbus (St) M. Aug 8
d. ?305. An old man, he was martyred at Anazarbus in Cilicia, Asia Minor, in the reign of Diocletian.

Marinus of Besalú (St)
B. R(OSB). Aug 19
d. *c*800. He was a Benedictine abbot-bishop at Besalú near Gerona, Spain.

Marinus of Cava (Bl) R(OSB). Dec 15
d. 1170. A Benedictine monk of La Cava near Salerno, Italy, he became abbot there in 1146. He was a friend both of several popes and of the kings of Sicily, and he acted as mediator between pope and king in 1156. His cultus was confirmed for La Cava in 1928.

Marinus of Chandor
(St) M. R(OSB). Nov 24
d. 731. An Italian, he migrated to the Maurienne valley in Savoy, France, and became a hermit near the monastery of Chandor. He was killed in a Muslim raid.

Marinus of Rome (St) M? Dec 26
d. 283. His legend describes him as the son of a Roman senator, beheaded under Numerian after having been miraculously delivered from various tortures and other means of death. His acta are romantic fiction, and his existence is questionable as there was no persecution in the period concerned.

Marius *see* **Maurus**

Marius (Maris), Martha, Audifax and Abachum *Jan 19*
d. ?270. They were allegedly a Persian nobleman, his wife and their two sons. Travelling to Rome on pilgrimage, when they got there they started to bury the bodies of those who were being martyred in the persecution of Claudius II. They were seized, the three men were beheaded and St Martha was drowned. This is dubious legend, and all that is known of them are their names and place of burial (the cemetery 'Ad Nymphas' in Rome). Their cultus was suppressed in 1969.

Marius-Francis Mouffle (Bl) *see* **September (Martyrs of)**

Mark (St) *see* **Faustinus, Lucius and Comps**

Mark *see* **John Mark**

Mark *see* **Marcius**

Mark (St) *see* **Priscus II of Capua and Comps**

Mark (St) *see* **Quintus, Quintilla and Comps**

Mark (St) *see* **Robustian and Mark**

Mark (St) *see* **Rufinus, Mark and Comps**

Mark (St) *see* **Theodosius, Lucius and Comps**

Mark (St) *see* **Theusetas, Horres and Comps**

Mark, Alphius, Alexander and Comps (SS) MM. Sep 28
d. ?303. According to the old Roman Martyrology, Mark was a shepherd of Antioch in Pisidia, Asia Minor, who converted Alphius, Alexander and Zosimus his brothers, also Nicon, Neon, Heliodorus, and thirty soldiers 'in various places', implying that several groups of martyrs were conflated in previous listings.

Mark and Marcellian (SS) MM. Jun 18
d. *c*290. The legend concerning these Roman martyrs describes them as twins, both deacons, who were martyred in the reign of Maximian Herculeus. Their underground basilica was rediscovered in 1902. Their cultus was confined to local calendars in 1969.

Mark, Marcian and Comps (SS) MM. Oct 4
d. ?304. The old Roman Martyrology has a confused entry for these Egyptian martyrs, describing them as two brothers and their companions as 'innumerable' and 'of all ages and both sexes'. The brothers seem to be a duplication of the second-named in **Nicander and Marcian** (q.v.), and the companions as the Egyptian martyrs of the persecution ordered by Diocletian and mentioned by Eusebius.

Mark, Mucian, Paul and Comp. (SS) MM. Jul 3
? They are listed in the old Roman Martyrology as two martyrs who were beheaded with two onlookers who were encouraging them, one an unnamed little boy and the other called Paul. The place and date is unknown.

Mark, Stephen and Melchior (SS) MM. Nov 22
d. ?305. They were martyred at Antioch in Pisidia, Asia Minor, in the reign of Galerius.

Mark and Timothy (SS) MM. Mar 24
d. *c*150. These Roman martyrs are mentioned by Pope St Pius I in a letter to a bishop of Vienne, but not much is known about them. They are patrons of Orte in Tuscany, Italy.

Mark I, Pope (St) Oct 7
d. 336. A Roman, he died in the year that he was elected pope. His cultus was confined to local calendars in 1969.

Mark of Arethusa (St) B. Mar 29
d. ?362. Bishop of Arethusa in Lebanon, he attended the synod of Sirmium in 351 and drew up a creed for which he was unjustly accused of Arianism by Baronius, who excluded his name from the old Roman Martyrology. He has since been vindicated by the Bollandists. He died shortly after he destroyed a pagan temple in his city, which action led to its congregation giving him a thorough beating.

Mark Barkworth (alias Lambert) (Bl) M. R(OSB). Feb 27
d. 1601. From Lincolnshire, he was educated at

Oxford before his conversion and then studied for the priesthood at Rome and Valladolid, Spain, in order to go on the English mission. While at Valladolid he became a Benedictine monk at the abbey of Hirache near Estella in Spanish Navarre. He was executed at Tyburn, London. *See* **England (Martyrs of)**.

Mark Caldeira (Bl*) see* **Ignatius de Azevedo and Comps**

Mark Criado (Bl) M. R. Sep 25
1522–1569. From Andújar near Cordoba, Spain, he became a Trinitarian in 1536 but was tortured and killed at Almería by a group of Muslims. His cultus was approved for Guadix and the Trinitarians in 1899.

Mark the Evangelist (St) Apr 25
d. ?75. He is probably the young man who ran away when Christ was arrested (Mk 14:51-2), and the 'John whose other name was Mark' of Acts 12:25. He accompanied SS Paul and Barnabas on their first missionary journey but turned back after Cyprus. By Roman tradition (possibly derived from the reference to 'my son Mark' in 1 Pet 5:13) he was St Peter's disciple and interpreter at Rome and wrote his gospel as a summary of the apostle's preaching. The Egyptian tradition is that he founded the church at Alexandria and was martyred there, but there is no historical evidence for this. His alleged relics were taken from Alexandria to Venice in the C9th and are in the cathedral there. His attribute is a winged lion.

Mark Fantucci (Bl) R(OFM). Apr 10
1405–1479. From Bologna, Italy, he was a law student before becoming a Franciscan Observant in 1430. He went on to become vicar-general and preached throughout Italy and the Croatian coast, also visiting the friars in Austria, Poland, Russia and the Middle East. He died at Piacenza and his cultus was approved for the Friars Minor in 1868.

Mark of Galilee (St) M. B. Apr 28
d. ?92. Allegedly a Galilean by descent and the first bishop of Atina in Lazio, Italy, he was apparently a missionary in the Abruzzi and was martyred in his city.

Mark of Jerusalem (St) M? B. Oct 22
d. ?156. He was the first bishop of Jerusalem not to be of Jewish extraction, and was allegedly bishop for twenty years before being martyred.

Mark Ji (Tianxiang) (St) M. L. Jul 7
1834–1900. From Yanzhuangtou in Hebei, China, he was the leader of the Catholics in his village and worked as a doctor. However, he became addicted to opium and was excommunicated as a result. The local magistrate was sympathetic to the Boxers and allowed them to behead eleven of St Mark's family before his eyes. He was offered his life in exchange for his faith and was beheaded when he refused. *See* **China (Martyrs of)**.

Mark Körösy of Košice (St*) see* **Košice (Martyrs of)**

Mark dei Marconi (Bl) R. Feb 24
1480–1510. From a poor family at Milliarino near Mantua, Italy, he joined the Hieronymite monastery of Bl Peter of Pisa at Mantua. His order is now extinct. His cultus was approved for Mantua in 1906.

Mark of Montegallo (Bl) R(OFM). Mar 20
1426–1497. From Montegallo near Ascoli Piceno, Italy, he was a doctor of medicine and happily married but he and his wife parted by mutual consent to become Franciscans. Ordained at Fabriano, he became a famous home missionary in Italy and established a chain of charitable pawnshops for the poor, known in Italy as 'Monti di Pieta'. His cultus was confirmed for Vicenza in 1839.

Mark Royer (Bl*) see* **September (Martyrs of)**

Mark of Sandomir (Bl*) see* **Sadoc of Sandomir and Comps**

Mark Scalabrini of Modena
(Bl) R(OP). Sep 23
d. 1498. From Modena, Italy, he became a Dominican and was a very successful preacher in north and central Italy. He died at his reform friary at Pesaro and had his cultus confirmed for there and for the Dominicans in 1857.

Mark Shinyemon (Bl) M. L. Aug 19
d. 1622. A Japanese merchant, he was with Bl Louis Flores and Comps. *See* **Japan (Martyrs of)**.

Mark Tyeng and Alexis Wu
(SS) MM LL. Mar 11
d. 1866. Mark was the royal master of games in Korea before his conversion and execution as a catechist when aged seventy. He was accompanied by Alexis, who was a convert aged nineteen whose parents had tried to make him abandon his faith by force. They were canonized in 1984.

Marmaduke Bowes (Bl) M. L. Nov 27
d. 1585. A farmer at Ingram Grange at Welbury, Yorks, he had sheltered Bl Hugh Taylor and had gone to York to help him after he had heard of his arrest. He was seized and executed without proper trial, and was beatified in 1987. *See* **England (Martyrs of)**.

Marnock (Marnanus, Marnan, Marnoc) (St) B. R. Mar 1
d. ?625. An Irish monk under St Columba at Iona, Scotland, he became a missionary bishop, died in Annandale and was venerated in the Scottish border regions. Kilmarnock in Ayrshire is named after him.

Maro (St) R. Feb 14
d. ?435. A Syrian hermit, he lived on the bank of the Orontes river between Emesa (Homs) and Apamea and was admired by St John Chrysostom and by Theodoret of Cyrrhus. The monastery of Beit-Marun was built around his shrine and became the focus of a Monothelite sect in the C7th. This fled to Lebanon to escape persecution, and later became the Catholics of the Maronite rite.

Maro, Eutyches and Victorinus (SS) MM. Apr 15
d. ?99. According to the unreliable legend of SS Nereus and Achilleus, they were of the household of St Flavia Domitilla and went with her into exile. Then they returned to Rome and were martyred in the reign of Trajan. The old Roman Martyrology lists Victorinus again on Sep 5 as a bishop, but it is not clear why.

Marolus (St) B. Apr 23
d. 423. From Syria, he became bishop of Milan, Italy, in 408. The Christian poet Ennodius wrote a poem in his honour.

Marotas (St) *see* **Zanitas and Comps**

Maroveus (St) R. Oct 22
d. *c*650. A monk of Bobbio in Lombardy, Italy, he became abbot-founder of the monastery of Precipiano near Tortona.

Marquard (St) M. B. R(OSB). Feb 2
d. 880. A monk at Corvey near Paderborn, Germany, he became bishop of Hildesheim in 874 and was killed with the **Ebstorf martyrs** (q.v.).

Martha (St) L. Jul 29
d. ?80. Sister of St Lazarus and of St Mary of Bethany (often identified in the West with St Mary Magdalen), she was Christ's hostess in their house at Bethany (Lk 10:38; Jn 11:2) and was 'anxious and troubled about many things'. Hence she is the patron of housewives, and is depicted with an attribute of housework such as a distaff or a bunch of keys. The legend of her subsequent journey to the south of France is worthless.

St Martha, Jul 29

Martha (St) *see* **Marius, Martha and Comps**

Martha, Saula and Comps (SS) VV. Oct 20
? The old Roman Martyrology listed them as having been martyred at Cologne, Germany, but they seem to be part of the worthless legend of St Ursula and Comps.

Martha of Astorga (St) V. Feb 23
d. 251. She was beheaded in the reign of Decius at Astorga, Spain, and is the patron of that city.

Martha-of-the-Good-Angel Cluse (Bl) *see* **Orange (Martyrs of)**

Martha Kim (St) *see* **Korea (Martyrs of)**

Martha Le Bouteiller (Bl) R. Mar 18
1806–1883. From near Coutances, France, in 1841 she joined the 'Sisters of Mercy of the Christian Schools' at Saint-Sauveur-le-Vicomte,

being received by St Mary-Magdalen Postel and having Bl Placida Viel as novice mistress. She spent forty years there as cook, gardener and cellarer, doing the domestic work and receiving guests with joy. Extremely charitable, she lived a fervent prayer life centred on the Eucharist and Our Lady. She was beatified in 1990.

Martha Poulin de la Forestrie (Bl) *see* **William Repin and Comps**

Martha Wang (Luomande)
(St) M. L. Jul 29
1802–1861. From Zunyi in Guizhou, China, she was a widow running an inn at Qingyian before her conversion. She was appointed chef at the new seminary at Yaojiaguan in 1857 and took letters from the imprisoned seminarians SS Joseph Zhang (Wenlan) and Paul Chen (Changpin) to their bishop. She was arrested and beheaded with them and St John-Baptist Luo (Tingying). *See* **China (Martyrs of)**.

Martia (St) *see* **Rufinus and Martia**

Martial (St) *see* **Marcellus of Tangier**

Martial (St) *see* **Seven Brothers**

Martial (St) *see* **Zaragoza (Eighteen Martyrs of)**

Martial, Laurence and Comps (SS) MM. Sep 28
? They are listed as twenty-two Roman African martyrs of Numidia, Algeria.

Martial, Saturninus, Epictetus, Maprilis, Felix and Comps
(SS) MM. Aug 22
d. ?300. They are mentioned in the unreliable acta of St Aurea of Ostia, and are otherwise unknown.

Martial of Limoges and Comps (SS) Jun 30
d. ?250. He was the alleged first bishop of Limoges, France, and apostle of the Limousin (where his veneration is popular) and (according to St Gregory of Tours) was one of seven missionary bishops sent from Rome to Gaul. His extant biography is a worthless medieval forgery. Alpinian and Austriclinian were his assistant priests.

Martin *see* **Marcius**

Martin (St) *see* **Willigod and Martin**

Martin I, Pope (St) M. Apr 13
d. 655. From Todi in Umbria, Italy, he was elected pope in 649. At once he condemned the Monothelite doctrine being promulgated by the reigning emperor Constans II, and was deported as a result to the Aegean island of Naxos in 653. The following year he was tried and condemned to death at Constantinople, but was exiled to the Crimea instead. There he died of starvation some months after his successor at Rome had been elected as pope.

St Martin, Apr 13

Martin of Arades (St) R. Nov 26
d. 726. A monk of Corbie in Picardy, France, he was chaplain to Charles Martel, the mayor (comptroller) of the Merovingian palace.

Martin of Braga (St) B. Mar 20
520–580. From Pannonia (now Hungary), he became a monk in the Holy Land and somehow ended up in north-west Spain as a missionary to the barbarian Suevi, whom he helped to convert from Arianism in 560. He was bishop first of Mondoñedo and then of Braga in Portugal, and introduced monasticism in the area. Several of his writings are still extant, and he seems to be responsible for the days of the week in modern Portuguese being numbered instead of having pagan names.

Martin of Camaldoli (Bl)
R(OSB Cam). Sep 13
d. 1259. He became abbot of Camaldoli, Italy, in 1248 and general of the Camaldolese congregation of monk-hermits, for which he wrote new constitutions.

Martin Cid (St) R(OCist). Oct 8
d. 1152. From Zamora, Spain, he became the abbot-founder of the Cistercian abbey of Valparaiso and was supplied with a community of monks from Clairvaux by St Bernard. His veneration is popular in Zamora.

Martin Gómez (Bl) M. T(OFM). Aug 16
d. 1627. He was a Japanese of Portuguese descent, beheaded at Nagasaki with BB Francis-of-St-Mary of Mancha and Comps. *See* **Japan (Martyrs of)**.

Martin de Hinojosa (St)
B. R(OCist). Sep 3
d. 1213. A Castilian nobleman, he became a Cistercian and was the abbot-founder of Huerta near Soria, Spain, in 1164. In 1185 he became bishop of Sigüenza but resigned in 1192 and went back to being a monk.

Martin-Luke Huin (St*) see* **Anthony Daveluy and Comps**

Martin of León (St) R(CR). Jan 12
d. 1203. From León, Spain, he became an Augustinian canon regular at the monastery of St Marcellus there before it was suppressed, and then at that of St Isidore. He was a prolific ascetical writer.

Martin Loublier (Bl*) see* **September (Martyrs of)**

Martin-of-the-Ascension Loynaz (St) M. R(OFM). Feb 6
d. 1597. From near Pamplona in Navarre, Spain, he became a Franciscan in 1586 and was a missionary in Mexico, at Manila and finally in Japan. He was crucified at Nagasaki with SS Paul Miki and Comps. *See* **Japan (Martyrs of)**.

Martin-of-St-Nicholas Lumberes Peralta and Melchior-of-St-Augustine Sánchez Pérez
(BB) MM. RR(OSA). Dec 11
d. 1632. Martin was born in 1599 at Zaragoza, Spain, and joined the Augustinian Recollects in 1619. Melchior was born in Granada, Spain, in 1598 and became a Recollect in 1617. They were missionaries in Mexico and at Manila in the Philippines and travelled together to Nagasaki, Japan, in September 1632. Arrested two months later, they were burned alive in public and their ashes were thrown into the sea. They were beatified in 1989. *See* **Japan (Martyrs of)**.

Martin Manuel (St) M. P. Jan 31
d. 1156. From near Coïmbra, Portugal, he became arch-priest of the church of Soure near that city but was kidnapped by the Muslims and died of ill-treatment in prison at Cordoba.

Martin Martínez Pascual (Bl*) see* **Peter Ruiz de los Paños y Angel and Comps**

Martin de Porres (St) R(OP). Nov 3
1569–1639. Born at Lima, Peru, his parents were a Spanish knight of Alcantara and a Negro or native American woman from Panama. He became a barber and studied surgery before becoming a Dominican lay brother at Lima. There he nursed the sick and soon became a friend of stray animals, maltreated slaves and the destitute and marginalized people of what was then one of the richest cities in the world. When he was dying the Spanish viceroy came to kneel by his bed and ask for his blessing. He was canonized in 1962.

Martin of Saujon (St) R. Dec 7
d. *c*400. He was with St Martin of Tours at Marmoutier before becoming the abbot-founder of Saujon near Saintes, France.

Martin Tho and Martin (Ta Duc) Tinh (SS) MM. Nov 8
d. 1840. The former was a tax-collector and the latter was an octogenarian priest, and were beheaded with SS Joseph (Nguyen Dinh) Nghi and Comps. *See* **Vietnam (Martyrs of)**.

Martin of Tongeren (St) B. Jun 21
d. ?350. He is alleged to have been an early missionary bishop of Tongeren, Belgium, but was possibly bishop of Trier, Germany, instead.

Martin of Tours (St) B. Nov 11
?316–397. From what is now Szombathely in Hungary, he was the son of a pagan Roman officer and was educated at Pavia before joining the imperial cavalry himself at the age of fifteen. He was baptized five years later (according to legend, this was the result of his sharing his cloak with a poor beggar and a subsequent vision of Christ as the same beggar). Leaving the army, he became a disciple of St Hilary of Poitiers and later founded a community of monk-hermits at Ligugé, allegedly the first monastery in Gaul. In 372 he reluctantly became bishop of Tours and founded another monastery near that city at Marmoutier as a base for himself. He was a zealous and charismatic bishop, to the extent that relations with his aristocratic and urbane fellow bishops of Gaul were never easy. He fought both heretics and the use of the secular authorities against them. His biography was written by Sulpicius Severus, who presented him as the West's answer to the great monastic fathers of the East. Around his popular pilgrimage shrine at Tours was built a vast Romanesque basilica, but this was destroyed in the French Revolution.

Martin of Trier (St) M? B. Jul 19
d. ?210. He is listed as the tenth bishop of Trier, Germany, but there is no evidence for the tradition that he was martyred.

Martin of Vertou (St) R. Oct 24
d. 601. The abbot-founder of Vertou near Nantes, France, he also founded several other monasteries in Poitou. His extant biography is mostly legendary.

Martin of Vienne (St) B. Jul 19
d. p132. He is alleged to have been sent to Vienne, France, as its third bishop by Pope St Alexander, but was probably of the late C3rd.

Martin-of-St-Felix Woodcock
(Bl) M. R(OFM). Aug 7
1603–1646. From near Preston and baptized as John, he was educated at Douai and Rome before joining the Franciscans at Douai in 1631. He went to England in 1644 and was immediately seized near Clayton-le-Woods, Lancs, imprisoned for two years at Lancaster and executed with BB Edward Bamber and Thomas Whitaker. They were beatified in 1987. *See* **England (Martyrs of)**.

Martin Wu (Xuesheng) (St) M. L. Feb 18
1817–1862. A farmer from Chuchangbo in Guizhou, China, he became a lay catechist and was imprisoned twice. He was then seized with SS St John-Peter Néel, John Zhang (Tianshen) and John Chen (Xianheng) and was beheaded with them at Kaiyang. *See* **China (Martyrs of)**.

Martina (St) V. Jan 30
d. ?228. Nothing is known about her except her name and the existence of an early cultus at Rome. There is a basilica dedicated to her in the Forum, where a sarcophagus containing her remains was found in 1634 and to which her cultus was confined in 1969. She is alleged to have been martyred in the reign of Alexander Severus, but her acta are a worthless forgery based on those of SS Prisca and Tatiana.

Martinian (St) *see* **Processus and Martinian**

Martinian, Saturian and Comps (SS) MM. Oct 16
d. 458. Four Roman African brothers, with a young woman called Maxima they were made slaves in the house of an Arian Vandal in what is now Algeria. By command of king Genseric they were dragged to death by horses, but Maxima died in peace in a nunnery.

Martinian of Caesarea (St)R. Feb 13
d. *c*400. According to his dubious story, he was a hermit living near Caesarea in the Holy Land who was the target of an attempt at seduction by Zoë, a promiscuous local woman. He persuaded the latter to become a nun at Bethlehem instead.

Martinian Meléndez Sánchez (Bl) *see* **Hospitaller Martyrs of Spain**

Martinian (Maternian) of Milan (St) B. Jan 2
d. ?435. He was bishop of Milan, Italy, from 423, was at the council of Ephesus in 431 and wrote against Nestorianism.

Martius (St) R. Apr 13
d. *c*530. A native of Auvergne, France, he became a hermit near Clermont-Ferrand and founded a monastery for his disciples.

Martyrius (Martory) (St) R. Jan 23
C6th. A hermit in the Abruzzi, Italy, he was mentioned in the *Dialogues* of St Gregory the Great.

Martyrius (St) *see* **Sisinius, Martyrius and Alexander**

Martyrius and Marcian
(SS) MM. Oct 25
d. 351. A sub-deacon and a chorister of Constantinople, they were executed there on a charge of sedition for preaching against Arianism in the reign of Valens.

Maruthas (St) B. Dec 4
d. ?415. One of the great Syrian fathers, he was bishop of Maiferkat (Martyropolis) in Persian Mesopotamia and reorganized the church in the western Sassanid empire after the vicious persecution of Shah Shapur II. He collected the relics of many martyrs (hence the name of his city), transcribed their acta and wrote liturgical hymns in their honour. St John Chrysostom was his friend.

Mary (St) Aug 15
C1st. The Virgin Mother of God features in the infancy narratives of the gospels of Matthew and Luke, and is referred to as having been present at the Crucifixion and at the descent of the Holy Spirit at Pentecost. There are two conflicting traditions concerning her subsequent life. One depends on Jn 29:25 in linking her with St John the Evangelist and thus having her die at Ephesus. The other describes her death ('dormition') on the site of the Dormition Abbey at Jerusalem, her burial in the tomb now venerated in the Kidron Valley and her being taken from there bodily into heaven (her 'assumption'). She has always had a special cultus, in Greek called 'hyperdulia' (extreme veneration) to distinguish it from the veneration paid to saints ('dulia') and the worship given to God ('latria'). The intensity of this cultus is Christological in basis, as witnessed at the ecumenical council of Ephesus in 351 when the teaching that Christ was fully God and fully human led her to be declared 'Mother of God' ('Theotokos'). The dogmatic implications of this have been developed through the Church's history, and the present situation is that her conception free from original sin, her lifelong physical virginity and her assumption into heaven are all integral parts of the deposit of Catholic faith. The first recorded of her apparitions was to St Gregory Thaumaturgus in *c*250, and these have featured in the Church's life ever since. Many of these (such as that at Lourdes) are celebrated with special feast-days, as are the principal events of her life, certain aspects of her special status and many of the varied representations of her. Individual apparitions notwithstanding, she is traditionally depicted in both East and West with head covered, shoes on and holding the Christ-Child.

St Mary the Virgin, Aug 15

Mary-of-the-Incarnation Acarie (Bl) R(OCD). Apr 18
1566–1618. A Parisian married to a French government official, when young she was nicknamed 'the beautiful Acarie' but her husband was imprisoned and their property confiscated. She arranged the introduction of the Discalced Carmelite nuns of St Teresa into France (at Paris) and became a lay sister at Amiens when widowed in 1613. She died at Pontoise and was beatified in 1791.

Mary of Albitina (St) *see* **Saturninus, Dativus and Comps**

Mary-Magdalen Albrizzi
(Bl) R(OSA). May 15
d. 1465. From Como, Italy, she entered a nunnery at Brunate near there, became prioress and affiliated it with the Augustinian friars. She advocated frequent communion for her community in an era when this was unusual. Her cultus was approved for Como in 1907.

Mary-of-St-Joseph Alvarado Cardozo (Bl) R. F. Apr 2
1875–1967. Born at Choroní in Venezuela, she made a private vow of virginity at her first communion, identifying with Our Lady's love for the Eucharist. When young she started

instructing children at home in Maracay and in the hospital founded by Fr Vincent López Aveledo, the parish priest. They founded the 'Augustinian Recollects of the Heart of Jesus' in 1901 to care for the sick, elderly and orphans:- 'Those no-one wants to take are ours'. She founded 37 houses in Venezuela, and was beatified in 1995.

Mary An (Guo) and Mary An (Linghua) (SS) *see* **Anne An (Xin) and Comps**

Mary-Clare-of-St-Rosalia du Bac (Bl) *see* **Orange (Martyrs of)**

Mary-Bartholomea Bagnesi
(Bl) R(OP). May 27
1511–1577. From Florence, Italy, she became a Dominican nun there in 1544 and was famous for the variety of her sufferings, including demonic obsessions. Her cultus was confirmed for Florence in 1804.

Mary-Antonia Bandrés y Elósegui (Bl) R. Apr 27
1898–1919. Born in the Basque country, Spain, of a very large family, when young she helped female factory workers with their problems. She joined the 'Daughters of Jesus' in Salamanca in 1915, and died while singing to Our Lady three years later. She was beatified in 1996.

Mary-Magdalen-Sophia Barat (St) R. F. May 25
1779–1865. From Joigny in Burgundy, France, she was the daughter of a vintner and received a vocation while studying in Paris. She founded the first house of her new congregation, the 'Society of the Sacred Heart of Jesus', at Amiens in 1801. A woman of great charm and enterprise, before her death she had established one hundred and five houses running schools for girls throughout Europe, America and Africa. She died at Paris and was canonized in 1925.

Mary-of-Jesus-Crucified Bawardy (Bl) R(OC). Aug 26
1846–1878. From Abellin near Nazareth in the Holy Land, her family were Catholics of the Melkite rite. She was orphaned when aged three and taken to Alexandria, where she avoided marriage by cropping her hair in response to a private vow. She went to Marseilles, France, and joined the Carmelites in 1867, being sent to a new foundation at Mangalore (India) in 1870. She had to return after problems with her health, and went back to the Holy Land where she founded a Carmel at Bethlehem in 1875. She died of a fall while working in the garden, and was beatified in 1983.

Bl Mary-of-Jesus-Crucified Bawardy, Aug 26

Mary-Anne-of-St-Joachim Béguin-Royal (Bl) *see* **Orange (Martyrs of)**

Mary-of-St-Cecilia Bélanger
(Bl) R. Sep 4
1897–1929.From Quebec City, Canada, she was a talented girl, especially at the piano. In 1921 she joined the 'Religious of Jesus and Mary' at Sillery (founded by Bl Claudia Thévenet) and taught music to the community, but had very poor health and died after only eight years of religious life. Her spiritual life was extremely rich, however, and she was granted mystical marriage and a mystical share in the Passion. She was beatified in 1993.

Mary-Clare-of-St-Martin Blanc (Bl) *see* **Orange (Martyrs of)**

Mary-Magdalen Blond (Bl) *see* **William Repin and Comps**

Mary-Anne Blondin (Bl) R.F. Jan 2
1809–1890. From a family in humble circumstances at Terrebonne in Quebec, Canada, in her twenties she became a domestic servant in a convent situated in her village. As such she managed to overcome her illiteracy, became a teacher and noticed that one reason for a high level of illiteracy among the Catholics

Bl Mary-of-St-Cecilia Bélanger, Sep 4

of Quebec was a policy of insisting on separate schools for boys and girls in the face of inadequate educational resources. As a result she founded the co-educational Sister of St Anne at Vaudreuil in 1850. Her congregation flourished, but in 1858 she was permanently excluded from any position of authority on the pretext that she was a poor administrator. She was beatified in 2001.

Mary-Bertilla Boscardin (St) R. Oct 20
1888–1922. From Vicenza, Italy, she joined the 'Teaching Sisters of St Dorothy and the Sacred Hearts' and lived a life of obedience in the care of sick people and of children. She died at Treviso and was canonized in 1961.

Mary-Anne-of-St-Louis Brideau (Bl) *see* **Compiègne (Carmelite Martyrs of)**

Mary-Dominica Brun Barbatini (Bl) R. F. May 12
1789–1868. From Lucca, Italy,, she was widowed with a son when aged 22 and took up her husband's business by day while helping derelict people by night. When her son died she worked wherever needed in Catholic activity. A Camillan priest taught her the charism of service to the sick, and she founded the 'Sisters, Servants of St Camillus'. She was beatified in 1995.

Mary-Bernarda Bütler
(Bl) R(OFM). F. May 19
1848–1924. Born in Aargau, Switzerland, she became a Poor Clare at Atstätten in 1869 and went on to be superior. Then she and six others obtained papal authorization in 1888 to go to Ecuador, and they founded the 'Franciscan Missionaries of Mary Help of Christians' at Chone. They had to leave that place in 1895 and move to Cartagena in Colombia, but other houses were founded in Austria and Brazil. She was beatified in 1995.

Mary de la Cabeza (Bl) L. Sep 9
d. ?1175. From Torrejon, Spain, she was the wife of St **Isidore the Farmer** (q.v.). Her cultus was confirmed for Toledo in 1697.

Mary-Magdalen Cady (Bl) *see* **William Repin and Comps**

Mary-Margaret Caiani
(Bl) T(OFM). F. Aug 8
1863–1921. From near Pistoia, Italy, she tried to become a Benedictine nun there but left when she realized that her vocation was outside the cloister. Opening a school at Podi a Caiano, her native village, she formed a community there in 1896 which became the 'Franciscan Tertiaries of the Sacred Heart'. When she died at Florence there were 21 houses. She was beatified in 1989.

Mary-of-the-Rosary Calpe Ibáñez (Bl) *see* **Angela-of-St-Joseph Lloret Martí and Comps**

Mary-Magdalen of Canossa
(St) R. F. May 8
1774–1835. From Verona, Italy, she was a daughter of the marquis of Canossa but he died when she was a child and her mother remarried, abandoning her children. She managed her late father's household till she was thirty-three. Then, after a brief period of hospital nursing in Venice in 1808, she founded the first house of the 'Daughters of Charity' at Verona for educating poor girls, nursing in hospitals and teaching the catechism in parishes. When she died at Verona several houses had been founded in north Italy, and the congregation is now worldwide. She was canonized in 1988.

Mary Cassin (Bl) *see* **William Repin and Comps**

Mary-Cecilia Cendoya Araquistain (Bl*) see* **Mary-Gabrielle de Hinojosa Naveros and Comps**

Mary de Cerevellon (St) R. Sep 19
d. 1290. From Barcelona, she became one of the first Mercedarian nuns at the new community there in 1264 and served as superior. She was especially famous for her charity, and was nicknamed 'Mary of Help'. Her cultus was confirmed for Barcelona in 1692.

Mary-of-Jesus Charransol (Bl*) see* **Orange (Martyrs of)**

Mary-Jane Chauvigné (Bl*) see* **William Repin and Comps**

Mary-Vincenza-of-St-Dorothy Chávez Orosco (Bl) R. F. Jul 21
1867–1949. From Cotija in Michoacán state, Mexico, she was treated at the parish hospital for pleurisy in 1892 and received a vocation to serve sick people. Starting at the same hospital, she went on to found the 'Servants of the Holy Trinity and the Poor' in 1905 and became the superior-general in 1913. The congregation spread in and around Guadalajara, but the anti-clerical Mexican revolution in 1911 raised a serious danger. This the sisters ignored, successfully continuing their religious life and work as usual. She died at Guadalajara and was beatified in 1997.

Mary Chi (Yu) (St*) see* **Lucy Wang (Cheng) and Comps**

Mary-Theresa Chiramel Mankidiyan (B1) R. F. Jun 6
1876–1926. from Puthenchira in Kerala, India, she was from a family which had once been wealthy but had become impoverished through paying dowries. After taking a private vow of chastity when aged ten, she had become a visionary and penitent. In 1913 she was allowed by her bishop to build a prayer-house, and soon attracted companions to her life of eremitic prayer and penance with service to needy people regardless of caste. This was the beginning of the 'Congregation of the Holy Family', which is now international. She died of complications caused by her diabetes and was beatified in 2000.

Mary-Magdalen Cho (St*) see* **Korea (Martyrs of)**

Mary-Raphaela Cimatti (Bl) R. Jun 23
1861–1945. From Ravenna, Italy, when little she taught her brothers and catechized in her parish, and went on to join the 'Hospitaller Sisters of Mercy' in 1890. She settled at Alatri near Rome as the superior, but ended up as an ordinary nun who nursed wounded soldiers in Second World War when aged 83. She was beatified in 1996.

Mary Clopas (St) L. Apr 9
C1st. The wife of Clopas or Alpheus (*see* Jn 19:25) and the mother of St James the Less, she was one of the 'three Marys' who followed Christ in his final journey to Jerusalem and who witnessed the Crucifixion. The legends about her subsequent life are worthless. She is depicted carrying a pot of ointment or a jar of spices.

Mary the Consoler (St) R? Aug 1
C8th. She was allegedly a sister of St Anno of Verona, Italy, and was herself a thaumaturge. Little is known about her.

Mary of Cordoba (St*) see* **Flora and Mary**

Mary-Rose Deloye (Bl*) see* **Orange (Martyrs of)**

Mary-of-Jesus Deluil-Martiny (Bl) R. F. Feb 27
1841–1884. From Marseilles, she founded the 'Daughters of the Heart of Jesus' to give consolation to the Sacred Heart of Jesus for the wrongs done to it. The mother-house was at Berchem-Anvers near Mecheln, Belgium, and the Rule was based on that of the Jesuits. She was killed by a gardener whom she had sacked for negligence, and was beatified in 1989.

Mary-Michaela-of-the-Blessed-Sacrament Desmaisières (St) R. F. Aug 24
1809–1865. The Viscountess of Jorbalán was born at Madrid, Spain, educated by the Ursulines and then lived with her family at Guadalajara. There she helped prostitutes and sufferers of epidemic disease, and to further her work for the former she founded the institute of 'Handmaids of the Blessed Sacrament and of Charity' in 1848. She died of cholera at Valencia after nursing her own nuns during an epidemic, and was canonized in 1934.

Mary-Anne-of-St-Francis Depeyre (Bl*) see* **Orange (Martyrs of)**

Mary-Adolphine Dierkx (St*) see* **Gregory Grassi and Comps**

Mary de la Dive (Bl*) see* **William Repin and Comps**

Mary-Henrietta Dominici (Bl) R. Feb 21
1829–1894. From near Turin, Italy, she joined the 'Sisters of St Anne and of Providence' in 1850 and became the superior in 1861, which she remained until death. A confidante of St John Bosco, she wrote an autobiography and was beatified in 1978.

Mary-Anne-of-St Michael Doux (Bl) *see* **Orange (Martyrs of)**

Mary-of-the-Divine-Heart Droste zu Vischering (Bl) R. Jun 8
1863–1899. A noblewoman born at Münster, Germany, she lacked the health to enter religious life until she recognized a vocation to help destitute and unchaste girls. She became a 'Good Shepherd Sister' at Münster when aged twenty-four, and was made superior at Oporto, Portugal, when aged thirty. Her visions of the Sacred Heart led Pope Leo XIII to consecrate the world to it in the year of her early death. She was a very beautiful woman. She was beatified in 1975.

Mary-Magdalen Du (Fengju) and Mary Du (Tian) (SS) MM. LL. Jun 29
1858 and 1881–1900. They were mother and daughter, from Du in Hebei, China. During a Boxer raid they hid in a pit near their village with two sons and another daughter of the family but were discovered. The daughters ran away but St Mary-Magdalen was caught and shot. St Mary and her two sons were killed in the pit. The villagers buried them, including St Mary-Magdalen who was still alive but who volunteered to be buried in order to go to heaven. *See* **China (Martyrs of)**.

Mary Du (Zhao) (St) M. L. Jul ?
1849–1900. From a Catholic family of Qifengzhuang in Hebei, China, she married and moved to Dujiatun. While visiting a cousin and his wife in Wangjiatian she was killed with them by a gang of Boxers. *See* **China (Martyrs of)**.

Mary-of-St-Martha Dufour (Bl) *see* **Compiègne (Carmelite Martyrs of)**

Mary-Rose Durocher (Bl) R. F. Oct 6
1811–1849. Born at Saint-Antoine-sur-Richelieu in Quebec, Canada, she helped her brother, a priest, in his parish work despite not having good health. She set up the first Marian sodality in Canada and founded the 'Sisters of the Sacred Name of Jesus' at Longueil, chiefly to care for girls. She was beatified in 1982.

Mary of Egypt (St) R. Apr 2
C5th ? According to her doubtful story, she was an Egyptian actress and high-class prostitute at Alexandria. She was converted at the Holy Sepulchre at Jerusalem (where there is a chapel dedicated to her) and then fled into the desert beyond the Jordan to spend the rest of her life doing penance. She was discovered by St Zosimus, who later buried her with the help of a lion. She is depicted naked but covered with her long hair and holding loaves, or with the lion that dug her grave, or kneeling before a skull.

Mary-of-the-Sacred-Heart Encarnación Rosal (Bl) R. F. Oct 27
1820–1886. Born at Quetzaltenango in Guatemala, in 1837 she joined the Bethlemite congregation founded there by Bl Peter de Betancur but discovered that the founder's charism was being lost. She became prioress in 1855 and revised the constitutions to restore the charism, but the older sisters refused to accept the changes and she left to found a new house in 1861. (This reformed 'Institute of Bethlemite Sisters' is now in thirteen countries.) She had a special devotion to the sorrows of the Sacred Heart and to reparation for humanity's sins, and was beatified in 1997.

Mary Fan (Kun) (St) *see* **Lucy Wang (Cheng) and Comps**

Mary-Teresa Fantou (Bl) *see* **Cambrai (Martyrs of)**

Mary-Teresa Fasce (Bl) R(OSA). Oct 12
1881–1947. From near Genoa, Italy, she entered the Augustinian nunnery of St Rita in Cascia in 1906. She became abbess in 1920, and was repeatedly re-elected until her death. Her life's work was the propagation of devotion to St Rita of Cascia, and she built up a great pilgrimage centre. Also around the shrine she founded an orphanage, a seminary, a hospital and a retreat house. Her health was very poor long before she died. She was beatified in 1997.

Mary Fausseuse (Bl) *see* **William Repin and Comps**

Mary-Magdalen Fontaine (Bl) *see* **Cambrai (Martyrs of)**

Mary-of-the-Angels Fontanella (Bl) R(OCD). Dec 16
1661–1717. A noblewoman born at Baldinero near Turin, Italy,, she became a Carmelite at Turin in 1616. For fourteen years she was tormented by violent temptations to blasphemy.

She founded the Carmel of Moncaglieri (which still exists) and was beatified in 1865.

Mary Forestier (Bl*)* *see* **William Repin and Comps**

Mary-Victoria Fornari Strata (Bl) R. F. Sep 12
1562–1617. A noblewoman of Genoa, Italy, she was married with six children but was widowed in 1589. After she had brought up her children she founded a congregation of contemplative nuns called the 'Blue Annunciades' with a charism based on the hidden life of Our Lady at Nazareth and with part of their habits in sky-blue. She was superior of the first house at Genoa, died there and was beatified in 1828.

Mary Fu (Guilin) (St) M. L. Jun 21
1863–1900. From Luopo in Hebei, China, she took a private vow of virginity and taught in the parish school at Liu. During a Boxer raid she was beheaded. *See* **China (Martyrs of)**.

Mary Gallard (Bl*)* *see* **William Repin and Comps**

Mary-Frances-of-the-Wounds-of-Our-Lord Gallo (St) T(OFM). Oct 6
1715–1791. From a bourgeois family of Naples, Italy, she had a father who was brutal and avaricious and who was especially cruel when she refused to marry the man he had chosen for her. In 1731 he let her become a Franciscan tertiary, and she lived with her parents until she found a priest who would employ her as his housekeeper. This she was for thirty-eight years before her death at Naples. She was favoured with extraordinary graces, including mystical marriage and the stigmata. She was canonized in 1867.

Mary Gasnier (Bl*)* *see* **William Repin and Comps**

Mary Gengoro (Bl) M. L. Aug 16
d. 1620. A Japanese, she was the wife of Bl Thomas Gengoro and mother of Bl James. The whole family was crucified at Kokura. *See* **Simon Kiyota and Comps** and **Japan (Martyrs of)**

Mary-Teresa-of-Jesus Gerhardinger (Bl) R. F. May 9
1797–1879. Born near Regensburg, Bavaria, she trained as a teacher and, when aged eighteen, was told by her bishop that she would be useful helping to found a community of teaching sisters not confined to monasteries but making the rounds of poor villages. This resulted in the 'School Sisters of Notre Dame'. She died at Munich after 46 years in vows, and was beatified in 1985.

Mary Gingueneau (Bl*)* *see* **William Repin and Comps**

Mary-of-Peace Giuliani (St*)* *see* **Gregory Grassi and Comps**

Mary Goretti (St) V. Jul 6
1890–1902. Born at Corinaldo near Ancona, Italy, she showed clear signs of youthful holiness despite being illiterate. She was being harassed by a youth who was sexually obsessed with her, and he attempted to rape her after the two of them were left alone when the rest of their village of Nettuno were working in the fields. She resisted successfully and he stabbed her to death. About forty miracles were ascribed to her intercession, and her canonization in 1950 was attended by her mother, family and repentant murderer.

St Mary Goretti, Oct 16

Mary Grillard (Bl*)* *see* **William Repin and Comps**

Mary-Hermina-of-Jesus Grivot (St*)* *see* **Gregory Grassi and Comps**

Mary-Magdalen-of-St-Melania de Guilhermirer (Bl*)* *see* **Orange (Martyrs of)**

Mary Guo (Li) (St) M. L. Jul 7
1835–1900. From Hujiache in Hebei, China, she had many children and grandchildren

whom she brought up to be Catholics. She was beheaded with two of her daughters-in-law, two grandsons and two grand-daughters by a gang of Boxers. *See* **China (Martyrs of)**.

Mary-of-the-Incarnation Guyart (Bl) R. Apr 30
1599–1672. Born in Tours, France, when aged nineteen she was left a widow with a small son. After involvement in business she joined the Ursulines in 1630 and went to Canada for the rest of her life nine years later. (The Ursulines were the first religious foundation in the colony, which was then French.) She was a noted mystic, and her autobiography and letters were published by her son (who became a Benedictine). She was beatified in 1980.

Mary-Anne Hacher du Bois (Bl*) see* **William Repin and Comps**

Mary-Magdalen Han (St*) see* **Korea (Martyrs of)**

Mary-Teresa-of-the-Sacred-Heart Haze (Bl) R. F. Jan 7
1782–1876. From Liege, Belgium, her family was rich and she had a happy childhood broken off by chaos and exile in the Revolution. She wanted to become a religious but the new civil law prevented this when she returned home, so

Bl Mary-Teresa-of-the-Sacred-Heart Haze, Jan 7

she opened a free school instead. In 1832 she finally founded the 'Daughters of the Cross', which spread worldwide to help orphans and women in prison and also to work in education and nursing. She died at Liege and was beatified in 1991.

Mary-Magdalen He (St*) see* **Korea (Martyrs of)**

Mary-Elizabeth Hesselblad (Bl) R.F. Jun 4
1870–1957. From Fåglavik in Västergötland, Sweden, she was raised as a Lutheran and was a housemaid before emigrating to the USA in 1888. As a nurse in New York she came into contact with Catholic patients and chaplains, her first contact with Catholics. A period as a house-nurse in a convent led evenutally to her conversion in 1902 and she moved back to Sweden to become a Brigittine in 1906. She founded houses of her order in Rome and Sweden, and was active in the ecumenical movement after the Second World War. She was beatified in 2000.

Mary-Gabrielle de Hinojosa Naveros and Comps (Bl) MM. RR. Nov 18
d. 1936. When the Spanish Civil War broke out in early 1936 the community of the Visitation at Madrid moved out of the city, leaving a group of six nuns in her charge. They tried to live unobtrusively but were noticed and harassed. Finally their apartment was raided by a patrol of anarchists and they were taken by van to a vacant site to be shot. The bullets missed Mary-Cecilia Cendoya Araquistan, who ran away but immediately gave herself up and was shot five days later. They were beatified in 1998. *See* **Spanish Civil War (Martyrs of)**.

Mary-Crescentia Höss (St) T(OFM). Apr 5
1682–1744. From Kaufbeuren in Bavaria, Germany, she had mystical experiences from an early age and was admitted to the Mayerhof convent of Franciscan tertiaries without a dowry in 1703 at the request of the Protestant mayor. This did not make her popular there, but her holiness overcame the resentment and she became novice-mistress and superior. She became famous for her sanctity, and was canonized in 2001.

Mary-Pilar Izquierdo Albero (Bl) R. F. (Aug 27)
1906–1945. From a poor family of Zaragoza in Spain, she became a worker in a shoe factory but fractured her pelvis by falling off a tram in

1926. Complications set in, leaving her blind and paralysed, but she became known for her spiritual discernment. In 1939 her health suddenly improved and she set about founding a missionary congregation. The first attempt was a failure; the second was in 1942 but she was forced out of the nascent congregation and was in the process of making a third attempt at Madrid when she died at San Sebastiano. Her disciples became the 'Missionary Workers of Jesus and Mary' in 1948, and she was beatified in 2001.

Mary-Bernardina Jabłońska
(Bl) T(OSF). Sep 23
1878–1940. From near Zamość in Poland, when young she joined a youth group founded by St Albert Chmielowski to help very poor people and became his chief helper in this work at Cracow. She was the first superior-general of the 'Albertine Sisters', an institute of Franciscan tertiaries founded by her spiritual father to bring together his female disciples. She died at Cracow and was beatified in 1997.

Mary-Amandina Jeuris (St) *see* Gregory **Grassi and Comps**

Mary-of-Succour Jiménez Baldoví (Bl) *see* **Angela-of-St-Joseph Lloret Martí and Comps**

Mary-of-the-Cross Jugan
(Bl) R. F. Aug 29
1846–1931. From St Malo, France, and baptized as Joanne, she joined the 'Eudist Third Order' and worked as a domestic and hospital servant in St Servan. With two others she set up an old peoples' home in 1839 and supported it by begging. Thus began the 'Little Sisters of the Poor'. She was initially the superior but proved incompetent in administration and was deposed, but her congregation had 177 houses at her death. She was beatified in 1982.

Mary-of-St-Henry de Justamond, Mary-Magdalen-of-the Blessed Sacrament de Justamond and Mary-Magdalen-of-the-Heart-of-Mary de Justamond (BB) *see* **Orange (Martyrs of)**

Mary-Restituta Kafka
(Bl) M. R. (Mar 30)
1894–1943. A shoemaker's daughter of what is now Brno in the Czech Republic, she grew up in Vienna, Austria, and joined the 'Franciscan Sisters of Christian Charity' in 1914, becoming a surgical nurse. After the 'Anschluss' she made her rejection of Nazism quite clear, and when she hung crucifixes in every room of a new wing of the hospital she was arrested. Charged with this and with writing a poem mocking Hitler, she was beheaded in 1942 and beatified in 1998.

Mary Karłowska (Bl) R. F. Jun 6
1865–1935. From Słupówka near Poznan in Poland (then Posen in Germany), she wished to help the prostitutes for which Posen was notorious by running refuges where they could experience God's love and learn a respectable trade. This led to her founding the 'Good Shepherd Sisters of Divine Providence' for that work, and these spread throughout Poland. She died near Toruń and was beatified in 1997.

Mary-Catherine Kasper (Bl) R. F. Feb 2
1820–1898. Born at Dernbach near Limburg, Germany, she collected a few companions in her home village to look after poor sick people and orphans. At the time of her death these had become the 'Poor Handmaids of Jesus Christ', an international congregation numbering in the thousands. Her charism was personal humility in service. She was beatified in 1978.

Mary-of-the-Holy-Birth Kerguin (St) *see* **Gregory Grassi and Comps**

Mary-Magdalen Kim (St) *see* **Korea (Martyrs of)**

Mary-Magdalen Kiyota (1)
(Bl) M. L. Aug 16
d. 1620. Wife of Bl Simon Kiyota, she was crucified with him and his companions at Kokura in Japan. *See* **Japan (Martyrs of)**.

Mary-Magdalen Kiyota (2)
(Bl) M. T(OP). Aug 17
d. 1627. A Japanese Dominican tertiary and a relative of the daimyos of Bungo, she was burnt at Nagasaki with BB Francis-of-St-Mary of Mancha and Comps for having received missionaries as guests. *See* **Japan (Martyrs of)**.

Mary of Korea (Bl) M. Sep 10
1622. Wife of Bl Anthony, she was beheaded at the 'Great Martyrdom' at Nagasaki, Japan, with her family. *See* **Japan (Martyrs of)**.

Mary-Faustina Kowalska
(St) R. Oct 5
1905–1938. Born in Glogowiec, Poland, of poor but devout peasants, she worked as a housemaid after leaving school at sixteen until she joined the 'Sisters of Our Lady of Mercy' in 1925. She lived in various Polish houses of her

order, and had many private revelations leading her to promote the devotion to the Divine Mercy. She died of tuberculosis at Cracow and was canonized in 2000.

Mary-Anne-of-St-Francis Lambert (Bl) *see* **Orange (Martyrs of)**

Mary-Frances Lanel (Bl) *see* **Cambrai (Martyrs of)**

Mary Lardeaux (Bl) *see* **William Repin and Comps**

Mary-Rose-of-St-Andrew Laye (Bl) *see* **Orange (Martyrs of)**

Mary-Teresa-of-Jesus Le Clerc (Bl) R(CR). F. Jan 9
1576–1622. From a wealthy family of Remiremont, Lorraine (now in France), when young she was hedonistic but then became a religious under the guidance of St Peter Fourier and founded the 'Congregation of Our Lady, Canonesses of St Augustine' in order to educate girls ('rich and poor alike'). Called 'a woman of profound silence', she was a noted mystic. Dying at Nancy, she was beatified in 1947. She is usually referred to as 'Alix', her baptismal name.

Mary-Engracia Lecuona Aramburu (Bl) *see* **Mary-Gabrielle de Hinojosa Naveros and Comps**

Mary Teresa Ledochowska (Bl) L. F. Jun 6
1863–1922. Born at Loosdorf, Austria, of a famous noble family of the Hapsburg Empire, she dedicated herself to the abolition of slavery and the evangelization of Africa and founded the 'Sodality of St Peter Claver for African Missions' in 1894 to the latter end. She was also much involved in publishing work for African catechesis. She was beatified in 1975.

Mary Lee (1) and Mary Lee (2) (SS) *see* **Korea (Martyrs of)**

Mary-Magdalen Lee (1) and Mary-Magdalen Lee (2) (SS) *see* **Korea (Martyrs of)**

Mary Lenéc (Bl) *see* **William Repin and Comps**

Mary of Lérida (St) *see* **Bernard, Mary and Comps**

Mary Leroy (1) and Mary Leroy (2) (BB) *see* **William Repin and Comps**

Mary Lhuilier (Bl) *see* **Laval (Martyrs of)**

Mary-of-Montserrat Llimona Planas (Bl) *see* **Angela-of-St-Joseph Lloret Martí and Comps**

Mary-Catherine-of-St-Augustine de Longpré (Bl) R(OSA). May 8
1623–1668. Born at Saint-Sauveur-le-Vicomte in Normandy, France, she joined the Augustinian Hospitaller nuns at the 'Hôtel-Dieu' at Bayonne when aged twelve. In 1648 she emigrated to their foundation in Quebec City, Canada, and (despite her youth) became noted for her prudence and intellect. Totally devoted to caring for sick people, she served as bursar and novice-mistress and was beatified in 1989.

Mary-of-Peace López García (Bl) *see* **Angela-of-St-Joseph Lloret Martí and Comps**

Mary-of-Jesus López de Rivas (Bl) R(OC). Sep 13
1560–1640. Born near Segovia, Spain, she became a disciple of St Teresa of Jesus and entered the reformed convent at Toledo where she stayed for 63 years, serving as prioress and novice mistress. She was beatified in 1976.

Mary-of-the-Cross Mackillop (Bl) R. F. Aug 8
1842–1909. From Melbourne, Australia, she started work as a governess when young in order to support her family and went to Penolia (S. A.). Finding that the Catholic children of the vast parish had no schooling whatever, she started the 'Sisters of St Joseph of the Sacred Heart' in 1866 in order to 'destroy the secular spirit of education among our schools'. The order multiplied in Australia and New Zealand, running schools, orphanages and nursing homes and relying entirely on donations. She suffered a lot of human opposition and poor health. She was beatified in 1995.

Mary Magdalen (St) L. Jul 22
C1st. One of the Galilean women who ministered to Christ, she had had 'seven devils' expelled from her (Mk 16:9) and was one of the first witnesses of Christ's Resurrection. The Western Church used to follow the opinion of St Gregory the Great in identifying her with the unnamed sinner in Lk 7:37; 8:2 and with Mary of Bethany, the sister of Martha and Lazarus. This led her to be depicted in the West as having long, unbound hair (usually blonde) and

St Mary-of-the-Cross Mackillop, Aug 8
(see p. 391)

carrying a jar of unguent. The Eastern tradition never accepted this identification and it is now discredited. The legend connecting her with France is worthless.

Mary Mancini of Pisa (Bl) T(OP). Dec 22
d. 1431. A noblewoman of Pisa, Italy, she received extraordinary mystical graces from childhood, for example the visibility of her Guardian Angel. She married when aged twelve and was left a widow with two children at sixteen. She married again, but lost her second husband eight years later. Then she became a Dominican tertiary and joined Bl Clare Gambacorta at her reformed foundation, succeeding her as prioress. Her cultus was confirmed for Pisa and the Dominicans in 1855.

Mary Mardosewicz and Comps
(BB) MM. RR. Sep 4
d. 1943. They were eleven sisters of the Holy Family of Nazareth at Nowogródek in eastern Poland, now Navahradak in Bielarus. Their convent had been founded in 1929, but the town was overrun by the Soviet Union in 1939 and by the Third Reich in 1941. The German policy was to destroy all aspects of Polish culture, and the sisters were summoned to Gestapo headquarters, driven to a wood near the town and shot. They were beatified in 2000. *See* list of national martyrs in appendix.

Mary-of-the-Conception Martí Lacal (Bl) *see* **Angela-of-St-Joseph Lloret Martí and Comps**

Mary-Magdalen Martinengo
(Bl) R(OFM Cap). Jul 27
1687–1737. From Brescia, Italy, she became a Capuchin nun there and was a capable novice-mistress and prioress. She was beatified in 1900.

Mary-Pilar-of-St-Francis-Borgia Martínez García and Comps
(BB) MM. R(OC). Jul 25
d. 1936. The city of Guadalajara, Spain, was captured in 1936 by the Republican militia during the Civil War, and the Carmelite community there dispersed to private houses in secular dress. Three of them together were recognized as religious by a militiaman they met on the road, and he took them at gun-point to his comrades and said that they were nuns and should be shot. His comrades obliged. Mary-Angels-of St-Joseph Valtierra Tordesillas died instantly, Mary-Pilar-of-St-Francis-Borgia Martínez García was mortally wounded and died clutching a crucifix, and Teresa-of-the-Child-Jesus García García was told to say 'Success to Communism' but replied 'Success to Jesus Christ' and was shot with a revolver. They were beatified in 1987. *See* **Spanish Civil War (Martyrs of)**.

Mary de Matthias (Bl) R. F. Aug 20
1805–1866. From Vallecorsa near Frosenone, Italy, when aged seventeen she was inspired by St Caspar del Bufalo to found a congregation of sisters teaching girls, corresponding to that which he was founding for teaching boys. In 1834 she opened her first school at Acuto, and this was the beginning of the 'Sisters, Adorers of the Precious Blood'. When she died they were running about seventy schools. She was beatified in 1950.

Mary-Dominica Mazzarello
(St) R. F. May 14
1837–1881. From a peasant family of Mornese near Acqui, Italy, she helped on the farm as a child and then joined the 'Pious Union of Mary Immaculate' to lead a life of charity. She attracted companions and thus her institute, the 'Daughters of Mary Auxiliatrix', came into being. Under the direction of St John Bosco it received full canonical formation and status, and undertook for girls what the Salesians were doing for boys. She reluctantly became the first superior general in 1874, died after a long illness at Nizza Monferrato and was canonized in 1951.

Mary-Eugenia-of-Jesus Milleret de Brou (Bl) R. F. Mar 10
1817–1898. From Metz, France, her home was irreligious and her family broke up in her teens. She received faith when aged seventeen and

founded her 'Congregation of Our Lady of the Assumption' five years later. Her charism was summarized in the latter's motto: 'Pray and Teach'. She was beatified in 1975.

Mary-Anne Mogas Fontcuberta
(Bl) R(OFM). F. Oct 6
1827–1886. An orphan girl, she was brought up in Barcelona, Spain, where she met three exclaustrated Capuchins trying to start a school. She joined them at Ripoll where the school was set up, and the 'Capuchins of the Divine Shepherdess' were thus founded. She died at her other foundation in Madrid after a monastic career inspired by love of Our Lady and was beatified in 1996.

Mary-of-the-Assumption Mogoche Homs (Bl) *see* **Angela-of-St-Joseph Lloret Martí and Comps**

Mary-Rose Molas y Vallvé
(St) R. F. Jun 11
1815–1876. From Reus near Tarragona, Spain, she saw her vocation as being in hospital work and ran away from home to join a sodality at the local hospital. She soon became their leader, and they also started teaching in local schools. In 1858 she founded the 'Sisters of Our Lady of Consolation' at Tortosa. She was canonized in 1988.

Mary-Sanctuary-of-St-Aloysius-Gonzaga Moragas Cantarero
(Bl) M. R(OC). Aug 16
1881–1936. Her father was the royal purveyor of pharmaceuticals at Madrid, Spain, and she qualified as a pharmacist herself. In 1915 she entered the Carmel at Madrid and served as prioress and as novice mistress. She was prioress for a second term when the convent was attacked by an anti-clerical mob on July 20 1936 on the outbreak of the Spanish Civil War, and the community dispersed for safety. On 14 August she was arrested, interrogated and shot the following day. She was beatified in 1998. *See* **Spanish Civil War (Martyrs of)**.

Mary-Magdalen-Catherine Morano (Bl) R. Nov 15
1847–1908. Born near Turin, Italy, when she was eight years old she had to start earning on the death of her father and became a teacher and catechist. In 1878 she entered the congregation of 'Daughters of Mary Auxiliatrix' founded six years previously by St John Bosco, and was sent to Sicily in 1881. She was a catechist in Catania diocese until her death, believing that the formation of a Christian conscience was the basis of personal maturity and of social improvement. She was beatified in 1994.

Mary-of-St-Justus Moreau (St) *see* **Gregory Grassi and Comps**

Mary, Mother of John Mark (St) L. Jun 29
C1st. She is mentioned in the Acts of the Apostles (12:12) as the mother of John, surnamed Mark. From the text it appears that her house in Jerusalem was a place of assembly for the apostles and the faithful generally. Subsequent traditions about her are conflicting.

Mary-Magdalen of Nagasaki
(St) M. T(OP). Sep 28
1610–1634. A Japanese virgin and Dominican tertiary, she was martyred at Nagasaki and was canonized in 1987. *See* **Japan (Martyrs of)**.

Mary-Clare Nanetti (St) *see* **Gregory Grassi and Comps**

Mary-Anne-of-Jesus Navarro de Guevara (Bl) R. Apr 27
1565–1624. Nicknamed the 'Lily of Madrid, Spain)', she was born in that city, became a Discalced Mercedarian there and was famous for her life of penance. She was beatified in 1783.

Mary of Oignies (Bl) R. Jun 23
d. 1213. From Nivelles, Belgium, she married when young but persuaded her husband not to consummate the marriage. They turned their house into a leper hospital where they nursed, and when she was widowed she became a hermit attached to the church at Oignies. Her cultus is unconfirmed.

Mary-Angela Olaizola Garagarza (Bl) *see* **Mary-Gabrielle de Hinojosa Naveros and Comps**

Mary-of-Suffrage Orts Baldó (Bl) *see* **Angela-of-St-Joseph Lloret Martí and Comps**

Mary-of-Jesus d'Oultremont d'Hooghvorst (Bl) R. F. Oct 11
1818–1878. A noblewoman from near Liege, Belgium, she was married with four children but was widowed in 1847 and refused to re-marry, choosing instead to found a new religious congregation. The 'Sisters of Mary Reparatrix' thus began at Strasbourg in 1887, with the aim of making the name of Jesus

better known and loved in the world. They spread through western Europe and were established in India and on the Mascarene Islands in the Indian Ocean. She died at Florence and was beatified in 1997.

Mary-Magdalen dei Panatieri
(Bl) T(OP). Oct 13
1443–1503. From Trino near Vercelli, Italy, she modelled herself on St Catherine of Siena, becoming a Dominican tertiary in her own home and being occupied with charitable works among her neighbours. Her cultus was approved for Trino in 1827.

Mary Pak and Mary-Magdalen Pak (SS) *see* **Korea (Martyrs of)**

Mary-Leonie Paradis (Bl) R. F. May 4
1840–1912. Born in Quebec, Canada, she joined the 'Marian Sisters of the Holy Cross' when she was fourteen and was a priests' housekeeper in Canada and the USA. In 1867 her congregation gave up housekeeping for priests, with the result that she founded the 'Poor Sisters of the Holy Family' at Côtes des Neiges, Quebec, for this work alone. She died at the convent at Sherbrook, and was beatified in 1984.

Bl. Mary-Leonie Paradis, May 4

Mary-Anne-of-Jesus Paredes y Flores (St) R. May 26
1618–1645. Nicknamed the 'Lily of Quito', she was of Spanish descent and was born at Quito, Ecuador. She tried her vocation as a consecrated religious, but failed and then lived as a hermit in the house of her brother-in-law. Her penitential practices were extreme, but she received mystical graces. During the earthquakes at Quito in 1645 she offered herself as a sacrificial victim in reparation for the city and died shortly afterwards. She was canonized in 1950.

Mary-Magdalen de' Pazzi
(St) R(OC). May 25
1566–1607. From Florence, Italy, when aged sixteen she became a Carmelite there. Throughout her life she was subject to remarkable mystical experiences (which she described in writing) and suffered both spiritually and physically. This did not prevent her being a capable worker and administrator at her nunnery. She was canonized in 1669.

Mary-of-St-Euphrasia Pelletier (St) R. F. Apr 24
1796–1868. From Noirmoutier in the Vendée, France, when aged eighteen she joined the 'Sisters of Our Lady of Charity' founded by St John Eudes and herself founded the first house of the 'Sisters of the Good Shepherd' at Angers in 1829 in order to re-educate delinquent girls and young women whose only future otherwise would be in prostitution. She died there and was canonized in 1940.

Mary-Henrietta-of-Providence Pelras (Bl) *see* **Compiègne (Carmelite Martyrs of)**

Mary-Magdalen Perrotin (Bl) *see* **William Repin and Comps**

Mary Phon (Bl) *see* **Thailand (Martyrs of)**

Mary Pichery (Bl) *see* **William Repin and Comps**

Mary-Miracles-of-Jesus Pidal y Chico de Guzmán (Bl) R(OCD). Dec 11
1891–1974. Born at Madrid, Spain, to a devout family in diplomatic service, she joined the Carmel at El Escorial in 1920 and was a founder-member of the Carmel at Cerro de los Ángeles in 1924. This was the founding house of several others in India. After the destruction of the Spanish Civil War she oversaw the foundation and restoration of thirteen Carmels, and was a great proponent of the Carmelite charism. She died at La Aldehuela and was beatified in 1998.

Mary-of-Jesus-Crucified Piedcourt (Bl) *see* **Compiègne (Carmelite Martyrs of)**

Mary Piou (Bl) *see* **William Repin and Comps**

Mary-Adeodata Pisani
(B1) R (OSB) Feb 25
1806–1855. Born in Naples of a noble Maltese family, she suffered the break-up of her family when her father was sentenced to exile and went back to Malta. In 1825 she and her mother also went to Malta, but the family did not come back together. She joined the Benedictine nuns at Medina in 1828 and served as novice mistress and abbess before her early death of heart disease. She was beatified in 2001.

Mary-Magdalen Postel (St) R. F. Jul 16
1756–1846. From Barfleur, France, when young she opened a school for girls but this was suppressed by the French Revolution. During the period of persecution she administered the Blessed Sacrament to the dying. In 1805 she reopened her school at Cherbourg, and this proved to be the origin of the 'Sisterhood of Christian Schools' which spread throughout the world after serious difficulties. She died at St-Sauveur-le-Vicomte and was canonized in 1925.

Mary-Genevieve Poulin de la Foresrie (Bl) *see* **William Repin and Comps**

Mary Poussepin (Bl) R(OP). F. Oct 14
1652–1744. Born at Dourdin near Paris, France, her family ran a stocking factory and she took this over in 1680. In 1691 she entered the Dominican Third Order and moved to Sainville nearby to help in nursing sufferers from repeated epidemics there. She founded the 'Dominican Sisters of Charity of the Presentation of the Blessed Virgin' in 1697 to help in teaching, nursing and catechesis. She hoped that the sisters would not be confined to an enclosed convent, but this freedom did not happen in her lifetime. She was beatified in 1994.

Mary-of-Mercy Prat y Prat
(Bl) M. R. Jul 24
1880–1936. Born in Barcelona, Spain, she joined the Society of St Teresa of Jesus at Tortosa in 1904 and was at the mother house at Barcelona from 1920. When the Civil War broke out the community decided to disperse and to meet up in a safer place. She was sent with a companion to stay with her sister, but they met a group of armed militia on the way. Being questioned, they declared themselves to be consecrated religious and so were seized, driven to a lonely place and shot. She died after some hours, praying for her executors, but her companion survived and gave witness. The beatification was in 1990.

Mary Rafols (Bl) R.F. Nov 5
1781–1853. Born near Barcelona, Spain, she joined a group of young women at Zaragoza who were dedicated to serving the most helpless people at a hospital there. They took vows in 1825 as the 'Sisters of Charity of St Anne', and cared for the wounded and mentally ill during the Napoleonic and Carlist wars (she was imprisoned during the latter). Then she ran a home for foundlings, where she died. She was beatified in 1994.

Mary Repetto (Bl) R. Jan 5
1807–1890. Born at Voltaggio near Genoa, Italy, when aged twenty-two she joined the 'Daughters of Our Lady of Refuge on Mount Calvary' at Brignolini. She was gatekeeper there for 61 years, only leaving the convent in order to nurse cholera sufferers, and impressed all sorts of people with her holiness and by the help she gave in advice and prayer. She was beatified in 1981.

Mary-Margaret-of-St-Sophia de Ripert d'Alauzier (Bl) *see* **Orange (Martyrs of)**

Mary-Anne Rivier (Bl) R. F. Feb 3
1768–1838. Born a cripple at Montpezat near Viviers, France, when aged eleven she was healed after praying to Our Lady and thus began her vocation. When aged twenty-two she started to teach and catechize the women and girls of her parish, and led the people in prayer and pious activity when the Revolution left the area bereft of priests and sacraments. To assist in this she gathered a group of helpers which became the 'Congregation of the Presentation of the Blessed Virgin Mary'. This had 137 houses when she died. She was beatified in 1982.

Mary Rochard (Bl) *see* **William Repin and Comps**

Mary-of-the-Angels du Rocher (Bl) *see* **Orange (Martyrs of)**

Mary-Emily de Rodat (St) R. F. Sep 19
1787–1852. From near Rodat in the Massif Central, France, she tried her vocation with three different congregations before starting a new teaching order in Villefranche in 1816 called the 'Congregation of the Holy Family'. This was to make up for the suppression of the Ursuline schools. She was helped by Fr Anthony Marty, who wrote the rule. She died at

Villefranche and was canonized in 1950.

Mary Roger (Bl) *see* **William Repin and Comps**

Mary of Rome (St) *see* **Eusebius, Marcellus and Comps**

Mary-of-Calvary Romero Clariana (Bl) *see* **Angela-of-St-Joseph Lloret Martí and Comps**

Mary-Anastasia-of-St-Gervase de Roquard (Bl) *see* **Orange (Martyrs of)**

Mary-Crucifixa di Rosa (St) R. F. Dec 15
1813–1855. A noblewoman from Brescia, Italy, from childhood she showed a lively piety and sympathy with the poor while running her father's household after her mother died. When cholera broke out in 1836 she was enthusiastic in nursing its sufferers, and in the course of this gathered the first companions of her institute, the 'Handmaids of Charity', which was founded in 1840. She died at Brescia and was canonized in 1954.

Mary-Joseph Rossello (St) R. F. Dec 7
1811–1888. From a poor family at Albisola near Savona, Italy, she wished to become a religious but her poor health and lack of a dowry prevented her and she became a Franciscan tertiary. In 1837 she founded a new institute, the 'Daughters of Our Lady of Mercy', which spread through Italy and South America. As superior she suffered from constant illness, but ruled her institute with heroic courage amid many difficulties until her death at Savona. She was canonized in 1949.

Mary-of-the-Holy-Spirit Roussel (Bl) *see* **Compiègne (Carmelite Martyrs of)**

Mary-Frances-of-Jesus Rubatto (Bl) R(OFM). F. Aug 9
1844–1904. From Carmagnola in Piedmont, Italy, she moved with her widowed mother to Turin and, while on holiday in Loano in Liguria, helped a workman injured while working on a new convent. The edification she gave led her to be persuaded to join it, and she became the superior and formation director. Thus started the 'Capuchin Sisters of Mother Rubatto', which spread to Argentina and Uruguay. As superior-general, she died while visiting the house at Montevideo and was beatified in 1993.

Mary-Gabrielle Sagheddu (Bl) R(OCSO). Apr 22
1914–1939. From Dorgali in Sardinia, she became a Trappestine at the nunnery at Grottaferrata (now moved to Viterbo), making profession in 1937. Supported by her community (who were influenced by the Abbe Couturier) she offered her life as a mystical sacrifice for church unity, especially between Catholics and Orthodox. Immediately she started suffering painful illnesses and severe spiritual trials, which only ended with her early death. She was beatified in 1983.

Bl Mary-Gabrielle Sagheddu, Mar 17

Mary-Magdalen Saillard d'Epinatz (Bl) *see* **William Repin and Comps**

Mary-Anne Sala (Bl) R. Nov 24
1829–1891. Born in Lombardy, Italy, she joined the 'Sisters of St Marcellina' (a teaching order) in 1848. She was a very good teacher, based mainly in Milan where she died and where her body was found to be incorrupt in 1921. She was beatified in 1980.

Mary-Magdalen Sallé (Bl) *see* **William Repin and Comps**

Mary-of-Mt-Carmel Sallés y Barangueras (Bl) R. F. Dec 6
1848–1911. From a prosperous family at Vich in Catalonia, Spain, when young she was aware

of the urgent need to help prostitutes and realized that their lack of education was a factor in their plight. So she devoted her life to educating women, and founded the 'Sisters of the Immaculate Conception' for that purpose. She died at Madrid and was beatified in 1998.

Mary Salome (St) L. Oct 22
C1st. One of the 'three Marys' (the others being Our Lady and Mary Salome), she was the wife of Zebedee and the mother of St James the Great and St John the Evangelist. One of the women who ministered to Christ during his public ministry, she also witnessed his crucifixion, burial and resurrection. She is depicted carrying a pot of ointment, a cruse or a pair of cruets.

Mary-of-Grace de San Antonio (Bl) *see* **Angela-of-St-Joseph Lloret Martí and Comps**

Mary-of-the-Heart-of-Jesus Sancho de Guerra (St) R. F. Mar 20
1842–1912. Born at Vitoria in the Basque Country, Spain, in 1864 she joined the 'Sisters, Servants of Mary for the Sick' which had just been founded by St Mary Torres Acosta. In 1871 she founded the 'Sisters, Servants of Jesus' at Bilbao under the bishop of Vitoria. She died after a long illness, and was canonized in 2000.

Mary-Magdalen Sanga (Bl) *see* **Great Martyrdom at Nagasaki**

Mary-Crucified Satellico
(Bl) R(OFM). Nov 8
1706–1745. Born in Venice, Italy, when aged nineteen she became a Poor Clare at Ostra Vetere. Working to become more like Jesus crucified, she enjoyed extraordinary mystical graces and took her authority as superior as being one of loving service to her community and of charity to poor people, as all were redeemed by the Cross. She was beatified in 1993.

Mary-Teresa Scherer (Bl) R. F. Jun 16
1825–1888. Born near Lucerne, Switzerland, in 1854 she joined Fr Theodosius Florentini (OFMCap) in his new foundation, the 'Sisters of Schools and the Care of the Poor', which was to educate poor girls. However he extended his concern to the social works of mercy and opened a hospital at Ingenbohl, which she ran. This was not acceptable to all the congregation and it split, Bl Mary becoming the superior of the 'Sisters of Mercy of the Holy Cross'. She was beatified in 1995.

Mary-Frances Schervier
(Bl) R. F. Dec 14
1819–1876. From Aachen, Germany, she was of a wealthy middle-class background. Practical concern for poor people led her to found the 'Franciscan Sisters of the Poor' in 1845. These were proved in service in the wars at the founding of the German Empire and comprised 41 houses in Europe and North America when she died at Aachen. She was beatified in 1974.

Mary-of-the-Sacred-Heart-of-Jesus Schininà (Bl) R. F. Jun 11
1844–1910. Born at Ragusa, Sicily, she was a rich noblewoman but she changed her life when aged twenty-five started to help the poor, sick and aged, to catechize and to propagate devotion to the Sacred Heart. This caused some scandal in the town. In 1889 she founded the 'Institute of the Sacred Heart of Jesus' to help her work, and she sometimes went begging for its support. She died in her home town and was beatified in 1990.

Mary Shoun (Bl) *see* **Great Martyrdom at Nagasaki**

Mary-of-Jesus-the-Good-Shepherd Siedliska (Bl) R. F. Nov 21
1842–1902. A Polish aristocrat, she was born near Warsaw but contracted tuberculosis as a girl and spent 1866–70 in Tyrol and Provence. She almost died in 1872, but unexpectedly recovered and went to Rome the next year to set about founding a new congregation, away from the Russians who were suppressing Latin consecrated life in Poland. The 'Sisters of the Holy Family of Nazareth', originally contemplative with the Augustinian rule but later with various apostolates, received many vocations from expatriate Poles and the mother house was founded at Cracow (under the Austrians) in 1880. She founded 29 other houses in Europe and the USA, died at Rome and was beatified in 1989.

Mary the Slave (St) L. Nov 1
d. *c*300. A slave-girl in the household of a Roman patrician in the reign of Diocletian, because she fasted against her mistress's will she was whipped and given to a soldier to be sexually abused. He let her escape instead, and she died in peace. She is mistakenly listed as a martyr.

Mary-of-Providence Smet (Bl) R. F. Feb 7
1825–1871. From Lille, France, she took the advice of St John Vianney to found the congregation of the 'Helpers of the Holy Souls' in order to make atonement on behalf of the souls in purgatory by works of charity. This she

did in Paris after 1856, writing a rule modelled on that of the Jesuits. The new and little congregation initially shared the material destitution of the people it helped but is now worldwide, being active in mission territories. She was noteworthy for her great patience in various difficulties, especially when she contracted terminal cancer. She died at Paris and was beatified in 1957.

Mary-Magdalen Sou (St) *see* **Korea (Martyrs of)**

Mary-Teresa de Soubiran La Louvière (Bl) R. F. Oct 20
1834–1889. A noblewoman from Castelnaudary near Carcassonne, France, she wanted to become a Carmelite nun but was advised to join to Beguines of Ghent and to found a house in her home village. This she did in 1855, and in 1864 she transferred the community to Toulouse and founded the 'Institute of Mary Auxiliatrix', which ran an orphanage and practised perpetual adoration of the Blessed Sacrament. As superior she was advised by her deputy to undertake a disastrous expansion of the institute, and through the machinations of the latter was then deposed and expelled. In 1868 she joined the 'Institute of Our Lady of Charity' and died as a member thereof. The truth then emerged and her treacherous deputy, who had become superior, was herself expelled. She was beatified in 1946.

Mary-Bernarda Soubirous (St) R. Apr 16
1844–1879. Universally known as 'Bernardette', she was the daughter of a destitute miller at Lourdes, France, and experienced a series of apparitions of Our Lady by the river just outside the town when aged fourteen. These established the famous shrine there. Eight years later she joined the 'Sisters of Charity of Our Lady' at Nevers, where she lived in obscurity until her death from tuberculosis. She was canonized in 1933.

Mary-Helen Stollenwerk (Bl) R. F. Nov 28
1852–1900. Born in the Eifel, Germany, and early wishing to go to China as a missionary, she was employed aged 29 as a mission-house domestic by Bl Arnold Janssen at Steyr, Netherlands. He was the founder of the 'Society of the Divine Word' and he also founded the 'Servants of the Holy Spirit' in 1889. In 1892 she joined the latter and became a contemplative in the cloistered branch in 1898, contracting tubercular meningitis three years later. She was beatified in 1995.

St Mary-Bernarda Soubirous, Apr 16

Mary-of-Sorrows Surís Brusola (Bl) *see* **Angela-of-St-Joseph Lloret Martí and Comps**

Mary Tanaka and Mary Tanaura (Bl) *see* **Great Martyrdom at Nagasaki**

Mary-of-the-Incarnation Thévenet (St) R. F. Feb 3
1774–1837. From Lyons, France, she was educated at a Benedictine convent school but her family was disrupted by the Revolution. Helping the victims of the 'Terror' led her to renounce marriage for the Church's sake, and this resulted in her founding the 'Religious of Jesus and Mary' in 1818. Her charism derived from the union of the Hearts of Jesus and Mary. She died at the mother-house at Fourvière and was canonized in 1993.

Mary Tokuan (Bl) *see* **Great Martyrdom at Nagasaki**

Mary-Desolata Torres Acosta (St) R. F. Oct 11
1826–1887. From a poor family of Madrid, Spain, she tried unsuccessfully to become a Dominican nun before founding an institute, the 'Handmaids of Mary, Ministers to the Sick'

in 1848 to care for sick people in their own homes. A subsequent priest-director of the new institute removed her and appointed another superior, with the result that the institute nearly failed. But she was re-appointed after inquiry by the bishop and went on to found forty-six houses before dying in Madrid. She was canonized in 1970.

Mary-Louise-of-Jesus Trichet (Bl) R. F. May 7
1684–1759. From Poitiers, France, when aged seventeen she became a disciple of St Louis Grignon de Montfort in that city. She entered the hospital for the poor in which he worked in 1703 and became the first of the 'Daughters of Wisdom'. This congregation received the approval of the bishop in 1715, just before St Louis died. She founded a number of houses between 1725 and 1748 and died at the mother-house at St Laurent-sur-Sèvre in 1759. She was beatified in 1993.

Mary-Catherine-of-St-Rose Troiani (Bl) R(OFM). F. May 6
1813–1887. An orphan, she was brought up in the Poor Clare convent at Ferentino near Rome and became a nun there in 1829. In 1859 she was one of a group who got permission to go to Cairo, Egypt, and to open a school. There they also cared for abandoned children. This foundation became the 'Franciscan Missionary Sisters of the Immaculate Heart of Mary', which had her as its first superior. She also opened a house in Jerusalem before dying in Cairo, being beatified in 1985.

Mary-Christina of the Two Sicilys, Queen (Bl) L. Jan 31
1812–1836. Born in Cagliari, Sardinia, she was a daughter of Victor Emmanuel, king of Savoy and of Mary Teresa, niece of the emperor Joseph II of Austria. In 1832 she married Ferdinand II, king of the Two Sicilys, and gave birth to a male heir before her early death. She was beatified in 1872.

Mary-Euthymia Üffing (Bl) R. (Sep 9)
1914–1955. From Halver in Westphalia, Germany, she came from a large farming family and joined the 'Sisters of Charity of Münster' in 1934. Her work was in nursing, and during the Second World War she nursed a large number of prisoners of war and indentured foreign workers with spiritual concern. After the war she ran the laundry at the central convent at Münster before dying of cancer. The memory of her kindliness and devotion to prayer led to her being beatified in 2001.

Mary-Anne Vaillot (Bl) *see* **William Repin and Comps**

Mary-Angels-of-St-Joseph Valtierra Tordesillas (Bl) *see* **Mary-Pillar-of-St-Francis-Borgia Martínez García**

Mary-Natalia-of-St-Louis Vanot (Bl) *see* **Valenciennes (Martyrs of)**

Mary Vas (Bl) M. T(OFM). Aug 16
d. 1627. A Japanese Franciscan tertiary, wife of Bl Caspar Vas, she was beheaded at Nagasaki with him and BB Francis-of-St-Mary of Mancha and Comps. *See* **Japan (Martyrs of)**.

Mary-of-Jesus-in-the-Sacrament Venegas de la Torre (St) R. F.
1868–1959. From a middle-class family of Zaplotanejo in Jalisco, Mexico, in 1905 with three companions she joined a group of pious women running a hospital. In 1910 she took religious vows and established the group as a new religious congregation, the 'Daughters of the Sacred Heart', in 1921. She was canonized in 2000.

Mary Wang (Li) (St) M. L. Jul ?
1851–1900. From Wei county in Hebei, China, she met a gang of Boxers on the road near Daning while trying to flee with her two children and was beheaded. *See* **China (Martyrs of)**.

Mary Won (St) *see* **Korea (Martyrs of)**

Mary-of-the-Apostles von Wüllenweber (Bl) T(OFM). F. (Dec 25)
1838–1907. A German baroness born near Gladbach, she had a pious upbringing but had difficulty in discerning the form of her religious vocation. She bought a house in Neuwerk in order to set up a community of Franciscan tertiaries dedicated to missionary work among women, but had trouble keeping it going at the time of the 'Kulturkampf'. Inspired by Fr John Jordan, the founder of the Salvatorians, she and five others moved to Rome and settled at Tivoli, despite not knowing the Italian language and customs. Thus began the 'Salvatorian Sisters', who had 25 other mission houses by the time she died. She was beatified in 1968.

Mary-Margaret d'Youville (St) R. F. Apr 11
1701–1771. Born at Varennes in French Canada, she married a government agent who was a swindling merchant but was widowed after eleven years and six children (two

survived infancy). She ran a shop to pay her husband's debts and performed works of charity with some companions. Thus started the congregation of the 'Grey Nuns', who later ran hospitals and orphanages but who initially suffered vicious persecution because people refused to believe that the widow of such a worthless man as her husband could herself do any good. She died at Montreal and was canonized in 1990.

St Mary-Margaret d'Youville, Apr 11

Mary Zhao (Guo) and Comps (SS) MM. LL. Jul 28
d. 1900. She was a sixty-year old woman of Zhaojiacun in Hebei, China, with two unmarried daughters, SS Mary and Rose Zhao. They hid in a well from a gang of Boxers, but were discovered and offered their lives if they denied their faith. They refused and were beheaded. *See* **China (Martyrs of)**.

Mary Zheng (Xu) (St) *see* **Lucy Wang (Cheng) and Comps**

Mary Zhu (Wu) (St) *see* **Ignatius Mangin and Comps**

Mary-Agnes Zudaire Galdeano (Bl) *see* **Mary-Gabrielle de Hinojosa Naveros and Comps**

Masculas (St) *see* **Armogastes and Saturus**

Massa Candida (SS) MM. Aug 24
d. *c*260. Meaning 'white mass', this name denotes a large group who were martyred at Utica, Roman Africa, in the reign of Gallienus and Valerian. The old Roman Martyrology asserts that they numbered three hundred and that the name referred to what was left of them after they had been thrown into a pit of quicklime. St Augustine, however, mentioned in a sermon that they numbered one hundred and fifty-three, and the name appears rather to refer to a locality near Utica.

Massalius (St) *see* **Corfu, Martyrs of**

Maternian *see* **Martinian**

Maternus of Cologne (St) B. Sep 14
d. ?325. He is the first bishop of Cologne mentioned in historical sources (in connection with the Donatist controversy). A medieval myth, invented to enhance the reputation of the diocese, identified him with the son of the widow of Naim and made him a disciple of St Peter.

Maternus of Milan (St) B. Jul 18
d. ?307. Elected by popular acclamation as bishop of Milan, Italy, in 295, he was imprisoned and tortured in the persecution of Diocletian but survived and died in peace.

Mathildis *see* **Matilda**

Matilda (Mathild, Maud) of Germany, Queen (St) L. Mar 14
d. 968. Wife of the German king Henry I and mother of Emperor Otto I and Duke Henry I of Bavaria, she was of a generous disposition and founded many monasteries. She was a widow for thirty years and had much trouble from her two sons, who relieved her of most of her possessions. She died at Quedlinburg nunnery, one of her foundations, and hence has been claimed as a Benedictine oblate.

Matrona (St) V. Mar 15
d. ?350. According to her unreliable acta, she was a serving-maid of a rich Jewish woman of Thessalonika, Greece, who ordered her to be whipped to death on discovering that she was a Christian.

Matrona (St) *see* **Alexandra of Amisus and Comps**

Matrona (St) *see* **Theodotus of Ancyra and Comps**

Matronian (St) R. Dec 14
? Nothing is known about this hermit of Milan, Italy.

Matthew (St) A. Sep 21
C1st. Matthew, or Levi, was a tax-collector at Capernaum before being called as an apostle, and is the author of the first gospel in the New Testament. The gospels provide the only trustworthy data concerning him. His career subsequent to Pentecost is unclear, as is whether or not he died a martyr, and the various traditions are unreliable. His attribute is a winged man (not an angel), and he may be depicted holding money, a bag of coins or a money-box.

Matthew of Albano
(Bl) B. R(OSB). Dec 25
d. 1134. A canon of Rheims, France, he became a Cluniac monk and prior at St-Martin-des-Champs in 1108. In 1125 he was created cardinal bishop of Albano and was papal legate in France and Germany. He was a strong supporter of the Cluniac ideal, and a great friend of St Peter the Venerable. His cultus is unconfirmed.

Matthew Alvarez (Bl) M. T(OP). Sep 8
d. 1628. A Japanese catechist and Dominican tertiary, he was burnt alive at Nagasaki with BB Dominic Castellet and Comps. *See* **Japan (Martyrs of)**.

Matthew of Beauvais (St) M. L. Mar 27
d. ?1098. From Beauvais, France, he went on the First Crusade with his bishop, was captured by the Muslims and was allegedly killed after he refused to convert to Islam.

Matthew Carreri (Bl) R(OP). Oct 7
d. 1470. From Mantua, Italy, he became a Dominican and spent his life in preaching throughout Italy. He died at Vigevano in Piedmont, and his cultus was confirmed for there in 1625.

Matthew Correa Magallanes (St) *see* **Mexico (Martyrs of)**

Matthew Feng (De) (St) *see* **Gregory Grassi and Comps**

Matthew Flathers (Bl) M. P. Mar 21
d. 1608. A farmer's son from Weston near Otley, Yorks, he was a graduate of Oxford and was ordained at Arras. He was a priest in Yorkshire (being banished once) until he was captured and executed at York. He was beatified in 1987. *See* **England (Martyrs of)**.

Matthew (Le van) Gam (St) M. L. May 11
1812–1847. A Vietnamese ship-owner, he used to ferry missionaries of the Paris Society from Singapore to Vietnam in his ship. He was imprisoned in 1846, tortured and beheaded. *See* **Vietnam (Martyrs of)**.

Matthew of Gniezno (St) *see* **Benedict of Gniezno and Comps**

Matthew Guimerá of Girgenti
(Bl) B. R(OFM Conv). Feb 3
d. 1450. From Girgenti, Sicily, he became a Conventual Franciscan but transferred to the Observants as a disciple of St Bernardine of Siena. He was forced by the pope to become bishop of Girgenti, but was not popular there. So he resigned and died in the Conventual friary at Palermo. His cultus was confirmed for Palermo and Girgenti in 1767.

Matthew-of-the-Rosary Kohioye (St) M. R(OP). Sep 28
d. 1633. A Japanese Dominican novice aged 18, he was a helper of St Luke Alonso and was martyred with him at Nagasaki. He was canonized in 1987. *See* **Japan (Martyrs of)**.

Matthew Lambert and Comps (BB) MM. LL. Jun 2
d. 1581. He and his three companions, BB Robert Mayler, Edward Cheevers and Patrick Cavenagh, were hanged at Wexford for conveying priests to France and were beatified in 1992. *See* **Ireland (Martyrs of)**.

Matthew (Nguyen van) Phuong (St) M. May 26
?1801–1861. Born at Ke-lav in Vietnam, he became a catechist and was beheaded near Dong-hoi. *See* **Vietnam (Martyrs of)**.

Matthew of Sandomir (Bl) *see* **Sadoc of Sandomir and Comps**

Matthia del Nazarei
(Bl) R(OSB)? Dec 30
d. ?1213. From Metalica in the Marches, Italy, she entered the nunnery of St Mary Magdalen there and went on to serve as abbess for forty years. The nunnery seems to have been Benedictine in her period (if the year of her death as given above is correct), but later transferred to the Poor Clares. Her cultus was confirmed for Camerino and Metalica in 1765.

Matthias (St) A. May 14
C1st. He was chosen by lot to take the place of Judas Iscariot among the apostles (Acts 1:21-22). The traditions concerning his later life are conflicting, but his relics were allegedly removed by St Helena from Jerusalem to what is

now St Matthias' Abbey at Trier, Germany. He is depicted as an elderly man holding (or being pierced by) a halberd.

Matthias Araki-Hyozaemon (Bl) M. L. Jul 12
d. 1626. Brother of Bl **Mancius Araki-Kyuzaburo** (q.v.), he was burnt alive at Nagasaki, Japan, for having accommodated European missionaries at his house. *See* **Japan (Martyrs of)**.

Matthias of Arima (Bl) M. L. May 27
d. 1622. A Japanese, he worked with the Jesuit missionaries in Japan as a catechist and was the provincial's servant. He refused to betray his master when interrogated in prison, was subjected to the water torture and died as a result. He was beatified in 1867. *See* **Japan (Martyrs of)**.

Matthias Cardona Meseguer (Bl*) see* **Dionysius Pamplona Polo and Comps**

Matthias of Jerusalem (St) B. Jan 30
d. ?120. Of Jewish descent, he was bishop of Jerusalem after that city's destruction by the Romans and probably had few people left in his diocese.

Matthias Kozaka (Bl*) see* **Thomas Koteda and Comps**

Matthias of Miyako (St) M. T(OFM). Feb 6
d. 1597. From Miyako in Japan, he became a Franciscan tertiary and was crucified at Nagasaki with SS Paul Miki and Comps. *See* **Japan (Martyrs of)**.

Matthias Mulumba (St) M. L. Jun 3
d. 1886. He was the chief of several villages in Buganda, Uganda, and had been a Muslim and then a Protestant before becoming a Catholic. He was executed on the orders of King Mwanga. *See* **Charles Lwanga and Comps**.

Matthias Nakano (Bl*) see* **Thomas Koteda and Comps**

Matthias Nogier (Bl*) see* **September (Martyrs of)**

Matthias of Sandomir (Bl*) see* **Sadoc of Sandomir and Comps**

Maturin (St) P. Nov 1
? According to his worthless legend he was from near Sens, France, and was converted and ordained by Polycarp, bishop of that city. Then he converted his parents and was a successful missionary in the area.

Maturin Deruelle and Maturin de la Villecrohain le Bous de Villeneuve (BB*) see* **September (Martyrs of)**

Maturus (St*) see* **Photinus, Sanctus and Comps**

Maud *see* **Mechtilde, Matilda or Mary Magdalen**

Maughan *see* **Meugant**

Maughold (Maccald) (St) B. Dec 28
d. ?488. He was allegedly an Irish brigand who was converted by St Patrick and sent to the Isle of Man as a missionary bishop.

Maura (St*) see* **Baya and Maura**

Maura (St*) see* **Fusca and Maura**

Maura (St*) see* **Timothy and Maura**

Maura and Brigid (Britta) (SS) RR. Jan 15
?C4th. According to St Gregory of Tours, the relics of these two obscure consecrated virgins were found during the episcopate of his predecessor St Euphronius and enshrined near Tours, France.

Maura of Byzantium (St) V. Nov 30
? She was martyred at Byzantium (Constantinople), but no details are extant. Her cultus was extremely popular in the patristic era.

Maura of Troyes (St) R. Sep 21
?827–850. From Troyes, France, and sister of a bishop there, she lived as a consecrated virgin in her parents' house.

Maurice (St*) see* **Leontius, Maurice and Comps**

Maurice (St*) see* **Theban Legion**

Maurice of Carnoët (St) R(OCist). Oct 13
?1114–1191. From Brittany, France, he became a Cistercian at Langonel and went on to be abbot-founder of Carnoët near Morlaix in 1177. He was an adviser of the dukes of Brittany.

Maurice McKenraghty (Bl) M. P. Jun 20
d. 1585. A diocesan priest, he was hanged at Clonmel and beatified in 1992. *See* **Ireland (Martyrs of)**.

Maurice-of-the-Infant-Jesus Macho Ródriguez (Bl) *see* **Nicephorus Díez Tejerina and Comps**

Maurice Tornay (Bl) M. R(OSA). Aug 12
1910–1949. Born in the Valais, Switzerland, he joined the 'Canons Regular of St Bernard' in 1931 and was sent to Yunnan in China in 1936. In 1945 he was appointed priest to Yerkalo, the only parish in Tibet (then autonomous). The local lamas expelled him and forced his people to apostatize. Going to Lhasa to intercede for them, he was ambushed and killed with his servant. He was beatified in 1993.

Maurilius of Angers (St) B. R. Sep 13
d. *c*430. From Milan, he migrated to France, became a disciple of St Martin of Tours and was made bishop of Angers in 407.

Maurilius of Cahors (St) B. Sep 3
d. 580. Bishop of Cahors, France, he was alleged to know the whole Bible by heart (an Egyptian monastic tradition).

Maurilius of Rouen (St) B. R(OSB). Aug 9
d. 1067. From Rheims, France, he became successively headmaster of the cathedral school at Halberstadt, a Benedictine monk at Fécamp in Normandy, abbot of St Mary's at Florence and archbishop of Rouen in 1055.

Maurinus (St) M? R? Jun 10
? The rebuilding of the church of St Pantaleon's Abbey at Cologne, Germany, in 966 allegedly uncovered his tomb with an epitaph describing him as abbot and martyr. There is no historical record of him.

Mauritius *see* **Maurice**

Mauronts (Maurontius, Mauruntius, Mauront) of Douai (St) R. May 5
d. 701. Eldest son of SS Adalbald and Rictrude, he was educated at the Frankish court and succeeded his father as lord of Douai, France. About to marry, he suddenly chose to become a monk at Marchiennes instead and was later the abbot-founder of Breuil-sur-Lys near Douai. He is the patron of Douai.

Maurontus of Marseilles (St) B. R. Oct 21
d. ?804. Abbot of St Victor at Marseilles, France, he was made bishop of the city in ?767.

Maurontus of St-Florent (St) R. Jan 9
d. *c*700. He was the abbot-founder of St-Florent-le-Vieil near Angers, France.

Maurus (St) *see* **Bonus and Comps**

Maurus (St) *see* **Claudius, Hilaria and Comps**

Maurus (St) *see* **Felix and Maurus**

Maurus (St) *see* **Papias and Maurus**

Maurus, Panteleimon and Sergius (SS) MM. Jul 27
d. ?117. They are alleged by their worthless acta to have been martyred at Bisceglie near Bari, Italy. Maurus is said to have been from Bethlehem and to have been sent by St Peter to be the first bishop of Bisceglia, but they were probably Roman martyrs whose relics were transferred.

Maurus and Placid (SS) RR(OSB). Jan 15
C6th. They feature in the second of the *Dialogues* of St Gregory the Great as young disciples of St Benedict at Subiaco. Apart from this reference, nothing is known about them. Maurus was alleged to have migrated to found the monastery of Glanfeuil near Angers, France, and Placid to have been martyred with some companions at Messina in Sicily by Muslim pirates. Both stories are worthless, the latter having been maliciously invented by a refugee Greek priest at Montecassino in 1115. Their cultus were confined to local or particular calendars in 1969, but they are still the patrons of Benedictine novices.

Maurus the African (St) M. Nov 22
d. *c*280. From a Christian family in Roman Africa, he travelled to Rome and was martyred there in the reign of Numerian. About ten different cities in Italy and France claimed to possess his relics as a result of his story being applied to various local saints.

Maurus (Marius, May) of Bodon (St) R. Jan 27
d. ?555. He was abbot-founder of Bodon near Sisteron in upper Provence, France.

Maurus of Cesena (St) B. R(OSB). Jan 20
d. 946. A Roman, he was ordained by Pope John IX, his uncle, and became a monk and abbot of Classe at Ravenna in 926. In 934 he was made bishop of Cesena, and the cell on a hill near the city which he built as a retreat for himself later grew into the Benedictine abbey of Santa Maria del Monte.

Maurus of Pećs (Bl) B. R(OSB). Oct 25
d. *c*1070. A Benedictine abbot, he was invited to Hungary by King St Stephen and joined the royal

foundation of Pannonhalma before becoming bishop of Pećs in 1036. He wrote biographies of SS Benedict Zorard and Andrew Szkalka. His cultus was confirmed for Pećs in 1848.

Maurus of Rheims and Comps (SS) MM. Aug 22
d. ?260 or 300 They are listed by the old Roman Martyrology as a priest and forty-nine others who were martyred at Rheims, France. The location is uncertain, as is the date.

Maurus of Sandomir (Bl*)* *see* **Sadoc of Sandomir and Comps**

Maurus Scott (Bl) M. R(OSB). May 30
d. 1612. Born at Chigwell, Essex, and baptized as William, he studied law at Cambridge but was converted by reading Catholic literature and received into the Church by Bl John Roberts, who sent him to the Benedictine abbey at Sahagún in Spain. He became a monk there in 1604, and after his ordination was sent back to England as a missionary. Shortly after his arrival he witnessed the martyrdom of his mentor, and shortly afterwards was captured and himself martyred at Tyburn. He was beatified in1929. *See* **England (Martyrs of)**.

Maurus of Verdun (St) B. Nov 8
d. 383. He became second bishop of Verdun, France, in 353, and his shrine was especially famous for miracles in the Dark Ages.

Maurus of Verona (St) B. R. Nov 21
d. *c*600. This bishop of Verona, Italy, apparently resigned when old to become a hermit.

Mavilus (Majulus) (St) M. Jan 4
d. 212. He was thrown to the wild animals in the arena at Adrumetum in Roman Africa in the reign of Caracalla.

Mawes (Maudetus, Maudez) (St) R. Nov 18
C6th? He was a Welsh hermit, based firstly across the estuary from Falmouth in Cornwall, England, where a small town is named after him, and then on the island of Modez in Brittany, France, where many churches are dedicated to him as St Maudez.

Mawgan *see* **Meugant**

Maxellend (St) V. Nov 13
d. *c*600. She was stabbed to death near Cambrai, France, by the lord of Solesmes because she wished to be a nun and refused to marry him.

Maxentia (St) V. Nov 20
? A young Irish or Scottish ('Scota') woman, she was allegedly a hermit near Senlis, France, and was killed at the place now called Pont-Sainte-Maxence after her. She is venerated at Beauvais.

Maxentiolus (Mezenceul) (St) R. Dec 17
C5th. A disciple of St Martin of Tours, France, he became the abbot-founder of Cunault.

Maxentius, Constantius, Crescentius, Justin and Comps (SS) MM. Dec 12
d. ?287. They were martyred at Trier, Germany, at the beginning of the reign of Diocletian.

Maxentius (Maixent) of Agde (St) R. Jun 26
?448–515. From Agde near Béziers, France, he was educated by St Severus and then became a monk and abbot of a monastery in Poitou. The place is now called Saint-Maixent-l'Ecole after him. He allegedly provided the local inhabitants with miraculous protection against the marauding Visigoths.

Maxima (St*)* *see* **Januarius, Maxima and Macaria**

Maxima (St*)* *see* **Martinian, Saturian, and Comps**

Maxima (St*)* *see* **Montanus and Maxima**

Maxima (St*)* *see* **Verissimus, Maxima and Julia**

Maxima, Donatilla and Secunda (SS) VV. Jul 30
d. 304. Three young women (Secunda was aged twelve), they were martyred at Tebourba in Roman Africa in the reign of Diocletian.

Maxima of Caillon (St) V? May 16
? She is venerated in the diocese of Fréjus, France, but nothing is known about her.

Maxima of Rome (St) M. Sep 2
d. 304. A Roman slave, she was whipped with St Ansanus. She died as a result but he survived and escaped.

Maximian (St*)* *see* **Bonosus and Maximian**

Maximian (St*)* *see* **Lucian, Maximian, and Julian**

Maximian of Bagae (St) B. Oct 3
d. 404. A Roman African convert from

Donatism, he was made bishop of Bagae in Numidia, Algeria, but the people there did not want him. When he took an important church from the Donatists he was attacked by them, seriously beaten and thrown from a tower. He recovered, emigrated to Italy (where he gained the sympathy of the emperor Honorius) and died in peace.

Maximian of Constantinople
(St) B. Apr 21
d. 434. Born at Rome, he emigrated to Constantinople when young, became a priest there and was made patriarch in 431.

Maximian of Ravenna (St) B. Feb 22
d. ?556. He became bishop of Ravenna, Italy, in 546, built the basilica of St Vitalis and is depicted on a mosaic therein.

Maximian of Syracuse (St) B. Jun 9
d. 594. A Sicilian, he became a monk of St Andrew's abbey on the Coelian Hill in Rome under St Gregory the Great. He represented him and his predecessor, Pope Pelagius, at Constantinople, and was made bishop of Syracuse and apostolic legate in Sicily in 591. This was an important responsibility, as the city of Rome as well as the papacy depended on food and revenue from the Sicilian estates of the Pope.

Maximilian-Mary Kolbe
(St) M. R(OFM Conv). Aug 14
1894–1941. Born at Zdunska-Wola in Poland (then in Russia), when young he became a Franciscan Conventual and worked hard as a missionary in Japan and in the newly independent Poland. He considered that the life of the Church depended on right devotion to Our Lady. During the German occupation after 1939 he sheltered over two thousand Jews and refugees and was at length sent to Auschwitz concentration camp. There he volunteered to take the place of a family man among a group selected to die of starvation in a punishment bunker, and was heard encouraging his fellow victims with hymns and prayers during the fortnight that this took. He was canonized in 1982.

Maximilian of Lorch
(St) M. B. Oct 12
d. 284. The 'Apostle of Noricum' (roughly modern Austria) was born at Cilli in Styria and became a missionary bishop with a base at Lorch near Passau. He was martyred at his home city in the reign of Numerian. His extant biography is unreliable, and the old Roman Martyrology duplicates him on Oct 29.

Maximilian (Mamilian)
of Thebeste (St) M. Mar 12
d. 295. He was conscripted into the army at Thebeste in Numidia, Africa, but refused to join because of the pagan ceremonies that were an integral part of army life. As a result he was executed. His acta are genuine. The old Roman Martyrology is erroneous in listing him as a martyr of Rome.

Maximinus (St) *see* **Juventinus and Maximinus**

Maximinus of Aix (St) B. Jun 8
C1st? Alleged to have been the first bishop of Aix in Provence, France, he features in the worthless legend concerning the journey of St Mary Magdalen to Marseilles. Further, he was imaginatively identified with the man born blind in the gospel of John, Ch.9.

Maximinus (Mesmin)
of Micy (St) R. Dec 15
d. ?520. From Verdun, France, he followed his uncle St Euspicius to Micy near Orléans and succeeded him as abbot there. He allegedly suppressed the local paganism which had survived two centuries of state Christianity (which apparently did not evangelize rural Gaul very well).

Maximinus of Trier (St) B. May 29
d. ?349. From near Poitiers, France, (his brother was St Maxentius of Poitiers), he succeeded St Agrecius, his teacher, as bishop of Trier, Germany, in 333 and was a powerful opponent of

St Maximilian-Mary Kolbe, Aug 14

imperial Arianism. He sheltered and defended St Athanasius of Alexandria and St Paul of Constantinople when they were exiled to Trier, and was mentioned with approbation by St Jerome.

Maximus (St) *see* **Cassius, Victorinus and Comps**

Maximus (St) *see* **Eusebius, Marcellus and Comps**

Maximus (St) *see* **Florus, Laurus and Comps**

Maximus (St) *see* **Liberatus, Boniface and Comps**

Maximus (St) *see* **Lucius, Silvanus and Comps**

Maximus *see* **Maginus**

Maximus (St) *see* **Magnus, Castus and Maximus**

Maximus *see* **Maximinus**

Maximus (St) *see* **Paul, Tatta and Comps**

Maximus (St) *see* **Quiriacus, Maximus and Comps**

Maximus (St) *see* **Sabinus, Julian and Comps**

Maximus (St) *see* **Tiburtius, Valerian and Maximus**

Maximus, Bassus and Fabius (SS) MM. May 11
d. 304. They were martyrs of Rome in the reign of Diocletian.

Maximus, Claudius, Praepedigna, Alexander and Cutias (SS) MM. Feb 18
d. ?295. They were allegedly martyred at Ostia near Rome in the reign of Diocletian, but their legend is worthless.

Maximus and Olympiades (SS) MM. Apr 15
d. 251. They are listed as Persian noblemen who were beaten to death with iron bars in the reign of Decius.

Maximus, Quintilian and Dadas (SS) MM. Apr 13
d. 303. Three brothers of Durostorum (now Silistra on the Danube in Bulgaria), they were beheaded at Ozobia in the reign of Diocletian.

Maximus, Theodore and Asclepiodotus (SS) MM. Sep 15
d. *c*310. They were from Marcianopolis in what is now Bulgaria, and were martyred at Adrianopolis (in European Turkey).

Maximus and Victorinus (SS) MM. May 25
d. ?384. They were allegedly brothers sent by Pope St Damasus as missionaries to the north of France who were killed by barbarians near Evreux. Their story is untrustworthy.

Maximus of Alexandria (St) B. Dec 27
d. 282. A priest of Alexandria, Egypt, he administered the patriarchate while St Dionysius was in exile from 261 and succeeded him in 282. He excommunicated Paul of Samosata for his adoptionist Christology.

Maximus of Apamea *see* **Maximus of Cuma**

Maximus of Chinon (St) R. Aug 20
d. *c*470. A disciple of St Martin, he became a hermit and then abbot-founder of Chinon near Tours, France.

Maximus the Confessor and Comps (SS) RR. Aug 13
580–662. A nobleman of Constantinople, he became a monk at Chrysopolis across the Bosporus with a disciple named Anastasius in 613. They migrated to Africa in 628, where he publicly opposed the imperial Monothelite doctrine being promulgated for political reasons. In 649 he visited Rome and supported the stand of Pope St Martin I against the same doctrine, but was seized with the pope in 653, tried at Constantinople and exiled. He refused to keep silence on the controverted subject and had his tongue and right hand amputated before a final exile to what is now Batum in Georgia with Anastasius and another disciple of the same name. He was a prolific and profound theological and spiritual writer, and is arguably the most important Church father not to have been declared a doctor.

Maximus of Cuma (St) M. Oct 30
d. 304. He was martyred at Cuma in Campania, Italy, but the old Roman Martyrology listed him as having been martyred at Apamea in Phrygia, Asia Minor.

Maximus of Ephesus (St) M. Apr 30
d. ?251. A merchant of Ephesus, Asia Minor, when the edict of Decius against the Christians was published in 250 he voluntarily gave himself up to the judge as a Christian and was

martyred. His acta are extant. He is also listed on Sep 28.

Maximus Hawryluk *see* **Podlasia (Martyrs of)**

Maximus of Jerusalem (St) B. May 5
d. *c*350. As a priest of Jerusalem he was blinded in one eye and lamed in one foot in the persecution of Diocletian. He succeeded St Macarius as bishop of Jerusalem in 333, but was persuaded by the Arian faction to join them against St Athanasius. This he repented of later, but he has never been venerated in the East.

Maximus of L'Aquila
(St) M. D. Oct 20
d. *c*250. This patron of L'Aquila in the Abruzzi, Italy, was a deacon there who was martyred in the reign of Decius by being thrown over a precipice.

Maximus of Mainz (St) B. Nov 18
d. 378. He became bishop of Mainz, Germany, in ?354, and as a bishop had a continual struggle against the Arian heresy. He wrote on the subject.

Maximus of Naples (St) M. B. Jun 10
C4th. He became the tenth bishop of Naples, Italy, in 359 but died in exile, allegedly as a martyr. His cultus was confirmed for Naples in 1872.

Maximus of Nola (St) B. Jan 15
d. *p*250. Bishop of Nola, Italy, he ordained St Felix. During the persecution of Decius in 250 he took to the hills and nearly died there of exposure and hunger. Being rescued by St Felix, he died at Nola shortly afterwards.

Maximus of Padua (St) B. Aug 2
C2nd. He was the successor of St Prosdocimus as bishop of Padua, Italy, and his alleged relics were found and enshrined in 1053 by Pope St Leo IX.

Maximus of Pavia (SS) BB. Jan 19
Pavia in Italy had two bishops of this name venerated as saints, one who succeeded St Crispin I in 270 and the other who succeeded St Epiphanius in 496 and who died in 511.

Maximus of Riez (St) B. R. Nov 27
d. 460. A monk of Lérins, France, he became abbot there in 426 and bishop of Riez in Provence reluctantly in 434. He was a prominent bishop of the time, and was allegedly a missionary in the area around Calais.

Maximus of Rome (St) M. Nov 19
d. ?255. He was martyred at Rome in the reign of Valerian.

Maximus of Turin (St) B. Jun 25
d. *c*420. Bishop of Turin, Italy, he has left a hundred and ten extant homilies which have been published in a critical edition and are of value. He has been confused with a namesake bishop of Turin who died about fifty years later.

Maximus of Verona (St) B. May 29
C6th? He was a bishop of Verona, Italy.

Mazota (St) R. Dec 23
C8th? She was the alleged superior of nineteen Irish nuns who settled at Abernethy near Perth, Scotland.

Mbaga-Tuzinde (St) M. L. Jun 3
d. 1886. A page at the court of King Mwanga of Buganda and adopted son of the chief executioner, he was burnt alive at Namuyongo and had to resist the pleas of his family to apostatize up to the time of his death. *See* **Charles Lwanga and Comps**

Mechtild of Diessen (St) R(OSB). May 31
1125–1160. From Andechs in Bavaria, Germany, and daughter of the count there, she was a child-oblate at the nunnery of Diessen and went on to become a nun there and then abbess. In 1153 she undertook the reform of the corrupt nunnery of Edelstetten on behalf of the bishop of Augsburg, which was no easy task. She was respected as a thaumaturge.

Mechtild of Hackeborn
(St) R(OSB). Nov 19
d. 1298. A noblewoman from Eisleben near Halle, Germany, she was a Benedictine child-oblate and ended up at the nunnery of Helfta where her sister was abbess. She was a noted mystic, and her experiences were recorded after her death by St Gertrude the Great (her former novice) in the *Book of Special Grace*. There was another mystic at Helfta with the same name at the same period, Mechtild of Magdeburg, who has not been canonized.

Mechtild of Spanheim *see* **Matilda of Spanheim**

Meda *see* **Ita**

Medan (St) *see* **Croidan, Medan and Comps**

Médard (St) B. Jun 8
*c*470–?558. A nobleman from Picardy, France,

he became bishop of Vermand in 530 and transferred the see to Noyon as the latter place was easier to defend. Later he also became bishop of Tournai, which remained united with Noyon until 1146. A legend similar to that of St Swithin is told about him.

Médard of Sandomir (Bl) *see* **Sadoc of Sandomir and Comps**

Mederic (Merry) (St) R. Aug 29
d. *c*700. From Autun, France, when aged thirteen he became a child-oblate at the abbey of St Martin there and went on to be abbot. Later he resigned and became a hermit locally and then near Paris, where the church of St Merry is now situated.

Medrald (Méerald, Méeraut) (St) R(OSB). Feb 23
d. *c*850. He was a monk at Ouche before becoming abbot of Vendôme, France.

Medran and Odran (SS) RR. Jul 7
C6th. Two brothers, they were disciples of St Kieran of Ossory, Ireland, at Saighir.

Meen *see* **Maine**

Megingaud (Mengold, Megingoz) (St) B. R. Mar 16
d. 794. A Frankish nobleman, he became a monk at Fritzlar in 738 and was a school-teacher before becoming abbot. Then he succeeded St Burchard as bishop of Würzburg, Germany, in ?754.

Meginhard (Meginher, Meginard) (Bl) R(OSB). Sep 26
d. 1059. Abbot of Hersfeld, Germany, from 1035, he rebuilt the monastery after it burned in 1037. He was one of the greatest biblical scholars of the early Middle Ages, but his relationship with the local bishop at Halberstadt was very poor. His cultus has not been confirmed.

Meginrat *see* **Meinrad**

Meinhard (Bl) B. R(CR). Apr 12
d. 1196. A Dutch Augustinian canon regular, he went to Livonia as a missionary, was made bishop in 1184 and lived at Ikškile on the Dvina. The see was moved to Riga, Latvia, in 1201 when that city was founded by the Knights of the Sword.

Meinrad (St) M. R(OSB). Jan 21
d. 861. A nobleman from near Tübingen, Germany, allegedly of the Hohenzollern family, he was a schoolboy and then a monk at Reichenau on the Rhine above Basel. Then he became a hermit for twenty-five years at the place in Switzerland later occupied by the abbey of Einsiedeln ('Hermitage'), but was murdered by robbers hoping to find hidden treasure in his cell. He is venerated as a martyr.

Meinulf (St) P. Oct 5
d. ?859. A Westphalian nobleman, he became a cathedral canon at Paderborn, Germany, and founded the abbey of Bödeken, where he died.

Meinwerk (Bl) B. Jun 5
d. 1036. A relative of Emperor St Henry II and his court chaplain, he became bishop of Paderborn, Germany, in 1099 and was an energetic builder in the city, being called its 'second founder' for providing it with walls.

Mel (Melchno) (St) B? Feb 6
d. ?488. According to the tradition he was one of the four nephews (Mel, Melchu, Munis and Rioch) of St Patrick, sons of Darerca (St Patrick's sister) and Conis. They accompanied St Patrick to Ireland as missionaries, Mel becoming the first abbot-bishop of Ardagh. The historical evidence concerning him and his brothers is hopelessly entangled and conflicting, however. He is the principal patron of the diocese of Ardagh, with its cathedral at Longford.

Melan (St) B. Jun 15
d. *p*549. He was bishop of Viviers near Montélimar, France, from 519.

Melangell (Monacella) (St) R. May 27
d. *c*590. She was apparently a hermit at Pennant Melangell in Powys, Wales, where her shrine has been reconstructed from fragments.

Melania the Elder (St) R. Jun 8
?342–?410. Of a Roman patrician family and a relative of St Paulinus of Nola, she was one of those caught up in the surge of interest in the ascetical life at Rome caused by the visit of the exiled St Athanasius and his companion monks in 340. Widowed when aged twenty-two, she was one of the first Roman women to visit the Holy Land and Egypt and founded a double monastery at Jerusalem in 378 with Rufinus of Aquilea. She incurred the enmity of St Jerome in the Origenist controversy.

Melania the Younger and Pinian (SS) RR. Dec 31
?383–438. A grand-daughter of St Melania the Elder, she was born in Rome and received a vast

inheritance. Marrying Pinian, a cousin, she had (and lost) two children before the couple decided to live in continence, turning their home into a pilgrims' hostel and giving their wealth to the poor. In ?406 they joined Rufinus in Sicily, from 410 they were in Roman Africa (where they got to know St Augustine) and finally settled in Jerusalem in 417. Pinian died in 431, and Melania founded a nunnery on the Mount of Olives in the following year. She died there.

Melanius *see* **Mellon**

Melanius of Rennes (St) B. Nov 6
d. ?535. From Brittany, France, he was bishop of Rennes when the Franks were conquering Gaul and won the friendship of King Clovis. He is alleged to have almost completely succeeded in extirpating rural paganism from his diocese (in contrast to the Gallic church in general), and tried to persuade his countrymen to abandon the Celtic church customs that they had brought from Britain.

Melas (Melantius) (St) B. Jan 16
d. ?385. An Egyptian monk, he was made bishop of Rhinocolura (now El-Arish) on the coast of Egypt, east of Port Said. He was imprisoned and banished on the orders of Emperor Valens for opposing Arianism.

Melasippus *see* **Meleusippus**

Melasippus, Carina and Anthony (Antoninus, Antonina) (SS) MM. Nov 7
d. 360. They were a couple with a son (or daughter), and were martyred at Ancyra, Asia Minor (now Ankara in Turkey) in the reign of Julian. The parents died under torture and the child was beheaded. This story conflicts with the declared policy of that emperor in not directly persecuting Christians.

Melchiades *see* **Miltiades**

Melchior (St) *see* **Magi**

Melchior (Bl) *see* **Mark, Stephen and Melchior**

Melchior Garcia Sampedro (St) M. B. Jul 28
d. 1858. He was the coadjutor of St Joseph Diaz Sanjurjo in central Tonkin, and was beheaded the year after him. *See* **Vietnam (Martyrs of)**.

Melchior Grodziecky (St) *see* **Košice (Martyrs of)**

Melchior-of-St-Augustine Sánchez Pérez (Bl) *see* **Martin of St Nicholas**

Meldon (Medon) (St) B. Feb 7
C6th. He was an obscure Irish hermit at Péronne near Amiens, France.

Meletius of Antioch (St) B. Feb 12
d. 381. From Melitene in Armenia, he became bishop of Sebaste in 358 and was exiled by the emperor Julian before being elected patriarch of Antioch, Syria, in 360. The church there had been in schism between a semi-Arian majority with its own bishop whom he replaced, and an orthodox minority whose bishop, St Eustathius, had been deposed. Meletius tried to reconcile the former group, but was himself exiled by the emperor Valens and replaced by a semi-Arian. The priest Paulinus was then consecrated for the Eustathian party, and this caused a schism between the Meletian and Eustathian factions in the city which lasted until 418 and which disturbed the entire Eastern church. Meletius returned in 378 and died while attending the first ecumenical council of Constantinople.

Meletius the Elect (St) B. Sep 21
? The martyrology of St Basil associates him with an alleged martyr called Isacius, and both are described as bishops in Cyprus.

Meletius of Sebastopolis (St) B. Dec 4
d. ?295. A bishop in Pontus, Asia Minor, he took refuge in the Holy Land during the persecution of Diocletian and became acquainted with Eusebius. The latter wrote that his name derived from 'Mel Atticum' (Attic honey), and was a description of his preaching style. If so, his real name is unknown.

Meletius Stratelates and Comps (SS) MM. May 24
C2nd? They are listed in the old Roman Martyrology as a general of the Roman army who was martyred with 252 companions. There is no other information about them, and their acta are fictitious.

Meleusippus (St) *see* **Speusippus, Eleusippus and Comps**

Melitina (St) V. Sep 15
d. *c*150. She was martyred at Marcianopolis (near Varna, Bulgaria) in the reign of Antoninus Pius.

Melito of Sardis (St) B. Apr 1
d. *c*180. He was a bishop of Sardis in Lydia, Asia Minor, but biographical details are scanty. He

was a well-known ecclesiastical writer of the period of the Apologists, but little of his work is extant apart from his famous paschal homily.

Mellanius *see* **Mellon**

Mellitus (St) B. R. Apr 24
d. 624. A Roman abbot, presumably from St Andrew's monastery on the Coelian Hill, he was sent to England in 601 by St Gregory the Great at the head of a group of monks intended as reinforcements for St Augustine. He spent three years in Kent before becoming a missionary bishop for the East Saxons based at London, but was exiled to France for excommunicating the apostate sons of their king. In 619 he succeeded St Laurence as archbishop of Canterbury.

Mellon (St) B. R? Oct 22
d. 314. The tradition alleges that the first bishop of Rouen, France, was a missionary from near Cardiff, Wales, where there is now a village named St Mellons after him.

Melor (St) M. Oct 1
d. *c*540. According to his legend he was a son of a ruler of Brittany, France, and was killed as a child by his brother who wanted no rival claimants to the throne. His shrine was at Lanmeur near Morlaix, and he was also venerated at Amesbury in Wiltshire, England. Even in the early Middle Ages the true facts about him were lost.

Memmius (Menge, Meinge) (St) B. Aug 5
d. *c*300. The traditional first bishop of Châlons-sur-Marne, France, was alleged to have been a disciple of St Peter in a typical pretence at apostolicity by the medieval French church, but the diocese was founded in the late C3rd at the earliest.

Memnon (St) *see* **Severus, Memnon and Comps**

Memorius (Mesmin) and Comps (SS) MM. Sep 7
d. 451. According to the untrustworthy tradition, he was a deacon of Troyes, France, when St Lupus was bishop and was sent with five companions on an embassy to Attila the Hun to ask that the city be spared. They were beheaded. Attila has been traditionally blamed for the killing of Christians by various barbarians at this time. The old Roman Martyrology misspells his name as 'Nemorius'.

Menalippus (St) *see* **Diomedes, Julian and Comps**

Menander (St) *see* **Cyril, Aquila and Comps**

Menander (St) *see* **Patrick, Acacius and Comps**

Menas, Hermogenes, and Eugraphus (SS) MM. Dec 10
d. ?312. They were beheaded at Alexandria, Egypt, in the reign of Diocletian. Their acta are worthless, and were falsely attributed to St Athanasius.

Menas of Constantinople (St) B. R. Aug 25
d. 552. From Alexandria, Egypt, he became superior of the hospice of St Samson at Constantinople and was made patriarch in 536. He condemned Origenism but endorsed the decrees of the emperor Justinian condemning the 'Three Chapters' at a time when the Western Church strongly opposed this policy, and was excommunicated by Pope Vigilius in 551. He withdrew his endorsement and was reconciled just before his death. The chapters were eventually condemned at the fifth ecumenical council, which caused a schism in the West.

Menas of Egypt (St) M. Nov 11
d. *c*300. He was alleged to have been an Egyptian officer in the imperial army martyred at Alexandria, and his cultus became extremely popular during the Christian era of Egypt. He had a shrine at Kotyaeum in Phrygia, which led to the erroneous tradition that he was martyred there. His main shrine was in the desert south of Alexandria at Abu-Mîna, and was a large complex including a basilica and monastery. The Coptic church ascribed the victory of the Allies at El Alamein during the Second World War to his intercession, and in thanksgiving his ruined shrine has been restored and is now a functioning pilgrimage centre.

Menas of Santomena (St) R. Nov 11
C6th. A Greek from Asia Minor, he became a hermit in the Abruzzi, Italy, probably at Santomena (of which place he is patron and which is named after him). St Gregory the Great mentions him in his *Dialogues*.

Mendez Valle (Bl) *see* **Peter Rodriguez and Comps**

Menedemus (St) *see* **Urban, Theodore, and Comps**

Menehould (Manehild) (St) R. Oct 14
C5th. She was a hermit near Châlons-sur-Marne, France, one of the seven saintly

daughters of a count of Perthes, and gave her name to the town of Ste-Menehould. *See* **Amata of Joinville**.

Menelaus (Ménelé, Mauvier) (St) R. Jul 22
d. *c*720. He was the abbot-founder of Menat near Clermont-Ferrand, France.

Meneus (Hymenaeus) and Capito (SS) MM. Jul 24
? They are listed in both the Roman and Byzantine martyrologies, but nothing is known about them.

Menignus (St) M. Mar 15
d. 251. From Parium on the Hellespont, Asia Minor, he was a dyer who tore down the town's publicly displayed copy of the imperial edict against the Christians. His fingers were cut off and he was later beheaded.

Menna (Manna) (St) R. Oct 3
d. *c*400. She was allegedly from Lorraine and became a nun at Châlons-sur-Marne, France, but her extant biography is unreliable.

Mennas *see* **Menas**

Menodora, Metrodora and Nymphodora (SS) VV. Sep 10
d. 306. Three sisters, they were martyred under Galerius near the Pythian hot springs in Bithynia, Asia Minor. These facts are certain, but their acta are worthless.

Menulf (Menou) (St) B. Jul 12
C7th. He is alleged to have been an Irish pilgrim who became bishop of Quimper in Brittany, France, and who died near Bourges while returning from Rome.

Mercedes-of-Jesus Molina (Bl) R. F. Jun 12
1828–83. Born in Los Rios, Ecuador, she made a private vow of chastity in 1849. While living in her sister's house she tried to help the poor, and in 1867 she went to work in an orphanage and in missionary work in the Andes with two companions. After several journeys they ended up at Rivibamba in 1872. There she founded the 'Congregation of Mary and Anne, Progenitors of Jesus' in order to help poor girls and lapsed women. She was beatified in 1985.

Mercolino *see* **Marcolino**

Mecuria (St) *see* **Ammonaria and Comps**.

Mercurialis (St) B. May 23
d. ?406. Allegedly from what is now Azerbaijan, he was the first bishop of Forli, Italy. His cultus is ancient but has inspired many fanciful legends.

Mercurius of Caesarea (St) M. Nov 25
d. *c*250. According to his untrustworthy acta, he was a Scythian officer in the imperial army and was martyred at Caesarea in Cappodocia, Asia Minor, in the reign of Decius. He is popular in the East as one of the great soldier-martyrs.

Mercurius of Lentini and Comps (SS) MM. Dec 10
d. ?300. A group of twenty soldiers, they were detailed to escort some Christian prisoners to their place of execution at Lentini, Sicily, and were so impressed with the behaviour of the prisoners that they declared themselves to be Christians also and were thus also beheaded.

Merewenna of Marhamchurch (St) R. Aug 13
? The patron of Marhamchurch near Bude in Cornwall, England, is alleged to have been one of the daughters of St Brychan.

Merewenna of Romsey (St) R(OSB). May 13
d. *c*970. She was abbess of Romsey nunnery in Hampshire, England, restored under King Edgar in 967.

Meriadec of Vannes (1) (St) B. R. Jun 7
d. ?686. Probably from Wales, he was a hermit at Vannes in Brittany, France, before becoming bishop there. His extant C12th biography is unreliable.

Meriadec of Vannes (2) (St) B. R. Jun 7
d. 1302. From Brittany, France, like his namesake he was a hermit who was made bishop of Vannes. He was famous for his charity to the poor.

Merin of Bangor (St) R. Jan 6
d. *c*600. A disciple of St Dunawd at Bangor Isycoed near Wrexham, Wales, he is commemorated by Bodferin in Gwynned and also by churches in Brittany.

Merin (Meadhran, Mirren) of Paisley (St) B. R. Sept 15
d. *c*620. Allegedly a disciple of St Comgall at Bangor, Ireland, he became a missionary bishop based at Paisley, Scotland, of which place he is the patron. The local soccer club is named after him.

Merililaun (Merolilaun) (St) M. May 18
C8th. A 'Scot' (from Scotland or Ireland), he was killed by robbers near Rheims, France, when on pilgrimage to Rome.

Merry *see* **Mederic**

Merulus (St) *see* **Anthony, Merulus and John**

Merwenna *see* **Merewenna**

Mesme *see* **Maximus**

Mesmin *see* **Memorius or Maximinus**

Mesopotamia (Martyrs of)
(SS) MM. May 23
d. ?307. This group was martyred in the region of Edessa (now Urfa in Turkey) in the reign of Galerius.

Mesrop the Teacher (St) B. R. Nov 25
?345–440. He was a monk and disciple of St Nerses the Great, Catholicos of Armenia, and was an auxiliary bishop under St Isaac the Great, his successor. He became Catholicos himself only six months before he died. The Armenians attribute to him the invention of their alphabet and the translation of the New Testament into Armenian, and he founded many schools and monasteries. This activity was in the context of Armenia having been annexed by the Persian Empire, and arguably saved the Armenians from extinction as a nation.

Messalina (St) V. Jan 19
d. ?251. According to her story, she was from Foligno, Italy, and was consecrated as a virgin by St Felician, bishop there. She visited him in prison, was spotted as a Christian and then clubbed to death.

Metellus (St) *see* **Mardonius, Musonius and Comps**

Methodius (St) *see* **Cyril and Methodius**

Methodius the Confessor
(St) B. R. Jun 14
d. 847. From Syracuse, Sicily, he was a civil servant at Constantinople before founding and joining a monastery on the Aegean island of Chios, Greece. When iconoclasm was re-introduced as imperial policy in 814 he joined the opposition and was imprisoned for seven years from 821. Finally the empress Theodora designated him patriarch of Constantinople in 842 in place of the deposed iconoclast John the Grammarian, and the synod that he then convoked marked the final end of iconoclasm.

Methodius of Olympus
(St) M. B. Sep 18
d. 311. He was bishop of Olympus in Lycia, Asia Minor, and possibly then of Tyre in Lebanon (if St Jerome's assertion is correct). He is alleged to have been martyred at Chalcis. An eminent theologian, he is known for his *Banquet of the Ten Virgins* (a Christian version of Plato's *Symposium*) and for his treatise on the resurrection against Origen.

Methodius Trčka (Bl)
M. R(CSSR). (Mar 23)
1886–1959. From near Ostravici, Czech Republic, he became a Redemptorist in 1902. He then went to work with the Greek Catholics of the Ukrainian and Ruthenian rites in what was then the north-eastern part of the Hapsburg Empire. (The Ruthenians are Slavs living south-west of the Carpathian mountains.) In 1921 he founded a mixed-rite Redemptorist community at Stropkov in Slovakia and a Ruthenian rite community at Michalovce where he became the superior. In 1949 the Communist government of Czechoslovakia suppressed his foundations; he was accused of collaboration with Bl Paul Gojdič and imprisoned. He eventually died of pneumonia after ill-treatment and was beatified as a martyr in 2001.

Metranus (Metras) (St) M. Jan 31
d. c250. From Alexandria, Egypt, he was martyred in the reign of Decius. St Dionysius of Alexandria, his bishop and contemporary, left an account of the martyrdom.

Metrobius (St) *see* **Lucian, Metrobius and Comps**

Metrodora (St) *see* **Menodora, Metrodora and Nymphodora**

Metrophanes (St) B. Jun 4
d. 325. Bishop of Byzantium from 313, he was apparently that city's first but very little is known about him. The town was previously in the diocese of Heraclea. It became Constantinople five years after his death.

Meugant (Mawgan, Morgan)
(St) R. Sep 26
C6th. He appears to have been a disciple of St Illtyd, to have lived as a hermit in several places and to have died on the island of Bardsey,

Wales. Several churches in Wales and Cornwall are dedicated to him.

Meuris and Thea (SS) VV. Dec 19
d. ?307. They were martyred at Gaza in the Holy Land, and are probably identical with SS Valentina and Comps.

Mewan *see* **Maine**

Mewrog (St) Sep 25
? Nothing is known about this Welsh saint.

Mexico (Martyrs of) (SS) MM. May 25
d. 1915–37. The Mexican Revolution of 1911 gave rise to the 'Constitution of Querétaro', which aimed at eliminating the Church from all aspects of the country's secular life. The period in office of President Calles (1924–8) saw an attempt at its enforcement, and all Catholic organizations and institutions were suppressed. The 'Cristero' rebellion in favour of the Church was defeated, and many priests as well as lay people were killed. Twenty-six were beatified in 1992, all of them priests except Bl Michael de la Mora (a cleric) and three lay companions of Bl Aloysius Batis: BB Emmanuel Morales, Salvator Lara and David Roldán. All but one were canonized in 2000. *See* lists of national martyrs in appendix.

Michael de Aozaraza (St) *see* **Laurence Ruiz and Comps**

Michael the Archangel (St) Sep 29
He is described in the Bible as 'one of the chief princes' of the angels (Dan 10:13) and as the leader of the heavenly armies in their battle against the forces of evil (Rev 12:7). He is mentioned also in the letter of Jude as 'rebuking the devil'. His veneration in both East and West is ancient, and his feast-day is probably the anniversary of the dedication of a church in his honour on the Salarian Way at Rome in the C6th. His most famous shrine is at Monte Gargano on the Adriatic coast of Italy. In northern Europe he often had churches dedicated to him on hilltops (e.g. at Glastonbury), apparently in order to supplant worship of the pagan god Wotan. He is depicted as an angel in full armour with a sword and a pair of scales, or piercing a dragon or devil with his lance. Since 1969 his feast-day on this date has been combined with those of SS Gabriel and Raphael.

Michael-of-the-Saints Argemir (St) R(OTrin). Apr 10
1591–1625. Born at Vich in Catalonia, Spain,

St Michael the Archangel, Sep 29

he joined the Calced Trinitarians at Barcelona in 1603 and took his vows at Zaragoza in 1607. The same year he transferred to the Discalced Trinitarians and renewed his vows at Alcalá. After his ordination he was twice superior at Valladolid, where he died. He was canonized in 1862.

Michael Binard (Bl) *see* **September (Martyrs of)**

Michael-Aloysius Brulard (Bl) *see* **John-Baptist Souzy and Comps**

Michael Carvalho and Comps (Bl) M. R(SJ). Aug 25
1577–1624. From Braga, Portugal, he became a Jesuit in 1597, taught theology at Goa for fifteen years and then went to Japan. He was burnt to death at Shimabara with BB Louis Baba, Louis Sasada, Louis Sotelo and Peter Vasquez. They were beatified in 1867. *See* **Japan (Martyrs of)**.

Michael Díaz Hori (Bl) M. l. Aug 19
d. 1622. He was a Spanish merchant accompanying BB Louis Flores and Comps and was beheaded at Nagasaki, Japan, with them. *See* **Japan (Martyrs of)**.

Michael Febres-Cordero Muñoz (St) R. Feb 9
1854–1910. From Ecuador, he became a de la Salle Brother and was their first indigenous vocation. A gifted teacher and author, he was much loved by his pupils and his literary and poetic works earned him membership of the Académie Française. A person full of charity and good humour, he led an intense life of personal prayer. He died near Barcelona, Spain, and owing to anti-clerical hostility his body was taken back to Ecuador in 1936. He was canonized in 1984.

Michael de la Gardette (Bl) *see* **September (Martyrs of)**

Michael Garicoïts (St) P. F. May 14
1797–1863. From a Basque peasant family of Ibarre near Bayonne, France, he became a domestic servant of his parish priest and then of the bishop of Bayonne in exchange for their educating him for the priesthood. He was ordained in 1823 and was appointed professor of philosophy at the diocesan seminary. He went on to become rector there, and as such he founded at Betharram in 1838 the congregation of 'Auxiliary Priests of the Sacred Heart' (the 'Betharram Fathers') for home mission work. After many initial difficulties the congregation became international in scope, being established in America. He was canonized in 1947.

Michael Gedroye (Bl) R(CR). May 4
d. 1485. A nobleman from near Vilna, Lithuania, he was a crippled dwarf and became a hermit in a cell adjoining the church of the Augustinian canons regular at Cracow, Poland. He spent his life there, being famous as a prophet and a thaumaturge. His cultus is not confirmed.

Michael Ghebre (Bl) M. R. Sep 1
1791–1855. From Mertule Maryam near the Blue Nile in Ethiopia, he became a monk of the native Ethiopian church and was a noted theologian. He met Bl Justin de Jacobis while in Cairo in 1841, which led to a visit to Rome and his conversion in 1844. With the help of the Vincentians he established a seminary at Gaula to train a native Catholic clergy, and translated many Catholic writings into the native languages. In 1851 he joined the Vincentians and was secretly ordained, but a persecution against the Ethiopian Catholics was started in 1855 by Theodore II, an usurper of the throne. Michael was arrested and died from ill-treatment while in custody. He was beatified in 1926.

Michael Himoyona (Bl) M. R(OP). Sep 16
d. 1628. A Japanese catechist and Dominican tertiary, he was beheaded at Nagasaki with his son, Bl Paul, and Bl Dominic Shobyoye. *See* **Japan (Martyrs of)**.

Michael (Ho Dinh) Hy (St) M. L. May 22
?1808–1857. From a Christian family of Nhu-Lam in south Vietnam, he became a great mandarin and superintendent of the royal silk mills in the reign of Tu-Duc. As a young man he was an agnostic, but converted and used his position to try and protect his fellow Christians. He was for this reason beheaded at An-Hoa near Hue. *See* **Vietnam (Martyrs of)**.

Michael Ichinose (Bl) M. T(OSA). Sep 28
d.1630. A Japanese Augustinian tertiary, he was beheaded at Nagasaki with BB John Chozaburo and Comps for having given shelter to the Augustinian missionaries. *See* **Japan (Martyrs of)**.

Michael Kizayemon (Bl) M. T(OFM). Aug 16
d. 1627. He was a Japanese Franciscan tertiary beheaded at Nagasaki with BB Francis-of-St-Mary of Mancha and Comps. *See* **Japan (Martyrs of)**.

Michael Kosaki (St) M. L. Feb 6
d. 1597. A Japanese catechist and hospital nurse, he worked with the Franciscan missionaries in Kyushu and was crucified at Nagasaki with SS Paul Miki and Comps (including his own son, St Thomas Kosaki). *See* **Japan (Martyrs of)**.

Michael Kozal (Bl) M. B. Jan 16
1893–1943. A Pole, when he was born his home town was Gniesen in Germany but it became Gniezno in Poland in 1919. He became a priest there, taught in the diocesan seminary and became auxiliary bishop in 1939. Two months later the Germans invaded Poland and re-annexed the area. They set out to destroy all manifestations of the Polish Church and culture there and sent him to the concentration camp at Dachau, where he used to celebrate the Mass in secret for his fellow inmates before his death. He was beatified as a martyr in 1987.

Michael Kurobioye (St) M. L. Aug 17
d. 1633. He was the assistant of St James Gorobioye, was martyred with him at Nagasaki, Japan, and was canonized in 1987. *See* **Japan (Martyrs of)**.

Michael Leber (Bl) *see* **September (Martyrs of)**

Michael-Bernard Marchand (Bl) *see* **John-Baptist Souzy and Comps**

Michael Masip González (Bl) *see* **Philip-of-Jesus Munárriz Azcona and Comps**

Michael de la Mora (St) *see* **Mexico (Martyrs of)**

Michael (Nguyen Huy) My (St) M. L. Aug 12
d. 1838. The married Vietnamese mayor of Ke-vinh, he was beheaded with St James Nam. *See* **Vietnam (Martyrs of)**.

Michael Nakashima (Bl) M. R(SJ). Dec 25
d. 1628. From near Nagasaki, he concealed missionaries in his house for years and became a Jesuit. In 1627 he was placed under house arrest, and in the following year was taken to Shimabara and tortured. Then he was finally taken to Unzen-dake, a volcano above the town, and had boiling water from the hot springs there poured upon him until he died. He was beatified in 1867. *See* **Japan (Martyrs of)**.

Michael Pini (Bl) R(OSB Cam). Jan 27
?1445–1522. From Florence, Italy, he was well placed at the court of Lorenzo de' Medici before becoming a Camaldolese hermit in 1502. After ordination he was walled up in his hermitage, where he remained until his death. His cultus is not confirmed.

Michael-Augustine Pro (Bl) R(SJ). Nov 23
1894–1927. Born of a wealthy family at Guadalupe near Zacatecas, Mexico, he joined the Jesuits in 1911, just in time for the viciously anti-clerical Mexican Revolution. He was in exile in Belgium from 1912 to 1926 and was ordained despite having serious problems with his stomach. On his return, he worked very hard in the persecuted Church until he was seized and executed on suspicion of plotting against President Obregón. He was beatified in 1988.

Michael Rua (Bl) R. Oct 29
1837–1910. From Turin, Italy, he was an early disciple of St John Bosco and succeeded him as superior-general of the Salesians in 1888. Nearly three hundred new houses of the institute were opened under him. He was beatified in 1972.

Michael Ruedas Mejías (Bl) *see* **Hospitaller Martyrs of Spain**

Michael Sakaguchi (Bl) M. L. Nov 27
1594–1619. A Japanese layman, he was related to the daimyos of Hirado-jima and was described as a very amiable man. He was beheaded at Nagasaki with BB Thomas Koteda and Comps. *See* **Japan (Martyrs of)**.

Michael of Sandomir (Bl) *see* **Sadoc of Sandomir and Comps**

Michael Sato (Bl) M. R(SJ). Sep 10
1589–1622. A Japanese, he started helping the Jesuit missionaries when only eight years old. He made his profession as a Jesuit to Bl Charles Spinola in prison at Omura just before they were burned in the 'Great Martyrdom' at Nagasaki. *See* **Japan (Martyrs of)**.

Michael of Synnada (St) B. May 23
d. ?820. He was a disciple of St Tarasius, patriarch of Constantinople, and was appointed by him bishop of Synnada in Phrygia, Asia Minor, in 787. He was a fearless opponent of iconoclasm, and when this heresy became imperial policy again under Emperor Leo IV he was exiled to Galatia, where he died.

Michael Tomachi (Bl) M. L. Sep 8
1613–1628. A Japanese teenager, he was beheaded at Nagasaki with his father, John, and his three brothers: Dominic, Paul and Thomas. *See* **Dominic Castellet and Comps** and **Japan (Martyrs of)**.

Michael Tozo (Bl) M. R(SJ). Jun 20
d. 1626. He was a Japanese catechist who worked with Bl Balthasar Torres and became a Jesuit just before his execution. *See* **Francis Pacheco and Comps** and **Japan (Martyrs of)**.

Michael Ulumbijski (St) *see* **John Zedazneli and Comps**

Michael Wawryszuk (Bl) *see* **Podlasia (Martyrs of)**

Michael Yamada (Bl) M. T(OP). Sep 8
d. 1628. A Japanese Dominican tertiary, he was beheaded at Nagasaki with BB Dominic Castellet and Comps. *See* **Japan (Martyrs of)**.

Michael Yamichi (Bl) M. L. Sep 10
1617–1622. The five-year-old son of Bl Damian Yamiki, he was beheaded at Nagasaki with his father in the 'Great Martyrdom'. *See* **Japan (Martyrs of)**.

Michael-Pius a Zerbo (Bl) *see* Liberatus **Weiss and Comps**

Michaela *see* **Mary-Michaela**

Michan (St)
? A church dedicated to this saint is in Dublin. A tradition claims that he was a Dane, but nothing is known.

Michelina Metelli of Pesaro
(Bl) T(OFM). Jun 20
1300–1356. A noblewoman from Pesaro, Italy, when aged twelve she married the duke of Malatesta but was widowed when she was twenty. Then her only child died and she became a Franciscan tertiary. Her disgusted parents treated her as a madwoman and imprisoned her for a while. On being released she gave her property to the poor and lived in asceticism for the rest of her life. Her cultus for Gubbio was confirmed in 1737.

Mida *see* **Ita**

Midan (Nidan) (St) R. Sep 30
d. *c*610. This alleged disciple of St Kentigern founded Llanidan in Anglesey, Wales, and was possibly a missionary near Aberdeen, Scotland (if there is no confusion between different saints).

Midnat *see* **Medana**

Migdonius and Mardonius
(SS) MM. Dec 23
d. 303. When the emperor Diocletian instigated his persecution in 303, the imperial court at Nicomedia was purged of Christian officials. These two refused to apostatize and were imprisoned and condemned. Migdonius was burnt alive and Mardonius was drowned in a well.

Miguel *see* **Michael**

Milburga (St) R. Feb 23
d. 715. Eldest daughter of St Ermenburga and sister of SS Mildred and Mildgyth, she became second abbess of the nunnery of Wenlock in Shropshire, England, founded by her father, the king of Mercia. St Theodore consecrated her as a nun, and the nunnery apparently flourished under her. (It became extinct in the Viking era and was re-founded after the Norman Conquest as a Cluniac priory, whereupon her alleged relics were discovered.) She was a thaumaturge and had a peculiar rapport with birds.

Mildgyth (St) R. Jan 17
d. ?676. The youngest of the three daughters of St Ermenburga, she either became a nun under her mother at Minster in Thanet, Kent, England, and succeeded her sister as abbess or she entered a nunnery in Northumbria, where she died. These contradictory traditions are both old.

Mildred of Thanet (St) R. Jul 13
d. *c*700. The middle of the three daughters of St Ermenburga, she was sent to be educated in the French nunnery of Chelles and, on her return, was consecrated as a nun by St Theodore at Minster in Thanet, Kent, England. She eventually succeeded her mother as abbess. The monks of St Augustine's Abbey in Canterbury stole her relics for their own monastery in 1030 (an account of the escapade survives), and they were taken to Deventer in the Netherlands after the Reformation. Part has now been returned to Minster. Her cultus was popular in the Middle Ages. Her attribute is a white deer.

St Mildred of Thanet, Jul 13

Miles Gerard (alias William Richardson) (Bl) M. P. Apr 30
d. 1590. From near Wigan, Lancs, he became a schoolteacher before studying for the priest-

hood at Rheims. He was ordained in 1583, executed at Rochester, Kent, and beatified in 1929. *See* **England (Martyrs of)**.

Milles (St) M. B. Apr 22
d. 380. Bishop of Susa in the Persian Empire, he was cut to pieces in the reign of Shah Shapur II.

Miltiades, Pope (St) Dec 10
d. 314. Perhaps a Roman African, he became pope in 311. He was reigning when the Edict of Milan was promulgated by Emperor Constantine, and was asked to arbitrate in the Donatist controversy in Africa by him. His name is often wrongly spelt 'Melchiades'. His cultus was confined to local calendars in 1969.

Miltiades Ramírez Zuluaga (Bl) *see* **Hospitaller Martyrs of Spain**

Minervinus (St) *see* **Stephen, Pontian and Comps**

Minervius, Eleazar and Comps (SS) MM. Aug 23
C3rd. Their surviving acta are worthless, but it seems that they were martyred at Lyons, France. They have been alleged to have been a married couple with eight children, or two men with the children belonging to one or the other. Eleazar is the one with uncertain gender.

Minias (Miniato) (St) M. Oct 25
d. *c*250. A Roman soldier at Florence, Italy, he tried to evangelize his comrades and was beheaded in the reign of Decius. A famous abbey grew around his shrine.

Minnborinus (St) R(OSB). Jul 18
d. 986. He was an Irish abbot of St Martin's Abbey at Cologne, Germany.

Minver (St) R. Nov 24
C6th? She was a hermit at Tredresick near Padstow in Cornwall, England, and has a holy well there.

Mirocles (St) B. Dec 3
d. 318. An archbishop of Milan, Italy, he was one of the authors of the Ambrosian liturgy used in that diocese.

Mirren *see* **Merin**

Mitrius (Mitre,Metre, Merre) (St) M. Nov 13
d. 314. A Greek slave at Aix-en-Provence, France, because he was a Christian he was savagely ill-treated by his master and his fellow slaves and ended up being beheaded.

Minason *see* **Jason**

Mo
Many names of Irish saints have this prefix, which is an honorific meaning 'My'. This has caused duplication in the past.

Mobeoc *see* **Beoc**

Mochelloc (Cellog, Mottelog, Motalogus) (St) Mar 26
d. ?639. He is the obscure patron of the town of Kilmallock in Co. Limerick, Ireland.

Mochoemoc (Mochaemhog, Pulcherius, Vulcanius) (St) R. Mar 13
d. ?656. From Munster, Ireland, he brought up by St Ita, his aunt, and became a monk of Bangor in Co. Down under St Comgall. Then he became the abbot-founder of Liath-Mochoemoc near Thurles in Co. Tipperary. Many legends are associated with him.

Mochta (Mochteus) (St) B. R. Aug 19
C6th. Allegedly from Britain, he founded the monastery of Louth in Ireland. The place is now a village but it gave its name to the county. His biography is full of miraculous legends.

Mochua *see* **Cuan**

Mochuda *see* **Carthage the Younger**

Modan (St) R. Feb 4
C6th? An Irish nobleman, he was a missionary in central Scotland between the Forth and the Clyde before becoming a hermit near Dumbarton when old.

Modanic (St) B. Nov 14
C8th. This Scottish bishop was venerated at Aberdeen, but no reliable information about him survives.

Moderan (Moderamnus, Moran) (St) B. Oct 22
d. *c*730. From Rennes, France, he became bishop there in 703. In *c*720 he made a pilgrimage to Rome, resigned as bishop and became a monk-hermit in the abbey of Berceto near Parma.

Modesta (St) *see* **Macedonius, Patricia and Modesta**

Modesta of Ohren (St) R. Nov 4
d. *c*680. She was the niece of St Modoald, who appointed her first abbess of the nunnery of Ohren which he had founded at Trier, Germany.

Modestinus-of-Jesus-and-Mary Mazzarella (Bl) R(OFM). Jul 24
1802–1854. From near Naples, he became a Franciscan there in 1822, serving as a preacher and confessor and as the guardian of two friaries. In 1839 he transferred to a friary in a Neapolitan slum, where he helped the poor and sick, defended newborn babies against neglect and spread devotion to Our Lady of Good Counsel in what was a post-Christian environment. He died of cholera while nursing victims of an epidemic, and was beatified in 1995.

Modestus (St) *see* **Tiberius, Modestus and Florentia**

Modestus (St) *see* **Vitus, Crescentia and Modestus**

Modestus (St) *see* **Zoticus, Rogatus and Comps**

Modestus and Ammonius (SS) MM. Feb 12
? They were listed as having been martyred at Alexandria, Egypt, but nothing is known about them.

Modestus and Julian (SS) MM. Feb 12
? Modestus was martyred at Carthage, Julian at Alexandria (in 160). The former is the patron of Cartagena, Spain. They were arbitrarily listed together in the old Roman Martyrology.

Modestus Andlauer (St) *see* **Remigius Isoré and Modestus Andlauer**

Modestus of Benevento (St) M. D. Feb 12
d. ?304. Allegedly a Sardinian deacon, he was martyred at an uncertain place in the reign of Diocletian. His shrine was established at Benevento, Italy.

Modestus of Carinthia (St) B. Feb 5
d. ?722. St Virgilius, bishop of Salzburg, at the invitation of their ruler, sent him as a missionary bishop with a group of clergy to the Carinthian Slavs. He was largely responsible for the evangelization of that people (whose territory spread to the north of what is now Carinthia in Austria).

Modestus of Trier (St) B. Feb 24
d. 489. He was bishop of Trier, Germany, from 486, when the city was being rebuilt under the rule of the Franks.

Modoald (St) B. May 12
d. 640. From Gascony, he was either a relative or a friend of most of the saints of the contemporary Merovingian church. He was an adviser of King Dagobert I before he became bishop of Trier, Germany, in 622.

Modoc *see* **Aidan of Ferns**

Modomnoc (Domnoc, Dominic) (St) B? R. Feb 13
d. *c*550. Allegedly descended from the Irish royal line of O'Neil, he was a disciple of St David at Menevia in Wales before becoming a hermit at Tibraghny near Kilkenny, Ireland. Some sources allege that he was bishop of Ossory, and that he was Ireland's first bee-keeper.

Modwenna (Edana, Medana, Monyna, Merryn, Modivene) (SS) RR. Jul 5
C7th? Several saints of this name are listed in different martyrologies, but their biographies are hopelessly confused. Three are notable. One succeeded St Hilda as abbess of Whitby and died ?695, another was a hermit near Burton-on-Trent (where she had her shrine) associated with the foundation of a nunnery at Polesworth in Warwickshire and who died *c*900, and another was the patron of St Merryn in Cornwall who seems to have had a connection with Brittany. *See* **Monenna**.

Moeliai (Moelray) (St) R. Jun 23
d. ?493. He was baptized by St Patrick and appointed abbot of the newly founded monastery of Nendrum on an island in the Strangford Lough in Co. Down, Ireland, where he had SS Finian of Moville and Colman of Dromore among his disciples.

Mogue *see* **Aidan**

Molagga (Laicin) (St) R. Jan 20
d. ?655. He spent some time with St David at Menevia, Wales, and founded a monastery at Fermoy in Co. Cork, Ireland.

Molaisse *see* **Laserian**

Moling (Mullin, Dairchilla) (St) B. R. Jun 17
d. 697. From Wexford, Ireland, he allegedly became a monk at Glendalough and then abbot at what is now St Mullin's on the River Barrow north of Waterford. Later he succeeded St

Aidan as bishop of Ferns, having the whole of Leinster as his diocese, but resigned some years before his death. His attribute is his pet fox.

Moloc (Molluog, Murlach, Lugaidh) (St) B. R. Jun 25
d. ?572. Allegedly a Scottish monk of Bangor monastery, Ireland, he became a missionary bishop in the Hebrides, Scotland, and was based apparently on the island of Lismore. He died at Rosemarkie on the Moray Firth and had his shrine at Mortlach near Dufftown.

Molonachus (St) B. Jun 25
C7th. A disciple of St Brendan, he became bishop on the island of Lismore in Argyle, Scotland.

Molua *see* **Lua**

Mommolinus *see* **Mummolinus**

Mommolus *see* **Mummolus**

Monacella *see* **Melangell**

Monaldus of Ancona and Comps (BB) MM. RR(OFM). Mar 15
d. 1286. With Anthony of Milan and Francis of Fermo he was killed at Erzincan on the Euphrates in western Armenia (now in Turkey) while on a missionary journey. The area was under the control of the Ilkhan Mongols of Persia. Their cultus is unconfirmed.

Monan (St) M. R. Mar 1
d. ?874. He was a missionary in Fife, Scotland, in association with St Adrian of May, and was also killed by the Danes. His shrine was at Abercrombie.

Monas (St) B. Oct 12
d. 249. He was bishop of Milan, Italy, from 193 and was noted as a philosopher.

Monegund (St) R. Jul 2
d. 570. A married woman of Chartres, France, when her two daughters died she became a hermit with the consent of her husband. To escape attention she migrated to Tours and lived in a cell near the tomb of St Martin, where she died and where her disciples founded a nunnery.

Monenna (St) Jul 6
d. ?518. By tradition she was the founder of the nunnery at Killeevy in Co. Armagh, Ireland, and was associated with SS Patrick and Brigid. She has been confused with St Modwenna.

Monessa (Ness) (St) R. Sep 4
d. 456. The daughter of a nobleman converted by St Patrick, she either died immediately on being baptized or became a hermit at Urney in Co. Tyrone, Ireland. Traditions differ.

Monica (St) L. Aug 27
332–387. From a Christian family of Carthage, Roman Africa, she married a pagan and had three children. The eldest of these was St Augustine, who did not imitate his mother's faith as a young man. Her patience converted her husband, and after his death she followed St Augustine to Italy. Her prayers contributed to her son being baptized a Catholic, which event took place in Milan in 387. She died the same year at Ostia near Rome, on the way back to Africa with him, and her shrine is in his church at Rome.

Monica Naizen (Bl) M. L. Jul 12
d. 1626. A Japanese laywoman, she was beheaded at Nagasaki with her husband, Bl John Naizen, and her son, Bl Louis, for having sheltered Bl John-Baptist Zola. *See* **Mancius Araki and Comps** and **Japan (Martyrs of)**.

Monica Pichery (Bl) *see* **William Repin and Comps**

Monitor (St) B. Nov 10
d. *c*490. Nothing is known about this bishop of Orléans, France.

Monon (St) M. R. Oct 18
d. ?645. A Scottish (or Irish) pilgrim, he settled as a hermit at Nassogne in the Ardennes, Belgium, and was murdered by some malefactors whom he had rebuked.

Montanus, Lucius, Julian, Victoricus, Flavian and Comps (SS) MM. Feb 24
d. 259. Ten disciples of St Cyprian of Carthage, Roman Africa, they were martyred in that city in the reign of Valerian. Their acta are authentic, as the story of their imprisonment was related by themselves and that of their martyrdom by eye-witnesses.

Montanus and Maxima (SS) MM. Mar 26
d. 304. A priest and his wife, they were martyred by being drowned in the River Save at Sirmium (now Srem Mitrovica in Serbia).

Montanus of Gaeta (St) M. Jun 17
d. *c*300. A Roman soldier, he was exiled to the island of Ponza off Gaeta, Italy, and later

thrown into the sea with a stone tied to his neck. His body was recovered and enshrined at Gaeta.

Montford Scott (Bl) M. P. Jul 1
d. 1591. A Suffolk landowner, he studied at Douai in the 1570s, started work in East Anglia while still a deacon and was ordained at Brussels in 1577. In 1584 he was captured at York while about to leave the country, imprisoned for seven years and executed at Tyburn with Bl George Beesley. He was beatified in 1987. *See* **England (Martyrs of)**.

Mooti Massabki (Bl) *see* **Emmanuel Ruiz and Comps**

Morand (St) R(OSB). Jun 3
d. ?1115. A nobleman from near Worms, Germany, he became a monk at Cluny under St Hugh the Great after a pilgrimage to Compostela. Eventually he became the first superior of the new Cluniac foundation at Altkirch near Mulhouse, France.

Moricus (Bl) R. Mar 30
d. 1236. A consecrated religious of the 'Cruciferi', he features in the biography of St Francis by St Bonaventure and is claimed as the fifth Franciscan recruit. He has an unconfirmed cultus at Orvieto, Italy, and among the Franciscans.

Moroc (St) B. Nov 8
C9th. He was abbot of Dunkeld, Scotland, and then bishop of Dunblane.

Morwenna (St) R. July 8
C5th? She was apparently a hermit who gave her name to Morwenstow near Bude in Cornwall, England, but there is confusion between several Cornish and Irish saints with similar names.

Moses (St) *see* **Cyrion, Bassian and Comps**

Moses (Moysetes) of Africa
(St) M. Dec 18
d. ?250. A Roman African, he was probably martyred in the reign of Decius.

Moses the Arab (St) B. R. Feb 7
d. ?372. He was an Arab hermit at what is now El-Arish on the Mediterranean coast of the Sinai Peninsula, and became a missionary bishop among his fellow Bedouin of the region.

Moses the Black (St) M. R. Aug 28
d. ?395. A Negro of enormous stature (none of it fat), he was born in slavery in Egypt and turned out to have such a nasty character that his master drove him from the household and he became the leader of a gang of robbers. As a fugitive from justice he took refuge among the hermits of Scetis (now the Wadi Natrun), was converted and joined them. He was ordained and became one of the most famous of the second generation of Egyptian desert fathers. When old he was murdered by barbarian raiders after refusing either to flee or to defend himself.

Moses of Rome (St) M. Nov 25
d. 251. A Roman priest, noted for his zeal against Novatianist rigorism, he was martyred in the reign of Decius.

Moses of Sandomir (Bl) *see* **Sadoc of Sandomir and Comps**

Moseus and Ammonius
(SS) MM. Jan 18
d. 250. For being Christians these two soldiers were sentenced to forced labour for life in the mines and later burnt alive at Astas in Bithynia, Asia Minor.

Movean (Biteus) (St) R. Jul 22
Late C5th? Allegedly a disciple of St Patrick, he was abbot of Iniscoosery in Co. Down, Ireland, and seems to have gone to Scotland as a missionary, dying as a hermit at Ween near Aberfeldy.

Mucian (St) *see* **Mark, Mucian and Comps**

Mucian-Mary Wiaux (Bl) R. Jan 30
1841–1917. From Mellet, Belgium, as a teenager he joined the Brothers of the Christian Schools with difficulty since he had little natural aptitude for teaching. But he then spent 55 years at a school in Malonne as a prefect and primary music teacher, with no great success but with such personal holiness that he was canonized in 1989.

Mucius (St) *see* **Parmenius and Comps**

Mucius (St) *see* **Silvanus, Luke and Mucius**

Mucius (Mocius) of Byzantium (St) M. P. May 13
d. 304. According to his doubtful acta, he was from a Roman family but was born at Byzantium and became a priest at Amphipolis in Macedonia. He was martyred at Byzantium (later Constantinople) in the reign of Diocletian for allegedly overturning a pagan altar.

Mugagga (St) M. L. Jun 3
d. 1886. He was an apprentice of the royal cloth-maker at the court of King Mwanga of Buganda, and was martyred on the latter's orders. *See* **Charles Lwanga and Comps**.

Muirchu (Maccutinus) (St) Jun 8
C7th. From Ireland, he wrote biographies of SS Brigid and St Patrick. Nothing is known about his own life.

Mukasa Kiriwawanvu (St) M. L. Jun 3
d. 1886. He waited at the table of King Mwanga of Buganda, Uganda, and was martyred on his orders. *See* **Charles Lwanga and Comps**.

Mullion *see* **Melanius**

Mummolin (Mommolin)
(St) B. R. Oct 16
d. ?686. From Constance, Germany, he became a monk at Luxeuil and then superior of the Old Monastery (later named St Mommolin after him) at St Omer, France. Then he transferred to Sithiu nearby, which had been founded by (and later named after) his friend St Bertinus. Finally he was made bishop of Noyon-Tournai in 660.

Mummolus (Mommolus, Mommolenus) (St) R. Aug 8
d. ?678. He was the second abbot of Fleury near Orléans, France. During his abbacy there was an alleged transfer of the relics of SS Benedict and Scholastica from Montecassino to Fleury (that this event took place is denied by the former monastery). Thus Fleury is now known as Saint-Benoît-sur-Loire.

Mummolus (Mumbolus, Momleolus, Momble) (St) R. Nov 18
d. *c*690. An Irishman, he accompanied St Fursey to Lagny near Paris, France, and succeeded him as abbot there.

Mun (St) B. Feb 6
C5th. According to his tradition he was a nephew of St Patrick, who ordained him as bishop for Co. Longford, Ireland, and who died as a hermit on an island in Lough Ree.

Mundus (Munde, Mund, Mond) (St) R. Apr 15
d. ?962. He was a monastic founder in Argyle, Scotland, but details are lacking.

Mungo *see* **Kentigern**

Munnu *see* **Fintan**

Mura MeFeredach (Muran, Murames) (St) R. Mar 12
d. ?645. From Co. Donegal, Ireland, he was appointed abbot of Fahan in Co. Derry by St Columba. He is the special patron saint of the O'Neills, and his monumental cross survives at Fahan.

Muredach (Murtagh) (St) B. Aug 12
C6th? Allegedly a disciple of St Patrick and the first bishop of Killala in Co. Mayo, Ireland, he either became a hermit on the island of Inishmurray in Donegal Bay or became involved with St Columba at Iona. Both traditions together cannot be correct. He is the principal patron of the diocese of Killala.

Muredhae *see* **Marianus Scotus**

Muritta (St) *see* **Eugene of Carthage and Comps**

Musa (St) L. Apr 2
C6th. A child mystic living in Rome, she is mentioned by St Gregory the Great in his *Dialogues*. She died very young.

Musonius (St) *see* **Mardonius, Musonius and Comps**

Mustiola (St) *see* **Irenaeus and Mustiola**

Mydwyn (St) *see* **Elvan and Mydwyn**

Myllin *see* **Molling**

Mylor *see* **Melor**

Myrbad (St) *see* **Winnow, Mancus and Myrbad**

Myron the Wonderworker (St) B. Aug 8
*c*250–350. From near Knossos in Crete, he became a bishop somewhere in that island and died a centenarian.

Myron of Cyzicus (St) M. P. Aug 17
d. *c*250. He was martyred at Cyzicus on the Sea of Marmara, Asia Minor, after having confronted some imperial officers directed to destroy his church by decree of the emperor Decius.

Myrope (St) M. July 13
d. ?251. A native of Chios in the Aegean Sea, Greece, she buried some martyrs of the Decian persecution, including St Isidore. Because of this she was whipped and died in prison as a result.

N

Naal *see* **Natalis**

Nabor (St) *see* **Basilides, Cyrinus and Comps**

Nabor (St) *see* **Januarius, Marinus and Comps**

Nabor and Felix (SS) MM. July 12
d. ?304. They were beheaded at Milan, Italy, in the reign of Diocletian and had their relics enshrined by St Ambrose almost a century later. Their cultus was confined to local calendars in 1969.

Najran (Martyrs of) (SS) Oct 24
d. 523. A large group of martyrs (numbering 340, according to the old Roman Martyrology), they were massacred at Najran in south-west Arabia by Jews and pagan Arabs at the instigation of a Jewish leader, Dhu Nowas (Dunaan). The head of the group was the chief of the Beni Harith, Abdullah ibn Kaab (the 'Aretas' of the Roman Martyrology). Religion in Arabia before Muhammed was an eclectic mixture of paganism and orthodox and heterodox versions of both Judaism and Christianity. This massacre left such a deep contemporary impression that Muhammed later mentioned it in the Koran (Sura 85).

Nahum (St) *see* **Clement of Ohrid and Comps**

Namatius (Namace) of Clermont (St) B. Oct 27
d. *p*462. He was a bishop of Clermont-Ferrand, France.

Namatius (Namasius, Naamat, Namat) of Vienne (St) B. Nov 17
d. ?599. He was a bishop of Vienne, France, whose cultus was confirmed in 1903.

Namphanion and Comps (SS) MM. Jul 4
d. ?180. A Roman African of Carthaginian descent, he was martyred with several companions at Madaura in Numidia (Algeria). Patristic African writers referred to him as 'the Arch-martyr', implying that he was the province's first.

Namphasius (Nauphary, N phrase) (St) R. Nov 12
d. *c*800. Allegedly a friend of Charlemagne, he fought as a soldier against the Arab raiders in southern France before becoming a hermit at Marcillac near Cahors.

Napoleon *see* **Neopolus**

Narcissa-of-Jesus Martillo Morán (Bl) L. Dec 8
1832–1869. Born at a little village near Guayaquil, Ecuador, when both parents died she went to that city to work as a cook, sharing her wages with the poor. She saw her vocation as one of reparative expiation to the Sacred Heart on behalf of the world and lived for a time with Bl Mercedes Molina, sharing her ideals. In 1868 she went to the monastery of Our Lady of Protection at Lima, Peru, but died before she could join. She was beatified in 1992.

Narcissus (St) *see* **Ampliatus, Urban and Narcissus**

Narcissus (St) *see* **Argeus, Narcissus, and Marcellinus**

Narcissus and Crescentio (SS) MM. Sep 17
d. *c*260. They are mentioned in the unreliable acta of St Laurence of Rome, who allegedly used to distribute alms to the poor in the house of Narcissus and there cured Crescentio of blindness. On the Salarian Way a cemetery bore the name of Crescentio, indicating his historical existence.

Narcissus and Felix (SS) MM. Mar 18
d. ?307. A bishop and his deacon, they are venerated as martyrs at Gerona, Spain.

Nothing else is known about them, as the story of their escape to, and their apostolate in, Germany and Switzerland (including their conversion of St Afra) is fictitious.

Narcissus of Jerusalem (St) B. R. Oct 29
d. ?222. A Greek, he became bishop of Jerusalem when already very old and supported the Alexandrine mode of computation of the date of Easter (used at Rome) against the earlier one linking it to the Passover. As a result he was calumniated, had to resign and apparently became a hermit but later returned and died as bishop.

Narnus of Bergamo (St) B. Aug 27
? According to the spurious legend, this alleged first bishop of Bergamo, Italy, was consecrated by St Barnabas.

Narses (St) *see* **Zanitas and Comps**

Narses of Suborgord (St) B. Jan 3
d. ?340. Bishop of Subogord in Persia, he was martyred with his disciple Joseph (possibly in the persecution of Shah Shapur II).

Narseus (St) *see* **Philip, Zeno and Comps**

Narzales (St) *see* **Scillitan Martyrs**

Natalia (St) *see* **George, Aurelius and Comps**

Natalia of Nicomedia (St) L. Dec 1
d. ?311. Wife of St Adrian of Nicomedia, Asia Minor, she imitated her husband in helping those imprisoned during the persecution of Diocletian. Surviving the persecution, she died in peace at Constantinople.

Natalia Vanot (Bl) *see* **Valenciennes (Martyrs of)**

Natalis (St) R. Jan 27
C6th. He was one of the founders of monasticism in the northern parts of Ireland, and a fellow-worker with St Columba.

Natalis of Casale (St) P. Sep 3
C6th. From Benevento, Italy, he was a priest at Casale in Piedmont.

Natalis Chabanel (Bl) *see* **John Brébeuf and Comps**

Natalis-Hilary Le Conte (Bl) *see* **John-Baptist Souzy and Comps**

Natalis of Milan (St) B. May 13
d. 751. He was archbishop of Milan, Italy, from 740.

Natalis (Noel) Pinot (Bl) M. P. Feb 21
1747–1794. From Angers, France, he was ordained as a diocesan priest there in 1771 and was parish priest of Louroux-Beconnais until the outbreak of the French Revolution. When he refused to take the oath recognizing the civil constitution of the clergy he was expelled from his parish but continued to minister to it, at first in secret and afterwards openly. In 1794 he was captured when about to say Mass and immediately guillotined, still wearing his vestments. He was beatified in 1926.

Nathalan (St) B. Jan 8
d. ?678. According to his legend he was a wealthy man who became a hermit near Aberdeen, Scotland, and supported himself by cultivating his smallholding 'which work approaches nearest to divine contemplation'. He became a missionary bishop based at Old Meldrum, and had his cultus confirmed in 1898.

Nathanael *see* **Bartholomew**

Nathy (David) (St) B. Aug 9
d. ?610. Disciple of St Finian of Clonard, he became the founder and abbot-bishop of a monastery at Achonry in Co. Sligo, Ireland, of which diocese he is the principal patron. His cultus was confirmed in 1903.

Navalis (St) *see* **Valentine, Concordius and Comps**

Nazaria-Ignatia-of-St-Teresa-of-Jesus March Mesa (Bl) R. F. Jul 6
1889–1943. From Madrid, Spain, she emigrated with her family to Mexico when aged twenty and joined the 'Sisters of Forsaken Old People'. After her noviciate in Spain she joined a group making a new foundation at Oruro in Bolivia and was extremely enthusiastic, despite knowing little about Bolivian culture. She was asked to found the first Bolivian religious congregation, the 'Crucified Missionaries of the Church', with an Ignatian spirituality and a special vow of obedience to the pope. They spread to Argentina, Uruguay and Spain. She died at Buenos Aires and was beatified in 1992.

Nazarius (St) *see* **Basilides, Cyrinus and Comps**

Nazarius and Celsus (SS) MM. Jul 28
d. ?68. According to their worthless acta, they

were beheaded at Milan, Italy, in the reign of Nero. St Ambrose searched for and discovered their alleged relics at Milan in 395. The cultus was confined to local calendars in 1969.

Nazarius of Lérins (St) R. Nov 18
d. *c*450. He was an abbot of Lérins in Provence, France.

Neachtain (St) B? May 2
C5th. According to tradition he was a near relative of St Patrick and was present at his death. He is associated with Fennor in Co. Meath, Ireland.

Nebridius (St) B. Feb 9
d. *p*527. He was bishop of the city of Egara (since destroyed) near Barcelona, Spain.

Nectan (St) M? R. Jun 17
C6th. Allegedly a son of St Brychan, he became a hermit at Hartland in Devon, England. He was later venerated as a martyr, for unknown reasons (the extant legend is untrustworthy). His shrine was in an Augustinian monastery and was a focus of pilgrimage in north Devon until the Reformation.

Nectarius of Autun (St) B. Sep 13
d. *c*550. He was a bishop of Autun, France, and a friend of St Germanus of Paris.

Nectarius of Constantinople
(St) B. Oct 11
d. 397. He succeeded St Gregory Nazianzen as bishop of Constantinople in 381, and became the first patriarch after the first council of Constantinople declared the see a patriarchate in the same year. He was succeeded by St John Chrysostom.

Nectarius of Vienne (St) B. May 5
d. ?445. He was a bishop of Vienne, France.

Nemesian and Comps
(SS) MM. BB. Sep 10
d. 257. Nine Roman African bishops of Numidia (Algeria) they were sentenced to slavery in the marble quarries of Sigum with many priests and lay people. There they were worked to death. The other bishops were: two named Felix, Lucius, Litteus, Polyanus, Victor, Jader and Dativus. A letter by St Cyprian to them survives.

Nemesius (St) *see* **Potamius and Nemesius**

Nemesius (St) *see* **Symphorosa of Tivoli and Comps**

Nemesius and Lucilla
(SS) MM. Aug 25
d. *c*260. According to their untrustworthy acta they were a Roman deacon and his daughter and were martyred at Rome in the reign of Valerian.

Nemesius of Alexandria
(St) M. Dec 19
d. 250. He was burnt at the stake between two thieves at Alexandria, Egypt, in the reign of Decius.

Nemesius of Liewen (St) Aug 1
? He is venerated around Lisieux, France, but nothing is known about him.

Nemorius *see* **Memorius**

Nennius (Ninnidh) (St) R. Jan 17
C6th. He was a disciple of St Finian of Clonard and is reckoned as one of the 'Twelve Apostles of Ireland', but why is not now known. He has been associated with Innismacsaint in Co. Fermanagh.

Nennoc (Nennocha, Ninnoc)
(St) R. Jun 4
d. ?467. According to tradition she was a daughter of St Brychan who migrated to Brittany, France, and founded a nunnery at Pleumeur. Her name as given means 'little nun' (her real name was apparently 'Gwen', meaning 'Blonde').

Nennus (Nenus, Nehemias)
(St) R. Jun 14
C7th. He succeeded St Enda as superior of his monastic foundations on the Aran Islands, Ireland.

Neomisia (St) *see* Aurelia and Neomisia

Neon (St) *see* **Claudius, Asterius and Comps**

Neon (St) *see* **Eusebius, Marcellus and Comps**

Neon (St) *see* **Eusebius, Neon and Comps**

Neon (St) *see* **Mark, Alphius and Comps**

Neophytus (St) *see* **Athanasius, Anthusa and Comps**

Neophytus of Nicaea (St) M. Jan 20
296–310. He was a teenager martyred at Nicaea, Asia Minor, in the reign of Galerius.

Neopolus (St) *see* **Saturninus, Neopolus and Comps**

Neopolus (Neapolysus, Napoleon) of Alexandria (St) M. Aug 15
d. *c*300. He was tortured at Alexandria, Egypt, in the reign of Diocletian and died of the effects immediately afterwards. The French emperor was named after him.

Neot (St) R. Jul 31
d. *c*880. According to his tradition he was a monk of Glastonbury, England (insofar as any monastic life survived there at the time) and became a hermit near Liskeard in Cornwall at the place now called St Neot. Apparently his relics were taken to a monastery in Cambridgeshire in the C10th, and this led to his name being given to the town of St Neot's there. There may have been two saints of the same name.

Neoterius (St) *see* **Ammon, Theophilus and Comps**

Nepotian of Altinum (St) P. May 4
d. 395. He was a nephew of St Heliodorus of Altinum, Italy, and was ordained by him after resigning as an officer of the imperial bodyguard. St Jerome admired him, and dedicated to him a treatise on the priestly life. It seems, however, that he has never had a public cultus.

Nepotian of Clermont (St) B. Oct 22
d. ?388. He was bishop of Clermont-Ferrand, France, from 386.

Nereus (St) *see* **Saturninus, Nereus and Comps**

Nereus and Achilles (SS) MM. May 12
d. *c*100. They were soldiers of the Praetorian Guard, according to the epitaph written by Pope St Damasus. Their acta are unreliable, alleging that they were baptized by St Peter and were exiled with St Flavia Domitilla to the island of Ponza and later to Terracina, where they were beheaded.

Nerses the Great (St) M. B. Nov 19
d. 373. An Armenian and a close relative of St Gregory the Illuminator, he was educated at Caesarea in Cappodocia, Asia Minor, and married to a princess of the Mamikonian family by whom he became the father of St Isaac the Great. On his return to Armenia he became a royal courtier before being made sixth Catholicos in 353, and as such he worked for the reform of the national church along the lines of what he had seen in Cappodocia. Some of this work displeased the king and he was exiled, but was recalled in 368 by the succeeding monarch. In the end he was apparently poisoned by the same.

Nerses Klayetsi (St) B. Aug 13
1102–1173. A Cilician Armenian, he became 'Catholicos' or head of the national Armenian church in 1166, fixing his residence at Hromkala on the Euphrates, where he died. He was nicknamed Shnorhali' (meaning 'the Gracious') because of his personal goodness and his agreeable literary style (he was a great poet and hymnographer as well as a theologian and exegete). As Catholicos he tried to bring about the union of the Byzantine and Armenian churches, but with no success. He was, however, in communion with Rome.

Nerses of Lambron (St) B. R. Jul 17
1153–1198. An Armenian nobleman from Cilicia, Asia Minor, he was related to St Nerses Klayetsi and was ordained by him at Hromkla. Then he was a hermit before being made archbishop of Tarsus in 1175, and was instrumental in bringing about the reconciliation of the kingdom of Little Armenia (i.e. Cilicia) with the Roman Catholic church in 1198, when King Leo II was crowned by the papal legate. He was a significant Armenian ecclesiastical writer, and also translated many patristic works into Armenian (such as the rule of St Benedict and St Gregory's *Dialogues*).

Nerses of Sahgerd and Comps (SS) MM. Nov 20
d. 343. A group of at least twelve Persian martyrs, including Nerses bishop of Sahgerd and four other bishops, they were killed by strangling, stoning, and beheading in the persecution of Shah Shapur II.

Nestabus (St) *see* **Eusebius, Nestabus and Comps**

Nestor (St) *see* **Basil, Ephrem and Comps**

Nestor (St) *see* **Eusebius, Nestabus and Comps**

Nestor of Magydos (St) M. B. Feb 26
d. 251. Bishop of Magydos in Pamphylia, Asia Minor, he was crucified at Perga in the reign of Decius.

Nestor of Thessalonika (St) M. Oct 8
d. ?304. He was martyred at Thessalonika, Greece, in the reign of Diocletian. His acta are worthless.

Nevolo (Bl) T(OSB Cam. or OFM) Jul 27
d. 1280. A married shoemaker of Faenza, Italy, he lived a frivolous life until a conversion when aged twenty-four, whereupon he became either a Franciscan tertiary or a Camaldolese lay brother (or was the latter after the former). His cultus was approved for Faenza in 1817, and is kept by both orders.

(?) Nezel (Bl) *see* **September (Martyrs of)**

Nicaeas and Paul (SS) MM. Aug 29
? They are listed as having been martyred at Antioch, Syria.

Nicander (St) *see* **Hieron, Nicander and Comps**

Nicander and Hermas (SS) MM. Nov 4
? Allegedly a bishop and a priest who were disciples of St Titus, they were martyred at Myra in Lycia, Asia Minor.

Nicander and Marcian (SS) MM. Jun 17
d. ?173 or 304. They are listed as two officers in the imperial army, martyred somewhere in present-day Bulgaria, and seem to be duplicates of Marcian and Nicanor.

Nicander of Egypt (St) M. Mar 15
d. ?304. He is listed as an Egyptian physician who ministered to Christians in prison and buried those martyred in the persecution of Diocletian. He was beheaded himself as a result.

Nicanor (St) *see* **Marcian, Nicanor and Comps**

Nicanor Ascanius (Bl) *see* **Emmanuel Ruiz and Comps**

Nicanor the Deacon (St) M? D. Jan 10
d. ?76. A Jew, he was one of the seven deacons of Jerusalem chosen by the apostles (Acts 6:5). The tradition is that he eventually went to Cyprus and was martyred there in the reign of Vespasian, but there is no historical evidence for this.

Nicarete (Niceras) (St) L. Dec 27
d. ?405. A noblewoman of Nicomedia, Asia Minor, resident at Constantinople, she became a loyal supporter of St John Chrysostom and was exiled with him.

Nicasius Jonson van Hez
(St) M. R(OFM). Jul 9
?1522–1572. Born in the castle of Hez in Brabant, he became a Franciscan licentiate of theology and was the author of several polemical works against Protestantism. He was based at the friary at Gorinchem when he was hanged with the other **Gorinchem martyrs** (q.v.).

Nicasius of Rheims and Comps (SS) MM. Dec 14
d. ?407 or 451. He was a bishop of Rheims, France, and was killed in his cathedral by invading barbarians, with his sister Eutropia, a consecrated virgin, and a number of priests and lay people. It is unclear which barbarians were responsible (possibly the Vandals or the Huns).

Nicasius of Rouen and Comps (SS) MM. Oct 11
d. ?250. According to his unreliable legend, he was a bishop of Rouen, France, who was killed on the way home from Paris with a priest Quirinus, a deacon Scubiculus and a consecrated virgin Pientia. There was no such bishop of the city, and he is probably a duplicate of Nicasius of Rheims.

Nicasius Sierra Ucar (Bl) *see* **Philip-of-Jesus Munárriz Azcona and Comps**

Nicephorus (St) *see* **Victorinus, Victor and Comps**

Nicephorus of Antioch (St) M. Feb 9
d. 260. The story of this alleged martyr of Antioch, Syria, in the reign of Valerian is probably a pious fiction, written to teach the necessity of forgiving one's enemies.

Nicephorus of Constantinople
(St) B. Mar 13
758–829. He had been imperial secretary at the court of Constantinople before retiring to a monastery for a while (without becoming a monk) and then running the city's largest almshouse. He was chosen patriarch in 806, despite being still a layman. Initially opposed by St Theodore Studites, he proved himself by standing firm against the revival of iconoclasm by the emperor Leo V in 815. He died in exile at a monastery which he had founded on the Bosporus.

Nicephorus Salvador del Río (Bl) *see* **Hospitaller Martyrs of Spain**

Nicephorus-of-Jesus-and-Mary-Díez Tejerina and Comps (BB) MM. RR(CP). Jul 23
d. 1936. They were the superior and brethren (mostly clerics studying philosophy) of the Passionist community at Daímiel near Ciudad

Real in Spain. During the Civil War the retreat was raided by a couple of hundred Republican soldiers on the night of June 21. Bl Nicephorus and 25 out of 30 of the others were taken away in groups and shot at various times and in various places nearby. They were beatified in 1989. *See* **Spanish Civil War (Martyrs of)**.

Niceta and Aquilina (SS) MM. Jul 24
? These names were originally Nicetas and Aquila, and were of two mythical soldier-martyrs. In the fictional acta of St Christopher the names were feminized and given to two prostitutes converted by him and executed with him.

Nicetas of Appolonias (St) B. Mar 20
d. ?735. Bishop of Apollonias in Bithynia, Asia Minor, he died in exile for opposing the iconoclast policy of the emperor Leo III.

Nicetas the Great (St) M. Sep 15
d. ?378. An Ostrogoth nobleman, he was converted with many of his nation (in what is now the Ukraine) by the Arian missionary Ulfilas, who probably also ordained him priest. A Gothic leader started a persecution of Christianity in 377, and Nicetas was burnt at the stake somewhere in Bessarabia (Moldova). His shrine was established at Mopsuestia near Antioch, Syria, and his veneration became popular in the East. It is virtually certain that he was an Arian, however.

Nicetas of Medikion (St) R. Apr 3
d. 824. He was abbot of Medikion, one of the monasteries of the great monastic colony on the Bithynian Olympus near Nicaea, Asia Minor, and stood out against the iconoclastic policy of the emperor Leo V. As a result he was imprisoned for six years on an island in the Sea of Marmara, but after the emperor's death was set free and died as a hermit near Constantinople.

Nicetas the Patrician (St) R. Oct 6
d. ?838. A nobleman of Paphlagonia, Asia Minor, he became prefect of Cilicia and then a monk at Constantinople. As a result of opposing the resurgence of iconoclasm by the emperors Leo V and Theophilus he died in exile.

Nicetas of Remesiana (St) B. Jan 7
d. ?414. He was a missionary bishop working among the barbarians on the Empire's Danube frontier, and seems to have been based at what is now Biela Palanka near Niš, Serbia. He was a distinguished church author, although his authorship of the ancient hymn called the *Te Deum* is doubtful.

Nicetius (Nizier) of Besançon
(St) B. Feb 8
d. 611. Bishop of Nyon on the Lake of Geneva, he re-established his see at Besançon, France, whence it had been transferred after the city's destruction by the Huns. He was a friend and supporter of St Columbanus and dedicated the abbey church at Luxeuil. His cultus was confirmed for Besançon in 1900.

Nicetius (Nizier) of Lyons (St) B. Apr 2
d. 573. He became bishop of Lyons, France, in 553.

Nicetius of Trier (St) B. Dec 5
d. 566. A monk and abbot of Auvergne, he became bishop of Trier, Germany, in 532 and was the last who was a Gallo-Roman rather than a Frank. He withstood the cruelty of the new Frankish rulers, excommunicated two kings for disgusting behaviour and was exiled for a year as a result. He also founded a school of clerical studies and rebuilt the cathedral.

Nicetus (St) B. May 5
d. *p*449. He was a bishop of Vienne, France.

Nicholas (St) *see* **Daniel, Samuel and Comps**

Nicholas I, Pope, 'the Great' (St) Nov 13
d. 867. A native priest of Rome, he was elected pope in 858 at a time when the Dark Ages in the West were taking a turn for the worse. His energy and courage in office, especially in dealing with bad bishops and rulers, led him to be the last of the popes to be nicknamed 'the Great'. He had to cope with the schism of Photius, patriarch of Constantinople, and tried to extend the influence of the Latin church in Scandinavia under St Ansgar as legate and in Bulgaria, where Khan Boris wished to convert his country to Christianity. His replies to a long list of questions by the khan survives. Both of these initiatives lacked success (Bulgaria opted for the Eastern church).

Nicholas Alberca (Bl) *see* **Emmanuel Ruiz and Comps**

Nicholas Albergati (Bl) B. R(OCart). May 9
1375–1443. From Bologna, Italy, he became a Carthusian in 1394 but was made bishop of Bologna (against his will) in 1418 and cardinal in 1426. He served as papal legate to France and Germany and also at the council of Basel, and was a generous benefactor of many Renaissance scholars. His cultus was confirmed for Bologna in 1744.

St Nicholas, Nov 13 *(see p. 427)*

Nicholas Appleine (Bl) R(CR). Aug 11
d. 1466. He was a canon of St-Marcel-de-Prémery near Nevers, France, and had his cultus locally approved by the bishop of Nevers in 1731.

Nicholas Barré (Bl) R. (May 31)
1621–1686. From Amiens, France, he became a Minim friar and was established at Rouen, where he began a movement offering education to ordinary people. This led to the foundation of the 'Charitable Teachers', a secular institution for both sexes, and he also influenced St John-Baptist de la Salle. He was beatified in 1999.

Nicholas Benoist and Nicholas Bize (BB) *see* **September (Martyrs of)**

Nicholas Bunkerd Kitbamrung (B1) M.P. Jan 12
1895–*a*1956. From a native Catholic family of Nakhon Pathom near Bangkok, Thailand, he was ordained priest at Bangkok in 1926 and served in several parishes in Thailand. However, there was a strong anti-catholic sentiment in Thailand arising partly from hostility to French interests in the area and partly from the identificatin of Thai nationalism with Buddhism. As result, B1 Nicholas was arrested in 1941, accused of having the bells of his church rung in violation of an official ban and sentenced to fifteen years in prison. He continued his priestly work in prison, but died of tuberculosis before his sentence was finished. He was beatified in 2000.

Nicholas Chrysoberges (St) B. Dec 16
d. 996. He was patriarch of Constantinople from 983, and oversaw the conversion of Russia.

Nicholas Clairet and Nicholas Colin (BB) *see* **September (Martyrs of)**

Nicholas Dinnis (Bl) *see* **Ignatius de Azevedo**

Nicholas Factor (Bl) R(OFM). Dec 23
1520–1582. Born at Valencia, Spain, he became a Franciscan there in 1537 and was an itinerant preacher of extreme asceticism, whipping himself before every sermon. He died at Valencia and was beatified in 1786.

Nicholas von Flüe (St) R. Mar 21
1417–1487. From a peasant family near Sarnen in Unterwalden canton, Switzerland, he married and had ten children. He became a judge and councillor for his canton as well as a soldier in its army, but when aged fifty he obtained the consent of his family to become a hermit at Ranft. It is alleged that he then went without any food except Holy Communion for nineteen years. Many sought his advice, especially civil magistrates. He was canonized in 1947 and is the patron of Switzerland, being nicknamed 'Bruder Klaus'.

Nicholas of Forca-Palena (Bl) R. Oct 1
1349–1449. From Palena near Sulmona, Italy, he founded the 'Hermits of St Jerome' and established houses at Naples, Rome (St Onufrius) and Florence. Afterwards he

amalgamated these with the Hieronymites founded by Bl Peter of Pisa (and not connected with the Spanish order of the same name). His cultus was approved for Rome locally and Sulmona in 1771.

Nicholas Garlicx (Bl) M. P. Jun 24
1555–1588. Born at Dinting in Derbyshire, he was ordained at Châlons-sur-Marne in 1582 and was a priest in Hampshire, Dorset and then Derbyshire. Being captured at Padley Hall with Bl Robert Ludlum, he was executed at Derby with him and Bl Richard Simpson. He was beatified in 1987. *See* **England (Martyrs of)**.

Nicholas Gaudreau (Bl) *see* **September (Martyrs of)**

Nicholas of Gesturi (Bl)
R(OFM Cap) (Jun 8)
1882–1958. From Gesturi on Sardinia, Italy, he became a Capuchin at Cagliari in 1911 and spent most of his life begging alms for the friary there. He was beatified in 1999.

Nicholas Giustiniani (Bl)
R(OSB). Nov 21
d. *p*1180. A nobleman of Venice, Italy, he became a Benedictine monk at the Lido. After all his brothers had been killed fighting for the Serene Republic the Doge obtained for Nicholas a papal dispensation from his vows so that he could marry and produce an heir for his family. He did so, but returned to his monastery when old. He has an unconfirmed cultus at Venice.

Nicholas Gross (Bl) M. L. (Jan 23)
1898–1945. From Niederwenigern near Essen, Germany, as a young coal-miner he joined the 'St Anthony's Miners' Association', an influential union for Catholic miners, and went on to become the editor of the union's newspaper. Settling at Bochum in the Ruhr, he married and had seven children. His religious convictions led him to oppose Nazism totally, and his newspaper was banned in 1938. But he continued to publish pamphlets aiming at strengthening the Christian faith among manual workers, and was eventually arrested on a false suspicion of involvement in the plot to assassinate Hitler. He was hanged in Berlin and was beatified in 2001.

Nicholas Hermanssön (Bl) B. Jul 24
1331–1391. A Swede, he was educated at Paris and Orléans before being ordained and appointed tutor to the sons of St Brigid of Sweden. Eventually he became bishop of Linköping. He was a great Swedish liturgist and poet. That he was canonized in 1414 is not now proveable.

Nicholas Horner (Bl) M. L. Mar 3
d. 1590. An old man born in Ripon and a tailor in London, he was imprisoned in Newgate and lost a leg through gangrene. He was bought out but was re-arrested and executed on Ash Wednesday with Bl Alexander Blake on the charge of aiding Bl Christopher Bales, a priest. He was beatified in 1987. *See* **England (Martyrs of)**.

Nicholas Janssen-Poppel (St) M. Jul 9
d. 1572. He was the curate of St Leonard Vechel, and both were among the **Gorinchem martyrs** (q.v.).

Nicholas of Myra (St) B. Dec 6
d. *c*350. All that is known about him is that he was a bishop of Myra in Lycia, Asia Minor, and that his relics were stolen by Italian merchants in 1087, being now enshrined at Bari. His veneration as one of the most popular saints in Christendom is based mainly on his accumulated legends, especially as narrated by Simon Metaphrastes in the C10th. These include the story of his revivifying three children killed and pickled in brine, which has led to his being a patron of children and is the remote cause of the legend of 'Santa Claus'. He is also a patron of prisoners, sailors and pawnbrokers (the three golden balls symbolizing the latter derive from another legend, of his having provided three bags of gold as a dowry for a poor girl) and is a principal patron of Russia. He is often depicted with the aforesaid children or balls, or with a ship or anchor.

Nicholas the Mystic (St) B. May 15
d. 925. He was made patriarch of Constantinople in 906, and received his surname because he was the oldest member of the 'mystic' (secret) council of the Byzantine court. He was deposed and exiled by the emperor Leo VI in 906 for refusing to allow him to marry a fourth time (this being forbidden in the Eastern church) but was recalled in 911.

Nicholas Owen ('Little John') (St) M. R(SJ). Mar 2
d. 1606. The details of his early life are unknown, although he is alleged to have been a servant of St Edmund Campion before being on record as a Jesuit lay brother imprisoned in London in 1582. After his release he constructed priests' hiding places in mansions throughout England with amazing ingenuity. He was finally captured just after hiding in one of these

with Bl Ralph Ashley at Hinlip Hall near Worcester. The Gunpowder Plot had just taken place, and he was racked for information at London with such severity that his abdomen burst and he died. He was canonized in 1970. *See* **England (Martyrs of)**.

Nicholas Paglia (Bl) R(OP). Feb 14
1197–1256. From near Bari, Italy, after hearing St Dominic preach at Bologna he became a Dominican and founded friaries at Perugia in 1233 and at Trani in 1254. He was also twice superior of the Roman province. Dying at Perugia, his cultus was confirmed for there and for the Dominicans in 1828.

Nicholas Peregrinus (St) L. Jun 2
1075–1094. Historically he appears as a teenage Greek immigrant in Apulia, Italy, who wandered about shouting 'Kyrie eleison' (Lord, have mercy). Crowds of people (especially children) followed and imitated him, and he was understandably regarded as mad. He died at Trani (of which place he is the patron), and so many miracles were alleged to have taken place at his tomb that he was canonized in 1098.

Nicholas Pieck (SS) M. R(OFM). Jul 9
d. 1572. A Dutchman and a former student at Louvain, he was the Franciscan guardian of the friary at Gorinchem. He had made the conversion of Calvinists his life's work, and was one of the **Gorinchem martyrs** (q.v.).

Nicholas Politi (Bl) R. Aug 17
1117–1167. From Adernò near Patti, Sicily, he allegedly abandoned his wife on his wedding night to become a hermit on Mt Etna. He has a cultus in the diocese of Patti.

Nicholas Postgate (Bl) M. P. Aug 7
1604–1679. Ordained at Douai, he had been a priest in Yorkshire for nearly fifty years when he was seized while baptizing a baby at Littlebeck and executed at York during the agitation caused by Titus Oates. He was beatified in 1987. *See* **England (Martyrs of)**.

Nicholas of Prussia (Bl) R(OSB). Feb 23
?1379–1456. From East Prussia, he was one of the original community at the reformed abbey of St Justina at Padua, Italy. Then he was at several other abbeys before ending up at the abbey of St Nicholas del Boschetto near Genoa, where he was novice-master and prior. His cultus is not confirmed.

Nicholas Roland (Bl). P. F. Apr 27
1642–78. Born at Rheims, France, he abandoned the prospect of a successful business career in order to become a priest, hoping to set up free schools for girls. Inspired by Nicholas Barré (a Minim of Rouen) and the ideals of spiritual childhood, he founded the 'Sisters of the Infant Jesus'. He died worn-out aged 35 and was beatified in 1994. His disciple, St John Baptist de la Salle, did the equivalent work for boys.

Nicholas Roussel (Bl) *see* **September (Martyrs of)**

Nicholas Saggio (Bl) R. Feb 12
d. 1709. From a poor family at Longobardi in Calabria, Italy, he became a Minim lay brother at Rome and was beatified in 1786.

Nicholas Savouret (Bl) *see* **John-Baptist Souzy and Comps**

Nicholas Stensen (Bl) B. Nov 25
1638–1686. He was from Copenhagen, Denmark, and his family had contained many Lutheran pastors. One of the most important pioneer anatomists of all time, he studied at Leyden (1660), Paris (1665) and Florence (1666) and also made discoveries in geology and palaeontology. In 1667 he became a Catholic, then was the royal anatomist in Denmark from 1672 and was ordained in Florence in 1675. He was quickly made vicar-apostolic for the Nordic missions and became auxiliary bishop of Münster in 1681. As a bishop he was a Tridentine reformer who strived for personal sanctification, but he left in protest at diocesan corruption and ended his life as a missionary in Schwerin. He was beatified in 1988.

Nicholas Studites (St) R. Feb 4
d. 863. From Kydonia in Crete, when young he became a monk at the Studion at Constantinople under St Theodore. During the iconoclastic persecution he accompanied the latter into exile and, after their return, succeeded him as abbot in 884. He was exiled again by the emperor Michael III for refusing to recognize Photius as patriarch and for condemning the emperor's morals, but was restored by the emperor Basil I. Thereupon he lived as an ordinary monk at the Studion.

Nicholas Tabouillot (Bl) *see* **John-Baptist Souzy and Comps**

Nicholas Tavelić and Comps
(SS) MM. RR(OFM). Dec 5
d. 1391. A Croat from Sibenik in Dalmatia, Croatia, he became a Franciscan near Assisi,

Italy, and was on mission in Bohemia (Czech Republic) before being sent to the Holy Land with BB Deodatus de Ruticinio, Peter of Narbonnne and Stephen of Cuneo. For preaching to Muslims they were imprisoned and dismembered. They were canonized in 1970.

Nicholas (Bui Duc) Thé
(St) M. L. Jun 13
d. 1839. A Vietnamese soldier, he was hacked in half with Bl Augustine (Phan Viet) Huy. *See* **Vietnam (Martyrs of)**.

Nicholas of Tolentino
(St) R(OSA). Sep 10
1245–1305. From Sant' Angelo near Fermo in the Marches, Italy, he became an Augustinian friar at Cingoli in 1263 and, after his ordination, made a resolution to preach daily to the people. This he did, first at Cingoli and then for thirty years at Tolentino, where he was an enormous success. He was canonized in 1446, and his cultus was confined to local calendars in 1969.

Nicholas of Vaucelles (Bl)
R(OCist). May 31
d. ?1163. He and his father were among those noblemen who became Cistercian monks at Clairvaux, France, under St Bernard, and he went on to be third abbot of Vaucelles near Dinant, Belgium. He has an unconfirmed cultus among the Cistercians.

Nicholas Verron (Bl) *see* **September (Martyrs of)**

Nicholas Woodfen (alias Wheeler) (Bl) M. P. Jan 21
d. 1586. Born in Leominster, Herefordshire, he studied at Douai and worked for St Swithin Wells in London after being ordained. He then ran a school in Wiltshire before being seized and executed at Tyburn with Bl Richard Stransham. He was beatified in 1987. *See* **England (Martyrs of)**.

Nicodemus (St) M? Aug 3
C1st. He is mentioned in the gospel of St John (3 and 7) as a secret follower of Christ, and helped St Joseph of Arimathaea in the entombing of Christ's body. There was an apocryphal gospel circulated under his name. By tradition he was martyred, and his alleged relics were found with those of SS Stephen, Gamaliel and Abibas.

Nicolino Magalotti (Bl) T(OFM). Nov 29
d. 1370. A Franciscan tertiary, he was a hermit near Camerino, Italy, for thirty years and had his cultus confirmed in 1856.

Nicomedes (St) M. P. Sep 15
d. ?90. A priest of Rome, he was allegedly martyred in the reign of Domitian. In legend he is connected with SS Nereus, Achilleus and Petronilla. His cultus was confined to local calendars in 1969.

Nicomedia (Martyrs of) (SS)
The old Roman Martyrology lists four anonymous groups of martyrs at Nicomedia, Asia Minor, which was the seat of government of the emperor Diocletian and which thus seems to have been the locality of especially intense persecution. The figures of thousands quoted are wildly exaggerated, and are probably divisible by fifty to a hundred to obtain an idea of how many actually died.

Mar 18
d. *c*300. Allegedly 10,000 were massacred following a fire in the imperial palace.

Jun 23
d. ?303. Allegedly 20,000 took to the hills, hid in caves and were hunted down.

Dec 23
d. ?304. A group of twenty martyrs is separately listed in the old Roman Martyrology.

Dec 25
d. 303. Allegedly 20,000 were burnt alive in the great basilica by order of the emperor while they were celebrating Christmas. (Christmas was not celebrated in the East on this date at the time).

Nicon (St) *see* **Mark, Alphius and Comps**

Nicon and Comps (SS)
MM. RR. Mar 23
d. *c*250. Their legend is that Nicon was a pagan imperial soldier from Naples, Italy, who travelled to the East, became a Christian and then was a monk in the Holy Land. He became superior of about two hundred disciples, and when persecution broke out in the reign of Decius they fled to Sicily and were martyred there. The old Roman Martyrology wrongly assigned them to Caesarea in the Holy Land, and the whole story is dubious.

Nicon Metanoite (St) R. Nov 26
d. 998. He was an Armenian monk at Khrysopetro in Pontus, Asia Minor, and became an itinerant preacher throughout present-day Greece, where his theme of 'metanoite!' (repent!) gave him his surname. He died near Sparta.

Nicostratus (St) *see* **Four Crowned Martyrs.**

Nicostratus, Antiochus and Comps (SS) MM. May 21
d. 303. A cohort of Roman soldiers, according to the unreliable acta of St Procopius they were martyred at Caesarea Philippi in the Holy Land in the reign of Diocletian. Nicostratus was their tribune.

Nidan *see* **Midan**

Nighton *see* **Nectan**

Nilammon (St) R. Jun 6
C5th. His story is that he was an Egyptian monk who was chosen to become a bishop and who barricaded his cell and died in prayer while the bishops due to ordain him were waiting outside. Forced ordination was a feature of the early Egyptian church, as was a strong opposition among monks to being ordained for pastoral duties among the laity.

Nilus (St) *see* **Peleus, Nilus and Comps**

Nilus (St) *see* **Tyrannio of Tyre and Comps**

Nilus the Elder (St) B. Nov 12
d. *c*430. His worthless tradition describes him as a courtier at Constantinople who became a monk on Mt Sinai with his son, but he was actually a bishop of Ancyra, Asia Minor, (now Ankara in Turkey) and a friend of St John Chrysostom. He was a prolific spiritual writer, and under his name some important treatises by Evagrius Ponticus survive. The tradition may have been invented to help preserve these writings on monastic spirituality after Evagrius's speculative theology had been condemned.

Nilus the Younger (St) R. Sep 26
d. 1004. A Greek of Rossano in Calabria, Italy, he became a hermit after losing his wife and family but Muslim raids drove him into the relative safety of the Byzantine-rite monastery of St Adrian near his home village. He became abbot there, but the community fled as refugees from further Muslim incursions and eventually settled near Gaeta. Just before he died he designated the permanent site of the new monastery to be at Grottaferrata near Frascati, which still survives as an abbey of the Italo-Greek rite using the rule of St Basil.

Nimatullah-Joseph Kassab Al-Hardini (Bl) R. Dec 14
1808–1859. From Hardin in the Lebanon, he became a Maronite monk at Qozhaya in 1828 and transferred to Kfifan as director of the house of studies there. In 1845 he became assistant-general, but refused to be appointed abbot-general. He was remembered for saying 'A monk's first concern should be not to hurt or trouble his brethren' and for his devotion to Our Lady. He died of pneumonia at Kfifan and was beatified in 1998.

Nimmia (St) *see* **Hilaria, Digna and Comps**

Ninian (St) B. Aug 26
C5th. According to St Bede, he was a Briton educated in Rome who founded a church at Whithorn ('Candida Casa' or the White House, so called because the church was built of white-painted stone) in Galloway, Scotland. The monastery attached to it became a missionary centre for evangelizing the northern Britons and the Picts. St Bede himself qualifies this information ('as they say'), and the connection with Rome is especially dubious. Archeological investigations have, however, revealed an early Christian settlement on the site. He is depicted with heavy chains about him or hanging from his arm.

Nino (St) R? Dec 15
d. *c*320. According to tradition, Christianity was brought to Georgia by a captive from Cappodocia, Asia Minor, who was a slave-girl in the royal household. She converted the royal family and built the first church in the country at Mtskhet near Tbilisi. She is a historic personage and is regarded as the apostle of Georgia, but her extant biography has many contradictory legends. The original compilers of the old Roman Martyrology did not know her name and listed her as 'Christiana'.

Nithard (St) M. R(OSB). Feb 4
d. 845. A monk of Corvey near Paderborn, Germany, he went to Sweden with St Ansgar as a missionary and was killed there.

Nivard of Rheims (St) B. Sep 1
d. *c*670. Brother-in-law of King Childeric II of Frankish Austrasia, he became archbishop of Rheims, France, restored the abbey of Hautvilliers and was buried there.

Nivard of Vaucelles (Bl) R(OCist). Feb 7
*c*1000–*p*1150. The youngest brother of St Bernard followed his brother to Clairvaux, France, and eventually became novice-master at Vaucelles. The information as to his later life is confused. His cultus among the Cistercians is unconfirmed.

Nizier *see* **Nicetius**

Noah Mawaggali (St) M. L. Jun 3
d. 1886. He was a potter at the court of King Mwanga of Buganda, at whose orders he was executed. *See* **Charles Lwanga and Comps**

Noel *see* **Natalis**

Nominanda (St) *see* **Donata and Comps**

Non (Nonna, Nonnita) (St) R? Mar 3
C5th. She was the mother of St David, patron of Wales, and was possibly of a ruling family in Dyfed (the legends concerning her early life are confused). A chapel and a well near her son's cathedral are named after her. She is also associated with Altarnum near Launceston, Cornwall, whither she may have migrated and where her alleged relics survived until the Reformation. She died in Brittany, according to a Breton tradition, and her alleged tomb is at Dirinon.

Nonius Alvarez Pereira
(Bl) R(OCD). Nov 6
1360–1431. A Portuguese nobleman, he became major-general in 1383 of the Portuguese forces successfully fighting to break their country's union with Spain. After the death of his wife in 1422 he became a Carmelite lay brother at Lisbon. His cultus was confirmed for Lisbon in 1918.

Nonna (St) L. Aug 5
d. 374. She was the wife of St Gregory Nazianzen the Elder, whom she converted. Their three children, Gorgonia, Gregory and Caesarius, are also saints.

Nonnosus (St) R. Sep 2
d. ?575. He was prior at the monastery of Monte Soracte near Rome, and his miracles were recounted by St Gregory the Great in his *Dialogues*. He has been claimed as a Benedictine. His shrine was established at Freising, Germany.

Nonnus (St) B. Dec 2
d. ?458. A Tabennesiote monk of Egypt, he was made bishop of Edessa, Syria (now Urfa, Turkey), in 448 but also seems to have been connected with the former pagan stronghold of Baalbek, Lebanon, where his missionary efforts had some success. He also features in the story of St Pelagia the Penitent.

Norbert (St) B. R. F. Jun 6
*c*1080–1134. Born into a princely family at Xanten near Cleves, Germany, he was at the courts of the emperor and the prince-bishop of Cologne, and became a sub-deacon and canon of Xanten so as to enjoy the benefice. Then he almost died in 1115 when he fell off his horse, and this caused a radical conversion. He tried to reform the chapter of canons at Xanten but was treated with contempt, so he became an itinerant preacher and founded a community of reformed canons regular under the rule of St Augustine at Prémontré near Laon, France, in 1121. This was the first house of the Premonstratensians (now usually called Norbertines), and the new order became very popular in Western Europe as it combined the priesthood with an austere common life. He was compelled to become archbishop of Magdeburg, where he reformed the clergy by force and where he died.

Nostrianus (St) B. Feb 14
d. *c*450. This bishop of Naples, Italy, opposed Arianism and Pelagianism and had his cultus confirmed for Naples in 1878.

Notburga of Cologne (St) R. Oct 3
d. ?714. She was a nun at the nunnery of St Mary in the Capitol at Cologne, Germany.

Notburga of Eben (St) L. Sep 14
d. 1313. She was born at Rottenburg near Innsbruck in the Tyrol, Austria, and was a serving-maid in the castle there most of her life, except for a period when she worked for a peasant at Eben (where her shrine is now established). She was remembered for her hard work, charity and piety and had her cultus confirmed for Brixen in the South Tyrol in 1862.

Nothelm (St) B. Oct 17
d. 739. Archbishop of Canterbury, England, he was a friend of St Bede and a correspondent of St Boniface.

Notker Balbulus (Bl) R(OSB). Apr 6
*c*840–912. His surname means 'the Stammerer'. Born at Elgg in the canton of Zurich, Switzerland, he became a child-oblate and then a monk at the Benedictine abbey of St Gall. There he spent his life, serving as librarian, guest-master and precentor. An excellent musician, he was famous as a composer of liturgical sequences. His cultus was confirmed in 1512.

Novatus (St) P? Jun 20
d. ?151. He was alleged to have been a brother of SS **Praxedes and Pudentiana** (q.v.), but this is false and he probably never existed.

Novellone *see* **Nevolo**

Noyala (St) V. Jul 6
? According to her worthless legend she was a British maiden who was beheaded at Bignan near Vannes in Brittany, France, and who then walked seventeen miles to Pontivy holding her head in her hands. She is popularly venerated in Brittany.

Numerian (Memorian) (St) B. R. Jul 5
d. ?666. A nobleman of Trier, Germany, he became a monk in France at Remiremont under St Arnulf, then transferred to Luxeuil under St Waldebert and finally became bishop of his native city.

Numidicus and Comps (SS) MM. Aug 9
d. ?251. Roman Africans, they were burnt at the stake at Carthage in the reign of Decius (not in that of Valerian, pace the old Roman Martyrology). Numidicus is alleged to have been dragged from the pyre while still alive and to have survived to be ordained priest by St Cyprian. The latter mentions a priest of that name in his letters, but this group of martyrs is not in the earliest sources.

Nunctus (Noint) (St) M. R. Oct 22
d. 668. Abbot of a monastery near Mérida in Extremadura, Spain, he was killed by robbers and then venerated as a martyr.

Nunilo and Alodia (SS) VV. Oct 22
d. 851. Two sisters from near Huesca, Spain, when most of Spain was under Arab rule, they had a Muslim father and a Christian mother and were raised as Christians. After the death of their father their mother married another Muslim, who brutally persecuted them and had them imprisoned. They were finally beheaded at Huesca.

Nuntius Sulprizio (Bl) L. May 5
1817–1836. From the Abruzzi, Italy, he became an apprentice blacksmith at Naples and died when only nineteen. However he was remembered for his patience and chastity and was beatified in 1963.

Nympha (St) *see* **Tryphon of Nicaea and Comps**

Nymphodora (St) *see* **Menodora, Metrodora and Nymphodora**

Nymphodora (St) *see* **Theusetas, Horres and Comps**

O

Obdulia (St) R? Sep 5
? She has a cultus as a virgin at Toledo, Spain, but nothing is known about her.

Obitius (St) T(OSB). Feb 4
d. ?1204. A knight of Brescia, Italy, he almost drowned in a river during a battle and had a vision of hell in the process. This led him to live the rest of his life in austere penance while working for the Benedictine nuns of St Julia at Brescia. His cultus was approved for Brescia in 1900.

Oceanus (St) *see* **Theodore, Oceanus and Comps**

Octavian and Comps (SS) MM. Mar 22
d. 484. He was archdeacon at Carthage, Roman Africa, and was martyred with many others (allegedly several thousand) at the instigation of the Arian Vandal king, Hunneric.

Octavian of Savona (Bl) B. R(OSB). Aug 6
*c*1060–1132. A Burgundian nobleman, he became a monk at the abbey of St Peter in Ciel d'Oro, Pavia, Italy, and was made bishop of Savona in 1129. His cultus was confirmed in 1793.

Octavius, Solutor and Adventor (SS) MM. Nov 20
d. ?297. They were martyred at Turin, Italy, of which place they are patrons. Later they were connected with the legend of the Theban Legion.

Oda of Aquitaine (St) L. Oct 23
d. ?723. A Burgundian princess, she was the widow of a duke of Aquitaine and was remembered for her charitable activity. Her shrine is at Amay near Liege, Belgium, and she is a patron of sick pigs.

Oda (Odo) the Good (St) B. R(OSB). Jul 4
d. 959. Born in East Anglia, England, of Danish parents, he became bishop of Ramsbury in Wessex and was a royal courtier before being made archbishop of Canterbury in 942. He was apparently clothed as a monk at Fleury, France, just beforehand (not by St Abbo, who had not been born then). He took an active part in the restoration of secular as well as ecclesiastical institutions after the destruction of the Danish period, and paved the way for the monastic restoration under SS Oswald (his nephew), Dunstan and Ethelwold.

Oddino Barrotti (Bl) T(OFM). Jul 21
1324–1400. From Fossano in Piedmont, Italy, he became parish priest there and a Franciscan tertiary. Later he resigned and turned his house into a hospital. His cultus was locally approved in 1808.

Oderisius de' Marsi (Bl) R(OSB). Dec 2
d. 1105. A nobleman from the Marsi region in the Abruzzi, Italy, he was educated at Montecassino and became a cardinal in 1059, firstly as a deacon and then as a priest. In 1087 he became abbot of Montecassino when his predecessor became pope as Bl Victor III. He was a poet and a patron of scholars and mediated between the crusaders and the Byzantine emperor Alexius I. His cultus is unconfirmed.

Odger (St) *see* **Wiro and Comps**

Odilia *see* **Ottilia**

Odilo of Cluny (St) R(OSB). May 11
?962–1049. A nobleman of the Auvergne, France, he was a canon at Brioude before becoming a monk at Cluny in 991. He was made coadjutor to the abbot, St Majolus, the following year and became abbot himself in 994. An affable and gentle man, he was also a great organizer and under his government the Cluniac congregation increased from thirty-seven to sixty-five houses. He was personally acquainted with most of those in high office in western Europe, secular and ecclesiastical. The commemoration of the faithful dead (All Souls'

Day) was initially introduced by him for Cluny but soon spread to the entire Church.

Odilo of Stavelot-Malmédy (Bl) R(OSB). Oct 15
d. *p*954. A Benedictine monk at Gorze in Lorraine, in 945 he was elected abbot of Stavelot-Malmédy, Belgium, and raised the standard of studies and observance in those great twin abbeys. *See* **Sigolin**.

Odo of Beauvais (St) B. R(OSB). Jan 28
801–880. From near Beauvais, France, he was a soldier before becoming a Benedictine monk at Corbie, where he was tutor to the sons of Emperor Charles the Bald. He succeeded St Paschasius Radbert as abbot in 851 and he was made bishop of Beauvais in 861, where his reforms were influential in the Church in northern France.

Odo of Cambrai (Bl) B. R(OSB). Jun 19
1050–1113. From Orléans, France, he became the headmaster of the cathedral school at Tournai, Belgium. In *c*1090 he was inspired by reading St Augustine on free will to become the abbot-restorer of St Martin's abbey at Tournai, and he was made bishop of Cambrai in 1105. Difficulties with lay investiture and with the deposed simoniac whom he had replaced caused his exile to the abbey of Anchin, where he died. He was one of the greatest French scholars of the eleventh century. His cultus is unconfirmed.

Odo of Canterbury *see* **Oda the Good**

Odo of Cluny (St) R(OSB). May 11
?879–942. A nobleman from Maine, France, he was educated at the cathedral school of Tours before becoming a monk at Baume under Bl Berno, the abbot-founder of Cluny, in 909. He became abbot of Baume in 924 and of Cluny in 927. A great abbot and monastic reformer, he arranged for Cluny to be free from any secular control and thus secured the monastery's rapid growth and flourishing life for the next few centuries. Under him Cluny began to exert its influence in France and Italy, including Rome, where he restored the abbey of St Paul-outside-the-Walls). He died at Tours, by the tomb of St Martin.

Odo of Novara (Bl) R(OCart). Jan 14
?1105–1200. From Novara in Piedmont, Italy, he became a Carthusian and was made prior of Geyrach in Slavonia, Croatia. Owing to difficulties with the bishop he resigned, and then became chaplain to a nunnery at Tagliacozzo in the Abruzzi, Italy. His cultus was confirmed for the Carthusians in 1859.

Odo of Urgell (St) B. Jul 7
d. 1122. A relative of the counts of Barcelona, Spain, he fought in the petty wars of Catalonia as a soldier before becoming a priest and archdeacon of Urgell. He was made bishop there in 1095, and was remembered as a reformer of a run-down diocese.

Odoric Mattiuzzi of Pordenone (Bl) R(OFM). Feb 3
1285–1331. From near Pordenone in Friuli, Italy, he became a Franciscan at Udine and spent some time as a hermit. Then he set out on an amazing missionary journey, from Trebizond (Trabzon) on the Black Sea along the Silk Road as far as Beijing and even into Tibet. This was possible after the great conquests of the Mongols had imposed an imperial peace on much of Asia. After sixteen years he returned to Europe to report to the pope at Avignon, but died at Udine and had his cultus confirmed for there in 1775.

Odran (St) *see* **Medran and Odran**

Odran the Martyr (St) M. Feb 19
d. ?452. From Offaly, Ireland, he became St Patrick's chariot-driver and (according to legend) was killed in an ambush meant for his master after realizing the danger and changing places with him in the chariot. He was the only martyr remembered of the early Irish church.

Odran of Waterford (St) B. May 8
? He was one of the early bishops of Waterford, Ireland.

Odulf (St) R(CR)? Jun 12
d. ?855. From North Brabant, Netherlands, he was made a canon of Utrecht by St Frederick, whom he assisted in the evangelization of Friesland. He allegedly founded a monastery of Augustinian canons at Stavoren on the Ijsselmeer, but this was probably a house of secular canons at first. His relics were allegedly stolen in 1034 and taken to England, firstly to London and then to Evesham Abbey, Worcs.

Oduvald (St) R. May 26
d. 698. A nobleman of Scotland, he became a monk at Melrose and went on to be made abbot. He was a contemporary of St Cuthbert.
Oengus *see* **Aengus**

Offa (St) R(OSB). Dec 31
d. *c*1070. She was abbess of the Benedictine nunnery of St Peter's at Benevento, Italy.

Ogerius (Ogler) (Bl) R(OCist). Sep 10
d. 1214. From Trino near Vercelli, Italy, he became a Cistercian and then abbot of Locedio nearby. He is famous for a series of sermons defending the doctrine of the Immaculate Conception. His cultus was confirmed for Vercelli and Trino in 1875.

Ogmund (St) B. Mar 8
d. 1121. He was first bishop of Holar in Iceland, and is counted as one of the apostles of that nation. He was canonized in 1201.

Olalla *see* **Eulalia of Merida**

Olav (Olaf, Tola) of Norway, King (St) M. Jul 29
995–1030. Son of King Harald of Norway, as a young man he was a raider in western Europe. The contact with Christianity led him to be baptized at Rouen, France, in 1010, and he helped King Ethelred of England against the Danes in 1013. In 1015 he became king of Norway and summoned missionaries (chiefly from England) to complete the Christianization of his country. He succeeded to some extent, but his harshness led to his deposition and exile. In an attempt to recover power he led an invasion which was defeated at the battle at Stiklestad, during which he was killed. His opponents were also Christians but he was regarded as a martyr and his veneration was popular in northern Europe (the city of London had four churches dedicated to him). In Norway he is regarded as a patron of national independence.

Olav of Sweden, King (St) M. Jul 30
d. ?950. He was allegedly a king of Sweden who was murdered by his rebellious pagan subjects for refusing to sacrifice to idols at what is now Stockholm.

Olcan *see* **Bolcan**

Olga (St) L. Jul 11
?879–969. She married of Igor I, prince of Kiev, Ukraine, in 903, and when he was assassinated in 945 she became regent for Svyatoslav, their infant son. In 958 she was baptized at Constantinople but had little success in introducing Christianity into Kievan Rus (apart from the settlements of Byzantine merchants at Kiev). The conversion of the country was achieved by St Vladimir, her grandson.

Oliva of Anagni (St) R. Jun 3
? She is venerated as a nun at Anagni near Rome, but nothing is known about her.

Oliva of Brescia (St) V. Mar 5
d. ?138. She has her shrine at Brescia, Italy, and was allegedly martyred in the reign of Hadrian.

Oliva (Olivia, Olive) of Palermo (St) V. Jun 10
C10th? She is the heroine of a fictitious story which describes her as a young woman who was kidnapped from Palermo, Sicily, by Muslim raiders and eventually martyred at Tunis after adventures among the natives there.

Oliver (Liberius) of Ancona (St) R(OSB). Feb 3
d. *c*1050. He was a Benedictine monk of Saint Mary of the New Gate at Ancona, Italy.

Oliver Lefebvre (Bl) *see* **September (Martyrs of)**

Oliver Plunket (St) M. B. T(OSB). Jul 11
1629–1681. From Loughcrew in Co. Meath, Ireland, he studied for the priesthood and was ordained in Rome in 1654. There he remained as professor of theology in the college 'de Propaganda Fide' until he was made archbishop of Armagh in 1669, whereupon he set about renewing the persecuted Church in Ireland. He was arrested on a patently false charge of treason and was brought for trial to London because the Irish judges refused to convict him. There the first trial collapsed for lack of evidence, but on a second trial he was found guilty of treason 'for propagating the Catholic religion'. While in prison with the

St Oliver Plunket, Jul 11

president of the English Benedictines he became a Benedictine oblate, which is why his body is now enshrined at Downside Abbey, Somerset (his head is enshrined at Drogheda, Ireland). He was the last Catholic to be martyred at Tyburn, and was canonized in 1975.

Ollegarius (Oldegar, Olegari) (St) B. R(CR). Mar 6
1060–1137. From Barcelona, Spain, he became an Augustinian canon regular and was prior in several houses in France before being made bishop of Barcelona in 1115. The following year he was transferred to the archbishopric of Tarragona, which city had just been conquered from the Muslims. He successfully restored Church life there. His cultus was confirmed for Barcelona in 1675.

Olympiades (St) *see* **Maximus and Olympiades**

Olympiades of Amelia (St) M. Dec 1
d. 303. He was allegedly consular prefect at Amelia in Umbria, Italy, and was martyred in the reign of Diocletian.

Olympias (St) L. Dec 17
d. 408. A noblewoman of Constantinople, she was the widow of a prefect of the city and became a deaconess (rather akin to a modern active female religious, but not in vows). She worked in the service of the Church with a community of like-minded women living with her. She was a loyal supporter of St John Chrysostom, and as a result was deprived of her property and exiled, her house being sold and her community disbanded. She died in exile in Nicomedia, Asia Minor.

Olympius (St) *see* **Symphronius of Rome and Comps**

Olympius of Aenos (St) B. Jun 12
d. *p*343. Bishop of Aenos (now Enez, at the western extremity of European Turkey), he was in solidarity with St Athanasius in opposing Arianism and was exiled as a result by the emperor Constantius.

Omer (Audomarus) (St) B. R. Sep 9
?595–670. From near Constance, Germany, he became a monk at Luxeuil, France, and bishop of Thérouanne (which missionary diocese then embraced what is now Flanders and the Pas-de-Calais) in ?637. In order to evangelize the area he enlisted the help of many missionary monks who founded numerous monasteries. He himself founded the monastery of Sithiu with St Bertin, and this was the nucleus of the future town of St Omer.

Oncho (Onchuo) (St) R. Feb 8
d. *c*600. An Irish pilgrim-wanderer, he was also a bard and a collector of holy relics. He died at Clonmore in Co. Carlow, Ireland, a monastery founded by St Maedhog, and was enshrined there with the relics he had collected.

Onesimus (St) M? B? Feb 16
d. ?90. A runaway slave, he was the reason for St Paul's letter to Philemon. The old Roman Martyrology wrongly alleged that he was bishop of Ephesus, Asia Minor, after St Timothy and was martyred (this seems to refer to another person).

Onesimus of Soissons (St) B. May 13
d. ?361. He was the fifth bishop of Soissons, France.

Onesiphorus and Porphyry (SS) MM. Sep 6
d. ?80. Onesiphorus is mentioned by St Paul in his second letter to Timothy (4:19). According to his legend, he accompanied St Paul to Spain and then back to the East, were he was tied to wild horses and torn to pieces somewhere on the Hellespont in the reign of Domitian. Porphyry was allegedly his servant who was martyred with him.

Onuphrius (Humphrey) (St) R. Jun 12
d. *c*400. According to his unreliable story, he was an Egyptian hermit for seventy years in the Thebaid (Upper Egypt). He was a very popular saint in the Middle Ages, both in East and in West, but his existence has been questioned. He is the patron saint of weavers, possibly because 'he was dressed only in his own abundant hair and a loin-cloth of leaves', and is depicted nude with his long beard protecting his modesty.

Onuphrius of Sandomir (Bl) *see* **Sadoc of Sandomir and Comps**

Onuphrius Wasyluk (Bl) *see* **Podlasia (Martyrs of)**

Opportuna (St) R. Apr 22
d. *c*770. From Exmes near Argentan, Normandy, she was a sister of St Chrodegang, bishop of Sées, and when young became a nun at Monteuil near her home. She went on to be abbess, and was described as 'a true mother to all her nuns'. Her veneration is popular in France.

Optatian of Brescia (St) B. Jul 14
d. ?505. He became bishop of Brescia, Italy, in ?451.

Optatus (St) *see* **Zaragoza (Eighteen Martyrs of)**

Optatus of Auxerre (St) B. Aug 31
d. ?532. He became bishop of Auxerre, France, in *c*530.

Optatus of Milevis (St) B. Jun 4
d. ?387. Bishop of Milevis in Numidia, Roman Africa, (now Algeria), he wrote six treatises against the native Donatist schismatics and is the principal authority on the history of Donatism. Nothing is known about his life.

Oran *see* **Odran**

Orange (Martyrs of) (BB) MM. RR. Jul 9
d. 1794. Thirty-two consecrated religious women, they were imprisoned at Orange, France, in October 1793 for refusing to take the civil oath demanded during the French Revolution. Two were Cistercians from Avignon, while the others were from Bollène north of Orange: sixteen Ursulines, thirteen Sacramentines and one Benedictine (Mary-Rose Deloye). They formed an impromptu religious community in prison, trying to lead a life of prayer as far as possible, until they were guillotined during the following July. *See* **French Revolution (Martyrs of)**.

Ordonius (Ordoño) (St) B. R(OSB). Feb 23
d. 1066. Monk of the Cluniac abbey of Sahagún near León, Spain, he became bishop of Astorga in 1062.

Orentius, Heros, Pharnacius, Firminus, Firmus, Cyriac and Longinus (SS) MM. Jun 24
d. ?304. According to the old Roman Martyrology, they were seven brothers who were soldiers in western Asia Minor but who were dismissed from the army by Maximian, sent into exile and died of hardship or were killed in various places.

Orentius and Patientia (SS) MM. May 1
d. *c*240. According to a Spanish tradition they were the parents of St Laurence of Rome and lived at Loret near Huesca, Spain.

Orentius (Orientius) of Auch (St) B. R. May 1
d. ?439. A nobleman, he became a hermit in the Lavedan valley near Tarbes, France, but was made bishop of Auch in 419 and proved an effective pastor, allegedly eliminating paganism from his diocese.

Orestes (St) *see* **Eustratius and Comps**

Orestes of Tyana (St) M. Nov 9
d. 304. From Tyana in Cappodocia, Asia Minor, he was tortured to death there in the reign of Diocletian.

Orgonne *see* **Aldegund**

Oria *see* **Aurea**

Oriculus and Comps (SS) MM. Nov 18
d. *c*430. They were martyred by the Arian Vandals in the province of Carthage, Roman Africa.

Oringa (Christiana)-of-the-Cross Menabuci (Bl) R(OSA). Jan 4
d. According to her unreliable story, she fled from her home at Castello di Santa Croce in Tuscany, Italy, in order to avoid marriage and became a serving-maid at Lucca. Then she returned to found an Augustinian nunnery. Her cultus was confirmed for San Miniato in 1776.

Ormond Chapt de Rastignac and Ormond de Foucauld de Pontbriand (BB) *see* **September (Martyrs of)**.

Orontius (St) *see* **Vincent, Orontius and Victor**

Orsisius *see* **Horsiesius**

Osanna *see* **Hosanna**

Osburga (Osberga) (St) R(OSB). Mar 30
d. ?1018. She was the first abbess of the nunnery founded by King Canute at Coventry, England. This later failed and was replaced by a Benedictine monastery after the Norman conquest, which itself became a cathedral priory. Her shrine there became a focus of pilgrimage, and her cultus was confirmed for Coventry in 1410. The cathedral with shrine was destroyed in the Reformation (the only English cathedral to be lost), and the present modern Anglican cathedral and its bombed-out predecessor (formerly a parish church) have no connection with it.

Oscar *see* **Ansgar**

Osith *see* **Osyth**

Osmanna (Osanna) of Jouarre (St) R. Jun 18
d. *c*700. She was a nun at Jouarre near Paris, France).

Osmanna (Argariarga) of Saint-Brieuc (St) R. Sep 9
d. *c*650. According to her unreliable story, she was an Irish maiden who emigrated to Brittany, France, and became a hermit near St Brieuc.

Osmund (St) B. Dec 4
d. 1099. A Norman nobleman, he accompanied his relative William the Conqueror on his expedition to England and became chancellor of the kingdom after the conquest. He was made bishop of Sarum in 1078, his diocese having been formed by uniting those of Sherborne and Ramsbury. He finished the cathedral at what is now Old Sarum (Salisbury did not then exist) and was formerly credited with a compilation of liturgical services for his diocese, now known as the *Sarum Rite*. His hobby was copying books and binding them. He was canonized in 1457.

Ostianus (St) P? Jun 30
? He is venerated as a priest at Viviers, France. Nothing is known about him.

Oswald of Northumbria, King (St) M. L. Aug 5
604–642. The son of King Ethelfrith of Northumbria, England, he fled to Scotland after his father's death in battle and the seizure of the throne by St Edwin. He was baptized at Iona, and after St Edwin was overthrown and killed in battle by the Cymric king Cadwalladr he returned, defeated the latter near Hexham and started his reign. His policy was the Christianization of his kingdom, and he was the patron of St Aidan in this. In 642 he was killed in battle against Penda, the pagan king of Mercia, and the dismemberment of his body led to his having a popular cultus in various places as a martyr. His head is still in St Cuthbert's coffin at Durham, and his attribute is a raven with a ring in its beak.

Oswald of Worcester (St) B. R(OSB). Feb 28
d. 992. A Danish nobleman born in England, he was educated under his uncle St Odo of Canterbury and became dean of Winchester. Having a monastic vocation at a time when the monastic life did not exist in England, he went to Fleury on the Loire, France, to become a monk and was made bishop of Worcester on his return in 961. He allied himself with St Dunstan and with St Ethelwold in their efforts to revive monastic life and ecclesiastical discipline in England, and founded the abbey of Ramsey in the Fens and the cathedral priory at Worcester. In 972 he became archbishop of York while remaining the bishop of Worcester, and died while still on his knees after having finished his daily practice of washing the feet of twelve poor men.

Oswin of Deira, King (St) M. L. Aug 20
d. 651. After the death of St Oswald in 642 the kingdom of Northumbria, England, was divided between the cousins Oswin and Oswiu, the former getting the southern part (roughly modern Yorkshire). He had been educated by St Aidan, and reigned nine years before being killed in cold blood at Gilling, Yorks, by order of his cousin. He was then regarded as a martyr, although his faith was not a motive for his murder. His shrine was at Tynemouth.

Osyth (Osith) (St) M? R. Oct 7
d. *c*700. A a minor Saxon princess, she married a sub-king of East Anglia, England, and apparently founded a nunnery at what is now St Osyth in Essex. According to her unreliable biography she was killed by robbers. St Bede does not mention her in his *History*. Her nunnery died out, but was re-founded as an Augustinian monastery containing her shrine in the early C12th. Her attribute is a white stag.

Othmar (Otmar, Audemar) (St) R. Nov 16
d. 759. A German priest, he was made superior of the then dilapidated monastery of St Gall, Switzerland, in 720. He introduced the Benedictine rule (the Columbanian rule had been used), and the abbey began to grow in prosperity. Some donations of land were disputed, however, so he was seized and imprisoned by two neighbouring noblemen and died in prison.

Otteran *see* **Odran**

Otteran (Odran) of Iona (St) R. Oct 27
d. ?563. Superior of a monastery at Tyfarnham in West Meath, Ireland, he emigrated to Iona, Scotland, with St Columba and was the first to die there. He is the principal patron of the diocese of Waterford, Ireland.

Ottilia (Odilia, Othilia, Adilia) (St) R. Dec 13
d. *c*720. According to her unreliable story, she

was a noblewoman of Alsace, France, who had been born blind. Rejected by her family, she was taken in as a child oblate by a nunnery. Miraculously recovering her sight, she eventually became abbess-founder of the nunneries of Odilienberg and Niedermünster. Her shrine is at the former.

Ottilia Baumgarten (Bl) *see* **William Repin and Comps**

Ottilien *see* **Ottilia**

Otto (St) *see* **Berard of Carbio and Comps**

Otto of Bamberg (St) B. Jul 2
?1062–1139. A nobleman of south Germany, he became chancellor of Emperor Henry IV in 1101 and was made bishop of Bamberg, Bavaria, in 1106. He tried hard to achieve reconciliation of the investiture controversy, but was more successful in his missionary activities among the Pomeranian Slavs and is regarded as their apostle. He was canonized in 1189.

Otto of Heidelberg (Bl) R(OSB). Dec 28
d. 1344. He was a monk at the Benedictine abbey of Niederaltaich in Bavaria, Germany, with his brother, Bl Herman of Heidelberg. After his brother's death in 1326 he inherited his cell and lived therein as a hermit.

Otto Neururer (Bl) M. P. May 30
1882–1940. Born to a peasant family of Piller, Austria, he became a priest and an active member of the 'Christian Social Movement'. As parish priest at Götzens in the Tyrol after the 'Anschlüss' in 1938, he advised a girl not to marry an immoral friend of the local Nazi gauleiter. As a result he was sent to Büchenwald and later hanged upside-down until he died. He was the first priest to die in a Nazi concentration camp, and was beatified in 1996.

Oudoceus (Eddogwy) (St) B. Jul 2
d. ?615. His biography as found in later Welsh chronicles may contain some truth. His family were apparently Breton emigrants to Wales, and he became a bishop with jurisdiction over an area roughly corresponding to the present Anglican diocese of Llandaff. His shrine was at Llandaff Cathedral until the Reformation.

Ouen (Audöenus, Aldwin, Owen, Dado) (St) B. Aug 24
*c*600–684. A Frankish courtier from near Soissons, France, he founded the abbey of Rebais in Brie and became bishop of Rouen in 641. He died at a place now named after him near Paris.

Owen (Owin, Ouini) (St) R. Mar 4
d. *c*670. After having been steward in the household of St Etheldreda he became a monk at Lastingham in Yorkshire, England, under St Chad and was known for his devotion to manual work. The latter became missionary bishop of Mercia and established a monastery at his base at Lichfield, where St Owen was one of the founder-members. There was a church dedicated to him at Gloucester.

Oyand *see* **Eugendus**

Oye *see* **Authaire or Eutychius**

P

Pabo Post-Prydain (St) R. Nov 9
d. ?510. The 'Bulwark of Pictland' was a nobleman of what is now the Scottish Borders, and was a soldier before being made a refugee. He went to Wales and founded the church at Llanbabo on Anglesey.

Pachomius (St) R. F. May 14
*c*290–346. From the Upper Thebaid in Egypt, he became a Christian after a period of military conscription in 313 and became a hermit three years later. In 320 he built his first monastery at Tabennesi north of Thebes on the east bank of the Nile, and subsequently founded several others. He governed them all rather like a superior-general nowadays, and wrote for them a rule for life under obedience in a monastic community. In this he was an innovator, as previous Egyptian consecrated life was eremitic. When he died in an epidemic he ruled at least eleven monasteries (two of them nunneries) allegedly containing thousands of monastics. His rule was translated into Latin by St Jerome and influenced later monastic founders.

Pachomius (St) *see* **Faustus, Didius and Comps**

Pacian (St) B. Mar 9
d. *c*390. He became bishop of Barcelona, Spain, in 365 and wrote much on ecclesiastical discipline, but most of his work is lost. His treatise on penance survives, as do three letters against Novatian. The first of these contains the famous tag: 'My name is Christian, my surname is Catholic'.

Pacificus Divini of San Severino (St) R(OFM). Sep 24
1653–1721. From San Severino near Ancona, Italy, he became a Franciscan at Forano and was a popular preacher in the badly evangelized rural districts of the Apennines. However, a serious illness in 1688 left him deaf, blind and severely disabled, and the rest of his life involved intense suffering and the receipt of supernatural charismata. He died at his home town and was canonized in 1839.

Pacificus Ramota of Cerano (Bl) R(OFM). Jun 8
1424–1482. From Cerano near Novara, Italy, he became a Franciscan at the latter place in 1445 and proved a popular preacher in country districts. He wrote the *Summa Pacifica* as a popular guide for priests hearing confessions. His cultus was approved for Novara in 1745.

Padarn *see* **Paternus**

Paduin (Pavin) (St) R. Nov 15
d. ?703. He was a monk at Le Mans, France, and first abbot of St Mary's there.

Paisius the Great (St) R. Jun 19
C4th. He was one of the early desert fathers at Scetis, Egypt, and was a disciple of St Pambo.

Palaemon (St) R. Jan 11
d. 325. A hermit in the Thebaid, Egypt, he taught St Pachomius about the eremitic life and eventually followed him to Tabennesi, where he died.

Palatias and Laurentia (SS) MM. Oct 8
d. 302. A noblewoman of Ancona, Italy, and her slave, the latter converted the former and both were martyred at Fermo near Ancona in the reign of Diocletian.

Palatinus (St) *see* **Sycus and Palatinus**

Paldo, Taso and Tato (SS) RR. Jan 11
C8th. Three brothers of Benevento, Italy, they became monks at Farfa in the Sabine Hills and eventually founded the monastery of San Vincenzo at the headwaters of the Volturno. They were abbots in turn there, Paldo dying *c*720, Taso *c*729 and Tato *c*739.

Palestine, Martyrs of *see* **Holy Land (Martyrs of)**

Palladia (St) *see* **Susanna, Marciana and Comps**

Palladius of Antioch (St) R. Jan 28
d. *c*390.A hermit near Antioch, Syria, and a friend of St Simeon the Ancient, he was allegedly accused of murder and raised the victim to life to prove his innocence.

Palladius of Auxerre (St) B. R. Apr 10
d. 661. He was abbot of St Germanus's Abbey at Auxerre, France,) before he was made bishop of that city in 622. He founded several monasteries.

Palladius of Ireland (St) B. Jul 7
C5th. According to St Prosper of Aquitaine, he was sent by Pope St Celestine I to Ireland in 430 as first bishop of the Christians there. He was either a deacon of Rome or (more probably) one from Auxerre who had accompanied St Germanus on his first visit to Britain. He seems to have landed and worked mainly in Co. Wicklow, but apparently soon left for Scotland and died at Fordoun (north of Montrose).

Palladius of Saintes (St) B. Oct 7
d. *c*590. He became bishop of Saintes, France, in 570 and was locally venerated, although he seems to have been unworthy of this.

Palmatius (St) *see* **Calepodius and Comps**

Palmatius of Trier and Comps
(SS) MM. Oct 5
d. ?287. They were alleged to have been martyred at Trier, Germany, in the reign of Maximian Herculeus, but their existence is doubtful as their cultus dates only from the C11th.

Pambo (St) R. Jul 18
d. *c*390. A native Egyptian, he was one of the first to join St Amoun at Nitria and was illiterate until he learnt to read the Scriptures in preparation for ordination as priest for the monastic settlement. He features in the *Apophthegmata Patrum* and when old was famous throughout the Roman Empire, being visited by the likes of St Athanasius, St Melania the Elder and Rufinus.

Pammachius (St) R. Aug 30
*c*340–410. A Roman senator, he was proconsul in 370. He was a friend of SS Jerome and Paulinus of Nola, married one of the daughters of St Paula but was left a widower in 395. Then he spent the rest of his life and his wealth in the personal service of the sick and the poor, meanwhile living an ascetic life. Remains of his house survive beneath the Roman church of SS John and Paul.

Pamphilus of Caesarea (St) M. P. Jun 1
*c*240–309. From Beirut, Lebanon, he studied at Alexandria, Egypt, under Pierius, a disciple of Origen. Later he became a priest at Caesarea in the Holy Land, was head of the theological school and catalogued Origen's library there. He was one of the greatest biblical scholars of his day, and while in prison awaiting martyrdom wrote an *Apology* to defend Origen's memory against charges of heresy. His disciple was Eusebius, who took the surname 'Pamphili' in admiration.

Pamphilus of Capua (St) B. Sep 7
d. *c*400. From Greece, he was consecrated bishop of Capua, Italy, by Pope St Siricius.

Pamphilus of Sulmona
(St) B. Apr 28
d. *c*700 Bishop of Sulmona (a diocese later merged with Valva) in the Abruzzi, Italy, he was accused before Pope St Sergius of being an Arian, allegedly because he celebrated Mass before daybreak on Sundays. He completely vindicated himself.

Pamphilus of Rome (St) M. Sep 21
? Nothing is known about this Roman martyr.

Panacea (Panexia, Panassia) de Muzzi (St) M. L. May 1
1378–1383. Born at Quarona near Novara, Italy, when aged five she was killed with a spindle by her stepmother while praying. Her cultus was confirmed for Novara in 1867.

Pancharius of Besançon
(St) B. Jul 22
d. ?356. Bishop of Besançon, France, he withstood Arianism and was hence persecuted by the officials of the emperor Constantius.

Pancharius of Nicomedia
(St) M. Mar 19
d. 303. A Roman senator, he was secretary to the emperor Maximian. When Christianity was proscribed he denied (or at any rate concealed) his faith but was then edified by a letter from his mother and sister. Thereupon he proclaimed his faith and was beheaded in Nicomedia, Asia Minor.

Pancras of Rome (St) M. May 12
d. ?304. Beyond the fact of his martyrdom at Rome and the antiquity of his cultus, nothing is

known about him (his extant acta are worthless). A church was dedicated to him at Canterbury by St Augustine, and relics of him were sent to the king of Northumbria in 664. Subsequently his cultus in England was very popular. The railway station in London is named after a nearby church dedicated to him.

Pancras (Pancratius) of Taormina (St) M. B. Apr 3
C1st? According to his unreliable tradition, he was from Antioch, Syria, and was consecrated bishop of Taormina, Sicily, by St Peter, only to be stoned to death by pagans.

Pandwyna (Pandonia) (St) R? Aug 26
d. ?904. A church at Eltisley in Cambridgeshire, England, is dedicated to her. Leland in his *Itinerary* apparently quotes from a lost biography in describing her as a 'daughter of a king of Scots' who fled to England to avoid marriage and died at Eltisley.

Pannonia (Martyrs of) (SS) Apr 9
? The old Roman Martyrology listed a group of seven who were martyred at Sirmium (Srem Mitrovica, Serbia). Nothing is known about them.

Pantaenus (St) L. Jul 7
d. *c*190. A Sicilian convert from Stoicism, he became the head of the catechetical school of Alexandria, Egypt, and made it the intellectual centre of the Christian East. His most famous pupil was Clement of Alexandria. He is alleged to have died as a missionary in 'India' (more probably somewhere around the southern Red Sea).

Pantagapes (St) *see* **Diomedes, Julian and Comps**

Pantagathus (St) B. Apr 17
475–540. He had been at the Frankish court of King Clovis before he became bishop of Vienne, France.

Panteleimon (Pantaleon) (St) M. Jul 27
d. ?305. His name is Greek for 'the all-compassionate', and this may have given rise to the untrustworthy legend that he was a doctor of medicine who did not charge for his services and who was martyred at Nicomedia, Asia Minor, in the reign of Diocletian. His cultus was confined to local calendars in 1969.

Panteleimon (St) *see* **Maurus, Panteleimon and Sergius**

Pantalus (St) M? B? Oct 12
? Allegedly a martyr-bishop of Basel, Switzerland, connected with St Ursula, his very dubious existence depends on a tomb-inscription found in the C12th and on the 'revelations' of St Elizabeth of Schönau.

Papas (St) M. Mar 16
d. *c*30. He was martyred in Lycaonia, Asia Minor, in the reign of Diocletian.

Paphnutius (St) R? Sep 25
d. ?480. The story of the girl-monk St Euphrosyne describes him as her father. He allegedly became a monk and abbot in Egypt and his veneration is popular in the East, but he probably never existed.

Paphnutius the Buffalo (St) R. Jul 20
305–*c*400. He was one of the great desert fathers at Scetis, Egypt, and never left his cell except to attend Mass at the chapel five miles away on Saturday and Sunday. He was visited by St John Cassian and features in the latter's *Conferences*. He was the only Egyptian monastic superior who allowed the encyclical of the patriarch Theophilus condemning anthropomorphism (the idea that God as such has a human form) to be read.

Paphnutius of Dendara and Comps (SS) MM. Sep 24
d. ?303. They were martyred in Egypt in the reign of Diocletian, at Dendara near Thebes according to their unreliable acta.

Paphnutius the Great (St) B. R. Sep 11
d. *c*360. An Egyptian, during the persecution under Maximinus Daza he had one eye gouged out and one leg hamstrung. He became a disciple of St Anthony in 311, but shortly afterwards was ordained bishop of an unknown town in the Upper Thebaid. Highly respected by the emperor Constantine, he attended the first council of Nicaea in 325, where he successfully moved that married priests should not have to divorce their wives. He was a strenuous opponent of Arianism.

Paphnutius of Jerusalem (St) M. P. Apr 19
? He is listed as a priest martyred at Jerusalem.

Papas (Papius) (St) M. June 28
d. *c*303. He was martyred in the reign of Diocletian, possibly in Sicily.

Papias (St) *see* **Peregrine, Lucian and Comps**

Papias (St) *see* **Publius, Victor and Comps**

Papias (St) *see* **Victorinus, Victor and Comps**

Papias, Diodore, Conon and Claudian (SS) MM. Feb 26
d. *c*250. Shepherds of Pamphylia, Asia Minor, they were tortured and martyred in the reign of Decius.

Papias and Maurus (SS) MM. Jan 29
d. ?303. They were Roman soldiers martyred at Rome in the reign of Maximian.

Papias of Hierapolis (St) B. Feb 22
d. *c*130. Bishop of Hierapolis in the valley of the Lycus in Phrygia, Asia Minor, he wrote the *Explanation of the Sayings of the Lord*, a lost work which was referred to by St Irenaeus and by Eusebius (who wrote a cutting comment about his intelligence). It is the source of the traditions that St Matthew wrote his gospel in Aramaic and that St Mark wrote his as a summary of St Peter's preaching. He is described as having heard St John preach and as being acquainted with St Polycarp, but no details are known about his life.

Papinianus and Mansuetus (SS) MM. Nov 28
C5th. They were Roman African bishops martyred under the Arian Vandal king Genseric.

Papolenus *see* **Babolenus**

Pappus *see* **Papias**

Papulus (Papoul) (St) M. P. Nov 3
d. *c*300. A missionary priest, he worked with St Saturninus around Toulouse, France, and the two were martyred in the reign of Diocletian. His shrine is at Toulouse.

Papylus (St) *see* **Carpus of Thyatira and Comps**

Paragrus (St) *see* **Samosata (Martyrs of)**

Paraguay (Martyrs of) (SS) RR(SJ). Nov 17
d. 1628. Three Spanish Jesuits – Roch (Roque) Gonzalez (born at Asunción, Paraguay), Alphonsus Rodriguez and John de Castillo – they founded the 'reduction' or mission of the Assumption at Itapúa on the Jiuhi river in Paraguay. In 1628 they established the new mission of All Saints at Caaró near the Uruguay river (now in Brazil), where they were murdered at the instigation of a local chief. They were canonized in 1988.

Paramon and Comps (SS) MM. Nov 29
d. 250. A group of three hundred and seventy-five, they are alleged to have martyred in Bithynia, Asia Minor, on the same day during the Decian persecution. Their veneration is popular in the East.

Parasceve (St) *see* **Photina and Comps**

Pardulf (Pardoux) (St) R. Oct 6
?658–738. A blind boy from near Guéret near Limoges, France, he was a hermit before becoming a monk and then abbot at Guéret. At the time of the Arab incursion which was defeated by Charles Martel he remained alone in the abbey, which he allegedly saved by prayer.

Paregorius (St) *see* **Leo and Paregorius**

Paris (St) B. Aug 5
d. 346. He was a Greek bishop of Teano near Naples, Italy.

Parisius (St) R(OSB Cam). Jun 11
1152–1267. Probably from Treviso, Italy, when aged twelve he became a Camaldolese monk and went on to be the chaplain of the Camaldolese nuns of St Christina there for seventy-seven years. His shrine is in the cathedral.

Parmenas (St) M. D. Jan 23
d. *c*100. He was one of the original seven deacons (Acts 6:5). According to tradition he was a missionary in Asia Minor and was martyred at Philippi in Greek Macedonia in the reign of Trajan.

Parmenius and Comps (SS) MM. Apr 22
d. *c* 250. The priests Parmenius, Helimenas and Chrysotelus and the deacons Luke and Mucius were allegedly beheaded near Babylon during the fictitious invasion of Persian Mesopotamia by the emperor Decius.

Parthenius (St) *see* **Calocerus and Parthenius**

Paschal I, Pope (St) R(OSB). May 14
d. 824. A Roman, he became abbot of the Benedictine monastery of St Stephen near the Vatican and was elected pope in 817. He protested against the revival of iconoclasm in the Byzantine Empire and helped the victims of the resulting persecution, as well as restoring

many Roman churches and transferring many relics of martyrs.

Paschal Baylon (St) R(OFM). May 17
1540–1592. A peasant from Torre Hermosa in Aragón, Spain, he was a shepherd before becoming a Franciscan lay brother of the Alcantarine reform in 1564. He spent his life mainly as a doorkeeper in various Spanish friaries, except for one journey through France in 1570. During this his intense love for the Eucharist led him to defend the Real Presence in polemical debate with Protestants, with such success that he was declared patron of all eucharistic confraternities and congresses in 1897. Canonized in 1690, his cultus was confined to local calendars in 1969.

Paschal Cada Saporta (Bl) *see* **Peter Ruiz de los Paños y Angel and Comps**

Pascharius (Pasquier) (St) B. Jul 10
d. *c*680. Bishop of Nantes, France, he founded the abbey of Aindre and made St Hermenland its first abbot.

Paschasia (St) V. Jan 9
d. ?190. The cultus of this virgin-martyr of Dijon, France, was already described as ancient by St Gregory of Tours. Later untrustworthy legends connected her with St Benignus of Dijon.

Paschasius (St) *see* **Arcadius, Probus and Comps**

Paschasius Radbert (St) R(OSB). Apr 26
*c*790–865. From near Soissons, France, he became a monk at Corbie in Flanders, France, under St Adalard and was novice-master and headmaster of the abbey school for many years, both at Corbie and at New Corvey near Paderborn, Germany, whither he accompanied his abbot in 822. He was made abbot of Corbie in 844, but was not suited to the post and resigned in 849. A noted scholar, he wrote much on biblical studies but his most famous book is on the Eucharist: *De Corpore et Sanguine Domini.*

Paschasius of Rome (St) D. May 31
d. ?512. A Roman deacon and church author, he is mentioned in the *Dialogues* of St Gregory the Great. His own writings have been lost.

Paschasius of Vienne (St) B. Feb 22
d. ?312. He was a bishop of Vienne, France.

Pasicrates, Valentio and Comps (SS) MM. May 25
d. ?302. They were four soldiers martyred at Silistra, Bulgaria, and belong to the group of St Julius of Durostorum and Comps.

Pastor (St) *see* **Justus and Pastor**

Pastor, Victorinus and Comps (SS) MM. Mar 29
d. ?311. They were a group of seven martyred at Nicomedia, Asia Minor, in the reign of Galerius.

Pastor of Orléans (St) B. Mar 30
C6th? This alleged bishop of Orléans, France, does not appear in the ancient lists.

Pastor of Rome (St) P. Jul 26
d. *c*160. A Roman priest and an alleged brother of Pope St Pius I, he founded the church of St Pudentiana in Rome.

Patapius (St) R. Dec 8
C7th. An Egyptian monk from the Thebaid, he migrated to Constantinople and became a hermit in the Blachernae suburb of that city. His veneration is popular in the East.

Paterius (St) B. Feb 21
d. 606. A Roman monk, he was a disciple and friend of St Gregory the Great and was the notary of the Roman church before becoming bishop of Brescia in Lombardy, Italy. He was a prolific commentator on the Bible.

Patermuthius, Copres and Alexander (SS) MM. Jul 9
d. ?363. What is known is that Copres was an Egyptian hermit who converted Patermuthius, a notorious robber who then became a hermit also. The old Roman Martyrology listed them as having been martyred with Alexander (a converted soldier) at the orders of the emperor Julian, but this is fiction (Julian was never in Egypt).

Paternian of Bologna (St) B. Jul 12
d. ?470. He was allegedly bishop of Bologna, Italy, from *c*450, but was probably identical with the following.

Paternian of Fano (St) B. Nov 23
d. ?343. He was a fugitive in the Apennines, Italy, during the persecution of Diocletian, and later became bishop of Fano on the Adriatic coast.

Paternus of Abdinghof (Bl) R(OSB). Apr 10
d. 1058. A Scot, he was one of the first monks at the Benedictine abbey of Abdinghof in

Paderborn, Germany, founded by Bl Meinwerk. Afterwards he became a hermit and died in his cell after refusing to leave it when the monastery was destroyed by fire. His cultus is unconfirmed.

Paternus of Auch (St) B. Sep 28
C2nd? Allegedly from Bilbao, Spain, he was one of the earliest bishops (if not the first) of Auch, France.

Paternus (Pair) of Avranches (St) B. R. Sep 23
d. ?574 (or 563). From Poitiers, France, he became a monk with St Scubilio at Saint-Jouin-de-Marnes south of Saumur, and later a hermit near Coutances. Eventually he became bishop of Avranches in Normandy and died at the village now named St Pair after him. He is often confused with St Paternus of Wales.

Paternus the Breton (St) R. Nov 12
d. ?726. Born in Brittany, France, he was a monk first at Cessier near Avranches and then at Saint-Pierre-le-Vif near Sens. He was murdered by robbers, allegedly because he had admonished them.

Paternus of Fondi (St) M. Aug 21
d. ?255. According to his unreliable acta, he was an Alexandrian returning from a pilgrimage to Rome who was arrested at Fondi, Italy, and died in prison there.

Paternus (Pern) of Vannes (St) B. Apr 15
d. *c*500. He was a bishop of Vannes in Brittany, France, often confused with St Paternus of Wales.

Paternus (Padarn) of Wales (St) B. R. Apr 15
C5th-6th. A Welsh missionary monk, he founded Llanbadarn Fawr ('the great monastery of Padarn') near Aberystwyth and was bishop for the region. His veneration was very popular in Wales in the Middle Ages.

Patiens of Lyons (St) B. Sep 11
d. ?491. Archbishop of Lyons, France, he gave his revenues to the poor during a famine and the invasion of the Visigoths and was commended by St Sidonius Apollinaris, his contemporary.

Patiens of Metz (St) B. Jan 8
C3rd? He was the fourth bishop of Metz, France.

Patientia (St) *see* **Orentius and Patientia**

Patricia (St) *see* **Macedonius, Patricia and Modesta**

Patricia of Naples (St) R. Aug 25
d. ?665. According to her legend she was a relative of the emperor Constans II and, in order to avoid marriage, went on a pilgrimage from Constantinople to Jerusalem and then to Rome where she became a nun. She allegedly died at Naples, Italy, and has her shrine there.

Patrician (St) B. Oct 10
C5th. He is described as a north British bishop who was made a refugee by the Saxon invaders and settled on the Isle of Man.

Patrick (St) B. Mar 17
?390–?461. A Roman Briton, when aged sixteen he was abducted by Irish slave-raiders from his home (where this was is uncertain) and was a shepherd during his six years of slavery in Antrim, Ireland. Then he escaped and obtained a monastic education in Gaul. In ?432 he returned to Ireland as a missionary bishop

St Patrick, Mar 17

and thoroughly established the Church there, to the extent that he is regarded as Ireland's apostle. His main base was apparently at Armagh, which became the primatial see. The extant biographies contain much contradictory and legendary material, but the wealth of this is a testimony of the impact that he had and his veneration has always been central to Irish nationality and culture throughout the world. He has one of the largest modern bibliographies of any saint, with works ranging from the scholarly to the demented. He is often depicted getting rid of snakes, and the shamrock is his attribute.

Patrick, Acacius, Menander and Polyaenus (SS) MM. Apr 28
? They were martyred at Brusa near the Sea of Marmara, Asia Minor, after being tortured with water from the hot springs there. The acta of Patrick are apparently authentic, and the names of the others were added in early martyrologies.

Patrick of Auvergne (St) B? Mar 16
? He is listed in the old Roman Martyrology as a bishop of Auvergne, France, but his name is not in the lists of bishops of that region and he is probably a duplicate of St Patrick of Ireland created by an ignorant copyist reading 'Auvergne' for 'Hibernia', Ireland. A further dubious tradition claims that he was previously a bishop of Malaga, Spain, who fled to the Auvergne in the reign of Diocletian.

Patrick of Bayeux (St) B. May 24
d. ?469. He was the fourth bishop of Bayeux, France.

Patrick Cavenagh (Bl) *see* **Matthew Lambert and Comps**

Patrick Dong (Bodi) (St) *see* **Gregory Grassi and Comps**

Patrick Magonius (St) R. Aug 24
d. *c*450. Nicknamed 'Sen-Patrick' (Patrick the Elder), he is mentioned in several legends as a relative and contemporary of St Patrick of Ireland. He was allegedly buried at Glastonbury, which English abbey later pretended that his shrine belonged to his more famous namesake. There is also a St Patrick, abbot of Nevers, France, commemorated on the same day. The data concerning these and other saints of the same name is hopelessly confused.

Patrick O'Healey and Comps (BB) MM. B. RR(OFM). Jun 20
d. 1579. The Franciscan bishop of Mayo, he was hanged at Killmalloch with Bl Conrad O'Rourke, a fellow Franciscan priest. They were beatified in 1992. *See* **Ireland (Martyrs of)**.

Patrick O'Loughlan (Bl) *see* **Conor O'Devany and Comp**

Patrick Salmon (Bl) M. L. Jul 4
d. 1594. A servant of Bl Thomas Bosgrave, he was seized with him and Bl John Craven for sheltering priests and executed with them and Bl John Cornelius at Dorchester. *See* **England (Martyrs of)**.

Patrobas (St) *see* **Philologus and Patrobas**

Patroclus (St) M. Jan 21
d. ?275 (or 259). He was a wealthy and charitable citizen of Troyes, France, and was martyred there. His relics were translated in 960 to Soest near Dortmund, Germany, which became a great pilgrimage shrine.

Patto (Pacificus) (St) B. R. Mar 30
d. ?788. A Scot, he emigrated to Lower Saxony, Germany, became abbot of a monastery there and was made bishop of Werden.

Paul
In Latin this name is Paulus; in Italian and Portuguese, Paolo; in Spanish, Pablo; in Catalan, Pau.

Paul (St) M. A. Jun 29
*c*3–65. Most of his career as an apostle (the 'apostle to the Gentiles') is familiar in outline from the Acts of the Apostles, and forms the greater part of that work. The thirteen letters by him in the New Testament give a good presentation of his theology, and attempts to dispute his authorship of many of them are not conclusive. (The letter to the Hebrews is, however, not by him). His conversion near Damascus was about the year 34, and his apostolic journeys were from 47 until his arrest in Jerusalem in 58. He was in Rome in 61. There is no evidence of his career apart from the New Testament, but it is noticeable that the areas in Asia Minor and modern Greece described as having been evangelized by him were strongholds of Christianity during the Roman persecutions. The year of his martyrdom at Rome is uncertain (he was traditionally beheaded near the Ostian Way where the church of Tre Fontane now stands), and nothing is known of his activities after his first visit to Rome. Some have postulated further missionary journeys. A very ancient icono-

graphic tradition, possibly based on his real appearance, shows him as a small, balding , thin-faced old man with a long, pointed dark beard.

St Paul the Apostle, Jun 29

Paul (St) *see* **Crescens of Rome and Comps**

Paul (St) *see* **Darius, Zozimus and Comps**

Paul (St) *see* **Dionysius, Faustus and Comps**

Paul (St) *see* **Heradius, Paul and Comps**

Paul (St) *see* **John and Paul**

Paul (St) *see* **Lucian, Metrobius and Comps**

Paul (St) *see* **Lucillian, Claudius and Comps**

Paul (St) *see* **Mark, Mucian, Paul and Comps**

Paul (St) *see* **Nicaeas and Paul**

Paul (St) *see* **Peter, Andrew and Comps**

Paul (St) *see* **Reverianus, Paul and Comps**

Paul (St) *see* **Valens of Caesarea and Comps**

Paul and Cyriac (SS) MM. Jun 20
? They were martyred at Tomi on the Black Sea coast of Romania.

Paul, Cyril, Eugene and Comps (SS) MM. Mar 20
? A group of seven, they were martyred in Syria.

Paul, Gerontius, Januarius, Saturninus, Successus, Julius, Catus, Pia and Germana (SS) MM. Jan 19
C2nd? They are listed as having been martyred in Numidia, Roman Africa (now Algeria), but with no details.

Paul, Heraclius, Secundilla and Januaria (SS) MM. Mar 2
d. ?305. They were martyred in the reign of Diocletian at Porto Romano at the mouth of the Tiber, Italy.

Paul and Juliana (SS) MM. Aug 17
d. *c*270. According to their unreliable acta they were a brother and sister beheaded at Ptolemais (Acre) in the Holy Land in the reign of Aurelian.

Paul, Lucius and Cyriac (SS) MM. Feb 8
? They were martyred at Rome.

Paul, Tatta, Sabinian, Maximus, Rufus, and Eugene (SS) MM. Sep 25
? A married couple with their four sons, they were tortured to death at their native city of Damascus, Syria.

Paul I, Pope (St) Jun 28
d. 767. A native Roman priest, he succeeded Stephen II (his brother) as pope in 757 and continued the policy of relying on the Frankish ruler as patron to protect the independence of the Papacy against threats from the Lombard kingdom. He also sheltered refugees from the iconoclast persecution of emperor Constantine V.

Paul Aurelian (St) B. R. Mar 12
d. ?575. Born in Wales, he was educated at Llantwit Major under St Illtyd with many other famous saints (e.g. David, Samson, Gildas). After spending some time on Caldey Island he emigrated to Brittany, France, with twelve companions and founded a monastery on the island of Ushant. Later he moved to what is now Saint-Pol-de-Léon and became bishop there.

Paul Aybara (Bl) M. T(OP). Sep 8
d. 1628. A Japanese catechist and Dominican tertiary, he was beheaded with Dominic Castellet and Comps at Nagasaki. *See* **Japan (Martyrs of)**.

Paul of Brusa (St) B. Mar 7
d. 840. Bishop of Brusa in Bithynia, Asia Minor, he opposed the iconoclast policy of the emperor Leo VI and died in exile. He had no connection with Egypt (pace the old Roman Martyrology), which was under Muslim rule.

Paul (Tong Viet) Buong (St) M. L. Oct 23
d. 1833. A soldier of the Vietnamese army, he was captain of the bodyguard of King Minh-Menh and was an associate of the Paris Society of Foreign Missions. He was arrested in 1832, degraded and beheaded. *See* **Vietnam (Martyrs of)**.

Paul Burali d'Arezzo (Bl) B. R. Jun 17
1511–1578. From Itri near Gaeta, Italy, he was a lawyer for ten years at Naples before becoming a royal counsellor in 1549. In 1558 he became a Theatine and was superior of the houses at Naples and Rome before being made cardinal and bishop of Piacenza. Finally he was transferred as bishop to Naples. He was beatified in 1772.

Paul-John Charles (Bl) *see* **John-Baptist Souzy and Comps**

Paul Chen (Changping) (St) M. L. Jul 29
1838–1861. From Xingren in Guizhou, China, he was brought up by a priest after his family broke up and became a seminarian at Yaojiaguan. He was beheaded with SS Joseph Zhang (Wenlan), John-Baptist Luo (Tingying) and Martha Wang (Luo). *See* **China (Martyrs of)**.

Paul Cheong (St) *see* **Korea (Martyrs of)**

Paul of Constantinople (St) M. B. Jun 7
d. 350. From Thessalonika, Greece, he was elected bishop of Constantinople in 336 but was exiled to Pontus in 337 by Emperor Constantine for opposing a conciliatory policy towards the Arians. Returning after the emperor's death, he was exiled to Trier, Germany, by the Arian emperor Constantius until 340, to Mesopotamia from 342 to 344 and finally to Cucusus in Armenia, where he was allegedly locked up without food for six days and then strangled.

Paul of Cordoba (St) *see* **Elias, Paul and Isidore**

Paul of Corinth (St) *see* **Codratus and Comps**

Paul of the Cross *see* **Paul-of-the-Cross Danei**

Paul of Cyprus (St) M. R. Mar 17
d. 775. A monk of Cyprus, during the iconoclast persecution of the emperor Constantine V he refused to trample on a crucifix and was hence hanged head downwards over a slow fire until he died.

Paul-of-the-Cross Danei
(St) R. F. Oct 19
1694–1775. Born at Ovada near Genoa, Italy, of an impoverished noble family, he was a pious youth and initially tried to join the Venetian army in order to fight the Turks. Then he had a series of visions in 1720 which inspired him to write the rule of a religious order (the Passionists) dedicated to propagating devotion to the passion of Christ especially by conducting missions, and this was approved by the bishop of Alessandria. The first 'retreat' (house) was at Monte Argentaro near Orbitello, and eleven other houses were founded in his lifetime throughout Italy. He also founded the congregation of the Passionist nuns. A great mystic, he died at Rome and was canonized in 1867.

St Paul-of-the-Cross Danei, Oct 19

Paul Denn (St) *see* **Ignatius Mangin and Comps**

Paul Duong (St) M. Jun 6
1862. He was a Vietnamese lay martyr. *See* **Vietnam (Martyrs of)**.

Paul of Gaza (St) M. Jul 25
d. 308. He was beheaded at Gaza in the Holy Land in the reign of Galerius.

Paul Ge (Tingzhu) (St) M. L. Aug 8
1839–1900. A peasant and the leader of the Catholics of Xiaotun in Hebei, China, he was going to work at sunrise when he was seized by a gang of Boxers, tied to a tree and disembowelled. *See* **China (Martyrs of)**.

Paul Giustiniani (Bl) R(OSB Cam). Jun 28
1476–1528. A nobleman of Venice, Italy, he became a Camaldolese monk and eventually established the new, notably austere congregation of Monte Corona. He is the most prolific Camaldolese writer and has an unconfirmed cultus among the Camaldolese.

Paul Gojdič (Bl) M. B. R. (Jul 17)
1888–1960. He was a son of a Greek Catholic parish priest of the Ruthenian rite near Prešov in eastern Slovakia, and followed his father's vocation to the priesthood. (The Ruthenians are Slavs living south-west of the Carpathian mountains.) He was ordained at Prešov in 1911 and became a Basilian monk in 1922. In 1926 he was appointed apostolic administrator of the diocese there, and was made bishop in 1940. He had to contend with the upheavals of the Second World War and with the suppression of the Greek Catholic Church of the Ruthenian rite by the Communists in 1950. He was imprisoned for continuing his pastoral ministry, died of cancer in prison and was beatified as a martyr in 2001.

Paul Hanh (St) M. L. May 28
d. 1859. From Cho-kuan in the Mekong delta of Vietnam, he was a lapsed Christian who joined a gang of brigands. After his arrest, however, he returned to the faith and was beheaded at Saigon after being viciously tortured. *See* **Vietnam (Martyrs of)**.

Paul He (St) *see* **Korea (Martyrs of)**

Paul-of-St-Mary-Magdalen Heath (Bl) M. R(OFM). Apr 17
d. 1643. Born in Peterborough, he was baptized as Henry. Educated at Cambridge, he became an Anglican minister but was converted by reading the Fathers and went to Douai. There he joined the new English province of the Franciscans at their friary of St Bonaventure, and served as guardian of the friary and superior of the province. Wanting to go on mission in England, he arrived penniless in London and was immediately arrested as a vagrant, but it was then realized that he was a priest and so he was executed at Tyburn. He was beatified in 1987. *See* **England (Martyrs of)**.

Paul the Hermit (St) R. Jan 10
*c*230–342. His biography by St Jerome is the sole source, and there is a suspicion that he never existed. The story is that he was a well-educated Egyptian who fled into the desert of Thebes to escape the persecution under Decius when aged twenty-two, and remained there as a hermit for ninety years. He was eventually found by St Anthony, who found him dead on a second visit and buried him. He is depicted dressed in rough garments made from leaves or skins with a bird bringing him food or a lion digging his grave. His cultus was confined to local or particular calendars in 1969.

Paul Himonoya (Bl) M. T(OP). Sep 16
d. 1628. He was beheaded at Nagasaki with Bl Michael Himonoya, his father, and Bl Dominic Shobyoye. *See* **Japan (Martyrs of)**.

Paul Hong (St) *see* **Korea (Martyrs of)**

Paul of Hungary (Bl) M? R(OP). Feb 10
d. 1223. A Hungarian canon lawyer at the University of Bologna, he was a disciple of St Dominic and became one of the first Dominicans in 1221. He established his order in Hungary and was allegedly killed with ninety companions on an expedition to the Cumans in Wallachia (now Romania). He has a cultus, not approved, in Hungary.

Paul (Phan Khac) Khoan (St) M. P. Apr 28
d. 1840. From north Vietnam, he was a priest of the Paris Society for Foreign Missions for forty years and was imprisoned for two years before being beheaded. *See* **Vietnam (Martyrs of)**.

Paul Lang (Fu) (St) M. L. Jul 20
1900. He was a victim of the Boxers in south-eastern Hebei, China. *See* **China (Martyrs of)**.

Paul of Latros (St) R. Dec 15
d. 956. Born near Pergamum, Asia Minor, he became a hermit on the Bithynian Olympus (a great monastic colony) and then in a cave on Mt Latros near Miletus. He died there after

spending some time on the island of Samos, and Latros became famous for its monks until the arrival of the Turks.

Paul-Mary-of-St-Joseph Leoz y Portillo (Bl) *see* **Nicephorus Díez Tejerina and Comps**

Paul Liu (Hanzhuo) (St) M. P. Feb 21
1778–1819. From a poor Catholic family of Lezi in Sichuan, China, he was a shepherd before being accepted into the seminary and was ordained in 1813. He was betrayed while staying at Dezhou, arrested while saying Mass and hanged. *See* **China (Martyrs of)**.

Paul Liu (Jinde) (St) M. L. Jul 20
1821–1900. An old peasant of Hengshui in south-eastern Hebei, China, he was killed at home by a gang of Boxers. *See* **China (Martyrs of)**.

Paul (Le van) Loc (St) M. P. Feb 13
1831–1859. From An-nhon in Vietnam, he was beheaded at Saigon shortly after his ordination. *See* **Vietnam (Martyrs of)**.

Paul Manna (Bl) P. (Sep 15)
1872–1952. From Avellino in Italy, he was ordained as a missionary priest at Milan in 1894 and went to Burma but had to return owing to ill-health. But his passion for missionary activity overseas led him to organize support for the foreign missions in various ways and to direct the formation of missionary priests. In 1916 he founded the Pontifical Missionary Union, and in 1926 was made superior of the pontifical missionary seminaries in Italy. He died at Naples and was beatified in 2001.

Paul Miki and Comps (SS) MM. Feb 6
1562–1597. From the Tsunokuni district of Kyushu, Japan, the son of a samurai, he was educated by the Jesuits and became one himself in 1580. He was famed as an orator and controversialist and was able to continue missionary activity even after the decree of banishment of foreign missionaries by the shogun Toyotomi Hideyoshi in 1587. Sharper measures followed in reaction to the activities of Spanish Franciscans from the Philippines in Kyushu, and the shogun ordered the execution of Paul, two other Japanese Jesuits, six Spanish Franciscans and seventeen Japanese laymen (including interpreters, cathechists and tertiaries) on the Nishizaka at Nagasaki. They were tied to crosses and stabbed to death, and were canonized as a group in 1862. *See* **Japan (Martyrs of)**.

Paul (Nguyen van) My (St) M. Dec 18
d. 1838. A Vietnamese associate of the Paris Society of Foreign Missions in Vietnam, he was executed by strangulation. *See* **Vietnam (Martyrs of)**.

Paul Nagaishi (BB) M. L. Sep 10
d. 1622. He was a Japanese burned in the 'Great Martyrdom' at Nagasaki. *See* **Charles Spinola and Comps** and **Japan (Martyrs of)**.

Paul of Narbonne (St) B. Mar 22
d. *p*250. According to St Gregory of Tours, he was a missionary priest from Rome who worked around Narbonne, France. A late and worthless legend identifies him with the Roman proconsul Sergius Paulus converted by St Paul the Apostle (Acts 13).

Paul Navarro and Comps
(BB) MM. Nov 1
d. 1622. An Italian Jesuit, as a scholastic he was sent to Goa, India, ordained there and then sent to Japan. He had complete success in learning the language, was made superior of the college at Yamaguchi and was a missionary around Nagasaki. He was burnt alive at Shimabara with two Jesuit juniors, Peter Onizuka and Dionysius Fujishima (who took vows in prison), and Clement Kyuyemon, a servant. *See* **Japan (Martyrs of)**.

Paul (Nguyen) Ngan (St) M. P. Nov 8
d. 1840. A Vietnamese priest, he was beheaded with SS Joseph (Nguyen Dinh) Nghi and Comps. *See* **Vietnam (Martyrs of)**.

Paul of St Zoilus (St) M. D. Jul 20
d. 851. A deacon of Cordoba, Spain, he was involved in the 'martyr movement' there and ministered to those imprisoned by the Muslim rulers. He was himself beheaded and his remains enshrined in the church of St Zoilus.

Paul of Sandomir (Bl) *see* **Sadoc of Sandomir and Comps**

Paul Sankichi (Bl) M. L. Aug 19
d. 1622. He was a Japanese sailor on board the ship carrying Bl Louis Flores and Comps and was beheaded with them at Nagasaki. *See* **Japan (Martyrs of)**.

Paul Shinsuke (Bl) M. R(SJ). Jun 20
d. 1626. A Japanese catechist, he worked with Bl Paul Navarro and became a Jesuit in prison just before he was burnt alive at Nagasaki with Francis Pacheco and Comps. *See* **Japan (Martyrs of)**.

Paul the Simple (St) R. Mar 7
d. ?339. An Egyptian farmer of the Thebaid, when aged sixty he discovered his wife in bed with a neighbour and immediately left home to become a hermit in the desert. A disciple of St Anthony, he became famous for his prompt obedience and the childlike disposition which gave him his nickname. He is mentioned by Rufinus and Palladius.

Paul Tanaka (Bl) M. L. Sep 10
d. 1622. He was the Japanese host of Bl Joseph of St Hyacinth and was burned with him in the 'Great Martyrdom' at Nagasaki. *See* **Charles Spinola and Comps** and **Japan (Martyrs of)**.

Paul (Le Bao) Tinh (St) M. P. Apr 6
d. 1857. From Trinh-ha in north Vietnam, he became a priest and was beheaded at Son-tay. *See* **Vietnam (Martyrs of)**.

Paul Tomachi (Bl) M. L. Sep 8
d. 1628. A seven-year-old, he was beheaded with Bl John Tomachi, his father, at Nagasaki, Japan. *See* **Dominic Castellet and Comps** and **Japan (Martyrs of)**.

Paul of Trois-Châteaux (St) B. Feb 1
d. ?405. From Rheims, France, as a refugee from the barbarians he became a hermit near Arles and eventually bishop of Trois-Châteaux (a diocese now extinct) in Dauphiné.

Paul of Verdun (St) B. R. Feb 8
d. ?649. Formerly a Frankish courtier from Autun, he was a hermit on the Paulsberg near Trier, Germany, before becoming a monk at Tholey in Saarland, where he was headmaster of the monastic school. He was made bishop of Verdun, *c*630.

Paul Wu (Anju) and Comps
(SS) MM. LL. Jun 29
1900. The sixty-two-year old head of a Catholic family of Xihetou in Hebei, China, he fled with nine of his relatives to Xiaoluyi during the Boxer uprising. They were, however, discovered hiding in some bushes by a gang and killed on the spot. St Paul has been canonized, with two of his grandsons: Paul Wu (Wanshu) and John-Baptist Wu (Mantang). *See* **China (Martyrs of)**.

Paul Wu (Wanshu) (St) *see* preceding entry

Paula (St) R. Jan 26
347–404. A Roman noblewoman, in 380 she was left a widow with five children, two of whom were SS Eustochium and Blesilla. She became a disciple of St Jerome, and when he left for the Holy Land after his enemies had questioned their relationship she followed suit and founded a nunnery and hospice near his monastery in Bethlehem. He wrote her biography.

Paula (St) *see* **Bassa, Paula and Agathonica**

Paula (St) *see* **Cyriac and Paula**

Paula (St) *see* **Sabinus, Julian and Comps**

Paula-Elizabeth Cerioli
(Bl) R. F. Dec 24
1816–1865. A noblewoman from Soncino near Cremona, Italy, she was educated by the Visitation nuns and wished to become a consecrated religious but her parents wanted her to marry and she did so. She had three children, but they and her husband had all died by 1854 and she then started to lodge and care for orphan girls at her house at Como. She educated these as farm-workers. Companions started to gather, and thus was founded the institute of the 'Sisters of the Holy Family', of which she was made superior. She founded a similar orphanage for boys in 1863. Dying early of heart disease at Comonte, she was beatified in 1950.

Paula Frassinetti (St) R. F. Jun 11
1809–1882. From Genoa, Italy, she lived with her brother who was parish-priest of the suburb of Quinto. There she taught poor children at their home, and this led to her founding the 'Congregation of St Dorothy' (Dorotheans) for the education of poor girls, which spread throughout Italy and to the New World in her lifetime. She died at Rome and was canonized in 1984.

Paula Gambara-Costa (Bl) L. Jan 31
1473–1515. A noblewoman of Brescia, Italy, when aged twelve she married a young nobleman who proved a bad husband, habitually adulterous. He also objected to her lavish charitable donations. By her heroic patience she won him over, and they passed the rest of their married life in peaceful wedlock with an austere lifestyle. She died worn out by self-imposed penances, and her cultus was confirmed for Monreale in 1867.

Paula von Mallinckrodt (Bl) R. F. Apr 30
1817–1881. Born near Paderborn, Germany, she lost her mother when she was a child and she had to care for her family until her father died in 1842. This left her with a great

compassion for sick, poor and blind children and in 1849 she founded the 'Sisters of Christian Charity, Daughters of Our Lady of the Immaculate Conception' to help them. She served as superior for 32 years, and was beatified in 1985.

Paula-of-St-Joseph-Calasantz Montal Fornés (St) R. F. Feb 26
1779–1889. Born near Barcelona, Spain, she had to leave school early in order to support her family as a lace-maker. However she became active in her parish as a catechist and, inspired by St Joseph Calasantz, she founded the 'Daughters of Mary of Religious Schools' in 1847. She never took high office, but remained an ordinary sister until her death. She was canonized in 2001.

Paula of Montaldo (Bl) R(OFM). Oct 29
1443–1514. From Montaldo near Mantua, Italy, when aged fifteen she joined the Poor Clares at the nunnery of St Lucy in Mantua, where she was later elected abbess three times. She was a noted mystic. Her cultus was approved for Mantua in 1866.

Paula of Nicomedia (St) M. Jun 3
d. ?273. According to one late and unreliable legend, she was the wife of St Lucillian and the mother of his four sons, all of whom were martyred at Byzantium. She is also described as a young woman of Nicomedia, Asia Minor, who visited the five mentioned above in prison where she was seized, tortured and beheaded. Probably none of these was martyred at Byzantium.

Paula-of-the-Heart-of-Jesus-in-Agony Wisenteiner (Bl) R. F. Jul 9
1865–1942. Born near Trent (then in Austria), her family emigrated to Brazil when she was ten and settled at Nova Trento in Santa Catarina state. She nursed at home and catechized children and went with a companion in 1890 to nurse a woman with cancer (who recovered) at her cottage. This was the start of the 'Poor Sisters of the Immaculate Conception', which institute moved to São Paolo in 1909. She died of diabetes as a simple sister after losing her eyesight and one arm, and was beatified in 1991.

Paulillus (St) *see* **Arcadius, Probus and Comps**

Paulillus (St) *see* **Cyriac, Paulillus and Comps**

Paulina (St) *see* **Artemius, Candida and Paulina**

Paulina (St) *see* **Donata and Comps**

Paulina (St) *see* **Eusebius, Marcellus and Comps**

Paulinus (St) *see* **Augustine and Paulinus**

Paulinus (St) *see* **Felicissimus, Heraclius and Paulinus**

Paulinus of Antioch and Comps (SS) MM. Jul 12
? According to his worthless C13th legend, the patron of Lucca in Tuscany, Italy, was a native of Antioch sent to Lucca by St Peter to be its first bishop but who was martyred there with a priest, a deacon and a soldier. There was a bishop of the city with this name in the C4th.

Paulinus of Aquileia (St) B. Jan 28
?726–802. From near Cividale in Friuli, Italy, he was well educated and became a courtier of Charlemagne after the destruction of the Lombard kingdom in 774. The emperor appointed him patriarch of Aquileia in 787 (the bishop of that city had taken the title 'Patriarch' while in schism from Rome over the question of the 'Three Chapters'). He wrote against adoptionism, was a notable poet and a firm supporter of the 'Filioque' doctrine. He also carried on missionary work among the Avars before they were exterminated by the Franks.

Paulinus of Brescia (St) B. Apr 29
d. ?545. He was bishop of Brescia, Italy, from ?524.

Paulinus of Capua (St) B. Oct 10
d. 843. According to his story he was an English pilgrim on his way to Jerusalem who stopped off at Capua, Italy, and was forced by the inhabitants to become their bishop in 835. He died as a refugee after the city was destroyed in a Muslim raid.

Paulinus of Cologne (St) M. May 4
? Nothing is known about this martyr, whose relics are enshrined at Cologne, Germany.

Paulinus of Nola (St) B. Jun 22
354–431. Born at Bordeaux, France, he was the son of a Roman patrician who was praetorian prefect in Gaul at the time. He was taught by the poet Ausonius and became prefect of Rome, but after the death of his only child in 390 he resigned and went to Spain, where the people of Barcelona compelled him to become a priest. Finally he settled as a hermit near Nola in Campania, Italy, and was made bishop there in

400. He proved to be very capable, especially during the invasion by the Goths under Alaric, and was friendly with most of the great teachers of the Church at that time, e.g. Ambrose, Jerome, Augustine, Martin of Tours. Most of his poems and a number of his letters are extant, showing him to have been a talented Christian poet and a fluent writer of Latin prose.

Paulinus of Trier (St) B. Aug 31
d. 358. From Gascony, France, he accompanied St Maximinus to Trier, Germany, and succeeded him as bishop in 349. He supported St Athanasius and was hence exiled to Phrygia by the Arian emperor Constantius in 355. He died in exile, but his relics were brought back to Trier in 396.

Paulinus of York (St) B. R. Oct 10
d. 644. A Roman monk, he was sent to England in 601 with SS Mellitus and Justus by Pope St Gregory the Great in order to reinforce St Augustine's mission. He spent twenty-four years in Kent, but the princess St Ethelburga was sent to Northumbria in 625 to marry King St Edwin and he was consecrated as bishop of York and sent with her. The new mission was a success and the king was converted and baptized in 627, but was then killed in battle. In the pagan reaction that followed Ethelburga and Paulinus fled back to Kent, where he was appointed bishop of Rochester. St James the Deacon was left behind to minister to the Christians left in Northumbria, but the mission there was later re-started from Iona, Scotland.

Paulinus (Polin, Pewlin, Paulhen) of Whitland (St) R. Nov 23
d. ?505. A monk under St Illtyd, he was the founder or an early superior of the monastery of Whitland in Dyfed, Wales. Among his disciples there were SS David and Teilo.

Pausides (St) *see* **Timolaus and Comps**

Pausilippus (St) *see* **Theodore and Pausilippus**

Peblig *see* **Byblig**

Pega (St) R. Jan 8
d. ?719. A sister of St Guthlac of Croyland, she imitated him in becoming a hermit in the Fens north of Peterborough, England, at a place now called Peakirk after her. She died at Rome while on a pilgrimage.

Pegasius (St) *see* **Acindynus, Pegasius and Comps**

Pelagia (St) *see* **Beronicus, Pelagia and Comps**

Pelagia (St) *see* **Domitius of Caesarea and Comps**

Pelagia (St) *see* **Januarius and Pelagia**

Pelagia of Antioch (St) V. Jun 9
d. ?311. A girl of fifteen, she was a disciple of St Lucian at Antioch, Syria. When soldiers were sent to arrest her she killed herself by leaping from the roof of her house in order to avoid being raped. St John Chrysostom praised her courage and attributed her action to divine inspiration, but St Augustine later expounded the Church's teaching that suicide in such circumstances is not permissible.

Pelagia the Penitent (St) R. Oct 8
d. ?457. According to her fictitious legend, she was an actress of Antioch, Syria, who was converted by St Nonnus and who spent the rest of her life disguised as a male hermit on the Mount of Olives at Jerusalem. There is a suspicion that the story was merely attached to the memory of St Pelagia of Antioch, but her cultus dates from the C6th at Jerusalem.

Pelagia of Tarsus (St) V. May 4
d. ?300. According to her fictitious legend, she was a maiden of Tarsus in Cilicia, Asia Minor, who was roasted to death for refusing to marry one of the sons of the emperor Diocletian. She never existed.

Pelagius, Arsenius and Sylvanus (SS) MM. RR. Aug 30
d. *c*950. According to an old tradition, they were hermits near Burgos, Spain, who were killed by Muslim raiders. Their cell was the origin of the Benedictine abbey of Artanza and they are venerated locally.

Pelagius of Aemonia (St) M. Aug 28
d. ?283. He was allegedly martyred at Aemonia in Istria in the reign of Numerian, and after that town was destroyed his relics were taken to Citta Nuovo (now Novigrad in Slovenia). Part of them were apparently taken to Constance in Germany, of which place he is the patron.

Pelagius of Alexandria (St) M. P. Apr 7
? He was listed in the Hieronomian martyrology as a priest martyred at Alexandria, Egypt.

Pelagius (Pelayo) of Cordoba (St) M. Jun 26
?912–925. A boy of eleven from Asturias,

Spain, he was left as a hostage with the dominant Muslim government at Cordoba. During his three years of imprisonment he was offered freedom and preferment if he would convert to Islam, but he refused and in the end he was tortured to death over a period of six hours. His relics were enshrined at Oviedo in Asturias in 985.

Pelagius of Laodicea (St) B. Mar 25
d. *p*381. A bishop of Laodicea, Asia Minor, he opposed the Arian policy of the emperor Valens and was exiled to Bostra, Syria. Recalled by the emperor Gratian, he was present at the council of Constantinople in 381 but there is no later record of him.

Peleus (St) *see* **Tyrannio of Tyre and Comps**

Peleus, Nilus, Elias and Comps (SS) MM. Sep 19
d. *c*310 They were either three Egyptian bishops together with many priests and laymen, or three priests with one layman. They were sentenced to be worked as slaves in quarrying, probably at Phunon near Petra, Jordan, and were finally burnt alive for celebrating Mass at their labour-camp. Nilus and Elias seem to be duplicated under 'Tyranno and Comps' in the old Roman Martyrology.

Peleusius (St) M? P. Apr7
? Nothing is known about this priest of Alexandria, Egypt.

Pelinus (St) M. B. Dec 5
d. 361. Allegedly from Durrës, Albania, he became bishop of Confinium, a town in the Abruzzi, Italy, now destroyed, and was martyred in the reign of Julian.

Pepin of Landen (Bl) L. Feb 21
d. ?646. The duke of Brabant, he was mayor of the palace under three Merovingian kings and was the ancestor of Charlemagne. His wife was Bl Ida of Nivelles and his daughters were SS Begga and Gertrude of Nivelles. He was described as 'a lover of peace and a constant defender of truth and justice'. He had a cultus at Nivelles, Belgium.

Peregrine (St) *see* **Eusebius, Pontian and Comps**

Peregrine (Bl) *see* **Evangelist and Peregrine**

Peregrine (St) *see* **Irenaeus, Peregrine and Irene**

Peregrine (St) *see* **Isaurus, Innocent and Comps**

Peregrine, Lucian, Astius and Comps (SS) MM. Jul 7
d. ?117. Astius was bishop of Dyrrachium (Durrës in Albania) and was crucified there in the reign of Trajan. The others were Italian refugees from persecution who expressed sympathy for him and were seized, loaded with chains, taken out to sea and thrown overboard. The companions were Pompeius, Hesychius, Papias, Saturninus and Germanus.

Peregrine, Maceratus and Viventius (SS) MM. Aug 4
C6th. According to their doubtful legend they were three Spanish brothers who went to France to rescue their enslaved sister and were killed there. They used to be venerated at Le Mans.

Peregrine (Cetheus) of Aquila (St) M. B. Jun 13
d. *c*600. Bishop of L'Aquila in the Abruzzi, Italy, he was drowned in a river by Arian Lombards because he interceded for a condemned prisoner.

Peregrine of Auxerre (St) M. B? May 16
? According to his dubious legend, he was a Roman missionary sent by Pope Sixtus II to be first bishop of Auxerre, France, and martyred in the reign of Diocletian. He was probably only a martyr at Bouhy near Nevers, where his shrine was initially established.

Peregrine of Falerone (Bl) R(OFM). Sep 6
d. 1240. From Falerone near Fermo, Italy, he was a disciple of St Francis of Assisi and became a lay brother at San Severino after a pilgrimage to the Holy Land. His cultus was confirmed for Fermo and San Severino in 1821.

Peregrine Laziosi (St) R(OSM). May 1
?1265–1345. A native of Forli near Rimini, Italy, he was a worldly youth until he slapped St Philip Benizi across the face during a popular revolt. He was converted on the spot when Philip turned the other cheek, and joined the Servites at Siena. He was sent back to Forli, where he spent the rest of his long life. While waiting to have his leg amputated because of cancer of the foot he was instantaneously cured as a result of a vision, and is thus invoked against cancer. He was canonized in 1726.

Peregrine of Lyons (St) R. Jul 28
C2nd? Apparently he was a priest of Lyons,

France, contemporary with St Irenaeus, and lived as a hermit on an island in the Saône river during a persecution in the reign of Severus.

Peregrine of Modena (St) R. Aug 1
d. 643. He was a 'Scot' (Irish or Scottish) pilgrim to Jerusalem who stopped off at Modena, Italy, on his return journey and became a hermit nearby for the rest of his life.

Peregrine of Terni (St) B. May 16
d. ?138. He was bishop of Terni in Umbria, Italy, and founder of its cathedral. His traditional year of death is almost certainly much too early.

Perfectus (St) M. Apr 18
d. 851. A priest of Cordoba, Spain, he spoke publicly against Islam and was beheaded on Easter Sunday, being the first of the 'martyr movement' to die in this way.

Pergentinus and Laurentinus (SS) MM. Jun 3
d. ?251. It is uncertain whether these two alleged brothers, martyred at Arezzo, Italy, in the reign of Decius, ever existed.

Peris (St) Dec 11
? Nothing is known about the patron of Llanberis in Gwynedd, Wales.

Perpetua, Felicity and Comps (SS) MM. Mar 7
d. 203. Vivia Perpetua was a young married noblewoman of Carthage, Roman Africa, and Felicity (also married) was a slave. They were catechumens together with Saturninus, Revocatus and Secundulus, while Saturus was possibly their instructor. All were imprisoned at Carthage under a law of Septimus Severus forbidding conversions to Christianity. Secundulus died in prison and the others were thrown to the wild animals in the amphitheatre during the games. Their acta are authentic, having been written by Saturus before his martyrdom and completed by an eyewitness (perhaps Tertullian). Perpetua and Felicity are mentioned in the Roman canon of the Mass.

Perpetua Hong (St) *see* **Korea (Martyrs of)**

Perpetua of Rome (St) L. Aug 4
d. ?80. According to her dubious legend, she was a married woman of Rome who was baptized by St Peter and who converted her husband and her son, St Nazarius. (*See* **Nazarius and Celsus**.) Her relics are at Milan and Cremona.

Perpetuus of Tours (St) B. Apr 8
d. *c*490. He was bishop of Tours, France, from *c*460. His alleged will is a C17th forgery.

Perreux *see* **Petroc**

Perseveranda (Pecinna, Pezaine) (St) R. Jun 26
d. ?726. According to her fictitious story, she was a Spanish maiden who emigrated with her two sisters to Poitiers, France, where they founded a nunnery. This was sacked by a brigand, so she fled and died of exhaustion at a place now named Ste Pezaine after her.

Persia (Martyrs of) (SS)
In its first two centuries the only place where Christianity penetrated beyond the Roman Empire was into the Parthian Empire of Persia (roughly modern Iraq and Iran). Nothing is known historically of how it arrived in Mesopotamia, although a large and prosperous Jewish population had lived there since the Exile. Christianity was tolerated by the Parthians but these were overthrown in 226 by the Sassanids, whose official policy was to hark back to the great days of Persia under the Achaemenids. This included the encouragement of Zoroastrianism as the state religion, and consequent suspicion of Christianity. The situation abruptly deteriorated when Christianity became the state religion of the Roman Empire under Constantine, as Persian Christians were then regarded as fifth-columnists. Persecution was especially vicious under Shah Shapur II (309–379) until the Persian church went into schism after the Council of Ephesus condemned Nestorianism, but it continued until a treaty of toleration in 422 and sporadically afterwards until the arrival of the Muslim Arabs. The old Roman Martyrology lists five anonymous groups of martyrs:

Mar 10
? A group of forty-two, about which nothing is known.

May 9
? A group of three hundred and ten, about whom nothing is known.

Apr 6
d. ?345 A group of one hundred and twenty, probably martyred in the reign of Shah Shapur II.

Apr 22
d. 376. A very large number killed in the reign of Shah Shapur II on Good Friday. Among them were about twenty-five bishops, two hundred and fifty priests and deacons and many monastics.

Feb 8
C6th? 'Martyrs slain under Cabas'.

Peter
The name Petrus is the latinized form of the Greek Petros, which means 'Rock'. In Italian it is Pietro; in Spanish and Portuguese, Pedro; in French, Pierre; in Catalan, Pere.

Peter (St) M. A. Jun 29
d. ?64. A married fisherman of Galilee, he was a disciple of St John the Baptist before being called by Christ to be an apostle with St Andrew, his brother. As the chief of the apostles and one of Christ's 'inner council' with SS James and John, the early part of his career is familiar from the Gospels and the first part of the Acts of the Apostles. From his imprisonment by Herod Agrippa (and his miraculous release) until his martyrdom at Rome his career is virtually unknown, however. He made a decisive intervention at the Council of Jerusalem, and St Paul described a difference with him at Antioch, Syria, in his letter to the Galatians. This attested visit to Antioch may account for the early tradition that he was the first bishop of Antioch. The tradition that he was crucified upside-down in the reign of Nero derives from Tertullian. Excavations under his basilica at Rome strongly suggest that he was buried there, but some sloppiness in archaeological technique have left loopholes for doubt. His authorship of the first letter bearing his name is not conclusively doubted, and the reference found therein to his being at Babylon is generally accepted to be a euphemism for Rome (this usage occurs in Jewish apocalyptic). The second letter is probably not by him, as it deals with themes apparently post-dating his martyrdom and depends on the letter of Jude. An ancient iconographic tradition has him as a sturdy old man with curly hair and a curly, square-cut beard. His attribute is the familiar pair of keys, one gold and one silver.

Peter (St) *see* **Amator, Peter and Louis**

Peter (St) *see* **Andrew, John and Comps**

Peter (St) *see* **Berard of Carbio and Comps**

Peter (St) *see* **Cyril, Aquila and Comps**

Peter (St) *see* **Dionysius, Faustus and Comps**

Peter (St) *see* **Marcellinus, Mannea and Comps**

Peter (St) *see* **Marcellinus and Peter**

Peter (St) *see* **Stephen the Younger and Comps**

Peter (St) *see* **Theodosius, Lucius and Comps**

Peter, Andrew, Paul and Dionysia (SS) MM. May 15
d. 251. Peter was a young man of Lampsacus on the Hellespont and martyred at Troas, Asia Minor, with the other three in the reign of Decius.

Peter and Aphrodisius (SS) MM. Mar 14
C5th. They were martyred by the Arian Vandals in Roman Africa, but no details are known.

Peter and Hermogenes (SS) MM. Apr 17
? A deacon and his servant, they were probably martyred at Antioch, Syria, at an unknown date.

Peter, Julian and Comps (SS) MM. Aug 7
d. *c*260. They were twenty or more Roman martyrs of the reign of Valerian and Gallienus. Julian should probably be Juliana.

Peter, Marcian, Jovinus, Thecla, Cassian and Comps (SS) MM. Mar 26
? Nothing is known about these Roman martyrs. 'Thecla' is also listed 'Theodula'.

Peter, Severus and Leucius (SS) MM. Jan 11
? Peter and Leucius are listed in the Hieronomian martyrology as confessors. To them the old Roman Martyrology adds Severus and describes all three as martyrs of Alexandria, Egypt.

Peter, Successus, Bassian, Primitivus and Comps (SS) MM. Dec 9
? Nothing is known about these Roman African martyrs.

Peter-Mary Alcalde Negredo (Bl) *see* **Hospitaller Martyrs of Spain**

Peter of Alcántara (St) R(OFM). F. Oct 19
1499–1562. From Alcántara in Extremadura, Spain, at the age of sixteen he became a Franciscan Observant at Manjarates and was made provincial in 1524. In 1555 he received papal approval to found a reform friary at Pedrosa, the first house of the Discalced or

Alcantarene Franciscans. This was marked by an intense austerity in imitation of the first Franciscans, forbidding the eating of meat, wearing of sandals (hence 'discalced') and keeping of libraries. He was a great mystic who wrote a famous treatise on prayer and was the confessor of St Teresa, whom he encouraged and defended. The latter admired him and described his austerities as 'incomprehensible to the human mind', as they had reduced him to looking 'as if he were made from the roots of trees'. He was canonized in 1669, is the patron of Brazil and had his cultus confined to local and particular calendars in 1969. His congregation was amalgamated to the Friars Minor in 1897.

Peter of Alexandria (St) M. B. Nov 26
d. ?311. Born in Alexandria, Egypt, as a young man he witnessed to the faith during the persecution by the emperor Diocletian and afterwards became the head of the catechetical school. As such he opposed Origenistic speculative theology. In 300 he became patriarch and had to oppose the Meletian schism and the first manifestations of Arianism. He was martyred in the reign of Galerius, and the Coptic church refer to him as 'the seal and complement of martyrs' because he was the last to be executed as a Christian by public authority at Alexandria. His cultus was confined to particular calendars in 1969.

Peter Almato Ribera
(St) M. R(OP). Nov 1
d. 1861. From near Vich, Spain, he became a Dominican, was sent to the Philippine Islands and thence to north Vietnam to assist Bl Jerome Hermosilla, with whom he was beheaded. *See* **Vietnam (Martyrs of)**.

Peter Amaître (St) *see* **Anthony Daveluy and Comps**

Peter of Anagni (St) B. R(OSB). Aug 3
d. 1105. From Salerno, Italy, he became a Benedictine monk there and was made bishop of Anagni in 1062 by Pope St Gregory VII. He built a new cathedral, took part in the First Crusade and was papal legate in Constantinople. He was canonized in 1109.

Peter Apselamus (Absalon)
(St) M. Jan 3
d. 311. According to his acta, Peter Apselamus (or Balsamus) was crucified at Aulona near Hebron in the Holy Land. Eusebius mentions a Peter Absalon (or Abselame) who was burnt at Caesarea. It is suspected that these are the same person.

Peter Araki-Chobyoye
(Bl) M. L. Jul 12
d. 1626. Cousin of Bl **Mancius Araki-Kyuzaburo** (q.v.), he was burnt alive at Nagasaki for having accommodated European missionaries at his house. *See* **Japan (Martyrs of)**.

Peter de Arbués (St)
M. R(CR). Sep 17
1442–1485. From Epila near Zaragoza, Spain, he was a student at Huesca and Bologna before becoming an Augustinian canon regular at Zaragoza in 1478. He was appointed inquisitor of Aragón by Torquemada in 1484. Allegations made about his cruelty are unsubstantiated, and not a single sentence of death or of torture can be ascribed to him. He was zealous, however, in investigating the persistence of non-Christian customs among those former Jews and Muslims who had been forcibly baptized or who had accepted baptism in order to avoid deportation, and this was resented. He was murdered in Zaragoza Cathedral and canonized in 1867.

Peter-of-the-Holy-Mother-of-God of Arima (Bl) M. R(OP). Jul 29
d. 1629. A Japanese catechist and a Dominican lay brother, he was burnt alive at Omura with BB Louis Bertrán and Comps. *See* **Japan (Martyrs of)**.

Peter-Paul-of-St-Clare of Arima (Bl) M. R(OFM). Sep 12
d. 1622. From Arima, Japan, he worked with Bl Apollinaris Franco as a catechist, became a Franciscan in prison and was burnt alive at Omura with Thomas Zumarraga and Comps. *See* **Japan (Martyrs of)**.

Peter Armengol (Bl) M. R. Apr 27
1238–1304. A nobleman related to the counts of Urgell in Catalonia, Spain, as a young man he lived recklessly but repented and joined the Mercedarians in 1528 in order to help ransom Christians enslaved by Muslim raiders from Africa. He offered himself as a hostage for eighteen Christian children in the Maghreb, and when the ransom was not paid by the stipulated date he was hanged. A few hours later the money arrived so he was cut down, found to be still alive and was released. This is the reason for his cultus as a martyr, despite his having died in peace at Tarragona. His cultus was confirmed for there in 1686.

Peter Arnaud (Bl) *see* **William Arnaud and Comps**

Peter van Asse (St) M. R(OFM). Jul 9
d. 1572. From Asse near Brussels, he became a Franciscan lay brother at Gorinchem, Netherlands, and was one of the martyrs there.

Peter de Avila (Bl) M. R(OFM). Sep 10
1562–1622. From Palomares in Castile, Spain, he was sent to Manila with Bl Louis Sotelo in 1617 and thence to Japan. He was burnt alive at Nagasaki in the 'Great Martyrdom'. *See* **Japan (Martyrs of)**.

Peter Balzac (Bl) *see* **September (Martyrs of)**

Peter Becchetti (Bl) *see* **John and Peter Becchetti**

Peter Berna (Bl) M. R(SJ). Jul 27
d. 1583. From Ascona near Locarno in Ticino canton, Switzerland, he studied at the German college in Rome and joined the Jesuits. He went to Goa, India, with Bl **Rudolf Acquaviva** (q.v.) and was martyred with him.

Peter-of-Alcantara Bernalte Calzado (Bl) *see* **Hospitaller Martyrs of Spain**

Peter-of-St-Joseph de Betancur (Bl) T(OFM). F. Apr 25
?1619–1667. A shepherd from Tenerife, Canary Islands, he went to Guatemala City hoping to be a missionary but became destitute and could not afford to study for the priesthood. As a casual worker on the margins of society he joined the Franciscan tertiaries, and started many institutions for poor people as well as catechizing them. His co-workers became, in time, the 'Congregation of Our Lady of Bethlehem' (the 'Bethlemites'). He was beatified in 1980.

Peter Bonilli (Bl) P. F. Jan 5
1841–1935. From near Terni in Umbria, Italy, he became a priest there in 1863 and was appointed to a small and poor parish called Cannaiola. There he stayed until 1897. In 1887 he opened a girls' orphanage and founded the 'Sisters of the Holy Family' the following year to run it. Then he opened a hospital for deaf, dumb and blind girls in 1893, which he moved to Spoleto where he was appointed seminary rector. He died there, and was beatified in 1988.

Peter Bonsé (Bl) *see* **September (Martyrs of)**

Peter of Braga (St) M. B. Apr 26
? According to the tradition he was associated with the apostolate of St James the Great in Spain, became the first bishop of Braga, Portugal, and was martyred. Historically he seems to have been a C5th or C6th bishop.

Peter Briquet and Peter Brisse (BB) *see* **September (Martyrs of)**

Peter de la Cadireta (Bl) M. R(OP). Dec 20
d. 1277. From Moya near Barcelona, Spain, he became a Dominican and was stoned to death by heretics while preaching at Urgell. His shrine is there, but his cultus is unconfirmed.

Peter Calungsod (Bl) R(OP) *see* **Diegeo-Aloysius de San Vitores** and **Peter Calungsod**

Peter Cambian de Ruffi (Bl) M. R(OP). Feb 2
d. 1365. A Dominican, he was made inquisitor general of Piedmont and Lombardy, Italy, in 1351 in response to the growth of the dualist heresy of the Waldenses. A group of these trapped and killed him at the Franciscan friary at Susa, and his cultus was approved for Turin and the Dominicans in 1856.

Peter Canisius (St) R(SJ). Dr. Dec 21
1521–1597. From Nijmegen, Netherlands, he became a Jesuit as a disciple of Bl Peter Faber at Mainz, Germany, in 1543. He was the leader of the Catholic counter-Reformation in Germany, attending the Council of Trent in 1547 and subsequently being engaged in preaching, teaching, writing and instructing in Germany, Austria, Switzerland, Bohemia and Poland. His short catechism in Latin and German had passed through two hundred editions before his death at Fribourg, Switzerland, and was translated into twelve European languages. He also wrote theological, ascetical and historical treatises. He has been called 'the Second Apostle of Germany' but was hated by the Protestants, who called him 'the dog' (which is what his surname means). He was canonized and declared a doctor of the Church in 1925.

Peter of Canterbury (St) R. Jan 6
d. ?607. A monk of St Andrew's, Rome, he was one of those sent to England with St Augustine by St Gregory the Great and became the first abbot of the monastery of SS Peter and Paul (afterwards St Augustine's), founded at Canterbury. While on a mission to France he was drowned at Ambleteuse near Boulogne. His cultus was confirmed in 1915.

Peter Capucci (Bl) R(OP). Oct 21
1390–1445. From Città di Castello, Italy, he joined the Dominicans at Cortona and became known as 'the preacher of death' because he used to preach with a skull in his hands. His cultus was confirmed for the Dominicans in 1816.

Peter-of-the-Birth-of-Mary Casani (Bl) R. Oct 16
1572–1649. Born in Lucca, Italy, he joined the 'Congregation of the Mother of God' founded there by St John Leonardi. When the latter died, his disciples offered assistance to the 'Piarists' of St Joseph Calasantz and temporarily joined them 1614–17. When they left, Bl Peter stayed and eventually became assistant general to St Joseph, dying just before him. Their charism together was a love of poverty combined with a preferential option for poor children. He was beatified in 1995.

Peter of Castelnau (Bl) M. R(OCist). Jan 15
d. 1208. Born near Montpellier, France, he became archdeacon of Maguelonne in 1199 and a Cistercian monk at Fontfroide in 1202. The following year Pope Innocent III appointed him apostolic legate and inquisitor in southern France in order to combat the Albigensian heresy prevalent there. He excommunicated Count Raymond VI of Toulouse (their main patron) who submitted, but the day following the submission, Bl Peter was killed by an official of the count at St Gilles near Nîmes. This act triggered the Albigensian Crusade.

Peter II of Cava (Bl) R(OSB). Mar 13
d. 1208. He became the ninth abbot of Cava near Salerno, Italy, in 1195 and was described as 'an enemy of all litigation' which, for monks of that era, was praise indeed. His cultus was confirmed in 1928.

Peter Celestine, Pope (St) R(OSB). F. May 19
?1215–1296. From Isernia in Molise, Italy, he became a priest-hermit and joined the abbey of Faizola in 1246. Becoming a hermit again at Morone near Sulmona in 1251, he attracted numerous disciples and founded the new Benedictine congregation of the Celestines (which was suppressed in the C18th). In 1294 he was elected pope as Celestine V because factionalism prevented any more obvious candidate being acceptable, and was a disaster owing to his simplicity and lack of political knowledge. The Curia fell into complete disorder. He resigned (the only pope to have done so) after nine months, and Pope Boniface VIII (his successor) kept him imprisoned until his death. He was canonized (as Peter) in 1313 but his cultus was confined to local calendars in 1969. Recent pathological evidence suggests that he was murdered.

Peter Chanel (St) M. P. Apr 28
1803–1840. The protomartyr of Oceania was from a peasant family at Cluet near Belley, France, and was ordained as a diocesan priest of Belley in 1827. He was parish priest of Crozet before transferring to the Marist Fathers in 1831, and was in the first group of missionaries sent to Oceania by that new society. He established himself on Futuna Island, north-east of Fiji, and was welcomed until he baptized the chief's son. Then he was killed. He was canonized in 1954.

Peter of Chavanon (St) R(CR). Sep 11
1003–1080. From Langeac in the Massif Central, France, he was a secular priest before becoming the prior-founder of an abbey of Augustinian canons regular at Pébrac in Auvergne.

Peter Cheng (Wen-chi) (St) *see* **Bartholomew Chieng (Moun-ho) and Comps**

Peter Choi (St) *see* **Korea (Martyrs of)**

Peter Choi (Chi-chieng) and John-Baptist Chieng (Seung-yen) (SS) MM. Mar 10
d. 1866. Two Korean helpers of St Simon Berneaux, both family men in their fifties, they were executed together in Seoul. *See* **Korea (Martyrs of)**.

Peter Chyo (Hoa-se) (St) *see* **Bartholomew Chieng (Moun-ho) and Comps**

Peter of Cordoba and Comps (SS) MM. Jun 7
d. 851. He was a priest at Cordoba, Spain, during the rule of the Umayyad emirs there, and was involved in the 'martyr movement'. With five companions (Wallabonsus, a deacon; Sabinian and Wistremund, monks of St Zoilus's; Habentius, a monk of St Christopher's and Jeremiah, the aged founder of the monastery of Tabanos near Cordoba) he publicly preached against Islam. They were beheaded, except Jeremiah who was whipped to death.

Peter Chrysologus (St) B. Dr. Jul 30
?406–*c*450. From Imola, Italy,, he was archdeacon of Ravenna before becoming arch-

bishop in ?433. The city was the capital of the western Roman Empire at the time. His skill in preaching earned him his surname, 'Golden Speech' (although he was a Latin, the nickname is Greek in imitation of St John Chrysostom). He died at Imola, where his shrine is located. A large number of his sermons are extant, and he was declared a doctor of the Church in 1729.

Peter Claver (St) R(SJ). Sep 9
1581–1654. From a peasant family of Verdù near Barcelona, Spain, he became a Jesuit in 1601 and went to Majorca, where he was inspired by St Alphonsus Rodriguez to work in America. He was sent to Bogota, Colombia, in 1610 and to Cartagena in 1616, where he remained for forty years. The city was the central slave-market for the Caribbean area, and he made a special vow to minister to the enslaved blacks there. He was alleged to have baptized and cared for over 300,000 of them. During the last four years of his life he was an invalid, and was often neglected by his brethren. Canonized in 1888, he was declared patron of all missions of the Church among black people in 1896.

Peter Corradini of Mogliano (Bl) R(OFM). Jul 30
d. 1490. From Mogliano near Fermo, Italy, he studied law at Perugia and joined the Observant Franciscans there. Later he became a companion missionary of St James Gangala della Marca. His cultus was confirmed for Camerino in 1760.

Peter-of-the-Assumption of Cuerva (Bl) M. R(OFM). May 22
d. 1617. From Cuerva near Toledo, Spain, he was one of fifty Franciscan missionaries sent to Japan in 1601 and was appointed guardian of the friary at Nagasaki. He was beheaded at Nagasaki with Bl John Machado , which martyrdom was the first in the great wave of persecution aimed at the Japanese church thereupon. *See* **Japan (Martyrs of)**.

Peter Cunill Padrós (Bl) *see* **Philip-of-Jesus Munárriz Azcona and Comps**

Peter Da (St) M. L. Jun 17
1862. He was a Vietnamese layman and martyr. *See* **Vietnam (Martyrs of)**.

Peter of Damascus (St) M. B. Oct 4
d. *c* 750. A bishop of Damascus, Syria, he preached against Islam and so had his tongue cut out and was exiled to Arabia. Later he was maimed, blinded, bound to a cross and beheaded.

Peter Damian (St) B. Dr. R(OSB). Feb 21
1007–1072. From Ravenna, Italy, the youngest of a large family, he was orphaned and allegedly left in the care of an elder brother who ill-treated him and made him look after his pigs. Another brother, the archpriest of Ravenna, took pity on him and paid for his education at Faenza and Parma. Then he taught at Ravenna, but became a monk at Fontavellana in 1035 and went on to be elected prior in 1043. He made the monastery the centre of a very strict monastic reform with an eremitic character, but also became involved in the contemporary moves to reform the Church and was in contact with the papal curia and the imperial German court. In 1057 he was forced to become cardinal bishop of Ostia, and was papal representative in various capacities. His literary output was prodigious and varied, including very capable Latin verse as well as theological and ascetical works. He died exhausted at Faenza and was declared a doctor of the Church in 1828. His monastic congregation eventually decayed and was joined to the Camaldolese in 1569.

Peter the Deacon (St) D. R? Mar 12
d. *p*605. He appears in the *Dialogues* of St Gregory the Great as the disciple and secretary to whom the various stories comprising that work were told, and may have been a literary device rather than a real person. Other legends about him are derivative. He is patron of Salussola near Vercelli, Italy.

Peter Délepine (Bl) *see* **William Repin and Comps**

Peter (Nguyen) Dich (St) M. L. Aug 12
d. 1838. A wealthy Vietnamese farmer, he helped the missionaries of the Paris Society and was beheaded for sheltering a priest, St James Nam. *See* **Vietnam (Martyrs of)**.

Peter Donders (Bl) R(CSSR). Jan 14
1809–1887. Born of a poor family at Tilburg, Netherlands, he tried his religious vocation without success before becoming a priest and going to Dutch Guiana (now Surinam) in 1842. There he was an outstanding success as a missionary, especially to lepers (he was nicknamed 'apostle of the lepers'). He joined the Redemptorists in 1867 after they had taken over the mission, and was beatified in 1982.

Peter Dorié (St) *see* **Simon Berneaux and Comps**

Peter de Dueñas (Bl) *see* **John de Cetina**

Peter Dumoulin-Bori and Comps (SS) MM. Nov 24
1808–1838. From Cors near Tulle, France, he joined the Paris Society for Foreign Missions in 1829 and was sent to north Vietnam after his ordination in 1832. In 1836 he was arrested, and while in prison was made vicar-apostolic of so-called 'West Tonkin' and titular bishop of Acanthus. He was beheaded at Dong-Hoi, and with him were strangled two Vietnamese priests, BB Peter (Vo Bang) Khoa and Vincent (Nguyen The) Diem. *See* **Vietnam (Martyrs of)**.

Peter Dung (St) M. Jun 6
1862. He was a Vietnamese lay martyr. *See* **Vietnam (Martyrs of)**.

Peter (Truong van) Duong (St) M. L. Dec 18
d. 1838. A north Vietnamese catechist, he was executed with St Peter (Vu van) Truat. *See* **Vietnam (Martyrs of)**.

Peter Esqueda Ramírez (St) *see* **Mexico (Martyrs of)**

Peter Julian Eymard (St) R. F. Aug 2
1811–1864. He was born and died at La Mure d'Isère near Grenoble, France. Being ordained as a diocesan priest in 1834, he joined the 'Marist Fathers' five years later. He then tried to organize a group of priests dedicated to the adoration of the Blessed Sacrament within this congregation, but was told that this activity did not match their charism. So he was allowed to leave, and founded the 'Blessed Sacrament Fathers' in Paris in 1856, the 'Sisters, Servants of the Blessed Sacrament' in 1858 and then a confraternity for seculars. He was canonized in 1963.

Peter Faber (Lefèvre) (Bl) R(SJ). Aug 1
1506–1546. From Villaret in Savoy, France, as a priest and a student at Paris he became one of the first disciples of St Ignatius of Loyola (by tradition the first) and said the Mass at Montmartre during which the first Jesuits took their vows. After 1540 he was mainly occupied in converting Protestants and reforming Catholics along the Rhine in Germany, especially at Cologne, and had St Peter Canisius as a disciple. He was an attractive character, with great ability and untiring energy. He died in Rome when about to leave for the council of Trent and his cultus was confirmed for Annecy in 1872.

Peter-Sulpicius-Christopher Faverge (Bl) *see* **John-Baptist Souzy and Comps**

St Peter Julian Eymard, Aug 2

Peter Fontura (Bl) *see* **Bl Ignatius de Azevedo and Comps**

Peter Fourier (St) R(CR). F. Dec 9
1565–1640. From Mirecourt in Lorraine, France, he became an Augustinian canon regular at Chaumousey and served as procurator and parish priest of the monastery after his ordination in 1585. In 1597 he was appointed to the neglected parish of Mattaincourt. There he founded two congregations for the education of children: the 'Augustinian Canonesses of Our Lady' for girls and the 'Augustinian Canons of Our Saviour' for boys. He was superior of the latter from 1632 until he fled to Gray in Spanish Burgundy to avoid taking an oath of allegiance to King Louis XIII in 1640, just before he died. He was canonized in 1897. His male congregation was first suppressed in the French Revolution, and then finally became extinct in 1919.

Peter-George Frassati (Bl) T(OP). Jul 4
1901–1925. From Turin, Italy, in 1918 he enrolled at Turin University to study engineering, specializing in tunnelling design. He aimed also at Christian perfection, joining several confraternities (including the Dominican tertiaries), and had a strong Marian piety. He had achieved his doctorate before dying of poliomyelitis, and was beatified in 1990.

Peter Frémond (Bl) *see* **William Repin and Comps**

Bl Peter George Frassati, Jul 4 *(see p. 463)*

Peter Friedhofen (Bl) R. F. Jun 25
1819–1860. From Vallendar near Koblenz, Germany, he was orphaned as a child, became a municipal street-cleaner and was made the foreman of the gang in 1842. He helped many families in difficulties (including that of his deceased brother) and set up sodalities of St Aloysius in several parishes. He also started a nursing home for invalids in Weitersburg which became the 'Brothers of Mercy of Mary Auxiliatrix'. He was beatified in 1985.

Peter Gabilhaud (Bl) *see* **John-Baptist Souzy and Comps**

Peter Gambacorta (Bl) R. F. J Jun 17
1355–1435. Born at either Pisa or Lucca, Italy, a son of the ruler of these cities, he was a reckless young man but repented and became a hermit at Montebello near Urbino. According to the story he converted twelve robbers there and thus founded the Italian Hieronomites (the 'Poor Brothers of St Jerome'). When his father and two brothers were murdered he refused to leave his cell and forgave the assassins. His sister was Bl Clare Gambacorta. His cultus was confirmed for Pisa in 1693.

Peter García Bernal (Bl) *see* **Philip-of-Jesus Munárriz Azcona and Comps**

Peter Garrigues and Peter Gaugain (BB) *see* **September (Martyrs of)**

Peter de Geremia (Bl) R(OP). Mar 10
1381–1452. From Palermo, Sicily, he was a student of law at Bologna when he decided to join the Dominicans and became famous as a preacher and missionary in central and southern Italy. He was prior at Palermo where he died, and had his cultus confirmed for there in 1784.

Peter Gervais (Bl) *see* **September (Martyrs of)**

Peter Ghisleni of Gubbio
(Bl) R(OSA). Mar 23
d. ?1350. From Gubbio in Umbria, Italy, he became an Augustinian friar and provincial of a small congregation based at Fano. His shrine is at Gubbio, and his cultus was confirmed for there in 1847.

Peter González ('Telmo')
(St) R(OP). Apr 14
1190–1246. A nobleman from Astorga, Spain, he became a cathedral canon at Palencia before joining the Dominicans. He was the confessor and court-chaplain of King St Ferdinand III of Castile, and in that position was influential in fostering the 'Reconquista' and in obtaining a policy of tolerance of the kingdom's new Muslim subjects when Cordoba and Seville were conquered. He also worked among the sailors and peasants of Galicia. Spanish sailors mistakenly call him Telmo or Elmo, thought to be a corruption of 'St Erasmus' (another patron of sailors).

Peter Guérin, Peter Guérin du Rocher and Peter Héncocq (BB) *see* **September (Martyrs of)**

Peter the Hermit (Bl) R(CR). Jul 8
?1055–1115. He was apparently from near Amiens, France, but his early career is obscure. He appeared as a vagabond preacher of the First Crusade in Italy, France and Germany and gathered an army of followers whom he led through Hungary and Constantinople to annihilation by the Turks in Asia Minor. Then he joined the professional soldiers on their expedition and was at the siege of Antioch (where he attempted to desert) and at the capture of Jerusalem. Then he returned to become prior of the Augustinian monastery of Neufmoutier at Huy near Liege, Belgium, where he died. He had an unconfirmed cultus in Flanders.

Peter (Nguyen van) Hieu
(St) M. L. Apr 28
d. 1840. A Vietnamese catechist attached to the Paris Society of Foreign Missions, he was beheaded with John-Baptist (Dinh van) Thanh and Paul (Phan Khac) Khoan. *See* **Vietnam (Martyrs of)**.

Peter Higgins (Bl) M. R(OP). Jun 20
d. 1653. A Dominican priest, he was a victim of the persecution by Cromwell and was beatified in 1992 *see* **Ireland (Martyrs of)**.

Peter Hong (St) *see* **Korea (Martyrs of)**

Peter Igneus (Bl)
B. R(OSB Vall). Feb 8
d. ?1089. A nobleman of Florence, Italy, he became a monk at Vallombrosa under St John Gualbert. According to the story, shortly afterwards he accused the bishop of Florence of simony and submitted to trial by ordeal to prove his case, walking uninjured through a fire. This gave him his nickname of Igneus, 'of the fire'. Later he became cardinal-bishop of Albano and served as papal legate. His cultus is unconfirmed.

Peter-Francis Jamet (Bl) P. Jan 12
1762–1845. From Fresnes in Normandy, France, he was ordained in 1787 and became the confessor in 1790 of the 'Daughters of the Good Saviour' at Caen, becoming the canonical superior in 1819. During the 'Terror' he was imprisoned but was released and ministered to the scattered sisters. Afterwards he helped them open schools, hospitals and dispensaries and is called their 'second founder'. He died at Caen and was beatified in 1987.

Peter Jarrige de la Morélie du Puyredon (Bl) *see* **John-Baptist Souzy and Comps**

Peter Joret (Bl) *see* **September (Martyrs of)**

Peter of Juilly (Bl) R(OCist). Jun 23
d. 1136. An Englishman, he was a companion monk of St Stephen Harding at Molesme, France, and became chaplain of the Benedictine nuns of Juilly-les-Nonnais (affiliated to Molesme) where St Bernard's sister, St Humbeline, was abbess. He was described as a great preacher and thaumaturge, and died at Juilly. He has an unconfirmed cultus among the Cistercians.

Peter Khanh (St) M. P. Jul 12
*c*1780–1842. A Vietnamese priest, he was beheaded at Con-co. *See* **Vietnam (Martyrs of)**

Peter (Phan Khac) Khoa and Peter (Vo Bang) Khoa (SS) *see* **Peter Dumoulin-Bori and Comps**

Peter of Korea (Bl) M. L. Sep 10
d. 1622. He was only three years old when he was beheaded with his mother Mary and brother John in the 'Great Martyrdom' at Nagasaki, Japan. His father Anthony was burned. *See* **Japan (Martyrs of)**.

Peter Kuhyoye (Bl) M. T(OSA). Sep 28
d. 1630. A Japanese Augustinian tertiary, he gave shelter to the Augustinian missionaries and was hence beheaded at Nagasaki with BB John Chozaburo and Comps. *See* **Japan (Martyrs of)**.

Peter Kwon (St) *see* **Korea (Martyrs of)**

Peter Landry (Bl) *see* **September (Martyrs of)**

Peter-of-the-Heart-of-Jesus Largo Redondo (Bl) *see* **Nicephorus Díez Tejerina and Comps**

Peter Leclerq (Bl) *see* **September (Martyrs of)**

Peter Lee (St) *see* **Korea (Martyrs of)**

Peter-Joseph Legroing de La Romagère (Bl) *see* **John-Baptist Souzy and Comps**

Peter Levita (Bl)
C6th. His cultus was confirmed for Biella, Italy, in 1866.

Peter Li (Quanhui) and Raymund Li (Quanzhen)
(SS) MM. LL. Jun 30
1837 and 1841–1900. Brothers, they were from Chentucun in Hebei, China. During the Boxer rebellion they were caught hiding in a marsh by a Boxer gang and taken to a Buddhist temple as an invitation to apostasy. There they were tortured and killed. *See* **China (Martyrs of)**.

Peter Liu (Wenyuan) (St) M. L. May 17
1760–1834. A vegetable farmer of Giuzhu county in Guizhou, China, he was converted when young and exiled as a result to Manchuria in 1800. After thirty years of slavery he was allowed to return home, but when his sons were imprisoned for the faith he tricked his way into prison to visit them, was apprehended and strangled. *See* **China (Martyrs of)**.

St Peter Martyr, Apr 29

Peter Liu (Zeyu) (St) M. L. Jul 17
1843–1900. From Zhujiaxie in Hebei, China, he was a worker in a pottery factory and refused to flee during the Boxer rebellion. He was seized on the orders of the local magistrate and, on declining to apostatize, was beheaded. *See* **China (Martyrs of)**.

Peter (Nguyen Van) Luu
(St) M. Apr 7
1861. He was a Vietnamese secular priest and martyr. *See* **Vietnam (Martyrs of)**.

Peter of Luxembourg (Bl) B. Jul 4
1369–1387. A nobleman from Ligny-en-Baurrois in Lorraine, France, as a boy he was interested in religion and so (in accordance to a common contemporary abuse) he was made a cathedral canon of Paris, Chartres and Cambrai and arch-deacon of Dreux. When aged fourteen he was made bishop of Metz, and at sixteen was created cardinal by the anti-pope Clement VII at Avignon. A young man of great holiness, he retired to the Carthusian monastery of Villeneuve-lès-Avignon and died there aged eighteen, being beatified in 1527.

Peter Maldonado Lucero (St) *see* **Mexico (Martyrs of)**

Peter Marginet (Bl) R(OCist). Mar 26
d. 1435. A Cistercian monk of Poblet near Tarragona, Spain, he was the cellarer before he apostatized and became the leader of a gang of bandits. After some years he repented, went back to the abbey and spent the rest of his life doing penance. His cultus is unconfirmed.

Peter Martinez of Mozonzo
(St) B. R(OSB). Sep 10
d. *c*1000. From Galicia, Spain, he became a Benedictine at the abbey of Mozonzo in 950. Later he was appointed abbot of St Martin de Antealtares at Compostela, and finally archbishop of that city in ?986. He is one of the heroes of the Spanish Reconquista, and also one of candidates for authorship of the *Salve Regina*.

Peter Martyr (St) M. R(OP). Apr 29
?1205–1252. From Verona, Italy, where his parents were Waldensian dualist heretics, he became a Dominican in 1221 and was appointed inquisitor of Lombardy, where Waldensians were then common. He preached successfully throughout northern and central Italy until he was ambushed and killed by two heretics on the road between Como and Milan. He was canonized in the following year as the first Dominican martyr. His attribute is the

large knife used to kill him, often shown in his head. His cultus was confined to local or particular calendars in 1969.

Peter Maubant (Bl) *see* **Laurence Imbert and Comps**

Peter Nagaishi (Bl) M. L. Sep 10
d. 1622. A seven-year-old Japanese boy , he was beheaded with his parents BB Paul and Thecla Nagaishi in the 'Great Martyrdom' at Nagasaki. *See* **Japan (Martyrs of)**.

Peter Nam (St) *see* **Korea (Martyrs of)**

Peter of Narbonne (St) *see* **Nicholas Tavelić and Comps**

Peter-Francis Néron (St) M. P. Nov 3
1818–1860. From Bornay in the Jura, France, he joined the Paris Society of Foreign Missions in 1846 and was ordained as a missionary priest two years later. He went to Vietnam via Hong Kong, and was the director of the central seminary until he was arrested, kept in a cage without food and beheaded at Sontay. *See* **Vietnam (Martyrs of)**.

Peter Ni (Mieng-se) (St) *see* Bartholomew **Chieng (Moun-ho) and Comps**

Peter of Nicomedia (St) M. Mar 12
d. 303. A chamberlain in the palace of Diocletian at Nicomedia, Asia Minor, he was one of the first victims of the persecution ordered by that emperor. Bits of his flesh were torn off, salt and vinegar were applied to the wounds and he was finally roasted to death over a slow fire.

Peter-Michael Noël (Bl) *see* **John-Baptist Souzy and Comps**

Peter Nolasco (St) R. F. Jan 28
?1182–1258. A native of Languedoc, he took part in the Albigensian crusade before becoming a courtier of King James I of Aragón at Barcelona, Spain. There he got to know St Raymund of Peñafort, and in about 1218 they reorganized a lay confraternity for ransoming captives from the Muslims with the help of the king. This became the Mercedarian order. He journeyed to the Maghreb twice, died at Barcelona and had his cultus confirmed for there in 1628. From 1664 to 1969 this was extended to the whole Church.

Peter Nuñez (Bl) *see* **Bl Ignatius de Azevedo and Comps**

Peter Onizuka (Bl) M. R(SJ). Nov 1
d. 1622. A Japanese from Arima, he became a Jesuit in prison before being burned alive with Bl Paul Navarro and Comps. *See* **Japan (Martyrs of)**.

Peter Orseolo (St) R(OSB). Jan 10
928–987. A nobleman of Venice, Italy, when aged twenty he became admiral of the fleet. In 976 he became Doge and was a successful ruler, but two years later he abandoned his office and family to become a monk at the Benedictine abbey of Cuxa in Roussillon, France. He was sacristan there until he became a hermit in his last years.

Peter of Osma (St) B. R(OSB). Aug 2
d. 1109. From Berry, France, he became a monk of Cluny and was one of the numerous Cluniac monks who settled in Spain from *c*1050 to *c*1130. He was archdeacon of Toledo before being made bishop of Osma in Old Castile in 1101, of which diocese he is the principal patron.

Peter Pappacarbone (St)
B. R(OSB). Mar 4
d. 1123. From Salerno, Italy, he became a monk of Cava under the second abbot, St Leo I. In ?1062 he was sent to Cluny in France for about six years, was made bishop of Policastro in 1079 but resigned and returned to Cava. There he became third abbot in 1075, but was thought too strict and withdrew to another monastery. Soon recalled, he showed himself more paternal and the abbey prospered (he allegedly took in over three thousand monks). When he died Cava was a congregation of twenty-nine subject abbeys, ninety priories and over three hundred and forty cells.

Peter Parenzi (St) M. L. May 22
d. 1199. A Roman, he was sent to Orvieto, Italy, as papal governor in 1199 in response to the growing success of dualist heresy there. He adopted severe measures, with the result that he was seized and killed. His shrine is in the cathedral.

Peter Pascual (St) M. B. Dec 6
1227–1300. From Valencia, Spain, he became tutor to Sancho, archbishop of Toledo and the son of King James I of Aragón, and administered the diocese for him. In 1296 he became bishop of Jaén, which was still under Muslim rule. He was zealous in ransoming captives and in preaching and writing against Islam, for which he was executed at Granada. His cultus was confirmed for Granada and Jaén in 1673.

Peter of Pavia (St) B. May 7
d. ?735. A relative of Luitprand, king of the Lombards, he was briefly bishop of Pavia (the Lombard capital in Italy).

Peter Pazery de Thorame (Bl) *see* **September (Martyrs of)**

Peter-James of Pesaro
(Bl) R(OSA). Jun 23
d. ?1496. He was an Augustinian friar at Pesaro, Italy, and his cultus was confirmed for there in 1848.

Peter Petroni (Bl) R(OCart). May 29
1311–1361. From Siena, Italy, he became a Carthusian at Maggiano nearby in 1328. His thoughtful charity helped in the conversion of Boccaccio. His cultus is unconfirmed.

Peter Ploquin (Bl) *see* **September (Martyrs of)**

Peter of Poitiers (St) B. Apr 4
d. 1115. He became bishop of Poitiers, France, in 1087, was a friend of Bl Robert Arbrissel and helped him in founding the double abbey of Fontrevault.

Peter Pottier (Bl) *see* **September (Martyrs of)**

Peter Poveda Castroverde (Bl) P. Jul 28
1874–1936. From Linares, Spain, he became a priest of Guadix in 1897 before moving to Madrid and founding the 'Teresian Association' for the spiritual and pastoral formation of teachers. He taught in seminaries, started periodicals and was a royal chaplain. Marked by simplicity and a constant devotion to study, he was beatified in 1993.

Peter Psalmon (Bl) *see* **September (Martyrs of)**

Peter (Doang Kong) Quy (St) M. P. Jul 31
d. 1859. A priest from Bung in Vietnam, he was beheaded near Chau-doc. *See* **Vietnam (Martyrs of)**.

Peter Regalado (St) R(OFM). Mar 30
1390–1456. A nobleman of Valladolid, Spain, he became a Franciscan there and instituted a reform movement starting at Aguilar, where he died. Many Spanish friaries joined this. He was canonized in 1746.

Peter Régnet (Bl) *see* **September (Martyrs of)**

Peter Rinsei (Bl) M. R(SJ). Jun 20
1589–1626. A Japanese, he was educated at the Jesuit seminary of Arima and worked with Bl Francis Pacheco as a catechist. The latter received his vows as a Jesuit while they were in prison before being burned together at Nagasaki. *See* **Francis Pacheco and Comps** and **Japan (Martyrs of)**.

Peter Riu *see* **Korea (Martyrs of)**

Peter-Louis de la Rochefoucault Maumont (Bl) *see* **September (Martyrs of)**

Peter Rodríguez and Comps
(BB) MM. Jun 11
d. 1242. He was the leader of a group of six Portuguese knights of Santiago and a merchant who were killed by their Muslim opponents during an armistice at Tavira in the Algarve, Portugal. The companions were Mendez Valle, Damian Vaz, Alvarez Garcia, Stephen Vasquez, Valerius de Ora and Garcia Rodriguez (the merchant). Their cultus has not been approved.

Peter Roque (Bl) M. R. Mar 1
1758–1796. From Vannes in Brittany, France, he became a Vincentian priest at Paris and was guillotined during the French Revolution for refusing to take the constitutional oath. He was beatified in 1934. *See* **French Revolution (Martyrs of)**.

Peter Ruiz de los Paños y Angel and Comps (BB) MM. Jul 23
1881–1936. From near Toledo, Spain, in 1881, he was fervent for priestly vocations and worked in various seminaries after ordination, founding the sisterhood of 'Disciples of Jesus' to help him. He became general director in Toledo of the 'Diocesan Worker Priests', and was killed with eight of his fellow members in Toledo during the Civil War. They were beatified in 1995. *See* **Spanish Civil War (Martyrs of)**.

Peter Ryou (Chieng-rioul)
(St) M. L. Feb 17
d. 1866. A married convert Korean layman aged fifty who had brought many others to the faith, he was seized during a bible-reading meeting, flogged and executed. *See* **Korea (Martyrs of)**.

Peter Saint-James (Bl) *see* **September (Martyrs of)**

Peter Sampo (Bl) M. R(SJ). Sep 10
d. 1622. A Japanese catechist, he was received

into the Jesuits by Bl Charles Spinola while they were in prison at Omura. They were burnt alive together at Nagasaki in the 'Great Martyrdom'. *See* **Japan (Martyrs of)**.

Peter of Sandomir (Bl) *see* **Sadoc of Sandomir and Comps**

Peter-Baptist of San Esteban (St) M. R(OFM). Feb 6
1545–1597. From near Avila, Spain, he became a Franciscan in 1567 and was sent to the Philippines, arriving there in 1583 after three years in Mexico. In 1593 he was sent to Japan as one of a group of Franciscan missionaries sponsored by the governor of the colony. The mission was initially a success, but the government were led to believe that it was in preparation for a Spanish invasion and St Peter was one of the companions of St Paul Miki crucified at Nagasaki in consequence. *See* **Japan (Martyrs of)**.

Peter Sanz i Jordá (St) M. B. R(OP). May 26
1680–1747. From Asco in Catalonia, Spain, he became a Dominican at Lerida in 1697 and was sent to China by way of the Philippines in 1713. In 1730 he was made vicar-apostolic of Fujian and titular bishop of Mauricastro, but in 1746 he was imprisoned and beheaded at Fuzhou after some years in hiding. *See* **China (Martyrs of)**.

Peter of Sassoferrato (Bl) *see* **John of Perugia**

Peter of Sebaste (St) B. Jan 9
d. ?391. The younger brother of SS Basil and Gregory of Nyssa, he succeeded St Basil as abbot of his monastic foundation on the Iris river. In 380 St Basil appointed him bishop of Sebaste in Armenia, and he attended the first ecumenical council of Constantinople in 381. (Not to be confused with another Peter who was bishop of Sebaste, who died *c*320 and who was also listed as a saint.)

Peter of Seville (St) M. Oct 8
? He has a cultus as a martyr at Seville, Spain, but nothing is known and the legends concerning him are worthless.

Peter Shichiyemon (Bl) M. L. Sep 11
d. 1622. The seven-year-old son of Bl Bartholomew Shichiyemon, he was martyred with BB Caspar Koteda and Comps at Nagasaki, Japan, the day after his father. *See* **Japan (Martyrs of)**.

Peter of Siena (Bl) *see* **Thomas of Tolentino and Comps**

Peter Snow (Bl) M. P. Jun 15
d. 1598. From Ripon, Yorks, he was ordained at Soissons in 1591 and was caught celebrating Mass at Nidd Hall near Knaresborough, the residence of Bl Ralph Grimston. They were executed at York and were beatified in 1987. *See* **England (Martyrs of)**.

Peter Soler (Bl) *see* **Emmanuel Ruiz and Comps**

Peter Son (Syen-chi) (St) *see* **Bartholomew Chieng (Moun-ho) and Comps**

Peter the Spaniard (St) R. Mar 11
? According to his story, he was a Spanish soldier who made a pilgrimage to Rome and then became a hermit at Babuco near Veroli, Italy. He wore a coat of mail next to his skin as a penance. His dates are unknown.

Peter of Subiaco (Bl) M. R(OSB). Dec 31
d. 1003. He was abbot of Subiaco near Rome, and for defending the feudal rights of his abbey he was blinded by the baron of Monticello and died in prison. He was locally venerated as a martyr.

Peter Sukejiro (St) M. T(OFM). Feb 6
d. 1597. He was a Japanese Franciscan tertiary, a catechist, domestic servant and sacristan to the Spanish Franciscan missionaries on Kyushu in Japan and was martyred with SS Paul Miki and Comps. *See* **Japan (Martyrs of)**.

Peter of Tarantaise (St) B. R(OCist). May 8
1102–1175. From near Vienne in Dauphiné, France, at the age of twelve he joined the Cistercians at Bonnevaux and was made first abbot of Tamiens in 1132. In 1142 he became archbishop of Tarantaise and was one of the most notable churchmen of his time, but according to the story he fled after thirteen years and was eventually found serving his novitiate as a lay brother in a remote Cistercian abbey in Switzerland. He was compelled to return, and died at Bellevaux while mediating between the kings of England and France. Pope St Innocent V had the same name before his election.

Peter Tecelano (Bl) R(OFM). Dec 10
d. 1289. From near Siena, Italy, he was initially a married comb-maker there but his wife died and he then joined the Franciscans as a lay

brother and carried on his craft in his friary at Rome for the remainder of his long life. He reached a high degree of mystical prayer. His cultus was confirmed locally for Rome in 1802.

Peter Tessier (Bl) *see* **William Repin and Comps**

Peter (Phan van) Thi (St) Dec 21
1763–1839. A Vietnamese priest, he was beheaded with St Andrew Dung Lac at Hanoi. *See* **Vietnam (Martyrs of)**.

Peter Thomas (1) (St) B. R(OC). Jan 25
1305–1366. From Breil in Gascony, France, he became a Carmelite at Condom in 1325 and was sent to Avignon as procurator of the order in 1342. There he entered the service of the papal curia and was sent on diplomatic missions to Italy, Serbia, Hungary and the Middle East, being appointed successively bishop of Patti-Lipari in 1354, of Coron in the Peloponnesus, Greece, in 1359, archbishop of Candia, Crete, in 1363 and titular Latin patriarch of Constantinople in 1364. With the support of King Peter I of Cyprus he led an unsuccessful crusade against Alexandria in Egypt, and died three months later at Cyprus (allegedly of wounds received). His cultus was confirmed in 1608.

Peter Thomas (2) (Bl) *see* **Laval (Martyrs of)**

Peter Thuan (St) M. Jun 6
1862. He was a Vietnamese layman and martyr. *See* **Vietnam (Martyrs of)**.

Peter To Rot (Bl) M. L. Jul 7
1912–1945. He was born at Rakunai on the Melanesian island of New Britain, which had been first evangelized by Methodists. His father was chief of the village and was one of several in the area who had asked to become the island's first Catholics in 1898. He became a catechist for Rakunai in 1933. Married with three children, he was left as the only spiritual guide for the district when the Japanese invaded and interned all the missionaries. The Japanese forbade Christian worship in 1942 and tried to enforce the old traditions, especially polygamy. He resisted this and was arrested, imprisoned and poisoned. He was beatified in 1995.

Peter of Tréia (Bl) R(OFM). Feb 20
d. 1304. From near Tréia in the Abruzzi, Italy, he was an early Franciscan and a disciple and fellow worker of Bl Conrad of Offida at Forano. He died at Sirolo near Ancona, and had his cultus confirmed in 1793.

Peter of Trevi (St) P. Aug 30
d. *c*1050. From Carsoli in the Abruzzi, Italy, he became a diocesan priest of Marsi and preached successfully to the peasants around Tivoli, Anagni and Subiaco. He died while still young at Trevi, near Subiaco, and was canonized in 1215.

Peter (Vu van) Truat (St) M. L. Dec 18
d. 1838. A north Vietnamese catechist, he was executed with St Peter (Truong van) Duong. *See* **Vietnam (Martyrs of)**.

Peter (Nguyen Khac) Tu (St) M. L. Jul 10
d. 1840. A Vietnamese catechist in central Vietnam, he was beheaded. *See* **Vietnam (Martyrs of)**.

Peter (Nguyen van) Tu (St) M. R(OP). Sep 5
d. 1838. A Vietnamese Dominican priest, he was beheaded at Ninh-Tai. *See* **Vietnam (Martyrs of)**.

Peter Tuan (St) M. P. Jul 15
1766–1838. A Vietnamese priest, he died in prison of wounds received before being beheaded. *See* **Vietnam (Martyrs of)**.

Peter de Turmenyes (Bl) *see* **September (Martyrs of)**

Peter (Le) Tuy (St) M. P. Oct 11
1763–1833. A Vietnamese priest, he was beheaded in the reign of King Minh-Mang. *See* **Vietnam (Martyrs of)**.

Peter (Doan van) Van (St) M. L. May 26
*c*1780–1857. A Vietnamese catechist, he was beheaded at Son-tay. *See* **Vietnam (Martyrs of)**.

Peter Vasquez (Bl) M. R(OP). Aug 25
d. 1624. From Galicia, Spain, he joined the Dominicans in Madrid, was sent to Japan and burnt alive at Shimabara with BB Michael Carvalho and Comps. *See* **Japan (Martyrs of)**.

Peter the Venerable (Bl) R(OSB). May 11
?1092–1156. A nobleman from the Auvergne, France, he became a monk at Cluny in 1109, prior of Vézelay in 1102 and abbot of Cluny in 1109. The abbey had experienced a period of setback, but during his long tenure of office he regulated the finances, raised the standard of scholarship (he was himself a poet and a theologian and had the Koran translated into

Latin) and restored its position as the Church's greatest and most influential monastery. He gave shelter to Abelard at the end of the latter's tempestuous career and was a contrast in many ways to his contemporary, friend and rival, St Bernard of Clairvaux. He has a cultus, never confirmed, at Arras and among the Benedictines.

Peter Verrier (Bl) *see* **September (Martyrs of)**

Peter-of-Alcantara Villanueva Larráyoz (Bl) *see* **Hospitaller Martyrs of Spain**

Peter Vincioli (St) R(OSB). Jul 10
d. 1007. A nobleman from near Perugia, Italy, he was the abbot-restorer of the monastery of St Peter at Perugia.

Peter Vitalis (Bl) *see* **September (Martyrs of)**

Peter Wang (Erman) (St) *see* **Gregory Grassi and Comps**

Peter Wang (Zuolung) (St) M. L. Jun 7
1842–1900. From a Catholic family of Shuangzhong in Hebei, China, he was captured by a Boxer gang in his village, hanged by his pigtail from a temple flagpole and tortured to induce apostasy. Failing, they killed him and left his body to be eaten by dogs. *See* **China (Martyrs of)**.

Peter Wright (Bl) M. R(SJ) May 19
d. 1651. From Slipton near Thrapston, Northants, he was a convert who studied for the priesthood at Ghent and at Rome. In 1629 he became a Jesuit and was a chaplain in the royalist army during the Civil War. He was executed at Tyburn, London. *See* **England (Martyrs of)**.

Peter Wu (Anbang) (St) *see* **Gregory Grassi and Comps**

Peter Wu (Guosheng) (St) M. L. Nov 7
1768–1814. Originally an innkeeper of Longping in Guizhou, China, on his conversion he became a catechist in his home town and instructed about six hundred people before being strangled at Chengdo in Sichuan. He was canonized in 2000. *See* **China (Martyrs of)**.

Peter Yriex Labrouhe de Laborderie (Bl) *see* **John-Baptist Souzy and Comps**

Peter Zhang (Banniu) (St) *see* **Gregory Grassi and Comps**

Peter Zhao (Mingzhen) and John-Baptist Zhao (Mingxi)
(SS) MM. LL. Jul 3
1839 and 1844–1900. They were brothers of a Catholic family of Beiwangtou in Hebei, China, and were massacred by Boxers together with sixteen relatives and friends.

Peter Zhu (Rixin) (St) *see* **Ignatius Mangin and Comps**

Peter Zuñiga (Bl) M. R(OSA). Aug 19
1585–1622. From Seville, Spain, he spent his youth in Mexico where his father was viceroy. On return to Spain he became an Augustinian at Seville and volunteered to be sent to Japan as a missionary. He arrived at Manila, Philippines, in 1610, set out for Japan in 1620 but his ship was captured and two years later he was burnt alive at Nagasaki with Bl Louis Flores and Comps. *See* **Japan (Martyrs of)**.

Petra Androuin, Petra Besson, Petra Bourigault, Petra Grille, Petra Laurent and Petra Ledoyen (BB) *see* **William Repin and Comps**

Petra Morosini (Bl) V. Apr 6
1931–1957. Born into a large family near Bergamo, Italy, she wanted to become a missionary but her family needed her earnings, so she learned dressmaking and started work in a factory some distance from home when she was fifteen. She continued her domestic and religious duties, made private vows when she was seventeen and joined several sodalities. She was walking back home one lunch-time when she was waylaid by a youth in a wood who wanted to have sexual intercourse. She reminded him of the requirements of moral behaviour, he tried to rape her and broke her neck in the struggle. She died two days later, and was beatified in 1987.

Petra-of-St-Joseph Pérez Florido (Bl) R. F. Oct 16
1845–1906. From Malaga, Spain, she had a great devotion to St Joseph and begged on behalf of the destitute when young. Being joined in this by three companions, she started the 'Congregation of the Mothers of the Helpless and of St Joseph of the Holy Mountain' in 1880. The sanctuary of the latter she founded at Barcelona in 1895. She was beatified in 1994.

Petra Phélyppeaux, Petra-Renata Potier and Petra-Jane Saillard d'Epinatz (BB) *see* **William Repin and Comps**

Petroc (Pedrog, Perreux)
(St) B? R. Jun 4
d. ?594. Allegedly the son of a Welsh prince, he studied in Ireland, settled in Cornwall, England, and was evidently very active as a missionary. He founded a monastery at a place later called Petrocston (Padstow) after him and another at Bodmin, where he died. In Brittany he is called Perreux. His attribute is a stag, and he is sometimes shown as a bishop holding a church.

Petronax (St) R. May 6
d. ?747. From Brescia, Italy, he was persuaded by Pope St Gregory II in 717 to visit St Benedict's old monastery of Montecassino (which had been destroyed by the Lombards in 580) with a view to restoring the cenobitical life there. He found a few hermits who elected him as their abbot and monastic life began again, using the Benedictine rule. St Willibald, bishop of Eichstatt, and St Sturmius of Fulda were monks under him. He is called 'the second founder of Montecassino'.

Petronilla (St) R. May 31
? She has an ancient cultus as a consecrated virgin at Rome, and later legends alleged that she helped look after St Peter there. The old Roman Martyrology describes her as the daughter of the apostle (which she certainly was not). Her cultus was confined to local calendars in 1969. Her attribute is a bunch of keys.

Petronius of Bologna (St) B. Oct 4
d. *c*450. Probably the son of a praetorian prefect in Gaul, as a young man he visited the monks and shrines in Egypt and the Holy Land. While in Italy on a mission from the emperor he was made bishop of Bologna in 432 and allegedly built the monastery of St Stephen there, modelled on the buildings of the holy places at Jerusalem. A fictitious biography increased his popularity in the Middle Ages.

Petronius of Die (St) B. R. Jan 10
d. ?463. The son of a senator of Avignon, France, he became a monk at Lérins and was bishop of Die in the Dauphiné from ?456.

Petronius of Verona (St) B. Sep 6
d. *c*450. He was a bishop of Verona, Italy.

Phaebadius (Fiari) (St) B. Apr 25
d. ?392. A Gascon bishop of Agen, France, he was a friend and ally of St Hilary of Poitiers in fighting Arianism in Gaul. One of the best known bishops of his time, he presided at several councils and St Jerome referred to him as one of 'the illustrious men of the Church'.

Phaganus *see* **Fugatius**

Phaina (St) *see* **Theodotus of Ancyra and Comps**

Phal *see* **Fidolus**

Phanurius (St) M. Aug 27
? Little is known about him except that he was martyred in Crete, but he is usually depicted as a warrior saint. He is traditionally invoked to help in the rediscovery of lost objects. His attribute is a cross with a burning candle on top of the shaft.

Phara *see* **Burgundofara**

Pharaildis (Varede, Verylde, Veerle) (St) L. Jan 4
d. ?740. Details concerning this patron of Ghent, Belgium, differ. Apparently a native of that city, she suffered abuse on the part of her husband either because he objected to her nocturnal visits to churches or because she refused to consummate the marriage, having been married against her will after making a private vow of virginity. The latter story has caused her to be venerated as a virgin.

Pharnacius (St) *see* **Orentius, Heros and Comps**

Pharo *see* **Faro**

Phiala (St) *see* **Fingar, Phiala and Comps**

Philadelphus (St) *see* **Alphius, Philadelphus and Cyrinus**

Philadelphus (St) *see* **Diomedes, Julian and Comps**

Philastrius (St) B. Jul 18
d. ?387. A Spaniard, he became bishop of Brescia, Italy, in 379 and wrote an extant work against the Arian heresy. St Gaudentius, his successor, praised him for his 'modesty, quietness and gentleness towards all'.

Phileas and Comps (SS) MM. Feb 4
d. ?305. Their martyrdom was described by the historian Eusebius, their contemporary. Phileas, a bishop of Thmuis in the Nile Delta, Egypt, was seized, imprisoned at Alexandria and beheaded with a Roman tribune named Philoromus and a number of other Christians from Thmuis. While in prison he wrote a letter to his church describing the sufferings of his fellow Christian prisoners. He was listed with SS

Faustus, Didius and Comps in error by the old Roman Martyrology.

Philemon and Apollonius (SS) MM. Mar 8
d. ?305. Philemon was an actor and musician at Antinoë, Egypt, and was converted by the deacon Apollonius of the same city. They were arrested, brought to Alexandria, tied up and thrown into the sea in the reign of Diocletian.

Philemon and Apphia (SS) MM. Nov 22
d. ?70. Philemon was the Christian of Colossae, Asia Minor, who owned the runaway slave Onesimus and to whom St Paul addressed a letter concerning the latter. Apphia is presumed to have been Philemon's wife, and both were allegedly stoned to death at their home.

Philemon and Domninus (SS) MM. Mar 21
? They are listed as Roman missionaries who worked in various parts of Italy. Their place of martyrdom is unknown.

Philetus, Lydia and Comps (SS) MM. Mar 27
d. ?121. They were martyred in present-day Bosnia in the reign of Hadrian. The old Roman Martyrology described Philetus as a senator, Lydia as his wife, Macedo and Theoprepius as their sons, Amphilochius as a captain and Cronidas as a notary. Their acta are not reliable.

Philibert (St) R. Aug 20
?608–?685. From Gascony, France, he was educated at the Merovingian court and became a monk when aged twenty at Rebais near Paris under St Agilus. Shortly afterwards he was made the abbot, but his inexperience led to a revolt and he left, visited several famous Columbanian houses (which were at that time starting to use the rule of St Benedict in their customaries) and then became the abbot-founder of Jumièges in Normandy. He opposed Ebroin (the mayor of the palace) and so was imprisoned and then exiled to Poitiers, where he founded Noirmoutier and restored Quinçay. He died at the former.

Philibert (St) *see* **Fabrician and Philibert**

Philibert Fougères (Bl) *see* **September (Martyrs of)**

Philip
This is the English form of the Latin Philippus. The French is Philippe; the Italian, Filippo; the Spanish, Felipe.

Philip (St) *see* **Diomedes, Julian and Comps**

Philip (St) *see* **Seven Brothers**

Philip (St) *see* **Straton, Philip and Eutvchian**

Philip, Severus, Eusebius and Hermes (SS) MM. Oct 22
d. 304. Philip was bishop of Heraclea near Byzantium, Severus was apparently deacon and Hermes was a priest. During the persecution by Diocletian they were arrested, put on trial and instructed to hand over the sacred books of their church to be burnt in accordance with the emperor's edict. On their refusal they were taken to Adrianople, European Turkey, and burnt at the stake. Their acta appear to be genuine. The old Roman Martyrology included a priest Eusebius, apparently in error.

Philip, Zeno, Narseus and Comps (SS) MM. Jul 15
? They are listed as three adult martyrs of Alexandria, Egypt, and ten small children.

Philip of Agirone (St) P? May 12
? He has a cultus at the little hill town of Agirone in Sicily as the first missionary sent to that island, but the story is full of contradictory and improbable statements.

Philip the Apostle (St) M? A. May 3
d. *c*80. From Bethsaida in Galilee, he is listed as fifth among the Twelve and is mentioned three times as a confidant of Christ in St John's gospel. His career after the Resurrection is obscure, and the traditions are late and conflicting. He has been confused with St Philip the Deacon in them. His attributes are a basket of loaves and a cross, sometimes T-shaped.

Philip Benizi (St) R(OSM). Aug 23
1233–1285. A nobleman of Florence, Italy, he studied medicine at Paris and Padua and became a physician at Florence. In 1253 he became a Servite lay brother by pretending to be ignorant, but was found out and was then compelled by his superiors to be ordained in 1259. He became known as one of the most able preachers in Italy. After being superior of several friaries he became the fifth superior-general of the order in 1267 and oversaw its rapid spread into Poland, Hungary and Germany. He was also influential in his attempts to maintain concord between the Guelfs and Ghibellines in northern Italy and took part in the council of Lyons in 1274. He died at Todi, was canonized in 1671 and had his cultus confined to local calendars in 1969.

St Philip Howard, Oct 19

Philip Berruyer (Bl) B. Jan 9
d. 1260. A nephew of St William of Bourges, he was bishop of Orléans, France, from 1221 and was transferred to Bourges in 1235.

Philip the Deacon (St) D. Jun 6
C1st. One of the first seven deacons ordained by the apostles (Acts 6:5), he worked in Samaria, baptized the Ethiopian eunuch (Acts 6:8) and (with his four daughters who were prophets) was the host of St Paul at Caesarea (Acts 21:9). Traditions concerning his subsequent career are unreliable, and he has been confused with St Philip the Apostle.

Philip Evans (St) M. R(SJ). Jul 22
1645–1679. From Gwent, Wales, he was educated at Saint-Omer, France, joined the Jesuits in 1665 and worked on the Welsh mission from 1675. He was a skilled harpist and a good real-tennis player. In consequence of the Oates plot he was imprisoned and executed at Cardiff, and was canonized in 1970. *See* **Wales (Martyrs of)**.

Philip of Fermo (St) M. B. Oct 22
d. *c*270. The shrine of this martyred bishop is at the cathedral at Fermo, Italy.

Philip Geryluk *see* **Podlasia (Martyrs of)**

Philip of Gortyna (St) B. Apr 11
d. *c*180. A bishop of Gortyna in Crete, he wrote a lost treatise against the Marcionite Gnostics.

Philip Howard (St) M. L. Oct 19
1557–1595. The Earl of Arundel and Surrey was of a recusant family but was initially rather indifferent to religious matters. He converted, however, and became a conscientious Catholic, which led to his arrest and imprisonment in the Tower of London in 1585. Four years later he was sentenced to death, but this was not implemented and he died in the Tower after another six years. His shrine is at Arundel Cathedral in Sussex. He was canonized in 1970, and his attribute is a greyhound. *See* **England (Martyrs of)**.

Philip-of-Jesus Casas Martínez
(St) M. R(OFM). Feb 6
d. 1597. Born into a Spanish family at Mexico City, he became a Franciscan at Puebla but left in 1589 and went to the Philippines as a merchant. He rejoined at Manila in 1590, and was on his way back to Mexico to be ordained when his ship was driven by a storm to Japan in 1596. He was arrested with St Peter-Baptist of San Esteban and crucified at Nagasaki. *See* **Paul Miki and Comps** and **Japan (Martyrs of)**.

Philip (Phan van) Minh
(St) M. P. Jul 3
1815–1853. Born at Caimong in Vietnam, he joined the Paris Society for Foreign Missions and was a priest based at Mac-Bat. He was beheaded at Vinh-hong. *See* **Vietnam (Martyrs of)**.

Philip-of-Jesus Munárriz Azcona and Comps (BB) MM. RR. Aug 23
d. 1936. At the start of the Spanish Civil War the superiors of the Claretian noviciate and seminary at Barbastro and all their charges, a total of fifty-one, were seized on June 20 and massacred by Republican forces after being kept in prison for three weeks. The superior, Bl Philip, and his two deputies, BB John Díaz Nosti and Leontius Pérez Ramos, were shot first in the cemetery, while the rest were shot during the middle of August at a place called Berbegal. They were beatified in 1992. *See* **Spanish Civil War (Martyrs of)**.

Philip Neri (St) P. F. May 26
1515–1595. The son of a lawyer of Florence, Italy, he was educated by the Dominicans before being apprenticed to his uncle's mercantile business when aged seventeen. Rejecting this in 1533, he migrated to Rome, became a tutor in the house of a Florentine nobleman there and studied for the priesthood, but abandoned this in turn and spent several years on his own as a layman among those of the city whom the corrupt and indifferent institutional clergy of the era were neglecting. In 1548 he gathered fourteen companions, the start of the 'Congregation of the Oratory', and was ordained in 1551. For thirty-three years he ran a popular mission centre (virtually the centre of local Roman church life) at the presbytery of S. Girolamo della Carità before moving to the Chiesa Nuova in 1583, which latter church he had rebuilt and where he had established his infant congregation of secular priests. He was cheerful and very friendly, was acquainted with most of the great saints of the counter-Reformation and was nicknamed the 'Second Apostle of Rome'. His congregation was already spreading through Italy by the time of his death at Rome, and he was canonized in 1622. A portrait from life by Guido Reni is the basis for all other representations, and his attribute is a lily.

St Philip Neri, May 26

Philip Oderisi (Bl) B. R. Sep 18
d. 1285. A monk of Fontavellana (then an independent monastic congregation), he was made bishop of Nocera in Umbria, Italy, in 1254. He was a friend and patron of the early Franciscans. His cultus is unconfirmed.

Philip Papon (Bl) *see* **John-Baptist Souzy and Comps**

Philip Powel (Bl) M. R(OSB). Jun 30
d. 1646. From Gwent, Wales, he was educated at Abergavenny grammar school before joining the Benedictines of St Gregory's at Douai (now Downside) in 1614, being ordained in 1621. In the following year he went on mission to England and worked chiefly in Devon (but also in Somerset and Cornwall) for twenty years. He was executed at Tyburn, London, and was beatified in 1929. *See* **England (Martyrs of)**.

Philip Rinaldi (Bl) R. Dec 5
1866–1931. Born at Lu Monferratone near Casale, Italy, as a boy he had St John Bosco as a

spiritual director and so joined the Salesians. After his final vows in 1880 he was sent to Spain and became inspector of the Iberian houses, returning to become vicar-general under Bl Michael Rua at Turin in 1901. He became the superior of the Salesians in 1922, and took care to foster the charism as laid down by the founder. He died suddenly in Turin and was beatified in 1990.

Philip Ripoll Morata (Bl) *see* **Anselm Polanco Fontecha**

Philip of Rome (St) M. Sep 13
C3rd? His existence is doubtful, since it depends on the witness of the worthless acta of St Eugenia in which he is described as her father.

Philip-of-St-Michael Ruiz Fraile (Bl) *see* **Nicephorus Díez Tejerina and Comps**

Philip of Sandomir (Bl) *see* **Sadoc of Sandomir and Comps**

Philip Siphong Onphithak (Bl) *see* **Thailand (Martyrs of)**

Philip Smaldone (Bl) P. F. Jun 4
1848–1923. Born in Naples, Italy, he early started his life's work of helping deaf-mutes and, as a priest in Lecce, founded the 'Salesian Sisters of the Sacred Heart' to this end. He became a cathedral canon there and a well-known spiritual director, being beatified in 1996.

Philip Suzanni (Bl) R(OSA). May 24
d. 1306. From Piacenza, Italy, he became an Augustinian friar there and was famous for his spirit of prayer and compunction. His cultus was approved for Piacenza in 1766.

Philip-of-the-Sacred-Heart-of-Mary Valcabado Granado (Bl) *see* **Nicephorus Díez Tejerina and Comps**

Philip of Vienne (St) B. Feb 3
d. ?578. He was bishop of Vienne, France, from *c*560.

Philip of Zell (St) R. May 3
d. *c*1770. An Anglo-Saxon pilgrim to Rome, he was ordained there and, on the way back, settled as a hermit near Worms, Germany. He organized the disciples whom he attracted into a monastery later named Zell or 'cell'.

Philip Zhang (Zhihe) (St) *see* **Gregory Grassi and Comps**

Philippa (St) *see* **Theodore of Perga and Comps**

Philippa Mareri (Bl) R(OFM). Feb 16
d. 1236. A noblewoman of the Abruzzi, Italy, she met St Francis of Assisi at her parents' home and was inspired to become a hermit on a mountain above Mareri. Eventually she founded a Franciscan nunnery at Rieti with the help of Bl Roger of Todi, and became its first superior. Her cultus is unconfirmed.

Philippian (St) *see* **Felician, Philippian and Comps**

Philippine Duchesne (St) R. Nov 17
1769–1852. From Grenoble, France, she became a Visitation nun there but the community were scattered in the French Revolution and she returned to her family home. After attracting disciples she took the advice of St Mary-Magdalen-Sophia Barat to join the new community to the 'Society of the Sacred Heart' and then emigrated to what was then French Louisiana in 1818. Arriving at New Orleans, she founded her first mission station at St Charles near St Louis in Missouri and went on to found six others. She died at St Charles and was canonized in 1988.

Philo and Agathopodes (Agathopus) (SS) DD. Apr 25
d. *c*150. Two deacons of Antioch, Syria, they accompanied their bishop St Ignatius on his journey to martyrdom at Rome in ?107, and returned to Antioch with such relics of him that they were able to recover. They are believed to have written his acta also. Their subsequent careers are unknown.

Philogonius (St) B. Dec 20
d. 324. A lawyer at Antioch, Syria, he was a confessor in the persecution of Licinius and later (after the death of his wife) became bishop of the city. As such he was one of the first to denounce Arianism. St John Chrysostom preached an extant panegyric in his honour.

Philologus and Patrobas (SS) Nov 4
C1st. They were Roman Christians saluted by St Paul in his letter to the Romans (16:14-18).

Philomena
In 1802 the bones of a young woman were discovered in a niche in the catacomb of St Priscilla on the Via Salaria at Rome in the course of an excavation for supposed relics of martyrs. The niche was closed by three tiles bearing the description 'LUMENA' 'PAX TECUM'

'FI'. Reading 'Filumena pax tecum' (Philomena, peace be with you), the conclusion was drawn that here was buried a martyr called St Philomena, and a shrine was set up at Mugnano near Nola, Italy. The cultus proved extremely popular, helped by a completely fictitious biography written by the parish priest, and spread throughout the world. Further archaeological investigation indicated, however, that the muddling of the tiles of the epitaph was a regular practice of the C4th whenever materials already engraved were being re-used, and this so as to indicate that they did not belong to the interment concerned. The shrine was dismantled and the cultus forbidden by a decree of the Magisterium in 1961, although some private veneration continues.

Philomena of San Severino (St) V? Jul 5
d. *a*500. Her relics were found and enshrined in the C16th at San Severino near Ancona, Italy, but nothing is known about her. By default she has a cultus as a virgin.

Philomenus (St) *see* **Clementinus, Theodotus and Philomenus**

Philomenus of Ancyra (St) M. Nov 29
d. He was martyred at Ancyra, Asia Minor, (now Ankara in Turkey), in the reign of Aurelian.

Philonilla (St) *see* **Zenais and Philonilla**

Philoromus (St) *see* **Phileas and Comps**

Philoterius (Philetaerus) (St) M. May 19
d. 303. A nobleman of Nicomedia, Asia Minor, he was martyred there in the reign of Diocletian. His acta are unreliable.

Philotheus (St) *see* **Domninus, Sylvanus and Comps**

Philotheus (St) *see* **Samosata (Martyrs of)**

Phlegon (St) *see* **Herodion, Asyncritus and Phlegon**

Phocas of Antioch (St) M? Mar 5
d. *c*320. An alleged martyr of Antioch, Syria, according to his unreliable acta he was suffocated in a steam-bath although this is also alleged of St Phocas of Sinope. He is also confused with St Phocas the Gardener, and the Eastern martyrologies do not list him.

Phocas the Gardener (St) M. Jul 23
d. ?303. A smallholder near Sinope on the Black Sea coast of Asia Minor, he was martyred in the reign of Diocletian. His existence, martyrdom and the antiquity of his cultus (which remains popular in the East) are established facts.

Phocas of Sinope (St) M? B? Jul 14
d. ?117. He was allegedly a bishop of Sinope who was martyred in the reign of Trajan, and is not identified with Phocas the Gardener in the Byzantine martyrology.

Phoebe (St) L. Sep 3
C1st. A married deaconess of Cenchreae near Corinth, Greece, she was the bearer of St Paul's letter to the Romans and was commended by him therein (Rom 16:1-3).

Photina and Comps (SS) MM. Mar 20
? According to the old Roman Martyrology as revised by Baronius, she was the Samaritan woman in the fourth chapter of St John's gospel and was martyred with her sons Joseph and Victor, together with Sebastian, Anatolius, Photius, Photis (Photides), Parasceve and Cyriaca. Their legend is both obscure and unreliable, and Baronius may have inserted them because he believed that the head of St Photina was preserved at St Paul's basilica at Rome.

Photinus (St) *see* **Anicetus, Photinus and Comps**

Photinus (Pothinus), Sanctius (Sanctus) and Comps (SS) MM. Jun 2
d. 177. They were martyred at Lyons, France, and the graphic details are preserved in an authentic letter (possibly written by St Irenaeus) sent by the churches of Vienne and Lyons to those of Asia. They were firstly attacked by a pagan lynch-mob in the reign of Marcus Aurelius, but were rescued and put on trial. Photinus was the bishop, aged ninety, and he died in prison from the beating he had received. The others, Vetius, Epagathus, Maturus, Ponticus, Biblis, Attalus, Alexander, Blandina and companions, were thrown to the wild animals in the amphitheatre at the next public games.

Photis (St) *see* **Photina and Comps**

Photius (St) *see* **Archelaus, Cyril and Photius**

Photius (St) *see* **Photina and Comps**

Pia (St) *see* **Paul, Gerontius and Comps**

Piaton (Piato, Piat) (St) M. P. Oct 1
d. ?286. According to his C10th biography he was from Benevento, Italy, became a missionary priest in the districts around Tournai and Chartres, France, and was martyred at the former place in the reign of Maximian.

Pientia (St) *see* **Nicasius of Rouen and Comps**

Pierius (St) P. Nov 4
d. *c*310. A priest of Alexandria, Egypt, he taught at the catechetical school there. His learning (he wrote several philosophical and theological treatises) and his voluntary poverty led him to be compared with Origen.

Pigmenius (St) M. P. Mar 24
d. 362. A priest at Rome, he was thrown into the Tiber by a pagan mob in the reign of Julian.

Pimen *see* **Poemen**

Pinian (St) *see* **Melania the Younger and Pinian**

Pinnock (St) Nov 6
? He is the putative patron of St Pinnock near Liskeard in Cornwall, England, but it is probable that Pinnock is a corruption of Winoc.

Pinytus (St) B. Oct 10
d. *p*180. A bishop of Knossos in Crete, he was praised by the historian Eusebius.

Pionius and Comps (SS) MM. Feb 1
d. 250. A priest of Smyrna, Asia Minor (now Izmir, Turkey), in the reign of Decius, he was seized with fifteen companions while celebrating the anniversary of the martyrdom of St Polycarp. They were burnt at the stake after a long cross-examination and after having been severely tortured. There is an extant eye-witness account of their death, which document was known to Eusebius.

Pior (St) R. Jan 17
d. ?395. An Egyptian desert father, he was a disciple of St Anthony before becoming one of the priests at Nitria. He was later at Scetis, and features in the *Apophthegmata Patrum*.

Piperion (St) *see* **Candidus, Piperion and Comps**

Piran (St) R. Mar 5
d. *c*480. A hermit near Padstow in Cornwall, England, he has Perranporth named after him and is the patron of Cornish tin miners. His flag, a vertical white cross on a black background, is now the national flag of Cornwall and is based on a fictitious legend wherein he discovered tin-smelting by finding the white metal in the ashes of his fire after he had used bits of ore to build a surround for it. He has been identified with St Kieran of Ossory, but this is unlikely.

Pirmin (St) B. R. Nov 3
d. 753. Apparently a Visigothic refugee from the Arab invasion of Spain, he founded several monasteries in southern Germany (notably Reichenau near Constance) and restored several others (notably Disentis). He was also a regionary bishop, but was never bishop of Metz nor of Meaux.

St Pius X Pope, Aug 21

Pistis *see* **Faith**

Pius I, Pope *Jul 11*
d. ?155. He was listed as pope from ?142, and may have been a brother of that Hermas who was the author of *The Shepherd*. If so, they were born into a family of slaves. His was a period of opposition to popular Gnosticism. He is first listed as a saint by the forger St Ado, and his cultus was suppressed in 1969.

Pius V, Pope (St) R(OP). Apr 30
1504–1572. Anthony Ghislieri was born at

Bosco in Piedmont, Italy, joined the Dominicans in 1518, was ordained in 1540, taught philosophy and theology for sixteen years and became bishop of Sutri and inquisitor for Lombardy in 1556. In 1557 he was made a cardinal, was transferred to the see of Mondovi in 1559 and was elected pope in 1565. Of an austere character, he was well suited to the necessary task of fighting the corruption endemic in many aspects of Church life at that time, including the Roman curia. He insisted (where he could) on the implementation of the decrees of the council of Trent, organized the Holy League against the Ottoman Turks which resulted in the victory of Lepanto in 1570, promoted ecclesiastical learning, reformed the liturgy (the Tridentine missal and breviary were promulgated in his time) and excommunicated Queen Elizabeth of England. He was canonized in 1712.

Pius IX, Pope (Bl) (Feb 7)
1792–1878. John-Mary Mastai Ferretti was born into a noble family of Senigallia, Italy, and after studying at Rome was ordained in 1819. His qualities as a pastor and his life of prayer were early recognized, and he was made archbishop of Spoleto in 1827. Transferring to Mastai in 1832, he was made cardinal in 1840 and was elected Pope in 1846. At that time, the popes still ruled central Italy (the 'Papal States') and the policy since the Napoleonic Wars had been one of strict adherence to the status quo ante. This had entailed incompetent and reactionary government by clerics, and Bl Pius was welcomed as a modernizer before the revolutions of 1848. He defined the dogma of the Immaculate Conception in 1854, convened the First Vatican Council in 1869 and lost his temporal power with the annexation of Rome by Italy in 1870. He did not accept this (the situation was only regularized in 1923). His pontificate was the longest in history.

Pius X, Pope (St) Aug 21
1835–1914. Joseph Sarto was born in 1835 at Riese near Venice, then part of the Austrian empire. His father was a postman and the family was poor, but he was accepted at the diocesan junior seminary at Treviso in 1850. After his ordination he became parish priest of Salzano in 1867, bishop of Mantua in 1884 and cardinal-patriarch of Venice in 1893. To his own surprise he was elected pope in 1903, and as pope he made it his principle 'to restore all things in Christ'. He encouraged early and frequent communion, liturgical reform and the teaching of the Catechism and also reorganized the Curia and started the very necessary codification of canon law. He was most famous for the condemnation of Modernism, which was a heterogeneous collection of ideas alleged to make the deposit of faith subordinate to the conclusions of secular scholarship and fashionable thought. His will read: 'I was born poor, I lived poor, I wish to die poor'. He was canonized in 1954.

Pius-of-St-Aloysius Campidelli
(Bl) R(CP). Nov 3
1868–1889. Born near Rimini, Italy, his peasant father died when he was a child and left the family in serious poverty, which frustrated his wish to enter the junior seminary. In 1882 he joined the Passionists at S. Maria de Casale and reached minor orders, but he died before he could be ordained as deacon. He was beatified in 1985.

Pius Forgione of Pietrelcina
(Bl) R(OFM) Sep 23
1887–1968. From Pietrelcina near Benevento, Italy, he became a Franciscan at Morcone in 1903. In 1916, after his ordination, he went to San Giovanni Rotundo where he remained all his life. The Mass as the recapitulation of the sacrificial passion of Christ was central to his ministry as a priest, the effectiveness of which was shown by the number of people who sought his help. He was in receipt of extraordinary mystical phenomena, most famously the stigmata, and has been the subject of worldwide popular devotion as 'Padre Pio' since his death. He was beatified in 1999 and due to be canonized in 2002.

Bl Pius Forgione of Pietrelcina, Sep 23

Placid (St) *see* **Anastasius, Placid and Comps**

Placid (St) *see* **Maurus and Placid**

Placid (St) *see* **Sigisbert and Placid**

Placid, Eutychius, Victorinus, Flavia and Comps *Oct 5*
d. *c*300. They were apparently martyred at Messina in Sicily in the reign of Diocletian, but their acta were lost. A refugee Greek priest at Montecassino in 1115 produced a maliciously forged document alleging that Placid was the disciple of St Benedict, that the others were his siblings, that they had been sent by St Benedict to Messina to found a monastery and that they had been killed by Muslim raiders *c*540 (before Muhammed was born!). In 1588 'relics' were conveniently found in a Roman cemetery at Messina. The unjustifiable cultus was suppressed in 1969.

Placid (Plait) of Autun (St) R. May 7
d. ?675. He was an abbot of St Symphorian at Autun, France.

Placid Riccardi (Bl) R(OSB). Mar 15
1844–1915. Born near Spoleto, Italy, he joined the abbey of St Paul's outside the Walls at Rome in 1864. He was thirteen years there, then ten years as chaplain to the Benedictine nuns at Amelia and finally the rest of his life he spent in charge of the shrine at Farfa. He had no special charism, but his prayer, penance and humility were such that he was beatified in 1955.

Placid of Rodi (Bl) R(OCist). Jun 12
d. 1248.From working-class family of Rodi on the Gargano promontory, Italy, he became a Cistercian monk at Corno, then a hermit at Ocre in the Abruzzi and finally the abbot-founder of the monastery of Santo Spirito nearby. It was alleged that he slept in a standing posture for thirty-seven years. His cultus is unconfirmed.

Placide Viel (Bl) R. Mar 4
1815–1877. Born on a farm in Normandy, France, through a family connection she got to know St Mary-Magdalen Postel, the first mother-general of the 'Sisters of the Christian Schools'. She joined them in 1833 and became assistant-general when aged twenty-six, which caused some resentment against her. Nevertheless on the death of St Mary-Magdalen in 1846 she succeeded her, and in 1859 obtained papal approval of the institute. Her work during the Franco-Prussian war was heroic and probably hastened her death at St Sauveur-le-Vicomte. She was beatified in 1951.

Placidia of Verona (St) R. Oct 11
d. *c*460. She is venerated as a virgin at Verona, Italy, and has been erroneously identified with Galla Placidia, the daughter of the emperor Valentinian III.

Plato of Ancyra (St) M. Jul 22
d. ?306. He was a rich young man martyred at Ancyra, Asia Minor (now Ankara in Turkey).

Plato of Constantinople (St) R. Apr 4
d. 813. From a rich family of Constantinople, he became a monk and abbot at Symboleon on the Bithynian Olympus, Asia Minor, and then at Sakkudion near Constantinople. He was prominent in opposing iconoclasm, being present at the second ecumenical council of Nicaea in 787, and appointed St Theodore Studites his successor before retiring in 794. He was subsequently imprisoned and exiled both by the emperor Constantine VI Porphyrogenitus for opposing his divorce and remarriage and by the emperor Nicephorus I for opposing the reconciliation of the priest who officiated at his predecessor's second marriage. However he died in peace at Constantinople.

Platonides and Comps (SS) RR. Apr 6
d. ?308. A deaconess, she founded a nunnery at Nisibis in Mesopotamia. The old Roman Martyrology listed her as a martyr of Ascalon in error. Nothing is known about her companions.

Plautilla (St) L. May 20
C1st. The alleged widowed mother of St Flavia Domitilla was, according to legend, baptized by St Peter and present at the martyrdom of St Paul.

Plautus (St) *see* **Eutychius, Plautus and Heracleas**

Plechelm (St) *see* **Wiro and Comps**

Plegmund (St) B. R. Aug 2
d. 914. He had been a hermit at Plemstall (named after him) near Chester, England, before becoming tutor to King Alfred the Great and a notable scholar. In 890 he became archbishop of Canterbury and reorganized the dioceses of Wessex. His cultus was never confirmed.

Plutarch of Alexandria and Comps (SS) MM. Jun 28
d. 202. They were pupils of Origen at the

catechetical school of Alexandria, Egypt, and were martyred there in the reign of Septimius Severus. The companions were a young woman called Potamioena (who was lowered slowly into a cauldron of boiling pitch), her mother Marcella, two called Serenus, Heraclides, Heron and Rhais.

Podius (St) B. R(CR). May 28
d. 1002. A son of the margrave of Tuscany, he became a canon regular and then bishop of Florence, Italy, in 990.

Podlasia (Martyrs of)
(BB) MM. LL. Jan 23
d. 1874. In the C19th the Imperial Russian government's policy was forcibly to convert all Byzantine-rite Catholics under its rule to Russian Orthodoxy, so the hierarchy of the remaining Polish ecclesiastical province of Chełm were deported to Siberia in 1874 and the churches were seized. In Pratulin in Podlasia (now eastern Poland) the congregation blockaded their church when an army detachment came to seize it, so they were fired upon and thirteen of them killed. They were ordinary laymen aged between 19 and 50, mostly married with families: Vincent Lewoniuk, Daniel Karmasz, Luke Bojko, Constantius Bojko, Bartholomew Osypiuk, Anacetus Hryeiuk, Philip Geryluk, Ignatius Franczuk, John Andrzejuk, Maxim Hawryluk and Onuphrius Wasyluk; Consantius Lukaszuk and Michael Wawryszuk died the next day. They were beatified in 1996.

Poemen (Pimen, Pastor)
(St) R. Aug 27
d. *c*450. His name means 'Shepherd'. Together with two of his brothers he was a monk at Scetis, Egypt, but they were driven out by barbarians in 407 and settled for a while at the abandoned pagan temple at Tereneuthis, the nearest point on the Nile. A substantial section of the *Apophthegmata Patrum* is in his name, and his disciples may have initiated that collection of sayings.

Pol de Léon *see* **Paul Aurelian**

Poland, Martyrs of the Nazi Occupation of (BB)
1939–45. Of the people killed in hatred of the faith in Nazi-occupied Poland during the Second World War, one hundred and eight were beatified in 1999. They comprise three bishops, 52 diocesan priests, 29 male religious, eight female religious, three seminarians and nine lay people.

Polius (St) *see* **Timothy, Polius and Eutychius**

Pollio (St) M. Apr 28
d. ?304. A reader in the church at Cybalae (now Vinkovci in Croatia), he was burnt alive in the reign of Diocletian.

Polyaenus (St) *see* **Hermas, Serapion and Polyaenus**

Polyaenus (St) *see* **Patrick, Acacius and Comps**

Polyanus (St) *see* **Nemesian and Comps**

Polycarp and Theodore
(SS) MM. Dec 7
? They were martyred at Antioch, Syria.

Polycarp of Alexandria (St) M. Apr 2
d. 303. He was tortured and beheaded at Alexandria, Egypt.

Polycarp of Rome (St) P. Feb 23
d. *c*300. He is mentioned in the acta of SS Mark and Marcellian and of St Sebastian as a Roman priest who ministered to those imprisoned for their faith.

Polycarp of Smyrna and Comps (SS) MM. Feb 23
?69–?155. According to St Ireneaus (who knew him) he had been a disciple of St John the Evangelist and became bishop of Smyrna, Asia Minor, in ?96. He opposed Gnosticism, had a letter written to him by St Ignatius of Antioch and wrote an extant letter to the church at Philippi which was read liturgically for three centuries. He was burned alive with twelve others in the amphitheatre at the instigation of the pagans in the reign of Marcus Aurelius. The authentic contemporary account of this is the earliest surviving acta of any martyr.

Polychronius (St) M. B. Feb 17
? According to the old Roman Martyrology, he was bishop of Babylon in the Persian Empire and was martyred on the orders of the emperor Decius. The difficulty with this is that Decius never invaded Persia. He may be a duplicate of St Polychronius of Nicaea.

Polychronius of Nicaea
(St) M. P. Dec 6
C4th. He was present at the council of Nicaea in 325 as a reader, became a priest and was killed by Arians in the reign of the emperor Constantius while he was celebrating Mass.

Polydore Plasden (Oliver Palmer) (St) M. P. Dec 10
1563–1591. A Londoner, he was educated for the priesthood at Rheims and in Rome and was ordained at Rome in 1588. He worked in London and Sussex before being captured with St Edmund Genings at the house of St Swithun Wells, and was executed at Tyburn with St Eustace White and Comps. He was canonized in 1970. *See* **England (Martyrs of)**.

Polyeuctus (St) M. Feb 13
d. ?259. A Roman officer, he was martyred at Melitene in Armenia in the reign of Valerian, allegedly after having destroyed some pagan idols.

Polyeuctus, Victorius and Donatus (SS) MM. May 21
? They are listed as martyrs of Caesarea in Cappodocia, Asia Minor, but nothing is known about them.

Polyxena (St) *see* **Xantippa and Polyxena**

Pompeius (St) *see* **Peregrine, Lucian and Comps**

Pompeius (St) *see* **Terence, Africanus and Comps**

Pompeius of Pavia (St) B. Dec 14
d. *c*290. He was a bishop of Pavia, Italy.

Pompilius-Mary-of-St-Nicholas Pirotti (St) R. Jul 15
1710–1756. From Montecalvo near Benevento, Italy, he joined the Piarist Fathers at Naples in 1727 and taught in schools run by them in Apulia, Naples and Ancona. He died near Lecce in Apulia and was canonized in 1934.

Pomponius (St) B. Apr 30
d. 536. Bishop of Naples from 508, he strongly opposed the court Arianism of Theodoric, the Ostrogothic king of Italy (which was more than the papacy did).

Pomposa (St) M. R. Sep 19
d. 835. A nun of Peñamelaria near Cordoba, Spain, she was involved in the 'martyr movement' and was beheaded by the Muslims at Cordoba.

Pons *see* **Pontius**

Pontian (St) *see* **Eusebius, Pontian and Comps**

Pontian (St) *see* **Stephen, Pontian and Comps**

Pontian (St) *see* **Trason, Pontian and Praetextatus**

Pontian, Pope (St) M. Aug 13
d. 235. He succeeded St Urban I as pope in 230 but was exiled by the emperor Maximinus Thrax as a slave to the mines of Sardinia about five years later, where the working conditions are thought to have killed him. He shares a feast day with St Hippolytus, his fellow exile.

Pontian Ngondwe (St) M. L. Jun 3
d. 1886. He was one of the royal guard of King Mwanga of Buganda, Uganda, by whose orders he was executed. *See* **Charles Lwanga and Comps**.

Pontian of Rome and Comps (SS) MM. Dec 2
d. ?259. Five Romans, they were martyred in the reign of Valerian.

Pontian of Spoleto (St) M. Jan 19
d. 169. He was martyred at Spoleto, Italy, in the reign of Marcus Aurelius. His acta are authentic in outline, although embellished.

Ponticus (St) *see* **Photinus, Sanctius and Comps**

Pontius of Balmey (Bl) B. R(OCart). Dec 13
d. 1140. A nobleman, he had been a cathedral canon of Lyons, France, before founding and joining a Carthusian monastery on his paternal estate at Meyriat. He was made bishop of Belley in 1121 but resigned to die at Meyriat. His cultus is unconfirmed.

Pontius of Carthage (St) D. Mar 8
d. *c*260. A deacon under St Cyprian at Carthage, Roman Africa, he was his attendant in exile and at his trial and execution and wrote a graphic account of his life and martyrdom.

Pontius of Cimiez (St) M. May 14
d. ?258. Apparently he was martyred at Cimiez near Nice, France, and had his relics transferred to St Pons (named after him) near Béziers. His acta are unreliable.

Pontius of Faucigny (Bl) R(CR). Nov 26
d. 1178. A Savoyard nobleman, at the age of twenty he became an Augustinian canon regular at Abondance in the Chablais, France, and was abbot there after being abbot-founder of St Sixtus. He was held in great veneration by

St Francis of Sales and had his cultus confirmed for Annecy in 1896.

Poppo (St) R(OSB). Jan 25
978–1048. He was initially a soldier without much thought for religion but converted, made a penitential pilgrimage to Jerusalem and Rome and then joined the Benedictine abbey of St Theodoric at Rheims in 1006. Two years later he migrated to St Vitonius's Abbey at Verdun and helped Bl Richard of Verdun in the revival of monastic discipline there. Then he was provost of St Vedast at Arras, became an adviser of Emperor St Henry II and was appointed by him abbot of Stavelot-Malmédy with responsibility for sixteen other abbeys of the Holy Roman Empire. Into some of these he introduced the Cluniac reform.

Porcarius and Comps
(SS) MM. RR. Aug 12
d. ?732. Abbot of Lérins, on its island off the coast of Provence, France, he was massacred with his entire community by Muslim pirates who also burned the abbey and remained in occupation for the next two centuries. The total number of dead, including lay employees, was reckoned as five hundred and only some boys and young monks previously sent to the mainland for safety escaped.

Porphyry (St) M. Sep 15
d. 362. According to his legend he was a horse-dealer and an actor who, while taking part in a parody of Christian baptism in the presence of the emperor Julian, suddenly declared himself a believer and was at once killed. The story is repeated of several alleged martyrs and seems to be a fiction.

Porphyry (St) *see* **Onesiphorus and Porphyry**

Porphyry and Seleucus (SS) MM. Feb 16
d. 309. They were martyred at Caesarea in the Holy Land, and were mentioned by the historian Eusebius.

Porphyry of Camerino (St) M. May 4
d. ?250. He never existed, as his name was transferred from the unreliable acta of St Agapitus of Palestrina to the equally fictitious acta of St Venantius. He was alleged to have been a priest martyred at Camerino in Umbria, Italy, in the reign of Decius.

Porphyry of Ephesus (St) M. Nov 4
d. 271. He was martyred at Ephesus, Asia Minor, in the reign of Aurelian.

Porphyry of Gaza (St) B. Feb 26
d. 420. From Thessalonika, Greece, he was wealthy but gave everything away and was a monk in Scetis, Egypt, and by the Jordan in the Holy Land before becoming cross-warden in Jerusalem. In 395 he was made bishop of Gaza, a stronghold of prosperous and aggressive paganism where Christianity had made little impact. His zeal and ability resulted in a flow of conversions, however. This caused persecution and attempts to kill him, so he appealed to the emperor Arcadius and the temples were eventually destroyed by imperial troops. His extant biography was written by his deacon, Mark.

Porphyry of Palestrina (St) M. Aug 20
? He features in the unreliable acta of St Agapitus of Palestrina, Italy.

Portianus (St) R. Nov 24
d. 533. He was a slave before becoming a monk and then abbot of Miranda in Auvergne, France, and was remembered for his courage in obtaining the release of his compatriots taken prisoner by the Merovingian king.

Possessor (St) B. May 11
d. ?485. He was a city magistrate of Verdun, France, before being made bishop there in 470, and had his diocese devastated by barbarian incursions (especially by the Franks).

Possidius (St) B. May 16
*c*370–*c*440. A friend and disciple of St Augustine of Hippo (whose biography he wrote), he became bishop of Calama in Numidia (Roman Africa, now Algeria) but was exiled by the Vandal invasion and died in Apulia, Italy. He was one of the most talented polemicists of his time against Donatism and Pelagianism.

Potamia (St) *see* **Julius, Potamia and Comps**

Potamioena the Elder (St) *see* **Plutarch of Alexandria and Comps**

Potamioena the Younger
(St) V. Jun 7
d. ?304. She was a young slave martyred at Alexandria, Egypt, in the reign of Diocletian.

Potamius and Nemesius
(SS) MM. Feb 20
? Nothing is known about them. The old Roman Martyrology lists them as martyred in Cyprus, but Eusebius associates them with Alexandria, Egypt.

Potamon (St) B. May 18
d. *c*340. Bishop of Heraclea in Upper Egypt, during the persecution of Maximinus Daza he was lamed in one leg, deprived of one eye and sent as a slave to the mines. Released after Constantine's edict of toleration, he was at the council of Nicaea and was a strong supporter of St Athanasius. As a result he was fiercely persecuted by the Arians, who eventually arranged his murder.

Potentian (St) *see* **Sabinian and Potentian**

Potentiana *see* **Pudentiana**

Potentinus, Simplicius and Felicius (BB) RR. Jun 18
C4th. Their relics were brought to Steinfeld monastery, Germany, in 920, and their cultus was confirmed for Cologne in 1908. Their legend states that they were Gascon pilgrims going to the Holy Land who settled instead with St Castor on the Moselle.

Pothinus *see* **Photinus**

Pothmius *see* **Potamius**

Potitus (St) M. Jan 13
? He is venerated as a boy-martyr at Naples, Italy, but his acta are legendary.

Praejectus (Priest, Prest, Preils, Prix) and Comps (SS) MM. Jan 25
d. 676. From Auvergne, France, he was an abbot before becoming bishop of Clermont-Ferrand in 666. A great administrator and patron of monasticism, he had cause to complain in person about a nobleman of Marseilles to the king and was assassinated as a result on his return at Volvic near Clermont, together with a hermit Amarinus and an acolyte Elidius.

Praepedigna (St) *see* **Maximus, Claudius and Comps**

Praesidius (St) *see* **Donatian, Praesidius and Comps**

Praetextatus (St) *see* **Trason, Pontian and Praetextatus**

Praetextatus (Prix) of Rouen (St) M. B. Feb 24
d. 586. He was bishop of Rouen, France, from 550, but became involved in politics, was accused of treason and was exiled in 577. He was restored in 584, against the wishes of Queen Fredegonda whose crimes he publicly denounced. As a result she had him assassinated in his cathedral on Easter Sunday.

Pragmatius (St) B. Nov 22
d. *c*520. He was a bishop of Autun, France.

Prague (Martyrs of) (BB) MM. RR(OSM). Aug 11
d. 1420. Four Servite friars from the nobility of Siena, Italy, Augustine Cennini, Bartholomew Sonati, John Baptist Petrucci and Laurence Nerucci, they were sent by the pope to Bohemia to help combat the Hussite heresy. With sixty other Servites they were burned in their church at Prague while singing the 'Te Deum'. Their cultus was approved for Prague, Czech Republic, in 1918.

Praxedes (St) R. Jul 21
C2nd? A church in Rome is dedicated to her, and probably stands on the site of her house. According to her unreliable legend she was a consecrated virgin, daughter of the Roman senator St Pudens and sister of St Pudentiana. Her cultus was confined to her church in 1969.

Priam (St) *see* **Emilius, Felix and Comps**

Prilidian (St) *see* **Babylas and Comps**

Primael (St) R. May 16
d. *c*450. From Britain, he migrated to Brittany, France, and became a hermit near Quimper.

Primian (St) *see* **Dominic, Victor and Comps**

Primitiva (St) V. Feb 24
? She was an early martyr, probably of Rome. Some old martyrologies list her as 'Primitivus', which would make her a he.

Primitiva (St) V. Jul 23
? She was an early martyr, probably of Rome and very probably identical with the above. She is also listed as 'Primitia' and 'Privata'.

Primitivus (St) *see* **Facundus and Primitivus**

Primitivus (St) *see* **Getulius, Amantius and Comps**

Primitivus (St) *see* **Peter, Successus and Comps**

Primitivus (St) *see* **Symphorosa of Tivoli and Comps**

Primitivus (St) *see* **Zaragoza (Eighteen Martyrs of)**

Primus (St) *see* **Cyrinus, Primus and Theogenes**

Primus, Cyril and Secundarius (SS) MM. Oct 2
? They are listed as having been martyred at Antioch, Syria, during an early persecution.

Primus and Donatus (SS) MM. Feb 9
d. 362. They were two Roman African deacons killed in an attempt by the local Donatist schismatics to take over the Catholic church at Lavallum during the reign of Julian.

Primus and Felician (SS) MM. Jun 9
d. ?297. Two old brothers of Rome, they were beheaded in the reign of Diocletian on the Via Nomentana and had a basilica built over their tomb. Their acta are not entirely reliable, but seem to be based on original sources. Their cultus was confined to local calendars in 1969.

Primus Martínez de San Vicente Castillo (Bl) *see* **Hospitaller Martyrs of Spain**

Principia (St) R. May 11
d. *c*420. She was a Roman consecrated virgin, a disciple of St Marcella.

Principius (St) B. Sep 25
d. ?505. The elder brother of St Remigius of Rheims, he became bishop of Soissons, France.

Prisca (St) V. Jan 18
C3rd? Allegedly a Roman virgin martyr, her cultus is ancient and she has a church dedicated to her on the Aventine, but nothing is known about her. In 1969 her cultus was confined to her church.

Priscian (St) *see* **Carponius, Evaristus and Comps**

Priscian (St) *see* **Evagrius, Priscian and Comps**

Priscilla (St) L. Jan 16
C1st. According to the legend, she was the widowed mother of St Pudens and was the hostess in Rome of St Peter, whose headquarters were at her villa near the Roman catacombs which are named after her.

Priscilla (St) *see* **Aquila and Priscilla**

Priscus (St) M. Sep 20
? He is listed as a native of Phrygia, Asia Minor, who was stabbed with daggers and then beheaded.

Priscus, Cottus and Comps (SS) MM. May 26
d. ?272. Priscus, a Roman military officer, several soldiers under his command and several citizens of Besançon, France, were martyred near Auxerre after fleeing persecution in the reign of Aurelian.

Priscus, Crescens and Evagrius (SS) MM. Oct 1
? They were martyred at Tomi, on the Black Sea coast of Romania.

Priscus, Malchus and Alexander (SS) MM. Mar 28
d. 260. They were thrown to the wild animals during some public games at Caesarea in the Holy Land in the reign of Valerian.

Priscus, Priscillian and Benedicta (SS) MM. Jan 4
? Their existence depends upon the untrustworthy acta of St Bibiana, which state that they were Christians buried by her father. The forger St Ado was responsible for listing them as martyrs.

Priscus I of Capua (St) M. B. Sep 1
d. ?66. According to the legend, he was a native of Jerusalem and a disciple of Christ who was sent to be the first bishop of Capua, Italy, by St Peter and who was martyred in the reign of Nero.

Priscus II of Capua and Comps (SS) Sep 1
C5th? The legend is that Priscus, a Roman African bishop, and his priests were set adrift in a rudderless boat by the Arian Vandal invaders. They reached Italy, where eventually Priscus became bishop of Capua and several of the others also became bishops. The acta are untrustworthy, however, and it seems that the companions of St Priscus (Castrensis, Tammarus, Rosius, Heraclius, Secundinus, Adjutor, Mark, Augustus, Elpidius, Canion and Vindonius) are Campanian saints unconnected with the story. It may be that the listing 'Priscus Castrensis' means 'Priscus, formerly Bishop of Castra in Africa'.

Privatus (St) *see* **Dionysius and Privatus**

Privatus of Gévaudan (St) M. B. Aug 21
d. 260. A regionary bishop of Gévaudan in the southern Massif Central, France, he was beaten to death by invading barbarians for refusing to tell them the place where some of his people were hiding.

Privatus of Rome (St) M. Sep 28
d. 223. A Roman, he was whipped to death in the reign of Alexander Severus.

Prix *see* **Praejectus**, or **Praetextatus**

Probus (St) *see* **Arcadius, Probus and Comps**

Probus (St) *see* **Tharacus, Probus and Andronicus**

Probus and Grace (SS) Jul 5
? These obscure saints, by tradition husband and wife, had churches dedicated to them at Probus and at Tressilian near Truro in Cornwall, England. Their existence is dubious.

Probus of Ravenna (St) B. Nov 10
d. ?175. A Roman, he was allegedly the sixth bishop of Ravenna, Italy, and has his shrine in the cathedral there. His traditional date as given is much too early.

Probus of Rieti (St) B. Mar 15
d. ?571. He was bishop of Rieti, Italy, and his death-bed visions feature in the *Dialogues* of St Gregory the Great.

Probus of Verona (St) B. Jan 12
d. *p*591. Nothing is known about this bishop of Verona, Italy.

Processus and Martinian (SS) MM. Jul 2
? Martyrs of Rome, they have an ancient cultus (confined to local calendars in 1969). Apparently originally buried on the Aurelian Way, they had their relics transferred to St Peter's in the C9th. Nothing is known about them, and the story associating them with SS Peter and Paul in the Mamertine prison is legendary.

Processus Ruiz Cascales (Bl) *see* **Hospitaller Martyrs of Spain**

Prochorus (St) M. B. Apr 9
C1st. He was one of the seven deacons ordained by the apostles, and according to tradition became bishop of Nicomedia, Asia Minor, and a martyr at Antioch.

Proclus and Hilarion (SS) MM. Jul 12
d. 115. They were martyred at Ancyra, Asia Minor, (now Ankara in Turkey) in the reign of Trajan.

Proclus of Constantinople (St) B. Oct 24
d. 447. A priest of Constantinople and a disciple of St John Chrysostom, he became patriarch in 434. He was a zealous supporter of St Cyril in the campaign against Nestorianism, but tempered zeal with gentleness. According to tradition he introduced the *Trisagion* into the liturgy. Some of his homilies and letters are extant, notably his famous homily on the Mother of God.

Procopius Decapolita (St) *see* **Basil of Constantinople**

Procopius the Great (St) M. Jul 8
d. 303. According to Eusebius he was from Jerusalem, was a reader in the church of Scythopolis and was beheaded at Caesarea in the Holy Land. He was the first local martyr of the persecution of Diocletian. His cultus is extremely popular in the East, and his story has attracted much later legend.

Procopius of Sázava (St) R. Jul 4
*c*980–1053. Born in Bohemia (Czech Republic), he was educated at a Basilian monastery at Prague, married and was then ordained in the Byzantine rite and became a cathedral canon. Later he became a hermit and finally abbot-founder of the Basilian abbey of Sázava near Prague. He was canonized in 1804.

Proculus (St) *see* **Florus, Laurus and Comps**

Proculus (St) *see* **Januarius of Benevento**

Proculus, Ephebus and Apollonius (SS) MM. Feb 14
d. 273. They are mentioned in the untrustworthy Acts of St Valentine of Terni, Italy, as having been martyred there, but Proclus seems to be a duplicate of the alleged bishop of Terni and the other two belong elsewhere.

Proculus of Autun (St) M. B. Nov 4
d. *p*717. This bishop of Autun, France, was alleged to have been killed in the invasion of the Huns in the C5th, but seems to be of later date.

Proculus of Bologna (1) (St) M. Jun 1
d. ?304. According to his unreliable acta he was a Roman officer martyred at Bologna, Italy, in the reign of Diocletian. His cultus is ancient.

Proculus of Bologna (2)
(St) M. B. Jul 12
d. 542. He was bishop of Bologna, Italy, from 540 until killed by the Ostrogothic leader Totila.

Proculus of Narni (St) M. B. Dec 1
d. ?542. He was allegedly either a bishop of Narni or of Terni in Umbria, Italy, who was killed by order of Totila, leader of the Ostrogoths.

Proculus of Terni (St) M. B. Apr 14
? He was allegedly a martyr-bishop of Terni in Umbria, Italy, in the reign of Maxentius, but his details are seriously confused. There are suspicious similarities with the Proculus of **Proculus, Ephebus and Apollonius**, also with **Proculus of Bologna (2)** and **Proculus of Narni**.

Proculus of Verona (St) B. Dec 9
d. *c*320. A bishop of Verona, Italy, he was a confessor during the persecution of Diocletian but died in peace.

Projectus (St) *see* **Thyrsus and Projectus**

Projectus *see* **Praejectus**

Prosdoce (St) *see* **Domnina, Berenice and Prosdoce**

Prosdocimus (St) B. Nov 7
d. ?100. He was listed as the first bishop of Padua, Italy, but the story that he was sent there from Antioch by St Peter is unhistorical.

Prosper of Aquitaine (St) L. Jul 7
*c*390–436. From Aquitaine, France, he was a layman, probably married and apparently lived in Provence. He was a capable theologian, a prolific writer and an enthusiastic disciple of St Augustine, becoming heavily involved in controversy with the local opponents of the latter's teaching on grace (the so-called semi-Pelagians).

Prosper of Orléans (St) B. Jul 29
d. ?453. A bishop of Orléans, France, he has been confused with the Prospers of Aquitaine and of Reggio.

Prosper of Reggio (St) B. Jun 25
d. ?466. He was a bishop of Reggio in Emilia, Italy, and is that city's principal patron, but little is known about him.

Prosper of Tarragona (St) B.
C4th or C5th. He is the third known bishop of Tarragona, Spain, and has a cultus in Genoa, Italy, which was confirmed in 1854.

Protase (St) *see* **Gervase and Protase**

Protase Cheong (St) *see* **Korea (Martyrs of)**

Protase of Cologne (St) M. Aug 4
? He has a cultus as a martyr at Cologne, Germany, but is probably identical with the companion of St Gervase.

Protase Cubells Minguel (Bl) *see* **Hospitaller Martyrs of Spain**

Protase of Milan (St) B. Nov 24
d. 352. He was bishop of Milan, Italy, from 331, and was one of the defenders of St Athanasius against the Arians.

Proterius (St) M. B. Feb 28
d. 458. After Dioscorus, patriarch of Alexandria, was deposed and disgraced at the council of Chalcedon in 451 for Monophysite leanings, Proterius was selected to succeed him from the few clergy in the city who accepted the council's decisions. The vast majority of the people were, however, violent in rejection and he had to rely on imperial troops for protection. After the death of the emperor Maurice he was killed by a lynch-mob on Good Friday, his body was dismembered and burnt and his place taken by the Monophysite called Timothy the Cat.

Prothadius (Protagius) (St) B. Feb 10
d. 624. The son of a Frankish courtier, he succeeded St Nicetius as bishop of Besançon, France, in 613 and was influential at the Merovingian court.

Protogenes (St) B. May 6
C4th. A priest of Carrhae in Syria (the Harran where Abraham stayed, now Altinbasak near Urfa in Turkey), he was exiled by the Arian emperor Valens but recalled by Theodosius I and ordained bishop. His city remained a stronghold of paganism until after the Muslim conquest.

Protolicus (St) *see* **Bassus, Anthony and Protolicus**

Protomartyrs of Rome (SS) MM. Jun 30
d. 64. When a large part of the city of Rome was burned in June 64, the emperor Nero accused the local Christians of starting the fire and ordered a pogrom. Some of them were sewn up in animal skins and had dogs set upon

them, while others were covered in pitch, tied to poles and used as living torches in the public gardens after sunset. It is not certain whether Nero started the fire himself to clear the ground for his palace, the 'Domus Aurea', and there is no evidence that the persecution spread outside the city.

Protomartyrs of the West
(SS) MM. Jul 22
d. ?60. They are venerated at Nepi in Tuscany, Italy, as a group of thirty-eight who were thrown over a precipice there before the persecution by Nero in Rome, but their existence is unhistorical and seems to depend on ecclesiastical one-upmanship.

Protus (St) *see* **Cantius and Comps**

Protus and Hyacinth (SS) MM. Sep 11
? According to their fictitious acta they were Roman brothers who were servants in the house of St Philip of Rome and who were martyred in the reign of Valerian. The genuine relics of St Hyacinth were, however, apparently discovered in the cemetery of St Basilla at Rome in 1845. There is apparently one church in Britain dedicated to them, at Blisland in Cornwall. Their cultus was confined to local calendars in 1969.

Protus and Januarius (SS) MM. Oct 25
d. 303. They were Roman missionaries, a priest and a deacon, in Sardinia and were beheaded at Porto Torres in the north of the island in the reign of Diocletian.

Provinus of Como (St) B. Mar 8
d. *c*420. From Gaul, he became a disciple of St Ambrose at Milan and then coadjutor to St Felix, bishop of Como. He became bishop himself in 391.

Prudentius Galindo (St) B. Apr 6
d. 861. A Spanish nobleman, he was a refugee from the Arabs at the court of France, became bishop of Troyes in 846 and played a prominent part in a controversy concerning predestination. He wrote works against Gottschalk and John Scotus Erigena, but his defence of double predestination (to damnation as well as salvation) was suspect. He had a cultus, not approved, at Troyes.

Prudentius of Tarazona
(St) B. R. Apr 28
d. *p*700. From the Basque province of Alava, Spain, he was a hermit for several years before becoming a priest of Tarazona (not Tarragona) in Aragón and then bishop there. He is patron of the diocese.

Psalmodius (Psalmet, Sauman) (St) R. Jun 14
C7th. A 'Scot' (Irish or Scottish), he was a disciple of St Brendan of Clonfert who emigrated to France and lived as a hermit near Limoges.

Ptolemy (St) *see* **Ammon, Zeno and Comps**

Ptolemy, Lucius and Companion (SS) MM. Oct 19
d. ?165. Ptolemy was a Roman sentenced to death for catechizing a woman in the reign of Antoninus Pius. Lucius and an unnamed man protested against the injustice of the sentence and were also martyred. St Justin Martyr, their contemporary, wrote an extant account of the event.

Ptolemy of Nepi (St) M. B. Aug 24
C1st? He was allegedly a disciple of St Peter and a martyr-bishop of Nepi in Tuscany, Italy.

Publia (St) R. Oct 9
d. 362. According to the story she was a widow of Antioch, Syria, who founded a community of consecrated virgins in her house. The emperor Julian happened to pass by on his way to the Persian front while they were singing Psalm 115:4: 'Their idols are silver and gold, the work of human hands'. This he took as a personal insult, his bodyguard beat up the singers and he promised their deaths when he returned. He was killed in battle.

Publicus *see* **Byblig**

Publius (St) *see* **Aurelius and Publius**

Publius (St) *see* **Zaragoza (Eighteen Martyrs of)**

Publius, Julian and Comps
(SS) MM. Feb 19
? They are listed merely as Roman African martyrs. The companions were: Marcellus, Manubius, another Julian, Baraceus, Tullius, Lampasius, Majolus, Julius, Paul and Maximilla.

Publius, Victor, Hermes and Papias (SS) MM. Nov 2
? They were Roman African martyrs.

Publius of Malta (St) M. B. Jan 21
d. ?112. The Publius who was 'chief man of the island' of Malta and who befriended the

castaways including St Paul (Acts 28:7) traditionally became bishop of Athens, Greece, and was martyred in the reign of Trajan. Other sources merely list him as the first bishop of Malta.

Publius of Zeugma (St) R. Jan 25
d. *c*380. A nobleman of Zeugma, Syria, he became a hermit in the hills nearby and attracted so many disciples that he founded a double monastery for Greek and Syriac speakers so that the liturgy could be celebrated in both languages.

Pudens (St) M. May 19
C3rd. A wealthy Roman Christian, he founded a church in his house known as the 'domus Pudentiana'. From this title was erroneously inferred the existence of a St Pudentiana, and spurious acta were written for her. Pudens was then identified as her father, a C1st senator baptized by the apostles, and also falsely identified with the Pudens mentioned by St Paul in 2 Tim 4:21.

Pudentiana (Potentiana) (St) May 19
? She is a mythical Roman virgin, daughter of St **Pudens** (q.v.). Her name does not occur in any ancient martyrology, and her cultus was suppressed as unhistorical in 1969 (except for her basilica in Rome).

Pulcheria, Empress (St) L. Sep 10
399–453. Daughter of the Eastern emperor Arcadius, she was regent during the minority of her brother Theodosius II and influenced the condemnation of Nestorianism in 431. However a Monophysite clique centred on the dowager empress Eudocia caused her withdrawal from court life until after the emperor's death in a hunting accident. Then she married the elderly senator Marcian, who thus became emperor, but apparently refused to consummate the marriage because of a private vow of virginity. Together they arranged the holding of the council of Chalcedon to condemn Monophysitism in 451.

Pupulus (St) *see* **Caerealis, Pupulus and Comps**

Pusicius (St) *see* **Simeon Barsabae and Comps**

Pusinna (St) R. Apr 23
C6th? She was allegedly one of the seven saintly daughters of a count of Perthes who became hermits near Châlons-sur-Marne, France. The others were Amata, Francula, Hoilde, Liberia, Lutrud and Menehould.

Pyran *see* **Piran**

Q

Quadragesimus (St) S. Oct 26
d. *c*590. He features in the *Dialogues* of St Gregory the Great as a shepherd and subdeacon who resurrected a dead man at Policastro south of Naples, Italy.

Quadratus (St) M. May 26
? St Augustine preached an extant panegyric in honour of this Roman African martyr at a church dedicated to him at what is now Bizerte, Tunisia, but without giving any historical details.

Quadratus, Theodosius, Emmanuel and Comps (SS) MM. Mar 26
d. ?304. Quadratus was a bishop somewhere in Asia Minor, and he was martyred with forty-two others in the reign of Diocletian.

Quadratus the Apologist (St) B? May 26
C2nd. He is the first known to have written a defence ('apology') of Christianity, which he addressed to the emperor Hadrian in ?124. He has been confused with an early bishop of Athens.

Quadratus of Hermopolis (St) M. May 7
d. 257. He was allegedly imprisoned for years at Nicomedia and Nicaea, Asia Minor, and Apamea, Syria, before being martyred at Hermopolis, Egypt, in the reign of Valerian. Possibly several martyrs have been conflated.

Quadratus of Utica (St) B. Aug 21
C3rd. Bishop of Utica in Roman Africa, he was highly praised by St Augustine: 'He taught his whole people, clergy and laity, to confess Christ'. His cultus was widespread in Africa.

Quartilla (St) *see* **Quintus, Quintilla and Comps**

Quartus (St) B? Nov 3
C1st. He was a Corinthian whom St Paul mentioned in his letter to the Romans (Rom 16:23) as 'greeting the Christians of Rome'. One tradition described him as one of the seventy-two disciples and others, which contradict, that he was a bishop.

Quartus and Quintus (SS) MM. May 10
? Two Roman citizens of Capua, Italy, they were arrested and (because of their status) condemned and executed in Rome. Their relics were enshrined at Capua.

Quenburga (St) *see* **Cuthburga and Quenburga**

Quentin (St) M. Oct 31
? According to his unreliable acta (which contain fanciful legendary material) he was a Roman who went as a missionary to the district round Amiens, France, before being martyred at the town on the Somme now called St Quentin. He is a historical person and his cultus is ancient, but nothing more than that is known about him. He is variously depicted either as a bishop or as a Roman soldier, and his attribute is a roasting-spit or two.

Quentin of Tours (St) M. L. Oct 4
d. *c*570. From Tours, France, he was a Frankish courtier who fended off an attempted seduction by a powerful woman (apparently the queen). Spurned, she had him assassinated on the Indrois river near Montrésor.

Queranus *see* **Kieran**

Quinidius (St) B. Feb 15
d. ?579. He was a hermit at Aix-en-Provence, France, before becoming bishop of Vaison near Orange.

Quinta *see* **Cointha**

Quintian (St) B. Jun 14
? He is listed in the old Roman Martyrology as a bishop of Rodez, France, but this is mistaken and his diocese in Gaul and date are unknown.

Quintian (St) *see* **Stephen, Pontian and Comps**

Quintian and Irenaeus (SS) MM. Apr 1
? Nothing is known about these martyrs of Roman Armenia.

Quintian, Lucius, Julian and Comps (SS) MM. May 23
d. *c*430. They were apparently nineteen Roman Africans (including several women) martyred in the reign of the Arian Vandal King Hunneric.

Quintian of Clermont (St) B. Nov 13
d. ?527. A Roman African refugee from the Arian Vandals, he became bishop of Rodez, France, but was again exiled, this time by the Arian Visigoths. Then St Euphrasius made him his successor as bishop of Clermont-Ferrand.

Quintilian (St) *see* **Maximus, Quintilian and Dadas**

Quintilian (St) *see* **Zaragoza (Eighteen Martyrs of)**

Quintilis and Capitolinus (St) MM. Mar 8
? They were martyrs of Nicomedia, Asia Minor. Capitolinus is not listed by the old Roman Martyrology, which lists Quintilis as a bishop.

Quintilla (St) *see* **Quintus, Quintilla and Comps**

Quintius, Arcontius and Donatus (SS) MM. Sep 5
? They were apparently martyred at Capua, Italy.

Quintus (St) *see* **Aquilinus, Geminus, Eugene and Comps**

Quintus, Quintilla, Quartilla, Mark and Comps (St) MM. Mar 19
? They are martyrs venerated at Sorrento near Naples, Italy, and the first three were perhaps a brother and two sisters.

Quintus, Simplicius and Comps (SS) MM. Dec 18
d. ?255. They were martyred in various places in Roman Africa in the reigns of Decius and Valerian.

Quiriacus *see* **Cyriac**

Quiriacus {St) *see* **Hilaria, Digna and Comps**

Quiriacus, Maximus, Archelaus and Comps (SS) MM. Aug 23
d. ?235 or 250. Allegedly a bishop, priest and deacon respectively of Ostia near Rome, they were martyred with some soldiers either in the reign of Alexander Severus or of Decius.

Quiricus (Cyr) and Julitta (SS) MM. Jun 16
d. 304. According to their fictitious acta, they were a widowed noblewoman from Iconium, Asia Minor (now Konya in Turkey) and her three-year-old son. He was beaten to death before her eyes because he had scratched the face of the examining magistrate at Tarsus, just before she herself was executed. She has been confused with Juliot, a Cornish saint.

Quirinus (St) *see* **Nicasius of Rouen and Comps**

Quirinus of Rome (1) (St) M. Mar 25
d. ?269. He features in the dubious acta of SS Marius, Martha and Comps as a Roman who was martyred in the reign of Claudius II.

Quirinus of Rome (2) (St) M. Mar 30
d. ?117. According to the fictitious acta of Pope St Alexander I, he was the pope's jailer and was converted with his daughter, St Balbina. He was martyred shortly afterwards in the reign of Hadrian.

Quirinus of Sisak (St) M. B. Jun 4
d. 308. Bishop of what is now Sisak, Croatia, according to his story he fled from his city to escape the persecution of Galerius, was captured, brought back and ordered to sacrifice to the gods. He refused, was thoroughly beaten and handed over to the provincial governor at Sabaria (now Szombathely in Hungary). There, on his continued refusal to apostatize, he was drowned in the river.

Quirinus of Tivoli (St) M. Jun 4
? He was martyred at Tivoli near Rome.

Quiteria (St) V. May 22
? She has a cultus as a virgin-martyr in the Basque regions straddling the Franco-Spanish border, but nothing is known about her and her traditional story is completely unreliable.

Quivox *see* **Kevoca**

Quodvultdeus (St) B. Feb 19
d. *c*450. A bishop of Carthage, Roman Africa, he was exiled by the Arian King Genseric of the Vandals after the capture of the city in 439. He died at Naples.

R

Rabanus Maurus (Bl) B. R(OSB). Feb 4
?776–856. From Mainz, Germany, he was a child-oblate at the abbey of Fulda but studied under Alcuin at Tours for two years. He was appointed headmaster of the abbey school in 799, was abbot from 822 to 847, then resigned and was immediately made archbishop of Mainz. An outstanding scholar for the time, he tried to improve the education of his clergy and was a prolific writer, producing many homilies and poems and being noted for works on biblical exegesis and hagiography.

Rachild (St) R(OSB). Nov 23
d. ?946. She was a hermit living in a walled-up cell near that of St Wiborada, both being associated with the abbey of St Gall, Switzerland.

Racho (Ragnobert) (St) B. Jan 25
d. *c*660. He was the first Frankish bishop of Autun, France.

Radbod (St) B. R(OSB)? Nov 29
d. 918. The great-grandson of the last pagan king of Friesland, he was raised in the household of an uncle who was archbishop of Cologne and studied at the imperial court and at Tours. In 900 he became bishop of Utrecht, Netherlands, but had to move the see to Deventer in the face of Norse raids. His cathedral at Utrecht was a Benedictine monastery of which he was nominally abbot, hence the tradition that he became a monk when made bishop.

Radegund, Queen (St) R. Aug 13
518–587. Daughter of a pagan king of Thuringia, when aged twelve she was abducted by the Frankish king Clotaire I who had her baptized and educated before marrying her in 536. He was an unfaithful and cruel husband, so she left him in 542, took vows at Noyon under the authority of St Médard and went on to found the monastery of the Holy Cross at Poitiers, France, using the rule of St Caesarius. During the thirty years she was there as a nun the nunnery became a noted centre of scholarship and initiated the fashion for royal Frankish patronage of monasticism. She was a friend of St Venantius Fortunatus.

Radegund of Wellenburg (St) L. Aug 13
d. *c*1300. A young domestic servant at the castle of Wellenburg near Augsburg, Bavaria, she practised works of charity in her spare time. While on the road to a neighbouring hospital in order to visit the sick she was caught by hungry wolves and eaten. Her cultus has not been approved.

Radingus *see* **Rodingus**

Radulphus *see* **Ralph**

Ralph
This is the English form of Radulf, which is Raoul in French. There are many other variants, e.g. Radult, Raul, Radolph, Randulph, Rodolfo, Rodolphe, Rollon, Ruph. The German form Rudolf is listed separately.

Ralph Ashley (Bl) M. R(SJ). Apr 7
d. 1606. A Jesuit lay brother, he was seized with Bl Edward Oldcorne and executed with him at Worcester. He was beatified in 1929. *See* **England (Martyrs of)**.

Ralph of Bourges (St) B. R(OSB). Jun 21
d. 866. A child-oblate at the abbey of Solignac near Limoges, France, he possibly became a monk there. He was abbot of several monasteries (notably that of St Médard at Soissons) before becoming bishop of Bourges in 840.

Ralph Corby (alias Corbington)
(Bl) M. R(SJ). Sep 7
d. 1644. Born in Dublin, he was educated at St Omer and then studied for the priesthood at Seville and Valladolid. In 1631 he became a Jesuit, was sent on mission to England and worked as a priest in Co. Durham. He was executed at Tyburn, London, and was beatified in 1929. *See* **England (Martyrs of)**.

Ralph Crockett (Bl) M. P. Oct 1
d. 1588. From Cheshire, he was educated at Cambridge and at Oxford before becoming a schoolmaster in East Anglia. After his conversion he studied for the priesthood at Rheims, where he was ordained in 1586. He went on the English mission, was executed at Chichester, Sussex, and was beatified in 1929. *See* **England (Martyrs of)**.

Ralph de la Futaye (de Flageio) (Bl) R(OSB). Aug 16
d. 1129. A Benedictine monk of St-Jouin-de-Marne, France, he helped Bl Robert of Arbrissel to found the great double monastery and congregation of Fontevrault and was himself the abbot-founder in 1092 of the double monastery (for monks and nuns) of St Sulpice near Rennes.

Ralph Grimston (Bl) M. L. Jun 15
d. 1598. He lived at Nidd Hall near Knaresborough, Yorks, and was known for sheltering priests. His house was raided on the feast day of SS Philip and James while Bl Peter Snow was celebrating Mass there, and the two of them were executed at York. He was beatified in 1987. *See* **England (Martyrs of)**.

Ralph Milner (Bl) M. L. Jul 7
d. 1591. A Hampshire small-holder, he was convicted of sheltering Bl Roger Dickenson and executed with him at Winchester. He was beatified in 1929. *See* **England (Martyrs of)**.

Ralph Sherwin (St) M. P. Dec 1
1550–1581. From Rodsley near Ashbourne in Derbyshire, he gained a fellowship as a classical scholar of distinction at Oxford University. After his conversion he studied for the priesthood at Douai and Rome, was ordained in 1577, returned to England in 1580 and was quickly arrested. Despite torture and an offer of preferment by Queen Elizabeth if would become a Protestant, he held on to his faith and was executed at Tyburn, London. He is the proto-martyr of the English College at Rome, and was canonized in 1970. *See* **England (Martyrs of)**.

Rambert (Ragnebert, Ragnobert) (St) M. L. Jun 13
d. *c*680. A Frankish nobleman, he was influential at the court of King Thierry III of Austrasia in northern France, but Ebroin, mayor (comptroller) of the palace, had him exiled and then ambushed and murdered in the Jura mountains. He was (with little justification) venerated as a martyr.

Rambold (Ramnold) (St) R(OSB). Jun 17
901–1001. A monk of St Maximinus's Abbey at Trier, Germany, he was summoned to Regensburg by St Wolfgang to be abbot of St Emmeram's Abbey there. He died at the age of one hundred.

Ramirus and Comps (SS) MM. Mar 13
d. ?554 or 630. He was prior of the monastery of St Claudius at León, Spain. His abbot, St Vincent, was killed in a persecution ordered by the Arian Visigothic king Leovegild, and two days later he was himself massacred with twelve of his brethren while chanting the Nicene (anti-Arian) creed in the abbey church. St Vincent has a separate feast-day on Sep 11.

Ramón *see* **Raymund**

Randoald (St) *see* **Germanus and Randoald**

Ranulf (Ragnulf) (St) M. L. May 27
d. *c*700. The father of St Hadulph, bishop of Arras-Cambrai, he was killed at Thélus near Arras, France.

Raphael the Archangel (St) Sep 29
The three archangels Michael, Gabriel and Raphael are liturgically venerated together. The last-named, 'the Healer of God', features in the deuterocanonical book of Tobit and is the only one of the three not to be mentioned in the New Testament. Because of his name, however, he has been traditionally identified with the angel of the sheep-pool in John 5: 1-4.

Raphael Arnaiz Barón (Bl) R(OCSO) Apr 26
1911–1938. Born at Burgos, Spain, his parents were wealthy and he went to Madrid University to study architecture. He loved beauty in nature, music and painting. Giving up a promising secular career, he joined the Trappists at Dueñas near Palencia in 1934. His health forced him to return home for two years after a few months there, but with no damage to his vocation. He considered his bad health to be a purgation of his soul, and he died at the monastery. He was beatified in 1991.

Raphael Briega Morales (Bl) *see* **Philip-of-Jesus Munárriz Azcona and Comps**

Raphael Chylinski (Bl) R(OFM Cap). Dec 2
1694–1741. Born near Poznan, Poland, he joined the Capuchins at Cracow in 1715. In 1728 he moved to Łagiewniki near Łódz where he stayed until death, apart from two years spent nursing sufferers of an epidemic at Cracow. He

was known for his preaching, moral catechesis and hearing of confessions, and he subjected himself to severe penances for the sins of the world. However he was joyful in the liturgy, in the care of the poor and in his chastity and love for Our Lady. He was beatified in 1991.

Raphael Flamarique Salinas (Bl) *see* **Hospitaller Martyrs of Spain**

Raphael Guizar Valencia (Bl) B. Oct 24
1878–1938. Born in Michoacán, Mexico, he became a priest of the diocese of Zamorra but persecution of the Church drove him underground and into exile. He returned and became bishop of Veracruz in 1919, re-founding the seminary there, but the government set out to destroy the Church and he went into exile again, assisting the hierarchies in neighbouring countries and keeping in touch with the underground Church in Mexico by letter. He was allowed to return just before he died, and was beatified in 1995.

Raphael-of-St-Joseph Kalinowski (St) R(OC). Nov 19
d. 1907. Born of Polish parents in Lithuania when this was part of the Russian Empire, he served in the army and civil service. But he took part in the Polish rebellion of 1863, was exiled to Siberia for ten years and became a Carmelite priest in Poland on his return. He had such success as a spiritual director that he became known as the 'martyr of the confessional'. He died at Wadowice and was canonized in 1991.

Raphael Massabki (Bl) *see* **Emmanuel Ruiz and Comps**

Raphael of Sandomir (Bl) *see* **Sadoc of Sandomir and Comps**

Raphaela Ybarra (Bl) L. F. Feb 23
1843–1898. Born in Bilbao, Spain, she married and had seven children (five survived). In 1885 she took religious vows in private with the consent of her husband, and became known as a 'mother of charity' through her benefactions. She had especial care for derelict young people, and founded the 'Sisters of the Guardian Angels' in order to help teenage girls facing the choice between prostitution and starvation. She was beatified in 1984.

Raphaela-Mary-of-the-Sacred-Heart Porras Ayllón (St) R. F. Jan 6
1850–1925. From Pedro Abad near Cordoba, Spain, with her sister she joined the 'Society of Mary Auxiliatrix' at the latter place in 1875, but stayed behind when the society had to leave the city. In 1877 she founded the 'Handmaids of the Sacred Heart' at Madrid, and became the first superior-general in 1887. The charism involved teaching and also adoration of the Blessed Sacrament in reparation for outrages against it. Six years later she resigned, and then lived a busy but anonymous life until her death in Rome. She was canonized in 1977.

Rasso (Ratho) (Bl) R(OSB). May 17
d. 953. Count of Andechs in Bavaria, Germany, he was a famous warrior and fought for the Bavarians against the raiding Magyars. In middle age he made a pilgrimage to the Holy Land and Rome, and on his return founded the abbey of Wörth in Bavaria (now named Grafrath after him) and became a monk there. His cultus is unconfirmed.

Rasyphus (St) M. July 23
? He has an ancient cultus as a martyr at Rome, and may be identical with a St Rasius whose relics are enshrined in the Pantheon there.

Rasyphus and Ravennus (SS) MM. RR. Jul 23
C5th. According to their dubious story, they were Roman Britons who fled from the Anglo-Saxon invaders, settled as hermits near Sées in Normandy, France, and were killed by order of a local nobleman. Their alleged relics are in Bayeux cathedral, and the legend was probably invented when these were discovered.

Ravennus (St) *see* **Rasyphus and Ravennus**

Raverranus (Raverianus) (St) B. R. Nov 7
d. 682. A bishop of Sées in Normandy, France, he resigned and became a monk at Fontenelle.

Raymund of Barbastro (St) B. R(CR). Jun 21
d. 1126. From Durban, south of Toulouse, France, he became an Augustinian canon regular at Pamiers and second bishop of Barbastro in Aragón, Spain, in 1104. The city had been recently conquered from the Muslims. He is its principal patron.

Raymund Carbonier and Raymund Costivan (BB) *see* **William Arnaud and Comps**

Raymund of Fitero (St) R(OCist). Mar 15
d. 1163. An Aragonese cathedral-canon of Tarazona, Spain, he became a Cistercian at the French abbey of Scala Dei and was sent to be

the abbot-founder of Fitero in Spanish Navarre. In 1158 the city of Calatrava in New Castile was abandoned by the Knights Templar and threatened by the Muslims, so he founded the military order of Calatrava for its defence. This utilized the Benedictine rule and the Cistercian customary and played a notable part in the 'Reconquista'. He died near Toledo and his cultus as a saint was confirmed in 1719.

Raymund Illa Salvía (Bl) *see* **Philip-of-Jesus Munárriz Azcona and Comps**

Raymund Li (Quanzhen) (St) *see* **Peter Li (Quanhui) and Raymund Li (Quanzhen)**.

Raymund Lull (Bl) T(OFM). Jul 3
?1232–?1315. From Palma on Majorca, Spain, he married young and was seneschal at the court of Aragón. When aged about thirty he was converted by a vision of Christ crucified, became a Franciscan tertiary and devoted his whole life to the conversion of the Muslims. To this end he travelled extensively in Italy, France, England and Germany, wrote copiously in Latin, Arabic (which he learned) and Catalan, and encouraged the study of oriental religion and culture. He was, however, unsuccessful in his attempts to interest the Holy See and the courts of Western Europe in his objective. He made three journeys to preach the gospel to the Muslims of Tunis and was allegedly stoned to death there, but there is no contemporary proof of this. He was a philosopher, a poet, an alchemist and a chemist as well as a theologian (nicknamed 'Doctor Illuminatus'), but he had no formal training in the scholastic theology of his age and invented his own method, which had a small but enthusiastic following in his time.

Raymund Nonnatus (St) R. Aug 31
d. 1240. According to his unreliable biography he was from an impoverished noble family of Catalonia and was cut out of his dead mother's womb (hence his surname, 'Unborn'). He joined the Mercedarian order, which had been recently founded in Spain for the ransoming of Christian captives from the Muslims of North Africa, and succeeded St Peter Nolasco as its second master-general. He surrendered himself as a hostage in exchange for a Christian slave when he was out of funds, and was very badly treated until ransomed in turn. He was created a cardinal in 1239 but died on his way to Rome. His cultus was confined to local calendars in 1969.

Raymund Novich Rabionet (Bl) *see* **Philip-of-Jesus Munárriz Azcona and Comps**

Raymund of Peñafort
(St) R(OP). Jan 7
*c*1180–1275. Related to the royal family of Aragón, he was born at Villafranca in Catalonia, Spain, and studied and taught at Barcelona, where he became a priest and archdeacon of the cathedral. In 1222 he became a Dominican and worked among the Muslims and the Albigenses until summoned to Rome by Pope Gregory IX. He became the pope's confessor, and was given the task of systematizing and codifying the contemporary canon law. This resulted in his five books of the *Decretals*, finished in 1234, which remained the most authoritative codification of ecclesiastical legislation until 1917. He became master-general of the Dominicans in 1238 and encouraged St Thomas Aquinas to write his *Contra Gentiles*. In later life he lived on Majorca, but died at Barcelona. He is alleged to have helped in the foundation of the Mercedarians, but this is debatable. He was canonized in 1601.

Raymund Petinaud de Jourgnac (Bl) *see* **John-Baptist Souzy and Comps**

Raymund of Toulouse (St) P. Jul 8
d. 1118. He had been a cantor in the church of St Sernin at Toulouse, France, before his wife died, whereupon he became a secular canon there and founded a hospice in the city later named after him. He was noted for his generosity to the poor and for his personal austerity.

Raymund delle Vigne of Capua (Bl) R(OP). Oct 5
d. 1399. From Capua, Italy, he joined the Dominicans and taught at Bologna, Rome and (from 1374) at Siena, where he was the spiritual director of St Catherine of Siena. Later he became master-general of the Dominicans and restored discipline with such success that he has been called the second founder of the order. He wrote biographies of St Catherine and of St Agnes of Montepulciano. His cultus was confirmed for the Dominicans and locally for Rome in 1899.

Raynald de Bar (Bl) R(OCist). Dec 16
d. 1151. A monk of Clairvaux, France, he was appointed abbot of Cîteaux in 1133 and compiled the first collection of Cistercian statutes. He was also instrumental in bringing about the union of the reformed Benedictine congregations of Obazine and Savigny with the Cistercians in 1147. These included nunneries, which the Cistercians had previously refused to accept, and the rigour of the original Cistercian

rule had to be mitigated to allow the newcomers to keep their tithes and serfs. His cultus is unconfirmed.

Raynald Concorrezzo (Bl) B. Aug 18
d. 1321. From Milan, Italy, he became a canon of Lodi, then bishop of Vicenza in 1296 and archbishop of Ravenna in 1303. He was a friend and defender of the Knights Templar. His cultus was confirmed for Ravenna in 1852.

Raynald of Nocera (St) B. R(OSB). Feb 9
d. 1225. Of German ancestry, he was born near Nocera in Umbria, Italy, became a monk at Fontavellana and was made bishop of Nocera in 1222, of which city he is the principal patron.

Raynerius of Aquila (St) B. Dec 30
d. 1077. He was a bishop of Aquila in the Abruzzi, Italy.

Raynerius (Raynier) of Beaulieu (St) R(OSB). Feb 22
d. ?967. He was a Benedictine monk at Beaulieu near Limoges, France.

Raynerius Mariani of Arezzo (Bl) R(OFM). Nov 3
d. 1304. From Arezzo, Italy, he became a Franciscan lay brother and died at Borgo San Sepolcro. His cultus was confirmed for there in 1802.

Raynerius (Raniero, Rainerius) Scacceri (St) T(OSB). Jun 17
d. 1160. From Pisa, Italy, after a dissipated youth he undertook several penitential pilgrimages to Jerusalem and afterwards lived as a conventual oblate in the Benedictine abbey of St Andrew at Pisa and then in that of St Vitus in the same city, where he died.

Raynerius of Split (St) M. R(OSB). Aug 4
d. 1180. A Camaldolese monk of Fontavellana, he was made bishop of Cagli, Italy, in 1156 and archbishop of Split in Dalmatia (Croatia) in 1175. His attempts to reclaim property alienated from his diocese led to his murder.

Reatrus (St) *see* **Datius, Reatrus and Comps**

Rebecca Ar Rayès de Himlaya (Bl) R. Mar 23
1832–1914. Born at Himlaya in the Lebanon, she joined the 'Religious of Our Lady' ('Marianettes') in 1853 and taught girls. There was a persecution by the Turks and her congregation had to leave the country, so she joined the 'Maronite Order of St Anthony' at Al-Qarn in 1871. She spent 26 years there, then went blind and moved to Ad-Dahr where she became paralyzed as well before her death. She was beatified in 1985.

Recared Centelles Abad (Bl) *see* **Peter Ruiz de los Paños y Angel and Comps**

Redempta (St) *see* **Romula, Redempta and Herundo**

Redemptus of Ferentini (St) B. Apr 8
d. 586. Bishop of Ferentini south of Rome, he was a friend of St Gregory the Great.

Redemptus-of-the-Cross Rodriguez da Cunha (Bl) *see* **Dionysius and Redemptus**

Regimbald (Reginbald, Regimbaut, Reginobald) (St) B. ROSB). Oct 13
d. 1039. A Benedictine monk of the abbey of SS Ulric and Afra at Augsburg, Germany, he transferred to the abbey of Edersberg before becoming abbot of Lorsch in 1022. As such he founded the abbey of Heiligenberg. In 1032 he was made bishop of Speyer.

Regina (Regnia, Reine) (St) V. Sep 7
d. ?286. She has an ancient cultus as a virgin-martyr in the diocese of Autun, France, but no reliable information about her survives.

Regina Protmann (Bl) R. F. (Jan 18)
1552–1613. From a bourgeois family of Braniewo in Warmia, Poland, she had an ordinary life appropriate to her background until the spread of Protestantism and the plague suddenly inspired her to leave her family in 1571 and found the Sisters of St Catherine of Alexandria for prayer, nursing and teaching without an enclosure (an innovation at the time). She died at her home town and was beatified in 1999.

Reginald of Picardy (St) R(CR). Sep 17
d. 1104. He was a canon regular at Soissons, France, before becoming a hermit at Melinais near La Flèche. King Henry II of England had an abbey built over his tomb. His cultus was confirmed for Angers in 1868.

Reginald of St Gilles (Bl) R(OP). Feb 1
1183–1220. From St Gilles near Nîmes, France, he taught canon law at the university of Paris from 1206 and was dean of the collegiate church of St Agnan in Orléans from 1211. He met St Dominic in Rome, became his disciple and helped to establish the Dominicans at

Bologna and at Paris. His cultus was confirmed for Paris and the Dominicans in 1885.

Regula (St) *see* **Felix and Regula**

Regulus of Lucca (St) M. B? R. Sep 1
d. ?545. A Roman African, possibly a bishop, he was exiled by the Arian Vandals and settled as a hermit on the coast of Tuscany, Italy. He appears to have been killed by order of the Ostrogothic leader Totila, and his relics were enshrined at Lucca.

Regulus (Reol) of Rheims
(St) B. R. Sep 3
d. 698. He was a monk at Rebais east of Paris, France, under St Philibert, and succeeded St Nivard as archbishop of Rheims in *c*670. He founded the abbey of Orbais in 680, where he was buried.

Regulus (Rieul) of Senlis (St) B. Mar 30
d. *c*260. Allegedly a Greek and the first bishop of Senlis, France, he is also linked with Arles.

Regulus (Rule) of St Andrew's (St) R. Oct 17
C4th? According to the C9th legend, he was a Greek abbot who brought some relics of St Andrew to Scotland and founded the church at St Andrew's in Fife. He was more likely a later Irish missionary.

Reine *see* **Regina**

Reineldis (Raineldis, Reinaldes) de Contich and Comps (SS) MM. Jul 16
d. *c*680. According to her dubious C11th biography she was a daughter of St Amelberga of Maubeuge, became a nun at Saintes near Brussels, Belgium, and was killed with a subdeacon Grimwald and her servant Gondulf by invading barbarians.

Reinold (Rainald, Reynold)
(St) M. R(OSB). Jan 7
d. ?960. According to his dubious story he was a relative of Charlemagne who became a Benedictine monk of St Pantaleon's Abbey at Cologne, Germany. While in charge of building operations there he had an argument with the stonemasons, who killed him with their hammers and threw his body into a pond.

Relinda (St) *see* **Herlinda and Relinda**

Remaclus of Maastricht (St) B. R. Sep 3
d. ?663. From Aquitaine, France, he was a courtier before becoming a monk-disciple of St Sulpicius at Bourges. He was the first abbot of Solignac near Limoges and then of Cougnon in Luxembourg before founding the twin abbeys of Stavelot-Malmédy in the Ardennes, Belgium, in 648. In 652 he became bishop of Maastricht, Netherlands, but resigned in 663 and died at Stavelot.

Rembert (St) B. R(OSB). Feb 4
d. 888. From Tourhout in Flanders, he was educated at the monastery founded there by St Ansgar, accompanied the latter on his missionary journeys and succeeded him as archbishop of Hamburg-Bremen in 865. He died at Bremen, Germany, and is remembered for a biography that he wrote of St Ansgar.

Remedius (St) B. Feb 3
? He was a bishop of Gap, France, but his dates are uncertain.

Rémy *see* **Remigius**

Remigius Isoré and Modestus Andlauer
(SS) MM. RR(SJ). Jun 19
d. 1900. Two French Jesuits, they were missonaries around the city of Xian in Hebei, China. St Modestus was pastor of Wuyi, while St Remigius was that of Zhoujiazhuang. The latter came to Wuyi on a journey, and the two were beaten to death in the church by Boxers. *See* **China (Martyrs of)**.

Remigius of Lyons (St) B. Oct 28
d. 875. He was royal chaplain to King Charles of Provence before being made archbishop of Lyons, France, in 852. As such he led the controversy against Gottschalk's doctrine on predestination.

Remigius of Rheims (St) B. Oct 1
d. ?533. The 'Apostle of the Franks' was a Gallo-Roman nobleman who was elected bishop of Rheims, France, in 459 when still a layman. He was the most influential bishop of Gaul during the seventy-four years of his episcopate, and was instrumental in the conversion to Catholicism of Clovis, king of the Franks. He baptized him at Rheims during the Easter vigil of 496. His cultus was confined to particular calendars in 1969.

Remigius of Rouen (St) B. Jan 19
d. ?772. An illegitimate son of Charles Martel, he became bishop of Rouen, France, in 755 and was successful in introducing the Roman rite and liturgical chant into France.

Remigius of Strasbourg
(Bl) B. R. Mar 20
d. 783. A son of a duke of Alsace and a nephew of St Ottilia, he was educated at the abbey of Münster near Colmar in Alsace, France, became a monk and abbot there and was made bishop of Strasbourg in 776. He has a cultus at Münster.

Remo *see* **Romulus**

Renata Bourgeais, Renata Cailleau, Renata-Mary Feillatreau, Renata Grillard, Renata Martin, Renata Rigault, Renata Seichet and Renata Valin (BB) *see* **William Repin and Comps**

Renatus (St) B. Nov 12
d. ?422. He was allegedly bishop at Angers, France, and then at Sorrento, Italy, but was probably a conflation of two separate persons.

Renatus-Louis Ambroise (Bl) *see* **Laval (Martyrs of)**

Renatus Andrieux (Bl) *see* **September (Martyrs of)**

Renatus Goupil (St) *see* **John de Brébeuf and Comps**

Renatus Lego (Bl) *see* **William Repin and Comps**

Renatus Massey, Renatus Nativelle, Renatus Poret and Renatus Urvoy (BB) *see* **September (Martyrs of)**

Renovatus (St) B. Mar 31
d. ?633. A converted Arian Visigoth, he was abbot of Cauliana before becoming bishop of Mérida, Spain, in ?611.

Reol *see* **Regulus**

Reparata (St) V. Oct 8
d. *c*250. She was a virgin-martyr of Caesarea in the Holy Land in the reign of Decius. Her acta are spurious.

Repositus (St) *see* **Vitalis, Sator and Repositus**

Respicius (St) *see* **Tryphon of Nicaea and Comps**

Restituta (St) V. May 17
d. 255 or 304. A Roman African maiden, she was martyred at Carthage in the reign of either Valerian or Diocletian. Her alleged relics are in the cathedral of Naples, Italy.

Restituta and Comps
(SS) MM. May 27
d. 272. According to her story she was a patrician maiden of Rome who fled to Sora in Campania, Italy, to escape persecution in the reign of Aurelian and who was martyred there with several companions.

Restitutus, Donatus, Valerian, Fructuosa and Comps
(SS) MM. Aug 23
d. ?305. They were listed by Florus of Lyons in *c*850 as a group of sixteen Syrians martyred at Antioch, but some may have been African.

Restitutus of Carthage
(St) M. B. Dec 9
? He was a martyred bishop of Carthage, Roman Africa, in whose honour St Augustine preached a sermon which is now lost.

Restitutus of Rome (St) M. May 29
d. ?299. He was a Roman martyr of the reign of Diocletian. His acta are unreliable.

Reverianus, Paul and Comps (SS) MM. Jun 1
d. 272. They were an Italian missionary bishop and priest who allegedly worked in the region around Autun, France, and were martyred with several companions in the reign of Aurelian.

Revocata (St) *see* **Saturninus, Theophilus and Revocata**

Revocatus (St) *see* **Perpetua, Felicity and Comps**

Revocatus (St) *see* **Vitalis, Revocatus and Fortunatus**

Reyne *see* **Regina**

Rhais *see* **Irais**

Rhais (St) *see* **Plutarch of Alexandria and Comps**

Rhediw (St) Nov 11
? The church at Llanllyfni in Gwynedd, Wales, is dedicated to this unknown saint.

Rheticus (Rheticius, Rhetice) (St) B. Jul 20
d. 334. A Gallo-Roman nobleman, he became bishop of Autun, France, about three years

before he attended the Roman synod which condemned Donatism in 313.

Rhian (Ranus, Rian) (St) R. Mar 8
? Llanrhian, near St David's, Wales, is named after him. There are no authentic details of his life.

Rhipsime (Ripsimis), Gaiana and Comps (SS) VV. Sep 29
d. *c*290. A group of virgin-martyrs, they have an ancient cultus as the first martyrs of the Armenian church. Their existence is certain but their acta are unreliable.

Rhodopianus (St) *see* **Diodore and Rhodopianus**

Rhuddlad (St) R. Sep 4
C7th? She is the patron of Llanrhyddlad on Anglesey, Wales.

Ribert (Raimbert) (St) B? R. Sep 15
C7th. He was abbot of St-Valéry-sur-Somme near Abbeville, France, and perhaps also a regionary bishop in Normandy and Picardy. He is the patron of numerous parishes in the diocese of Rouen.

Ribert (Ribarius) (St) R. Dec 19
d. *c*790. He was abbot of St Oyend and is venerated in Franche-Comté, France. He has been confused with the Ribert of the preceeding entry.

Richard of Andria (St) B. Jun 9
d. *p*1196. He was an English bishop of Andria near Bari, Italy. The assertion that he was of the C5th is erroneous.

Richard Bere (Bl) M. R(OCart). Aug 9
d. 1537. From Glastonbury, Somerset, he was educated at Oxford and the Inns of Court in London before becoming a Carthusian at the London Charterhouse. He was among those of that community starved to death in Newgate prison for refusing the spiritual supremacy of Henry VIII. *See* **England (Martyrs of)**.

Richard-of-St-Anne of Brussels (Bl) M. R(OFM). Sep 10
1585–1622. Born of Spanish parents in Flanders, he was a tailor at Brussels before becoming a Franciscan lay brother. He was sent as a missionary firstly to Mexico and then to the Philippines in 1611, where he was ordained on Cebu. In 1613 he went to Japan and was martyred at Nagasaki on the day of the 'Great Martyrdom'. *See* **Charles Spinola and Comps** and **Japan (Martyrs of)**.

Richard Featherston (Bl) M. P. Jul 30
d. 1540. Educated at Cambridge, he was appointed archdeacon of Brecon, tutor to Princess Mary and was one of the chaplains of Queen Catherine of Aragón. He defended the validity of her marriage to King Henry VIII, refused the latter's oath of supremacy and was executed at Smithfield, London, with BB Edward Powell and Thomas Abel. He was beatified in 1929. *See* **England (Martyrs of)**.

Richard Flower (Bl) M. L. Aug 30
d. 1588. He was born on Anglesey, Wales, of a Catholic family called Lloyd (of which 'Flower' was an English mispronunciation). His brother Owen was a priest. Condemned for giving shelter to priests, he was executed at Tyburn, London, with St Margaret Ward and BB Richard Leigh, Edward Shelley, Richard Martin and John Roche. He was beatified in 1987. *See* **England (Martyrs of)**.

Richard Gwyn (alias White) (St) M. L. Oct 17
1537–1584. From Llanidloes in Powys, Wales, he was educated at St John's College, Cambridge before converting, marrying and working as a schoolteacher at Overton in Clwyd. He was imprisoned for four years (during which he wrote many religious poems in Welsh) before he was executed at Wrexham. He is the protomartyr of the Reformation in Wales, and was canonized in 1970. *See* **Wales (Martyrs of)**.

St Richard Gwyn, Oct 17

Richard Herst (Hurst, Hayhurst) (Bl) M. L. Aug 29
d. 1628. From near Preston, Lancs, he was a farmer there and, because he was a Catholic, was falsely found guilty and hanged at Lancaster for murder. He was beatified in 1929. *See* **England (Martyrs of)**.

Richard Hill and Richard Holliday (BB) *see* **Edmund Duke and Comps**

Richard 'the King' (St) L. Feb 7
d. ?720. The earlier Italian legend describes him as a prince of Wessex, England, father of SS Willibald, Winebald and Walburga, who died at Lucca on a pilgrimage to Rome. The later legend describes him as a duke of Swabia, Germany. Both are fictitious.

Richard Kirkman (Bl) M. P. Aug 22
d. 1582. From Addingham near Skipton, Yorks, he was educated at Douai, ordained in 1579 and was a tutor at Scrivelsby Manor near Hornchurch, Lincs. He was executed at York with Bl William Lacey and was beatified in 1886. *See* **England (Martyrs of)**.

Richard Langhorne (Bl) M. L. Jul 14
d. 1679. From Bedfordshire, he was a law student at the Inner Temple in London and became a barrister in 1654. He was executed at Tyburn for alleged involvement in the Oates plot and was beatified in 1929. *See* **England (Martyrs of)**.

Richard Langley (Bl) M. L. Dec 1
d. 1586. A landowner at Ousethorpe near Pocklington, Yorks, he was hanged at York for sheltering priests in his house. He was beatified in 1929. *See* **England (Martyrs of)**.

Richard Leigh (alias Garth or Earth) (Bl) Aug 30
d. 1588. A Londoner, he was educated at Rheims and Rome, was ordained in 1586 and was executed at Tyburn together with St Margaret Ward and BB Edward Shelley, John Roche, Richard Flower and Richard Martin. He was beatified in 1929. *See* **England (Martyrs of)**.

Richard Martin (BB) M. L. Aug 30
d. 1588. He was a Shropshire landowner and was executed at Tyburn, London, for sheltering priests together with St Margaret Ward and BB Edward Shelley, John Roche, Richard Flower and Richard Leigh. He was beatified in 1929. *See* **England (Martyrs of)**.

Richard Newport (alias Smith) (Bl) M. P. May 30
d. 1612. From Harringworth in Northamptonshire, he was educated for the priesthood at Rome, ordained in 1597 and worked in the London district until his execution at Tyburn. *See* **England (Martyrs of)**.

Richard Pampuri (St) R. Mar 1
1897–1930. Born at Trivolzio near Pavia, Italy, he studied medicine before the First World War and was a paramedic during it. Afterwards he qualified as a surgeon and, wishing to combine the vocations of ministering to sick bodies and to needy souls, he helped poor people and catechized in his spare time. He was led to join the 'Hospitaller Order of St John of God' in 1927. He was canonized in 1989.

Richard Reynolds (1) (St) M. R. May 4
?1492–1535. From Devon, he studied at Cambridge, became a fellow of Corpus Christi College and was appointed university preacher in 1513. In the same year he became a Bridgettine monk at Syon Abbey near Isleworth, Middlesex, a recently-founded double house for nuns and monks famous for its spiritual and intellectual fervour. He refused to take the oath of spiritual supremacy demanded by King Henry VIII and was executed at Tyburn with three Carthusians. He was canonized in 1970. His community fled into exile, and is now in Devon. *See* **England (Martyrs of)**.

Richard Reynolds (alias Green) (2) (Bl) M. P. Jan 31
d. 1642. From Oxford, he was educated for the priesthood at Rheims, France, and at Valladolid and Seville, Spain. After his ordination in 1592 he returned to England and was on mission for nearly fifty years. He must have been an octogenarian when he was hanged at Tyburn with Bl Alban-Bartholomew Roe. He was beatified in 1929. *See* **England (Martyrs of)**.

Richard Sergeant (alias Lee or Long) (Bl) M. P. Apr 20
d. 1586. Born in Gloucestershire, he was ordained at Douai, France, and was a priest in London. He was executed at Tyburn with Bl William Thompson, and was beatified in 1987. *See* **England (Martyrs of)**.

Richard Simpson (Bl) M. P. Jun 24
d. 1588. Born near Ripon, Yorks, he was a convert Anglican minister who was probably an Oxford graduate. Ordained in Brussels in 1577, he was a priest in the North for three years and was caught travelling between

Lancashire and Derbyshire. He was executed at Derby with BB Nicholas Garlicx and Robert Ludlum, and was beatified in 1987. *See* **England (Martyrs of)**.

Richard Thirkeld (Thirkild) (Bl) M. P. May 29
d. 1583. From Co. Durham, he was educated at the Queen's College, Oxford, and as an old man completed his studies for the priesthood at Douai and Rheims, being ordained in 1579. He worked in Yorkshire and was executed at York, being beatified in 1886. *See* **England (Martyrs of)**.

Richard of Vaucelles (St) R(OCist). Jan 28
d. 1169. An English disciple of St Bernard of Clairvaux, he was made second abbot of Vaucelles near Cambrai, France.

Richard of Verdun (Bl) R(OSB). Jun 14
d. 1046. He was dean of the cathedral of Rheims, France, before becoming a Benedictine at St Vannes at Verdun. Later he was abbot at Arras. He was a friend of St Odilo of Cluny and of the emperor Henry III, and was nicknamed 'Gratia Dei' from his frequent habit of thanking God. His cultus is unconfirmed.

Richard Whiting (Bl) *see* **Benedictine Martyrs of the Reformation**

Richard de Wych (St) B. Apr 3
1197–1253. From Droitwich near Worcester, England, he studied at Oxford, Paris and Bologna before becoming chancellor of Oxford University in 1235. Then he was legal adviser to two archbishops of Canterbury, St Edmund Rich (with whom he shared exile in France) and St Boniface of Savoy. Having been ordained in France, he became bishop of Chichester in 1244 (although King Henry III sequestered his revenues for two years because the election was disputed). He died at Dover while preaching a crusade. Being remembered as a model pastor, he was canonized in 1262 and his pilgrimage shrine was at Chichester Cathedral until the Reformation. His attribute is a chalice lying on its side on the ground at his feet.

Richard Yaxley (Bl) M. P. Jul 7
1560–1589. Born at Boston, Lincs, he was ordained at Rheims in 1586, went to Oxford and was seized on his arrival with BB Humphrey Pritchard, Thomas Belson and George Nichols. They were executed together in Oxford and were beatified in 1987. *See* **England (Martyrs of)**.

Richardis, Empress (St) L. Sep 18
d. ?895. Daughter of a count of Alsace, France, in 862 she married the emperor Charles the Fat but nineteen years later was accused of adultery with the chancellor. She was vindicated but retired to the nunnery of Andlau which she had founded near Strasbourg, and died there. She has been claimed as a Benedictine oblate.

Richarius (Riquier) (St) R. Apr 26
d. ?645. From Celles near Amiens, France, he became a priest and was at the Frankish court and in England before founding an abbey in his native village. He was famous for ransoming those kidnapped by invading barbarians. After some years as abbot he resigned and spent the rest of his life as a hermit. His shrine was at St-Riquier, near Abbeville.

Richimir (St) R. Jan 17
d. ?715. From near Tours, France, he was helped by the bishop of Le Mans to found a monastery in that diocese, later named St-Rigomer-des-Bois after him.

Rictrude (St) R. May 12
d. 688. A Gascon noblewoman, she married St Adalbald d'Ostrevant and had four children who all became saints (Mauruntius, Eusebia, Clotsindis and Adalsindis). After her husband's murder she founded the nunnery of Marchiennes near Douai, France, with the help of St Amandus of Elnone, and was abbess there for forty years.

Rieul *see* Regulus

Rigobert (St) B. R. Jan 4
d. ?745. He was abbot of Orbais near Rheims, France, before he became archbishop of the latter place in 696. In 721 he was ejected by Charles Martel for opposing the sequestration of Church lands and returned to his abbey. Later he became a hermit, and died near Soissons.

Ringan *see* **Ninian**

Rioch (St) R. Aug 1
d. *c*480. He was allegedly a nephew of St Patrick and abbot of Innisboffin in Co. Longford, Ireland, but this is not certain.

Riquier *see* **Richarius**

Rita of Cascia (St) R(OSA). May 22
1381–1457. From Roccaporena near Cascia in Umbria, Italy, she married a brutal man who ended up being murdered. Her two sons swore a

vendetta against the killers, but she prayed that they would not persevere and they died shortly afterwards having expressed forgiveness. Then she entered an Augustinian nunnery at Cascia, where she suffered from a permanent maggoty ulcer on her forehead after a vision of Christ crowned with thorns. She was canonized in 1900, and is the patron of desperate or impossible problems. Her name is a diminutive of 'Margaret'.

Rita-of-the-Sorrowing-Virgin Pujalte Sánchez and Frances-of-the-Sacred-Heart Aldea Araujo (BB) MM. RR. Jul 20
d. 1936. The former, from near Alicante, Spain, joined the 'Sisters of Charity of the Sacred Heart of Jesus' in 1888 and was their superior-general from 1900 to 1928. Then she retired to St Susanna's College at Madrid. The latter was an orphan brought up at the same college who took vows in 1903 and became Bl Rita's general secretary. During the Spanish Civil War the college was attacked by an anti-clerical mob, and the two sick religious were misguidedly advised to take refuge in a nearby flat. Two hours after they did so they were seized, driven out of the city and shot. They were beatified in 1998. *See* **Spanish Civil War (Martyrs of)**.

Ritbert (St) R. Sep 15
d. *c*690. A disciple of St Ouen, he became abbot of a monastery at Varennes, France.

Rixius Varus (Rictiovarus) (St) M. Jul 6
d. ?260. According to the old Roman Martyrology in its entry for 'Lucy, Antoninus and Comps', he was a persecuting prefect who ordered the killing of hundreds of Christians before his conversion by Lucy and his martyrdom with her. He almost certainly never existed.

Rizzerio (Richerius) (Bl) R(OFM). Feb 7
d. 1236. From near Camerino in the Marches, Italy, he was a student at Bologna when he heard St Francis preaching. He at once became his disciple and friend and was present at his death. He later became Franciscan provincial of the Marches. His cultus was confirmed for Camerino in 1838.

Ro *see* **Maelrubha**

Robert *also see* **Rupert**

Robert Anderton (Bl) M. P. Apr 25
d. 1586. From Chorley, Lancs, he was educated at Brasenose College in Oxford before his conversion. Then he studied at Rheims, France, was ordained in1585 and was executed on the Isle of Wight in the following year. He was beatified in 1929. *See* **England (Martyrs of)**.

Robert of Arbrissel (Bl) R(OSB). Feb 24
d. 1117. From Arbrissel in Brittany, France, the son of a priest, he studied at the university of Paris and then became vicar-general at Rennes in 1085, but his preaching and attempts at reform were so unpopular there that he had to flee Brittany. In 1092 he became a hermit in the forest of Craon near Angers, and he founded the Augustinian monastery of La Roë there. However, Pope Urban II visited Angers in 1096 and commissioned him as an itinerant preacher. In 1099 he founded a Benedictine double monastery for monks and nuns at Fontevrault near Saumur, and this was the first house of a new congregation over which the abbess of Fontevrault had supreme jurisdiction. He died there.

Robert Bellarmine (St) B. Dr. R(SJ). Sep 17
1542–1621. From Montepulciano in Tuscany, Italy, he was educated by the Jesuits and joined them in 1560. From 1570 he taught Greek, Hebrew and theology at Louvain, Belgium, and became famous there as an effective polemicist against Protestantism. His opponents in the Netherlands hated him to the extent that his name was later given to a style of pot-bellied pottery wine jug. From 1576 he taught in Rome, and was the provincial superior at Naples before being made cardinal in 1598 and archbishop of Capua in 1602. Recalled to Rome in 1605, he became head of the Vatican library and theological adviser to the pope. His interventions against Galileo were disastrously mistaken. He was canonized in 1930, and declared a doctor of the Church in the following year.

Robert Bickerdyke (Bl) M. L. (Aug ?)
d. 1586. Born near Knaresborough, Yorks, while apprenticed at York he was spotted drinking in a pub with a known priest and paying for the beer. This was regarded as 'harbouring a priest' and, after three trials, he was executed at York on an uncertain date. He was beatified in 1987 *see* **England (Martyrs of)**.

Robert of Bury St Edmunds (St) M. L. Mar 25
d. 1181. A young boy, he was allegedly crucified by Jews on Good Friday at Bury St

Edmunds in Suffolk, England. His shrine was established at the Benedictine abbey there. The story is a common anti-semitic legend and the cultus was never approved (the abbey was exempt from the authority of the local bishop).

Robert Dalby (Bl) M. P. Mar 15
d. 1589. From Hemingborough near Selby, Yorks, he became an Anglican minister but converted and was ordained priest at Rheims, France, in 1588. He was hanged at York in the following year. *See* **England (Martyrs of)**.

Robert Dibdale (Bl) M. P. Aug 10
d. 1586. Born at Stratford-upon-Avon, he was ordained at Rheims, France, and became chaplain at Denham to Sir George Peckham. He was executed at Tyburn with BB John Adams and John Love and was beatified in 1987. *See* **England (Martyrs of)**.

Robert Drury (Bl) M. P. Feb 26
1568–1607. A Buckinghamshire landowner, he studied at Rheims, France, and at the new college at Valladolid, Spain, being ordained there in 1595. He was a priest in London, was arrested near Fleet Street and was executed at Tyburn. He was beatified in 1987. *See* **England (Martyrs of)**.

Robert Flower (Bl) R. Sep 24
d. ?1218 or 1235. From York, England, he became a postulant at the Cistercian abbey of Newminster, but left and became a hermit in a cave by the river Nidd near Knaresborough, Yorks. His local cultus was not confirmed.

Robert of Frassinoro (St) R(OSB). Jun 8
d. *p*1070. He was abbot of the Benedictine monastery of Frassinoro near Modena, Italy.

Robert Grissold (Bl) *see* **John Sugar and Robert Grissold**

Robert Gruthuysen of Bruges (Bl) R(OCist). Apr 29
d. 1157. From Bruges, Belgium, as a disciple of St Bernard he became a monk at Clairvaux, France, in 1131, and was made the first Cistercian abbot of Dunes near Dunkirk in 1139. In 1153 he succeeded St Bernard as abbot of Clairvaux. His cultus among the Cistercians is unconfirmed.

Robert Guérin du Rocher (Bl) *see* **September (Martyrs of)**

Robert Hardesty (Bl) M. L. Sep 24
d. 1589. From York, possibly a clothier, he was seized while acting as a guide to Bl Robert Dibdale on the road to Ripon. Since they were not caught together he was charged with having previously aided Catholic prisoners at York Castle and was executed at York. He was beatified in 1987. *See* **England (Martyrs of)**.

Robert Johnson (Bl) M. P. May 28
d. 1582. From Shropshire, he was educated at Rome and Douai, France, was ordained in 1576 and was able to work in London for two years before being executed at Tyburn. He was beatified in 1886. *See* **England (Martyrs of)**.

Robert Lawrence (St) M. R(OCart). May 4
d. 1535. Prior of the Carthusian monastery at Beauvale, Notts, he was executed at Tyburn, London, with SS Augustine Webster and John Houghton (fellow Carthusian priors) and with St Richard Reynolds and Bl John Haile. He was canonized in 1970. *See* **England (Martyrs of)**.

Robert Le Bis (Bl) *see* **September (Martyrs of)**

Robert Ludlum (Bl). M. P. Jun 24
d. 1588. Born in Derbyshire, he studied at Oxford and was ordained at Rheims, France, in 1581. After being on the mission for six years in the North of England he was captured at Padley Hall with Bl Nicholas Garlicx and executed at Derby with him and Bl Robert Dibdale. He was beatified in 1987. *See* **England (Martyrs of)**.

Robert Mayler (Bl) *see* **Matthew Lambert and Comps**

Robert Middleton (Bl) M. R(SJ). Apr 3
1571–1601. Born in York (a relative of St Margaret Clitherow), he converted when he was eighteen and was ordained at Rome in 1598. He was captured in the Fylde (near what is now Blackpool), and there followed an attempt to free him by ambush in which Bl Thurstan Hunt was also captured They were executed together at Lancaster. He became a Jesuit in prison and was beatified in 1987. *See* **England (Martyrs of)**.

Robert of Molesmes (St) R(OSB). F. Apr 29
1027–1110. From near Troyes in Champagne, France, he became a Benedictine monk at Moutier-la-Celle and was made abbot of Tonnerre. He left this monastery to become the superior of some hermits in the forest of Collan, and founded with them the monastery of Molesmes near Tonnerre in 1075. As the

community grew he became dissatisfied with the standard of observance and withdrew to a hermitage at Or. He was recalled but left again, this time in the company of SS Stephen Harding and Alberic. In 1098 they founded at Cîteaux a new monastery which corresponded more with their monastic ideals and he was the first superior, but the monks of Molesmes appealed to Rome and obtained his recall as their abbot, which he remained until his death. He is counted as one of the founders of the Cistercians.

Robert Morton (Bl) M. P. Aug 28
d. 1588. From Bawtry, Yorks, he studied for the priesthood at Rheims, France, and Rome, was ordained in 1587 but was quickly apprehended on his return to England and executed at Lincoln's Inn Fields, London. He was beatified in 1929. *See* **England (Martyrs of)**.

Robert of Newminster (St) R(OCist). Jun 7
1100–1159. He was a parish priest in north Yorkshire before becoming a Benedictine monk at Whitby, but in 1132 he joined the new reformed monastery at Fountains, founded from St Mary's Abbey at York. This quickly became Cistercian. Newminster Abbey at Morpeth, Northumberland, was founded from it in 1137, and he became the first abbot. His shrine there was a centre of pilgrimage and his abbey became important, but few remnants survive.

Robert Nutter (Bl) M. R(OP). Jul 26
d. 1600. From Burnley, Lancs, the brother of Bl John Nutter, he was ordained at Rheims, France, in 1582, was in the Tower of London by 1584 and was deported back to France. Then he acted as an escort for priests crossing the Channel to England, but was captured on board ship off Gravesend and sent to the concentration camp at Wisbech. He joined the Dominicans there before escaping and going back to Burnley. Re-captured, he was executed at Lancaster with Bl Edward Thwing. He was beatified in 1987. *See* **England (Martyrs of)**.

Robert Salt (Bl) M. R(OCart). Jun 9
d. 1537. A Carthusian lay brother at the London Charterhouse, he was starved to death with six of his brethren in Newgate prison at the instigation of King Henry VIII. He was beatified in 1886. *See* **England (Martyrs of)** and **Carthusian Martyrs**.

Robert Southwell (St) M. R(SJ). Feb 21
1561–1595. From Horsham St Faith's in Norfolk, when aged seventeen he became a Jesuit at Rome and worked as a priest in London from 1584 to 1592. He was betrayed and spent three years in prison (being tortured thirteen times) before being executed at Tyburn. He was a notable religious poet. He was canonized in 1970. *See* **England (Martyrs of)**.

Robert Sutton (1) (Bl) M. P. Jul 27
d. 1588. Born in Burton-upon-Trent, he studied at Oxford and became the Anglican rector of Lutterworth, Leics. He was converted in 1577, was ordained at Rheims and was a priest in Staffordshire. He was executed at Stafford and was beatified in 1987. *See* **England (Martyrs of)**.

Robert Sutton (2) (Bl) M. L. Oct 5
d. 1588. From Kegworth, Leics, he was a schoolmaster in London and was hanged at Clerkenwell for having converted to the Catholic church. He was beatified in 1929. *See* **England (Martyrs of)**.

Robert of Syracuse (St) R(OSB). Apr 25
d. *c*1000. He was abbot of a Benedictine monastery founded at Syracuse, Sicily, after the conquest of the island by the Normans from the Muslims.

Robert Thorpe (Bl) M. P. May 31
1591. A Yorkshireman who was ordained at Rheims, France, he was a priest in his native county for six years before his capture while saying a Palm Sunday Mass at Menthorp. A servant was spotted collecting flowering sallow for use as palm, and this tipped off the pursuivants. He was executed at York with Bl Thomas Watkinson and was beatified in 1987. *See* **England (Martyrs of)**.

Robert de Turlande (St) R(OSB). Apr 17
d. 1067. From the Auvergne, France, he became a priest and canon at Brioude where he founded a hospice. After spending some time at Cluny under St Odilo he made a pilgrimage to Rome and then became a hermit near Brioude, where he was joined by many disciples. Thus was founded the great Benedictine abbey of Chaise-Dieu (housing some three hundred monks) and this became the mother-house of a Benedictine congregation of some three hundred monasteries.

Robert Watkinson (Bl) M. P. Apr 20
1579–1602. From Hemingborough, Yorks, he studied for the priesthood at Douai, France, and Rome and was ordained in 1602. He was immediately captured on his return to England and executed at Tyburn, London. *See* **England (Martyrs of)**.

Robert Widmerpool and Robert Wilcox (BB) MM. Oct 1
d. 1588. The former was from a Nottinghamshire landowning family and was a schoolmaster in Kent after having been educated at Oxford. The former was from Chester, studied for the priesthood at Rheims, France, and was ordained there in 1585. They were executed together at Canterbury and beatified in 1929. *See* **England (Martyrs of)**.

Robustian (St) M. May 24
? Nothing is known about this early martyr of Milan, Italy, who is possibly a duplicate of the Robustian of the next entry.

Robustian and Mark (SS) MM. Aug 31
? They had an early cultus at Milan, Italy, but nothing is known about them.

Roch (St) L. Aug 16
1350–1380. According to his legendary biography he was from Montpellier, France, and went to Italy as a pilgrim. There he nursed those suffering from plague in various places before dying at Angera on Lake Maggiore (he did not return home to die in prison under suspicion of being a spy, as alleged). He is invoked against epidemic diseases. In Italy he is Rocco; in Spain, Roque; in Scotland Rollock, Rollox or Seemirookie. He is depicted dressed as a pilgrim with a plague bubo (boil) on his thigh, sometimes with a dog licking it.

Roch (Roque) Gonzalez (St) *see* **Paraguay (Martyrs of)**

Roderick *see* **Ruderic**

Roderick Aguilar Alemán (St) *see* **Mexico (Martyrs of)**

Roding (Rouin) (St) R. Sep 17
d. *c*690. An Irish missionary monk, he preached in Germany and joined the abbey of Tholey near Trier. Disturbed by the visits of his converts, he left and became a hermit in the forest of Argonne where he became the abbot-founder of Beaulieu.

Rodolf *see* **Rudolf**

Rodrigo *see* **Roderick**

Rogatian (St) *see* **Castor, Victor and Rogatian**

Rogatian (St) *see* **Donatian and Rogatian**

St Roch, Aug 16

Rogatian (St) *see* **Saturninus, Dativus and Comps**

Rogatian and Felicissimus (SS) MM? Oct 26
d. 256. They were a priest and a layman at Carthage, Roman Africa, and were described by St Cyprian as having 'witnessed a good confession for Christ'. This perhaps referred to their martyrdom.

Rogatus (St) *see* **Aresius, Rogatus and Comps**

Rogatus (St) *see* **Liberatus, Boniface and Comps**

Rogatus (St) *see* **Lucius, Rogatus and Comps**

Rogatus (St) *see* **Zoticus, Rogatus and Comps**

Rogatus and Rogatus (St) *see* **Cyril, Rogatus and Comps**

Rogatus, Successus and Comps (SS) MM. Mar 28
? They are listed as eighteen martyrs of Roman Africa.

Rogellus and Servusdei (SS) MM. Sep 16
d. 852. A monk of Cordoba, Spain, and his young disciple, they belonged to the 'martyr movement' and were executed for invading the city's Friday Mosque and denouncing Islam.

Roger Cadwallador (Bl) M. P. Aug 27
d. 1610. A farmer's son from Stretton Sugwas, Herefordshire, he studied at Rheims, France, and Valladolid, Spain, and was ordained at the latter place in 1593. He was a priest in Herefordshire and Powys for 16 years before being seized near Hereford and executed at Leominster. He was beatified in 1987. *See* **England (Martyrs of)**.

Roger Dickenson (Bl) M. P. Jul 7
d. 1591. From Lincoln, he was educated for the priesthood at Rheims, France, and ordained there in 1583. He was hanged at Winchester with Bl Ralph Milner, a layman who had sheltered him, and was beatified in 1929. *See* **England (Martyrs of)**.

Roger Filcock (Bl) M. R(SJ). Feb 27
d. 1601. From Sandwich in Kent, he studied at Rheims, France, and was ordained at Valladolid, Spain, in 1597. After being a priest in London for two years he was about to leave for the Jesuit noviciate when he was arrested, but he became a Jesuit in prison. He was executed at Tyburn with St Anne Line and Bl Mark Barkworth and was beatified in 1987. *See* **England (Martyrs of)**.

Roger James (Bl) *see* **Benedictine Martyrs of the Reformation**

Roger Lefort (Bl) B. Mar 1
d. 1367. A nobleman of the Limousin, France, he became a jurist and while a sub-deacon was elected bishop of Orléans in 1321. In 1328 he transferred to Limoges, and to Bourges in 1343. He introduced a liturgical feast in honour of Our Lady's conception, and in his will left all his property for the education of poor boys. His cultus is unconfirmed.

Roger Wrenn (Bl) *see* **John Thules and Roger Wrenn**

Roland de' Medici (Bl) R. Sep 15
d. 1386. Related to the famous ruling family of Florence, he lived without any shelter for twenty-six years in the forests around Parma, Italy. He died at Borgone and had his cultus confirmed for Borgo San Donnino in 1852.

Rolende (St) L. May 13
End C7th. A French princess, she died while on a pilgrimage to Cologne and was buried at Gerpinnes, Belgium. She is venerated there.

Rollock *see* **Roch**

Romana (St) R. Feb 23
?306–?324. According to the legendary biography of Pope St Sylvester, she was a Roman maiden who lived as a hermit in a cave (or ruined cellar) on the banks of the Tiber.

Romanus (St) *see* **Samosata (Martyrs of)**

Romanus and Barulas (SS) MM. Nov 18
d. 304. The former was a young deacon martyred at Antioch, Syria, in the reign of Diocletian. His companion was listed in the old Roman Martyrology as a young boy, but nothing is known about him.

Romanus and David *see* **Boris and Gleb**

Romanus Adame Rosales (St) *see* **Mexico (Martyrs of)**

Romanus Aibara (Bl) M. T(OP). Sep 8
d. 1628. A Japanese Dominican tertiary, he was beheaded at Nagasaki with his father Paul and brother Leo. *See* **Dominic Castellet and Comps** and **Japan (Martyrs of)**.

Romanus of Auxerre (St) M. B. Oct 6
d. ?564. The existence of this alleged bishop of Auxerre, France, is doubtful.

Romanus of Condat (St) R. Feb 28
d. *c*460. A Gallo-Roman, when aged thirty-five he went to live as a hermit in the Jura mountains, France, and was joined by St Lupicinus, his brother. They attracted disciples and thus were founded the abbeys of Condat (later known as St-Oyend) and Leuconne. They were joint superiors of these, and also founded the nunnery of La Beaume (afterwards St-Romain-de-la-Roche) where their sister was superior.

Romanus of Le Mans (St) P. Nov 24
d. 385. A Gallo-Roman missionary priest, he worked along the estuary of the Gironde north of Bordeaux, France, and died at Blaye. He is a patron of sailors.

Romanus the Melodist (St) P. Oct 1
d. *c*540. From Syria, he was a deacon at Beirut before becoming a priest at Constantinople. He was the greatest Byzantine hymnographer, and allegedly wrote a thousand hymns. Some eighty of these are extant, and some may be misattributed. Their literary quality is very high.

Romanus Motoyama
(Bl) M. L. Nov 27
d. 1619. A Japanese layman related to the rulers of Hirado-jima, he was born at Omura and beheaded at Nagasaki. *See* **Thomas Koteda and Comps** and **Japan (Martyrs of)**.

Romanus of Nepi (St) M. B. Aug 24
C1st? He was allegedly a disciple of St Ptolemy of Nepi, succeeded him as bishop of that place in Tuscany, Italy, and was himself martyred.

Romanus Ostiarius (St) M. Aug 9
d. 258. There are no reliable data concerning him. He was martyred at about the same time as St Laurence, and one legend describes him as a soldier converted by the latter. He was probably a Roman church doorkeeper, as is indicated by his surname. His cultus was confined to local calendars in 1969.

Romanus of Rouen (St) B. Oct 23
d. ?640. A Frankish nobleman and courtier, he became bishop of Rouen, France, in ?629 and had a special concern for prisoners. He also set about eliminating paganism from his diocese, especially in rural areas (a task not seriously attempted by his Gallo-Roman predecessors).

Romanus of Subiaco (St) R. May 22
d. *c*560. According to the biography of St Benedict in the *Dialogues* of St Gregory the Great, he was a monk (not an abbot) in a monastery near Subiaco who discovered St Benedict as a hermit in a cave when the latter first fled the world. Thereupon he brought him food and instructed him in the monastic life. There is no other historical evidence concerning him.

Romanus Touceda Fernández (Bl) *see* **Hospitaller Martyrs of Spain**

Romaric (St) R. Dec 8
d. 653. A Merovingian nobleman and courtier, he became a monk and disciple of St Amatus at Luxeuil, France, and founded the double monastery on his estate on the River Moselle later named Remiremont after him. St Amatus was the first abbot and St Romaric the second. The Divine Office was celebrated there continuously, the monastics taking turns in choir in seven shifts.

Rome (Martyrs of) (SS)
Despite its importance in the Church as a whole, the Church at Rome was marginal to the general life of the city for much of the imperial period. Rome was a stronghold of paganism until the C5th, and Christianity was probably regarded with suspicion and contempt by most of the population there as well as by the imperial government. Thus the Church was especially vulnerable to persecution. Apart from the **Protomartyrs of Rome** (q.v.), the old Roman Martyrology listed sixteen anonymous groups of martyrs, as follows:-

Mar 25
? A group of two hundred and sixty-two martyrs, they were probably identical with those in the year 269.

Jun 17
? A group of two hundred and sixty-two, they were alleged to have been martyred in the reign of Diocletian and to have been buried on the Via Salaria but were apparently identical with the above and with those of the year 269.

Mar 14
d. ?67. According to the unreliable acta of SS Processus and Martinian, forty-seven were baptized by St Peter and martyred the same day in the reign of Nero.

Jul 2
d. ?68. Three soldiers, according to the legend they were converted during the execution of St Paul and were themselves martyred.

Apr 10
d. ?115. According to the probably fictional narrative, several criminals imprisoned with Pope St Alexander were baptized by him and were subsequently taken to Ostia and put on board an old boat which was then taken out to sea and scuttled.

Mar 2
d. 219. A large number were martyred in the reign of Alexander Severus by the prefect Ulpian.

Feb 10
d. ?250. Ten soldiers were martyred on the Via Lavicana.

Mar 4
d. ?260. Nine hundred martyrs were buried in the catacombs of Callistus on the Appian Way, concerning whom no details are extant.

Jan 13
d. 262. Forty soldiers were martyred on the Via Lavicana in the reign of Gallienus.

Mar 1
d.269. Two hundred and sixty were put to work as slaves in sand-pits on the Salarian Way and then used for archery practice in the amphitheatre in the reign of Claudius II.

Oct 25
d. 269. Forty-six soldiers and one hundred and twenty-one civilians were martyred in the reign of Claudius II.

Aug 10
d. 274. One hundred and sixty-five were martyred in the reign of Aurelian.

Jan 2
d. ?303. Many were martyred in the reign of Diocletian for refusing to hand over sacred texts.

Aug 5
d. 303. Twenty-three were martyred on the Salarian Way in the reign of Diocletian.

Dec 22
d. ?303. A group of thirty were martyred in the reign of Diocletian and buried on the Via Lavicana 'between the two laurels'.

Jan 1
d. ?304. Thirty soldiers were martyred in the reign of Diocletian.

Romedius (St) Jan 15
C4th. He was a hermit at Tavo near Trent, Italy, where his shrine is now established. His cultus was confirmed for Trent in 1907.

Romeo (Romaeus) (Bl) R(OC). Mar 4
d. 1380. An Italian Carmelite lay brother, he accompanied St Avertanus on pilgrimage to the Holy Land from Limoges, France, but they both apparently died of plague at Lucca, Italy. His cultus was confirmed for the Carmelites in 1842.

Romuald (St) R(OSB Cam). F. Jun 19
?951–1027. A nobleman of Ravenna, Italy, in his youth he saw his father commit a murder and resolved to make vicarious atonement by becoming a monk at the Benedictine abbey of Classe near Ravenna. In 996 he was elected abbot, but he resigned in 999 and thereupon led a wandering life in northern Italy and southern France, founding hermitages and monasteries. The best known of these is Camaldoli near Arezzo, Italy, founded in 1009, which became the mother-house of a Benedictine congregation combining the eremitic life of an Eastern laura with the cenobitic monachism of the West. He made repeated attempts to undertake missionary work among the Magyars and Slavs. He died at Val di Castro near Camaldoli.

Romula, Redempta and Herundo (SS) RR. Jul 23
d. *c*580. Three Roman maidens, they lived an austere life of prayer and solitude near the church of St Mary Major in Rome. St Gregory the Great had high regard for them.

Romulus (St) M. Sep 5
d. ?112. An court official of the Roman emperor Trajan, he was allegedly whipped and beheaded after rebuking him for persecuting Christians while on campaign at Melitene in Armenia.

Romulus (St) *see* **Donatus, Secundian and Comps**

Romulus (St) *see* **Timolaus and Comps**

Romulus and Conindrus (SS) BB. Dec 28
d. *c*450. They were two missionary bishops on the Isle of Man, allegedly contemporaries of St Patrick.

Romulus and Secundus (SS) MM. Mar 24
? They were listed as two brothers who were martyred in Roman Africa. Secundus also appears as Secundulus.

Romulus of Fiesole and Comps (SS) MM. Jul 6
d. ?90. According to his fictitious acta he was made first bishop of Fiesole near Florence, Italy, by St Peter and was martyred with several companions in the reign of Domitian.

Romulus (Remo) of Genoa (St) B. Oct 13
d. *p*641. There is no reliable evidence concerning this bishop of Genoa, Italy. He died at the Riviera town later named San Remo after him.

Romulus of Saissy (St) R. Mar 27
d. *c*730. He was abbot of St Baudilius's Abbey near Nîmes, France, but Arab raids drove the community away and they settled in a ruined monastery at Saissy-les-Bois near Nevers.

Ronald (St) M. L. Aug 20
d. 1158. An earl of Orkney, Scotland, he built the cathedral of St Magnus at Kirkwall but was assassinated by rebels and was then venerated as a martyr.

Ronan (St) B. R. Jun 1
C6th? He was a missionary bishop in Cornwall, England, and Brittany, France, but there are about a dozen other Celtic saints listed of this name and the evidence is very confused. *See* **Rumon**.

Roque *see* **Roch**

Rosalia-Clotilde-of-St-Pelagia Bès (Bl) *see* **Orange (Martyrs of)**

Rosalia of Palermo (St) R. Sep 4
d. ?1160. According to her tomb inscription, discovered with her relics in 1624, she was a hermit in a cave on Mt Coschina near Bivona and later in another cave on Mt Pellegrino near Palermo, Sicily. She is a patron of the latter place. The old Roman Martyrology listed her twice in error, also on July 15.

Rosalia du Verdier de la Sorinière (Bl) *see* **William Repin and Comps**

Rose Chen (Anjie) (St) *see* **Teresa Chen (Jinjie) and Rose Chen (Anjie)**

Rose-Philippine Duchesne *see* **Philippine Duchesne**

Rose Fan (Hui) (St) M. L. Aug 15
1855–1900. From Fan in Hebei, China, she became a schoolteacher but her school was closed during the Boxer Uprising and she hid in the village's fields. She was betrayed, however, and a gang of Boxers slashed her with knives and threw her into a river to drown. *See* **China (Martyrs of)**.

Rose Flores of Lima
(St) T(OP). Aug 23
1586–1617. Born of Spanish parents at Lima in Peru, from childhood she set out to imitate St Catherine of Siena while living at her family home as a Dominican tertiary. Her physical austerities were such as to amount to self-torture, and she suffered from mental as well as physical sickness. She was, however, favoured with extraordinary mystical graces. She was the first American to be canonized (in 1671) and is the patron of South America. Her attribute is a thorny rose or roses, and she is sometimes depicted with the Holy Infant.

Rose Kim (St) *see* **Korea (Martyrs of)**

Rose Quenion (Bl) *see* **William Repin and Comps**

Rose-of-St-Xavier Talieu (Bl) *see* **Orange (Martyrs of)**

Rose of Viterbo (St) L. Sep 4
1234–1252. Born at Viterbo, Italy, her family was poor. Even as a little girl she received mystical graces, and used to speak out in the streets against the Ghibellines (the anti-papal faction) and in favour of the pope. This caused her and her family to be expelled from the city for a time. She tried to join the Poor Clare nunnery in the city and was repeatedly refused, but she was buried there after her death by order of the pope. She was canonized in 1457.

Rose Venerini (Bl) R. F. May 7
1656–1728. After her fiancé died she had to start caring for her widowed mother, so she began to teach religion to women and girls at her home in Verona, Italy, and opened a free school there in 1685 with three companions. This was the beginning of the 'Verona Sisters', which had forty houses by the time she died at Rome. Their special charism is in maintaining liason between school, child and parents. She was beatified in 1952.

Rose Zhao (Guo) (St) M. L. Jul 20
d. 1900. She was a victim of the Boxers in south-eastern Hebei, China. *See* **China (Martyrs of)**.

Roseline de Villeneuve
(Bl) R(OCart). Jan 17
d. 1329. A noblewoman from near Fréjus in Provence, France, she became a Carthusian nun at Bertrand and then prioress of Celle-Roubaud. She had frequent visions and other mystical graces, and her cultus was confirmed in 1851.

Rosendo *see* **Rudesind**

Rosius (St) *see* **Priscus II of Capua and Comps**

Rosula (St) *see* **Crescentian, Victor and Comps**

Roswinda (St) *see* **Einhilde and Roswinda**

Rotrude (St) R. Jun 22
d. ?869. Her shrine was at St Bertin's Abbey at St Omer, France, and she was allegedly a close relative of Charlemagne, but her cultus dates from the C11th and she probably never existed.

Rouin *see* **Rodingus**

Ruadan (Ruadhan, Rodan) (St) R. Apr 15
d. ?584. He was one of the leading disciples of St Finian of Clonard, Ireland, and founded the monastery of Lothra in Co. Tipperary, but the data concerning him are seriously confused and may refer to more than one person of this name.

Ruben-of Jesus López Aguilar (Bl) *see* **Hospitaller Martyrs of Spain**

Ruderic (Roderick) and Solomon (Salomon) (SS) MM. Mar 13
d. 857. The former was a priest at Cordoba, Spain, who was accused by his brother of apostasy from Islam. In prison he met the latter, accused of the same charge, and they were executed together.

Rudesind (Rosendo) (St) B. R(OSB). Mar 1
907–977. A nobleman of Galicia, Spain, he became bishop of Mondoñedo when aged eighteen but was transferred to Compostela after the deposition of an unworthy bishop there. He had to organize resistance to raids by Norsemen and Muslims before being ejected in turn by the one deposed, after which he founded the Benedictine abbey of Celanova, became a monk there and founded other monasteries. He died as second abbot of Celanova and was canonized in 1195.

Rudolf Acquaviva and Comps (BB) MM. RR(SJ). Jul 27
d. 1583. Born at Atri near Pescara, Italy, in 1550, a nephew of a Jesuit general, he became a Jesuit himself and taught philosophy at Goa in India from 1578 to 1580. Goa was the centre of the Portuguese mercantile empire in the Far East and of corresponding missionary activity. He was at the court of the Mughal emperor Akbar from 1580, and was killed with four fellow missionaries on the island of Salsette next to Bombay, which the Portuguese were trying to bring under their rule. The others were Alphonsus Pacheco, Anthony Francisco, Francis Aranha and Peter Berna. They were beatified in 1893.

Rudolf of Gubbio (St) B. R(OSB). Oct 17
d. ?1066. A monk of Fontavellana under St Peter Damian, he became bishop of Gubbio, Italy, in 1061 while still a young man and was famous for his unselfishness.

Rudolf of Vallombrosa (Bl) R(OSB Vall). Aug 1
d. 1076. He was guest-master at the abbey of Vallombrosa near Florence, Italy, when the founder St John Gualbert was abbot, and succeeded him as abbot. His cultus is unconfirmed.

Ruellin (St) B. Feb 28
C6th. He succeeded St Tudwal as bishop of Treguier in Brittany, France.

Ruffin (St) *see* **Wulfhad and Ruffin**

Rufillus (Ruffilius) (St) B. Jul 18
d. 382. He was the alleged first bishop of Forlimpopoli near Forli in Emilia, Italy.

Rufina (St) *see* **Justa and Rufina**

Rufina (St) *see* **Theodotus of Caesarea and Ammia**

Rufina, Moderata, Romana, Secundus and Seven Comps (SS)MM. Apr 6
C4th. They were allegedly martyred at Sirmium (now Srem Mitrovica, Serbia).

Rufina and Secunda (SS) VV. Jul 10
d. 257. They were martyred in the reign of Valerian and buried on the Aurelian Way. Their acta are unreliable.

Rufinian (St) *see* **Rufinus and Rufinian**

Rufinus (St) *see* **Epiphanius, Donatus and Comps**

Rufinus (St) *see* **Macarius, Rufinus and Comps**

Rufinus (St) *see* **Valerius and Rufinus**

Rufinus, Mark, Valerius and Comps (SS) MM. Nov 16
? They were martyrs of Roman Africa.

Rufinus and Martia (SS) MM. Jun 21
? They were early martyrs at Syracuse, Sicily.

Rufinus and Rufinian (SS) MM. Sep 9
? They are listed as brothers who were martyred together, but nothing else is known.

Rufinus and Secundus (SS) MM. Jul 10
? These Roman martyrs were buried on the Via Cornelia and had their relics transferred to the Lateran basilica in the C12th. Nothing is known about them. Since 1969 their cultus has been confined to local calendars.

Rufinus, Silvanus and Vitalicus (SS) MM. Sep 4
? They are listed as three children who were among a large group of martyrs at Ancyra, Asia Minor, (now Ankara in Turkey).

Rufinus of Assisi (St) M. Jul 30
? He was an early martyr at Assisi, Italy.

Rufinus of Capua (St) B. Aug 27
C5th. He was a bishop of Capua, Italy, and has his shrine in the cathedral there.

Rufinus Lasheras Aizcorbe (Bl) *see* **Hospitaller Martyrs of Spain**

Rufinus of Mantua (St) P? Aug 19
? He has an ancient cultus at Mantua, Italy, but nothing is known about him except that he may have been a priest.

Rufinus of the Marsi and Comps (SS) MM. Aug 11
? He is listed in the old Roman Martyrology as 'bishop of the Marsi', but may be the same as St Rufinus of Assisi. Nothing is known about his companions.

Rufus (St) *see* **Cyril, Aquila and Comps**

Rufus (St) *see* **Hermogenes of Melitene and Comps**

Rufus (St) *see* **Paul, Tatta and Comps**

Rufus and Carpophorus (SS) MM. Aug 27
d. 295. They were martyred in the reign of Diocletian. Their acta are unreliable and nothing is known about them.

Rufus and Zosimus (SS) MM. Dec 18
d. ?107. From Philippi in Macedonia, Greece, they were taken to Rome with St Ignatius of Antioch and thrown to the wild animals in the amphitheatre two days before the latter's own martyrdom.

Rufus of Avignon (St) B. Nov 12
d. *c*200. Allegedly the first bishop of Avignon, France, he certainly existed but the extant biographies are unhistorical.

Rufus of Capua (St) M. Aug 27
? The old Roman Martyrology listed him as a bishop of Capua, Italy, and disciple of St Apollinaris of Ravenna, but he is either a duplicate of Rufus the companion of Carpophorus (not a bishop) or of Rufinus of Capua.

Rufus of Glendalough (St) B? R. Apr 2
C6th? He was a hermit at Glendalough in Co. Wicklow, Ireland, where he was buried, and may have been a bishop.

Rufus Ishimoto (Bl) M. L. Sep 10
1622. A Japanese layman, he was beheaded at Nagasaki in the 'Great Martyrdom'. *See* **Charles Spinola and Comps** and **Japan (Martyrs of)**.

Rufus of Metz (St) B. Nov 7
d. *c*400. He was bishop of Metz, France, for about twenty-nine years, and is perhaps identical with the Rufus of Metz mentioned in 386 in connection within the Priscillianist controversy.

Rufus of Rome (1) (St) B? Nov 21
d. *c*90. He is mentioned by St Paul in Rom 16:13, and a guess is that he was the son of Simon of Cyrene mentioned in Mk 15:21. A later tradition makes him a bishop in the East.

Rufus of Rome (2) and Comps (SS) MM. Nov 28
d. 304. A Roman, he was martyred with his entire household in the reign of Diocletian.

Rule *see* **Regulus**

Rumold (Rumbold, Rombauld) (St) M. B. R. Jun 24
d. ?775. As far as can be ascertained from his unreliable biography he was a monk, probably an Anglo-Saxon, who became a missionary bishop and worked under St Willibrord in Holland and Brabant. He was murdered near Mechelen near Brussels, Belgium, and is patron of the cathedral there. The old Roman Martyrology alleged that he was an Irish bishop of Dublin, which seems to be a confusion with another of the same name.

Rumon (St) B? R? Aug 30
C6th? Allegedly a missionary bishop, he had his shrine in Tavistock Abbey, Devon, and is also patron of three villages called Ruan in Cornwall. Nothing is known about him, and various legends confuse him with other saints named Ronan and Ruadan.

Rumwold (St) L. Aug 28
d. ?650. According to his weird legend, he was a three-day-old baby prince of Northumbria who, immediately after baptism, spoke like an adult in making a profession of faith and then died at King's Sutton in Northants. He had a popular cultus centred on Brackley, Northants,

and Buckingham before the Reformation, but the story is possibly a fictional tale in defence of infant baptism.

Rupert and Bertha (SS) RR. May 15
C9th. A young nobleman and his mother, they became hermits on a hill near Bingen, Germany, later named Rupertsberg after him. St Hildegard fostered their cultus.

Rupert Mayer (Bl) R(SJ). Nov 3
1876–1945. Born in Stuttgart, Germany, he became a priest at Rottenburg in 1899 but joined the Jesuits a year later. From 1906 to 1912 he worked in various parts of Germany, noting the social effects of rapid industrialization, and became the chaplain for new immigrants to Munich in danger of losing touch with the Church. In 1939 the Nazis sent him to Sachsenhausen but did not want him to become a martyr and put him in isolation in the Benedictine abbey of Ettal instead. He died there of a stroke and was beatified in 1987.

Rupert of Ottobeuren
(Bl) R(OSB). Aug 15
d. 1145. He was prior of St George's Abbey in the Black Forest, Germany, before transferring to the Bavarian monastery of Ottobeuren as abbot in 1102. He introduced the Hirschau reform there, and the abbey prospered during his long abbacy. His cultus is unconfirmed.

Rupert (Hrodbert, Robert) of Salzburg (St) B. R. Mar 27
d. ?717. Apparently from France, he became missionary bishop at Worms, Germany, and worked at Regensburg and down the Danube. The Duke of Bavaria gave him the ruined town of Iuvavum which he rebuilt as Salzburg, Austria, becoming the first archbishop and founding St Peter's Abbey (with school and church attached) and the nunnery of Nonnberg, for which he made his niece St Erentrude abbess. He is venerated as an apostle of Bavaria and Austria.

Rustica (St) *see* **Donata and Comps**

Rusticus (St) *see* **Dionysius of Paris and Comps**

Rusticus (St) *see* **Firmus and Rusticus**

Rusticus (St) *see* **Liberatus, Boniface and Comps**

Rusticus of Cahors (St) M. B. Aug 19
d. 629. From Albi, France, he was archdeacon at Rodez before becoming bishop of Cahors in 622. He was killed by malefactors and thrown into a river, being succeeded by his brother St Desiderius.

Rusticus of Clermont (St) B. Sep 24
d. 446. He became bishop of Clermont-Ferrand, France, in 426.

Rusticus of Narbonne (St) B. Oct 26
d. ?462. A monk of Lérins, he became bishop of Narbonne, France, and was present at the council of Ephesus in 431.

Rusticus of Sirmium (St) M. Aug 9
C4th? He was martyred at Sirmium, (now Srem Mitrovica, Serbia).

Rusticus of Trier (St) B. Oct 14
d. 574. Bishop of Trier, Germany, he was allegedly accused of sexual impurity by St Goar so resigned and retired to the latter's hermitage. This is probably a fable.

Rutilius (St) M. Aug 2
d. 250. A Roman African in what is now Algeria, during the persecution of Decius he became a fugitive and paid money to obtain exemption from sacrifice but was at length arrested and bravely witnessed to his faith. The story was given by Tertullian in his *De Fuga in Persecutione*.

Rutilus (St) *see* **Lucius, Silvanus and Comps**

Rutilus and Comps (SS) MM. Jun 4
? They were martyred at Sabaria, (now Szombathely, Hungary).

S

Sabas (St) *see* **Isaias, Sabas and Comps**

Sabas the Goth and Comps (1) (SS) MM. Apr 24
d. 272. A Christian officer of Gothic descent, he was allegedly martyred with seventy companions at Rome in the reign of Aurelian. They may be a duplicate of those in the next entry.

Sabas the Goth and Comps (2) (SS) MM. Apr 12
d. 372. A Visigoth and a church reader in what is now Romania, he was captured by pagan soldiers and refused to eat food which had been sacrificed to idols. Then he was tortured to death and thrown into the river Mussovo near Tirgovişti, upstream from Bucharest. Several others died with him.

Sabas the Great (St) R. Dec 5
439–532. A Cappodocian, when young he fled a family quarrel and became a monk at various places in the Judaean Desert in the Holy Land. He eventually founded a famous laura there, which was named Mar Saba after him and which has been a functioning monastery from his time to the present. It has been a major source of Eastern monastic custom. He was appointed archimandrite over all the monasteries of the Holy Land, and as such was important in the local campaign against Monophysitism. His incorrupt body, which had been stolen by the Venetians, was returned to his monastery (now Orthodox) in 1965 as an ecumenical gesture. His cultus was confined to local calendars in 1969.

Sabas of Ohrid (St) *see* **Clement of Ohrid and Comps**

Sabas Reyes Salazar (St) *see* **Mexico (Martyrs of)**

Sabbatius (St) *see* **Trophimus, Sabbatius, and Dorymedon**

Sabel (St) *see* **Manuel, Sabel and Ismael**

Sabina (St) *see* **Vincent, Sabina and Christeta**

Sabina (Savina) of Milan (St) L. Jan 30
d. 311. A married woman of Milan, Italy, during the persecution of Diocletian she visited the martyrs in prison and buried their bodies after execution. According to her legend she died while praying at the tomb of SS Nabor and Felix.

Sabina Petrilli (Bl) R. F. Apr 18
1851–1923. From Siena, Italy, she had to help to educate and catechize her younger siblings and this helped to give her a precocious vocation to help poor girls. She founded the 'Sisters of St Catherine of Siena' in 1874 when aged 23, although they only took formal vows in 1900. She died very slowly of cancer from 1890, and was beatified in 1988.

Sabina of Rome (St) M? Aug 29
? A famous basilica on the Aventine in Rome is dedicated to her, and she was probably a rich noblewoman who founded it in the third or fourth century and not (as her unreliable acta assert) a martyr. Nothing is known about her and her cultus was confined to her basilica in 1969.

Sabina of Troyes (St) L. Aug 29
d. ?275. Alleged to have been the sister of St Sabinian of Troyes, France, she has a cultus as a virgin at that place but little is known about her.

Sabinian (St) *see* **Honoratus, Fortunatus and Comps**

Sabinian (St) *see* **Paul, Tatta and Comps**

Sabinian (St) *see* **Peter of Cordoba and Comps**

Sabinian and Potentian
(SS) MM. BB. Dec 31
d. *c*300. According to tradition they were the first and second bishops of Sens, France, and were martyred. The legend that they were disciples of St Peter is worthless. They are patrons of the diocese.

Sabinian de Chaumillac
(St) R. Nov 22
d. ?720 or 770. He was the third abbot of Moutier-St-Chaffre near Le Puy, France.

Sabinian (Savinien) of Troyes (St) M. Jan 29
d. ? 275. He was allegedly martyred at Troyes, France, in one of the early persecutions (perhaps in the reign of Aurelian). The local tradition is that he and St Sabina, his sister, were refugees from Samos in the Aegean Sea.

Sabinus (St) *see* **Donatus, Sabinus and Agape**

Sabinus (Savinus) and Cyprian (SS) MM. Jul 11
? They are listed in the old Roman Martyrology as brothers who were martyred at 'Brixia'. This is either Brescia, Italy, or La Bresse in Poitou, France, and they are venerated in both places.

Sabinus, Exuperantius, Marcellus and Comps
(SS) MM. Dec 30
d. 303. Sabinus was allegedly a bishop martyred near Spoleto, Italy, with two deacons, Exuperantius and Marcellus, and also Venustian and his family, converts. His see is unknown, but Faenza, Assisi, Spoleto and Chiusi each claims him.

Sabinus, Julian and Comps
(SS) MM. Jul 20
? They were sixteen Syrians martyred at Damascus. Maximus, Macrobius, Cassia and Paula are also listed.

Sabinus of Canosa (St) B. Feb 9
d. ?566. Bishop of Canosa in Apulia, Italy, he features in the *Dialogues* of St Gregory the Great as a friend of St Benedict. If it was the same person, he was papal legate of Pope St Agapitus I at the court of Emperor Justinian I for a year from 535. When his city was destroyed his relics were taken to Bari, of which place he is the patron.

Sabinus of Catania (St) B. R. Oct 15
d. *c*760. He was bishop of Catania, Sicily, for a few years before resigning to become a hermit.

Sabinus of Hermopolis (St) M. L. Mar 13
d. 287. A nobleman of Egypt, he was drowned in the Nile at Antinoë in the reign of Diocletian.

Sabinus of Piacenza (St) B. Dec 11
d. 420. While a deacon at Milan he was sent by Pope St Damasus to help resolve the Meletian schism at Antioch, Syria. Then he became bishop of Piacenza, Italy, and a friend of St Ambrose, who used to send him his writings for revision.

Sabinus of Poitiers (St) M? Jul 11
C5th. Allegedly a disciple of St Germanus of Auxerre and a martyr at Poitiers, France, he is venerated locally.

Sabinus (Savin) of Tarbes (St) R. Oct 9
d. ?820. According to the dubious tradition he was born at Barcelona, Spain, educated at Poitiers, France, became a monk at Ligugé and died as a hermit at Tarbes in the Pyrenees, France.

Sacer (Mosacra) (St) R. Mar 3
C7th. He was the abbot-founder of the monastery of Saggart in Co. Dublin, Ireland.

Sacerdos (Sardot, Serdot) of Limoges (St) B. R. May 4
670–*c*720. From Périgord, France, he became a monk and eventually the abbot-founder of Calabre before being made bishop of Limoges.

Sacerdos of Lyons (St) B. Sep 12
d. 551. He became bishop of Lyons, France, in 544 and was an adviser of King Childebert. He presided at the council of Orléans in 549.

Sacerdos of Sigüenza (St) B. May 5
d. *c*560. He was allegedly a bishop of Sigüenza near Guadalajara, Spain, but nothing is known about him.

Sadoc of Sandomir and Comps (BB) MM. RR(OP). Jun 2
d. 1260. He was a disciple of St Dominic, who sent him to Hungary. Later he passed on to Poland where he founded a Dominican friary at Sandomir and became its prior. The town was destroyed in a Mongol raid and he and the other forty-eight brethren were massacred in their church while singing the *Salve Regina*. Their cultus was confirmed for the Dominicans in 1807. *See* **Poland** in lists of national martyrs in appendix.

Sadoc (Sadoth, Shadhost) of Seleucia and Comps (SS) MM. Feb 20
d. 345 or 342. The metropolitan of Seleucia-Ctesiphon in Persian Mesopotamia and head of

the Persian Church, he was arrested in the persecution of Shah Shapur II with one hundred and twenty-eight others. Most of these were martyred at once, but he was kept with eight companions for five months in a filthy prison at Bei-Lapat before being executed.

Sadwrn (Sadwen) (St) R. Nov 29
C6th. Brother of St Illtyd, he was a disciple of St Cadfan. There are churches in Wales dedicated to him.

Sagar (St) M. B. Oct 6
d. *c*175. Bishop of Laodicea in Phrygia, Asia Minor, he was martyred in the reign of Marcus Aurelius. The tradition that he was a disciple of St Paul is false.

Saintin Huré (Bl) *see* **September (Martyrs of)**

Sair *see* **Servan**

Salaberga (St) R. Sep 22
d. ?665. From near Langres, France, as a young widow she married St Blandinus and had five children, including SS Anstrudis and Baldwin of Laon. The couple separated to become consecrated religious and she founded the great double monastery of St John the Baptist at Laon, dying there as abbess.

Salaun (Salomon) (St) R. Nov 1
d. 1358. A poor man of Lesneven in western Brittany, France, he was a 'fool for Christ's sake' and reached a high level of contemplative prayer. His shrine at Le Folgoët nearby is still a centre of pilgrimage.

Sallustia (St) *see* **Caerealis and Sallustia**

Sallustian (St) Jun 8
? He has an ancient cultus in Sardinia, but the sources differ as to whether he was a martyr or a hermit.

Salome *see* **Mary Salome**

Salome and Judith (SS) RR. Jun 29
C9th. According to the legend Salome was an Anglo-Saxon princess (identity uncertain) in exile in Bavaria, Germany, who was met by a widowed childhood friend named Judith. Both of them then became hermits attached to a Benedictine abbey, Oberaltaich or Niederaltaich (the sources differ).

Salome of Galicia (Bl) R(OFM). Nov 17
?1219–1268. Daughter of Prince Lesko of Poland, when aged three she was betrothed to Prince Coloman of Galicia (in what is now the western Ukraine). In 1241 her husband was killed in the Mongol incursion, whereupon she founded a Poor Clare nunnery at Strala and died as a nun there. Her shrine is at the Poor Clare nunnery at Cracow, and her cultus was confirmed for there and Galicia in 1673.

Salomon *see* **Solomon**

Salonius (Solomon) of Genoa (St) B. Sep 28
d. *p*269. He was the first bishop of Genoa, Italy, and is more generally known as 'Salomon' or 'Solomon' owing to an early scribal error.

Salutaris (St) *see* **Eugene of Carthage and Comps**

Salvator Grionesos of Horta (St) R(OFM). Mar 18
1520–1567. From Santa Coloma de Farnés near Gerona, Spain, he was a shoemaker before becoming a Franciscan lay brother at Barcelona. He spent most of his life as cook at the friary of Horta near Tortosa, but died at the friary of Cagliari in Sardinia. He was canonized in 1940.

Salvator Lara Puente (St) *see* **Mexico (Martyrs of)**

Salvator Lilli and Comps (BB) MM. R(OFM). Nov 22
1853–1895. Born in the Abruzzi, Italy, he became a Franciscan in 1870 and went to the Holy Land. Then he was sent to the region of Kahramurasc in Turkey (north-east of Aleppo) and became pastor at the mission of Mujuk-Deresi, where his people were mostly Armenian. Starting in 1894, the Ottoman government carried out a systematic policy of massacre and repression of the native Christians of eastern Anatolia. In 1895 a detachment of Turkish soldiers arrived at the mission, offered Bl Salvator and some others the choice between conversion to Islam or death and, on their refusal, shot them and burned their bodies. They were beatified in 1982. The government policy culminated in the Armenian genocide in the First World War, and led to the deaths of between one and three million Christians. The companions were: Baldji Oghlou Ohannes, Khodianin Oghlou Kadir, Dimbalac Oghlou Wartavar, Jeremias Oghlou Boghos, Toros Oghlou David, Kouradji Oghlou Ziroun and David Oghlou David.

Salvator Pigem Serra (Bl) *see* **Philip-of-Jesus Munárriz Azcona and Comps**

Salvius and 'Superius' (SS) MM. Jun 26
d. ?768. Salvius was a regionary bishop in the district of Angoulême, France, who went to Valenciennes to evangelize the Flemish. He was seized, imprisoned, killed and buried with an anonymous companion by a relative of the local count, and when the bodies were exhumed the latter was on top (hence the nickname 'one on top').

Salvius of Albi (St) B. R. Sep 10
d. 584. He was in turn a lawyer, a monk, an abbot and a hermit before becoming bishop of Albi, France, in 574. He allegedly died as a result of nursing sufferers of an epidemic.

Salvius (Salve, Sauve) of Amiens (St) B. Jan 11
d. ?625. He was a bishop of Amiens, France, and had his shrine at Montreuil-sur-Mer near Boulogne. The old Roman Martyrology listed him as a martyr in error, and he has been confused with the others of the same name.

Salvius of Carthage (St) M. Jan 11
? A Roman African martyr, he had his shrine at Carthage.

Samonas (St) *see* **Gurias and Samonas**

Samosata (Martyrs of) (SS) Dec 9
d. ?311. They were two magistrates, Hipparchus and Philotheus and their converts James, Paragrus, Abibus, Romanus and Lollian. They were crucified at Samosata on the Euphrates, Syria, for refusing to join in the public festivities (which included pagan rites) after a victory by emperor Maximinus over the Persians.

Samson (Sampson) of Caldey (St) B. R. Jul 28
*c*490–?565. Born in Wales, he was a disciple of St Illtyd before becoming a monk and then abbot of the monastery on Caldey Island. After a visit to Ireland he was ordained as a missionary bishop by St Dubricius, spent some time in Cornwall and finally went to Brittany, France. There he spent the rest of life, fixing his missionary headquarters at a monastery at Dol (although no permanent diocese was established there for many centuries to come). His veneration is very popular in Brittany and Wales.

Samson (Sampson) Xenodochius (St) P. Jun 27
d. *c*530. A rich citizen of Constantinople, he was ordained and studied medicine in order to devote his life to the spiritual and physical care of the sick and destitute (his surname means 'the Hospitable') . He founded a hospital near Hagia Sophia.

Samthann (St) R. Dec 18
C6th. She was first abbess of her foundation at Clonbroney in Co. Longford, Ireland.

Samuel (St) *see* **Daniel, Samuel and Comps**

Samuel (St) *see* **Elias, Jeremias and Comps**

Samuel of Edessa (St) P. Aug 9
d. *p*496. He was a priest of Edessa, Syria, (now Urfa in Turkey) and died at Constantinople. He wrote in Syriac against the Nestorians and Monophysites and is remembered as the author of the dogmatic letter to Ibas, one of the *Three Chapters* condemned at the second ecumenical council of Constantinople in 553.

Samuel Marzorati (Bl) *see* **Liberatus Weiss and Comps**

Sancha (Sanctia) of Portugal (St) R(OCist). Mar 13
*c*1180–1229. Daughter of King Sancho I of Portugal and sister of BB Teresa and Mafalda, she helped the Franciscans and Dominicans establish themselves in Portugal and herself became a Cistercian nun at Cellas in 1223. Her cultus was approved for Portugal in 1705.

Sancho (Sanctius, Sancius) (St) M. L. Jun 5
d. 851. From Albi, France, he was captured in a Muslim raid and brought to Cordoba, Spain, as a prisoner of war. There he was educated at the court of the Umayyad emir and was enrolled into his bodyguard, but refused to convert to Islam and was impaled (an act contrary to Muslim law).

Sanctes Brancasino (Bl) R(OFM). Aug 14
d. 1390. From Monte Fabri near Urbino, Italy, he became a Franciscan lay brother at Scotamento, where he spent most of his life. His cultus was approved for Urbino in 1770.

Sanctes of Cori (Bl) R(OSA). Oct 5
d. 1390. From Cori, near Velletri, Italy, he became an Augustinian friar and was famous as a home missionary. His cultus was confirmed for Cori and Velletri in 1888.

Sanctian (St) *see* **Augustine, Sanctian and Beata**

Sanctinus (St) B. Sep 22
d. *c*300. The alleged first bishop of Meux,

France, and disciple of St Dionysius of Paris is probably identical with one of the same name whose shrine is at Verdun.

Sanctus (St) *see* **Photinus, Sanctus and Comps**

Sandila (Sandalus) (St) M. Sep 3
d. ?855. He was allegedly martyred at Cordoba, Spain, under the Umayyads, but details are lacking.

Sandratus (St) R(OSB). Aug 24
d. 986. A monk at St Maximinus's Abbey at Trier, Germany, he was sent by the emperor Otto I in 972 to restore monastic observance at St Gall, Switzerland. Shortly afterwards he was made abbot of Gladbach, and also abbot of Weissenburg in 981. He died at Gladbach.

Santiago *see* **James the Great**

Santuccia Terrebotti
(Bl) R(OSB). Mar 21
d. 1305. From Gubbio in Umbria, Italy, she married and had a daughter who died young, whereupon the bereaved couple decided to become consecrated religious. She became a Benedictine at Gubbio, was elected abbess and moved the community to Santa Maria in Via Lata, Rome, where they were nicknamed 'Le Santuccie'. Her cultus is not confirmed.

Sapientia *see* **Sophia**

Sapor *see* **Shapur**

Saragossa *see* **Zaragoza**

Sardon *see* **Sacerdos**

Sarmata (St) M. R. Oct 11
d. 357. An Egyptian disciple of St Anthony, he was killed in his monastery during a raid by barbarian nomads and was venerated as a martyr.

Sator (St) *see* **Vitalis, Sator and Repositus**

Saturian (St) *see* **Martinian, Saturian and Comps**

Saturnina (St) V. Jun 4
? According to her legend she was a young German woman who fled from her impending marriage to the area of Arras, France, but was pursued by her betrothed and killed. She probably never existed.

Saturninus (St) *see* **Basileus, Auxilius and Saturninus**

Saturninus (St) *see* **Corfu (Martyrs of)**

Saturninus (St) *see* **Dominic, Victor and Comps**

Saturninus (St) *see* **Irenaeus, Anthony and Comps**

Saturninus (St) *see* **Marcellus, Castus and Comps**

Saturninus (St) *see* **Martial, Saturninus and Comps**

Saturninus (St) *see* **Paul, Gerontius and Comps**

Saturninus (St) *see* **Peregrine, Lucian and Comps**

Saturninus (St) *see* **Perpetua, Felicity and Comps**

Saturninus (St) *see* **Theodulus, Saturninus and Comps**

Saturninus (SS) *see* **Zaragoza (Eighteen Martyrs of)**

Saturninus, Castulus, Magnus and Lucius (SS) MM. Feb 15
d. ?273. They were allegedly martyred at Terni, Italy, when St Valentine was bishop there.

Saturninus, Dativus, Felix and Comps (SS) MM. Feb 11
d. 304. A group of forty-six from Albitina in Roman Africa, they were seized while celebrating Mass, taken to Carthage for interrogation and apparently all died in prison. Saturninus was the priest and had with him his four children: Saturninus and Felix (readers), Mary (a virgin) and Hilarion (a young boy). Dativus and another Felix were senators, and others named were Thelica, Ampelius, Emeritus, Rogatian and Victoria. The child Hilarion, when threatened by the magistrates while his companions were being tortured, replied: 'Yes, torture me, too; anyway, I am a Christian'. Their acta appear to be genuine.

Saturninus and Lupus
(SS) MM. Oct 14
? They were martyred at Caesarea in Cappodocia, Asia Minor.

Saturninus, Neopolus, Germanus and Celestine (SS) MM. May 2
d. 304. Saturninus was martyred at Alexandria, Egypt, in the reign of Diocletian, not at Rome as stated in the old Roman Martyrology. Nothing is known about the others.

Saturninus, Nereus and Comps (SS) MM. Oct 16
d. *c*450. They are listed as some three hundred and sixty-five who were martyred in Roman Africa in the reign of the Vandal king Genseric, but they may be a duplicate of **Martinian, Saturian and Comps**.

Saturninus and Sisinnius (SS) MM. Nov 29
d. ?304. According to their legend they were a Carthaginian priest at Rome and his deacon who were sentenced to hard labour and subsequently martyred. All that is known is that Saturninus was an early martyr buried along the Salerian Way, and there is no connection with SS Cyriacus, Largus and Smaragdus, as has been alleged. Their cultus was confined to local calendars in 1969. *See* **Apronian**.

Saturninus, Theophilus and Revocata (SS) MM. Feb 6
? Nothing is known about these martyrs.

Saturninus, Thyrsus and Victor (SS) MM. Jan 31
d. *c*250. They were martyred at Alexandria, Egypt.

Saturninus of Cagliari (St) M. Oct 30
d. 303. He was martyred at Cagliari, Sardinia, in the reign of Diocletian. According to his untrustworthy acta this was during a festival of Jupiter.

Saturninus of Numidia and Comps (SS) MM. Mar 22
? They were a group of ten Roman African martyrs in what is now Algeria.

Saturninus (Sernin) of Toulouse (St) M. B. Nov 29
d. ?257. A Roman missionary, he worked in the district around Pamplona, Spain, and then in and around Toulouse, France, of which city he was apparently the first bishop. He was allegedly martyred in the persecution of Valerian by being tied behind a wild bull which dragged him about until his body disintegrated.

Saturninus of Verona (St) B. Apr 7
C4th. Nothing is known about this bishop of Verona, Italy.

Saturus (St) *see* **Armogastes and Saturus**

Saturus (St) *see* **Perpetua, Felicity and Comps**

Satyrus (St) M. Jan 12
? An Arab, he was martyred either in Achaia, Greece, or at Antioch, Syria, for insulting an idol. Another version of the legend alleges that the idol fell to the ground when he made the sign of the cross over it. The sources are extremely confused.

Satyrus of Milan (St) L. Sep 17
d. ?376. The elder brother of St Ambrose of Milan, he was a lawyer and then prefect of Liguria, Italy, before taking over the administration of his brother's property on the latter's election as bishop of Milan. The sermon preached by St Ambrose at his funeral, 'On the death of a brother', survives.

Saula (St) *see* **Martha, Saula and Comps**

Sauman *see* **Psalmodius**

Sauve *see* **Salvius**

Savina *see* **Sabina**

Savinian *see* **Sabinian**

Savinus *see* **Sabinus**

Sawl (St) R? Jan 15
C6th. A Welsh nobleman, he was father of St Asaph. The traditions concerning him are very obscure.

Sazan (St) *see* **Aizan and Sazan**

Scannal (St) R. May 3
d. *p*563. He was a disciple of St Columba and accompanied him to Iona, Scotland.

Scarthin *see* **Schotin**

Scholastica (St) R(OSB). Feb 10
*c*480–?543. The *Dialogues* of St Gregory the Great are the only source concerning her, and describe her as a sister (according to later tradition, the twin) of St Benedict who followed him to Montecassino, Italy, and lived a life of prayer nearby. The tradition that she was the first Benedictine nun dates from the C11th, and she is usually depicted as an abbess. Her attribute is a dove flying from her mouth. Her alleged relics are at Montecassino, with a rival set at Le Mans, France.

Scholastica (St) *see* **Injuriosus and Scholastica**

Scholastica-of-St-James Leroux (Bl) *see* **Valenciennes (Martyrs of)**

Scillitan Martyrs (SS) Jul 17
d. 180. Seven men and five women, they were martyred at Scillium in Roman Africa in the reign of Septimius Severus. Their names were Speratus, Narzales, Cythinus, Veturius, Felix, Acyllinus, Laetantius, Januaria, Generosa, Vestina, Donata and Secunda. The official record of the proceedings is extant, and is an important historical source. St Augustine preached three sermons in their honour at their tomb.

Scipio-Jerome Brigéat de Lambert (Bl) *see* **John-Baptist Souzy and Comps**

Scothin (Scarthin) (St) R. Jan 6
C6th. As a young man he left Ireland to become a disciple of St David in Wales, and on his return became a hermit on Mt Mairge in Co. Laois. He is alleged to have founded a school for boys at Kilkenny.

Scubiculus (St) *see* **Nicasius of Rouen and Comps**

Scubilio (St) R. Apr 16
d. 575. He was a companion of St Paternus of Avranches at Saint-Jouin-de-Marnes south of Saumur, France.

Scubilio Rousseau (Bl) R. Dec 20
1797–1867. Born at Annay-le-Côte in Burgundy, France, his father was a mason and he was a great help to a new parish priest when young, especially in the parish school. This led to his joining the 'Brothers of the Christian Schools' in 1822, and he went to Réunion in the Indian Ocean in 1833. He was there until his death, for 23 years, and was beatified in 1987.

Seachnall (Sechnall, Secundinus) (St) B. Nov 27
d. 457. A disciple of St Patrick, he became first bishop of Dunshauglin in Co. Meath, Ireland, in 433 and was later assistant bishop of Armagh. He wrote an alphabetical hymn in honour of St Patrick, the earliest extant Latin poem of the Irish church.

Sebald (St) R. Aug 19
d. *c*770. Apparently an Anglo-Saxon missionary and one of St Willibald's helpers, he became a hermit in the Reichswald near Nuremberg, Bavaria, of which city he is a patron.

Sebaste (Martyrs of) *see* **Forty Armenian Martyrs**

Sebastia (St) *see* **Innocent, Sebastia and Comps**

Sebastian (St) *see* **Dionysius, Emilian and Sebastian**

Sebastian (St) *see* **Photina and Comps**

Sebastian de Aparicio (Bl) R(OFM). Feb 25
1502–1600. From Galicia, Spain, he was a farm-worker and then a gentleman's valet before emigrating to Mexico, where he was contracted by the government to maintain roads and run the postal service between Mexico City and Zacateca. After the death of his second wife, when he was seventy-two years old, he became a Franciscan lay brother at Puebla. He lived for another twenty-six years, his chief occupation being to beg alms for the community. He was beatified in 1789.

Sebastian Calvo Martinez (Bl) *see* **Philip-of-Jesus Munárriz Azcona and Comps**

Sebastian Desbrielles (Bl) *see* **September (Martyrs of)**

Sebastian of Esztergom (Bl) B. R(OSB). Dec 30
d. ?1036. Apparently a Benedictine monk, he became archbishop of Esztergom and primate of Hungary in 1002, during the reign of King St Stephen.

Sebastian Kimura (Bl) M. R(SJ). Sep 10
d. 1622. A grandson of the first Japanese to be baptized by St Francis Xavier, when aged eighteen he became a Jesuit and worked as a catechist at Miyako before becoming the first Japanese to be ordained. After two years imprisonment at Omura he was burnt alive with Bl Charles Spinola and Comps in the 'Great Martyrdom' and was beatified in 1867. *See* **Japan (Martyrs of)**.

Sebastian Loup Hunot (Bl) *see* **John-Baptist Souzy and Comps**

Sebastian Maggi (Bl) R(OP). Dec 16
d. 1494. From Brescia, Italy, he became a Dominican and was famous for his penitential sermons and for his zeal in reform. He was vicar of the Lombard province twice, and was Savonarola's confessor for a time. He died at Genoa and his cultus was confirmed for there in 1760.

Sebastian Nam (St) *see* **Korea (Martyrs of)**

Sebastian Newdigate (Bl)
M. R(OCart). Jun 19
d. 1535. From Harefield near Uxbridge, Middlesex, he was educated at Cambridge and became a Carthusian monk at the London Charterhouse. He was executed at Tyburn with two brethren, BB Humphrey Middlemore and William Exmew, for denying the royal supremacy of King Henry VIII and was beatified in 1886. *See* **England (Martyrs of)**.

Sebastian Riera Coromina (Bl) *see* **Philip-of-Jesus Munárriz Azcona and Comps**

Sebastian of Rome (St) M. Jan 20
d. ?288. He is one of the most famous of the Roman martyrs with a cultus dating from the C4th, but his C5th acta are not reliable. According to them he was a favourite army officer of the emperor Diocletian until his Christianity was discovered. Then he was tied to a tree, used for archery practice and finally clubbed to death. Pope St Damasus built a basilica over his tomb on the Appian Way in 367. His attribute is a bundle of arrows, or he is depicted as a naked youth tied to a tree and pierced with arrows.

Sebastian-of-Jesus Sillero
(Bl) R(OFM). Oct 15
1665–134. From Montalban near Teruel, Spain, he became a Franciscan lay brother at Seville and his cultus was confirmed for there in 1776.

Sebastian Valfré (Bl) P. Jan 30
1629–1710. From Verduno near Alba, Italy, he joined the Oratorians at Turin after his ordination and spent the rest of his life there, becoming prefect of the Oratory and a famous spiritual director. He was beatified in 1834.

Sebbi (Sebba, Sebbe) (St) R. Aug 29
664–694. He was king of the East Saxons at the time of the Heptarchy in England. After a peaceful reign of thirty years he became a monk at London and died shortly afterwards, being buried in old St Paul's Cathedral. There was no cultus, and his name was inserted in the old Roman Martyrology by Baronius on the grounds of St Bede's description of him.

Secunda (St) *see* **Maxima, Donatilla and Secunda**

Secunda (St) *see* **Rufina and Secunda**

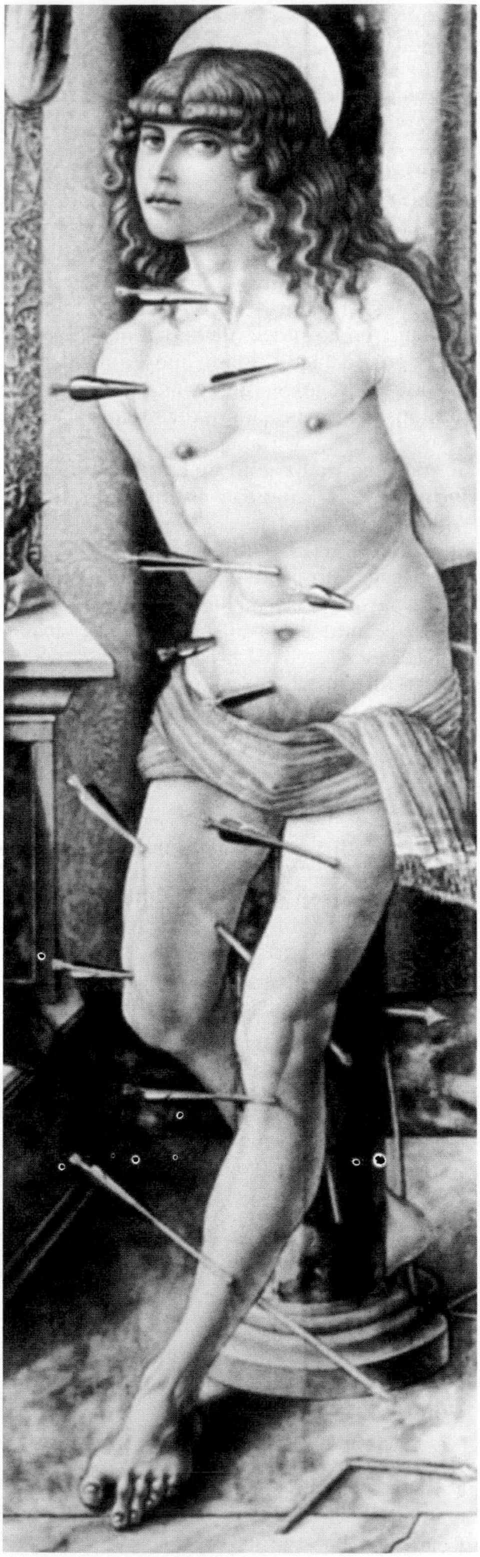

St Sebastian, Jan 20

Secunda (St) *see* **Scillitan Martyrs**

Secundarius (St) *see* **Primus, Cyril and Secundarius**

Secundel (St) *see* **Friard and Secundel**

Secundian (St) *see* **Donatus, Secundian and Comps**

Secundian, Marcellian and Verian (SS) MM. Aug 9
d. 250. They were martyred near Civitavecchia in Tuscany, Italy, in the reign of Decius. Secundian was apparently a prominent government official and the others are listed as 'scholastics', but this information is uncertain.

Secundilla (St) *see* **Paul, Heraclius and Comps**

Secundina (St) V. Jan 15
d. *c*250. She was a maiden whipped to death at Fondi near Rome in the persecution of Decius.

Secundinus (St) *see* **Agapius of Cirta and Comps**

Secundinus (St) *see* **Auxilius, Isserninus and Secundinus**

Secundinus (St) *see* **Castus and Secundinus**

Secundinus (St) *see* **Lucius, Silvanus and Comps**

Secundinus (St) *see* **Priscus II of Capua and Comps**

Secundinus, Agrippinus, Maximus, Fortunatus and Martialis (SS) MM. Jul 15
C4th? They are listed as martyrs of Pannonia, in the Danube basin.

Secundinus of Cordoba (St) M. May 21
d. ?306. He was martyred at Cordoba, Spain, in the reign of Diocletian.

Secundinus-Mary Ortega-García (Bl) *see* **Philip-of-Jesus Munárriz Azcona and Comps**

Secundulus (St) *see* **Perpetua, Felicity and Comps**

Secundus (St) *see* **Carpophorus of Como and Comps**

Secundus (St) *see* **Cyriac, Paulillus and Comps**

Secundus (St) *see* **Darius, Zosimus and Comps**

Secundus (St) *see* **Democritus, Secundus and Dionysius**

Secundus (St) *see* **Dominic, Victor and Comps**

Secundus (St) *see* **Epictetus, Jucundus and Comps**

Secundus (St) *see* **Romulus and Secundus**

Secundus (St) *see* **Torquatus, Ctesiphon and Comps**

Secundus, Fidentian and Varicus (SS) MM. Nov 15
? Nothing is known about these Roman African martyrs.

Secundus of Alexandria and Comps (SS) MM. May 21
d. 357. When St Athanasius was driven into exile (his third) by the emperor Constantius in 356 he was replaced as patriarch of Alexandria by an Arian, George. The latter established himself with violence and Secundus, a priest, was killed in the process with many other clergy and laity, including many women.

Secundus of Asti (St) M. Mar 29
d. 119. A patrician of Asti in Piedmont, Italy, and a subaltern officer in the imperial army, he was beheaded at Asti in the reign of Hadrian. He is depicted as a soldier-martyr, often with a horse.

Secundus of Amelia (St) M. Jun 1
d. 304. He was an alleged martyr of Amelia in Umbria, Italy, who was drowned in the Tiber in the reign of Diocletian. He is the patron of several places in central Italy, but his historical existence cannot be proved.

Secundus Pollo (Bl) P. (Dec 26)
1908–41. From Caresanablot near Vercelli, Italy, he entered the minor seminary of the archdiocese of Vercelli and became a diocesan priest in due course. He served as a curate and parish priest, as a professor of theology and philosophy, as the spiritual director at the major seminary, as prison chaplain and as chaplain to the youth of Catholic Action. In 1941 he was conscripted as an army chaplain and sent to

Montenegro but was quickly killed in battle. He was beatified in 1998.

Secundus of Ventimiglia (St) M. Aug 26
C3rd. According to the legend he was an officer of the **Theban Legion** (q.v.) who fled its massacre but was captured and executed near Ventimiglia, Italy.

Securus (St) *see* **Severus, Securus and Comps**

Sedna (St) B. R. Mar 10
d. *c*570. Bishop of Ossory in Co. Offaly, Ireland, he was a friend of St Lua.

Sedopha (St) *see* **Marinus, Theodotus and Sedopha**

Seduinus *see* **Swithin**

Seemie-Rookie *see* **Roch**

Seine *see* **Sequanus**

Seiriol (St) R. Feb 1
C6th. He founded monasteries (remains of which are extant) at Penmon on Anglesey, Wales, and on the island named Ynys-Seiriol after him, off the eastern tip of Anglesey.

Seleucus (St) M? Mar 24
? He was a Syrian but nothing else is known, not even whether he was a martyr.

Seleucus (St) *see* **Hieronides, Leontius and Comps**

Seleucus (St) *see* **Porphyrius and Seleucus**

Selyf (St) R? Jun 25
C6th? The alleged founder of Lansallos near Fowey in Cornwall, England, he may be a duplicate of St Solomon III of Brittany or of St Levan.

Sempronia (St) *see* **Juliana and Sempronia**

Senach (St) B. Aug 3
C6th. A disciple of St Finian, he succeeded him as abbot of Clonard in Co. Meath, Ireland.

Senan (St) R. Apr 29
C7th. He was apparently a hermit in north Wales. There are at least a dozen other Irish saints with the same name and yet others with similar names, and there is serious confusion between them.

Senan of Scattery (St) B. Mar 8
d. *c*540. A monk of Kilmanagh in Co. Kilkenny, Ireland, he apparently founded a monastery at Enniscorthy in Co. Wexford, then went on pilgrimage to Rome and stayed with St David in Wales on his way back. Then he founded several more monasteries, notably one at Inishcarra near Cork, before settling on Scattery Island in the Shannon estuary. He died and was buried there.

Senator of Albanum (St) M? Sep 26
? He is merely listed as a saint of 'Albanum', which may be Albano near Rome or Apt (the ancient Alba Helvetiorum), in the south of France.

Senator of Milan (St) B. May 28
d. 480. When still a young priest of Milan, Italy, he attended the council of Chalcedon as a legate of Pope St Leo the Great, and became archbishop in 477.

Sennen (St) *see* **Abdon and Sennen**

Señorina (St) R(OSB). Apr 22
d. 982. A relative of St Rudesind of Mondonedo, she was educated at the nunnery of Vieyra where her aunt was abbess, became abbess herself and moved the community to Basto near Braga, Portugal.

September (Martyrs of) (BB) Sep 2
d. 1792. One hundred and ninety-one martyrs were massacred by the mob in Paris on September 2 and 3 after having been imprisoned by the Legislative Assembly of the French Revolution for refusing the oath to support the civil constitution of the clergy. They were three bishops, one hundred and twenty-four secular priests, twenty-three former Jesuits, twelve Sulpicians, eighteen other religious (including Ambrose Chevreaux, the superior-general of the Maurist Benedictines), five deacons, a cleric and five laymen. Ninety-five died at the Carmelite church in the rue de Rennes, seventy-two at the Vincentian seminary of St Firman, twenty-one at the Abbey of St Germain des Prés and three at La Force. They were beatified in 1926. *See* **French Revolution (Martyrs of)**.

Septiminus, Januarius and Felix (SS) *see* **Twelve Brothers**

Septimus (St) *see* **Liberatus, Boniface and Comps**

Sepulchre
Old churches in England called 'St Sepulchre's'

are commemorating Christ's tomb and not any saint of that name.

Sequanus (Seine, Sigo) (St) R. Sep 19
d. *c*580. He was the abbot-founder of a monastery near Dijon, France, which was later named St Seine after him.

Seraphia *see* **Serapia**

Seraphina (St) V. Jul 29
? The old Roman Martyrology placed her at 'Civitas Mamiensis', which is unknown. Armenia, Spain or Italy are suggestions.

Seraphina (Fina) of San Gimignano (St) T(OSB)? Mar 12
d. 1253. Born into a poor family at San Gimignano in Tuscany, Italy, she was never a nun but lived at home (possibly as a Benedictine tertiary). She suffered a repulsive and paralyzing breakdown in health when young and took six years to die in a state of serious neglect, being remembered for her patience.

Seraphina Sforza (Bl) R(OFM). Sep 9
1434–1478. From Urbino, Italy, the daughter of the count there, she married Alexander Sforza, Duke of Pesaro in 1448 but the marriage was a disaster. He treated her with cruelty before ejecting her from their home at Pesaro, whereupon she took refuge at a local Poor Clare nunnery. She eventually became a nun there, and was later abbess. Her cultus was confirmed for Pesaro in 1754.

Seraphinus de Nicola
(St) R(OFM Cap). Oct 12
1540–1604. A shepherd from Montegranaro in the Marches, Italy, he became a Capuchin lay brother at Ascoli Piceno in 1556 and spent an outwardly uneventful life there. However he became a thaumaturge and, despite being illiterate, was allegedly the spiritual director of important people in Church and society. He was canonized in 1767.

Serapia (St) V. Jul 29
d. ?119. She features in the legendary acta of St Sabina as a Syrian slave who converted her to the faith and was beheaded in the reign of Hadrian.

Serapion (St) M. Jul 13
d. ?195. He was martyred somewhere in the East in the reign of Septimus Severus, probably in Macedonia.

Serapion (St) *see* **Caerealis, Pupulus and Comps**

Serapion (St) *see* **Marcellinus, Mannea and Comps**

Serapion (St) *see* **Victorinus, Victor and Comps**

Serapion of Alexandria (St) M. Nov 14
d. 252. A citizen of Alexandria, Egypt, he died after his house was sacked in an anti-Christian riot. He was thrown from the roof after being tortured.

Serapion of Antioch (St) B. Oct 30
d. 211. A bishop of Antioch, Syria, he was praised by Eusebius and St Jerome for his theological writings but only small fragments of these survive.

Serapion of Arsinoe (St) R. Mar 21
C4th? According to the old Roman Martyrology he was a notable desert father of Egypt, being superior over ten thousand monks in the desert

St Seraphina of San Gimignano, Mar 12

who supported themselves and many poor people of Alexandria by manual work.

Serapion the Mercedarian (St) M. R. Nov 14
d. 1240. Allegedly an English soldier, he served in the army of Castile in Spain before joining the Mercedarian order in order to help ransom Christians taken captive by the Muslims. He surrendered himself as a hostage to this end at Algiers, but was crucified for preaching to Muslims while awaiting his ransom. His cultus as a saint was confirmed for Gerona and Barcelona in 1728.

Serapion the Sindonite (St) R. May 21
d. ?356. An Egyptian desert father, he was famous for his charity and his complete lack of possessions. He had only a linen sheet (a 'sindon') to wear, hence his nickname.

Serapion of Thmuis (St) B. R. Mar 21
d. *c*370. An Egyptian monk, he became bishop of Thmuis in Lower Egypt in ?339 and was a leading opponent of Arianism as well as a friend of St Athanasius and of St Anthony. He was exiled to the desert in 359. Among his several extant works the *Sacramentary* is important in liturgical history.

Serdot *see* **Sacerdos**

Serena (St) L. Aug 16
d. ?290. According to the old Roman Martyrology she was a wife of the emperor Diocletian and a secret Christian who died of a fever at Rome, but this information derives from the spurious acta of St Cyriac and is unhistorical.

Serenedus and Serenicus (SS) RR. May 7
d. ?669. According to their story they were two brothers, noblemen of Spoleto, Italy, who became monks at Montecassino and migrated to France to become hermits at Charnie near Le Mans. Serenicus then founded a monastery at Hyesmes near Alençon with the disciples that he had attracted. One problem with this story is that Montecassino was in ruins at the time.

Serenus (St) *see* **Plutarch of Alexandria and Comps**

Serenus of Marseilles (St) B. Aug 9
d. 606. As bishop of Marseilles, France, he was the recipient of several letters from St Gregory the Great, who commended to his care the Roman missionaries travelling to England and who twice reprimanded him for his iconoclastic tendencies.

Serenus (Cerneuf, Sirenus) of Sirmium (St) M. Feb 23
d. ?303. According to his story he was from Greece but fled to Sirmium (now Srem Mitrovica in Serbia) during the persecution of Diocletian and became a gardener. But he was involved in a dispute with a pagan neighbour, admitted to being a Christian in court and was martyred.

Serf *see* **Servan**

Sergius (St) *see* **John, Sergius and Comps**

Sergius (St) *see* **Maurus, Panteleimon and Sergius**

Sergius and Bacchus *Oct 7*
d. ?303. According to the story they were senior Roman army officers in Syria who refused to join in pagan sacrifices. As a result they were dressed in women's clothes and paraded through the streets of Arabissus in Cappadocia, Asia Minor. Then Bacchus was beaten to death and Sergius was beheaded a week later. Their cultus was suppressed in 1969.

Sergius I, Pope (St) Sep 8
d. 701. He was born at Palermo in Sicily of refugee Syrian parents, became a priest at Rome and was made pope in 687. He was one of the Greek-speaking clergy who dominated Roman church life at the period, but was adamantly opposed to the imposition of Eastern church customs by the Empire and refused to sign the decrees of the 'Quinisext' council at Constantinople in 692. One of these prohibited the representation of Christ as a lamb, so he introduced the 'Agnus Dei' into the Roman eucharistic rite. He supported the English missionary monks in Friesland and Germany and baptized King St Ceadwalla of Wessex in 689.

Sergius of Caesarea (St) M. R. Feb 24
d. 304. He may have been a priest before becoming a hermit near Caesarea in Cappodocia, Asia Minor, where he was martyred in the reign of Diocletian. His alleged relics are at Ubeda near Tarragona, Spain.

Serlo of Savigny (Bl) R(OCist). Sep 10
d. 1158. A Benedictine monk of Cherisy near Chartres, France, he became abbot of Savigny in 1140. This was the mother-house of a reform Benedictine congregation, which he arranged to be united to the Cistercians in 1147. This involved the latter accepting the

Savignac nunneries as Cistercian as well as the appropriation of tithes and the ownership of manors with feudal rights, all of which involved a mitigation of the original Cistercian ideals.

Sernin *see* **Saturninus**

Serotina (St) *see* **Donata and Comps**

Servan (Serf, Sair) (St) B. R. Jul 1
C8th? He was a missionary bishop in West Fife, Scotland, and died and was buried at Culross, but the traditions concerning him are contradictory and extravagant.

Servandus and Germanus
(SS) MM. Oct 23
d. ?305. They were allegedly two of the twelve sons of St **Marcellus of Tangier** (q.v.) who were martyred at Cadiz, Spain.

Servatus (Servais) (St) B. May 13
d. 384. He was bishop of Tongeren near Liege, Belgium, and showed hospitality to St Athanasius when the latter was an exile in the West.

Servilian (St) *see* **Sulpicius and Servilian**

Servilius (St) *see* **Zoellus, Servilius and Comps**

Servulus (St) L. Dec 23
d. *c*590. A tetraplegic beggar in Rome based at the door of the church of St Clement in Rome, he shared what he received with other beggars. St Gregory the Great, who probably knew him personally, described his edifying death in an extant homily.

Servus (St) *see* **Liberatus, Boniface and Comps**

Servus of Tuburbum (St) M. Dec 7
d. 483. A Roman African nobleman of what is now Algeria, he was seized and tortured to death in the reign of the Arian Vandal king Hunneric.

Servusdei (St) *see* **Gumesind and Servusdei**

Servusdei (St) *see* **Rogellus and Servusdei**

Sethrida (Saethrith) (St) R. Jan 20
d. *c*660. A step-daughter of Anna, king of the East Angles, England, and thus a half-sister of St Etheldreda, she became a nun at Faremoutier-en-Brie, France, under St Fara and succeeded her as abbess.

Servites, Founders of
(SS) RR(OSM). FF. Feb 17
Noblemen of Florence, Italy, and members of the 'Confraternity of Our Lady', they withdrew to a hermitage on Mt Senario in revolt at the materialism and moral laxity of their city and founded there the order of the 'Servants of Mary'. These became known as the Servite Friars, with a rule based on those of St Augustine and of the Dominicans, and were approved in 1304. Bonfilius Monaldi was the first superior general, Bonajuncta Manetti the second and Manettus dell' Antella the fourth. Bartholomew degli' Amedei was first prior of Carfaggio. Hugh dei Lippi-Uguccioni and Sosthenes Sostegni established the order in France and Germany respectively. Alexis Falconieri was a lay brother and was the last to die, in 1310. They were canonized together in 1887.

Seven Archangels (SS) Apr 20
As well as SS Michael, Gabriel and Raphael, four other archangels have traditionally been given names derived from apocryphal writings. They are Uriel, Shealtiel, Jehudiel and Berachiel. The seven together have a local cultus at Palermo, Sicily.

Seven Brothers *Jul 10*
d. ?150. The old Roman Martyrology alleges that they were the seven sons of St Felicity of Rome, martyred in the reign of Antoninus Pius in the following ways: Januarius, Felix and Philip, scourged to death; Silvanus, thrown over a precipice; Alexander, Vitalis and Martial, beheaded. This is fiction, and they seem to be seven early martyrs, not brothers and probably unconnected, about whom nothing definite is known. That they shared the same feast-day was the probable motivation for the writing of the legend. Their cultus was suppressed in 1969.

Seven Robbers *see* **Corfu (Martyrs of)**

Seven Sleepers *Jul 27*
Their legend is that they were seven young men of Ephesus, Asia Minor, who were walled up in a cave where they had taken refuge from the persecution of Decius in 250 and were found there alive in 362, having been sleeping in the meantime. There are several different lists of names (the old Roman Martyrology giving them as John, Maximian, Constantine, Mortian, Malchus, Serapion and Dionysius) and various versions of the legend, which probably arose from the discovery of some relics in a cave. Cardinal Baronius left their entry in the old Roman Martyrology, despite his having

expressed doubts about the legend, but the cultus is now suppressed.

Severa of Aquitaine (St) R. Jul 20
d. *c*680. Sister of St Modoald, bishop of Trier, she was the first abbess of the nunnery later named after her at Villeneuve near Bourges, France.

Severa of Oehren (St) R. Jul 20
d. *c*750. She was abbess of Oehren nunnery at Trier, Germany.

Severian (St) *see* **Four Crowned Martyrs**

Severian (St) *see* **Victor, Zoticus and Comps**

Severian and Aquila (SS) MM. Jan 23
? A husband and wife, Roman Africans, they were martyred at Julia Caesarea in what is now Morocco.

Severian of Scythopolis
(St) M. B. Feb 21
d. ?452. A bishop of Scythopolis (now Bet Shean) in the Holy Land, he attended the council of Chalcedon in 451 and supported its decrees against Monophysitism. For this he was killed on his return by partisans of Theophilus, the Monophysite intruded as bishop of Jerusalem in place of Juvenal.

Severian of Sebaste (St) M. Sep 9
d. 320. A senator at Sebaste in Armenia, according to his legend he witnessed the martyrdom of the Forty Armenian Martyrs, openly professed his Christianity and was torn with iron rakes until he died.

Severinus (St) *see* **Lucy, Antoninus and Comps**

Severinus (St) *see* **Carpophorus of Como and Comps**

Severinus, Exuperius and Felician (SS) MM. Nov 19
d. 170. They were martyred in the reign of Marcus Aurelius, probably at Vienne, France, although they are also claimed by Viviers.

Severinus of Agaunum
(St) R. Feb 11
d. ?507. A Burgundian, he allegedly became abbot in 476 of Agaunum (now St Maurice in the Valais, Switzerland), cured the gout of Clovis, king of the Franks and died near Sens. The historical evidence for these assertions is not good.

Severinus Boethius *see* **Boethius**

Severinus (Seurin) of Bordeaux (St) B. Oct 23
d. *c*420. Allegedly from the East, he became bishop of Bordeaux, France, in ?405.

Severinus of Cologne (St) B? Oct 10
d. ?403. He was allegedly a bishop of Cologne, Germany, from Bordeaux and a prominent opponent of Arianism. The evidence is confused; he is also alleged to have died at Bordeaux, France.

Severinus Girault (Bl) *see* **September (Martyrs of)**

Severinus of Naples (St) B. Jan 8
? The old Roman Martyrology listed him as a bishop of Naples, Italy, but he is a result of confusion between his namesakes of Noricum and Septempeda and never existed.

Severinus of Noricum (St) R. Jan 8
d. 482. Apparently a monk from the East, he settled on the Danube in what is now Austria and founded several monasteries including those at Passau and at Favianae near Vienna, which was his base and where he died. He organised help for the local people being harassed by the invasions of the Huns and other barbarians, but six years after his death these incursions escalated and his community fled with his relics. These were eventually enshrined at the abbey named after him at Naples, Italy.

Severinus of Paris (St) R. Nov 27
d. *c*540. He was allegedly a hermit at Paris, France, who died where the church dedicated to him now stands, but he may be a duplicate of St Severinus of Agaunum.

Severinus of Septempeda (St) B. Jun 8
d. 540. He and his brother St Victorinus of Camerino were noblemen who distributed their wealth among the poor and became hermits at Montenero near Livorno, Italy. However, Pope Vigilius forced St Severinus to become bishop of Septempeda in the Marches in 540, which place is now named Sanseverino after him.

Severinus of Tivoli (St) R. Nov 1
d. ?699. He was a hermit at Tivoli near Rome and has his shrine in the church of St Laurence there.

Severinus of Trier (St) B. Oct 23
d. *c*300. He was bishop of Trier, Germany, but transferred to Bordeaux, France, and died there.

Severus (St) *see* **Mansuetus, Severus and Comps**

Severus (St) *see* **Peter, Severus and Leucius**

Severus (St) *see* **Philip, Severus and Comps**

Severus, Securus, Januarius and Victorinus (SS) MM. Dec 2
d. *c*450. They were Roman Africans martyred by the Arian Vandals.

Severus, Memnon and Comps (SS) MM. Aug 20
d. *c*300. A priest and a centurion respectively at Bizya in Thrace (European Turkey), they were beheaded but thirty-seven soldiers with them from Philippopolis (Plovdiv in Bulgaria) were burned in a furnace.

Severus of Avranches (St) B. R. Feb 1
d. *c*690. According to his untrustworthy legend, he was from a poor family in the Cotentin peninsula, France, and was a shepherd before becoming successively a priest, an abbot and bishop of Avranches. Before his death he resigned and returned to monastic life.

Severus of Barcelona (St) M. B. Nov 6
d. 633. Bishop of Barcelona, Spain, he was killed by the Arian Visigoths who hammered nails into his head. He is a minor patron of Barcelona.

Severus of Münstermaifeld (St) P. Feb 15
d. *c*530. St Gregory the Great described this parish priest of Interocrea (Androcca) in the Abruzzi, Italy, as having neglected to ensure that he was present to administer viaticum to a dying man, and so brought him back to life so that he might do so. His relics were transferred to Münstermaifeld near Koblenz, Germany, in the C10th.

Severus of Naples (St) B. Apr 29
d. 409. Bishop of Naples, Italy, he was a famous thaumaturge and (according to the legend) revived a dead man so that he could bear witness for his persecuted widow.

Severus of Orvieto (St) P. Oct 1
? He is listed by the old Roman Martyrology as a priest at Orvieto, Italy, but seems to be a duplicate of St Severus of Münstermaifeld.

Severus of Prague (Bl) B. R(OSB). Dec 9
d. 1067. A Benedictine of Brevnov, Czech Republic, he became bishop of Prague in 1031 and built many churches in Bohemia. His local cultus is unconfirmed.

Severus of Ravenna (St) B. Feb 1
d. ?348. A weaver of Ravenna, Italy, he was made bishop there in 283 and was assistant papal legate at the synod of Sardica in 344. His relics ended up at Erfurt in Thuringia, Germany, and he is a patron of weavers.

Severus of Rustan (St) P. Aug 1
d. *c*500. A nobleman who became a priest, he has an ancient cultus at the village near Tarbes, France, named St Sever de Rustan after him.

Severus of Sirmium and Comps (SS) MM. Feb 21
C3rd-C4th. They were sixty-three martyrs of Sirmium (Srem Mitrovica in Serbia).

Severus of Trier (St) B. Oct 15
d. ?455. A Gallo-Roman, he was a disciple of St Lupus of Troyes and of St Germanus of Auxerre and allegedly accompanied the latter to Britain to oppose the Pelagian heresy. He was a missionary among the Germans on the lower Moselle and became bishop of Trier, Germany, in 446.

Severus of Vienne (St) P. Aug 8
d. *p*445. He was a missionary priest based in Vienne, Gaul, who had migrated from the East (allegedly from 'India', meaning perhaps the Yemen).

Sexburga (St) R. Jul 6
?635–?699. Daughter of King Anna of the East Angles, sister of SS Etheldreda, Ethelburga and Withburga and half-sister of St Sethrida, she married King Erconbert of Kent and became the mother of SS Ermengilda and Ercongotha. As queen she founded the nunnery of Minster in Sheppey, Kent, and became abbess there. In 679 she succeeded her sister St Etheldreda as abbess of Ely. Her shrine was established there.

Sextus (St) *see* **Stephen, Pontian and Comps**

Shadost *see* **Sadoc**

Shapur, Isaac and Comps (SS) MM. Nov 30
d. 339. They were among the many martyrs during the reign of Shah Shapur II of Persia. Shapur and Isaac were bishops, the former dying in prison and the latter being stoned to death. SS Mahanes, Abraham and Simeon were martyred at the same time.

Sharbel (Sarbel, Tuthail) and Barbea (Bebaia) (SS) MM. Jan 29
d. 101. Brother and sister, they were martyred at Edessa, Syria (now Urfa in Turkey), in the reign of Trajan. Sharbel had been a pagan high-priest there before their conversion. They were tortured with red-hot irons before having nails hammered into their heads.

Shealtiel (St) *see* **Seven Archangels**

Shenoute (St) R. Jul 1
d. *c*450. A native Egyptian, he became a monk at the White Monastery at Sohag in 370 and was made abbot in ?388. According to ancient sources he had charge of 2,200 monks and 1,800 nuns in several houses. His rule was very strict, featuring beatings and imprisonment even for minor offences. He seems to have been the first monastic superior to have used a written charter of profession for his monastics and this practice (as well as that of encouraging experienced monastics to live as hermits) influenced the rule of St Benedict. He attended the council of Ephesus in 431. He is a pioneer figure in early monasticism, but many of the writings formerly attributed to him seem to be spurious.

Siagrius *see* **Syagrius**

Siard (St) R(OPraem). Nov 13
d. 1230. He became Premonstratensian abbot of Mariengaarden in Friesland, Netherlands, in 1196.

Sibyllina Biscossi (Bl) T(OP). Mar 23
1287–1367. An orphan of Pavia, Italy, when aged twelve she became blind and was adopted by a community of Dominican tertiaries. In 1302 she retired to a cell near the Dominican friary and lived as a hermit there for the rest of her long and penitential life, becoming famous as a thaumaturge. Her cultus was approved for Pavia and the Dominicans in 1853.

Sidney Hodgson (Bl) M. L. Dec 10
d. 1591. A convert layman, he was hanged at Tyburn, London, with St Eustace White and Comps for sheltering priests. He was beatified in 1929. *See* **England (Martyrs of)**.

Sidonius Apollinaris (St) B. Aug 23
?432–?488. Gaius Sollius Apollinaris Sidonius, a Gallo-Roman aristocrat from Lyons, France, was at first a soldier and married the daughter of Avitus, emperor of the West, in 455. He was prefect of Rome 468-9 and then retired to his estate, but was made bishop of Clermont-Ferrand while still a layman in 472. As bishop he had to deal with the Gothic invasion under Alaric, using diplomacy and also a cycle of public prayers called 'Rogation Days' (his invention). His main fame derives from his twenty-four Latin poems (of some quality) and his collected letters. He is one of the last examples in the West of an intellectual formed in the classic Roman culture which was in the process of alteration by the barbarian invasions.

Sidonius (Saëns) of Jumièges (St) R. Nov 14
d. *c*690. From Ireland, he became a monk at Jumièges in Normandy, France, under St Philibert in 644. Later he became first abbot of a monastery founded by St Ouen near Rouen, at the place later named St Saëns after him.

Sidronius (St) M. Jul 11
d. *c*270. He was allegedly a Roman martyr of the reign of Aurelian and had his relics transferred to Mesen south of Ypres, Belgium, in the Middle Ages. Another St Sidronius is venerated at Sens in France. These two have been confused, and the traditions concerning them are untrustworthy.

Sidwell (Sativola) (St) V. Aug 2
? She was apparently a Celt living in Devon, England, and has traditionally been venerated as a virgin-martyr who had her head cut off and thrown down a well by reapers incited by her stepmother. She may not have existed. The centre of the cultus was the church dedicated to her at Exeter. Her attribute is a scythe.

Siffred (Siffrein, Syffroy) (St) B. R. Nov 27
d. ?540 or 660. From Albano near Rome, he became a monk at Lérins and later bishop of Carpentras near Avignon, France, of which diocese he is the principal patron.

Sigebert III of Austrasia, King (St) L. Feb 1
631–656. A son of King Dagobert I of the Franks, when aged three he was made king of Austrasia (straddling the present French-German border, with a capital at Metz). He was baptized by St Amandus of Elnone and had St Cunibert of Cologne and Bl Pepin of Landen as regents. His reign is not well documented, but he was venerated as the founder of various religious institutions and for his justice and moral probity, even though he was a failure as a warrior and was later to be known as the first of the Merovingian 'rois fainéants' (incapable kings).

Sigebert of East Anglia, King (St) M. R. Sep 27
d. ?635. The first Christian king of East Anglia, England, he was baptized while an exile in France and was aided by SS Felix and Fursey in Christianizing his kingdom. He tried to retire and become a monk (possibly at Dunwich) but was forced to leave his monastery and lead the army against the invasion by King Penda of Mercia. He died in battle and was venerated as a martyr on the dubious grounds that Penda was a pagan.

Sigfrid of Växjö (St) B. R(OSB). Feb 15
d. ?1045. A monk of England (probably of Glastonbury), he went to Norway as a missionary at the invitation of King St Olav and passed over to Sweden, where he became a bishop based at Växjö in the south of the country. He died there. His work was successful and he baptized the Swedish king who was also called Olav. He was allegedly canonized in 1158, but documentary proof is lacking.

Sigfrid of Wearmouth (St) R. Aug 22
d. 688. As a disciple of St Benet Biscop he was made abbot of Wearmouth (now Sunderland, England, in 686, and was remembered as a biblical scholar.

Sigibald (St) B. Oct 26
d. *c*740. He became bishop of Metz, France, in 716, and as such promoted scholarship and founded schools and the abbeys of Neuweiter and Saint Avold. He died at the latter.

Sigiran (Cyran, Siran, Sigram) (St) R. Dec 5
d. ?655 or 690. A Frankish nobleman, he was at first cup-bearer at the Merovingian court and then archdeacon of Tours, France, of which city his father was bishop. Later he became a monk and abbot-founder of Méobecq near Châteauroux and of Lonrey near Bourges, which latter was later named St Cyran after him.

Sigisbert and Placid (SS) RR. Jul 11
d. ?650 or 750. The former was the abbot-founder of the abbey of Disentis in Graubünden, Switzerland. This had been built on land donated by the latter, a wealthy landowner who then became a monk there and was allegedly killed for being outspoken in defence of the abbey's privileges. The two existed but their dates are uncertain. Their cultus was approved for the Benedictines in 1905.

Sigismund of Burgundy, King (St) M. L. May 1
d. 523. A Vandal by descent, he was converted from Arianism by St Avitus of Vienne just before he became king of Burgundy, France, in 515. He founded the great abbey of Agaunun (now St Maurice) in the Valais, Switzerland, and did penance there after having his son strangled at the instigation of his second wife. He was defeated by the Franks and the story is that he then fled, disguised himself as a monk and hid in a cell near the above abbey, only to be taken prisoner and killed. He has been venerated as a martyr.

Sigolena (Segouleme) (St) R. Jul 24
d. ?769. A noblewoman of Aquitaine, France, she was widowed when young and became a nun and later abbess at Troclar near Albi. She is a patron of the latter place.

Sigolin (Sighelm) (St) R. Oct 29
d. *c*670. He was an abbot of Stavelot-Malmédy, Belgium, twin monasteries founded by King St Sigebert III of Austrasia. Four other later abbots are venerated with him, namely Godwin, Anglin, Alberic and Odilo.

Sigrada (St) R. Aug 8
d. ?678. Mother of SS Leodegar and Gerin, she founded a nunnery at Soissons, France, and became a nun there after her banishment by Ebroin, mayor (comptroller) of the palace. She died shortly after he had her two sons killed.

Silas (St) B? Jul 13
C1st. He is mentioned in the Acts of the Apostles as a disciple from Jerusalem who accompanied St Paul on his second missionary journey as far as Corinth (15:22 ; 18:5). According to legend he was the first bishop of that city. The Roman tradition identifies him with the Silvanus mentioned in 2 Cor 1:19; 1 Thess 1:1-2; 2 Thess 1:1; 1 Pet 5:12, but this identification is not accepted in the East.

Silaus (Silave, Silanus) (St) B. May 17
d. ?1100. He was allegedly an Irish bishop who died at Lucca, Italy, on his way back from a pilgrimage to Rome, but his extant biography is replete with legendary material and his dates are uncertain.

Silin (Sulian) (St) R. Jul 29
C6th. A legendary abbot of Brittany, he may have founded a monastery at Luxulyan in Cornwall, England.

Sillan (Silvan) (St) R. Feb 28
d. ?610. A disciple of St Comgall, he was his second successor as abbot of Bangor in Co.

Down, Ireland. There are at least fourteen other Irish saints listed with the same name.

Silvanus (St) *see* **Bianor and Silvanus**

Silvanus (St) *see* **Cyril, Rogatus and Comps**

Silvanus (St) *see* **Domninus, Silvanus and Comps**

Silvanus (St) *see* **Lucius, Silvanus and Comps**

Silvanus (St) *see* **Rufinus, Silvanus and Vitalicus**

Silvanus (St) *see* **Seven Brothers**

Silvanus *see* **Silas**

Silvanus (St) *see* **Zoellus, Servilius and Comps**

Silvanus, Luke and Mucius (SS) MM. Feb 6
d. 312. They were bishop, deacon and reader respectively at Emesa in Syria (now Homs) and were martyred in the reign of Maximian after a long imprisonment. The old Roman Martyrology listed Silvanus again with St Tyrannio in error.

Silvanus of Gaza and Comps (SS) MM. May 4
d. ?311. Bishop of Gaza, he was sentenced to work as a slave in the mines of the Holy Land but proved too old for the purpose and was beheaded instead. Forty others from Egypt and the Holy Land who also proved incapable were killed with him, and Eusebius left an account of their martyrdom.

Silvanus of Levroux (St) Sep 22
? He had an ancient cultus at Levroux near Châteauroux, France, but nothing is known about him. His legend identified him with the Zacchaeus of the gospel account set in Jericho.

Silvanus of Rome (St) M. May 5
? He was a martyr of Rome.

Silvanus of Tabennisi (St) R. May 15
C4th. He was an actor before becoming a monk at Tabennisi, Egypt, under St Pachomius. After twenty years of monastic life he became lax and was excommunicated by the latter, but repented and henceforth lived a life of serious penance. He is venerated in the East.

Silvanus of Terracina (St) B. Feb 10
? Bishop of Terracina, Italy, he is listed as a 'confessor' with the original meaning of someone who had survived imprisonment or torture during a persecution.

Silvanus of Troas (St) B. Dec 2
d. *c*450. He was a rhetorician at Constantinople before becoming an ascetic and being made bishop of Philippopolis (now Plovdiv in Bulgaria). But he could not endure the cold weather there so was made bishop of Troas on the Dardanelles instead.

Silverius, Pope (St) M. Jun 20
d. 537. Born at Frosinone in Campania, Italy, a son of Pope St Hormisdas, he was only a subdeacon when the Ostrogothic king appointed him pope. But Vigilius, the papal ambassador at Constantinople, promised the empress Theodora that he would rehabilitate Anthimos, the excommunicated Monophysite patriarch of Constantinople, if he were made pope instead. Silverius was accused of treason and deported to Anatolia after Belisarius, the imperial general, had captured Rome from the Ostrogoths, and Vigilius became pope in 537. Emperor Justinian repented, however, and sent Silverius back to Rome for a proper trial, only for Vigilius arrange his imprisonment on the island of Ponza (off Gaeta) where he died of malnutrition. His cultus was confined to local calendars in 1969.

Silvester *see* **Sylvester**

Silvinus of Brescia (St) B. Sep 28
d. 444. He became bishop of Brescia, Italy, in 440 in extreme old age.

Silvinus of Thérouanne (St) B. R. Feb 17
d. *c*720. A Frankish courtier, he was consecrated as a missionary bishop at Rome and evangelized the district round Thérouanne in Picardy, France, for forty years, being active in ransoming those enslaved in barbarian raids. At the end of his life he became a monk at Auchy-les-Moines near Arras.

Silvinus of Verona (St) B. Sep 12
d. *c*550. Nothing is known about this bishop of Verona, Italy.

Silvius (St) *see* **Arator of Alexandria and Comps**

Simbert (Simpert, Sintbert) (St) B. R. Oct 13
d. ?809. He was educated at the abbey of Murbach near Colmar in Alsace, France,

became a monk there and was made abbot. In 778 he was made bishop of Augsburg by Charlemagne (remaining abbot of Murbach) and was a notable restorer of Church life. He was canonized in 1468.

Simeon the Ancient (St) R. Jan 28
d. *c*390. When young he was a hermit in a cave in Syria, then migrated and founded two monasteries on Mt Sinai. He often visited his friend Palladius.

Simeon Barsabae and Comps (SS) Apr 21
d. 341. He was bishop of Seleucia-Ctesiphon, the patriarchal see of the Persian church situated in central Mesopotamia, and was martyred in the reign of Shah Shapur II together with Abdechalas and Ananias (priests), Usthazanes the Shah's tutor (a repentant apostate), Pusicius the overseer of the king's workmen and his unmarried daughter and over one hundred other Christians including bishops, priests and clerics. The acta are authentic.

Simeon of Cava (Bl) R(OSB). Nov 16
d. 1141. Abbot of the great Benedictine abbey of La Cava near Salerno, Italy, from 1124, he was highly regarded by Pope Innocent II and by King Roger II of Sicily. During his abbacy Cava reached the peak of its splendour. His cultus was confirmed for there in 1928.

Simeon Metaphrastes (St) L? Nov 9
C10th. He is the most famous Byzantine hagiographer, and his collection of lives of the saints (the *Menologion*) has been regarded as a standard work in the East since his lifetime. Nothing is now known about his own life, however.

Simeon the New Theologian (St) R. Mar 12
949–1022. A Studite monk at Constantinople, he became abbot of St Mamas there in 981. His spiritual teachings caused controversy, so he resigned and was later exiled. Although he was pardoned he remained away from the city. He is one of the greatest Byzantine mystics and wrote much on the divine light manifested at the Transfiguration, thus being influential in the development of hesychastic prayer in the East.

Simeon of Polirone (St) R(OSB). Jul 26
d. 1016. Allegedly an Armenian hermit, he went on pilgrimage to Jerusalem, Rome, Compostela, in Spain and Tours in France and became famous as a thaumaturge. Finally he settled at the Cluniac abbey of Polirone near Padua, Italy, where he died.

Simeon Salus (St) R. Jul 1
d. *p*588. Apparently from Emesa (now Homs) in Syria, he was at the monastery of St Gerasimus on the Jordan for twenty-eight years before returning to Emesa. There he pretended to be sub-normal in order not to be praised, hence his surname which means 'fool'. He was alive when an earthquake destroyed the city but nothing is known about him afterwards.

Simeon of Sandomir (Bl) *see* **Sadoc of Sandomir and Comps**

Simeon Senex (St) L. Oct 8
C1st. The prophecy which he made when the infant Jesus was presented at the Temple in Jerusalem is described in Lk 2:25-35. His surname means 'Elder', although the text of the Gospel merely describes him as a righteous and devout man without indication of age. The legends concerning him are worthless.

Simeon Stylites the Elder (St) R. Jan 5
*c*390–459. From Sisan near Aleppo, Syria, he was a shepherd like his father until he became a monk at the Syrian monastery of Tel Ada. He was ejected because of his excessive austerities and became a hermit at Telanissos in the hills west of Aleppo, attaching himself by chains to a rock, but many visitors disturbed his solitude so he started living on a platform mounted on a pillar. He gradually raised the height of this until it reached sixty-six feet and he spent the remaining thirty-seven years of his life on the platform, about a yard in width. His surname means 'on a pillar', and he was imitated by many in Syria and elsewhere. He became famous throughout the Roman Empire, being consulted by all sorts of people from emperors to the local nomads, and he was influential in support of the council of Chalcedon. After his death his pillar became the focus of a pilgrimage centre containing four basilicas, and the ruins of this form the most important Christian monument in Syria.

Simeon Stylites the Younger (St) R. Sep 3
521–597. From Antioch, Syria, as a child he became a monk and as a young man became a stylite like his elder namesake. He was on a pillar situated on the 'Wonderful Mountain' (near the pagan shrine of Daphne) for forty-five years, and while he was still alive a great basilica was built

round him there. The ruins of this survive near Antioch, which is now in Turkey.

Simeon of Trier (St) R. Jun 1
d. 1035. A Greek from Syracuse, Sicily, he studied at Constantinople and was in turn a hermit by the Jordan and a monk at Bethlehem. Then he migrated to St Catherine's on Sinai and again became a hermit, first in a cave near the Red Sea and then on the summit of Sinai. But he was chosen to go on a trip to Europe to collect alms, and after a series of adventures he settled at Trier, Germany, as a hermit affiliated to the Benedictine abbey of St Martin. The abbot of this monastery was at his deathbed and wrote his biography. He was canonized in 1042.

Similian (Sambin) (St) B. Jun 16
d. 310. This bishop of Nantes, France, was highly regarded by St Gregory of Tours.

Simitrius and Comps (SS) MM. May 26
d. ?159. A priest and his congregation of twenty-two, they were seized while assembled at the church of St Praxedis at Rome and beheaded without trial.

Simon Acosta (Bl) *see* **Ignatius de Azevedo and Comps**

Simon Ballachi (Bl) R(OP). Nov 3
d. 1319. A nobleman from near Rimini, Italy, he was a nephew of two archbishops of that city. When aged twenty-seven he became a Dominican lay brother at Rimini and was famous for his extraordinary austerities. His cultus was confirmed for there in 1820.

Simon Berneaux and Comps (SS) MM. B. PP. Mar 8
d. 1866. Born near Le Mans, France, he became a priest of the Paris Foreign Mission Society and went to Manchuria in 1840. He was coadjutor to the Vicar-Apostolic there before becoming Vicar-Apostolic of Korea. He was seized in Seoul with three fellow priests, accused of corrupting Korean customs, imprisoned, tortured and beheaded. His companions were Justus Ranfer de Brenières, who was a 28-year-old nobleman from Chalon-sur-Saône; Louis Beaulieu of the same age from Bordeaux and Peter Dorié from Luçon, aged 27. They were canonized in 1984. *See* **Korea (Martyrs of)**.

Simon Chen (Ximan) (St) *see* **Gregory Grassi and Comps**

Simon of Créspy (St) R(OSB). Sep 18
d. *c*1080. Count of Créspy in Valois, France, he was a descendant of Charlemagne and was brought up at the court of William the Conqueror. The sight of his father's decomposing body caused a conversion and he went on pilgrimage to Rome but stopped off on the way at the Benedictine abbey of St Claude in the Jura. He became a monk there in 1070, but was called to Rome by Pope St Gregory VII in 1080 to act as a papal ambassador. He died at Rome.

Simon Fidati of Cascia (Bl) R(OSA). Feb 3
d. 1348. From Cascia in Umbria, Italy, he became an Augustinian friar and was a prominent figure as a writer, preacher and spiritual director in the life of most of the cities of central Italy. Scholars have claimed to find in his book *De Gestis Domini Salvatoris* a source of several of Luther's doctrines. His cultus was confirmed for the Augustinian friars in 1883.

Simon (Phan Dac) Hoa (St) M. L. Dec 12
d. 1840. A Vietnamese physician in the Mekong Delta and mayor of his village, he was affiliated to the Paris Foreign Mission Society. As a result he was viciously tortured and beheaded. *See* **Vietnam (Martyrs of)**.

Simon of Jerusalem (St) M. B. Feb 18
d. ?107. He was the son of Clopas and relative of Christ mentioned in Matt 13:55, Mk 6:3 and Jn I9:25. The tradition is that he succeeded St James the Less as bishop of Jerusalem and was crucified in extreme old age in the reign of Trajan. His attribute is a fish. His cultus was confined to local calendars in 1969.

Simon Kiyota Bokusai and Comps (BB) MM. Aug 16
d. 1620. An army officer from Bungo in Japan, he became a catechist and was crucified at Kokura on Kyushu when aged sixty together with his wife, Mary-Magdalen Kiyota, and a family of three who had been his servants: Thomas and Mary Gengoro and their son, James. They were beatified in 1867. *See* **Japan (Martyrs of)**.

Simon of Lipnicza (Bl) R(OFM). Jul 30
d. 1482. From Lipnicza in Poland, he was inspired to become a Franciscan after hearing a sermon by St John de Capistrano and was a famous preacher of the Holy Name. He died of the plague while nursing those suffering at Cracow during an epidemic, and had his cultus confirmed for there in 1685.

Simon López (Bl) *see* **Ignatius de Azevedo and Comps**

Simon Rinalducci (Bl) R(OSA). Apr 20
d. 1322. From Todi, Italy, he became an Augustinian friar and a famous preacher and was provincial superior of Umbria for a time. He kept silence in face of an unjust accusation rather than cause scandal among his brethren. He died at Bologna and had his cultus confirmed for the Augustinian friars in 1833.

Simon de Rojas (St) R. Sep 28
1522–1624. From Valladolid, Spain, he became a Trinitarian and was superior-general as well as a famous missionary. Later he was confessor at the court of King Philip III of Spain and tutor to the royal family. Dying at Madrid, he was canonized in 1988.

Simon Stock (St) R(OC). May 16
d. 1265. An English superior-general of the Carmelites, he was elected ?1234, had a reputation for sanctity and died at Bordeaux, France. Nothing more is known about him from contemporary sources. He was not responsible for converting the Carmelites from hermits to friars, as that had been done before he was elected. The famous legend wherein he is alleged to have been given the scapular (his attribute) by Our Lady is based on a C17th forgery. He is venerated as a saint by the Carmelites and at Bordeaux but his cultus has not been formally confirmed.

Simon Qin (Qunfu) (St) *see* **Elizabeth Qin (Bian) and Simon Qin (Qunfu)**

Simon of Trent *Mar 24*
d. 1474. A child aged two of Trent in Austria (now Italy), he was allegedly ritually tortured to death by Jews on Good Friday. The confessions of those accused were obtained under torture and the actual events are uncertain, but the trial was reviewed by the pope in 1478 and no objections raised. In 1588 Simon became the only alleged victim of Jewish ritual murder to be inserted into the Roman Martyrology as a saint after several miracles were reported at his shrine, but the cultus was suppressed in 1965 as being scandalous.

Simon Yempo (Bl) M. L. Dec 4
d. 1623. A Japanese Buddhist bonze, he converted to Christianity with the rest of his community and become a lay catechist. He was burnt alive at Edo (now Tokyo) with BB Francis Galvez and Jerome de Angelis. He was beatified in 1867. *See* **Japan (Martyrs of)**.

Simon the Zealot (St) A. Oct 28
C1st. In the New Testament he is only referred to in the lists of the apostles with the surname 'Cananean' meaning 'Zealot' (not a 'native of Cana', pace St Jerome and later tradition in the West). The traditions concerning his career after the Resurrection are conflicting and nothing is known about his life. He has various attributes: a fish or two, a boat, an oar or a saw. He is also depicted being sawn in half lengthwise.

Simone Chauvigné (Bl) *see* **William Repin and Comps**

Simplician (St) *see* **Stephen, Pontian and Comps**

Simplician of Milan (St) B. Aug 16
d. 400. A friend and adviser of St Ambrose, he succeeded him as archbishop of Milan, Italy, but was elderly and died three years later. He played a leading part in the conversion of St Augustine by whom he was remembered with gratitude.

Simplicius (St) *see* **Calepodius and Comps**

Simplicius (St) *see* **Four Crowned Martyrs**

Simplicius (St) *see* **Quintus, Simplicius and Comps**

Simplicius, Pope (St) Mar 10
d. 483. From Tivoli near Rome, he became pope in 468 and upheld the council of Chalcedon against three successive Eastern emperors who sought a modus vivendi with the Monophysites in Egypt and Syria. The last Western emperor was deposed during his reign in 476 by the Arian King Odoacer.

Simplicius, Constantius and Victorian (SS) MM. Aug 26
? According to the old Roman Martyrology they were a father and his two sons who were martyred in the reign of Aurelian. However they seem to be a mistaken grouping of Simplicius of Rome, Victorianus of Amiternum and Constantius of Perugia.

Simplicius, Faustinus and Beatrice (SS) MM. Jul 29
d. ?303. They were allegedly three siblings, two brothers and a sister, who were martyred at Rome in the reign of Diocletian. Their acta are untrustworthy and their cultus was confined to local calendars in 1969.

Simplicius of Autun (St) B. Jun 24
d. *c*360. He was married but was allegedly abstaining from sexual relations when he

became bishop of Autun, France. He worked zealously and successfully for the conversion of pagans.

Simplicius of Bourges (St) B. Jun 16
d. 477. A Gallo-Roman nobleman, he was already married with a large family when he was chosen to be the bishop of Bourges, France. He fought against Arianism and simony.

Simplicius of Montecassino (St) R(OSB). Oct 22
d. *c*570. He was allegedly the third abbot of Montecassino, Italy, St Benedict being the first.

Simplicius of Tempio Pausania (St) M. B? May 15
d. 304. He was allegedly a bishop in the north of Sardinia who was buried alive in the reign of Diocletian.

Simplicius of Verona (St) B. Nov 20
d. ?535. He was bishop of Verona, Italy.

Sincheall the Elder (St) R . Mar 26
C5th. A disciple of St Patrick, he was the abbot-founder of a monastery and school at Killeigh in Co. Offaly, Ireland, where his community had one hundred and fifty monks.

Sincheall the Younger (St) R. Jun 25
C5th. He succeeded the above as abbot of Killeigh in Co. Offaly, Ireland.

Sindimius (St) *see* **Cyriac, Paulillus and Comps**

Sindulf of Rheims (St) R. Oct 20
d. 660. From Gascony, he became a hermit at Aussonce near Rheims, France.

Sindulf of Vienne (St) B. Dec 10
d. ?669. He was a bishop of Vienne, France.

Siran *see* **Sigiran**

Siricius, Pope (St) Nov 26
d. 399. A Roman, he succeeded St Damasus as pope in 384. A collection of his letters are regarded as the first papal decretals, and the consolidation of papal authority was also manifest in the foundation of a vicariate at Thessalonica, Greece, in opposition to the patriarchate of Constantinople.

Siridion (St) B. Jan 2
? This entry in the old Roman Martyrology is probably a copyist's error for 'Isidore of Antioch'.

Sirmium (Martyrs of) (SS) Feb 23, Apr 9
d. ?303 The old Roman Martyrology lists two anonymous groups of martyrs at Sirmium (now Srem Mitrovica in Serbia) in the rule of Diocletian. One numbered seventy-two and the other comprised seven maidens. They were probably martyred in the same year.

Sisebut (St) R(OSB). Mar 15
d. 1082. He was abbot of the Benedictine monastery of Cardena near Burgos, Spain, which was an important centre of contemporary ecclesiastical and civil life. He gave shelter to El Cid, the famous hero of the 'Reconquista', when the latter was exiled by the king.

Sisenand (St) M. D. Jul 16
d. 851. Allegedly from Badajoz in Extremadura, Spain, he was a deacon at Cordoba and was beheaded in the reign of Emir Abderrahman II.

Sisinnius (St) *see* **Saturninus and Sisinnius**

Sisinnius, Diocletius and Florentius (SS) MM. May 11
d. 303. They were stoned to death at Osimo near Ancona, Italy, in the reign of Diocletian.

Sisinnius, Martyrius and Alexander (SS) MM. May 29
d. 397. According to their story, they were missionaries from Cappodocia, Asia Minor, who were welcomed by St Vigilius of Trent on the recommendation of St Ambrose and sent to evangelize the Tyrol. They were lynched by a mob during a pagan festival in the Val di Non.

Sisinnius of Cyzicus (St) B. Nov 23
d. *p*325. Bishop of Cyzicus on the south shore of the Sea of Marmara, Asia Minor, during the persecution of Diocletian he was seized and tied behind an unbroken horse which was then turned loose. He managed to survive somehow and was present at the council of Nicaea in 325.

Sisoes the Great (St) R. Jul 4
d. ?429. He was one of the desert fathers of Egypt and was initially a hermit at Scetis. Finding this monastic settlement becoming too crowded, he went off and settled at St Anthony's 'Interior Mountain' in the desert east of the Nile, which he found deserted and where he remained for over seventy years.

Sithian *see* **Swithin**

Siviard (St) R. Mar 1
d. ?729. A monk at Saint-Calais near Le Mans, France, he succeeded his own father as abbot

and wrote a biography of St Carilefus, founder of the monastery.

Sixtus I, 'Pope' (St) Apr 3
d. 127. He was allegedly pope from 117 and a martyr but there are no acta and the list of popes by St Irenaeus makes no mention of martyrdom. That his name corresponds with his being sixth on the list has raised suspicions that the early names thereon are spurious.

Sixtus II, Pope and Comps
(St) MM. Aug 7
d. 258. A Greek, he was pope for one year. While preaching during Mass in the catacomb of Praetextatus he was seized with his deacons Felicissimus and Agapitus and martyred. His name is in the Roman canon of the Mass. The old Roman Martyrology lists Januarius, Magnus, Vincent and Stephen (sub-deacons) and Quartus as having been martyred with him. Quartus owes his existence to a bad manuscript in which 'diaconus Quartus' was written for 'diacones quattuor', which implies that St Sixtus was martyred with six of his deacons while the seventh, St Laurence, was martyred later.

Sixtus III, Pope (St) Mar 28
d. 440. A Roman, he became pope in 432. He opposed Nestorianism and Pelagianism and restored the basilica of St Mary Major in thanksgiving for the declaration at the Council of Ephesus that Our Lady is the Mother of God.

Sixtus of Rheims (St) B. Sep 1
d. *c*300. He was a Roman missionary who became first bishop of Rheims, France, in *c*290. He had previously established his base at Soissons before moving to Rheims.

Slebhene (Slebhine) (St) R. Mar 2
d. 767. An Irish monk, he was abbot of Iona, Scotland, from 752.

Smaragdus (St) *see* **Cyriac, Largus and Comps**

Sobel (St) *see* **Cantidius, Cantidian and Sobel**

Socrates and Dionysius (SS) MM. Apr 19
d. 275. They were killed with lances at Perga in Pamphylia, Asia Minor, in the reign of Aurelian.

Socrates and Stephen (SS) MM. Sep 17
? The old Roman Martyrology listed them as martyrs of Britain in the reign of Diocletian, but it is probable that 'Britain' is a copyist's error either for Abretania or for Bithynia, both in Asia Minor.

Sola (Sol, Suolo) (St) R.. Dec 3
d. 794. An Anglo-Saxon missionary monk, he followed St Boniface to Germany and lived as a hermit near the abbey of Fulda. Then Charlemagne gave him some land near Eichstätt on which he founded a monastery later named Solnhofen after him.

Solangia (Solange) (St) V. May 10
d. *c*880. A peasant's daughter of Villemont near Bourges, France, when shepherding her father's sheep she was sexually assaulted by a local nobleman and murdered when she resisted.

Solemnis (Soleine) (St) B. Sep 25
d. ?511. He was made bishop of Chartres, France, in *c*490 and assisted at the baptism of Clovis, king of the Franks.

Solina (St) V. Oct 17
d. *c*290. According to her legend she was a young woman from a pagan family of Gascony, France, who fled to Chartres to escape an arranged marriage but was captured and beheaded there.

Solochon, Pamphamer and Pamphalon (SS) MM. May 17
d. 305. Three Egyptian soldiers in the Roman army, stationed at Chalcedon on the Bosporus, Asia Minor, they were clubbed to death in the reign of Maximian.

Solomon (St) *see* **Ruderic and Solomon**

Solomon *see* **Salonius**

Solomon I of Brittany
(St) M. L. Jun 25
C5th. According to the legend he was born in Cornwall, England, was the husband of St Gwen and father of St Cybi. He emigrated to Brittany, France, became a ruler there and was assassinated by pagan rebels.

Solomon (Selyf) III of Brittany (St) M. L. Jun 25
d. 874. King of Brittany, France, he was a brave (though at times brutal) warrior who fought the Franks, Norse and his own rebellious subjects. He did penance for the crimes of his youth and when he was assassinated was counted as a martyr. The Bretons regard him as a national hero.

Solomon Leclercq (Bl) *see* **September (Martyrs of)**

Solutor (St) *see* **Octavius, Solutor and Adventor**

Solutor (St) *see* **Valentine, Solutor and Victor**

Sopatra (St) *see* **Eustolia and Sopatra**

Sophia
The famous church in Constantinople has often been referred to in the West as St Sophia's. This does not commemorate a saint but is a corruption of the Greek 'Hagia Sofia' or Holy Wisdom.

Sophia and Irene (SS) MM. Sep 18
d. ?200. They were beheaded in Egypt.

Sophia of Fermo (St) V. Apr 30
d. *c*250. She was a maiden martyred at Fermo, Italy, in the reign of Decius.

Sophia of Rome (St) L. Sep 30
d. ?117. According to the legend she was the widowed mother of the three unmarried sisters Faith, Hope and Charity who were martyred at Rome in the reign of Hadrian. Three days later she visited their tomb and died there. The story is apparently a fictional Eastern allegory of God's wisdom ('sophia') from which come the virtues of faith, hope and charity.

Sophronius of Cyprus (St) B. Dec 8
C6th. The old Roman Martyrology alleged that he was a bishop of Cyprus but there is no evidence supporting this.

Sophronius of Jerusalem
(St) B. Mar 11
d. ?639. From Damascus, Syria, as a monk he accompanied John Moschus on his journeys to the various monastic sites in the Middle East. (The latter wrote a description of them, the extant *Spiritual Meadow*.) He was at the monastery of St Theodosius near Bethlehem from 616 and became patriarch of Jerusalem in 634. A noted ecclesiastical writer, he was in the forefront of the struggle against the Monothelite policy of the imperial government. The Muslims took Jerusalem in 637 and he fled to Alexandria, where he died.

Sosipater (St) B? Jun 25
C2nd. The relative that St Paul mentioned in Rom 16:21 has been hypothetically identified with the Sosipater of Beroea who accompanied him on the initial stage of his final return to Jerusalem from Greece (Acts 20:4). Conflicting traditions allege that he either became bishop of Iconium in Asia Minor or evangelized Corfu with St Jason.

Sosius (St) *see* **Januarius of Benevento and Comps**

Sosthenes and Victor (SS) MM. Sep 10
C4th? They were martyred at Chalcedon on the Bosporus in the reign of Maximian. In the unreliable acta of St Euphemia they featured among the executioners appointed to torture her, being converted through her prayers and example.

Sosthenes of Corinth (St) B? Nov 28
C1st. He is the ruler of the synagogue at Corinth mentioned in Acts 18:17 who became a disciple of St Paul and is possibly the 'brother' mentioned in 1 Cor 1:1. Byzantine tradition made him the first bishop of Colophon in Ionia.

Sosthenes Sostegni (St) *see* **Servites, Founders of**

Sostratus, Spirus, Eraclius, Eperentius and Cecilia (SS) MM. Jul 8
C4th.? They were martyred at Sirmium (now Srem Mitrovica in Serbia).

Soter, Pope *Apr 22*
d. ?174. An Italian, he is eleventh in St Irenaeus's list of early popes and Eusebius referred to his correspondence with the church of Corinth. In his time Easter was fixed as an annual festival, to be celebrated on the Sunday following the Jewish Passover. There is no evidence that he was a martyr and his cultus was suppressed in 1969.

Soteris (St) V. Feb 10
d. 304. A Roman maiden, she was martyred in the reign of Diocletian and seems to have been a sister of the great-grandmother of St Ambrose. The latter mentioned her in writing several times.

Sozon (St) M. Sep 7
d. ?304. According to the legend he was a shepherd of Cilicia, Asia Minor, who pulled a hand off an idol made of gold being displayed at a pagan festival, broke it up and distributed the pieces among the poor. He was burnt at the stake.

Spanish Civil War (Martyrs of)
1934–9. The election of a Republican government in Spain in 1931 initiated a policy of

government hostility towards the Church that was a consequence of the radical anti-clericalism that had been a feature of Spanish politics in the C19th. Persecution soon grew vicious, especially in areas controlled by Communist or Anarchist factions, and this was a factor leading to the rebellion by Nationalist forces under General Franco and the consequent civil war which saw the defeat of the Republicans. Many victims of massacre have been beatified. These were mostly killed during the early stages of the war in 1936, but some before it started. In total, 4,184 priests, and 283 female and 2,365 male consecrated religious were reported to have been killed in cold blood, along with many lay members of the Church. Up to 2001, 17 had been canonized and 212 beatified; a further 233 were beatified in that year. *See* lists of national martyrs in the appendix.

Speciosus (St) R(OSB). Mar 15
d. ?555. According to the second *Dialogue* of St Gregory the Great he was from Rome and became a disciple of St Benedict at Montecassino with his brother, Gregory. They were then sent to found a monastery at Terracina, but he died at Capua while on an errand connected with this.

Sperandea (Sperandia)
(St) R(OSB). Sep 11
d. 1276. A relative of St Ubald Baldassini, she became a Benedictine nun at Cingoli in the Marches, Italy, going on to become abbess. She is the patron of Cingoli.

Speratus (St) *see* **Scillitan Martyrs**

Spes (St) R. Mar 28
d. ?513. He was the abbot-founder of a monastery at Campi near Norcia, Italy, and was totally blind for forty years, but fifteen days before his death his eyesight returned. This was considered remarkable but is medically explicable.

Speusippus, Eleusippus, Meleusippus and Leonilla
(SS) MM. Jan 17
d. ?175. According to the legend, probably fictional, they were triplet brothers of Cappodocia, Asia Minor, who were martyred with their grandmother in the reign of Marcus Aurelius. Their alleged relics were taken to Langres, France, in the C6th.

Spinulus (Spinula, Spin) (St) R. Nov 5
d. ?707 or 720. A monk of Moyenmoutier in the Jura, France, under St Hidulf of Trier, later he became the abbot-founder of St Blasien in the Black Forest, Germany.

Spiridion (St) B. Dec 14
d. ?348. He was a shepherd before becoming bishop of Tremithus on his native Cyprus. In the persecution of Diocletian he had one eye removed and was made a slave in the copper mines, but survived. He was allegedly one of the 'confessors of the Faith' present at the council of Nicaea and a strong opponent of Arianism there, although his name is not among the list of signatories. He was, however, definitely present at the council of Sardica in 343.

Stachys (St) B? Oct 31
C1st. St Paul referred to him as 'my beloved Stachys' in Rom 16:9. The unreliable tradition concerning the apostolic foundation of the church at Constantinople makes him the first bishop of Byzantium, ordained by St Andrew.

Stacteus (St) *see* **Symphorosa of Tivoli and Comps**

Stacteus of Rome (St) M. Sep 28
? Nothing is known about this martyr of Rome.

Stanislaus Kazimierczyk
(Bl) R(CR). May 3
1433–1489. Born near Cracow, Poland, he studied in the Jagełłonian University there and became a canon regular in 1456. He was a well-known preacher who stressed the centrality of the Eucharist in the Christian life and has left many spiritual writings. His cultus was confirmed for Poland in1993.

Stanislaus Kostka (St) R(SJ). Nov 13
1550–1568. A young nobleman from Rostków in Poland, in 1563 he went to study at the Jesuit college at Vienna, Austria, and (despite the fierce opposition of his family) fled to St Peter Canisius at Augsburg, Bavaria, in order to become a Jesuit himself. He was received into the noviciate at Rome by St Francis Borgia in 1567 and died as a novice after having quickly acquired a reputation for moral purity. He was canonized in 1726.

Stanislaus Szczepanowsky
(St) M. B. Apr 11
1030–1079. From near Cracow, Poland, he was educated at Gniezno and Paris and became bishop of Cracow in 1072. He excommunicated King Boleslaus II for his evil life and the king killed him with a sword as a result while he was celebrating Mass. Pope St Gregory VII laid an

interdict upon Poland, the king fled to Hungary and died in exile. Stanislaus was canonized in 1253, although there is a disputed theory that the assassination was as a result of his plotting to dethrone the king. He is often depicted being hacked in pieces at the foot of the altar.

St Stanislaus Szczepanowsky, Apr 11

Stephana de Quinzani (Bl) T(OP). Jan 2
1457–1530. From Brescia, Italy, she became a Dominican tertiary when aged fifteen and lived at the family home for many years. Then she founded, and was first superior of, a monastery at Soncino near Cremona, where she died. She was noted for her ecstasies and for having the stigmata, which were attested by many eye-witnesses. Her cultus was confirmed for Cremona in 1740.

Stephen
Deviant vernacular forms of the original Greek 'Stefanos' (meaning 'crowned') are: French, Etienne; Spanish, Esteban; Hungarian, Istvan.

Stephen (St) *see* **Castor and Stephen**

Stephen (St) *see* **Claudius, Crispin and Comps**

Stephen (St) *see* **Honorius, Eutychius and Stephen**

Stephen (St) *see* **Mark and Stephen**

Stephen (St) *see* **Socrates and Stephen**

Stephen (St) *see* **Victor and Stephen**

Stephen and Hildebrand
(BB) RR(OCist). Apr 11
d. 1209. They were Cistercians (an abbot and a monk) killed by the Albigenses at Saint-Gilles in Languedoc, France, where they have an unconfirmed cultus.

Stephen, Pontian and Comps (SS) MM. Dec 31
? They are listed as martyrs of Catania, Sicily. Also named are Attalus, Fabian, Cornelius, Sextus, Flos, Quintian, Minervinus and Simplician.

Stephen I, Pope (St) Aug 2
d. 257. A nobleman of Rome, he was made pope in 254 and maintained the validity of baptism by heretics against the rigorist position held by St Cyprian of Carthage and others. According to the unreliable legend (contradicted by early evidence and now discarded) he was beheaded while seated in his chair during the celebration of Mass in the catacombs. His cultus was confined to local calendars in 1969.

Stephen of Antioch (St) M. B. Apr 25
d. 481. He was elected patriarch of Antioch, Syria, in 478 after the Monophysite Peter the Fuller had been exiled. The partisans of the latter refused to accept him, and eventually assassinated him in one of the city's churches and threw his body into the river.

Stephen of Apt (St) B. Nov 6
975–1046. From Agde near Montpellier, France, he became bishop of Apt in 1010 and rebuilt the cathedral there.

Stephen Bandelli (Bl) R(OP). Jun 12
d. 1450. From Castelnuovo near Piacenza, Italy, he became a Dominican at the latter place and was famous as a preacher and reformer. He died at Saluzzo and his cultus was confirmed for there and for the Dominicans in 1856.

Stephen Bellesini (Bl) R(OSA). Feb 3
1774–1840. From Trent, Austria (now Italy), he became an Augustinian friar at Bologna, Italy, and studied there and at Rome. When the French Revolution brought war he fled back to Trent and became the government inspector of schools after the religious orders were suppressed. As soon as it was possible he became a

friar again and was novice master at Rome and parish priest at the shrine of our Lady at Genazzano, where he died as a result of nursing cholera sufferers. He was beatified in 1904.

Stephen du Bourg (St) R(OCart). Jan 4
d. 1118. He had been a canon at Valence, France, before becoming a hermit near Langres, and then became one of the first companions of St Bruno at the foundation of the Grande-Chartreuse in 1084. In 1116 he was sent to found the Carthusian monastery of Meyria, where he died.

Stephen of Caiazzo (St)
B. R(OSB). Oct 29
935–1023. From Macerata near Ancona, Italy, he was abbot of San Salvatore Maggiore before becoming bishop of Caiazzo near Naples in 979. He is the principal patron of the city and diocese.

Stephen of Cardena and Comps (SS) MM. RR(OSB). Aug 6
d. ?872. He was allegedly abbot of Cardena near Burgos, Spain, and was massacred with his community of two hundred by Muslim raiders. The cultus was approved in 1603, but the earliest evidence for their existence is an inscription of the C13th which does not give the name of the abbot.

Stephen Casadevall Puig (Bl) *see* **Philip-of-Jesus Munárriz Azcona and Comps**

Stephen of Chatillon (St)
B. R(OCart). Sep 7
d. 1208. A nobleman from Lyons, France, he became a Carthusian at Portes and was made prior in 1196. In 1203 he became bishop of Dié, where he died. His cultus was approved in 1907.

Stephen of Corvey (St)
M. B. R(OSB). Jun 2
d. ?1075. A monk of Corvey in Lower Saxony, Germany, he was consecrated as a missionary bishop for Sweden by the archbishop of Bremen and worked around Uppsala and Stockholm (the seat of royal power) and to the north. He was killed in a pagan reaction, probably at Nora.

Stephen Cuénot (St) M. B. Nov 14
1802–1861. From Beaulieu in Franche Comté, France, he joined the Paris Society for Foreign Missions and was sent to Vietnam. In 1833 he was appointed Vicar-Apostolic of 'East Cochin-China' (the area around Saigon). He was one of the first to be arrested on the outbreak of persecution in 1861 and died in prison (perhaps from poison) shortly before the date fixed for his execution. *See* **Vietnam (Martyrs of)**.

Stephen of Cuneo (St) *see* **Nicholas Tavelić and Comps**

Stephen Gillet (Bl) *see* **September (Martyrs of)**

Stephen Harding (St)
R(OCist). Jan 26
d. 1134. A monk (or student) of Sherborne Abbey, England, after a pilgrimage to Rome he joined St Robert at Molesmes and migrated to Cîteaux with him. There he was successively sub-prior under St Robert, prior under St Alberic and third abbot from 1109. He initiated the unified congregational structure of the Cistercians but was not the author of the original constitutions (as previously thought). He received St Bernard as a novice at Cîteaux and sent him to become the abbot-founder of Clairvaux two years later, thus starting the spectacular success of the Cistercians in Europe. He was canonized in 1623.

Stephen of Hungary, King (St) L. Aug 16
d. ?935–1038. Born at Esztergom, Hungary, he was baptized when young, succeeded as duke of the Magyars in 997 and made his life's work the Christianization of his people. In this he was aided by the connections made by his marriage to Gisela, a sister of Emperor St Henry II, and he obtained the title of king from the pope in 1000 (the original crown used in his coronation survives). He organized dioceses and founded several abbeys (the greatest being Pannonhalma, which survives), successfully suppressed revolts motivated by pagan reaction and gave his kingdom the civil organization which survived until the incursion of the Ottomans. His son, St Emeric, predeceased him and the later years of his reign were very difficult. He was canonized in 1083 and is the patron of Hungary and the Magyar people.

Stephen del Lupo (St) R(OSB). Jul 19
d. 1191. He was the abbot-founder of the Benedictine abbey of St Peter Vallebona at Manoppello near Pescara, Italy. He allegedly befriended a wolf, hence his surname.

Stephen of Lyons (St) B. Feb 13
d. 512. He was a bishop of Lyons, France, who was instrumental in converting the Arian Burgundians to orthodoxy.

Stephen Maya Gutierrez (Bl) *see* **Hospitaller Martyrs of Spain**

Stephen Min (St) *see* **Korea (Martyrs of)**

Stephen of Muret (St) R. F. Feb 8
1046–1124. A son of a nobleman of the Auvergne, France, when aged twelve he went on pilgrimage with his father to Bari, Italy, but fell ill at Benevento and had to stay behind. Then he lived with hermits in Calabria before returning to France and becoming a hermit himself at Muret in the Limousin in 1076. He attracted many hermit-disciples and he became their informal superior, dying as such but apparently not having formally taken religious vows. The brethren then moved to Grandmont near Lodève and became the nucleus of a new monastic order, the Grandmontines. This was not Benedictine, as their 'Rule of St Stephen' was written from reminiscences of his teachings. The order was suppressed before (not by) the French Revolution.

Stephen of Obazine (Bl) R(OCist). Mar 8
d. 1154. With another priest he withdrew into the forest of Obazine near Tulle, France, to be a hermit, but disciples joined them and they built a monastery. This became a congregation (which included a nunnery) and he arranged for its affiliation to the Cistercian order in 1147. He died at Bonaigne, one of his foundations. His cultus was not confirmed.

Stephen of Perugia (St) R(OSB). Sep 16
d. 1026. He was abbot of the Benedictine monastery of St Peter at Perugia, Italy, where he had an unconfirmed cultus.

Stephen Pongrácz (St) *see* **Košice (Martyrs of)**

Stephen the Protomartyr (St) M. D. Dec 26
d. ?35. He was one of the first seven deacons of the infant church in Jerusalem and was stoned to death by a lynch-mob after being interrogated by the Sanhedrin (Acts 6,7). His attribute is a number of stones.

Stephen de Ravinel (Bl) *see* **September (Martyrs of)**

Stephen of Reggio (St) M? B? Jul 5
C1st? According to a C10th Byzantine tradition he was consecrated as first bishop of Reggio in Calabria, Italy, by St Paul and was martyred in the reign of Nero. There was no such tradition in the city itself until the C17th, and he probably never existed.

Stephen of Rieti (St) R. Feb 13
d. *c*590. He was an abbot at Rieti, Italy, whom St Gregory the Great described as 'rough in speech but cultured in life'.

Stephen Rowsham (Bl) M. P. (Mar)
d. 1587. Born in Oxfordshire, he was an Oxford graduate and vicar of St Mary's Church there before his conversion. Ordained in 1881 at Soissons, he was captured immediately on his return to England and kept for 18 months in 'Little Ease' (reputedly a cell of 64 cubic feet) in the Tower of London before being deported. Returning, he was executed at Gloucester on an uncertain date and was beatified in 1987. *See* **England (Martyrs of)**.

Stephen de Saint-Thibéry (Bl) *see* **William Arnaud and Comps**

Stephen of Sandomir (Bl) *see* **Sadoc of Sandomir and Comps**

Stephen Vasquez (Bl) *see* **Peter Rodriguez and Comps**

St Stephen the Protomartyr, Dec 26

Stephen (Nguyen van) Vinh (St) M. T(OP). Dec 19
d. 1839. A Vietnamese peasant and a Dominican tertiary, he was strangled at Ninh-Tai with Augustine (Nguyen van) Moi, Dominic (Bui van) Uy, Francis-Xavier (Ha Trong) Mau and Thomas (Nguyen van) De. *See* **Vietnam (Martyrs of)**.

Stephen the Younger and Comps (SS) MM. RR. Nov 28
714–764. A native of Constantinople, he became a monk at St Auxentius's Abbey there in 730 and was made abbot in 744. He resigned and became a hermit on the outbreak of the iconoclast controversy, but his opposition to the imperial policy led to his monastery being destroyed by the emperor Constantine V and he was exiled in 754. Later he was brought back and imprisoned, but was dragged from prison and lynched by a mob with Andrew, Basil, Peter and allegedly 339 other monks.

Stephen de Zudaira (Bl) *see* **Ignatius de Azevedo and Comps**

Stercatius (St) *see* **Victor, Stercatius and Antinogenes**

Stilla (Bl) R. Jul 19
d. ?1141. A relative of the counts of Abenberg near Nuremberg, Bavaria, as a hermit she founded a chapel near her home and was buried there. Nothing else is known. Her cultus was confirmed for Eichstätt in 1927.

Straton (St) M. Sep 9
? He is listed as having been martyred by having his ankles tied to two young trees which were bent towards each other and then let go. Nothing else is known.

Straton (St) *see* **Hieronides, Leontius and Comps**

Straton, Philip and Eutychian (SS) MM. Aug 17
d. ?301. From Nicomedia, Asia Minor, they were allegedly burnt at the stake there but their acta are worthless. Most sources add a fourth martyr, Cyprian.

Stratonicus (St) *see* **Hermylus and Stratonicus**

Sturmi (St) R. Dec 17
d. 779. The first German to follow the Benedictine rule was born to Christian parents, educated by St Wigbert in the abbey of Fritzlar and became one of the favourite disciples of St Boniface. As a missionary he worked in Hesse and founded the abbey of Fulda for St Boniface as a central mission base there in 744. For a year from 747 he was at Montecassino, Italy, to learn the monastic observance there before becoming abbot of Fulda. He was with Charlemagne on the latter's campaign against the Saxons in the year that he died. He was canonized in 1139.

Stylianos (St) R. Nov 28
d. 390. He was a hermit near Adrianople in Paphlagonia, Asia Minor, but his extant biography is legendary. He is probably identical with Alypius the Stylite.

Styriacus (St) *see* **Carterius and Comps**

Suairlech (St) B. Mar 27
d. *c*750. He was the first bishop of Fore in Co. Westmeath, Ireland. Another of the same name was abbot at Magheralin in Co. Down.

Successus (St) *see* **Paul, Gerontius and Comps**

Successus (St) *see* **Peter, Successus and Comps**

Successus (St) *see* **Rogatus, Successus and Comps**

Successus (St) *see* **Zaragoza (Eighteen Martyrs of)**

Sulinus *see* **Silin**

Sulpicius and Servilian (SS) MM. Apr 20
d. ?117. They were Roman martyrs traditionally associated with St Flavia Domitilla and beheaded in the reign of Trajan.

Sulpicius of Bayeux (St) M. B. Sep 4
d. 843. Bishop of Bayeux, France, from ?838, he was killed by the Norsemen at Livry in the Paris suburbs.

Sulpicius I of Bourges 'Severus' (St) B. Jan 29
d. 591. He became archbishop of Bourges, France, in 584 and has been confused with the writer Sulpicius Severus. This resulted in the latter being inserted in the old Roman Martyrology.

Sulpicius II of Bourges 'Pius' (St) B. Jan 17
d. 647. An nobleman from near Béziers, France, he became archbishop of Bourges in

624. He is commemorated by the church and seminary of St Sulpice in Paris.

Sunaman (St) *see* **Winaman, Unaman and Sunaman**

Sunniva (Sunnifa) (St) V. Jul 8
C10th? According to the legend, which seems to be a fiction based on that of St Ursula, she was an Irish princess who became a refugee with her brother Alban and a number of other maidens. They were shipwrecked off the island of Selje in Norway and were killed there by people from the mainland. Their alleged relics, probably remains of anonymous victims of shipwreck, were enshrined at Bergen.

Superius (St) *see* **Salvius and Superius**

Suranus (St) R. Jan 24
d. *c*580. According to St Gregory the Great in his *Dialogues*, he was the abbot of a monastery at Sora in Umbria, Italy. When the Lombards invaded he distributed all the possessions of the monastery among the refugees so that the invaders had nothing to plunder when they arrived. They killed him as soon as they realized this.

Susanna (St) *see* **Archelais, Thecla and Susanna**

Susanna, Marciana, Palladia and Comps (SS) MM. May 24
C2nd? According to their legendary acta, they were the wives and children of certain soldiers belonging to the military unit commanded by St Meletius Stratelates and were killed with other Christians in Galatia, Asia Minor.

Susanna Androuin (Bl) *see* **William Repin and Comps**

Susanna Chobyoye (Bl) M. L. Jul 12
d. 1628. The wife of Bl Peter Araki Chobyoye, she was beheaded with her husband at Nagasaki. Six months earlier she had been hanged naked by her hair from a tree for eight hours. *See* **Mancius Araki Kyuzaburo and Comps** and **Japan (Martyrs of)**.

Susanna of Eleutheropolis (St) V. Sep 19
d. 362. According to the old Roman Martyrology she was the daughter of a pagan priest and a Jewish woman. Being converted after their deaths, she became a deaconess at Eleutheropolis between Jerusalem and Gaza and was martyred there in the reign of Julian.

Susanna Ou (St) *see* **Korea (Martyrs of)**

Susanna of Rome (St) V. Aug 11
d. ?295. Her acta are worthless, but there probably was a Roman martyr of this name and the Roman church of St Susanna is dedicated to her. She had no connection with St Tiburtius who is commemorated on the same day. Since 1969 her cultus has been confined to her basilica in Rome.

Swithbert the Elder (St) B. R. Mar 1
?647–713. A Northumbrian, he was one of twelve missionary monks who went with St Willibrord to Friesland in 690. Three years later he returned to be consecrated as a regionary bishop by St Wilfrid and was then active around what is now the Ruhr, Germany. Saxon incursions destroyed his work, and he retired to the small island of Kaiserswerth in the Rhine, near Düsseldorf, where he founded a monastery and where he died.

Swithbert the Younger (St) B. Apr 30
d. 807. He was an English bishop of Werden in Westphalia, Germany, and has been confused with his elder namesake. The claim that he was a missionary monk is suspect.

Swithin (Swithun) of Winchester (St) B. Jul 2
d. 862. From Wessex, England, he was educated at the cathedral at Winchester and, after being ordained, was chaplain to King Egbert of Wessex and tutor to the crown-prince. In 852 he was appointed bishop of Winchester, and during the decade for which he was bishop the kingdom of Wessex attained the height of its power and influence. On his death, at his request, he was buried in the cemetery outside the cathedral but his body was moved into the cathedral in 971. According to legend his disapproval was shown by a downpour, which gave rise to the absurd but popular saying 'If it rains on St Swithin's day it will rain for the following forty days'. His shrine was destroyed at the Reformation.

Swithin Wells (St) M. L. Dec 10
d. 1591. From a landowning family at Brambridge, Hants, he ran a Catholic school in Wiltshire until 1582 and then was involved with his wife in helping priests working in secret. He was arrested at his house in Gray's Inn Road, London, together with St Edmund Genings and was hanged, drawn and quartered with him at Gray's Inn Fields. His wife died in prison. He was canonized in 1970. *See* **England (Martyrs of)**.

Syagrius (Siacre) of Autun
(St) B. Aug 27
d. 600. A Gallo-Roman nobleman, he became bishop of Autun, France, in *c*560 and was one of the most influential men in the contemporary Gallic church. He showed hospitality to St Augustine and his companions on their way to England.

Syagrius (Siacre) of Nice
(St) B. May 23
d. ?787. A relative of Charlemagne, he became a monk at Lérins and then abbot-founder of the monastery of St Pons at Cimiez in Provence, France. In 777 he was made bishop of Nice.

Sycus and Palatinus (SS) MM. May 30
? They are listed as two martyrs of Antioch, Syria, but the original entry was probably 'Hesychius Palatinus' (one person).

Sylvanus *see* **Silvanus**

Sylvester, Pope (St) Dec 31
d. 335. A Roman, he became pope in 314, just after the emperor Constantine had granted imperial toleration to Christianity in the edict of Milan in 313. Very little that is historically certain is known about his life, though there are various unreliable legends connecting him with Constantine. He did not baptize the emperor, which event only took place after his death. During his pontificate the first ecumenical council of Nicaea was convened to deal with the Arian heresy, and he was represented by bishop Hosius of Cordoba. The greater part of his relics are at San Silvestro in Capite, Rome. His attribute is a small dragon in his hand or on a chain.

Sylvester of Chalon-sur-Saône (St) B. Nov 20
d. ?525. Bishop of Chalon-sur-Saône, France, from ?484, he was praised by St Gregory of Tours.

Sylvester Gozzolini (St)
R(OSB Silv). F. Nov 26
1177–1267. From Osimo near Ancona, Italy, he studied law at Padua and Bologna before becoming a secular priest and canon at Osimo. Later he became a hermit at Montefano near Fabriano. There he had a vision of St Benedict in 1231, which led him to found a new reformed Benedictine congregation initially known as the Blue Benedictines (from the colour of their habits) and later as the Silvestrines. This had a centralized structure, was approved in 1247 and had eleven monasteries by the time of his death as abbot-general. He was listed in the Roman Martyrology as a saint in 1598, but had his cultus confined to particular calendars in 1969.

Sylvester of Ireland (St) B. Mar 20
C5th. He was a companion of St Palladius in Ireland, being associated with Co. Wicklow.

Sylvester of Réome (St) R. Apr 15
d. ?625. He was the second abbot of Moûtier-Saint-Jean (originally Réome) near Dijon, France.

Sylvester Ventura (Bl)
R(OSB Cam). Jun 9
d. 1348. From Florence, Italy, he worked at preparing wool for spinning before becoming a Camaldolese lay brother at S. Maria degli Angeli when aged forty. He was the monastery cook and experienced ecstasies and visions, it being alleged that angels would come and do his cooking for him. His spiritual advice was highly regarded in the city. His cultus is unconfirmed.

Sylvia (St) L. Nov 3
d. ?572. She was the mother of Pope St Gregory the Great and had a chapel dedicated to her on the site of her house on the Coelian Hill at Rome. The assertion that she persuaded her husband, Gordianus, to donate his lands to the abbey of Montecassino is false and was possibly maliciously invented there in furtherance of legal claims.

Symmachus, Pope (St) Jul 19
d. 514. A pagan convert from Sardinia, he was elected pope in 498 by the Roman clerical faction determined not to grant any concessions to the patriarchate of Constantinople in order to end the Acacian schism. The aristocratic opponents of this policy, wanting reconciliation with the Emperor, elected an anti-pope called Laurence. Both factions were violently competing in Rome until Theodoric, the Arian king of the Ostrogoths, was appealed to and made judgment in favour of Symmachus in 506. He was not listed in any martyrology before the C16th.

Symphorian (St) *see* **Claudius, Nicostratus and Comps**

Symphorian (St) *see* **Four Crowned Martyrs**

Symphorian of Autun (St) M. Aug 22
d. *c*200. A nobleman of Autun, France, he was martyred in the reign of Marcus Aurelius for refusing to sacrifice to the goddess Cybele. He is

one of the most famous martyrs of Gaul but his cultus was confined to local calendars in 1969.

Symphorosa (St) *see* **Ariston and Comps**

Symphorosa of Tivoli and Comps *Jul 18*
C2nd? She was possibly a martyr at Tivoli near Rome in the reign of Hadrian. According to her worthless acta (an adaptation of the story of the mother with seven sons in the second book of the Maccabees) she was the widow of the martyr St Getulius and the mother of seven martyred brothers: Crescens, Julian, Nemesius, Primitivus, Justin, Stacteus and Eugene. She was not the mother of these seven, they were not brothers and they were not martyred together. Their cultus was suppressed in 1969.

Symphronius (St) *see* **Felix, Symphronius and Comps**

Symphronius of Rome and Comps (SS) MM. Jul 26
d. 257. He was a Roman slave who converted the tribune Olympius, the latter's wife Exuperia and their son Theodulus. They were all burnt to death in the reign of Valerian.

Syncletica of Alexandria (St) R. Jan 5
d. *c*400. A wealthy inhabitant of Alexandria, Egypt, she fled the city to live as a hermit in a tomb until her eighty-fourth year. For a long time she suffered from temptations and spiritual aridity, and in her latter years from cancer and tuberculosis.

Syncrotas of Sirmium and Comps (SS) MM. Feb 23
C4th. They were martyred at Sirmium (Srem Mitrovica in Serbia). Also listed are Antigonus, Rutilus, Libius, Senerotas and Rogatianus.

Synesius *see* **Theopemptus and Theonas**

Synesius of Rome (St) M. Dec 12
d. 275. He was a Roman church reader martyred in the reign of Aurelian.

Syntyche of Philippi (St) L. Jul 22
C1st. She is referred to by St Paul in Phil 4:2-3.

Syra (Syria) of Troyes (St) R. Jun 8
C7th. She was allegedly a sister of St Fiacre who followed him from Ireland to France and became a hermit at Troyes.

Syra of Châlons-sur-Marne (St) R. Oct 23
d. *c*660. She was a nun at Faremoutier before becoming abbess of the nunnery at Châlons-sur-Marne, France.

Syrus of Genoa (St) B. June 29
d. *c*380. He was bishop of Genoa, Italy, from ?324 and is the principal patron of the city and diocese.

Syrian Monks (SS) MM. Jul 31
d. 517. They were a group of three hundred and fifty monks of Syria massacred by Monophysites for defending the decrees of the council of Chalcedon.

Syrian Women (SS) MM. Nov 14
d. 773. They were allegedly a large number of women viciously killed at Emesa (now Homs) in Syria by Muslim invaders.

Syrus (St) M. B. Dec 9
? The alleged first bishop of Pavia, Italy, the city's principal patron, probably belongs to the C3rd or C4th. Unreliable legends attempt to place him in the C1st. *See* **Juventius of Pavia**.

Sytha *see* **Osyth**

T

Tabitha (Dorcas) (St) L. Oct 25
C1st. The resurrection of this widow of Joppa by St Peter is described in Acts 9:36-43.

Talarican (St) B. Oct 30
C6th? According to his unreliable biography he was a Pictish missionary bishop consecrated by Pope St Gregory the Great. Several churches in Scotland were dedicated to him, notably at Kiltarlity near Beauly.

Talida (St) R. Jan 5
C4th. Palladius mentioned her in his *Lausiac History* as an abbess of one of the twelve nunneries at Antinoë, Egypt. She had been a nun for eighty years when he visited her.

Tammarus (St) *see* **Priscus II of Capua and Comps**

Tanca (St) V. Oct 10
d. ?637. The daughter of Syrian refugees, she was killed when she resisted an attempt at rape at Arcis north of Troyes, France. She is venerated at the latter place.

Tanco (Tancho, Tatta)
(St) M. B. Feb 6
d. 808. An Irish monk, he was abbot of a German monastery called Amalbarich in Lower Saxony (site uncertain) before becoming bishop of Werden. He was lynched by a pagan mob whose savage customs he had denounced.

Tancred, Torthred and Tova (SS) MM. RR. Sep 30
d. 870. They were hermits, two men and a woman, who were killed during a raid by the Danes at Thorney in Lincolnshire, England. SS Hedda of Peterborough and Comps died in the same raid.

Taracus *see* **Tharacus**

Taraghta *see* **Amacta**

Tarasius (St) B. Feb 25
d. 806. A nobleman of Constantinople, he was the secretary of Empress Irene during her regency for her son, Emperor Constantine VI. He was chosen to be patriarch in 784 while still a layman, and he accepted on condition that a general council be convened to end iconoclasm. The second council of Nicaea took place in 787. Shortly after, however, Constantine VI divorced his wife and remarried, and St Theodore the Studite and his followers condemned Tarasios of being too lenient in the resultant 'Moechian controversy'.

Tarbula (Tarbo, Tarba) (St) V. Apr 22
d. 345. Sister of St Simeon Barsabae, she was a consecrated virgin. After her brother's martyrdom she was accused by Jews of having made the wife of Shah Shapur II fall ill through witchcraft, and was killed by being sawn in half.

Tarkin *see* **Talarican**

Tarsicia (Tarsitia) (St) R. Jan 15
d. *c*600. Allegedly of royal descent, she was a sister of St Ferreolus of Uzès and was a hermit near Rodez, France. Her shrine is in the cathedral there.

Tarsicius, Zoticus, Cyriac and Comps (SS) MM. Jan 31
? They are listed as martyrs at Alexandria, Egypt.

Tarsicius of Rome (St) M. D? Aug 15
C3rd-4th. According to the inscription upon his tomb, written by Pope St Damasus, he was carrying the blessed sacrament (perhaps to Christians in prison) when he was ambushed by a pagan mob. He chose to die rather than let the sacred elements be profaned. He was probably a deacon.

Tarsilla (St) R. Dec 24
d. ?581. She was an aunt of Pope St Gregory the Great and sister of St Emiliana, and lived a life of seclusion and mortification in her family home.

Tarsus (Martyrs of) (SS) Jun 6
d. ?290. The listing in the old Roman Martyrology of twenty martyrs at Tarsus in Cilicia, Asia Minor, in the reign of Diocletian seems to depend on the fictitious acta of St Boniface of Tarsus.

Tassach (St) B. Apr 14
d. ?495. One of St Patrick's earliest disciples, he was first bishop of Raholp in Co. Down, Ireland, and was remembered as a craftsman who made crosses, croziers and shrines for St Patrick.

Tassilo (Bl) R. Dec 13
d. *p*794. Duke of Bavaria, Germany, he founded many monasteries and churches before becoming a monk at Jumièges in France and then at Lorsch near Frankfurt, where he died.

Taso (St) *see* **Paldo, Taso and Tato**

Tate *see* **Ethelburga**

Tathai (Tathan, Tathar, Athaeus) (St) R. Dec 26
Early C6th. Allegedly from Ireland, he founded a monastery at what is now St Athan's near Cardiff, Wales, and a school at Caerwent in Gwent.

Tatian (St) *see* **Hilary, Tatian and Comps**

Tatian Dulas *see* **Dulas**

Tatian (St) *see* **Macedonius, Theodulus and Tatian**

Tatiana (St) M. Jan 12
d. *c*230. According to the old Roman Martyrology she was martyred at Rome in the reign of Alexander Severus. The Byzantine martyrology add Euthasia and Mertius as companions. Her acta are unreliable.

Tation (St) M. Aug 24
d. ?304. He was beheaded at Claudipolis in Bithynia, Asia Minor, in the reign of Diocletian.

Tato (St) *see* **Paldo, Taso and Tato**

Tatta (St) *see* **Paul, Tatta and Comps**

Tatwin (St) B. Jul 30
d. 734. A monk of 'Briudun' (Bredon or Brenton?) in Mercia, England, he was highly regarded by St Bede. He succeeded St Brithwald as archbishop of Canterbury in 731. Some of his riddles and his *Grammar* are extant.

Taurinus (St) B. Aug 11
d. ?412. He was a bishop of Evreux in Normandy, France. The legend connecting him with St Dionysius of Paris is a worthless medieval forgery.

Taurion (St) *see* **Auctus, Taurion and Thessalonika**

Teath *see* **Ita**

Teath (Teatha, Eatha) (St) Jan 15
? She is the patron of the church of St Teath near Camelford in Cornwall, England, and has been claimed as one of the daughters of St Brychan.

Tegla (Thecla) (St) R? Jun 1
? She is the patron of the church and holy well at Llandegla near Ruthin in Clwyd, Wales, and has been claimed as one of the companions of St Breaca.

Teilo (St) B. R. Feb 9
C6th. Born probably at Penally near Tenby, Wales, according to his C12th biography he was educated by St Dyfrig and was a companion of SS David and Samson. He became the founder and abbot-bishop of a monastery at Llandeilo Fawr in Dyfed and was buried in Llandaff cathedral. There are many variants of his name, e.g. Teilio, Teilus, Thelian, Teilan, Teilou, Teliou, Dillo, Dillon.

Telemachus *see* **Almachius**

Telesphorus, Pope *Jan 5*
d. ?137. A Calabrian Greek, he was pope for ten years. According to a discredited tradition he was martyred in the reign of Hadrian. His cultus was suppressed in 1969.

Tenenan (St) B. Jul 16
C7th cent. A Briton by birth, he was a hermit in Brittany, France, and eventually became bishop of Léon there. His shrine was at Ploabennec.

Terence (St) *see* **Fidentius and Terence**

Terence, Africanus, Pompeius and Comps (SS) MM. Apr 10
d. 250. A group of fifty Roman Africans, they were beheaded at Carthage in the reign of Decius. Beforehand they had been imprisoned with a number of snakes and scorpions which did not harm them, a fact which was regarded as miraculous by those ignorant of how those creatures actually behave when unmolested.

Terence of Iconium (St) M. B. Jun 21
C1st. He was a very early bishop of Iconium, Asia Minor (now Konya in Turkey). His identification with the Tertius mentioned by St Paul in Rom 16:22 is based on a guess.

Terence of Luni (St) M. B. Jul 15
C9th. A bishop of Sarzana near La Spezia, Italy, he was killed by robbers on a journey and venerated as a martyr.

Terence of Metz (St) B. Oct 29
d. 520. He was a bishop of Metz, France.

Terence-Albert O'Brien
(Bl) M. B. Jun 20
d. 1651. The bishop of Emly, he was hanged after the siege of Limerick and was beatified in 1992. *See* **Ireland (Martyrs of)**.

Terentian (St) M. B. Sep 1
d. ?118. Bishop of Todi in Umbria, Italy, he was allegedly racked, had his tongue cut out and was then beheaded in the reign of Hadrian.

Teresa Bracco (Bl) V. Aug 30
1924–1944. Of a pious peasant family at Santa Giulia near Acqui, Italy, she became known as a schoolgirl for her piety and modesty. After Italy was invaded by the Allies in 1943 during the Second World War, guerilla warfare against the Germans broke out behind the front line. Santa Giulia was suspected of being a partisan stronghold and so the Germans raided it. A soldier seized her and took her into the woods in order to rape her, but her resistance was so vigorous that he strangled and shot her instead. She was beatified in 1998.

Teresa-Mary Cavestany y Anduaga (Bl) *see* **Mary-Gabrielle de Hinojosa Naveros and Comps**

Teresa-of-Jesus Cepeda de Ahumada (St) Dr. R(OCD). F. Oct 15
1515–1582. From Avila near Madrid, Spain, she entered the local Carmelite nunnery when aged eighteen and found that the observance there had grown lax. This, together with a series of profound spiritual experiences, led her to undertake the reform of the Carmelite order and she opened her first reformed nunnery of St Joseph at Avila in 1562. From then on until her death she was always travelling and opening new houses (fifteen directly and seventeen through others). She had to ameliorate difficulties for her nuns and placate those in authority (both clerical and lay), who often opposed her and called her the 'roving nun'. During all this her remarkable mystical experiences continued and these she described (under obedience) in treatises which led her to be declared a doctor of the Church in 1970. She was a woman of sound common sense, of sane good humour and of generous ideals. Dying at Alba de Tormes, she was canonized in 1622. She is often depicted with her heart being pierced by an arrow held by an angel, as in the famous sculpture of her at Rome by Bernini.

St Teresa-of-Jesus Cepeda de Ahumada, Oct 15

Teresa Chen (Jinjie) and Rose Chen (Anjie) (SS) MM. LL. Jul 5
1875 and 1878–1900. They were sisters at Feng in Hebei, China, and tried to flee the Boxers with a group of relatives and friends. They were, however, caught and three of the party were killed and two wounded. St Teresa was also killed, but St Rose survived being stabbed for a few hours. *See* **China (Martyrs of)**.

Teresa Couderc (St) R. F. Sep 26
1805–1885. From Sablières in Ardèche, France, when aged twenty she joined a new teaching congregation at Apt and was sent to open a hostel for women pilgrims at La Louvesc near Valence. Thus was founded the 'Society of Our Lady of the Cenacle', which became a separate congregation in 1836. Her intention was to attract pilgrims to the tomb of St John Francis Regis there and to help them to spend time in recollection. The institute developed as one of retreat houses for women and rapidly spread

throughout Europe and to America. She had to resign as superior in 1835 owing to illness, but lived for another fifty years under superiors whose incompetence almost destroyed the congregation. She was canonized in 1970.

Teresa-of-St-Joseph Duart Roig (Bl) *see* **Angela-of-St-Joseph Lloret Martí and Comps**

Teresa-of-Jesus Fernández Solar of Los Andes (St) R(OC). Apr 12
1900–1920. Born in Santiago, Chile, she was a very pious child who loved Our Lady. Being influenced by St Teresa of the Child Jesus and Bl Elizabeth of the Trinity, she entered the Carmel at Los Andes in 1919 but died of typhus the following year, being allowed to make her profession beforehand. She was canonized in 1993.

Teresa-of-the-Child-Jesus García García (Bl) *see* **Mary-Pillar-of-St-Francis-Borgia Martínez García**

Teresa Grillo Michel (Bl) R. F. Jan 26
1855–1944. She was from a well-placed family (her father was head physician of the hospital) of Alessandria in Piedmont, Italy. In 1877 she married an army officer, but was widowed in 1891 and became prey to depression which only lifted when she decided to spend her life in helping the poor. In 1893 she founded the 'Little Shelter of Divine Providence' at Alessandria, and became founder-superior of the 'Little Sisters of Divine Providence' in 1899. By the time she died these had twenty-five houses in Italy, nineteen in Brazil and seven in Argentina. She was beatified in 1998.

Teresa-of-the-Heart-of-Mary Hanisset (Bl) *see* **Compiègne (Carmelite Martyrs of)**

Teresa-of-Jesus Jornet Ibars (St) R. F. Aug 26
1843–1897. She was brought up on a farm at Aytona near Lérida, Spain, but managed to qualify as a teacher at the latter place. Trying her vocation at several religious institutions and failing, she then took the advice of her spiritual director and started one of her own at Barbastro in 1872. Her deep spiritual insight, firmness of spirit, unflagging energy and endurance were responsible for the foundation of fifty-eight houses of the 'Little Sisters of the Poor' in her lifetime. She died at Liria near Valencia and was canonized in 1974.

Teresa Kim, Teresa Lee and Teresa Lee (SS) *see* **Korea (Martyrs of)**

Teresa-of-St-Augustine Lidoine (Bl) *see* **Compiègne (Carmelite Martyrs of)**

Teresa-Mary-of-the-Cross Manetti (Bl) T(OCD). F. Apr 23
1846–1910. Born near Florence, Italy, she started common life at home with two companions in 1868, and moved to St Justus in Florence in 1874. There they opened an orphanage, and became the 'Tertiary Sisters of the Order of Discalced Carmel' in 1885. Other houses were opened in Tuscany, also a house of perpetual adoration in Florence and a foundation at Carmel in the Holy Land. She suffered painfully from illness before she died, and was beatified in 1985.

Teresa-of-the-Child-Jesus Martin (St) Dr. R(OCD). Oct 1
1873–1897. Born at Alençon, France, she was one of five sisters in a pious bourgeois family which later moved to Lisieux. An initially happy childhood was marked by the death of her mother from cancer, the entry of her oldest sister into the local Carmel and the mental deterioration of her father (later to lead to

St Teresa-of-the-Child-Jesus Martin, Oct 1

complete insanity). She entered the Carmel herself in 1888 when aged only fifteen, despite serious opposition on account of her age. This initially seemed justified, as she died in agony of disseminated tuberculosis nine years later after having served as assistant novice-mistress. Her subsequent fame rests entirely on her spiritual autobiography, written under obedience and containing her doctrine of the 'Little Way' of spiritual childhood, which was published after her death. She was canonized in 1925, declared co-patron of foreign missions (with St Francis Xavier), co-patron of France (with St Joan of Arc) and finally doctor of the Church in 1997. Her attribute is a rose or rose petals. Photographs of her have survived, and the fact that many extant artistic representations of her do not much resemble these is owing to attempts at portraiture by one of her sisters.

Teresa (Tarasia) of Portugal
(St) R(OCist). Jun 17
d. 1250. Daughter of King Sancho I of Portugal, she married her cousin Alphonsus IX, king of León, but the marriage was annulled on the grounds of consanguinity. Returning to Portugal, she became a Cistercian nun at Lorvao near Coïmbra and died there. Her cultus as a saint was confirmed in 1705 for Portugal.

Teresa-Margaret-of-the-Sacred-Heart Redi (St) R(OCD). Mar 7
1747–1770. From Arezzo, Italy, she became a Discalced Carmelite nun at Florence in 1765 and only lived another five years, but her witness of penance and prayer led her to be canonized in 1934.

Teresa Soiron (Bl) *see* **Compiègne (Carmelite Martyrs of)**

Teresa-Benedicta-of-the-Cross Stein (St) R(OC). Oct 11
1891–1942. Born in Breslau, Germany (now Wroclaw, Poland), of a rich and devout Jewish family, Edith Stein lost her faith early in life. She studied philosophy under Husserl at Göttingen University and became a noted philosopher in her own right, being converted to Catholicism by reading the works of St Teresa of Jesus. Baptized in 1922, she entered the Carmel at Cologne in 1933. Her main work was in synthesizing Thomism with modern philosophy (especially phenomenology). She moved to Echt, Netherlands, in 1938, but was taken from there to Auschwitz by the Nazis and gassed. She was canonized in 1998 and declared a patron of Europe in 2000.

St-Teresa-Benedicta-of-the-Cross Stein, Oct 11

Teresa-of-St-Ignatius Trézelle (Bl) *see* **Compiègne (Carmelite Martyrs of)**

Teresa-Eustochium Verzeri
(Bl) R. F. Mar 3
1801–1852. A noblewoman of Bergamo, Italy, she attempted three times to become a Benedictine nun but failed and took to teaching young girls at home instead. This led her to found the 'Daughters of the Sacred Heart' in 1831. Both the numbers and the scope of the institute grew so as to include a wide range of charitable works. The bishop of Bergamo, at first favourable, turned against her but approval was given by Rome in 1841. She died comparatively young, worn out by her activities, at Brescia and was beatified in 1946.

Teresa Zhang (He) (St) M. L. Jul 16
1864–1900. From a Catholic family of Yuan in south-eastern Hebei, China, she was seized while working in a vegetable garden by a Boxer gang and taken to the village temple. She refused to worship and was stabbed with her son and daughter. *See* **China (Martyrs of)**.

Ternan (St) B. Jun 12
C5th? He was an early missionary bishop among the Picts in Scotland, allegedly ordained by St Palladius and based at Abernethy. He is the reputed founder of the abbey of Culross in Fife.

Ternatius (Terniscus) (St) B. Aug 8
d. *c*680. He was a bishop of Besançon, France.

Tertius (St) *see* **Dionysia, Dativa and Comps**

Tertulla (St) *see* **Agapius of Cirta and Comps**

Tertullian (St) B. Apr 27
d. ?490. He was a bishop of Bologna, Italy. (His famous namesake among the Latin Fathers is not a saint, having died in heresy.)

Tertullinus (St) M. P. Aug 4
d. 257. A Roman priest, he was martyred in the reign of Valerian two days after his ordination.

Tertricus of Langres (St) B. Mar 20
d. 572. Son of St Gregory of Langres, France, and uncle of St Gregory of Tours, he succeeded his father as bishop in *c*540.

Tetricus of Auxerre (St) M. B. Apr 12
d. 707. He was abbot of the monastery of St Germanus at Auxerre, France, before becoming bishop there, but was stabbed to death by his archdeacon while asleep on a bench.

Tetta (St) R. Sep 28
d. ?772. Abbess of Wimborne in Dorset, England, she helped St Boniface in the German missions by sending him several groups of missionary nuns from her community (allegedly numbering about five hundred), among whom were SS Lioba and Thecla.

Thaddeus *see* **Jude**

Thaddeus Liu (Ruiting)
(St) M. P. Nov 24
1773–1823. From Qunglai county in Sichuan, China, he was a poor peasant until he became a priest's helper and was recommended for ordination. After this took place in 1807 he worked in north-east Sichuan until he was captured, imprisoned for two years and then hanged. *See* **China (Martyrs of)**.

Thaddeus (Tadhg) McCarthy (Bl) B. Oct 25
d. 1497. He was made bishop of Ross in Co. Wexford, Ireland, in 1482 but was exiled in 1488. The pope then nominated him bishop of Cork and Cloyne, but he was not allowed into the diocese. So he returned to Rome to plead his cause personally, but died on his way home at Ivrea in Piedmont, Italy. His cultus was approved for Ivrea and Ireland in 1910.

Thaddeus of Sandomir (Bl) *see* **Sadoc of Sandomir and Comps**

Thailand (Martyrs of) (BB) MM. Dec 16
d. 1940. Thailand has never been a European colony but the eastern regions, bordered by the Mekong river and French Indo-China, were considered a French sphere of influence before the Second World War. Ecclesiastically they were part of the Vicariate of Laos. In 1940 there was a reaction against Christianity in favour of Buddhism, and persecution was violent in these areas. At Song-Khon, a station of the Paris Mission Society, seven native Catholics were shot after the missionaries were expelled. They were Philip Siphong Onphithak, a local family man and the schoolmaster, aged 33; Agnes Phila and Lucy Khambang, teachers and religious of the 'Sisters, Lovers of the Cross', aged 30 and 23 respectively; Agatha Phutta, the sister's cook, aged 59, and four teenage girls of the village: Cecilia Butsi, Bibiana Hampai and Mary Phon. They were beatified in 1989.

Thaïs the Penitent (St) R. Oct 8
C4th? According to her story, which seems to be fictional, she was a wealthy and beautiful prostitute of Alexandria, Egypt, who was converted by St Paphnutius (other accounts allege St Bessarion or St Serapion) and joined a nunnery, where she was walled up for three years in a cell. Only towards the end of her life was she allowed to live with the other nuns.

Thalassius and Limnaeus
(SS) RR. Feb 22
C5th. Theodoret of Cyrrhus described these two Syrian hermits, whom he knew personally, as living in a cave near Cyrrhus, north of Antioch.

Thalelaeus of Aegae and Comps (SS) MM. May 20
d. ?284. He was a physician who allegedly treated his patients free of charge at Anazarbus in Cilicia, Asia Minor, and was martyred at Aegae, a town on the coast nearby (not at Edessa). The old Roman Martyrology listed with him Asterius and Alexander, two of his executioners, and others of the spectators who were converted by his example.

Thalelaeus Epiclautos (St) R. Feb 27
d. *c*450. A hermit, he lived at Gabala in Syria next to a pagan temple and converted many of the pagan pilgrims. For many years he lived in an open barrel. His surname means 'weeping much'.

Thalus (St) *see* **Trophimus and Thalus**

Thamel and Comps (SS) MM. Sep 4
d. ?125. He is listed as a convert pagan priest who was martyred with four or five others (one of them his sister) somewhere in the East in the reign of Hadrian.

Tharacus (Tarachus), Probus and Andronicus (SS) MM. Oct 11
d. 304. According to their dubious acta they were a retired Roman army officer and two civilians from Pamphilia and Ephesus respectively. They were beheaded near Tarsus in Cilicia, Asia Minor, in the reign of Diocletian.

Tharasius *see* **Tarasius**

Thaw *see* **Lythan**

Thea (St) *see* **Meuris and Thea**

Theau *see* **Tillo**

Theban Legion (SS) MM. Sep 22
d. ?287. According to the developed legend, this was a legion of 6,600 Christians recruited in Upper Egypt for the army of Maximian Herculeus. When that emperor took his army across the Alps to suppress a revolt in Gaul he camped on the Rhône in the Valais, Switzerland, and prepared for battle with public sacrifices. The Christian legion refused to attend (another version says that they refused to attack innocent people) and were in consequence twice decimated. When they persevered in their refusal they were massacred. Those named are Maurice the 'primicerius', Exuperius, Candidus, Innocent, Vitalis, two Victors, Alexander (at Bergamo) and Gereon (at Cologne). A basilica was built on the site in the late C4th (where the town of St Maurice now is), which indicates that the story is based on truth. Perhaps a large number of soldiers were massacred there, but not a whole legion. Their cultus was confined to particular calendars in 1969.

Thecla (St) *see* **Archelais, Thecla and Susanna**

Thecla (St) *see* **Boniface and Thecla**

Thecla (St) *see* **Euphemia, Dorothea and Comps**

Thecla (St) *see* **Peter, Marcian and Comps**

Thecla (St) *see* **Timothy, Thecla and Agapius**

Thecla the Apostolic *Sep 23*
C1st. According to the work of pious fiction entitled the 'Acts of Paul and Thecla', which contains extravagant legends and is not doctrinally sound, she was a maiden of Iconium, Asia Minor, who heard St Paul preaching while she sat at her window, became a Christian as a result and followed him dressed in boy's clothes. Several times she was viciously tortured, and finally died as a hermit at Seleucia. It is not possible to disentangle truth (if any) from fiction in her case. Her cultus was suppressed in 1969.

Thecla of Kitzingen (St) R. Oct 15
d. *c*790. A nun of Wimborne in Dorset, England, under St Tetta, she was one of the group which set out for the German missions under St Lioba. She was chosen by St Boniface as first abbess of Ochsenfurt near Würzburg and then of Kitzingen on the Main river, over which monastery she ruled for many years.

Thecla Nagaishi (Bl) M. L. Sep 10
d. 1622. A Japanese woman, she was beheaded at Nagasaki in the 'Great Martyrdom' with her husband Paul and son, Peter. *See* **Charles Spinola and Comps** and **Japan (Martyrs of)**.

Thecusa (St) *see* **Theodotus of Ancyra and Comps**

Thelica (St) *see* **Saturninus, Dativus and Comps**

Themistocles and Dioscorus (SS) MM. Dec 21
d. 253. The former was a shepherd of Myra in Lycia, Asia Minor, who was beheaded for refusing to reveal the hiding-place of the latter. Their attribute is a set of caltrops (spikes used to cripple horses in battle).

Theneva (Thenew, Thenova, Dwynwen) (St) L. Jul 18
C7th. She is venerated at Glasgow, Scotland, as the mother of St Kentigern but her biography is legendary.

Theobald of Marly (St) R(OCist). Jul 27
d. 1247. A nobleman born at Marly near Laon, France, he was a knight at the court of King Philip Augustus before abandoning his career and becoming a Cistercian monk at Vaux-de-Cernay near Paris in 1220. He was made abbot there in 1235, and was esteemed by King St Louis IX.

Theobald (Thibaut) of Provins (St) R(OSB Cam). Jun 30
1017–1066. A nobleman from Brie, France, he was a soldier as a teenager but converted and became a pilgrim with a companion, Walter, at the age of eighteen. After a time as hermits at Pettingen in Luxembourg they settled at Salanigo near Vicenza, Italy, and attracted disciples who settled around them. This was the start of a Camaldolese monastery. He was canonized in 1073.

Theobald Roggeri (Bl) L. Jun 1
d. 1150. From Vico in Liguria, Italy, allegedly of a wealthy family, he left home and worked as a cobbler at Alba in Piedmont. After a pilgrimage to Compostela he earned his living as a carrier and shared his wages with the poor. His shrine is at Alba but his cultus is unconfirmed.

Theobald (Thibaud) of Vienne (St) B. May 21
d. 1001. He was archbishop of Vienne, France, from 970 and had his cultus confirmed for Grenoble in 1903.

Theoctista of Lesbos (St) R. Nov 10
C10th. She was allegedly a nun of Lesbos in the Aegean who became a hermit on Paros in the Cyclades after escaping a Muslim slave-raid. The story of her last holy communion appears to be an adaptation from the biography of St Mary of Egypt.

Theoctista-Mary Pelissier (Bl) *see* **Orange (Martyrs of)**

Theodard of Maastricht (St) M. B. Sep 10
d. *c*670. He succeeded St Remaclus as abbot of Stavelot-Malmédy, Belgium, in 653 and became bishop of Maastricht in 663. He was on his way to the Frankish court to seek justice in a legal dispute when he was ambushed in the Bienwald near Speyer, Germany, and killed.

Theodard (Audard) of Narbonne (St) B. R(OSB)? May 1
d. 893. From Montauban, France, he was educated at the Benedictine abbey of St Martin at Montauriol and became archbishop of Narbonne. He died at the same abbey (later named St Audard after him), allegedly having become a monk there just beforehand.

Theodemir of Carmona (St) M. R. Jul 25
d. 851. A monk from Carmona near Cordoba, Spain, he was beheaded at the latter place in the reign of Emir Abd-er-Rahman II.

Theodemir-Joaquim Sáiz Sáiz (Bl) *see* **Aurelius-Mary Villalón Acebrón and Comps**

Theodichild (Telchild) (St) R. Jun 28
d. *p*660. A nun of Faremoutier, she became the first abbess of the great double monastery of Jouarre near Meaux, France.

Theodora (St) *see* **Flavia Domitilla, Euphrosyne and Theodora**

Theodora (St) *see* **Theusetas, Horres and Comps**

Theodora and Didymus (SS) MM. Apr 28
d. 304. The former was a maiden of Alexandria, Egypt, who was sentenced to be a sex-slave in a brothel but was rescued by the latter who was still a pagan. This led to his conversion, and the two were martyred together. The acta seem to be genuine.

Theodora, Empress (St) R. Feb 11
d. 867. From 830 to his death in 842 she was the wife of the last iconoclast emperor, Theophilus. Then she was regent for her son, Michael III 'the Drunkard', and put an end to iconoclasm by having the decrees of the second ecumenical council of Nicaea (787) confirmed in 842 with the assistance of St Methodius the Confessor, whom she had appointed patriarch of Constantinople. Her son deposed her in 856 and sent her to a monastery, where she died. Her veneration as a saint in the East derives from her doctrinal action rather than her personal morality.

Theodora-Anne-Teresa Guérin (Bl) R. (May 14)
1798–1856. From Etables, France, she joined the 'Sisters of Providence' at Ruillé-sur-Loire in 1823 and became a noted teacher and nurse. In 1839 she was the head of a group of six sisters who were sent to the diocese of Vincennes in Indiana, USA to make a foundation at St Mary of the Woods. The area was then mostly still undeveloped and the new community had enormous problems establishing itself, but by the time of her death it had established schools throughout Indiana. She was beatified in 1998.

Theodora the Penitent (St) R. Sep 11
d. 491. Her developed story is similar to that of St Pelagia of Antioch, but the old Roman Martyrology merely describes her as a woman of Alexandria, Egypt, who sinned but repented and remained as a consecrated hermit until her death.

Theodora of Rome (1) (St) M? Apr 1
d. ?120. According to the worthless acta of Pope St Alexander I, she was a sister of St Hermes of Rome and assisted him when he was in prison and being tortured. She was herself martyred some months later, and brother and sister were buried side by side.

Theodora of Rome (2) (St) L. Sep 17
d. ?305. A wealthy Roman noblewoman, she was remembered for assisting those being persecuted in the reign of Diocletian.

Theodore (St) *see* **Alexander and Theodore**

Theodore (St) *see* **Drusus, Zosimus and Theodore**

Theodore (St) *see* **Faustus, Didius and Comps**

Theodore (St) *see* **Irenaeus, Anthony and Comps**

Theodore (St) *see* **Lucilla, Flora and Comps**

Theodore (St) *see* **Maximus, Theodore and Asclepiodotus**

Theodore (St) *see* **Polycarp and Theodore**

Theodore (St) *see* **Urban, Theodore and Comps**

Theodore (St) *see* **Zeno, Concordius and Theodore**

Theodore, Oceanus, Ammianus and Julian (SS) MM. Sep 4
d. *c*310. They were burnt at the stake somewhere in the eastern Roman Empire, probably in the reign of Maximian Herculeus.

Theodore and Pausilippus (SS) MM. Apr 9
d. *c*130. They were martyred near Byzantium (Constantinople) in the reign of Hadrian.

Theodore of Bologna (St) B. May 5
d. *c*550. He was bishop of Bologna, Italy, from *c*530.

Theodore of Canterbury (St) B. Sep 19
?602–690. An Asiatic Greek from Tarsus in Cilicia, Asia Minor, he spent some time at Athens and apparently became a monk at Rome. He was in his sixties when Pope Vitalian chose him in 666 to be archbishop of Canterbury at the suggestion of St Adrian, who went to England with him as adviser. He is arguably the unifier of the Anglo-Saxon church, as he made the first visitation of most of the country as archbishop and held the first national council at Hatfield in 672. He tried to rationalize the boundaries of the extant dioceses and created several new ones, but this policy was opposed by St Wilfrid. The school that he opened at Canterbury with St Adrian became nationally important and he was a noted scholar in his own right, but none of his writings survives.

Theodore of Crowland and Comps (SS) MM. RR. Apr 5
d. 870. Abbot of Crowland in the Lincolnshire fens, England, he was killed with his community when the monastery was sacked in the same Danish raid as caused the deaths of Hedda and Comps at Peterborough, Tancred and Comps at Thorney and Beocca and Comps at Chertsey. Also mentioned by name in the account are Askega, prior; Swethin, sub-prior; Elfgete, deacon; Savinus, sub-deacon; Egdred and Ulrick, acolytes and Grimkeld and Agamund (Argamund), both centenarians.

Theodore of Cyrene (St) M. B. Jul 4
d. *c*310. Bishop of Cyrene in Libya, he was a skilled copyist and was allegedly tortured and martyred in the reign of Diocletian for refusing to surrender manuscripts of the Bible in his possession. There is confusion with St Theodore of Pentapolis.

Theodore of Egypt (St) R. Jan 7
C4th. He was one of the disciples of St Ammon the Great at Nitria, Egypt.

Theodore Graptus and Theophanes Graptus (SS) M. R. Dec 27
d. ?841. Brothers, they were monks at Mar Saba in the Holy Land and then at Constantinople. They were fervent opponents of the renewal of iconoclasm after the second ecumenical council of Nicaea, and the emperor Theophilus ordered that they be whipped and their faces tattooed with insulting verses before being exiled (hence their nickname). Theodore died of ill-treatment in exile at Apamea in Syria, but Theophanes survived and was allegedly made bishop of Nicaea by Empress St Theodora.

Theodore of Pavia (St) B. May 20
d. 778. Bishop of Pavia near Milan, Italy, in 743, he was harassed and exiled by the Arian Lombard kings (whose capital it was) until the kingdom was conquered by Charlemagne.

Theodore of Pentapolis and Comps (SS) 'MM'. Mar 26
d. *c*310. He was allegedly bishop of Pentapolis in Libya (this was actually a region, not a city) and had his tongue cut out in the reign of Gallienus with Irenaeus, his deacon, and Serapion and Ammonius, two church readers. They survived and died in peace, yet were listed as martyrs. There is confusion with St Theodore of Cyrene.

Theodore of Perga and Comps (SS) MM. Sep 20
d. 220. Theodore and Socrates were soldiers, Dionysius was a former pagan priest and Philippa was Theodore's mother. They were crucified at Perga in Pamphylia, Asia Minor, in the reign of Eliogabalus, and allegedly took three days to die.

Theodore Ruiz de Larrinaga (Bl) *see* **Philip-of-Jesus Munárriz Azcona and Comps**

Theodore the Sacristan (St) L. Dec 26
C6th. He was sacristan at St Peter's in Rome and a contemporary of Pope St Gregory the Great, who wrote about him.

Theodore Stratelates (St) M. Feb 7
C4th. He was allegedly a general ('stratelates') in the army of emperor Licinius, by whose order he was tortured and crucified at Heraclea in Thrace (European Turkey). He is identical with St Theodore Tyro.

Theodore Studites (St) R. Nov 11
759–826. From Constantinople, he became a monk at Saccudion where his uncle St Plato was abbot and succeeded him in 794. His community opposed Emperor Constantine VI in the 'moechian controversy' and they were dispersed and exiled, but he was recalled by Irene and re-founded his monastery at Studios in 799. This became a lasting source of monastic revival in the East, its influence reaching to Mt Athos and later to Russia, Romania and Bulgaria, and was famous for its liturgical prayer, community life, enclosure, poverty, studies and manual work (the monks excelled in calligraphy). It was also a powerful centre of opposition to the revival of iconoclasm, and he was again exiled because of this before his death at Chalcis. His monastery church survived (latterly as a mosque) until its roof fell in during a snowfall in 1912.

Theodore of Sykeon (St) B. Apr 22
d. 613. Born at Sykeon in Galatia, Asia Minor, where his parents ran a way-station for the imperial postal service, he became a monk at Jerusalem and was later the abbot-founder of several monasteries in his native province. About 590 he was made bishop of Anastasiopolis in Galatia but resigned before he died. He was a great promoter of the cultus of St George.

Theodore of Tabennesis (St) R. Apr 27
?314–?368. From near Thebes, Egypt, he joined the cenobites of Tabennesis and was a favourite disciple of St Pachomius. He had to replace St Horsiesius as superior in 351 when there was a revolt among the brethren, but he always regarded this as a temporary expedient. He oversaw, with sorrow, the growing wealth of the congregation. When he died, St Horsiesius became superior again.

Theodore Trichinas (St) R. Apr 20
d. *p*330. From Constantinople, he became a hermit near his city and was nicknamed Trichinas, 'the hairy', because his only garment was a rough hair shirt.

Theodore Tyro (St) M. Nov 9
C4th. According to his story he was a recruit ('tyro') in the Roman army who set fire to the temple of Cybele at Euchaita near Amasea in Pontus, Asia Minor, and was himself burnt alive at the same place. He is almost certainly identical with St Theodore Stratelates. In the East he is venerated as one of the 'three soldier saints' (George, Demetrius and Theodore) but his cultus in the Roman rite was confined to local calendars in 1969.

Theodore (Theudar, Chef) of Vienne (St) R. Oct 29
d. ?575. A disciple of St Caesarius of Arles, he was abbot of one of the monasteries of Vienne, France, and founded several monasteries in the neighbourhood before dying as a hermit in the city.

Theodoret (Theodore) of Antioch (St) M. P. Oct 23
d. 362. A priest of Antioch, Syria, and treasurer to the great church there, he was beheaded in the reign of Julian for refusing to hand over church property formerly belonging to pagan institutions. He was highly regarded by St John Chrysostom.

Theodoric Balat (St) *see* **Gregory Grassi and Comps**

Theodoric of Cambrai (St) B. Aug 5
d. 863. He was bishop of Cambrai-Arras, France, from *c*830.

Theodoric van Emden (St)
M. R(OFM). Oct 9
d. 1572. A Dutch Franciscan, he was confessor to the Franciscan nuns at **Gorinchem** (q.v.) and one of the martyrs there.

Theodoric (Thierry) of Mont d'Or (St) R. Jul 1
d. ?533. He was educated by St Remigius of Rheims, France, by whom he was appointed abbot of Mont d'Or near that city.

Theodoric of Ninden (St) M. B. Feb 2
d. 880. Bishop of Ninden, he was one of those who died at Ebstorf. *See* **Ebstorf (Martyrs of)**.

Theodoric II of Orléans
(St) B. R(OSB). Jan 27
d. 1022. He was a monk at Saint-Pierre-le-Vif at Sens, France, and was a royal counsellor before being made bishop of Orléans. He died at Tonnerre on his way to Rome.

Theodoric (Thierry) of St-Hubert (Bl) R(OSB). Oct 25
d. 1087. Educated at Maubeuge in Flanders, France, he became a Benedictine at Lobbes and was made abbot of St Hubert in the Ardennes, Belgium, in 1055. Here and at the neighbouring twin abbeys of Stavelot-Malmédy he successfully introduced the Cluniac observance. His cultus was not confirmed.

Theodoric (Tewdric) of Tintern (St) M. R. Apr 1
C5th or C6th. Allegedly a prince of Glamorgan, Wales, he was a hermit at Tintern, Gwent, and was killed in a Saxon raid. He was buried at Mathern.

Theodosia (St) *see* **Alexandra of Amisus and Comps**

Theodosia (St) *see* **Domitius of Caesarea and Comps**

Theodosia of Caesarea Philippi and Comps (SS) MM. May 29
d. ?303. According to the legend, probably a fabrication, she was the mother of St Procopius the Great and was martyred at Caesarea Philippi in the Holy Land with twelve other women in the reign of Diocletian.

Theodosia of Constantinople
(St) M. R. May 29
d. 745. A nun of St Anastasia at Constantinople, she led a group of other nuns in a violent attempt to prevent the destruction of the icon of Christ over the main door of their monastery by soldiers sent on the orders of the iconoclast emperor, Constantine V. She died of torture in prison.

Theodosia of Tyre (St) V. Apr 2
290–308 A teenager of Tyre, Lebanon, she was on a visit to Caesarea in the Holy Land when she asked some martyrs on their way to execution to pray for her. She was overheard, seized, tortured and finally thrown into the sea.

Theodosius (St) *see* **Quadratus, Theodosius and Comps**

Theodosius, Lucius, Mark and Peter (SS) MM. Oct 25
d. 269. They were among fifty soldiers martyred at Rome in the reign of Claudius II.

Theodosius of Antioch (St) R. Jan 11
d. ?412. A nobleman of Antioch, Syria, he became a hermit and founded a monastery near Rhosus in Cilicia, Asia Minor. He died and was buried at Antioch.

Theodosius of Auxerre (St) B. Jul 17
d. 516. He was bishop of Auxerre, France, from ?507.

Theodosius the Cenobiarch
(St) R. Jan 11
423–529. A Cappodocian, he went to Jerusalem to be a monk and joined a monastery on the road to Bethlehem, but then fled in order to avoid being made abbot and settled as a hermit in the desert east of Bethlehem in 479. He attracted disciples and founded the largest and most thoroughly organized of the Judaean monasteries with several hundred monks. He built a church for each of three language groups (Greeks, Armenians and Arabs), and made the monastery famous for its hospitality and charitable works. The patriarch of Jerusalem appointed him visitor to all the cenobitical communities in the Holy Land (St Sabas was responsible for the hermits), and as such he was forceful in support of the council of Chalcedon against the Monophysites. His monastery has been refounded, but is now surrounded by a suburb.

Theodosius of Vaison (St) B. Feb 14
d. 554. He was predecessor of St Quinidius as bishop of Vaison near Orange, France.

Theodota of Constantinople
(St) M. L. Jul 17
d. ?735. A noblewoman of Constantinople, she was executed for having hidden three icons to

save them from destruction by the officials of the iconoclastic emperor Leo III.

Theodota of Nicaea and Comps (SS) MM. Aug 2
d. ?304. According to their untrustworthy acta they were a mother and three sons (Evodius, Hermogenes and Callistus) who were martyred at Nicaea, Asia Minor, by being thrown into a furnace.

Theodota the Penitent (St) L. Sep 29
d. *c*318. According to her untrustworthy acta she was a penitent prostitute who was martyred at Philippopolis (now Plovdiv in Bulgaria) after being subject to an imaginative variety of tortures.

Theodotus (St) *see* **Aquilinus, Geminus, Eugene and Comps**

Theodotus (St) *see* **Clementinus, Theodotus and Philomenus**

Theodotus (St) *see* **Marinus, Theodotus and Sedopha**

Theodotus of Ancyra and Comps (SS) MM. May 18
d. ?304. According to their acta, which are probably fictional, he was an innkeeper of Ancyra, Asia Minor (now Ankara in Turkey), who was martyred there in the reign of Diocletian for burying the bodies of the seven martyred consecrated virgins Thecusa, Alexandra, Claudia, Phaina, Euphrasia, Matrona and Julitta.

Theodotus of Caesarea and Comps (SS) MM. Aug 31
d. ?270. According to the unreliable acta of St Mamas (the only source) they were the martyr's father, mother (Rufina) and foster-mother (Ammia) and were themselves martyred at Caesarea in Cappodocia, Asia Minor, in the reign of Aurelian.

Theodotus of Cyrenia (St) B. May 6
d. ?325. He was bishop of Cyrenia in Cyprus and suffered a long term of imprisonment in the reign of Licinius.

Theodotus of Laodicea (St) B. Nov 2
d. 334. A bishop of Laodicea (Latakia in Syria), he was an Arian and a friend of the historian Eusebius but signed the decrees of the council of Nicaea. Afterwards he sided with the Arian leader Eusebius of Nicomedia. His insertion in the Roman Martyrology was an error.

Theodula *see* **Dula**

Theodulf (Thiou) of Lobbes (St) B. R. Jun 24
d. 776. He was the third abbot-bishop of Lobbes near Liege, Belgium.

Theodulus (St) *see* **Agathopodes and Theodulus**

Theodulus (St) *see* **Alexander, Eventius and Theodulus**

Theodulus (St) *see* **Exuperius, Zoë and Comps**

Theodulus (St) *see* **Leontius, Hyparius and Theodulus**

Theodulus (St) *see* **Macedonius, Theodulus and Tatian**

Theodulus (St) *see* **Symphronius of Rome and Comps**

Theodulus, Anesius, Felix, Cornelia and Comps (SS) MM. Mar 31
? They were Roman African martyrs.

Theodulus, Saturninus and Comps (SS) MM. Dec 23
d. 250. They were ten martyrs of Crete in the reign of Decius, the others being Euporus, Gelasius, Eunician, Zeticus, Cleomenes (Leomenes), Agathopus, Basilides and Evaristus

Theodulus (Theodore, Theodoric) of Antioch (St) P. Mar 23
? He is listed as a priest of Antioch, Syria, but with no further information.

Theodulus of Caesarea (St) M. Feb 17
d. 309. He was an old servant in the household of Firmilian, governor of the Holy Land, who ordered him to be crucified.

Theodulus (Theodore) of Grammont (St) B. Aug 17
C4th. He was an early bishop in Valais, Switzerland, and was venerated in Switzerland and Savoy. A later biography placed him in the C9th century and has caused confusion about his identity.

Theofrid (Theofroy, Chaffre) of Carmery (St) R. Oct 19
d. 728. From Orange, France, he joined the abbey of Carmery-en-Velay near Le Puy and

became its abbot. He died as a result of injuries received in an Arab raid and was regarded as a martyr. The abbey was renamed St Chaffre after him.

Theofrid (Theofroy) of Corbie (St) B. R. Jan 26
d. *c*690. A monk of Luxeuil, he became abbot of Corbie near Amiens, France, in 622 and a bishop (perhaps at Amiens) in 670.

Theogenes (St) *see* **Cyrinus, Primus and Theogenes**

Theoger (Theogar, Diethger) (Bl) B. R(OSB). Apr 29
d. 1120. Probably an Alsatian, he was in turn a canon of Mainz, Germany, a monk at Hirsau, prior of Reichenbach, abbot of Sankt-Georgen in the Black Forest from 1090 and finally bishop of Metz in 1118. He never went to his diocese, however, but died at Cluny, France.

Theogonius (St) *see* **Bassa and Sons**

Theonas (St) *see* **Theopemptus and Theonas**

Theonas (St) *see* **Victor, Zoticus and Comps**

Theonas of Alexandria (St) B. Aug 23
d. 300. He became patriarch of Alexandria, Egypt, in 281, supported the famous catechetical school there and opposed Sabellianism (which denied any real distinctions between the persons of the Trinity).

Theonas of Egypt (St) R. Apr 4
d. ?395. An Egyptian desert father, he was a hermit near Oxyrinchus for thirty years.

Theonestus (St) M. B? Oct 30
d. 425. Allegedly a refugee bishop of Philippi in Greek Macedonia in exile from the Arians, he was sent by the pope with several companions (including St Alban of Mainz) as missionaries to Germany. They were at Mainz but had to flee the invading Vandals, and Theonestus was martyred at Altino near Venice, Italy. He was probably a local martyr having no connection with the others.

Theonilla (St) *see* **Claudius, Asterius and Comps**

Theopemptus and Theonas (SS) MM. Jan 3
d. 284. According to their worthless acta (probably written about real martyrs) they were a bishop of Nicomedia, Asia Minor, and a magician respectively, the latter converted by the martyrdom of the former and himself then martyred. The old Roman Martyrology listed them again in error on May 21, as 'Theopompus and Synesius'.

Theophanes, Papias, Strategius and Jacob (SS) MM. Dec 4
d. ?815. Four officials at the court of Leo V at Constantinople, they were imprisoned and tortured for their opposition to iconoclasm. Theophanes died under torture but the others survived and eventually became monks.

Theophanes the Confessor (St) R. Mar 12
d. 818. From Constantinople, as an orphan he was educated at the imperial court and married young but the couple separated to enter monastic life in 780. He became a monk at Polychronion and was later abbot-founder of Mt Sigriana near Cyzicus. He was a determined opponent of the revival of iconoclasm by Emperor Leo V and was exiled to the island of Samothrace, where he died from ill-treatment.

Theophanes Graptus (St) *see* **Theodore Graptus**

Theophanes Vénard (St) M. P. Feb 2
1829–1861. From near Poitiers, France, he joined the Paris Society for Foreign Missions, was ordained in 1852 and went to Vietnam two years later. After teaching in a seminary he secretly worked west of Hanoi during the persecution that started in 1857, but was captured and executed. *See* **Vietnam (Martyrs of)**.

Theophila (St) *see* **Indes, Domna and Comps**

Theophilus (St) *see* **Ammon, Theophilus and Comps**

Theophilus (St) *see* **Ammon, Zeno and Comps**

Theophilus (St) *see* **Germanus, Theophilus and Comps**

Theophilus (St) *see* **Macarius, Rufinus and Comps**

Theophilus (St) *see* **Saturninus, Theophilus and Revocata**

Theophilus *see* **Theophylact**

Theophilus (St) *see* **Trophimus and Theophilus**

Theophilus and Helladius (SS) MM. Jan 8
? A deacon and a layman, they were tortured and thrown into a furnace in Libya, Roman Africa.

Theophilus the Apologist (St) B. Oct 13
d. 181. An Eastern philosopher, he read the scriptures with the intention of rebutting them but was converted and became bishop of Antioch, Syria. He wrote an extant *Apology* in three volumes, in which he contrasted the pagan myths of Greece with the Biblical account of creation. His work developed the idea of the Logos or Word of God.

Theophilus of Brescia (St) B. Apr 27
d. *p*427. He succeeded St Gaudentius as bishop of Brescia, Italy.

Theophilus of Caesarea (St) B. Mar 5
d. ?195. Bishop of Caesarea in Palestine, he opposed the Quartodecimans, a sect which celebrated Easter on the Jewish Passover day regardless of whether it fell on a Sunday or not.

Theophilus the New Martyr (St) M. Jul 22
d. 789. He was an officer of the imperial forces stationed in Cyprus when the Arabs invaded the island, was taken prisoner after battle and was executed after a year for refusing to become a Muslim.

Theophilus the Penitent (St) P. Feb 4
d. ?538. The legend (according to Simon Metaphrastes) alleges that he was the archdeacon of Adana in Cilicia, Asia Minor. Having been deposed through calumny he made a written pact with the devil but repented, whereupon Our Lady appeared to him and returned the document. This was then torn up and publicly burnt. Goethe made use of this legend in his *Faust*.

Theophilus Scholasticus (St) M. Feb 6
d. ?300. According to the legend of St Dorothy he was a lawyer beheaded at Caesarea in Cappodocia, Asia Minor.

Theophilus of Seleution (St) R. Oct 2
d. *c*750. A Bulgarian, he became a monk of a monastery on Mt Seleution in Asia Minor, where the Western rule of St Benedict was allegedly kept. For opposing iconoclasm he was persecuted and exiled by the emperor Leo IV.

Theophilus de Signori of Corte (St) R(OFM). May 19
1676–1740. From Corte in Corsica, he became a Franciscan in 1693, was ordained at Naples and taught theology at Civitella near Rome. Later he became a famous missioner in Italy and Corsica and was zealous for Franciscan reform. He died at Fucecchio and was canonized in 1930.

Theophylact (St) B. Mar 7
d. 845. He was a monk from Asia Minor and became bishop of Nicomedia, Asia Minor, in 816. He helped in the opposition to the iconoclastic policy of Emperor Leo V and was exiled to Caria, where he died thirty years later. He was mistakenly listed as Theophilus in the old Roman Martyrology.

Theopistes and Theopistus (SS) *see* **Eustace of Rome and Comps**

Theopompus *see* **Theopemptus and Theonas**

Theoprepius (St) *see* **Philetus, Lydia and Comps**

Theorogitha *see* **Thordgith**

Theoticus (St) *see* **Arian, Theoticus and Comps**

Theotimus (St) *see* **Domninus, Silvanus and Comps**

Theotimus (St) *see* **Lucian, Metrobius and Comps**

Theotimus and Basilian (SS) MM. Dec 18
? They were martyred at Laodicea (Latakia) in Syria.

Theotimus of Tomi (St) B. Apr 20
d. 407. Bishop of Tomi (on the coast of Romania), he defended the writings of Origen against St Epiphanius of Salamis and evangelized the barbarian tribes of the Lower Danube then migrating into imperial territory.

Theotonius (St) R(CR). Feb 18
1086–1166. From Galicia, Spain, he was educated at Coïmbra, Portugal, and became archpriest of Viseu but resigned to go on pilgrimage to the Holy Land. On returning he joined the Augustinian Canons Regular at Coïmbra and was highly regarded by the first ruler of the new kingdom of Portugal.

Theresa *see* **Teresa**

Thespesius (St) M. Jun 1
d. *c*230. He was martyred in Cappodocia, Asia Minor, in the reign of Alexander Severus.

Thespesius (St) *see* **Eustace, Thespesius and Anatolius**

Thessalonika (St) *see* **Auctus, Taurion and Thessalonika**

Thethmar (Theodemar)
(St) R(OPraem)? May 17
d. 1152. From Bremen, Germany, he was a missionary with St Vicelin among the Wagrian Slavs and may have been a Premonstratensian. He died at Neumünster.

Theuderius *see* **Theodore**

Theusetas, Horres and Comps (SS) MM. Mar 13
? According to the old Roman Martyrology, they were a father and his young son who were martyred at Nicaea, Asia Minor, together with Theodora, Nymphodora, Mark and Arabia. Earlier martyrologies have a much longer list of martyrs, and Horres is variantly given as Choris, a virgin.

Thiemo (Theodmar)
(Bl) M. B. R(OSB). Sep 28
d. 1102. A nobleman of Bavaria, Germany, he became a Benedictine at Niederaltaich and was famous as a metalworker, painter and sculptor. In 1077 he became abbot of St Peter's, Salzburg, Austria, and was made archbishop of the same city in 1090. He was imprisoned and exiled for upholding the Gregorian reforms, so joined the first crusade and was captured by the Seljuk Turks. After imprisonment at Ascalon he was killed, allegedly for refusing to apostatize to Islam. His cultus is unconfirmed.

Thiento and Comps (BB)
MM. RR(OSB). Aug 10
d. 955. An abbot of Wessobrunn in Bavaria, he was killed with six of his community in a raid by the Magyars. Their cultus is unconfirmed.

Thierry *see* **Theodoric**

Thillo *see* **Tillo**

Thiou *see* **Theodulf**

Thomais (St) M. Apr 14
d. 476. The wife of a fisherman at Alexandria, Egypt, she was murdered by her father-in-law after she had rejected an indecent proposal that he had made.

Thomas Abell (Bl) M. P. Jul 30
d. 1540. He obtained a doctorate at Oxford University before becoming a chaplain to Queen Catherine of Aragon. As such he defended the validity of her marriage to King Henry VIII and was imprisoned in the Tower of London for six years before being executed at Smithfield for refusing to acknowledge the king's spiritual supremacy. He was beatified in 1886. *See* **England (Martyrs of)**.

Thomas Akahoshi (Bl) M. L. Sep 10
d. 1622. A Japanese nobleman, he worked as a catechist with Bl Leonard Kimura and was burnt alive in the 'Great Martyrdom' at Nagasaki with BB Charles Spinola and Comps. *See* **Japan (Martyrs of)**.

Thomas Alfield (Bl) M. P. Jul 6
d. 1585. From Gloucester, he was educated at Eton and King's College, Cambridge, before his conversion. Then he studied for the priesthood at Douai and Rheims and was ordained in 1581. After his return to England he was arrested while engaged in distributing copies of Dr Allen's *True and Modest Defence*, and was hanged at Tyburn for this. He was beatified in 1929. *See* **England (Martyrs of)**.

Thomas of Antioch (St) R. Nov 18
d. 782. He was a Syrian monk in a monastery near Antioch, and is a patron against epidemics.

Thomas the Apostle (St) M. A. July 3
C1st. He is surnamed 'Didymus', meaning 'the twin'. All that is known for certain about him is in the gospels, where he chiefly features in the episode concerning his unbelief and subsequent profession of faith in Christ's resurrection (Jn 20:24-29). According to an ancient tradition (important to the native churches but lacking proof) he went as a missionary to Kerala in south India and was martyred there. His name was later attached to apocryphal writings of the C2nd-4th such as the Gospel of Thomas. His attribute is a lance.

Thomas Aquinas (St) Dr. R(OP). Jan 28
?1225–1274. Born at Roccasecca near Aquino in Campania, Italy, the son of a local nobleman, he was educated at Montecassino and then joined the recently founded Dominicans (despite the opposition of his family). After becoming doctor of theology at the university

of Paris he taught at Paris (1252–1260), at Orvieto to 1264, at Rome to 1267, at Viterbo in 1268, at Paris again to 1271 and finally at Naples to 1274. He died at Fossanova near Rome while on his way to the council of Lyons. His systematic philosophical and theological writings, especially the *Summa Theologiae*, have had a profound influence up to the present day and were a successful synthesis of Christian and Aristotelian thought (western Christian philosophy having previously been Platonic, mediated through Augustine). As a person he was humble and prayerful, and very fat. He was canonized in 1323, declared a doctor of the Church in 1567 and patron of Catholic centres of study in 1880. His special attribute is a star or rays of light on his breast.

St Thomas Aquinas, Jan 28

Thomas Atkinson (Bl) M. P. Mar 11
d. 1616. From the East Riding of Yorkshire, he was ordained at Rheims in 1588 and was a priest in Yorkshire. He was very charitable, and travelled on foot until a leg broken by slipping on ice forced him to rely on a horse. He was captured at Willitoft and was executed at York, being beatified in 1987. *See* **England (Martyrs of)**.

Thomas Becket (St) M. B. Dec 29
1118–1170. His father was a Norman merchant in London and he studied at Paris before entering the service of the archbishop of Canterbury, who made him his archdeacon in 1154. He was a close friend of King Henry II, who made him royal chancellor in the following year and archbishop of Canterbury in 1162. Previously he had lived a rather worldly life, but as archbishop he concentrated on his pastoral duties and insisted on the independence of the Church from the jurisdiction of the Crown. He went into exile in 1164, returned in 1170 and was assassinated in Canterbury Cathedral by four royal knights who thought they were acting on the king's wishes. He was canonized as a martyr in 1173, and his tomb became one of the foremost pilgrimage shrines in western Christendom until its destruction by King Henry VIII. He is often depicted with a wounded head, or holding an inverted sword or a crosier with a battle-axe head on it.

Thomas Bellacci (Bl) R(OFM Conv). Oct 31
1370–1447. From Florence, Italy, he became a conventual Franciscan lay brother at Fiesole and was novice-master there before successfully introducing reform measures to the Franciscans in Corsica and southern Italy and withstanding the heretical Fraticelli in Tuscany. When over seventy he went to preach in Syria where (to his sorrow) he narrowly escaped being killed by the Muslims. He died at Rieti and his cultus was approved for there and for the conventual Franciscans in 1771.

Thomas Belson (Bl) M. L. Jul 7
1565–1589. Born at Brill of a recusant Buckinghamshire landowning family, he studied at Oxford and Rheims and was seized when the Catherine Wheel Inn in Oxford (the city's centre of Catholic activity) was raided. He was executed at Oxford with those captured with him, BB Humphrey Pritchard, George Nichols and Richard Yaxley, and was beatified in 1987. *See* **England (Martyrs of)**.

Thomas Bosgrave (Bl) M. L. Jul 4
d. 1594. A Dorset landowner, he was hanged at Dorchester with two of his servants, BB John Carey and Patrick Salmon, for aiding Catholic priests. Bl John Cornelius was executed with them. He was beatified in 1929. *See* **England (Martyrs of)**.

Thomas de Cantalupe (St) B. Oct 3
?1218–1282. A nobleman from Hambleden near Great Marlow, Bucks, he studied at Oxford and Paris and became chancellor of Oxford University in 1261 (serving for a time as chancellor of England). He was made bishop of Hereford in 1275. The seven years of his

episcopate he spent in continually fighting the mismanagement and neglect of his diocese (caused especially by civil war) and in untiring pastoral activities. He died at Montefiascone in Italy after setting out to appeal to the pope as he had quarrelled with John Peckham, archbishop of Canterbury, and had been excommunicated by him. Some relics were returned to Hereford and a popular cultus grew up based on his personal holiness and pastoral zeal and overlooking his irascibility and the fact that he died technically excommunicate. He was canonized in 1320.

Thomas Capdevila Miró (Bl) *see* **Philip-of-Jesus Munárriz Azcona and Comps**

Thomas of Cori (St) R(OFM) Jan 19
1653–1729. From near Velletri, Italy, he was a shepherd in the Roman Campagna before becoming an Observant Franciscan in 1675. After his ordination he was at Civitella near Subiaco and spent the rest of his life in ministering to the inhabitants of the mountains round about. He was beatified in 1786 and canonized in 1999.

Thomas Corsini (Bl) R(OSM). Jun 23
d. 1343. Born in Orvieto, Italy, he became a Servite lay brother there and spent his life collecting alms for his friary, where he died. He had many visions. His cultus was confirmed for Orvieto in 1768.

Thomas (Thomasius) of Costacciaro (Bl) R(OSB Cam). Mar 25
d. 1337. From Costacciaro in Umbria, Italy, the son of poor peasants, he joined the Camaldolese at Sitria and then became a hermit on Monte Cupo. He has an unconfirmed cultus at Gubbio.

Thomas Cottam (Bl) M.R(SJ). May 30
1549–1582. From Dilworth near Preston, Lancs, his family were Protestants but after his graduation at Oxford university he was converted and studied for the priesthood at Douai and Rome. At Rome he became a Jesuit and returned to England in 1580, but was arrested on landing at Dover and imprisoned in the Tower of London. Two years later he was hanged at Tyburn with St Luke Kirby and BB Laurence Richardson and William Filby, and was beatified in 1886. *See* **England (Martyrs of)**.

Thomas-of-the-Blessed-Sacrament Cuartero Gascón (Bl) *see* **Nicephorus Díez Tejerina and Comps**

Thomas Dangi (St) M. T(OFM). Feb 6
d. 1597. A Japanese Franciscan tertiary, he worked with the Franciscan missionaries in Kyushu, Japan, as a catechist and interpreter. He was crucified at Nagasaki with SS Paul Miki and Comps. *See* **Japan (Martyrs of)**.

Thomas (Nguyen van) De (St) T(OP). Dec 19
d. 1839. From north Vietnam, a tailor by trade and a Dominican tertiary, he was strangled at Ninh-Tai with four companions (Augustine (Nguyen van) Moi, Dominic (Bui van) Uy, Francis-Xavier (Ha Trong) Mau and Stephen (Nguyen van) Vinh). *See* **Vietnam (Martyrs of)**.

Thomas of Dover *see* **Thomas Hales**

Thomas (Dinh Viet) Du (St) M. T(OP). May 31
1774–1839. A Vietnamese priest and Dominican tertiary, he worked in the province of Nam-Dinh before being arrested, tortured and beheaded. *See* **Vietnam (Martyrs of)**.

Thomas Dubray and Thomas Dubuisson (BB) *see* **September (Martyrs of)**

Thomas of Farfa (St) R. Dec 10
d. *c*720. From Maurienne in Savoy, he went on pilgrimage to the Holy Land and on his return became a hermit near Farfa, Italy. With the help of the Duke of Spoleto he restored the abbey there to its former splendour. His cultus was confirmed for Farfa in 1921.

Thomas Felton (Bl) M. R(OMinim). Aug 28
1568–1588. From Bermondsey, London, son of Bl John Felton, he was educated at Rheims and became a Minim Friar. He was hanged at Isleworth in his twentieth year and beatified in 1929. *See* **England (Martyrs of)**.

Thomas Ford (Bl) M. P. May 28
d. 1582. From Devon, he was at Trinity College, Oxford when he converted and then studied for the priesthood at Douai. After ordination in 1573 he worked in Oxfordshire and Berkshire until his arrest and execution at Tyburn with BB John Shert and Robert Johnson. He was beatified in 1886. *See* **England (Martyrs of)**.

Thomas-Mary Fusco (Bl) P.F. Feb 24
1831–1891. From a middle-class family of Pagani near Salerno, Italy, he was orphaned as a child and was ordained priest in 1855. In 1857 he became an itinerant missionary in southern Italy and, in 1860, he became

chaplain at the Marian shrine at Pagani. There he founded the 'Daughters of Charity of the Precious Blood' in 1873 in order to run orphanages for poor girls. He died of liver failure and was beatified in 2001.

Thomas Garnet (St) M. R(SJ). Jun 23
?1575–1608. From Southwark, London, a nephew of the famous Fr Henry Garnet SJ, he was educated for the priesthood at St Omer and Valladolid. At first he was on the English mission as a secular priest but became a Jesuit in 1604. He was hanged at Tyburn as a result of returning after being exiled and was canonized in 1970. *See* **England (Martyrs of)**.

Thomas Gengoro (Bl) M. L. Aug 18
d. 1620. A Japanese layman, he was a servant of Bl Simon Kiyota Bokusai and had a wife, Mary, and two-year-old son, James. They were crucified at Kokura and beatified in 1867. *See* **Japan (Martyrs of)**.

Thomas Green (Greenwood)
(Bl) M. R(OCart). Jun 15
d. 1537. He was a fellow of St John's College, Cambridge, before becoming a Carthusian monk at the London Charterhouse, and was one of the seven of that community who were starved to death at Newgate prison for refusing to take the oath of spiritual supremacy demanded by King Henry VIII. *See* **England (Martyrs of)**.

Thomas Hales of Dover *Aug 2*
d. 1295. He was a Benedictine monk of Dover Priory, a dependency of Canterbury Cathedral Priory. In 1295 there was a French raid on Dover, England, and his brethren fled, leaving him in bed as he was old and infirm. The raiders ordered him to disclose the whereabouts of the priory's valuables, he refused and was then murdered. Miracles were alleged at his tomb and a local cultus grew up, but attempted canonization was abortive and his status as a martyr is dubious. The alleged altar dedicated to him in Dover Priory church was probably only nicknamed after him, and other evidence of a cultus since the Reformation is as a result of wishful thinking.

Thomas Hélye (Bl) P. Oct 19
1187–1257. From Biville in Normandy, France, he led an ascetic life in the house of his parents and spent some of his time teaching the catechism to the poor. He accepted ordination at the request of his bishop and became an itinerant preacher in Normandy before being made the royal almoner. He died at the castle of Vauville, Manche, and had his cultus for Coutances confirmed in 1859.

Thomas Hemerford (Bl) M. P. Feb 12
d. 1584. From Dorset, he was at the University of Oxford and studied for the priesthood at the English College, Rome, where he was ordained in 1583. The following year he was hanged at Tyburn, London, with BB George Haydock, James Fenn, John Munden and John Nutter. He was beatified in 1929. *See* **England (Martyrs of)**.

Thomas of Hereford *see* **Thomas de Cantalupe**

Thomas Holford (alias Acton, Bude) (Bl) M. P. Aug 28
d. 1588. From Acton near Nantwich, Cheshire, his family was Protestant and he became a schoolmaster in Herefordshire before his conversion. Then he studied for the priesthood and was ordained at Rheims in 1583. After being on mission in Cheshire he was hanged at Clerkenwell, London, and was beatified in 1929. *See* **England (Martyrs of)**.

Thomas Holland (alias Sanderson, Hammond)
(Bl) M. R(SJ). Dec 12
d. 1642. From Sutton near Prescot, Lancs, he was educated at St Omer and Valladolid and became a Jesuit in 1624. He was hanged at Tyburn, London, and was beatified in 1929. *See* **England (Martyrs of)**.

Thomas Hunt (Bl) M. P. Jul 7
1577–1600. From Norfolk, he was among the first students of St Gregory's College at Seville in Spain and was ordained there in 1599. On his arrival at London he was captured and sent to the concentration camp at Wisbech, but he escaped and was re-captured at the Saracen's Head Inn at Lincoln with Bl Thomas Sprott. They were executed together in that city, and were beatified in 1987. *See* **England (Martyrs of)**.

Thomas Jinyemono (Bl) M. L. Aug 16
d. 1627. A Japanese layman, for sheltering missionaries he was beheaded at Nagasaki with BB Francis-of-St-Mary of Mancha and Comps. *See* **Japan (Martyrs of)**.

Thomas Johnson (Bl) R(OCart). Sep 20
d. 1537. A Carthusian at the London Charterhouse, he was one of that community starved to death in Newgate prison for refusing to take the oath of spiritual supremacy demanded by King Henry VIII. *See* **England (Martyrs of)**.

Thomas Kahyoye (Bl) M. T(OSA) Sep 28
d. 1630. A Japanese Augustinian tertiary, he was beheaded at Nagasaki with BB John Chozaburo and Comps. *See* **Japan (Martyrs of)**.

Thomas Khuong (St) M. T(OP). Jan 30
1861. He was a Vietnamese secular priest and martyr. *See* **Vietnam (Martyrs of)**.

Thomas Kosaki (St) M. L. Feb 6
d. 1597. He was a Japanese teenager aged fifteen, the son of St Michael Cozaki, and served at Mass for the Franciscan missionaries in Kyushu, Japan. He was crucified at Nagasaki with his father and Paul Miki and Comps. *See* **Japan (Martyrs of)**.

Thomas Koteda and Comps
(BB) MM. Nov 27
d. 1619. Related to the ruling family on the Japanese island of Hirado-jima, he was educated by the Jesuits and lived in exile at Nagasaki, where he was ultimately beheaded with ten companions: Alexis Nakamura, Anthony Kimura, Bartholomew Seki, John Iwanaga, John Motoyama, Leo Nakanishi, Matthias Kozaka, Matthias Nakano, Michael Sakaguchi and Romanus Motoyama. They were beatified in 1867. *See* **Japan (Martyrs of)**.

Thomas Koyanagi (Bl) M. L. Aug 19
d. 1622. He was a Japanese passenger on the ship carrying BB Louis Flores and Comps and was beheaded with them at Nagasaki. *See* **Japan (Martyrs of)**.

Thomas Loup (Bl) *see* **September (Martyrs of)**

Thomas Maxfield (Bl) M. P. Jul 1
d. 1616. A native of Enville near Stourbridge, Staffs, he was educated for the priesthood at Douai and ordained in 1615 but was captured and hanged at Tyburn, London, the year after. He was beatified in 1929. *See* **England (Martyrs of)**.

Thomas Monsaint (Bl) *see* **September (Martyrs of)**

Thomas More (St) M. L. Jun 22
1478–1535. A Londoner, he studied at Oxford University and became a barrister in London in 1501. Married twice, he was a good husband, devoted to wife and children, devout, cheerful and charitable. In 1516 he published his *Utopia*, which earned him a European reputation as a scholar and humanist. He was highly regarded by King Henry VIII and

St Thomas More, Jun 22

Cardinal Wolsey, and succeeded the latter in 1529 as Lord Chancellor. He did not accept the king's wish to divorce Queen Catherine, however, so resigned and, on refusing to take the oath of spiritual supremacy demanded by the king, was imprisoned in the Tower of London for fifteen months. Then he was condemned for treason and beheaded on Tower Hill. He was canonized with St John Fisher in 1935. *See* **England (Martyrs of)**.

Thomas-of-the-Holy-Rosary of Nagasaki (Bl) M. R(OP). Sep 10
d. 1622. A Japanese Dominican lay brother, he worked as a catechist before being beheaded in the 'Great Martyrdom' at Nagasaki with BB Charles Spinola and Comps. *See* **Japan (Martyrs of)**.

Thomas-of-St-Hyacinth of Nagasaki (Bl) M. R(OP). Sep 8
d. 1628. A Japanese catechist and Dominican lay brother, he was burnt alive at Nagasaki with BB Dominic Castellet and Comps. *See* **Japan (Martyrs of)**.

Thomas Netter of Walden (Bl) R(OC). Nov 2
?1375–1430. From Saffron Walden in Essex, England, he became a Carmelite, was an active opponent of the Lollards and attended the council of Constance. He was the confessor of King Henry V and was at the king's deathbed. He died at Rouen, France. His cultus is unconfirmed.

Thomas Palaser and Comps (Bl) M. S. Sep 8
d. 1600. Born at Ellerton on Swale, Yorks, he studied at Rheims and was ordained at Valladolid in 1596. He was a priest for three years in Yorkshire before being picked up on suspicion near Raven's Hall at Laymsley, a known recusant house. His vestments and books were then found there and he was executed at Durham with the owner of the house, Bl John Norton and his guest, Bl John Talbot from Thornton le Street. They were beatified in 1987. *See* **England (Martyrs of)**.

Thomas Percy (Bl) M. L. Aug 22
1528–1572. As Earl of Northumberland he was leader of the Catholic gentry of the North of England, and was condemned to death and executed at York for his part in the insurrection in favour of Mary, Queen of Scots. He was in prison for nearly three years before being executed, and was repeatedly offered his freedom on condition of his apostasy to Protestantism. He was beatified in 1896. *See* **England (Martyrs of)**.

Thomas Pickering (Bl) M. R(OSB). May 9
d. 1679. From Westmoreland, he became a Benedictine lay brother at St Gregory's, Douai (the precursor of Downside Abbey), in 1660 and was sent to England to join the small community of Benedictine chaplains who served the Chapel Royal. He was falsely accused in the Oates plot, was hanged at Tyburn and beatified in 1929. *See* **England (Martyrs of)**.

Thomas Pilcher (Bl) M. P. Mar 21
1557–1587. Born in Battle in Sussex, he studied at Oxford and Rheims and was ordained at Laon, France. Then he was a priest in Dorset and Hampshire before being deported, but returned to Dorset. He was recognized and captured while on a visit to London and was executed at Dorchester by a butcher (no hangman being available). He was beatified in 1987. *See* **England (Martyrs of)**.

Thomas Plumtree (Bl) M. P. Jan 4
d. 1570. From Lincolnshire, he was at the University of Oxford and became rector of Stubton in the reign of the Catholic Queen Mary I. After the Protestant Queen Elizabeth I succeeded to the throne, he became chaplain to the insurgents of the North and was executed in the market-place at Durham after refusing an offer of clemency if he would become a Protestant. He was beatified in 1886. *See* **England (Martyrs of)**.

Thomas Pormont (Bl) M. P. Feb 20
1560–1592. Born near Brocklesby, he was of the Lincolnshire gentry and his family were fervent Anglicans (John Whitgift, later Archbishop of Canterbury, was his godfather). He converted, however, was ordained at Rome and taught at the Swiss College. His return to London was quickly followed by his capture and execution, and he was beatified in 1987. *See* **England (Martyrs of)**.

Thomas Reding (Bl) M. R(OCart). Jun 15
d. 1537. A Carthusian lay brother at the London Charterhouse, he was one of the seven of that community who were starved to death at Newgate prison for refusing to take the oath of spiritual supremacy demanded by King Henry VIII. *See* **England (Martyrs of)**.

Thomas Reggio (Bl) B. F. (Nov 22)
1818–1901. A nobleman from Genoa, Italy, he

was ordained in 1841 despite the promise of a brilliant secular career and became bishop of Ventimiglia in 1877. He revitalized that poor diocese and founded the 'Sisters of St Martha' in 1878. In 1892 he was made archbishop of his home city of Genoa and was one of the great C19th bishops seeking to implement the social teaching of the Church. He died at Ventimiglia and was beatified in 2000.

Thomas-of-St-Hyacinth Rokuzaymon (St) M. R(OP). Sep 28
d. 1634. A Japanese Dominican priest from Hirado, he worked in Taiwan before being martyred in Nagasaki. He was left in a pit to die (which took a week) and was canonized in 1987. *See* **Japan (Martyrs of)**.

Thomas of Sandomir (Bl) *see* **Sadoc of Sandomir and Comps**

Thomas Scryven (Bl) M. R(OCart). Jun 15
d. 1537. A Carthusian lay brother at the London Charterhouse, he was one of the seven of that community who were starved to death at Newgate prison for refusing to take the oath of spiritual supremacy demanded by King Henry VIII. *See* **England (Martyrs of)**.

Thomas Shen (Jihe) (St) *see* **Gregory Grassi and Comps**

Thomas Sherwood (Bl) M. L. Feb 7
1551–1578. A Londoner, he was preparing to go to Douai to study for the priesthood when he was betrayed, imprisoned and racked in the Tower of London in order to force him to reveal the place where he had been going to Mass. He was finally executed at Tyburn on the charge of denying the Queen's ecclesiastical supremacy and was beatified in 1886. *See* **England (Martyrs of)**.

Thomas Shiquiro (Bl) M. L. Sep 10
d. 1622. A seventy-year old Japanese layman with a sound reputation, he was beheaded in the 'Great Martyrdom' at Nagasaki with BB Charles Spinola and Comps. *See* **Japan (Martyrs of)**.

Thomas Somers (Wilson) (Bl) M. P. Dec 10
d. 1610. From Skelsmergh near Kendal in Cumbria, he was a schoolmaster before studying and being ordained at Douai. He was on the London mission, was hanged at Tyburn with Bl John Roberts and was beatified in 1929. *See* **England (Martyrs of)**.

Thomas Son (Cha-sien) (St) M. L. Mar 30
d. 1866. He was a married Korean layman who was viciously tortured in prison before his execution. *See* **Korea (Martyrs of)**.

Thomas Sprott (Bl) M. P. Jul 1
d. 1600. Born near Kendal, he was ordained at Rheims in 1596 but was captured in Holland on his way to England and was forwarded by the Dutch to London. He escaped but was recaptured at the Saracen's Head Inn at Lincoln with Bl Thomas Hunt. They were executed together and were beatified in 1987. *See* **England (Martyrs of)**.

Thomas (Tran van) Thien (St) M. L. Sep 21
1820–1838. A Vietnamese catechist attached to the Paris Society for Foreign Missions in the Mekong delta, he was studying for the priesthood when he was viciously whipped and strangled with St Francis Jacquard. *See* **Vietnam (Martyrs of)**.

Thomas Thwing (Thweng) (Bl) M. P. Oct 23
d. 1680. From Heworth near York, he was educated for the priesthood at Douai, was ordained in 1665 and was fifteen years on the Yorkshire mission. He was executed at York for alleged involvement in the Oates plot, and was beatified in 1929. *See* **England (Martyrs of)**.

Thomas Toan (St) T(OP). Jun 27
1767–1840. A Vietnamese Dominican tertiary, he worked in north Vietnam. After being arrested he initially apostatized but quickly repented and was in consequence whipped and exposed to the sun and insects without food or drink for twelve days until his death. *See* **Vietnam (Martyrs of)**.

Thomas of Tolentino and Comps (SS) MM. RR(OFM). Apr 9
d. 1321. From Tolentino, Italy, he became a Franciscan and travelled as a missionary to Armenia and Persia. He was on his way to Ceylon, intending eventually to go to China, when he was shipwrecked at Tana near Bombay with three companions: BB James of Padua and Peter of Siena, Franciscans, and Demetrius of Tbilisi, a layman. They were beheaded by native Muslims and had their cultus approved for Tolentino in 1894.

Thomas Tomachi (Bl) M. L. Sep 8
d. 1628. He was a ten-year-old Japanese boy, and when his father, Bl John Tomachi, was

burned with Bl Dominic Castellet he was beheaded with his three brothers: Dominic, Michael and Paul. *See* **Japan (Martyrs of)**.

Thomas Tsuji (Bl) M. R(SJ). Sep 7
d. 1627. A Japanese, he was educated by the Jesuits at Arima and joined them in 1589, becoming famous as a preacher. He was exiled to Macao in 1614, but returned to Japan in disguise. Becoming discouraged, he abandoned his vocation for one day but repented and was eventually captured and burnt alive at Nagasaki with his housekeeper and son, BB Louis and John Maki. He was beatified in 1867. *See* **Japan (Martyrs of)**.

Thomas Tunstal (Helmes)
(Bl) M. R(OSB). Jul 13
d. 1616. From Whinfell near Kendal in Cumbria, he was educated for the priesthood at Douai, ordained there in 1609, sent to the English mission in 1610 and arrested almost at once. He spent six years in prison, becoming a Benedictine meanwhile, before being hanged at Norwich. He was beatified in 1929. *See* **England (Martyrs of)**.

Thomas Urdanoz Aldaz (Bl) *see* **Hospitaller Martyrs of Spain**

Thomas of Villanueva
(St) B. R(OSA). Sep 22
1486–1555. From Fuellana near Villanueva, Spain, he was a miller's son who joined the Augustinian friars at Salamanca in 1516 and was prior successively of the Augustinian friars of Salamanca (where he taught moral theology in the university), Burgos and Valladolid. Later he was in turn provincial superior of Andalucia and Castile, court chaplain and finally archbishop of Valencia in 1544. As archbishop he was known as the 'grand almoner of the poor'. He has left a number of theological writings. Canonized in 1658, his cultus was confined to particular calendars in 1969.

Thomas Warcop (Bl) M. L. Jul 4
d. 1597. A Yorkshire landowner, he was hanged at York with BB Edward Fulthrop, Henry Abbot and William Andleby for sheltering Catholic priests. He was beatified in 1929. *See* **England (Martyrs of)**.

Thomas Watkinson (Bl) M. L. May 31
d. 1591. A widower living at Menthorp, Yorks, he was seized at home with Bl Robert Thorpe when the latter was saying Mass for Palm Sunday. They were executed together at York. He was beatified in 1987. *See* **England (Martyrs of)**.

Thomas Welbourne (Bl) M. L. Aug 1
d. 1605. From Hutton Bushel near Scarborough, Yorks, he was a schoolmaster who was hanged at York for proselytizing Protestants. He was beatified in 1929. *See* **England (Martyrs of)**.

Thomas Whitaker (Bl) M. P. Aug 7
d. 1646. The son of a Burnley schoolmaster, he studied at St Omer and Valladolid and was ordained in 1638. He was a priest in Lancashire until caught at Goosnargh and executed at Lancaster with BB Edward Bamber and Martin Woodcock. They were beatified in 1987. *See* **England (Martyrs of)**.

Thomas Whitbread (alias Harcourt) and Comps
(Bl) M. R(SJ). Jun 20
d. 1679. From Essex, he was educated at St Omer, France, and became a Jesuit in 1635. He became provincial superior of the English mission, and at the time of the Oates Plot was convicted with four other Jesuits (BB Anthony Turner, John Fenwick, John Gavan and William Harcourt) on a bogus charge of conspiring to murder King Charles II. They were hanged at Tyburn and beatified in 1929. *See* **England (Martyrs of)**.

Thomas Woodhouse (Bl) M. R(SJ) Jun 19
d. 1573. A secular priest in Lincolnshire, he was also a private tutor in Wales. In 1561 he was imprisoned in the Fleet prison in London for eleven years before being executed at Tyburn. During his imprisonment he was admitted by letter to the Society of Jesus. He was beatified in 1886. *See* **England (Martyrs of)**.

Thomas-of-the-Holy-Spirit Zumarraga and Comps
(BB) M. R(OP). Sep 12
1575–1622. From Vitoria in the Basque Country, Spain, he became a Dominican missionary in Japan and was imprisoned for three years at Omura before being burned there with BB Mancius-of-St-Thomas Shibata and Dominic Magaoshichi de Hyuga (who became Dominicans in prison with him) and the Franciscans BB Apollinaris Franco, Francis-of-St-Bonventure of Musashino and Peter-Paul-of-St-Clare of Arima. They were beatified in 1867. *See* **Japan (Martyrs of)**.

Thomasius *see* **Thomas of Costacciaro**

Thomian (St) B. Jan 10
d. *c*660. Archbishop of Armagh, Ireland, from 623, he wrote a letter to the Holy See on the controversy concerning the date of Easter.

Thordgith (Thorctgyd, Theorigitha) (St) R. Jan 26
d. *c*700. Novice-mistress at the abbey of Barking in Essex, England, under St Ethelburga, she was described as a miracle of patience in the face of suffering.

Thorlák Thórhallsson (St) B. R(CR). Dec 23
1133–1193. From Iceland, he was ordained priest when aged eighteen and studied at Paris before becoming a canon regular at Thykkvibaer, being made abbot there in 1172. In 1174 he became bishop of Sklholt and was vigorous against simony and clerical concubinage. He was declared a saint in 1198 by the Althing (the Icelandic parliament), but his cultus has not been confirmed.

Thrace (Martyrs of) (SS) Aug 20
? They were listed as a group numbering thirty-seven who were thrown into a furnace somewhere in Thrace, south-eastern Balkans, after having their hands and feet cut off.

Thraseas (St) M. B. Oct 5
d. *c*170. Bishop of Eumenia in Phrygia, Asia Minor, and an opponent of the Montanist heretics, he was martyred at Smyrna.

Thrasilla *see* **Tarsilla**

Thurstan Hunt (Bl) M. P. Apr 3
d. 1601. Born at Carlton Hall near Leeds, he had been a priest on mission for fifteen years when he heard that Bl Robert Middleton had been captured near Preston. With four laymen he ambushed the posse taking Bl Robert to Lancaster but was himself captured and they were executed together, being beatified in 1987. *See* **England (Martyrs of)**.

Thyrsus (St) *see* **Andochius, Thyrsus and Felix**

Thyrsus (St) *see* **Saturninus, Thyrsus and Victor**

Thyrsus, Leucius and Callinicus (SS) MM. Jan 28
d. 251. They were martyred at Apollonia in Phrygia, Asia Minor, and their alleged relics were taken to Constantinople and thence to Spain and France.

Thyrsus and Projectus (SS) MM. Jan 24
? Nothing is known about these martyrs.

Tibba (St) *see* **Kyneburga, Kyneswith and Tibba**

Tiberius, Modestus and Florentia (SS) MM. Nov 10
d. ?303. They were martyred in the reign of Diocletian at Agde near Montpellier, France.

Tiburtius (St) *see* **Hyacinth, Alexander and Tiburtius**

Tiburtius, Valerian and Maximus (SS) MM. Apr 14
C3rd? They occur in the unreliable acta of St Cecilia as her brother-in-law, her husband and an official, but may have been authentic martyrs whose names were used by the author. Their alleged tombs were in the cemetery of Praetextatus, and their cultus was confined to local calendars in 1969.

Tiburtius of Rome (St) M. Aug 11
C3rd? This Roman martyr had an ancient cultus based on his tomb on the Via Lavicana, but nothing is known about him and the connection with St Sebastian was a later invention. His cultus was confined to local calendars in 1969.

Tigernach (Tigernake, Tierney, Tierry) (St) B. Apr 4
d. 549. He was allegedly an abbot of the monastery of Clones, Ireland, who became bishop of Clogher, but the extant biography is unhistorical.

Tigides and Remedius (SS) B. Feb 3
C6th? The latter succeeded the former as bishop of Gap, France.

Tigridia (Trigidia) (St) R(OSB). Nov 22
d. ?925. She was a daughter of a nobleman of Old Castile, Spain, who founded for her the Benedictine nunnery of Oña near Burgos (which later became a monastery of monks). She is venerated in the province of Burgos.

Tigrius and Eutropius (SS) MM. Jan 12
d. 404–5. A priest and reader respectively of Constantinople, they were disciples of St John Chrysostom. When the latter was banished they were falsely accused of setting fire to the cathedral and senate-house of the city and were tortured. Eutropius died as a result, while Tigrius apparently survived and was exiled to Asia Minor.

Tilbert (Gilbert) (St) B. R. Sep 7
d. 789. Nothing is known about him except that he became bishop of Hexham in Northumberland, England, in 781.

Tillo (St) R. Jan 7
d. ?702. From Lower Saxony, Germany, he was kidnapped in a raid and sold as a slave in the Low Countries, where he was bought by St Eligius of Noyon. He became a monk at Solignac, and after his ordination evangelized the district round Tournai and Courtrai, Belgium). He returned to Solignac and died as a hermit nearby. His name has many variants, e.g. Thillo, Thielman, Theau, Tilloine, Tillon, Tilman, Hillonius.

Timolaus and Comps (SS) MM. Mar 24
d. 303. A group of eight, they were beheaded at Caesarea in the Holy Land in the reign of Diocletian. Eusebius listed the names of the others: Dionysius (two), Romulus, Pausdes, Alexander (two) and Agapius.

Timon (St) M? D. Apr 19
C1st. He was one of the first seven deacons chosen by the apostles (Acts 6:5), but the traditions concerning his subsequent career conflict.

Timothy (St) M. B. Jan 26
d. ?97. He features in the Acts of the Apostles (16:1-3) as a companion of St Paul on the latter's missionary journeys, and two letters of St Paul are addressed to him. Eusebius wrote that he became bishop at Ephesus and an ancient tradition describes him as having been stoned to death for denouncing the worship of Dionysius.

Timothy (St) *see* **Apollinaris and Timothy**

Timothy (St) *see* **Artaxus and Comps**

Timothy (St) *see* **Faustinus, Timothy and Venustus**

Timothy (St) *see* **Mark and Timothy**

Timothy and Diogenes
(SS) MM. Apr 6
d. ?345. They were martyred at Philippi in Macedonia, Greece, probably by Arians.

Timothy and Faustus (SS) MM. Sep 8
? They were martyred at Antioch, Syria.

Timothy and Maura (SS) MM. May 3
d. 298. Husband and wife, married for only three weeks, they were martyred at Antinoë in Egypt by being nailed to a wall. They lingered for nine days while consoling each other. Timothy (who was a church reader) had been condemned for refusing to hand over the sacred books for burning.

Timothy, Polius and Eutychius (SS) MM. May 21
? They were three deacons martyred in the Roman African province of Mauretania (now Morocco) in the reign of Diocletian.

Timothy, Thecla and Agapius (SS) MM. Aug 19
d. 304. Timothy was bishop of Gaza in the Holy Land and was burnt alive in that city, while Thecla was thrown to the wild animals at the games. Agapius was mistakenly listed with them, as he was thrown into the sea at Caesarea in the Holy Land in 306.

Timothy of Africa (St) M. D. Dec 19
d. *c*250. He was a Roman African deacon burnt alive in the reign of Decius.

Timothy of Brusa (St) M. B. Jun 10
d. 362. Bishop of Brusa, Asia Minor (now Bursa in Turkey), he was martyred in the reign of Julian.

Timothy Giaccardo (Bl) R. Jan 24
1896–1948. Born near Alba in Piedmont, Italy, he entered the seminary there but discerned his vocation to be in the apostolate of social communications and joined the 'Society of St Paul' (which had been newly founded at Alba for this work). He was ordained in 1919 and was their first priest, master of students and vicar-general. He founded the mother-house in Rome and built the Society up to become worldwide. He died of leukaemia at Rome and was beatified in 1989.

Timothy of Montecchio
(Bl) R(OFM). Aug 26
1414–1504. From Montecchio near Aquila, Italy, he became a Franciscan Observant and was known for his humility. He died at Fossa and had his cultus confirmed for Aquila in 1870.

Timothy of Rome (St) M. Aug 22
d. ?306. A Roman, he was martyred in the reign of Diocletian and had his shrine near St Paul's-outside-the-Walls. His cultus was confined to local calendars in 1969.

Timothy of Sandomir (Bl) *see* **Sadoc of Sandomir and Comps**

Titian of Brescia (St) B. Mar 3
d. ?536. Allegedly a German, he was bishop of Brescia, Italy.

Titian of Oderzo (St) B. Jan 16
d. 650. He was bishop for thirty years at Oderzo near Venice, Italy. His diocese is now extinct

Titus (St) B. Jan 26
C1st. He was a helper and disciple of St Paul, who addressed a letter to him concerning the organization of the church in Crete. Later he was sent to Dalmatia, Croatia, but the tradition is that he returned to Crete and (according to Eusebius) died as a bishop there. His alleged relics were at the cathedral of Gortyna before the island was conquered by the Muslims.

Titus Brandsma (Bl) M. R(OC). Jul 26
1881–1942. Born in Bolsward in Friesland, Netherlands, he joined the Carmelites when aged seventeen and taught in the Catholic University of Nijmegen, becoming rector there in 1923. When the Germans occupied the Netherlands in 1940 he adhered to the teaching of the Church in refusing to dismiss Jewish pupils or to propagate Nazi doctrine. He was arrested, taken to the concentration camp at Dachau and killed with an injection of phenol. He was beatified in 1985.

Bl Titus Brandsma, Jul 26

Titus of Rome (St) M. D. Aug 16
d. ?410 or 426. A Roman deacon, he was killed by a barbarian soldier during one of the two sacks of Rome in the C5th while distributing aid to the starving population.

Tobias (St) *see* **Carterius and Comps**

Tobias Borrás Romeau (Bl) *see* **Hospitaller Martyrs of Spain**

Tobias of Sandomir (Bl) *see* **Sadoc of Sandomir and Comps**

Tochumra (St) R. Jun 11
? She was venerated as a virgin in the former diocese of Kilmore in Co. Cavan, Ireland, and was a patron of women in childbirth.

Toiman *see* **Thomian**

Tola (St) B. R. Mar 30
d. ?733. He was an abbot-bishop of Disert Tola in Co. Meath, Ireland.

Tooley *see* **Olav**

Torannan *see* **Ternan**

Torello (Bl) R. Mar 16
1201–1282. From Poppi in Tuscany, Italy), he was led astray by evil companions in his youth but repented and became a hermit. He lived for sixty years walled up in his cell and was buried in the Vallumbrosan monastery of San Fedele. The Vallumbrosans and Franciscans have both claimed him as a tertiary, but these claims lack evidence. His cultus is unconfirmed.

Toros Oghlou David (Bl) *see* **Salvator Lilli and Comps**

Torpes (St) M. Apr 29
C1st? He was allegedly martyred at Pisa, Italy, in the reign of Nero, but his extant acta are worthless.

Torquatus, Ctesiphon and Comps (SS) MM. May 15
C1st? Their fairly recent tradition is as follows. They were disciples of the apostles, were sent to evangelize Spain and worked chiefly in the South: Torquatus at Guadix, near Granada; Ctesiphon at Verga (Vierzoa); Secundus at Avila; Indaletius at Urci, near Almeria; Caecilius at Granada; Hesychius at Gibraltar and Euphrasius at Andujar. Most of them were martyred. The Mozarabic liturgy had a common feast-day for all seven.

Totnan (St) *see* **Kilian, Colman and Totnan**

Tozzo (St) B. R(OSB). Jan 16
d. ?777. A monk of Murbach, Germany, he became bishop of Augsburg in ?772.

Tranquillinus of Rome (St) M. Jul 6
d. ?288. A Roman martyr, he features in the legend of St Sebastian.

Tranquillinus Ubiarco Robles (St) *see* **Mexico (Martyrs of)**

Trason, Pontian and Praetextatus (SS) MM. Dec 11
d. ?302. They were Romans executed in the reign of Diocletian for ministering to the Christian prisoners awaiting martyrdom.

Trea (St) R. Aug 3
C5th. Allegedly one of St Patrick's converts, she was a hermit at the place in Co. Derry, Ireland, named Ardtrea after her.

Tremorus (St) M. Nov 7
C6th. He was a small child murdered by his step-father, a local nobleman, at Carhaix in Brittany, France. He is patron of that place.

Tressan (Trésain) (St) R. Feb 7
d. 550. An Irish missionary, he was ordained priest by St Remigius of Rheims, France, and was based at Mareuil on the Marne.

Triduana (Tradwell, Trallen) (St) R. Oct 8
C8th? According to legend she came to Scotland with St Regulus of St Andrew's in the C4th, but was more likely to have been a later Irish hermit. Her tomb at Restalrig near Edinburgh was a notable Scottish pilgrimage shrine before its destruction in 1560.

Trier (Martyrs of) (SS) Oct 6
d. 287. According to the old Roman Martyrology, very many were martyred on the orders of the governor Rictiovarus at Trier, Germany, in the reign of Diocletian.

Trillo (Drillo, Drel) (St) R? Jun 15
C6th. Nothing is known about him. He is patron of the two villages in Wales called Llandrillo, one near Corwen and the other near Colwyn Bay.

Triphina (St) *see* **Agatho and Triphina**

Triphina of Carhaix (St) R. Jul 5
C6th. She was the mother of St **Tremorus** (q.v.), and allegedly became a nun.

Triphyllius (St) B. Jun 13
d. *c*370. A convert lawyer, he was a disciple of St Spiridion and became bishop of what is now Nicosia in Cyprus. As a loyal supporter of St Athanasius he was seriously harassed by the Arians, and was at the council of Sardica in 347.

Tripos (St) *see* **Basilides, Tripos and Comps**

Triverius (St) R. Jan 16
d. *c*550. From a Gallo-Roman family, he was apparently a hermit near the monastery of Thérouanne in the Pas de Calais, France, before he moved to the Pays de Dombes north of Lyons. Two villages named Saint Trivier commemorate him, and he is venerated locally at Lyons and in the diocese of Belley.

Troadius (St) M. Dec 28
d. 250. He was martyred at Neocaesarea in Pontus, Asia Minor, in the reign of Decius.

Trojan (Troyen) (St) B. Nov 30
d. 533. He allegedly had a Jewish father and a Muslim mother and was a disciple of St Vivian of Saintes, France, whom he succeeded as bishop.

Trond *see* **Trudo**

Trophimus and Eucarpius (SS) MM. Mar 18
d. ?304. Two pagan soldiers, they were employed in hunting out Christians but converted and were themselves burnt alive at Nicomedia, Asia Minor, in the reign of Diocletian.

Trophimus, Sabbatius and Dorymedon (SS) MM. Sep 19
d. ?277. They were martyred in the reign of Probus, probably at Antioch, Syria.

Trophimus and Thalus (SS) MM. Mar 11
d. *c*300. They were crucified at Laodicea (Latakia in Syria) in the reign of Diocletian.

Trophimus and Theophilus (SS) MM. Jul 23
d. ?302. They were beheaded at Rome in the reign of Diocletian.

Trophimus of Arles (St) B. Dec 29
d. *c*280. He was sent from Rome to be the first bishop of Arles, France, in *c*240–260. Since the C5th he has been falsely identified with St Trophimus the Ephesian, the disciple of St Paul.

Trophimus the Ephesian
(St) M. Dec 29
d. ?65. He accompanied St Paul to Jerusalem, and his presence there was the motivation for the riot which caused the latter's arrest (Acts 21:29). By one tradition he was beheaded at Rome in the reign of Nero. The allegation in the old Roman Martyrology that he was the first bishop of Arles is false.

Trudo (Truiden, Trond)
(St) R. Nov 23
d. ?695. He was a monk at Stavelot-Malmédy, Belgium, under St Remaclus, was ordained by St Clodulf of Metz and eventually became the abbot-founder of a monastery on his family's estate where the town of St Truiden, Belgium, now is.

Trudpert (St) R. Apr 26
d. ?644. He was a hermit in the Breisgau, Germany, on the site where the abbey of St Trudpert was later founded. According to the legend he was an Irishman who was murdered by workmen building his chapel.

Trumwin (St) B. R. Feb 10
d. ?704. A monk of Whiby, England, he was consecrated bishop for the southern Picts in 681 by St Theodore of Canterbury and made his base at a monastery at Abercorn near Linlithgow, Scotland. Lothian was then ruled by Northumbria, but the king was killed in battle by the Picts and Trumwin and his community had to flee. He died as a monk at Whitby.

Tryphaena (Triphenes) of Cyzicus (St) M. Jan 31
? A married woman of Cyzicus on the Sea of Marmara, Asia Minor, she was tortured and then thrown to a wild bull to be gored to death.

Tryphenna and Tryphosa
(SS) LL. Nov 10
C1st. They are mentioned by St Paul in his letter to the Romans (16:12). The unreliable legend of St Thecla describes them as converts of Iconium, Asia Minor.

Tryphon (St) *see* **Aquilinus, Geminus and Comps**

Tryphon of Alexandria and Comps (SS) MM. Jul 3
? A group of thirteen, they were martyred at Alexandria, Egypt.

Tryphon of Nicaea and Comps *Nov 10*
d. ?251. He allegedly kept geese at Campsada near Apamea, Syria, and was martyred at Nicaea, Asia Minor, in the reign of Decius. Respicius and Nympha have been linked with him only since the C11th, and are otherwise unknown. Their cultus was suppressed in 1969.

Tryphonia (St) M. Oct 18
C3rd. A Roman widow martyr, according to her worthless acta she was the wife either of the emperor Decius or of his son.

Tryphosa (St) *see* **Tryphenna and Tryphosa**

Tuda (St) B. R. Oct 21
d. 664. When St Colman of Lindisfarne, England, returned to Ireland rather than accept the Roman customs prescribed for the Anglo-Saxon Church by the Synod of Whitby, Tuda (an Irish monk) took his place as bishop but died within the year in an epidemic. There is no evidence of an early cultus.

Tude *see* **Antidius**

Tudinus *see* **Tudy**

Tudno (St) R. Jun 5
C6th. The patron of Llandudno in Gwynedd, Wales, according to his legend he was a monk at Bangor Isycoed.

Tudwal (Tugdual) (St) B. Dec 1
C6th. A British monk, he emigrated to Brittany, France, and became bishop of Tréguier. Three places in the Lleyn Peninsula, Wales, are named after him.

Tudy (Tegwin, Thetgo)
(St) R. May 11
C5th. A Breton, possibly a disciple of St Brieuc, he was a hermit near Landevennec in Brittany, France, and then abbot there. He apparently spent some time in Cornwall, England, where a village is named after him.

Tugdual *see* **Tudwal**

Turiaf (Turiav) (St) B. Jul 13
d. *c*750. From Brittany, France, he succeeded St Samson as bishop of Dol.

Turibius of Astorga (St) B. Apr 16
d. *c*460. Bishop of Astorga, Spain, at a time when that place was ruled by the barbarian Suevi, he was troubled by the Priscillianist heretics and obtained a condemnation of them from the pope.

Turibius de Mongrovejo
(St) B. Mar 23
1538–1606. From Mayorga de Campos in the province of León, Spain, he was professor of law at Salamanca and was made president of the Inquisition at Granada while still a layman. King Philip II made him archbishop of Lima in Peru in 1580, and he zealously set out to reform the corruptions and abuses prevalent in Church life in what was then one of the richest cities in the world. He especially tried to protect the native Americans against exploitation by Spanish immigrants. He was canonized in 1726.

Turibius of Palencia
(St) B? R. Apr 16
d. ?528. The abbot-founder of Liébana in Asturias (Spain) was probably a bishop, but has been confused with Turibus of Astorga.

Turibius Romo González (Bl) *see* **Mexico (Martyrs of)**

Turketil (St) R(OSB). Jul 11
887–975. A nephew of King Edred of England and the royal chancellor, he became a monk in 948 and then the abbot-restorer of Crowland in the Lincolnshire Fens (the monastery had been destroyed by the Vikings).

Turnin (St) R. Jul 17
C8th. An Irish missionary, he was with St Foillan in the Low Countries and worked round Antwerp, Belgium.

Tutilo (St) R(OSB). Mar 28
d. ?915. A monk of St Gall, Switzerland, he was famous as a polymath. Handsome, a giant in strength and stature, eloquent, quick-witted, a poet, orator, architect, painter, sculptor, metal worker, mechanic and musician who played and taught several instruments at the abbey school, he was nevertheless known for his obedience and life of prayer.

Tuto (Totto) of Ottobeuren
(Bl) R. Nov 19
d. 815. He became abbot-founder of Ottobeuren in Bavaria (still a functioning Benedictine abbey) in 764. His cultus there is unconfirmed.

Tuto (Totto) of Regensburg
(Bl) B. R(OSB). May 14
d. 930. He was a monk and abbot of St Emmeram at Regensburg, Germany, before becoming bishop of that city and imperial secretary. His cultus is unconfirmed.

Twelve Brothers *Sep 1*
Early C4th. The alleged relics of four groups of southern Italian martyrs were brought together and enshrined at Benevento in 760. A spurious legend subsequently grew up that they were the remains of the twelve sons of SS Boniface and Thecla and had been arrested in Africa and martyred in Italy. The four groups concerned are: (1) At Potenza in Basilicata on Aug 27, Arontius (Orontius), Honoratus, Fortunatus and Sabinian. (2) At Venosa in Apulia on Aug 28, Septiminus, Januarius and Felix. (3) At Velleianum in Apulia on Aug 29, Vitalis, Sator (Satyrus) and Repositus. (4) At Sentianum in Apulia on Sep 1, Donatus and another Felix. The cultus was suppressed in 1969.

Tybie (Tudy, Tudclyd)
(St) R. Jan 30
C5th? She was one of the alleged daughters of St Brychan (perhaps a relative or descendant), and Llandybie near Llandeilo in Dyfed, Wales, is named after her.

Tychicus (St) B. Apr 29
C1st. He was a disciple of St Paul (Acts 20:4; 21:29) and his fellow-worker (Col 4:7; Eph 6:21), and by tradition became bishop of Paphos in Cyprus.

Tychon (St) B. Jun 16
d. *c*450. Bishop of Amathus in Cyprus, he energetically fought against the surviving paganism in the island, especially the cult of Aphrodite based at Paphos.

Tydecho (St) R. Dec 17
C6th. Allegedly a Breton, he was on the island of Bardsey, Wales, with his cousin St Cadfan and then settled in Merioneth with his sister and two brothers. He is patron of several Welsh churches.

Tydfil (St) M. Aug 23
d. ?480. Allegedly of the clan of St Brychan, she was apparently killed by Pictish or Saxon invaders where the Welsh town of Merthyr Tydfil now stands, The story may be based on a false etymology of 'Merthyr', taken to mean 'martyr' when it probably means 'shrine'.

Tyrannio of Tyre and Comps (SS) MM. Feb 20
d. ?304. The old Roman Martyrology named these five among the martyrs of Tyre, Lebanon. However, Tyrannio and Zenobius were martyred at Antioch in 310, Silvanus at Emesa and Peleus and Nilus were (according to Eusebius) Egyptian bishops among those

enslaved and martyred in the quarries of the Holy Land.

Tyre (Martyrs of) (SS) Feb 20
d. 302–310. The old Roman Martyrology referred to a large number of martyrs at Tyre, Lebanon, in the reign of Diocletian, including Tyrannio and Comps in error (see above).

Tysilio (Tyssel, Tyssilo, Suliau) (St) R. Nov 8
C7th. A Welsh prince, he became abbot of Meifod in Powys and founded several churches in other parts of Wales. In Brittany the village of Saint-Suliac may commemorate him or another of the same name.

U

Ubald Adimari (Bl) R(OSM). Apr 9
1246–1315. A nobleman of Florence, Italy, he was a leader of the anti-papal Ghibelline party and was notoriously dissolute. In 1276 he was converted by St Philip Benizi, however, then became a Servite and spent the rest of his life as a penitential hermit on Mt Senario. His cultus was confirmed for the Servites in 1821.

Ubald Baldassini (St) B. May 16
?1080–1160. From Gubbio near Ancona, Italy, as dean of the cathedral there he re-organized the chapter around a rule of common life. He became bishop in 1128 and was famous for being both gentle and brave (which helped him in dealing with Emperor Frederick Barbarossa). He was canonized in 1192, but his cultus was confined to local calendars in 1969.

Ubric *see* **Ulric**

Uda *see* **Tudy**

Uganda (Martyrs of) *see* **Charles Lwanga and Comps**

Uguzo (Lucius) (St) M. L. Aug 16
? According to his story he was a poor shepherd of Cavargna, in the Alps of Italy near Lake Como, who gave away much of his earnings in charity. His master drove him away in envy, then killed him when he found another employer. His dates are unknown, but his cultus at Milan existed in 1280.

Ulched (Ulchad, Ylched) (St) Apr 6
? Nothing is known about the patron of Llechylched on Anglesey, Wales.

Ulfrid (Wolfred, Wilfrid) (St) M. Jan 18
d. 1028. One of the late Anglo-Saxon missionaries in Sweden, he was martyred after destroying an image of the pagan war-god Thor.

Ulmar *see* **Wulmar**

Ulphia (Wulfia, Olfe, Wulfe) (St) R. Jan 31
C8th. She was allegedly a hermit-disciple of St Domitius of Amiens at Saint-Acheuil and has her shrine in the cathedral at Amiens, France.

Ulpian *see* **Vulpian**

Ulric *see* **Wulfric**

Ulric (Udalric) of Augsburg (St) B. Jul 4
*c*890–973. From Augsburg, Bavaria, he was educated at the abbey of St Gall, Switzerland, and became bishop of his native city and its secular ruler in 923. He was the protector of his people against the invading Magyars and a friend and supporter of the emperor Otto I. When old he retired to St Gall and took one of his nephews as his coadjutor, but does not seem to have taken religious vows. He was canonized in 993, the first formal canonization at Rome.

Ulric of Einsiedeln (Bl) R(OSB). May 29
d. *p*978. A son of St Gerold, he became a monk at his father's abbey of Einsiedeln, Switzerland, and served as treasurer. After his father's death he became a hermit in his turn in the latter's cell. He has an unconfirmed cultus at Einsiedeln.

Ulric of Zell (St) R(OSB). Jul 14
1029–1093. From Regensburg, Germany, he became archdeacon of Freising and then went on a pilgrimage to Rome and Jerusalem. On his return he became a monk at Cluny, France, under St Hugh in 1061, and was in turn novice master (as such he wrote the Cluniac Customary) and superior of several dependent monasteries before he became prior-founder of Zell in the Black Forest, Bavaria. He suffered from migraines all his life.

Ulrica Nisch (Bl) R. May 8
1882–1913. She was born in Württemberg, Germany, and her family was very poor. In 1898 she became a domestic servant and went

to Rorschach in Switzerland, where she fell seriously ill in 1904. She had already been thinking about a religious vocation, and her being nursed by the 'Sisters of Charity of the Holy Cross' led her to join them at Baden in 1907. She was a model religious for six years despite her bad health, and treated her work in the kitchen as a holy exercise. She was beatified in 1987.

Ultan of Ardbraccan (St) B. Sep 4
d. 657. Bishop of Ardbraccan in Co. Meath, Ireland, he was remembered for his fondness for children and for collecting the alleged writings of St Brigid.

Ultan of Fosse (St) R May 2
C7th. From Ireland, he was a brother of SS Fursey and Foillan and was a monk with them at Burgh Castle in Norfolk, England. Then he emigrated to Belgium, was chaplain and choirmaster at the nunnery of St Gertrude of Nivelles and then succeeded his brother St Foillan as abbot of Fosses and Peronne. He died at the latter place, but his shrine was at Fosses. There are about twenty other Irish saints named Ultan listed, most of them extremely obscure.

Ultius *see* **Wulsin**

Unaman (St) *see* **Winaman, Unaman and Sunaman**

Unni (Uni, Huno, Wimo)
(St) B. R. Sep 17
d. 936. A monk at New Corvey near Paderborn, Germany, he became bishop of Hamburg-Bremen in 917 and was a successful missionary in Denmark and Sweden. He died at Björkä in Sweden.

Urban (St) *see* **Ampliatus, Urban and Narcissus**

Urban (St) *see* **Ariston and Comps**

Urban (St) *see* **Babylas and Comps**

Urban (St) *see* **Cyril, Rogatus and Comps**

Urban (St) *see* **Valerian, Urban and Comps**

Urban (St) *see* **Zaragoza (Eighteen Martyrs of)**

Urban, Theodore, Menedemus and Comps (SS) MM. Sep 5
d. 370. They were a group of eighty priests and clerics of Constantinople who, in the reign of the Arian emperor Valens, were left to die in a burning ship for having appealed to the emperor against the persecution of Catholics.

Urban I, Pope May 25
d. 230. A Roman, he succeeded St Callistus I as pope in 222. During his pontificate there was apparently no serious persecution of the Church at Rome. His cultus was suppressed in 1969.

Urban II, Pope (Bl) R(OSB). Jul 29
1042–1099. Odo of Lagery was a nobleman from Châtillon-sur-Marne, France, who studied at Rheims under St Bruno (the founder of the Carthusians) and became archdeacon there. In 1070 he became a monk at Cluny and was grand prior under St Hugh, then was made cardinal bishop of Ostia in 1080 and pope in 1088. A strong advocate of the Gregorian policy of ecclesiastical reform, he had St Bruno as an adviser and is remembered as the promoter of the first crusade at the council of Clermont in 1095. His cultus was confirmed for Rheims in 1881.

Urban V, Pope (Bl) R(OSB). Dec 19
1309–1370. William of Grimoard was from Languedoc, France, and was educated at the universities of Montpellier and Toulouse. He became a Benedictine at the priory of Chirac, was abbot of St Germanus at Auxerre from 1352 and of St Victor at Marseilles in 1361. Later that year he was sent as papal legate to Italy (the papacy then being at Avignon) and in the following year (although not a cardinal) was elected pope. He succeeded in transferring the papacy back to Rome, but was forced to return to Avignon in 1370 just before he died. His cultus was confirmed for Marseilles in 1870.

Urban of Langres (St) B. Apr 2
d. *c*390. He became bishop of Langres in Burgundy, France, in 374, and is a local patron of vine-dressers.

Urban Lefebvre (Bl) *see* **September (Martyrs of)**

Urban of Penalba (St) R(OSB). Apr 6
d. *c*940. He was abbot of the monastery of Penalba near Astorga, Spain, and helped St Gennadius of Astorga in his monastic revival.

Urban Salin de Niart (Bl) *see* **September (Martyrs of)**

Urban of Teano (St) B. Dec 7
d. ?356. He was a bishop of Teano in Campania, Italy.

Urbitius of Metz (St) B. Mar 20
d. *c*420. He was bishop of Metz, France.

Urbitius (Úrbez) of Nocito (St) R. Dec 15
d. ?805. He was allegedly born at Bordeaux, became a monk in France and was taken prisoner in a Spanish Muslim raid. Escaping, he became a hermit in the valley of Nocito in the Pyrenees near Huesca, Spain. His extant biography is unreliable, but his local cultus is still popular.

Urciscenus (St) B. Jun 21
d. ?216. He allegedly became the seventh bishop of Pavia, Italy, in 183, but his dates are probably much later.

Urith of Chittlehampton (St) R? Jul 8
? She was allegedly a hermit at Chittlehampton in Devon, England, and was venerated there.

Urpasian (St) M. Mar 13
d. 295. A servant in the imperial household of Diocletian at Nicomedia, Asia Minor, he was burnt alive.

Ursacius *see* **Arsacius**

Ursicinus of Brescia (St) B. Dec 1
d. *p*347. A bishop of Brescia in Lombardy, Italy, he was at the council of Sardica in 347.

Ursicinus of Cahors (St) B. Dec 20
d. ?585. He was a Frankish courtier and then bishop of Cahors, France, being mentioned by the historian St Gregory of Tours.

Ursicinus of Chur (St) B. R. Oct 2
d. 760. He was abbot of Disentis in Switzerland before becoming bishop of Chur in 754. In 758 he resigned and became a hermit.

Ursicinus of Luxeuil (St) R. Dec 20
d. ?625. An Irish monk at Luxeuil, France, he left that monastery with St Columban when the latter went into exile. Instead of going to Italy with him he settled as a hermit at the place later named St Ursanne, in the Jura canton of Switzerland.

Ursicinus of Ravenna (St) M. Jun 19
C2nd? According to his unreliable acta he was a physician at Ravenna, Italy, who wavered in his faith after being sentenced to death but repented and was martyred. He was probably martyred elsewhere and his relics transferred to Ravenna. Another saint of the same name was archbishop of the city in the C6th.

Ursicinus of Sens (St) B. Jul 24
d. *c*380.This bishop of Sens, France, was an opponent of Arianism and a friend of St Hilary of Poitiers.

Ursicius (St) M. Aug 14
d. 304. An Illyrian tribune in the imperial army, he was beheaded at Nicomedia, Asia Minor, in the reign of Diocletian.

Ursinus (St) B. Nov 9
C3rd. Though alleged to have been one of several disciples of Christ sent by the apostles to be bishops in Gaul, it is clear that he lived in the C3rd and was the first bishop of Bourges, France.

Ursmar (St) B. R. Apr 18
d. 713. He was abbot and missionary bishop of the Benedictine abbey of Lobbes on the river Sambre, Belgium, and founder of the abbeys of Aulne and Wallers. His missionary work in Flanders was of great importance.

Ursula and Comps *Oct 21*
C4th. The fantastic legend, as fully developed, alleges that she was a British virgin who was about to be married when a storm drove her and 11,000 virgin companions on board ship to the Low Countries. They visited Rome before returning to Cologne and being martyred by the Huns. The basis of this story is an inscription of *c*400 recording the restoration of a church by Clematius in honour of some local early virgin-martyrs whose number and names are not given. By the C9th they were claimed to have been a large number martyred in the reign of Maximian, and the discovery of an old cemetery at Cologne in 1155 provided a vast number of bones as spurious relics. The cultus was very popular in northern France, the Rhineland and the Low Countries in the Middle Ages but subsequently proved an embarrassment to the Church and was suppressed in 1969. The medieval artistic legacy concerning her is rich; she is depicted as being shot with arrows while her companions are killed in various grotesque ways.

Ursula-of-St-Bernardine Bourla (Bl) *see* **Valenciennes (Martyrs of)**

Ursula Ledochówska (Bl) R. F. May 29
1865–1939. She was born in Loosdorf, Austria, of a famous noble family of the Hapsburg

Empire. In 1886 she joined the Ursulines in Cracow, Poland, became the superior and founded the first university college of theology for girls in the Polish lands. She moved to St Petersburg, Russia, and did the same there in 1906, and then worked among the Lutherans of Finland and Scandinavia. In 1923 she founded the 'Ursuline Sisters of the Heart of Jesus in Agony' and worked in the Polish borderlands. She had great charity in ecumenical matters, and was beatified in 1983.

Ursulina (Bl) L. Apr 7
1375–1410. She was a young woman of Parma, Italy, who, alleging supernatural visions, visited the rival popes Clement VII at Avignon and Boniface IX at Rome in order to try and resolve the papal schism. After a pilgrimage to the Holy Land she was ejected from Parma and had to go to Bologna, where she died. She has, however, an unconfirmed cultus as a virgin at Parma.

Ursus (St) *see* **Victor and Ursus**

Ursus of Aosta (St) P. Feb 1
C6th. According to his unreliable biography he was an Irish missionary who preached against the Arians in the South of France and became archdeacon of Aosta in the Alps, Italy.

Ursus of Auxerre (St) B. R. Jul 30
d. 508. He was a hermit at the church of St Amator of Auxerre, France, and was made bishop of that city when aged seventy-five.

Ursus of Ravenna (St) B. Apr 13
d. 396. A pagan Sicilian nobleman, he became a convert and fled from his father's anger to Ravenna, Italy, where he became bishop in 378.

Ust (Just) (St) Aug 12
? Possibly the patron of the village of St Just near Land's End in Cornwall, England, he is described variously as a hermit, a martyr, and a bishop. Possibly several persons of the same name have been amalgamated.

Usthazanes (St) *see* **Simeon Barsabae and Comps**

Utto (Bl) R. Oct 3
*c*750–820. From Milan, he was abbot-founder of the Benedictine monastery of Metten in Bavaria, Germany. His cultus was confirmed for Regensburg in 1909.

Uval *see* **Eval**

V

Vaast *see* **Vedast**

Vacz (Bl) R. Nov 26
C11th. A hermit at Visegrád near Pilis, Hungary, he was regarded by the Hungarian Pauline order as being the forerunner of their founder, Bl Eusebius of Esztergom. His cultus is unconfirmed.

Valenciennes (Martyrs of)
(BB) MM. RR. Oct 17
d. 1794. The Ursuline convent and school at Valenciennes in northern France were shut by the French Revolution in 1792, and the community moved to Mons in the Austrian Netherlands. The Austrians captured Valenciennes in 1793 and the sisters returned and reopened their school. When the revolutionary forces returned, Bl Clotilde Joseph of St Francis Borgia Poillot (the superior) and seven of her community were condemned as returned emigrées and guillotined in two groups, including Bl Cordelia Joseph of St Dominic Barré, a lay sister who was overlooked when the tumbril was departing for the guillotine and who jumped on board herself. Two former Bridgettines and one former Poor Clare, who had joined the Ursulines when their own houses were suppressed, were also executed. *See* **French Revolution (Martyrs of)**.

Valens of Auxerre and
Comps (SS) MM. May 21
? He is listed as a bishop martyred at Auxerre, France, with three boys.

Valens of Caesarea and
Comps (SS) MM. Jun 1
d. 309. Companions of St Pamphilus, they were martyred at Caesarea in the Holy Land in the reign of Diocletian. Valens was an old deacon of Jerusalem, and a Paul is also mentioned.

Valens of Verona (St) B. Jul 26
d. 531. He was bishop of Verona, Italy, from 524.

Valentina and Comps (SS) VV. Jul 25
d. 308. They are listed as virgin-martyrs of the Holy Land in the reign of Galerius, but seem to be identical with SS Meuris and Thea.

Valentine (St) B. Oct 29
? He is listed as a bishop in the old Roman Martyrology but nothing is known about him and he may be a duplicate of Valentine of Passau.

Valentine (St) *see* **Fructus, Valentine and Engratia**

Valentine, Concordius, Navalis
and Agricola (SS) MM. Dec 16
d. ?305. They were allegedly martyred at Ravenna, Italy, in the reign of Diocletian. St Peter Chrysologus (d. *c*450) wrote, however, that St Apollinaris was the only martyr of Ravenna, which implies that they were martyred elsewhere and had their relics transferred to Ravenna.

Valentine, Felician and
Victorinus (SS) MM. Nov 11
d. ?305. They are most probably duplicates of SS Valentine, Concordius and Comps.

Valentine and Hilary (SS) MM. Nov 3
d. ?304. A priest and his deacon, they were beheaded at Viterbo near Rome in the reign of Diocletian.

Valentine, Solutor and
Victor (SS) MM. Nov 13
d. ?305. They are most probably duplicates of SS Valentine, Concordius and Comps.

Valentine Berrio-Ochoa
(St) M. B. R(OP). Nov 1
1827–1861. From Ellorio near Vitoria, Spain, he became a Dominican and was a missionary in the Philippines before going to Vietnam as vicar-apostolic of Central Tonkin (the area around Hanoi). He was beheaded with St Jerome Hermosilla. *See* **Vietnam (Martyrs of)**.

Valentine of Genoa (St) B. May 2
d. ?307. He was bishop of Genoa, Italy, from *c*295.

Valentine of Passau (St) B. Jan 17
d. *c*470. He was a missionary bishop in the region around Passau, Austria, of which place he is the principal patron.

Valentine of Rome (St) M. Feb 14
d. ?269. According to his unreliable acta he was a priest and physician at Rome. He was possibly martyred in the reign of Claudius II and buried on the Flaminian Way, and a church was built over his tomb in 350. The custom of sending 'Valentines' on his feast-day is based on the medieval belief that perching birds begin courtship then. His cultus was confined to local calendars in 1969.

Valentine of Sandomir (Bl) *see* **Sadoc of Sandomir and Comps**

Valentine of Strasbourg (St) B. Sep 2
C4th. He was an early bishop of Strasbourg, France.

Valentine of Terni (St) M. B. Feb 14
d. ?269. According to his unreliable acta he was a bishop of Terni near Rome who was martyred in the reign of Claudius II. It seems very probable that he is identical with Valentine of Rome.

Valentine of Trier (St) M. B. Jul 16
d. ?305. He was a bishop martyred in the reign of Diocletian, listed as of Trier, Germany, but more probably of Tongeren, Belgium.

Valentinian (St) B. Nov 3
d. *c*500. He was bishop of Salerno, Italy.

Valentio (St) *see* **Pasicrates, Valentio and Comps**

Valeria (St) *see* **Zenais, Dyria and Comps**

Valeria of Limoges (St) V. Dec 9
d. ?250. She was allegedly converted by St Martial of Limoges, France, and beheaded there, but she only features in his worthless acta and probably never existed.

Valeria (Martyrs of) (SS) RR. Mar 14
C5th. St Gregory the Great described them in his *Dialogues* as two monks who were hanged by the invading Lombards in the Italian province of Valeria and who were heard singing psalms after they had died.

Valeria of Milan *Apr 28*
C1st? She was the alleged wife of St Vitalis of Milan and mother of SS Gervase and Protase, but she never existed and her story is fictitious. Her cultus has been suppressed.

Valerian (St) *see* **Hieronides, Leontius and Comps**

Valerian (St) *see* **Restitutus, Donatus and Comps**

Valerian (St) *see* **Tiburtius, Valerian and Maximus**

Valerian, Macrinus and Gordian (SS) MM. Sept 17
? They are listed as having been martyred at 'Noviodunum', which has been variously located near the Danube delta, at Nyon in Berne canton, Switzerland, and at Nevers and at Noyon, France.

Valerian, Urban and Comps (SS) BB. Nov 28
C5th. Roman African bishops, they were sent into exile by the Arian Vandal King Genseric and died there. The others were Crescens, Eustace, Cresconius, Crescentian, Felix, Hortulanus and Florentian.

Valerian of Abbenza (St) M. B. Dec 15
d. 457. Bishop of Abbenza in Roman Africa, when aged over eighty he refused to hand over his church's sacred vessels to the Arians patronized by Genseric, king of the Vandals. As a result he was driven into the desert and left to die of exposure.

Valerian of Aquileia (St) B. Nov 27
d. 389. He succeeded an Arian as bishop of Aquileia near Venice, Italy, and had to re-establish orthodoxy in his diocese.

Valerian of Auxerre (St) B. May 13
d. *c*350. Bishop of Auxerre, France, he opposed Arianism and was at the council of Sardica.

Valerian of Cimiez (St) B. Jul 23
d. *c*460. A monk of Lérins, he became bishop of Cimeiz near Nice, France. A collection of his homilies is extant.

Valerian of Lyons (St) M. Sep 15
d. 178. He was with SS Photinus and Comps in prison at Lyons, France, but escaped to the mountains and was a missionary there. He was recaptured at Tournus near Autun and beheaded.

Valerius (St) *see* **Lambert and Valerius**

Valerius (St) *see* **Rufinus, Mark and Comps**

Valerius and Rufinus
(SS) MM. Jun 14
d. ?287. Roman missionaries, they were martyred at Soissons, France.

Valerius of Antibes (St) B. Feb 19
d. *p*450. He was bishop of Antibes on the Riviera, France.

Valerius of Astorga (St) R. Feb 21
d. 695. From Astorga, Spain, he became a monk and abbot of San Pedro de Montes. Several spiritual writings of his are extant, and he is regarded as the last author of the Isidorian revival in Spain.

Valerius of Conserans (St) B. Feb 20
? He was mentioned by St Gregory of Tours as the first bishop of Conserans in the Pyrenees, France.

Valerius-Bernard Herrero Martínez (Bl) *see* **Aurelius-Mary Villalón Acebrón and Comps**

Valerius de Ora (Bl) *see* **Peter Rodriguez and Comps**

Valerius of Sorrento (St) B. R. Jan 16
d. ?453. He was a hermit before becoming bishop of Sorrento, Italy, and quickly went back to being a hermit again.

Valerius of Trier (St) B. Jan 29
d. *c*320. According to legend he was the second bishop of Trier, Germany, and a disciple of St Peter, but more probably he was bishop there at the beginning of the C4th.

Valerius of Zaragoza (St) B. Jan 28
d. 315. He was the bishop of Zaragoza, Spain, when St Vincent was a deacon there. Arrested and exiled in the reign of Diocletian, he survived the persecution and died in peace in his city.

Valéry *see* **Waleric**

Vandrille *see* **Wandrille**

Vanne *see* **Vitonus**

Varelde *see* **Pharaildis**

Varicus (St) *see* **Secundus, Fidentian and Varicus**

Varus (St) M. Oct 19
d. 307. A Roman soldier in Upper Egypt, he was on guard at a prison containing some monks condemned to death. When he discovered that one of them had died he insisted on taking his place and was immediately hanged from a tree. The acta are genuine.

Vasius (Vaise, Vaize) (St) M. Apr 16
d. *c*500. A rich citizen of Saintes, France, he was murdered by his relatives for giving his property to the poor.

Vedast (Vaast, Vaat, Gaston, Foster) (St) B. Feb 6
d. 539. A fellow-worker with St Remigius of Rheims, France, in the conversion of the Franks, he was bishop of the combined dioceses of Arras-Cambrai for almost forty years. He renewed the Church therein and instructed King Clovis the Frank for his baptism by St Remigius. Several churches in England are dedicated to him, notably the one in the City of London. He is depicted with a wolf and a goose, the latter of which he raises to life.

Veep (Veepy, Wimp, Wennap) (St) R? Jul 1
C6th? Nothing is known about the patron of St Veep and Gwennap in Cornwall, England, although she has been claimed as one of the clan of St Brychan.

Veho *see* **Vouga**

Velleicus (Willeic) (St) R. Aug 29
C8th. An Anglo-Saxon monk, he followed St Swithbert the Elder to Germany and became abbot of Kaiserswerth near Düsseldorf.

Venantius (St) M. B. Apr 1
d. ?255. He was a bishop in Dalmatia, Croatia, but his era and diocese are uncertain. His body was taken from Split to the Lateran basilica in Rome in 641.

Venantius of Arles (St) R. May 30
d. *c*400. He was the elder brother of St Honoratus, the founder of the monastery of Lérins, France. They lived together as hermits on an island near Cannes before travelling the East to learn more about the monastic life. Venantius died at Modon in the Pelopponese, Greece.

Venantius of Camerino
(St) M. May 18
d. ?250. According to his spurious acta, written in the C13th, he was a teenager aged fifteen

who was martyred at Camerino near Ancona, Italy, in the reign of Decius. He is not listed in the ancient martyrologies, and his cultus was confined to local calendars in 1969.

Venantius Fortunatus (St) B. Dec 14
*c*530–610. From near Treviso, Italy, he migrated to Poitiers, France, when aged thirty, was ordained and became a friend of the Frankish Queen St Radegund. He became bishop of Poitiers in ?594. His fame is owing to his large number of extant hymns and poems, notably the *Vexilla Regis* and *Pange Lingua Gloriosi*, which had a major influence on later Christian hymnography and poetry.

Venantius of Tours (St) R. Oct 13
C5th. He was abbot of the monastery of St Martin at Tours, France.

Venantius of Viviers (St) B. Aug 5
d. 544. He became bishop of Viviers, France, in 517 and his cultus was popular, but his C12th biography is worthless.

Veneranda (St) V. Nov 14
C2nd. She is listed in the old Roman Martyrology as a virgin-martyr of Gaul, but apparently Veneranda is a corruption of Venera from 'dies veneris' (Friday), itself the Latin equivalent of 'Parasceves' in Greek. She is thus probably the same as the St Parasceve of Iconium found in the Byzantine martyrology on July 26.

Venerandus of Clermont
(St) B. Dec 24
d. 423. A nobleman of Clermont-Ferrand in Auvergne, France, he became bishop there in 385.

Venerandus of Troyes (St) M. Nov 14
d. 275. An influential citizen of Troyes, France, he was martyred in the reign of Aurelian.

Venerius of Milan (St) B. May 4
d. 409. Ordained deacon by St Ambrose, he eventually became bishop of Milan, Italy. He was a loyal supporter of St John Chrysostom.

Venerius of Tino (St) R. Sep 13
C7th or C9th. He was a hermit and then abbot-founder of a monastery on the island of Tino in the Gulf of Genoa, Italy. His extant biography is unreliable.

Ventura Spellucci (Bl) R. May 31
C12th. From Spello near Assisi, Italy, he joined the Cruciferi (an Italian order using the Benedictine rule, now extinct) and eventually built an abbey and hospice on his family estate. He was abbot until his death. His cultus is unconfirmed.

Venturinus of Bergamo
(Bl) R(OP). Mar 28
1304–1346. From Bergamo, Italy, he was a famous Dominican preacher in Lombardy. He preached a crusade against the Turks in Asia Minor in 1343 and died at Smyrna after accompanying the expedition. His cultus is unconfirmed.

Venustian (St) *see* **Sabinus, Exuperantius and Comps**

Venustus (St) *see* **Faustinus, Timothy and Venustus**

Venustus (St) *see* **Heliodorus, Venustus and Comps**

Veranus of Cavaillon (St) B. Oct 19
d. 590. From near Avignon, France, he became bishop of the local town of Cavaillon.

Veranus of Lyons (St) B. Nov 11
C5th? The old Roman Martyrology lists him as a bishop of Lyons, France, but he is probably a duplicate of St Veranus of Vence.

Veranus of Vence (St) B. R. Sep 10
d. *c*480. Son of St Eucherius of Lyons, France, he was a monk at Lérins and then bishop of Vence near Nice.

Verda (St) *see* **Daniel and Verda**

Verecundus of Verona (St) B. Oct 22
d. 522. He was a bishop of Verona, Italy.

Veremund Arborio (Bl) B. Aug 9
d. ?1011. Born at Vercelli, Italy, he became bishop of Ivrea in Piedmont in 969. His cultus was confirmed for there in 1857.

Veremund of Hierache
(St) R(OSB). Mar 8
d. 1092. A native of Navarre (now in Spain, then independent), he entered the Benedictine abbey of Hirache and became its abbot. Under him the monastery was the most influential religious centre of Navarre, and he was a royal adviser. He was famous for his charity towards the poor and for his zeal for the accurate recitation of the divine office, and he helped forestall the papal intention to suppress the local Mozarabic rite as part of the Gregorian reform.

Verena (St) R. Sep 1
C3rd? According to her legend she was an Egyptian maiden, related to a soldier of the Theban Legion, who travelled to Switzerland in search of him and settled as a hermit near Zurich. Her cultus is very ancient.

Vergil *see* **Virgil**

Verian (St) *see* **Secundian, Marcellian, and Verian**

Veridiana (St) T(OSB Vall). Feb 1
d. 1242. A maiden of Castelfiorentino in Tuscany, Italy, she went on pilgrimage to Compostela and was then walled up as a hermit in her native town, where she lived for thirty-four years as an affiliate of a Vallumbrosan abbey. Her cultus was approved in 1533.

Verissimus, Maxima and Julia (SS) MM. Oct 1
d. ?302. They were martyred at Lisbon, Portugal, in the reign of Diocletian.

Veronica (St) L. Jul 12
The legend is that she was a woman (identified with several in the Gospels) who took pity on Christ on his way to crucifixion and wiped his face with a cloth, on which an image of his face was left imprinted. This story seems to have been supplied in the C14th as a background to a relic called the 'veil of Veronica' which has been enshrined at St Peter's at Rome since the C8th, and she is not listed in any of the ancient martyrologies or in the old Roman Martyrology. There is now no trace of any image on the relic. She features in the 'Stations of the Cross', a devotion propagated by the Franciscans at Jerusalem only since the C18th.

Veronica of Binasco (Bl) R(OSA). Jan 13
d. 1497. From Binasco near Milan, Italy, she was the daughter of poor peasants and a worker on their farm before becoming an Augustinian lay sister at Milan. She spent her life collecting alms for her community in the streets of the city. Her cultus was confirmed in 1517.

Veronica Giuliani (St) R(OFM Cap). Jul 9
1660–1727. From Mercatello near Urbino, Italy, she spent her life as a Capuchin nun at Città di Castello in Urbino, being novice-mistress for thirty-four years. Her amazing mystical experiences, including continual visions, revelations and the stigmata, were described by eyewitnesses and described in her extant diary but did not prevent her having a practical and level-headed personality. She was canonized in 1839.

Verulus, Secundinus and Comps (SS) MM. Feb 21
d. ?434. According to the old Roman Martyrology they were twenty-six martyred at Hadrumetum in Roman Africa by the Vandals. They probably died in an earlier persecution. Also named are Siricius, Felix, Servulus, Saturninus and Fortunatus.

Verus of Arles (St) B. Aug 1
d. *p*314. A bishop of Vienne, France, he was at the synod of Arles in 314.

Verus of Salerno (St) B. Oct 23
C4th. He was the third bishop of Salerno, Italy.

Vestina (St) *see* **Scillitan Martyrs**

Vetius (St) *see* **Photinus, Sanctius and Comps**

Veturius (St) *see* **Scillitan Martyrs**

Vial *see* **Vitalis**

Viator and Amor (SS) MM. Aug 9
C3rd? They were allegedly officers of the Theban legion martyred at what is now St Amour in Franche Comté, France, but nothing is actually known about them.

Viator of Bergamo (St) B. Dec 14
d. ?378. The local tradition alleges that he was one of the first bishops of Brescia, Italy, and transferred to Bergamo during the C1st, but it seems that he was bishop of Bergamo only from 344.

Viator of Lyons (St) R. Oct 21
d. ?390. He was a disciple of St Justus, archbishop of Lyons, France, and went with him to Egypt to be a hermit.

Vibiana (St) V. Sep 1
? Her remains were brought from the Roman catacombs to the cathedral of Los Angeles, USA, by the bishop in 1858. She is the city's principal patron. The assertion that she was a virgin-martyr is unsupported by any evidence, as is the case with all the alleged relics of 'martyrs' removed from the catacombs in the C19th, and the name was given to her arbitrarily.

Vicelin (St) B. Dec 12
1090–1154. From Hameln, Germany, he became a cathedral-canon at Bremen and a

St Veronica, Jul 12

disciple of St Norbert. From 1126 he worked among the Wagrian Slavs of what is now Holstein, but his efforts were frustrated by the great rebellion of the Slavs against German colonization in 1147. In 1149 he was made bishop of Oldenburg (now Stargard, Poland). He died at Neumünster, an Augustinian monastery that he had founded.

Victor (St) *see* **Adrio, Victor and Basilla**

Victor (St) *see* **Ambicus, Victor and Julius**

Victor (St) *see* **Castor, Victor and Rogatian**

Victor (St) *see* **Crescentian, Victor and Comps**

Victor (St) *see* **Dominic, Victor and Comps**

Victor (St) *see* **Domninus, Victor and Comps**

Victor (St) *see* **Irenaeus, Anthony and Comps**

Victor (St) *see* **Nemesian and Comps**

Victor (St) *see* **Photina and Comps**

Victor (St) *see* **Publius, Victor and Comps**

Victor (St) *see* **Saturninus, Thyrsus and Victor**

Victor (St) *see* **Sosthenes and Victor**

Victor (SS) *see* **Theban Legion**

Victor (St) *see* **Valentine, Solutor and Victor**

Victor (St) *see* **Victorinus, Victor and Comps**

Victor (St) *see* **Victurus, Victor and Comps**

Victor (St) *see* **Vincent, Orontius and Victor**

Victor, Alexander and Marianus (SS) MM. Oct 17
d. 303. They were martyred at Nicomedia, Asia Minor, in the reign of Diocletian.

Victor and Corona (SS) MM. May 14
d. ?176. Apparently they were a married couple martyred in Syria, but their acta are unreliable.

Victor and Stephen (SS) MM. Apr 1
? They were martyred in Egypt.

Victor, Stercatius and Antinogenes (SS) MM. Jul 24
d. 304. They were allegedly three brothers martyred at Mérida in Extremadura, Spain, but probably only Victor belonged there. The other two were probably among a group listed in the Hieronomian martyrology as having been martyred at Sebaste in Armenia.

Victor, Victorinus and Comps (SS) MM. Mar 6
? They are listed as Bithynians who died in prison at Nicomedia, Asia Minor. The others were Claudian and Bassa (a married couple).

Victor and Ursus (SS) MM. Sep 30
d. ?286. They were alleged soldiers of the Theban Legion captured and executed at Solothurn in Switzerland.

Victor, Zoticus and Comps (SS) MM. Apr 20
d. ?303. They were martyred at Nicomedia, Asia Minor, and feature in the unreliable acta of St George. The others were Zeno, Acindynus, Caesareus, Severian, Chrysophorus, Theonas and Antoninus.

Victor I, Pope *Jul 28*
d. 198. From Roman Africa, he became pope in 188 and excommunicated several Eastern churches for not keeping the date of Easter according to the Roman practice (for which act he was rebuked by St Irenaeus). His cultus was suppressed in 1969.

Victor III, Pope (St) R(OSB). Sep 16
?1027–1087. From Benevento, Italy, and related to the Norman rulers there, Desiderius Danfari became a monk in the face of his family's opposition and was at various monasteries before becoming abbot of Montecassino in 1057. The abbey flourished under his rule and he became one of the great churchmen of Italy. On the death of Pope St Gregory VII he was elected pope by the cardinals meeting at Montecassino in 1086. Initially he refused, was not consecrated for a year and died after another four months without having been able to stay at Rome (the city was occupied by an anti-pope). His cultus as a saint was confirmed in 1887.

Victor the African (St) M. Mar 10
? A Roman African, he was possibly martyred in the reign of Decius. He is mentioned in St Augustine's commentary on Psalm 116.

Victor of Braga (St) M. Apr 12
d. *c*300. A catechumen, he was martyred at

Braga, Portugal, in the reign of Diocletian and is an example of 'red baptism' (being baptized with one's own blood).

Victor of Capua (St) M. B. Apr 2
d. 554. Bishop of Capua, Italy, he was an ecclesiastical writer.

Victor (Vitores) of Cereso (St) M. Aug 26
? According to the acta written in the C15th, he was a priest at Cereso near Burgos, Spain, and was martyred in *c*950 for converting Muslims. Older documents refer to him as a Roman African martyred at Caesarea in Mauretania in one of the early persecutions.

Victor of Marseilles and Comps (SS) MM. Jul 21
d. *c*290. A Roman army officer stationed at Marseilles, France, he was martyred there with three prison-guards, Alexander, Felician and Longinus, whom he had converted. In the C4th St John Cassian built a monastery over their tomb. His attribute is a windmill.

Victor the Moor (St) M. May 8
d. 303. A soldier from Mauritania (now Morocco) in Roman Africa, he was martyred at Milan, Italy, in the reign of Maximian. He was associated by St Ambrose with SS Nabor and Felix.

Victor of Piacenza (St) B. Dec 7
d. 375. He was the first bishop of Piacenza, Italy, and a notable opponent of Arianism.

Victor of Plancy (St) R. Feb 26
C6th. From Troyes, France, he became a hermit at Arcis-sur-Aube in Champagne. St Bernard of Clairvaux wrote a hymn in his honour, but his extant acta are worthless.

Victor of Vita (St) B. Aug 23
d. ?535. From Carthage, Roman Africa, he was bishop either there or (as stated in the old Roman Martyrology) at Utica. Baronius identified him (without proof) with the Victor of Vita who wrote an account of the persecution by King Huneric.

Victor of Xanten and Comps (SS) MM. Oct 10
d. ?286. They were allegedly three hundred and thirty soldiers of the Theban Legion martyred at Xanten on the Rhine, Germany.

Victoria (St) *see* **Acislus and Victoria**

Victoria (St) *see* **Saturninus, Dativus and Comps**

Victoria and Anatolia (SS) VV. Dec 23
d. ?250. According to their worthless acta they were two sisters martyred at Rome for refusing to marry pagans. Anatolia was not listed in the old Roman Martyrology.

Victoria Bauduceau (Bl) *see* **William Repin and Comps**

Victoria Diez y Bustos de Molina (Bl) M. L. Aug 20
1903–1936. Born in Seville, Spain, she became a state teacher and was deeply influenced by the Teresian Association of Bl. Peter Poveda Castroverde, desiring to join holiness and apostolicity in her career. She worked at Hornachudos, where she was a great help to the parish priest and was very charitable to her needier pupils. She was thrown down a mineshaft at Rincón during the Civil War along with seventeen other Catholics, and was beatified in 1993. *See* **Spanish Civil War (Martyrs of)**.

Victoria Gusteau (Bl) *see* **William Repin and Comps**

Victoria Rasoamanarivo (Bl) L. Aug 24
1848–1894. Born in Antananarivo, the capital of the native kingdom of Madagascar, she was a noblewoman of the highest rank. Her family was pagan but they sent her to be taught by the 'Sisters of St Joseph of Cluny' and she was baptized in 1863. Then she was married off to a drunken and vicious cousin, but she insisted on the marriage being solemnized and later refused divorce as being against Church teaching. (Rather she prayed for his conversion, which took place after a drunken fall in 1887 which proved fatal.) In 1883 the government tried to suppress the Church and expelled the missionaries. Bl Victoria's position enabled her to obtain many concessions and to support the laity, so that the missionaries found healthy churches on their return three years after. Then she retired into obscurity. She was beatified in 1989.

Victorian (St) *see* **Aquilinus and Victorian**

Victorian (St) *see* **Simplicius, Constantius and Victorian**

Victorian, Frumentius and Comps (SS) MM. Mar 23
d. 484. Victorian, a former pro-consul in Roman Africa, and four wealthy merchants were martyred at Adrumetum in the reign of the Vandal King Hunneric for refusing to become Arians.

Victorian of Asan (St) R. Jan 12
d. *c*560. An Italian, he went to France and then to Aragón, Spain, where he became the abbot-founder of Asan (later named San Victorian after him) in the Pyrenees near Barbastro. He was praised by St Venantius Fortunatus.

Victoricus (St) *see* **Montanus, Lucius and Comps**

Victoricus, Fuscian and Gentian (SS) MM. Dec 11
d. ?287. The first two were allegedly Roman missionaries who were martyred near Amiens, France, while the last was an old man killed while trying to protect them when they were arrested.

Victorinus (St) *see* **Cassius, Victorinus and Comps**

Victorinus (St) *see* **Four Crowned Martyrs**

Victorinus (St) *see* **Maro, Eutyches and Victorinus**

Victorinus (St) *see* **Pastor, Victorinus and Comps**

Victorinus (St) *see* **Placid, Eutychius and Comps**

Victorinus (St) *see* **Severus, Securus and Comps**

Victorinus (St) *see* **Valentine, Felician and Victorinus**

Victorinus (St) *see* **Victor, Victorinus and Comps**

Victorinus (St) *see* **Victurus, Victor and Comps**

Victorinus, Victor and Comps (SS) MM. Feb 25
d. ?284. According to the old Roman Martyrology they were citizens of Corinth, Greece, who were exiled to Egypt in 249 in the reign of Numerian and martyred with great brutality at Diospolis in the Thebaid. The others were Nicephorus, Claudian, Dioscorus, Serapion and Papias. Their acta are untrustworthy, and the historical details confused.

Victorianus-Pius Bernabé Cano (St) *see* **Cyril-Bertrand Sanz Tejedor and Comps**

Victorinus of Camerino (St) B? R. Jun 8
d. 543. Brother of St Severinus of Septempeda, he was a hermit with him at Montenero near Livorno, Italy, and apparently became bishop of Camerino, where he died.

Victorinus of Como (St) B. Sep 5
d. 644. He was bishop of Como, Italy, and a great opponent of the Arianism imported into Italy by the Goths.

Victorinus of Pettau (St) M. B. Nov 2
d. ?304. Bishop of Pettau (now Ptuj in Slovenia), he is the earliest known biblical exegete of the Western church, his commentary on the Apocalypse being extant. He was martyred in the reign of Diocletian.

Victorius (St) *see* **Claudius, Lupercus and Victorius**

Victorius (St) *see* **Polyeuctus, Victorius and Donatus**

Victorius of Le Mans (St) B. Sep 1
d. *c*490. A disciple of St Martin of Tours, he became bishop of Le Mans, France, in ?453.

Victricius (St) B. Aug 7
d. 407. A Roman army officer, he resigned because he thought military service incompatible with Christianity. He was sentenced to death, but the sentence was commuted and he became a missionary among the northern tribes of Gaul, being made bishop of Rouen, France, while still a layman in 380.

Victurus, Victor, Victorinus, Adjutor, Quartus and Comps (SS) Dec 18
? Thirty-five Roman Africans, they were martyred in what is now Morocco.

Vietnam (Martyrs of) (SS) MM. Nov 24
1798–1862. The first missionaries arrived in Vietnam in the 1530s, but great success followed only after the foundation of the Jesuit mission at Hanoi in 1615. Christianity was not compatible with State Confucianism, and the first persecution was in 1698. The country was in chaos between 1772 and 1802, but persecution intensified on its reunification and foreign missionaries were killed, especially in the reigns of Kings Minh Mang (1820–41) and Tu Duc (1847–83). The country was then conquered by France. 117 of the martyrs (the total of whom is allegedly in six figures) were canonized in 1988, this being the largest mass canonization in the Church's history. Another was beatified in 2000. (N.B. The names 'Tonkin',

'Annam' and 'Cochin China' were colonial names for the three main parts of the country, north to south, and were not used by the Vietnamese themselves.) *See* lists of national martyrs in appendix.

Vigean *see* **Fechin**

Vigilius of Auxerre (St) M. B. Mar 11
d. 685. He succeeded St Palladius as bishop of Auxerre, France, in 661, but was assassinated in a forest near Compiègne by order of the mayor of the palace of the Merovingian king.

Vigilius of Brescia (St) B. Sep 26
d. *p*506. He was a bishop of Brescia in Lombardy, Italy.

Vigilius of Trent (St) M. B. Jun 26
d. 405. A Roman nobleman, he studied at Athens and then emigrated with his family to Trent, Italy. He became bishop and took effective measures against the local paganism until he was stoned to death for toppling a statue of Saturn in the Val di Rendena.

Vigor (St) B. Nov 1
d. ?537. A disciple of St Vedast, he was a hermit and then a diocesan priest before becoming bishop of Bayeux, France. He was remembered for opposing the surviving paganism.

Villana de' Botti (Bl) T(OP). Feb 28
d. *c*1360. Daughter of a rich merchant of Florence, Italy, when young she wanted to become a nun but was opposed by her father, so she married and led a life of worldliness and pleasure. Then she converted completely and became a Dominican tertiary devoted to penance and charity, allegedly because she saw the face of a demon instead of her own face in a mirror one day. Her cultus was confirmed for Florence in 1824.

Villanus (St) B. R(OSB). May 7
d. 1237. From Gubbio, Italy, he became a monk at Fontavellana and bishop of his native city in 1206.

Villicus (St) B. Apr 17
d. 568. He was bishop of Metz, France, from 543 and was praised by Venantius Fortunatus.

Vilmos *see* **William**

Vimin (Wynnin, Gwynnin) (St) B. Jan 21
C6th. A bishop of Scotland, he allegedly founded the monastery of Holywood near Dumfries but the evidence is very confused.

Vimius (St) *see* **Marinus, Vimius and Zimius**

Vincent (St) *see* **Datius, Julian and Comps**

Vincent (St) *see* **Eusebius, Pontian and Comps**

Vincent (St) *see* **Marcellinus, Vincent and Domninus**

Vincent (St) *see* **Sixtus II, Pope and Comps**

Vincent and Laetus (SS) MM. Sep 1
C5th? The old Roman Martyrology ascribes these martyrs to Spain and they are further alleged to belong to Toledo, but apparently they were the first bishop of Dax in Gascony, France) and one of his deacons.

Vincent, Orontius and Victor (SS) MM. Jan 22
d. 305. The first two were brothers of Cimiez near Nice, France, and went as missionaries to the Spanish Pyrenees. They were martyred with St Victor at Puigcerda near Gerona and their shrine subsequently established at Embrun near Gap, France.

Vincent, Sabina and Christeta (SS) MM. Oct 27
d. 303. They were martyred at Avila, Spain, but their acta are unreliable.

Vincent Abraham (Bl) *see* **September (Martyrs of)**

Vincent of Agen (St) M. D. Jun 9
d. ?292. He was a deacon allegedly killed at Agen in Gascony, France, for having interrupted a feast of the Druids. His date is uncertain.

Vincent of Aquila (Bl) R(OFM). Aug 7
d. 1504. From Aquila, Italy, he became a Franciscan lay brother there and was famous for his mystical gifts. His cultus was approved for Aquila in 1785.

Vincent of Astorga (St) R(OSB). May 9
d. *c*950. He was a disciple of St Gennadius of Astorga and succeeded him as abbot of San Pedro de Montes near Astorga, Spain.

Vincent-of-St-Joseph of Ayamonte (Bl) M. R(OFM). Sep 10
1596–1622. From Ayamonte near Huelva, Spain, he emigrated to Mexico and became a Franciscan lay brother in 1615. In 1618 he

accompanied Bl Louis Sotelo to Manila and was sent to Japan in 1619. He was arrested in 1620 and, after two years of inhuman imprisonment, was burnt alive in the 'Great Martyrdom' at Nagasaki with BB Charles Spinola and Comps. *See* **Japan (Martyrs of)**.

Vincent of Bevagna (St) M. B. Jun 6
d. 303. The first bishop of Bevagna in Umbria, Italy, he was martyred in the reign of Diocletian.

Vincent-de-Paul Canelles Vives (Bl) *see* **Hospitaller Martyrs of Spain**

Vincent Carvalho (Bl) M. R(OSA). Sep 3
d. 1632. From near Lisbon, Portugal, he became an Augustinian friar there, was sent to Mexico in 1621 and to Japan in 1623. He was burnt alive at Nagasaki with BB Anthony Ishida and Comps. *See* **Japan (Martyrs of)**.

Vincent Caum (Bl) M. R(SJ). Jun 20
d. 1626. From Seoul in Korea, he was taken to Japan as a prisoner of war in 1591. There he became a Christian and entered the Jesuit seminary at Arima, spending thirty years as a catechist in Japan and in China. He was burnt alive at Nagasaki with BB Francis Pacheco and Comps. *See* **Japan (Martyrs of)**.

Vincent of Collioure (St) M. Apr 19
d. ?304. He was allegedly martyred at Collioure near Perpignan, France, in the reign of Diocletian, but his acta are worthless and he may be a duplicate of St Vincent the Deacon.

Vincent the Deacon (St) M. D. Jan 22
d. 304. From Huesca, Spain, he became a deacon under St Valerius at Zaragoza and was martyred at Valencia in the reign of Diocletian. St Augustine, Pope St Leo I and Prudentius all wrote in his honour, but details of his martyrdom are lacking. He is a local patron of vine-dressers and is depicted being torn with hooks, carrying his intestines or having ravens defending his body. His attributes are a set of cruets or a millstone.

Vincent (Nguyen The) Diem (Bl) M. Nov 24
d. 1838. A Vietnamese priest, he worked in north Vietnam and was beheaded with Peter Dumoulin-Bori and Comps. *See* **Vietnam (Martyrs of)**.

Vincent Duong (St) M. Jun 6
1862. He was a Vietnamese layman and martyr. *See* **Vietnam (Martyrs of)**.

Vincent Ferrer (St) R(OP). Apr 5
*c*1350–1419. Born in Valencia in Spain (his father was English), when young he joined the Dominicans and soon became the adviser of the King of Aragón and of the Avignon anti-pope, with whom he sided in good faith. In 1399 he started travelling through Spain, France, Switzerland and Italy preaching penance (he was convinced that the end of the world was imminent), working miracles and converting thousands. He had an extraordinary gift for learning languages. He realized that the Avignon anti-pope needed to resign for the good of the Church and played a vital role at the council of Constance in 1414. He died at Vannes in Britanny. He is represented as a Dominican holding an open book while preaching, sometimes with a cardinal's hat, wings or a crucifix.

Vincent Frelichowski (Bl) P. Feb 23
1913–1945. From Chelmża, Poland, he became a priest of the diocese of Pelplin in 1937 and served as curate at Toruń. Immediately after the German invasion of Poland in 1939 he was arrested and sent in turn to the concentration camps at Stuthoff, Sachsenhausen and Dachau. He engaged in clandestine pastoral work, and died of typhus at Dachau after nursing sufferers of that disease. He was beatified in 1999.

Vincent Grossi (Bl) P. F. Nov 7
1845–1917. Born near Cremona, Italy, he became a parish priest of that diocese and remained one all his life, being an exemplary pastor. In 1885 he founded the 'Daughters of the Oratory' to assist in catechizing young people according to the principles of St Philip Neri. He was beatified in 1975.

Vincent Kadlubek (Bl) B. R(OCist). Mar 8
d. 1223. A German from the Palatinate, he studied in France and Italy and was made provost at Sandomir in Poland. In 1208 he became bishop of Cracow, but resigned in 1218 and became a Cistercian at Jendrzejó. He is one of the earliest Polish chroniclers, and had his cultus approved for Cracow in 1764.

Vincent of León (St) *see* **Ramirus and Comps**

Vincent of Lérins (St) R. May 24
d. ?445. Possibly a Gallo-Roman nobleman, he was a soldier before he became a monk on the island of Lérins off the Riviera coast, France. He is remembered as the author of the *Commonitorium* concerning the development of

Church doctrine, and in which is the famous precept (the 'Vincentian canon') that the only true doctrines are those adhered to 'everywhere, always and by all'.

Vincent Lewoniuk *see* **Podlasia (Martyrs of)**

Vincent (Le Quang) Liem
(St) M. R(OP). Nov 7
d. 1773. A Vietnamese nobleman, he became a Dominican priest and worked with St Hyacinth Castaneda in north Vietnam until his beheading. *See* **Vietnam (Martyrs of)**.

Vincent Madelgar (St) R. Sep 20
d. ?687. A Frankish nobleman named Madelgar from Strepy near Mons, Belgium, he married and his wife Waldetrude and his four children, Aldetrude, Dentlin, Landeric and Madalberta, are saints also. In ?653 the couple separated to become consecrated religious and he took the name Vincent as a monk in the monastery of Haumont which he had founded. Later he founded another abbey at Soignies, where he became abbot and where he died.

Vincent Pallotti (St) P. F. Jan 23
1795–1850. A Roman, his father was a grocer and he became a secular priest in 1820. After a short period of theological teaching he took up pastoral work in Rome and became famous for his zeal (especially during the cholera epidemic of 1837) and his austerities. He founded his society of missionary priests, the 'Pallotines', in 1835 and a corresponding congregation of sisters in 1843. In 1836 he started the keeping of an octave of prayer after the Epiphany for the reunion of the Eastern churches with Rome, and was also very interested in the English mission. He died at Rome and was canonized in 1963.

Vincent de Paul (St) P. F. Sep 27
1581–1660. From Ranquine (now renamed after him) in Gascony, France, he studied at Toulouse and was ordained in 1600. According to legend he was captured by Muslim pirates in 1605 and was sold as a slave at Tunis, but escaped in 1607. He was a court chaplain at Paris while carrying out his life's work of active charity for all sorts of deprived people, e.g. abandoned orphans, sick children, prostitutes, the destitute, the blind and the insane. He also preached missions and retreats, and enlisted a number of priests for this work who formed the nucleus of a new religious institute, the 'Lazarists' or 'Vincentian Fathers', in 1625. In 1633 he founded the congregation of the 'Sisters of Charity' who have become an integral feature of Church life worldwide. Dying at Paris, he was canonized in 1737 and is the patron of organizations devoted to charitable works.

Vincent Pinilla (Bl) *see* **Vincent Soller and Comps**

Vincent of Porto (St) M. May 24
? He was martyred at Porto Romano, the ancient port of Rome at the mouth of the Tiber.

Vincent Romano (Bl) P. Dec 20
1751–1836. He was born at Tor' del Greco near Naples, Italy, and lived there all his life, being rather like St John Vianney in character. He had great care for orphans and deprived people, but was persecuted by the French in the Napoleonic period and by anti-clericals afterwards. He was beatified in 1963.

Vincent of Rome (St) M. Jul 24
? He was a Roman martyred outside the walls of the city on the road to Tivoli.

Vincent le Rousseau (Bl) *see* **September (Martyrs of)**

Vincent-of-the-Cross Shiwozuka (St) *see* **Laurence Ruiz and Comps**

Vincent Soler and Comps (BB) MM.
d. 1936. They were seven Augustinian recollects (Vincent Soler, Deogratias Palacios, Leo Inchausti, Joseph Rada, Vincent Pinilla, Julian Moreno and Joseph-Richard Díez) and the parish priest (Emmanuel Martin Sierra) of Motril near Granada, Spain. After the Spanish Republican government came to power, there were violent popular demonstrations against the Church in the town. On July 25 BB Deogracias, Leo, Joseph, Julian and Joseph-Richard were summarily seized and shot; the following day, Bl Manuel was machine-gunned at the door of his church with Bl Vincent Pinilla. Bl Vincent Soller went into hiding, but was betrayed and captured and was shot on August 15 with 28 others. *See* **Spanish Civil War (Martyrs of)**.

Vincent-Mary Strambi (St)
B. R(CP). Jan 1
1745–1824. From Civitavecchia near Rome, he was ordained in 1767 and then joined the Passionists. He filled almost all the offices of his order and was also an effective home-missioner. He was made bishop of Macerata and Tolentino in 1801, but was exiled in 1808 for refusing to take the oath of allegiance to Napoleon. At the

end of his life he was appointed papal adviser to Pope Leo XII. Dying at Rome, he was canonized in 1950.

Vincent of Troyes (St) B. Feb 4
d. ?546. He became bishop of Troyes, France in ?536.

Vincent Tuong (St) M. Jun 16
1862. He was a Vietnamese layman and martyr. *See* **Vietnam (Martyrs of)**.

Vincent Vilar David (Bl) M. L. Feb 14
1889–1937. Born near Valencia, Spain, he worked as an industrial engineer in his family's ceramics firm and held municipal office. As a Catholic he was involved in parish activities and in youth and workers' groups, and tried to help persecuted priests and religious after the outbreak of the Civil War. He was shot as a result, and beatified in 1995. *See* **Spanish Civil War (Martyrs of)**.

Vincent (Do) Yen (St) M. R(OP). Jun 30
?1765–1838. A Vietnamese, he became a Dominican in 1808. After his ordination he worked in north Vietnam for forty years, the last six in hiding after the edict of persecution in 1832. He was betrayed and beheaded at Hai-Duong. *See* **Vietnam (Martyrs of)**.

Vincentian (Viance, Viants) (St) R. Jan 2
d. *c*730. He was allegedly a disciple of St Menelaus who became a hermit near Tulle, France, but his extant biography is an C11th forgery.

Vincenza Gerosa (St) R. Jun 28
1784–1847. She was born and died at Lovere near Bergamo, Italy, and until her fortieth year led an undistinguished domestic life in the context of a wealthy but disfunctional family. Then she became acquainted with St Bartolomea Capitanio and joined her work in founding the 'Sisters of Charity of Lovere' at Lovere. When St Bartolomea died in 1833 St Vincenza succeeded her as superior, and oversaw the massive growth of the institute. She was canonized in 1950.

Vincenza-Mary López Vicuña (St) R. F. Jan 18
1847–1890. From a bourgeois family of Cascante in Navarre, Spain, she was sent to Madrid for her education and lodged with an aunt who ran a hostel for casually employed female domestic servants. This importance of this work impressed her, and she started living a life in common with her aunt and some others in 1871 (despite her family wanting her to get married). This was the start of the 'Daughters of Mary Immaculate' which taught domestic science and ran hospices for young women servants in danger of becoming prostitutes. She became the first superior, died at Madrid of overwork and was canonized in 1975.

Vindemialis, Eugene and Longinus (SS) MM. BB. May 2
d. ?485. They were Roman African bishops executed on the orders of the Arian Vandal King Hunneric after having been viciously tortured.

Vindician (St) B. Mar 11
d. ?712. A disciple of St Eligius, he became bishop of Arras-Cambrai, France, in 675. He protested at the crimes of the degenerate Merovingian kings and the powerful mayors of the palace (especially the murder of St Leodegar) with great courage. He died at Brussels.

Vindonius (St) *see* **Priscus II of Capua and Comps**

Vintila (St) R(OSB). Dec 23
d. 890. A Benedictine monk, he died as a hermit at Pugino near Orense in Galicia, Spain.

Virgil of Arles (St) B. R. Mar 5
d. ?610. A monk of Lérins, he became archbishop of Arles, France, in 580 and was probably the consecrator of St Augustine as bishop of Canterbury at the request of Pope St Gregory the Great. The latter had to rebuke him for trying to convert Jews by force.

Virgil (Fergal) of Salzburg (St) B. R. Nov 27
d. 784. An Irish monk, he was allegedly abbot of Aghadoe in Co. Kerry before going on pilgrimage and ending up in Bavaria in 745. He continued the work of St Rupert and was made bishop of Salzburg in Austria (where he consecrated the first cathedral) and abbot of St Peter's in *c*765. He was regarded as one of the foremost scholars of the period, but St Boniface complained to Rome about some of his ideas and this may have been a continuation of the friction between Celtic and Roman traditions. He is venerated as the apostle of Carinthia and was canonized in 1233.

Virginia Centurione Bracelli (Bl) R. Dec 15
1587–1651. Born in Genoa, Italy, she wanted to become a nun but her parents forced her to

marry Gaspar Bracelli, a noble so addicted to vice that he ruined his health and left her a widow in 1607 (after she had helped him die in grace). Then she made private vows and performed the social works of mercy. After 1624, during social chaos caused by famine and war, she took in fifty young refugee girls and then opened four other houses in the city to cater for others like them. She was very much loved by her city, and was beatified in 1985.

Viridiana *see* **Veridiana**

Virila (St) R(OSB). Oct 1
d. *c*1000. He was abbot of the Benedictine abbey of St Saviour at Leyre in Navarre, Spain, and certainly existed, but his biography contains much legendary material.

Vissia (St) V. Apr 12
d. *c*250. She was martyred at Fermo near Ancona, Italy, in the reign of Decius.

Vitalian, Pope (St) Jan 27
d. 672. He was pope from 657 and tried to resolve the Monothelite controversy. He sent St Theodore to England as archbishop of Canterbury in 668.

Vitalian of Capua (St) B. July 16
? He was a bishop of Capua, Italy.

Vitalian of Osimo (St) B. Jul 16
d. 776. He was a bishop of Osimo, Italy.

Vitalicus (St) *see* **Rufinus, Silvanus and Vitalicus**

Vitalis (St) *see* **Arator of Alexandria and Comps**

Vitalis (St) *see* **Ariston and Comps**

Vitalis (St) *see* **Epictetus, Jucundus and Comps**

Vitalis (St) *see* **Germanus, Theophilus and Comps**

Vitalis (St) *see* **Seven Brothers**

Vitalis (St) *see* **Theban Legion**

Vitalis and Agricola (SS) MM. Nov 4
d. ?304. According to the legend they were martyred at Bologna, Italy, in the reign of Diocletian. Vitalis was a slave of Agricola, and was martyred in the presence of his master with such courage that the latter was inspired to accept death also. Their veneration started when SS Ambrose of Milan and Eusebius of Bologna discovered some alleged relics of martyrs, and the legend was invented to explain these. The cultus was confined to local calendars in 1969.

Vitalis, Felicula and Zeno
(SS) MM. Feb 14
? They were probably Roman martyrs, but nothing is known about them.

Vitalis, Revocatus and Fortunatus (SS) MM. Jan 9
? Apparently a bishop and two deacons, they were martyred at Smyrna, Asia Minor.

Vitalis, Sator and Repositus
(SS) MM. Aug 29
C3rd or C4th? They were martyred at Velleianum in Apulia, Italy, and were included in the legend of the **Twelve Brothers** (q.v.).

Vitalis of Gaza (St) R. Jan 11
d. ?625. An old monk of Gaza in the Holy Land, he left his monastery and set about trying to convert prostitutes, causing great scandal by associating with them. He was vindicated after his death.

Vitalis of Milan *Apr 28*
C1st? The alleged father of SS Gervase and Protase and husband of St Valeria probably never existed. His acta are spurious and his cultus was suppressed in 1969.

Vitalis of Montesubasio
(St) R(OSB). May 31
d. ?1370. He was a Benedictine monk at Monte Subasio near Assisi, Italy, and then a hermit at Santa Maria delle Viole for twenty years.

Vitalis (Vial) of Noirmoutier
(St) R. Oct 16
d. ?740. Apparently an Anglo-Saxon, he joined the monastery of Noirmoutier at the mouth of the Loire river, France, and later became a hermit on Mt Scobrit nearby.

Vitalis of Salzburg (St) B. R. Oct 20
d. 745. He was St Rupert's successor as archbishop of Salzburg, Austria, and abbot of St Peter's there in 717.

Vitalis of Savigny (Bl) R(OSB). Sep 16
?1063–1122. From near Bayeux in Normandy, France, when young he was chaplain to a relative of William the Conqueror but then became a hermit and itinerant preacher for

seventeen years. Being acquainted with Bl Robert of Arbrissel he followed his example, settled in the forest of Savigny and founded a reform Benedictine monastery in 1112. This became the nucleus of a new congregation which had spread through France and into England by the time of its incorporation into the Cistercians in 1147.

Vitonus (Vanne, Vaune) (St) B. Nov 9
d. ?525. He was bishop of Verdun, France, from *c*500, and had his shrine in a monastery named after him which became the mother-house of the Benedictine congregation of St Vanne in 1600.

Vitus (Guy), Crescentia and Modestus (SS) MM. Jun 15
d. ?303. Their cultus is ancient, but their acta (in various versions) are legendary and they are described in them as a child, his nurse and her husband respectively who were martyred in the reign of Diocletian. The latter two are fictional characters, however, and their cultus has been suppressed, while that of St Vitus has been confined to local calendars from 1969. St Vitus is a patron of epileptics, and the nervous disorder called St Vitus's dance is named after him.

Vitus of Pontida (St) R(OSB). Sep 5
d. ?1095. He was a Benedictine monk at the abbey of Pontida near Bergamo, Italy, under its founder, St Albert.

Vivald (Ubaldo, Gualdo) (St) T(OFM) May 11
d. 1300. He was a disciple and companion of Bl Bartholomew Buonpedoni and nursed him as a leper for twenty years. Then he became a hermit in a hollow chestnut tree at Boscotondo near Montone in Tuscany, Italy, allegedly as a Franciscan tertiary. His cultus was approved for Volterra in 1908.

Viventiolus (St) B. R. Jul 12
d. 524. He was a monk of St Oyend at Condat before becoming archbishop of Lyons, France, and was a friend of St Avitus of Vienne.

Viventius (St) *see* **Peregrine, Maceratus and Viventius**

Viventius of Poitiers (St) R. Jan 13
d. *c*400. Allegedly a refugee born in Samaria who spent some time with St Martin of Tours on the Ligurian island of Gallinara, he became a disciple of St Hilary at Poitiers, France, and died as a hermit at Sables d'Olonne in the Vendée. His C10th biography is unreliable.

Vivian *see* **Bibiana or Vimin**

Vivian of Saintes (St) B. Aug 28
d. *c*460. He succeeded St Ambrose as bishop of Saintes, France. His extant biography is spurious.

Vivina *see* **Wivina**

Vladimir (St) L. Jul 15
956–1015. Of the princely house of Rurik ruling at Kiev, Ukraine, and a grandson of St Olga, he was a pagan when he became Grand Prince of Kievan Rus in 972 but was baptized before his marriage to the sister of the Byzantine emperor Basil II in 987. Previously licentious and immoral, he took his new faith seriously, invited Byzantine missionaries to evangelize his country and is counted as the founder of the Russian Orthodox Church. His two sons SS Boris and Gleb were killed after his death and are venerated as martyrs.

Vodoald (Voel, Vodalus, Vodalis) (St) R. Feb 5
d. ?725. According to his unreliable biography he was an Irish or Scottish monk who emigrated to France as a missionary and died as a hermit near Soissons.

Volker (Bl) M. R(OSB). Mar 7
d. 1132. A Benedictine monk of Siegburg near Bonn, Germany, he went as a missionary to the Obotrite Slavs of Mecklenburg and was killed by them. His cultus is unconfirmed.

Voloc (St) B. Jan 29
d. ?725. He was an Irish missionary bishop in Scotland.

Volusian (St) B. Jan 18
d. ?498. A senator of Tours, France, who was married to a memorably bad-tempered wife, he was chosen to be bishop in 491 and shortly after exiled by the Arian Visigoths. He died at Toulouse.

Votus (St) *see* **John de Atarés and Comps**

Vouga (Vougar, Veho, Feock, Fiech) (St) B. R. Jun 15
C6th. An Irish bishop, he emigrated to Brittany, France, and lived as a hermit in a cell near Lesneven.

Vulcherius *see* **Mochoemoc**

Vulgan (St) R. Nov 3
d. ?704. An Irishman or Welshman, he

emigrated to northern France as a missionary and settled as a hermit at Arras, being affiliated to the abbey of St Vaast.

Vulgis (St) B. R. Feb 4
d. *c*760. He was a regionary bishop and abbot of the monastery of Lobbes in Hainault, Belgium.

Vulliermus de Leaval (Bl) Feb 7
His cultus was confirmed for Aosta in 1877.

Vulmar *see* **Wulmar**

Vulphy (Wulflagius) (St) R. Jun 7
d. ?643. A parish priest at Rue near Abbeville, France, he became a hermit and has his shrine at Montreuil-sur-Mer.

Vulpian (St) M. Apr 3
d. ?304. A Syrian, he was martyred at Tyre, Lebanon, in the reign of Diocletian, allegedly by being sewn up in a leather sack with a dog and a snake before being thrown into the sea.

Vulsin *see* **Wulsin**

Vyevain (Bl) B. Aug 26
d. 1285. This archbishop of York, England, was venerated at the Cistercian abbey of Pontigny, France.

W

Waccar, Gundekar, Elleher and Hadulf (SS) MM. RR. Jun 5
d. 755. These monks are mentioned by name among the fifty-two companions killed with St Boniface.

Walbert (Vaubert) (St) May 11
d. ?678. Duke of Lorraine, France, and count of Hainault, he was the husband of St Bertilia and father of SS Waldetrude and Aldegund.

Walburga (St) R. Feb 25
?710-779. Sister of SS Willibald and Winebald, she became a nun at Wimborne in Dorset, England, under St Tatta and followed St Lioba to Germany at the invitation of St Boniface. She died as abbess of Heidenheim in Württemberg (a double monastery) and her relics were taken to Eichstätt. A liquid that oozes from the rock beneath the shrine, known as 'St Walburga's oil', is reputed to have curative properties.

Waldalenus (St) R. May 15
C7th. He was abbot-founder of the monastery of Bèze near Dijon, France.

Waldebert (Walbert, Gaubert) (St) R. May 2
d. ?668. A Frankish nobleman, he was a soldier before becoming a monk at the Columbanian monastery of Luxeuil in the Vosges, France. In ?628 he became abbot and introduced the Benedictine rule into the abbey's customary. Under him the monastery reached the peak of its religious and cultural influence in western Europe. He helped St Salaberga to found her monastery at Laon.

Waldetrude (Vaudru) (St) R. Apr 9
d. ?688. She was daughter of SS Walbert and Bertilla, wife of St Vincent Madelgar and mother of SS Landeric, Dentelin, Madalberta and Aldetrude. When her husband became a monk she founded a nunnery at Mons in Belgium (around which the town grew up) and became a nun there.

Waldrada (St) R. May 5
d. *c*620. She was the first abbess of the nunnery of Saint-Pierre-aux-Nonnais at Metz, France.

Waleric (Valéry) (St) R. Apr 1
d. ?622. From the Auvergne, France, he was a monk under St Columban at Luxeuil before becoming a missionary in northern France, where he became the abbot-founder of Leuconay at the mouth of the Somme. Two settlements in that district are called Saint-Valéry after him.

Wales (Martyrs of)
The Reformation was a disaster for Christianity in Wales as well as for Welsh culture, because the Latin in the liturgy was replaced by English (which was a foreign language for the majority of the people). There was not much Catholic missionary activity in Wales in penal times compared with that in England, but six martyrs have been recognized. They are: Bl Charles Meehan, an Irish Franciscan executed at Ruthin in 1679 after being shipwrecked; St David Lewis, executed at Usk in the same year; SS John Lloyd and Philip Evans, executed together at Cardiff in the same year; St Richard Gwyn, executed at Wrexham in 1584 and Bl William Davies, executed at Beaumaris in 1593.

Walfrid (Gualfredo) della Gherardesca (St) R(OSB). Feb 15
d. ?765. A married nobleman of Pisa, Italy, with five sons and one daughter, in middle age he joined with two other married men in founding the abbey of Palazzuolo (between Volterra and Piombino) and a nunnery nearby for their wives and Walfrid's daughter. He was Palazzuolo's first abbot and was succeeded by one of his sons. His cultus was confirmed for Pisa and the Benedictines in 1861.

Walhere (St) M. P. Jun 23
C8th? His story is that he was from near Dinant, Belgium, became parish priest at Onhaye nearby and was killed by a nephew (priest of the

neighbouring parish of Hastière) whom he had reproved for his immoral life. He is locally venerated as a martyr.

Wallabonsus (St) *see* **Peter of Cordoba and Comps**

Walpurgis *see* **Walburga**

Walstan (St) R. May 30
C11th? Possibly from Bawburgh in Norfolk, England, according to his legend he was a farm-worker at Taverham and Costessey nearby and was famous for his charity. This may be historical, unlike the assertion that he was a prince who exiled himself to live with ordinary people. He had a locally popular shrine at Bawburgh before the Reformation, and is depicted as a king with scythe and sceptre and accompanied by calves.

Walter *see* **Gaucherius**

Walter of Bruges (Bl)
B. R(OFM). Jan 22
d. 1307. From Bruges, Belgium, he became a Franciscan and was provincial at Tours, France, before being made bishop of Poitiers. He excommunicated his metropolitan, Bernand de Got, but the latter became pope as Clement V and deposed him. Then he went back to being an ordinary Franciscan and was vindicated after his death. His cultus is unconfirmed.

Walter of Fontenelle (St)
R(OSB). Jun 4
d. 1150. An Englishman, he became abbot of Fontenelle in Normandy, France, and was commended for his humility, piety and zeal by Pope Innocent II. His feast-day is uncertain, as his cultus is extinct.

Walter of Guimarães (Bl)
R(OFM). Aug 2
d. ?1258. One of the first Franciscan companions of St Francis, he was sent by the latter to establish the order in Portugal and died at Guemarães near Braga. His cultus is unconfirmed.

Walter (Gualterius, Gautier) of Himerode (Bl) R(OCist). Jan 22
d. 1222. From Brabant in the Low Countries, he was a knight and a noted participant at tournaments before he became a Cistercian at Himerode. As guest master there he attracted many to the monastic life by his affability and tact. He died at Villers, Belgium. His cultus is unconfirmed.

Walter of L'Esterp (St) R(CR). May 11
d. 1070. He was abbot of the Augustinian monastery of L'Esterp in the Limousin, France.

Walter Pierson (Bl) M. R(OCart). Jun 6
d. 1537. A Carthusian lay brother of the London Charterhouse, he was one of seven of that community starved to death at the Newgate prison for refusing the oath of supremacy demanded by King Henry VIII. *See* **England (Martyrs of)**.

Walter of Pontoise (St) R(OSB). Apr 8
d. 1099. From Picardy, France, he was a professor of philosophy and rhetoric but tired of his fame and became a Benedictine at Rebais. Against his will he was made abbot of Pontoise and fled the responsibility several times, once to Cluny and on the last occasion to Rome where the pope refused his resignation and ordered him to return.

Walter of Serviliano (St) R(OSB). Jun 4
d. *c*1250. A Roman, he became a hermit at Serviliano in the Marches, Italy, and founded a monastery there. His extant biography is spurious.

Waltheof (Walthen, Waldef)
(St) R(OCist). Aug 4
*c*1100-11. An English nobleman, he was educated at the court of Scotland after his widowed mother married King David and became a close friend of St Aelred. Initially joining the Augustinian canons at Nostell in Yorkshire, England, he transferred to the Cistercians and eventually became abbot of Melrose which was rebuilt for him by King David of Scotland, his stepfather. He was famous for his cheerfulness and generosity to the poor. His cultus was never confirmed.

Waltman (Bl) R(OPraem). Apr 11
d. 1138. He was a disciple of St Norbert, whom he accompanied to Cambrai, France, to preach against the heresy of Tanchelm. He became first abbot of the Premonstratensian abbey of St Michael there.

Waltram (Bl) *see* **Lantfrid, Waltram and Elilantus**

Wando (Vando) (St) R. Apr 17
d. ?756. Monk and abbot of Fontenelle in Normandy, France, as a result of a false accusation he was exiled to Troyes but reinstated after his innocence had been proved. He died at Fontenelle.

Wandrille (Wandregisilus) (St) R. Jul 22
*c*600-668. From near Verdun, France, he was a royal courtier and became count of the palace of King Dagobert I. He married, but after a pilgrimage to Rome the couple separated to become consecrated religious and he was a monk in various places before founding the monastery of Fontenelle in Normandy in 648. This became the missionary centre of the district as well as a school of arts and crafts, and it soon had a community of over three hundred monks. It survives as an abbey.

Waning (Vaneng) (St) R. Jan 9
d. ?686. From near Rouen, France, he was a royal courtier of King Clothair III before becoming a monk and helping his friend St Wandrille in the foundation of Fontenelle. Then he himself founded Fécamp, which became a great abbey.

Warin *see* **Guarin**

Wastrada (St) R? Jul 21
d. *c*760. The mother of St Gregory of Utrecht, she possibly became a nun and abbess of Susteren near Maastricht, Netherlands, as an old widow, although contemporary evidence of this is lacking.

Wenceslas (Vatslav) (St) M. L. Sep 28
907-929. Born near Prague, Czech Republic, he was raised as a Christian by his grandmother St Ludmilla and became duke of Bohemia in 922 at the time of a pagan and anti-German reaction. He met this with patience and tolerance, but was eventually conspired against and assassinated at the door of the church at Stara-Boleslav by his brother Boleslav. He is the patron of the Czech Republic. The incidents recorded in the popular carol 'Good King Wenceslas looked out' are fictional.

Wenceslas-Mary Clarís Vilaregut (Bl) *see* **Philip-of-Jesus Munárriz Azcona and Comps**

Wendolin (Wendelin, Wendel) (St) L. Oct 21
d. ?607 or 650. All that is known is that he was a shepherd who had a shrine at St Wendel in the Saarland, Germany. An unreliable legend describes him as an Irish hermit who became abbot of Tholey nearby.

Wenn *see* **Gwen**

Wennap *see* **Veep**

Wenog (Gwenog) (St) Jan 3
? Nothing is known about this Welsh saint, patron of Llanwenog near Lampeter.

Weonard *see* **Gwrnerth**

Werburga of Chester (St) R. Feb 3
d. ?699. Traditionally the daughter of St Ermenilda and of King Wulfhere of Mercia, England, she became a nun at Ely under St Etheldreda and later founded the nunneries of Hanbury near Tutbury, Staffs, Trentham (near Stoke-on-Trent) and Weedon, Northants. She died at Trentham but her body was transferred to the abbey (now Anglican cathedral) of Chester, of which city she is the patron.

Werburga of Mercia (St) R. Feb 3
d. ?785. She was allegedly wife of King Ceolred of Mercia, England, and became a nun when widowed (possibly at Bardney, Lincs).

Werenfrid (St) R. Aug 14
d. *c*760. An Anglo-Saxon missionary monk, he worked with St Willibrord among the Frisians and died at Arnhem, Netherlands.

Werner (St) M. Apr 18
?1273-1287. According to his very dubious legend, he was a teenage boy who was employed by a Jewish vineyard owner at Oberwesel in the Rhineland, Germany, and who was killed by him in hatred of the faith at Easter. The story is part of the 'Blood Libel' told against Jews in medieval times.

Wiborada (Guiborat, Weibrath) (St) R(OSB). May 2
d. 926. A noblewoman from the Aargau, Switzerland, she became a hermit walled up in a cell near the abbey of St Gall, to which she was affiliated. She worked as a bookbinder for the abbey library and was killed in a Magyar raid, being canonized in 1047.

Wicterp (Wiho, Wicho) (St) B. R. Apr 18
d. 749. Abbot of Ellwangen near Ulm, Germany, he helped in the foundation of the abbeys of Füssen, Wessobrünn and Kempten (all famous in medieval Germany) before becoming bishop of Augsburg.

Widrad (Waré) (St) R. Oct 3
d. 747. He restored the abbey of Flavigny in Burgundy, France, and founded that of Saulieu near Autun.

Widukind *see* **Wittikund**

Wifred (Bl) R(OSB). Dec 13
d. 1021. He was abbot of the Benedictine abbey of St Victor at Marseilles, France, from 1005.

Wigbert the Elder (St) R. Apr 12
d. 690. An Anglo-Saxon monk, he became a disciple in Ireland of St Egbert of Iona and spent two years as a missionary in Friesland, Netherlands, but returned to Ireland to die.

Wigbert of Fritzlar (St) R. Aug 13
d. ?738. An Anglo-Saxon monk, he went to the missions in Germany under St Boniface and was appointed by the latter abbot of Fritzlar near Kassel. A few years later he transferred to Ohrdruf in Thuringia, but returned to Fritzlar before his death.

Wilfetrude (St) R. Nov 23
d. *p*670. She succeeded her aunt St Gertrude (the founder) as abbess of the nunnery of Nivelles, Belgium.

Wilfrid of York (St) B. Oct 12
633-709. A Northumbrian nobleman from Ripon in Yorkshire, England, he was educated at Lindisfarne under the Celtic monastic observance before going to Rome in 653 to learn Roman church customs. Returning to Northumbria in 657, he founded the abbey of Ripon with a customary based exclusively on the rule of St Benedict (which he claimed as the first such in England) and played a leading part in the council of Whitby in 664 at which Roman usages were adopted for the English church. He was then consecrated bishop of York at Compiègne, but only started ruling his diocese in 669 when his rival St Chad had withdrawn. He exalted his position as bishop into one of great power, wealth and display and St Theodore divided his diocese into four as a result. He was eventually vindicated in appealing to Rome against this (the first such appeal in English history) after several periods of exile, and did missionary work among the Frisians and South Saxons meanwhile. He died at Oundle, Northants, after apparently founding several monasteries in Mercia. His model of the secular dignity of bishops has been criticized as a corrupting influence within the Church.

Wilfrid the Younger
(St) B. R. Apr 29
d. 744. He was educated by St Hilda at Whitby, became a disciple of St John of Beverley and was appointed superior of the cathedral community at York, England. He succeeded his master as archbishop of York in 718, but resigned to die in a monastery (possibly Ripon).

Wilfrida *see* **Wulftrude**

Wilgefortis *Jul 20*
? According to her legend she was one of sextuplet sisters and miraculously grew a beard in order to escape marriage. This strange story was possibly invented in the Middle Ages to explain earlier representations of Christ on the cross clothed in a tunic (a loincloth having become the usual garment depicted). She is depicted as a maiden with a long beard, carrying a T-shaped cross or crucified. Her name is derived from 'Virgo fortis', and she was known as Uncumber in England, Ontkommena in the Netherlands, Kümmernis in Germany, Livrade in Gascony and Librada in Spain. Her cultus is extinct.

Willehad of Bremen (St) B. R. Nov 8
d. ?789. A Northumbrian monk educated at York, England, he went as a missionary to Friesland, Netherlands, in 766. Charlemagne sent him to evangelize the Saxons in 780, but was lucky to escape death in the Saxon revolt two years later. He was at the abbey of Echternacht during the bloody suppression of the revolt, and then became the first bishop of Bremen in 787. He died there.

Willehad of Denmark
(St) R(OFM). Jul 9
1482-1572. A Danish Franciscan, he was exiled when Denmark became Lutheran and went to the friary at **Gorinchem** (q.v.) in the Netherlands. He was one of the martyrs there.

Willeic (Willaik) (St) R. Mar 7
d. 726. He was a disciple of St Swithbert the Elder and prior under him of the abbey of Kaiserswerth near Düsseldorf, Germany.

William
This is the English form of the Germanic Wilhelm, which has been Latinized into Gulielmus or Guilielmus whence in turn the Italian Gulielmo, the French Guillaume and the Spanish Guillermo. In Hungarian it is Vilmos.

William (St) *see* **Acheric and William**

William of Aebelholt
(St) R(CR) Apr 6
d. 1203. A French Augustinian canon regular at St Genevieve's in Paris, he was sent to Denmark in 1171 to reform the monastery at Eskilsø on Ise Fjord, Zealand, and then founded the abbey of Aebelholt on the same island. He was canonized in 1224.

William Andleby (Bl) M. L. Jul 4
d. 1597. From Etton near Beverley, Yorks, he was educated at St John's College, Cambridge before converting, studying for the priesthood and being ordained in 1577. He was on the Yorkshire mission for twenty years before being executed at York with BB Edward Fulthrop, Henry Abbot and Thomas Warcop. He was beatified in 1929. *See* **England (Martyrs of)**.

William Apor (Bl) M. B. May 23
1892-1945. A nobleman from Segesvár, Hungary, he was ordained for the Nagyvárad diocese in 1915 and was a successful parish priest at Gyula. In 1941 he was made bishop of Győr and worked hard to alleviate the suffering caused by war. He also fought against the Nazi persecution of the Jews. When the Red Army invaded Hungary many female refugees gathered at the bishop's palace for security from molestation. On Good Friday in 1945 a gang of drunken soldiers tried to abduct them but was confronted by the bishop. He was shot, the soldiers fled and he died on Easter Monday, being beatified in 1997.

William Arnaud and Comps (BB) MM. May 29
d. 1242. A Dominican, he was chosen by the papal legate to be Inquisitor-General for southern France in order to suppress the Catharist heresy. In the year that the Count of Toulouse (the protector of the Cathars) broke with the French king, the Inquisitor's party went on a tour during which they stayed at the castle of Avignonet (between Toulouse and Carcassonne). The castle bailiff, with the probable connivance of the Count, arranged their massacre by enthusiastic knights and local people. The others killed were Stephen de Saint-Thibéry, OFM and assistant Inquisitor; Garcia d'Aure and Bernard de Roquefort, OP; Raymond Carbonier, the bishop's representative; Raymond Costivan, archdeacon; Peter Arnaud, a lay notary; an unidentified Franciscan and two Benedictines, the prior of Avignonet and a monk of Chiusa. Their cultus was confirmed for Toulouse and the Dominicans in 1866.

William of Breteuil (St) R(OSB). Jul 14
d. 1130. He was abbot-restorer of the monastery of Breteuil, near Beauvais, France, which had been destroyed by the Norsemen.

William Browne (Bl) M. L. Sep 5
d. 1605. A layman from Northamptonshire, he was executed at Ripon, Yorks, and beatified in 1929. *See* **England (Martyrs of)**.

William Carter (Bl) M. L. Jan 12
1550–1584. A Londoner, he ran a printing and bookbinding business and used this to disseminate Catholic publications. Being persecuted for this, he was finally condemned and executed at Tyburn for 'persuading to popery' after he was found to be holding sacred vessels and vestments in safe-keeping. He was beatified in 1987. *See* **England (Martyrs of)**.

William-Joseph Chaminade (Bl) P. F. (Jan 22)
1761–1850. From Périgueux, France, he was ordained in 1785 and settled at Bordeaux for most of his life, apart from some time in exile during the French Revolution. He was committed to the rechristianization of France under the guidance of Our Lady and attracted disciples who became a secular sodality (later to be called Marianists). He also helped to found the 'Daughters of Mary Immaculate' and the 'Society of Mary'. He was beatified in 2000.

William Courtet (St) *see* **Laurence Ruiz and Comps**

William Cufitella (Bl) T(OFM). Apr 7
d. 1411. From Noto in Sicily, he was a hermit and a Franciscan tertiary at Sciacca for seventy years. His cultus was approved in 1537.

William Davies (Bl) M. P. Jul 27
d. 1593. Born near Colwyn Bay, Wales, he studied at Oxford and was ordained at Rheims in 1595. After being a priest for five years in north Wales he was captured in 1592 and imprisoned at Beaumaris for a year before execution. He was beatified in 1987. *See* **Wales (Martyrs of)**.

William Dean (St) M. P. Aug 28
d. 1588. From Linton in Craven, Yorks, he was a Protestant minister before his conversion and was ordained at Rheims, France, in 1581. He was executed at Mile End Green, East London and was beatified in 1929. *See* **England (Martyrs of)**.

William Delfaut (Bl) *see* **September (Martyrs of)**

William of Dijon (St) R(OSB). Jan 1
962–1031. A nobleman from Novara, Italy, he became a Benedictine at Locedio near Vercelli and transferred to Cluny in France in 987. Sent to restore the abbey of St Benignus at Dijon, France, he made this a centre from which he extended the Cluniac observance throughout Burgundy, Normandy, Lorraine and northern

Italy. Gentle with the poor, he was remarkably firm in dealing with important people. Towards the end of his life he refounded the abbey of Fécamp, where he died.

William de Donjeon (St)
B. R(OCist). Jan 10
d. 1209. From Nevers, France, as a priest he was a canon at Soissons and at Paris before becoming a monk at Grandmont and transferring to the Cistercians of Pontigny. He was successively abbot of Fontaine-Jean near Sens, abbot of Châlis near Senlis and bishop of Bourges from 1200. He converted many Cathars. He was canonized in 1218.

William Exmew (Bl) M. R(OCart). Jun 19
d. 1535. Educated at Christ's College, Cambridge, he became a Carthusian at London and was sub-prior there. He was executed with BB Humphrey Middlemore and Sebastian Newdigate. *See* **England (Martyrs of)**.

William of Fenoli (Bl)
R(OCart). Dec 19
d. ?1205. He was a Carthusian lay brother at Casotto in Lombardy, Italy. His cultus was confirmed for the Carthusians in 1860.

William Filby (Bl) M. P. May 30
d. 1582. From Oxfordshire, he was at the University of Oxford and, after his conversion, studied for the priesthood at Rheims where he was ordained in 1581. He was executed at Tyburn with St Luke Kirby and BB Laurence Richardson and Thomas Cottam, and was beatified in 1886. *See* **England (Martyrs of)**.

William Firmatus (St) R. Apr 24
d. ?1095. From Tours, France, he became a canon at St Venance and practised medicine before receiving a divine warning against avarice. Then he gave his property to the poor and spent the rest of his life on pilgrimages and as a hermit at Savigny and at Mantilly near Le Mans, where he died.

William Fitzherbert (Thwayt) (St) B. Jun 8
d. 1154. A nephew of King Stephen, he became a canon of York, England, in 1130 and was appointed archbishop there in 1142 at the request of the king. The rival candidate was Murdac, a Cistercian monk, and powerful enemies (chiefly the Cistercians supported by St Bernard of Clairvaux) declared the appointment to be simonical. The pope initially found in his favour and he was consecrated in 1143, but his partisans burnt Fountains Abbey (Murdac's monastery), so he was deposed and his rival consecrated. He went into retirement at Winchester and lived a very penitential life of patience and resignation until he was finally restored after the death of Murdac. He died, perhaps of poison, almost immediately and was canonized in 1226.

William Freeman (Mason)
(Bl) M. P. Aug 13
d. 1595. From Yorkshire, he was at Magdalen College, Oxford, before his conversion. He was ordained at Rheims in I587 and worked in Worcestershire and Warwickshire until his execution at Warwick. He was beatified in 1929. *See* **England (Martyrs of)**.

William of Gellone (St) R. May 28
755–812. As the duke of Aquitaine and a knight at the court of Charlemagne he took part in campaigns against Muslim insurgency in the south of France. Afterwards he built a monastery near Montpellier as an offshoot of the nearby abbey of Aniane and joined the new community as a lay brother. Later the abbey was named Saint-Guilhem-du-Désert after him. He was canonized in 1066.

William Gibson (Bl) M. L. Nov 29
d. 1593. From Ripon, Yorks, he was imprisoned for many years at York for recusancy before being executed with Bl William Knight. He was beatified in 1987. *See* **England (Martyrs of)**.

William Greenwood (Bl)
M. R(OCart). Jun 16
d. 1537. A Carthusian lay brother of the London Charterhouse, he was one of the six of that community starved to death at Newgate prison for refusing the oath of supremacy demanded by King Henry VIII.

William Gunter (Bl) M. P. Aug 28
d. 1588. From Raglan in Gwent, he was educated at Rheims and ordained there in 1587. He was hanged at Shoreditch, London, and was beatified in 1929. *See* **England (Martyrs of)**.

William Harcourt (Bl) M. R(SJ). Jun 20
d. 1679. A Lancastrian, he became a Jesuit at St Omer, France, in 1632 and was on the English mission from 1645, chiefly in London. He was executed at Tyburn with BB Thomas Whitbread and Comps. *See* **England (Martyrs of)**.

William Harrington (Bl) M. P. Feb 18
1567–1594. From Felixkirk near Thirsk, Yorks, he studied at Rheims, was ordained there in

1592 and was hanged, drawn and quartered at Tyburn, London. He was beatified in 1929. *See* **England (Martyrs of)**.

William Hart (Bl) M. P. Mar 15
d. 1583. From Wells, Somerset, he was educated the University of Oxford before converting and studying for the priesthood at Douai, Rheims and Rome. After his ordination in 1581 he returned to England, was betrayed by an apostate in the house of Bl Margaret Clitherow and was executed at York. He was beatified in 1886. *See* **England (Martyrs of)**.

William Hartley (Bl) M. P. Oct 5
d. 1588. From Church Wilne near Derby, he was educated at St John's College, Oxford, and became an Anglican minister. After his conversion he studied for the priesthood at Rheims, was ordained there in 1580 and was hanged at Shoreditch, London. He was beatified in 1929. *See* **England (Martyrs of)**.

William of Hirsau (Bl) R(OSB). Jul 4
d. 1091. A monk at Regensburg, Bavaria, he was appointed abbot of the recently restored abbey of Hirsau in Württemberg and introduced the Cluniac observance there. He founded a monastic school, restored the scriptorium, paid attention to the spiritual and temporal well-being of the tenants and serfs of the abbey estates, supported Pope St Gregory VII against Emperor Henry IV, wrote works of scholarship and founded seven new abbeys. He was also remembered for his personal holiness. His cultus was not confirmed.

William Horne (Bl) M. R(OCart). Aug 4
d. 1540. A Carthusian lay brother of the London Charterhouse, he was executed at Tyburn with two companions. He was beatified in 1886, but his companions have not yet been. *See* **England (Martyrs of)**.

William Howard (Bl) M. L. Dec 29
1616-1680. Grandson of St Philip Howard and viscount of Stafford, he was accused of being involved in the Oates Plot and was beheaded on Tower Hill after two years' imprisonment. He was beatified in 1929. *See* **England (Martyrs of)**.

William Ireland (Iremonger)
(Bl) M. R(SJ) Jan 24
d. 1679. From Lincolnshire, he was educated at St Omer, France, became a Jesuit there in 1655 and was executed at Tyburn, London, for alleged complicity in the Oates Plot, being beatified in 1929. *See* **England (Martyrs of)**.

William Knight (Bl) M. L. Nov 29
1573-1596. From South Duffield, Yorks, he was the orphan of a yeoman farmer and was denounced for recusancy when he grew up by a relative who coveted his inheritance. While imprisoned at York he was convicted of trying to convert a renegade Anglican minister imprisoned with him and was executed with Bl William Gibson. He was beatified in 1987. *See* **England (Martyrs of)**.

William Lacey (Bl) M. P. Aug 22
d. 1582. From Horton in Ribblesdale, Yorks, he was a wealthy recusant landowner. After fourteen years of his married life his second wife died, so he went to Rheims, in France to study for the priesthood and was ordained at Rome. He worked around York and was secretly chaplain to the Catholics in York prison for two years until he was spotted, arrested and executed with Bl Richard Kirkman. He was beatified in 1886. *See* **England (Martyrs of)**.

William Lampley (Bl) M. L. (?)
d. 1588. A poor glovemaker, he was condemned at Gloucester for 'persuading to Popery' and was offered a reprieve if he attended a Protestant service. He preferred to die, and was beatified in 1987. His date of execution is unknown. *See* **England (Martyrs of)**.

William Llop Gayá (Bl) *see* **Hospitaller Martyrs of Spain**

William of Maleval (St) R. F. Feb 10
d. 1157. Apparently a French soldier, he went on pilgrimage to the Holy Land and was made superior on his return of an abbey near Pisa, Italy. Failing to maintain discipline there (as well as at a foundation of his own on Monte Bruno), he became a hermit at Maleval near Siena in 1155 and attracted disciples. This was the beginning of the monastic order of the Williamites, which made use of the Benedictine rule but was later mostly absorbed by the Augustinian friars.

William Marsden (Bl) M. P. Apr 25
d. 1586. A Lancastrian, he was educated at St Mary Hall, Oxford, studied for the priesthood at Rheims, France, and was ordained there in 1585. The following year he was executed on the Isle of Wight. He was beatified in 1929. *See* **England (Martyrs of)**.

William of Montevergine
(St) R. F. Jun 25
1085-1142. From Vercelli, Italy, after a pilgrimage to Compostela he became a hermit

on the summit of what is now Montevergine between Nola and Benevento. He attracted disciples, founded a monastery and gave it a rule based on that of St Benedict. Then he founded other monasteries and formed a new monastic congregation, which became definitively Benedictine under his successor. He died at the daughter house of Guglieto near Nusco. Only the monastery of Montevergine survives of his congregation, and this now belongs to the Subiaco Benedictines. His cultus was confined to local calendars in 1969.

William de Naurose (Bl) R(OSA). May 18
1297-1369. From Toulouse, France, he became an Augustinian friar and was famous as a home missioner specializing in preaching on purgatory. His cultus was confirmed for Toulouse in 1893.

William of Norwich *Mar 26*
d. 1144. A twelve-year-old apprentice tanner at Norwich, he was found murdered in Thorpe Wood just outside the city. Two Jews were accused of having killed him in a parody of the Crucifixion, which makes him the first case of alleged 'Jewish ritual murder'. His shrine at Norwich Cathedral (which lacked a proper saint) was popular in the Middle Ages, but his cultus was never approved. He is depicted as a boy crowned with thorns with a knife piercing his side, with wounded extremities and holding a cross and nails.

William Patenson (Bl) M. P. Jan 22
d. 1592. From Durham, he studied for the priesthood at Rheims, France, and was ordained there in 1587. He was hanged, drawn and quartered at Tyburn, London, and beatified in 1929. *See* **England (Martyrs of)**.

William of Peñacorada
(St) R(OSB). Mar 20
d. ?1042. He was a monk at the Cluniac monastery of Sahagún near León, Spain, but the community fled from Muslim raids in 988. He settled as a hermit at Peñacorada and founded a monastery later named after him.

William Pinchon (St) B. Jul 29
d. 1234. A Breton nobleman, he was a canon of Saint-Brieuc before becoming bishop there in 1220. He was exiled for a time to Poitiers by the Duke of Brittany for defending the independence of the Church. He was canonized in 1253.

William Pike (Bl) M. L. (?)
d. 1591. From Christchurch, Hants, he was a carpenter and a family man who was executed outside Dorchester for denying the Royal supremacy in spiritual matters. His date of execution is unknown. He was beatified in 1987.

William Plaza Hernández (Bl) *see* **Peter Ruiz de los Paños y Angel and Comps**

William of Pontoise (St) P. May 10
d. 1192. Apparently an English priest, he settled at Pontoise near Paris, France, and was highly regarded by King Philip Augustus. He died in the latter's palace at Pontoise. There is no proof that he was a monk.

William Repin and
Comps (BB) MM. Feb 1
d. 1793–4. The period known as the 'Terror' during the French Revolution saw an anti-Catholic pogrom in the Vendée around Angers and about 2,000 people were guillotined, burnt or beaten to death. Ninety-nine were beatified in 1983, comprising William Repin, eleven other priests, three female religious, four laymen and the rest laywomen. *See* **French Revolution (Martyrs of)**.

William Richardson
(Anderson) (Bl) M. P. Feb 17
d. 1603. From Wales near Sheffield in Yorkshire, he was educated for the priesthood at Valladolid and at Seville, where he was ordained in 1594. He was executed at Tyburn and beatified in 1929. *See* **England (Martyrs of)**.

William of Rochester (St) M. L. May 23
d. 1201. Allegedly a baker or fisherman of Perth, Scotland, he was on his way to the Holy Land when he was robbed and murdered at Rochester, Kent, by his servant. Owing to miracles being reported he became the focus of popular veneration, and his shrine was at Rochester Cathedral before the Reformation.

William of Roskilde (St) B. Sep 2
d. 1067. An Anglo-Saxon, he was chaplain to King Canute who ruled both England and Denmark and who made him bishop of Roskilde on Zealand, Denmark. He was a successful missionary, and had to resist the anti-Christian policies of King Sweyn Estridsen who succeeded Canute in Denmark,

William Saultemouche (Bl) *see* **James Sales**

William Scott *see* **Maurus Scott**

William Southerne (Bl) M. P. (Apr)
d. 1618. From Ketton near Darlington, he was ordained in Spain at Valladolid and was a priest

among the poor Catholics of Northumberland for fourteen years before being captured and executed at Newcastle. The date of his execution is uncertain. He was beatified in 1987. *See* **England (Martyrs of)**.

William Spencer (Bl) M. P. Sep 24
d. 1589. From Gisburgh, Yorks, he became a fellow of Trinity College, Oxford, but converted, went to Rheims, France, and was ordained in 1583. He was a priest at York but was seized on the road to Ripon with his guide, Bl Robert Hardesty, and was executed with him at York. He was beatified in 1987. *See* **England (Martyrs of)**.

William Thompson (Bl) M. P. Apr 20
*c*1560–1586. From Blackburn, Lancs, he was ordained in France at Douai and was a priest in London before being seized at Harrow and executed at Tyburn with Bl Richard Sergeant. He was beatified in 1987. *See* **England (Martyrs of)**.

William Tirry (Bl) M. R(OSA). Jun 20
d. 1654. An Augustinian priest, he was hanged at Clonmel in the persecution by Cromwell and was beatified in 1992. *See* **Ireland (Martyrs of)**.

William Ward (Webster)
(Bl) M. L. Jul 26
d. 1641. From Westmorland, he was educated in France at Douai and ordained there in 1608. He spent thirty-three years on the English mission (twenty of them in prison) and was executed at Tyburn, London. He was beatified in 1929. *See* **England (Martyrs of)**.

William Way (Bl) M. P. Sep 23
d. 1588. From Devon, England, he was educated for the priesthood in France at Rheims, ordained there in 1586 and executed at Kingston-on-Thames, Surrey. He was beatified in 1929. *See* **England (Martyrs of)**.

Willibald (Willebald) (St) B. R. Jul 7
*c*700–781. From Wessex, England, he was a brother of SS Winebald and Walburga and a relative of St Boniface. When aged five he became a child-oblate at the monastery of Bishop's Waltham, Hants, and in 722 went with his brother on a long journey via Rome, to the Holy Land, and to many famous monastic centres of the East and Constantinople. In 730 he settled at the newly re-founded Italian monastery of Montecassino under St Petronax for ten years, but the pope then sent him to Germany to help St Boniface. He was made bishop of Eichstätt, Germany, in 742 and founded the double abbey of Heidenheim with his brother St Winebald, making their sister St Walburga the first abbess. His shrine is at Eichstätt Cathedral. He was canonized in 938.

Willibrord (St) B. R. Nov 7
?658–739. A Northumbrian, he was educated by St Wilfrid at Ripon, England, and also spent twelve years under St Egbert of Iona in Ireland. From there he went to Friesland, Netherlands, with eleven other Anglo-Saxon monks in *c*690, and became missionary archbishop of Utrecht in 696. His work in the Low Countries (he also went on mission to Denmark and the island of Heligoland) was of lasting success in the areas ruled by the Franks. He founded the monastery of Echternach in Luxembourg in 698, where he died and where he has his shrine.

Willigis (St) B. Feb 23
d. 1011. The son of a wheelwright of Schöningen near Brunswick, Germany, he became a canon of Hildesheim and then chaplain to Emperor Otto III and chancellor of the Empire in 971. He was made archbishop of Mainz in 975 as well as papal vicar-apostolic for Germany. He campaigned for the election of Emperor St Henry II and crowned him in 1002. His attribute is a wheel, which he chose to adorn his shield in memory of his father.

Willigod and Martin (SS)
RR(OSB). Sep 28
d. ?690. Monks of Moyenmoutier, they became co-founders and successive abbots of the monastery of Romont near Fribourg, Switzerland.

Wiltrude (Bl) R(OSB). Jan 6
d. ?986. The widow of a duke of Bavaria, Germany, she founded the Benedictine nunnery of Bergen near Ingolstadt on the Danube and became its first abbess. She was famous for her skill at handicrafts.

Winaman, Unaman and
Sunaman (SS) MM. RR(OSB). Feb 15
d. *c*1040. Missionary monks from an English monastery (possibly Glastonbury), they were nephews of St Sigfrid of Växjö and accompanied him to Scandinavia. They were killed by robbers at Växjö, Sweden.

Winebald (Winnibald) of
Heidenheim (St) R. Dec 18
d. 761. Brother of SS Willibald and Walburga, he accompanied the former on his journey to the East but fell ill and remained at Rome,

where he studied for seven years. Eventually he returned to England, collected some disciples and went to Germany at the invitation of St Boniface. Later he became the superior of the monks of Heidenheim, a double monastery founded by his brother (then bishop of Eichstätt) and where his sister was abbess. There he died.

Winebald (Vinebaud) of Troyes (St) R. Apr 6
d. *c*650. At first a hermit near Noyon, France, he then joined the monastery of St Loup at Troyes and became abbot there.

Winewald (St) R. Apr 27
d. ?731. He succeeded St Bercthun as abbot of Beverley in Yorkshire, England.

Winefride (Wenefrida, Gwenfrewi, Guinevra) (St) V. Nov 3
C7th. According to her late legend she was a niece of St Beuno from Holywell, Wales, and was beheaded by a suitor near there for refusing his amorous proposal. A spring of water emerged from the spot where her head fell, and this was the alleged origin of the famous Holy Well which has been an ancient focus of pilgrimage. A gloss on the legend adds that she was restored to life by St Beuno and became abbess of Gwytherin in Clwyd. She was a real person, but historical details are obscure. Her shrine was at Shrewsbury Abbey.

Winin *see* **Finian**

Winnoc (St) R. Nov 6
d. ?717. Probably from Wales, he became a monk of Sithiu at St Omer, France, under St Bertin and was sent to become abbot-founder of the monastery at Wormhoudt near Dunkirk. He was famously devoted to manual work. The Cornish village of St Winnow probably commemorates him (see next entry).

Winnow, Mancus and Myrbad (SS) RR. May 31
C6th? They were allegedly Irish hermits living together in Cornwall, England. There is a village called St Winnow near Fowey, but this may be a corruption of Winnoc.

Winwaloe (St) R. Mar 3
C6th. From Brittany, France, he became a disciple of St Budoc and abbot-founder of Landevennec near Brest. Several Cornish churches are dedicated to him, indicating a possible connection with Cornwall (they may have received portions of his relics after the Viking invasions). He is depicted as carrying a church on his shoulders or ringing a bell, and has many variants on his name: Guengaloeus, Gwenno, Wonnow, Wynwallow, Valois.

Wiomad (Weomad, Wiomagus) (St) B. R. Nov 8
d. *c*790. Monk of St Maximinus's Abbey at Trier, Germany, he became abbot of Mettlach and bishop of Trier in *c*750.

Wiro and Comps (SS) RR. May 8
d. ?753. A Northumbrian monk, he went to the Friesland mission in the Netherlands and was made bishop of Utrecht by St Boniface in *c*741. He and his two companions, Plechelm and Odger, founded a monastery at Odiliënberg near Roermond, Netherlands, and their shrine was established there.

Wistan (St) M. L. Jun 1
d. 850. According to his legend he was a prince of Mercia, England, who was murdered by a cousin for thwarting his wish to marry Wistan's mother, the Queen Regent. He was probably killed at Wistow, Leics, rather than at Wistanstow in Shropshire, and eventually had his shrine established at Evesham Abbey.

Wistremund (St) *see* **Peter of Cordoba and Comps**

Withburga (St) R. Jul 8
d. ?743. Youngest daughter of King Anna of East Anglia, England, after her father had died in battle she became a hermit at Holkham and then a nun at her foundation at East Dereham in Norfolk. After her death the monastery of Ely mounted a raid to steal her body for their own church, where her shrine was until the Reformation. Her attribute is a doe.

Wita *see* **Candida**

Witta *see* **Albinus**

Wittikund (Bl) L. Jan 7
d. ?804. From Enger near Herford in Westphalia, Germany, as the duke of the Saxons he was a bitter enemy of the Franks and of Christianity until defeated by Charlemagne in a vicious war. It was alleged that he was then converted by a miraculous vision and baptized in 785, thereafter being zealous in propagating Christianity. He died in battle with the Suevi and had his shrine at Enger until the Reformation.

Wivina (Vivina) (St) R(OSB). Dec 17
d. 1170. A Flemish noblewoman, when aged

twenty-two she secretly left the family home and became a hermit in a wood called Grand-Bigard near Brussels, Belgium. There she founded a nunnery, affiliated it to the Benedictine abbey of Affligem and became the first abbess.

Wolfgang (St) B. R(OSB). Oct 31
924–994. From Swabia, Germany, he was educated at the abbey of Reichenau and, after being dean of the cathedral school at Trier, became a Benedictine at Einsiedeln in 964. He was headmaster of the abbey school and a missionary to the Magyars before being made bishop of Regensburg in Bavaria in 972. He restored abbeys (notably that of St Emmeram at Regensburg), improved the standard of education, reformed ecclesiastical discipline and was a great benefactor of the poor. He was canonized in 1052.

Wolfhard *see* **Gualfard**

Wolfhelm (Bl) R(OSB). Apr 22
d. 1091. A Rhinelander, he joined the Benedictine abbey of St Maximinus at Trier, Germany, transferred to St Pantaleon's Abbey at Cologne and was abbot successively of Gladbach, Siegburg and Brauweiler. He died at Brauweiler, and was described as a great biblical scholar and a lover of the monastic life. His cultus is unconfirmed.

Woolos *see* **Gwynllyw**

Wulfhad and Ruffin (SS) MM. Jul 24
? According to their legend they were two royal princes of Mercia, England, who were baptized by St Chad and killed as a result by their father the king (still a pagan) at Stone, Staffs. This story conflicts with known historical facts, and the legend was perhaps invented for two early saints venerated at Stone whose story was forgotten by the time of the Middle Ages.

Wulfhilda (St) R. Sep 9
d. *c*1000. When she was a novice at the abbey of Wilton, England, King Edgar wished to make her his mistress and tried to abduct her with the connivance of her aunt, the abbess of Wherwell. She escaped and the king relented, making her abbess of Barking, Essex, and being content with her cousin St Wulftrude instead. In 973 she was ejected and lived at Horton abbey, Dorset, until reinstated in 993.

Wulfram (St) B. R. Mar 20
C7th. From near Fontainebleau, France, he was one of the Merovingian court clergy and was made bishop of Sens in 683. In 685 he resigned, spent some time at the abbey of Fontenelle and went on mission to Friesland, Netherlands, for many years with some of the monks. He died at Fontenelle and has his shrine at Abbeville.

Wulfric (St) R. Feb 20
*c*1080-1154. A secular priest, he led a lax life before converting and becoming a hermit at Haselbury Plucknett near Crewkerne in Somerset, England. The Cistercians falsely alleged that he was affiliated to them, and the Cistercian abbot John of Ford wrote his biography.

Wulftrude (St) R. Sep 9
d. ?988. She was a nun at Wilton, England, when she became the mistress of King Edgar, giving birth to St Edith of Wilton as a result. Then she went back to being a nun and was later abbess of Wilton. She has been confused with St Wulfhilda, a cousin of hers who was also the object of King Edgar's attentions.

Wulmar (St) R. Jul 20
d. *c*700. From near Boulogne, France, he married but the couple were forcibly separated and he then became a lay brother at the abbey of Haumont in Hainault, Belgium. Initially a cowherd and wood-chopper, he was later ordained and eventually became the abbot-founder of Samer near Boulogne, afterwards called St Vulmaire after him. He also founded the nunnery at Wierre-aux-Bois. His name has many variants, e.g. Ulmar, Ulmer, Vilmarus, Volmar, Vilmer.

Wulsin (St) B. R(OSB). Jan 8
d. 1002. From London, England, he was a disciple of St Dunstan and when the latter restored Westminster Abbey he appointed him abbot in 980. In 993 he became bishop of Sherborne while remaining abbot of Westminster.

Wulstan (Wulfstan, Ulfstan, Wolstan) (St) B. R(OSB). Jan 19
?1008-1095. From Itchington, Warwickshire, England, he studied at the abbeys of Evesham and Peterborough and became a monk at the cathedral priory of Worcester where he was precentor and prior. Finally he was made bishop of Worcester in 1062, and his success was such that he was the only Anglo-Saxon bishop who was allowed to remain in place after the Norman Conquest. He rebuilt his cathedral and was the first English bishop to hold a regular visitation of his diocese. He was canonized in 1203.

Wynnin *see* **Vimin**

X, Y, Z

Xantippa and Polyxena (SS) Sep 23
C1st? The old Roman Martyrology listed them as virgins who were disciples of the Apostles but nothing is known about them.

Xavier-Aloysius Bandréz Jímenez (Bl) *see* **Philip-of-Jesus Munárriz Azcona and Comps**

Xystus *see* **Sixtus**

Ymar (St) M. R. Nov 12
d. ?830. A monk at Reculver near Herne Bay in Kent, England, he was killed in a Danish raid.

Yolanda *see* **Helen of Poland**

Yon *see* **Jonas**

Yrchard (Yarcard) (St) B. Aug 24
C5th. Allegedly from Kincardine O'Neill near Aberdeen, Scotland, he was consecrated as missionary bishop by St Ternan to share his work among the Picts.

Yrieix *see* **Aredius**

Ysarn (St) R(OSB). Sep 24
d. 1043. From near Toulouse, France, he became a Benedictine monk and then abbot of St Victor's Abbey at Marseilles. Under him the abbey became the centre of a Benedictine congregation with monasteries in southern France and Catalonia.

Ytha *see* **Ita**

Yvo *see* **Ivo**

Ywi (St) D. R. Oct 8
d. *c*690. A monk of Lindisfarne in Northumberland, England, he was a disciple of St Cuthbert. According to his legend he emigrated to Brittany, France, and died there but had his relics brought back to England *c*950, where they were enshrined at Wilton near Salisbury.

Zacchaeus (St) *see* **Alphaeus and Zacchaeus**

Zacchaeus of Jerusalem (St) B. Aug 23
d. ?116. Patristic sources list him (variantly as Zacharias) as the fourth bishop of Jerusalem.

Zacharias, Pope (St) Mar 15
d. 752. Born at San Severino in Calabria of a Greek family, he became pope in 741 and successfully negotiated a peace between the Lombards and the imperial exarchate at Ravenna. The iconoclastic policy of Emperor Constantine V led him to look to the Franks for support, however, and he permitted the coronation of Pepin. He also encouraged the German missions of St Boniface and part of their correspondence is extant.

Zacharias of Nicomedia (St) M. Jun 10
? He is listed as a martyr of Nicomedia, Asia Minor.

Zacharias the Prophet (St) Nov 5
C1st. The only available information on the father of St John the Baptist is in the first chapter of the gospel of St Luke.

Zacharias of Vienne (St) M. B. May 26
d. ?106. He was alleged to have been the second bishop of Vienne, France, and to have been martyred in the reign of Trajan.

Zama (St) B. Jan 24
d. ?268. He is the first recorded bishop of Bologna, Italy, allegedly consecrated by St Dionysius in *c*260.

Zambdas (Zabdas, Bazas) (St) B. Feb 19
d. ?304. He was allegedly a bishop of Jerusalem and features in the legend of the Theban legion.

Zanitas and Comps (SS) MM. Mar 27
d. 326. He was martyred in the reign of the Persian Shah Shapur II with Abibos, Elias, Lazarus, Mares, Marotas, Narses, Sembeeth and Sabas.

Zaragoza (Eighteen Martyrs of) (SS) Apr 16
d. ?304. They were martyred at Zaragoza, Spain, under the prefect Dacian in the reign of the emperor Diocletian. Prudentius (who lived at Zaragoza later in the century) described their martyrdom. Their names were Apodemius, Caecilian, Eventius, Felix, Fronto, Julia, Lupercus, Martial, Optatus, Primitivus, Publius, Quintilian, Successus, Urban and four named Saturninus.

Zaragoza (Innumerable Martyrs of) (SS) Nov 3
d. ?304. As well as the eighteen martyrs named by Prudentius, very many were killed at Zaragoza by the prefect Dacian who had been sent to Spain to enforce the decrees of Emperor Diocletian against Christianity. He published an edict expelling all Christians from the city, and while they were leaving he ordered the garrison to massacre them.

Zdislava Berka (St) T(OP). Jan 1
d. 1252. A Czech noblewoman born at Krizanov, she married and had four children. Her generosity to the poor was resented by her husband but she won him over by her heroic patience. She died as a Dominican tertiary in the priory of St Lawrence at Jabbone which she had founded and was canonized in 1995.

Zebinas (St) *see* **Antoninus of Caesarea and Comps**

Zebinus (St) R. Feb 23
C5th. A hermit of Cyrrhus near Antioch, Syria, he trained St Maro, St Polychronius and others in the monastic life.

Zechariah-of-the-Blessed-Sacrament Fernández Crespo (Bl) *see* **Nicephorus Díez Tejerina and Comps**

Zenais, Cyria, Valeria and Marcia (SS) MM. Jun 5
? Zenais was apparently martyred at Constantinople and was not connected with the other three, who were traditionally disciples of Christ martyred at Caesarea in the Holy Land.

Zenais and Philonilla (SS) MM. Oct 11
C1st? Their story is that they were two sisters of Tarsus related to St Paul who were stoned by pagans at Demetrias in Thessaly, Greece.

Zenas (St) *see* **Zeno and Zenas**

Zeno (St) M. Apr 5
? He was burnt alive, but it is not known where or when.

Zeno (St) *see* **Ammon, Zeno and Comps**

Zeno (St) *see* **Eudoxius, Zeno and Comps**

Zeno (St) *see* **Eusebius, Nestabus, and Zeno**

Zeno (St) *see* **Philip, Zeno and Comps**

Zeno (St) *see* **Victor, Zoticus and Comps**

Zeno (St) *see* **Vitalis, Felicula and Zeno**

Zeno and Chariton (SS) MM. Sep 3
d. 303. They were martyred somewhere in the East in the reign of Diocletian.

Zeno, Concordius and Theodore (SS) MM. Sep 2
d. 302. A father and his two sons, they were martyred at Nicomedia, Asia Minor, in the reign of Diocletian.

Zeno and Zenas (SS) MM. Jun 23
d. ?304. Their story is that Zeno was a wealthy citizen of Philadelphia near the Dead Sea who freed all his slaves and gave his property to the poor. Zenas, one of the former slaves, remained with him as a servant and both were beheaded in the reign of Diocletian.

Zeno of Gaza (St) B. Dec 26
d. ?399. He was allegedly related to the Eusebius, Nestabus and Comps who destroyed the main temple at Gaza in the Holy Land and were lynched as a result. He himself became bishop of Gaza.

Zeno of Nicomedia (St) M. Dec 22
d. 303. A soldier based at the imperial capital of Nicomedia, Asia Minor, he laughed during the offering of a sacrifice to Ceres by the emperor Diocletian. As a result his jaw was broken and he was beheaded.

Zeno of Rome and Comps (SS) MM. Jul 9
d. *c*300. He was apparently the spokesman of the Christians enslaved to work on the public baths built at Rome on the orders of the emperor Diocletian, who ordered their massacre when the project was completed. The old Roman Martyrology asserted that they numbered 10,204 (a gross exaggeration).

Zeno of Verona (St) B. Apr 12
d. 371. From Roman Africa, he was bishop of Verona, Italy, from 362 and was a fervent opponent of Arianism. He also corrected liturgical abuses and encouraged consecrated virgins living at home. His attribute is a fish.

Zenobia (St) *see* **Zenobius and Zenobia**

Zenobius (St) *see* **Lucian, Metrobius and Comps**

Zenobius (St) *see* **Tyrannio of Tyre and Comps**

Zenobius and Zenobia (SS) MM. Oct 30
d. ?285. He was allegedly bishop and physician at Aegae (now Alexandretta on the Turkish coast near Syria) and is probably identical with St Zenobius of Antioch, in which case his martyrdom took place later than the year given. Zenobia was alleged to have been his sister.

Zenobius of Antioch (St) M. P. Oct 29
d. 310. A priest and physician from Sidon, Lebanon, he was tortured with iron hooks at Antioch in the reign of Diocletian and died as a result.

Zenobius of Florence (St) B. May 25
d. ?390. He was bishop of Florence, Italy, and a friend of St Ambrose and of Pope St Damasus, by whom he was sent as papal representative to Constantinople in connection with the Arian controversy. He is sometimes depicted raising a dead child to life.

Zephyrinus, Pope *Aug 26*
d. 217. He was pope from 198 and had to contend with an adoptionist heresy disturbing the Church at Rome. His cultus was suppressed in 1969.

Zephyrinus Agostini (Bl) P. (Apr 6)
1813–1896. From Verona, Italy, he was ordained as a diocesan priest there in 1837 and was appointed to the large and poor city parish of St Nazarius, where he remained all his life. He took a special interest in the moral and material poverty of the local young women, and set up a pious society on Ursuline principles to help them. This he established as the 'Ursuline Congregation of Daughters of Mary Immacuate' in 1869. He was beatified in 1998.

Zephyrinus Giménez Malla (Bl) M. L. May 4
1861–1938. A gypsy from Fraga in Huesca, Spain, he married and became a flourishing horse-dealer at Barbastro. He was a model Christian, honest in his business dealings and charitable, and was esteemed for his wisdom despite his illiteracy. He was arrested at the start of the Civil War for defending a priest who was being attacked in the street, and was offered his freedom on condition that he stop saying the Rosary. He refused, was shot and was beatified in 1997 (the first gypsy to be honoured thus). *See* **Spanish Civil War (Martyrs of)**.

Zeticus (St) *see* **Theodulus, Saturninus and Comps**

Zhang Huailu (St) M. L. Jun 9
1843–1900. From Zhukotian in Hebei, China, he was the first of his family to become a Catholic catechumen. When a gang of Boxers visited his village the Catholics fled but he was too old and infirm to keep up and was captured. He insisted that he was a Christian and was beheaded in consequence, witnessing to his faith by his death despite not being baptized. *See* **China (Martyrs of)**.

Zimius (St) *see* **Marinus, Vimius and Zimius**

Zita (St) L. Apr 27
1218–1278. From Monsagrati near Lucca, Italy, when aged twelve she started work as a domestic servant at a household at Lucca and remained there all her life. She would give her food and clothing to the poor, and also her employer's when she had none. For this she was initially misunderstood and treated harshly, but she eventually became respected by the whole household. Her cultus was confirmed for Lucca in 1696 and she is the patron of domestic servants. Thus she is depicted in working clothes with a bag, keys, loaves or a rosary.

Zoë (St) *see* **Exuperius, Zoë and Comps**

Zoë (St) *see* **Martinian of Caesarea**

Zoë (Zoa) of Rome (St) M. Jul 5
d. ?286. She was allegedly a Roman martyr who was the wife of a high official of the imperial court, but she possibly never existed.

Zoëllus, Servilius, Felix, Silvanus and Diocles
(SS) MM. May 24
? They are listed as martyrs of Istria, which may be a mistake for Syria.

Zoerard *see* **Andrew Zoerard**

Zoilus and Comps (SS) MM. Jun 27
d. ?304. He was allegedly a young man martyred at Cordoba, Spain, in the reign of Diocletian. The Benedictine abbey of San Zoil de Carrión near León was founded to enshrine his relics, together with those of nineteen other dubious martyrs.

Zosima (St) *see* **Eutropius, Zosima and Bonosa**

Zosimus (St) R. Apr 4
C5th. He features in the story of St Mary of Egypt as a hermit who lived on the banks of the River Jordan and who discovered her in the desert before she died.

Zosimus (St) *see* **Darius, Zosimus and Comps**

Zosimus (St) *see* **Drusus, Zosimus and Theodore**

Zosimus (St) *see* **Mark, Alphius and Comps**

Zosimus (St) *see* **Rufus and Zosimus**

Zosimus and Athanasius
(SS) MM? RR? Jan 3
d. 303. One story describes them as martyrs of Cilicia, Asia Minor, in the reign of Diocletian, but another alleges that Zosimus was put to the torture and that Athanasius (a spectator) was converted and immediately tortured also, but that both survived and died in peace as hermits.

Zosimus, Pope (St) Dec 26
d. 418. A Greek, he was pope for a year and his short pontificate was marked by a high view of papal authority linked to tactlessness and personality clashes in which he seems to have been usually wrong.

Zosimus of Spoleto (St) M. Jun 19
d. 110. He was martyred at Spoleto in Umbria, Italy, in the reign of Trajan.

Zosimus of Syracuse
(St) B. R. Mar 30
*c*570–*c*660. A Sicilian, when aged seven he became a child-oblate at the monastery of St Lucia (of uncertain rite) near Syracuse. After being a monk for thirty years he became abbot and then bishop of the city.

Zosimus the Thaumaturge
(St) R. Nov 30
C6th. He was a hermit in the Holy Land, famous as a wonder-worker.

Zoticus (St) *see* **Agathonicus, Zoticus and Comps**

Zoticus (St) *see* **Dasius, Zoticus and Comps**

Zoticus (St) *see* **Tarsicius, Zoticus and Comps**

Zoticus (St) *see* **Victor, Zoticus and Comps**

Zoticus, Irenaeus, Hyacinth, Amantius and Comps
(SS) MM. Feb 10
d. 120. A group of ten soldiers, they were martyred at Rome and buried on the Via Lavicana there.

Zoticus, Rogatus, Modestus, Castulus and Comps
(SS) MM. Jan 12
? A group of between forty and fifty soldiers, they were martyred in Roman Africa.

Zoticus of Comana (St) M. B. Jul 21
d. ?204. This alleged martyr-bishop of Comana in Cappodocia, Asia Minor, was inserted into the old Roman Martyrology by Baronius, on what authority is unclear.

Zoticus of Constantinople
(St) M. P. Dec 31
d. *c*350. A Roman priest, he emigrated to Constantinople when Constantine made that city the capital of the Empire and founded a hospital for the poor and for orphans. He was allegedly tied to wild horses in the reign of the Arian emperor Constantius and dragged to death.

Zoticus of Tivoli (St) M. Jan 12
d. *c*120. This alleged martyr of Tivoli near Rome is an erroneous duplication of St Getulius.

Bibliography

Acta Apostolicae Sedis, Vatican 1884 to date. (The Church's official record of the workings of the Magisterium, including canonizations and beatifications. In Latin.)

Acta Sanctorum, 64 vv, Antwerp, 1643-. (This vast compendium of Bollandist scholarship is still valuable as a source, but is in Latin and will only be found in the greater libraries.)

Bibliotheca Sanctorum, 12 vv, Vatican 1960-70. (The latest product of Bollandist scholarship is in Italian.)

Butler's *Lives of the Saints*, 12 vv, B & O 1995-. (This classic has been thoroughly revised and contains individual biographies of saints listed by feast-day.)

Catholic University of America, *New Catholic Encyclopaedia*, 1967– with supplementary vols.

Chitty, D., *The Desert a City*, Mowbrays 1966. (The standard work on the history of the desert fathers.)

Congregatio Pro Causis Sanctorum, *Index ac Status Causarum*, Vatican 1988. (Lists of canonizations, beatifications, confirmations of cultus and processes pending.)

Cross and Livingstone, *Oxford Dictionary of the Christian Church*, Oxford 1978.

Ellwood Post, W., *Saints, Signs and Symbols*, SPCK 1964. (The best short introduction to hagiographical symbols available.)

Farmer, D. H., *The Oxford Dictionary of Saints*, Oxford 1978. (Gives alphabetical entries for *c*1000 saints known in the British Isles, each with an individual biography. Excellent, but with a few errors.)

Holweck, F. G., *A Biographical Dictionary of the Saints*, Herder 1924. (Almost eighty years old and containing many errors, this is still the only attempt at a full alphabetical listing of all saints, including those of the Eastern churches. It has been recently reprinted in the USA.)

Jedin, H. (ed), *History of the Church*, 10 vv, B&O 1962–.

Kalberer, A., *Lives of the Saints*, Franciscan Herald 1983. (A useful alternative to the Roman Martyrology for reading in religious communities.)

Lawrence, C.H., *Medieval Monasticism*, Longman 1989. (A good modern introduction to the subject for Western Europe.)

Meinardus, O., *The Saints of Greece*, Athens 1970. (Contains many post-schism Greek Orthodox saints.)

Sacra Congregatio pro Sacramentis, *Notitiae*, Vatican 1964 to date. (Official periodical including matters pertaining to liturgical veneration of saints. Has included useful biographies. In Latin.)

Roman Martyrology, B & O 1937. (This is the old Roman Martyrology as referred to in the text of this book. *See* glossary entry.)

Roman Martyrology Libreria Editrice Vaticana 2001. (Just published, in Latin. It is the definitive list of saints officially recognized by the Roman Catholic Church as a whole.)

Sayings of the Desert Fathers, Mowbray 1981. (Alphabetically listed according to name.)

The Times, *Atlas of the World*, Comprehensive Edition, 1987.

Velimirovic, N., *Prologue from Ochrid*, Lazarica 1985 (The Serbian Orthodox equivalent of Butler).

List of Websites

http://alapadre.net/
Website of Catholic interest with international listing of churches and various online resources

http://www.allaboutsaints.com/
A site with plenty of useful information about saints

http://www.archangelbooks.com/saintsquizi.htm
A quiz to test your knowledge on Catholic Saints

http://www.botsands.com/religious/christian/
A useful site with links to many Catholic topics

http://www.bridgebulding.com
Wide variety of images. Each image is accompanied by a short story about the Saint.

http://www.catholic-forum.com/saints
Patron Saints listed. Further useful information on site.

http://www.catholic-forum.com/saints/indexsnt.htm
Patron Saints index. Search facility helps you search by topic or by name. Site includes image gallery of various saints.

http://www.catholicgoldmine.com/people/saints/index.html
Explores the lives of numerous Saints.

http://www.catholic-pages.com/dir/saints.asp
Alphabetical listing of Saints. Many useful links.

http://www.catholic-pages.com/saints/
Basic questions relating to Saints are answered including 'What is a Saint' and 'How does one become a Saint?'

http://www.catholic-pages.com/dir/link.asp?ref=186
A list of saints and their symbols

http://www.catholic-pages.com/dir/link.asp?ref=21400
Explains the process of beatification and canonization

http://www.catholic-pages.com/dir/link.asp?ref=13193
Biographies of Saints canonized from 1993-1999

http://www.catholic-pages.com/dir/link.asp?ref=13762
Article written by Mgr. P.E. Hallett on the canonization of saints

http://www.catholicyouth.freeservers.com/saints/index.htm
Biographies of younger Saints

http://www.christusrex.org/
Various links to saint-related sites

http://www.cwnews.com/
The Catholic World News site. One of the features is the Saint of the Day page.

http://www.ewtn.com/
Site for EWTN, a US-based Catholic radio station providing various links to saint-related matter.

http://disciplesnow.com/catholic/index.html
Extensive Catholic-related topics are examined on this site.

http://www.domestic-church.com/
A beautifully illustrated site. Splits Saints up into seasons and includes lengthy and informative entries.

http://elvis.rowan.edu/~kilroy/JEK/home.html
Day by day listings of saints. Includes Saints' biographies and prayers.

http://festivals.com/01-01-january/patronsaint/map.cfm
A directory of Patron Saint festivals around the world

http://www.fordham.edu/halsall/sbook3.html
Internet Medieval sourcebook on saints' lives. Numerous useful links.

http://www.ixeh.net/faith/Treasure/vc-menu.html
A virtual online chapel containing various images and prayers

http://www.kbr.be/~socboll
The Bollandists' website gives a good introduction to hagiography. It has a useful bibliography and extensive links.

http://www.lifeteen.com/SaintOftheWeek.asp
Saints of the week are featured with biographical information and illustrations.

http://luckymojo.com/patronsaints.html
Patron Saints for various occupations and conditions

http://www.mcgill.pvt.k12.al.us/jerryd/cm/saints.htm
Listings of saints and many links

http://www.mcgill.pvt.k12.al.us/jerryd/cm/saints/papal.htm
Various Papal documents on Saints

http://orb.rhodes.edu/encyclop/religion/hagiography/hagindex.html
Comprehensive hagiography site

http://www.op.org/domcentral/trad/#saints
Dominican site on saints

http://www.opusdei.org/
Opus Dei is a personal prelature of the Catholic church. It was founded by Blessed Josemaria Escriva.

http://www.newadvent.org/cathen/04171a.htm
Site concentrating on the Communion of Saints

tp://www.newadvent.org/cathen/02364b.htm
Site explaining the Beatification and Canonization process

http://www.rc.net/africa/catholicafrica/saints.htm
List of African Saints

http://saints.catholic.org/stsindex.html
Alphabetical listings and resources on Saints

http://www.scborromeo.org/index.htm
A variety of images of Saints produced in different mediums

http://users.erols.com/saintpat/ss/ss-index.htm
Index of Saints compiled by St Patrick's Church, Washington D.C.

http://www.theworkofgod.org/
A well organized site listing various apparitions and biographies on Saints

http://wordbytes.org/saints/names.htm
A listing of various Saints containing useful information

Glossary

Acta
When Christians were martyred in the days of the Roman Empire their brethren in the local church often wrote down what happened in order to inform other churches. These written 'acta' survive in several cases, e.g. Polycarp, Perpetua and Felicity. Many must have been lost in later persecutions, and many were probably never written down. Later, after persecution ceased, the tendency was to provide spurious acta where genuine ones were lacking and many famous martyrs have them. These inventions vary from an embroidery on what seems actually to have happened to absurd pieces of fiction repeating stock themes. A common example of the latter is the martyr who proves invulnerable to various grotesque attempts at execution until he or she is beheaded.

Africa
In the martyrologies this refers to Roman Africa, which comprised what is now known as the Maghreb (Morocco, Algeria, Tunisia and Libya). The Church there (concerning the foundation of which absolutely nothing is known) was the first to use Latin in its liturgy. It suffered seriously in persecutions, especially during that of Diocletian, and disagreements about how to deal with apostates led to the Donatist schism. After the arrival of Islam in the C7th the African Church became extinct in circumstances which are obscure.

Apophthegmata Patrum
These are the collected sayings of the early desert fathers in Egypt. The most famous collection is the 'alphabetical' where the sayings are attributed to famous individuals, although there are also anonymous ones ordered according to subject.

Apostles
There are fourteen saints liturgically venerated as apostles: the Twelve (including St Matthias), St Paul and St Barnabas. Of these, St James the Great was martyred in NT times, St James the Less just afterwards and SS Peter, Paul, Andrew, John, Barnabas and Thomas have strong traditions associating them with certain local churches. St Matthew was an evangelist. The others (SS Philip, Bartholomew, Simon, Matthias and Jude) have left no old traditions of apostolic journeys or activity, which is probably significant since a claim to apostolic foundation was of advantage to any local church in later centuries. All five have late and conflicting traditions ascribed to them and all the apostles, except St John, are venerated as martyrs. They are usually depicted without shoes (*see* Mt 10:10) and holding books.

Assyrian Church
This is the nickname of the 'Ancient Church of the East', the descendent of the church in the pre-Muslim Persian Empire. It went out of communion with the rest of Christianity after 431 when it did not accept the Council of Ephesus, and has been pejoratively referred to as 'Nestorian'. It has its own ancient calendar of saints. The corresponding Catholic rite is the Chaldean.

Attributes
After the art of portraiture was lost in the West in the Dark Ages, representations of saints were identified either by a personal characteristic or by some object or objects associated with the saint concerned. These latter are called attributes, and are either generic (e.g. palm branches for martyrs) or specific (e.g. stones for St Stephen).

Augustinians
The Rule of St Augustine, based on two letters written by him, emerged at the start of the Middle Ages as an alternative to the Rule of St Benedict. Various different religious orders have used it, notably the Canons and Canonesses Regular (monastic) and the Augustinian Friars (apostolic). The official name of the latter is the 'Hermits of St Augustine', but this derives from their early history and not their charism.

Barefoot Saints

In much religious art, saints are represented with bare feet, often inappropriately. Usually the symbolism intended is that of heavenly status, but this is properly shown by the halo. Apostles are traditionally represented with bare feet because of the apparent prohibition of footwear expressed to them by Christ in Mt 10:10 (actually a ban on carrying a spare pair). Certain founders of apostolic congregations initially tried to imitate them, such as St Ignatius Loyola and St Paul-of-the-Cross Danei. Monks and hermits in patristic times often went barefoot as a sign of poverty, and this was imitated by the early Franciscans. Only the Poor Clares reformed by St Colette maintained the practice, however. It is to be noted that 'discalced' means 'without shoes' and not 'barefoot'. For example, the 'Discalced Carmelites' reformed by St Teresa of Jesus have worn straw sandals, as distinct from the 'Calced' Carmelites who wear shoes or boots. St Teresa disapproved of habitually going barefoot as a penitential practice; it is only so in cold weather and otherwise can become physically stimulating once the soles harden.

Beatification

By this act of the Magisterium a person is declared to be worthy of a local or particular public cultus (the latter usually being within a religious congregation). It is often an intermediate stage to canonization if this is considered of advantage to the Church as a whole. The act is permissive, not prescriptive, and is not infallible (although no beatification has ever been rescinded). In recent years the number of beatifications has been substantially in excess of canonizations, showing the Church's recognition of the value of such local venerations.

Benedictines

From 817, when the Monastic Capitulary imposed the Benedictine Rule on all monasteries of the Carolingian Empire, until the rise of the Augustinian Canons Regular in the early Middle Ages (to be followed by the various orders of friars) virtually all Western European monasticism was Benedictine. Many saints before 817 have, however, been claimed for the Order.

The traditional position is as follows: when Montecassino was destroyed in *c*570 and its monks took refuge in Rome, the Rule of St Benedict quickly took over Roman monasticism. This meant that St Gregory was a Benedictine, as were the missionaries he sent to England with St Augustine and, through them, all of Roman-rite Saxon monasticism with its saints. Further, the Benedictine rule replaced other rules in Europe as the seventh and eighth centuries progressed, so that all the monasteries were Benedictine by the time of Charlemagne.

The historical evidence is as follows: there is no evidence of a cultus of St Benedict at Rome before the C10th (except that three popes were named Benedict), and the writings of St Gregory the Great show no acquaintance with the Rule of St Benedict (the famous *Dialogue* featuring St Benedict may not have been by him). No direct evidence survives that pre-Viking Saxon monasticism was exclusively Benedictine, although much of it probably was (especially the houses associated with St Wilfrid, who claimed to have introduced the full observance of the Rule to England). Finally, rather than a process of one rule replacing another taking place, European monasticism before Charlemagne was eclectic with the tendency being for monastic customaries to make use of more than one rule. Especially popular was a conflation of the Benedictine and Columbanian rules known as the 'Mixed Rule'. The Benedictine rule gradually came to dominate, but the process was not complete by 817 as several abbeys resisted the imposition of the full rule even then.

Calced *see* **Barefoot Saints**

Calendar (Revision of)

The general liturgical calendar of the Latin rite was thoroughly revised in 1969, and it is well known that several saints of ancient veneration (mostly martyrs of the Roman Empire) had their cultus suppressed then. This was not primarily a judgment on their existence, as is often alleged, although many of them are historically dubious and this was a factor in the suppression. Rather, the Church had decided that their veneration was no longer of any advantage, especially since the old calendar had been rather cluttered with the feast-days of saints (especially of obscure martyrs).

The Eastern rites have their own calendars in which many of these saints are still venerated. Other saints in the former general calendar had their veneration restricted to local or particular calendars at the same time. The cultus of Simon of Trent was unusual in being suppressed because of scandal.

Canons

These are priests who live a life in common. They can be secular (e.g. cathedral canons) or regular (e.g. Augustinians or Premon- stratensians).

Canonization

By this act of the Magisterium a person is declared to be a saint and worthy of a cultus in the Church as a whole. The act is prescriptive, in that the cultus is mandatory. It is infallible, in that the person is declared without possibility of error to be in heaven and to be worthy of veneration. Such an act cannot be rescinded and a saint cannot be unmade.

Carmelites
This religious order was founded in the early C13th when the Latin-rite hermits on Mount Carmel were organized under a rule. Originally the order claimed the prophet Elijah as its historical founder, and several Biblical characters and early saints were claimed as Carmelites (e.g. St Cyril of Alexandria). This fiction was strenuously defended up to the C19th. The order was divided in 1580 and the Discalced Carmelite saints after then are separately noted.

Catacomb Saints
The necessity to build new churches to match the growth in world population in the C19th, especially in America, led to an increased demand for relics of saints to place under their altars. The catacombs in Rome, where Christians had been buried during the era of the Roman Empire, were considered to be a suitable source of these. This was so because it was thought that the graves of martyrs could be easily identified, for example by a burial being accompanied by a small glass bottle. Such confidence was misplaced, and 'St' Philomena is only the most notorious of the doubtful relics of martyrs which were excavated from the catacombs before the necessary archaeological knowledge was available to make a proper judgment of them.

Catholicos
Originally, this was a bishop of territorial jurisdiction subordinate to a patriarch (q.v.). The title was taken by the heads of the churches of Georgia and Armenia, and by a historical quirk the latter now has two independent catholicates of Etchmiadzin and Sis with three subordinate patriarchates at Constantinople, Jerusalem and Aghtamar (extinct).

Child-Oblate
It was an early tradition in Western monasticism (one accepted by St Benedict) to allow parents of young children to give their children to monasteries to be brought up as monks or nuns. Initially such a donation was regarded as being binding on the child as if the latter had taken vows, but the problems caused by oblates without vocations later led the Church to condemn this insistence as an abuse and to require the oblate to make a free choice of monastic life on reaching the age of discretion. This was done by a papal decretal of 1198.

Cistercians
They started out as a Benedictine reform movement but became a separate monastic order. In the Middle Ages several saintly churchmen retired to Cistercian monasteries to die, and claims that they became Cistercian monks need to be treated with caution. After many tribulations two separate orders were established in 1892, the Common Observance and the Strict Observance ('Trappists'), and saints and blesseds belonging to the latter are separately noted.

Confessor
In the old Roman Martyrology all male saints are listed either as martyrs or confessors. This latter category (so wide now as to be useless) derived from the latter persecutions of the Roman Empire when those Christians who witnessed for their faith and suffered for it, but were not killed, were given great honour and accepted as equal to the martyrs so that they were listed in the martyrologies when they died.

Confirmation
An ancient local cultus (one claimed to date from before the reservation of the process of canonization to the Holy See) can be presented to the Magisterium for confirmation. This usually involves confirmation of beatification but sometimes of canonization. There are many local venerations which have not been so confirmed and these are tolerated, but cannot be regarded as approved by the Church and (in principle) are liable to suppression by the local Ordinary.

Cultus
This is the public liturgical veneration paid to saints and to those beatified (and has been rendered as 'cult' in English, although that now means something more pejorative). The latter is confined to local churches and congregations. It may be noted that 'veneration' is quite distinct from 'worship', which is something paid to God alone.

Desert Fathers
This is the generic term for the first hermit-monks in Egypt, as distinct from the cenobites founded by St Pachomius. The first of them was traditionally St Anthony, and the two great monastic centres were at Nitria on the edge of the Nile Delta (being near Alexandria, it was influenced by Greek thought and culture) and at Scetis, now known as the Wadi Natrun (this

was, and is, the stronghold of native Coptic monasticism). Their importance in the early development of monastic theory and practice cannot be exaggerated, although the greatest systematizer of their doctrine on prayer, Evagrius Ponticus of Nitria, fell into disfavour because of his Origenist speculations.

Dies Natalis *see* **Feast Day**

Discalced *see* **Barefoot Saints**

Doctors
Those pastors of the Church whose writings are especially important in the elucidation of the deposit of faith have been formally declared to be doctors (with the original meaning of 'teachers'). They can be of either sex. Such a declaration can be the equivalent of canonization if the person concerned was a blessed, for example St Albert the Great was equivalently canonized when declared a doctor in 1931. The teaching in good faith of doctrines later condemned can prevent a Church father being declared a doctor, for example certain Origenist ideas that St Gregory of Nyssa accepted.

The following are the doctors of the Church: Albert the Great, Alphonsus-Mary Liguori, Ambrose of Milan, Anselm of Canterbury, Anthony of Padua, Athanasius of Alexandria, Augustine of Hippo, Basil the Great, Bede the Venerable, Bernard of Clairvaux, Bonaventure, Catherine of Siena, Cyril of Alexandria, Cyril of Jerusalem, Ephraem the Syrian, Francis de Sales, Gregory I, Pope 'the Great', Gregory of Nazianzen, Hilary of Poitiers, Isidore of Seville, Jerome, John Chrysostom, John Damascene, John-of-the-Cross de Yepes, Laurence of Brindisi, Leo I Pope 'the Great', Peter Canisius, Peter Chrysologus, Peter Damian, Robert Bellarmine, Teresa-of-Jesus Cepeda de Ahumada, Teresa-of-the-Child-Jesus Martin and Thomas Aquinas.

Eastern Churches *see* **Assyrians, Oriental Orthodox, Orthodox**

Eastern Rites
The Latin rite is only one of nineteen rites of the Roman Catholic Church which are of equal dignity. Each of these has its own calendar. Most of them, apart from the Latin and the Maronite, are descended from Eastern churches out of communion with Rome and derive their calendars from them.

Enclosure
This is the part of a monastery which is closed to persons of the opposite sex. For some nunneries, the nuns are not allowed to leave this area except in an emergency.

Evangelists
These are the four authors of the Gospels: Matthew, Mark, Luke and John. Mark and Luke are not apostles but are given the same liturgical veneration.

Feast Day
Originally all saints were liturgically commemorated on the anniversaries of their deaths (each of these being referred to as the 'dies natalis' or 'birthday' into heaven). They are still listed under these in martyrologies. However, the inconvenience of having saints' days clashing with more important feasts or with penitential seasons such as Lent led to many feast days being transferred, sometimes to the nearest suitable day and sometimes to another date significant to the saint (e.g. anniversary of ordination or of transfer of relics).

Franciscans
The heroic charism of St Francis of Assisi has called for repeated revitalization among his followers throughout their history. In 1517 the Franciscan order split into Conventuals and Observants, and the Capuchins were founded in 1525. The Observants themselves split into various reform movements until they were finally reunited as the Friars Minor in 1897. Thus there are three male Franciscan orders today. The Conventuals after 1517 and the Capuchins are noted separately. The Franciscan nuns are usually known as 'Poor Clares', and there are many tertiary congregations.

Friar
This is a male religious whose vows are to a religious institute, rather than to a monastery as in the case of a monk. He does not have to be a priest.

General Calendar
This is the liturgical calendar for the Roman Catholic Church of the Latin Rite as a whole, ignoring local differences. It used to be known as the 'Universal Calendar'.

Gothic Revival
During the C19th it was fashionable to imitate medieval forms in church buildings and furnishings, and this activity has left many artistic representations of saints. These need to be regarded with caution, however. Some of the proponents of romantic medievalism had an uncritical attitude to medieval devotions and sought to revitalize the extinct veneration of dubious and unauthorized local saints (*see* Kenelm, Thomas Hales of Dover). Further, it was sometimes pretended that a medieval per-

son was a saint when there had never been any sort of veneration in the first place (*see* Bertha).

Halo
This was originally meant to be the nimbus surrounding a holy person, and became stylized into the circular region round the head in iconography. When perspective was re-discovered in the West artists had difficulty with halos and they tended to mutate into pie-pans and the horizontal rings familiar in cartoon imagery.

Hermit
This is a consecrated religious living in solitude, sometimes referred to as an anchorite or a solitary. For some reason the word has not been used in the past for women, who have been generally referred to as anchoresses.

Incorruptibility
From early days the refusal of a person's corpse to decay has been taken as an indication of that person's sanctity. This still tends to be the case in the Eastern churches, especially if a sweet odour is noticed. Forensic medicine has, however, noted many cases where incorruption has occurred naturally, and this is especially associated with the condition known as adipocere in which the body's fat turns to wax. Thus no conclusive importance is nowadays attached to the condition of the body of a candidate for canonization in the West.

Islam
Apart from certain civic disabilities, Shahira law actually forbids the active persecution of its Christian subjects by a Muslim government. Apart from those killed by corrupt and vicious Muslim rulers, martyrs under Islam mostly fall into two categories proscribed by this law. Publicly speaking against Islam ('blasphemy') and converting from Islam to Christianity ('apostasy') are both punishable by death, and in the latter case includes those considered to be Muslim because their fathers were.

Jewish Ritual Murders
There are at least thirteen cases in western Europe of children venerated as martyrs who were allegedly killed by Jews out of hatred for Christianity, in several cases in a parody of the Crucifixion on Good Friday. These allegations form part of the notorious 'Blood Libel' which has been a major feature of anti-semitism, and it is certain that the liturgical veneration was an expression of such prejudice in most or all cases. It is possible that black magic involving human sacrifice lay behind some of the events. Only one of them, Simon of Trent, was canonized (his cultus was suppressed in 1965) but Andrew of Rinn, Christopher of Guardia and Laurentinus Sossius also had their veneration as beati confirmed.

Liturgical Categories
The liturgical celebration of saints in the Latin rite has always maintained an extremely conservative categorization, basically continuing that which pertained at the end of the Roman Empire. This categorization in the old Roman Martyrology is quite different for the two sexes. 'Martyrs' are of either sex, but other men are 'confessors' whereas women are 'virgins', 'widows' or 'matrons' according to their marital status at death. It may be noted that there is no separate category for consecrated religious.

Martyr
In the early Church, the only saints venerated were martyrs. The requirement for being one was to have been killed out of hatred for the faith, and this condition used to be strictly applied (and distinguished from political motivations). In the early Middle Ages, however, many saints were accepted as martyrs who did not fit this condition (perhaps because there were few genuine martyrs in that period). There were those who chose the injustice of being killed rather than acquiesce in an injustice being done to others (*see* Alphege, Boris and Gleb). Others were ecclesiastical personages who were killed in the course of robbery (*see* Boniface).

Starting with the canonization of St Maximilian Kolbe in 1982, the condition has been relaxed to include Catholics killed (or whose deaths were expedited) as a result of systematic denial of the moral status of the human individual by totalitarian governments.

Martyr Movement of Cordoba
During the C9th most of Spain was ruled by the Ummayad Arab emirate of Cordoba. Among Christian monastic circles in and around the capital arose the idea that it would be virtuous to seek martyrdom by publicly preaching against Islam, and several achieved that fate by doing so in the reign of Abderrahman II. These were (and are) locally venerated as martyrs. It may be noted that they did not die in the context of any persecution of the Church by the Muslim government, nor were they necessarily executed out of hatred of Christianity. *See* **Islam**.

Matron
This is the category into which the old Roman Martyrology put married non-martyr women

saints whose husbands were still alive when they died. There are not many of them.

Mental Illness
The traditional, and nowadays offensive, stigma attached to mental illness has caused a lack of proper attention to be paid to its occurrence among saints. Hagiographical works have tended either to ignore manifestations of mental illness among saints or to try to explain them away. On the other hand, polemical works by writers hostile to the veneration of saints have emphasized such manifestations as being a reproach. Neither approach is fitting. It is clear that many saints, for example St Margaret-Mary Alacoque and St Rose Flores of Lima, were seriously mentally ill. However this is no bar to sanctity, and may even be a means to it, as long as the subject has the capacity for moral behaviour presumed in the practice of heroic virtue.

Miracles
The process of canonization requires two miracles for confirmation, one before beatification and one before final canonization. These are usually (although not necessarily) ones of healing, and a process can be halted indefinitely for lack of them. They are not necessary in cases of martyrs. Unlike the Eastern churches the Catholic church does not accept miracles as sole proof of sanctity. It did so in past ages, until the scandals caused by 'miracles' occurring at the shrines of wholly unsuitable people (e.g. King Edward II of England).

Monk
This is a consecrated male religious who lives a community life in a monastery and who makes a vow of stability thereto. He does not have to be a priest, although for much of the Church's history most have been.

Nun
This is a consecrated female religious who lives a community life in a monastery (a nunnery) and who makes a vow of stability thereto. Active female religious, whose stability is in the congregation, are called 'sisters'.

Oblates *see* **Tertiaries** or **Child-Oblates**

Old Testament
Apart from litanies, the Latin rite does not liturgically venerate any of the people featured in the Old Testament except for the archangels Michael, Gabriel and Raphael. The old Roman Martyrology lists several of the more famous figures, but these are not included in this book so as to avoid involvement in questions of biblical exegesis (those interested are advised to refer to an encyclopaedia of the Bible).

Oriental Orthodox
These are the Eastern churches which refused to accept the Council of Chalcedon in 451 and have hence been called Monophysite. They are the Coptic, Syrian and Armenian churches. Apart from the Orthodox Syrian Church, recently established in India, each has its own ancient calendar of saints.

Origen
This Egyptian genius was head of the Alexandrian catechetical school in the C3rd and was the greatest biblical exegete of the patristic era if not of all time. His influence on subsequent church fathers was profound, but he was condemned posthumously because his theological speculations proved incompatible with Christianity and most of his vast opus has been lost.

Orthodox
These are the Eastern churches which went out of communion with Rome after 1056. There are generally accepted to be fifteen of them, each of which has its own calendar and can canonize its own saints. In theory at least, all the Orthodox churches accept each others' saints as well as those Western saints before the acceptance of the 'Filioque' into the Latin Creed (at different times in different places). The ancient calendars of saints are the Byzantine from Constantinople, the Russian, the Serbian and the Georgian. The rest are derivative.

Patriarch
By ancient tradition this is the title given to the bishops of the four great cities of the Roman Empire, namely Rome, Constantinople, Alexandria and Antioch. It implies territorial jurisdiction over a wide area. Jerusalem became a patriarchate also in 451. After the schism between Rome and the Eastern churches, Latin-rite patriarchates were set up for the four latter cities but only Jerusalem survives. As churches of various **Eastern Rites** (q.v.) were set up in communion with Rome, some became patriarchates, and so also did many independent national Orthodox churches such as the Russian. There are patriarchates in the Western church at Lisbon, Venice and Goa but for these the title is an empty honorific.

Patrons
Local churches and settlements have always had their own patron saints. Since the Middle Ages many trades, crafts and states of life have also had

their own patrons. The Church can declare a saint or a blessed to be a patron of any such, and for a blessed this is equivalent to canonization (e.g. 'Fra Angelico' or John Faesulanus was declared patron of artists in 1984 while still a beatus).

Persecutions

From AD100, when it broke from Judaism, until the edict of toleration in 313, Christianity was a proscribed religion in the Roman Empire. There was little attempt at any central co-ordination of persecution early on, however, when local pogroms could alternate with periods of toleration. The emperor Decius attempted to eliminate Christianity from the Empire in 250, but his reign ended before any lasting damage was done. The major persecution was by Diocletian, whose re-ordering of the social and economic structures of Empire had no place for Christianity and who ordered a determined campaign of extirpation from 303. This lasted longer in some places than in others, until 313. Then there was a vicious series of persecutions in the Persian Empire until the mid C5th.

Active persecutions of Catholic Christianity by hostile governments wanting to destroy it have, since then, mostly been a feature of the post-medieval world. These have led to mass beatifications and canonizations for Imperial China, England and Wales, Revolutionary France, Republican Spain, Ireland, Japan, the kingdom of Korea, revolutionary Mexico, Buganda in Uganda and the kingdom of Vietnam.

Notable recent persecutions awaiting such recognition have been in the Stalinist Soviet Union, Khmer-Rouge Cambodia, North Korea, Communist Albania and Equatorial Guinea (especially barbaric).

Process of Canonization

This seems to be extremely complex, but is fairly straightforward in outline. A local church or religious congregation proposes to the Magisterium at Rome that a person is fit to be canonized (or only beatified, if the cultus sought is local).

The first stage is the discernment as to whether the person was either martyred in hatred of the faith or lived the Christian virtues in a heroic manner. If so, then he or she is declared 'Venerable'.

Subsequent is an extremely painstaking investigation into the person's life, writings, reported sayings and actions, and all possible objections are entertained. For a non-martyr a verified miracle is also required before beatification. After beatification the investigation is repeated and another miracle required before canonization. The process can be aborted by unauthorized public veneration taking place.

In 1983 the process was reformed so as to make it less legalistic, quicker, cheaper and more scholarly (among other changes, the office of the so-called 'devil's advocate' was abolished).

Reformation

None of the various communions arising as a result of the Protestant Reformation has maintained the ability to canonize its own saints.

Relics

These are what remains of a saint, basically the body or bits of it. 'Second-class relics' are things (usually bits of cloth) which have touched these. *See* **Incorruptibility**.

Religious (Consecrated)

Apart from the martyr, the most common type of saint is the consecrated religious (monk, friar, nun, sister, hermit) nowadays defined as one making vows of poverty, chastity and obedience. Surprisingly, they are not liturgically venerated as such. Males are 'confessors' while females are either 'widows', 'matrons', or 'virgins' if previously unmarried.

Religious Institutes

In the Eastern churches the tradition has been that consecrated religious are regarded as either hermits or cenobitic monks and nuns without any further categorization arising from different charisms and types of work undertaken. This state of affairs also obtained in the Western church until the onset of the Middle Ages, and no attempt is made in this book to categorize saints who were consecrated religious before 817 (when the Benedictine rule was imposed on the monasteries of the Carolingian Empire). In the late C11th there began a proliferation of different institutes mostly arising either from the wish to reform a form of religious life already existing or to create new institutes in response to perceived needs, usually apostolic. The older-established institutes, with a greater number of saints, are noted in the entries. One unfortunate past result of the pluralism has been a certain competitiveness as institutes claimed various saints as having belonged to them, with resulting distortions in the historical witness and some outright forgery. Institutes can be called 'orders', 'congregations' or 'societies' according to the descending gravity of obligation formerly incurred in their vows.

Roman Martyrology
A martyrology is a list of saints (initially only martyrs) in feast-day order, and the Roman Martyrology is the official list of all the saints recognized as such by the Roman Catholic Church of the Latin rite. Attempts at a historical listing of saints date back to St Bede and were initially apparently conscientious. However, St Ado of Vienne in 865 drew up a martyrology which he claimed was based on an ancient Roman one but which was forged by him and which contained many grave errors. This was utilized in the martyrology of Usuard, which was used by the Roman church until 1584. Then a new martyrology (unfortunately still containing errors, but a creditable attempt at historical accuracy for the time) was published (and amended by Cardinal Baronius in 1586), and this was the Roman Martyrology for the next 417 years. It was revised several times, lastly in 1924 but never thoroughly, and became obsolete when the church's calendar was revised in 1969. The new edition was finally published in October 2001.

Scots
Many saints of the Dark Ages and early Middle Ages are described as 'Scoti' in the contemporary records. This term is applied to the Celtic people of Northern Ireland and south-west Scotland. It is thus equivocal, meaning either Irish or Scottish, and it is often not now possible to discern which country is meant.

Sister
This is a female consecrated religious whose vows are to a religious institute with no fixed geographical location. In this she contrasts with a nun who is established at one place, in her monastery.

Sub-deacon
This used to be a clerical rank below that of deacon before its suppression in the Latin rite after the Second Vatican Council. There are very few saints who were sub-deacons only.

Tertiaries
These are people associated with monasteries or religious congregations by virtue of a promise of self or by temporary vows where no permanent vows are intended. They are not consecrated religious but usually live in the world while intending to share in the graces and to practise the particular virtues of the congregation concerned. In the past many congregations of sisters were tertiaries so as to avoid the necessity of the monastic enclosure and physical virginity which used to be required of female religious. They are also known as 'oblates'.

Translation
An obsolescent term concerning relics, meaning a transfer.

Venerable
This is the first stage in the process of canonization. It is when a person is declared either to have been martyred in hatred of the faith or to have practised the Christian virtues to a heroic degree. Private individuals can ask the intercession of any such, but public veneration is not permitted (and would abort the process).

Virgin
The consecrated virgin has an ancient history in the Roman church, and was a woman who chose and vowed to remain unmarried for love of God. The ceremony of receiving the veil on making such a vow existed by the C4th, paralleling the veiling of the bride in the contemporary rite of marriage. Such virgins either lived with relatives or together in communities and in the latter case the evolution to consecrated religious life as nowadays understood was straightforward, especially after Egyptian monachism became known in Rome in the C4th. The two states are not nowadays equivalent, however. Consecrated religious life requires three vows: poverty, chastity (not necessarily virginity) and obedience. Consecrated virginity merely requires a vow of chastity while in a state of virginity. Traditionally all unmarried women saints, including consecrated religious, have been liturgically celebrated as virgins.

Virgin Martyr
Some very popular Roman women martyrs are also venerated as virgins, especially if their wish to remain virgins had something to do with their martyrdom (*see* Agnes). In this category are included virgins who have resisted attempted rape at the cost of their lives, even if no vow of virginity was previously made (*see* Mary Goretti), and several such have been recently beatified. Suicide to avoid rape is, however, impermissible.

Widow
This is one of the three categories into which non-martyr women saints are put in the old Roman Martyrology.

Lists of National Martyrs

CANARY ISLANDS

Ignatius de Azevedo and Comps

Alexis Delgado
Alphonsus de Vaena
Alvarez Mendez
Anthony Correa
Anthony Fernandez
Anthony Suarez
Aymarus Vaz
Benedict de Castro
Caspar Alvarez
Diego Andrade
Diego Pérez
Dominic Fernandez
Emmanuel Alvarez
Emmanuel Fernández
Emmanuel Pacheco
Emmanuel Rodríguez
Ferdinand Sanchez
Francis Alvarez
Francis Magellanes
Francis Perez Godoy
Gregory Escrivano
Gundisalvus Hendriquez
Ignatius de Azevedo
James Andrade
Joanninus de San Juan
John de Baeza
John Fernandez of Braga
John Fernandez of Lisbon
John de Mavorga
John de San Martin
John de Zafra
Louis Correa
Mark Caldeira
Nicholas Dinnis
Peter Nuñez
Peter Fontura
Simon Acosta
Simon López
Stephen de Zudaira
(plus one other)

CHINA

Saints (121)

Agatha Lin (Zhao)	14/12/1857
Agnes Cao (Guiying)	25/01/1856
Alberic Crescitelli	21/07/1900
Aloysius Versiglia	25/02/1930
Andrew Bauer	09/07/1900
Andrew Wang (Tiangqing)	22/07/1900
Anne An (Jiao)	11/07/1900
Anne An (Xin)	11/07/1900
Anne Wang	22/07/1900
Anthony Fantosati	07/07/1900
Augustine Zhao Rong	00/00/1815
Augustus Chapdelaine	26/02/1856
Barbara Cui (Lian)	19/07/1900
Caesidius Giacomantonio	04/07/1900
Callistus Caravario	25/02/1930
Chi Zhuzi	??/07/1900
Elias Facchini	09/07/1900
Elizabeth Qin (Bian)	19/07/1900
Francis-Ferdinand de Capillas	15/01/1648
Francis Diaz del Rincón	28/10/1748
Francis Fogolla	09/07/1900
Francis Regis Clet	18/02/1820
Francis Serrano Frias	28/10/1748
Francis Zhang (Rong)	09/07/1900
Gabriel-John Taurin Dufresse	14/10/1815
Gregory Grassi	09/07/1900
Ignatius Mangin	20/07/1900
James Zhao (Quanxin)	09/07/1900
James Yan (Guodong)	09/07/1900
Jerome Lu (Tingmei)	14/12/1857
Joachim Hao (Kaizhi)	29/05/1839
Joachim Royo Péréz	28/10/1748
John Alcober Figuera	28/10/1748
John Chen (Xianheng)	18/02/1862
John Lantrua of Triora	07/02/1816
John-Baptist Luo (Tingying)	29/07/1861
John-Peter Néel	18/02/1862
John-Gabriel Perboyre	11/10/1840
John Wang (Guiju)	13/07/1900
John Wang (Rui)	09/07/1900

John-Baptist Wu (Mantang)	29/06/1900
John Wu (Wenyin)	05/07/1900
John Zhang (Huan)	09/07/1900
John Zhang (Jingguang)	09/07/1900
John Zhang (Tianshen)	18/02/1862
John-Baptist Zhao (Mingxi)	03/07/1900
John-Baptist Zhu (Wurui)	18/08/1900
Joseph Zhang (Wenlan)	29/07/1861
Joseph Gambaro	07/07/1900
Joseph Ma (Taishun)	??/07/1900
Joseph Wang (Guixin)	13/07/1900
Joseph Wang (Yumei)	21/07/1900
Joseph Yuan (Gengyin)	??/07/1900
Joseph Yuan (Zaide)	09/05/1817
Joseph Zhang (Dapeng)	02/02/1815
Lang Yang	00/07/1900
Laurence Bai (Xiaoman)	25/02/1856
Laurence Wang (Bing)	14/12/1857
Lucy Wang (Cheng)	28/06/1900
Lucy Wang (Wang)	22/07/1900
Lucy Yi (Zhenmei)	19/02/1862
Mark Ji (Tianxiang)	08/07/1900
Martha Wang (Luomande)	29/07/1861
Martin Wu (Xuesheng)	18/02/1862
Mary An (Guo)	11/07/1900
Mary An (Linghua)	11/07/1900
Mary Chi (Yu)	28/06/1900
Mary-Adolphine Dierkx	09/07/1900
Mary Du (Zhao)	??/07/1900
Mary-Magdalen Du (Fengju)	29/06/1900
Mary Du (Tian)	29/06/1900
Mary Fan (Kun)	28/06/1900
Mary Fu (Guilin)	21/06/1900
Mary-of-Peace Giuliani	09/07/1900
Mary-Hermina-of-Jesus Grivo	09/07/1900
Mary-Amandina Jeuris	09/07/1900
Mary-of-the-Holy-Birth Kerguin	09/07/1900
Mary Guo (Li)	07/07/1900
Mary-of-St-Justus Moreau	09/07/1900
Mary-Clare Nanetti	09/07/1900
Mary Wang (Li)	??/07/1900
Mary Zhao	28/07/1900
Mary Zhao (Guo)	28/07/1900
Mary Zheng (Xu)	28/06/1900
Mary Zhu (Wu)	20/07/1900
Matthew Feng (De)	09/07/1900
Modestus Andlauer	19/07/1900
Patrick Dong (Bodi)	09/07/1900
Paul Chen (Changpin)	29/07/1861
Paul Denn	20/07/1900
Paul Ge (Tingzhu)	08/08/1900
Paul Lang (Fu)	00/07/1900
Paul Liu (Jinde)	13/07/1900
Paul Liu (Hanzhuo)	21/02/1819
Paul Wu (Anju)	29/06/1900
Paul Wu (Wanshu)	29/06/1900
Peter Li (Quanhui)	30/06/1900
Peter Liu (Wenyuan)	17/05/1834
Peter Liu (Zeyu)	17/07/1900
Peter Sanz i Jordá	26/05/1747
Peter Wang (Erman)	09/07/1900
Peter Wang (Zuolung)	07/06/1900
Peter Wu (Gosheng)	07/11/1814
Peter Wu (Anbang)	09/07/1900
Peter Zhang (Banniu)	09/07/1900
Philip Zhang (Zhihe)	09/07/1900
Peter Zhao (Mingzhen)	03/07/1900
Peter Zhu (Rixin)	20/07/1900
Raymund Li (Quanzhen)	30/06/1900
Remigius Isoré	20/07/1900
Rose Chen (Anjie)	05/07/1900
Rose Fan (Hui)	00/07/1900
Rose Zhao (Guo)	28/07/1900
Simon Chen (Ximan)	09/07/1900
Simon Qin (Qunfu)	19/07/1900
Teresa Chen (Jinjie)	05/07/1900
Teresa Zhang (He)	16/07/1900
Thaddeus Liu (Ruiting)	30/11/1823
Theodoric Balat	09/07/1900
Thomas Shen (Jihe)	09/07/1900
Zhang Huailu	00/07/1900

ENGLAND

Saints (38)

Alban Bartholomew Roe	31/01/1642
Alexander Briant	01/12/1581
Ambrose Edward Barlow	10/09/1641
Anne Line	27/02/1601
Augustine Webster	04/05/1535
Cuthbert Mayne	30/11/1577
Edmund Campion	01/12/1581
Edmund Arrowsmith	28/08/1628
Edmund Gennings	10/12/1591
Eustace White	10/12/1591
Henry Walpole	07/04/1595
Henry Morse	01/02/1645
Joachim Wall	22/08/1679
John Almond	05/12/1612
John Boste	24/07/1594
John Fisher	22/06/1535
John Houghton	04/05/1535
John Jones	12/07/1598
John Kemble	22/08/1679
John Payne	02/04/1582
John Plessington	19/07/1679
John Rigby	21/06/1600
John Roberts	10/12/1610
John Southworth	28/06/1654
John Stone	??/12/1539
Luke Kirby	30/05/1582
Margaret Clitherow	25/03/1586
Margaret Ward	30/08/1588
Nicholas Owen	02/03/1606

Philip Howard	19/10/1595
Polydore Plasden	10/12/1591
Ralph Sherwin	01/12/1581
Richard Reynolds (1)	04/05/1535
Robert Lawrence	04/05/1535
Robert Southwell	21/02/1595
Swithin Wells	10/12/1591
Thomas Garnet	23/06/1608
Thomas More	22/06/1535

Beati (240)

* *These were beatified in 1987.*

Adrian Fortescue	09/07/1539
Alexander Blake	04/03/1590 *
Alexander Crow	30/11/1586 *
Alexander Rawlins	07/04/1595
Anthony Middleton	06/05/1590
Anthony Page	20/04/1593 *
Anthony Turner	20/06/1679
Arthur Bell	11/12/1643 *
Brian Lacey	10/12/1591
Christopher Bales	04/03/1590
Christopher Buxton	01/10/1588
Christopher Robinson	??/03/1597 *
Christopher Wharton	28/03/1600 *
David Gonson	12/07/1541
Edmund Duke	27/05/1590 *
Edmund Sykes	23/03/1588 *
Edward Bamber	07/08/1646 *
Edward Burden	29/11/1588 *
Edward Campion	01/10/1588
Edward Catherick	13/04/1642
Edward Coleman	03/12/1678
Edward Fulthrop	04/07/1597
Edward James	01/10/1588
Edward Jones	06/05/1590
Edward Oldcorne	07/04/1606
Edward Osbaldeston	16/11/1594 *
Edward Powell	30/06/1540
Edward Shelley	30/08/1588
Edward Stransham	21/01/1586
Edward Thwing	26/07/1600 *
Edward Waterson	08/01/1593
Everard Hanse	31/07/1581
Francis Dickenson	30/04/1590
Francis Ingleby	03/06/1586 *
Francis Page	20/04/1602
George Beesley	01/07/1591 *
George Douglas	09/09/1587 *
George Errington	29/11/1596 *
George Gervase	11/04/1608
George Haydock	12/02/1584 *
George Napper	09/11/1610
George Nichols	05/07/1589 *
George Swallowell	26/07/1594
Henry Abbot	04/07/1597
Henry Heath	17/04/1643 *
Henry Webley	28/08/1588 *
Hugh Faringdon	15/11/1539
Hugh Green	19/08/1642
Hugh More	28/08/1588
Hugh Taylor	26/11/1585 *
Humphrey Middlemore	19/06/1535
Humphrey Pritchard	05/07/1589 *
James Bell	10/04/1584
James Bird	25/03/1593
James Claxton	28/08/1588
James Duckett	19/04/1602
James Fenn	12/02/1584
James Thompson	28/11/1582
James Walworth	11/05/1537
Jermyn Gardiner	07/03/1544
John Adams	08/10/1586 *
John Amias	15/03/ 1589
John Beche	01/12/1539
John Bodey	02/11/1583
John Bretton	01/04/1598 *
John Carey	04/07/1594
John Cornelius	04/07/1594
John Davy	08/06/1537
John Duckett	07/09/1644
John Eynon	15/11/1539
John Felton	08/08/1570
John Fenwick	20/06/1679
John Finch	10/04/1584
John Fingley	08/08/1586 *
John Forest	22/05/1538
John Gavan	20/06/1679
John Grove	24/01/1679
John Haile	04/05/1535
John Hambley	??/03/1587 *
John Hewett	05/10/1588
John Hogg	27/03/1590 *
John Holiday	27/05/1590 *
John Houghton	04/05/1535
John Ingram	26/07/1594
John Ireland	07/03/1544
John Larke	07/03/1544
John Lockwood	13/04/1642
John Love	08/10/1586 *
John Mason	10/12/1591
John Munden	12/02/1584
John Nelson	03/02/1578
John Norton	08/09/1600 *
John Nutter	12/02/1584
John Payne	02/04/1582
John Pibush	18/02/1601
John Robinson	01/10/1588
John Roche	30/08/1588
John Rochester	11/05/1537
John Rugg	15/11/1539
John Sandys	11/08/1586 *
John Shert	28/05/1582
John Slade	30/10/1583
John Speed	04/02/1594
John Storey	01/06/1571
John Sugar	16/07/1604 *

John Talbot	08/09/1600 *
John Thorne	15/11/1539
John Thules	18/03/1616 *
John Woodcock	07/08/1646 *
Joseph Lambton	31/07/1592 *
Laurence Humphrey	07/07/1591
Laurence Richardson	30/05/1582
Margaret Pole	28/05/1541
Mark Barkworth	27/02/1601
Marmaduke Bowes	27/11/1585 *
Matthew Flathers	21/03/1608 *
Montford Scott	01/07/1591 *
Miles Gerard	30/04/1590
Nicholas Garlicx	24/07/1588 *
Nicholas Horner	04/03/1590 *
Nicholas Postgate	07/08/1679 *
Nicholas Woodfen	27/01/1586 *
Patrick Salmon	04/07/1594
Peter Snow	15/06/1598 *
Peter Wright	19/05/1651
Philip Powel	30/06/1646
Ralph Ashley	07/04/1606
Ralph Corby	07/09/1644
Ralph Crockett	01/10/1588
Ralph Grimston	15/06/1598 *
Ralph Milner	07/07/1591
Richard Bere	09/08/1537
Richard Fetherston	30/07/1540
Richard Flower	30/08/1588 *
Richard Herst	29/08/1628
Richard Hill	27/05/1590 *
Richard Kirkman	22/08/1582
Richard Langhorne	14/07/1679
Richard Langley	10/12/1596
Richard Leigh	30/08/1588
Richard Martin	30/08/1588
Richard Newport	30/05/1612
Richard Reynolds (2)	31/01/1642
Richard Sergeant	20/04/1586 *
Richard Simpson	24/07/158 *
Richard Thirkeld	29/05/1583
Richard Whiting	15/11/1539
Richard Yaxley	05/07/1589 *
Robert Anderton	25/04/1586
Robert Bickerdyke	??/08/1586 *
Robert Dalby	15/03/1589
Robert Dibdale	08/10/1586 *
Robert Drury	26/02/1607 *
Robert Grissold	16/07/1604 *
Robert Hardesty	24/09/1589 *
Robert Johnson	28/05/1582
Robert Ludlam	24/07/1588 *
Robert Middleton	03/04/1601 *
Robert Morton	28/08/1588
Robert Nutter	26/07/1600 *
Robert Thorpe	31/05/1591
Robert Salt	09/06/1537
Robert Sutton (1)	27/07/1588 *
Robert Sutton (2)	05/10/1588
Robert Watkinson	20/04/1602
Robert Widmerpool	01/10/1588
Robert Wilcox	01/10/1588
Roger Cadwallador	27/08/1610 *
Roger Dickenson	07/07/1591 *
Roger Filcock	27/02/1601 *
Roger James	15/11/1539
Roger Wrenn	18/03/1616 *
Sebastian Newdigate	19/06/1535
Sidney Hodgson	10/12/1591
Stephen Rowsham	??/03/1587
Thomas Abel	30/07/1540
Thomas Alfield	06/07/1585
Thomas Atkinson	11/05/1616 *
Thomas Belson	05/07/1589 *
Thomas Bosgrave	04/07/1594
Thomas Bullaker	12/10/1642 *
Thomas Cottam	30/05/1582
Thomas Felton	28/08/1588
Thomas Ford	28/05/1582
Thomas Green	10/06/1537
Thomas Hemerford	12/02/1584
Thomas Holford	28/08/1588
Thomas Holland	12/12/1642
Thomas Hunt	01/07/1600 *
Thomas Johnson	20/09/1537
Thomas Maxfield	01/07/1616
Thomas Palaser	08/09/1600 *
Thomas Percy	22/08/1572
Thomas Pickering	09/05/1679
Thomas Pilcher	21/03/1587 *
Thomas Plumtree	04/01/1570
Thomas Pormont	20/02/1592 *
Thomas Redyng	16/06/1537
Thomas Scriven	15/06/1537
Thomas Sherwood	07/02/1578
Thomas Somers	10/12/1610
Thomas Sprott	01/07/1600 *
Thomas Thwing	23/10/1680
Thomas Tunstal	13/07/1616
Thomas Warcop	04/07/1597
Thomas Watkinson	31/05/1591 *
Thomas Welbourne	01/08/1605
Thomas Whitaker	07/08/1646 *
Thomas Whitbread	20/06/1679
Thomas Woodhouse	19/06/1573
Thurston Hunt	03/04/1601 *
Walter Pierson	10/06/1537
William Andleby	04/07/1597
William Browne	05/09/1605
William Carter	12/01/1584 *
William Dean	28/08/1588
William Exmew	19/06/1535
William Filby	30/05/1582
William Freeman	13/08/1595
William Gibson	29/11/1596 *
William Greenwood	06/06/1537
William Gunter	28/08/1588
William Harcourt	20/06/1679

William Harrington 18/02/1594
William Hart 15/03/1583
William Hartley 05/10/1588
William Horne 04/08/1540
William Howard 29/12/1680
William Ireland 24/01/1679
William Knight 29/11/1596 *
William Lacey 22/08/1582
William Lampley ? 1588 *
William Marsden 25/04/1586 *
William Patenson 22/01/1592
William Pike ? 1591 *
William Richardson 17/02/1603
William Scott 30/05/1612
William Southerne ??/04/1618 *
William Spenser 24/09/1589 *
William Thompson 20/04/1586 *
William Ward 26/07/1641
William Way 23/09/1588

FRENCH REVOLUTION

Beati (438)

Cambrai, Martyrs of (26/06/1794) (Daughters of Charity of Arras)

Jane Gérard
Mary-Teresa Fantou
Mary-Magdalen Fontaine
Mary-Frances Lanel

Valenciennes, Ursuline Martyrs of (17/10/1794)

Anne-Mary Erraux
Anne-Josephine Leroux
Augustina-of-the-Sacred-Heart Dejardin
Clotilde-of-St-Francis-Borgia Paillot
Cordula-of-St-Dominic Barré
Frances Lecroix
Laurentina-of-St-Stanislaus Prin
Louise-of-St-Francis-of-Assisi Ducrez
Mary-Natalia-of-St-Louis Vanot
Scholastica-of-St-James Leroux
Ursula-of-St-Bernardine Bourla

Compiègne, Carmelite Martyrs of (17/07/1794)

Catherine Soiron
Charlotte-of-the-Resurrection Thouret
Constance Meunier
Euphrasia-of-the-Immaculate-Conception Brard
Henrietta-of-Jesus de Croissy
Julia-of-Jesus de la Neuville
Juliette-of-St-Francis Verolot
Mary-Anne-of-St-Louis Brideau
Mary-of-St-Martha Dufour
Mary-Henrietta-of-Providence Pelras
Mary-of-Jesus-Crucified Piedcourt
Mary-of-the-Holy-Spirit Roussel
Teresa-of-the-Heart-of-Mary Hanisset
Teresa-of-St-Augustine Lidoine
Teresa Soiron
Teresa-of-St-Ignatius Trézelle

John-Baptist Souzy and Comps (1794)

Aloysius-Armand-Joseph Adam OFM Conv 13/07
Aloysius-Francis Lebrun OSB 20/08
Aloysius Wulphy Huppy 29/08
Andrew-Joseph Marchandon 22/09
Anthony Auriel 16/06
Anthony Bannassat 18/08
Augustine-Joseph Desgardin OCist 06/07
Bartholomew Jarrige de la Morélie de Biars 13/07
Charles-Anthony-Nicholas Ancel 29/07
Charles-Renatus Collas de Bignon 03/06
Charles-Arnold Hanus 28/08
Claudius Béguignot OCart 16/07
Claudius Dumonet 13/09
Claudius-Joseph Jouffret de Bonnefont 10/08
Claudius Laplace 14/09
Claudius-Barnabas Laurent de Mascloux 07/09
Claudius Richard OSB 09/08
Elias Leymarie de Laroche 22/08
Florentius Dumontet de Cardaillac 05/09
Francis D'Oudinot de la Boissière 07/09
Francis François OFM Cap 10/08
Francis Hunot 06/10
Francis Mayaudon 11/09
Gabriel Pergaud CR 21/07
George Edme René 02/10
Gervase-Protase Brunel OCist 20/08
James Cagnot OCD 10/09
James Lombardie 22/07
James Morelle Dupas 21/06
James Retouret OC 26/08
John Bourdon OFM Cap 23/08
John-Baptist de Bruxelles 18/09
John-Nicholas Cordier SJ 30/09
John-Baptist Duverneuil OCD 01/07
John-Baptist Guillaume 27/08
John Hunot 07/10
John-Francis Jarrige de la Morélie du Breuil 21/07
John-Joseph Jugé de Saint Martin 07/07
John-Baptist Laborier du Vivier 26/09
John-Baptist Loir OFM Cap 19/05
John-Baptist Menestrel 16/08
John Mopinot 21/05
John-George Rehm OP 11/08
John-Baptist Souzy 27/08
John-Baptist Vernoy de Montjournal 01/06
Joseph Imbert SJ 09/06
Lazarus Tiersot OCist 10/08

Marcellus Gaucher Labiche de Reignefort 26/07
Michael-Aloysius Brulard OCD 25/07
Michael-Bernard Marchand 15/07
Natalis-Hilary Le Conte 17/08
Nicholas Savouret OFM Conv 16/07
Nicholas Tabouillot (1795) 23/02
Paul-John Charles OCist 25/08
Peter Sulpicius Christopher Faverge 12/09
Peter Gabilhaud 13/08
Peter Jarrige de la Morélie du Puyredon 10/08
Peter Yriex Labrouhe de Laborderie 01/07
Peter-Joseph Legroing de La Romagère 26/07
Peter-Michael Noël 05/08
Philip Papon 17/06
Raymund Petinaud de Jourgnac 26/06
Scipio-Jerome Brigéat de Lambert 04/09
Sebastian Loup Hunot 17/11

Laval, (Martyrs of) (1794)

Secular Priests 21/01
Andrew Duliou
Augustine-Emmanuel Philippot
Francis Duchesne
Francis Migoret Lambeardière
James André
John-Baptist Turpin du Cormier
John-Mary Gallot
Joseph Pellé
Julian-Francis Morin de la Girardière
Julian Moulé
Louis Gastineau
Peter Thomas
Renatus-Louis Ambroise

Religious
Frances Mézière (private vows) 05/02
Frances Tréhet (OL of Charity, Evron) 13/03
Jane Véron (OL of Charity, Evron) 20/03
John-Baptist Triquerie OFM Conv 21/01
Mary-of-St-Monica Lhuilier (Hospitaller of Mercy of Jesus) 25/06

Layman
James Burin 17/10

Orange (Martyrs of) (1794)

Benedictine
Mary-Rose Deloye 06/07

Cistercians
Mary-of-St-Henry de Justamond 12/07
Mary-Magdalen-of-the-Heart-of-Mary de Justamond 16/07

Sacramentines
Amata-of-Jesus de Gordon 16/07
Anne-of-St-Alexis Minutte 13/07
Henrietta-of-the-Annunciation Faurie 13/07
Iphigenia-of-St-Matthew de Gaillard 07/07
Margaret-of-St-Augustine Bonnet 26/07
Martha-of-the-Good-Angel Cluse 12/07
Mary-Anne-of-St-Joachim Béguin-Royal 16/07
Mary-Clare-of-St-Martin Blanc 11/07
Mary-of-Jesus Charransol 16/07
Mary-Magdalen-of-the-Mother-of-God Verchière 13/07
Rosalia-Clotilde-of-St-Pelagia Bès 11/07
Rose-of-St-Xavier Talieu 12/07
Theoctista-Mary Pelissier 11/07

Ursulines
Agnes-of-St-Louis de Romillon 10/07
Anne-of-St-Basil Cartier 26/07
Catherine-of-Jesus de Justamond 16/07
Elizabeth-Teresa-of-the-Heart-of-Jesus Consolin 26/07
Jane-Mary-of-St-Bernard de Romillon 12/07
Margaret-of-St-Sophia D'Albarède 11/07
Mary-Clare-of-St-Rosalia du Bac 26/07
Mary-Anne-of-St-Francis Depeyre 13/07
Mary-Anne-of-St Michael Doux 16/07
Mary-Magdalen-of-St-Melania de Guilhermirer 10/07
Mary-Magdalen-of-Blessed-Sacrament de Justamond 26/07
Mary-Anne-of-St-Francis Lambert 13/07
Mary-Rose-of-St-Andrew Laye 16/07
Mary-Margaret-of-St-Sophia de Ripert d'Alauzier 10/07
Mary-of-the-Angels du Rocher 10/07
Mary-Anastasia-of-St-Gervase de Roquard 13/07

September (Martyrs of) (02/09/1792)

Bishops
Francis-Joseph de la Rochefoucault Maumont, of Beauvais
John-Mary du Lau d'Alleman, of Arles
Peter-Louis de la Rochefoucault Maumont, of Saintes

Secular priests
Andrew Alricy
Andrew Angar
Andrew Grasset de Saint-Sauveur
Anthony Boucharenc de Chaumeils
Anthony de Bouzet
Bertrand de Caupenne
Caspar Maignien

Charles Carnus
Claudius Chaudet
Claudius Colin
Claudius Fontaine
Claudius Marmotant
Claudius Mayneud de Bisefranc
Daniel-Andrew des Pommerayes
Dionysius Duval
Francis Dardin
Francis Dumasrambaud de Calandelle
Francis Londiveau
Francis Méallet de Fargues
Francis Monnier
Francis Pey
Gabriel Desprez de Roche
George Girous
Gilbert Fautrel
Gilbert Lanchon
Henry Ermès
Henry Millet
Henry Samson
Ivo Guillon de Keranrum
Ivo Rey de Kervisic
James Dufour
James de la Lande
James Lejardinier des Landes
James de Lubersac
James Menuret
James le Meunier
James Rabé
James Schmid
John Aubert
John Bangue
John Bottex
John Bousquet
John Capeau
John Caron
John Goizet
John Guilleminet
John Jannin
John le Laisant
John Lanier
John de Lavèze Belay
John Lecan
John Legrand
John Lemaitre
John Leroy
John Marchand
John-Baptist Nativelle
John Phillipot
John Quéneau
John Rateau
John de Saint-Clair
John Séguin
John Simon
Joseph Bécavin
Joseph Falcoz
Joseph Gros
Joseph Oviefve
Joseph Pazery de Thorame
Julian Hédouin
Julian Le Laisant
Julian Poulain de Launay
Julius Pazery de Thorame
(?) Laurent
Louis Barret
Louis-Remigius Benoist
Louis le Danois
Louis Gaultier
Louis Longuet
Louis Maudit
Marius-Francis Mouffle
Mark Royer
Martin Loublier
Mathurin Deruelle
Matthias Nogier
Michael Binard
Michael de la Gardette
Michael Leber
Nicholas Benoist
Nicholas Bize
Nicholas Clairet
Nicholas Colin
Nicholas Gaudreau
Nicholas Roussel
Oliver Lefebvre
Ormond Chapt de Rastignac
Ormond de Foucauld de Pontbriand
Peter Balzac
Peter Bonsé
Peter Briquet
Peter Brisse
Peter Garrigues
Peter Gervais
Peter Héncocq
Peter Joret
Peter Landry
Peter Leclerq
Peter Pazery de Thorame
Peter Ploquin
Peter Régnet
Peter Saint-James
Peter de Turmenyes
Peter Verrier
Peter Vitalis
Philibert Fougères
Renatus Nativelle
Renatus Poret
Renatus Urvoy
Robert Le Bis
Saintin Huré
Stephen Gillet
Thomas Dubuisson
Thomas Monsaint
Urban Lefebvre (MEP)
Urban Salin de Niart
Vincent Abraham

Former Jesuits
Anne-Alexander Lanfant
Charles Bérard de Pérou
Charles le Gué
Claudius Cagnières des Granges
Claudius Cayx-Dumas
Claudius Laporte
Eligius Herque du Roule
Francis Balmain
Francis le Livec de Tresurin
Francis Vareilhe-Duteil
James Bonnaud
James Friteyre-Durvé
John Benoît
John Charton de Millou
John Seconds
Mathurin de la Villecrohain le Bous de Villeneuve
Nicholas Verron
Peter Guérin du Rocher
Renatus Andrieux
Robert Guérin du Rocher
Thomas Loup
Vincent le Rousseau
William Delfaut

Sulpicians
Bernard Cucsac
Claudius Rousseau
Henry Luzeau de la Mullonière
James Galais
James Hourrier
John Pontus
John Savine
John Tessier
Peter Gaugain
Peter Guérin
Peter Psalmon
Thomas Dubray

Other Religious
Ambrose Chevreaux (OSB Maur)
Apollinaris Morel (OFM Cap)
Charles Hurtel (Minim)
Claudius Bochot (Doctrinarian)
Claudius Ponse (CR)
Eustace Félix (Doctrinarian)
Francis Hébert (Eudist)
Francis Lefranc (Eudist)
John Bernard (CR)
John Bonnel de Pradal (CR)
John Burté (OFM Conv)
John Gruyer (Vincentian)
Louis Barreau de la Touche (OSB Maur)
Louis François (Vincentian)
Peter Pottier (Eudist)
Renatus Massey (OSB Maur)
Severinus Girault (Tert OSF)
Solomon Leclercq (Xn Bro)

Deacons
Charles Veret
James-Robert de Lezardière
Louis Boubert
Louis Hurtrel
Stephen de Ravinel

Cleric
(?) Nezel

Laymen
Charles Régis de la Calmette
John Duval
Louis Rigot
John de Villette
Sebastian Desbrielles

William Repin and Comps (1793-4)
Fr Andrew Fardeau
Anne Hamard
Anne Maugrin
Anne-Frances de Villeneuve
Anthony Fournier
Carol Davy
Caroline Lucas
Catherine Coltenceau
Catherine du Verdier de la Sorinière
Felicity Pricet
Frances Bellanger
Frances Bonneau
Frances Michau
Frances Michineau
Frances Pagis
Frances Suhard
Fr Francis-Louis Chartier
Fr Francis Peltier
Gabrielle Androuin
Fr James Laigneau de Langellerie
Fr James Ledoyen
Jane Bourigault
Jane Fouchard
Jane Gourdon
Jane Gruget
Jane-Mary Leduc
Jane Monnier
Jane Onillon
Jane-Mary Saillard d'Epinatz
Jane Thomas
Fr John-Michael Langevin
Fr John-Baptist Lego
John Ménard
Fr Joseph Moreau
Fr Laurence Bâtard
Louise-Amata Dean de Luigné
Louise Bessay de la Voûle
Louise Poirier
Louise Raillier de la Tertinière
Margaret Rivière
Margaret Robin
Martha Poulin de la Forestrie
Mary-Magdalen Blond

Mary-Magdalen Cady
Mary Cassin
Mary-Jane Chauvigné
Mary de la Dive
Mary Fausseuse
Mary Forestier
Mary Gallard
Mary Gasnier
Mary Gingueneau
Mary Grillard
Mary-Anne Hacher du Bois
Mary Lardeaux
Mary Lenéc
Mary Leroy (1)
Mary Leroy (2)
Mary-Magdalen Perrotin
Mary Pichery
Mary Piou
Mary-Genevieve Poulin de la Foresrie
Mary Rochard
Mary Roger
Mary Rouault
Mary-Magdalen Saillard d'Epinatz
Mary-Magdalen Sallé
Sr Mary-Anne Vaillot
Mary-Louise du Verdier de la Sorinière
Monica Pichery
Sr Ottilia Baumgarten
Peter Délepine
Peter Frémond
Fr Peter Tessier
Petra Androuin
Petra Besson
Petra Bourigault
Petra Grille
Petra Laurent
Petra Ledoyen
Petra Phélyppeaux
Petra-Renata Potier
Petra-Jane Saillard d'Epinatz
Renata Bourgeais
Renata Cailleau
Renata-Mary Feillatreau
Renata Grillard
Renata Martin
Renata Rigault
Renata Seichet
Renata Valin
Fr Renatus Lego
Sr Rosalia du Verdier de la Sorinière
Rose Quenion
Simone Chauvigné
Susan Androuin
Victoria Bauduceau
Victoria Gusteau
Fr William Repin

Others
Natalis Pinot
Peter Roque

IRELAND

Conor O'Devany
Conrad O'Rourke
Dermitius O'Hurley
Dominic Collins
Edward Cheevers
Francis Taylor
John Kearney
Margaret Bermingham
Matthew Lambert
Maurice McKenraghty
Patrick O'Healey
Patrick Cavenagh
Patrick O'Loughlan
Peter Higgins
Robert Mayler
Terence-Albert O'Brien
William Tirry

JAPAN

Saints (42)

St Paul Miki and Comps 05/02/1597
Anthony Deynan
Bonaventure of Miyako
Cosmas Takeya
Francis Blanco OFM
Francis of Nagasaki
Francis the Carpenter
Francis-of-St-Michael of Parilla OFM
Gabriel of Ise
Gundisalvus Garcia OFM
James Kisai SJ
Joachim Sakakibara
John (Leo?) Kinuya
John Soan de Goto SJ
Leo Karasumaru
Louis Ibaraki
Martin-of-the-Ascension Loynaz OFM
Matthias of Miyako
Michael Kosaki
Paul Ibaraki
Paul Miki SJ
Paul Suzuki
Peter-Baptist of San Esteban OFM
Peter Sukejiro
Philip-of-Jesus Casas Martínez OFM
Thomas Dangi
Thomas Kosaki

St Laurence Ruiz and Comps

Anthony González	24/10/1637
Dominic Ibañez de Eriquicia	14/08/1633
Francis Shoyemon	14/08/1633

James Gorobiyoye	17/08/1633
Jordan Ansalone	17/11/1634
Laurence Ruiz	28/09/1637
Lazarus of Kyoto	28/09/1637
Luke Alonso	19/10/1633
Marina of Omura	11/11/1634
Mary-Magdalen of Nagasaki	15/10/1634
Matthew Kohiyoye	19/10/1633
Michael de Aozaraza	28/09/1637
Michael Kurobioye	28/09/1637
Thomas Rokuzayemon	17/11/1634
Vincent Shiwozuka	28/09/1637
William Courtet	28/09/1637

Beati (207)
** These died in the 'Great Martyrdom'.*

*Agnes Takeya	10/09/1622
*Alexius of Nagasaki OP	10/09/1622
Alexius Nakamura	27/11/1619
*Alphonsus de Mena OP	20/09/1622
Alphonsus Navarete OP	01/06/1617
Ambrose Fernandez SJ	06/01/1620
Andrew Tokuan	18/11/1619
Andrew Yakichi	02/10/1622
Andrew Yoshida	01/10/1617
*Angelus Orsucci OP	10/09/1622
Anthony Ishida SJ	03/09/1632
Anthony Kimura	27/11/1619
*Anthony Kiuni SJ	10/09/1622
*Anthony of Korea	10/09/1622
Anthony-of-St-Dominic of Nagasaki OP	08/09/1628
Anthony-of-St-Francis of Nagasaki OFM	16/08/1627
*Anthony Ono	10/09/1622
Anthony-of-St-Bonaventure of Tuy OFM	08/09/1628
*Anthony Sanga	10/09/1622
Anthony Yamada	19/08/1622
Apollinaris Franco OFM	12/09/1622
*Apollonia of Nagasaki	10/09/1622
Augustine Ota SJ	10/08/1622
Balthasar de Torres SJ	20/06/1626
Bartholomew Guttierez OSA	03/09/1632
Bartholomew Laurel OFM	16/08/1627
Bartholomew Mohyoye	19/08/1622
Bartholomew Seki	27/11/1619
*Bartholomew Shichiyemon	10/09/1622
Camillus Costanzo SJ	15/10/1622
Caspar Hikojiro	01/10/1617
Caspar Koteda	11/10/1622
Caspar Sadamatsu SJ	20/06/1626
Caspar Vas	16/08/1627
*Catherine of Nagasaki	10/09/1622
Catherine Tanaka	12/07/1626
*Charles Spinola SJ	10/09/1622
*Clare Yamada	10/09/1622
Clement Kyuyemon	01/11/1622
*Clement Ono	10/09/1622
Cosmas Takeya	18/11/1619
*Damian Yamichi	10/09/1622
Diego Carvalho SJ	22/02/1624
Dionysius Fujishima SJ	01/11/1622
Dominic Castellet OP	08/09/1628
Dominic Magoshichi de Hyuga OP	12/09/1622
Dominic Jorge	18/11/1619
Dominic of Nagasaki OFM	08/09/1628
*Dominic-of-the-Holy-Rosary of Nagasaki OP	10/09/1622
*Dominic Nakano	10/09/1622
Dominic Nihachi	08/09/1628
Dominic Shobyoye	16/09/1628
Dominic Tomachi	08/09/1628
*Dominic Yamada	10/09/1622
*Dominica Ogata	10/09/1622
Ferdinand-of-St-Joseph Ayala OSA	01/06/1617
Frances Bisoka	16/08/1627
Francis Galvez OSF	04/12/1623
Francis Kuhyoye	16/08/1627
Francis Kurobyoye	16/08/1627
Francis de Morales OP	20/09/1622
Francis Nihachi	08/09/1628
Francis-of-Jesus Ortega OSA	03/09/1632
Francis Pacheco SJ	20/06/1626
Francis-of-St-Bonaventure of Musashino OFM	12/09/1622
Francis-of-St-Mary of Mancha OFM	16/08/1627
Francis Takeya	11/09/1622
Francis Yakichi	02/10/1622
Gabriel-of-St-Mary-Magdalen of Fonseca OFM	03/09/1632
Gaius Jinyemon	16/08/1627
Gaius of Korea	15/11/1624
*Gundisalvus Fusai SJ	10/09/1622
*Hyacinth Orfanel OP	10/09/1622
*Ignatius Jorjes	10/09/1622
*Isabella Fernandez	10/09/1622
James Denji	19/08/1622
James Gengoro	16/08/1620
James Hayashi	08/09/1628
Jerome de Angelis SJ	04/12/1623
Jerome-of-the-Cross de Torres	03/09/1632
Joachim Hirayama Diaz	19/08/1622
John Chozaburo OSA	28/09/1630
*John Chugoku	10/09/1622
John Inamura	08/09/1628
John Iwanaga	27/11/1619
John Kisaku SJ	20/06/1626
*John of Korea	10/09/1622
John-Baptist Machado SJ	22/05/1617

John Maki	07/09/1627
John Matashichi	19/08/1622
John Motoyama	27/11/1619
John Naizen	12/07/1626
John-of-St-Dominic of Omura OP	19/03/1619
John-of-St-Martha of Prados OFM	16/08/1618
John Shoun	18/11/1619
John Soyemon	19/08/1622
John Tanaka	12/07/1626
John Tomachi	08/09/1628
John Yago	19/08/1622
John-Baptist Zola SJ	20/06/1626
*Joseph-of-St-Hyacinth of Villareal OP	10/09/1622
Laurence Hachizo OSA	16/09/1628
Laurence Rokuyemon	19/08/1622
Laurence Yamada	08/09/1628
Leo Aibara	08/09/1628
Leo Nakanishi	27/11/1619
Leo Tanaka	01/06/1617
*Leo Satsuma	10/09/1622
Leo Sukuyemon	19/08/1622
Leonard Kimura SJ	18/11/1619
Louis Baba OSF	25/08/1624
Louis Bertrán OP	29/07/1627
Louis Flores OP	19/08/1622
*Louis Kawara SJ	10/09/1622
Louis Maki	07/09/1627
Louis Matsuo	16/08/1627
Louis Naizen	12/07/1626
Louis Nihachi	08/09/1628
Louis Sasada OSF	25/08/1624
Louis Sotelo OSF	25/08/1624
Louis Yakichi	02/10/1622
Louise of Omura	08/09/1628
*Lucy de Freitas	10/09/1622
Lucy Yakichi	02/10/1622
Luke Kiyemon	16/08/1627
Mancius Araki	12/07/1626
Mancius Ichizayemon OSA	16/09/1628
Mancius-of-the-Holy-Cross of Omura	29/07/1627
Mancius-of-St-Thomas Shibata OP	12/09/1622
Mark Shinyemon	19/08/1622
Martin Gomez	16/08/1627
Martin-of-St-Nicholas Lumberes Peralta	11/12/1632
Mary Gengoro	16/08/1620
Mary Magdalen Kiyota (1)	16/08/1620
Mary Magdalen Kiyota (2)	16/08/1627
*Mary of Korea	10/09/1622
*Mary Magdalen Sanga	10/09/1622
*Mary Shoun	10/09/1622
*Mary Tanaka	10/09/1622
*Mary Tanaura	10/09/1622
*Mary Tokuan	10/09/1622
Mary Vaz	16/08/1627
Matthew Alvarez	08/09/1628
Matthias Araki	12/07/1626
Matthias of Arima	27/05/1620
Matthias Kozaka	27/11/1619
Matthias Nakano	27/11/1619
Melchior-of-St-Augustine Sánchez Pérez	11/12/1632
Michael Carvalho SJ	25/08/1624
Michael Diaz	19/08/1622
Michael Himonoya	16/09/1628
Michael Kizaiyemon	16/08/1627
Michael Nakashima SJ	25/12/1628
Michael Sakaguchi	27/11/1619
*Michael Sato SJ	10/09/1622
Michael Sukizayemon OSA	16/09/1628
Michael Tomachi	08/09/1628
Michael Tozo SJ	20/06/1626
Michael Yamada	08/09/1628
*Michael Yamichi	10/09/1622
Monica Naizen	12/07/1626
Paul Aibara	08/09/1628
Paul Himonoya	16/09/1628
Paul Navarro SJ	01/11/1622
*Paul Nagaishi	10/09/1622
Paul Sankichi	19/08/1622
Paul Shinsuke SJ	20/06/1626
*Paul Tanaka	10/09/1622
Paul Tomachi	08/09/1628
Peter Araki Chobyoye	12/07/1626
Peter-Paul-of-St-Clare of Arima	12/09/1622
*Peter de Avila OFM	10/09/1622
Peter-of-the-Assumption of Cuerva OFM	22/05/1617
*Peter of Korea	10/09/1622
Peter Kuhyoye OSA	16/09/1628
*Peter Nagaishi	10/09/1622
Peter-of-the-Holy-Mother-of-God of Omura OP	29/07/1627
Peter Onizuka SJ	01/11/1622
Peter Rinsei SJ	20/06/1626
*Peter Sampo SJ	10/09/1622
Peter Shichiyemon	11/09/1622
Peter Vasquez OP	25/08/1624
Peter Zuñiga OSA	19/08/1622
*Richard-of-St-Ann of Brussels OFM	10/09/1622
Romanus Aibara	08/09/1628
Romanus Motoyama	27/11/1619
*Rufus Ishimoto	10/09/1622
*Sebastian Kimura SJ	10/09/1622
Simon Kiyota Bokusai	16/08/1620
Simon Yempo SJ	04/12/1623
Susanna Chobyoye	12/07/1626
*Thecla Nagaishi	10/09/1622
*Thomas Akahoshi SJ	10/09/1622
Thomas Gengoro	16/08/1620
Thomas Jinyemono	16/08/1627

Thomas Kahyoye OSA	16/09/1628
Thomas Koteda	27/1/1619
Thomas Koyanagi	19/08/1622
*Thomas-of-the-Holy-Rosary of Nagasaki OP	10/09/1622
Thomas-of-St-Hyacinth of Nagasaki OP	08/09/1628
*Thomas Shikiro	10/09/1622
Thomas Tomachi	08/09/1628
Thomas Tsuji SJ	07/09/1627
Thomas Zumarraga OP	12/09/1622
Vincent Carvalho OSA	03/09/1632
Vincent Caum SJ	20/06/1626
*Vincent-of-St-Joseph of Ayamonte OFM	10/09/1622

KOREA

Saints (103)

Agatha Jeon
Agatha Kim
Agatha Kwon
Agatha Lee (1)
Agatha Lee (2)
Agatha Lee (3)
Agatha Lee (4)
Agnes Kim
Alexis Wu (Syei-hpil)
Andrew Kim
Andrew Cheong
Anne Kim
Anne Pak
Anthony Daveluy
Anthony Kim
Augustine Lee
Augustine Pak
Augustine Ryou
Barbara Cho
Barbara Choi
Barbara Han
Barbara Kim
Barbara Ko
Barbara Kwon
Barbara Lee (1)
Barbara Lee (2)
Bartholomew Chieng (Moun-ho)
Benedicta Hyon
Catherine Cheong
Catherine Lee
Cecilia Ryou
Charles Cho
Charles Hyen
Columba Kim
Damian Nam
Elizabeth Cheong
Francis Choi
Ignatius Kim
James Chastan
John-Baptist Chieng (Seung-yen)
John Lee
John-Baptist Lee
John-Baptist Nam (Thiong-sam)
John Ni (Youn-Il)
John Pak
Joseph Chang
Joseph Chiang (Nak-syo)
Joseph Cho (Youn-o)
Joseph Han (Wen-sye)
Joseph Rim
Julitta Kim
Justus Ranfer de Brenières
Laurence Imbert
Laurence Han
Louis Beaulieu
Lucy Kim (1)
Lucy Kim (2)
Lucy Pak
Luke Hoang (Chai-ken)
Mark Tyeng
Martha Kim
Martin-Luke Huin
Mary-Magdalen Cho
Mary-Magdalen Han
Mary-Magdalen He
Mary-Magdalen Kim
Mary Lee (1)
Mary Lee (2)
Mary-Magdalen Lee (1)
Mary-Magdalen Lee (2)
Mary Pak
Mary-Magdalen Pak
Mary-Magdalen Sou
Mary Won
Paul Cheong
Paul He
Paul Hong
Perpetua Hong
Peter Amaître
Peter Cheng (Wen-chi)
Peter Choi
Peter Choi (Chi-chieng)
Peter Chyo (Hoa-se)
Peter Dorié
Peter Hong
Peter Kwon
Peter Lee
Peter Maubant
Peter Nam
Peter Ni (Mieng-se)
Peter Ryou
Peter Ryou (Chieng-rioul)
Peter Son (Syen-chi)
Protase Cheong
Rose Kim
Sebastian Nam
Simon Berneaux
Stephen Min
Susanna Ou

Teresa Kim (1)
Teresa Kim (2)
Teresa Lee
Thomas Son (Cha-sien)

MEXICO

Saints (25)

Chihuahua
Peter-of-Jesus Maldonado Lucero 21/02/37

Chilpancingo
David Uribe Velasco 12/04/27
Margaritus Flores García 12/11/27

Colima
Michael de la Mora 07/08/27

Guadalajara
Atilanus Cruz Alvarado 01/07/28
Augustine Caloca Cortés 25/05/27
Christopher Magallanes Jara 25/05/27
David Galván Bermúdez 30/01/15
Januarius Sánchez Delgadillo 17/01/27
Joseph-Isabel Flores Varela 21/07/27
Joseph-Mary Robles Hurtado 26/06/27
Julius Álvarez Mendoza 30/03/27
Justin Orona Madrigal 01/07/28
Peter Esqueda Ramírez 22/11/27
Roderick Aguilar Alemán 28/10/28
Romanus Adame Rosales 21/04/27
Sabas Reyes Salazar 13/04/27
Tranquillinus Ubiarco Robles 05/10/28
Turibius Romo González 25/02/28

Durango
Aloysius Batis Sainz 15/08/26
David Roldán Lara 15/08/26
Emmanuel Morales 15/08/26
Matthew Correa Magallanes 06/02/27
Salvator Lara Puente 15/08/26

Morelia
Jesus Méndez Montoya 05/02/28

Beati (2)

Jesuit
Michael-Augustine Pro 23/11/27

Augustinian friar
Elias-del-Socorro Nieves 10/03/28

NETHERLANDS

Saints (19)

Gorinchem, Martyrs of
Adrian van Hilvarenbeek OPrem
Andrew Wouters van Heynoert
Anthony van Hornaer OFM
Anthony Weerden OFM
Cornelius van Wijk OFM
Francis Rod OFM
Godfrey van Duyen
Godfrey of Merville OFM
James Lacops OPrem
Jerome Weerden OFM
John of Cologne OP
John van Oosterwijk CR
Leonard Vechel
Nicasius Jonson van Hez OFM
Nicholas Janssen-Poppel
Nicholas Pieck OFM
Peter of Asse OFM
Theodoric van Emden OFM
Willehad of Denmark OFM

POLAND

Mary Mardosewicz and Comps
Mary-Felicita Borowik
Mary-Canuta-of-Jesus-in-the-Garden Chrobot
Mary-Gwidona-of-the-Mercy-of-God Cierpka
Mary-Daniela-of-Jesus-and-Mary-Immaculate Jóźwik
Mary-Raymund-of-Jesus-and-Mary Koklowicz
Mary-Canisia Mackiewicz
Mary-Stella-of-the-Blesed-Sacrament Mardosewicz
Mary-Heliodora Matuszewska
Mary-Boromea Narmontowicz
Mary-Sergia-of-the-Sorrowful-Mother-of-God Rapiej
Mary-Imelda-of-Jesus-in-the-Host Źak

Beati (49)

Sadoc of Sandomir and Comps
Priests
Abel
Andrew
Barnabas
Bartholomew
Clement
Elias
James
John (1)
Luke
Malachy
Matthew
Paul
Peter
Philip
Sadoc
Simeon

Deacons

Joachim
Stephen
Joseph

Sub-deacons
Abraham
Basil
Moses
Thaddeus

Clerics
Aaron
Benedict
David
Dominic
Matthias
Michael
Onuphrius
Timothy

Novices
Christopher
Daniel
Donatus
Felician
Gervase
Gordianus
Isaias
John (2)
Macarius
Mark
Maurus
Medardus
Raphael
Tobias
Valentine

Lay brothers
Cyril
Jeremias
Thomas

There are 108 other beatified martyrs of the Nazi occupation of Poland, but the official list has not yet been published.

SPANISH CIVIL WAR

Saints

James-Hilary Barbal Cosán	18/01/1937

Cyril-Bertrand Sanz Tejedor and Comps (09/10/1934)
Anicetus-Adolf Seco Gutierrez
Augustus-Andrew Martín Fernandez
Benedict-of-Jesus Valdivieso Saez
Benjamin-Julian Alfonsus Andrés
Cyril-Bertrand Sanz Tejedor
Innocent-of-Mary-Immaculate Canoura Arna
Julian-Alfred Fernández Zapico
Marcian-Joseph López López
Victorianus-Pius Bernabé Cano

Beati

Angela Lloret Martí and Comps (20/11/1936)
Amparo Rosat y Balasch
Angela-of-St-Joseph Lloret Martí
Elizabeth Ferrer Sabría
Heart-of-Jesus Gómez Vives
Ignatia-of-the-Bl.-Sacrament Pascual Pallardó
Marcella-of-St-Thomas Navarro
Mary-of-the-Rosary Calpe Ibáñez
Mary-of-Succour Jiménez Baldoví
Mary-of-Montserrat Llimona Planas
Mary-of-Peace López García
Mary-of-the-Conception Martí Lacal
Mary-of-the-Assumption Mogoche Homs
Mary-of-Suffrage Orts Baldó
Mary-of-Calvary Romero Clariana
Mary-of-Grace de San Antonio
Mary-of-Sorrows Surís Brusola
Teresa-of-St-Joseph Duart Roig

Aurelius-Mary Villalón Acebrón and Comps (16/11/1936)
Aurelius-Mary Villalón Acebrón
Edmigius Primo Rodríguez
Emilian Zariquiegui Mendoza
Evincius-Richard Alonso Uyarra
Joseph-Cecil Rodríguez Gonzalez
Theodemar-Joaquim Sáiz Sáiz
Valerius-Bernard Herrero Martínez

Dionysius Pamplona Polo and Comps (22/09/1936)

Alfred Parte Saiz	27/12/1936
Charles Navarro Miquel	22/09/1936
David Carlos Marañón	28/07/1936
Dionysius Pamplona Polo	25/07/1936
Emmanuel Segura López	27/07/1936
Faustinus Oteiza Segura	09/08/1936
Florentinus Felipe Naya	09/08/1936
Francis Carceller Galindo	02/10/1936
Henry Canadell Quintana	17/08/1936
Ignatius Casanovas Perramon	26/09/1936
John Agramunt Riera	14/08/1936
Joseph Ferrer Esteve	09/12/1936
Matthias Cardona Meseguer	20/08/1936

Hospitaller Martyrs (30/07/1936)

Talavera de la Reina, Toledo, Jul 25
Frederick Rubio Alvarez
Jerome Ochoa Urdangarin
John-of-the-Cross Delgado Pastor
Primus Martínez de San Vicente Castillo

Calafell, Tarragona, Jul 30
Anthony Llauradó Parisi
Anthony Sanchez Silvestre
Benedict-Joseph-Labre Mañoso González
Braulius-Mary Corres Diaz de Cerio
Constantius Roca Huguet
Dominic Pitarch Gurrea
Emmanuel Jímenez Salado
Emmanuel López Orbara
Eusebius Forcades Ferraté
Henry Betrán Llorca
Ignatius Tejero Molina
Julian Carrasquer Fos
Raphael Flamarique Salinas
Thomas Urdanoz Aldaz
Vincent de Paul Canelles Vives

Colombians at Barcelona, Aug 9
Arthur Ayala Niño
Caspar Páez Perdomo
Eugene Ramirez Salazar
John-Baptist Velázquez Peláez
Melchiades Ramírez Zuluaga
Ruben-of Jesus López Aguilar
Stephen Maya Gutierrez

Carabanchal Alto, Madrid, Sep 1
Benjamin Cobos Celada
Caesareus Niño Pérez
Caecilius López López
Canute Franco Gómez
Carmelus Gil Arano
Christinus Roca Huguet
Cosmas Brun Arará
Dositheus Rubio Alonso
Euthymius Aramendía García
Faustinus Villanueva Igual
Processus Ruiz Cascales
Rufinus Lasheras Aizcorbe

Ciemposuelos Hospital, Madrid, Nov 28
Angelus Sostre Corporales
Clement Díez Sahagún
Edward Bautista Jímenez
Flavius Argüeso González
Francis Arias Martín
Hilary Delgado Vílchez
Isidore Martínez Izquierdo
John-Jesus Adradas Gonzalo
John Alcalde Alcalde
Joseph Mora Velasco
Joseph Ruiz Cuesta
Julian Palazaola Artola
Lazarus Múgica Goiburu
Martinian Meléndez Sánchez
Peter-Mary Alcalde Negredo
Peter-of-Alcantara Bernalte Calzado
Tobias Borrás Romeau
William Llop Gayá
Ciemposuelos Hospital, Madrid, Nov 30
Anthony Martinez Gil-Leonis
Arthur Donoso Murillo
Diego-of-Cadiz García Molina
Jesus Gesta de Piquer
Michael Ruedas Mejías
Romanus Touceda Fernández

Barcelona, killed on different dates
Acisclus Piña Piazuelo
Francis-Xavier Ponsa Casallach
John-Anthony Burró Más
John-Baptist Egozcuezábel Aldaz
Peter-of-Alcantara Villanueva Larráyoz
Protase Cubells Minguell

Castile, different places and times
Gonzalus Gonzalo Gonzalo
Hyacinth Hoyuelos González
Nicephorus Salvador del Río

Mary-Gabrielle de Hinojosa Naveros and Comps (18/11/1936)
Josephine-Mary Barrera Izaguirre
Mary-Cecilia Cendoya Araquistain
Mary-Gabrielle de Hinojosa Naveros
Mary-Engracia Lecuona Aramburu
Mary-Angela Olaizola Garagarza
Mary-Agnes Zudaire Galdeano
Teresa-Mary Cavestany y Anduaga

Nicephorus Díez Tejerina and Comps (23/07/1936)
Abilius-of-the-Cross Ramos y Ramos
Anacarius-of-the-Immaculate Benito Nozal
Benedict-of-the-Virgin-del-Villar Solana Ruiz
Epiphanius-of-St-Michael Sierra Conde
Euphrasius-of-the-Merciful-Love de Celis Santos
Felix-of-the-Five-Wounds Ugalde Irurzun
Fulgentius-of-the-Heart-of-Mary Calvo Sánchez
Germanus-of-Jesus-and-Mary Pérez Gímenez
Honorius-of-the-Sorrowing-Virgin Carracedo Ramos
Ildephonsus-of-the-Cross Garcia Nozal
John-Peter-of-St-Anthony Bengoa Aranguren
Joseph-of-the-Sacred-Heart Estalayo García
Joseph-of-Jesus-and-Mary Osés Sainz
Joseph-Mary-of-Jesus Cuartero Gascón
Joseph-Mary-of-Jesus-Dying Ruiz Martínez
Julius-of-the-Sacred-Heart Mediavilla Concejero
Justin-of-St-Gabriel-O.L.-Sorrows Cuesta Redondo
Laurianus-of-Jesus-Crucified Proaño Cuesta
Maurice-of-the-Infant-Jesus Macho Ródriguez
Nicephorus-of-Jesus-and-Mary Díez Tejerina

Paul-Mary-of-St-Joseph Leoz y Portillo
Peter-of-the-Heart-of-Jesus Largo Redondo
Philip-of-St-Michael Ruiz Fraile
Philip-of-Sacred-Heart-Mary Valcabado Granado
Thomas-of-the-Blessed-Sacrament Cuartero Gascón
Zechariah-of-Blessed-Sacrament Fernández Crespo

Peter Ruiz de los Paños y Angel and Comps (23/07/1936)

Anthony Perulles Estíval	12/08
Isidore Bover Oliver	02/10
Joseph-Mary Peris Polo	15/08
Joseph Sala Picó	24/06
Martin Martínez Pascual	18/08
Paschal Cada Saporta	04/09
Peter Ruiz de los Paños y Angel	24/06
Recared Centelles Abad	25/10
William Plaza Hernández	09/08

Philip-of-Jesus-Munárriz Azcona and Comps (1936)

11/08
John Díaz Nosti
Leontius Pérez Ramos
Philip-of-Jesus-Munárriz Azcona

12/08
Gregory Chirivás Lacambra
Joseph Pavón Bueno
Nicasius Sierra Ucar
Peter Cunill Padrós
Sebastian Calvo Martinez
Wenceslas-Mary Claris Vilaregut

13/08
Alphonsus Miquel Garriga
Anthony-Mary Dalmau Rosich
Antonillus-Mary Calvo Calvo
Emmanuel Buil Lalueza
Emmanuel Torras Sais
Eusebius Codina Millá
Hilary-Mary Llorente
John Codinachs Tuneu
John Echarri Vique
John Sánchez Munárriz
Joseph Brengaret Pujol
Joseph-Mary Ormo Seró
Peter García Bernal
Raymund Novich Rabionet
Salvator Pigem Serra
Secundinus-Mary Ortega-García
Stephen Casadevall Puig
Theodore Ruiz de Larrinaga Martín
Thomas Capdevila Miró
Xavier-Aloysius Bandréz Jímenez

15/08
Aloysius Escalé Binefa
Aloysius Lladó Teixidó
Aloysius Masferrer Vila
Alphonsus Sorribes Teixidó
Edward Ripoll Diego
Emmanuel Martínez Jarauta
Faustinus Perez García
Francis Castan Messeguer
Francis-Mary Roura Farró
Jesus-Augustine Viela Ezcurdia
John Baixeras Berenguer
Joseph-Mary Amorós Hernández
Joseph-Mary Badía Mateai
Joseph-Mary Blasco Juan
Joseph Figuero Beltrán
Joseph-Mary Ros Florensa
Michael Masip González
Raphael Briega Morales
Raymund Illa Salvía
Sebastian Riera Coromina

18/08
Athanasius Vidauretta Labra
James Falgarona Vilanova

Vincent Soler and Comps (1936)

25/07
Deogratias Palacios
Leo Inchausti
Joseph-Richard Díez
Joseph Rada
Julian Moreno

26/07
Emmanuel Martin Sierra
Vincent Pinilla

15/08
Vincent Soler

Others

Anselm Polanco Fontecha	07/02/1939
Charles Eraña Guruceta	18/09/1936
Diego Ventaja Milán	29/08/1936
Emmanuel Medina Olmos	29/08/1936
Fidelis Fuidio Rodríguez	20/09/1936
Florentinus Asensio Barroso	09/08/1936
Frances-of-the-S.H. Aldea Araujo	20/07/1936
Jesus Hita Miranda	18/09/1936
Mary-Pillar Martínez García	25/07/1936
Mary-Sanctuary Moragas Cantarero	15/08/1936
Mary-Angels Valtierra Tordesillas	25/07/1936
Philip Ripoll Morata	07/02/1939
Rita-Dolores Pujalte Sánchez	20/07/1936
Teresa García García	25/07/1936

Victoria Diez y Bustos de Molina 11/08/1936
Zephyrinus Giménez Malla 04/05/1936

Beatified in 2001

Archdiocese of Valencia, Diocesan Priests

Alphonsus Sebastiá Viñals 01/09/36
Anthony Silvestre Moya 07/08/36
Carmel Sastre Sastre 15/08/36
Diego Llorca Llopis 06/09/36
Elias Carbonell Mollá 02/10/36
Felix Yuste Cava 14/08/36
Ferdinard Garcia Sendra 18/09/36
Ferdinard González Añón 27/12/36
Francis Ibáñez Ibáñez 19/08/36
Francis Sendra Ivars 04/09/36
Germanus Gozalbo Andreu 22/09/36
Gundesalvus Viñes Masip 10/12/36
Henry Juan Requena 29/12/36
Henry Morant Pellicer 03/10/36
Joachim Vilanova Camallonga 29/07/36
John Carbonell Mollá 02/10/36
John Ventura Solsona 17/09/36
Joseph Aparicio Sanz 29/12/36
Joseph Canet Giner 04/10/36
Joseph Fenellosa Alcayna 27/09/36
Joseph-Mary Ferrándiz Hernández 24/06/36
Joseph Garcia Mas 18/09/36
Joseph González Huguet 12/10/36
Joseph Ruiz Bruixola 29/10/36
Joseph-Mary Segura Penadés 11/09/36
Joseph Toledo Pellicer 10/08/36
Paschal Ferrer Botella 24/09/36
Paschal Penadés Jornet 15/10/36
Raymund-Stephen Bou Pascual 15/10/36
Raymund Marti Soriano 27/08/36
Salvator Estrugo Solves 18/09/36
Salvator Ferrandis Segui 03/08/36
Vincent Ballester Far 23/06/36
Vincent-Mary Izquierdo Alcón 18/08/36
Vincent Pelufo Corts 11/09/36
Vincent Rubiols Castelló 04/08/36
Vincent Sicluna Hernándex 22/09/36

Archdiocese of Valencia, Members of Catholic Action

Amelia Abad Casasempere 21/09/36
Anne-Mary Aranda Riera 14/10/36
Arthur Ros Monalt 28/08/36
Charles Diaz Gandia 11/08/36
Charles López Vidal 06/08/36
Crescentia Valls Espi 20/09/36
Emmanuel Torró Garcia 21/09/36
Florence Caerols Martinez 02/10/36
Francis de Paula Castelló y Aleu (diocese of Lleida) 29/09/36
Francisca Culladó Baixauli 19/09/36
Herminia Martinez Amigó 26/09/36
Incarnation Gil Valls 24/09/36
Ishmael Escrihuela Esteve 09/09/36
John-Baptist Faubel Cano 28/08/36
John Gonga Martinez 13/11/36
Joseph-Mary Corbin Ferrer 27/12/36
Joseph-Raymund Ferragud Girbés 24/09/36
Joseph Medes Ferris 12/11/36
Joseph Perpiñá Nácher 29/12/36
Joseph-Mary Zabal Blasco 08/12/36
Josephine Moscardó Montalvá
Louise-Mary Frias Cañizares 06/12/36
Marinus Blanes Giner 08/09/36
Mary Climent Mateau 20/08/36
Mary-Teresa Ferragud Roig
Mary Jordá Botella 27/09/36
Mary-Louise Montesinos Orduña 31/07/37
Mary-of-Olvido Noguera Albeda 30/11/36
Mary-of-the-Purification Vidal Pastor 21/09/36
Mary-of-Carmen Viel Ferrando 04/11/36
Paschal Torres Lloret 06/09/36
Paul Meléndez Gonzalo 23/12/36
Pilar Villalonga Villalba 11/12/36
Raphael Alonso Gutiérrez 11/08/36
Salvator-Damian Enguix Garés 29/10/36
Sophia Ximénez Ximénex 23/09/36
Tarsilla Córdoba Belda 17/10/36
Vincent Galbis Gironés 21/09/36

Dominicans of Zaragoza

Anthony López Couceiro 29/07/36
Constantine Fernández Alvarez 29/08/36
Emmanuel Albert Ginés 29/07/36
Felicissimus Diez González 29/07/36
Francis Calvo Burillo 02/08/36
Francis Monzón Romeo 29/08/36
Gumersind Soto Barros 29/07/36
Hyacinth Serrano López 25/11/36
James Meseguer Burillo ??/11/36
Joachim Prats Baltueña 30/07/36
Joseph-Mary Muro Sanmiguel 30/07/36
Joseph-Mary Vidal Segú ??/09/36
Lambert de Navascués y de Juan 29/07/36
Louis Urbano Lanaspa 25/08/36
Lucius Martinez Mancebo 29/07/36
Raphael Pardo Molina 26/09/36
Raymund Peiró Victori 21/08/36
Saturus Rey Robles 29/07/36
Thyrsus Manrique Melero 29/07/36
Zosimus Izquierdo Gil 30/07/36

Franciscans, Capuchin

Ambrose Valls Matamales 24/08/36

Aurelius Ample Alcaide	28/08/36
Berard Bleda Grau	04/09/36
Bonaventure Esteve Flors	26/09/36
Fidelis Clement Sanchis	27/09/36
Henry Garcia Beltrán	16/08/36
Germanus Garrigues Hernández	09/08/36
James Mesre Iborra	29/09/36
Joachim Ferrer Adell	30/08/36
Modestus Garcia Marti	13/08/36
Pacificus Salcedo Puchades	12/10/36
Peter Mas Ginester	26/08/36

Franciscans, Conventual

Alphonsus López López	03/08/36
Dionysius Vicente Ramos	31/07/36
Francis Remón Játiva	31/07/36
Michael Remón Salvador	03/08/36
Modestus Vegas Vegas	27/07/36
Peter Rivera Rivera	01/09/36

Franciscans, Friars Minor

Alfred Pellicer Muñoz	04/10/36
Paschal Fortuño Almela	07/09/36
Placid Garcia Gilabert	16/08/36
Salvator Mollar Ventura	26/10/36

Poor Clare Capuchinesses

Elizabeth Calduch Rovira	14/04/37
Mary-Felicity Masia Ferragud	25/10/36
Mary-of-Jesus Masia Ferragud	25/10/36
Mary-Veronica Masia Ferragud	25/10/36
Miracles Ortells Gimeno	20/11/36

Discalced Augustinian Nun

Josepha-of-the-Purificacion Masia Ferragud	25/10/36

Jesuits

Alfred Simón Colomina	29/11/36
Constantine Carbonell Sempere	23/08/36
Darius Hernández Morató	29/09/36
John-Baptist Ferreres Boluda	29/12/36
Joseph Tarrats Comaposada	28/09/36
Louis Campos Górriz	28/11/36
Narcissus Basté Basté	15/10/36
Paul Bori Puig	29/09/36
Peter Gelabert Amer	23/08/36
Raymund Grimaltós Monllor	23/08/36
Thomas Sitjar Fortiá	19/08/36
Vincent Sales Genovés	29/09/36

Salesians

Alexander Planas Sauri	19/11/36
Alvarez Sanjuan Canet	02/10/36
Angelus Ramos Velázquez	11/10/36
Anthony Martin Hernández	
Augustine Garcia Calvo	
Elisha Garcia Garcia	19/11/36
Felix Vivet Trabal	25/08/36
Francis Bandrés Sánchez	03/08/36
Giles Rodicio Rodicio	04/08/36
James Bonet Nadal	18/08/36
James Buch Canals	29/07/36
James Oriz Alzueta	27/07/36
John Martorell Soria	10/08/36
Joseph Batalla Parramón	04/08/36
Joseph Bonet Nadal	13/08/36
Joseph Calasanz Marqués	29/07/36
Joseph Caselles Moncho	27/07/36
Joseph Castell Camps	28/07/36
Joseph Giménez López	
Joseph Otin Aquilé	01/11/36
Joseph Rabasa Bentanachs	
Julian Rodriguez Sánchez	
Julius Junyer Padern	26/04/36
Michael Domingo Cendra	12/08/36
Peter Mesonero Rodriguez	??/08/36
Philip Hernández Martinez	27/07/36
Recared de los Rios Fabregat	
Sergius Cid Paso	30/07/36
Xavier Bordás Piferer	23/07/36
Zacharias Abadia Buesa	27/07/36

Daughters of Mary, Help of Christians

Mary-Amparo Carbonell Muñoz	06/09/36
Mary-of-Carmen Moreno Benitez	06/09/36

Third Order Capuchins of Our Lady of Sorrows

Augustine Hurtado Soler	15/08/36
Carmen Garcia Moyon	30/01/37
Crescentius Garcia Pobo	03/10/36
Emmanuel Ferrer Jordá	16/09/36
Emmanuel Legua Marti	26/09/36
Florentinus Pérez Romero	23/08/36
Francis Tomás Serer	02/08/36
Joseph Arahal de Miguel	01/08/36
Joseph-Mary Llópez Mora	18/09/36
Joseph Llosá Balaguer	07/10/36
Joseph-Mary Sanchis Monpó	16/08/36
Justus Lerman Martinez	18/09/36
Paul Martinez Robles	16/09/36
Salvator Chulia Ferrandis	18/09/36
Salvator Ferrer Cardet	16/09/36
Timothy Valero Pérez	17/09/36
Urban Gil Sáez	23/08/36
Vincent Cabanes Badenas	30/08/36
Vincent Gay Zarzo	18/09/36
Vincent Jaunzarás Gómez	18/09/36

Priest of the Sacred Heart

Marianus-John-Mary-of-the-Cross Garcia Méndez	23/08/36

Brothers of the Christian Schools

Ambrose-Leo Lorente Vicente	23/10/36
Bertrand-Francis Lahoz Moliner	14/12/36

Elias-Julian Torrijo Sánchez	22/11/36
Florentius-Martin Ibáñez Lázaro	23/10/36
Honoratus-Andrew Zorraquino Herrero	23/10/36
Leonard Olivera Buera	23/10/36

Carmelite Sisters of Charity

Agueda Hernández Amorós	19/08/36
Antonia Gosens Sáez	24/11/36
Ascension Lloret Marco	07/09/36
Candida Cayuso González	24/11/36
Clare Ezcurra Urrutia	24/11/36
Conception Odriozola Zabalia	24/11/36
Conception Rodriguez Fernández	24/11/36
Consuelo Cuñado González	24/11/36
Daria Campillo Paniagua	24/11/36
Elvira Torrentallé Paraire	19/08/36
Erundina Colino Vega	24/11/36
Feliciana de Uribe Orbe	24/11/36
Francisca de Amezúa Ibaibarriaga	19/08/36
Justa Maiza Goicoechea	24/11/36
Mary Calaf Miracle	19/08/36
Mary-of-the-Snows Crespo López	19/08/36
Mary-of-the-Helpless Giner Lister	19/08/36
Mary-Josepha del Rio Messa	23/09/36
Mary-of-Sorrows Vidal Cervera	19/08/36
Mary-of-the-Purification Ximénez Ximénez	23/09/36
Niceta Playa Xifra	24/11/36
Paula Isla Alonso	24/11/36
Rose Pedret Rull	19/08/36
Teresa Chambó Palés	19/08/36

Servant of Mary

Mary-of-Guadalupe Ricart Olmos	02/12/36

Sisters of the Pious Schools

Carmen-of-St-Philip-Neri Gomez Lezaun	08/08/36
Clementia-of-St-John-Baptist Riba Mestres	08/08/36
Consuelo Aguiar-Mella Diaz (lay person)	19/06/36
Dolores Aguiar-Mella Diaz (lay person)	19/09/36
Mary-of-the-Child-Jesus Baldillou Bullit	08/08/36
Mary-Louise-of-Jesus Girón Romera	08/08/36
Mary-of-Jesus de la Yglesia de Varo	19/09/36
Presentation-of-the-Holy-Family Gallén Marti	08/08/36

Claretian Sister

Mary Giner Gomis de San Juan	13/11/36

Little Sisters of the Abandoned Elderly

Dolores-of-St-Eualalia Puig Bonany	08/09/36
Josepha-of-St-John Ruano Garcia	08/09/36

Third Order Capuchin Sisters of the Holy Family

Emmanuelle Fernández Ibero	22/08/36
Mary Fenollosa Alcaina	27/09/36
Mary-Victoria Quintana Argos	22/08/36

UGANDA

Saints (22)

Charles Lwanga and Comps

Achilleus Kiwanuka	03/06/1886
Adolphus Mukasa Ludigo	03/06/1886
Aloysius Gonzaga Gonza	00/05/1886
Ambrose Kibuka	03/06/1886
Anatolius Kiriggwajjo	03/06/1886
Andrew Kaggwa	00/05/1886
Athanasius Bazzekuketta	00/05/1886
Bruno Serunkuma	03/06/1886
Charles Lwanga	03/06/1886
Dionysius Ssebuggwawo	25/05/1886
Gyavira	03/06/1886
James Buzabaliawo	03/06/1886
John Mary Muzeyi	27/01/1887
Joseph Mkasa	15/11/1885
Kizito	03/06/1886
Luke Banabakintu	03/06/1886
Matthias Mulumba	00/05/1886
Mbaga-Tuzinde	03/06/1886
Mugagga	03/06/1886
Mukasa Kiriwawanvu	03/06/1886
Noah Mawaggali	00/05/1886
Pontian Ngondwe	00/05/1886

UKRAINE

Bishops

Basil Velychkovsky	30/06/73
Gregory Khomyshyn	17/01/47
Gregory Lakota	12/11/50
John Sleziuk	02/12/73
Josaphat Kotsylovsky	17/11/47
Joseph Bilczewski	20/03/23
Michael Charnetsky	02/04/59
Nicetas Budka	01/10/49
Simeon Lukach	22/08/64
Theodore Romzha	01/11/47

Priests

Alexis Zarytskyi	30/10/63
Andrew Ishchak	26/06/41
Emilian Kovch	25/03/44

Michael Conrad	26/06/41
Michael Tsehelskyi	25/05/51
Peter Verhun	07/02/37
Romanus Lysko	14/10/49
Religious	
Clement Sheptysky	01/05/51
Joachim Senkivskyi	29/06/41
John Ziatyk	17/05/52
Laurentia Herasimiv	28/08/52
Leonidas Feodorov	07/03/35
Olympia Bida	28/01/52
Severian Baranyk	26/06/41
Tarsicia Matskiv	17/07/44
Vitalius Bairak	??/03/46
Zenobius Kovalyk	??/??/41
Layman	
Vladimir Pryjma	26/06/41

VIETNAM

Saints (117)

Agnes (Le Thi) Thanh	12/07/1841
Alphonsus Leciniana OP	22/01/1745
Andrew (Dung) Lac	21/12/1839
Andrew (Nguyen Kim) Thong	15/07/1855
Andrew (Tran van) Trong	28/11/1835
Andrew Tuong	16/06/1862
Anthony (Nguyen Huu) Quynh	10/07/1840
Augustine (Phan Viet) Huy	13/06/1839
Augustine (Nguyen van) Moi	19/12/1839
Augustine Schöffler	01/05/1851
Bernard (Vu van) Due	01/08/1838
Dominic Cam	11/03/1859
Dominic (Dinh) Dat	18/07/1839
Dominic (Nguyen van) Hanh OP	01/08/1838
Dominic Henares OP	25/06/1838
Dominic Huyen	05/06/1862
Dominic (Pham Trong) Kham	13/01/1859
Dominic Mao	16/06/1862
Dominic Mau OP	05/11/1858
Dominic Nguen	16/06/1862
Dominic Nhi	16/06/1862
Dominic Ninh	02/06/1862
Dominic Toai	05/06/1862
Dominic Trach OP	18/09/1840
Dominic Tuoc OP	02/04/1839
Dominic (Bui van) Uy	19/12/1839
Dominic (Nguyen van) Xuyen OP	26/11/1839
Emmanuel (Le van) Phung	31/07/1859
Emmanuel (Nguyen van) Trieu	17/09/1798
Francis-Xavier Can	20/11/1837
Francis (Do van) Chieu	25/06/1838
Francis-Isidore Gagelin	17/10/1833
Francis Gil de Federich OP	22/01/1745
Francis Jaccard	21/09/1838
Francis-Xavier (Ha Trong) Mau	19/12/1839
Francis (Phan van) Trung	06/10/1858
Hyacinth Castañeda OP	07/11/1773
Ignatius Delgado y Cebrian OP	12/07/1838
James (Do Mai) Nam	12/08/1838
Jerome Hermosilla OP	01/11/1861
John-Louis Bonnard	01/05/1852
John-Baptist Con	08/11/1840
John-Charles Cornay	20/09/1837
John Dat	28/10/1798
John-Baptist (Dinh van) Thanh	28/04/1840
Joseph (Hoang Luong) Canh	05/09/1838
Joseph Diaz Sanjurjo OP	20/07/1857
Joseph Fernandez OP	24/07/1838
Joseph (Do Quang) Hien OP	09/05/1840
Joseph (Doan Trinh) Hoan	26/05/1861
Joseph (Nguyen Duy) Khang	06/11/1861
Joseph (Nguyen van) Luu	02/05/1854
Joseph Marchand	30/11/1835
Joseph (Nguyen Dinh) Nghi	08/11/1840
Joseph (Pham Trong) Ta	13/01/1859
Joseph (Le Dang) Thi	24/10/1860
Joseph Tuan (1) OP	30/04/1861
Joseph Tuan (2)	07/01/1862
Joseph Tuc	01/06/1862
Joseph (Nguyen Dinh) Uyen	03/07/1838
Joseph (Dang Dinh) Vien	21/08/1838
Laurence (Nguyen van) Huong	27/04/1856
Laurence Ngon	22/05/1862
Luke (Vu Ba) Loan	05/06/1840
Luke (Pham Trong) Thin	13/01/1859
Martin (Ta Duc) Thinh	08/11/1840
Martin Tho	08/11/1840
Matthew (Le van) Gam	11/05/1847
Matthew (Nguyen van) Phuong	26/05/1861
Melchior Garcia Sampedro OP	28/07/1858
Michael (Ho Dinh) Hy	22/05/1857
Michael (Nguyen Huy) My	12/08/1838
Nicholas (Bui Duc) The	13/06/1839
Paul (Tong Viet) Buong	23/10/1833
Paul Duong	03/06/1862
Paul Hanh	28/05/1859
Paul (Phan Khac) Khoan	28/04/1840
Paul (Le van) Loc	13/02/1859
Paul (Nguyen van) My	18/12/1838

Paul (Nguyen) Ngan	08/11/1840
Paul (Le Bao) Tinh	06/04/1857
Peter Alamato Ribera OP	01/11/1861
Peter Da	17/06/1862
Peter (Nguyen) Dich	12/08/1838
Peter Dumoulin-Borie	24/11/1838
Peter Dung	06/06/1862
Peter (Truong van) Duong	18/12/1838
Peter (Nguyen van) Hieu	28/04/1840
Peter Khanh	12/07/1842
Peter (Vo Bang) Khoa	24/11/1838
Peter (Nguyen van) Luu	07/04/1861
Peter-Francis Neron	03/11/1860
Peter (Doang Cong) Quy	31/07/1859
Peter (Phan van) Thi	21/12/1839
Peter Thuan	06/06/1862
Peter (Vu van) Truat	18/12/1838
Peter (Nguyen Khac) Tu	10/07/1840
Peter (Nguyen van) Tu OP	05/09/1838
Peter (Nguyen Ba) Tuan	15/07/1838
Peter (Le) Tuy	11/10/1833
Peter (Doan van) Van	25/05/1857
Philip (Phan van) Minh	03/07/1853
Simon (Phan Dac) Hoa	12/12/1840
Stephen Cuénot	14/11/1861
Stephen (Nguyen van) Vinh	19/12/1839
Theophanes Venard	02/02/1861
Thomas (Nguyen van) De	19/12/1839
Thomas (Dinh Viet) Du OP	26/11/1839
Thomas Khuong	30/01/1861
Thomas (Tran van) Thien	21/09/1838
Thomas Toan	21/07/1840
Valentine Berrio Ochoa OP	01/11/1861
Vincent (Nguyen The) Diem	24/11/1838
Vincent Duong	06/06/1862
Vincent (Le Quang) Liem OP	07/11/1773
Vincent Tuong	16/06/1862
Vincent (Do) Yen OP	30/06/1838

Beatus

Andrew Phú Yên

WALES

Saints (4)

David Lewis	27/08/1679
John Lloyd	22/07/1679
Philip Evans	22/07/1679
Richard Gwyn	17/10/1584

Beati (2)

Charles Meehan	12/08/1679
William Davies	27/07/1593